PHILOSOPHICAL INQUIRY

Classic and Contemporary Readings

PHILOSOPHICAL INQUIRY

Classic and Contemporary Readings

Edited by

Jonathan E. Adler
Catherine Z. Elgin

Hackett Publishing Company, Inc.
Indianapolis/Cambridge

15   14   13   12   11   10   2   3   4   5   6   7

For further information, please address
  Hackett Publishing Company, Inc.
  P.O. Box 44937
  Indianapolis, Indiana 46244-0937

  www.hackettpublishing.com

Cover design by Abigail Coyle
Interior design by Elizabeth L. Wilson
Composition by Agnew's, Inc.
Printed at Victor Graphics, Inc.
Cover photograph: Getty Images

Library of Congress Cataloging-in-Publication Data

Adler, Jonathan Eric, 1948–
    Philosophical inquiry: classic and contemporary readings / Jonathan E. Adler
and Catherine Z. Elgin.
        p. cm.
    Includes bibliographical references.
    ISBN-13: 978-0-87220-868-1 (cloth)
    ISBN-13: 978-0-87220-867-4 (pbk.)
    1. Philosophy. I. Elgin, Catherine Z., 1948– II. Title.
    BD21.A25 2007
    100—dc22
                                                    2007014143

The paper used in this publication meets the minimum requirements of American National
Standard for Information Sciences—Permanence of Paper for Printed Library Materials,
ANSI Z39.48–1984.
                              ∞

ACKNOWLEDGMENTS

IT IS NOT EASY deciding what to include in a work like this one. We thank the following people for helpful advice: Joshua Cohen, Peter Hylton, Christine Korsgaard, Alexander Nehamas, Harvey Siegel, Eric Steinberg, Kenneth Winkler, Roslyn Weiss, and several anonymous referees. Our thanks also to Alicia Redemske for help preparing the manuscript. We are grateful to all of you.

For Emily, Jeff, and Sam

CONTENTS

METAPHYSICS

形而上学

Causation and the Nature of Reality

Identity and Personal Identity

Freedom of the Will

PHILOSOPHY OF MIND

精神哲学

ETHICS 伦理学

Aesthetics 美学

A support page for this title can be found at www.hackettpublishing.com

*Titles marked with an asterisk have been provided by the editors to clarify the contents of the relevant selection. These titles are not part of the original work.

WHY STUDY PHILOSOPHY?

'THE AIM OF PHILOSOPHY, abstractly formulated, is to understand how things in the broadest possible sense of the term hang together in the broadest possible sense of the term'.[1] To achieve such an understanding, philosophy asks very basic questions and evaluates proposed answers to them. It scrutinizes and assesses fundamental presuppositions. Ideas that we take for granted in everyday life and in the other disciplines are starting points for philosophy.

A biologist might wonder how to explain a particular observation. The philosopher wonders about the nature of scientific explanation: How do we determine that something has been adequately explained? She also wonders about more basic questions: What is it to explain? Why do we want to explain? What is it to observe? How does observation relate to reality? The biologist might wonder whether a virus is alive. The philosopher wants to know what life is: What does it mean to say that something is alive? What do all living things have in common that nonliving things lack? Before the biologist can begin to answer his question, he has to presuppose an answer to the philosopher's question. It is crucial to know whether his presupposition is sound, for if it is not, his results may be unfounded. The philosopher's question leads to others: Do we have obligations to living things that we do not have to nonliving things? Does it matter what quality of life the things possess?

A coach may be vitally interested in whether some player is a good athlete. The philosopher wants to know what kind of human excellence athletic ability is. Unless the coach presupposes some answer to the philosopher's question, he will be unable to tell a good athlete from a klutz. If he accepts the wrong answer, he may pass over good players and settle for mediocre ones. The philosopher also wants to know what makes athletic excellence worth pursuing. Many people value athletic prowess. But is it genuinely valuable? If so, what makes it so? How is it like other valuable abilities?

A legislator might want to know whether a particular revision in the tax code is just. The philosopher asks: What is justice? What is a good society, and how can we achieve it? How does an individual's good relate to the common good? What constitutes a fair balance between liberty and equality?

The biologist, the coach, and the legislator take it for granted that they know their subjects pretty well. They can generally tell living from nonliving things, athletes from klutzes, just from unjust laws. They simply have problems with a few special cases. The philosopher takes as little for granted as possible. She worries about what the few special cases reveal. Each time an answer is given, the philosopher wants to know what justifies it. The philosopher then is like a little kid asking 'why?' 'why?' 'why?' But, as is evident even to two-year-olds, just asking 'why?' 'why?' 'why?' is not an effective way of getting acceptable answers. The

---

1. Wilfrid Sellars, 'Philosophy and the Scientific Image of Man', *Science, Perception, and Reality,* London: Routledge and Kegan Paul, 1963, p. 1.

philosopher thus attempts to develop methods for investigating fundamental problems so that her questions can force the data to yield answers. This requires assessing methods and standards as well as substantive assumptions. To validate empirical science, for example, we need to establish when and why and to what extent observation is a good source of evidence. To validate a moral requirement, we need to figure out what makes right acts right.

We end up asking the most basic questions. What is the nature of reality: Are there such things as electrons, as numbers, as God? What do we commit ourselves to when we say that we believe in such things? When, if ever, are we right to believe in them? What is knowledge: How does knowledge differ from belief? How does knowledge relate to understanding? How does it differ from faith? What is good: Is morality a matter of what we know, of how we feel, of what we do? How, if at all, is morality related to religion? These questions turn out to be very difficult indeed.

One might be tempted to dismiss such questions on the grounds that the presuppositions we have been using work quite well. Why mess with them now? The answer is twofold: (1) So long as we take our presuppositions for granted, they are mere prejudices. They might be justifiable, but we do not know how to justify them. Our suspicion of prejudice stems precisely from the fact that it is not justified and perhaps cannot be justified. Once we justify our presuppositions, they become warranted beliefs. To the extent that they are warranted, it is reasonable and responsible to count on them. (2) If we look at history, we can discover a number of firmly held presuppositions that have turned out to be wrong—the conviction that the sun orbits the earth, that slavery is morally permissible, that species do not evolve. In light of the history of smart, thoughtful people who have been wrong about such matters, we would be unwise to be confident that we are right.

Still, one might argue, most of our fundamental beliefs must be at least roughly correct. Otherwise they would not have worked so well for so long. This is a fairly powerful argument. Our worldview probably is not entirely wrong or totally beside the point, but our worldview clearly is not totally successful as it stands either. Normally we know the difference between right and wrong well enough. We have been taught that certainly. But major ethical problems arise when there is a conflict of rights or a conflict of duties. For example, a physician is morally obliged to prolong life and to alleviate suffering. Usually this presents no difficulty. But sometimes the only way to prolong a life is to cause, or at least tolerate, suffering; and the only way to alleviate suffering is to shorten a life. In that case the physician's knowledge that he is supposed to do both—alleviate suffering and prolong life—is insufficient. He needs to know what he is supposed to do when he cannot do both. Another problem is this: Disagreements about the permissibility of abortion often turn on the question of whether a fetus is a person. Normally we are pretty good at telling whether something is a person or not. But a fetus seems to be a borderline case. Unless we have a more adequate understanding of what it is to be a person than common sense provides, we do not know how to answer the question. And even when we have an answer, we still have to ask whether the permissibility of abortion is determined by whether a fetus is or is not a person. Are there other issues that come into play?

In the clear cases that our concepts evolved to deal with, philosophical problems are normally not acute. But there are borderline cases and complicating factors, and it is here that philosophical problems become practical problems. Unless we know how to critically analyze a situation, we do not know what or how to think about it. And if we do not know what or how to think about it, we are unlikely to know what to do.

Once a branch of Philosophy has amassed enough truth it becomes its own school)

Nevertheless it would be wrong to construe philosophy mainly as an underlaborer to science[2] or a tool for crisis management. And it would be wrong to think that philosophical questions are only in the purview of professional philosophers or that those in every field, such as the biologist discussed earlier, do not in their professional pursuits engage with philosophical questions. It is an intellectual enterprise whose goal is a broad and deep understanding of the world and our place in it. That is something worth valuing for its own sake.

One might object that the fruits of philosophical labor are sparse. Unlike physics or biology, philosophy cannot point to a large stock of truths that it has firmly established. This is true. Little in philosophy is beyond dispute. Part of the reason stems from the sociology of knowledge. Once a branch of philosophy begins to amass a body of established truths, it spins off and becomes a science. Newton called his enterprise 'natural philosophy'. We call it 'physics'. Much of what used to belong to the philosophy of mind has morphed into psychology or cognitive science. If successes come to be called something else, philosophy is left with the outstanding problems.

When students first study philosophy, they often complain, 'There is no answer!' For fundamental problems such as whether we have free will, the complaint is on target to this extent: There is no widely accepted answer. But does the lack of a widely accepted answer constitute an objection?

The lack of a solution after long efforts may be a clue to the difficulty and depth of a problem. In many cases, even if no solution has been widely accepted, reflection on the problem has taught us much. In the case of free will, for example, we have gained clarification (e.g., that an event's being fated is not the same as its being caused). We have learned that some paths are dead ends and that others are questionable (e.g., that every event has a cause). And we have reached some substantive, if not wholly uncontroversial, conclusions (e.g., that the free will that matters must be compatible with scientific understanding of how changes take place in the world).

We may also gain an appreciation of our limits. As Kant suggests, our ability to pose problems may outrun our ability to solve them.

> Human reason has this particular fate. . . . It is troubled by questions that it cannot dismiss because they are posed by the nature of reason itself, but that it also cannot answer, because they surpass human reason's every ability.[3]

Kant holds that the limits are built into reason itself. If so, some of our failings are inevitable. But there are other possibilities as well. If a question currently lacks an answer, it might be because we have not yet developed the resources to figure out the answer. Such questions might someday be answered (e.g., after several hundred years of failure, Fermat's last theorem was finally proved). Or the question might be a bad question (like, 'In outer space, which way is up and which way is down?'). Since we usually do not know what explains our lack of an answer, the possibility that a question is unanswerable should not dissuade us from looking for one.

---

2. John Locke, *An Essay Concerning Human Understanding,* Indianapolis: Hackett Publishing Co., 1996, p. 3.

3. Immanuel Kant, *Critique of Pure Reason,* Indianapolis: Hackett Publishing Co., 1996, p. 5.

Even if a question as posed cannot be answered, the lack of an answer does not entail a lack of progress. In Plato's *Meno* (7–23), for example, a central question is, What is virtue? Despite an extensive investigation, Socrates and Meno never reach a satisfactory answer. In his closing words, Socrates returns to the very same task specified early in the dialogue—'to first try to find out what virtue itself is'. Still they have learned much, even if the main task remains undone. Meno's first attempt to define virtue is a list of virtues specific to different social roles: 'There is virtue for every action and every age, for every task of ours and every one of us' (72a). Socrates persuades him to reject this sort of answer: 'Even if [the virtues] are many and various, all of them have one and the same form which makes them virtues, and it is right to look to this when one is asked to make clear what virtue is' (72c–d). Meno then offers the right kind of answer: Virtue is 'to be able to rule over men, if you are seeking one description to fit them all'. This is the right kind of answer, for it attributes a shared characteristic to all the virtues. But whether it is the right answer is immediately disputed. Socrates says, 'You say that virtue is to be able to rule. Shall we now add to this *justly and not unjustly?*' (73d–e; emphasis added). Meno accepts this qualification, which leads to additional problems. The dialogue continues with further attempts at a viable definition and further failures. But at each step our understanding of the problem deepens. In the tiny fragment so far glimpsed, there is progress, even if it is largely negative. *If* Socrates' demand for a single concept that applies to all virtues is legitimate, a list of virtues won't do. *If* virtue is a kind of power to rule, that power to rule will only be virtuous if the ruler rules justly; so virtue and power are not the same thing. To cite these marks of progress is not to claim that they are sacrosanct. As we signal by expressing them as conditionals—'if-then' statements—their antecedents are accepted tentatively and are open to challenge in turn.

Still there is some truth to the charge that philosophy delivers few fixed and final answers. If nothing is beyond question, we can hardly be certain that any particular answer, however well supported, is sound. This, according to Russell, is an asset, not a flaw.

> The value of philosophy is, in fact, to be sought largely in its very uncertainty. The man who has no tincture of philosophy goes through life imprisoned in the prejudices derived from common sense, from the habitual beliefs of his age or his nation, and from convictions which have grown up in his mind without the cooperation or consent of his deliberate reason. To such a man the world tends to become definite, finite, obvious; common objects rouse no questions, and unfamiliar possibilities are contemptuously rejected. . . . Philosophy, though unable to tell us with certainty what is the true answer to the doubts which it raises, is able to suggest many possibilities which enlarge our thoughts and free them from the tyranny of custom. Thus, while diminishing our feeling of certainty as to what things are, it greatly increases our knowledge as to what they may be; it removes the somewhat arrogant dogmatism of those who have never traveled into the region of liberating doubt, and it keeps alive our sense of wonder by showing familiar things in an unfamiliar aspect.[4]

Russell's point is not merely that the man imprisoned in his prejudices might be wrong but also that, even if he is right, he is apt to be missing something significant. There are more as-

---

4. Bertrand Russell, *The Problems of Philosophy,* Indianapolis: Hackett Publishing Co., 1990, pp. 156–7.

pects to things than meets any particular eye. If we reexamine our assumptions, we may come up with ways to view matters differently, hence discover more truths about them than common sense or contemporary science delivers. If the cost of such an activity is a loss of certainty, it is a cost worth paying. Certainty may be unfounded, and even when well founded it may be excessively constricting.

Plato's 'Myth of the Cave' (23–6) describes our predicament.

> Imagine human beings living in an underground, cavelike dwelling, with an entrance a long way up, which is both open to the light and as wide as the cave itself. They've been there since childhood, fixed in the same place, with their necks and legs fettered, able to see only in front of them, because their bonds prevent them from turning their heads around. Light is provided by a fire burning far above and behind them. Also behind them, but on higher ground, there is a path stretching between them and the fire. Imagine that along this path a low wall has been built, like the screen in front of puppeteers above which they show their puppets. . . . Also imagine that there are people along the wall, carrying all kinds of artifacts that project above it—statues of people and other animals, made of stone, wood, and every material. And, as you'd expect, some of the carriers are talking, and some are silent.[5]

The prisoners in the cave see only appearances—the shadows that are reflected on the wall in front of them. They never see things as they really are. And given that they are chained and cannot turn around, there is nothing in their perception to demonstrate that they are looking only at shadows. There is nothing about the appearances that would tell the perceivers that they are not seeing the world as it really is. So the practice of awarding 'honors, praises, or prizes for the one who was sharpest at identifying the shadows as they passed by and who best remembered which usually came earlier, which later, and which simultaneously, and who could thus best divine the future'[6] is not trivial. For the findings that earn these rewards are science. What the award-winning cave dwellers are doing is attempting to provide order to their perceptions—to both explain and predict the passing show.

Plato claims that if someone could escape his fetters, ascend out of the cave, and see things as they really are, he would understand the essential natures of things. He would realize that what he had formerly believed to be real was a mere illusion. And because he now knew reality, he would be able to recognize the illusion for what it is and explain its force. Plato thus believes that the goal of philosophy is to lead us out of the cave in which we ordinarily live, to see the reality that lies behind our illusions. What is the cave in which we are trapped? Our bodies. All knowledge of reality comes to us through our sense organs. And our sense organs are capable of directly conveying information only about how things appear, not about how they really are. We always see things from one perspective or another, from one distance or another, under some light or other. This information—the data of our sense of sight—tells us only how the visible object appears to us, and only under limited conditions. But appearances can be deceiving. What looks round from one perspective looks elliptical from another.

---

5. Plato, *Republic,* Indianapolis: Hackett Publishing Co., 1992, 514a–515a.

6. Ibid., 516c–d.

What looks green in one light looks blue in another. There is no perspective from which the thing in itself can be viewed without distortion, as it is in itself. The thing in itself never appears in public without its makeup.

Our predicament, however, is even worse than the problem Plato's captives face. We cannot escape our fetters and climb out of the cave. Trapped in our bodies, we must discover that what is given by the senses is just appearance, and we must determine how to find the reality behind the appearances *without ever leaving the cave.* The problem of appearance and reality then is that of determining the nature of reality on the basis of the appearances that are presented to the senses. When we have done so, we will explain to the scientists in the cave how to do more than predict the passing show. We will give them the resources to understand how the passing show can be explained on the basis of the reality that lies behind it.

KNOWLEDGE

A T THE BEGINNING OF his *Meditations,* Descartes explains that although he had the best education in the world, he had come to realize that much of what he had been taught was false. He therefore decides to embark on a systematic investigation to see if he can discover when or indeed whether knowledge is possible. We face a similar predicament. We have dutifully learned what we have been taught. But we are now in a position to realize that much of what we have been taught is suspect. It is incomplete, or shallow, or oversimplified. Some of it is simply false. This leads to questions: What can we know, and how can we know it? Is it possible to know the way the world is?

To answer these questions, Descartes adopts the 'method of doubt'. By doubting every belief that could possibly be false, he hopes to discover whether he can be certain of anything. Since, he thinks, knowledge requires certainty, the method of doubt will reveal whether knowledge is possible. Initially it appears that the enterprise will founder, as more and more of his beliefs succumb to the method of doubt: His senses might err (by, e.g., illusion); he might be dreaming; an evil demon, of unlimited power and cunning, might deceive him. Even when he engages in so simple an act as inferring $2 + 3 = 5$, he cannot exclude the possibility that an evil demon has manipulated his mind so that he adds wrong. Is then certainty or a foundation for knowledge impossible?

Finally he discovers an indubitable truth: A person can be absolutely certain that he exists each time he thinks. If you think that you think, then you think. So you cannot be wrong about the fact that you think. But if you think, then you exist, since you would not be thinking if you did not exist. So the very fact that you are thinking proves that you exist. 'I think therefore I am' (*cogito ergo sum*) is true whenever it is thought. The guarantee conferred by the cogito ('I think') proves only the existence of one's mind. If an evil demon is deceiving me, I can be mistaken in believing that I have two arms, and I can be mistaken that another person is thinking or even that he exists. So the immediate payoff is slight. But it does show that knowledge is possible.

Why does the cogito argument work? Descartes thinks that it does because we 'clearly and distinctly' perceive its soundness. This leads him to conclude that clarity and distinctness is the criterion of certain truth. But then Descartes faces a version of the 'problem of the criterion' (Chisholm, 77–85). What guarantees that the criterion works? Descartes argues that the solution lies in his proof that God exists and is not a deceiver. Since God secures the truth of clear and distinct ideas, you cannot be wrong about what you clearly and distinctly perceive. But unless the soundness of the proof of God's existence is clearly and distinctly perceived, the proof is untrustworthy. Descartes seems to be presupposing his criterion in order to validate it. The problem of the criterion is circularity.

The effectiveness of skeptical arguments like Descartes' is controversial. Peirce urges that Cartesian doubt is unlike real doubt in that it has neither a specific reason nor practical consequences. As I write this section, I am certain that I am looking at a computer screen. I ignore the possibility that my experience is just an extraordinarily realistic dream. Peirce argues that global doubt and specific doubts that are mere consequences of global doubt are not genuine doubts since they do not, and should not, affect practice. Is this correct?

Descartes stresses that his attempt to provide a foundation for the sciences is a theoretical project, not a practical one. The high standard of certainty is only appropriate where we seek to ground knowledge. When going to meet a friend for lunch, I would be crazy to stop to wonder, without special reason, whether the friend is real or a dream, or whether I really made the date or it is a delusion. But, Descartes thinks, where the goal is unshakeable knowledge, the possibilities that we rightly ignore in everyday life can no longer be dismissed.

Is there ever an inquiry into knowledge that is so totally free of practicalities, even in the most rigorous of scientific research? Do scientists ever contend that their conclusions could not possibly be wrong? If not, are their positive results knowledge?

One might also question the basic form of Descartes' skeptical arguments:

1. I know that there is a computer screen in front of me.

2. If I know that there is a computer screen in front of me, I know that I am not dreaming that there is a computer screen in front of me.

3. But I don't know that I'm not dreaming that there is a computer screen in front of me.

So, 4. I don't know that there is a computer screen in front of me.

Whereas the usual challenge to this valid argument is to premise 3, Nozick (44–9) questions premise 2. Why do I have to know that I am not dreaming in order to know that there is a computer screen in front of me? The answer is presumably that if I were dreaming that there was a computer screen in front of me, I would not see a computer screen, so it would likely be false that there is a computer screen in front of me. In that case, I wouldn't know it. But that answer relies on a further principle:

If I know that p and I know that q implies not-p, then I know that not-q.

In the case at hand: p = There is a computer screen in front of me (that I see);
q = I am dreaming that there is a computer screen in front of me.

Nozick defends an account of knowledge that denies that principle and so blocks Descartes' skeptical reasoning at its (implicit) second step.

The crux of Nozick's analysis of knowledge is the *subjunctive* or *counterfactual* condition that:

Were p false, X would not believe that p.

When we consider p as false in order to test whether or not X would still believe it, we are to examine only the closest or nearest ways for p to be false, not all the ways. The nearest way for my computer not to be in front of me is, for example, if I moved it to another room. It is a way-out way for p to be false that I am only dreaming that p, and so it does not bear on the truth of Nozick's condition.

Nozick's reply to the skeptical argument comes with a heavy price: If you know something and deduce a conclusion from it and believe the conclusion as a result, it does not follow that you thereby know the conclusion. Yet deduction preserves truth and a core condition of knowledge is truth. From 'John knows that Harry is in France' it follows that 'Harry is in France'.

What besides truth is required for knowledge? A traditional answer emerges from Plato's *Meno* (7–23). Knowledge is justified true belief. If you believe that Foolish Pleasure will win tomorrow's race only because it is your birthday, then even if Foolish Pleasure wins, you still did not know that Foolish Pleasure would win, because its being your birthday has nothing to do with who wins. Your reason is not a good one. It provides no justification.

Is the justified true belief sufficient for knowledge? Gettier (43–4) provides counterexamples anticipated in the following vivid case: Because you are looking at your trustworthy clock, which reads 1:10, you believe the time is 1:10. In fact it is. Since the clock has always been trustworthy, your belief is justified. However, what you do not know is that the battery went dead at 1:10, exactly twelve hours ago. Although your belief is true and justified, you do not know the time. Why not?

One fairly obvious reason is that it is *accidental* that your belief is true—had you looked at the clock two minutes earlier or six minutes later, as you easily might have, you still would have believed that it was 1:10. What modified or new condition would capture the insight in the proposal that to know, it must be non-accidental that one is correct?

Some philosophers believe that the justification condition must be strengthened, perhaps by ruling out all possibilities of error. Although that would block the counterexamples, the cost is steep. It seems not to leave room, as Gettier (43–4) explicitly does, for fallibility. And it threatens to lead to skepticism, since rarely, if ever, are we in a position to exclude all possibilities of error.

A different route taken by Nozick (44–9), Goldman (168–75), and others replaces the justification requirement with a reliability requirement. For a belief to be knowledge is for it to be formed or sustained by a reliable process. They hold that knowledge is a relation between belief and the world. It does not depend on the agent's grasping that relation.

Goldman assimilates knowing to the kind of lawful processes that underlie reliable mechanisms like watches or clocks. A clock whose hands specifying that it is 8:05 is accurate because the mechanisms that regularly move them correspond to seconds, minutes, and hours. (Other models include a thermostat or thermometer.) Knowledge, Goldman maintains, requires a similar reliable connection between beliefs and what in the world makes them true. A young child looks out the window, sees a yellow car, and comes to believe that there is a yellow car in front of his house. His belief, it seems, is knowledge because he acquires it by vision, a highly reliable process for generating such beliefs. It makes no difference that he cannot say how he knows.

Perception is the paradigm case of reliable processes. Our generally successful dependence on perception lends credence to *empiricism*—the view, in its unqualified form, that all knowledge derives from experience. By contrast *rationalism* emphasizes the role of reason, unaided by sensory experience. Its paradigm is mathematics. Although the debate between rationalists and empiricists was important in the history of philosophy, most contemporary commentators think the empiricism-rationalism contrast is too crude to do justice to the complexity of the problems and even to the work of the historical figures who endorsed it.

If all knowledge of the external world comes by way of the senses, it is important to determine exactly what the senses deliver. Well, we see colors, shapes, and sizes. They seem to present themselves directly and immediately. Should we conclude then that the world contains things of various colors, shapes, and sizes? Not so fast! The colors of things look different under different lights. Color-blind people cannot tell red and green apart. So saying that color is 'out there' in the world is problematic. Which color—the color the shirt looks in daylight, or the color it looks in the store, or the color it looks to the person who cannot tell whether it is red or green? Locke concluded that *secondary qualities*—such as colors, odors, flavors, and tones—depend not only on what is in the world but also on the conditions of the perceiver. So we cannot take them as accurate representations of the way the world is. By contrast *primary qualities*—size, shape, and motion, for example—are not so dependent. When we perceive them, we discern aspects of the mind-independent world. If there were no sensing creatures, there would be no colors, flavors, or odors. But there would still be sizes and shapes.

Although we perceive only properties, Locke denies that we should think that the world consists only of unanchored properties. There must be something that the properties are properties of. He calls the possessor of properties 'substance' and concedes that it is 'something we know not what'. In principle we cannot know what it is, since we only know properties it has. But, Locke believes, it must exist.

Berkeley argues that primary qualities are as dependent on the perceiver as secondary qualities. Apparent shape depends on perspective. A tilted coin's appearance elongates in the direction of sight. We have then no perceptions that provide unmediated access to the mind-independent world. As an empiricist, Berkeley repudiates Locke's substance. Our sensory experiences, he maintains, give us no reason to believe there is such a thing. All we have evidence of is impressions, ideas, and the minds that have those impressions and ideas.

But impressions and ideas are fleeting. If we do not postulate material substances that exist independently of us and retain their properties whether we perceive them or not, what accounts for the order and regularity in our perceptions? Dreams and hallucinations—that is, unanchored impressions—display no such order. Why, if Berkeley is right, isn't all experience dreamlike? Berkeley replies, *our* ideas are fleeting and disorderly. But God's are not. Reality consists not in mind-independent material substances but in the robust, regular, and orderly ideas in the mind of God. When we perceive what God does, our perceptions are orderly and regular. When we perceive on our own, they are not.

Such *idealism* seems incredible. But it solves important problems that Berkeley's predecessors could not solve. One set of problems derives from dualism. If, as Descartes and Locke believe, there are two sorts of things, minds and material objects, what is the connection between them? How can changes in one sort of substance cause changes in the other? If, as Berkeley maintains, the only causality is mental causality, these problems do not arise. A second problem is the 'veil of perception'. On Locke's account, we immediately and directly know our perceptions, which represent the way things are in the mind-independent world. But how can we tell whether the representations are accurate? We can never lift the veil to find out. Berkeley evades this problem by saying that all we have and all we need is order and regularity within perception and that we can tell when we have that.

Like Locke and Berkeley, Hume is an empiricist. Unlike them, he refuses to appeal to God or to 'something we know not what' to underwrite beliefs. He argues that the ordinary objects of experience are constructs grounded in our impressions and ideas. But all our impressions and ideas have taken place in the past. How can we form any reasonable expectations about the future? Take your ordinary expectation that your car will start when you next turn the key in the ignition. That expectation is grounded in experience. In the past each time you turned the key in the ignition, the car started. The two events—the turning of the key and the car starting—have been in your experience constantly conjoined. This, Hume believes, led you to form the habit of expecting the car to start when the key is turned.

Is that expectation well founded? Hume answers no. The fact that two events were constantly conjoined in the past gives us no reason to think that the pattern will continue into the future. To infer that the future will be like the past requires us to assume the uniformity of nature. But what evidence do we have of that? Well, we have evidence that in the past nature has been uniform. But without an independent reason to think that the future will be like the past, the past uniformity of nature gives us no good reason to think that nature will continue to be uniform in the future. Evidently we cannot vindicate induction without the uniformity of nature hypothesis, and we cannot secure the uniformity of nature hypothesis without using induction. So attempts to vindicate induction are circular. (One attempt to evade this conclusion is to argue that there is a formal—e.g., a probabilistic—relation that holds only in cases where constant conjunction is a reliable indicator of the future. Goodman [220–26] shows that this maneuver does not succeed.)

Why can't we simply reason as follows?

> If the key is turned in the ignition, the car will start.
> The key is turned.
> So the car starts.

Such an argument would yield knowledge only if the first premise were necessary. For if it merely happened to hold, there would be no reason to trust that it will continue to hold. If the first premise were necessary, then given that the key was turned, there would be no possibility that the car would fail to start. But there is such a possibility. Regardless of how many times it has started in the past, it might not start. There is, Hume maintains, no necessary connection among matters of fact. The only necessity is conceptual (or logical) necessity. The first premise is not conceptually necessary. If it were, 'The key turned in the ignition and the car did not start' would be a contradiction, which it is not.

The recognition of analytic or conceptual truths leads to a slight restriction on empiricism. Hume does not think that our knowledge that, for example, a square has four sides is based on experience. We need experience of course to learn the concepts. But we need only grasp the concepts to recognize that it is true that a square has four sides. The relation between the concept of a square and the concept of having four sides is, Hume maintains, 'a relation of ideas', not 'a matter of fact'. Truths that are relations of ideas are *a priori*. We know them simply by understanding the concepts involved. Hume's view suggests the following identification:

> Relations of ideas = analytic truths = what is knowable a priori = logical truths
> or definitions

Such truths are necessary but information-poor, since they convey no more information than is needed simply to understand them. By contrast, matters of fact (or synthetic statements), such as 'The Earth travels around the sun', are *a posteriori*. Knowledge of their truth depends on evidence about the way the world is. The correlative and contrasting identification is:

> Matters of fact = synthetic statements = what is knowable only a posteriori =
> contingent truths

Such truths are informative. To learn that a synthetic sentence is true is to learn more than how its terms or concepts relate to each other.

Hume believes that only analytic truths are a priori and necessary. He denies that 'every event has a cause' is necessary, since there is no contradiction in imagining an uncaused event. Kant, by contrast, argues that besides analytic a priori truths and synthetic a posteriori truths, there are synthetic a priori truths. 'Every event has a cause' is one; '7 +5 = 12' is another. Such truths are, he maintains, necessary and knowable independently of experience. But their denial is not a contradiction.

Kant agrees with Hume that necessary conditions cannot be found in the world. Perception reveals only what is the case, not what must be the case. But, Kant maintains, some connections—such as the connection between cause and effect—are necessary if we are to have the experiences of the world that we in fact have. Even though there is no contradiction in imagining uncaused events, human rationality is such that we could not experience events as uncaused (although we often experience events for which we do not know the causes). That every event has a cause then is a necessary condition for the possibility of human reason. Since human reason exists, anything that is necessary for it also exists.

Kripke (35–42) insists that the distinction between necessity and contingency and the distinction between the a priori and the a posteriori are distinct. The distinction between necessary and contingent propositions is a distinction between truths—the domain of metaphysics. The distinction between the a priori and the a posteriori is a distinction about knowledge—an epistemological distinction. It is epistemologically possible—compatible with what we know or have good reason to believe—that a person could be decomposed by a machine and 'beamed' down and reconstructed on another planet; yet such a process may not be physically or metaphysically possible. Another example: Having long believed that Mark Twain and Samuel Clemens were two different people, we might meet at a party the man who goes by both names. Being grounded in experience, our knowledge that Mark Twain is Samuel Clemens is a posteriori. But since the names 'Mark Twain' and 'Samuel Clemens' only serve to pick out someone, they continue to pick out the same object (person), regardless of the variations that are possible in that object. If, for example, we imagine that Mark Twain is shorter, then we thereby imagine that Samuel Clemens is shorter. Since under no possible alteration will 'Mark Twain' and 'Samuel Clemens' pick out different objects, it is metaphysically necessary that Mark Twain and Samuel Clemens are identical. Prior to the discovery, of course, someone might easily believe that Samuel Clemens and Mark Twain are two different people. But though it is easy to conceive, such a situation, Kripke maintains, is really—metaphysically—impossible.

The Nature of Knowledge

Plato

Meno

Meno: Can you tell me, Socrates, can virtue be taught?
70 Or is it not teachable but the result of practice, or is it neither of these, but men possess it by nature or in some other way?

Socrates: Before now, Meno, Thessalians had a high reputation among the Greeks and were admired for their horsemanship and their wealth, but now, it seems
b to me, they are also admired for their wisdom, not least the fellow citizens of your friend Aristippus of Larissa. The responsibility for this reputation of yours lies with Gorgias, for when he came to your city he found that the leading Aleuadae, your lover Aristippus among them, loved him for his wisdom, and so did the other leading Thessalians. In particular, he accustomed you to give a bold and grand answer to any question you may
c be asked, as experts are likely to do. Indeed, he himself was ready to answer any Greek who wished to question him, and every question was answered. But here in Athens, my dear Meno, the opposite is the case, as if there were a dearth of wisdom, and wisdom seems to
71 have departed hence to go to you. If then you want to ask one of us that sort of question, everyone will laugh and say: "Good stranger, you must think me happy indeed if you think I know whether virtue can be taught or how it comes to be; I am so far from knowing whether virtue can be taught or not that I do not even have any knowledge of what virtue itself is."

b I myself, Meno, am as poor as my fellow citizens in this matter, and I blame myself for my complete ignorance about virtue. If I do not know what something is, how could I know what qualities it possesses? Or do you think that someone who does not know at all who Meno is could know whether he is good-looking or rich or well-born, or the opposite of these? Do you think that is possible?

Meno: I do not; but, Socrates, do you really not know what virtue is? Are we to report this to the folk back c home about you?

Socrates: Not only that, my friend, but also that, as I believe, I have never yet met anyone else who did know.

Meno: How so? Did you not meet Gorgias when he was here?

Socrates: I did.

Meno: Did you then not think that he knew?

Socrates: I do not altogether remember, Meno, so that I cannot tell you now what I thought then. Perhaps he does know; you know what he used to say, so you re- d mind me of what he said. You tell me yourself, if you are willing, for surely you share his views.—I do.

Socrates: Let us leave Gorgias out of it, since he is not here. But Meno, by the gods, what do you yourself say that virtue is? Speak and do not begrudge us, so that I may have spoken a most unfortunate untruth when I said that I had never met anyone who knew, if you and Gorgias are shown to know.

Meno: It is not hard to tell you, Socrates. First, if you e want the virtue of a man, it is easy to say that a man's virtue consists of being able to manage public affairs and in so doing to benefit his friends and harm his enemies and to be careful that no harm comes to himself; if you want the virtue of a woman, it is not difficult to describe: she must manage the home well, preserve its possessions, and be submissive to her husband; the virtue of a child, whether male or female, is different again, and

From Plato, *Five Dialogues (Second Edition),* translated by G. M. A. Grube, revised by John M. Cooper (Indianapolis: Hackett Publishing Company, 2002). Reprinted by permission of the publisher.

so is that of an elderly man, if you want that, or if you want that of a free man or a slave. And there are very many other virtues, so that one is not at a loss to say what virtue is. There is virtue for every action and every age, for every task of ours and every one of us—and, Socrates, the same is true for wickedness.

Socrates: I seem to be in great luck, Meno; while I am looking for one virtue, I have found you to have a whole swarm of them. But, Meno, to follow up the image of swarms, if I were asking you what is the nature of bees, and you said that they are many and of all kinds, what would you answer if I asked you: "Do you mean that they are many and varied and different from one another insofar as they are bees? Or are they no different in that regard, but in some other respect, in their beauty, for example, or their size or in some other such way?" Tell me, what would you answer if thus questioned?

Meno: I would say that they do not differ from one another in being bees.

Socrates: If I went on to say: "Tell me, what is this very thing, Meno, in which they are all the same and do not differ from one another?" Would you be able to tell me?

Meno: I would.

Socrates: The same is true in the case of the virtues. Even if they are many and various, all of them have one and the same form which makes them virtues, and it is right to look to this when one is asked to make clear what virtue is. Or do you not understand what I mean?

Meno: I think I understand, but I certainly do not grasp the meaning of the question as fully as I want to.

Socrates: I am asking whether you think it is only in the case of virtue that there is one for man, another for woman, and so on, or is the same true in the case of health and size and strength? Do you think that there is one health for man and another for woman? Or, if it is health, does it have the same form everywhere, whether in man or in anything else whatever?

Meno: The health of a man seems to me the same as that of a woman.

Socrates: And so with size and strength? If a woman is strong, that strength will be the same and have the same form, for by "the same" I mean that strength is no different as far as being strength, whether in a man or a woman. Or do you think there is a difference?

Meno: I do not think so.

Socrates: And will there be any difference in the case

of virtue, as far as being virtue is concerned, whether it be in a child or an old man, in a woman or in a man?

Meno: I think, Socrates, that somehow this is no longer like those other cases.

Socrates: How so? Did you not say that the virtue of a man consists of managing the city well, and that of a woman of managing the household?—I did.

Socrates: Is it possible to manage a city well, or a household, or anything else, while not managing it moderately and justly?—Certainly not.

Socrates: Then if they manage justly and moderately, they must do so with justice and moderation?—Necessarily.

Socrates: So both the man and the woman, if they are to be good, need the same things, justice and moderation.—So it seems.

Socrates: What about a child and an old man? Can they possibly be good if they are intemperate and unjust?—Certainly not.

Socrates: But if they are moderate and just?—Yes.

Socrates: So all human beings are good in the same way, for they become good by acquiring the same qualities.—It seems so.

Socrates: And they would not be good in the same way if they did not have the same virtue.—They certainly would not be.

Socrates: Since then the virtue of all is the same, try to tell me and to remember what Gorgias, and you with him, said that that same thing is.

Meno: What else but to be able to rule over people, if you are seeking one description to fit them all.

Socrates: That is indeed what I am seeking, but, Meno, is virtue the same in the case of a child or a slave, namely, for them to be able to rule over a master, and do you think that he who rules is still a slave?—I do not think so at all, Socrates.

Socrates: It is not likely, my good man. Consider this further point: you say that virtue is to be able to rule. Shall we not add to this *justly and not unjustly?*

Meno: I think so, Socrates, for justice is virtue.

Socrates: Is it virtue, Meno, or a virtue?—What do you mean?

Socrates: As with anything else. For example, if you wish, take roundness, about which I would say that it is a shape, but not simply that it is shape. I would not so speak of it because there are other shapes.

Meno: You are quite right. So I too say that not only justice is a virtue but there are many other virtues.

Socrates: What are they? Tell me, as I could mention 74 other shapes to you if you bade me do so, so do you mention other virtues.

Meno: I think courage is a virtue, and moderation, wisdom, and munificence, and very many others.

Socrates: We are having the same trouble again, Meno, though in another way; we have found many virtues while looking for one, but we cannot find the one which covers all the others.

Meno: I cannot yet find, Socrates, what you are look-b ing for, one virtue for them all, as in the other cases.

Socrates: That is likely, but I am eager, if I can, that we should make progress, for you understand that the same applies to everything. If someone asked you what I mentioned just now: "What is shape, Meno?" and you told him that it was roundness, and if then he said to you what I did: "Is roundness shape or a shape?" you would surely tell him that it is a shape?—I certainly would.

Socrates: That would be because there are other c shapes?—Yes.

Socrates: And if he asked you further what they were, you would tell him?—I would.

Socrates: So too, if he asked you what color is, and you said it is white, and your questioner interrupted you, "Is white color or a color?" you would say that it is a color, because there are also other colors?—I would.

Socrates: And if he bade you mention other colors, you would mention others that are no less colors than d white is?—Yes.

Socrates: Then if he pursued the argument as I did and said: "We always arrive at the many; do not talk to me in that way, but since you call all these many by one name, and say that no one of them is not a shape even though they are opposites, tell me what this is which applies as much to the round as to the straight and e which you call shape, as you say the round is as much a shape as the straight." Do you not say that?—I do.

Socrates: When you speak like that, do you assert that the round is no more round than it is straight, and that the straight is no more straight than it is round?

Meno: Certainly not, Socrates.

Socrates: Yet you say that the round is no more a shape than the straight is, nor the one more than the other.— That is true.

Socrates: What then is this to which the name shape applies? Try to tell me. If then you answered the man who was questioning about shape or color: "I do not under- 75 stand what you want, my man, nor what you mean," he would probably wonder and say: "You do not understand that I am seeking that which is the same in all these cases?" Would you still have nothing to say, Meno, if one asked you: "What is this which applies to the round and the straight and the other things which you call shapes and which is the same in them all?" Try to say, that you may practice for your answer about virtue.

Meno: No, Socrates, but you tell me. b

Socrates: Do you want me to do you this favor?

Meno: I certainly do.

Socrates: And you will then be willing to tell me about virtue?

Meno: I will.

Socrates: We must certainly press on. The subject is worth it.

Meno: It surely is.

Socrates: Come then, let us try to tell you what shape is. See whether you will accept that it is this: Let us say that shape is that which alone of existing things always follows color. Is that satisfactory to you, or do you look c for it in some other way? I should be satisfied if you defined virtue in this way.

Meno: But that is foolish, Socrates.

Socrates: How do you mean?

Meno: That shape, you say, always follows color. Well then, if someone were to say that he did not know what color is, but that he had the same difficulty as he had about shape, what do you think your answer would be?

Socrates: A true one, surely, and if my questioner was one of those clever and disputatious debaters, I would say to him: "I have given my answer; if it is wrong, it is your job to refute it." But if they are friends as you and I are, d and want to discuss with each other, they must answer in a manner more gentle and more proper to discussion. By this I mean that the answers must not only be true, but in terms admittedly known to the questioner. I too will try to speak in these terms. Do you call something "the end"? I mean such a thing as a limit or boundary, for all e those are, I say, the same thing. Prodicus might disagree with us, but you surely call something "finished" or "completed"—that is what I want to express, nothing elaborate.

Meno: I do, and I think I understand what you mean.

Socrates: Further, you call something a plane, and
76 something else a solid, as in geometry?

Meno: I do.

Socrates: From this you may understand what I mean
by shape, for I say this of every shape, that a shape is that
which limits a solid; in a word, a shape is the limit of a
solid.

Meno: And what do you say color is, Socrates?

Socrates: You are outrageous, Meno. You bother an
old man to answer questions, but you yourself are not
b willing to recall and to tell me what Gorgias says that
virtue is.

Meno: After you have answered this, Socrates, I will
tell you.

Socrates: Even someone who was blindfolded would
know from your conversation that you are handsome
and still have lovers.

Meno: Why so?

Socrates: Because you are forever giving orders in a
discussion, as spoiled people do, who behave like tyrants
as long as they are young. And perhaps you have recog-
c nized that I am at a disadvantage with handsome people,
so I will do you the favor of an answer.

Meno: By all means do me that favor.

Socrates: Do you want me to answer after the manner
of Gorgias, which you would most easily follow?

Meno: Of course I want that.

Socrates: Do you both say there are effluvia of things,
as Empedocles does?—Certainly.

Socrates: And that there are channels through which
the effluvia make their way?—Definitely.

d   *Socrates:* And some effluvia fit some of the channels,
while others are too small or too big?—That is so.

Socrates: And there is something which you call sight?
—There is.

Socrates: From this, "comprehend what I state," as
Pindar said; for color is an effluvium from shapes which
fits the sight and is perceived.

Meno: That seems to me to be an excellent answer,
Socrates.

Socrates: Perhaps it was given in the manner to which
you are accustomed. At the same time I think that you
e can deduce from this answer what sound is, and smell,
and many such things.—Quite so.

Socrates: It is a theatrical answer so it pleases you,
Meno, more than that about shape.—It does.

Socrates: It is not better, son of Alexidemus, but I am
convinced that the other is, and I think you would
agree, if you did not have to go away before the mysteries as you told me yesterday, but could remain and be
initiated.

Meno: I would stay, Socrates, if you could tell me
many things like these.   77

Socrates: I shall certainly not be lacking in eagerness
to tell you such things, both for your sake and my own,
but I may not be able to tell you many. Come now, you
too try to fulfill your promise to me and tell me the nature of virtue as a whole and stop making many out of
one, as jokers say whenever someone breaks something;
but allow virtue to remain whole and sound, and tell b
me what it is, for I have given you examples.

Meno: I think, Socrates, that virtue is, as the poet says,
"to find joy in beautiful things and have power." So I
say that virtue is to desire beautiful things and have the
power to acquire them.

Socrates: Do you mean that the man who desires
beautiful things desires good things?—Most certainly.

Socrates: Do you assume that there are people who
desire bad things, and others who desire good things? c
Do you not think, my good man, that all men desire
good things?

Meno: I do not.

Socrates: But some desire bad things?—Yes.

Socrates: Do you mean that they believe the bad
things to be good, or that they know they are bad and
nevertheless desire them?—I think there are both kinds.

Socrates: Do you think, Meno, that anyone, knowing
that bad things are bad, nevertheless desires them?—I
certainly do.

Socrates: What do you mean by desiring? Is it to secure for oneself?—What else?

Socrates: Does he think that the bad things benefit him
who possesses them, or does he know they harm him? d

Meno: There are some who believe that the bad things
benefit them, others who know that the bad things harm
them.

Socrates: And do you think that those who believe
that bad things benefit them know that they are bad?

Meno: No, that I cannot altogether believe.

Socrates: It is clear then that those who do not know
things to be bad do not desire what is bad, but they desire those things that they believe to be good but that e

are in fact bad. It follows that those who have no knowledge of these things and believe them to be good clearly
desire good things. Is that not so?—It is likely.

Socrates: Well then, those who you say desire bad
things, believing that bad things harm their possessor,
know that they will be harmed by them?—Necessarily.

Socrates: And do they not think that those who are
78 harmed are miserable to the extent that they are harmed?
—That too is inevitable.

Socrates: And that those who are miserable are unhappy?—I think so.

Socrates: Does anyone wish to be miserable and unhappy?—I do not think so, Socrates.

Socrates: No one then wants what is bad, Meno, unless he wants to be such. For what else is being miserable but to desire bad things and secure them?

Meno: You are probably right, Socrates, and no one
b wants what is bad.

Socrates: Were you not saying just now that virtue is
to desire good things and have the power to secure
them?—Yes, I was.

Socrates: The desiring part of this statement is common to everybody, and one man is no better than another in this?—So it appears.

Socrates: Clearly then, if one man is better than another, he must be better at securing them.—Quite so.

Socrates: This then is virtue according to your argu-
c ment, the power of securing good things.

Meno: I think, Socrates, that the case is altogether as
you now understand it.

Socrates: Let us see then whether what you say is true,
for you may well be right. You say that the capacity to
acquire good things is virtue?—I do.

Socrates: And by good things you mean, for example,
health and wealth?

Meno: Yes, and also to acquire gold and silver, also
honors and offices in the city.

Socrates: By good things you do not mean other
goods than these?

Meno: No, but I mean all things of this kind.

d *Socrates:* Very well. According to Meno, the hereditary guest friend of the Great King, virtue is the acquisition of gold and silver. Do you add to this acquiring,
Meno, the words justly and piously, or does it make no
difference to you but even if one secures these things
unjustly, you call it virtue nonetheless?

Meno: Certainly not, Socrates.

Socrates: You would then call it wickedness?—Indeed
I would.

Socrates: It seems then that the acquisition must be
accompanied by justice or moderation or piety or some e
other part of virtue; if it is not, it will not be virtue, even
though it provides good things.

Meno: How could there be virtue without these?

Socrates: Then failing to secure gold and silver, whenever it would not be just to do so, either for oneself or
another, is not this failure to secure them also virtue?

Meno: So it seems.

Socrates: Then to provide these goods would not
be virtue any more than not to provide them, but ap- 79
parently whatever is done with justice will be virtue,
and what is done without anything of the kind is
wickedness.

Meno: I think it must necessarily be as you say.

Socrates: We said a little while ago that each of these
things was a part of virtue, namely, justice and moderation and all such things?—Yes.

Socrates: Then you are playing with me, Meno.
—How so, Socrates?

Socrates: Because I begged you just now not to break
up or fragment virtue, and I gave examples of how you
should answer. You paid no attention, but you tell me
that virtue is to be able to secure good things with jus- b
tice, and justice, you say, is a part of virtue.

Meno: I do.

Socrates: It follows then from what you agree to, that
to act in whatever you do with a part of virtue is virtue,
for you say that justice is a part of virtue, as are all such
qualities. Why do I say this? Because when I begged you
to tell me about virtue as a whole, you are far from
telling me what it is. Rather, you say that every action
is virtue if it is performed with a part of virtue, as if you
had said what virtue is as a whole, so I would already c
know that, even if you fragment it into parts. I think you
must face the same question from the beginning, my
dear Meno, namely, what is virtue, if every action performed with a part of virtue is virtue? For that is what
one is saying when he says that every action performed
with justice is virtue. Do you not think you should face
the same question again, or do you think one knows
what a part of virtue is if one does not know virtue itself?—I do not think so.

Socrates: If you remember, when I was answering you
d about shape, we rejected the kind of answer that tried to
answer in terms still being the subject of inquiry and not
yet agreed upon.—And we were right to reject them.

Socrates: Then surely, my good sir, you must not think,
while the nature of virtue as a whole is still under inquiry, that by answering in terms of the parts of virtue
you can make its nature clear to anyone or make anything else clear by speaking in this way, but only that the
same question must be put to you again—what do you
e take the nature of virtue to be when you say what
you say? Or do you think there is no point in what I
am saying?—I think what you say is right.

Socrates: Answer me again then from the beginning:
What do you and your friend say that virtue is?

Meno: Socrates, before I even met you I used to hear
80 that you are always in a state of perplexity and that you
bring others to the same state, and now I think you are
bewitching and beguiling me, simply putting me under
a spell, so that I am quite perplexed. Indeed, if a joke is
in order, you seem, in appearance and in every other way,
to be like the broad torpedo fish, for it too makes any-
b one who comes close and touches it feel numb, and you
now seem to have had that kind of effect on me, for both
my mind and my tongue are numb, and I have no answer to give you. Yet I have made many speeches about
virtue before large audiences on a thousand occasions,
very good speeches as I thought, but now I cannot even
say what it is. I think you are wise not to sail away from
Athens to go and stay elsewhere, for if you were to behave like this as a stranger in another city, you would be
driven away for practicing sorcery.

Socrates: You are a rascal, Meno, and you nearly deceived me.

Meno: Why so particularly, Socrates?

c *Socrates:* I know why you drew this image of me.

Meno: Why do you think I did?

Socrates: So that I should draw an image of you in return. I know that all handsome men rejoice in images
of themselves; it is to their advantage, for I think that the
images of beautiful people are also beautiful, but I will
draw no image of you in turn. Now if the torpedo fish
is itself numb and so makes others numb, then I resemble it, but not otherwise, for I myself do not have the
answer when I perplex others, but I am more perplexed
than anyone when I cause perplexity in others. So now

I do not know what virtue is; perhaps you knew before d
you contacted me, but now you are certainly like one
who does not know. Nevertheless, I want to examine
and seek together with you what it may be.

Meno: How will you look for it, Socrates, when you
do not know at all what it is? How will you aim to
search for something you do not know at all? If you
should meet with it, how will you know that this is the
thing that you did not know?

Socrates: I know what you want to say, Meno. Do you e
realize what a debater's argument you are bringing up,
that a man cannot search either for what he knows or
for what he does not know? He cannot search for what
he knows—since he knows it, there is no need to
search—nor for what he does not know, for he does not
know what to look for.

Meno: Does that argument not seem sound to you, 81
Socrates?

Socrates: Not to me.

Meno: Can you tell me why?

Socrates: I can. I have heard wise men and women talk
about divine matters . . .

Meno: What did they say?

Socrates: What was, I thought, both true and beautiful.

Meno: What was it, and who were they?

Socrates: The speakers were among the priests and
priestesses whose care it is to be able to give an account
of their practices. Pindar too says it, and many others of b
the divine among our poets. What they say is this; see
whether you think they speak the truth: They say that
the human soul is immortal; at times it comes to an end,
which they call dying; at times it is reborn, but it is never
destroyed, and one must therefore live one's life as piously as possible:

> *Persephone will return to the sun above in the*
> *   ninth year*
> *the souls of those from whom*
> *she will exact punishment for old miseries,*
> *and from these come noble kings,*
> *mighty in strength and greatest in wisdom,*
> *and for the rest of time men will call them sacred heroes.*

As the soul is immortal, has been born often, and has
seen all things here and in the underworld, there is nothing which it has not learned; so it is in no way surpris-

ing that it can recollect the things it knew before, both
d about virtue and other things. As the whole of nature is akin, and the soul has learned everything, nothing prevents a man, after recalling one thing only—a process men call learning—discovering everything else for himself, if he is brave and does not tire of the search, for searching and learning are, as a whole, recollection. We must, therefore, not believe that debater's argument, for it would make us idle, and fainthearted men like to hear
e it, whereas my argument makes them energetic and keen on the search. I trust that this is true, and I want to inquire along with you into the nature of virtue.

Meno: Yes, Socrates, but how do you mean that we do not learn, but that what we call learning is recollection? Can you teach me that this is so?

Socrates: As I said just now, Meno, you are a rascal. You
82 now ask me if I can teach you, when I say there is no teaching but recollection, in order to show me up at once as contradicting myself.

Meno: No, by Zeus, Socrates, that was not my intention when I spoke, but just a habit. If you can somehow show me that things are as you say, please do so.

Socrates: It is not easy, but I am nevertheless willing
b to do my best for your sake. Call one of these many attendants of yours, whichever you like, that I may prove it to you in his case.

Meno: Certainly. You there come forward.

Socrates: Is he a Greek? Does he speak Greek?

Meno: Very much so. He was born in our household.

Socrates: Pay attention then whether you think he is recollecting or learning from me.

Meno: I will pay attention.

Socrates: Tell me now, boy, you know that a square figure is like this?—I do.
c *Socrates:* A square then is a figure in which all these four sides are equal?—Yes indeed.

Socrates: And it also has these lines through the middle equal?[1]—Yes.

Socrates: And such a figure could be larger or smaller? —Certainly.

Socrates: If then this side were two feet, and this other side two feet, how many feet would the whole be? Con-

sider it this way: If it were two feet this way, and only one foot that way, the figure would be once two feet?—Yes.

Socrates: But if it is two feet also that way, it would surely be twice two feet?—Yes.   *d*

Socrates: How many feet is twice two feet? Work it out and tell me.—Four, Socrates.

Socrates: Now we could have another figure twice the size of this one, with the four sides equal like this one.— Yes.

Socrates: How many feet will that be?—Eight.

Socrates: Come now, try to tell me how long each side of this will be. The side of this is two feet. What about each side of the one which is its double?—Obviously, *e* Socrates, it will be twice the length.

Socrates: You see, Meno, that I am not teaching the boy anything, but all I do is question him. And now he thinks he knows the length of the line on which an eight-foot figure is based. Do you agree?

Meno: I do.

Socrates: And does he know?

Meno: Certainly not.

Socrates: He thinks it is a line twice the length?

Meno: Yes.

Socrates: Watch him now recollecting things in order, as one must recollect. Tell me, boy, do you say that a figure double the size is based on a line double the length? Now I mean such a figure as this, not long on one side *83* and short on the other, but equal in every direction like this one, and double the size, that is, eight feet. See whether you still believe that it will be based on a line double the length.—I do.

Socrates: Now the line becomes double its length if we add another of the same length here?—Yes indeed.

---

which also go through the center of the square, namely EF and GH.

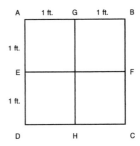

---

1. Socrates draws a square ABCD. The "lines through the middle" are the lines joining the middle of these sides,

Socrates: And the eight-foot square will be based on it, if there are four lines of that length?—Yes.

Socrates: Well, let us draw from it four equal lines, and

b surely that is what you say is the eight-foot square?—Certainly.

Socrates: And within this figure are four squares, each of which is equal to the four-foot square?—Yes.

Socrates: How big is it then? Is it not four times as big?—Of course.

Socrates: Is this square then, which is four times as big, its double?—No, by Zeus.

Socrates: How many times bigger is it?—Four times.

c *Socrates:* Then, my boy, the figure based on a line twice the length is not double but four times as big?—You are right.

Socrates: And four times four is sixteen, is it not?—Yes.

Socrates: On how long a line should the eight-foot square be based? On *this* line we have a square that is four times bigger, do we not?—Yes.

Socrates: Now this four-foot square is based on this line here, half the length?—Yes.

Socrates: Very well. Is the eight-foot square not double this one and half that one?[2]—Yes.

Socrates: Will it not be based on a line longer than this

d one and shorter than that one? Is that not so?—I think so.

Socrates: Good, you answer what you think. And tell me, was this one not two-feet long, and that one four feet?—Yes.

Socrates: The line on which the eight-foot square is based must then be longer than this one of two feet, and shorter than that one of four feet?—It must be.

e *Socrates:* Try to tell me then how long a line you say it is.—Three feet.

Socrates: Then if it is three feet, let us add the half of this one, and it will be three feet? For these are two feet, and the other is one. And here, similarly, these are two feet and that one is one foot, and so the figure you mention comes to be?—Yes.

Socrates: Now if it is three feet this way and three feet that way, will the whole figure be three times three feet?—So it seems.

---

2. I.e., the eight-foot square is double the four-foot square and half the sixteen-foot square—double the square based on a line two feet long and half the square based on a four-foot side.

Socrates: How much is three times three feet?—Nine feet.

Socrates: And the double square was to be how many feet?—Eight.

Socrates: So the eight-foot figure cannot be based on the three-foot line?—Clearly not.

Socrates: But on how long a line? Try to tell us exactly, and if you do not want to work it out, show me 84 from what line.—By Zeus, Socrates, I do not know.

Socrates: You realize, Meno, what point he has reached in his recollection. At first he did not know what the basic line of the eight-foot square was; even now he does not yet know, but then he thought he knew, and answered confidently as if he did know, and he did not think himself at a loss, but now he does think himself at a loss, and as he does not know, neither does he think he knows. b

Meno: That is true.

Socrates: So he is now in a better position with regard to the matter he does not know?

Meno: I agree with that too.

Socrates: Have we done him any harm by making him perplexed and numb as the torpedo fish does?

Meno: I do not think so.

Socrates: Indeed, we have probably achieved something relevant to finding out how matters stand, for now, as he does not know, he would be glad to find out, whereas before he thought he could easily make many fine speeches to large audiences about the square of double size and said that it must have a base twice as long. c

Meno: So it seems.

Socrates: Do you think that before he would have tried to find out that which he thought he knew though he did not, before he fell into perplexity and realized he did not know and longed to know?

Meno: I do not think so, Socrates.

Socrates: Has he then benefited from being numbed?

Meno: I think so.

Socrates: Look then how he will come out of his perplexity while searching along with me. I shall do nothing more than ask questions and not teach him. Watch whether you find me teaching and explaining things to d him instead of asking for his opinion.

Socrates: You tell me, is this not a four-foot figure? You understand?—I do.

Socrates: We add to it this figure which is equal to it?—Yes.

Socrates: And we add this third figure equal to each of them?—Yes.

Socrates: Could we then fill in the space in the corner?—Certainly.[3]

e *Socrates:* So we have these four equal figures?—Yes.
Socrates: Well then, how many times is the whole figure larger than this one?[4]—Four times.

Socrates: But we should have had one that was twice as large, or do you not remember?—I certainly do.

85 *Socrates:* Does not this line from one corner to the other cut each of these figures in two?[5]—Yes.

Socrates: So these are four equal lines which enclose this figure?[6]—They are.

Socrates: Consider now: How large is the figure?—I do not understand.

Socrates: Within these four figures, each line cuts off half of each, does it not?—Yes.

---

3. Socrates now builds up his sixteen-foot square by joining two four-foot squares, then a third, like this:

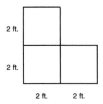

Filling "the space in the corner" will give another four-foot square, which completes the sixteen-foot square containing four four-foot squares.

4. "This one" is any one of the inside squares of four feet.

5. Socrates now draws the diagonals of the four inside squares, namely, FH, HE, EG, and GF, which together form the square GFHE.

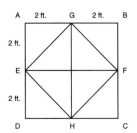

6. I.e., GFHE.

Socrates: How many of this size are there in this figure?[7]—Four.

Socrates: How many in this?[8]—Two.

Socrates: What is the relation of four to two?—Double. b

Socrates: How many feet in this?[9]—Eight.

Socrates: Based on what line?—This one.

Socrates: That is, on the line that stretches from corner to corner of the four-foot figure?—Yes.—Clever men call this the diagonal, so that if diagonal is its name, you say that the double figure would be that based on the diagonal?—Most certainly, Socrates.

Socrates: What do you think, Meno? Has he, in his answers, expressed any opinion that was not his own? c

Meno: No, they were all his own.

Socrates: And yet, as we said a short time ago, he did not know?—That is true.

Socrates: So these opinions were in him, were they not?—Yes.

Socrates: So the man who does not know has within himself true opinions about the things that he does not know?—So it appears.

Socrates: These opinions have now just been stirred up like a dream, but if he were repeatedly asked about these same things in various ways, you know that in the end his knowledge about these things would be as ac- d
curate as anyone's.—It is likely.

Socrates: And he will know it without having been taught but only questioned, and find the knowledge within himself?—Yes.

Socrates: And is not finding knowledge within oneself recollection?—Certainly.

Socrates: Must he not either have at some time acquired the knowledge he now possesses, or else have always possessed it?—Yes.

Socrates: If he always had it, he would always have known. If he acquired it, he cannot have done so in his e
present life. Or has someone taught him geometry? For he will perform in the same way about all geometry, and all other knowledge. Has someone taught him

---

7. Again, GFHE: Socrates is asking how many of the triangles "cut off from inside" there are inside GFHE.

8. I.e., any of the interior squares.

9. GFHE again.

everything? You should know, especially as he has been born and brought up in your house.

Meno: But I know that no one has taught him.

Socrates: Yet he has these opinions, or doesn't he?

Meno: That seems indisputable, Socrates.

86 *Socrates:* If he has not acquired them in his present life, is it not clear that he had them and had learned them at some other time?—It seems so.

Socrates: Then that was the time when he was not a human being?—Yes.

Socrates: If then, during the time he exists and is not a human being he will have true opinions which, when stirred by questioning, become knowledge, will not his soul have learned during all time? For it is clear that during all time he exists, either as a man or not.—So it seems.

b *Socrates:* Then if the truth about reality is always in our soul, the soul would be immortal so that you should always confidently try to seek out and recollect what you do not know at present—that is, what you do not recollect?

Meno: Somehow, Socrates, I think that what you say is right.

Socrates: I think so too, Meno. I do not insist that my argument is right in all other respects, but I would contend at all costs in both word and deed as far as I could that we will be better men, braver and less idle, if we be-
c lieve that one must search for the things one does not know, rather than if we believe that it is not possible to find out what we do not know and that we must not look for it.

Meno: In this too I think you are right, Socrates.

Socrates: Since we are of one mind that one should seek to find out what one does not know, shall we try to find out together what virtue is?

Meno: Certainly. But Socrates, I should be most pleased to investigate and hear your answer to my original question, whether we should try to find out on the
d assumption that virtue is something teachable, or is a natural gift, or in whatever way it comes to men.

Socrates: If I were directing you, Meno, and not only myself, we would not investigate whether virtue is teachable or not before we investigated what virtue itself is. But because you do not even attempt to rule yourself, in order that you may be free, but you try to rule me and do so, I will agree with you—for what can I do? So we must, it appears, inquire into the qualities of

something the nature of which we do not yet know. e However, please relax your rule a little bit for me and agree to investigate whether it is teachable or not by means of a hypothesis. I mean the way geometers often carry on their investigations. For example, if they are asked whether a specific area can be inscribed in the 87 form of a triangle within a given circle, one of them might say: "I do not yet know whether that area has that property, but I think I have, as it were, a hypothesis that is of use for the problem, namely this: If that area is such that when one has applied it as a rectangle to the given straight line in the circle, it is deficient by a figure similar to the very figure which is applied, then I think one b alternative results, whereas another results if it is impossible for this to happen. So, by using this hypothesis, I am willing to tell you what results with regard to inscribing it in the circle—that is, whether it is impossible or not." So let us speak about virtue also, since we do not know either what it is or what qualities it possesses, and let us investigate whether it is teachable or not by means of a hypothesis, and say this: Among the things existing in the soul, of what sort is virtue, that it should be teachable or not? First, if it is another sort than knowledge, is it teachable or not, or, as we were just saying, recollectable? Let it make no difference to us which term we use: Is it c teachable? Or is it plain to anyone that men cannot be taught anything but knowledge?—I think so.

Socrates: But, if virtue is a kind of knowledge, it is clear that it could be taught.—Of course.

Socrates: We have dealt with that question quickly, that if it is of one kind it can be taught; if it is of a different kind, it cannot.—We have indeed.

Socrates: The next point to consider seems to be whether virtue is knowledge or something else.—That does seem to be the next point to consider.   d

Socrates: Well now, do we say that virtue is itself something good, and will this hypothesis stand firm for us, that it is something good?—Of course.

Socrates: If then there is anything else good that is different and separate from knowledge, virtue might well not be a kind of knowledge; but if there is nothing good that knowledge does not encompass, we would be right to suspect that it is a kind of knowledge.—That is so.

Socrates: Surely virtue makes us good?—Yes.   e

Socrates: And if we are good, we are beneficent, for all that is good is beneficial. Is that not so?—Yes.

Socrates: So virtue is something beneficial?

Meno: That necessarily follows from what has been agreed.

Socrates: Let us then examine what kinds of things benefit us, taking them up one by one: health, we say, and strength, and beauty, and also wealth. We say that these things, and others of the same kind, benefit us, do we not?—We do.

Socrates: Yet we say that these same things also some-88 times harm one. Do you agree or not?—I do.

Socrates: Look then, what directing factor determines in each case whether these things benefit or harm us? Is it not the right use of them that benefits us, and the wrong use that harms us?—Certainly.

Socrates: Let us now look at the qualities of the soul. There is something you call moderation, and justice, courage, mental quickness, memory, munificence, and all such things?—There is.

b *Socrates:* Consider whichever of these you believe not to be knowledge but different from it; do they not at times harm us, at other times benefit us? Courage, for example, when it is not wisdom but like a kind of recklessness: when a man is reckless without understanding, he is harmed; when with understanding, he is benefited.—Yes.

Socrates: The same is true of moderation and mental quickness; when they are learned and disciplined with understanding they are beneficial, but without understanding they are harmful?—Very much so.

c *Socrates:* Therefore, in a word, all that the soul undertakes and endures, if directed by wisdom, ends in happiness, but if directed by ignorance, it ends in the opposite?—That is likely.

Socrates: If then virtue is something in the soul and it must be beneficial, it must be knowledge, since all the qualities of the soul are in themselves neither beneficial d nor harmful, but accompanied by wisdom or folly they become harmful or beneficial. This argument shows that virtue, being beneficial, must be a kind of wisdom. —I agree.

Socrates: Furthermore, those other things we were mentioning just now, wealth and the like, are at times good and times harmful. Just as for the rest of the soul the direction of wisdom makes things beneficial, but harmful if directed by folly, so in these cases, if the soul e uses and directs them right it makes them beneficial, but bad use makes them harmful?—Quite so.

Socrates: The wise soul directs them right, the foolish soul wrongly?—That is so.

Socrates: So one may say this about everything; all other human activities depend on the soul, and those of the soul itself depend on wisdom if they are to be good. According to this argument the beneficial would be wis-89 dom, and we say that virtue is beneficial?—Certainly.

Socrates: Then we say that virtue is wisdom, either the whole or a part of it?

Meno: What you say, Socrates, seems to me quite right.

Socrates: Then, if that is so, the good are not so by nature?—I do not think they are.

Socrates: For if they were, this would follow: If the good were so by nature, we would have people who knew b which among the young were by nature good; we would take those whom they had pointed out and guard them in the Acropolis, sealing them up there much more carefully than gold so that no one could corrupt them, and when they reached maturity they would be useful to their cities.—Reasonable enough, Socrates.

Socrates: Since the good are not good by nature, does learning make them so?

Meno: Necessarily, as I now think, Socrates, and clearly, on our hypothesis, if virtue is knowledge, it can be taught.

Socrates: Perhaps, by Zeus, but may it be that we were not right to agree to this?

Meno: Yet it seemed to be right at the time.

Socrates: We should not only think it right at the time, but also now and in the future if it is to be at all sound.

Meno: What is the difficulty? What do you have in mind that you do not like about it and doubt that virtue d is knowledge?

Socrates: I will tell you, Meno. I am not saying that it is wrong to say that virtue is teachable if it is knowledge, but look whether it is reasonable of me to doubt whether it is knowledge. Tell me this: If not only virtue but anything whatever can be taught, should there not be of necessity people who teach it and people who learn it?—I think so.

Socrates: Then again, if on the contrary there are no e teachers or learners of something, we should be right to assume that the subject cannot be taught?

Meno: Quite so, but do you think that there are no teachers of virtue?

Socrates: I have often tried to find out whether there were any teachers of it, but in spite of all my efforts I cannot find any. And yet I have searched for them with the help of many people, especially those whom I believed to be most experienced in this matter. And now, Meno, Anytus here has opportunely come to sit down 90 by us. Let us share our search with him. It would be reasonable for us to do so, for Anytus, in the first place, is the son of Anthemion, a man of wealth and wisdom, who did not become rich automatically or as the result of a gift like Ismenias the Theban, who recently acquired the possessions of Polycrates, but through his own wisdom and efforts. Further, he did not seem to be b an arrogant or puffed up or offensive citizen in other ways, but he was a well-mannered and well-behaved man. Also he gave our friend here a good upbringing and education, as the majority of Athenians believe, for they are electing him to the highest offices. It is right then to look for the teachers of virtue with the help of men such as he, whether there are any and if so who they are. Therefore, Anytus, please join me and your guest friend Meno here, in our inquiry as to who are the teachers of virtue. Look at it in this way: If we c wanted Meno to become a good physician, to what teachers would we send him? Would we not send him to the physicians?

Anytus: Certainly.

Socrates: And if we wanted him to be a good shoemaker, to shoemakers?—Yes.

Socrates: And so with other pursuits?—Certainly.

Socrates: Tell me again on this same topic, like this: We say that we would be right to send him to the physi- d cians if we want him to become a physician; whenever we say that, we mean that it would be reasonable to send him to those who practice the craft rather than to those who do not, and to those who exact fees for this very practice and have shown themselves to be teachers of anyone who wishes to come to them and learn. Is it not with this in mind that we would be right to send him? —Yes.

Socrates: And the same is true about flute-playing and the other crafts? It would be very foolish for those who e want to make someone a flute-player to refuse to send him to those who profess to teach the craft and make money at it, but to send him to make trouble for others by seeking to learn from those who do not claim to be teachers or have a single pupil in that subject which we want the one we send to learn from them? Do you not

think it very unreasonable to do so?—By Zeus, I do, and also very ignorant.

Socrates: Quite right. However, you can now deliberate with me about our guest friend Meno here. He has been telling me for some time, Anytus, that he longs to acquire that wisdom and virtue which enables men to 91 manage their households and their cities well, to take care of their parents, to know how to welcome and to send away both citizens and strangers as a good man should. Consider to whom we should be right to send b him to learn this virtue. Or is it obvious in view of what was said just now that we should send him to those who profess to be teachers of virtue and have shown themselves to be available to any Greek who wishes to learn, and for this fix a fee and exact it?

Anytus: And who do you say these are, Socrates?

Socrates: You surely know yourself that they are those whom men call sophists.

Anytus: By Heracles, hush, Socrates. May no one of my household or friends, whether citizen or stranger, c be mad enough to go to these people and be harmed by them, for they clearly cause the ruin and corruption of their followers.

Socrates: How do you mean, Anytus? Are these people, alone of those who claim the knowledge to benefit one, so different from the others that they not only do not benefit what one entrusts to them but on the contrary corrupt it, even though they obviously expect to make d money from the process? I find I cannot believe you, for I know that one man, Protagoras, made more money from this knowledge of his than Phidias who made such notably fine works, and ten other sculptors. Surely what you say is extraordinary, if those who mend old sandals and restore clothes would be found out within the month if they returned the clothes and sandals in a worse e state than they received them; if they did this they would soon die of starvation, but the whole of Greece has not noticed for forty years that Protagoras corrupts those who frequent him and sends them away in a worse moral condition than he received them. I believe that he was nearly seventy when he died and had practiced his craft for forty years. During all that time to this very day his reputation has stood high; and not only Protagoras but a great many 92 others, some born before him and some still alive today. Are we to say that you maintain that they deceive and harm the young knowingly, or that they themselves are not aware of it? Are we to deem those whom some people consider the wisest of men to be so mad as that?

Anytus: They are far from being mad, Socrates. It is much rather those among the young who pay their fees who are mad, and even more the relatives who entrust their young to them and most of all the cities who allow them to come in and do not drive out any citizen or stranger who attempts to behave in this manner.

Socrates: Has some sophist wronged you, Anytus, or why are you so hard on them?

Anytus: No, by Zeus, I have never met one of them, nor would I allow any one of my people to do so.

Socrates: Are you then altogether without any experience of these men?

Anytus: And may I remain so.

Socrates: How then, my good sir, can you know whether there is any good in their instruction or not, if you are altogether without experience of it?

Anytus: Easily, for I know who they are, whether I have experience of them or not.

Socrates: Perhaps you are a wizard, Anytus, for I wonder, from what you yourself say, how else you know about these things. However, let us not try to find out who the men are whose company would make Meno wicked—let them be the sophists if you like—but tell us, and benefit your family friend here by telling him, to whom he should go in so large a city to acquire, to any worthwhile degree, the virtue I was just now describing.

Anytus: Why did you not tell him yourself?

Socrates: I did mention those whom I thought to be teachers of it, but you say I am wrong, and perhaps you are right. You tell him in your turn to whom among the Athenians he should go. Tell him the name of anyone you want.

Anytus: Why give him the name of one individual? Any Athenian gentleman he may meet, if he is willing to be persuaded, will make him a better man than the sophists would.

Socrates: And have these gentlemen become virtuous automatically, without learning from anyone, and are they able to teach others what they themselves never learned?

Anytus: I believe that these men have learned from those who were gentlemen before them; or do you not think that there are many good men in this city?

Socrates: I believe, Anytus, that there are many men here who are good at public affairs, and that there have been as many in the past, but have they been good teachers of their own virtue? That is the point we are discussing, not whether there are good men here or not, or whether there have been in the past, but we have been investigating for some time whether virtue can be taught. And in the course of that investigation we are inquiring whether the good men of today and of the past knew how to pass on to another the virtue they themselves possessed, or whether a man cannot pass it on or receive it from another. This is what Meno and I have been investigating for some time. Look at it this way, from what you yourself have said. Would you not say that Themistocles was a good man?—Yes. Even the best of men.

Socrates: And therefore a good teacher of his own virtue if anyone was?

Anytus: I think so, if he wanted to be.

Socrates: But do you think he did not want some other people to be worthy men, and especially his own son? Or do you think he begrudged him this, and deliberately did not pass on to him his own virtue? Have you not heard that Themistocles taught his son Cleophantus to be a good horseman? He could remain standing upright on horseback and shoot javelins from that position and do many other remarkable things which his father had him taught and made skillful at, all of which required good teachers. Have you not heard this from your elders?—I have.

Socrates: So one could not blame the poor natural talents of the son for his failure in virtue?—Perhaps not.

Socrates: But have you ever heard anyone, young or old, say that Cleophantus, the son of Themistocles, was a good and wise man at the same pursuits as his father? —Never.

Socrates: Are we to believe that he wanted to educate his son in those other things but not to do better than his neighbors in that skill which he himself possessed, if indeed virtue can be taught?—Perhaps not, by Zeus.

Socrates: And yet he was, as you yourself agree, among the best teachers of virtue in the past. Let us consider another man, Aristides, the son of Lysimachus. Do you not agree that he was good?—I very definitely do.

Socrates: He too gave his own son Lysimachus the best Athenian education in matters which are the business of teachers, and do you think he made him a better man than anyone else? For you have been in his company and seen the kind of man he is. Or take Pericles, a man of such magnificent wisdom. You know that he brought up two sons, Paralus and Xanthippus?—I know.

Socrates: You also know that he taught them to be as good horsemen as any Athenian, that he educated them in the arts, in gymnastics, and in all else that was a matter of skill not to be inferior to anyone, but did he not want to make them good men? I think he did, but this could not be taught. And lest you think that only a few most inferior Athenians are incapable in this respect, re- c flect that Thucydides too brought up two sons, Melesias and Stephanus, that he educated them well in all other things. They were the best wrestlers in Athens— he entrusted the one to Xanthias and the other to Eudorus, who were thought to be the best wrestlers of the day, or do you not remember?

Anytus: I remember I have heard that said.

d   *Socrates:* It is surely clear that he would not have taught his boys what it costs money to teach, but have failed to teach them what costs nothing—making them good men—if that could be taught? Or was Thucydides perhaps an inferior person who had not many friends among the Athenians and the allies? He belonged to a great house; he had great influence in the city and among the other Greeks, so that if virtue could be taught he would have found the man who could make his sons good men, be it a citizen or a stranger, if he himself did e not have the time because of his public concerns. But, friend Anytus, virtue can certainly not be taught.

Anytus: I think, Socrates, that you easily speak ill of people. I would advise you, if you will listen to me, to be careful. Perhaps also in another city, and certainly here, it is easier to injure people than to benefit them. 95 I think you know that yourself.

Socrates: I think, Meno, that Anytus is angry, and I am not at all surprised. He thinks, to begin with, that I am slandering those men, and then he believes himself to be one of them. If he ever realizes what slander is, he will cease from anger, but he does not know it now. You tell me, are there not worthy men among your people? —Certainly.

Socrates: Well now, are they willing to offer themselves b to the young as teachers? Do they agree they are teachers, and that virtue can be taught?

Meno: No, by Zeus, Socrates, but sometimes you would hear them say that it can be taught, at other times, that it cannot.

Socrates: Should we say that they are teachers of this subject, when they do not even agree on this point?— I do not think so, Socrates.

Socrates: Further, do you think that these sophists, who alone profess to be so, are teachers of virtue?

Meno: I admire this most in Gorgias, Socrates, that you would never hear him promising this. Indeed, he ridicules c the others when he hears them making this claim. He thinks one should make people clever speakers.

Socrates: You do not think then that the sophists are teachers?

Meno: I cannot tell, Socrates; like most people, at times I think they are; at other times I think that they are not.

Socrates: Do you know that not only you and the other public men at times think that it can be taught, at other times that it cannot, but that the poet Theognis d says the same thing?—Where?

Socrates: In his elegiacs: "Eat and drink with these men, and keep their company. Please those whose power is great, for you will learn goodness from the good. If e you mingle with bad men you will lose even what wit you possess." You see that here he speaks as if virtue can be taught?—So it appears.

Socrates: Elsewhere, he changes somewhat: "If this could be done," he says, "and intelligence could be instilled," somehow those who could do this "would collect large and numerous fees," and further: "Never would a bad son be born of a good father, for he would be per- suaded by wise words, but you will never make a bad man 96 good by teaching." You realize that the poet is contradicting himself on the same subject?—He seems to be.

Socrates: Can you mention any other subject of which those who claim to be teachers not only are not recognized to be teachers of others but are not recognized to have knowledge of it themselves, and are thought to be b poor in the very matter which they profess to teach? Or any other subject of which those who are recognized as worthy teachers at one time say it can be taught and at other times that it cannot? Would you say that people who are so confused about a subject can be effective teachers of it?—No, by Zeus, I would not.

Socrates: If then neither the sophists nor the worthy people themselves are teachers of this subject, clearly there would be no others?—I do not think there are.

Socrates: If there are no teachers, neither are there c pupils?—As you say.

Socrates: And we agreed that a subject that has neither teachers nor pupils is not teachable?—We have so agreed.

Socrates: Now there seem to be no teachers of virtue anywhere?—That is so.

Socrates: If there are no teachers, there are no learners?—That seems so.

Socrates: Then virtue cannot be taught?

d *Meno:* Apparently not, if we have investigated this correctly. I certainly wonder, Socrates, whether there are no good men either, or in what way good men come to be.

Socrates: We are probably poor specimens, you and I, Meno. Gorgias has not adequately educated you, nor Prodicus me. We must then at all costs turn our atten-
e tion to ourselves and find someone who will in some way make us better. I say this in view of our recent investigation, for it is ridiculous that we failed to see that it is not only under the direction of knowledge that men succeed in their affairs, and that is perhaps why the knowledge of how good men come to be escapes us.

Meno: How do you mean, Socrates?

Socrates: I mean this: We were right to agree that good men must be beneficent, and that this could not be otherwise. Is that not so?—Yes.

Socrates: And that they will be beneficent if they give us correct direction in our affairs. To this too we were
97 right to agree?—Yes.

Socrates: But that one cannot give correct direction if one does not have knowledge; to this our agreement is likely to be incorrect.—How do you mean?

Socrates: I will tell you. A man who knew the way to Larissa, or anywhere else you like, and went there and directed others would surely lead them well and correctly?—Certainly.

Socrates: What if someone had had a correct opinion
b as to which was the way but had not gone there nor indeed had knowledge of it, would he not also lead correctly?—Certainly.

Socrates: And as long as he has the right opinion about that of which the other has knowledge, he will not be a worse guide than the one who knows, as he has a true opinion, though not knowledge.—In no way worse.

Socrates: So true opinion is in no way a worse guide for correct action than knowledge. It is this that we omitted in our investigation of the nature of virtue,
c when we said that only knowledge can guide correct action, for true opinion can do so also.—So it seems.

Socrates: So correct opinion is no less useful than knowledge?

Meno: Yes, to this extent, Socrates. But the man who has knowledge will always succeed, whereas he who has true opinion will only succeed at times.

Socrates: How do you mean? Will he who has the right opinion not always succeed, as long as his opinion is right?

Meno: That appears to be so of necessity, and it makes me wonder, Socrates, this being the case, why knowledge is prized far more highly than right opinion, and *d*
why they are different.

Socrates: Do you know why you wonder, or shall I tell you?—By all means tell me.

Socrates: It is because you have paid no attention to the statues of Daedalus, but perhaps there are none in Thessaly.

Meno: What do you have in mind when you say this?

Socrates: That they too run away and escape if one does not tie them down but remain in place if tied *e*
down.—So what?

Socrates: To acquire an untied work of Daedalus is not worth much, like acquiring a runaway slave, for it does not remain, but it is worth much if tied down, for his works are very beautiful. What am I thinking of when I say this? True opinions. For true opinions, as long as they remain, are a fine thing and all they do is good, but they are not willing to remain long, and they escape *98*
from a man's mind, so that they are not worth much until one ties them down by [giving] an account of the reason why. And that, Meno, my friend, is recollection, as we previously agreed. After they are tied down, in the first place they become knowledge, and then they remain in place. That is why knowledge is prized higher than correct opinion, and knowledge differs from correct opinion in being tied down.

Meno: Yes, by Zeus, Socrates, it seems to be something like that.

Socrates: Indeed, I too speak as one who does not have *b*
knowledge but is guessing. However, I certainly do not think I am guessing that right opinion is a different thing from knowledge. If I claim to know anything else —and I would make that claim about few things—I would put this down as one of the things I know.—Rightly so, Socrates.

Socrates: Well then, is it not correct that when true opinion guides the course of every action, it does no worse than knowledge?—I think you are right in this too.

c   *Socrates:* Correct opinion is then neither inferior to knowledge nor less useful in directing actions, nor is the man who has it less so than he who has knowledge.—That is so.

Socrates: And we agreed that the good man is beneficent.—Yes.

Socrates: Since then it is not only through knowledge but also through right opinion that men are good, *d* and beneficial to their cities when they are, and neither knowledge nor true opinion come to men by nature but are acquired—or do you think either of these comes by nature?—I do not think so.

Socrates: Then if they do not come by nature, men are not so by nature either.—Surely not.

Socrates: As goodness does not come by nature, we inquired next whether it could be taught.—Yes.

Socrates: We thought it could be taught, if it was knowledge?—Yes.

Socrates: And that it was knowledge if it could be taught?—Quite so.

Socrates: And that if there were teachers of it, it could *e* be taught, but if there were not, it was not teachable?—That is so.

Socrates: And then we agreed that there were no teachers of it?—We did.

Socrates: So we agreed that it was neither teachable nor knowledge?—Quite so.

Socrates: But we certainly agree that virtue is a good thing?—Yes.

Socrates: And that which guides correctly is both useful and good?—Certainly.

Socrates: And that only these two things, true belief and *99* knowledge, guide correctly, and that if a man possesses these he gives correct guidance. The things that turn out right by some chance are not due to human guidance, but where there is correct human guidance it is due to two things, true belief or knowledge.—I think that is so.

Socrates: Now because it cannot be taught, virtue no longer seems to be knowledge?—It seems not.

Socrates: So one of the two good and useful things has *b* been excluded, and knowledge is not the guide in public affairs.—I do not think so.

Socrates: So it is not by some kind of wisdom, or by being wise, that such men lead their cities, those such as

Themistocles and those mentioned by Anytus just now? That is the reason why they cannot make others be like themselves, because it is not knowledge which makes them what they are.

Meno: It is likely to be as you say, Socrates.

Socrates: Therefore, if it is not through knowledge, the only alternative is that it is through right opinion that statesmen follow the right course for their cities. As re- *c* gards knowledge, they are no different from soothsayers and prophets. They too say many true things when inspired, but they have no knowledge of what they are saying.—That is probably so.

Socrates: And so, Meno, is it right to call divine these men who, without any understanding, are right in much that is of importance in what they say and do?—Certainly.

Socrates: We should be right to call divine also those soothsayers and prophets whom we just mentioned, and all the poets, and we should call no less divine and inspired those public men who are no less under the gods' *d* influence and possession, as their speeches lead to success in many important matters, though they have no knowledge of what they are saying.—Quite so.

Socrates: Women too, Meno, call good men divine, and the Spartans, when they eulogize someone, say "This man is divine."

Meno: And they appear to be right, Socrates, though *e* perhaps Anytus here will be annoyed with you for saying so.

Socrates: I do not mind that; we shall talk to him again, but if we were right in the way in which we spoke and investigated in this whole discussion, virtue would be neither an inborn quality nor taught, but comes to those who possess it as a gift from the gods which is not ac- *100* companied by understanding, unless there is someone among our statesmen who can make another into a statesman. If there were one, he could be said to be among the living as Homer said Tiresias was among the dead, namely, that "he alone retained his wits while the others flitted about like shadows." In the same manner such a man would, as far as virtue is concerned, here also be the only true reality compared, as it were, with shadows.

Meno: I think that is an excellent way to put it, *b* Socrates.

Socrates: It follows from this reasoning, Meno, that virtue appears to be present in those of us who may possess it as a gift from the gods. We shall have clear knowledge of this when, before we investigate how it comes to be present in men, we first try to find out what virtue in itself is. But now the time has come for me to go. You convince your guest friend Anytus here of these very things of which you have yourself been convinced, in order that he may be more amenable. If you succeed, you will also confer a benefit upon the Athenians.

Plato

The Myth of the Cave An allegory for Socrates

Book VII

[...C]ompare the effect of education and of the lack of it on our nature to an experience like this: Imagine human beings living in an underground, cavelike dwelling, with an entrance a long way up, which is both open to the light and as wide as the cave itself. They've been there since childhood, fixed in the same place, with their necks and legs fettered, able to see only in front of them, because their bonds prevent them from turning their heads around. *b* Light is provided by a fire burning far above and behind them. Also behind them, but on higher ground, there is a path stretching between them and the fire. Imagine that along this path a low wall has been built, like the screen in front of puppeteers above which they show their puppets.

I'm imagining it.

Then also imagine that there are people along the wall, carrying all kinds of artifacts that project above it *c* —statues of people and other animals, made out of stone, wood, and every material. And, as you'd expect, *515* some of the carriers are talking, and some are silent.

It's a strange image you're describing, and strange prisoners.

They're like us. Do you suppose, first of all, that these prisoners see anything of themselves and one another besides the shadows that the fire casts on the wall in front of them?

How could they, if they have to keep their heads motionless throughout life? *b*

What about the things being carried along the wall? Isn't the same true of them?

Of course.

And if they could talk to one another, don't you think they'd suppose that the names they used applied to the things they see passing before them?

They'd have to.

And what if their prison also had an echo from the wall facing them? Don't you think they'd believe that the shadows passing in front of them were talking whenever one of the carriers passing along the wall was doing so?

I certainly do.

Then the prisoners would in every way believe that the truth is nothing other than the shadows of those *c* artifacts.

They must surely believe that.

Consider, then, what being released from their bonds and cured of their ignorance would naturally be like, if something like this came to pass. When one of them was freed and suddenly compelled to stand up, turn his head, walk, and look up toward the light, he'd be pained and dazzled and unable to see the things whose shadows he'd seen before. What do you think he'd say, if we told him that what he'd seen before was inconsequen- *d* tial, but that now—because he is a bit closer to the things that are and is turned towards things that are more—he sees more correctly? Or, to put it another way, if we pointed to each of the things passing by, asked

From Plato, *Republic,* translated by G. M. A. Grube, revised by C. D. C. Reeve (Indianapolis: Hackett Publishing Company, 1992). Reprinted by permission of the publisher.

him what each of them is, and compelled him to answer, don't you think he'd be at a loss and that he'd believe that the things he saw earlier were truer than the ones he was now being shown?

Much truer.

And if someone compelled him to look at the light itself, wouldn't his eyes hurt, and wouldn't he turn
e around and flee towards the things he's able to see, believing that they're really clearer than the ones he's being shown?

He would.

And if someone dragged him away from there by force, up the rough, steep path, and didn't let him go until he had dragged him into the sunlight, wouldn't he be pained and irritated at being treated that way? And when he came into the light, with the sun filling his
516 eyes, wouldn't he be unable to see a single one of the things now said to be true?

He would be unable to see them, at least at first.

I suppose, then, that he'd need time to get adjusted before he could see things in the world above. At first, he'd see shadows most easily, then images of men and other things in water, then the things themselves. Of these, he'd be able to study the things in the sky and the
b sky itself more easily at night, looking at the light of the stars and the moon, than during the day, looking at the sun and the light of the sun.

Of course.

Finally, I suppose, he'd be able to see the sun, not images of it in water or some alien place, but the sun itself, in its own place, and be able to study it.

Necessarily so.

And at this point he would infer and conclude that the sun provides the seasons and the years, governs
c everything in the visible world, and is in some way the cause of all the things that he used to see.

It's clear that would be his next step.

What about when he reminds himself of his first dwelling place, his fellow prisoners, and what passed for wisdom there? Don't you think that he'd count himself happy for the change and pity the others?

Certainly.

And if there had been any honors, praises, or prizes among them for the one who was sharpest at identifying the shadows as they passed by and who best remembered
d which usually came earlier, which later, and which si-

multaneously, and who could thus best divine the future, do you think that our man would desire these rewards or envy those among the prisoners who were honored and held power? Instead, wouldn't he feel, with Homer, that he'd much prefer to "work the earth as a serf to another, one without possessions," and go through any sufferings, rather than share their opinions and live as they do?

I suppose he would rather suffer anything than live *e* like that.

Consider this too. If this man went down into the cave again and sat down in his same seat, wouldn't his eyes—coming suddenly out of the sun like that—be filled with darkness?

They certainly would.

And before his eyes had recovered—and the adjustment would not be quick—while his vision was still dim, if he had to compete again with the perpetual pris- *517* oners in recognizing the shadows, wouldn't he invite ridicule? Wouldn't it be said of him that he'd returned from his upward journey with his eyesight ruined and that it isn't worthwhile even to try to travel upward? And, as for anyone who tried to free them and lead them upward, if they could somehow get their hands on him, wouldn't they kill him?

They certainly would.

This whole image, Glaucon, must be fitted together with what we said before. The visible realm should be *b* likened to the prison dwelling, and the light of the fire inside it to the power of the sun. And if you interpret the upward journey and the study of things above as the upward journey of the soul to the intelligible realm, you'll grasp what I hope to convey, since that is what you wanted to hear about. Whether it's true or not, only the god knows. But this is how I see it: In the knowable realm, the form of the good is the last thing to be seen, and it is reached only with difficulty. Once one has seen it, however, one must conclude that it is the cause of all that is correct and beautiful in anything, that it produces both light and its source in the visible realm, and that in *c* the intelligible realm it controls and provides truth and understanding, so that anyone who is to act sensibly in private or public must see it.

I have the same thought, at least as far as I'm able.

Come, then, share with me this thought also: It isn't surprising that the ones who get to this point are unwilling to occupy themselves with human affairs and that

their souls are always pressing upwards, eager to spend their time above, for, after all, this is surely what we'd ex-
d pect, if indeed things fit the image I described before.

It is.

What about what happens when someone **turns** from divine study to the evils of human life? Do you think it's surprising, since his sight is still dim, and he hasn't yet become accustomed to the darkness around him, that he behaves awkwardly and appears completely ridiculous if he's compelled, either in the courts or elsewhere, to contend about the shadows of justice or the statues of which they are the shadows and to dispute about the way these things are understood by people
e who have never seen justice itself?

That's not surprising at all.

No, it isn't. But anyone with any understanding
518 would remember that the eyes may be confused in two ways and from two causes, namely, when they've come from the light into the darkness *and* when they've come from the darkness into the light. Realizing that the same applies to the soul, when someone sees a soul disturbed and unable to see something, he won't laugh mindlessly, but he'll take into consideration whether it has come from a brighter life and is dimmed through not having yet become accustomed to the dark or whether it has come from greater ignorance into greater light and is dazzled by the increased brilliance. Then he'll declare the first soul happy in its experience and life, and he'll pity the latter—but even if he chose to make fun of it,
b at least he'd be less ridiculous than if he laughed at a soul that has come from the light above.

What you say is very reasonable.

If that's true, then here's what we must think about these matters: Education isn't what some people declare it to be, namely, putting knowledge into souls that lack
c it, like putting sight into blind eyes.

They do say that.

But our present discussion, on the other hand, shows that the power to learn is present in everyone's soul and that the instrument with which each learns is like an eye that cannot be turned around from darkness to light without turning the whole body. This instrument cannot be turned around from that which is coming into being without turning the whole soul until it is able to study that which is and the brightest thing that is,
d namely, the one we call the good. Isn't that right?

Yes.

Then education is the craft concerned with doing this very thing, this turning around, and with how the soul can most easily and effectively be made to do it. It isn't the craft of putting sight into the soul. Education takes for granted that sight is there but that it isn't turned the right way or looking where it ought to look, and it tries to redirect it appropriately.

So it seems.

Now, it looks as though the other so-called virtues of the soul are akin to those of the body, for they really aren't there beforehand but are added later by habit and *e* practice. However, the virtue of reason seems to belong above all to something more divine, which never loses its power but is either useful and beneficial or useless and harmful, depending on the way it is turned. Or have *519* you never noticed this about people who are said to be vicious but clever, how keen the vision of their little souls is and how sharply it distinguishes the things it is turned towards? This shows that its sight isn't inferior but rather is forced to serve evil ends, so that the sharper it sees, the more evil it accomplishes.

Absolutely.

However, if a nature of this sort had been hammered at from childhood and freed from the bonds of kinship with becoming, which have been fastened to it by feasting, greed, and other such pleasures and which, like leaden weights, pull its vision downwards—if, being rid of these, *b* it turned to look at true things, then I say that the same soul of the same person would see these most sharply, just as it now does the things it is presently turned towards.

Probably so.

And what about the uneducated who have no experience of truth? Isn't it likely—indeed, doesn't it follow necessarily from what was said before—that they will never adequately govern a city? But neither would those who've been allowed to spend their whole lives being educated. The former would fail because they don't *c* have a single goal at which all their actions, public and private, inevitably aim; the latter would fail because they'd refuse to act, thinking that they had settled while still alive in the faraway Isles of the Blessed.

That's true.

It is our task to compel the best natures to reach the study we said before is the most important, namely, to make the ascent and see the good. But when they've *d* made it and looked sufficiently, we mustn't allow them to do what they're allowed to do today.

What's that?

To stay there and refuse to go down again to the prisoners in the cave and share their labors and honors, whether they are of less worth or of greater.

Then are we to do them an injustice by making them live a worse life when they could live a better one?

You are forgetting again that it isn't the law's concern *e* to make any one class in the city outstandingly happy but to contrive to spread happiness throughout the city by bringing the citizens into harmony with each other through persuasion or compulsion and by making them share with each other the benefits that each class can confer on the community. The law produces such 520 people in the city, not in order to allow them to turn in whatever direction they want, but to make use of them to bind the city together.

That's true, I had forgotten.

Observe, then, Glaucon, that we won't be doing an injustice to those who've become philosophers in our city and that what we'll say to them, when we compel them to guard and care for the others, will be just. We'll say: "When people like you come to be in other cities, they're justified in not sharing in their city's labors, for *b* they've grown there spontaneously, against the will of the constitution. And what grows of its own accord and owes no debt for its upbringing has justice on its side when it isn't keen to pay anyone for that upbringing. But we've made you kings in our city and leaders of the swarm, as it were, both for yourselves and for the rest of the city. You're better and more completely educated than the others and are better able to share in both types *c* of life. Therefore each of you in turn must go down to live in the common dwelling place of the others and grow accustomed to seeing in the dark. When you are used to it, you'll see vastly better than the people there. And because you've seen the truth about fine, just, and good things, you'll know each image for what it is and also that of which it is the image. Thus, for you and for us, the city will be governed, not like the majority of cities nowadays, by people who fight over shadows and struggle against one another in order to rule—as if that were a great good—but by people who are awake rather than dreaming, for the truth is surely this: A city whose

prospective rulers are least eager to rule must of neces- *d* sity be most free from civil war, whereas a city with the opposite kind of rulers is governed in the opposite way."

Absolutely.

Then do you think that those we've nurtured will disobey us and refuse to share the labors of the city, each in turn, while living the greater part of their time with one another in the pure realm?

It isn't possible, for we'll be giving just orders to just people. Each of them will certainly go to rule as to some- *e* thing compulsory, however, which is exactly the opposite of what's done by those who now rule in each city.

This is how it is. If you can find a way of life that's better than ruling for the prospective rulers, your well-governed city will become a possibility, for only in it will *521* the truly rich rule—not those who are rich in gold but those who are rich in the wealth that the happy must have, namely, a good and rational life. But if beggars hungry for private goods go into public life, thinking that the good is there for the seizing, then the well-governed city is impossible, for then ruling is something fought over, and this civil and domestic war destroys these people and the rest of the city as well.

That's very true.

Can you name any life that despises political rule be- *b* sides that of the true philosopher?

No, by god, I can't.

But surely it is those who are not lovers of ruling who must rule, for if they don't, the lovers of it, who are rivals, will fight over it.

Of course.

Then who will you compel to become guardians of the city, if not those who have the best understanding of what matters for good government and who have other honors than political ones, and a better life as well?

No one.

Do you want us to consider now how such people will come to be in our city and how—just as some are *c* said to have gone up from Hades to the gods—we'll lead them up to the light?

Of course I do.

This isn't, it seems, a matter of tossing a coin, but of turning a soul from a day that is a kind of night to the true day—the ascent to what is, which we say is true philosophy. [. . .]

Immanuel Kant

The Nature of Knowledge

B1

Introduction
[Second Edition]

I. On the Distinction between Pure and Empirical Cognition

There can be no doubt that all our cognition begins with experience. For what else might rouse our cognitive power to its operation if objects stirring our senses did not do so? In part these objects by themselves bring about presentations. In part they set in motion our understanding's activity, by which it compares these presentations, connects or separates them, and thus processes the raw material of sense impressions into a cognition of objects that is called experience. *In terms of time,* therefore, no cognition in us precedes experience, and all our cognition begins with experience.

But even though all our cognition starts with experience, that does not mean that all of it arises from experience. For it might well be that even our experiential cognition is composite, consisting of what we receive through impressions and what our own cognitive power supplies from itself (sense impressions merely prompting it to do so). If our cognitive power does make such an addition, we may not be able to distin-*B2* guish it from that basic material until long practice has made us attentive to it and skilled in separating it from the basic material.

This question, then, whether there is such a cognition that is independent of experience and even of all impressions of the senses, is one that cannot be disposed of as soon as it comes to light, but that at least still needs closer investigation. Such cognitions are called *a priori cog-*

From Immanuel Kant, *Critique of Pure Reason,* translated by Werner S. Pluhar (Indianapolis: Hackett Publishing Company, 1996). Reprinted by permission of the publisher.

nitions; they are distinguished from empirical cognitions, whose sources are a posteriori, namely, in experience.

But that expression, [viz., *a priori,*] is not yet determinate enough to indicate adequately the full meaning of the question just posed. For it is customary, I suppose, to say of much cognition derived from experiential sources that we can or do partake of it a priori. We say this because we derive the cognition not directly from experience but from a universal rule, even though that rule itself was indeed borrowed by us from experience. Thus if someone has undermined the foundation of his house, we say that he could have known a priori that the house would cave in, i.e., he did not have to wait for the experience of its actually caving in. And yet he could not have known this completely a priori. For he did first have to find out through experience that bodies have weight and hence fall when their support is withdrawn.

In what follows, therefore, we shall mean by a priori cognitions not those that occur independently of this *B3* or that experience, but those that occur *absolutely* independently of all experience. They contrast with empirical cognitions, which are those that are possible only a posteriori, i.e., through experience. But we call a priori cognitions *pure* if nothing empirical whatsoever is mixed in with them. Thus, e.g., the proposition, Every change has its cause, is an a priori proposition; yet it is not pure, because change is a concept that can be obtained only from experience.

· · · · ·

IV. On the Distinction between Analytic and Synthetic Judgments

In all judgments in which we think the relation of a subject to the predicate (I here consider affirmative judgments only, because the application to negative judgments is easy afterwards), this relation is possible in two ways. Either the predicate B belongs to the subject

A as something that is (covertly) contained in this concept A; or B, though connected with concept A, lies
A7 quite outside it. In the first case I call the judgment *analytic;* in the second, *synthetic.* Hence (affirmative) analytic judgments are those in which the predicate's connection with the subject is thought by [thinking] identity, whereas those judgments in which this con-
B11 nection is thought without [thinking] identity are to be called synthetic. Analytic judgments could also be called *elucidatory.* For they do not through the predicate add anything to the concept of the subject; rather, they only dissect the concept, breaking it up into its component concepts which had already been thought in it (although thought confusedly). Synthetic judgments, on the other hand, could also be called *expansive.* For they do add to the concept of the subject a predicate that had not been thought in that concept at all and could not have been extracted from it by any dissection. For example, if I say: All bodies are extended—then this is an analytic judgment. For I do not need to go beyond the concept that I link with the word body in order to find that extension is connected with it. All I need to do in order to find this predicate in the concept is to dissect the concept, i.e., become conscious of the manifold that I always think in it. Hence the judgment is analytic. By contrast, if I say: All bodies are heavy—then the predicate is something quite different from what I think in the mere concept of a body as such. Hence adding such a predicate yields a synthetic judgment.

Experiential judgments, as such, are one and all synthetic. For to base an analytic judgment on experience would be absurd, because in its case I can formulate my judgment without going outside my concept, and hence do not need for it any testimony of experience. Thus the [analytic] proposition that bodies are extended is one that holds a priori and is not an experiential judgment.
B12 For before I turn to experience, I already have in the concept [of body] all the conditions required for my judgment. I have only to extract from it, in accordance with the principle of contradiction, the predicate [of extension]; in doing so, I can at the same time become conscious of the judgment's necessity, of which experience would not even inform me. On the other hand, though in the concept of a body as such I do not at all include the predicate of heaviness, yet the concept designates an object of experience by means of part of this

experience; hence I can [synthetically] add to this part further parts, of the same experience, in addition to those that belonged to the concept of a body as such. I can begin by cognizing the concept of a body *analytically* through the characteristics of extension, impenetrability, shape, etc., all of which are thought in this concept. But then I expand my cognition: by looking back to the experience from which I have abstracted this concept of body, I also find heaviness to be always connected with the above characteristics; and so I add it, as a predicate, to that concept *synthetically.* Hence experience is what makes possible the synthesis of the predicate of heaviness with the concept of body. For although neither of the two concepts is contained in the other, yet they belong to each other, though only contingently, as parts of a whole; that whole is experience, which is itself a synthetic combination of intuitions.

In synthetic judgments that are a priori, however, this   *A9* remedy is entirely lacking. If I am to go beyond the   *B13* concept A in order to cognize another concept B as combined with it, I rely on something that makes the synthesis possible: what is that something, considering that here I do not have the advantage of looking around for it in the realm of experience? Take the proposition: Everything that happens has its cause.—In the concept of something that happens I do indeed think an existence preceded by a time, etc., and from this one can obtain analytic judgments. But the concept of a cause lies quite outside that earlier concept and indicates something different from what happens; hence it is not part of what is contained in this latter presentation. In speaking generally of what happens, how can I say about it something quite different from it, and cognize as belonging to it—indeed, belonging to it necessarily—the concept of cause, even though this concept is not contained in the concept of what happens? What is here the unknown = X on which the understanding relies when it believes that it discovers, outside the concept A, a predicate B that is foreign to concept A but that the understanding considers nonetheless to be connected with that concept? This unknown cannot be experience. For in adding the presentation of cause to the presentation of what happens, the above principle does so not only with greater universality than experience can provide, but also with the necessity's being expressed; hence it does so entirely a priori and on the basis of mere concepts. Now, on such synthetic, i.e., expansive, principles depends the whole final aim of our speculative a priori cognition. For, analytic principles are indeed exceedingly important and needed, but only for attaining that distinctness in concepts which is required for a secure and extensive synthesis that, as such, will actually be a new acquisition [of cognition].

V. ALL THEORETICAL SCIENCES OF REASON CONTAIN SYNTHETIC A PRIORI JUDGMENTS AS PRINCIPLES

1. *Mathematical judgments are one and all synthetic.* Although this proposition is incontestably certain and has very important consequences, it seems thus far to have escaped the notice of those who have analyzed human reason; indeed, it seems to be directly opposed to all their conjectures. For they found that all the inferences made by mathematicians proceed (as the nature of all apodeictic certainty requires) according to the principle of contradiction; and thus they came to be persuaded that the principle of contradiction is also the basis on which we recognize the principles [of mathematics]. In this they were mistaken. For though we can indeed gain insight into a synthetic proposition according to the principle of contradiction, we can never do so [by considering] that proposition by itself, but can do so only by presupposing another synthetic proposition from which it can be deduced.

We must note, first of all, that mathematical propositions, properly so called, are always a priori judgments rather than empirical ones; for they carry with them necessity, which we could never glean from experience. But if anyone refuses to grant that all such propositions are a priori—all right: then I restrict my assertion to *pure mathematics,* in the very concept of which is implied that it contains not empirical but only pure a priori cognition.

It is true that one might at first think that the proposition 7 + 5 = 12 is a merely analytic one that follows, by the principle of contradiction, from the concept of a sum of seven and five. Yet if we look more closely, we find that the concept of the sum of 7 and 5 contains nothing more than the union of the two numbers into one; but in [thinking] that union we are not thinking in any way at all what that single number is that unites

the two. In thinking merely that union of seven and five, I have by no means already thought the concept of twelve; and no matter how long I dissect my concept of such a possible sum, still I shall never find in it that twelve. We must go beyond these concepts and avail ourselves of the intuition corresponding to one of the two: e.g., our five fingers, or five dots. In this way we must gradually add, to the concept of seven, the units of the five given in intuition. For I start by taking the number 7. Then, for the concept of the 5, I avail myself of the fingers of my hand as intuition. Thus, in that image of mine, I gradually add to the number 7 the units that I previously gathered together in order to make up the number 5. In this way I see the number 12 arise. That 5 *were to be added* to 7, this I had indeed already thought in the concept of a sum = 7 + 5, but not that this sum is equal to the number 12. Arithmetic propositions are therefore always synthetic. We become aware of this all the more distinctly if we take larger numbers. For then it is very evident that, no matter how much we twist and turn our concepts, we can never find the [number of the] sum by merely dissecting our concepts, i.e., without availing ourselves of intuition.

Just as little are any principles of pure geometry analytic. That the straight line between two points is the shortest is a synthetic proposition. For my concept of *straight* contains nothing about magnitude, but contains only a quality. Therefore the concept of shortest is entirely added to the concept of a straight line and cannot be extracted from it by any dissection. Hence we must here avail ourselves of intuition; only by means of it is the synthesis possible.

It is true that a few propositions presupposed by geometricians are actually analytic and based on the principle of contradiction. But, like identical propositions, they serve not as principles but only [as links in] the chain of method. Examples are a = a; the whole is equal to itself; or (a + b) > a, i.e., the whole is greater than its part. And yet even these principles, although they hold according to mere concepts, are admitted in mathematics only because they can be exhibited in intuition. [As for mathematics generally,] what commonly leads us to believe that the predicate of its apodeitic judgments is contained in our very concept, and that the judgment is therefore analytic, is merely the ambiguity with which we express ourselves. For we say that we *are to* add in thought a certain predicate to a given concept, and this necessity adheres indeed to the very concepts. But here the question is not what we *are to* add in thought to the given concept, but what we *actually* think in the concept, even if only obscurely; and there we find that, although the predicate does indeed adhere necessarily to such concept, [. . .] yet it does so not as something thought in the concept itself, but by means of an intuition that must be added to the concept.

2. *Natural science (physica) contains synthetic a priori judgments as principles.* Let me cite as examples just a few propositions: e.g., the proposition that in all changes in the corporeal world the quantity of matter remains unchanged; or the proposition that in all communication of motion, action and reaction must always be equal to each other. Both propositions are clearly not only necessary, and hence of a priori origin, but also synthetic. *B18* For in the concept of matter I do not think permanence, but think merely the matter's being present in space insofar as it occupies space. Hence I do actually go beyond the concept of matter, in order to add to it a priori in thought something that I have not thought *in it.* Hence the proposition is thought not analytically but synthetically and yet a priori, and the same occurs in the remaining propositions of the pure part of natural science.

3. *Metaphysics* is to *contain synthetic a priori cognitions.* This holds even if metaphysics is viewed as a science that thus far has merely been attempted, but that because of the nature of human reason is nonetheless indispensable. Metaphysics is not at all concerned merely to dissect concepts of things that we frame a priori, and thereby to elucidate them analytically. Rather, in metaphysics we want to expand our a priori cognition. In order to do this, we must use principles which go beyond the given concept and which add to it something that was not contained in it; and, by means of such synthetic a priori judgments, we must presumably go so far beyond such concepts that even experience can no longer follow us; as in the proposition: The world must have a first beginning—and others like that. And hence metaphysics consists, at least *in terms of its purpose,* of nothing but synthetic a priori propositions.

VI. THE GENERAL PROBLEM OF PURE REASON   *B19*

Much is gained already when we can bring a multitude of inquiries under the formula of a single problem. For we thereby facilitate not only our own business by defining it precisely, but also—for anyone else who wants to examine it—the judgment as to whether or not we have carried out our project adequately. Now the proper problem of pure reason is contained in this question:

How are synthetic judgments possible a priori?

That metaphysics has thus far remained in such a shaky state of uncertainty and contradictions is attributable to a sole cause: the fact that this problem, and perhaps even the distinction between *analytic* and *synthetic* judgments, has not previously occurred to anyone. Whether metaphysics stands or falls depends on the solution of this problem, or on an adequate proof that the possibility which metaphysics demands to see explained does not exist at all. *David Hume* at least came closer to this problem than any other philosopher. Yet he did not think of it nearly determinately enough and in its universality, but merely remained with the synthetic proposition about the connection of an effect with its causes. He believed he had discovered that such a proposition is quite impossible a priori. Thus, according to his conclusions, everything that we call metaphysics would amount to no more than the delusion of a supposed rational insight into what in fact is merely borrowed from experience and has, through habit, acquired a seeming necessity. This assertion, which destroys all pure philosophy, would never have entered Hume's mind if he had envisaged our problem in its universality. For he would then have seen that by his argument there could be no pure mathematics either, since it certainly does contain synthetic a priori propositions: and from such an assertion his good sense would surely have saved him.

In solving the above problem we solve at the same time another one, concerning the possibility of the pure use of reason in establishing and carrying out all sciences that contain theoretical a priori cognition of objects; i.e., we also answer these questions:

How is pure mathematics possible?
How is pure natural science possible?

Since these sciences are actually given [as existent], it is surely proper for us to ask how they are possible; for that they must be possible is proved by their being actual. As regards *metaphysics,* however, there are grounds on which everyone must doubt its possibility: its progress thus far has been poor; and thus far not a single metaphysics has been put forth of which we can say, as far as the essential purpose of metaphysics is concerned, that it is actually at hand.

Yet in a certain sense this *kind of cognition* must likewise be regarded as given; and although metaphysics is not actual as a science, yet it is actual as a natural predisposition. For human reason, impelled by its own need rather than moved by the mere vanity of gaining a lot of knowledge, proceeds irresistibly to such questions as cannot be answered by any experiential use of reason and any principles taken from such use. And thus all human beings, once their reason has expanded to [the point where it can] speculate, actually have always had in them, and always will have in them, some metaphysics. Now concerning it, too, there is this question:

How is metaphysics as a natural predisposition possible?

I.e., how, from the nature of universal human reason, do the questions arise that pure reason poses to itself and is impelled, by its own need, to answer as best it can?

Thus far, however, all attempts to answer these natural questions—e.g., whether the world has a beginning or has been there from eternity, etc.—have met with unavoidable contradictions. Hence we cannot settle for our mere natural predisposition for metaphysics, i.e., our pure power of reason itself, even though some metaphysics or other (whichever it might be) always arises from it. Rather, it must be possible, by means of this predisposition to attain certainty either concerning our knowledge or lack of knowledge of the objects [of metaphysics], i.e., either concerning a decision about the objects that its questions deal with, or certainty concerning the ability or inability of reason to make judgments about these objects. In other words, it must be possible to expand our pure reason in a reliable way, or to set for it limits that are determinate and safe. This last question, which flows from the general problem above, may rightly be stated thus:

How is metaphysics as science possible?

Ultimately, therefore, critique of pure reason leads necessarily to science; the dogmatic use of pure reason without critique, on the other hand, to baseless assertions that always be opposed by others that seem equally plausible, and hence to *skepticism.*

This science, however, cannot be overly, forbiddingly voluminous. For it deals not with objects of reason, which are infinitely diverse, but merely with [reason] itself. [Here reason] deals with problems that issue entirely from its own womb; they are posed to it not by the nature of things distinct from it, but by its own nature. And thus, once it has become completely acquainted with its own ability regarding the objects that it may encounter in experience, reason must find it easy to determine, completely and safely, the range and the bounds of its use [when] attempted beyond all bounds of experience. [. . .]

Bertrand Russell

How A Priori *Knowledge Is Possible*

Immanuel Kant is generally regarded as the greatest of the modern philosophers. Though he lived through the Seven Years War and the French Revolution, he never interrupted his teachings of philosophy at Königsberg in East Prussia. His most distinctive contribution was the invention of what he called the 'critical' philosophy, which, assuming as a datum that there is knowledge of various kinds, inquired how such knowledge comes to be possible, and deduced, from the answer to this inquiry, many metaphysical results as to the nature of the world. Whether these results were valid may well be doubted. But Kant undoubtedly deserves credit for two things: first, for having perceived that we have *a priori* knowledge which is not purely 'analytic', i.e. such that the opposite would be self-contradictory; and secondly, for having made evident the philosophical importance of the theory of knowledge.

Before the time of Kant, it was generally held that whatever knowledge was *a priori* must be 'analytic'. What this word means will be best illustrated by examples. If I say, 'A bald man is a man', 'A plane figure is a figure', 'A bad poet is a poet', I make a purely analytic judgement: the subject spoken about is given as having at least two properties, of which one is singled out to be asserted of it. Such propositions as the above are trivial, and would never be enunciated in real life except by an orator preparing the way for a piece of sophistry. They are called 'analytic' because the predicate is obtained by merely analysing the subject. Before the time of Kant it was thought that all judgements of which we could be certain *a priori* were of this kind: that in all of them there was a predicate which was only part of the subject of which it was asserted. If this were so, we should be involved in a definite contradiction if we at-

tempted to deny anything that could be known *a priori*. 'A bald man is not bald' would assert and deny baldness of the same man, and would therefore contradict itself. Thus according to the philosophers before Kant, the law of contradiction, which asserts that nothing can at the same time have and not have a certain property, sufficed to establish the truth of all *a priori* knowledge.

Hume, who preceded Kant, accepting the usual view as to what makes knowledge *a priori,* discovered that, in many cases which had previously been supposed analytic, and notably in the case of cause and effect, the connexion was really synthetic. Before Hume, rationalists at least had supposed that the effect could be logically deduced from the cause, if only we had sufficient knowledge. Hume argued—correctly, as would now be generally admitted—that this could not be done. Hence he inferred the far more doubtful proposition that nothing could be known *a priori* about the connexion of cause and effect. Kant, who had been educated in the rationalist tradition, was much perturbed by Hume's scepticism, and endeavoured to find an answer to it. He perceived that not only the connexion of cause and effect, but all the propositions of arithmetic and geometry, are 'synthetic', i.e. not analytic: in all these propositions, no analysis of the subject will reveal the predicate. His stock instance was the proposition $7 + 5 = 12$. He pointed out, quite truly, that 7 and 5 have to be put together to give 12: the idea of 12 is not *contained* in them, nor even in the idea of adding them together. Thus he was led to the conclusion that all pure mathematics, though *a priori,* is synthetic; and this conclusion raised a new problem of which he endeavoured to find the solution.

The question which Kant put at the beginning of his philosophy, namely 'How is pure mathematics possible?' is an interesting and difficult one, to which every philosophy which is not purely sceptical must find some answer. The answer of the pure empiricists, that our mathematical knowledge is derived by induction from particular instances, we have already seen to be inadequate, for two reasons: first, that the validity of the inductive principle itself cannot be proved by induction; secondly, that the general propositions of mathematics, such as 'two and two always make four', can obviously be known with certainty by consideration of a single instance, and gain nothing by enumeration of other cases in which they have been found to be true. Thus our knowledge of the general propositions of mathematics (and the same applies to logic) must be accounted for otherwise than our (merely probable) knowledge of empirical generalizations such as 'all men are mortal'.

The problem arises through the fact that such knowledge is general, whereas all experience is particular. It seems strange that we should apparently be able to know some truths in advance about particular things of which we have as yet no experience; but it cannot easily be doubted that logic and arithmetic will apply to such things. We do not know who will be the inhabitants of London a hundred years hence; but we know that any two of them and any other two of them will make four of them. This apparent power of anticipating facts about things of which we have no experience is certainly surprising. Kant's solution of the problem, though not valid in my opinion, is interesting. It is, however, very difficult, and is differently understood by different philosophers. We can, therefore, only give the merest outline of it, and even that will be thought misleading by many exponents of Kant's system.

What Kant maintained was that in all our experience there are two elements to be distinguished, the one due to the object (i.e. to what we have called the 'physical object'), the other due to our own nature. We saw, in discussing matter and sense-data, that the physical object is different from the associated sense-data, and that the sense-data are to be regarded as resulting from an interaction between the physical object and ourselves. So far, we are in agreement with Kant. But what is distinctive of Kant is the way in which he apportions the shares of ourselves and the physical object respectively. He considers that the crude material given in sensation —the colour, hardness, etc.—is due to the object, and that what we supply is the arrangement in space and time, and all the relations between sense-data which result from comparison or from considering one as the cause of the other or in any other way. His chief reason

in favour of this view is that we seem to have *a priori* knowledge as to space and time and causality and comparison, but not as to the actual crude material of sensation. We can be sure, he says, that anything we shall ever experience must show the characteristics affirmed of it in our *a priori* knowledge, because these characteristics are due to our own nature, and therefore nothing can ever come into our experience without acquiring these characteristics.

The physical object, which he calls the 'thing in itself', he regards as essentially unknowable; what can be known is the object as we have it in experience, which he calls the 'phenomenon'. The phenomenon, being a joint product of us and the things in itself, is sure to have those characteristics which are due to us, and is therefore sure to conform to our *a priori* knowledge. Hence this knowledge, though true of all actual and possible experience, must not be supposed to apply outside experience. Thus in spite of the existence of *a priori* knowledge, we cannot know anything about the thing in itself or about what is not an actual or possible object of experience. In this way he tries to reconcile and harmonize the contentions of the rationalists with the arguments of the empiricists.

Apart from minor grounds on which Kant's philosophy may be criticized, there is one main objection which seems fatal to any attempt to deal with the problem of *a priori* knowledge by his method. The thing to be accounted for is our certainty that the facts must always conform to logic and arithmetic. To say that logic and arithmetic are contributed by us does not account for this. Our nature is as much a fact of the existing world as anything, and there can be no certainty that it will remain constant. It might happen, if Kant is right, that to-morrow our nature would so change as to make two and two become five. This possibility seems never to have occurred to him, yet it is one which utterly destroys the certainty and universality which he is anxious to vindicate for arithmetical propositions. It is true that this possibility, formally, is inconsistent with the Kantian view that time itself is a form imposed by the subject upon phenomena, so that our real Self is not in time and has no to-morrow. But he will still have to suppose that the time-order of phenomena is determined by characteristics of what is behind phenomena, and this suffices for the substance of our argument.

Reflection, moreover, seems to make it clear that, if there is any truth in our arithmetical beliefs, they must apply to things equally whether we think of them or not. Two physical objects and two other physical objects must make four physical objects, even if physical objects cannot be experienced. To assert this is certainly within the scope of what we mean when we state that two and two are four. Its truth is just as indubitable as the truth of the assertion that two phenomena and two other phenomena make four phenomena. Thus Kant's solution unduly limits the scope of *a priori* propositions, in addition to failing in the attempt at explaining their certainty.

Apart from the special doctrines advocated by Kant, it is very common among philosophers to regard what is *a priori* as in some sense mental, as concerned rather with the way we must think than with any fact of the outer world. We noted in the preceding chapter the three principles commonly called 'laws of thought'. The view which led to their being so named is a natural one, but there are strong reasons for thinking that it is erroneous. Let us take as an illustration the law of contradiction. This is commonly stated in the form 'Nothing can both be and not be', which is intended to express the fact that nothing can at once have and not have a given quality. Thus, for example, if a tree is a beech it cannot also be not a beech; if my table is rectangular it cannot also be not rectangular, and so on.

Now what makes it natural to call this principle a law of *thought* is that it is by thought rather than by outward observation that we persuade ourselves of its necessary truth. When we have seen that a tree is a beech, we do not need to look again in order to ascertain whether it is also not a beech; thought alone makes us know that this is impossible. But the conclusion that the law of contradiction is a law of *thought* is nevertheless erroneous. What we believe, when we believe the law of contradiction, is not that the mind is so made that it must believe the law of contradiction. *This* belief is a subsequent result of psychological reflection, which presupposes the belief in the law of contradiction. The belief in the law of contradiction is a belief about things, not only about thoughts. It is not, e.g., the belief that if we *think* a certain tree is a beech, we cannot at the same time *think* that it is not a beech; it is the belief that if the tree *is* a beech, it cannot at the same time *be* not a beech. Thus the law

of contradiction is about things, and not merely about thoughts; and although belief in the law of contradiction is a thought, the law of contradiction itself is not a thought, but a fact concerning the things in the world. If this, which we believe when we believe the law of contradiction, were not true of the things in the world, the fact that we were compelled to *think* it true would not save the law of contradiction from being false; and this shows that the law is not a law of *thought*.

A similar argument applies to any other *a priori* judgement. When we judge that two and two are four, we are not making a judgement about our thoughts, but about all actual or possible couples. The fact that our minds are so constituted as to believe that two and two are four, though it is true, is emphatically not what we assert when we assert that two and two are four. And no fact about the constitution of our minds could make it *true* that two and two are four. Thus our *a priori* knowledge, if it is not erroneous, is not merely knowledge about the constitution of our minds, but is applicable to whatever the world may contain, both what is mental and what is non-mental.

The fact seems to be that all our *a priori* knowledge is concerned with entities which do not, properly speaking, *exist*, either in the mental or in the physical world. These entities are such as can be named by parts of speech which are not substantives; they are such entities as qualities and relations. Suppose, for instance, that I am in my room. I exist, and my room exists; but does 'in' exist? Yet obviously the word 'in' has a meaning; it denotes a relation which holds between me and my room. This relation is something, although we cannot say that it exists *in the same sense* in which I and my room exist. The relation 'in' is something which we can think about and understand, for, if we could not understand it, we could not understand the sentence 'I am in my room'. Many philosophers, following Kant, have maintained that relations are the work of the mind, that things in themselves have no relations, but that the mind brings them together in one act of thought and thus produces the relations which it judges them to have.

This view, however, seems open to objections similar to those which we urged before against Kant. It seems plain that it is not thought which produces the truth of the proposition 'I am in my room'. It may be true that an earwig is in my room, even if neither I nor the earwig nor any one else is aware of this truth; for this truth concerns only the earwig and the room, and does not depend upon anything else. Thus relations [...] must

be placed in a world which is neither mental nor physical. This world is of great importance to philosophy, and in particular to the problems of *a priori* knowledge.

Saul Kripke

The A Priori *and the Necessary*

... [W]hat is the relation between names and descriptions? There is a well known doctrine of John Stuart Mill, in his book *A System of Logic,* that names have denotation but not connotation. To use one of his examples, when we use the name 'Dartmouth' to describe a certain locality in England, it may be so called because it lies at the mouth of the Dart. But even, he says, had the Dart (that's a river) changed its course so that Dartmouth no longer lay at the mouth of the Dart, we could still with propriety call this place 'Dartmouth', even though the name may suggest that it lies at the mouth of the Dart. Changing Mill's terminology, perhaps we should say that a name such as 'Dartmouth' *does* have a 'connotation' to some people, namely, it *does* connote (not to me—I never thought of this) that any place called 'Dartmouth' lies at the mouth of the Dart. But then in some way it doesn't have a 'sense'. At least, it is not part of the *meaning* of the name 'Dartmouth' that the town so named lies at the mouth of the Dart. Someone who said that Dartmouth did not lie at the Dart's mouth would not contradict himself.

It should not be thought that every phrase of the form 'the *x* such that *Fx*' is always used in English as a description rather than a name. I guess everyone has heard about The Holy Roman Empire, which was neither holy, Roman nor an empire. Today we have The

United Nations. Here it would seem that since these things can be so-called even though they are not Holy Roman United Nations, these phrases should be regarded not as definite descriptions, but as names. In the case of some terms, people might have doubts as to whether they're names or descriptions; like 'God'— does it describe God as the unique divine being or is it a name of God? But such cases needn't necessarily bother us.

Now here I am making a distinction which is certainly made in language. But the classical tradition of modern logic has gone very strongly against Mill's view. Frege and Russell both thought, and seemed to arrive at these conclusions independently of each other, that Mill was wrong in a very strong sense: really a proper name, properly used, simply was a definite description abbreviated or disguised. Frege specifically said that such a description gave the sense of the name.

Now the reasons against Mill's view and in favor of the alternative view adopted by Frege and Russell are really very powerful; and it is hard to see—though one may be suspicious of this view because names don't seem to be disguised descriptions—how the Frege-Russell view, or some suitable variant, can fail to be the case.

Let me give an example of some of the arguments which seem conclusive in favor of the view of Frege and Russell. The basic problem for any view such as Mill's is how we can determine what the referent of a name, as used by a given speaker, is. According to the description view, the answer is clear. If 'Joe Doakes' is just short

---

Saul Kripke, *Naming and Necessity.* Copyright © 1980 by Saul Kripke. Reprinted with the permission of Harvard University Press and Blackwell Publishing, Ltd.

for 'the man who corrupted Hadleyburg', then who-ever corrupted Hadleyburg uniquely is the referent of the name 'Joe Doakes'. However, if there is *not* such a descriptive content to the name, then how do people ever use names to refer to things at all? Well, they may be in a position to point to some things and thus de-termine the references of certain names ostensively. This is what Russell's doctrine of acquaintance, which he thought the so-called genuine or proper names sat-isfied. But of course ordinary names refer to all sorts of people, like Walter Scott, to whom we can't possibly point. And our reference here seems to be determined by our knowledge of them. Whatever we know about them determines the referent of the name as the unique thing satisfying those properties. For example, if I use the name 'Napoleon', and someone asks, 'To whom are you referring?', I will answer something like, 'Napoleon was emperor of the French in the early part of the nine-teenth century; he was eventually defeated at Waterloo', thus giving a uniquely identifying description to deter-mine the referent of the name. Frege and Russell, then, appear to give the natural account of how reference is determined here; Mill appears to give none.

There are subsidiary arguments which, though they are based on more specialized problems, are also motiva-tions for accepting the view. One is that sometimes we may discover that two names have the same referent, and express this by an identity statement. So, for example (I guess this is a hackneyed example), you see a star in the evening and it's called 'Hesperus'. (That's what we call it in the evening, is that right?—I hope it's not the other way around.) We see a star in the morning and call it 'Phosphorus'. Well, then, in fact we find that it's not a star, but is the planet Venus and that Hesperus and Phospho-rus are in fact the same. So we express this by 'Hesperus is Phosphorus'. Here we're certainly not just saying of an object that it's identical with itself. This is something that we discovered. A very natural thing is to say that the real content [is that] the star which we saw in the evening is the star which we saw in the morning (or, more accu-rately, that the thing which we saw in the evening is the thing which we saw in the morning). This, then, gives the real meaning of the identity statement in question; and the analysis in terms of descriptions does this.

Also we may raise the question whether a name has any reference at all when we ask, e.g., whether Aristotle

ever existed. It seems natural here to think that what is questioned is not whether this *thing* (man) existed. Once we've *got* the thing, we know that it existed. What really is queried is whether anything answers to the properties we associate with the name—in the case of Aristotle, whether any one Greek philosopher produced certain works, or at least a suitable number of them.

It would be nice to answer all of these arguments. I am not entirely able to see my way clear through every problem of this sort that can be raised. Furthermore, I'm pretty sure that I won't have time to discuss all these questions in these lectures. Nevertheless, I think it's pretty certain that the view of Frege and Russell is false.

Many people have said that the theory of Frege and Russell is false, but, in my opinion, they have abandoned its letter while retaining its spirit, namely, they have used the notion of a cluster concept. Well, what is this? The obvious problem for Frege and Russell, the one which comes immediately to mind, is already mentioned by Frege himself. He said,

> In the case of genuinely proper names like 'Aris-totle' opinions as regards their sense may diverge. As such may, e.g., be suggested: Plato's disciple and the teacher of Alexander the Great. Whoever ac-cepts this sense will interpret the meaning of the statement 'Aristotle was born in Stagira', differ-ently from one who interpreted the sense of 'Aristotle' as the Stagirite teacher of Alexander the Great. As long as the nominatum remains the same, the fluctuations in sense are tolerable. But they should be avoided in the system of a demon-strative science and should not appear in a perfect language.[1]

So, according to Frege, there is some sort of looseness or weakness in our language. Some people may give one sense to the name 'Aristotle', others may give another. But of course it is not only that; even a single speaker when asked 'What description are you willing to substi-tute for the name?' may be quite at a loss. In fact, he may

---

1. Gottlob Frege, 'On Sense and Nominatum', translated by Herbert Feigl in *Readings in Philosophical Analysis* (ed. by Herbert Feigl and Wilfrid Sellars), Appleton Century Crofts, 1949, p. 86.

know many things about him; but any particular thing that he knows he may feel clearly expresses a contingent property of the object. If 'Aristotle' meant *the man who taught Alexander the Great,* then saying 'Aristotle was a teacher of Alexander the Great' would be a mere tautology. But surely it isn't; it expresses the fact that Aristotle taught Alexander the Great, something we could discover to be false. So, *being the teacher of Alexander the Great* cannot be part of [the sense of] the name.

The most common way out of this difficulty is to say 'really it is not a weakness in ordinary language that we can't substitute a *particular* description for the name; that's all right. What we really associate with the name is a *family* of descriptions'. A good example of this is (if I can find it) in *Philosophical Investigations,* where the idea of family resemblances is introduced and with great power.

> Consider this example. If one says 'Moses did not exist', this may mean various things. It may mean: the Israelites did not have a *single* leader when they withdrew from Egypt—or: their leader was not called Moses—or: there cannot have been anyone who accomplished all that the Bible relates of Moses—. . . But when I make a statement about Moses,—am I always ready to substitute some *one* of those descriptions for 'Moses'? I shall perhaps say: by 'Moses' I understand the man who did what the Bible relates of Moses, or at any rate, a good deal of it. But how much? Have I decided how much must be proved false for me to give up my proposition as false? Has the name 'Moses' got a fixed and unequivocal use for me in all possible cases?[2]

According to this view, and a *locus classicus* of it is Searle's article on proper names,[3] the referent of a name is determined not by a single description but by some cluster or family. Whatever in some sense satisfies enough or most of the family is the referent of the name. I shall return to this view later. It may seem, as an analysis of ordinary language, quite a bit more plausible than that

of Frege and Russell. It may seem to keep all the virtues and remove the defects of this theory.

Let me say (and this will introduce us to another new topic before I really consider this theory of naming) that there are two ways in which the cluster concept theory, or even the theory which require a single description, can be viewed. One way of regarding it says that the cluster or the single description actually gives the meaning of the name; and when someone says 'Walter Scott', he means *the man such that such and such and such and such*.

Now another view might be that even though the description in some sense doesn't give the *meaning* of the name, it is what *determines its reference* and although the phrase 'Walter Scott' isn't *synonymous* with 'the man such that such and such and such and such', or even maybe with the family (if something can be synonymous with a family), the family or the single description is what is used to determine to whom someone is referring when he says 'Walter Scott'. Of course, if when we hear his beliefs about Walter Scott we find that they are actually much more nearly true of Salvador Dali, then according to this theory the reference of this name is going to be Mr. Dali, not Scott. There are writers, I think, who explicitly deny that names have meaning at all even more strongly than I would but still use this picture of how the referent of the name gets determined. [. . .]

The difference between using this theory as a theory of meaning and using it as a theory of reference will come out a little more clearly later on. But some of the attractiveness of the theory is lost if it isn't supposed to give the meaning of the name; for some of the solutions of problems that I've just mentioned will not be right, or at least won't clearly be right, if the description doesn't give the meaning of the name. For example, if someone said 'Aristotle does not exist' *means* 'there is no man doing such and such', or in the example from Wittgenstein, 'Moses does not exist', *means* 'no man did such and such', that might depend (and in fact, I think, does depend) on taking the theory in question as a theory of the meaning of the name 'Moses', not just as a theory of its reference. Well, I don't know. Perhaps all that is immediate now is the other way around: if 'Moses' means the same as 'the man who did such and such' then to say that Moses did not exist is to say that the man who did such and such did not exist, that is, that no one person did such and such. If, on the other

---

2. Ludwig Wittgenstein, *Philosophical Investigations,* translated by G. E. M. Anscombe, MacMillan, 1953, § 79.

3. John R. Searle, 'Proper Names', *Mind* 67 (1958), 166–73.

hand, 'Moses' is not synonymous with any description, then even if its reference is in some sense determined by a description, statements containing the name cannot in general be *analyzed* by replacing the name by a description, though they may be materially equivalent to statements containing a description. So the analysis of singular existence statements mentioned above will have to be given up, unless it is established by some special argument, independent of a general theory of the meaning of names; and the same applies to identity statements. In any case, I think it's false that 'Moses exists' means that at all. So we won't have to see if such a special argument can be drawn up.

Before I go any further into this problem, I want to talk about another distinction which will be important in the methodology of these talks. Philosophers have talked (and, of course, there has been considerable controversy in recent years over the meaningfulness of these notions) [about] various categories of truth, which are called *'a priori'*, 'analytic', 'necessary'—and sometimes even 'certain' is thrown into this batch. The terms are often used as if *whether* there are things answering to these concepts is an interesting question, but we might as well regard them all as meaning the same thing. Now, everyone remembers Kant (a bit) as making a distinction between *'a priori'* and 'analytic'. So maybe this distinction is still made. In contemporary discussion very few people, if any, distinguish between the concepts of statements being *a priori* and their being necessary. At any rate I shall *not* use the terms *'a priori'* and 'necessary' interchangeably here.

Consider what the traditional characterizations of such terms as *'a priori'* and 'necessary' are. First the notion of a prioricity is a concept of epistemology. I guess the traditional characterization from Kant goes something like: *a priori* truths are those which can be known independently of any experience. This introduces another problem before we get off the ground, because there's another modality in the characterization of *'a priori'*, namely, it is supposed to be something which *can* be known independently of any experience. That means that in some sense it's *possible* (whether we do or do not in fact know it independently of any experience) to know this independently of any experience. And possible for whom? For God? For the Martians? Or just for people with minds like ours? To make this all clear might [involve] a host of problems all of its own about what sort of possibility is in question here. It might be best there-

fore, instead of using the phrase *'a priori* truth', to the extent that one uses it at all, to stick to the question of whether a particular person or knower knows something *a priori* or believes it true on the basis of *a priori* evidence.

I won't go further too much into the problems that might arise with the notion of a prioricity here. I will say that some philosophers somehow change the modality in this characterization from *can* to *must*. They think that if something belongs to the realm of *a priori* knowledge, it couldn't possibly be known empirically. This is just a mistake. Something may belong in the realm of such statements that *can* be known *a priori* but still may be known by particular people on the basis of experience. To give a really common sense example: anyone who has worked with a computing machine knows that the computing machine may give an answer to whether such and such a number is prime. No one has calculated or proved that the number is prime; but the machine has given the answer: this number is prime. We, then, if we believe that the number is prime, believe it on the basis of our knowledge of the laws of physics, the construction of the machine, and so on. We therefore do not believe this on the basis of purely *a priori* evidence. We believe it (if anything is *a posteriori* at all) on the basis of *a posteriori* evidence. Nevertheless, maybe this could be known *a priori* by someone who made the requisite calculations. So *'can* be known *a priori'* doesn't mean *'must* be known *a priori'*.

The second concept which is in question is that of necessity. Sometimes this is used in an epistemological way and might then just mean *a priori*. And of course, sometimes it is used in a physical way when people distinguish between physical and logical necessity. But what I am concerned with here is a notion which is not a notion of epistemology but of metaphysics, in some (I hope) nonpejorative sense. We ask whether something might have been true, or might have been false. Well, if something is false, it's obviously not necessarily true. If it is true, might it have been otherwise? Is it possible that, in this respect, the world should have been different from the way it is? If the answer is 'no', then this fact about the world is a necessary one. If the answer is 'yes', then this fact about the world is a contingent one. This in and of itself has nothing to do with anyone's knowledge of anything. It's certainly a philosophical thesis, and not a matter of obvious definitional equivalence, either that everything *a priori* is necessary or that everything necessary is *a priori*. Both concepts may be vague. That may be another problem. But at any rate they are dealing with two different domains, two different areas, the epistemological and the metaphysical. Consider, say, Fermat's last theorem—or the Goldbach conjecture. The Goldbach conjecture says that an even number greater than 2 must be the sum of two prime numbers. If this is true, it is presumably necessary, and if it is false, presumably necessarily false. We are taking the classical view of mathematics here and assume that in mathematical reality it is either true or false.

If the Goldbach conjecture is false, then there is an even number, *n,* greater than 2, such that for no primes p_1 and p_2, both < *n,* does $n = p_1 + p_2$. This fact about *n,* if true, is verifiable by direct computation, and thus is necessary if the results of arithmetical computations are necessary. On the other hand, if the conjecture is true, then every even number exceeding 2 is the sum of two primes. Could it then be the case that, although in fact every such even number is the sum of two primes, there might have been such an even number which was not the sum of two primes? What would that mean? Such a number would have to be one of 4, 6, 8, 10, . . .; and, by hypothesis, since we are assuming Goldbach's conjecture to be true, each of these can be shown, again by direct computation, to be the sum of two primes. Goldbach's conjecture, then, cannot be contingently true or false; whatever truth-value it has belongs to it by necessity.

But what we can say, of course, is that right now, as far as we know, the question can come out either way. So, in the absence of a mathematical proof deciding this question, none of us has any *a priori* knowledge about this question in either direction. We don't know whether Goldbach's conjecture is true or false. So right now we certainly don't know anything *a priori* about it.

Perhaps it will be alleged that we *can* in principle know *a priori* whether it is true. Well, maybe we can. Of course an infinite mind which can search through all the numbers can or could. But I don't know whether a finite mind can or could. Maybe there just is no mathematical proof whatsoever which decides the conjecture. At any rate this might or might not be the case. [. . .] At any rate, and this is the important thing, the question is not trivial; even though someone said that it's necessary, if true at all, that every even number is the sum of two primes, it doesn't follow that anyone knows anything *a priori* about it. It doesn't even seem to me to follow with-

out some further philosophical argument (it is an interesting philosophical question) that anyone *could* know anything *a priori* about it. The 'could', as I said, involves some other modality. We mean that even if no one, perhaps even in the future, knows or will know *a priori* whether Goldbach's conjecture is right, in principle there is a way, which *could* have been used, of answering the question *a priori*. This assertion is not trivial.

The terms 'necessary ' and '*a priori*', then, as applied to statements, are *not* obvious synonyms. There may be a philosophical argument connecting them, perhaps even identifying them; but an argument is required, not simply the observation that the two terms are clearly interchangeable. [. . .]

I think people have thought that these two things must mean the same for these reasons:

First, if something not only happens to be true in the actual world but is also true in all possible worlds, then, of course, just by running though all the possible worlds in our heads, we ought to be able with enough effort to see, if a statement is necessary, that it is necessary, and thus know it *a priori*. But really this is not so obviously feasible at all.

Second, I guess it's thought that, conversely, if something is known *a priori* it must be necessary, because it was known without looking at the world. If it depended on some contingent feature of the actual world, how could you know it without looking? Maybe the actual world is one of the possible worlds in which it would have been false. This depends on the thesis that there can't be a way of knowing about the actual world without looking that wouldn't be a way of knowing the same thing about every possible world. This involves problems of epistemology and the nature of knowledge; and of course it is very vague as stated. But it is not really *trivial* either. More important than any particular example of something which is alleged to be necessary and not *a priori* or *a priori* and not necessary, is to see that the notions are different, that it's not trivial to argue on the basis of something's being something which maybe we can only know *a posteriori,* that it's not a necessary truth. It's not trivial, just because something is known in some sense *a priori,* that what is known is a necessary truth. [. . .]

I think the next topic I shall want to talk about is that of statements of identity. Are these necessary or contingent? The matter has been in some dispute in recent philosophy. First, everyone agrees that descriptions can be used to make contingent identity statements. If it is true that the man who invented bifocals was the first Postmaster General of the United States—that these were one and the same—it's contingently true. That is, it might have been the case that one man invented bifocals and another was the first Postmaster General of the United States. So certainly when you make identity statements using descriptions—when you say 'the x such that φx and the x such that ψx are one and the same'—that can be a contingent fact. But philosophers have been interested also in the question of identity statements between names. When we say 'Hesperus is Phosphorus' or 'Cicero is Tully', is what we are saying necessary or contingent? Further, they've been interested in another type of identity statement, which comes from scientific theory. We identify, for example, light with electromagnetic radiation between certain limits of wavelengths, or with a stream of photons. We identify heat with the motion of molecules; sound with a certain sort of wave disturbance in the air; and so on. Concerning such statements the following thesis is commonly held. First, that these are obviously contingent identities: we've found out that light is a stream of photons, but of course it might not have been a stream of photons. Heat is in fact the motion of molecules; we found that out, but heat might not have been the motion of molecules, Secondly, many philosophers feel damned lucky that these examples are around. Now, why? These philosophers, whose views are expounded in a vast literature, hold to a thesis called 'the identity thesis' with respect to some psychological concepts. They think, say, that pain is just a certain material state of the brain or of the body, or what have you—say the stimulation of C-fibers. (It doesn't matter what.) Some people have then objected, 'Well, look, there's perhaps a *correlation* between pain and these states of the body; but this must just be a contingent correlation between two different things, because it was an empirical discovery that this correlation ever held. Therefore, by 'pain' we must mean something different from this state of the body or brain; and, therefore, they must be two different things'.

Then it's said, 'Ah, but you see, this is wrong! Everyone knows that there can be contingent identities'. First, as in the bifocals and Postmaster General case, which I have mentioned before. Second, in the case, be-

lieved closer to the present paradigm, of theoretical identifications, such as light and a stream of photons, or water and a certain compound of hydrogen and oxygen. These are all contingent identities. They might have been false. It's no surprise, therefore, that it can be true as a matter of contingent fact and not of any necessity that feeling pain, or seeing red, is just a certain state of the human body. Such psychophysical identifications can be contingent facts just as the other identities are contingent facts. And of course there are widespread motivations—ideological, or just not wanting to have the 'nomological dangler' of mysterious connections not accounted for by the laws of physics, one to one correlations between two different kinds of thing, material states, and things of an entirely different kind, which lead people to want to believe this thesis.

I guess the main thing I'll talk about first is identity statements between names. But I hold the following about the general case. First, that characteristic theoretical identifications like 'Heat is the motion of molecules', are not contingent truths but necessary truths, and here of course I don't mean just physically necessary, but necessary in the highest degree—whatever that means. (Physical necessity, *might* turn out to be necessity in the highest degree. But that's a question which I don't wish to prejudge. At least for this sort of example, it might be that when something's physically necessary, it always is necessary *tout court*.) Second, that the way in which these have turned out to be necessary truths does not seem to me to be a way in which the mind-brain identities could turn out to be either necessary or contingently true. So this analogy has to go. It's hard to see what to put in its place. It's hard to see therefore how to avoid concluding that the two are actually different.

Let me go back to the more mundane case about proper names. This is already mysterious enough. There's a dispute about this between Quine and Ruth Barcan Marcus.[4] Marcus says that identities between names are necessary. If someone thinks that Cicero is Tully, and really uses 'Cicero' and 'Tully' as names, he is

---

4. Ruth Barcan Marcus, 'Modalities and Intensional Languages' (comments by W. V. Quine, plus discussion) *Boston Studies in the Philosophy of Science,* volume I, Reidel, Dordrecht, Holland, 1963, pp. 77–116.

thereby committed to holding that his belief is a necessary truth. She uses the term 'mere tag'. Quine replies as follows, 'We may tag the planet Venus, some fine evening, with the proper name 'Hesperus'. We may tag the same planet again, some day before sunrise, with the proper name 'Phosphorus'. When we discover that we have tagged the same planet twice our discovery is empirical. And not because the proper names were descriptions'.[5] First, as Quine says when we discovered that we tagged the same planet twice, our discovery was empirical. Another example I think Quine gives in another book is that the same mountain seen from Nepal and from Tibet, or something like that, is from one angle called 'Mt. Everest' (you've heard of that); from another it's supposed to be called 'Gaurisanker'. It can actually be an empirical discovery that Gaurisanker is Everest. (Quine says that the example is actually false. He got the example from Erwin Schrödinger. You wouldn't think the inventor of wave mechanics got things wrong. I don't know where the mistake is supposed to come from. One could certainly imagine this situation as having been the case; and it's another good illustration of the sort of thing that Quine has in mind.)

What about it? I wanted to find a good quote on the other side from Marcus in this book but I am having trouble locating one. Being present at that discussion, I remember[6] that she advocated the view that if you really have names, a good dictionary should be able to tell you whether they have the same reference. So someone should be able, by looking in the dictionary, to say that Hesperus and Phosphorus are the same. Now this does not seem to be true. It does seem, to many people, to be a consequence of the view that identities between names are necessary. Therefore the view that identity statements between names are necessary has usually been rejected. [. . .]

What should we think about this? First, it's true that someone can use the name 'Cicero' to refer to Cicero and the name 'Tully' to refer to Cicero also, and not know that Cicero is Tully. So it seems that we do not necessarily know *a priori* that an identity statement between names is true. It doesn't follow from this that

the statement so expressed is a contingent one if true. This is what I've emphasized in my first lecture. There is a very strong feeling that leads one to think that, if you can't know something by *a priori* ratiocination, then it's got to be contingent: it might have turned out otherwise; but nevertheless I think this feeling is wrong.

Let's suppose we refer to the same heavenly body twice, as 'Hesperus' and 'Phosphorus'. We say: Hesperus is that star over there in the evening; Phosphorus is that star over there in the morning. Actually, Hesperus is Phosphorus. Are there really circumstances under which Hesperus wouldn't have been Phosphorus? Supposing that Hesperus is Phosphorus, let's try to describe a possible situation in which it would not have been. Well, it's easy. Someone goes by and he calls two *different* stars 'Hesperus' and 'Phosphorus'. It may even be under the same conditions as prevailed when we introduced the names 'Hesperus' and 'Phosphorus'. But are those circumstances in which Hesperus is not Phosphorus or would not have been Phosphorus? It seems to me that they are not.

Now, of course I'm committed to saying that they're not, by saying that such terms as 'Hesperus' and 'Phosphorus', when used as names, are rigid designators. They refer in every possible world to the planet Venus. Therefore, in that possible world too, the planet Venus is the planet Venus and it doesn't matter what any other person has said in this other possible world. How should *we* describe this situation? He can't have pointed to Venus twice, and in the one case called it 'Hesperus' and in the other 'Phosphorus', as we did. If he did so, then 'Hesperus is Phosphorus' would have been true in that situation too. He pointed maybe neither time to the planet Venus—at least one time he didn't point to the planet Venus, let's say when he pointed to the body he called 'Phosphorus'. Then in that case we can certainly say that the name 'Phosphorus' might not have referred to Phosphorus. We can even say that in the very position when viewed in the morning that we found Phosphorus, it might have been the case that Phosphorus was not there—that something else was there, and that even, under certain circumstances it would have been *called* 'Phosphorus'. But that still is not a case in which Phosphorus was not Hesperus. There might be a possible world in which, a possible counterfactual situation in

5. p. 101.
6. p. 115.

which, 'Hesperus' and 'Phosphorus' weren't names of the things they in fact are names of. Someone, if he did determine their reference by identifying descriptions, might even have used the very identifying descriptions we used. But still that's not a case in which Hesperus wasn't Phosphorus. For there couldn't have been such a case, given that Hesperus is Phosphorus.

Now this seems very strange because in advance, we are inclined to say, the answer to the question whether Hesperus is Phosphorus might have turned out either way. So aren't there really two possible worlds—one in which Hesperus was Phosphorus, the other in which Hesperus wasn't Phosphorus—in advance of our discovering that these were the same? First, there's one sense in which things might turn out either way, in which it's clear that that doesn't imply that the way it finally turns out isn't necessary. For example, the four color theorem might turn out to be true and might turn out to be false. It might turn out either way. It still doesn't mean that the way it turns out is not necessary. Obviously, the 'might' here is purely 'epistemic'—it merely expresses our present state of ignorance, or uncertainty.

But it seems that in the Hesperus-Phosphorus case, something even stronger is true. The evidence I have before I know that Hesperus is Phosphorus is that I see a certain star or a certain heavenly body in the evening and call it 'Hesperus', and in the morning call it 'Phosphorus'. I know these things. There certainly is a possible world in which a man should have seen a certain star at a certain position in the evening and called it 'Hesperus' and a certain star in the morning and called it 'Phosphorus'; and should have concluded—should have found out by empirical investigation—that he names two different stars, or two different heavenly bodies. At least one of these stars or heavenly bodies was not Phosphorus, otherwise it couldn't have come out that way. But that's true. And so it's true that given the evidence that someone has antecedent to his empirical investigation, he can be placed in a sense in exactly the same situation, that is a qualitatively identical epistemic situation, and call two heavenly bodies 'Hesperus' and 'Phosphorus', without their being identical. So in that

sense we can say that it might have turned out either way. Not that it might have turned out either way as to Hesperus's being Phosphorus. Though for all we knew in advance, Hesperus wasn't Phosphorus, that couldn't have turned out any other way, in a sense. But being put in a situation where we have exactly the same evidence, qualitatively speaking, it could have turned out that Hesperus was not Phosphorus; that is, in a counterfactual world in which 'Hesperus' and 'Phosphorus' were not used in the way that we use them, as names of this planet, but as names of some other objects, one could have had qualitatively identical evidence and concluded that 'Hesperus' and 'Phosphorus' named two different objects. But we, using the names as we do right now, can say in advance, that if Hesperus and Phosphorus are one and the same, then in no other possible world can they be different. We use 'Hesperus' as the name of a certain body and 'Phosphorus' as the name of a certain body. We use them as names of those bodies in all possible worlds. If, in fact, they are the *same* body, then in any other possible world we have to use them as a name of that object. And so in any other possible world it will be true that Hesperus is Phosphorus. So two things are true: first, that we do not know *a priori* that Hesperus is Phosphorus, and are in no position to find out the answer except empirically. Second, this is so because we could have evidence qualitatively indistinguishable from the evidence we have and determine the reference of the two names by the positions of two planets in the sky, without the planets being the same.

Of course, it is only a contingent truth (not true in every other possible world) that the star seen over there in the evening is the star seen over there in the morning, because there are possible worlds in which Phosphorus was not visible in the morning. But that contingent truth shouldn't be identified with the statement that Hesperus is Phosphorus. It could only be so identified if you though that it was a necessary truth that Hesperus is visible over there in the evening or that Phosphorus is visible over there in the morning. But neither of those are necessary truths even if that's the way we pick out the planet. These are the contingent marks by which we identify a certain planet and give it a name.

Edmund L. Gettier

Is Justified True Belief Knowledge?

Various attempts have been made in recent years to state necessary and sufficient conditions for someone's knowing a given proposition. The attempts have often been such that they can be stated in a form similar to the following:

(a) S knows that P   *IFF*   (i) P is true,
  (ii) S believes that P, and
  (iii) S is justified in believing that P.

For example, Chisholm has held that the following gives the necessary and sufficient conditions for knowledge:[1]

(b) S knows that P   *IFF*   (i) S accepts P,
  (ii) S has adequate evidence for P, and
  (iii) P is true.

Ayer has stated the necessary and sufficient conditions for knowledge as follows:[2]

(c) S knows that P   *IFF*   (i) P is true,
  (ii) S is sure that P is true, and
  (iii) S has the right to be sure that P is true.

I shall argue that (a) is false in that the conditions stated therein do not constitute a *sufficient* condition for the

Edmund Gettier, "Is Justified True Belief Knowledge?" from *Analysis,* 23 (1963). Reprinted with permission of Blackwell Publishing, Ltd.

1. Roderick M. Chisholm, *Perceiving: A Philosophical Study,* Cornell University Press (Ithaca, New York, 1957), p. 16.
2. A. J. Ayer, *The Problem of Knowledge,* Macmillan (London, 1956), p. 34.

truth of the proposition that S knows that P. The same argument will show that (b) and (c) fail if 'has adequate evidence for' or 'has the right to be sure that' is substituted for 'is justified in believing that' throughout.

I shall begin by noting two points. First, in that sense of 'justified' in which S's being justified in believing P is a necessary condition of S's knowing that P, it is possible for a person to be justified in believing a proposition that is in fact false. Secondly, for any proposition P, if S is justified in believing P, and P entails Q, and S deduced Q from P and accepts Q as a result of this deduction, then S is justified in believing Q. Keeping these two points in mind, I shall now present two cases in which the conditions stated in (a) are true for some proposition, though it is at the same time false that the person in question knows that proposition.

Case I:

Suppose that Smith and Jones have applied for a certain job. And suppose that Smith has strong evidence for the following conjunctive proposition:

(d) Jones is the man who will get the job, and Jones has ten coins in his pocket.

Smith's evidence for (d) might be that the president of the company assured him that Jones would in the end be selected, and that he, Smith, had counted the coins in Jones's pocket ten minutes ago. Proposition (d) entails:

(e) The man who will get the job has ten coins in his pocket.

Let us suppose that Smith sees the entailment from (d) to (e), and accepts (e) on the grounds of (d), for which he has strong evidence. In this case, Smith is clearly justified in believing that (e) is true.

But imagine, further, that unknown to Smith, he himself, not Jones, will get the job. And, also, unknown to Smith, he himself has ten coins in his pocket. Proposition (e) is then true, though proposition (d) from which

Smith inferred (e), is false. In our example, then, all of the following are true: (*i*) (e) is true, (*ii*) Smith believes that (e) is true, and (*iii*) Smith is justified in believing that (e) is true. But it is equally clear that Smith does not *know* that (e) is true; for (e) is true in virtue of the number of coins in Smith's pocket, while Smith does not know how many coins are in Smith's pocket, and bases his belief in (e) on a count of the coins in Jones's pocket, whom he falsely believes to be the man who will get the job.

Case II:

Let us suppose that Smith has strong evidence for the following proposition:

(f) Jones owns a Ford.

Smith's evidence might be that Jones has at all times in the past within Smith's memory owned a car, and always a Ford, and that Jones has just offered Smith a ride while driving a Ford. Let us imagine, now, that Smith has another friend, Brown, of whose whereabouts he is totally ignorant. Smith selects three place-names quite at random, and constructs the following three propositions:

(g) Either Jones owns a Ford, or Brown is in Boston;

(h) Either Jones owns a Ford, or Brown is in Barcelona;

(i) Either Jones owns a Ford, or Brown is in Brest-Litovsk.

Each of these propositions is entailed by (f). Imagine that Smith realizes the entailment of each of these propositions he has constructed by (f), and proceeds to accept (g), (h), and (i) on the basis of (f). Smith has correctly inferred (g), (h), and (i) from a proposition for which he has strong evidence. Smith is therefore completely justified in believing each of these three propositions. Smith, of course, has no idea where Brown is.

But imagine now that two further conditions hold. First, Jones does *not* own a Ford, but is at present driving a rented car. And secondly, by the sheerest coincidence, and entirely unknown to Smith, the place mentioned in proposition (h) happens really to be the place where Brown is. If these two conditions hold then Smith does *not* know that (h) is true, even though (*i*) (h) *is* true, (*ii*) Smith does believe that (h) is true, and (*iii*) Smith is justified in believing that (h) is true.

These two examples show that definition (a) does not state a *sufficient* condition for someone's knowing a given proposition. The same cases, with appropriate changes, will suffice to show that neither definition (b) nor definition (c) do so either.

Robert Nozick

An Analysis of Knowledge

You think you are seeing these words, but could you not be hallucinating or dreaming or having your brain stimulated to give you the experience of seeing these marks on paper although no such thing is before you? More extremely, could you not be floating in a tank while super-psychologists stimulate your brain electrochemically to produce exactly the same experiences as you are now having, or even to produce the whole sequence of experiences you have had in your lifetime thus far? If one of these other things was happening, your experience would be exactly the same as it now is. So how can you know none of them is happening? Yet if you do not know these possibilities don't hold, how can you know you are reading this book now? If you do not know you haven't always been floating in the tank at the mercy of the psychologists, how can you know anything—what your name is, who your parents were, where you come from?

Reprinted by permission of the publisher from "Knowledge and Skepticism" in *Philosophical Explanations* by Robert Nozick, Cambridge, Mass.: The Belknap Press of Harvard University Press. Copyright © 1981 by Robert Nozick.

The skeptic argues that we do not know what we think we do. Even when he leaves us unconverted, he leaves us confused. Granting that we do know, how *can* we? Given these other possibilities he poses, how is knowledge possible? In answering this question, we do not seek to convince the skeptic, but rather to formulate hypotheses about knowledge and our connection to facts that show how knowledge can exist even given the skeptic's possibilities. These hypotheses must reconcile our belief that we know things with our belief that the skeptical possibilities are logical possibilities.

The skeptical possibilities, and the threats they pose to our knowledge, depend upon our knowing things (if we do) mediately, through or by way of something else. Our thinking or believing that some fact *p* holds is connected somehow to the fact that *p*, but is not itself identical with that fact. Intermediate links establish the connection. This leaves room for the possibility of these intermediate stages holding and producing our belief that *p*, without the fact that *p* being at the other end. The intermediate stages arise in a completely different manner, one not involving the fact that *p* although giving rise to the appearance that *p* holds true.

Are the skeptic's possibilities indeed logically possible? Imagine reading a science fiction story in which someone is raised from birth floating in a tank with psychologists stimulating his brain. The story could go on to tell of the person's reactions when he is brought out of the tank, of how the psychologists convince him of what had been happening to him, or how they fail to do so. This story is coherent, there is nothing self-contradictory or otherwise impossible about it. Nor is there anything incoherent in imagining that you are now in this situation, at a time before being taken out of the tank. To ease the transition out, to prepare the way, perhaps the psychologists will give the person in the tank thoughts of whether floating in the tank is possible, or the experience of reading a book that discusses this possibility, even one that discusses their easing this transition. (Free will presents no insuperable problem for this possibility. Perhaps the psychologists caused all your experiences of choice, including the feeling of freely choosing; or perhaps you do freely choose to act while they, cutting the effector circuit, continue the scenario from there.)

Some philosophers have attempted to demonstrate there is no such coherent possibility of this sort. However, for any reasoning that purports to show this skeptical possibility cannot occur, we can imagine the psychologists of our science fiction story feeding *it* to their tank-subject, along with the (inaccurate) feeling that the reasoning is cogent. So how much trust can be placed in the apparent cogency of an argument to show the skeptical possibility isn't coherent?

The skeptic's possibility is a logically coherent one, in tension with the existence of (almost all) knowledge; so we seek a hypothesis to explain how, even given the skeptic's possibilities, knowledge is possible. We may worry that such explanatory hypotheses are ad hoc, but this worry will lessen if they yield other facts as well, fit in with other things we believe, and so forth. Indeed, the theory of knowledge that follows was not developed in order to explain how knowledge is possible. Rather, the motivation was external to epistemology; only after the account of knowledge was developed for another purpose did I notice its consequences for skepticism, for understanding how knowledge is possible. So whatever other defects the explanation might have, it can hardly be called ad hoc.

My original aim was to make progress on the topic of free will. Early in the flurry of journal articles presenting counterexamples to increasingly complicated accounts of knowledge, stimulated by Edward Gettier's counterexample to the traditional account of knowledge as justified true belief, I despaired of anyone's getting it exactly right. So messy did it all seem that I just stopped reading that literature. I was led back to the task of formulating conditions for knowledge, by the following line of reasoning.

In knowledge, a belief is linked somehow to the fact believed; without this linkage there may be true belief but there will not be knowledge. Plato first made the point that knowledge is not simply a belief that is true; if someone knowing nothing about the matter separately tells you and me contradictory things, getting one of us to believe *p* while the other believes not-*p*, although one of us will have a belief that happens to be true, neither of us will have knowledge. Something more is needed for a person S to know that *p*, to go alongside

(1)　　*p* is true

(2)　　S believes that *p*.

This something more, I think, is not simply an additional fact, but a way that 1 and 2 are linked. Thus, consider the traditional third condition stemming from Plato's account: S is justified in believing that *p*, or S has adequate evidence that *p*. Here, a two-part linkage connects S's belief that *p* with the fact that *p*: the link between the fact that *p* and the evidence, and the link between the evidence and the belief that *p*.

Recently it has been urged, with some plausibility, that the requisite linkage of belief to facts is a causal one, that the third condition is something like: the fact that *p* (partially) causes S to believe that *p*, that is, 2 because 1. A drunk who hallucinates a pink elephant in a bar where, behind a screen, there is a pink elephant does not know there is a pink elephant there. The elephant's being there is not a cause of his believing it there. Whereas, in tracing back through the causes of your believing there now is a book before you, we eventually reach the fact that there *is* a book before you. The causal account of knowledge thus has a certain plausibility. Since, on this view, the causation (in a certain way) of our beliefs is necessary for us to have knowledge, such causation therefore is desirable. To be sure, there are difficulties with the causal account of knowledge, most noticeably with mathematical knowledge and ethical knowledge but elsewhere as well. In these cases, the appropriate kind of causal connection fails to hold. Yet where it does hold, when a belief is caused appropriately by the fact, that connection appears desirable and plausibly is held to constitute knowledge.

In contrast, we strongly feel that the causal determination of action threatens responsibility and is undesirable. It is puzzling that what is desirable for belief, perhaps even necessary for knowledge, is threatening for action. Might not there be a way for action to parallel belief, to be so connected to the world, even causally, in a way that is desirable? At the least, it would be instructive to see where and why the parallel fails. If it did not fail, causality of action would be rendered harmless—determinism would be defanged.

The idea is to investigate how action is to be connected to the world, to parallel the connection of belief to fact when there is knowledge. This need not assume a causal account of knowledge. The causal linkage which appears to be a constituent in knowledge may be merely one way of realizing a more general linkage that constitutes knowledge. This would leave some room for ethical and mathematical knowledge, and perhaps even for a noncausal connection of action to the world that is not undercut by causality, just as mathematical knowledge, presumably, is not undercut by belief's being caused. To see if our actions desirably can be like knowledge, the first task is to see precisely what connection of belief to fact knowledge involves—then we shall know what it is that action must parallel.

It was this line of thought, this project of paralleling, that led me to investigate the details of the knowledge-link in the hope that it could be put to use later. What started as a means to another topic provided, along the way, an explanation of how knowledge is possible. This side result is especially fortunate in view of the free will problem's intractability.

• • • • •

Conditions for Knowledge

Our task is to formulate further conditions to go alongside

(1)   *p* is true

(2)   S believes that *p*.

We would like each condition to be necessary for knowledge, so any case that fails to satisfy it will not be an instance of knowledge. Furthermore, we would like the conditions to be jointly sufficient for knowledge, so any case that satisfies all of them will be an instance of knowledge. We first shall formulate conditions that seem to handle ordinary cases correctly, classifying as knowledge cases which are knowledge, and as nonknowledge cases which are not; then we shall check to see how these conditions handle some difficult cases discussed in the literature.

The causal condition on knowledge, previously mentioned, provides an inhospitable environment for mathematical and ethical knowledge; also there are well-known difficulties in specifying the type of causal connection. If someone floating in a tank oblivious to everything around him is given (by direct electrical and chemical stimulation of the brain) the belief that he is floating in a tank with his brain being stimulated, then even though that fact is part of the cause of his belief, still he does not know that it is true.

Let us consider a different third condition:

(3)   If p weren't true, S wouldn't believe that p.

Throughout this work, let us write the subjunctive 'if-then' by an arrow, and the negation of a sentence by prefacing "not-" to it. The above condition thus is rewritten as:

(3)   not-p → not-(S believes that p).

This subjunctive condition is not unrelated to the causal condition. Often when the fact that p (partially) causes someone to believe that p, the fact also will be causally necessary for his having the belief—without the cause, the effect would not occur. In that case, the subjunctive condition 3 also will be satisfied. Yet this condition is not equivalent to the causal condition. For the causal condition will be satisfied in cases of causal overdetermination, where either two sufficient causes of the effect actually operate, or a back-up cause (of the same effect) would operate if the first one didn't; whereas the subjunctive condition need not hold for these cases. When the two conditions do agree, causality indicates knowledge because it acts in a manner that makes the subjunctive 3 true.

The subjunctive condition 3 serves to exclude cases of the sort first described by Edward Gettier, such as the following. Two other people are in my office and I am justified on the basis of much evidence in believing the first owns a Ford car; though he (now) does not, the second person (a stranger to me) owns one. I believe truly and justifiably that someone (or other) in my office owns a Ford car, but I do not know someone does. Concluded Gettier, knowledge is not simply justified true belief.

The following subjunctive, which specifies condition 3 for this Gettier case, is not satisfied: if no one in my office owned a Ford car, I wouldn't believe that someone did. The situation that would obtain if no one in my office owned a Ford is one where the stranger does not (or where he is not in the office); and in that situation I still would believe, as before, that someone in my office does own a Ford, namely the first person. So the

subjunctive condition 3 excludes this Gettier case as a case of knowledge.

The subjunctive condition is powerful and intuitive, not so easy to satisfy, yet not so powerful as to rule out everything as an instance of knowledge. A subjunctive conditional "if p were true, q would be true," p→q, does not say that p entails q or that it is logically impossible that p yet not-q. It says that in the situation that would obtain if p were true, q also would be true. This point is brought out especially clearly in recent 'possible-worlds' accounts of subjunctives: the subjunctive is true when (roughly) in all those worlds in which p holds true that are closest to the actual world, q also is true. (Examine those worlds in which p holds true closest to the actual world, and see if q holds true in all these.) Whether or not q is true in p worlds that are still farther away from the actual world is irrelevant to the truth of the subjunctive. I do not mean to endorse any particular possible-worlds account of subjunctives, nor am I committed to this type of account. I sometimes shall use it, though, when it illustrates points in an especially clear way.

The subjunctive condition 3 also handles nicely cases that cause difficulties for the view that you know that p when you can rule out the relevant alternatives to p in the context. For, as Gail Stine writes, "what makes an alternative relevant in one context and not another? ... if on the basis of visual appearances obtained under optimum conditions while driving through the countryside Henry identifies an object as a barn, normally we say that Henry knows that it is a barn. Let us suppose, however, that unknown to Henry, the region is full of expertly made papier-mâché facsimiles of barns. In that case, we would not say that Henry knows that the object is a barn, unless he has evidence against it being a papier-mâché facsimile, which is now a relevant alternative. So much is clear, but what if no such facsimiles exist in Henry's surroundings, although they once did? Are either of these circumstances sufficient to make the hypothesis (that it's a papier-mâché object) relevant? Probably not, but the situation is not so clear."[1] Let p be the statement that the object in the field is a (real) barn, and q the one that the object in the field is a papier-mâché barn. When papier-mâché barns are scattered

---

1. G. C. Stine, "Skepticism, Relevant Alternatives and Deductive Closure," *Philosophical Studies* 29 (1976), p. 252.

through the area, if p were false, q would be true or might be. Since in this case (we are supposing) the person still would believe p, the subjunctive

(3)   not-p → not-(S believes that p)

is not satisfied, and so he doesn't know that p. However, when papier-mâché barns are or were scattered around another country, even if p were false q wouldn't be true, and so (for all we have been told) the person may well know that p. A hypothesis q contrary to p clearly is relevant when if p weren't true, q would be true; when not-p → q. It clearly is irrelevant when if p weren't true, q also would not be true; when not-p → not-q. The remaining possibility is that neither of these opposed subjunctives holds; q might (or might not) be true if p weren't true. In this case, q also will be relevant, according to an account of knowledge incorporating condition 3 and treating subjunctives along the lines sketched above. Thus, condition 3 handles cases that befuddle the "relevant alternatives" account; though that account can adopt the above subjunctive criterion for when an alternative is relevant, it then becomes merely an alternate and longer way of stating condition 3.

Despite the power and intuitive force of the condition that if p weren't true the person would not believe it, this condition does not (in conjunction with the first two conditions) rule out every problem case. There remains, for example, the case of the person in the tank who is brought to believe, by direct electrical and chemical stimulation of his brain, that he is in the tank and is being brought to believe things in this way; he does not know this is true. However, the subjunctive condition is satisfied: if he weren't floating in the tank, he wouldn't believe he was.

The person in the tank does not know he is there, because his belief is not sensitive to the truth. Although it is caused by the fact that is its content, it is not sensitive to that fact. The operators of the tank could have produced any belief, including the false belief that he wasn't in the tank; if they had, he would have believed that. Perfect sensitivity would involve beliefs and facts varying together. We already have one portion of that variation, subjunctively at least: if p were false he wouldn't believe it. This sensitivity as specified by a subjunctive does not have the belief vary with the truth or

falsity of p in all possible situations, merely in the ones that would or might obtain if p were false.

The subjunctive condition

(3)   not-p → not-(S believes that p)

tells us only half the story about how his belief is sensitive to the truth-value of p. It tells us how his belief state is sensitive to p's falsity, but not how it is sensitive to p's truth; it tells us what his belief state would be if p were false, but not what it would be if p were true.

To be sure, conditions 1 and 2 tell us that p is true and he does believe it, but it does not follow that his believing p is sensitive to p's being true. This additional sensitivity is given to us by a further subjunctive: if p were true, he would believe it.

(4) p → S believes that p.

Not only is p true and S believes it, but if it were true he would believe it. Compare: not only was the photon emitted and did it go to the left, but (it was then true that): if it were emitted it would go to the left. The truth of antecedent and consequent is not alone sufficient for the truth of a subjunctive; 4 says more than 1 and 2. Thus, we presuppose some (or another) suitable account of subjunctives. According to the suggestion tentatively made above, 4 holds true if not only does he actually truly believe p, but in the "close" worlds where p is true, he also believes it. He believes that p for some distance out in the p neighborhood of the actual world; similarly, condition 3 speaks not of the whole not-p neighborhood of the actual world, but only of the first portion of it. (If, as is likely, these explanations do not help, please use your own intuitive understanding of the subjunctives 3 and 4.)

The person in the tank does not satisfy the subjunctive condition 4. Imagine as actual a world in which he is in the tank and is stimulated to believe he is, and consider what subjunctives are true in that world. It is not true of him there that if he were in the tank he would believe it; for in the close world (or situation) to his own where he is in the tank but they don't give him the belief that he is (much less instill the belief that he isn't) he doesn't believe he is in the tank. Of the person actually in the tank and believing it, it is not true to make the further statement that if he were in the tank he would believe it—so he does not know he is in the tank.

The subjunctive condition 4 also handles a case presented by Gilbert Harman.[2] The dictator of a country is killed; in their first edition, newspapers print the story, but later all the country's newspapers and other media deny the story, falsely. Everyone who encounters the denial believes it (or does not know what to believe and so suspends judgment). Only one person in the country fails to hear any denial and he continues to believe the truth. He satisfies conditions 1 through 3 (and the causal condition about belief) yet we are reluctant to say he knows the truth. The reason is that if he had heard the denials, he too would have believed them, just like everyone else. His belief is not sensitively tuned to the truth, he doesn't satisfy the condition that if it were true he would believe it. Condition 4 is not satisfied.

There is a pleasing symmetry about how this account of knowledge relates conditions 3 and 4, and connects them to the first two conditions. The account has the following form.

(1)

(2)

(3)   not-1 → not-2

(4)   1 → 2

I am not inclined, however, to make too much of this symmetry, for I found also that with other conditions experimented with as a possible fourth condition there was some way to construe the resulting third and fourth conditions as symmetrical answers to some symmetrical looking questions, so that they appeared to arise in parallel fashion from similar questions about the components of true belief.

Symmetry, it seems is a feature of a mode of presentation, not of the contents presented. A uniform transformation of symmetrical statements can leave the results nonsymmetrical. But if symmetry attaches to a mode of presentation, how can it possibly be a deep feature of, for instance, laws of nature that they exhibit symmetry? (One of my favorite examples of symmetry is due to Groucho Marx. On his radio program he spoofed a commercial, and ended, "And if you are not completely satisfied, return the unused portion of our product and we will return the unused portion of your money.") Still, to present our subject symmetrically makes the connection of knowledge to true belief especially perspicuous. It seems to me that symmetrical formulation is a sign of our understanding, rather than a mark of truth. If we cannot understand an asymmetry as arising from an underlying symmetry through the operation of a particular factor, we will not understand why that asymmetry exists in that direction. (But do we also need to understand why the underlying asymmetrical factor holds instead of the opposite?)

A person knows that *p* when he not only does truly believe it, but also would truly believe it and wouldn't falsely believe it. He not only actually has a true belief, he subjunctively has one. It is true that *p* and he believes it; if it weren't true, he wouldn't believe it, and if it were true he would believe it. To know that *p* is to be someone who would believe it if it were true, and who wouldn't believe it if it were false.

It will be useful to have a term for this situation when a person's belief is thus subjunctively connected to the fact. Let us say of a person who believes that *p*, which is true, that when 3 and 4 hold, his belief *tracks* the truth that *p*. To know is to have a belief that tracks the truth. Knowledge is a particular was of being connected to the world, having a specific real factual connection to the world: tracking it.

One refinement is needed in condition 4. It may be possible for someone to have contradictory beliefs, to believe *p* and also believe not-*p*. We do not mean such a person to easily satisfy 4, and in any case we want his belief-state, sensitive to the truth of *p*, to focus upon *p*. So let us rewrite our fourth condition as:

(4)   *p* → S believes that *p* and not-(S believes that not-*p*). [. . .]

2. Gilbert Harman, *Thought*. Princeton: Princeton University Press, 1973, pp. 142–54.

Skepticism and the Scope of Knowledge

René Descartes

Meditations on First Philosophy

Meditation One: Concerning Those Things That Can Be Called into Doubt

Several years have now passed since I first realized how numerous were the false opinions that in my youth I had taken to be true, and thus how doubtful were all those that I had subsequently built upon them. And thus I realized that once in my life I had to raze everything to the ground and begin again from the original foundations, if I wanted to establish anything firm and lasting in the sciences. But the task seemed enormous, and I was waiting until I reached a point in my life that was so timely that no more suitable time for undertaking these plans of action would come to pass. For this reason, I procrastinated for so long that I would henceforth be at fault, were I to waste the time that remains for carrying out the project by brooding over it. Accordingly, I have today suitably freed my mind of all cares, secured for myself a period of leisurely tranquillity, and am withdrawing into solitude. At last I will apply myself earnestly and unreservedly to this general demolition of my opinions.

Yet to bring this about I will not need to show that all my opinions are false, which is perhaps something I could never accomplish. But reason now persuades me that I should withhold my assent no less carefully from opinions that are not completely certain and indubitable than I would from those that are patently false. For this reason, it will suffice for the rejection of all of these opinions, if I find in each of them some reason for doubt. Nor therefore need I survey each opinion individually, a task that would be endless. Rather, because undermining the foundations will cause whatever has been built upon them to crumble of its own accord, I will attack straightaway those principles which supported everything I once believed.

Surely whatever I had admitted until now as most true I received either from the senses or through the senses. However, I have noticed that the senses are sometimes deceptive; and it is a mark of prudence never to place our complete trust in those who have deceived us even once.

But perhaps, even though the senses do sometimes deceive us when it is a question of very small and distant things, still there are many other matters concerning which one simply cannot doubt, even though they are derived from the very same senses: for example, that I am sitting here next to the fire, wearing my winter dressing gown, that I am holding this sheet of paper in my hands, and the like. But on what grounds could one deny that these hands and this entire body are mine? Unless perhaps I were to liken myself to the insane, whose brains are impaired by such an unrelenting vapor of black bile that they steadfastly insist that they are kings when they are utter paupers, or that they are arrayed in purple robes when they are naked, or that they have heads made of clay, or that they are gourds, or that they are made of glass. But such people are mad, and I would appear no less mad, were I to take their behavior as an example for myself.

This would all be well and good, were I not a man who is accustomed to sleeping at night, and to experiencing in my dreams the very same things, or now and then even less plausible ones, as these insane people do

From René Descartes, *Meditations on First Philosophy,* translated by Donald A. Cress (Indianapolis: Hackett Publishing Company, 1993). Reprinted by permission of the publisher.

when they are awake. How often does my evening slumber persuade me of such ordinary things as these: that I am here, clothed in my dressing gown, seated next to the fireplace—when in fact I am lying undressed in bed! But right now my eyes are certainly wide awake when I gaze upon this sheet of paper. This head which I am shaking is not heavy with sleep. I extend this hand consciously and deliberately, and I feel it. Such things would not be so distinct for someone who is asleep. As if I did not recall having been deceived on other occasions even by similar thoughts in my dreams! As I consider these matters more carefully, I see so plainly that there are no definitive signs by which to distinguish being awake from being asleep. As a result, I am becoming quite dizzy, and this dizziness nearly convinces me that I am asleep.

Let us assume then, for the sake of argument, that we are dreaming and that such particulars as these are not true: that we are opening our eyes, moving our head, and extending our hands. Perhaps we do not even have such hands, or any such body at all. Nevertheless, it surely must be admitted that the things seen during slumber are, as it were, like painted images, which could only have been produced in the likeness of true things, and that therefore at least these general things—eyes, head, hands, and the whole body—are not imaginary things, but are true and exist. For indeed when painters themselves wish to represent sirens and satyrs by means of especially bizarre forms, they surely cannot assign to them utterly new natures. Rather, they simply fuse together the members of various animals. Or if perhaps they concoct something so utterly novel that nothing like it has ever been seen before (and thus is something utterly fictitious and false), yet certainly at the very least the colors from which they fashion it ought to be true. And by the same token, although even these general things—eyes, head, hands and the like—could be imaginary, still one has to admit that at least certain other things that are even more simple and universal are true. It is from these components, as if from true colors, that all those images of things that are in our thought are fashioned, be they true or false.

This class of things appears to include corporeal nature in general, together with its extension; the shape of extended things; their quantity, that is, their size and number; as well as the place where they exist; the time through which they endure, and the like.

Thus it is not improper to conclude from this that physics, astronomy, medicine, and all the other disciplines that are dependent upon the consideration of composite things are doubtful, and that, on the other hand, arithmetic, geometry, and other such disciplines, which treat of nothing but the simplest and most general things and which are indifferent as to whether these things do or do not in fact exist, contain something certain and indubitable. For whether I am awake or asleep, two plus three make five, and a square does not have more than four sides. It does not seem possible that such obvious truths should be subject to the suspicion of being false.

Be that as it may, there is fixed in my mind a certain opinion of long standing, namely that there exists a God who is able to do anything and by whom I, such as I am, have been created. How do I know that he did not bring it about that there is no earth at all, no heavens, no extended thing, no shape, no size, no place, and yet bringing it about that all these things appear to me to exist precisely as they do now? Moreover, since I judge that others sometimes make mistakes in matters that they believe they know most perfectly, may I not, in like fashion, be deceived every time I add two and three or count the sides of a square, or perform an even simpler operation, if that can be imagined? But perhaps God has not willed that I be deceived in this way, for he is said to be supremely good. Nonetheless, if it were repugnant to his goodness to have created me such that I be deceived all the time, it would also seem foreign to that same goodness to permit me to be deceived even occasionally. But we cannot make this last assertion.

Perhaps there are some who would rather deny so powerful a God than believe that everything else is uncertain. Let us not oppose them; rather, let us grant that everything said here about God is fictitious. Now they suppose that I came to be what I am either by fate, or by chance, or by a connected chain of events, or by some other way. But because being deceived and being mistaken appear to be a certain imperfection, the less powerful they take the author of my origin to be, the more probable it will be that I am so imperfect that I am always deceived. I have nothing to say in response to these arguments. But eventually I am forced to admit that there is nothing among the things I once believed to be true which it is not permissible to doubt—and not out of frivolity or lack of forethought, but for valid and considered reasons. Thus I must be no less careful to withhold assent henceforth even from these beliefs than I would from those that are patently false, if I wish to find anything certain.

But it is not enough simply to have realized these things; I must take steps to keep myself mindful of them. For long-standing opinions keep returning, and, almost against my will, they take advantage of my credulity, as if it were bound over to them by long use and the claims of intimacy. Nor will I ever get out of the habit of assenting to them and believing in them, so long as I take them to be exactly what they are, namely, in some respects doubtful, as has just now been shown, but nevertheless highly probable, so that it is much more consonant with reason to believe them than to deny them. Hence, it seems to me I would do well to deceive myself by turning my will in completely the opposite direction and pretend for a time that these opinions are wholly false and imaginary, until finally, as if with prejudices weighing down each side equally, no bad habit should turn my judgment any further from the correct perception of things. For indeed I know that meanwhile there is no danger or error in following this procedure, and that it is impossible for me to indulge in too much distrust, since I am now concentrating only on knowledge, not on action. Accordingly, I will suppose not a supremely good God, the source of truth, but rather an evil genius, supremely powerful and clever, who has directed his entire effort at deceiving me. I will regard the heavens, the air, the earth, colors, shapes, sounds, and all external things as nothing but the bedeviling hoaxes of my dreams, with which he lays snares for my credulity. I will regard myself as not having hands, or eyes, or flesh, or blood, or any senses, but as nevertheless falsely believing that I possess all these things. I will remain resolute and steadfast in this meditation, and even if it is not within my power to know anything true, it certainly is within my power to take care resolutely to withhold my assent to what is false, lest this deceiver, however powerful, however clever he may be, have any effect on me. But this undertaking is arduous, and a certain laziness brings me back to my customary way of living. I am not unlike a prisoner who enjoyed an imaginary freedom during his sleep, but, when he later begins to suspect that he is dreaming, fears being awakened and nonchalantly conspires with these pleasant illusions. In

just the same way, I fall back of my own accord into my old opinions, and dread being awakened, lest the toilsome wakefulness which follows upon a peaceful rest must be spent thenceforward not in the light but among the inextricable shadows of the difficulties now brought forward.

Meditation Two: Concerning the Nature of the Human Mind: That It Is Better Known than the Body

Yesterday's meditation has thrown me into such doubts that I can no longer ignore them, yet I fail to see how they are to be resolved. It is as if I had suddenly fallen into a deep whirlpool; I am so tossed about that I can neither touch bottom with my foot, nor swim up to the top. Nevertheless I will work my way up and will once again attempt the same path I entered upon yesterday. I will accomplish this by putting aside everything that admits of the least doubt, as if I had discovered it to be completely false. I will stay on this course until I know something certain, or, if nothing else, until I at least know for certain that nothing is certain. Archimedes sought but one firm and immovable point in order to move the entire earth from one place to another. Just so, great things are also to be hoped for if I succeed in finding just one thing, however slight, that is certain and unshaken.

Therefore I suppose that everything I see is false. I believe that none of what my deceitful memory represents ever existed. I have no senses whatever. Body, shape, extension, movement, and place are all chimeras. What then will be true? Perhaps just the single fact that nothing is certain.

But how do I know there is not something else, over and above all those things that I have just reviewed, concerning which there is not even the slightest occasion for doubt? Is there not some God, or by whatever name I might call him, who instills these very thoughts in me? But why would I think that, since I myself could perhaps be the author of these thoughts? Am I not then at least something? But I have already denied that I have any senses and any body. Still I hesitate; for what follows from this? Am I so tied to a body and to the senses that I cannot exist without them? But I have persuaded myself that there is absolutely nothing in the world: no sky, no earth, no minds, no bodies. Is it then the case that I too do not exist? But doubtless I did exist, if I persuaded myself of something. But there is some deceiver or other who is supremely powerful and supremely sly and who is always deliberately deceiving me. Then too there is no doubt that I exist, if he is deceiving me. And let him do his best at deception, he will never bring it about that I am nothing so long as I shall think that I am something. Thus, after everything has been most carefully weighed, it must finally be established that this pronouncement "I am, I exist" is necessarily true every time I utter it or conceive it in my mind.

But I do not yet understand sufficiently what I am—I, who now necessarily exist. And so from this point on, I must be careful lest I unwittingly mistake something else for myself, and thus err in that very item of knowledge that I claim to be the most certain and evident of all. Thus, I will meditate once more on what I once believed myself to be, prior to embarking upon these thoughts. For this reason, then, I will set aside whatever can be weakened even to the slightest degree by the arguments brought forward, so that eventually all that remains is precisely nothing but what is certain and unshaken.

What then did I use to think I was? A man, of course. But what is a man? Might I not say a "rational animal"? No, because then I would have to inquire what "animal" and "rational" mean. And thus from one question I would slide into many more difficult ones. Nor do I now have enough free time that I want to waste it on subtleties of this sort. Instead, permit me to focus here on what came spontaneously and naturally into my thinking whenever I pondered what I was. Now it occurred to me first that I had a face, hands, arms, and this entire mechanism of bodily members: the very same as are discerned in a corpse, and which I referred to by the name "body." It next occurred to me that I took in food, that I walked about, and that I sensed and thought various things; these actions I used to attribute to the soul. But as to what this soul might be, I either did not think about it or else I imagined it a rarified I-know-not-what, like a wind, or a fire, or ether, which had been infused into my coarser parts. But as to the body I was not in any doubt. On the contrary, I was under the impression that I knew its nature distinctly. Were I perhaps tempted to describe this nature such as I conceived it in my mind, I would have described it thus: by "body," I understand all that is capable of being bounded by some shape, of being enclosed in a place, and of filling up a space in such a way as to exclude any other body from it; of being perceived by touch, sight, hearing, taste, or smell; of being moved in several ways, not, of course, by itself, but by whatever else impinges upon it. For it was my view that the power of self-motion, and likewise of sensing or of thinking, in no way belonged to the nature of the body. Indeed I used rather to marvel that such faculties were to be found in certain bodies.

But now what am I, when I suppose that there is some supremely powerful and, if I may be permitted to say so, malicious deceiver who deliberately tries to fool me in any way he can? Can I not affirm that I possess at least a small measure of all those things which I have already said belong to the nature of the body? I focus my attention on them, I think about them, I review them again, but nothing comes to mind. I am tired of repeating this to no purpose. But what about those things I ascribed to the soul? What about being nourished or moving about? Since I now do not have a body, these are surely nothing but fictions. What about sensing? Surely this too does not take place without a body; and I seemed to have sensed in my dreams many things that I later realized I did not sense. What about thinking? Here I make my discovery: thought exists; it alone cannot be separated from me. I am; I exist—this is certain. But for how long? For as long as I am thinking; for perhaps it could also come to pass that if I were to cease all thinking I would then utterly cease to exist. At this time I admit nothing that is not necessarily true. I am therefore precisely nothing but a thinking thing; that is, a mind, or intellect, or understanding, or reason—words of whose meanings I was previously ignorant. Yet I am a true thing and am truly existing; but what kind of thing? I have said it already: a thinking thing.

What else am I? I will set my imagination in motion. I am not that concatenation of members we call the human body. Neither am I even some subtle air infused into these members, nor a wind, nor a fire, nor a vapor, nor a breath, nor anything I devise for myself. For I have supposed these things to be nothing. The assumption still stands; yet nevertheless I am something. But is it perhaps the case that these very things which I take to be nothing, because they are unknown to me, nevertheless are in fact no different from that "me" that I know? This I do not know, and I will not quarrel about it now. I can make a judgment only about things that are known to me. I know that I exist; I ask now who is this "I" whom I know? Most certainly, in the strict sense the knowledge of this "I" does not depend upon things of whose existence I do not yet have knowledge. Therefore it is not dependent upon any of those things that I simulate in my imagination. But this word "simulate" warns me of my error. For I would indeed be simulating were I to "imagine" that I was something, because imagining is merely the contemplating of the shape or image of a corporeal thing. But I now know with certainty that I am and also that all these images—and, generally, everything belonging to the nature of the body—could turn out to be nothing but dreams. Once I have realized this, I would seem to be speaking no less foolishly were I to say: "I will use my imagination in order to recognize more distinctly who I am," than were I to say: "Now I surely am awake, and I see something true; but since I do not yet see it clearly enough, I will deliberately fall asleep so that my dreams might represent it to me more truly and more clearly." Thus I realize that none of what I can grasp by means of the imagination pertains to this knowledge that I have of myself. Moreover, I realize that I must be most diligent about withdrawing my mind from these things so that it can perceive its nature as distinctly as possible.

But what then am I? A thing that thinks. What is that? A thing that doubts, understands, affirms, denies, wills, refuses, and that also imagines and senses.

Indeed it is no small matter if all of these things belong to me. But why should they not belong to me? Is it not the very same "I" who now doubts almost everything, who nevertheless understands something, who affirms that this one thing is true, who denies other things, who desires to know more, who wishes not to be deceived, who imagines many things even against my will, who also notices many things which appear to come from the senses? What is there in all of this that is not every bit as true as the fact that I exist—even if I am always asleep or even if my creator makes every effort to mislead me? Which of these things is distinct from my thought? Which of them can be said to be separate from myself? For it is so obvious that it is I who

doubt, I who understand, and I who will, that there is nothing by which it could be explained more clearly. But indeed it is also the same "I" who imagines; for although perhaps, as I supposed before, absolutely nothing that I imagined is true, still the very power of imagining really does exist, and constitutes a part of my thought. Finally, it is this same "I" who senses or who is cognizant of bodily things as if through the senses. For example, I now see a light, I hear a noise, I feel heat. These things are false, since I am asleep. Yet I certainly do seem to see, hear, and feel warmth. This cannot be false. Properly speaking, this is what in me is called "sensing." But this, precisely so taken, is nothing other than thinking.

From these considerations I am beginning to know a little better what I am. But it still seems (and I cannot resist believing) that corporeal things—whose images are formed by thought, and which the senses themselves examine—are much more distinctly known than this mysterious "I" which does not fall within the imagination. And yet it would be strange indeed were I to grasp the very things I consider to be doubtful, unknown, and foreign to me more distinctly than what is true, what is known—than, in short, myself. But I see what is happening: my mind loves to wander and does not yet permit itself to be restricted within the confines of truth. So be it then; let us just this once allow it completely free rein, so that, a little while later, when the time has come to pull in the reins, the mind may more readily permit itself to be controlled.

Let us consider those things which are commonly believed to be the most distinctly grasped of all: namely the bodies we touch and see. Not bodies in general, mind you, for these general perceptions are apt to be somewhat more confused, but one body in particular. Let us take, for instance, this piece of wax. It has been taken quite recently from the honeycomb; it has not yet lost all the honey flavor. It retains some of the scent of the flowers from which it was collected. Its color, shape, and size are manifest. It is hard and cold; it is easy to touch. If you rap on it with your knuckle it will emit a sound. In short, everything is present in it that appears needed to enable a body to be known as distinctly as possible. But notice that, as I am speaking, I am bringing it close to the fire. The remaining traces of the honey flavor are disappearing; the scent is vanishing; the color is changing; the original shape is disappearing. Its size is increasing; it is becoming liquid and hot; you can hardly touch it. And now, when you rap on it, it no longer emits any sound. Does the same wax still remain? I must confess that it does; no one denies it; no one thinks otherwise. So what was there in the wax that was so distinctly grasped? Certainly none of the aspects that I reached by means of the senses. For whatever came under the senses of taste, smell, sight, touch or hearing has now changed; and yet the wax remains.

Perhaps the wax was what I now think it is: namely that the wax itself never really was the sweetness of the honey, nor the fragrance of the flowers, nor the whiteness, nor the shape, nor the sound, but instead was a body that a short time ago manifested itself to me in these ways, and now does so in other ways. But just what precisely is this thing that I thus imagine? Let us focus our attention on this and see what remains after we have removed everything that does not belong to the wax: only that it is something extended, flexible, and mutable. But what is it to be flexible and mutable? Is it what my imagination shows it to be: namely, that this piece of wax can change from a round to a square shape, or from the latter to a triangular shape? Not at all; for I grasp that the wax is capable of innumerable changes of this sort, even though I am incapable of running through these innumerable changes by using my imagination. Therefore this insight is not achieved by the faculty of imagination. What is it to be extended? Is this thing's extension also unknown? For it becomes greater in wax that is beginning to melt, greater in boiling wax, and greater still as the heat is increased. And I would not judge correctly what the wax is if I did not believe that it takes on an even greater variety of dimensions than I could ever grasp with the imagination. It remains then for me to concede that I do not grasp what this wax is through the imagination; rather, I perceive it through the mind alone. The point I am making refers to this particular piece of wax, for the case of wax in general is clearer still. But what is this piece of wax which is perceived only by the mind? Surely it is the same piece of wax that I see, touch, and imagine; in short it is the same piece of wax I took it to be from the very beginning. But I need to realize that the perception of the wax is neither a seeing, nor a touching, nor an imagining. Nor has it ever been, even though it previously seemed so;

rather it is an inspection on the part of the mind alone. This inspection can be imperfect and confused, as it was before, or clear and distinct, as it is now, depending on how closely I pay attention to the things in which the piece of wax consists.

But meanwhile I marvel at how prone my mind is to errors. For although I am considering these things within myself silently and without words, nevertheless I seize upon words themselves and I am nearly deceived by the ways in which people commonly speak. For we say that we see the wax itself, if it is present, and not that we judge it to be present from its color or shape. Whence I might conclude straightaway that I know the wax through the vision had by the eye, and not through an inspection on the part of the mind alone. But then were I perchance to look out my window and observe men crossing the square, I would ordinarily say I see the men themselves just as I say I see the wax. But what do I see aside from hats and clothes, which could conceal automata? Yet I judge them to be men. Thus what I thought I had seen with my eyes, I actually grasped solely with the faculty of judgment, which is in my mind.

But a person who seeks to know more than the common crowd ought to be ashamed of himself for looking for doubt in common ways of speaking. Let us then go forward and inquire when it was that I perceived more perfectly and evidently what the piece of wax was. Was it when I first saw it and believed I knew it by the external sense, or at least by the so-called common sense, that is, the power of imagination? Or do I have more perfect knowledge now, when I have diligently examined both what the wax is and how it is known? Surely it is absurd to be in doubt about this matter. For what was there in my initial perception that was distinct? What was there that any animal seemed incapable of possessing? But indeed when I distinguish the wax from its external forms, as if stripping it of its clothing, and look at the wax in its nakedness, then, even though there can be still an error in my judgment, nevertheless I cannot perceive it thus without a human mind.

But what am I to say about this mind, that is, about myself? For as yet I admit nothing else to be in me over and above the mind. What, I ask, am I who seem to perceive this wax so distinctly? Do I not know myself not only much more truly and with greater certainty, but also much more distinctly and evidently? For if I judge that the wax exists from the fact that I see it, certainly from this same fact that I see the wax it follows much more evidently that I myself exist. For it could happen that what I see is not truly wax. It could happen that I have no eyes with which to see anything. But it is utterly impossible that, while I see or think I see (I do not now distinguish these two), I who think am not something. Likewise, if I judge that the wax exists from the fact that I touch it, the same outcome will again obtain, namely that I exist. If I judge that the wax exists from the fact that I imagine it, or for any other reason, plainly the same thing follows. But what I note regarding the wax applies to everything else that is external to me. Furthermore, if my perception of the wax seemed more distinct after it became known to me not only on account of sight or touch, but on account of many reasons, one has to admit how much more distinctly I am now known to myself. For there is not a single consideration that can aid in my perception of the wax or of any other body that fails to make even more manifest the nature of my mind. But there are still so many other things in the mind itself on the basis of which my knowledge of it can be rendered more distinct that it hardly seems worth enumerating those things which emanate to it from the body.

But lo and behold, I have returned on my own to where I wanted to be. For since I now know that even bodies are not, properly speaking, perceived by the senses or by the faculty of imagination, but by the intellect alone, and that they are not perceived through their being touched or seen, but only through their being understood, I manifestly know that nothing can be perceived more easily and more evidently than my own mind. But since the tendency to hang on to long-held beliefs cannot be put aside so quickly, I want to stop here, so that by the length of my meditation this new knowledge may be more deeply impressed upon my memory.

Meditation Three: Concerning God, That He Exists

I will now shut my eyes, stop up my ears, and withdraw all my senses. I will also blot out from my thoughts all images of corporeal things, or rather, since the latter is hardly possible, I will regard these images as empty, false and worthless. And as I converse with myself alone and look more deeply into myself, I will attempt to render myself gradually better known and more familiar to myself. I am a thing that thinks, that is to say, a thing that doubts, affirms, denies, understands a few things, is ignorant of many things, wills, refrains from willing, and also imagines and senses. For as I observed earlier, even though these things that I sense or imagine may perhaps be nothing at all outside me, nevertheless I am certain that these modes of thinking, which are cases of what I call sensing and imagining, insofar as they are merely modes of thinking, do exist within me.

In these few words, I have reviewed everything I truly know, or at least what so far I have noticed that I know. Now I will ponder more carefully to see whether perhaps there may be other things belonging to me that up until now I have failed to notice. I am certain that I am a thinking thing. But do I not therefore also know what is required for me to be certain of anything? Surely in this first instance of knowledge, there is nothing but a certain clear and distinct perception of what I affirm. Yet this would hardly be enough to render me certain of the truth of a thing, if it could ever happen that something that I perceived so clearly and distinctly were false. And thus I now seem able to posit as a general rule that everything I very clearly and distinctly perceive is true.

Be that as it may, I have previously admitted many things as wholly certain and evident that nevertheless I later discovered to be doubtful. What sort of things were these? Why, the earth, the sky, the stars, and all the other things I perceived by means of the senses. But what was it about these things that I clearly perceived? Surely the fact that the ideas or thoughts of these things were hovering before my mind. But even now I do not deny that these ideas are in me. Yet there was something else I used to affirm, which, owing to my habitual tendency to believe it, I used to think was something I clearly perceived, even though I actually did not perceive it at all: namely, that certain things existed outside me, things from which those ideas proceeded and which those ideas completely resembled. But on this point I was mistaken; or rather, if my judgment was a true one, it was not the result of the force of my perception.

But what about when I considered something very simple and easy in the areas of arithmetic or geometry, for example that two plus three make five, and the like? Did I not intuit them at least clearly enough so as to affirm them as true? To be sure, I did decide later on that I must doubt these things, but that was only because it occurred to me that some God could perhaps have given me a nature such that I might be deceived even about matters that seemed most evident. But whenever this preconceived opinion about the supreme power of God occurs to me, I cannot help admitting that, were he to wish it, it would be easy for him to cause me to err even in those matters that I think I intuit as clearly as possible with the eyes of the mind. On the other hand, whenever I turn my attention to those very things that I think I perceive with such great clarity, I am so completely persuaded by them that I spontaneously blurt out these words: "let anyone who can do so deceive me; so long as I think that I am something, he will never bring it about that I am nothing. Nor will he one day make it true that I never existed, for it is true now that I do exist. Nor will he even bring it about that perhaps two plus three might equal more or less than five, or similar items in which I recognize an obvious contradiction." And certainly, because I have no reason for thinking that there is a God who is a deceiver (and of course I do not yet sufficiently know whether there even is a God), the basis for doubting, depending as it does merely on the above hypothesis, is very tenuous and, so to speak, metaphysical. But in order to remove even this basis for doubt, I should at the first opportunity inquire whether there is a God, and, if there is, whether or not he can be a deceiver. For if I am ignorant of this, it appears I am never capable of being completely certain about anything else.

However, at this stage good order seems to demand that I first group all my thoughts into certain classes, and ask in which of them truth or falsity properly resides. Some of these thoughts are like images of things; to these alone does the word "idea" properly apply, as when I think of a man, or a chimera, or the sky, or an angel, or God. Again there are other thoughts that take different forms: for example, when I will, or fear, or affirm, or deny, there is always some thing that I grasp as the subject of my thought, yet I embrace in my thought something more than the likeness of that thing. Some of these thoughts are called volitions or affects, while others are called judgments.

Now as far as ideas are concerned, if they are considered alone and in their own right, without being referred to something else, they cannot, properly speaking, be false. For whether it is a she-goat or a chimera that I am imagining, it is no less true that I imagine the one than the other. Moreover, we need not fear that there is falsity in the will itself or in the affects, for although I can choose evil things or even things that are utterly non-existent, I cannot conclude from this that it is untrue that I do choose these things. Thus there remain only judgments in which I must take care not to be mistaken. Now the principal and most frequent error to be found in judgments consists in the fact that I judge that the ideas which are in me are similar to or in conformity with certain things outside me. Obviously, if I were to consider these ideas merely as certain modes of my thought, and were not to refer them to anything else, they could hardly give me any subject matter for error.

Among these ideas, some appear to me to be innate, some adventitious, and some produced by me. For I understand what a thing is, what truth is, what thought is, and I appear to have derived this exclusively from my very own nature. But say I am now hearing a noise, or looking at the sun, or feeling the fire; up until now I judged that these things proceeded from certain things outside me, and finally, that sirens, hippogriffs, and the like are made by me. Or perhaps I can even think of all these ideas as being adventitious, or as being innate, or as fabrications, for I have not yet clearly ascertained their true origin.

But here I must inquire particularly into those ideas that I believe to be derived from things existing outside me. Just what reason do I have for believing that these ideas resemble those things? Well, I do seem to have been so taught by nature. Moreover, I do know from experience that these ideas do not depend upon my will, nor consequently upon myself, for I often notice them even against my will. Now, for example, whether or not I will it, I feel heat. It is for this reason that I believe this feeling or idea of heat comes to me from something other than myself, namely from the heat of the fire by which I am sitting. Nothing is more obvious than the judgment that this thing is sending its likeness rather than something else into me.

I will now see whether these reasons are powerful enough. When I say here "I have been so taught by nature," all I have in mind is that I am driven by a spontaneous impulse to believe this, and not that some light of nature is showing me that it is true. These are two very different things. For whatever is shown me by this light of nature, for example, that from the fact that I doubt, it follows that I am, and the like, cannot in any way be doubtful. This is owing to the fact that there can be no other faculty that I can trust as much as this light and which could teach that these things are not true. But as far as natural impulses are concerned, in the past I have often judged myself to have been driven by them to make the poorer choice when it was a question of choosing a good; and I fail to see why I should place any greater faith in them than in other matters.

Again, although these ideas do not depend upon my will, it does not follow that they necessarily proceed from things existing outside me. For just as these impulses about which I spoke just now seem to be different from my will, even though they are in me, so too perhaps there is also in me some other faculty, one not yet sufficiently known to me, which produces these ideas, just as it has always seemed up to now that ideas are formed in me without any help from external things when I am asleep.

And finally, even if these ideas did proceed from things other than myself, it does not therefore follow that they must resemble those things. Indeed it seems I have frequently noticed a vast difference in many respects. For example, I find within myself two distinct ideas of the sun. One idea is drawn, as it were, from the senses. Now it is this idea which, of all those that I take to be derived from outside me, is most in need of examination. By means of this idea the sun appears to me to be quite small. But there is another idea, one derived from astronomical reasoning, that is, it is elicited from certain notions that are innate in me, or else is fashioned by me in some other way. Through this idea the sun is shown to be several times larger than the earth. Both ideas surely cannot resemble the same sun existing outside me; and reason convinces me that the idea that seems to have emanated from the sun itself from so close is the very one that least resembles the sun.

All these points demonstrate sufficiently that up to this point it was not a well-founded judgment but only a blind impulse that formed the basis of my belief that things existing outside me send ideas or images of themselves to me through the sense organs or by some other means.

But still another way occurs to me for inquiring whether some of the things of which there are ideas in me do exist outside me: insofar as these ideas are merely modes of thought, I see no inequality among them; they all seem to proceed from me in the same manner. But insofar as one idea represents one thing and another idea another thing, it is obvious that they do differ very greatly from one another. Unquestionably, those ideas that display substances to me are something more and, if I may say so, contain within themselves more objective reality than those which represent only modes or accidents. Again, the idea that enables me to understand a supreme deity, eternal, infinite, omniscient, omnipotent, and creator of all things other than himself, clearly has more objective reality within it than do those ideas through which finite substances are displayed.

Now it is indeed evident by the light of nature that there must be at least as much [reality] in the efficient and total cause as there is in the effect of that same cause. For whence, I ask, could an effect get its reality, if not from its cause? And how could the cause give that reality to the effect, unless it also possessed that reality? Hence it follows that something cannot come into being out of nothing, and also that what is more perfect (that is, what contains in itself more reality) cannot come into being from what is less perfect. But this is manifestly true not merely for those effects whose reality is actual or formal, but also for ideas in which only objective reality is considered. For example, not only can a stone which did not exist previously not now begin to exist unless it is produced by something in which there is, either formally or eminently, everything that is in the stone; nor heat be introduced into a subject which was not already hot unless it is done by something that is of at least as perfect an order as heat—and the same for the rest—but it is also true that there can be in me no idea of heat, or of a stone, unless it is placed in me by some cause that has at least as much reality as I conceive to be in the heat or in the stone. For although this cause conveys none of its actual or formal reality to my idea, it should not be thought for that reason that it must be less real. Rather, the very nature of an idea is such that of itself it needs no formal reality other than what it borrows from my thought, of which it is a mode. But that a particular idea contains this as opposed to that objective reality is surely owing to some cause in which there is at least as much formal reality as there is objective reality contained in the idea. For if we assume that something is found in the idea that was not in its cause, then the idea gets that something from nothing. Yet as imperfect a mode of being as this is by which a thing exists in the intellect objectively through an idea, nevertheless it is plainly not nothing; hence it cannot get its being from nothing.

Moreover, even though the reality that I am considering in my ideas is merely objective reality, I ought not on that account to suspect that there is no need for the same reality to be formally in the causes of these ideas, but that it suffices for it to be in them objectively. For just as the objective mode of being belongs to ideas by their very nature, so the formal mode of being belongs to the causes of ideas, at least to the first and preeminent ones, by their very nature. And although one idea can perhaps issue from another, nevertheless no infinite regress is permitted here; eventually some first idea must be reached whose cause is a sort of archetype that contains formally all the reality that is in the idea merely objectively. Thus it is clear to me by the light of nature that the ideas that are in me are like images that can easily fail to match the perfection of the things from which they have been drawn, but which can contain nothing greater or more perfect.

And the longer and more attentively I examine all these points, the more clearly and distinctly I know they are true. But what am I ultimately to conclude? If the objective reality of any of my ideas is found to be so great that I am certain that the same reality was not in me, either formally or eminently, and that therefore I myself cannot be the cause of the idea, then it necessarily follows that I am not alone in the world, but that something else, which is the cause of this idea, also exists. But if no such idea is found in me, I will have no argument whatsoever to make me certain of the existence of anything other than myself, for I have conscientiously reviewed all these arguments, and so far I have been unable to find any other.

Among my ideas, in addition to the one that displays me to myself (about which there can be no difficulty at this point), are others that represent God, corporeal and inanimate things, angels, animals, and finally other men like myself.

As to the ideas that display other men, or animals, or angels, I easily understand that they could be fashioned from the ideas that I have of myself, of corporeal things, and of God—even if no men (except myself), no animals, and no angels existed in the world.

As to the ideas of corporeal things, there is nothing in them that is so great that it seems incapable of having originated from me. For if I investigate them thoroughly and examine each one individually in the way I examined the idea of wax yesterday, I notice that there are only a very few things in them that I perceive clearly and distinctly: namely, size, or extension in length, breadth, and depth; shape, which arises from the limits of this extension; position, which various things possessing shape have in relation to one another; and motion, or alteration in position. To these can be added substance, duration, and number. But as for the remaining items, such as light and colors, sounds, odors, tastes, heat and cold and other tactile qualities, I think of these only in a very confused and obscure manner, to the extent that I do not even know whether they are true or false, that is, whether the ideas I have of them are ideas of things or ideas of non-things. For although a short time ago I noted that falsity properly so called (or "formal" falsity) is to be found only in judgments, nevertheless there is another kind of falsity (called "material" falsity) which is found in ideas whenever they represent a non-thing as if it were a thing. For example, the ideas I have of heat and cold fall so far short of being clear and distinct that I cannot tell from them whether cold is merely the privation of heat or whether heat is the privation of cold, or whether both are real qualities, or whether neither is. And because ideas can only be, as it were, of things, if it is true that cold is merely the absence of heat, then an idea that represents cold to me as something real and positive will not inappropriately be called false. The same holds for other similar ideas.

Assuredly I need not assign to these ideas an author distinct from myself. For if they were false, that is, if they were to represent non-things, I know by the light of nature that they proceed from nothing; that is, they are in me for no other reason than that something is lacking in my nature, and that my nature is not entirely perfect. If, on the other hand, these ideas are true, then because they exhibit so little reality to me that I cannot distinguish it from a non-thing, I see no reason why they cannot get their being from me.

As for what is clear and distinct in the ideas of corporeal things, it appears I could have borrowed some of these from the idea of myself: namely, substance, duration, number, and whatever else there may be of this type. For instance, I think that a stone is a substance, that is to say, a thing that is suitable for existing in itself; and likewise I think that I too am a substance. Despite the fact that I conceive myself to be a thinking thing and not an extended thing, whereas I conceive of a stone as an extended thing and not a thinking thing, and hence there is the greatest diversity between these two concepts, nevertheless they seem to agree with one another when considered under the rubric of substance. Furthermore, I perceive that I now exist and recall that I have previously existed for some time. And I have various thoughts and know how many of them there are. It is in doing these things that I acquire the ideas of duration and number, which I can then apply to other things. However, none of the other components out of which the ideas of corporeal things are fashioned (namely extension, shape, position, and motion) are contained in me formally, since I am merely a thinking thing. But since these are only certain modes of a substance, whereas I am a substance, it seems possible that they are contained in me eminently.

Thus there remains only the idea of God. I must consider whether there is anything in this idea that could not have originated from me. I understand by the name "God" a certain substance that is infinite, independent, supremely intelligent and supremely powerful, and that created me along with everything else that exists—if anything else exists. Indeed all these are such that, the more carefully I focus my attention on them, the less possible it seems they could have arisen from myself alone. Thus, from what has been said, I must conclude that God necessarily exists.

For although the idea of substance is in me by virtue of the fact that I am a substance, that fact is not sufficient to explain my having the idea of an infinite substance, since I am finite, unless this idea proceeded from some substance which really was infinite.

Nor should I think that I do not perceive the infinite by means of a true idea, but only through a negation of the finite, just as I perceive rest and darkness by means of a negation of motion and light. On the contrary, I clearly understand that there is more reality in an infinite substance than there is in a finite one. Thus the perception of the infinite is somehow prior in me to the perception of the finite, that is, my perception of God is prior to my perception of myself. For how would I understand that I doubt and that I desire, that is, that I lack something and that I am not wholly perfect, unless there were some idea in me of a more perfect being, by comparison with which I might recognize my defects?

Nor can it be said that this idea of God is perhaps materially false and thus can originate from nothing, as I remarked just now about the ideas of heat and cold, and the like. On the contrary, because it is the most clear and distinct and because it contains more objective reality than any other idea, no idea is in and of itself truer and has less of a basis for being suspected of falsehood. I maintain that this idea of a being that is supremely perfect and infinite is true in the highest degree. For although I could perhaps pretend that such a being does not exist, nevertheless I could not pretend that the idea of such a being discloses to me nothing real, as was the case with the idea of cold which I referred to earlier. It is indeed an idea that is utterly clear and distinct; for whatever I clearly and distinctly perceive to be real and true and to involve some perfection is wholly contained in that idea. It is no objection that I do not comprehend the infinite or that there are countless other things in God that I can in no way either comprehend or perhaps even touch with my thought. For the nature of the infinite is such that it is not comprehended by a being such as I, who am finite. And it is sufficient that I understand this very point and judge that all those things that I clearly perceive and that I know to contain some perfection—and perhaps even countless other things of which I am ignorant—are in God either formally or eminently. The result is that, of all the ideas that are in me, the idea that I have of God is the most true, the most clear and distinct.

But perhaps I am something greater than I myself understand. Perhaps all these perfections that I am attributing to God are somehow in me potentially, although they do no yet assert themselves and are not yet actualized. For I now observe that my knowledge is gradually being increased, and I see nothing standing in the way of its being increased more and more to infinity. Moreover, I see no reason why, with my knowledge thus increased, I could not acquire all the remaining perfections of God. And, finally, if the potential for these perfections is in me already, I see no reason why this potential would not suffice to produce the idea of these perfections.

Yet none of these things can be the case. First, while it is true that my knowledge is gradually being increased and that there are many things in me potentially that are not yet actual, nevertheless, none of these pertains to the idea of God, in which there is nothing whatever that is potential. Indeed this gradual increase is itself a most certain proof of imperfection. Moreover, although my knowledge may always increase more and more, nevertheless I understand that this knowledge will never by this means be actually infinite, because it will never reach a point where it is incapable of greater increase. On the contrary, I judge God to be actually infinite, so that nothing can be added to his perfection. Finally, I perceive that the objective being of an idea cannot be produced by a merely potential being (which, strictly speaking, is nothing), but only by an actual or formal being.

Indeed there is nothing in all these things that is not manifest by the light of nature to one who is conscientious and attentive. But when I am less attentive, and the images of sensible things blind the mind's eye, I do not so easily recall why the idea of a being more perfect than me necessarily proceeds from a being that really is more perfect. This being the case, it is appropriate to ask further whether I myself who have this idea could exist, if such a being did not exist.

From what source, then, do I derive my existence? Why, from myself, or from my parents, or from whatever other things there are that are less perfect than God. For nothing more perfect than God, or even as perfect as God, can be thought or imagined.

But if I got my being from myself, I would not doubt, nor would I desire, nor would I lack anything at all. For I would have given myself all the perfections of which I have some idea; in so doing, I myself would be God! I must not think that the things I lack could perhaps be more difficult to acquire than the ones I have now. On the contrary, it is obvious that it would have been much more difficult for me (that is, a thing or substance that thinks) to emerge out of nothing than it would be to

acquire the knowledge of many things about which I am ignorant (these items of knowledge being merely accidents of that substance). Certainly, if I got this greater thing from myself, I would not have denied myself at least those things that can be had more easily. Nor would I have denied myself any of those other things that I perceive to be contained in the idea of God, for surely none of them seem to me more difficult to bring about. But if any of them were more difficult to bring about, they would certainly also seem more difficult to me, even if the remaining ones that I possess I got from myself, since it would be on account of them that I would experience that my power is limited.

Nor am I avoiding the force of these arguments, if I suppose that perhaps I have always existed as I do now, as if it then followed that no author of my existence need be sought. For because the entire span of one's life can be divided into countless parts, each one wholly independent of the rest, it does not follow from the fact that I existed a short time ago that I must exist now, unless some cause, as it were, creates me all over again at this moment, that is to say, which preserves me. For it is obvious to one who pays close attention to the nature of time that plainly the same force and action are needed to preserve anything at each individual moment that it lasts as would be required to create that same thing anew, were it not yet inexistence. Thus conservation differs from creation solely by virtue of a distinction of reason; this too is one of those things that are manifest by the light of nature.

Therefore I must now ask myself whether I possess some power by which I can bring it about that I myself, who now exist, will also exist a little later on. For since I am nothing but a thinking thing—or at least since I am now dealing simply and precisely with that part of me which is a thinking thing—if such a power were in me, then I would certainly be aware of it. But I observe that there is no such power; and from this very fact I know most clearly that I depend upon some being other than myself.

But perhaps this being is not God, and I have been produced either by my parents or by some other causes less perfect than God. On the contrary, as I said before, it is obvious that there must be at least as much in the cause as there is in the effect. Thus, regardless of what it is that eventually is assigned as my cause, because I am a thinking thing and have within me a certain idea of God, it must be granted that what caused me is also a thinking thing and it too has an idea of all the perfections which I attribute to God. And I can again inquire of this cause whether it got its existence from itself or from another cause. For if it got its existence from itself, it is evident from what has been said that it is itself God, because, having the power of existing in and of itself, it unquestionably also has the power of actually possessing all the perfections of which it has in itself an idea—that is, all the perfections that I conceive to be in God. However, if it got its existence from another cause, I will once again inquire in similar fashion about this other cause: whether it got its existence from itself or from another cause, until finally I arrive at the ultimate cause, which will be God. For it is apparent enough that there can be no infinite regress here, especially since I am not dealing here merely with the cause that once produced me, but also and most especially with the cause that preserves me at the present time.

Nor can one fancy that perhaps several partial causes have concurred in bringing me into being, and that I have taken the ideas of the various perfections I attribute to God from a variety of causes, so that all of these perfections are found somewhere in the universe, but not all joined together in a single being—God. On the contrary, the unity, the simplicity, that is, the inseparability of all those features that are in God is one of the chief perfections that I understand to be in him. Certainly the idea of the unity of all his perfections could not have been placed in me by any cause from which I did not also get the ideas of the other perfections; for neither could some cause have made me understand them joined together and inseparable from one another, unless it also caused me to recognize what they were.

Finally, as to my parents, even if everything that I ever believed about them were true, still it is certainly not they who preserve me; nor is it they who in any way brought me into being, insofar as I am a thinking thing. Rather, they merely placed certain dispositions in the matter which I judged to contain me, that is, a mind, which now is the only thing I take myself to be. And thus there can be no difficulty here concerning my parents. Indeed I have no choice but to conclude that the mere fact of my existing and of there being in me an idea of a most perfect being, that is, God, demonstrates most evidently that God too exists.

All that remains for me is to ask how I received this idea of God. For I did not draw it from the senses; it never came upon me unexpectedly, as is usually the case with the ideas of sensible things when these things present themselves (or seem to present themselves) to the external sense organs. Nor was it made by me, for I plainly can neither subtract anything from it nor add anything to it. Thus the only option remaining is that this idea is innate in me, just as the idea of myself is innate in me.

To be sure, it is not astonishing that in creating me, God should have endowed me with this idea, so that it would be like the mark of the craftsman impressed upon his work, although this mark need not be something distinct from the work itself. But the mere fact that God created me makes it highly plausible that I have somehow been made in his image and likeness, and that I perceive this likeness, in which the idea of God is contained, by means of the same faculty by which I perceive myself. That is, when I turn the mind's eye toward myself, I understand not only that I am something incomplete and dependent upon another, something aspiring indefinitely for greater and greater or better things, but also that the being on whom I depend has in himself all those greater things—not merely indefinitely and potentially, but infinitely and actually, and thus that he is God. The whole force of the argument rests on the fact that I recognize that it would be impossible for me to exist, being of such a nature as I am (namely, having in me the idea of God), unless God did in fact exist. God, I say, that same being the idea of whom is in me: a being having all those perfections that I cannot comprehend, but can somehow touch with my thought, and a being subject to no defects whatever. From these considerations it is quite obvious that he cannot be a deceiver, for it is manifest by the light of nature that all fraud and deception depend on some defect.

But before examining this idea more closely and at the same time inquiring into other truths that can be gathered from it, at this point I want to spend some time contemplating this God, to ponder his attributes and, so far as the eye of my darkened mind can take me, to gaze upon, to admire, and to adore the beauty of this immense light. For just as we believe by faith that the greatest felicity of the next life consists solely in this contemplation of the divine majesty, so too we now experience that from the same contemplation, although it is much less perfect, the greatest pleasure of which we are capable in this life can be perceived.

Meditation Four: Concerning the True and the False

Lately I have become accustomed to withdrawing my mind from the senses, and I have carefully taken note of the fact that very few things are truly perceived regarding corporeal things, although a great many more things are known regarding the human mind, and still many more things regarding God. The upshot is that I now have no difficulty directing my thought away from things that can be imagined to things that can be grasped only by the understanding and are wholly separate from matter. In fact the idea I clearly have of the human mind—insofar as it is a thinking thing, not extended in length, breadth or depth, and having nothing else from the body—is far more distinct than the idea of any corporeal thing. And when I take note of the fact that I doubt, or that I am a thing that is incomplete and dependent, there comes to mind a clear and distinct idea of a being that is independent and complete, that is, an idea of God. And from the mere fact that such an idea is in me, or that I who have this idea exist, I draw the obvious conclusion that God also exists, and that my existence depends entirely upon him at each and every moment. This conclusion is so obvious that I am confident that the human mind can know nothing more evident or more certain. And now I seem to see a way by which I might progress from this contemplation of the true God, in whom, namely, are hidden all the treasures of the sciences and wisdom, to the knowledge of other things.

To begin with, I acknowledge that it is impossible for God ever to deceive me, for trickery or deception is always indicative of some imperfection. And although the ability to deceive seems to be an indication of cleverness or power, the will to deceive undoubtedly attests to maliciousness or weakness. Accordingly, deception is incompatible with God.

Next I experience that there is in me a certain faculty of judgment, which, like everything else that is in me, I undoubtedly received from God. And since he does not wish to deceive me, he assuredly has not given me the sort of faculty with which I could ever make a mistake, when I use it properly.

No doubt regarding this matter would remain, but for the fact that it seems to follow from this that I am never capable of making a mistake. For if everything that is in me I got from God, and he gave me no faculty for making mistakes, it seems I am incapable of ever erring. And thus, so long as I think exclusively about God and focus my attention exclusively on him, I discern no cause of error or falsity. But once I turn my attention back on myself, I nevertheless experience that I am subject to countless errors. As I seek a cause of these errors, I notice that passing before me is not only a real and positive idea of God (that is, of a supremely perfect being), but also, as it were, a certain negative idea of nothingness (that is, of what is at the greatest possible distance from any perfection), and that I have been so constituted as a kind of middle ground between God and nothingness, or between the supreme being and non-being. Thus insofar as I have been created by the supreme being, there is nothing in me by means of which I might be deceived or be led into error; but insofar as I participate in nothingness or non-being, that is, insofar as I am not the supreme being and lack a great many things, it is not surprising that I make mistakes. Thus I certainly understand that error as such is not something real that depends upon God, but rather is merely a defect. And thus there is no need to account for my errors by positing a faculty given to me by God for this purpose. Rather, it just so happens that I make mistakes because the faculty of judging the truth, which I got from God, is not, in my case, infinite.

Still this is not yet altogether satisfactory; for error is not a pure negation, but rather a privation or a lack of some knowledge that somehow ought to be in me. And when I attend to the nature of God, it seems impossible that he would have placed in me a faculty that is not perfect in its kind or that is lacking some perfection it ought to have. For if it is true that the more expert the craftsman, the more perfect the works he produces, what can that supreme creator of all things make that is not perfect in all respects? No doubt God could have created me such that I never erred. No doubt, again, God always wills what is best. Is it then better that I should be in error rather than not?

As I mull these things over more carefully, it occurs to me first that there is no reason to marvel at the fact that God should bring about certain things the reasons for which I do not understand. Nor is his existence therefore to be doubted because I happen to experience other things of which I fail to grasp why and how he made them. For since I know now that my nature is very weak and limited, whereas the nature of God is immense, incomprehensible, and infinite, this is sufficient for me also to know that he can make innumerable things whose causes escape me. For this reason alone the entire class of causes which people customarily derive from a thing's "end," I judge to be utterly useless in physics. It is not without rashness that I think myself capable of inquiring into the ends of God.

It also occurs to me that whenever we ask whether the works of God are perfect, we should keep in view not simply some one creature in isolation from the rest, but the universe as a whole. For perhaps something might rightfully appear very imperfect if it were all by itself, and yet be most perfect, to the extent that it has the status of a part in the universe. And although subsequent to having decided to doubt everything, I have come to know with certainty only that I and God exist, nevertheless, after having taken note of the immense power of God, I cannot deny that many other things have been made by him, or at least could have been made by him. Thus I may have the status of a part in the universal scheme of things.

Next, as I focus more closely on myself and inquire into the nature of my errors (the only things that are indicative of some imperfection in me), I note that these errors depend on the simultaneous concurrence of two causes: the faculty of knowing that is in me and the faculty of choosing, that is, the free choice of the will, in other words, simultaneously on the intellect and will. Through the intellect alone I merely perceive ideas, about which I can render a judgment. Strictly speaking, no error is to be found in the intellect when properly viewed in this manner. For although perhaps there may exist countless things about which I have no idea, nevertheless it must not be said that, strictly speaking, I

am deprived of these ideas but only that I lack them in a negative sense. This is because I cannot adduce an argument to prove that God ought to have given me a greater faculty of knowing than he did. No matter how expert a craftsman I understand him to be, still I do not for that reason believe he ought to have bestowed on each one of his works all the perfections that he can put into some. Nor, on the other hand, can I complain that the will or free choice I have received from God is insufficiently ample or perfect, since I experience that it is limited by no boundaries whatever. In fact, it seems to be especially worth noting that no other things in me are so perfect or so great but that I understand that they can be still more perfect or greater. If, for example, I consider the faculty of understanding, I immediately recognize that in my case it is very small and quite limited, and at the very same time I form an idea of another much greater faculty of understanding—in fact, an understanding which is consummately great and infinite; and from the fact that I can form an idea of this faculty, I perceive that it pertains to the nature of God. Similarly, were I to examine the faculty of memory or imagination, or any of the other faculties, I would understand that in my case each of these is without exception feeble and limited, whereas in the case of God I understand each faculty to be boundless. It is only the will or free choice that I experience to be so great in me that I cannot grasp the idea of any greater faculty. This is so much the case that the will is the chief basis for my understanding that I bear a certain image and likeness of God. For although the faculty of willing is incomparably greater in God than it is in me, both by virtue of the knowledge and power that are joined to it and that render it more resolute and efficacious and by virtue of its object inasmuch as the divine will stretches over a greater number of things, nevertheless, when viewed in itself formally and precisely, God's faculty of willing does not appear to be any greater. This is owing to the fact that willing is merely a matter of being able to do or not do the same thing, that is, of being able to affirm or deny, to pursue or to shun; or better still, the will consists solely in the fact that when something is proposed to us by our intellect either to affirm or deny, to pursue or to shun, we are moved in such a way that we sense that we are determined to it by no external force. In order to be free I need not be capable of being moved in each direction; on the contrary, the more I am inclined toward one direction—either because I clearly understand that there is in it an aspect of the good and the true, or because God has thus disposed the inner recesses of my thought—the more freely do I choose that direction. Nor indeed does divine grace or natural knowledge ever diminish one's freedom; rather, they increase and strengthen it. However, the indifference that I experience when there is no reason moving me more in one direction than in another is the lowest grade of freedom; it is indicative not of any perfection in freedom, but rather of a defect, that is, a certain negation in knowledge. Were I always to see clearly what is true and good, I would never deliberate about what is to be judged or chosen. In that event, although I would be entirely free, I could never be indifferent.

But from these considerations I perceive that the power of willing, which I got from God, is not, taken by itself, the cause of my errors, for it is most ample as well as perfect in its kind. Nor is my power of understanding the cause of my errors. For since I got my power of understanding from God, whatever I understand I doubtless understand rightly, and it is impossible for me to be deceived in this. What then is the source of my errors? They are owing simply to the fact that, since the will extends further than the intellect, I do not contain the will within the same boundaries; rather, I also extend it to things I do not understand. Because the will is indifferent in regard to such matters, it easily turns away from the true and the good; and in this way I am deceived and I sin.

For example, during these last few days I was examining whether anything in the world exists, and I noticed that, from the very fact that I was making this examination, it obviously followed that I exist. Nevertheless, I could not help judging that what I understood so clearly was true; not that I was coerced into making this judgment because of some external force, but because a great light in my intellect gave way to a great inclination in my will, and the less indifferent I was, the more spontaneously and freely did I believe it. But now, in addition to my knowing that I exist, insofar as I am a certain thinking thing, I also observe a certain idea of corporeal nature. It happens that I am in doubt as to whether the thinking nature which is in me, or rather which I am, is something different from this corporeal nature, or whether both natures are one and the same

thing. And I assume that as yet no consideration has occurred to my intellect to convince me of the one alternative rather than the other. Certainly in virtue of this very fact I am indifferent about whether to affirm or to deny either alternative, or even whether to make no judgment at all in the matter.

Moreover, this indifference extends not merely to things about which the intellect knows absolutely nothing, but extends generally to everything of which the intellect does not have a clear enough knowledge at the very time when the will is deliberating on them. For although probable guesses may pull me in one direction, the mere knowledge that they are only guesses and not certain and indubitable proofs is all it takes to push my assent in the opposite direction. These last few days have provided me with ample experience on this point. For all the beliefs that I had once held to be most true I have supposed to be utterly false, and for the sole reason that I determined that I could somehow raise doubts about them.

But if I hold off from making a judgment when I do not perceive what is true with sufficient clarity and distinctness, it is clear that I am acting properly and am not committing an error. But if instead I were to make an assertion or a denial, then I am not using my freedom properly. Were I to select the alternative that is false, then obviously I will be in error. But were I to embrace the other alternative, it will be by sheer luck that I happen upon the truth; but I will still not be without fault, for it is manifest by the light of nature that a perception on the part of the intellect must always precede a determination on the part of the will. Inherent in this incorrect use of free will is the privation that constitutes the very essence of error: the privation, I say, present in this operation insofar as the operation proceeds from me, but not in the faculty given to me by God, nor even in its operation insofar as it depends upon him.

Indeed I have no cause for complaint on the grounds that God has not given me a greater power of understanding or a greater light of nature than he has, for it is of the essence of a finite intellect not to understand many things, and it is of the essence of a created intellect to be finite. Actually, instead of thinking that he has withheld from me or deprived me of those things that he has not given me, I ought to thank God, who never owed me anything, for what he has bestowed upon me.

Again, I have no cause for complaint on the grounds that God has given me a will that has a wider scope than my intellect. For since the will consists of merely one thing, something indivisible, as it were, it does not seem that its nature could withstand anything being removed from it. Indeed, the more ample the will is, the more I ought to thank the one who gave it to me.

Finally, I should not complain because God concurs with me in eliciting those acts of the will, that is those judgments, in which I am mistaken. For insofar as those acts depend on God, they are absolutely true and good; and in a certain sense, there is greater perfection in me in being able to elicit those acts than in not being able to do so. But privation, in which alone the defining characteristic of falsehood and wrong-doing is to be found, has no need whatever for God's concurrence, since a privation is not a thing, nor, when it is related to God as its cause, is it to be called a privation, but simply a negation. For it is surely no imperfection in God that he has given me the freedom to give or withhold my assent in those instances where he has not placed a clear and distinct perception in my intellect. But surely it is an imperfection in me that I do not use my freedom well and that I make judgments about things I do not properly understand. Nevertheless, I see that God could easily have brought it about that, while still being free and having finite knowledge, I should nonetheless never make a mistake. This result could have been achieved either by his endowing my intellect with a clear and distinct perception of everything about which I would ever deliberate, or by simply impressing the following rule so firmly upon my memory that I could never forget it: I should never judge anything that I do not clearly and distinctly understand. I readily understand that, considered as a totality, I would have been more perfect than I am now, had God made me that way. But I cannot therefore deny that it may somehow be a greater perfection in the universe as a whole that some of its parts are not immune to error, while others are, than if all of them were exactly alike. And I have no right to complain that the part God has wished me to play is not the principal and most perfect one of all.

Furthermore, even if I cannot abstain from errors in the first way mentioned above, which depends upon a clear perception of everything about which I must de-liberate, nevertheless I can avoid error in the other way, which depends solely on my remembering to abstain from making judgments whenever the truth of a given matter is not apparent. For although I experience a certain infirmity in myself, namely that I am unable to keep my attention constantly focused on one and the same item of knowledge, nevertheless, by attentive and often repeated meditation, I can bring it about that I call this rule to mind whenever the situation calls for it, and thus I would acquire a certain habit of not erring.

Since herein lies the greatest and chief perfection of man, I think today's meditation, in which I investigated the cause of error and falsity, was quite profitable. Nor can this cause be anything other than the one I have de-scribed; for as often as I restrain my will when I make judgments, so that it extends only to those matters that the intellect clearly and distinctly discloses to it, it plainly cannot happen that I err. For every clear and dis-tinct perception is surely something, and hence it can-not come from nothing. On the contrary, it must necessarily have God for its author: God, I say, that supremely perfect being to whom it is repugnant to be a deceiver. Therefore the perception is most assuredly true. Today I have learned not merely what I must avoid so as never to make a mistake, but at the same time what I must do to attain truth. For I will indeed attain it, if only I pay enough attention to all the things that I per-fectly understand, and separate them off from the rest, which I apprehend more confusedly and more ob-scurely. I will be conscientious about this in the future.

Meditation Five: Concerning the Essence of Material Things, and Again Concerning God, That He Exists

Several matters remain for me to examine concerning the attributes of God and myself, that is, concerning the nature of my mind. But perhaps I will take these up at some other time. For now, since I have noted what to avoid and what to do in order to attain the truth, noth-ing seems more pressing than that I try to free myself from the doubts into which I fell a few days ago, and that I see whether anything certain is to be had con-cerning material things.

Yet, before inquiring whether any such things exist outside me, I surely ought to consider the ideas of these things, insofar as they exist in my thought, and see which ones are distinct and which ones are confused.

I do indeed distinctly imagine the quantity that philosophers commonly call "continuous," that is, the extension of this quantity, or rather of the thing quantified in length, breadth and depth. I enumerate the various parts in it. I ascribe to these parts any sizes, shapes, positions, and local movements whatever; to these movements I ascribe any durations whatever.

Not only are these things manifestly known and transparent to me, viewed thus in a general way, but also, when I focus my attention on them, I perceive countless particulars concerning shapes, number, movement, and the like. Their truth is so open and so much in accord with my nature that, when I first discover them, it seems I am not so much learning something new as recalling something I knew beforehand. In other words, it seems as though I am noticing things for the first time that were in fact in me for a long while, although I had not previously directed a mental gaze upon them.

What I believe must be considered above all here is the fact that I find within me countless ideas of certain things, that, even if perhaps they do not exist anywhere outside me, still cannot be said to be nothing. And although, in a sense, I think them at will, nevertheless they are not something I have fabricated; rather they have their own true and immutable natures. For example, when I imagine a triangle, even if perhaps no such figure exists outside my thought anywhere in the world and never has, the triangle still has a certain determinate nature, essence, or form which is unchangeable and eternal, which I did not fabricate, and which does not depend on my mind. This is evident from the fact that various properties can be demonstrated regarding this triangle: namely, that its three angles are equal to two right angles, that its longest side is opposite its largest angle, and so on. These are properties I now clearly acknowledge, whether I want to or not, even if I previously had given them no thought whatever when I imagined the triangle. For this reason, then, they were not fabricated by me.

It is irrelevant for me to say that perhaps the idea of a triangle came to me from external things through the sense organs because of course I have on occasion seen triangle-shaped bodies. For I can think of countless other figures, concerning which there can be no suspicion of their ever having entered me through the senses, and yet I can demonstrate various properties of these figures, no less than I can those of the triangle. All these properties are patently true because I know them clearly, and thus they are something and not merely nothing. For it is obvious that whatever is true is something, and I have already demonstrated at some length that all that I know clearly is true. And even if I had not demonstrated this, certainly the nature of my mind is such that nevertheless I cannot refrain from assenting to these things, at least while I perceive them clearly. And I recall that even before now, when I used to keep my attention glued to the objects of the senses, I always took the truths I clearly recognized regarding figures, numbers, or other things pertaining to arithmetic, geometry or, in general, to pure and abstract mathematics to be the most certain of all.

But if, from the mere fact that I can bring forth from my thought the idea of something, it follows that all that I clearly and distinctly perceive to belong to that thing really does belong to it, then cannot this too be a basis for an argument proving the existence of God? Clearly the idea of God, that is, the idea of a supremely perfect being, is one I discover to be no less within me than the idea of any figure or number. And that it belongs to God's nature that he always exists is something I understand no less clearly and distinctly than is the case when I demonstrate in regard to some figure or number that something also belongs to the nature of that figure or number. Thus, even if not everything that I have meditated upon during these last few days were true, still the existence of God ought to have for me at least the same degree of certainty that truths of mathematics had until now.

However, this point is not wholly obvious at first glance, but has a certain look of a sophism about it. Since in all other matters I have become accustomed to distinguishing existence from essence, I easily convince myself that it can even be separated from God's essence, and hence that God can be thought of as not existing. But nevertheless, it is obvious to anyone who pays close attention that existence can no more be separated from God's essence than its having three angles equal to two right angles can be separated from the essence of a triangle, or than that the idea of a valley can be separated from the idea of a mountain. Thus it is no less[1] contradictory to think of God (that is, a supremely perfect being) lacking existence (that is, lacking some perfection) than it is to think of a mountain without a valley.

But granted I can no more think of God as not existing than I can think of a mountain without a valley, nevertheless it surely does not follow from the fact that I think of a mountain without a valley that a mountain exists in the world. Likewise, from the fact that I think of God as existing, it does not seem to follow that God exists, for my thought imposes no necessity on things. And just as one may imagine a winged horse, without there being a horse that has wings, in the same way perhaps I can attach existence to God, even though no God exists.

But there is a sophism lurking here. From the fact that I am unable to think of a mountain with a valley, it does not follow that a mountain or a valley exists anywhere, but only that, whether they exist or not, a mountain and a valley are inseparable from one another. But from the fact that I cannot think of God except as existing, it follows that existence is inseparable from God, and that for this reason he really exists. Not that my thought brings this about or imposes any necessity on anything; but rather the necessity of the thing itself, namely of the existence of God, forces me to think this. For I am not free to think of God without existence, that is, a supremely perfect being without a supreme perfection, as I am to imagine a horse with or without wings.

Further, it should not be said here that even though I surely need to assent to the existence of God once I have asserted that God has all perfections and that existence is one of these perfections, nevertheless that earlier assertion need not have been made. Likewise, I need not believe that all four-sided figures can be inscribed in a circle; but given that I posit this, it would then be necessary for me to admit that a rhombus can be inscribed in a circle. Yet this is obviously false. For although it is not necessary that I should ever happen

upon any thought of God, nevertheless whenever I am of a mind to think of a being that is first and supreme, and bring forth the idea of God as it were from the storehouse of my mind, I must of necessity ascribe all perfections to him, even if I do not at that time enumerate them all or take notice of each one individually. This necessity plainly suffices so that afterwards, when I realize that existence is a perfection, I rightly conclude that a first and supreme being exists. In the same way, there is no necessity for me ever to imagine a triangle, but whenever I do wish to consider a rectilinear figure having but three angles, I must ascribe to it those properties on the basis of which one rightly infers that the three angles of this figure are no greater than two right angles, even though I do not take note of this at the time. But when I inquire as to the figures that may be inscribed in a circle, there is absolutely no need whatever for my thinking that all four-sided figures are of this sort; for that matter, I cannot even fabricate such a thing, so long as I am of a mind to admit only what I clearly and distinctly understand. Consequently, there is a great difference between false assumptions of this sort and the true ideas that are inborn in me, the first and chief of which is the idea of God. For there are a great many ways in which I understand that this idea is not an invention that is dependent upon my thought, but is an image of a true and immutable nature. First, I cannot think of anything aside from God alone to whose essence existence belongs. Next, I cannot understand how there could be two or more Gods of this kind. Again, once I have asserted that one God now exists, I plainly see that it is necessary that he has existed from eternity and will endure for eternity. Finally, I perceive many other features in God, none of which I can remove or change.

But, whatever type of argument I use, it always comes down to the fact that the only things that fully convince me are those that I clearly and distinctly perceive. And although some of these things I thus perceive are obvious to everyone, while others are discovered only by those who look more closely and inquire carefully, nevertheless, once they have been discovered, they are considered no less certain than the others. For example, in the case of a right triangle, although it is not so readily apparent that the square of the hypotenuse is equal to the sum of the squares of the other two sides as it is

---

1. A literal translation of the Latin text (*non magis*) is "no more." This is obviously a misstatement on Descartes' part, since it contradicts his own clearly stated views.

that the hypotenuse is opposite the largest angle, nevertheless, once the former has been ascertained, it is no less believed. However, as far as God is concerned, if I were not overwhelmed by prejudices and if the images of sensible things were not besieging my thought from all directions, I would certainly acknowledge nothing sooner or more easily than him. For what, in and of itself, is more manifest than that a supreme being exists, that is, that God, to whose essence alone existence belongs, exists?

And although I needed to pay close attention in order to perceive this, nevertheless I now am just as certain about this as I am about everything else that seems most certain. Moreover, I observe also that certitude about other things is so dependent on this, that without it nothing can ever be perfectly known.

For I am indeed of such a nature that, while I perceive something very clearly and distinctly, I cannot help believing it to be true. Nevertheless, my nature is also such that I cannot focus my mental gaze always on the same thing, so as to perceive it clearly. Often the memory of a previously made judgment may return when I am no longer attending to the arguments on account of which I made such a judgment. Thus, other arguments can be brought forward that would easily make me change my opinion, were I ignorant of God. And thus I would never have true and certain knowledge about anything, but merely fickle and changeable opinions. Thus, for example, when I consider the nature of a triangle, it appears most evident to me, steeped as I am in the principles of geometry, that its three angles are equal to two right angles. And so long as I attend to its demonstration I cannot help believing this to be true. But no sooner do I turn the mind's eye away from the demonstration, than, however much I still recall that I had observed it most clearly, nevertheless, it can easily happen that I entertain doubts about whether it is true, were I ignorant of God. For I can convince myself that I have been so constituted by nature that I might occasionally be mistaken about those things I believe I perceive most evidently, especially when I recall that I have often taken many things to be true and certain, which other arguments have subsequently led me to judge to be false.

But once I perceived that there is a God, and also understood at the same time that everything else depends on him, and that he is not a deceiver, I then concluded that everything that I clearly and distinctly perceive is necessarily true. Hence even if I no longer attend to the reasons leading me to judge this to be true, so long as I merely recall that I did clearly and distinctly observe it, no counter-argument can be brought forward that might force me to doubt it. On the contrary, I have a true and certain knowledge of it. And not just of this one fact, but of everything else that I recall once having demonstrated, as in geometry, and so on. For what objections can now be raised against me? That I have been made such that I am often mistaken? But I now know that I cannot be mistaken in matters I plainly understand. That I have taken many things to be true and certain which subsequently I recognized to be false? But none of these were things I clearly and distinctly perceived. But I was ignorant of this rule for determining the truth, and I believed these things perhaps for other reasons which I later discovered were less firm. What then remains to be said? That perhaps I am dreaming, as I recently objected against myself, in other words, that everything I am now thinking of is no truer than what occurs to someone who is asleep? Be that as it may, this changes nothing; for certainly, even if I were dreaming, if anything is evident to my intellect, then it is entirely true.

And thus I see plainly that the certainty and truth of every science depends exclusively upon the knowledge of the true God, to the extent that, prior to my becoming aware of him, I was incapable of achieving perfect knowledge about anything else. But now it is possible for me to achieve full and certain knowledge about countless things, both about God and other intellectual matters, as well as about the entirety of that corporeal nature which is the object of pure mathematics.

Meditation Six: Concerning the Existence of Material Things, and the Real Distinction between Mind and Body

It remains for me to examine whether material things exist. Indeed I now know that they can exist, at least insofar as they are the object of pure mathematics, since I clearly and distinctly perceive them. For no doubt God is capable of bringing about everything that I am capable of perceiving in this way. And I have never judged that God was incapable of something, except when it was incompatible with my perceiving it distinctly. Moreover, from the faculty of imagination, which I notice I use while dealing with material things, it seems to follow that they exist. For to anyone paying very close attention to what imagination is, it appears to be simply a certain application of the knowing faculty to a body intimately present to it, and which therefore exists.

To make this clear, I first examine the difference between imagination and pure intellection. So, for example, when I imagine a triangle, I not only understand that it is a figure bounded by three lines, but at the same time I also envisage with the mind's eye those lines as if they were present; and this is what I call "imagining." On the other hand, if I want to think about a chiliagon, I certainly understand that it is a figure consisting of a thousand sides, just as well as I understand that a triangle is a figure consisting of three sides, yet I do not imagine those thousand sides in the same way, or envisage them as if they were present. And although in that case—because of force of habit I always imagine something whenever I think about a corporeal thing—I may perchance represent to myself some figure in a confused fashion, nevertheless this figure is obviously not a chiliagon. For this figure is really no different from the figure I would represent to myself, were I thinking of a myriagon or any other figure with a large number of sides. Nor is this figure of any help in knowing the properties that differentiate a chiliagon from other polygons. But if the figure in question is a pentagon, I surely can understand its figure, just as was the case with the chiliagon, without the help of my imagination. But I can also imagine a pentagon by turning the mind's eye both to its five sides and at the same time to the area bounded by those sides. At this point I am manifestly aware that I am in need of a peculiar sort of effort on the part of the mind in order to imagine, one that I do not employ in order to understand. This new effort on the part of the mind clearly shows the difference between imagination and pure intellection.

Moreover, I consider that this power of imagining that is in me, insofar as it differs from the power of understanding, is not required for my own essence, that is, the essence of my mind. For were I to be lacking this power, I would nevertheless undoubtedly remain the same entity I am now. Thus it seems to follow that the power of imagining depends upon something distinct from me. And I readily understand that, were a body to exist to which a mind is so joined that it may apply itself in order, as it were, to look at it any time it wishes, it could happen that it is by means of this very body that I imagine corporeal things. As a result, this mode of thinking may differ from pure intellection only in the sense that the mind, when it understands, in a sense turns toward itself and looks at one of the ideas that are in it; whereas when it imagines, it turns toward the body, and intuits in the body something that conforms to an idea either understood by the mind or perceived by sense. To be sure, I easily understand that the imagination can be actualized in this way, provided a body does exist. And since I can think of no other way of explaining imagination that is equally appropriate, I make a probable conjecture from this that a body exists. But this is only a probability. And even though I may examine everything carefully, nevertheless I do not yet see how the distinct idea of corporeal nature that I find in my imagination can enable me to develop an argument which necessarily concludes that some body exists.

But I am in the habit of imagining many other things, over and above that corporeal nature which is the object of pure mathematics, such as colors, sounds, tastes, pain, and the like, though not so distinctly. And I perceive these things better by means of the senses, from which, with the aid of the memory, they seem to have arrived at the imagination. Thus I should pay the same degree of attention to the senses, so that I might deal with them more appropriately. I must see whether I can obtain any reliable argument for the existence of corporeal things from those things that are perceived by the mode of thinking that I call "sense."

First of all, to be sure, I will review here all the things I previously believed to be true because I had perceived them by means of the senses and the causes I had for thinking this. Next I will assess the causes why I later called them into doubt. Finally, I will consider what I must now believe about these things.

So first, I sensed that I had a head, hands, feet, and other members that comprised this body which I viewed as part of me, or perhaps even as the whole of me. I sensed that this body was found among many other bodies, by which my body can be affected in various beneficial or harmful ways. I gauged what was opportune by means of a certain sensation of pleasure, and what was inopportune by a sensation of pain. In addition to pain and pleasure, I also sensed within me hunger, thirst, and other such appetites, as well as certain bodily tendencies toward mirth, sadness, anger, and other such affects. And externally, besides the extension, shapes, and motions of bodies, I also sensed their hardness, heat, and other tactile qualities. I also sensed light, colors, odors, tastes, and sounds, on the basis of whose variety I distinguished the sky, the earth, the seas, and the other bodies, one from the other. Now given the ideas of all these qualities that presented themselves to my thought, and which were all that I properly and immediately sensed, still it was surely not without reason that I thought I sensed things that were manifestly different from my thought, namely, the bodies from which these ideas proceeded. For I knew by experience that these ideas came upon me utterly without my consent, to the extent that, wish as I may, I could not sense any object unless it was present to a sense organ. Nor could I fail to sense it when it was present. And since the ideas perceived by sense were much more vivid and explicit and even, in their own way, more distinct than any of those that I deliberately and knowingly formed through meditation or that I found impressed on my memory, it seemed impossible that they came from myself. Thus the remaining alternative was that they came from other things. Since I had no knowledge of such things except from those same ideas themselves, I could not help entertaining the thought that they were similar to those ideas. Moreover, I also recalled that the use of the senses antedated the use of reason. And since I saw that the ideas that I myself fashioned were not as explicit as those that I perceived through the faculty of sense, and were for the most part composed of parts of the latter, I easily convinced myself that I had absolutely no idea in the intellect that I did not have beforehand in the sense faculty. Not without reason did I judge that this body, which by a certain special right I called "mine," belongs more to me than did any other. For I could never be separated from it in the same way I could be from other bodies. I sensed all appetites and feelings in and on behalf of it. Finally, I noticed pain and pleasurable excitement in its parts, but not in other bodies external to it.

But why should a certain sadness of spirit arise from some sensation or other of pain, and why should a certain elation arise from a sensation of excitement, or why should that peculiar twitching in the stomach, which I call hunger, warn me to have something to eat, or why should dryness in the throat warn me to take something to drink, and so on? I plainly had no explanation other than that I had been taught this way by nature. For there is no affinity whatsoever, at least none I am aware of, between this twitching in the stomach and the will to have something to eat, or between the sensation of something causing pain and the thought of sadness arising from this sensation. But nature also seems to have taught me everything else as well that I judged concerning the objects of the senses, for I had already convinced myself that this was how things were, prior to my assessing any of the arguments that might prove it.

Afterwards, however, many experiences gradually weakened any faith that I had in the senses. Towers that had seemed round from afar occasionally appeared square at close quarters. Very large statues mounted on their pedestals did not seem large to someone looking at them from ground level. And in countless other such instances I determined that judgments in matters of the external senses were in error. And not just the external senses, but the internal senses as well. For what can be more intimate than pain? But I had sometimes heard it said by people whose leg or arm had been amputated that it seemed to them that they still occasionally sensed pain in the very limb they had lost. Thus, even in my own case it did not seem to be entirely certain that some bodily member was causing me pain, even though I did sense pain in it. To these causes for doubt I recently added two quite general ones. The first was that everything I ever thought I sensed while awake I could believe I also sometimes sensed while asleep, and since I do not believe that what I seem to sense in my dreams comes to me from things external to me, I saw no reason why I should hold this belief about those things I seem to be sensing while awake. The second was that, since I was still ignorant of the author of my origin (or at least pretended to be ignorant of it), I saw nothing to prevent my having been so constituted by nature that I should be mistaken even about what seemed to me most true. As to the arguments that used to convince me of the truth of sensible things, I found no difficulty responding to them. For since I seemed driven by nature toward many things about which reason tried to dissuade me, I did not think that what I was taught by nature deserved much credence. And even though the perceptions of the senses did not depend on my will, I did not think that we must therefore conclude that they came from things distinct from me, since perhaps there is some faculty in me, as yet unknown to me, that produces these perceptions.

But now, having begun to have a better knowledge of myself and the author of my origin, I am of the opinion that I must not rashly admit everything that I seem to derive from the senses; but neither, for that matter, should I call everything into doubt.

First, I know that all the things that I clearly and distinctly understand can be made by God such as I understand them. For this reason, my ability clearly and distinctly to understand one thing without another suffices to make me certain that the one thing is different from the other, since they can be separated from each other, at least by God. The question as to the sort of power that might effect such a separation is not relevant to their being thought to be different. For this reason, from the fact that I know that I exist, and that at the same time I judge that obviously nothing else belongs to my nature or essence except that I am a thinking thing, I rightly conclude that my essence consists entirely in my being a thinking thing. And although perhaps (or rather, as I shall soon say, assuredly) I have a body that is very closely joined to me, nevertheless, because on the one hand I have a clear and distinct idea of myself, insofar as I am merely a thinking thing and not an extended thing, and because on the other hand I have a distinct idea of a body, insofar as it is merely an extended thing and not a thinking thing, it is certain that I am really distinct from my body, and can exist without it.

Moreover, I find in myself faculties for certain special modes of thinking, namely the faculties of imagining and sensing. I can clearly and distinctly understand myself in my entirety without these faculties, but not vice versa: I cannot understand them clearly and distinctly without me, that is, without a substance endowed with understanding in which they inhere, for they include an act of understanding in their formal concept. Thus I perceive them to be distinguished from

me as modes from a thing. I also acknowledge that there are certain other faculties, such as those of moving from one place to another, of taking on various shapes, and so on, that, like sensing or imagining, cannot be understood apart from some substance in which they inhere, and hence without which they cannot exist. But it is clear that these faculties, if in fact they exist, must be in a corporeal or extended substance, not in a substance endowed with understanding. For some extension is contained in a clear and distinct concept of them, though certainly not any understanding. Now there clearly is in me a passive faculty of sensing, that is, a faculty for receiving and knowing the ideas of sensible things; but I could not use it unless there also existed, either in me or in something else, a certain active faculty of producing or bringing about these ideas. But this faculty surely cannot be in me, since it clearly presupposes no act of understanding, and these ideas are produced without my cooperation and often even against my will. Therefore the only alternative is that it is in some substance different from me, containing either formally or eminently all the reality that exists objectively in the ideas produced by that faculty, as I have just noted above. Hence this substance is either a body, that is, a corporeal nature, which contains formally all that is contained objectively in the ideas, or else it is God, or some other creature more noble than a body, which contains eminently all that is contained objectively in the ideas. But since God is not a deceiver, it is patently obvious that he does not send me these ideas either immediately by himself, or even through the mediation of some creature that contains the objective reality of these ideas not formally but only eminently. For since God has given me no faculty whatsoever for making this determination, but instead has given me a great inclination to believe that these ideas issue from corporeal things, I fail to see how God could be understood not to be a deceiver, if these ideas were to issue from a source other than corporeal things. And consequently corporeal things exist. Nevertheless, perhaps not all bodies exist exactly as I grasp them by sense, since this sensory grasp is in many cases very obscure and confused. But at least they do contain everything I clearly and distinctly understand—that is, everything, considered in a general sense, that is encompassed in the object of pure mathematics.

As far as the remaining matters are concerned, which are either merely particular (for example, that the sun is of such and such a size or shape, and so on) or less clearly understood (for example, light, sound, pain, and the like), even though these matters are very doubtful and uncertain, nevertheless the fact that God is no deceiver (and thus no falsity can be found in my opinions, unless there is also in me a faculty given me by God for the purpose of rectifying this falsity) offers me a definite hope of reaching the truth even in these matters. And surely there is no doubt that all that I am taught by nature has some truth to it; for by "nature," taken generally, I understand nothing other than God himself or the ordered network of created things which was instituted by God. By my own particular nature I understand nothing other than the combination of all the things bestowed upon me by God.

There is nothing that this nature teaches me more explicitly than that I have a body that is ill-disposed when I feel pain, that needs food and drink when I suffer hunger or thirst, and the like. Therefore, I should not doubt that there is some truth in this.

By means of these sensations of pain, hunger, thirst and so on, nature also teaches that I am present not merely to my body in the way a sailor is present in a ship, but that I am most tightly joined and, so to speak, commingled with it, so much so that I and the body constitute one single thing. For if this were not the case, then I, who am only a thinking thing, would not sense pain when the body is injured; rather, I would perceive the wound by means of the pure intellect, just as a sailor perceives by sight whether anything in his ship is broken. And when the body is in need of food or drink, I should understand this explicitly, instead of having confused sensations of hunger and thirst. For clearly these sensations of thirst, hunger, pain, and so on are nothing but certain confused modes of thinking arising from the union and, as it were, the commingling of the mind with the body.

Moreover, I am also taught by nature that various other bodies exist around my body, some of which are to be pursued, while others are to be avoided. And to be sure, from the fact that I sense a wide variety of colors, sounds, odors, tastes, levels of heat, and grades of roughness, and the like, I rightly conclude that in the bodies from which these different perceptions of the senses proceed there are differences corresponding to the different perceptions—though perhaps the latter do not resemble the former. And from the fact that some of these perceptions are pleasant while others are unpleasant, it is plainly certain that my body, or rather my whole self, insofar as I am comprised of a body and a mind, can be affected by various beneficial and harmful bodies in the vicinity.

Granted, there are many other things that I seem to have been taught by nature; nevertheless it was not really nature that taught them to me but a certain habit of making reckless judgments. And thus it could easily happen that these judgments are false: for example, that any space where there is absolutely nothing happening to move my senses is empty; or that there is something in a hot body that bears an exact likeness to the idea of heat that is in me; or that in a white or green body there is the same whiteness or greenness that I sense; or that in a bitter or sweet body there is the same taste, and so on; or that stars and towers and any other distant bodies have the same size and shape that they present to my senses, and other things of this sort. But to ensure that my perceptions in this matter are sufficiently distinct, I ought to define more precisely what exactly I mean when I say that I am "taught something by nature." For I am taking "nature" here more narrowly than the combination of everything bestowed on me by God. For this combination embraces many things that belong exclusively to my mind, such as my perceiving that what has been done cannot be undone, and everything else that is known by the light of nature. That is not what I am talking about here. There are also many things that belong exclusively to the body, such as that it tends to move downward, and so on. I am not dealing with these either, but only with what God has bestowed on me insofar as I am composed of mind and body. Accordingly, it is this nature that teaches me to avoid things that produce a sensation of pain and to pursue things that produce a sensation of pleasure, and the like. But it does not appear that nature teaches us to conclude anything, besides these things, from these sense perceptions unless the intellect has first conducted its own inquiry regarding things external to us. For it seems to belong exclusively to the mind, and not to the composite of mind and body, to know the truth in these matters. Thus, although a star affects my eye no more than does the flame from a small torch, still there is no real or positive tendency in my eye toward believing that the star is no larger than the flame. Yet, ever since my youth, I have made this judgment without any reason for doing so. And although I feel heat as I draw closer to the fire, and I also feel pain upon drawing too close to it, there is not a single argument that persuades me that there is something in the fire similar to that heat, any more than to that pain. On the contrary, I am convinced only that there is something in the fire that, regardless of what it finally turns out to be, causes in us those sensations of heat or pain. And although there may be nothing in a given space that moves the senses, it does not therefore follow that there is no body in it. But I see that in these and many other instances I have been in the habit of subverting the order of nature. For admittedly I use the perceptions of the senses (which are properly given by nature only for signifying to the mind what things are useful or harmful to the composite of which it is a part, and to that extent they are clear and distinct enough) as reliable rules for immediately discerning what is the essence of bodies located outside us. Yet they signify nothing about that except quite obscurely and confusedly.

I have already examined in sufficient detail how it could happen that my judgments are false, despite the goodness of God. But a new difficulty now arises regarding those very things that nature shows me are either to be sought out or avoided, as well as the internal sensations where I seem to have detected errors, as for example, when someone is deluded by a food's pleasant taste to eat the poison hidden inside it. In this case, however, he is driven by nature only toward desiring the thing in which the pleasurable taste is found, but not toward the poison, of which he obviously is unaware. I can only conclude that this nature is not omniscient. This is not remarkable, since man is a limited thing, and thus only what is of limited perfection befits him.

But we not infrequently err even in those things to which nature impels us. Take, for example, the case of those who are ill and who desire food or drink that will soon afterwards be injurious to them. Perhaps it could be said here that they erred because their nature was corrupt. However, this does not remove our difficulty, for a sick man is no less a creature of God than a healthy one, and thus it seems no less inconsistent that the sick man got a deception-prone nature from God. And a clock made of wheels and counter-weights follows all the laws of nature no less closely when it has been badly constructed and does not tell time accurately than it does when it completely satisfies the wish of its maker. Likewise, I might regard a man's body as a kind of mechanism that is outfitted with and composed of bones, nerves, muscles, veins, blood and skin in such a way that, even if no mind existed in it, the man's body would still exhibit all the same motions that are in it now except for those motions that proceed either from a command of the will or, consequently, from the mind. I easily recognize that it would be natural for this body, were it, say, suffering from dropsy and experiencing dryness in the throat (which typically produces a thirst sensation in the mind), and also so disposed by its nerves and other parts to take something to drink, the result of which would be to exacerbate the illness. This is as natural as for a body without any such illness to be moved by the same dryness in the throat to take something to drink that is useful to it. And given the intended purpose of the clock, I could say that it deviates from its nature when it fails to tell the right time. And similarly, considering the mechanism of the human body in terms of its being equipped for the motions that typically occur in it, I may think that it too is deviating from its nature, if its throat were dry when having something to drink is not beneficial to its conservation. Nevertheless, I am well aware that this last use of "nature" differs greatly from the other. For this latter "nature" is merely a designation dependent on my thought, since it compares a man in poor health and a poorly constructed clock with the ideas of a healthy man and of a well-made clock, a designation extrinsic to the things to which it is applied. But by "nature" taken in the former sense, I understand something that is really in things, and thus is not without some truth.

When we say, then, in the case of the body suffering from dropsy, that its "nature" is corrupt, given the fact that it has a parched throat and yet does not need something to drink, "nature" obviously is merely an extrinsic designation. Nevertheless, in the case of the composite, that is, of a mind joined to such a body, it is not a mere designation, but a true error of nature that this body should be thirsty when having something to drink would be harmful to it. It therefore remains to inquire here how the goodness of God does not prevent "nature," thus considered, from being deceptive.

Now my first observation here is that there is a great difference between a mind and a body in that a body, by its very nature, is always divisible. On the other hand, the mind is utterly indivisible. For when I consider the mind, that is, myself insofar as I am only a thinking thing, I cannot distinguish any parts within me; rather, I understand myself to be manifestly one complete thing. Although the entire mind seems to be united to the entire body, nevertheless, were a foot or an arm or any other bodily part to be amputated, I know that nothing has been taken away from the mind on that account. Nor can the faculties of willing, sensing, understanding, and so on be called "parts" of the mind, since it is one and the same mind that wills, senses, and understands. On the other hand, there is no corporeal or extended thing I can think of that I may not in my thought easily divide into parts; and in this way I understand that it is divisible. This consideration alone would suffice to teach me that the mind is wholly diverse from the body, had I not yet known it well enough in any other way.

My second observation is that my mind is not immediately affected by all the parts of the body, but only by the brain, or perhaps even by just one small part of the brain, namely, by that part where the "common" sense is said to reside. Whenever this part of the brain is disposed in the same manner, it presents the same thing to the mind, even if the other parts of the body are able meanwhile to be related in diverse ways. Countless experiments show this, none of which need be reviewed here.

My next observation is that the nature of the body is such that whenever any of its parts can be moved by another part some distance away, it can also be moved in the same manner by any of the parts that lie between them, even if this more distant part is doing nothing. For example, in the cord ABCD, if the final part D is pulled, the first part A would be moved in exactly the same manner as it could be, if one of the intermediate parts B or C were pulled, while the end part D remained immobile. Likewise, when I feel a pain in my foot, physics teaches me that this sensation took place by means of nerves distributed throughout the foot, like stretched cords extending from the foot all the way to the brain. When these nerves are pulled in the foot, they also pull on the inner parts of the brain to which they extend, and produce a certain motion in them. This motion has been constituted by nature so as to affect the mind with a sensation of pain, as if it occurred in the foot. But because these nerves need to pass through the shin, thigh, loins, back, and neck to get from the foot to the brain, it can happen that even if it is not the part in the foot but merely one of the intermediate parts that is being struck, the very same movement will occur in the brain that would occur were the foot badly injured. The inevitable result will be that the mind feels the same pain. The same opinion should hold for any other sensation.

My final observation is that, since any given motion occurring in that part of the brain immediately affecting the mind produces but one sensation in it, I can think of no better arrangement than that it produces the one sensation that, of all the ones it is able to produce, is most especially and most often conducive to the maintenance of a healthy man. Moreover, experience shows that all the sensations bestowed on us by nature are like this. Hence there is absolutely nothing to be found in them that does not bear witness to God's power and goodness. Thus, for example, when the nerves in the foot are agitated in a violent and unusual manner, this motion of theirs extends through the marrow of the spine to the inner reaches of the brain, where it gives the mind the sign to sense something, namely, the pain as if it is occurring in the foot. This provokes the mind to do its utmost to move away from the cause of the pain, since it is seen as harmful to the foot. But the nature of man could have been so constituted by God that this same motion in the brain might have indicated something else to the mind: for example, either the motion itself as it occurs in the brain, or in the foot, or in someplace in between, or something else entirely different. But nothing else would have served so well the maintenance of the body. Similarly, when we need something to drink, a certain dryness arises in the throat that moves the nerves in the throat, and, by means of them, the inner parts of the brain. And this motion affects the mind with a sensation of thirst, because in this entire affair nothing is more useful for us to know than that we need something to drink in order to maintain our health; the same holds in the other cases.

From these considerations it is utterly apparent that, notwithstanding the immense goodness of God, the nature of man, insofar as it is composed of mind and body, cannot help being sometimes mistaken. For if some cause, not in the foot but in some other part through which the nerves extend from the foot to the brain, or perhaps even in the brain itself, were to produce the same motion that would normally be produced by a badly injured foot, the pain will be felt as if it were in the foot, and the senses will naturally be deceived. For since an identical motion in the brain can only bring about an identical sensation in the mind, and it is more frequently the case that this motion is wont to arise on account of a cause that harms the foot than on account of some other thing existing elsewhere, it is reasonable that the motion should always show pain to the mind as something belonging to the foot rather than to some other part. And if dryness in the throat does not arise, as is normal, because taking something to drink contributes to bodily health, but from a contrary cause, as happens in the case of someone with dropsy, then it is far better that it should deceive on that occasion than that it should always be deceptive when the body is in good health. The same holds for the other cases.

This consideration is most helpful, not only for my noticing all the errors to which my nature is liable, but also for enabling me to correct or avoid them without difficulty. To be sure, I know that all the senses set forth what is true more frequently than what is false regarding what concerns the welfare of the body. Moreover, I can nearly always make use of several of them in order to examine the same thing. Furthermore, I can use my

memory, which connects current happenings with past ones, and my intellect, which now has examined all the causes of error. Hence I should no longer fear that those things that are daily shown me by the senses are false. On the contrary, the hyperbolic doubts of the last few days ought to be rejected as ludicrous. This goes especially for the chief reason for doubting, which dealt with my failure to distinguish being asleep from being awake. For I now notice that there is a considerable difference between these two; dreams are never joined by the memory with all the other actions of life, as is the case with those actions that occur when one is awake. For surely, if, while I am awake, someone were suddenly to appear to me and then immediately disappear, as occurs in dreams, so that I see neither where he came from nor where he went, it is not without reason that I would judge him to be a ghost or a phantom conjured up in my brain, rather than a true man. But when these things happen, and I notice distinctly where they come from, where they are now, and when they come to me, and when I connect my perception of them without interruption with the whole rest of my life, I am clearly certain that these perceptions have happened to me not while I was dreaming but while I was awake. Nor ought I have even the least doubt regarding the truth of these things, if, having mustered all the senses, in addition to my memory and my intellect, in order to examine them, nothing is passed on to me by one of these sources that conflicts with the others. For from the fact that God is no deceiver, it follows that I am in no way mistaken in these matters. But because the need to get things done does not always permit us the leisure for such a careful inquiry, we must confess that the life of man is apt to commit errors regarding particular things, and we must acknowledge the infirmity of our nature.

Roderick Chisholm

The Problem of the Criterion

1

"The problem of the criterion" seems to me to be one of the most important and one of the most difficult of all the problems of philosophy. I am tempted to say that one has not begun to philosophize until one has faced this problem and has recognized how unappealing, in the end, each of the possible solutions is. [. . .]

2

What is the problem, then? It is the ancient problem of "the diallelus"—the problem of "the wheel" or "the vicious circle." It was put very neatly by Montaigne in his *Essays.* So let us begin by paraphrasing his formulation of the puzzle. To know whether things really are as they seem to be, we must have a *procedure* for distinguishing appearances that are true from appearances that are false. But to know whether our procedure is a good procedure, we have to know whether it really *succeeds* in distinguishing appearances that are true from appearances that are false. And we cannot know whether it does really succeed unless we already know which appearances are *true* and which ones are *false*. And so we are caught in a circle.[1]

Let us try to see how one gets into a situation of this sort.

The puzzles begin to form when you ask yourself, "What can I really know about the world?" We all are acquainted with people who think they know a lot more than in fact they do know. I'm thinking of fanatics, bigots, mystics, various types of dogmatists. And we have all heard of people who claim at least to know a lot less than what in fact they do know. I'm thinking of those people who call themselves "skeptics" and who like to say that people cannot know what the world is really like. People tend to become skeptics, temporarily, after reading books on popular science: the authors tell us we cannot know what things are like really (but they make use of a vast amount of knowledge, or a vast amount of what is claimed to be knowledge, to support this skeptical conclusion). And as we know, people tend to become dogmatists, temporarily, as a result of the effects of alcohol, or drugs, or religious and emotional experiences. Then they claim to have an inside view of the world and they think they have a deep kind of knowledge giving them a key to the entire workings of the universe.

If you have a healthy common sense, you will feel that something is wrong with both of these extremes and that the truth is somewhere in the middle: we can know far more than the skeptic says we can know and far less then the dogmatist or the mystic says that he can know. But how are we to decide these things?

3

How do we decide, in any particular case, whether we have a genuine item of knowledge? Most of us are ready to confess that our beliefs far transcend what we really know. There are things we believe that we don't in fact know. And we can say of many of these things that we know that we don't know them. I believe that Mrs. Jones is honest, say, but I don't know it, and I know that I don't know it. There are other things that we don't know, but they are such that we don't know that we don't know them. Last week, say, I thought I knew that Mr. Smith was honest, but he turned out to be a thief. I didn't know that he was a thief, and, moreover, I didn't know that I didn't know that he was a thief; I

1. Book 2, Chapter 12 ("An Apologie of Raymond Sebond"); p. 544 of the Modern Library edition of *The Essays of Montaigne.*

thought I knew that he was honest. And so the problem is: How are we to distinguish the real cases of knowledge from what only seem to be cases of knowledge? Or, as I put it before, how are we to decide in any particular case whether we have genuine items of knowledge?

What would be a satisfactory solution to our problem? Let me quote in detail what Cardinal Mercier says:

> If there is any knowledge which bears the mark of truth, if the intellect does have a way of distinguishing the true and the false, in short, *if there is* a criterion of truth, then this criterion should satisfy three conditions: it should be *internal, objective,* and *immediate.*
>
> It should be *internal.* No reason or rule of truth that is provided by and *external authority* can serve as an ultimate criterion. For the reflective doubts that are essential to criteriology can and should be applied to this authority itself. The mind cannot attain to certainty until it has found *within itself* a sufficient reason for adhering to the testimony of such an authority.
>
> The criterion should be *objective.* The ultimate reason for believing cannot be a merely *subjective* state of the thinking subject. A man is aware that he can reflect upon his psychological states in order to control them. Knowing that he has this ability, he does not, so long as he has not made use of it, have the right to be sure. The ultimate ground of certitude cannot consist in a subjective feeling. It can be found only in that which, objectively, produces this feeling and is adequate to reason.
>
> Finally, the criterion must be *immediate.* To be sure, a certain conviction may rest upon many different reasons some of which are subordinate to others. But if we are to avoid an infinite regress, then we must find a ground of assent that presupposes no other. We must find an *immediate* criterion of certitude.
>
> Is there a criterion of truth that satisfies these three conditions? If so, what is it?[2]

2. Cardinal D. J. Mercier. *Critériologie Générale ou Théorie Générale de la Certitude,* Paris: Félix Alcan, 1884, p. 234.

4

To see how perplexing our problem is, let us consider a figure that Descartes had suggested and that Coffey takes up in his dealings with the problem of the criterion.[3] Descartes' figures come to this.

Let us suppose that you have a pile of apples and you want to sort out the good ones from the bad ones. You want to put the good ones in a pile by themselves and throw the bad ones away. This is a useful thing to do, obviously, because the bad apples tend to infect the good ones and then the good ones become bad, too. Descartes thought our beliefs were like this. The bad ones tend to infect the good ones, so we should look them over very carefully, throw out the bad ones if we can, and then—or so Descartes hoped—we would be left with just a stock of good beliefs on which we could rely completely. But how are we to do the sorting? If we are to sort out the good ones from the bad ones, then, of course, we must have a way of recognizing the good ones. Or at least we must have a way of recognizing the bad ones. And—again, of course—you and I do have a way of recognizing good apples and also of recognizing bad ones. The good ones have their own special feel, look, and taste, and so do the bad ones.

But when we turn from apples to beliefs, the matter is quite different. In the case of the apples, we have a method—a criterion—for distinguishing the good ones from the bad ones. But in the case of the beliefs, we do not have a method or a criterion for distinguishing the good ones from the bad ones. Or, at least, we don't have one yet. The question we started with was: How *are* we to tell the good ones from the bad ones? In other words, we were asking: What is the proper method for deciding which are the good beliefs and which are the bad ones—which beliefs are genuine cases of knowledge and which beliefs are not?

And now, you see, we are on the wheel. First, we want to find out which are the good beliefs and which are

3. See his reply to the VIIth set of Objections and P. Coffey, *Epistemology and the Theory of Knowledge.* London: Longmans, Green and Co., 1917, vol. 1, p. 127.

the bad ones. To find this out we have to have some way—some method—of deciding which are the good ones and which are the bad ones. But there are good and bad methods—good and bad ways—of sorting out the good beliefs from the bad ones. And so we now have a new problem: How are we to decide which are the good methods and which are the bad ones?

If we could fix on a good method for distinguishing between good and bad methods, we might be all set. But this, of course, just moves the problem to a different level. How are we to distinguish between a good method for choosing good methods? If we continue in this way, of course, we are led to an infinite regress and we will never have the answer to our original question.

What do we do in fact? We do know that there are fairly reliable ways of sorting out good beliefs from bad ones. Most people will tell you, for example, that if you follow the procedures of science and common sense—if you tend carefully to your observations and if you makes use of the canons of logic, induction, and the theory of probability—you will be following the best possible procedure for making sure that you will have more good beliefs than bad ones. This is doubtless true. But how do we know that it is? How do we know that the procedures of science, reason, and common sense are the best methods that we have?

If we do know this, it is because we know that these procedures work. It is because we know that these procedures do in fact enable us to distinguish the good beliefs from the bad ones. We say: "See—these methods turn out good beliefs." But *how* do we know that they do? It can only be that we already know how to tell the difference between the good beliefs and the bad ones.

And now you can see where the skeptic comes in. He'll say this: "You said you wanted to sort out the good beliefs from the bad ones. Then to do this, you apply the canons of science, common sense, and reason. And now, in answer to the question, 'How do you know that that's the right way to do it?', you say 'Why, I can see that the ones it picks out are the good ones and the ones it leaves behind are the bad ones.' But if you can *see* which ones are the good ones and which ones are the bad ones, why do you think you need a general method for sorting them out?"

5

We can formulate some of the philosophical issues that are involved here by distinguishing two pairs of questions. They are:

A) "*What* do we know? What is the *extent* of our knowledge?"

B) "How are we to decide *whether* we know? What are the *criteria* of knowledge?"

If you happen to know the answers to the first of these pairs of questions, you may have some hope of being able to answer the second. Thus, if you happen to know which are the good apples and which are the bad ones, then maybe you could explain to some other person how he could go about deciding whether or not he has a good apple or a bad one. But if you don't know the answer to the first of these pairs of questions—if you don't know what things you know or how far your knowledge extends—it is difficult to see how you could possibly figure out an answer to the second.

On the other hand, *if,* somehow, you already know the answers to the second of these pairs of questions, then you may have some hope of being able to answer the first. Thus, if you happen to have a good set of directions for telling whether apples are good or bad, then maybe you can go about finding a good one—assuming, of course, that there are some good apples to be found. But if you don't know the answer to the second of these pairs of questions—if you don't know how to go about deciding whether or not you know, if you don't know what the criteria of knowing are—it is difficult to see how you could possibly figure out an answer to the first.

And so we can formulate the position of *the skeptic* on these matters. He will say: "You cannot answer question A until you have answered question B. And you cannot answer question B until you have answered question A. Therefore you cannot answer either question. You cannot know what, if anything, you know, and there is no possible way for you to decide in any particular case." Is there any reply to this?

6

Broadly speaking, there are at least two other possible views. So we may choose among three possibilities.

There are people—philosophers—who think that they do have an answer to B and that, given their answer to B, they can then figure out their answer to A. And there are other people—other philosophers—who have it the other way around: they think that they have an answer to A and that, given their answer to A, they can then figure out the answer to B.

There don't seem to be any generally accepted names for these two different philosophical positions. (Perhaps this is just as well. There are more than enough names, as it is, for possible philosophical views.) I suggest, for the moment, we use the expressions "methodists" and "particularists." By "methodists," I mean, not the followers of John Wesley's version of Christianity, but those who think they have an answer to B, and who then, in terms of it, work out their answer to A. By "particularists," I mean those who have it the other way around.

7

Thus John Locke was a methodist—in our present, rather special sense of the term. He was able to arrive—somehow—at an answer to B. He said, in effect: "The way you decide whether or not a belief is a good belief—that is to say, the way you decide whether a belief is likely to be a genuine case of knowledge—is to see whether it is derived from sense experience, to see, for example, whether it bears certain relations to your sensations." Just what these relations to our sensations might be is a matter we may leave open, for present purposes. The point is: Locke felt that if a belief is to be credible, it must bear certain relations to the believer's sensations—but he never told us *how* he happened to arrive at this conclusion. This, of course, is the view that has come to be known as "empiricism." David Hume followed Locke in this empiricism and said that empiricism gives us an effective criterion for distinguishing the good apples from the bad ones. You can take this criterion to the library, he said. Suppose you find a book in which the author makes assertions that do not conform to the empirical criterion. Hume said: "Commit it to the flames: for it can contain nothing but sophistry and illusion."

8

Empiricism, then, was a form of what I have called "methodism." The empiricist—like other types of methodist—begins with a criterion and then he uses it to throw out the bad apples. There are two objections, I would say, to empiricism. The first—which applies to every form of methodism (in our present sense of the word)—is that the criterion is very broad and far-reaching and at the same time completely arbitrary. How can one *begin* with a broad generalization? It seems especially odd that the empiricist—who wants to proceed cautiously, step by step, from experience—begins with such a generalization. He leaves us completely in the dark so far as concerns what *reasons* he may have for adopting this particular criterion rather than some other. The second objection applies to empiricism in particular. When we apply the empirical criterion—at least, as it was developed by Hume, as well as by many of those in the nineteenth and twentieth centuries who have called themselves "empiricists"—we seem to throw out, not only the bad apples but the good ones as well, and we are left, in effect, with just a few parings or skins with no meat behind them. Thus Hume virtually conceded that, if you are going to be empiricist, the only matters of fact that you can really know about pertain to the existence of sensations. "'Tis vain," he said, "to ask whether there be body." He meant you cannot know whether any physical things exist—whether there are trees, or houses, or bodies, much less whether there are atoms or other such microscopic particles. All you can know is that there are and have been certain sensations. You cannot know whether there is any you who experiences those sensations—much less whether any other people exist who experience sensations. And I think, if he had been consistent in his empiricism, he would also have said you cannot really be sure whether there have been any sensations in the past; you can know only that certain sensations exist here and now.

9

The great Scottish philosopher, Thomas Reid, reflected on all this in the eighteenth century. He was serious about philosophy and man's place in the world. He finds

Hume saying things implying that we can know only of the existence of certain sensations here and now. One can imagine him saying: "Good Lord! What kind of nonsense is this?" What he did say, among other things, was this: "A traveler of good judgment may mistake his way, and be unawares led into a wrong track; and while the road is fair before him, he may go on without suspicion and be followed by others but, when it ends in a coal pit, it requires no great judgment to know that he hath gone wrong, nor perhaps to find out what misled him." [4]

Thus Reid, as I interpret him, was not an empiricist; nor was he, more generally, what I have called a "methodist." He was a "particularist." That is to say, he thought that he had an answer to question A, and in terms of the answer to question A, he then worked out a kind of answer to question B. An even better example of a "particularist" is the great twentieth century English philosopher, G. E. Moore.

Suppose, for a moment, you were tempted to go along with Hume and say, "The only thing about the world I can really know is that there are now sensations of a certain sort. There's a sensation of a man, there's the sound of a voice, and there's a feeling of bewilderment or boredom. But that's all I can really know about." What would Reid say? I can imagine him saying something like this: "Well, you can talk that way if you want to. But you know very well that it isn't true. You know that you are there, that you have a body of such and such a sort and that other people are here, too. And you know about this building and where you were this morning and all kinds of other things as well." G. E. Moore would raise his hand at this point and say: "I know very well this is a hand, and so do you. If you come across some philosophical theory that implies that you and I cannot know that this is a hand, then so much the worse for the theory." I think that Reid and Moore are right, myself, and I'm inclined to think that the "methodists" are wrong.

Going back to our questions A and B, we may summarize the three possible views as follows: there is skepticism (you cannot answer either question without presupposing an answer to the other, and therefore the questions cannot be answered at all); there is "methodism" (you begin with an answer to B); and there is "particularism" (you begin with an answer to A). I suggest that the third possibility is the most reasonable.

10

I would say—and many reputable philosophers would disagree with me—that, to find out whether you know such a thing as that this is a hand, you don't have to apply any test or criterion. Spinoza has it right. "In order to know," he said, "there is no need to know that we know, much less to know that we know that we know." [5]

This is part of the answer, it seems to me, to the puzzle about the diallelus. There are many things that quite obviously, we do know to be true. If I report to you the things I now see and hear and feel—or, if you prefer, the things I now think I see and hear and feel—the chances are that my report will be correct; I will be telling you something I know. And so, too, if you report the things that you think you now see and hear and feel. To be sure, there are hallucinations and illusions. People often think they see or hear or feel things that in fact they do not see or hear or feel. But from this fact—that our senses do sometimes deceive us—it hardly follows that your sense and mine are deceiving you and me right now. One may say similar things about what we remember.

Having these good apples before us, we can look them over and formulate certain criteria of goodness. Consider the senses, for example. One important criterion—one epistemological principle—was formulated by St. Augustine. It is more reasonable, he said, to trust the senses that to distrust them. Even though there have been illusions and hallucinations, the wise thing, when everything seems all right, is to accept the testimony of the senses. I say "when everything seems all right." If on a particular occasion something about *that* particular occasion makes you suspect that particular report of the senses, if, say, you seem to remember having been drugged or hypnotized, or brainwashed, then perhaps

---

4. Thomas Reid, *Inquiry into the Human Mind,* chap. 1, sec. 8.

5. *On Improvement of the Understanding,* in *Chief Works of Benedict de Spinoza,* vol. 2, trans. R. H. M. Elwes, rev. ed. (London: George Bell and Sons, 1898), p. 13.

you should have some doubts about what you think you see, or hear, or feel, or smell. But if nothing about this particular occasion leads you to suspect what the senses report of this particular occasion, then the wise thing is to take such a report at is face value. In short the senses should be regarded as innocent until there is some positive reason, on some particular occasion, for thinking that they are guilty on that particular occasion.

One might say the same thing of memory. If, on any occasion, you think you remember that such-and-such an event occurred, then the wise things is to assume that that particular event did occur—unless something special about this particular occasion leads you to suspect your memory.

We have then a kind of answer to the puzzle about the diallelus. We start with particular cases of knowledge and then from those we generalize and formulate criteria of goodness—criteria telling us what it is for a belief to be epistemologically respectable. Let us now try to sketch somewhat more precisely this approach to the problem of the criterion.

11

The theory of evidence, like ethics and the theory of value, presupposes an objective right and wrong. To explicate the requisite senses of "right" and "wrong," we need the concept of *right preference*—or, more exactly, the concept of one state of mind being *preferable,* epistemically, to another. One state of mind may be *better,* epistemically, than another. This concept of epistemic preferability is what Cardinal Mercier called an *objective* concept. It is one thing to say, objectively, that one state of mind is *to be preferred* to another. It is quite another thing to say, subjectively, that one state of mind is in fact preferred to another—that someone or other happens to prefer the one state of mind to the other. If a state of mind A is to be preferred to a state of mind B, if it is, as I would like to say, intrinsically preferable to B, then anyone who prefers B to A is *mistaken* in his preference.

Given this concept of epistemic preferability, we can readily explicate the basic concepts of the theory of evidence. We could say, for example, that a proposition *p* is *beyond reasonable doubt t* provided only that believing *p* is then epistemically preferable for S to withholding *p*—

where by "withholding *p*" we mean the state of neither accepting *p* nor its negation. It is evident to me, for example, that many people are here. This means it is epistemically preferable for me to believe that many people are here than for me neither to believe nor to disbelieve that many are people here.

A proposition is *evident* for a person if it is beyond reasonable doubt for that person and is such that his including it among the propositions upon which he bases his decisions is preferable to his not so including it. A proposition is *acceptable* if withholding it is *not* preferable to believing it. And a proposition is *unacceptable* if withholding it *is* preferable to believing it.

Again, some propositions are not beyond reasonable doubt but they may be said to have *some presumption in their favor.* I suppose that the proposition that each of us will be alive an hour from now is one that has some presumption in its favor. We could say that a proposition is of this sort provided only that believing the proposition is epistemically preferable to believing its negation.

Moving in the other direction in the epistemic hierarchy, we could say that a proposition is *certain,* absolutely certain, for a given subject at a given time, if that proposition is then evident to that subject and if there is no other proposition that is such that believing that other proposition is then epistemically preferable for him to believing the given proposition. It is certain for me, I would say, that there seem to be many people here and that 7 and 5 are 12. If this is so, then each of the two propositions is evident to me and there are no other propositions that are such that it would be even better, epistemically, if I were to believe those other propositions.

This concept of epistemic preferability can be axiomatized and made the basis of a system of epistemic logic exhibiting the relations among these and other concepts of the theory of evidence.[6] For present purposes, let us simply note how they may be applied in our approach to the problem of the criterion.

---

6. The logic of these concepts, though with a somewhat different vocabulary, is set forth in Roderick M. Chisholm and Robert Keim, "A System of Epistemic Logic," *Ratio,* 15 (1973).

12

Let us begin with the most difficult of the concepts to which we have just referred—that of a proposition being *certain* for a man at a given time. Can we formulate *criteria* of such certainty? I think we can.

Leibniz had said that there are two kinds of immediately evident proposition—the "first truths of fact" and the "first truths of reason." Let us consider each of these in turn.

Among the "first truths of fact," for any man at any given time, I would say, are various propositions about his own state of mind at that time—his thinking certain thoughts, his entertaining certain beliefs, his being in a certain sensory or emotional state. These propositions all pertain to certain states of the man that may be said to manifest or present themselves to him at that time. We could use Meinong's term and say that certain states are "self-presenting," where this concept might be marked off in the following way.

A man's being in a certain state is *self-presenting* to him at a given time provided only that (i) he is in that state at that time and (ii) it is necessarily true that if he is in that state at that time then it is evident to him that he is in that state at that time.

The states of mind just referred to are of this character. Wishing, say, that one were on the moon is a state that is such that a man cannot be in that state without it being evident to him that he is in that state. And so, too, for thinking certain thoughts and having certain sensory or emotional experiences. These states present themselves and are, so to speak, marks of their own evidence. They cannot occur unless it is evident that they occur. I think they are properly called the "first truths of fact." Thus St. Thomas could say that "the intellect knows that it possesses the truth by reflecting on itself."[7]

Perceiving external things and remembering are not states that present themselves. But thinking that one perceives (or seeming to perceive) and thinking that one remembers (or seeming to remember) *are* states of mind that present themselves. And in presenting themselves they may, at least under certain favorable conditions, present something else as well.

Coffey quotes Hobbes as saying that "the inn of evidence has no sign-board."[8] I would prefer saying that these self-presenting states are sign-boards—of the inn of indirect evidence. But these sign-boards need no further sign-boards in order to be presented, for they present themselves.

13

What of the first truths of reason? These are the propositions that some philosophers have called "a priori" and that Leibniz, following Locke, referred to as "maxims" or "axioms." These propositions are all necessary and have a further characteristic that Leibniz described in this way: "You will find in a hundred places that the Scholastics have said that these propositions are evident, *ex terminis,* as soon as the terms are understood, so that they were persuaded that the force of conviction was grounded in the nature of the terms, i.e., in the connection of their ideas."[9] Thus St. Thomas referred to propositions that are "manifest through themselves."[10]

An axiom, one might say, is a necessary proposition such that one cannot understand it without thereby knowing that it is true. Since one cannot know a proposition unless it is evident and one believes it, and since one cannot believe a proposition unless one understands it, we might characterize these first truths of reason in the following way:

A proposition is *axiomatic* for a given subject at a given time provided only that (i) the proposition is one that is necessarily true and (ii) it is also necessarily true that if the person then believes that proposition, the proposition is then evident to him.

We might now characterize the *a priori* somewhat more broadly by saying that a proposition is a priori for a given subject at a given time provided that one or the

---

7. *The Disputed Questions on Truth,* Question One, Article 9; trans. Robert W. Mulligan (Chicago: Henry Regnery Company, 1952).

8. Coffey, vol. 1, p. 146. I have been unable to find this quotation in Hobbes.

9. *New Essays concerning Human Understanding,* book 4, chap. 7, n. 1.

10. *Exposition of the Posterior Analytics of Aristotle,* Lectio 4, No. 10; trans. Pierre Conway (Quebec: M. Doyan, 1956).

other of these two things is true: either (i) the proposition is one that is axiomatic for that subject at that time, or else (ii) the proposition is one such that it is evident to the man at that time that the proposition is entailed by a set of propositions that are axiomatic for him at that time.

In characterizing the "first truths of fact" and the "first truths of reason," I have used the expression "evident." But I think it is clear that such truths are not only evident but also certain. And they may be said to be *directly,* or *immediately,* evident.

What, then, of the indirectly evident?

14

I have suggested in rather general terms above what we might say about memory and the senses. These ostensible sources of knowledge are to be treated as innocent until there is positive ground for thinking them guilty. I will not attempt to develop a theory of the indirectly evident at this point. But I will note at least the *kind* of principle to which we might appeal in developing such a theory.

We could *begin* by considering the following two principles, M and P; M referring to memory, and P referring to perception or the senses.

M) For any subject S, if it is evident to S that she seems to remember that *a* was F, then it is beyond reasonable doubt for S that *a* was F.

P) For any subject S, if it is evident to S that she thinks she perceives that *a* is F, then it is evident to S that *a* is F.

"She seems to remember" and "she thinks she perceives" here refer to certain self-presenting states that, in the figure I used above, could be said to serve as signboards for the inn of indirect evidence.

But principles M and P, as they stand, are much to latitudinarian. We will find that it is necessary to make qualifications and add more and more conditions. Some of these will refer to the subject's sensory state; some will refer to certain of her other beliefs; and some will refer to the relations of confirmation and mutual support. To set them forth in adequate detail would require a complete epistemology.

So far as our problem of the criterion is concerned, the essential thing to note is this. In formulating such principles we will simply proceed as Aristotle did when he formulated his rules for the syllogism. As "particularists" in our approach to the problem of the criterion, we will fit our rules to the cases—to the apples we know to be good and to the apples we know to be bad. Knowing what we do about ourselves and the world, we have at our disposal certain instances that our rules or principles should countenance, and certain other instances that our rules or principles should rule out or forbid. And, as rational beings, we assume that they by investigating these instances we can formulate criteria that any instance must satisfy if it is to be countenanced and we can formulate other criteria that any instance must satisfy if it is to be ruled out or forbidden.

If we proceed in this way we will have satisfied Cardinal Mercier's criteria for a theory of evidence or, as he called it, a theory of certitude. He said that any criterion, or any adequate set of criteria, should be internal, objective, and immediate. The type of criteria I have referred to are certainly *internal,* in his sense of the term. We have not appealed to any external authority as constituting the ultimate test of evidence. (Thus we haven't appealed to "science" or to "the scientists of our culture circle" as constituting the touchstone of what we know.) I would say that our criteria are *objective.* We have formulated them in terms of the concept of epistemic preferability—where the location "*p* is epistemically preferable to *q* for S" is taken to refer to an objective relation that obtains independently of the actual preferences of any particular subject. The criteria that we formulate, if they are adequate, will be principles that are necessarily true. And they are also *immediate.* Each of them is such that, if it is applicable at any particular time, then the fact that it is then applicable is capable of being directly evident to that particular subject at that particular time.

15

But in all of this I have presupposed the approach I have called "particularism." The "methodist" and the "skeptic" will tell us that we have started in the wrong place.

If now we try to reason with them, then, I am afraid, we will be back on the wheel.

What few philosophers have had the courage to recognize is this: we can deal with the problem only by begging the question. It seems to me that, if we do recognize this fact, as we should, then it is unseemly for us to try to pretend that it isn't so.

One may object: "Doesn't this mean, then, that the skeptic is right after all?" I would answer: "Not at all. His view is only one of the three possibilities and in itself has no more to recommend it than the others do. And in favor of our approach there is the fact that we *do* know many things, after all."

C. S. Peirce

How to Make Our Ideas Clear

i.

Whoever has looked into a modern treatise on logic of the common sort, will doubtless remember the two distinctions between *clear* and *obscure* conceptions, and between *distinct* and *confused* conceptions. They have lain in the books now for nigh two centuries, unimproved and unmodified, and are generally reckoned by logicians as among the gems of their doctrine.

A clear idea is defined as one which is so apprehended that it will be recognized wherever it is met with, and so that no other will be mistaken for it. If it fails of this clearness, it is said to be obscure.

This is rather a neat bit of philosophical terminology; yet, since it is clearness that they were defining, I wish the logicians had made their definition a little more plain. Never to fail to recognize an idea, and under no circumstances to mistake another for it, let it come in how recondite a form it may, would indeed imply such prodigious force and clearness of intellect as is seldom met with in this world. On the other hand, merely to have such an acquaintance with the idea as to have become familiar with it, and to have lost all hesitancy in recognizing it in ordinary cases, hardly seems to deserve the name of clearness of apprehension, since after all it only amounts to a subjective feeling of mastery which may be entirely mistaken. I take it, however, that when the logicians speak of "clearness," they mean nothing more than such a familiarity with an idea, since they regard the quality as but a small merit, which needs to be supplemented by another, which they call *distinctness*.

A distinct idea is defined as one which contains nothing which is not clear. This is technical language; by the *contents* of an idea logicians understand whatever is contained in its definition. So that an idea is *distinctly* apprehended, according to them, when we can give a precise definition of it, in abstract terms. Here the professional logicians leave the subject; and I would not have troubled the reader with what they have to say if it were not such a striking example of how they have been slumbering through ages of intellectual activity, listlessly disregarding the enginery of modern thought, and never dreaming of applying its lessons to the improvement of logic. It is easy to show that the doctrine that familiar use and abstract distinctness make the perfection of apprehension, has its only true place in philosophies which have long been extinct; and it is now time to formulate the method of attaining to a more perfect clearness of thought, such as we see and admire in the thinkers of our own time.

When Descartes set about the reconstruction of philosophy, his first step was to (theoretically) permit

From C. S. Peirce, "How to Make Our Ideas Clear" from *Popular Science Monthly* (1878).

skepticism and to discard the practice of the schoolmen of looking to authority as the ultimate source of truth. That done, he sought a more natural fountain of true principles, and professed to find it in the human mind; thus passing, in the directest way, from the method of authority to that of *a priority*. Self-consciousness was to furnish us with our fundamental truths, and to decide what was agreeable to reason. But since, evidently, not all ideas are true, he was led to note, as the first condition of infallibility, that they must be clear. The distinction between an idea *seeming* clear and really being so, never occurred to him. Trusting to introspection, as he did, even for a knowledge of external things, why should he question its testimony in respect to the contents of our own minds? But then I suppose, seeing men, who seemed to be quite clear and positive, holding opposite opinions upon fundamental principles, he was further led to say that clearness of ideas is not sufficient, but that they need also to be distinct, i.e., to have nothing unclear about them. What he probably meant by this (for he did not explain himself with precision) was that they must sustain the test of dialectical examination; that they must not only seem clear at the outset, but that discussion must never be able to bring to light points of obscurity connected with them.

Such was the distinction of Descartes, and one sees that it was precisely on the level of his philosophy. It was somewhat developed by Leibniz. This great and singular genius was as remarkable for what he failed to see as for what he saw. That a piece of mechanism could not do work perpetually without being fed with power in some form, was a thing perfectly apparent to him; yet he did not understand that the machinery of the mind can only transform knowledge, but never originate it, unless it be fed with facts of observation. He thus missed the most essential point of the Cartesian philosophy, which is, that to accept propositions which seem perfectly evident to us is a thing which, whether it be logical or illogical, we cannot help doing. Instead of regarding the matter in this way, he sought to reduce the first principles of science to formulas which cannot be denied without self-contradiction and was apparently unaware of the great difference between his position and that of Descartes. So he reverted to the old formalities of logic, and, above all, abstract definitions played a great part in his philosophy. It was quite natural, there-

fore that on observing that the method of Descartes labored under the difficulty that we may seem to ourselves to have clear apprehensions of ideas which in truth are very hazy, no better remedy occurred to him than to require an abstract definition of every important term. Accordingly, in adopting the distinction of *clear* and *distinct* notions, he described the latter quality as the clear apprehension of everything contained in the definition; and the books have ever since copied his words. There is no danger that his chimerical scheme will ever again be overvalued. Nothing new can ever be learned by analyzing definitions. Nevertheless, our existing beliefs can be set in order by this process, and order is an essential element of intellectual economy, as of every other. It may be acknowledged, therefore, that the books are right in making familiarity with a notion the first step toward clearness of apprehension, and the defining of it the second. But in omitting all mention of any higher perspicuity of thought, they simply mirror a philosophy which was exploded a hundred years ago. That much-admired "ornament of logic"—the doctrine of clearness and distinctness—may be pretty enough, but it is high time to relegate to our cabinet of curiosities the antique *bijou,* and to wear about us something better adapted to modern uses.

The very first lesson that we have a right to demand that logic shall teach us is how to make our ideas clear; and a most important one it is, depreciated only by minds who stand in need of it. To know what we think, to be masters of our own meaning, will make a solid foundation for great and weighty thought. It is most easily learned by those whose ideas are meager and restricted; and far happier they than such as wallow helplessly in a rich mud of conceptions. A nation, it is true, may, in the course of generations, overcome the disadvantage of an excessive wealth of language and its natural concomitant, a vast, unfathomable deep of ideas. We may see it in history, slowly perfecting its literary forms, sloughing at length its metaphysics, and, by virtue of the untirable patience which is often a compensation, attaining great excellence in every branch of mental acquirement. The page of history is not yet unrolled which is to tell us whether such a people will or will not in the long run prevail over one whose ideas (like the words of their language) are few, but which possesses a wonderful mastery over those which it has. For an individual, however, there can be no question that a few clear ideas are worth more than many confused ones. A young man would hardly be persuaded to sacrifice the greater part of his thoughts to save the rest; and the muddled head is the least apt to see the necessity of such a sacrifice. Him we can usually only commiserate, as a person with a congenital defect. Time will help him, but intellectual maturity with regard to clearness comes rather late, an unfortunate arrangement of nature, inasmuch as clearness is of less use to a man settled in life, whose errors have in great measure had their effect, than it would be to one whose path lies before him. It is terrible to see how a single unclear idea, a single formula without meaning, lurking in a young man's head, will sometimes act like an obstruction of inert matter in an artery, hindering the nutrition of the brain, and condemning its victim to pine away in the fullness of his intellectual vigor and in the midst of intellectual plenty. Many a man has cherished for years as his hobby some vague shadow of an idea, too meaningless to be positively false; he has, nevertheless, passionately loved it, has made it his companion by day and by night, and has given to it his strength and his life, leaving all other occupations for its sake, and in short has lived with it and for it, until it has become, as it were, flesh of his flesh and bone of his bone; and then he has waked up some bright morning to find it gone, clean vanished away like the beautiful Melusina of the fable, and the essence of his life gone with it. I have myself known such a man; and who can tell how many histories of circle squarers, metaphysicians, astrologers, and what not may not be told in the old German story?

ii.

The principles set forth in the first of these papers lead, at once, to a method of reaching a clearness of thought of a far higher grade than the "distinctness" of the logicians. We have there found that the action of thought is excited by the irritation of doubt, and ceases when belief is attained; so that the production of belief is the sole function of thought. All these words, however, are too strong for my purpose. It is as if I had described the phenomena as they appear under a mental microscope. Doubt and Belief, as the words are commonly employed,

relate to religious or other grave discussions. But here I use them to designate the starting of any question, no matter how small or how great, and the resolution of it. If, for instance, in a horsecar, I pull out my purse and find a five-cent nickel and five coppers, I decide, while my hand is going to the purse, in which way I will pay my fare. To call such a question Doubt, and my decision Belief, is certainly to use words very disproportionate to the occasion. To speak of such a doubt as causing an irritation which needs to be appeased, suggests a temper which is uncomfortable to the verge of insanity. Yet, looking at the matter minutely, it must be admitted that, if there is the least hesitation as to whether I shall pay the five coppers or the nickel (as there will be sure to be, unless I act from some previously contracted habit in the matter), though irritation is too strong a word, yet I am excited to such small mental activity as may be necessary to deciding how I shall act. Most frequently doubts arise from some indecision, however momentary, in our action. Sometimes it is not so. I have, for example, to wait in a railway station, and to pass the time I read the advertisements on the walls, I compare the advantages of different trains and different routes which I never expect to take, merely fancying myself to be in a state of hesitancy, because I am bored with having nothing to trouble me. Feigned hesitancy, whether feigned for mere amusement or with a lofty purpose, plays a great part in the production of scientific inquiry. However the doubt may originate, it stimulates the mind to an activity which may be slight or energetic, calm or turbulent. Images pass rapidly through consciousness, one incessantly melting into another, until at last, when all is over—it may be in a fraction of a second, in an hour, or after long years—we find ourselves decided as to how we should act under such circumstances as those which occasioned our hesitation. In other words, we have attained belief.

In this process we observe two sorts of elements of consciousness, the distinction between which may best be made clear by means of an illustration. In a piece of music there are the separate notes, and there is the air. A single tone may be prolonged for an hour or a day, and it exists as perfectly in each second of that time as in the whole taken together; so that, as long as it is sounding, it might be present to a sense from which everything in the past was as completely absent as the future itself. But it is different with the air, the performance of which occupies a certain time, during the portions of which only portions of it are played. It consists in an orderliness in the succession of sounds which strike the ear at different times; and to perceive it there must be some continuity of consciousness which makes the events of a lapse of time present to us. We certainly only perceive the air by hearing the separate notes; yet we cannot be said to directly hear it, for we hear only what is present at the instant, and an orderliness of succession cannot exist in an instant. These two sorts of objects, what we are *immediately* conscious of and what we are *mediately* conscious of, are found in all consciousness. Some elements (the sensations) are completely present at every instant so long as they last, while others (like thought) are actions having beginning, middle, and end and consist in a congruence in the succession of sensations which flow through the mind. They cannot be immediately present to us, but must cover some portion of the past or future. Thought is a thread of melody running through the succession of our sensations.

We may add that just as a piece of music may be written in parts, each part having its own air, so various systems of relationship of succession subsist together between the same sensations. These different systems are distinguished by having different motives, ideas, or functions. Thought is only one such system; for its sole motive, idea, and function is to produce belief, and whatever does not concern that purpose belongs to some other system of relations. The action of thinking may incidentally have other results. It may serve to amuse us, for example, and among *dilettanti* it is not rare to find those who have so perverted thought to the purposes of pleasure that it seems to vex them to think that the questions upon which they delight to exercise it may ever get finally settled; and a positive discovery which takes a favorite subject out of the arena of literary debate is met with ill-concealed dislike. This disposition is the very debauchery of thought. But the soul and meaning of thought, abstracted from the other elements which accompany it, though it may be voluntarily thwarted, can never be made to direct itself toward anything but the production of belief. Thought in action has for its only possible motive the attainment of thought at rest; and whatever does not refer to belief is no part of the thought itself.

And what, then, is belief? It is the demicadence which closes a musical phrase in the symphony of our intellectual life. We have seen that it has just three properties: first, it is something that we are aware of; second, it appeases the irritation of doubt; and, third, it involves the establishment in our nature of a rule of action, or, say for short, a *habit*. As it appeases the irritation of doubt, which is the motive for thinking, thought relaxes, and comes to rest for a moment when belief is reached. But, since belief is a rule for action, the application of which involves further doubt and further thought, at the same time that it is a stopping place, it is also a new starting place for thought. That is why I have permitted myself to call it thought at rest, although thought is essentially an action. The *final* upshot of thinking is the exercise of volition, and of this thought no longer forms a part; but belief is only a stadium of mental action, an effect upon our nature due to thought, which will influence future thinking.

The essence of belief is the establishment of a habit, and different beliefs are distinguished by the different modes of action to which they give rise. If beliefs do not differ in this respect, if they appease the same doubt by producing the same rule of action, then no mere differences in the manner of consciousness of them can make them different beliefs, any more than playing a tune in different keys is drawn between beliefs which differ only in their mode of expression—the wrangling which ensues is real enough, however. To believe that any objects are arranged . . . as in Fig. 1, and to believe that they are arranged as in Fig. 2, are one and the same belief; yet it

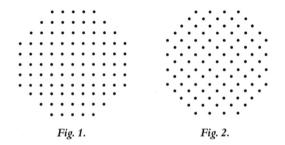

Fig. 1.   *Fig. 2.*

is conceivable that a man should assert one proposition and deny the other. Such false distinctions do as much harm as the confusion of beliefs really different, and are among the pitfalls of which we ought constantly to beware, especially when we are upon metaphysical ground. One singular deception of this sort, which often occurs, is to mistake the sensation produced by our own unclearness of thought for a character of the object we are thinking. Instead of perceiving that the obscurity is purely subjective, we fancy that we contemplate a quality of the object which is essentially mysterious; and if our conception be afterward presented to us in a clear form we do not recognize it as the same, owing to the absence of the feeling of unintelligibility. So long as this deception lasts, it obviously puts an impassable barrier in the way of perspicuous thinking; so that it equally interests the opponents of rational thought to perpetuate it, and its adherents to guard against it.

Another such deception is to mistake a mere difference in the grammatical construction of two words for a distinction between the ideas they express. In this pedantic age when the general mob of writers attend so much more to words than to things, this error is common enough. When I just said that thought is an *action,* and that it consists in a *relation,* although a person performs an action but not a relation, which can only be the result of an action, yet there was no inconsistency in what I said, but only a grammatical vagueness.

From all these sophisms we shall be perfectly safe so long as we reflect that the whole function of thought is to produce habits of action, and that whatever there is connected with a thought, but irrelevant to its purpose, is an accretion to it, but no part of it. If there be a unity among our sensations which has no reference to how we shall act on a given occasion, as when we listen to a piece of music, why, we do not call that thinking. To develop its meaning, we have, therefore, simply to determine what habits it involves. Now, the identity of a habit depends on how it might lead us to act, not merely under such circumstances as are likely to arise, but under such as might possibly occur, no matter how improbable they may be. What the habit is depends on *when* and *how* it causes us to act. As for the *when,* every stimulus to action is derived from perception; as for the *how,* every purpose of action is to produce some sensible result. Thus, we come down to what is tangible and practical as the root of every real distinction of thought, no matter how subtle it may be; and there is no distinction of meaning so fine as to consist in anything but a possible difference of practice.

To see what this principle leads to, consider in the light of it such a doctrine as that of transubstantiation. The Protestant churches generally hold that the elements of the sacrament are flesh and blood only in a tropical sense; they nourish our souls as meat and the juice of it would our bodies. But the Catholics maintain that they are literally just that, meat and blood, although they possess all the sensible qualities of wafer cakes and diluted wine. But we can have no conception of wine except what may enter into a belief, either—

1. That this, that, or the other, is wine; or,

2. That wine possesses certain properties.

Such beliefs are nothing but self-notifications that we should, upon occasion, act in regard to such things as we believe to be wine according to the qualities which we believe wine to possess. The occasion of such action would be some sensible perception, the motive of it to produce some sensible result. Thus our action has exclusive reference to what affects the senses, our habit has the same bearing as our action, our belief the same as our habit, our conception the same as our belief; and we can consequently mean nothing by wine but what has certain effects, direct or indirect, upon our senses; and to talk of something as having all the sensible characters of wine, yet being in reality blood, is senseless jargon. Now, it is not my object to pursue the theological question; and having used it as a logical example I drop it, without caring to anticipate the theologian's reply. I only desire to point out how impossible it is that we should have an idea in our minds which relates to anything but conceived sensible effects of things. Our idea of anything *is* our idea of its sensible effects; and if we fancy that we have any other we deceive ourselves, and mistake a mere sensation accompanying the thought for a part of the thought itself. It is absurd to say that thought has any meaning unrelated to its only function. It is foolish for Catholics and Protestants to fancy themselves in disagreement about the elements of the sacrament, if they agree in regard to all their sensible effects, here or hereafter.

It appears, then, that the rule for attaining the third grade of clearness of apprehension is as follows: consider what effects which might conceivably have practical bearings we conceive the object of our conception to have. Then, our conception of these effects is the whole of our conception of the object.

iii.

Let us illustrate this rule by some examples; and, to begin with the simplest one possible, let us ask what we mean by calling a thing *hard*. Evidently that it will not be scratched by many other substances. The whole conception of this quality, as of every other, lies in its conceived effects. There is absolutely no difference between a hard thing and a soft thing so long as they are not brought to the test. Suppose, then, that a diamond could be crystallized in the midst of a cushion of soft cotton, and should remain there until it was finally burned up. Would it be false to say that that diamond was soft? This seems a foolish question, and would be so, in fact, except in the realm of logic. There such questions are often of the greatest utility as serving to bring logical principles into sharper relief than real discussions ever could. In studying logic we must not put them aside with hasty answers, but must consider them with attentive care, in order to make out the principles involved. We may, in the present case, modify our question, and ask what prevents us from saying that all hard bodies remain perfectly soft until they are touched, when their hardness increases with the pressure until they are scratched. Reflection will show that the reply is this: there would be no *falsity* in such modes of speech. They would involve a modification of our present usage of speech with regard to the words "hard" and "soft," but not of their meanings. For they represent no fact to be different from what it is; only they involve arrangements of facts which would be exceedingly maladroit. This leads us to remark that the question of what would occur under circumstances which do not actually arise is not a question of fact, but only of the most perspicuous arrangement of them. For example, the question of free will and fate in its simplest form, stripped of verbiage, is something like this: I have done something of which I am ashamed; could I, by an effort of the will, have resisted the temptation, and done otherwise? The philosophical reply is that this is not a question of fact, but only of the arrangement of facts. Arranging them so as to exhibit what is particularly pertinent to my question—

namely, that I ought to blame myself for having done wrong—it is perfectly true to say that, if I had willed to do otherwise than I did, I should have done otherwise. On the other hand, arranging the facts so as to exhibit another important consideration, it is equally true that when a temptation has once been allowed to work, it will, if it has a certain force, produce its effect, let me struggle how I may. There is no objection to a contradiction in what would result from a false supposition. The *reductio ad absurdum* consists in showing that contradictory results would follow from a hypothesis which is consequently judged to be false. Many questions are involved in the free-will discussion, and I am far from desiring to say that both sides are equally right. On the contrary, I am of opinion that one side denies important facts, and that the other does not. But what I do say is that the above single question was the origin of the whole doubt; that, had it not been for this question, the controversy would never have arisen; and that this question is perfectly solved in the manner which I have indicated.

Let us next seek a clear idea of Weight. This is another very easy case. To say that a body is heavy means simply that, in the absence of opposing force, it will fall. This (neglecting certain specifications of how it will fall, etc., which exist in the mind of the physicist who uses the word) is evidently the whole conception of weight. It is a fair question whether some particular facts may not *account* for gravity; but what we mean by the force itself is completely involved in its effects.

This leads us to undertake an account of the idea of Force in general. This is the great conception which, developed in the early part of the seventeenth century from the rude idea of a cause, and, constantly improved upon since, has shown us how to explain all the changes of motion which bodies experience, and how to think about all physical phenomena; which has given birth to modern science, and changed the face of the globe; and which, aside from its more special uses, has played a principal part in directing the course of modern thought, and in furthering modern social development. It is, therefore, worth some pains to comprehend it. According to our rule, we must begin by asking what is the immediate use of thinking about force; and the answer is that we thus account for changes of motion. If bodies were left to themselves, without the intervention of forces, every motion would continue unchanged both in velocity and in direction. Furthermore, change of motion never takes place abruptly; if its direction is changed, it is always through a curve without angles; if its velocity alters, it is by degrees. The gradual changes which are constantly taking place are conceived by geometers to be compounded together according to the rules of the parallelogram of forces. If the reader does not already know what this is, he will find it, I hope, to his advantage to endeavor to follow the following explanation; but if mathematics are insupportable to him, pray let him skip three paragraphs rather than that we should part company here.

A *path* is a line whose beginning and end are distinguished. Two paths are considered to be equivalent, which, beginning at the same point, lead to the same point. Thus the two paths, *A–B–C–D–E* and *A–F–G–H–E* [Fig. 3], are equivalent. Paths which do *not* begin at the same point are considered to be equivalent, provided that, on moving either of them without turning it, but keeping it always parallel to its original position when its beginning coincides with that of the other path, the ends also coincide. Paths are considered as geometrically added together, when one begins where the other ends; thus the path *A–E* is conceived to be a sum of *A–B, B–C, C–D,* and *D–E.* In the parallelogram of Fig. 4 the diagonal *A–C* is the sum of *A–B* and *B–C;* or, since *A–D* is geometrically equivalent to *B–C, A–C* is the geometrical sum of *A–B* and *A–D.*

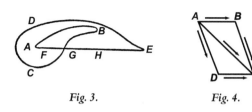

Fig. 3.   Fig. 4.

All this is purely conventional. It simply amounts to this: that we choose to call paths having the relations I have described equal or added. But, though it is a convention, it is a convention with a good reason. The rule for geometrical addition may be applied not only to paths, but to any other things which can be represented by paths. Now, as a path is determined by the varying direction and distance of the point which moves over it from the starting point, it follows that anything which

from its beginning to its end is determined by a varying direction and a varying magnitude is capable of being represented by a line. Accordingly, *velocities* may be represented by lines, for they have only directions and rates. The same thing is true of *accelerations,* or changes of velocities. This is evident enough in the case of velocities; and it becomes evident for accelerations if we consider that precisely what velocities are to positions—namely, states of change of them—that accelerations are to velocities.

The so-called "parallelogram of forces" is simply a rule for compounding accelerations. The rule is, to represent the accelerations by paths, and then to geometrically add the paths. The geometers however, not only use the "parallelogram of forces" to compound different accelerations, but also to resolve one acceleration into a sum of several. Let *A–B* [Fig. 5] be the path which rep-

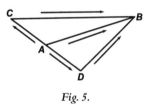

Fig. 5.

resents a certain acceleration—say, such a change in the motion of a body that at the end of one second the body will, under the influence of that change, be in a position different from what it would have had if its motion had continued unchanged such that a path equivalent to *A–B* would lead from the latter position to the former. This acceleration may be considered as the sum of the accelerations represented by *A–C* and *C–B.* It may also be considered as the sum of the very different accelerations represented by *A–D* and *C–B.* It may also be considered as the sum of the very different accelerations represented by *A–D* and *D–B,* where *A–D* is almost the opposite of *A–C.* And it is clear that there is an immense variety of ways in which *A–B* might be resolved into sum of two accelerations.

After this tedious explanation, which I hope, in view of the extraordinary interest of the conception of force, may not have exhausted the reader's patience, we are prepared at last to state the grand fact which this conception embodies. This fact is that if the actual changes of motion which the different particles of bodies experience are each resolved in its appropriate way, each component acceleration is precisely such as is prescribed by a certain law of Nature, according to which bodies in the relative positions which the bodies in question actually have at the moment,[1] always receive certain accelerations, which, being compounded by geometrical addition, give the acceleration which the body actually experiences.

This is the only fact which the idea of force represents, and whoever will take the trouble clearly to apprehend what this fact is perfectly comprehends what force is. Whether we ought to say that a force *is* an acceleration, or that it *causes* an acceleration, is a mere question of propriety of language, which has no more to do with our real meaning than the difference between the French idiom *"Il fait froid"* and its English equivalent *"It is cold."* Yet it is surprising to see how this simple affair has muddled men's minds. In how many profound treatises is not force spoken of as a "mysterious entity," which seems to be only a way of confessing that the author despairs of ever getting a clear notion of what the word means! In a recent, admired work on *Analytic Mechanics* it is stated that we understand precisely the effect of force, but what force itself is we do not understand! This is simply a self-contradiction. The idea which the word "force" excites in our minds has no other function than to affect our actions, and these actions can have no reference to force otherwise than through its effects. Consequently, if we know what the effects of force are, we are acquainted with every fact which is implied in saying that a force exists, and there is nothing more to know. The truth is, there is some vague notion afloat that a question may mean something which the mind cannot conceive; and when some hair-splitting philosophers have been confronted with the absurdity of such a view, they have invented an empty distinction between positive and negative conceptions, in the attempt to give their nonidea a form not obviously nonsensical. The nullity of it is sufficiently plain from the considerations given a few pages back; and, apart from those considerations, the quibbling character of the distinction must have struck every mind accustomed to real thinking.

---

1. Possibly the velocities also have to be taken into account.

iv.

Let us now approach the subject of logic and consider a conception which particularly concerns it, that of *reality*. Taking clearness in the sense of familiarity, no idea could be clearer than this. Every child uses it with perfect confidence, never dreaming that he does not understand it. As for clearness in its second grade, however, it would probably puzzle most men, even among those of a reflective turn of mind, to give an abstract definition of the real. Yet such a definition may perhaps be reached by considering, the points of difference between reality and its opposite, fiction. A figment is a product of somebody's imagination; it has such characters as his thought impresses upon it. That those characters are independent of how you or I think is an external reality. There are, however, phenomena within our own minds, dependent upon our thought, which are at the same time real in the sense that we really think them. But though their characters depend on how we think, they do not depend on what we think those characters to be. Thus, a dream has a real existence as a mental phenomenon if somebody has really dreamt it; that he dreamt so and so does not depend on what anybody thinks was dreamt but is completely independent of all opinion on the subject. On the other hand, considering, not the fact of dreaming, but the thing dreamt, it retains its peculiarities by virtue of no other fact than that it was dreamt to possess them. Thus we may define the real as that whose characters are independent of what anybody may think them to be.

But, however satisfactory such a definition may be found, it would be a great mistake to suppose that it makes the idea of reality perfectly clear. Here, then, let us apply our rules. According to them, reality, like every other quality, consists in the peculiar, sensible effects which things partaking of it produce. The only effect which real things have is to cause belief, for all the sensations which they excite emerge into consciousness in the form of beliefs. The question, therefore, is, how is true belief (or belief in the real) distinguished from false belief (or belief in fiction). Now, as we have seen in the former paper, the idea of truth and falsehood, in their full development, appertain exclusively to the scientific method of settling opinion. A person who arbitrarily chooses the propositions which he will adopt can use the word truth only to emphasize the expression of his determination to hold on to his choice. Of course, the method of tenacity never prevailed exclusively; reason is too natural to men for that. But in the literature of the Dark Ages we find some fine examples of it. When Scotus Erigena is commenting upon a poetical passage in which hellebore is spoken of as having caused the death of Socrates, he does not hesitate to inform the inquiring reader that Helleborus and Socrates were two eminent Greek philosophers; and that the latter having been overcome in argument by the former took the matter to heart and died of it! What sort of an idea of truth could a man have who could adopt and teach, without the qualification of a "perhaps," an opinion taken so entirely at random? The real spirit of Socrates, who I hope would have been delighted to have been "overcome in argument," because he would have learned something by it, is in curious contrast with the naïve idea of the glossist, for whom . . . discussion would seem to have been simply a struggle. When philosophy began to awake from its long slumber, and before theology completely dominated it, the practice seems to have been for each professor to seize upon any philosophical position he found unoccupied and which seemed a strong one, to intrench himself in it, and to sally forth from time to time to give battle to the others. Thus, even the scanty records we possess of those disputes enable us to make out a dozen or more opinions held by different teachers at one time concerning the question of nominalism and realism. Read the opening part of the *Historia Calamitatum* of Abélard, who was certainly as philosophical as any of his contemporaries, and see the spirit of combat which it breathes. For him, the truth is simply his particular stronghold. When the method of authority prevailed, the truth meant little more than the Catholic faith. All the efforts of the scholastic doctors are directed toward harmonizing their faith in Aristotle and their faith in the Church, and one may search their ponderous folios through without finding an argument which goes any further. It is noticeable that where different faiths flourish side by side, renegades are looked upon with contempt even by the party whose belief they adopt; so completely has the idea of loyalty replaced that of truth seeking. Since the time of Descartes, the defect in the conception of truth has been less apparent. Still, it will sometimes strike a scientific man that the philosophers have been less intent on finding out

what the facts are than on inquiring what belief is most in harmony with their system. It is hard to convince a follower of the *a priori* method by adducing facts; but show him that an opinion he is defending is inconsistent with what he has laid down elsewhere, and he will be very apt to retract it. These minds do not seem to believe that disputation is ever to cease; they seem to think that the opinion which is natural for one man is not so for another, and that belief will, consequently, never be settled. In contenting themselves with fixing their own opinions by a method which would lead another man to a different result, they betray their feeble hold of the conception of what truth is.

On the other hand, all the followers of science are fully persuaded that the processes of investigation, if only pushed far enough, will give one certain solution to each question to which they can be applied. One man may investigate the velocity of light by studying the transits of Venus and the aberration of the stars; another by the oppositions of Mars and the eclipses of Jupiter's satellites; a third by the method of Fizeau; a fourth by that of Foucault; a fifth by the motions of the curves of Lissajous; a sixth, a seventh, an eighth, and a ninth may follow the different methods of comparing the measures of statical and dynamical electricity. They may at first obtain different results, but, as each perfects his method and his processes, the results will move steadily together toward a destined center. So with all scientific research. Different minds may set out with the most antagonistic views, but the progress of investigation carries them by a force outside of themselves to one and the same conclusion. This activity of thought by which we are carried, not where we wish, but to a foreordained goal, is like the operation of destiny. No modification of the point of view taken, no selection of other facts for study, no natural bent of mind even, can enable a man to escape the predestinate opinion. This great law is embodied in the conception of truth and reality. The opinion which is fated[2] to be ultimately

---

2. Fate means merely that which is sure to come true, and can nohow be avoided. It is a superstition to suppose that a certain sort of events are ever fated, and it is another to suppose that the word "fate" can never be freed from its superstitious taint. We are all fated to die.

agreed to by all who investigate is what we mean by the truth, and the object represented in this opinion is the real. That is the way I would explain reality.

But it may be said that this view is directly opposed to the abstract definition which we have given of reality, inasmuch as it makes the characters of the real depend on what is ultimately thought about them. But the answer to this is that, on the one hand, reality is independent, not necessarily of thought in general, but only of what you or I or any finite number of men may think about it; and that, on the other hand, though the object of the final opinion depends on what that opinion is, yet what that opinion is does not depend on what you or I or any man thinks. Our perversity and that of others may indefinitely postpone the settlement of opinion; it might even conceivably cause an arbitrary proposition to be universally accepted as long as the human race should last. Yet even that would not change the nature of the belief, which alone could be the result of investigation carried sufficiently far; and if, after the extinction of our race, another should arise with faculties and disposition for investigation, that true opinion must be the one which they would ultimately come to. "Truth crushed to earth shall rise again," and the opinion which would finally result from investigation does not depend on how anybody may actually think. But the reality of that which is real does depend on the real fact that investigation is destined to lead, at last, if continued long enough, to a belief in it.

But I may be asked what I have to say to all the minute facts of history, forgotten never to be recovered, to the lost books of the ancients, to the buried secrets.

Full many a gem of purest ray serene
  The dark, unfathomed caves of ocean bear;
Full many a flower is born to blush unseen,
  And waste its sweetness on the desert air.

Do these things not really exist because they are hopelessly beyond the reach of our knowledge? And then, after the universe is dead (according to the prediction of some scientists), and all life has ceased forever, will not the shock of atoms continue though there will be no mind to know it? To this I reply that, though in no possible state of knowledge can any number be great enough to express the relation between the amount of what rests unknown to the amount of the known, yet it is unphilosophical to suppose that, with regard to any given question (which has any clear meaning), investigation would not bring forth a solution of it, if it were carried far enough. Who would have said, a few years ago, that we could ever know of what substances stars are made whose light may have been longer in reaching us than the human race has existed? Who can be sure of what we shall not know in a few hundred years? Who can guess what would be the result of continuing the pursuit of science for ten thousand years, with the activity of the last hundred? And if it were to go on for a million, or a billion, or any number of years you please, how is it possible to say that there is any question which might not ultimately be solved?

But it may be objected, "Why make so much of these remote considerations, especially when it is your principle that only practical distinctions have a meaning?" Well, I must confess that it makes very little difference whether we say that a stone on the bottom of the ocean, in complete darkness, is brilliant or not—that is to say, that it *probably* makes no difference, remembering always that that stone *may* be fished up tomorrow. But that there are gems at the bottom of the sea, flowers in the untraveled desert, etc., are propositions which, like that about a diamond being hard when it is not pressed, concern much more the arrangement of our language than they do the meaning of our ideas.

It seems to me, however, that we have, by the application of our rule, reached so clear an apprehension of what we mean by reality, and of the fact which the idea rests on, that we should not, perhaps, be making a pretension so presumptuous as it would be singular, if we were to offer a metaphysical theory of existence for universal acceptance among those who employ the scientific method of fixing belief. However, as metaphysics is a subject much more curious than useful, the knowledge of which, like that of a sunken reef, serves chiefly to enable us to keep clear of it, I will not trouble the reader with any more Ontology at this moment. I have already been led much further into that path than I should have desired; and I have given the reader such a dose of mathematics, psychology, and all that is most abstruse, that I fear he may already have left me, and that what I am now writing is for the compositor and proofreader exclusively. I trusted to the importance of the subject. There is no royal road to logic, and really valuable ideas can only be had at the price of close attention. [. . .]

We have, hitherto, not crossed the threshold of scientific logic. It is certainly important to know how to make our ideas clear, but they may be ever so clear without being true. How to give birth to those vital and pro-creative ideas which multiply into a thousand forms and diffuse themselves everywhere, advancing civilization and making the dignity of man, is an art not yet reduced to rules, but of the secret of which the history of science affords some hints.

Barry Stroud

Philosophical Scepticism and Everyday Life

I think that when we first encounter sceptical reasoning we find it immediately gripping. It appeals to something deep in our nature and seems to raise a real problem about the human condition. It is natural to feel that either we must accept the literal truth of the conclusion that we can know nothing about the world around us, or else we must somehow show that it is not true. Accepting it and holding to it consistently seem disastrous, and yet rejecting it seems impossible. But what *is* the 'literal truth' of that conclusion? Both responses depend on a firm understanding of what it says and means; without that there would be nothing determinate to accept as true or to reject as false. That proper understanding of the sceptical conclusion is what I want to concentrate on. That is why I suggest we look to the source of that conclusion—how it is arrived at and how it becomes so unavoidable—and in particular at just how closely Descartes's requirement that the dream-possibility must always be eliminated corresponds to our ordinary standards or requirements for knowledge in everyday life.

In suggesting that we try to determine exactly what the sceptical reasoning manages to establish I do not mean to deny that it does raise deep problems about the human condition and can reveal something of great significance about human knowledge. It might seem as if that is not so, since it might seem that as soon as we even glance in the direction of the standards and procedures we follow in everyday life we will find that there is nothing at all in Descartes's argument. It is obvious that we do not always insist that people know they are not dreaming before we allow that they know something in everyday life, or even in science or a court of law, where the standards are presumably stricter. So it can easily look as if Descartes reaches his sceptical conclusion only by violating our ordinary standards and requirements for knowledge, perhaps substituting a new and different set of his own. If that were so his conclusion would not have the consequences it seems to have for our everyday and scientific knowledge and beliefs. So understood, it would not have the significance we originally take it to have.

One example of a diagnosis of scepticism along these lines goes as follows. Suppose someone makes the quite startling announcement that there are no physicians in the city of New York. That certainly seems to go against something we all thought we knew to be true. It would really be astonishing if there were no physicians at all in a city that size. When we ask how the remarkable discovery was made, and how long this deplorable state of affairs has obtained, suppose we find that the bearer of the startling news says it is true because, as he explains, what he means by 'physician' is a person who has a medical degree and can cure any conceivable illness in less than two minutes.[1] We are no longer surprised by his announcement, nor do we find that it contradicts anything we all thought we knew to be true. We find it quite believable that there is no one in the whole city who fulfils all the conditions of that peculiar 're-definition' of 'physician'. Once we understand it as it was meant to be understood, there is nothing startling about the announcement except perhaps the form in which it was expressed. It does not deny what on first sight it might seem to deny, and it poses no threat to our original belief that there are thousands and thousands of physicians in New York.

The suggestion is that the sceptical conclusion is in the same boat. It too is said to rest on a misunderstanding or distortion of the meanings of the words in which it is expressed. It is at first astonishing to be told that no one can ever know anything about the world around us, but once we learn that the 'knowledge' in question is 'knowledge' that requires the fulfillment of a condition which is not in fact required for the everyday or scientific knowledge we are interested in, we will no longer be surprised or disturbed by that announcement. We do not insist that the dream-possibility must always be known not to obtain in order to know things in everyday or scientific life. When we find that Descartes's sceptical reasoning does insist on that requirement, we will find that his sceptical conclusion does not contradict anything we thought we knew at the outset. We might find it quite believable that there is no knowledge of the world fulfilling all the conditions of Descartes's special 're-definition' of knowledge. But properly understood, his conclusion would not deny what its peculiar linguistic form originally led us to suppose it denies, and it would pose no threat to our everyday knowledge and beliefs. Any exhilaration or disquiet we might have felt on first encountering it must therefore have been due to nothing but illusion.

If there were nothing more behind Descartes's sceptical conclusion than there is behind the peculiar an-

nouncement about physicians in New York it would indeed be profoundly uninteresting. If Descartes simply imposes on knowledge an unreasonable or outrageous requirement, and then points out (even quite correctly) that it can never be fulfilled, there will be no reason to go along with him, even temporarily. What he says would reveal nothing more about the everyday or scientific knowledge that we want a philosophical theory to illuminate than that crazy announcement manages to reveal about physicians in New York. Someone is no less a physician even though there are many patients he never happens to cure, and if Descartes is simply distorting the requirements for knowledge, what we possess in everyday life and in science will be no less knowledge even though we do not usually fulfill the outrageous condition that we must know we are not dreaming. I think many philosophers find philosophical scepticism uninteresting and the study of it unprofitable on grounds such as these. Descartes's assessment of his own position is thought to deviate so radically and so obviously from our familiar assessments that it cannot be expected to reveal anything of deep or lasting significance about the human knowledge we are interested in.

It is perhaps not so immediately obvious that a change or distortion of meaning has occurred in the philosophical case as it is in the announcement about physicians in New York. If we are at all taken in by the sceptical reasoning, the misunderstanding must be to that extent hidden from us, just as it is presumably hidden from the sceptical philosopher himself. Giving that special meaning to the word 'physician' is nothing more than a crazy whim. But the philosopher's alleged change in the meaning of the word 'know' might not be unmotivated; certainly it is not just a personal whim. What lies behind the sceptical conclusion might therefore turn out to be more interesting and more worthy of investigation than what lies behind that 're-definition' of 'physician'.

But still, it will be felt, the philosophical case will be interesting only to the extent to which it is interesting to find out how and why philosophers so persistently go wrong—why they continue to insist, as they apparently do, on misunderstanding or distorting the meanings of the familiar words they examine and use. The investigation of philosophical scepticism would then be of pathological interest only. Aside from revealing how

---

1. See P. Edwards, 'Bertrand Russell's Doubts About Induction' in A. Flew (ed.), *Logic and Language,* First Series (Oxford, 1955).

easy it is for philosophers to fall into confusion or make mistakes, it could not be expected to reveal anything deep or of lasting significance about human knowledge itself.

J. L. Austin, for example, thought an inquiry into the sources of the sceptical conclusion was 'a matter of un-picking, one by one, a mass of seductive (mainly verbal) fallacies, or exposing a wide variety of concealed mo-tives—an operation which leaves us, in a sense, just where we began'.[2] In a positive vein, he thought we might at most learn something about the meanings of certain English words that are interesting in their own right.[3] Many recent philosophers who care less than Austin did about the meanings of those English words would hold that if we simply keep our wits about us and guard against the errors that have led older philosophers astray we will find no reason to follow them down the garden path to philosophical scepticism. The misguided sceptical conclusion is held to reveal nothing about our everyday or scientific knowledge and beliefs because it is not really about that knowledge or those beliefs at all, any more than that crazy announcement is really about the physicians in New York.

I have tried so far to suggest that the best strategy in the face of the sceptical argument is to examine more carefully the requirement that we must know we are not dreaming if we are to know anything about the world around us. I think that is much more promising than ac-cepting Descartes's condition as a genuine condition of knowledge and trying to show that it can be fulfilled; I argued that that strategy cannot succeed. If it is in gen-eral a necessary condition of our knowing something about the world around us that we know we are not dreaming, it follows that we can never know that we are not dreaming. That is why I think the only hope lies in avoiding that condition. But I do not share the impres-sion that what Descartes says is a condition of knowl-edge of the world is obviously no such condition at all. There seems to me to be no question that the meaning of 'physician' has been changed in that trivial example, but in Descartes's reasoning I think much deeper and more complex issues are raised. And what is at stake is more than simply a mass of avoidable mistakes or con-fusions by traditional philosophers. I think the right kind of investigation into the sources of Descartes's re-quirement promises to illuminate something about our actual conception of knowledge, or about what we seek when we try to understand it, or perhaps even about human knowledge itself.

Let us suppose for the moment that the critics are right, and that what Descartes says is a requirement for knowledge of the world is really no such requirement at all. How could that be known, if it were true? What shows or would show that Descartes is or must be dis-torting or misunderstanding what knowledge is when he insists that we must know we are not dreaming if we are to know anything about the world around us? When critics of Descartes's conclusion argue that the meaning of 'know' does not in fact require what Descartes ap-parently requires of it, that knowledge is not 'closed un-der logical consequence', or that the word 'know' does not 'penetrate' to all the logical consequences of what is known or to what are known to be its logical conse-quences, or even to what are known to be the conse-quences of knowing it, how are such claims about knowledge or about the meaning of the word 'know' themselves to be supported? I will try to bring out some of the difficulties this question raises by looking at one of the most persuasive and most influential versions of that line of criticism.

The sceptical conclusion is reached in the course of an assessment of our knowledge of the world—an in-vestigation of how we know the things we think we know about the world around us. J. L. Austin thinks philosophers in the course of such assessments have not paid sufficient attention to 'what sort of thing does ac-tually happen when ordinary people are asked "How do you know?"',[4] and in his 'Other Minds' he tries to show how the typical philosophical investigation deviates from our normal practices.

If asked how I know there is a goldfinch in the gar-den, for example, I might reply by explaining how I have come to know about goldfinches, or about small British birds in general, or I might explain how I came

---

2. J. L. Austin, *Sense and Sensibilia* (Oxford, 1962), pp. 4–5.
3. *Sense and Sensibilia*, p. 5.

4. J. L. Austin, 'Other Minds', in his *Philosophical Papers* (Oxford, 1961), p. 45. (Hereafter cited as OM.)

to be in a position to recognize and hence to know about the goldfinch in the garden in this particular case. This second kind of reply to the question 'How do you know?' might be inadequate because my system of classification is wrong—what I think are goldfinches are really something else—or my response might be challenged on the grounds that what I have said about how I know is not enough. If I said I knew it was a goldfinch by its red head, it might be objected 'But that's not enough: plenty of other birds have red heads. What you say doesn't prove it. For all you know, it may be a woodpecker' (OM, 51). This amounts to raising a possibility compatible with everything I have said but which, if actual, would imply that I do not know that there is a goldfinch in the garden. It therefore brings us close to the kind of objection Descartes raises against our ordinary knowledge of the world around us.

Austin thinks philosophers in their assessments tend to concentrate on questions about 'reality' and to some extent about 'sureness and certainty', and that although questions of those kinds are of course raised about knowledge in everyday life, the philosopher's special investigation of knowledge distorts or abandons our everyday procedures for answering them. In objecting to a piece of putative knowledge on the grounds that what has been said is not enough or does not prove what is claimed to be known, he says, we all ordinarily accept that:

(a) If you say 'That's not enough', then you must have in mind some more or less definite lack.... If there is no definite lack, which you are at least prepared to specify on being pressed, then it's silly (outrageous) just to go on saying 'That's not enough'.

(b) Enough is enough; it doesn't mean everything. Enough means enough to show that (within reason, and for present intents and purposes) it 'can't' be anything else, there is no room for an alternative, competing description of it. It does *not* mean, for example, enough to show it isn't a *stuffed* goldfinch. (OM, 52.)

When philosophers go on to raise questions about 'reality' ('But do you know it's a *real* goldfinch?') they intend to question the reliability of the 'facts' put forward in support of the original claim to know. That too,

of course, is something we do in everyday life. Austin thinks philosophers do not always satisfy the above conditions when they press our ordinary knowledge-claims in this way.

> The doubt or question 'But is it a *real* one?' has always (must have) a special basis, there must be some 'reason for suggesting' that it isn't real, in the sense of some specific way, or limited number of specific ways, in which it is suggested that this experience or item may be phoney. Sometimes (usually) the context makes it clear what the suggestion is: ... If the context doesn't make it clear, then I am entitled to ask 'How do you mean? Do you mean it may be stuffed or what? *What are you suggesting?*' (OM, 55.)

Austin suggests that a philosopher interested in knowledge—or at any rate someone he calls 'the metaphysician'—does not fulfill this condition in his typical challenges. His 'wile' consists in asking 'Is it a real table?' without specifying or limiting the ways he has in mind in which it might not be real. This leaves us at a loss in trying to answer him, just as we are left baffled and uneasy by the conjurer's invitation 'Will some gentleman kindly satisfy himself that this is a perfectly ordinary hat?' (OM, 55n). It is no wonder we feel the philosophical objection to our ordinary knowledge cannot be met if this is what it trades on.

It should be clear that this unflattering description of the philosopher's or 'metaphysician's' procedure does not apply to Descartes's argument. In his assessment of his claim to know that he is sitting by the fire with a piece of paper in his hand he does not simply complain in general terms that his grounds are not sufficient to prove that he is really sitting there. He is fully prepared to specify, in fact the whole force of his argument turns on his explicitly specifying, a particular way in which his grounds are inadequate, a particular possibility compatible with the facts he is relying on but incompatible with his knowing that he is really sitting there. His grounds are found inadequate in a perfectly determinate way; he might be dreaming. The 'wile of the metaphysician' as Austin describes it cannot explain why it is difficult or impossible to meet Descartes's objection to our knowledge of the world.

Austin might still be right that Descartes does violate our ordinary standards or procedures in another closely-related way. Once it has been made determinate precisely what question must be answered before one can be said to know in a particular case, Austin says, the question can then be answered 'by means of recognized procedures (more or less roughly recognized, of course) appropriate to the particular type of case' (OM, 55). In fact Austin strongly suggests, without saying so explicitly, that the existence of such 'recognized procedures' is a simple consequence of the determinateness of the original criticism of the knowledge-claim; as soon as it is made clear what doubt or deficiency the critic of knowledge has in mind (e.g., 'How do you know you are not dreaming?'), it will follow that there are recognized procedures for making up the deficiency or allaying the doubt.[5] 'There are recognized ways of distinguishing between dreaming and waking', Austin says, '(how otherwise should we know how to use and to contrast the words?), and of deciding whether a thing is stuffed or live, and so forth' (OM, 55).

Austin does not say much about what he thinks the 'procedures' or 'recognized ways' of telling that one is not dreaming actually are. He seems content with the idea that there must be such procedures or else we would not be able to use and to contrast the words 'dreaming' and 'waking' as we do. I find that particular claim dubious, or at the very least difficult to establish, partly for reasons I will return to later. The reason he

gives in his lectures is even less persuasive. In *Sense and Sensibilia* he denies the philosopher's contention that there is no 'qualitative difference' between normal waking experience and dream experience. He argues that actually being presented to the Pope is not 'qualitatively indistinguishable' from dreaming that I am being presented to the Pope on the grounds that:

> After all, we have the phrase 'a dream-like quality'; some waking experiences are said to have this dream-like quality, and some artists and writers occasionally try to impart it, usually with scant success, to their works. But of course, if the fact here alleged *were* a fact, the phrase would be perfectly meaningless, because applicable to everything. If dreams were not 'qualitatively' different from waking experiences, then *every* waking experience would be like a dream; the dream-like quality would be, not difficult to capture, but impossible to avoid.[6]

Someone who believed that our ability to tell that we are not dreaming on particular occasions is guaranteed by the very meaningfulness of certain English expressions would perhaps feel little need to describe those 'procedures' carefully or to explain exactly how they work. He would already be convinced that they must work, so even without a detailed description of those 'procedures' he would seem to be directly in conflict with Descartes's reasoning. For Descartes at the end of his first *Meditation* it is impossible to know that we are not dreaming, so it might look as if the whole issue between him and Austin turns on the cogency of this appeal to the meaningfulness of the expression 'a dream-like quality' or to our ability to use and to contrast the words 'dreaming' and 'waking' as we do. But in fact I think Austin's real opposition to the sceptical philosophical conclusion is to be found elsewhere.

Descartes's conclusion rests on the general requirement that we must know that we are not dreaming if we are to know anything at all about the world about us. That requirement is what renders inadequate any tests or procedures for determining that one is not

---

5. Austin's reason for believing that this connection holds is probably to be found in his conception of what he calls 'the normal procedure of language', which he 'schematizes' as follows: if that complex of features originally taken to be sufficient for saying 'This is a C' comes to be 'accompanied or followed in definite circumstances by another special and distinctive feature or complex of features, which makes it seem desirable to revise our ideas' we will 'draw a distinction between "This looks like a C, but in fact is only a dummy, &c." and "This is a real C (live, genuine, &c.)."' . . . If the special distinctive feature is one which does not have to manifest itself in *any* definite circumstances (on application of some specific test, after some limited lapse of time, &c.) then it is not a suitable feature on which to base a distinction between "real" and "dummy, imaginary, &c." ' (OM, 57).

6. *Sense and Sensibilia*, pp. 48–9.

dreaming; one would have to know that one was not simply dreaming that one was performing the test, and not dreaming that one was performing any of the other tests used to determine *that,* and so on. For Austin it is precisely in insisting on that strong general condition for knowledge that the real distortion or unreasonableness comes in. If it is not in general a condition of knowing things about the world around us that we must know that we are not dreaming, not only will Descartes have failed to show that we can never know that we are not dreaming (and that there can be no 'procedures' of the kind Austin has in mind), he will not have begun to show that we cannot know anything about the world around us either. Without Descartes's condition for knowledge, philosophical scepticism about the external world would be completely disarmed. Austin attacks what is really the heart of Descartes's position. Can it be shown that in insisting on his strong general condition for knowledge of the world Descartes is violating or abandoning the ordinary conditions or standards of knowledge?

I have already said that a moment's reflection seems enough to convince us that Descartes's condition is not in fact a condition of knowledge in everyday or scientific life. After thinking about philosophical scepticism for some time we often tend to forget or distort what we actually do in everyday life, but if we insist on returning to a realistic account of how we actually behave there seems little doubt that we do not in fact impose that general condition on our knowledge-claims.

For example, suppose I remark to the bird-lovers at my cocktail party that a goldfinch has just appeared in the garden. 'Really? How do you know?', one of them asks, and I reply that I just saw it hop from one limb to another in that large pine tree.'How do you know you're not dreaming?', asks another, in what would obviously be no better than a feeble attempt at a joke.There is no reason to take what he says seriously, and none of us would.We do not regard it as a threat to my knowledge. Suppose I am in a bird-recognition contest. I examine my specimen carefully, noting its differences from birds of similar but distinct species, and I announce that I now know that this one is a goldfinch. Could one of the judges at that point ask me how I know I didn't simply dream it, and then reject my answer because I cannot give a satisfactory defence? That would be perfectly out-

rageous, and I would feel no necessity to answer the question in order for my original claim to stand.

These are trivial examples, but the inappropriateness of insisting on Descartes's condition does not stem from the relative unimportance of the knowledge in question. Even when it matters a great deal, when it is literally a matter of life or death, as in a court of law, it is simply not true that the dream-possibility is always allowed as a relevant consideration for the claim to know some particular thing. If I testify on the witness stand that I spent the day with the defendant, that I went to the museum and then had dinner with him, and left him about midnight, my testimony under normal circumstances would not be affected in any way by my inability to answer if the prosecutor were then to ask 'How do you know you didn't dream the whole thing?'.The question is outrageous; it has no tendency to undermine my knowledge. It is nothing more than the desperate reaction of a hard-pressed lawyer with no case. Nor do we ever expect to find a careful report of the procedures and results of an elaborate experiment in chemistry followed by an account of how the experimenter determined that he was not simply dreaming that he was conducting the experiment. No such thing was in question; the issue is never raised, let alone settled.The point is obvious, and the multiplication of further examples is unnecessary. It seems clear that we simply do not insist on fulfilling Descartes's condition in order to know things in real life. Nor do we insist that someone cure every conceivable illness in less than two minutes in order to be regarded as a physician.

Of course it is sometimes relevant to ask how or whether we know we are not dreaming.When that is a relevant criticism of a claim to know something, failure to answer the question satisfactorily would imply that we do not know what we claim to know. If I am lying half-awake in bed early in the morning after a late night and seem to hear someone calling my name from outside the window, I might not be sure whether there really is someone out there or I am only dreaming that I hear the call. I do not know whether there is someone out there or not. But from the fact that that possibility is sometimes relevant it does not follow that on every occasion we must know that it does not obtain if we are to know anything about the world around us.When the alarm-clock has sounded and I have reached out and turned it off and got out of bed and gone over to the window and opened the curtains and found my friend calling and gesticulating in the garden, there is no question at that point that I might be dreaming or that I should check to see whether I am dreaming before I can know that he is really there—even though I can truly say to him that I didn't know he was there a few minutes ago because I didn't know whether or not I was dreaming.

As Austin puts it in the case of the goldfinch:

> Knowing it's a 'real' goldfinch isn't in question in the ordinary case when I say I know it's a goldfinch: reasonable precautions only are taken. But when it *is* called in question, in *special* cases, then I make sure it's a real goldfinch in ways essentially similar to those in which I made sure it was a goldfinch, . . . (OM, 56.)

That there are such ways of making sure that it is a real goldfinch does not of course guarantee that we can always tell that it is, nor is it a proof against 'miracles or outrages of nature' (OM, 56). Something might still go wrong, something completely unexpected might happen to the bird, but that by itself is no bar to saying, or having been right to say, that we know it is a real goldfinch.

It is only in *special* circumstances that certain kinds of possibilities are relevant to claims to know something. Austin makes the point in connection with claims to know something about the mind or feelings of another person. Worries about deception, or about whether the person is sufficiently like us to be feeling what we would feel, or about whether he is quite inadvertently behaving as he does, all arise only in 'special cases'. Again, there are (more or less roughly) established procedures for dealing with such cases when they arise, but:

> These special cases where doubts arise and require resolving, are contrasted with the normal cases which hold the field[7] *unless* there is some special suggestion that deceit &c., is involved, and deceit, moreover, of an intelligible kind in the

circumstances, that is, of a kind that can be looked into because motive, &c., is specially suggested. There is no suggestion that I *never* know what other people's emotions are, nor yet that in particular cases I might be wrong for no special reason or in no special way.

Austin's stress here on the need for special reasons to doubt when questions of 'reality' are at issue is not the same as the earlier point that there must always be some 'special basis' for the doubt or question 'But is it a *real* one?' That requirement was expressed as the demand that the critic have 'some "reason for suggesting" that it isn't real, in the sense of some specific way, or limited number of specific ways, in which it is suggested that this experience or item may be phoney' (OM, 55). Descartes in his reasoning meets that requirement as stated: he specifies dreaming as the way the experience might be 'phoney'. But here Austin is arguing that even if the way the experience or item might be 'phoney' has been specified, the doubt or question 'But is it a *real* one?' is relevant to the original knowledge-claim and must be answered only if there is some special reason for suggesting that that specified possibility might obtain. It is not simply that the critic of the knowledge-claim must specify some way in which knowledge would not be present on the occasion in question; he must also have some reason for thinking or suggesting that the possible deficiency he has in mind might be present on that occasion. In the absence of such a reason—that is, in the normal or non-special case—knowing it is a real goldfinch, for example, is not in question. The 'reasonable precautions' said to be taken in the ordinary case are precautions against only those possibilities that there is some special reason to think might obtain in that case. Whether or not such possibilities obtain is all that is in question.

The need for a special reason for doubt is also present when we cite authorities or rely on the testimony of others—a rich source of knowledge not much studied by philosophers.

> Naturally, we are judicious: we don't say we know (at second hand) if there is any special reason to doubt the testimony: but there has to be *some* reason. It is fundamental in talking (as in other

---

7. [Austin's footnote: 'You cannot fool all of the people all of the time' is 'analytic'.] (OM, 81.)

matters) that we are entitled to trust others, except in so far as there is some concrete reason to distrust them. (OM, 50.)

The same holds for any other possibility of error or mistake. There can be no doubt that human beings are inherently liable to be mistaken in particular claims to know things—and not just things we know 'at second hand' or from testimony. But the question 'How do you know?' is not a successful challenge if it is based only on such general human fallibility. That is not to deny that knowledge precludes error or mistake.

'When you know you can't be wrong' is perfectly good sense. You are prohibited from saying 'I know it is so, but I may be wrong', just as you are prohibited from saying 'I promise I will, but I may fail'. If you are aware you may be mistaken, you ought not to say you know, ... But of course, being aware that you may be mistaken doesn't mean merely being aware that you are a fallible human being: it means that you have some concrete reason to suppose that you may be mistaken in this case.... It is naturally *always* possible ('humanly' possible) that I may be mistaken or may break my word, but that by itself is no bar against using the expressions 'I know' and 'I promise' as we do in fact use them. (OM, 66.)

It would be no easy matter to give a precise formulation of the requirement that there must be some special reason to think a certain possibility might obtain before the raising of that possibility is allowed as a relevant criticism of a claim to know something. Is it enough for there simply to be such a reason, or must someone actually have that reason, and raise the possibility for that reason? How concrete or specific must the reason be, and how good a reason must there be for thinking something is amiss in the particular case? I want to leave aside all such questions of detail and ask about the conflict between *any* requirement along those general lines and the condition that Descartes insists on for knowledge about the world around us. I therefore want to grant everything Austin says about what sort of thing does actually happen when ordinary people are asked 'How do you know?', and everything else that could be discovered about how we

respond to the questions or would-be challenges of others with respect to our knowledge. I want to concentrate on the question: do such facts about our everyday and scientific practices show that Descartes's reasoning deviates from our everyday procedures and standards for acquiring and assessing knowledge?

It certainly looks as if Descartes could not be right in insisting that we must rule out the dream-possibility in order to know something about the world around us if Austin is right about how the raising of such possibilities can work against our knowledge in everyday life. If there must be some special reason for suggesting or suspecting that one is dreaming before that reason for doubt is even allowed as relevant in everyday life, the most that is true of the dream-possibility with respect to our knowledge of the world is that it must be known not to obtain whenever there is some special reason to think it might obtain. That is to say, if there is some special or concrete reason to believe that one might be dreaming, one cannot know some particular thing about the world around us unless one knows that one is not dreaming. That is obviously weaker than Descartes's general requirement which says that one cannot know any particular thing about the world around us unless one knows that one is not dreaming. Descartes's reasoning imposes a condition on knowledge of the world which must be fulfilled in every case, whether there is any special reason to believe one might be dreaming or not. The weaker requirement says that that condition must be fulfilled only in some cases, when the 'special reason' condition is also fulfilled, but that otherwise the dream-possibility is not even relevant to our claims to know things about the world around us.

Another way to put the difference is that the weaker requirement allows for the possibility of knowledge of the world in a way that Descartes's requirement does not. I have tried to show how Descartes's requirement is strong enough to make knowledge of the world around us impossible; it precludes fulfillment of the very condition it holds to be necessary for knowledge of the world. For all the weaker requirement says, one *could* know things about the world around us without knowing that one is not dreaming. With no special reason to think one might be dreaming, that alleged possibility is simply not in question at all, so the possibility Descartes invokes would present no obstacle to knowing things about the world in those cases. It therefore looks as if the sceptical reasoning cannot succeed if only the weaker require-ment, and not Descartes's condition for knowledge, is what is true of our ordinary conception of knowledge.

Descartes's reasoning itself cannot be said to fulfill only the weaker requirement. He considers his knowledge of the world around him in general by considering the par-ticular case of his sitting by the fire with a piece of paper in his hand. That single case is chosen to serve as a repre-sentative of all of our knowledge of the world. It could sustain a quite general conclusion about all of our knowl-edge of the world only if it were a perfectly normal case, without special features. If Descartes had had some spe-cial reason to doubt the deliverances of his senses at that particular time and place—if it were early morning, for example, and he was not quite sure whether he was fully awake or not—his verdict could not support the kind of general conclusion he draws from it about our sensory knowledge in general. It would just be one special, non-representative case in which, as it turns out, he fails to know. But if there is nothing special about the case, if he had no special reason to think he might be dreaming at that particular time and place, his challenge 'How do I know I am not dreaming?' will have no special basis. The possibility will be raised without any special or concrete reason for supposing in this case that he might be dream-ing, so it would seem that it must violate what Austin says is a condition of its being a serious or even a relevant chal-lenge to a knowledge-claim in everyday life.

Despite this apparently obvious conflict between our everyday practices and Descartes's requirement I still want to press the question whether all the facts about how we speak and respond to the questions or would-be challenges of others in everyday life are enough to show that Descartes in his reasoning deviates from our everyday standards and procedures and changes or dis-torts the meaning of the word 'know' or any of the other words he uses. I think those facts would not have that anti-sceptical consequence if a certain conception of everyday life, and hence a certain conception of the re-lation between the philosophical problem of the exter-nal world and what goes on in everyday life, were correct. In looking at the significance of those facts I will therefore be looking from a different angle at the significance of the philosophical problem itself and at what, if anything, it can reveal about our position and procedures in everyday life. If the philosophical sceptic's conception of everyday life is intelligible, everything that goes on in everyday life and in science would be compatible with the literal truth of the conclusion that no one knows anything about the world around us.

If only Austin's weaker, and not Descartes's stronger, re-quirement is true of our ordinary conception of knowl-edge, it nevertheless should state a truth about *knowledge*. What I mean by such an obvious remark is this. If we have a conception of knowledge that we employ in everyday life prior to and independently of all philosophizing, and if Descartes or some other philosopher is to be shown to have changed or distorted that conception in the course of his philosophizing, it must be shown that it is that very conception that he has distorted, and that that con-ception is a conception of knowledge. Austin's weaker requirement, for example, will state a condition of knowl-edge only if it implies that in those cases in which there is no special reason to think one might be dreaming, and one fulfils all the other conditions for knowing, one does indeed *know* something about the world around us with-out knowing that one is not dreaming. I stress the point because I think that speaking very strictly, or on a certain conception of our linguistic and other behaviour in everyday life, facts of the kind cited by Austin do not ac-tually have that implication.

What Austin reminds us of are facts of speech, of lin-guistic usage. When he describes what sort of thing does actually happen when ordinary people are asked 'How do you know?' he tells us what people say, and what conditions must be fulfilled in order for them to say it, or to be speaking correctly in saying it. In the passages already quoted, for example, he says:

> If there is no definite lack, which you are at least prepared to specify on being pressed, then it's silly (outrageous) just to go on *saying* 'That's not enough'.
>
> Knowing it's a 'real' goldfinch isn't in question in the ordinary case when I *say* I know it's a goldfinch: we don't *say* we know . . . if there is any special reason to doubt. . . .
>
> If you are aware you may be mistaken, you ought not to *say* you know. . . .
>
> [Its being always possible that I may be mis-taken] is no bar against *using the expressions* 'I know' and 'I promise' as we do in fact use them.

I have italicized the crucial words to show that in each case what is in question is how certain expressions are or should be used. Similar facts are appealed to when Austin says:

> we are often right to say we *know* even in cases where we turn out subsequently to have been mistaken. (OM, 66.)
>
> we may be perfectly justified in saying we know or we promise, in spite of the fact that things 'may' turn out badly, and it's a more or less serious matter for us if they do. (OM, 69.)

I have said that I want to grant all facts of the kind Austin here describes. But in order to move from such facts about the use of the expressions 'I know' or 'He knows' or 'How do you know?' to conclusions about knowledge we must at least know *why* those expressions are used as they are on those occasions.

There are also facts about our reactions to the raising of various possibilities in ordinary circumstances that seem to support Austin's conclusion. I pointed out in earlier examples that we simply ignore, perhaps with some embarrassment, the party guest's question how I know I didn't dream the goldfinch in the garden. We find the bird-contest judge's challenge incomprehensible, and do not regard it as affecting in any way the truth or reasonableness of my identification. We immediately throw out of court the desperate prosecutor's ridiculous challenge and proceed as if it never had been made. We do not expect, and would be astonished to find, dream-elimination tests appended to laboratory reports; they would not affect one way or the other our acceptance of the results reported. When something serious is in question we usually find it silly (outrageous) for someone to persist in asking how we know we are not dreaming and to insist that we don't know what we thought we knew until we can answer the question satisfactorily. These all seem to me undeniable facts of everyday life.

The question is whether all this linguistic and other behaviour is generated by or warranted by or even required by our everyday conception of knowledge. Whether that is so or not depends on why we behave in those ways in everyday life. It is admittedly bizarre, silly, outrageous, perhaps even incomprehensible, to raise the dream-possibility as a criticism of ordinary claims to know things in everyday and scientific life, but exactly what kind of outrageousness or inappropriateness is it? What is its source? Is it derived from our very conception of knowledge itself? Is anyone who raises the possibility in normal circumstances necessarily violating or rejecting the everyday meaning of the word 'know'?

These questions arise because there are two apparently distinct questions that can be asked about what someone says. We can ask whether it is true, or we can ask whether it was appropriately or reasonably said. The two questions do not always get the same answer; certainly it is possible for them to differ. All the conditions sufficient for appropriate or reasonable utterance can be fulfilled when what is said is not literally true. The distinction even more obviously can be made in the other direction; there are countless things that are now true which no one is now in a position reasonably to assert or believe—many people are busily engaged in trying to find out what some of them are. I do not mean to suggest that there is or must be some sort of conflict or opposition, let alone an unbridgeable gap, between reasonable utterance and truth. There is nothing in the distinction itself which suggests that the truth is forever —or ever—beyond us. Normally, we believe, the conditions of reasonable utterance coincide with the conditions of truth. We usually take it for granted that what we are in a good position to assert is in fact true and what we are in a good position to deny is in fact false. In trying to find out whether or not some particular thing is true we try to get into the best possible position for accepting and asserting it, or for rejecting and denying it. The point is only that the two sets of conditions can be distinguished. From the fact that someone carefully, reasonably and appropriately asserts something on a particular occasion it does not directly follow that what he says is true, and from the fact that someone quite inappropriately and with no good reason says something it does not immediately follow that what he says is false. This holds just as much for assertions or denials of knowledge as for other assertions and denials.

For example, suppose I am at a party and my host asks me if I know whether my friend John, who was ill last week, will be coming to the party. I reply that I know he will be there, and when asked how I know I explain that he has now recovered, I have just talked to him on the telephone and he said he was coming right over; there is someone at the party he is interested in talking to and he wouldn't miss it for anything. Suppose further that John is well-known to be generally trustworthy, reliable, and also a careful, sober driver—and he doesn't live very far away. All this puts my assertion that I know John will be at the party beyond criticism. There could hardly be more favourable grounds for claiming knowledge about something not currently under my direct observation. Suppose now that John for some reason unknown to me nevertheless fails to show up at the party. My saying he would be there, in fact that I knew he would be there, was justified, reasonable, and appropriate in the circumstances, but it has turned out that what I said is not true. John is not at the party, so I did not know what I said I knew. The best possible conditions for asserting something, or that I knew something, did not coincide with the conditions under which what I said is true.

Suppose that as I am leaving the party at the end of the evening and John has still not appeared my host turns on me and says 'You should be more careful about what you claim to know. You said you knew John would be here and he isn't. You didn't know any such thing!' I think we find that response simply outrageous. It is absurd and improper and completely unjustified. It is difficult to find the right words to describe its degree of insensitivity and social obtuseness. It perhaps even shows incomprehension of how and why we claim to know things in the face of the normal vicissitudes of life. But aside from the unreasonable abuse and insensitivity conveyed by it, the remark cannot be said to be totally false or without foundation. Part of what the host said was 'You said you knew John would be here and he isn't. You didn't know any such thing', and that is, at least, the literal truth, however harsh or inappropriate it might have been for him to say it. I did say I knew, and I didn't know. What the cruel host says is an accurate description of my position.

It is clear that the host's remarks are outrageous or unreasonable as criticisms of me, or of my having *said* that I know John will be there. My response when asked whether I knew John would be at the party was justified, reasonable, appropriate, and perfectly proper. It is not open to the kind of attack the host tries to subject it to. But what is invulnerable to those absurd attacks is my act of *saying* something, and also perhaps my coming to believe or to accept something. My asserting it is beyond criticism even if what I assert is (of course unknown to me) not true. And the host's remark about the state of my knowledge is true even if his making it is outrageous, unreasonable, and unjustified. So even if we know that a certain attempt to criticize a knowledge-claim is outrageous or unreasonable or would not be listened to in everyday life, we cannot immediately infer that the knowledge-claim does not suffer from the deficiency stated in the criticism, or that the person does nevertheless know what he claims to know. Whether that is so or not will depend on the nature and source of the outrageousness or inappropriateness in question. The inappropriately-asserted objection to the knowledge-claim might not be an outrageous violation of the conditions of knowledge, but rather an outrageous violation of the conditions for the appropriate assessment and acceptance of *assertions* of knowledge. John's being at the party is an admitted condition of my knowing that he will be at the party—since he is not there I do not know what I said I knew—but his not being there does not warrant any and all criticisms of my saying or believing what I did. My saying and believing in those circumstances is beyond criticism. But still I did not know.

Suppose that in fact the reason John never arrived at the party was that just as he stepped out the front door he was struck down by a meteorite, the only one of lethal size known to have hit the earth in a century and a half. Of course there was no special reason—no reason at all—for me or for anyone else to expect such a thing. Certainly I never thought of it (nor of its not happening) when I said I knew John would be at the party, and it is safe to say that no one else at the party did either. If the news of John's fate had been conveyed to all of us just as I was about to leave the party, the host's parting shot as I described it a moment ago would be if anything even more outrageous and inappropriate. When we all discover why John never got to the party and hence why I failed to know, and we see how bizarre and how completely unforeseeable his not getting there was, it is even more difficult to understand what the host could think he was doing in saying to me 'You said you knew John would be here and he isn't. You didn't know any such thing!' But I think it cannot be denied that one thing the host was doing was speaking the truth. [. . .]

The doubts or possibilities considered by the philosopher investigating human knowledge are not put forward as relevant to such practical questions as whether to assert something or to say that you know it or to raise an objection to what someone else has said. They are thought relevant only to the question of whether one knows something—whether it is true that one knows—and not whether it is appropriate or reasonable to say that one knows. And if the dream-possibility, for example, is a possibility that one must know not to obtain if one is to know some particular thing about the world around us, then one will simply not know that thing about the world if one has not been able to eliminate that possibility—even though it might be completely inappropriate or unreasonable on particular occasions in everyday life to insist on ruling out that possibility before saying that one knows.

One way to bring out what I think is the sceptical philosopher's conception of everyday life in relation to his epistemological project is to consider in some detail the following story adapted from an example of Thompson Clarke's.[8] Suppose that in wartime people must be trained to identify aircraft and they are given a quick, uncomplicated course on the distinguishing features of different planes and how to recognize them. They learn from their manuals, for example, that if a plane has features x, y, and w it is an E, and if it has x, y, and z it is an F. A fully-trained and careful spotter on the job will not say that a particular plane is an F until he has found all three features, x, y, z. If at a certain point he has found only x and y and cannot yet tell what other features the plane has got, he does not know whether it is an F or an E. Once he finds that it also has feature z he can report that the plane in the sky is an F. He might even be asked how he knows it is an F and reply 'Because it has x, y, z'. He has observed the plane in the sky very carefully, he has followed his training to the letter, and he is right that it has x, y, z. There seems no doubt that he knows the plane is an F.

Suppose that there are in fact some other airplanes, Gs say, which also have features x, y, z. The trainees were never told about them because it would have made the recognition of Fs too difficult; it is almost impossible to distinguish an F from a G from the ground. The policy of simplifying the whole operation by not mentioning Gs in the training manual might be justified by the fact that there are not many of them, or that they are only reconnaissance planes, or that in some other ways they are not as directly dangerous as Fs; it does not matter as much whether they fly over our territory.

When we are given this additional information I think we immediately see that even the most careful airplane-spotter does not know that a plane he sees is an F even though he knows that it has x, y, z. For all he knows, it might be a G. Just as he did not know the plane was an F when he had found only features x and y—for all he knew then, it might have been an E—so he does not know now that it is an F because all the features he has now found are also present on another kind of airplane. Of course there would be no point in telling him that he does not know; the same good reasons for not even mentioning Gs in the training manual would still apply. In saying that he does not know it is an F we would be making no criticism of his performance; he has followed his training perfectly and conscientiously. We ourselves might not even care whether the plane in the sky is an F or a G; it is precisely because Gs are not worth worrying about in the same way that the manual was written as it was. But I think it must nevertheless be admitted that the spotter does not know that the plane is an F.

In saying that he does not know the plane is an F I do not mean to deny that he can be said to know 'for all practical purposes'. Whether it is an F or a G does not matter much; that is why the training could afford to ignore the differences between them. All things considered, it is best to have a policy of not distinguishing between the two kinds of planes when deciding what to do, how to respond to their presence. So as a contribution to the war effort his recognition is beyond criticism. We might even be tempted to say something like 'As far as his training goes, he knows it is an F', or 'He knows that according to his manual it is an F'. But if we know the facts about Gs I think we cannot say simply 'He knows it is an F'. When I say that we cannot say

---

8. Thompson Clarke, 'The Legacy of Scepticism', *The Journal of Philosophy*, 1972, pp. 759ff.

that he knows it is an F I mean that we recognize that that would not be true. We recognize that he does not know it is an F even though there is absolutely nothing to be gained by pointing his ignorance out to him or to anyone else. For all practical purposes we can accept his saying that he knows it's an F. He can perhaps be said to know-for-all-practical-purposes. After all, there are more important things in wartime—and even in peacetime everyday life—than knowledge.

I think the sceptical philosopher sees our position in everyday life as analogous to that of the airplane-spotters. There might be very good reasons why we do not normally eliminate or even consider countless possibilities which nevertheless strictly speaking must be known not to obtain if we are to know the sorts of things we claim to know. We therefore cannot conclude simply from our having carefully and conscientiously followed the standards and procedures of everyday life that we thereby know the things we ordinarily claim to know. The philosophical investigation of our knowledge is concerned with whether and how it is true that we know, whether and how the conditions necessary and sufficient for our knowing things about the world are fulfilled. Descartes's argument turned on its being a condition of our knowing any particular thing about the world around us that we know we are not dreaming, and on this conception the admitted fact that we do not insist on eliminating that possibility in everyday life does not show that we do not need to eliminate it in order to know things about the world. The well-trained airplane-spotter is not required to rule out the possibility that the plane he sees with features x, y, z is a G; nor do his teachers or his fellow spotters insist on that possibility's being eliminated. But we recognize that it is nevertheless a condition of knowing that the plane is an F on the basis of x, y, z that one know that it is not a G. Facts about the way we speak and the procedures we follow in everyday life do not show that the sceptical philosopher has misunderstood or distorted the nature of knowledge if this conception of our everyday practices and procedures is correct.

The point is worth stressing. Many people are apparently disposed to think that if the philosopher holds that a certain condition must be met in order to know something, and we do not insist on that condition's being met in everyday life, then the philosopher simply *must* be imposing new or higher standards on knowledge or changing the meaning of the word 'know' or some other word. But if our position in everyday life is like that of the airplane-spotters that is not so. When we who know the facts about Gs say that the careful spotter does not really know that the plane he sees is an F I do not think we are imposing on him or inventing for ourselves some new and unreasonably strict conception of knowledge. If we explained the situation to the spotter himself (which admittedly would not help the war effort) he too would agree that he did not know whether the plane was an F or a G. Just as he recognized earlier that the presence of x and y alone was not enough to settle the question whether the plane was an F, so he would see, with the new information, that even $x, y,$ and z are not enough. He would see that he has to do more in order to know that it is an F. The fact that there is nothing more that a mere airplane-spotter can do—that it is almost impossible to distinguish an F from a G from the ground—would not alter that judgement. He would see that with the resources currently available to him he simply cannot know whether a plane in the sky is an F or not. But in coming to that conclusion he would not have altered the conception of knowledge with which he began. He originally understood the word 'know' and applied that conception of knowledge fully reasonably and justifiably in particular cases, but (as we knew all along and he now would come to realize) he never knew on any of those occasions that the plane in the sky was an F.

That is how I think the philosopher who investigates human knowledge sees the relation between what he concludes about knowledge and the way we speak about knowledge in everyday life. We do not ordinarily insist on the dream-possibility's being ruled out unless there is some special reason to think it might obtain; the philosopher insists that it must always be known not to obtain in order to know anything about the world around us. But on his understanding of everyday life that difference is not to be explained by the philosopher's insisting on or inventing a conception of knowledge stricter or more demanding than that of the scientist or the lawyer or the plain man. Rather he claims to share with all of us one and the same conception of knowledge—that very conception that operates in everyday and scientific life. [. . .]

Robert Nozick

Skepticism

The skeptic about knowledge argues that we know very little or nothing of what we think we know, or at any rate that this position is no less reasonable than the belief in knowledge. The history of philosophy exhibits a number of different attempts to refute the skeptic: to prove him wrong or show that in arguing against knowledge he presupposes there is some and so refutes himself. Others attempt to show that accepting skepticism is unreasonable, since it is more likely that the skeptic's extreme conclusion is false than that of all his premises are true, or simply because reasonableness of belief just means proceeding in an anti-skeptical way. Even when these counterarguments satisfy their inventors, they fail to satisfy others, as is shown by the persistent attempts against skepticism. The continuing felt need to refute skepticism, and the difficulty in doing so, attests to the power of the skeptic's position, the depth of his worries.

Our goal is not, however, to refute skepticism, to prove it is wrong, or even to argue that it is wrong. [...] Our task here is to explain how knowledge is possible, given what the skeptic says that we do accept (for example, that it is logically possible that we are dreaming or are floating in the tank). In doing this, we need not convince the skeptic, and we may introduce explanatory hypotheses that he would reject. What is important for our task of explanation and understanding is that *we* find those hypotheses acceptable or plausible, and that they show us how the existence of knowledge fits together with the logical possibilities the skeptic points to, so that these are reconciled within our own belief system. These hypotheses are to explain to ourselves how knowledge is possible, not to prove to someone else that knowledge *is* possible.

Skeptical Possibilities

The skeptic often refers to possibilities in which a person would believe something even though it was false: really, the person is cleverly deceived by others, perhaps by an evil demon, or the person is dreaming or he is floating in a tank near Alpha Centauri with his brain being stimulated. In each case, the p he believes is false, and he believes it even though it is false.

How do these possibilities adduced by the skeptic show that someone does not know that p? Suppose that someone is you; how do these possibilities count against your knowing that p? One way might be the following. (I shall consider other ways later.) If there is a possible situation where p is false yet you believe that p, then in that situation you believe that p even though it is false. So it appears you do not satisfy condition 3 for knowledge.

(3) If p were false, S wouldn't believe that p.

For a situation has been described in which you do believe that p even though p is false. How then can it also be true that if p were false, you wouldn't believe it? If the skeptic's possible situation shows that 3 is false, and if 3 is a necessary condition for knowledge, then the skeptic's possible situation shows that there isn't knowledge.

So construed, the skeptic's argument plays on condition 3; it aims to show that condition 3 is not satisfied. The skeptic may seem to be putting forth

R: Even if p were false, S still would believe p.

This conditional, with the same antecedent as 3 and the contradictory consequent, is incompatible with the truth of 3. If 3 is true, then R is not. However, R is stronger than the skeptic needs in order to show 3 is false. For 3 is false when if p were false, S might believe that p. This last conditional is weaker than R, and is merely 3's denial:

T: not-[not-p → not-(S believes that p)].

Whereas R does not simply deny 3, it asserts an opposing subjunctive of its own. Perhaps the possibility the skeptic adduces is not enough to show that R is true, but it appears at least to establish the weaker T; since this T denies 3, the skeptic's possibility appears to show that 3 is false.

However, the truth of 3 is not incompatible with the existence of a possible situation where the person believes p though it is false. The subjunctive

(3) not-p → not-(S believes p)

does not talk of all possible situations in which p is false (in which not-p is true). It does not say that in all possible situations where not-p holds, S doesn't believe p. To say there is no possible situation in which not-p yet S believes p, would be to say that not-p entails not-(S believes p), or logically implies it. But subjunctive conditionals differ from entailments; the subjunctive 3 is not a statement of entailment. So the existence of a possible situation in which p is false yet S believes p does not show that 3 is false; 3 can be true even though there is a possible situation where not-p and S believes that p.

What the subjunctive 3 speaks of is the situation that would hold if p were false. Not every possible situation in which p is false is the situation that would hold if p were false. To fall into possible worlds talk, the subjunctive 3 speaks of the not-p world that is closest to the actual world, or of those not-p worlds that are closest to the actual world, or more strongly (according to my suggestion) of the not-p neighborhood of the actual world. And it is of this or these not-p worlds that it says (in them) S does not believe that p. What happens in yet other more distant not-p worlds is no concern of the subjunctive 3.

The skeptic's possibilities (let us refer to them as SK), of the person's being deceived by a demon or dreaming or floating in a tank, count against the subjunctive

(3) if p were false then S wouldn't believe that p

only if (one of) these possibilities would or might obtain if p were false; only if one of these possibilities is in the not-p neighborhood of the actual world. Condition 3 says: if p were false, S still would not believe p. And

this can hold even though there is some situation SK described by the skeptic in which p is false and S believes p. If p were false S still would not believe p, even though there is a situation SK in which p is false and S does believe p, provided that this situation SK wouldn't obtain if p were false. If the skeptic describes a situation SK which would not hold even if p were false then this situation SK doesn't show that 3 is false and so does not (in this way at least) undercut knowledge. Condition C acts to rule out skeptical hypotheses.

C: not-p → SK does not obtain.

Any skeptical situation SK which satisfies condition C is ruled out. For a skeptical situation SK to show that we don't know that p, it must fail to satisfy C which excludes it; instead it must be a situation that might obtain if p did not, and so satisfy C's denial:

not-(not-p → SK doesn't obtain).

Although the skeptic's imagined situations appear to show that 3 is false, they do not; they satisfy condition C and so are excluded.

The skeptic might go on to ask whether we know that his imagined situations SK are excluded by condition C, whether we know that if p were false SK would not obtain. However, typically he asks something stronger: do we know that his imagined situation SK does not actually obtain? Do we know that we are not being deceived by a demon, dreaming, or floating in a tank? And if we do not know this, how can we know that p? Thus we are led to the second way his imagined situations might show that we do not know that p.

Skeptical Results

According to our account of knowledge, S knows that the skeptic's situation SK doesn't hold if and only if

(1) SK doesn't hold

(2) S believes that SK doesn't hold

(3) If SK were to hold, S would not believe that SK doesn't hold

(4) If SK were not to hold, S would believe it does not.

Let us focus on the third of these conditions. The skeptic has carefully chosen his situations SK so that if they held we (still) would believe they did not. We would believe we weren't dreaming, weren't being deceived, and so on, even if we were. He has chosen situations SK such that if SK were to hold, S would (still) believe that SK doesn't hold—and this is incompatible with the truth of 3.

Since condition 3 is a necessary condition for knowledge, it follows that we do not know that SK doesn't hold. If it were true that an evil demon was deceiving us, if we were having a particular dream, if we were floating in a tank with our brains stimulated in a specified way, we would still believe we were not. So, we do not know we're not being deceived by an evil demon, we do not know we're not in that tank, and we do not know we're not having that dream. So says the skeptic, and so says our account. And also so we say—don't we? For how could we know we are not being deceived that way, dreaming that dream? If those things *were* happening to us, everything would seem the same to us. There is no way we can know it is not happening for there is no way we could tell if it were happening; and if it were happening we would believe exactly what we do now—in particular, we still would believe that it was not. For this reason, we feel, and correctly, that we don't know—how could we?—that it is not happening to us. It is a virtue of our account that it yields, and explains, this result.

The skeptic asserts we do not know his possibilities don't obtain, and he is right. Attempts to avoid skepticism by claiming we do know these things are bound to fail. The skeptic's possibilities make us uneasy because, as we deeply realize, we do not know they don't obtain; it is not surprising that attempts to show we do know these things leave us suspicious, strike us even as bad faith. Nor has the skeptic merely pointed out something obvious and trivial. It comes as a surprise to realize that we do not know his possibilities don't obtain. It is startling, shocking. For we would have thought, before the skeptic got us to focus on it, that we did know those things, that we did know we were not being deceived by a demon, or dreaming that dream, or stimu-

lated that way in that tank. The skeptic has pointed out that we do not know things we would have confidently said we knew. And if we don't know these things, what can we know? So much for the supposed obviousness of what the skeptic tells us.

Let us say that a situation (or world) is doxically identical for S to the actual situation when if S were in that situation, he would have exactly the beliefs (*doxa*) he actually does have. More generally, two situations are doxically identical for S if and only if he would have exactly the same beliefs in them. It might be merely a curiosity to be told there are nonactual situations doxically identical to the actual one. The skeptic, however, describes worlds doxically identical to the actual world in which almost everything believed is false.[1]

Such worlds are possible because we know mediately, not directly. This leaves room for a divergence between our beliefs and the truth. It is as though we possessed only two-dimensional plane projections of three-dimensional objects. Different three-dimensional objects, oriented appropriately, have the same two-dimensional plane projection. Similarly, different situations or worlds will lead to our having the very same beliefs. What is surprising is how very different the doxically identical world can be—different enough for almost everything believed in it to be false. Whether or not the mere fact that knowledge is mediated always makes room for such a very different doxically identical worlds, it does so in our case, as the skeptic's possibilities show. To be shown this is nontrivial, especially when we recall that we do not know the skeptic's possibility doesn't obtain: we do not know that we are not living in a doxically identical world wherein almost everything we believe is false.

What more could the skeptic ask for or hope to show? Even readers who sympathized with my desire not to dismiss the skeptic too quickly may feel this has gone too far, that we have not merely acknowledged the force of the skeptic's position but have succumbed to it.

---

1. I say almost everything, because there still could be some true beliefs such as "I exist." More limited skeptical possibilities present worlds doxically identical to the actual world in which almost every belief of a certain sort is false, for example, about the past, or about other people's mental states. See the discussion below in the section on narrower skepticisms.

The skeptic maintains that we know almost none of what we think we know. He has shown, much to our initial surprise, that we do not know his (nontrivial) possibility SK doesn't obtain. Thus, he has shown of one thing we thought we knew, that we didn't and don't. To the conclusion that we know almost nothing, it appears but a short step. For if we do not know we are not dreaming or being deceived by a demon or floating in a tank, then how can I know, for example, that I am sitting before a page writing with a pen, and how can you know that you are reading a page of a book?

However, although our account of knowledge agrees with the skeptic in saying that we do not know that not-SK, it places no formidable barriers before my knowing that I am writing on a page with a pen. It is true that I am, believe I am, if I weren't I wouldn't believe I was, and if I were, I would believe it. (I leave out the reference to method.) Also, it is true that you are reading a page (please, don't stop now!), you believe you are, if you weren't reading a page you wouldn't believe you were, and if you were reading a page you would believe you were. So according to the account, I do know that I am writing on a page with a pen, and you do know that you are reading a page. The account does not lead to any general skepticism.

Yet we must grant that it appears that if the skeptic is right that we don't know we are not dreaming or being deceived or floating in the tank, then it cannot be that I know I am writing with a pen or that you know you are reading a page. So we must scrutinize with special care the skeptic's "short step" to the conclusion that we don't know these things, for either this step cannot be taken or our account of knowledge is incoherent.

Nonclosure

In taking the "short step", the skeptic assumes that if S knows that p and he knows that 'p entails q' then he also knows that q. In the terminology of the logicians, the skeptic assumes that knowledge is closed under known logical implication; that the operation of moving from something known to something else known to be entailed by it does not take us outside of the (closed) area of knowledge. He intends, of course, to work things backwards, arguing that since the person does not know

that q, assuming (at least for the purposes of argument) that he does know that p entails q, it follows that he does not know that p. For if he did know that p, he would also know that q, which he doesn't.

The details of different skeptical arguments vary in their structure, but each one will assume some variant of the principle that knowledge is closed under known logical implication. If we abbreviate "knowledge that p" by "Kp" and abbreviate "entails" by the fishhook sign "$\rightarrow\hspace{-0.6em}\mathrel{3}$", we can write this principle of closure as the subjunctive principle

P: K(p $\rightarrow\hspace{-0.6em}\mathrel{3}$ q) & Kp $\rightarrow$ Kq.

If a person were to know that p entails q and he were to know that p then he would know that q. The statement that q follows by modus ponens from the other two stated as known in the antecedent of the subjunctive principle P; this principle counts on the person to draw the inference to q.

You know that your being in a tank on Alpha Centauri entails your not being in place X where you are (I assume here a limited readership). And you know also the contrapositive, that your being at place X entails that you are not then in a tank on Alpha Centauri. If you knew you were at X you would know you're not in a tank (of a specified sort) at Alpha Centauri. But you do not know this last fact (the skeptic has argued and we have agreed) and so (he argues) you don't know the first. Another intuitive way of putting the skeptic's argument is as follows. If you know that two statements are incompatible and you know the first is true then you know the denial of the second. You know that your being at X and your being in a tank on Alpha Centauri are incompatible; so if you knew you were at X you would know you were not in the (specified) tank on Alpha Centauri. Since you do not know the second, you don't know the first.

No doubt, it is possible to argue over the details of principle P, to point out it is incorrect as it stands. Perhaps, though, Kp, the person does not know that he knows that p (that is, not-KKp) and so does not draw the inference to q. Or perhaps he doesn't draw the inference because not-KK(p $\rightarrow\hspace{-0.6em}\mathrel{3}$ q). Other similar principles face their own difficulties: for example, the principle that K(p $\rightarrow$ q) $\rightarrow$ (Kp $\rightarrow$ Kq) fails if Kp stops

$p \rightarrow q$ from being true, that is, if $Kp \rightarrow$ not-$(p \rightarrow q)$; the principle that $K(p \rightarrow q) \rightarrow K(Kp \rightarrow Kq)$ faces difficulties if Kp makes the person forget that $(p \rightarrow q)$ and so he fails to draw the inference to q. We seem forced to pile K upon K until we reach something like $KK(p \rightarrow q)$ & $KKp \rightarrow Kq$; this involves strengthening considerably the antecedent of P and so is not useful for the skeptic's argument that p is not known. (From a principle altered thus, it would follow at best that it is not known that p is known.)

We would be ill-advised, however, to quibble over the details of P. Although these details are difficult to get straight, it will continue to appear that something like P is correct. If S knows that 'p entails q' and he knows that p and knows that '$(p$ and p entails $q)$ entails q' and he does draw the inference to q from all this and believes q via the process of drawing this inference, then will he not know that q? And what is wrong with simplifying this mass of detail by writing merely principle P, provided we apply it only to cases where the mass of detail holds, as it surely does in the skeptical cases under consideration? For example, I do realize that my being in the Van Leer Foundation Building in Jerusalem entails that I am not in a tank on Alpha Centauri; I am capable of drawing inferences now; I do believe I am not in a tank on Alpha Centauri (though not solely via this inference, surely); and so forth. Won't this satisfy the correctly detailed principle, and shouldn't it follow that I know I am not (in that tank) on Alpha Centauri? The skeptic agrees it should follow; so he concludes from the fact that I don't know I am not floating in the tank on Alpha Centauri that I don't know I am in Jerusalem. Uncovering difficulties in the details of particular formulations of P will not weaken the principle's intuitive appeal; such quibbling will seem at best like a wasp attacking a steamroller, at worst like an effort in bad faith to avoid being pulled along by the skeptic's argument.

Principle P is wrong, however, and not merely in detail. Knowledge is not closed under known logical implication. S knows that p when S has a true belief that p, and S wouldn't have a false belief that p (condition 3) and S would have a true belief that p (condition 4). Neither of these latter two conditions is closed under known logical implication.

Let us begin with condition

(3) if p were false, S wouldn't believe that p.

When S knows that p, his belief that p is contingent on the truth of p, contingent in the way the subjunctive condition 3 describes. Now it might be that p entails q (and S knows this), that S's belief that p is subjunctively contingent on the truth of p, that S believes q, yet his belief that q is not subjunctively dependent on the truth of q, in that it (or he) does not satisfy:

(3') if q were false, S wouldn't believe that q.

For 3' talks of what S would believe if q were false, and this may be a very different situation than the one that would hold if p were false, even though p entails q. That you were born in a certain city entails that you were born on earth. Yet contemplating what (actually) would be the situation if you were not born in that city is very different from contemplating what situation would hold if you weren't born on earth. Just as those possibilities are very different, so what is believed in them may be very different. When p entails q (and not the other way around) p will be a stronger statement than q, and so not-q (which is the antecedent of 3') will be a stronger statement than not-p (which is the antecedent of 3). There is no reason to assume you will have the same beliefs in these two cases, under these suppositions of differing strengths.

There is no reason to assume the (closest) not-p world and the (closest) not-q world are doxically identical for you, and no reason to assume, even though p entails q, that your beliefs in one of these worlds would be a (proper) subset of your beliefs in the other.

Consider now the two statements:

p = I am awake and sitting on a chair in Jerusalem;

q = I am not floating in a tank on Alpha Centauri being stimulated by electrochemical means to believe that p.

The first one entails the second: p entails q. Also, I know that p entails q; and I know that p. If p were false, I would be standing or lying down in the same city, or perhaps sleeping there, or perhaps in a neighboring city or town. If *q* were false, I would be floating in a tank on Alpha Centauri. Clearly these are very different situations, leading to great differences in what I then would believe. If *p* were false, if I weren't awake and sitting on a chair in Jerusalem, I would not believe that *p*. Yet if *q* were false, if I was floating in a tank on Alpha Centauri, I would believe that *q*, that I was not in the tank, and indeed, in that case, I would still believe that *p*. According to our account of knowledge, I know that *p* yet I do not know that *q*, even though (I know) *p* entails *q*.

This failure of knowledge to be closed under known logical implication stems from the fact that condition 3 is not closed under known logical implication; condition 3 can hold of one statement believed while not of another known to be entailed by the first. It is clear that any account that includes as a necessary condition for knowledge the subjunctive condition 3, not-*p* → not-(S believes that *p*), will have the consequence that knowledge is not closed under known logical implication.

When *p* entails *q* and you believe each of them, if you do not have a false belief that *p* (since *p* is true) then you do not have a false belief that *q*. However, if you are to know something not only don't you have a false belief about it, but also you wouldn't have a false belief about it. Yet, we have seen how it may be that *p* entails *q* and you believe each and you wouldn't have a false belief that *p* yet you might have a false belief that *q* (that is, it is not the case that you wouldn't have one). Knowledge is not closed under the known logical implication because "wouldn't have a false belief that" is not closed under known logical implication.

If knowledge were the same as (simply) true belief then it would be closed under known logical implication (provided the implied statements were believed). Knowledge is not simply true belief, however; additional conditions are needed. These further conditions will make knowledge open under known logical implication, even when the entailed statement is believed, when at least one of the further conditions itself is open. Knowledge stays closed (only) if all of the additional conditions are closed. I lack a general nontrivial characterization of those conditions that are closed under known logical implication; possessing such an illuminating characterization, one

might attempt to prove that no additional conditions of that sort could proved an adequate analysis of knowledge.

Still, we can say the following. A belief that *p* is knowledge that *p* only if it somehow varies with the truth of *p*. The causal condition for knowledge specified that the belief was "produced by" the fact, but that condition did not provide the right sort of varying with the fact. The subjunctive conditions 3 and 4 are our attempt to specify that varying. But however an account spells this out, it will hold that whether a belief that *p* is knowledge partly depends on what goes on with the belief in some situations when *p* is false. An account that says nothing about what is believed in any situation when *p* is false cannot give us any mode of varying with the fact.

Because what is preserved under logical implication is truth, any condition that is preserved under known logical implication is most likely to speak only of what happens when *p*, and *q*, are true, without speaking at all of what happens when either one is false. Such a condition is incapable of providing "varies with"; so adding only such conditions to true belief cannot yield an adequate account of knowledge.

A belief's somehow varying with the truth of what is believed is not closed under known logical implication. Since knowledge that *p* involves such variation, knowledge also is not closed under known logical implication. The skeptic cannot easily deny that knowledge involves such variation, for his argument that we don't know that we're not floating in that tank, for example, uses the fact that knowledge does involve variation. ("If you were floating in the tank you would still think you weren't, so you don't know that you're not.") Yet, though one part of his argument uses that fact that knowledge involves such variation, another part of his argument presupposes that knowledge does not involve any such variation. This latter is the part that depends upon knowledge being closed under known logical implication, as when the skeptic argues that since you don't know that not-SK, you don't know you are not floating in the tank, then you also don't know, for example, that you are now reading a book. That closure can hold only if the variation does not. The skeptic cannot be right both times. According to our view he is right when he holds that knowledge involves such variation and so concludes that we don't know, for example, that we are not floating in that tank; but he is wrong when he assumes knowledge is closed under known logical implication and concludes that we know hardly anything.

Knowledge is a real factual relation, subjunctively specifiable, whose structure admits our standing in this relation, tracking, to p without standing in it to some q which we know p to entail. Any relation embodying some variation of belief with the fact, with the truth (value), will exhibit this structural feature. The skeptic is right that we don't track some particular truths—the ones stating that his skeptical possibilities SK don't hold—but wrong that we don't stand in the real knowledge-relation of tracking to many other truths, including ones that entail these first mentioned truths we believe but don't know.

The literature on skepticism contains writers who endorse these skeptical arguments (or similar narrower ones), but confess their inability to maintain their skeptical beliefs at times when they are not focusing explicitly on the reasoning that led them to skeptical conclusions. The most notable example of this is Hume:

> I am ready to reject all belief and reasoning, and can look upon no opinion even as more probable or likely than another. . . . Most fortunately it happens that since reason is incapable of dispelling these clouds, nature herself suffices to that purpose, and cures me of this philosophical melancholy and delirium, either by relaxing this bent of mind, or by some avocation, and lively impression of my senses, which obliterate all these chimeras. I dine, I play a game of backgammon, I converse, and am merry with my friends; and when after three or four hours' amusement, I would return to these speculations, they appear so cold, and strained, and ridiculous, that I cannot find in my heart to enter into them any farther. (*A Treatise of Human Nature*, Book I, Part IV, section VII)

> The great subverter of Pyrrhonism or the excessive principles of skepticism is action, and employment, and the occupations of common life. These principles may flourish and triumph in the schools; where it is, indeed, difficult, if not impossible, to refute them. But as soon as they leave the shade, and by the presence of the real objects, which actuate our passions and sentiments, are put in opposition to the more powerful principles of our nature, they vanish like smoke, and leave the most determined skeptic in the same condition as other mortals. . . . And though a Pyrrhonian may throw himself or others into a momentary amazement and confusion by his profound reasonings; the first and most trivial event in life will put to flight all his doubts and scruples, and leave him the same, in every point of action and speculation, with the philosophers of every other sect, or with those who never concerned themselves in any philosophical researches. When he awakes from his dream, he will be the first to join in the laugh against himself, and to confess that all his objections are mere amusement. (*An Enquiry Concerning Human Understanding*, Section XII, Part II)

The theory of knowledge we have presented explains why skeptics of various sorts have had such difficulties in sticking to their far-reaching skeptical conclusions "outside the study", or even inside it when they are not thinking specifically about skeptical arguments and possibilities SK.

The skeptic's arguments do show (but show only) that we don't know the skeptic's possibilities SK do not hold; and he is right that we don't track the fact that SK does not hold. (If it were to hold, we would still think it didn't.) However, the skeptic's arguments don't show we do not know other facts (including facts that entail not-SK) for we do track these other facts (and knowledge is not closed under known logical entailment). Since we do track these other facts—you, for example, the fact that you are reading a book; I, the fact that I am writing on a page—and the skeptic tracks such facts too, it is not surprising that when he focuses on them, on his relationship to such facts, the skeptic finds it hard to remember or maintain his view that he does not know those facts. Only by shifting his attention back to his relationship to the (different) fact that not-SK, which relationship is not tracking, can he revive his skeptical belief and make it salient. However, this skeptical triumph is evanescent, it vanishes when his attention turns to other facts. Only by fixating on the skeptical possibilities SK can he maintain his skeptical virtue; otherwise, unsurprisingly, he is forced to confess to sins of credulity. [. . .]

Perceptual and Inductive Knowledge

John Locke

Origins of Our Ideas and Knowledge

Book II

Chap. I: Of Ideas in General, and Their Original.

1. Idea *is the object of thinking.* Every man being conscious to himself, that he thinks, and that which his mind is employed about whilst thinking being the *ideas,* that are there, 'tis past doubt, that men have in their minds several *ideas,* such as are those expressed by the words, *whiteness, hardness, sweetness, thinking, motion, man, elephant, army, drunkenness,* and others: it is in the first place then to be inquired, how he comes by them? [. . .]

2. *All* ideas *come from sensation or reflection.* Let us then suppose the mind to be, as we say, white paper, void of all characters, without any *ideas;* how comes it to be furnished? Whence comes it by that vast store, which the busy and boundless fancy of man has painted on it, with an almost endless variety? Whence has it all the materials of reason and knowledge? To this I answer, in one word, from *experience:* in that, all our knowledge is founded; and from that it ultimately derives itself. Our observation employed either about *external, sensible objects; or about the internal operations of our minds, perceived and reflected on by ourselves, is that which supplies our understandings with all the materials of thinking.* These two are the fountains of knowledge, from whence all the *ideas* we have, or can naturally have, do spring.

3. *The objects of sensation one source of* ideas. First, *our senses,* conversant about particular sensible objects, do *convey into the mind,* several distinct *perceptions* of things, according to those various ways, wherein those objects do affect them: and thus we come by those *ideas,* we have of *yellow, white, heat, cold, soft, hard, bitter, sweet,* and all those which we call sensible qualities, which when I say the senses convey into the mind, I mean, they from external objects convey into the mind what produces there those *perceptions.* This great source, of most of the *ideas* we have, depending wholly upon our senses, and derived by them to the understanding, I call *SENSATION.*

4. *The operations of our minds, the other source of them.* Secondly, the other fountain, from which experience furnishes the understanding with *ideas,* is the *perception of the operations of our own minds* within us, as it is employed about the *ideas* it has got; which operations, when the soul comes to reflect on, and consider, do furnish the understanding with another set of *ideas,* which could not be had from things without: and such are, *perception, thinking, doubting, believing, reasoning, knowing, willing,* and all the different actings of our own minds; which we being conscious of, and observing in ourselves, do from these receive into our understandings, as distinct *ideas,* as we do from bodies affecting ours senses. This source of *ideas,* every man has wholly in himself: and though it be not sense, as having nothing to do with external objects; yet it is very like it, and might properly enough be called internal sense. But as I call the other *sensation,* so I call this *REFLECTION,* the *ideas* it affords being such only, as the mind gets by reflecting on its own operations within itself. By *REFLECTION* then, in the following part of this discourse, I would be understood to mean, that notice which the mind takes of its own operations, and the manner of them, by reason whereof,

---

From John Locke, *An Essay Concerning Human Understanding,* abridged and edited by Kenneth Winkler (Indianapolis: Hackett Publishing Company, 1996). Reprinted by permission of the publisher.

there come to be *ideas* of these operations in the understanding. These two, I say, *viz.* external, material things, as the objects of *SENSATION;* and the operations of our own minds within, as the objects of *REFLECTION,* are, to me, the only originals, from whence all our *ideas* take their beginnings. The term *operations* here, I use in a large sense, as comprehending not barely the actions of the mind about its ideas, but some sort of passions arising sometimes from them, such as is the satisfaction or uneasiness arising from any thought.

5. *All our* ideas *are of the one or the other of these.* The understanding seems to me, not to have the least glimmering of any *ideas,* which it does not receive from one of these two. *External objects furnish the mind with the* ideas *of sensible qualities,* which are all those different perceptions they produce in us: and the *mind furnishes the understanding with* ideas *of its own operations.* These, when we have taken a full survey of them, and their several modes, combinations, and relations, we shall find to contain all our whole stock of *ideas;* and that we have nothing in our minds, which did not come in, one of these two ways. Let anyone examine his own thoughts, and thoroughly search into his understanding, and then let him tell me, whether all the original *ideas* he has there, are any other than that of objects of his *senses;* or of the operations of his mind, considered as objects of his *reflection:* and how great a mass of knowledge soever he imagines to be lodged there, he will, upon taking a strict view, see, that he has *not any* idea *in his mind, but what one of these two have imprinted;* though, perhaps, with infinite variety compounded and enlarged by the understanding, as we shall see hereafter.

6. *Observable in children.* He that attentively considers the state of a *child,* at his first coming into the world, will have little reason to think him stored with plenty of *ideas,* that are to be the matter of his future knowledge.... If a child were kept in a place, where he never saw any other but black and white, till he were a man, he would have no more *ideas* of scarlet or green, than he that from his childhood never tasted and oyster, or a pineapple, has of those particular relishes.

7. *Men are differently furnished with these, according to the different objects they converse with.* Men then come to be furnished with fewer or more simple *ideas* from without, according as the *objects,* they converse with, afford

greater or less variety; and from the operation of their minds within, according as they more or less *reflect* on them. For, though he that contemplates the operations of his mind, cannot but have plain and clear *ideas* of them; yet unless he turns his thoughts that way, and considers them *attentively,* he will no more have clear and distinct *ideas* of all the *operations of his mind,* and all that may be observed therein, than he will have all the particular *ideas* of any landscape, or of the parts and motion of a clock, who will not turn his eyes to it, and with attention heed all the parts of it....

8. Ideas *of reflection later, because they need attention.* And hence we see the reason why 'tis pretty late, before most children get *ideas* of the operations of their own minds; and some have not any very clear, or perfect *ideas* of the greatest part of them all their lives. Because, though they pass there continually; yet like floating visions, they make not deep impressions enough, to leave in the mind clear distinct lasting *ideas,* till the understanding turns inwards upon itself, *reflects* on its own *operations,* and makes them the object of its own contemplation....

9. *The soul begins to have* ideas, *when it beings to perceive.* To ask, *at what time a man has first any* ideas, is to ask, when he begins to perceive, having *ideas* and perception being the same thing. I know it is an opinion, that the soul always thinks, and that it has the actual perception of *ideas* in itself constantly, as long as it exists; and that actual thinking is as inseparable form the soul, as actual extension is from the body; which if true, to inquire after the beginning of a man's *ideas,* is the same, as to inquire after the beginning of his soul. For by this account, soul and its *ideas,* as body and its extension, will begin to exist both at the same time.

10. *The soul thinks not always, for this wants proofs.* But whether the soul be supposed to exist antecedent to, or coeval with, or some time after the first rudiments of organization, or the beginnings of life in the body, I leave to be disputed by those, who have better thought of that matter. I confess myself to have one of those dull souls, that does not perceive itself always to contemplate *ideas,* nor can it conceive it any more necessary for the *soul always to think,* that for the body always to move: the perception of *ideas* being (as I conceive) to the soul, what motion is to the body, not its essence, but one of its operations: and therefore, though thinking be sup-

posed never so much the proper action of the soul; yet it is not necessary, to suppose, that it should be always thinking, always in action. That, perhaps, is the privilege of the infinite author and preserver of things, *who never slumbers or sleeps;* but is not competent to any finite being, at least not to the soul of man. We know certainly by experience, that we sometimes think, and thence draw this infallible consequence, that there is something in us, that has a power to think: but whether that substance perpetually thinks, or no, we can be no farther assured, than experience informs us. . . .

11. *It is not always conscious of it.* I grant that the soul in a waking man is never without thought, because it is the condition of being awake: but whether sleeping without dreaming be not an affection of the whole man, mind as well as body, may be worth a waking man's consideration; it being hard to conceive, that anything should think, and not be conscious of it. If the *soul* does *think in a sleeping man,* without being conscious of it, I ask, whether during such thinking, it has any pleasure or pain, or be capable of happiness or misery? I am sure the man is not, no more than the bed or earth he lies on. For to be happy or miserable without being conscious of it, seems to me utterly inconsistent and impossible. Or if it be possible, that the soul can, whilst the body is sleeping, have its thinking, enjoyments, and concerns, its pleasure or pain apart, which the man is not conscious of, nor partakes in, it is certain that *Socrates* asleep, and *Socrates* awake, is not the same person; but his soul when he sleeps, and *Socrates* the man consisting of body and soul when he is waking, are two persons: since waking *Socrates,* has no knowledge of, or concernment for that happiness, or misery of his soul, which it enjoys alone by itself whilst he sleeps, without perceiving anything of it. . . . For if we take wholly away all consciousness of our actions and sensations, especially of pleasure and pain, and the concernment that accompanies it, it will be hard to know wherein to place personal identity.

12. *If a sleeping man thinks without knowing it, the sleeping and waking man are two persons.* The soul, during sound sleep, thinks, say these men. *Whilst it thinks* and perceives, it is capable certainly of those of delight or trouble, as well as any other perceptions; and *it must necessarily be conscious of its own perceptions.* But it has all this

apart: the sleeping man, 'tis plain, is conscious of nothing of all this. Let us suppose then the soul of *Castor,* whilst he is sleeping, retired from his body, which is no impossible supposition for the men I have here to do with, who so liberally allow life, without a thinking soul to all other animals. These men cannot then judge it impossible, or a contradiction, that the body should live without the soul; nor that the soul should subsist and think, or have perception, even perception of happiness or misery, without the body. Let us then, as I say, suppose the soul of *Castor* separated, during his sleep, from his body, to think apart. Let us suppose too, that it chooses for its scene of thinking, the body of another man, *v.g. Pollux,* who is sleeping without a soul: for if *Castor's* soul can think while *Castor* is asleep, what *Castor* is never conscious of, 'tis no matter what place it chooses to think in. We have here then the bodies of two men with only one soul between them, which we will suppose to sleep and wake by turns; and the soul still thinking in the waking man, whereof the sleeping man is never conscious, has never the least perception. I ask then, whether *Castor* and *Pollux,* thus, with only one soul between them, which thinks and perceives in one, what the other is never conscious of, nor is concerned for, are not two as distinct persons, as *Castor* and *Hercules;* or as *Socrates* and *Plato* were? And whether one of them might not be very happy, and the other miserable? Just by the same reason, they make the soul and the man two persons, who make the soul think apart, what the man is not conscious of. For, I suppose, nobody will make identity of persons, to consist in the soul's being united to the very same numerical particles of matter: for if that be necessary to identity, 'twill be impossible, in that constant flux of the particles of our bodies, that any man should be the same person, two days, or two moments together.

13. *Impossible to convince those that sleep without dreaming, that they think.* Thus, methinks every drowsy nod shakes their doctrine, who teach, that the soul is always thinking. . . .

14. *That men dream without remembering it, in vain urged.* 'Twill perhaps be said, that the *soul thinks,* even *in* the soundest *sleep, but the memory retains it not.* That the soul in a sleeping man should be this moment busy athinking, and the next moment in a waking man, not remember,

nor be able to recollect one jot of all these thoughts, is very hard to be conceived, and would need some better proof than bare assertion to make it be believed. . . .

. . . . .

19. *That a man should be busy in thinking, and yet not retain it the next moment, very improbable.* To suppose the soul to think, and the man not to perceive it, is, as has been said, to make two persons in one man: and if one considers well these men's way of speaking, one shall be led into a suspicion, that they do so. For they who tell us, that the soul always thinks, do never, that I remember, say, that a man always thinks. Can the soul think, and not the man? Or a man think, and not be conscious of it? This, perhaps, would be suspected of *jargon* in others. If they say, the man thinks always, but is not always conscious of it; they may as well say, his body is extended without having parts. For 'tis altogether as intelligible to say, that a body is extended without parts, as that anything *thinks without being conscious of it,* or perceiving, that it does so. They who talk thus, may, with as much reason, if it be necessary to their hypothesis, say, that a man is always hungry, but that he does not always feel it: whereas hunger consists in that very sensation, as thinking consists in being conscious that one thinks. . . .

20. *No ideas but from sensation or reflection, evident, if we observe children.* I see no reason therefore to believe, that the *soul thinks before the senses have furnished it with ideas* to think on; and as those are increased, and retained; so it comes, by exercise, to improve its faculty of thinking in the several parts of it, as well as afterwards, by compounding those *ideas,* and reflecting on its own operations, it increases its stock as well as facility, in remembering, imagining, reasoning, and other modes of thinking.

. . . . .

23. If it shall be demanded then, *when a man begins to have any ideas?* I think, the true answer is, when he first has any *sensation.* For since there appear not to be any *ideas* in the mind, before the senses have conveyed any in, I conceive that *ideas* in the understanding, are coeval with *sensation;* which is such an impression or motion, made in some part of the body, as produces some perception in the understanding.

24. *The original of all our knowledge.* The *impressions* then, that are made on our *senses* by outward objects, that are extrinsical to the mind, and *its own operations,* about the impressions, *reflected* on by itself, as proper objects to be contemplated by it, are, I conceive, *the original of all knowledge;* and the first capacity of human intellect, is, that the mind is fitted to receive the impressions made on it; either, through the *senses,* by outward objects, or by its own operations, when it *reflects* on them. This is the first step a man makes towards the discovery of anything, and the groundwork, whereon to build all those notions, which ever he shall have naturally in this world. All those sublime thoughts, which tower above the clouds, and reach as high as heaven itself, take their rise and footing here: in all that great extent wherein the mind wanders, in those remote speculations, it may seem to be elevated with, it stirs not one jot beyond those *ideas,* which *sense* or *reflection,* have offered for its contemplation.

25. *In the reception of simple* ideas, *the understanding is for the most part passive.* In this part, the *understanding* is merely *passive;* and whether or not, it will have these beginnings, and as it were materials of knowledge, is not in its own power. For the objects of our senses, do, many of them, obtrude their particular *ideas* upon our minds, whether we will or no: and the operations of our minds, will not let us be without, at least some obscure notions of them. No man, can be wholly ignorant of what he does, when he thinks. These *simple ideas,* when offered to the mind, *the understanding can* no more refuse to have, nor alter, when they are imprinted, nor blot them out, and make new ones in itself, than a mirror can refuse, alter, or obliterate the images or *ideas,* which, the objects set before it, do therein produce. As the bodies that surround us, do diversely affect our organs, the mind is forced to receive the impressions; and cannot avoid the perception of those *ideas* that are annexed to them.

Chap. II: Of Simple Ideas.

1. *Uncompounded appearances.* The better to understand the nature, manner, and extent of our knowledge, one thing is carefully to be observed, concerning the *ideas* we have; and that is, that *some* of them are *simple,* and *some complex.*

Though the qualities that affect our senses, are, in the things themselves, so united and blended, that there is no separation, no distance between them; yet 'tis plain, the *ideas* they produce in the mind, enter by the senses simple and unmixed. For though the sight and touch often take in from the same object, at the same time, different *ideas;* as a man sees at once motion and color; the hand feels softness and warmth in the same piece of wax: yet the simple *ideas* thus united in the same object, are a perfectly distinct, as those that come in by different senses. The coldness and hardness, which a man feels in a piece of *ice,* being as distinct *ideas* in the mind, as the smell and whiteness of a lily; or as the taste of sugar, and smell of a rose: and there is nothing can be plainer to a man, than the clear and distinct perception he has of those simple *ideas;* which being each in itself uncompounded, contains in it nothing but *one uniform appearance,* or conception in the mind, and is not distinguishable into different ideas.

2. *The mind can neither make nor destroy them.* These simple ideas, the materials of all our knowledge, are suggested and furnished to the mind, only by those two ways above mentioned, *viz. sensation* and *reflection.* When the understanding is once stored with these simple *ideas,* it has the power to repeat, compare, and unite them even to an almost infinite variety, and so can make at pleasure new complex *ideas.* But it is not in the power of the most exalted wit, or enlarged understanding, by any quickness or variety of thought, to *invent or frame one new simple* idea in the mind, not taken in by the ways before mentioned: nor can any force of the understanding, *destroy* those that are there. . . .

3. This is the reason why, though we cannot believe it impossible to God, to make a creature with other organs, and more ways to convey into the understanding the notice of corporeal things, than those five, as they are usually counted, which he has given to man: yet I think, it is *not possible,* for anyone *to imagine* any other *qualities* in bodies, howsoever constituted, whereby they can be taken notice of, besides sounds, tastes, smells, visible and tangible qualities. And had mankind been made with but four senses, the qualities, then, which are the object of the fifth sense, had been as far from our notice, imagination, and conception, as now any *belonging to a sixth, seventh, or eighth sense,* can possibly be: which, whether yet some other creatures, in some other parts of this vast, and stupendous universe, may not have, will be a great presumption to deny. . . .

Chap. III: Of Ideas of One Sense.

1. *Division of simple* ideas. Ideas *of one sense.* The better to conceive the *ideas,* we receive from sensation, it may not be amiss for us to consider them, in reference to the different ways, whereby they make their approaches to our minds, and make themselves perceivable by us.

First then, there are some, which come into our minds *by one sense* only.

Secondly, there are others, that convey themselves into the mind *by more senses than one.*

Thirdly, others that are had from *reflection* only.

Fourthly, there are some that make themselves way, and are suggested to the mind *by all the ways of sensation and reflection.*

We shall consider them apart under these several heads.

First, there are *some* ideas, *which have admittance only through one sense,* which is peculiarly adapted to receive them. Thus light and colors, as white, red, yellow, blue; with their several degrees or shades, and mixtures, as green, scarlet, purple, sea-green, and the rest, come in only by the eyes: all kinds of noises, sounds, and tones only by the ears: the several tastes and smells, by the nose and palate. And if these organs, or the nerves which are the conduits, to convey them from without to their audience in the brain, the mind's presence-room (as I may so call it) are any of them so disordered, as not to perform their functions, they have no postern to be admitted by; no other way to bring themselves into view, and be perceived by the understanding.

The most considerable of those, belonging to the touch, are heat and cold, and solidity; all the rest, consisting almost wholly in the sensible configuration, as smooth and rough; or else more, or less firm adhesion of the parts, as hard and soft, tough and brittle, are obvious enough. [. . .]

Chap. V: Of Simple Ideas of Divers Senses.

The *ideas* we get by more than one sense, are of *space,* or *extension, figure, rest,* and *motion:* for these make perceivable impressions, both on the eyes and touch; and we can receive and convey into our minds the *ideas* of the extension, figure, motion, and rest of bodies, both by seeing and feeling. But having occasion to speak more at large of these in another place, I here only enumerate them.

Chap. VI: Of Simple Ideas of Reflection.

1. *Are the operations of the mind about its other* ideas. The mind receiving the *ideas,* mentioned in the foregoing chapters, from without, when it turns its view, inward upon itself, and observes its own actions about those *ideas* it has, takes from thence other *ideas,* which are as capable to the objects of its contemplation, as any of those it received from foreign things.

2. *The* idea *of perception, and* idea *of willing, we have from reflection.* The two great and principal actions of the mind . . . are these two:

Perception, or *thinking,* and
Volition, or *willing.*

The power of thinking is called the *understanding,* and the power of volition is called the *will,* and these two powers or abilities in the mind are denominated *faculties.* Of some of the modes of the simple *ideas* of reflection, such as are *remembrance, discerning, reasoning, judging, knowledge, faith &c.* [. . .]

Chap. VII: Of Simple Ideas of Both Sensation and Reflection.

1. *Pleasure and pain.* There be other simple *ideas,* which convey themselves into the mind, by all the ways of sensation and reflection, *viz.*

Pleasure, or *delight,* and its opposite.

Pain, or *uneasiness.*

Power.

Existence.

Unity.

2. *Delight,* or *uneasiness,* one or other of them join themselves to almost all our *ideas,* both of sensation and reflection: and there is scarce any affection of our senses from without, any retired thought of our mind within, which is not able to produce in us *pleasure* or *pain.* By *pleasure* and *pain,* I would be understood to signify, what-

soever delights or molests us; whether it arises from the thoughts of our minds, or anything operating on our bodies. . . .

• • • • •

7. *Existence and unity. Existence* and *unity,* are two other *ideas,* that are suggested to the understanding, by every object without, and every *Idea* within. When *ideas* are in our minds, we consider them as being actually there, as well as we consider things to be actually without us; which is, that they exist, or have *existence;* and whatever we can consider as one thing, whether a real being, or *idea,* suggests to the understanding, the *idea of unity.*

8. *Power. Power* also is another of those simple *ideas,* which we receive from *sensation and reflection.* For observing in ourselves, that we do, and can think; and that we can, at pleasure, move several parts of our bodies, which were at rest; the effects also, that natural bodies are able to produce in one another, occurring every moment to our senses, we both these ways get the *idea* of *power.*

9. *Succession.* Besides these, there is another *idea,* which though suggested by our senses, yet is more constantly offered us, by what passes in our own minds; and that is the *idea* of *succession.* For if we look immediately into ourselves, and reflect on what is observable there, we shall find our *ideas* always, whilst we are awake, or have any thought, passing in train, one going, and another coming, without intermission.

10. *Simple* ideas *the materials of all our knowledge.* These, if they are not all, are at least (as I think) the most considerable of those *simple ideas* which the mind has, and out of which is made all its other knowledge; all which it receives, only by the two forementioned ways of *sensation* and *reflection.*

Nor let anyone think these two narrow bounds for the capacious mind of man to expatiate in, which takes its flight farther than the stars, and cannot be confined by the limits of the world; that extends its thoughts often, even beyond the utmost expansion of matter, and makes excursions into that incomprehensible *inane.* I grant all this, but desire anyone to assign any *simple idea,* which is not *received from* one of *those inlets* before-mentioned, or any *complex idea not made out of those simple ones.* Nor will it be so strange, to think these few simple *ideas* sufficient to employ the quickest thought, or largest capacity; and to furnish the materials of all that various knowledge, and more various fancies and opinions of all mankind, if we consider how many words may be made out of the various composition of 24 letters; or if going one step farther, we will but reflect on the variety of combinations may be made, with barely one of the above-mentioned *ideas, viz.* number, whose stock is inexhaustible, and truly infinite: and what a large and immense field, does extension alone afford the mathematicians?

Chap. VIII: Some Farther Considerations Concerning Our Simple Ideas.

1. *Positive* ideas *from privative causes.* Concerning the simple *ideas* of sensation 'tis to be considered, that whatsoever is so constituted in nature, as to be able, by affecting our senses, to cause any perception in the mind, does thereby produce in the understanding a simple *idea;* which, whatever be the external cause of it, when it comes to be taken notice of, by our discerning faculty, it is by the mind looked on and considered there, to be a real *positive idea* in the understanding, as much as any other whatsoever; though, perhaps, the cause of it be but a privation in the subject.

2. Thus the *ideas* of heat and cold, light and darkness, white and black, motion or rest, are equally clear and *positive ideas* in the mind; though, perhaps, some of *the causes* which produce them, are barely *privations* in those subjects, from whence our senses derives those *ideas.* These the understanding, in its view of them, considers all as distinct positive *ideas,* without taking notice of the causes that produce them: which is an inquiry not belonging to the *idea,* as it is in the understanding; but to the nature of the things existing without us. These are two very different things, and carefully to be distinguished; it being one thing to perceive, and know the *idea* of white or black, and quite another to examine what kind of particles they must be, and how ranged in the superficies, to make any object appear white or black.

3. A painter or dyer, who never inquired into their causes, has the *ideas* of white and black, and other colors, as clearly, perfectly, and distinctly in his understanding, and perhaps more distinctly, than the philosopher, who has busied himself in considering their natures, and thinks he knows how far either of them is in its cause positive or privative; and the *idea of black* is no less *positive* in his mind, than that of white, *however the cause* of that color in the external object, may *be only a privation.*

4. If it were the design of my present undertaking, to inquire into the natural causes and manner of perception, I should offer this as a reason *why a privative cause might,* in some cases at least, *produce a positive idea, viz.* that all sensation being produced in us, only by different degrees and modes of motion in our animal spirits, variously agitated by external objects, the abatement of any former motion, must as necessarily produce a new sensation, as the variation or increase of it; and so introduces a new *idea,* which depends only on a different motion of the animal spirits in that organ.

5. But whether this be so, or no, I will not here determine, but appeal to everyone's own experience, whether the shadow of a man, though it consists of nothing but the absence of light (and the more the absence of light is, the more discernible is the shadow) does not, when a man looks on it, cause as clear and positive an *idea* in his mind, as a man himself, though covered over with clear sunshine? And the picture of a shadow, is a positive thing. Indeed, we have *negative names,* which stand not directly for positive *ideas,* but for their absence, such as *insipid, silence, nihil, &c.* which words denote positive *ideas; v.g. taste, sounds, being,* with a signification of their absence.

6. And thus one may truly be said to see darkness. For supposing a hole perfectly dark, from whence no light is reflected, 'tis certain one may see the figure of it, or it may be painted; or whether the ink, I write with, makes any other *idea,* is a question. The privative causes I have here assigned of positive *ideas,* are according to the common opinion; but in truth it will be hard to determine, whether there be really any *ideas* from a privative cause, till it be determined, *whether rest be any more a privation than motion.*

7. Ideas *in the mind, qualities in bodies.* To discover the nature of our *ideas* the better, and to discourse of them intelligibly, it will be convenient to distinguish them, as they are *ideas* or perceptions in our minds; and as they are modifications of matter in the bodies that cause such

perceptions in us: that so we *may not* think (as perhaps usually is done) that they are exactly the images, and *resemblances* of something inherent in the subject; most of those of sensation being in the mind no more the likeness of something existing without us, than the names, that stand for them are the likeness of our *ideas,* which yet upon hearing, they are apt to excite in us.

8. Whatsoever the mind perceives in itself, or is the immediate object of perception, thought, or understanding, that I call *idea;* and the power to produce any *idea* in our mind, I call *quality* of the subject wherein that power is. Thus a snowball having the power to produce in us the *ideas* of *white, cold,* and *round,* the powers to produce those *ideas* in us, as they are in the snowball, I call *qualities;* and as they are sensations, or perceptions, in our understandings, I call them *ideas:* which *ideas,* if I speak of sometimes, as in the things themselves, I would be understood to mean those qualities in the objects which produce them in us.

9. *Primary and secondary qualities.* Qualities thus considered in bodies are, first such as are utterly inseparable from the body, in what estate soever it be; such as in all the alterations and changes it suffers, all the force can be used upon it, it constantly keeps; and such as sense constantly finds in every particle of matter, which has bulk enough to be perceived, and the mind finds inseparable from every particle of matter, though less than to make itself singly be perceived by our senses. *v.g.* Take a grain of wheat, divide it into two parts, each part has still *solidity, extension, figure,* and *mobility;* divide it again, and it retains still the same qualities; and so divide it on, till the parts become insensible, they must retain still each of them all those qualities. For division (which is all that a mill, or pestle, or any other body, does upon another, in reducing it to insensible parts) can never take away either solidity, extension, figure, or mobility from any body, but only makes two, or more distinct masses, reckoned as so many distinct bodies, after division make a certain number. These I call *original* or *primary qualities* of body, which I think we may observe to produce simple *ideas* in us, *viz.* solidity, extension, motion, or rest and number.

10. *2dly.* Such *qualities,* which in truth are nothing in the objects themselves, but powers to produce various sensations in us by their *primary qualities, i.e.,* by the

bulk, figure, texture, and motion of their insensible parts, as colors, sounds, tastes, *&c.* These I call *secondary qualities.* To these might be added a third sort which are allowed to be barely powers though they are as much real qualities in the subject, as those which I to comply with the common way of speaking call *qualities,* but for distinction *secondary qualities.* For the power in fire to produce a new color, or consistency in wax or clay by its primary qualities, is as much a quality in fire, as the power it has to produce in me a new *idea* or sensation of warmth or burning, which I felt not before, by the same primary qualities, *viz.* the bulk, texture and motion of its insensible parts.

11. *How primary qualities produce their* ideas. The next thing to be considered, is how *bodies* produce *ideas* in us, and that is manifestly *by impulse,* the only way which we can conceive bodies operate in.

12. If then external objects be not united to our minds, when they produce *ideas* in it; and yet we perceive *these original qualities* in such of them as singly fall under our senses, 'tis evident, that some motion must be thence continued by our nerves, or animal spirits, by some parts of our bodies, to the brains or the seat of sensation, there to *produce in our minds the particular* ideas *we have of them.* And since the extension, figure, number, and motion of bodies of an observable bigness, may be perceived at a distance *by* the sight, 'tis evident some singly imperceptible bodies must come from them to the eyes, and thereby convey to the brain some *motion,* which produces these *ideas,* which we have of them in us.

13. *How secondary.* After the same manner, that the *ideas* of these original qualities are produced in us, we may conceive, that the *ideas of secondary qualities* are also *produced, viz. by the operation of insensible particles on our senses.* For it being manifest, that there are bodies, and good store of bodies, each whereof is so small, that we cannot, by any of our senses discover either their bulk, figure, or motion, as is evident in the particles of the air and water, and other extremely smaller than those, perhaps, as much smaller than the particles of air, or water, as the particles of air or water, are smaller than peas or hail-stones. Let us suppose at present, that the different motions and figures, bulk and number of such particles, affecting the several organs of our senses, produce in us those different sensations, which we have from the col-

ors and smells of bodies, *v.g.* that a violet, by the impulse of such insensible particles of matter of peculiar figures, and bulks, and in different degrees and modifications of their motions, causes the *ideas* of the blue color, and sweet scent of that flower to be produced in our minds. It being no more impossible, to conceive, that God should annex such *ideas* to such motions, with which they have no similitude; than that he should annex the *idea* of pain to the motion of a piece of steel dividing our flesh, with which that *idea* has no resemblance.

14. What I have said concerning *colors* and *smells,* may be understood also of *tastes* and *sounds, and other the like sensible qualities;* which, whatever reality we, by mistake, attribute to them, are in truth nothing in the objects themselves, but powers to produce various sensations in us, and depend *on those primary qualities, viz.* bulk, figure, texture and motion of parts; as I have said.

15. Ideas *of primary qualities are resemblances; of secondary, not.* From whence I think it is easy to draw this observation, that the *ideas of primary qualities* of bodies, *are resemblances* of them, and their patterns do really exist in the bodies themselves; but the *ideas, produced* in us *by* these *secondary qualities, have no resemblance* of them at all. There is nothing like our *ideas,* existing in the bodies themselves. They are in the bodies, we denominate from them, only a power to produce those sensations in us: and what is sweet, blue, or warm in *idea,* is but the certain bulk, figure, and motion of the insensible parts in the bodies themselves, which we call so.

16. *Flame* is denominated *hot* and *light; snow white* and *cold;* and *manna white* and *sweet,* from the *ideas* they produce in us. Which qualities are commonly thought to be the same in those bodies, that those *ideas* are in us, the one the perfect resemblance of the other, as they are in a mirror; and it would by most men be judged very extravagant, if one should say otherwise. And yet he, that will consider, that *the same fire,* that at one distance *produces* in us the sensation of *warmth,* does at a nearer approach, produce in us the far different sensation of *pain,* ought to bethink himself, what reason he has to say, that his *idea* of *warmth,* which was produced in him by the fire, is actually *in the fire;* and his *idea* of *pain,* which the same fire produced in him in the same way, is *not* in the *fire.* Why is whiteness and coldness in snow, and pain not, when it produces the one and the other *idea* in us;

and can do neither, but by the bulk, figure, number, and motion of its solid parts?

17. The particular *bulk, number, figure, and motion of the parts of fire, or snow, are really in them,* whether anyone's senses perceive them or no: and therefore they may be called *real qualities,* because they really exist in those bodies. But *light, heat, whiteness,* or *coldness, are no more really in them, than sickness or pain is in* manna. Take away the sensation of them; let not the eyes see light, or colors, nor the ears hear sounds; let the palate not taste, nor the nose smell, and all colors, tastes, odors, and sounds, as they are such particular *ideas,* vanish and cease, and are reduced to their causes, *i.e.,* bulk, figure, and motion of parts.

18. A piece of *manna* of a sensible bulk, is able to produce in us the *idea* of a round or square figure; and, by being removed from one place to another, the *idea* of motion. This *idea* of motion represents it, as it really is in the *manna* moving: a circle or square are the same, whether in *idea* or existence; in the mind, or in the *manna:* and this, both *motion and figure are really in the manna,* whether we take notice of them or no: this everybody is ready to agree to. Besides, *manna* by the bulk, figure, texture, and motion of its parts, has a power to produce the sensations of sickness, and sometimes of acute pains, or gripings in us. That these *ideas of sickness and pain are not in the* manna, but effects of its operations on us, and are nowhere when we feel them not: this also everyone readily agrees to. And yet men are hardly to be brought to think, that *sweetness and whiteness are not really in manna;* which are but the effects of the operations of *manna,* by the motion, size, and figure of its particles on the eyes and palate; as the pain and sickness caused by *manna,* are confessedly nothing, but the effects of its operations on the stomach and guts, by the size, motion, and figure of its insensible parts; (for by nothing else can a body operate, as has been proved:) as if it could not operate on the eyes and palate, and thereby produce in the mind particular distinct *ideas,* which in itself it has not, as well as we allow it can operate on the guts and stomach, and thereby produce distinct *ideas,* which in itself it has not. These *ideas* being all effects of the operations of *manna,* on several parts of our bodies, by the size, figure, number, and motion of its parts, why those produced by the eyes and palate,

should rather be thought to be really in the *manna,* than those produced by the stomach and guts; or why the pain and sickness, *ideas* that are the effects of *manna,* should be thought to be nowhere, when they are not felt; and yet the sweetness and whiteness, effects of the same *manna* on other parts of the body, by ways equally as unknown, should be thought to exist in the *manna,* when they are not seen nor tasted, would need some reason to explain.

19. Let us consider the red and white colors in *porphyry:* hinder light but from striking on it, and its colors vanish; it no longer produces any such *ideas* in us: upon the return of light, it produces these appearances on us again. Can anyone think any real alterations are made in the *porphyry,* by the presence or absence of light; and that those *ideas* of whiteness and redness, are really in *porphyry* in the light, when 'tis plain *it has no color in the dark?* It has, indeed, such a configuration of particles, both night and day, as are apt by the rays of light rebounding from some parts of that hard stone, to produce in us the *idea* of redness, and from others the *idea* of whiteness: but whiteness or redness are not in it at any time, but such a texture, that has the power to produce such a sensation in us.

20. Pound an almond, and the clear white *color* will be altered into a dirty one, and the sweet *taste* into an oily one. What real alteration can the beating of the pestle make in any body, but an alteration of the *texture* of it?

21. *Ideas* being thus distinguished and understood, we may be able to give an account, how the same water, at the same time, may produce the *idea* of cold by one hand, and of heat by the other: whereas it is impossible, that the same water, if those *ideas* were really in it, should at the same time be both hot and cold. For if we imagine *warmth,* as it is *in our hands,* to be *nothing but a certain sort and degree of motion in the minute particles of our nerves, or animal spirits,* we may understand, how it is possible, that the same water may at the same time produce the sensation of heat in one hand, and cold in the other; which yet figure never does, that never producing the *idea* of a square by one hand, which has produced the *idea* of globe by another. But if the sensation of heat and cold, be nothing but the increase or diminution of the motion of the minute parts of our bodies, caused by the corpuscles of any other body, it is easy to be understood,

that if the motion be greater in one hand, than in the other; if a body be applied to the two hands, which has in its minute particles a greater motion, than in those of one of the hands, and a less, than in those of the other, it will increase the motion of the one hand, and lessen it is the other, and so cause the different sensations of heat and cold, that depend thereon.

22. I have in what just goes before, been engaged in physical inquires a little farther than, perhaps, I intended. But it being necessary, to make the nature of sensation a little understood, and to make the *difference between the qualities in bodies, and the* ideas *produced by them in the mind,* to be distinctly conceived, without which it were impossible to discourse intelligibly of them; I hope, I shall be pardoned this little excursion into natural philosophy, it being necessary in our present inquiry, to distinguish the *primary,* and *real qualities* of bodies, which are always in them, (*viz.* solidity, extension, figure, number, and motion, or rest; and are sometimes perceived by us, *viz.* when the bodies they are in, are big enough singly to be discerned) from those *secondary* and *imputed qualities,* which are but the powers of several combinations of those primary ones, when they operate, without being distinctly discerned; whereby we also may come to know what *ideas* are, and what are not resemblances of something really existing in the bodies, we denominate from them.

23. *Three sorts of qualities in bodies.* The *qualities* then that are in *bodies* rightly considered, are of *three sorts.*

First, the *bulk, figure, number, situation,* and *motion, or rest* of their solid parts; those are in them, whether we perceive them or no; and when they are of that size, that we can discover them, we have by these an *idea* of the thing, as it is in itself, as is plain in artificial things. These I call *primary qualities.*

Secondly, the *power* that is in any body, by reason of *its* insensible *primary qualities,* to operate after a peculiar manner on any of our senses, and thereby *produce in us* the *different ideas* of several colors, sounds, smells, tastes, &c. These are usually called sensible qualities.

Thirdly, the *power* that is in any body, *by* reason of the particular constitution of *its primary qualities, to* make such a *change in the bulk, figure, texture, and motion of another body,* as to make it operate on our senses, differently from what it did before. Thus the sun has a power to make wax white, and fire to make lead fluid. These *are* usually called powers.

The first of these, as has been said, I think, may be properly called *real original,* or *primary qualities,* because they are in the things themselves, whether they are perceived or no: and upon their different modifications it is, that the secondary qualities depend.

The other two, are only powers to act differently upon other things, which powers result from the different modifications of those primary qualities.

24. *The* 1st *are resemblances. The* 2d *thought resemblances, but are not. The* 3d *neither are nor are thought so.* But though *these two later sorts of qualities are powers barely,* and nothing but powers, relating to several other bodies, and resulting from the different modifications of the original qualities; yet they are generally otherwise thought of. For *the second sort, viz.* the powers to produce several *ideas* in us by our senses, *are looked upon as real qualities, in the things* thus affecting us: but *the third sort are called, and esteemed barely powers, v.g.* the *idea* of heat, or light, which we receive by our eyes, or touch from the sun, are commonly thought *real qualities* existing in the sun, and something more than mere powers in it. But when we consider the sun, in reference to wax, which it melts or blanches, we look upon the whiteness and softness produced in the wax, not as qualities in the sun, but effects produced by *powers* in it: whereas, if rightly considered, these qualities of light and warmth, which are perceptions in me when I am warmed, or enlightened by the sun, are not otherwise in the sun, than the changes made in the wax, when it is blanched or melted, are in the sun. They are all of them equally powers in the sun, depending on its primary qualities; whereby it is able in the one case, so to alter the bulk, figure, texture, or motion of some of the insensible parts of my eyes, or hands, as thereby to produce in me the *ideas* of light or heat; and in the other, it is able so to alter the bulk, figure, texture, or motion of the insensible parts of the wax, as to make them fit to produce in me the distinct *ideas* of white and fluid.

25. The reason, *why the one are ordinarily taken for real qualities, and the other only for bare powers,* seems to be, because the *ideas* we have of distinct colors, sounds *&c.* containing nothing at all in them, of bulk, figure, or motion, we are not apt to think them the effects of these primary qualities, which appear not to our senses to operate in their production; and with which, they have not any apparent congruity, or conceivable connection. Hence it is, that we are so forward to imagine, that those *ideas* are the resemblances of something really existing in the objects themselves: since sensation discovers nothing of bulk, figure, or the motion of parts in their production; nor can reason show, how bodies by their bulk, figure, and motion, should produce in the mind the *ideas* of blue, or yellow, *&c.* But in the other case, in the operations of bodies, changing the qualities one of another, we plainly discover, that the quality produced, has commonly no resemblance with anything in the thing producing it; wherefore we look on it as a bare effect of power. For though receiving the *idea* of heat, or light, from the sun, we are apt to think, 'tis a perception and resemblance of such a quality in the sun: yet when we see wax, or a fair face, receive change of color from the sun, we cannot imagine, that to be the reception or resemblance of anything in the sun, because we find not those different colors in the sun itself. For our senses, being able to observe a likeness, or unlikeness of sensible qualities in two different external objects, we forwardly enough conclude the production of any sensible quality in any subject, to be an effect of bare power, and not the communication of any quality, which was really in the efficient, when we find no such sensible quality in the thing that produced it. But our senses, not being able to discover any unlikeness between the *idea* produced in us, and the quality of the object producing it, we are apt to imagine, that our *ideas* are resemblances of something in the objects, and not the effects of certain powers, placed in the modifications of their primary qualities, with which primary qualities the *ideas* produced in us have no resemblance. [. . .]

Chap. IX: Of Perception.

1. *It is the first simple* idea *of reflection. Perception,* as it is the first faculty of the mind, exercised about our *ideas;* so it is the first and simplest *idea* we have from reflection, and is by some called thinking in general. Though thinking, in the propriety of the *English* tongue, signifies that sort of operation of the mind about its *ideas,* wherein the mind is active; where it with some degree of voluntary attention, considers anything. For in bare

naked *perception,* the mind is, for the most part, only passive; and what is perceives, it cannot avoid perceiving.

2. *Perception is only when the mind receives the impression. What perception is,* everyone will know better by reflecting on what he does himself, when he sees, hears, feels, *&c.* or thinks, than by any discourse of mine. Whoever reflects on what passes in his own mind, cannot miss it: and if he does not reflect, all the words in the world, cannot make him have any notion of it.

3. This is certain, that whatever alterations are made in the body, if they reach not the mind; whatever impressions are made on the outward parts, if they are not taken notice of within, there is no perception. Fire may burn our bodies, with no other effect, than it does a billet, unless the motion be continued to the brain, and there the sense of heat, or *ideas* of pain, be produced in the mind, wherein consists *actual perception.*

4. How often may a man observe in himself, that whilst his mind is intently employed in the contemplation of some objects; and curiously surveying some *ideas* that are there, it takes no notice of impressions of sounding bodies, made upon the organ of hearing, with the same alteration, that uses to be for the producing the *idea* of a sound? A sufficient impulse there may be on one organ; but it not reaching the observation of the mind, there follows no perception. . . . Want of sensation in this case, is not through any defect in the organ, or that the man's ears are less affected, than at other times, when he does hear: but that which uses to produce the *idea,* though conveyed in by the usual organ, not being taken notice of in the understanding, and so imprinting no *idea* on the mind, there follows no sensation. *So that wherever there is sense,* or *perception, there some* idea *is actually produced, and present in the understanding.*

5. *Children, though they have* Ideas, *in the womb, have none innate.* Therefore I doubt not but *children,* by the exercise of their senses about objects, that affect them *in the womb, receive some few ideas,* before they are born, as the unavoidable effects, either of the bodies that environ them, or else of those wants or diseases they suffer; amongst which, (if one may conjecture concerning things not very capable of examination) I think the *ideas* of hunger and warmth are two: which probably are some of the first that children have, and which they scarce ever part with again.

6. But though it be reasonable to imagine, that *children* receive some *ideas* before they come into the world, yet these simple *ideas* are *far from* those *innate principles,* which some contend for, and we above have rejected. These here mentioned, being the effects of sensation, are only from some affections of the body, which happen to them there, and so depend on something exterior to the mind; no otherwise differing in their manner of production from other *ideas* derived from sense, but only in the precedency of time: whereas those innate principles are supposed to be of quite another nature; not coming into the mind by any accidental alterations in, or operations on the body; but, as it were, original characters impressed upon it, in the very first moment of its being and constitution.

• • • • •

8. Ideas *of sensation changed by judgment.* We are farther to consider concerning perception, that the *ideas we receive by sensation, are often* in grown people *altered by the judgment,* without our taking notice of it. When we set before our eyes a round globe, of any uniform color, *v.g.* gold, alabaster, or jet, 'tis certain, that the *idea* thereby imprinted in our mind, is of a flat circle variously shadowed, with several degrees of light and brightness coming to our eyes. But we having by use been accustomed to perceive, what kind of appearance convex bodies are wont to make in us; what alterations are made in the reflections of light, by the difference of the sensible figures of bodies, the judgment presently, by an habitual custom, alters the appearances into their causes: so that from that, which truly is variety of shadow or color, collecting the figure, it makes it pass for a mark of figure, and frames to itself the perception of a convex figure, and an uniform color; when the *idea* we receive from thence, is only a plane variously colored, as is evident in painting. To which purpose I shall here insert a problem of that very ingenious and studious promoter of real knowledge, the learned and worthy Mr. *Molyneux,* which he was pleased to send me in a letter some months since; and it is this: *Suppose a man born blind, and now adult, and taught by his touch to distinguish between a cube, and a sphere of the same metal, and nighly of the same bigness, so as to tell, when he felt one and t'other, which is the cube, which the sphere. Suppose then the cube and sphere placed on a table, and the blind man*

to be made to see. Quaere, whether by his sight, before he touched them, he could now distinguish, and tell, which is the globe, which the cube. To which the acute and judicious proposer answers: *Not. For though he has obtained the experience of, how a globe, how a cube affects his touch; yet he has not yet attained the experience, that what affects his touch so or so, must affect his sight so or so; or that a protuberant angled in the cube, that pressed his hand unequally, shall appear to his eye, as it does in the cube.* I agree with this thinking gent. whom I am proud to call my friend, in his answer to this his problem; and am of opinion, that the blind man, at first sight, would not be able with certainty to say, which was the globe, which the cube, whilst he only saw them: though he could unerringly name them by his touch, and certainly distinguish them by the difference of their figures felt. This I have set down, and leave with my reader, as an occasion for him to consider, how much he may beholden to experience, improvement, and acquired notions, where he thinks, he has not the least use of, or help from them: and the rather, because this observing gent. farther adds, that *having upon the occasion of my book, proposed this to divers very ingenious men, he hardly ever met with one, that at first gave the answer to it, which he thinks true, till by hearing his reasons they were convinced.*

9. But this is not, I think, usual in any of our *ideas,* but those received by *sight:* because sight, the most comprehensive of all our senses, conveying to our minds, the *ideas* of light and colors, which are peculiar only to that sense; and also the far different *ideas* of space, figure, and motion, the several varieties whereof change the appearances of its proper object, *viz.* light and colors, we bring ourselves by use, to judge of the one by the other. This in many cases, by a settled habit, in things whereof we have frequent experience, is performed so constantly and so quick, that we take that for the perception of our sensation, which is an *idea* formed by our judgment; so that one, *viz.* that of sensation, serves only to excite the other, and is scarce taken notice of itself; as a man who reads or hears with attention and understanding, takes little notice of the characters, or sounds, but of the *ideas,* that are excited in him by them.

• • • • •

11. *Perception puts the difference between animals and inferior beings.* This faculty of *perception,* seems to me to be

that, which *puts the distinction betwixt the animal kingdom, and the inferior parts of nature.* For however vegetables have, many of them, some degrees of motion, and upon the different application of other bodies to them, do very briskly alter their figures and motions, and so have obtained the name of sensitive plants, from a motion, which has some resemblance to that, which in animals follows upon sensation: yet, I suppose, it is all bare mechanism; and no otherwise produced, than the turning of a wild oat-beard, by the insinuation of the particles of moisture; or the shortening of a rope, by the affusion of water. All which is done without any sensation in the subject, or the having or receiving any *ideas.*

12. *Perception,* I believe is, in some degree, *in all sorts of animals;* though in some, possibly, the avenues, provided by nature for the reception of sensations are so few, and the perception, they are received with, so obscure and dull, that it comes extremely short of the quickness and variety of sensations, which is in other animals. . . .

• • • • •

Chap. X: Of Retention.

1. *Contemplation.* The next faculty of mind, whereby it makes a farther progress towards knowledge, is that which I call *retention,* or the keeping of those simple *ideas,* which from sensation or reflection it has received. This is done two ways. First, by keeping the *idea,* which is brought into it, for some time actually in view, which is called *contemplation.*

2. *Memory.* The other way of retention is the power to revive again in our minds those *ideas,* which after imprinting have disappeared, or have been as it were laid out of sight: and thus we do, when we conceive heat or light, yellow or sweet, the object being removed. This is *memory,* which is as it were the storehouse of our *ideas.* For the narrow mind of man, not being capable of having many *ideas* under view and consideration at once, it was necessary to have a repository, to lay up those *ideas,* which at another time it might have use of. But our *ideas* being nothing, but actual perceptions in the mind, which cease to be anything, when there is no perception of them, this *laying up* of our *ideas* in the repository of the memory, signifies no more but this, that the mind

has a power, in many cases, to revive perceptions, which it has once had, with this additional perception annexed to them, that it has had them before. And in this sense it is, that our *ideas* are said to be in our memories, when indeed, they are actually nowhere, but only there is an ability in the mind, when it will, to revive them again; and as it were paint them anew on itself, though some with more, some with less difficulty; some more lively, and others more obscurely. And thus it is, by the assistance of this faculty, that we are said to have all those *ideas* in our understandings, which though we do not actually contemplate, yet we can bring in sight, and make appear again, and be the objects of our thoughts, without the help of those sensible qualities, which first imprinted them there.

· · · · ·

5. Ideas *fade in the memory. . . . The pictures drawn in our minds, are laid in fading colors;* and if not sometimes refreshed, vanish and disappear. How much the constitution of our bodies, and the make of our animal spirits, are concerned in this; and whether the temper of the brain make this difference, that in some it retains the characters drawn on it like marble, in others like freestone, and in others little better than sand, I shall not here inquire, though it may seem probable, that the constitution of the body does sometimes influence the memory; since we oftentimes find a disease quite strip the mind of all its *ideas,* and the flames of a fever, in a few days, calcine all those images to dust and confusion, which seemed to be as lasting, as if carved in marble.

6. *Constantly repeated* ideas *can scarce be lost.* But concerning the ideas themselves, it is easy to remark, that those that are *oftenest refreshed* (amongst which are those that are conveyed into the mind by more ways than one) by a frequent return of the objects or actions that produce them, *fix themselves best in the memory,* and remain clearest and longest there: and therefore those, which are the original qualities of bodies, *viz. solidity, extension, figure, motion,* and *rest,* and those that almost constantly affect our bodies, as *heat* and *cold;* and those which are the affectations of all kinds of beings, as *existence, duration,* and *number,* which almost every object that affects our senses, every thought which employs our minds,

bring along with them: these, I say, and the like *ideas,* are seldom quite lost, whilst the mind retains any *ideas* at all.

7. *In remembering the mind is often active.* In this secondary perception, as I may so call it, or viewing again of ideas, that are lodged *in the memory, the mind is oftentimes more than barely passive,* the appearance of those dormant pictures, depending sometimes on the will. The mind very often sets itself on working in search of some hidden *idea,* and turns, as it were, the eye of the soul upon it; though sometimes too they start up in our minds of their own accord, and offer themselves to the understanding; and very often are roused and tumbled out of their dark cells, into open daylight, by some turbulent and tempestuous passion; our affections bringing *ideas* to our memory, which had otherwise lain quiet and unregarded. This farther is to be observed, concerning *ideas* lodged in the memory, and upon occasion revived by the mind, that they are not only (as the word *revive* imports) none of them new ones; but also that the mind takes notice of them, as of a former impression, and renews its acquaintance with them, as with *ideas* it had known before. So that though *ideas* formerly imprinted are not all constantly in view, yet in remembrance they are constantly known to be such, as have been formerly imprinted, *i.e.,* in view, and taken notice of before by the understanding.

8. *Two defects in the memory, oblivion and slowness.* Memory, in an intellectual creature, is necessary in the next degree to perception. It is of so great moment, that where it is wanting, all the rest of our faculties are in great measure useless: and we in our thoughts, reasoning, and knowledge, could not proceed beyond present objects, were it not for the assistance of our memories, wherein there may be *two defects.*

First, that it *loses the idea* quite, and so far it produces perfect ignorance. For since we can know nothing farther, than we have the *idea* of it, when that is gone, we are in perfect *ignorance.*

Second, that it moves slowly, and *retrieves not the ideas,* that it has, and are laid up in store, *quick enough* to serve the mind upon occasions. . . .

· · · · ·

10. *Brutes have memory.* This faculty of laying up, and retaining the *ideas,* that are brought into the mind, several *other animals* seem to have, to a great degree, as well as

man. For to pass by other instances, birds learning of tunes, and the endeavors one may observe in them, to hit the notes right, put it past doubt with me, that they have perception, and retain *ideas* in their memories, and use them for patterns. For it seems to me impossible, that they should endeavor to conform their voices to notes (as 'tis plain they do) of which they had *ideas.* For though I should grant sound may mechanically cause a certain motion of the animal spirits, in the brains of those birds, whilst the tune is actually playing; and that motion may be continued on to the muscles of the wings, and so the bird mechanically be driven away by certain noises, because this may tend to the bird's preservation: yet that can never be supposed a reason, why it should cause mechanically, either whilst the tune was playing, much less after it has ceased, such a motion in the organs of the bird's voice, as should conform it to the notes of a foreign sound, which imitation can be of no use to the bird's preservation. But which is more, it cannot with any appearance of reason, be supposed (much less proved) that birds, without sense and memory, can approach their notes, nearer and nearer by degrees, to a tune played yesterday; which if they have no *idea* of in their memory, is now nowhere, nor can be a pattern for them to imitate, or which any repeated essays can bring them nearer to. Since there is no reason why the sound of a pipe should leave traces in their brains, which not at first, but by their after-endeavors, should produce the like sounds; and why the sounds they make themselves, should not make trace which they should follow, as well as those of the pipe, is impossible to conceive.

Chap. XI: Of Discerning, and Other Operations of the Mind

1. *No knowledge without it.* Another faculty, we may take notice of in our minds, is that of *discerning* and distinguishing between the several *ideas* it has. . . . On this faculty of distinguishing one thing from another, depends the *evidence and certainty* of several even very general propositions, which have passed for innate truths; because men over-looking the true cause, why those propositions find universal assent, impute it wholly to native uniform impressions; whereas it in truth *depends on this clear discerning faculty.* . . .

• • • • •

4. *Comparing.* The *COMPARING* them one with another, in respect of extent, degrees, time, place, or any other circumstances, is another operation of the mind about its *ideas,* and is that upon which depends all that large tribe of *ideas,* comprehended under *relation;* which of how vast an extent it is, I shall have occasion to consider hereafter.

• • • • •

6. *Compounding.* The next operation we may observe in the mind about its *ideas,* is *COMPOSITION;* whereby it puts together several of those simple ones it has received from sensation and reflection, and combines them into complex ones. Under this of composition, may be reckoned also that of *ENLARGING;* wherein though the composition does not so much appear as in more complex ones, yet it is nevertheless a putting several *ideas* together, though of the same kind. . . .

• • • • •

8. *Naming.* When children have, by repeated sensations, got *ideas* fixed in their memories, they begin, by degrees, to learn the use of signs. And when they have got the skill to apply the organs of speech to the framing of articulate sounds, they begin to make *use of words,* to signify their *ideas* to others: these verbal signs they sometimes borrow from others, and sometimes make themselves, as one may observe among the new and unusual names children often give to things in their first use of language.

9. *Abstraction.* The use of words then begin to stand as outward marks of our internal *ideas,* and those *ideas* being taken from particular things, if every particular *idea* that we take in, should have a distinct name, names must be endless. To prevent this, the mind makes the particular *ideas,* received from particular objects, to become general; which is done by considering them as they are in the minds such appearances, separate from all other existences, and the circumstances of real existence, as time, place, or any other concomitant *ideas.* This is called *ABSTRACTION,* whereby *ideas* taken from particular

beings, become general representatives of all of the same kind; and their names general names, applicable to whatever exists conformable to such abstract *ideas*. Such precise, naked appearances in the mind, without considering, how, whence, or with what others they came there, the understanding lays up (with names commonly annexed to them) as the standards to rank real existences into sorts, as they agree with those patters, and to *denominate* them accordingly. Thus the same color being observed today in chalk or snow, which the mind yesterday received from milk, it considers that appearance alone, makes it a representative of all that kind; and having given it the name *whiteness,* it by that sound signifies the same quality wheresoever to be imagined or me with; and thus universals, whether *ideas* or terms, are made.

10. *Brutes abstract not.* If it may be doubted, whether *beasts* compound and enlarge their *ideas* that way, to any degree: this, I think, I may be positive in, that the power of *abstracting* is not at all in them; and that the having of general *ideas,* is that which puts a perfect distinction betwixt man and brutes; and is an excellency which the faculties of brutes do by no means attain to. For it is evident, we observe no footsteps in them, of making use of general signs for universal *ideas;* from which we have reason to imagine, that they have not the faculty of abstracting, or making general *ideas,* since they have no use of words, or any other general signs.

11. Nor can it be imputed to their want of fit organs, to frame articulate sounds, that they have no use, or knowledge of general words; since many of them, we find, can fashion such sounds, and pronounce words distinctly enough, but never with any such application. And on the other side, men, who through some defect in the organs, want words, yet fail not to express their universal *ideas* by signs, which serve them instead of general words, a faculty which we see beasts come short in. And therefore I think we may suppose, that 'tis in this, that the species of *brutes* are discriminated from man; and 'tis that proper difference wherein they are wholly separated, and which at last widens to so vast a distance. For if they have any *ideas* at all, and are not bare machines (as some would have them) we cannot deny them to have some reason. It seems as evident to me, that they do some of them in certain instances reason,

as that they have sense; but it is only in particular *ideas,* just as they received them from their senses. They are the best of them tied up within those narrow bounds, and *have not* (as I think) the faculty to enlarge them by any kind of *abstraction*.

• • • • •

15. *These are the beginnings of human knowledge.* And thus I have given a short, and, I think, true *history of the first beginnings of human knowledge;* whence the mind has its first objects, and by what steps it makes its progress to the laying in, and storing up those *ideas,* out of which is to be framed all the knowledge it is capable of; wherein I must appeal to experience and observation, whether I am in the right: the best way to come to truth, being to examine things as they really are, and not to conclude they are, as we fancy of ourselves, or have been taught by others to imagine.

• • • • •

17. *Dark room.* I pretend not to teach, but to inquire; and therefore cannot but confess here again, that external and internal sensation, are the only passages that I can find, of knowledge, to the understanding. These alone, as far as I can discover, are the windows by which light is let into this *dark room.* For, methinks, the *understanding* is not much unlike a closet wholly shut from light, with only some little opening left, to let in external visible resemblances, or *ideas* of things without; would the pictures coming into such a dark room but stay there, and lie so orderly as to be found upon occasion, it would very much resemble the understanding of a man, in reference to all objects of sight, and the *ideas* of them.

These are my guesses concerning the minds whereby the understanding comes to have, and retain simple *ideas,* and the modes of them, with some other operations about them. I proceed now to examine some of these simple *ideas,* and their modes, a little more particularly.

Chap. XII: Of Complex Ideas.

1. *Made by the mind out of simple ones.* We have hitherto considered those *ideas,* in the reception whereof, the

mind is only passive, which are those simple ones received from *sensation* and *reflection* before-mentioned, whereof the mind cannot make any one to itself, nor have any *idea* which does not wholly consist of them. But as the mind is wholly passive in the reception of all its simple *ideas,* so it exerts several acts of its own, whereby out of its simple *ideas,* as the materials and foundations of the rest, the other are framed. The acts of the mind wherein it exerts its power over its simple *ideas* are chiefly these three, 1. Combining several simple *ideas* into one compound one, and thus all complex *ideas* are made. 2. The *2d.* is bring two *ideas,* whether simple or complex, together; and setting them by one another, so as to take a view of them at once, without uniting them into one; by which way it gets all its *ideas* of relations. 3. The *3d.* is separating them from all other *ideas* that accompany them in their real existence; this is called *abstraction:* and thus all its general *ideas* are made. This shows man's power and its ways of operation to be much what the same in the material and intellectual world. For the materials in both being such as he has no power over, either to make or destroy, all that man can do is either to unite them together, or to set them by one another or wholly separate them. I shall here begin with the first of these in the consideration of complex *ideas,* and come to the other two in their due places. As simple *ideas* are observed to exist in several combinations united together; so the mind has a power to consider several of them united together, as one *idea;* and that not only as they are united in external objects, but as itself has joined them. *Ideas* thus made up of several simple ones put together, I call *complex;* such as are *beauty, gratitude, a man, an army, the universe;* which though complicated of various simple *ideas,* or *complex ideas* made up of simple ones, yet are, when the mind pleases, considered each by itself, as one entire thing, and signified by one name.

2. *Made voluntarily.* In this faculty of repeating and joining together its *ideas,* the mind has great power in varying and multiplying the objects of its thoughts, infinitely beyond what *sensation* or *reflection* furnished it with: but all this still confined to those simple *ideas,* which it received from those two sources, and which are the ultimate materials of all its compositions. For simple *ideas* are all from things themselves; and of these *the mind can* have no more, nor other than what are suggested to it.

It can have no other *ideas* of sensible qualities, than what come from without by the senses; nor any *ideas* of other kind of operations of a thinking substance, than what it finds in itself: but when it has once got these simple *ideas,* it is not confined barely to observation, and what offers itself from without; it can, by its own power, put together those *ideas* it has, and *make new complex ones,* which it never received so united.

3. *Are either modes, substances, or relations. Complex ideas,* however compounded and decompounded, though their number be infinite, and the variety endless, wherewith they fill, and entertain the thoughts of men; yet, I think, they may be all reduced under these three heads.

1. *Modes.*

2. *Substances.*

3. *Relations.*

4. *Modes.* First, *modes* I call such complex *ideas,* which however compounded, contain not in them the supposition of subsisting by themselves, but are considered as dependences on, or affections of substances; such are the *ideas* signified by the words *triangle, gratitude, murder, &c.* And it in this I use the word *mode,* in somewhat a different sense from its ordinary signification, I beg pardon; it being unavoidable in discourses, differing from the ordinary received notions, either to make new words, or to use old words in somewhat a new signification, the latter whereof, in our present case, is perhaps the more tolerable of the two.

5. *Simple and mixed modes.* Of these *modes,* there are two sorts, which deserve distinct consideration. First, there are some which are only variations, or different combinations of the same simple *idea,* without the mixture of any other, as a dozen, or score; which are nothing but the *ideas* of so many distinct units added together, and these I call *simple modes,* as being contained within the bounds of one simple *idea.* Secondly, there are others compounded of simple *ideas* of several kinds, put together to make one complex one; *v.g. beauty,* consisting of a certain composition of color and figure, causing delight in the beholder; *theft,* which being the concealed change of the possession of anything, without the consent of the proprietor, contains, as is visible, a

combination of several *ideas* of several kinds; and these I call *mixed modes.*

6. *Substances single or collective.* Secondly, the *ideas of substances* are such combinations of simple *ideas,* as are taken to represent distinct particular things subsisting by themselves; in which the supposed, or confused *idea* of substance, such as it is, is always the first and chief. Thus if to substance be joined the simple *idea* of a certain dull whitish color, with certain degrees of weight, hardness, ductility, and fusibility, we have the *idea of lead;* and a combination of the *ideas* of a certain sort of figure, with the powers of motion, thought, and reasoning, joined to substance, make the ordinary *idea of a man.* Now of substances also, there are two sorts of *ideas;* one of single substances, as they exist separately, as of *a man,* or *a sheep;* the other of several of those put together, as an *army* of men, or *flock* of sheep; which *collective* ideas *of several substances* thus put together, are as much each of them one single *idea,* as that of a man, or an unit.

7. *Relation.* Thirdly, the last sort of complex *idea,* is that we call *relation,* which consists in the consideration and comparing one *idea* with another: of these several kinds we shall treat in their order.

8. *The abstrusest* ideas *from the two sources.* If we will trace the progress of our minds, and with attention observe how it repeats, adds together, and unites its simple *ideas* received from sensation or reflection, it will lead us farther than at first, perhaps, we should have imagined. And, I believe, we shall find, if we warily observe the originals of our notions, that even *the most abstruse* ideas, how remote soever they may seem from sense, or from any operation of our own minds, are yet only such, as the understanding frames to itself, by repeating and joining together *ideas,* that it had either from objects of sense, or from its own operations about them: so that those even large *and abstract* ideas *are derived from sensation, or reflection,* being no other than what the mind, by the ordinary use of its own faculties, employed about *ideas,* received from objects of sense, or from the operations it observes in itself about them, may, and does attain unto. This I shall endeavor to show in the *ideas* we have of *space, time,* and *infinity,* and some few other, that seem the most remote from those originals.

• • • • •

Book IV

Chap. III: Of the Extent of Human Knowledge.

1. *First, no farther than we have* ideas. Knowledge, as has been said, lying in the perception of the agreement, or disagreement, of any of our *ideas,* it follows from hence that,

> *First, no farther than we have* ideas. *First,* we can have *knowledge* no farther than we have *ideas.*

2. *Secondly, no farther than we can perceive their agreement or disagreement. Secondly,* that we can have no *knowledge* farther, than we can have perception of that agreement, or disagreement: which perception being, 1. either by *intuition,* or the immediate comparing any two *ideas;* or, 2. by *reason,* examining the agreement, or disagreement of two *ideas,* by the intervention of some others: or, 3. by *sensation,* perceiving the existence of particular things. Hence, it also follows,

3. *Thirdly, intuitive knowledge extends itself not to all the relations of all our* ideas. *Thirdly,* that we cannot have an *intuitive knowledge,* that shall extend itself to all our *ideas,* and all that we would know about them; because we cannot examine and perceive all the relations they have one to another by *juxta*position, or an immediate comparison one with another. Thus having the *ideas* of an obtuse, and an acute-angled triangle, both drawn from equal bases, and between parallels, I can by intuitive knowledge, perceive the one not to be the other; but cannot that way know, whether they be equal, or no; because of their agreement, or disagreement in equality, can never be perceived by an immediate comparing them: the difference of figure makes their parts uncapable of an exact immediate application; and therefore there is need of some intervening qualities to measure them by, which is demonstration, or rational knowledge.

4. *Fourthly, nor demonstrative knowledge. Fourthly,* it follows also, from what is above observed, that our *rational knowledge,* cannot reach to the whole extent of our *ideas.* Because between two different *ideas* we would examine, we cannot always find such *mediums,* as we can con-

nect one to another with an intuitive knowledge, in all the parts of the deduction; and wherever that fails, we come short of knowledge and demonstration.

5. *Fifthly, sensitive knowledge narrower than either. Fifthly, sensitive knowledge* reaching no farther than the existence of things actually present to our senses, is yet much narrower than either of the former.

6. *Sixthly, our knowledge therefore narrower than our* ideas. From all which it is evident, that *the extent of our knowledge* comes not only short of the reality of things, but even of the extent of our own *ideas.* Though our knowledge be limited to our *ideas,* and cannot exceed them either in extent, or perfection; and though these be very narrow bounds, in respect of the extent of all being, and far short of what we may justly imagine to be in some even created understandings, not tied down to the dull and narrow information, is to be received from some few, and not very acute ways of perception, such as are our senses; yet it would be well with us, if our knowledge were but as large as our *ideas,* and there were not many doubts and inquiries concerning the *ideas* we have, whereof we are not, nor I believe ever shall be in this world, resolved. Nevertheless, I do not question, but that human knowledge, under the present circumstances of our beings and constitutions may be carried much farther, than it hitherto has been, if men would sincerely, and with freedom of mind, employ all that industry and labor of thought, in improving the means of discovering truth, which they do for the coloring or support of falsehood, to maintain a system, interest, or party, they are once engaged in. But yet after all, I think I may, without injury to human perfection, be confident, that our knowledge would never reach to all we might desire to know concerning those *ideas* we have; nor be able to surmount all the difficulties, and resolve all the questions that might arise concerning any of them. We have the *ideas* of a *square,* a *circle,* and *equality;* and yet, perhaps, shall never be able to find a circle equal to a square, and certainly know that it is so. We have the *ideas* of *matter* an *thinking,* but possibly shall never be able to know, whether any mere material being thinks, or no; it being impossible for us, by the contemplation of our own *ideas,* without revelation, to discover, whether omnipotency has not given to some systems of matter fitly disposed, a power to perceive and think, or else joined and fixed to matter so disposed, a thinking immaterial substance: it being, in respect of our notions, not much more remote from our comprehension to conceive, that GOD can, if he pleases, superadd to matter a faculty of thinking, than that he should superadd to it another substance, with a faculty of thinking; since we know not wherein thinking consists, nor to what sort of substances the almighty has been pleased to give that power, which cannot be in any created being, but merely by the good pleasure and bounty of the creator. For I see no contradiction in it, that the first eternal thinking being or omnipotent spirit should, if he pleased, give to certain systems of created senseless matter, put together as he thinks fit, some degrees of sense, perception, and thought: though, as I think, I have proved, *Bk. IV.* c. xth it is no less than a contradiction to suppose matter (which is evidently in its own nature void of sense and thought) should be that eternal first thinking being. What certainty of knowledge can anyone have that some perceptions, such as, *v.g.* pleasure and pain, should not be in some bodies themselves, after a certain manner modified and moved, as well as that they should be in an immaterial substance, upon the motion of the parts of body: body as far as we can conceive being able only to strike and affect body; and motion, according to the utmost reach of our *ideas,* being able to produce nothing but motion, so that when we allow it to produce pleasure or pain, or the *idea* of a color, or sound, we are fain to quit our reason, go beyond our *ideas,* and attribute it wholly to the good pleasure of our maker. For since we must allow he has annexed effects to motion, which we can no way conceive motion able to produce, what reason have we to conclude, that he could not order them as well to be produced in a subject we cannot conceive capable of them, as well as in a subject we cannot conceive the motion of matter can any way operate upon? I say not this, that I would any way lessen the belief of the soul's immateriality: I am not here speaking of probability, but knowledge; and I think not only, that it becomes the modesty of philosophy, not to pronounce magisterially, where we want that evidence that can produce knowledge; but also, that it is of use to us to discern how far our knowledge does reach; for the state we are at present in, not being that of vision, we must, in many things, content ourselves with faith and probability: and in the present question, about the immateriality of the soul, if our

faculties cannot arrive at demonstrative certainty, we need not think it strange. All the great ends of morality and religion, are well enough secured, without philosophical proofs of the soul's immateriality; since it is evident, that he who made us at the beginning to subsist here, sensible intelligent beings, and for several years continued us in such a state, can and will restore us to the like state of sensibility in another world, and make us capable there to receive the retribution he has designed to men, according to their doings in this life. And therefore 'tis not of such mighty necessity to determine one way or t'other, as some over-zealous for, or against the immateriality of the soul, have been forward to make the world believe. Who, either on the one side, indulging too much to their thoughts immersed altogether in matter, can allow no existence to what is not material: or, who on the other side, finding not *cogitation* within the natural powers of matter, examined over and over again, by the utmost intention of mind, have the confidence to conclude, that omnipotency itself, cannot give perception and thought to a substance which has the modification of solidity. He that considers how hardly sensation is, in our thoughts, reconcilable to extended matter; or existence to anything that has no extension at all, will confess, that he is very far from certainly knowing what his soul is. 'Tis a point, which seems to me, to be put out of the reach of our knowledge: and he who will give himself leave to consider freely, and look into the dark and intricate part of each hypothesis, will scarce find his reason able to determine him fixedly for, or against the soul's materiality. Since on which side soever he views it, either as an unextended substance, or as a thinking extended matter; the difficulty to conceive either, will, whilst either alone is in his thoughts, still drive him to the contrary side. An unfair way which some men take with themselves: who, because of the inconceivableness of something they find in one, throw themselves violently into the contrary hypothesis, though altogether as unintelligible to an unbiased understanding. This serves, not only to show the weakness and the scantiness of our knowledge, but the insignificant triumph of such sort of arguments, which, drawn from our own views, may satisfy us that we can find no certainty on one side of the question; but do not at all thereby help us to truth, by running into the opposite opinion, which, on examination, will be found clogged with equal difficulties. For

what safety, what advantage to anyone is it, for the avoiding the seeming absurdities, and, to him, unsurmountable rubs he meets with in one opinion, to take refuge in the contrary, which is built on something altogether as inexplicable, and as far remote from his comprehension? 'Tis past controversy, that we have in us something that thinks, our very doubts about what it is, confirm the certainty of its being, though we must content ourselves in the ignorance of what *kind* of being it is: and 'tis in vain to go about to be skeptical in this, as it is unreasonable in most other cases to be positive against the being of anything, because we cannot comprehend its nature. For I would fain know what substance exists that has not something in it, which manifestly baffles our understandings. Other spirits, who see and know the nature and inward constitution of things, how much must they exceed us in knowledge? To which if we add larger comprehension, which enables them at one glance to see the connection and agreement of very many *ideas,* and readily supplies to them the intermediate proofs, which we by single and slow steps, and long poring in the dark, hardly at last find out, and are often ready to forget one before we have hunted out another, we may guess at some part of the happiness of superior ranks of spirits, who have a quicker and more penetrating sight, as well as a larger field of knowledge. But to return to the argument in hand, our *knowledge,* I say, is not only limited to the paucity and imperfections of the *ideas* we have, and which we employ it about, but even comes short of that too: but how far it reaches let us now inquire.

7. *How far our knowledge reaches.* The affirmations or negations we make concerning the *ideas* we have, may, as I have before intimated in general, be reduced to these four sorts, *viz.* identity, coexistence, relation, and real existence. I shall examine how far our knowledge extends in each of these:

8. *First, our knowledge of identity and diversity, as far as our* ideas. *First, as to identity and diversity,* in this way of agreement, or disagreement of our *ideas, our intuitive knowledge is as far extended as our ideas* themselves: and there can be no *idea* in the mind, which it does not presently, by an intuitive knowledge, perceive to be what it is, and to be different from any other.

9. *Secondly, of coexistence a very little way. Secondly, as to the* second sort, which is *the agreement, or disagreement* of our

ideas in coexistence, in this our knowledge is very short, though in this consists the greatest and most material part of our knowledge concerning substances. For our *ideas* of the species of substances, being, as I have showed, nothing but certain collections of simple *ideas* united in one subject, and so coexisting together: *v.g.* our *idea* of *flame* is a body hot, luminous, and moving upward, of *gold,* a body heavy to a certain degree, yellow, malleable, and fusible. These or some such complex *ideas* as these in men's minds, do these two names of the different substances, *flame* and *gold,* stand for. When we would know anything farther concerning these, or any other sort of substances, what do we inquire but what other qualities, or powers, these substances have, or have not? which is nothing else but to know, what other simple *ideas* do, or do not coexist with those that make up that complex *idea.*

10. *Because the connection between most simple* ideas *is unknown.* This, how weighty and considerable a part soever of human science, is yet very narrow, and scarce any at all. The reason whereof is, that the simple *ideas* whereof our complex *ideas* of substances are made up, are, for the most part such, as carry with them, in their own nature, no visible necessary connection, or inconsistency with any other simple *ideas,* whose coexistence with them we would inform ourselves about.

11. *Especially of secondary qualities.* The *ideas,* that our complex ones of substances are made up of, and about which our knowledge, concerning substances, is most employed, are those of their *secondary qualities;* which depending all (as has been shown) upon the primary qualities of their minute and insensible parts; or if not upon them, upon something yet more remote from our comprehension, 'tis impossible we should know, which have a necessary union or inconsistency one with another: for not knowing the root they spring from, not knowing what size, figure, and texture of parts they are, on which depend and from which result those qualities which make our complex *idea* of gold, 'tis impossible we should know what other qualities result from, our are incompatible with the same constitution of the insensible parts of *gold;* and so consequently must always coexist with that complex *idea* we have of it, or else are *inconsistent* with it.

12. *Because all connection between any secondary and primary qualities is undiscoverable.* Besides this ignorance of the primary qualities of the insensible parts of bodies, on which depend all their secondary qualities, there is yet another and more incurable part of ignorance, which sets us more remote from a certain knowledge of the *coexistence,* or incoexistence (if I may so say) of different *ideas* in the same subject; and that is, that there is no discoverable connection between any *secondary quality, and those primary qualities* that it depends on.

13. That the size, figure and motion of one body should cause a change in the size, figure and motion of another body, is not beyond our conception; the separation of the parts of one body, upon the intrusion of another; and the change from rest to motion, upon impulse; these, and the like, seem to have some *connection* one with another. And if we knew these primary qualities of bodies, we might have reason to hope, we might be able to know a great deal more of these operations of them one upon another: but our minds not being able to discover any *connection* betwixt these primary qualities of bodies, and the sensations that are produced in us by them, we can never be able to establish certain and undoubted rules, of the consequence or *coexistence* of any secondary qualities, though we could discover the size, figure, or motion of those invisible parts, which immediately produce them. We are so far from knowing what figure, size, or motion of parts produce a yellow color, a sweet taste, or a sharp sounds, that we can by no means conceive how any *size, figure, or motion* of any particles, can possibly produce in us the *idea* of any *color, taste,* or *sound* whatsoever; there is no conceivable *connection* betwixt the one and the other.

14. In vain therefore shall we endeavor to discover by our *ideas,* (the only true way of certain and universal knowledge) what other *ideas* are to be found constantly joined with that of our complex *idea* of any substance: since we neither know the real constitution of the minute parts, on which their qualities do depend; nor did we know them, could we discover any necessary *connection* between them, and any of the *secondary qualities:* which is necessary to be done, before we can certainly know their *necessary coexistence.* So that let our complex *idea* of any species of substances, be what it will, we can hardly, from the simple *ideas* contained in it, certainly determine the *necessary coexistence* of any other quality whatsoever. Our knowledge in all these

inquires, reaches very little farther than our experience. Indeed, some few of the primary qualities have a necessary dependence, and visible connection one with another, as figure necessarily supposes extension, receiving or communicating motion by impulse, supposes solidity. But though these, and perhaps some others of our *ideas* have: yet there are so *few* of them, that have a *visible connection* one with another, that we can by intuition or demonstration, discover the coexistence of very few of the qualities are to be found united in substances: and we are left only to the assistance of our senses, to make known to us, what qualities they contain. For of all the qualities that are *coexistent* in any subject, without this dependence and evident connection of their *ideas* one with another, we cannot know certainly any two to *coexist* any farther, than experience, by our sense, informs us. Thus though we see the yellow color, and upon trial find the weight, malleableness, fusibility, and fixedness, that are united in a piece of gold; yet because no one of these *ideas* has any evident *dependence,* or necessary connection with the other, we cannot certainly know, that where any four of these are, the fifth will be there also, how highly probably soever it may be: because the highest probability, amounts not to certainty; without which, there can be no true knowledge. For this *coexistence* can be no farther known, that it is perceived; and it cannot be perceived but either in particular subjects, by the observation of our senses, or in general, by the necessary *connection* of the *ideas* themselves.

15. *Of repugnancy to coexist larger. As to incompatibility or repugnancy to coexistence,* we may know, that any subject may have of each sort of primary qualities, but one particular at once; *v.g.* each particular extension, figure, number of parts, motion, excludes all other of each kind. The like also is certain of all sensible *ideas* peculiar to each sense; for whatever of each kind is present in any subject, excludes all other of that sort; *v.g.* no one subject can have two smells, or two colors, at the same time. . . .

16. *Of the coexistence of powers a very little way.* But *as to the powers of substances* to change the sensible qualities of other bodies, which make a great part of our inquiries about them, and is no inconsiderable branch of our knowledge; I doubt, as to these, whether *our knowledge reaches* much farther than our experience; or whether

we can come to the discovery of most of these powers, and be certain that they are in any subject by the connection with any of those *ideas,* which to us make its essence. Because the active and passive powers of bodies, and their ways of operating, consisting in a texture and motion of parts, which we cannot by any means come to discover: 'tis but in very few cases, we can be able to perceive their dependence on, or repugnance to any of those *ideas,* which make our complex one of that sort of things. I have here instanced in the corpuscularian hypothesis, as that which is through to go farthest in an intelligible explication of the qualities of bodies; and I fear the weakness of human understanding is scarce able to substitute another, which will afford us a fuller and clearer discovery of the necessary connection, and *coexistence,* of the powers, which are to be observed united in several sorts of them. This at least is certain, that whichever hypothesis be clearest and truest, (for of that it is not my business to determine) our knowledge concerning corporal substances, will be very little advanced by any of them, till we are made to see, what qualities and powers of bodies have a *necessary connection or repugnancy* one with another; which in the present state of philosophy, I think, we know but to a very small degree: and, I doubt, whether with those faculties we have, we shall ever be able to carry our general knowledge (I say no particular experience) in this part must farther. Experience is that, which in this part we must depend on. And it were to be wished, that it were more improved. . . .

17. *Of spirits yet narrower.* If we are at a loss in respect of the powers, and operations of bodies, I think it is easy to conclude, *we are much more in the dark in reference to spirits;* whereof we naturally have no *ideas,* but what we draw from that of our own, by reflecting on the operations of our own souls within us, as far as they can come within our observation. But how inconsiderable a rank the spirits that inhabit our bodies hold amongst those various, and possibly innumerable, kinds of nobler beings; and how far short they come of the endowments and perfections of cherubims, and seraphims, and infinite sorts of spirits above us, is what by a transient hint, in another place, I have offered to my reader's consideration.

18. *Thirdly, of other relations it is not easy to say how far. Morality capable of demonstration.* As to the third sort of

our knowledge, *viz.* the *agreement or disagreement of any of our* ideas *in any other relation:* this, as it is the largest field of our knowledge, so it is hard to determine how far it may extend: because the advances that are made in this part of knowledge, depending on our sagacity, in finding intermediate *ideas,* that may show the *relations* and *habitudes* of *ideas,* whose coexistence is not considered, 'tis a hard matter to tell, when we are at an end of such discoveries; and when reason has all the helps it is capable of, for the finding of proofs, or examining the agreement or disagreement of remote *ideas.* They that are ignorant of *algebra* cannot imagine the wonders in this kind are to be done by it: and what farther improvements and helps, advantageous to other parts of knowledge, the sagacious mind of man may yet find out, 'tis not easy to determine. This at least I believe, that the *ideas* of quantity are not those alone that are capable of demonstration and knowledge; and that other, and perhaps more useful parts of contemplation, would afford us certainty, if vices, passions, and domineering interest did not oppose or menace such endeavors.

The *idea* of a supreme being, infinite in power, goodness, and wisdom, whose workmanship we are, and on whom we depend; and the *idea* of ourselves, as understanding, rational creatures, being such as are clear in us, would, I suppose, if duly considered, and pursued, afford such foundations of our duty and rules of action, as might place *morality amongst the sciences capable of demonstration:* wherein I doubt not, but from self-evident propositions, by necessary consequences, as incontestable as those in mathematics, the measures of right and wrong might be made out, to anyone that will apply himself with the same indifferency and attention to the one, as he does to the other of these sciences. The *relation* of other *modes* may certainly be perceived, as well as those of number and extension: and I cannot see, why they should not also be capable of demonstration, if due methods were thought on to examine, or pursue their agreement or disagreement. *Where there is no property, there is no injustice,* is a proposition as certain as any demonstration in *Euclid:* for the *idea* of *property,* being a right to any thing; and the *idea* to which the name *injustice* is given, being the invasion or violation of that right; it is evident, that these *ideas* being thus established, and these names annexed to them, I can as certainly know this proposition to be true, as that a triangle has

three angles equal to two right ones. Again, *no government allows absolute liberty:* the *idea* of government being the establishment of society upon certain rules or laws, which require conformity to them; and the *idea* of absolute liberty being for anyone to do whatever he pleases; I am as capable of being certain of the truth of this proposition, as of any in mathematics.

19. *Two things have made moral* ideas *though uncapable of demonstration. Their complexedness, and want of sensible representations.* That which in this respect has given the advantage to the *ideas* of quantity, and made them thought more capable of certainty and demonstration, is,

First, that they can be set down, and represented by sensible marks, which have a greater and nearer correspondence with them than any words or sounds whatsoever. Diagrams drawn of paper are copies of the *ideas* in the mind, and not liable to the uncertainty that words carry in their signification. An angle, circle, or square, drawn in lines, lies open to the view, and cannot be mistaken: it remains unchangeable, and may at leisure be considered, and examined, and the demonstration be revised, and all the parts of it may be gone over more than once, without any danger of the least change in the *ideas.* This cannot be thus done in *moral ideas,* we have no sensible marks that resemble them, whereby we can set them down; we have nothing but words to express them by; which though, when written, they remain the same, yet the *ideas* they stand for, may change in the same man; and 'tis very seldom, that they are not different in different persons.

Secondly, another thing that makes the greater difficulty in *ethics,* is, that *moral ideas* are commonly more complex that those of the figures ordinarily considered in mathematics. From whence these two inconveniencies follow. *First,* that their names are of more uncertain signification, the precise collection of simple *ideas* they stand for not being so easily agreed on, and so the sign, that is used for them in communication always, and in thinking often, does not steadily carry with it the same *idea.* . . . *Secondly,* from the complexedness of these moral *ideas* there follows another inconvenience, (*viz.*) that the mind cannot easily retain those precise combinations, so exactly and perfectly, as is necessary in the examination of the habitudes and correspondencies, agreements or disagreements, of several of them one with another; especially where it is to be judged of by long deductions, and the intervention of several other complex *ideas,* to show the agreement or disagreement of two remote ones.

• • • • •

20. *Remedies of those difficulties.* One part of *these disadvantages,* in moral *ideas,* which has made them be thought not capable of demonstration, may in a good measure be *remedied* by definitions, setting down that collection of simple *ideas,* which every term shall stand for; and then using the terms steadily and constantly for that precise collection. . . .

21. *Fourthly, of real existence we have an intuitive knowledge of our own, demonstrative of God's, sensible of some few other things.* As to the fourth sort of our knowledge, *viz. of the real, actual, existence* of things, we have an intuitive knowledge of our own *existence;* and a demonstrative knowledge of the *existence* of a God; of the *existence* of anything else, we have no other but a sensitive knowledge, which extends not beyond the objects present to our senses.

22. *Our ignorance great.* Our knowledge being so narrow, as I have showed, it will, perhaps, give us some light into the present state of our minds, if we look a little into the dark side, and take a view of *our ignorance:* which being infinitely larger than our knowledge, may sever much to the quieting of disputes, and improvement of useful knowledge; if discovering how far we have clear and distinct *ideas,* we confine our thoughts within the contemplation of those things, that are within the reach of our understandings, and launch not out into that abyss of darkness (where we have not eyes to see, nor faculties to perceive anything) out of a presumption, that nothing is beyond our comprehension. But to be satisfied of the folly of such a conceit, we need not go far. He that knows anything, knows this in the first place, that he need not seek long for instances of his ignorance. The meanest, and most obvious things that come in our way, have dark sides, that the quickest sight cannot penetrate into. The clearest, and most enlarged understandings of thinking men find themselves puzzled, and at a loss, in every particle of matter. We shall the less wonder to find it so, when we consider the *causes of our ignorance:* which, from what has been said, I suppose, will be found to be these three:

First, want of *ideas.*

Secondly, want of a discoverable connection between the *ideas* we have.

Thirdly, want of tracing, and examining our *ideas.*

23. *First, one cause of it want of* ideas, *wither such as we have no conception of, or such as particularly we have not. First,* there are some things, and those not a few, that we are ignorant of for *want of ideas.*

First, all the simple *ideas* we have are confined (as I have shown) to the observation of our senses, and the operations of our own minds, that we are conscious of in ourselves. But how much these few and narrow inlets are disproportionate to the vast whole extent of all beings, will not be hard to persuade those, who are not so foolish, as to think their span the measure of all things. What other simple *ideas* 'tis possible the creatures in other parts of the universe may have, but the assistance of senses and faculties more or perfecter, than we have, or different from ours, 'tis not for us to determine. But to say, or think there are no such, because we conceive nothing of them, is no better an argument, that if a blind man should be positive in it, that there was no such thing as sight and colors, because he had no manner of *idea,* of any such thing, nor could by any means frame to himself any notions about seeing. . . .

24. *Because of their remoteness. Secondly,* another great cause of ignorance, is the *want of* ideas *we are capable of.* As the want of *ideas,* which our faculties are not able to give us, shuts us wholly from those views of things, which 'tis reasonable to think other beings, perfecter than we, have, of which we know nothing; so the want of *ideas,* I now speak of, keeps us in ignorance of things, we conceive capable of being known to us. *Bulk, figure,* and *motion,* we have *ideas* of. But though we are not without *ideas* of these primary qualities of bodies in general, yet not knowing what is the particular *bulk, figure,* and *motion,* of the greatest part of the bodies of the universe, we are ignorant of the several powers, efficacies, and ways of operation, whereby the effects, which we daily see, are produced. These are hid from us in some things, by being *too remote; and* in others, by being too *minute.* . . .

25. *Because of their minuteness.* If a great, nay far the greatest part of the several ranks of *bodies* in the uni-

verse, scape our notice by their remoteness, there are others that are no less concealed from us by their *minuteness*. These insensible corpuscles, being the active parts of matter, and the great instruments of nature, on which depend not only all their secondary qualities, but also most of their natural operations, our want of precise distinct *ideas* of their primary qualities, keeps us in an uncurable ignorance of what we desire to know about them. I doubt not but if we could discover the figure, size, texture, and motion of the minute constituent parts of any two bodies, we should know without trial several of their operations one upon another, as we do now the properties of a square, or a triangle. Did we know the mechanical affections of the particles of *rhubarb, hemlock, opium,* and a *man,* as a watchmaker does those of a watch, whereby it performs its operations, and of a files which by rubbing on them will alter the figure of any of the wheels, we should be able to tell beforehand that *rhubarb* will purge, *hemlock* kill, and *opium* make a man sleep; as well as a watchmaker can, that a little piece of paper laid on the balance, will keep the watch from going, till it be removed; or that some small part of it, being rubbed by a file, the machine would quite lose its motion, and the watch go no more. The dissolving of silver in *aqua fortis,* and gold in *aqua regia,* and not *vice versa,* would be then, perhaps, no more difficult to know, than it is to a smith to understand, why the turning of one key will open a lock, and not the turning of another. But whilst we are destitute of senses acute enough, to discover the minute particles of bodies, and to give us *ideas* of their mechanical affections, we must be content to be ignorant of their properties and ways of operation; nor can we be assured about them any farther, than some few trials we make, are able to reach. But whether they will succeed again another time, we cannot be certain. This hinders our certain knowledge of universal truths concerning natural bodies: and our reason carries us herein very little beyond particular matter of fact.

26. *Hence no science of bodies.* And therefore I am apt to doubt, how far soever human industry may advance useful and *experimental* philosophy *in physical things, scientifical* will still be out of our reach: because we want perfect and adequate *ideas* of those very bodies, which are nearest to us, and most under our command. Those which we have ranked into classes under names, and we

think ourselves best acquainted with, we have but very imperfect, and incomplete *ideas* of. Distinct *ideas* of the several sorts of bodies, that fall under the examination of our senses, perhaps, we may have: but adequate *ideas,* I suspect, we have not of any one amongst them. And though the former of these will serve us for common use and discourse: yet whilst we want the latter, we are not capable of *scientifical knowledge;* nor shall ever be able to discover general instructive, unquestionable truths concerning them. *Certainty* and *demonstration* are things we must not, in these matters, pretend to. . . .

· · · · ·

28. *Secondly, want of a discoverable connection between* ideas *we have. Secondly,* what a small part of the substantial beings, that are in the universe, the want of *ideas* leaves open to our knowledge, we have seen. In the next place, another cause of ignorance, of no less moment, is a want of a *discoverable connection* between those *ideas* we have. For wherever we want that, we are utterly uncapable of universal and certain knowledge; and are, as in the former case, left only to observation and experiment: which how narrow and confined it is, how far from general knowledge, we need not be told. I shall give some few instances of this cause of our ignorance and so leave it. 'Tis evident that the bulk, figure, and motion of several bodies about us, produce in us several sensations, as of colors, sounds, tastes, or smells, pleasure and pain, &c. These mechanical affections of bodies, having no affinity at all with those *ideas,* they produce in us, (there being no conceivable connection between any impulse of any sort of body, and any perception of a color, or smell, which we find in our minds) we can have no distinct knowledge of such operations beyond our experience; and can reason no otherwise about them, than as effects produced by the appointment of an infinitely wise agent, which perfectly surpass our comprehensions. As the *ideas* of sensible secondary qualities, which we have in our minds, can, by us, be no way deduced from bodily causes, nor any correspondence or connection be found between them and those primary qualities which (experience shows us) produce them in us; so on the other side, the operation of our minds upon our bodies is as unconceivable. How any thought should produce a motion in body is as remote

from the nature of our *ideas,* as how any body should produce any thought in the mind. That it is so, if experience did not convince us, the consideration of the things themselves would never be able, in the least, to discover to us. These, and the like, though they have a constant and regular connection, in the ordinary course of things: yet that connection being not discoverable in the *ideas* themselves, which appearing to have no necessary dependence one on another, we can attribute their connection to nothing else, but the arbitrary determination of that all-wise agent, who has made them to be, and to operate as they do, in a way wholly above our weak understandings to conceive.

29. *Instances.* In some of our *ideas* there are certain relations, habitudes, and connections, so visibly included in the nature of the *ideas* themselves, that we cannot conceive them separable from them, by any power whatsoever. And in these only, we are capable of certain and universal knowledge. Thus the *idea* of a right-lined triangle necessarily carries with it an equality of its angles to two right ones. Nor can we conceive this relation, this connection of these two *ideas,* to be possibly mutable, or to depend on any arbitrary power, which of choice made it thus, or could make it otherwise. But the coherence and continuity of the parts of matter; the production of sensation in us of colors and sounds, *&c.* by impulse and motion; nay, the original rules and communication of motion being such, wherein we can discover no natural connection with any *ideas* we have, we cannot but ascribe them to the arbitrary will and good pleasure of the wise architect. I need not, I think, here mention the resurrection of the dead, the future state of this globe of earth, and such other things, which are by everyone acknowledge to depend wholly on the determination of a free agent. The things that, as far as our observation reaches, we constantly find to proceed regularly, we may conclude, do act by a law set them; but yet by a law, that we know not; whereby, thought causes work steadily, and effects constantly flow from them, yet their *connections* and *dependencies* being not discoverable in our *ideas,* we can have by an experimental knowledge of them. . . . Several effects come every day within the notice of our senses, of which we have so far *sensitive knowledge:* but the causes, manner, and certainty of their production, for the two foregoing reasons, we must be content to be ignorant of. In these we can go no farther than particular

experience informs us of matter of fact, and by analogy to guess what effects the like bodies are, upon other trials, like to produce. But as to a perfect *science* of natural bodies, (not to mention spiritual beings) we are, I think, so far some being capable of any such thing, that I conclude it lost labor to seek after it.

30. *Thirdly, want of tracing our* ideas. *Thirdly,* where we have adequate *ideas,* and where there is a certain and discoverable connection between them, yet we are often ignorant, for want of *tracing* those *ideas* which we have, or may have; and for want of finding out those intermediate *ideas,* which may show us, what habitude of agreement or disagreement they have one with another. And this many are ignorant of mathematical truths, not out of any imperfection of their faculties, or uncertainty in the things themselves; but for want of application in acquiring, examining, and by due ways comparing those *ideas.* That which has most contributed to hinder the due *tracing* of our *ideas,* and finding out their relations, and agreements or disagreements one with another, has been, I suppose, the ill use of *words.* It is impossible that men should ever truly seek, or certainly discover the agreement or disagreement of *ideas* themselves, whilst their thoughts flutter about, or stick only in sounds of doubtful and uncertain significations. . . .

31. *Extent in respect of universality.* Hitherto we have examined the *extent* of our knowledge, in respect of the several sorts of beings that are. There is another *extent of it, in respect of universality,* which will also deserve to be considered: and in this regard, our knowledge follows the nature of our *ideas.* If the *ideas* are abstract, whose agreement or disagreement we perceive, our knowledge is universal. For what is known of such general *ideas,* will be true of every particular thing, in whom that essence, *i.e.,* that abstract *idea* it to be found: and what is once known of such *ideas,* will be perpetually, and forever true. So that as to all general knowledge, we must search and find it only in our minds, and 'tis only the examining of our own *ideas,* that furnishes us with that. Truths belonging to essences of things, (that is, to abstract *ideas*) are eternal, and are to be found out by the contemplation only of those essences: as the existence of things is to be known only from experience. But having more to say of this in the chapters, where I shall speak of general and real knowledge, this may here suffice, as to the universality of our knowledge in general.

George Berkeley

Three Dialogues between Hylas and Philonous

Preface

If the principles, which I here endeavor to propagate, are admitted for true; the consequences which, I think, evidently flow from thence, are, that *atheism* and *scepticism* will be utterly destroyed, many intricate points made plain, great difficulties solved, several useless parts of science retrenched, speculation referred to practice, and men reduced from paradoxes to common sense.

And although it may, perhaps, seem an uneasy reflection to some, that when they have taken a circuit through so many refined and unvulgar notions, they should at last come to think like other men: yet, methinks, this return to the simple dictates of nature, after having wandered through the wild mazes of philosophy, is not unpleasant. It is like coming home from a long voyage: a man reflects with pleasure on the many difficulties and perplexities he has passed through, sets his heart at ease, and enjoys himself with more satisfaction for the future.

As it was my intention to convince *sceptics* and *infidels* by reason, so it has been my endeavor strictly to observe the most rigid laws of reasoning. And, to an impartial reader, I hope, it will be manifest, that the sublime notion of a God, and the comfortable expectation of immortality, do naturally arise from a close and methodical application of thought: whatever may be the result of that loose, rambling way, not altogether improperly termed *free-thinking,* by certain libertines in thought, who can no more endure the restraints of *logic,* than those of *religion,* or *government.*

It will, perhaps, be objected to my design, that so far as it tends to ease the mind of difficult and useless inquiries, it can affect only a few speculative persons; but, if by their speculations rightly placed, the study of

From George Berkeley, *Three Dialogues between Hylas and Philonous,* edited by Robert Merrihew Adams (Indianapolis: Hackett Publishing Company, 1979). Reprinted by permission of the publisher.

morality and the law of nature were brought more into fashion among men of parts and genius, the discouragements that draw to *scepticism* removed, the measures of right and wrong accurately defined, and the principles of natural religion reduced into regular systems, as artfully disposed and clearly connected as those of some other sciences: there are grounds to think, these effects would not only have a gradual influence in repairing the too much defaced sense of virtue in the world; but also, by showing, that such parts of revelation, as lie within the reach of human inquiry, are most agreeable to right reason, would dispose all prudent, unprejudiced persons, to a modest and wary treatment of those sacred mysteries, which are above the comprehension of our faculties. [. . .]

Three Dialogues Between Hylas And Philonous In Opposition To Sceptics And Atheists

The First Dialogue

Philonous. Good morrow, Hylas: I did not expect to find you abroad so early.

Hylas. It is indeed something unusual; but my thoughts were so taken up with a subject I was discoursing of last night, that finding I could not sleep, I resolved to rise and take a turn in the garden.

Phil. It happened well, to let you see what innocent and agreeable pleasures you lose every morning. Can there be a pleasanter time of the day, or a more delightful season of the year? That purple sky, these wild but sweet notes of birds, the fragrant bloom upon the trees and flowers, the gentle influence of the rising sun, these and a thousand nameless beauties of nature inspire the soul with secret transports; its faculties too being at this time fresh and lively, are fit for those meditations, which the solitude of a garden and tranquility of the

morning naturally dispose us to. But I am afraid I interrupt your thoughts: for you seemed very intent on
something.

Hyl. It is true, I was, and shall be obliged to you if
you will permit me to go on in the same vein; not that
I would by any means deprive myself of your company,
for my thoughts always flow more easily in conversation with a friend, than when I am alone: but my request
is, that you would suffer me to impart my reflections to
you.

Phil. With all my heart, it is what I should have re-
quested myself, if you had not prevented me.

Hyl. I was considering the odd fate of those men
who have in all ages, through an affectation of being distinguished from the vulgar, or some unaccountable turn
of thought, pretended either to believe nothing at all,
or to believe the most extravagant things in the world.
This however might be borne, if their paradoxes and
scepticism did not draw after them some consequences
of general disadvantage to mankind. But the mischief
lies here; that when men of less leisure see them who
are supposed to have spent their whole time in the pursuits of knowledge, professing an entire ignorance of all
things, or advancing such notions as are repugnant to
plain and commonly received principles, they will be
tempted to entertain suspicions concerning the most
important truths, which they had hitherto held sacred
and unquestionable.

Phil. I entirely agree with you, as to the ill tendency
of the affected doubts of some philosophers, and fantastical conceits of others. I am even so far gone of late
in this way of thinking, that I have quitted several of the
sublime notions I had got in their schools for vulgar
opinions. And I give it you on my word, since this revolt from metaphysical notions to the plain dictates of
nature and common sense, I find my understanding
strangely enlightened, so that I can now easily comprehend a great many things which before were all mystery and riddle.

Hyl. I am glad to find there was nothing in the accounts I heard of you.

Phil. Pray, what were those?

Hyl. You were represented in last night's conversation, as one who maintained the most extravagant opinion that ever entered into the mind of man, to wit, that
there is no such thing as *material substance* in the world.

Phil. That there is no such thing as what philosophers
call *material substance,* I am seriously persuaded: but if I
were made to see anything absurd or sceptical in this, I
should then have the same reason to renounce this, that
I imagine I have now to reject the contrary opinion.

Hyl. What! Can anything be more fantastical, more
repugnant to common sense, or a more manifest piece
of scepticism, than to believe there is no such thing as
matter?

Phil. Softly, good Hylas. What if it should prove, that
you, who hold there is, are by virtue of that opinion a
greater *sceptic,* and maintain more paradoxes and repug-
nancies to common sense, than I who believe no such
thing?

Hyl. You may as soon persuade me, the part is greater
than the whole, as that, in order to avoid absurdity and
scepticism, I should ever be obliged to give up my opinion in this point.

Phil. Well, then, are you content to admit that opinion for true, which upon examination shall appear most
agreeable to common sense, and remote from scepticism?

Hyl. With all my heart. Since you are for raising disputes about the plainest things in nature, I am content
for once to hear what you have to say.

Phil. Pray, Hylas, what do you mean by a *sceptic?*

Hyl. I mean what all men mean, one that doubts of
everything.

Phil. He then who entertains no doubt concerning
some particular point, with regard to that point cannot
be thought a *sceptic.*

Hyl. I agree with you.

Phil. Whether does doubting consist in embracing
the affirmative or negative side of a question?

Hyl. In neither; for whoever understands English,
cannot but know that *doubting* signifies a suspense between both.

Phil. He then that denies any point, can no more be
said to doubt of it, than he who affirms it with the same
degree of assurance.

Hyl. True.

Phil. And consequently, for such his denial is no more
to be esteemed a *sceptic* than the other.

Hyl. I acknowledge it.

Phil. How comes it then, Hylas, that you pronounce
me a *sceptic,* because I deny what you affirm, to wit, the

existence of matter? Since, for aught you can tell, I am as peremptory in my denial, as you in your affirmation.

Hyl. Hold, Philonous, I have been a little out in my definition; but every false step a man makes in discourse is not to be insisted on. I said indeed, that a *sceptic* was one who doubted of everything; but I should have added, or who denies the reality and truth of things.

Phil. What things? Do you mean the principles and theorems of sciences? But these you know are universal intellectual notions, and consequently independent of matter; the denial therefore of this doth not imply the denying them.

Hyl. I grant it. But are there no other things? What think you of distrusting the senses, of denying the real existence of sensible things, or pretending to know nothing of them. Is not this sufficient to denominate a man a *sceptic?*

Phil. Shall we therefore examine which of us it is that denies the reality of sensible things, or professes the greatest ignorance of them; since, if I take you rightly, he is to be esteemed the greatest *sceptic?*

Hyl. That is what I desire.

Phil. What mean you by sensible things?

Hyl. Those things which are perceived by the senses. Can you imagine that I mean anything else?

Phil. Pardon me, Hylas, if I am desirous clearly to apprehend your notions, since this may much shorten our inquiry. Suffer me then to ask you this farther question. Are those things only perceived by the senses which are perceived immediately? Or, may those things properly be said to be *sensible,* which are perceived mediately, or not without the intervention of others?

Hyl. I do not sufficiently understand you.

Phil. In reading a book, what I immediately perceive are the letters, but mediately, or by means of these, are suggested to my mind the notions of God, virtue, truth, &c. Now, that the letters are truly sensible things, or perceived by sense, there is no doubt: but I would know whether you take the things suggested by them to be so too.

Hyl. No certainly, it were absurd to think God or *virtue* sensible things, though they may be signified and suggested to the mind by sensible marks, with which they have an arbitrary connection.

Phil. It seems then, that by *sensible things* you mean those only which can be perceived immediately by sense.

Hyl. Right.

Phil. Does it not follow from this, that though I see one part of the sky red, and another blue, and that my reason doth thence evidently conclude there must be some cause of that diversity of colors, yet that cause cannot be said to be a sensible thing, or perceived by the sense of seeing?

Hyl. It does.

Phil. In like manner, though I hear variety of sounds yet I cannot be said to hear the causes of those sounds.

Hyl. You cannot.

Phil. And when by my touch I perceive a thing to be hot and heavy, I cannot say with any truth or propriety, that I feel the cause of its heat or weight.

Hyl. To prevent any more questions of this kind, I tell you once for all, that by *sensible things* I mean those only which are perceived by sense, and that in truth the senses perceive nothing which they do not perceive immediately: for they make no inferences. The deducing therefore of causes or occasions from effects and appearances, which alone are perceived by sense, entirely relates to reason.

Phil. This point then is agreed between us, that *sensible things are those only which are immediately perceived by sense.* You will farther inform me, whether we immediately perceive by sight anything beside light, and colors, and figures: or by hearing anything but sounds: by the palate, anything beside tastes: by the smell, beside odors: or by the touch, more than tangible qualities.

Hyl. We do not.

Phil. It seems therefore, that if you take away all sensible qualities, there remains nothing sensible.

Hyl. I grant it.

Phil. Sensible things therefore are nothing else but so many sensible qualities, or combinations of sensible qualities.

Hyl. Nothing else.

Phil. Heat then is a sensible thing.

Hyl. Certainly.

Phil. Does the reality of sensible things consist in being perceived? Or, is it something distinct from their being perceived, and that bears no relation to the mind?

Hyl. To *exist* is one thing, and to be *perceived* is another.

Phil. I speak with regard to sensible things only: and of these I ask, whether by their real existence you mean a subsistence exterior to the mind, and distinct from their being perceived?

Hyl. I mean a real absolute being, distinct from, and without any relation to, their being perceived.

Phil. Heat therefore, if it be allowed a real being, must exist without the mind.

Hyl. It must.

Phil. Tell me, Hylas, is this real existence equally compatible to all degrees of heat, which we perceive: or is there any reason why we should attribute it to some, and deny it to others? And if there be, pray let me know that reason.

Hyl. Whatever degree of heat we perceive by sense, we may be sure the same exists in the object that occasions it.

Phil. What, the greatest as well as the least?

Hyl. I tell you, the reason is plainly the same in respect of both: they are both perceived by sense; nay, the greater degree of heat is more sensibly perceived; and consequently, if there is any difference, we are more certain of its real existence than we can be of the reality of a lesser degree.

Phil. But is not the most vehement and intense degree of heat a very great pain?

Hyl. No one can deny it.

Phil. And is any unperceiving thing capable of pain or pleasure?

Hyl. No, certainly.

Phil. Is your material substance a senseless being, or a being endowed with sense and perception?

Hyl. It is senseless, without doubt.

Phil. It cannot therefore be the subject of pain.

Hyl. By no means.

Phil. Nor consequently of the greatest heat perceived by sense, since you acknowledge this to be no small pain.

Hyl. I grant it.

Phil. What shall we say then of your external object; is it a material substance, or no?

Hyl. It is a material substance with the sensible qualities inhering in it.

Phil. How then can a great heat exist in it, since you own it cannot in a material substance? I desire you would clear this point.

Hyl. Hold, Philonous, I fear I was out in yielding intense heat to be a pain. It should seem rather, that pain is something distinct front heat, and the consequence or effect of it.

Phil. Upon putting your hand near the fire, do you perceive one simple uniform sensation, or two distinct sensations?

Hyl. But one simple sensation.

Phil. Is not the heat immediately perceived?

Hyl. It is.

Phil. And the pain?

Hyl. True.

Phil. Seeing therefore they are both immediately perceived at the same time, and the fire affects you only with one simple, or uncompounded idea, it follows that this same simple idea is both the intense heat immediately perceived, and the pain; and consequently, that the intense heat immediately perceived, is nothing distinct from a particular sort of pain.

Hyl. It seems so.

Phil. Again, try in your thoughts, Hylas, if you can conceive a vehement sensation to be without pain, or pleasure.

Hyl. I cannot.

Phil. Or can you frame to yourself an idea of sensible pain or pleasure in general, abstracted from every particular idea of heat, cold, tastes, smells? &c.

Hyl.—I do not find that I can.

Phil. Does it not therefore follow, that sensible pain is nothing distinct from those sensations or ideas, in an intense degree?

Hyl. It is undeniable; and to speak the truth, I begin to suspect a very great heat cannot exist but in a mind perceiving it.

Phil. What! Are you then in that *sceptical* state of suspense, between affirming and denying?

Hyl. I think I may be positive in the point. A very violent and painful heat cannot exist without the mind.

Phil. It has not therefore, according to you, any real being.

Hyl. I own it.

Phil. Is it therefore certain, that there is no body in nature really hot?

Hyl. I have not denied there is any real heat in bodies. I only say, there is no such thing as an intense real heat.

Phil. But did you not say before, that all degrees of heat were equally real: or if there was any difference, that the greater were more undoubtedly real than the lesser?

Hyl. True: but it was, because I did not then consider the ground there is for distinguishing between them, which I now plainly see. And it is this: because intense heat is nothing else but a particular kind of painful sensation; and pain cannot exist but in a perceiving being; it follows that no intense heat can really exist in an unperceiving corporeal substance. But this is no reason why we should deny heat in an inferior degree to exist in such a substance.

Phil. But how shall we be able to discern those degrees of heat which exist only in the mind, from those which exist without it?

Hyl. That is no difficult matter. You know, the least pain cannot exist unperceived; whatever, therefore, degree of heat is a pain, exists only in the mind. But as for all other degrees of heat, nothing obliges us to think the same of them.

Phil. I think you granted before, that no unperceiving being was capable of pleasure, any more than of pain.

Hyl. I did.

Phil. And is not warmth, or a more gentle degree of heat than what causes uneasiness, a pleasure?

Hyl. What then?

Phil. Consequently it cannot exist without the mind in any unperceiving substance, or body.

Hyl. So it seems.

Phil. Since therefore, as well those degrees of heat that are not painful, as those that are, can exist only in a thinking substance; may we not conclude that external bodies are absolutely incapable of any degree of heat whatsoever?

Hyl. On second thoughts, I do not think it so evident that warmth is a pleasure, as that a great degree of heat is a pain.

Phil. I do not pretend that warmth is as great a pleasure as heat is a pain. But if you grant it to be even a small pleasure, it serves to make good my conclusion.

Hyl. I could rather call it an *indolence.* It seems to be nothing more than a privation of both pain and pleasure. And that such a quality or state as this may agree to an unthinking substance, I hope you will not deny.

Phil. If you are resolved to maintain that warmth, or a gentle degree of heat, is no pleasure, I know not how to convince you otherwise than by appealing to your own sense. But what think you of cold?

Hyl. The same that I do of heat. An intense degree of cold is a pain; for to feel a very great cold, is to perceive a great uneasiness: it cannot therefore exist without the mind; but a lesser degree of cold may, as well as a lesser degree of heat.

Phil. Those bodies, therefore, upon whose application to our own, we perceive a moderate degree of heat, must be concluded to have a moderate degree of heat or warmth in them: and those, upon whose application we feel a like degree of cold, must be thought to have cold in them.

Hyl. They must.

Phil. Can any doctrine be true that necessarily leads a man into an absurdity?

Hyl. Without doubt it cannot.

Phil. Is it not an absurdity to think that the same thing should be at the same time both cold and warm?

Hyl. It is.

Phil. Suppose now one of your hands hot, and the other cold, and that they are both at once put into the same vessel of water, in an intermediate state; will not the water seem cold to one hand, and warm to the other?

Hyl. It will.

Phil. Ought we not therefore by your principles to conclude, it is really both cold and warm at the same time, that is, according to your own concession, to believe an absurdity?

Hyl. I confess it seems so.

Phil. Consequently, the principles themselves are false, since you have granted that no true principle leads to an absurdity.

Hyl. But after all, can anything be more absurd than to say, *there is no heat in the fire?*

Phil. To make the point still clearer; tell me, whether in two cases exactly alike, we ought not to make the same judgment?

Hyl. We ought.

Phil. When a pin pricks your finger, does it not rend and divide the fibres of your flesh?

Hyl. It does.

Phil. And when a coal burns your finger, does it any more?

Hyl. It does not.

Phil. Since therefore you neither judge the sensation itself occasioned by the pin, nor anything like it to be in the pin; you should not, conformably to what you have now granted, judge the sensation occasioned by the fire, or anything like it, to be in the fire.

Hyl. Well, since it must be so, I am content to yield this point, and acknowledge, that heat and cold are only sensations existing in our minds: but there still remain qualities enough to secure the reality of external things.

Phil. But what will you say, Hylas, if it shall appear that the case is the same with regard to all other sensible qualities, and that they can no more be supposed to exist without the mind, than heat and cold?

Hyl. Then indeed you will have done something to the purpose; but that is what I despair of seeing proved.

Phil. Let us examine them in order. What think you of tastes, do they exist without the mind, or no?

Hyl. Can any man in his senses doubt whether sugar is sweet, or wormwood bitter?

Phil. Inform me, Hylas. Is a sweet taste a particular kind of pleasure or pleasant sensation, or is it not?

Hyl. It is.

Phil. And is not bitterness some kind of uneasiness or pain?

Hyl. I grant it.

Phil. If therefore sugar and wormwood are unthinking corporeal substances existing without the mind, how can sweetness and bitterness, that is, pleasure and pain, agree to them?

Hyl. Hold, Philonous, I now see what it was deluded me all this time. You asked whether heat and cold, sweetness and bitterness, were not particular sorts of pleasure and pain; to which I answered simply, that they were. Whereas I should have thus distinguished: those qualities, as perceived by us, are pleasures or pains, but not as existing in the external objects. We must not therefore conclude absolutely, that there is no heat in the fire, or sweetness in the sugar, but only that heat or sweetness, as perceived by us, are not in the fire or sugar. What say you to this?

Phil. I say it is nothing to the purpose. Our discourse proceeded altogether concerning sensible things, which you defined to be the things we *immediately perceived by our senses.* Whatever other qualities therefore you speak of, as distinct from these, I know nothing of them, neither do they at all belong to the point in dispute. You may indeed pretend to have discovered certain qualities which you do not perceive, and assert those insensible qualities exist in fire and sugar. But what use can be made of this to your present purpose, I am at a loss to conceive. Tell me then once more, do you acknowledge

that heat and cold, sweetness and bitterness, (meaning those qualities which are perceived by the senses) do not exist without the mind?

Hyl. I see it is to no purpose to hold out, so I give up the cause as to those mentioned qualities. Though I profess it sounds oddly, to say that sugar is not sweet.

Phil. But for your farther satisfaction, take this along with you: that which at other times seems sweet, shall to a distempered palate appear bitter. And nothing can be plainer, than that diverse persons perceive different tastes in the same food, since that which one man delights in, another abhors. And how could this be, if the taste was something really inherent in the food?

Hyl. I acknowledge I know not how.

Phil. In the next place, odors are to be considered. And, with regard to these, I would fain know whether what has been said of tastes does not exactly agree to them? Are they not so many pleasing or displeasing sensations?

Hyl. They are.

Phil. Can you then conceive it possible that they should exist in an unperceiving thing?

Hyl. I cannot.

Phil. Or can you imagine, that filth and ordure affect those brute animals that feed on them out of choice, with the same smells which we perceive in them?

Hyl. By no means.

Phil. May we not therefore conclude of smells, as of the other forementioned qualities, that they cannot exist in any but a perceiving substance or mind?

Hyl. I think so.

Phil. Then as to sounds, what must we think of them: are they accidents really inherent in external bodies, or not?

Hyl. That they inhere not in the sonorous bodies, is plain from hence; because a bell struck in the exhausted receiver of an air-pump, sends forth no sound. The air therefore must be thought the subject of sound.

Phil. What reason is there for that, Hylas?

Hyl. Because when any motion is raised in the air, we perceive a sound greater or lesser, to the air's motion; but without some motion in the air, we never hear any sound at all.

Phil. And granting that we never hear a sound but when some motion is produced in the air, yet I do not see how you can infer from thence, that the sound itself is in the air.

Hyl. It is this very motion in the external air, that produces in the mind the sensation of *sound*. For, striking on the drum of the ear, it causes a vibration, which by the auditory nerves being communicated to the brain, the soul is thereupon affected with the sensation called *sound*.

Phil. What! Is sound then a sensation?

Hyl. I tell you, as perceived by us, it is a particular sensation in the mind.

Phil. And can any sensation exist without the mind?

Hyl. No certainly.

Phil. How then can sound, being a sensation, exist in the air, if by the *air* you mean a senseless substance existing without the mind?

Hyl. You must distinguish, Philonous, between sound as it is perceived by us, and as it is in itself; or (which is the same thing) between the sound we immediately perceive and that which exists without us. The former indeed is a particular kind of sensation, but the latter is merely a vibrative or undulatory motion in the air.

Phil. I thought I had already obviated that distinction by the answer I gave when you were applying it in a like case before. But to say no more of that; are you sure then that sound is really nothing but motion?

Hyl. I am.

Phil. Whatever therefore agrees to real sound, may with truth be attributed to motion.

Hyl. It may.

Phil. It is then good sense to speak of *motion,* as of a thing that is *loud, sweet, acute,* or *grave.*

Hyl. I see you are resolved not to understand me. Is it not evident, those accidents or modes belong only to sensible sound, or *sound* in the common acceptation of the word, but not to *sound* in the real and philosophic sense, which, as I just now told you, is nothing but a certain motion of the air?

Phil. It seems then there are two sorts of sound, the one vulgar, or that which is heard, the other philosophical and real.

Hyl. Even so.

Phil. And the latter consists in motion.

Hyl. I told you so before.

Phil. Tell me, Hylas, to which of the senses, think you, the idea of motion belongs: to the hearing?

Hyl. No certainly, but to the sight and touch.

Phil. It should follow then, that according to you, real sounds may possibly be *seen* or *felt,* but never *heard.*

Hyl. Look you, Philonous, you may if you please make a jest of my opinion, but that will not alter the truth of things. I own indeed, the inferences you draw me into, sound something oddly; but common language, you know, is framed by, and for the use of, the vulgar: we must not therefore wonder, if expressions adapted to exact philosophic notions, seem uncouth and out of the way.

Phil. Is it come to that? I assure, you, I imagine myself to have gained no small point, since you make so light of departing from common phrases and opinions; it being a main part of our inquiry, to examine whose notions are widest of the common road, and most repugnant to the general sense of the world. But can you think it no more than a philosophical paradox, to say that *real sounds are never heard,* and that the idea of them is obtained by some other sense. And is there nothing in this contrary to nature and the truth of things?

Hyl. To deal ingenuously, I do not like it. And after the concessions already made, I had as well grant that sounds too have no real being without the mind.

Phil. And I hope you will make no difficulty to acknowledge the same of colors.

Hyl. Pardon me: the case of colors is very different. Can anything be plainer, than that we see them on the objects?

Phil. The objects you speak of are, I suppose, corporeal substances existing without the mind.

Hyl. They are.

Phil. And have true and real colors inhering in them?

Hyl. Each visible object has that color which we see in it.

Phil. How! Is there anything visible but what we perceive by sight.

Hyl. There is not.

Phil. And do we perceive anything by sense, which we do not perceive immediately?

Hyl. How often must I be obliged to repeat the same thing? I tell you, we do not.

Phil. Have patience, good Hylas; and tell me once more, whether there is anything immediately perceived by the senses, except sensible qualities. I know you asserted there was not: but I would now be informed, whether you still persist in the same opinion.

Hyl. I do.

Phil. Pray, is your corporeal substance either a sensible quality, or made up of sensible qualities?

Hyl. What a question that is! Who ever thought it was?

Phil. My reason for asking was, because in saying, *Each visible object has that color which we see in it,* you make visible objects to be corporeal substances; which implies either that corporeal substances are sensible qualities, or else that there is something beside sensible qualities perceived by sight: but as this point was formerly agreed between us, and is still maintained by you, it is a clear consequence, that your corporeal substance is nothing distinct from sensible qualities.

Hyl. You may draw as many absurd consequences as you please, and endeavor to perplex the plainest things; but you shall never persuade me out of my senses. I clearly understand my own meaning.

Phil. I wish you would make me understand it too. But since you are unwilling to have your notion of corporeal substance examined, I shall urge that point no farther. Only be pleased to let me know, whether the same colors which we see, exist in external bodies, or some other.

Hyl. The very same.

Phil. What! Are then the beautiful red and purple we see on yonder clouds, really in them? Or do you imagine they have in themselves any other form, than that of a dark mist or vapor?

Hyl. I must own, Philonous, those colors are not really in the clouds as they seem to be at this distance. They are only apparent colors.

Phil. Apparent call you them? How shall we distinguish these apparent colors from real?

Hyl. Very easily. Those are to be thought apparent, which appearing only at a distance, vanish upon a nearer approach.

Phil. And those I suppose are to be thought real, which are discovered by the most near and exact survey.

Hyl. Right.

Phil. Is the nearest and exactest survey made by the help of a microscope, or by the naked eye?

Hyl. By a microscope, doubtless.

Phil. But a microscope often discovers colors in an object different from those perceived by the unassisted sight. And in case we had microscopes magnifying to any assigned degree; it is certain, that no object whatsoever, viewed through them, would appear in the same color which it exhibits to the naked eye.

Hyl. And what will you conclude from all this? You cannot argue that there are really and naturally no colors on objects: because by artificial managements they may be altered, or made to vanish.

Phil. I think it may evidently be concluded from your own concessions, that all the colors we see with our naked eyes, are only apparent as those on the clouds, since they vanish upon a more close and accurate inspection, which is afforded us by a microscope. Then as to what you say by way of prevention: I ask you, whether the real and natural state of an object is better discovered by a very sharp and piercing sight, or by one which is less sharp?

Hyl. By the former without doubt.

Phil. Is it not plain from *Dioptrics,* that microscopes make the sight more penetrating, and represent objects as they would appear to the eye in case it were naturally endowed with a most exquisite sharpness?

Hyl. It is.

Phil. Consequently the microscopical representation is to be thought that which best sets forth the real nature of the thing, or what it is in itself. The colors, therefore, by it perceived, are more genuine and real, than those perceived otherwise.

Hyl. I confess there is something in what you say.

Phil. Besides, it is not only possible but manifest, that there actually are animals, whose eyes are by nature framed to perceive those things, which by reason of their minuteness escape our sight. What think you of those inconceivably small animals perceived by glasses? Must we suppose they are all stark blind? Or, in case they see, can it be imagined their sight has not the same use in preserving their bodies from injuries, which appears in that of all other animals? And if it hath, is it not evident, they must see particles less than their own bodies, which will present them with a far different view in each object, from that which strikes our senses? Even our own eyes do not always represent objects to us after the same manner. In the *jaundice,* everyone knows that all things seem yellow. Is it not therefore highly probable, those animals in whose eyes we discern a very different texture from that of ours, and whose bodies abound with different humors, do not see the same colors in every object that we do? From all which, should it not seem to follow, that all colors are equally apparent, and that none of those which we perceive are really inherent in any outward object?

Hyl. It should.

Phil. The point will be past all doubt, if you consider, that in case colors were real properties or affections inherent in external bodies, they could admit of no alteration, without some change wrought in the very bodies themselves: but is it not evident from what has been said, that upon the use of microscopes, upon a change happening in the humors of the eye, or a variation of distance, without any manner of real alteration in the thing itself, the colors of any object are either changed, or totally disappear? Nay, all other circumstances remaining the same, change but the situation of some objects, and they shall present different colors to the eye. The same thing happens upon viewing an object in various degrees of light. And what is more known, than that the same bodies appear differently colored by candle-light from what they do in the open day? Add to these the experiment of a prism, which separating the heterogeneous rays of light, alters the color of any object; and will cause the whitest to appear of a deep blue or red to the naked eye. And now tell me, whether you are still of opinion that every body has its true real color inhering in it: and if you think it has, I would fain know farther from you, what certain distance and position of the object, what peculiar texture and formation of the eye, what degree or kind of light is necessary for ascertaining that true color, and distinguishing it from apparent ones.

Hyl. I own myself entirely satisfied, that they are all equally apparent; and that there is no such thing as color really inhering in external bodies, but that it is altogether in the light. And what confirms me in this opinion is, that in proportion to the light, colors are still more or less vivid; and if there be no light, then are there no colors perceived. Besides, allowing there are colors on external objects, yet how is it possible for us to perceive them? For no external body affects the mind, unless it act first on our organs of sense. But the only action of bodies is motion; and motion cannot be communicated otherwise than by impulse. A distant object therefore cannot act on the eye, nor consequently make itself or its properties perceivable to the soul. Whence it

plainly follows, that it is immediately some contiguous substance, which operating on the eye occasions a perception of colors: and such is light.

Phil. How! Is light then a substance?

Hyl. I tell you, Philonous, external light is nothing but a thin fluid substance, whose minute particles being agitated with a brisk motion, and in various manners reflected from the different surfaces of outward objects to the eyes, communicate different motions to the optic nerves; which, being propagated to the brain, cause therein various impressions: and these are attended with the sensations of red, blue, yellow, &c.

Phil. It seems then, the light does no more than shake the optic nerves.

Hyl. Nothing else.

Phil. And consequent to each particular motion of the nerves, the mind is affected with a sensation, which is some particular color.

Hyl. Right.

Phil. And these sensations have no existence without the mind.

Hyl. They have not.

Phil. How then do you affirm that colors are in the light, since by *light* you understand a corporeal substance external to the mind?

Hyl. Light and colors, as immediately perceived by us, I grant cannot exist without the mind. But in themselves they are only the motions and configurations of certain insensible particles of matter.

Phil. Colors then, in the vulgar sense, or taken for the immediate objects of sight, cannot agree to any but a perceiving substance.

Hyl. That is what I say.

Phil. Well then, since you give up the point as to those sensible qualities which are alone thought colors by all mankind beside, you may hold what you please with regard to those invisible ones of the philosophers. It is not my business to dispute about them; only I would advise you to bethink yourself, whether considering the inquiry we are upon, it be prudent for you to affirm, *The red and blue which we see are not real colors, but certain unknown motions and figures which no man ever did or can see are truly so.* Are not these shocking notions and are not they subject to as many ridiculous inferences, as those you were obliged to renounce before in the case of sounds?

Hyl. I frankly own, Philonous, that it is in vain to stand out any longer. Colors, sounds, tastes, in a word, all those termed *secondary qualities,* have certainly no existence without the mind. But by this acknowledgment I must not be supposed to derogate anything from the reality of matter or external objects, seeing it is no more than several philosophers maintain, who nevertheless are the farthest imaginable from denying matter. For the clearer understanding of this, you must know sensible qualities are by philosophers divided into *primary* and *secondary.* The former are extension, figure, solidity, gravity, motion, and rest. And these they hold exist really in bodies. The latter are those above enumerated; or briefly, all sensible qualities beside the primary, which they assert are only so many sensations or ideas existing nowhere but in the mind. But all this, I doubt not, you are already apprised of. For my part, I have been a long time sensible there was such an opinion current among philosophers, but was never thoroughly convinced of its truth till now.

Phil. You are still then of opinion that extension and figures are inherent in external unthinking substances.

Hyl. I am.

Phil. But what if the same arguments which are brought against secondary qualities, will hold good against these also?

Hyl. Why then I shall be obliged to think, they too exist only in the mind.

Phil. Is it your opinion, the very figure and extension which you perceive by sense, exist in the outward object or material substance?

Hyl. It is.

Phil. Have all other animals as good grounds to think the same of the figure and extension which they see and feel?

Hyl. Without doubt, if they have any thought at all.

Phil. Answer me, Hylas. Think you the senses were bestowed upon all animals for their preservation and well-being in life? Or were they given to men alone for this end?

Hyl. I make no question but they have the same use in all other animals.

Phil. If so, is it not necessary they should be enabled by them to perceive their own limbs, and those bodies which are capable of harming them?

Hyl. Certainly.

Phil. A mite therefore must be supposed to see his own foot, and things equal or even less than it, as bodies of some considerable dimension; though at the same time they appear to you scarce discernible, or at best as so many visible points.

Hyl. I cannot deny it.

Phil. And to creatures less than the mite they will seem yet larger.

Hyl. They will.

Phil. Insomuch that what you can hardly discern, will to another extremely minute animal appear as some huge mountain.

Hyl. All this I grant.

Phil. Can one and the same thing be at the same time in itself of different dimensions?

Hyl. That were absurd to imagine.

Phil. But from what you have laid down it follows, that both the extension by you perceived, and that perceived by the mite itself, as likewise all those perceived by lesser animals, are each of them the true extension of the mite's foot; that is to say, by your own principles you are led into an absurdity.

Hyl. There seems to be some difficulty in the point.

Phil. Again, have you not acknowledged that no real inherent property of any object can be changed, without some change in the thing itself?

Hyl. I have.

Phil. But as we approach to or recede from an object, the visible extension varies, being at one distance ten or a hundred times greater than at another. Does it not therefore follow from hence likewise, that it is not really inherent in the object?

Hyl. I own I am at a loss what to think.

Phil. Your judgment will soon be determined, if you will venture to think as freely concerning this quality, as you have done concerning the rest. Was it not admitted as a good argument, that neither heat nor cold was in the water, because it seemed warm to one hand, and cold to the other?

Hyl. It was.

Phil. Is it not the very same reasoning to conclude, there is no extension or figure in an object, because to one eye it shall seem little, smooth, and round, when at the same time it appears to the other, great, uneven, and angular?

Hyl. The very same. But does this latter fact ever happen?

Phil. You may at any time make the experiment, by looking with one eye bare, and with the other through a microscope.

Hyl. I know not how to maintain it, and yet I am loath to give up *extension,* I see so many odd consequences following upon such a concession.

Phil. Odd, say you? After the concessions already made, I hope you will stick at nothing for its oddness. But on the other hand should it not seem very odd, if the general reasoning which includes all other sensible qualities did not also include extension? If it be allowed that no idea nor anything like an idea can exist in an unperceiving substance, then surely it follows, that no figure or mode of extension, which we can either perceive or imagine, or have any idea of, can be really inherent in matter; not to mention the peculiar difficulty there must be, in conceiving a material substance, prior to and distinct from extension, to be the *substratum* of extension. Be the sensible quality what it will, figure, or sound, or color; it seems alike impossible it should subsist in that which doth not perceive it.

Hyl. I give up the point for the present, reserving still a right to retract my opinion, in case I shall hereafter discover any false step in my progress to it.

Phil. That is a right you cannot be denied. Figures and extension being dispatched, we proceed next to *motion.* Can a real motion in any external body be at the same time both very swift and very slow?

Hyl. It cannot.

Phil. Is not the motion of a body swift in a reciprocal proportion to the time it takes up in describing any given space? Thus a body that describes a mile in an hour, moves three times faster than it would in case it described only a mile in three hours.

Hyl. I agree with you.

Phil. And is not time measured by the succession of ideas in our minds?

Hyl. It is.

Phil. And is it not possible ideas should succeed one another twice as fast in your mind, as they do in mine, or in that of some spirit of another kind?

Hyl. I own it.

Phil. Consequently the same body may to another seem to perform its motion over any space in half the time that it does to you. And the same reasoning will hold as to any other proportion: that is to say, according to your principles (since the motions perceived are both really in the object) it is possible one and the same body shall be really moved the same way at once, both very swift and very slow. How is this consistent either with common sense, or with what you just now granted?

Hyl. I have nothing to say to it.

Phil. Then as for *solidity;* either you do not mean any sensible quality by that word, and so it is beside our inquiry: or if you do, it must be either hardness or resistance. But both the one and the other are plainly relative to our senses: it being evident, that what seems hard to one animal, may appear soft to another, who hath greater force and firmness of limbs. Nor is it less plain, that the resistance I feel is not in the body.

Hyl. I own the very sensation of resistance, which is all you immediately perceive, is not in the *body;* but the cause of that sensation is.

Phil. But the causes of our sensations are not things immediately perceived, and therefore not sensible. This point I thought had been already determined.

Hyl. I own it was; but you will pardon me if I seem a little embarrassed: I know not how to quit my old notions.

Phil. To help you out, do but consider that if extension be once acknowledged to have no existence without the mind, the same must necessarily be granted of motion, solidity, and gravity, since they all evidently suppose extension. It is therefore superfluous to inquire particularly concerning each of them. In denying extension, you have denied them all to have any real existence.

Hyl. I wonder, Philonous, if what you say be true, why those philosophers who deny the secondary qualities any real existence, should yet attribute it to the primary. If there is no difference between them, how can this be accounted for?

Phil. It is not my business to account for every opinion of the philosophers. But among other reasons which may be assigned for this, it seems probable, that pleasure and pain being rather annexed to the former than the latter, may be one. Heat and cold, tastes and smells, have something more vividly pleasing or disagreeable than the ideas of extension, figure, and motion, affect us with. And it being too visibly absurd to hold, that pain or pleasure can be in an unperceiving substance, men are more easily weaned from believing the external existence of the secondary, than the primary qualities. You will be satisfied there is something in this, if you recollect the difference you made between an intense and more moderate degree of heat, allowing the one a real existence, while you denied it to the other. But after all, there is no rational ground for that distinction; for surely an indifferent sensation is as truly *a sensation,* as one more pleasing or painful; and consequently should not any more than they be supposed to exist in an unthinking subject.

Hyl. It is just come into my head, Philonous, that I have somewhere heard of a distinction between absolute and sensible extension. Now though it be acknowledged that *great* and *small,* consisting merely in the relation which other extended beings have to the parts of our own bodies, do not really inhere in the substances themselves; yet nothing obliges us to hold the same with regard to *absolute extension,* which is something abstracted from *great* and *small,* from this or that particular magnitude or figure. So likewise as to motion, *swift* and *slow* are altogether relative to the succession of ideas in our own minds. But it does not follow, because those modifications of motion exist not without the mind, that therefore absolute motion abstracted from them does not.

Phil. Pray what is it that distinguishes one motion, or one part of extension, from another? Is it not something sensible, as some degree of swiftness or slowness, some certain magnitude or figure peculiar to each?

Hyl. I think so.

Phil. These qualities, therefore, stripped of all sensible properties, are without all specific and numerical differences, as the schools call them.

Hyl. They are.

Phil. That is to say, they are extension in general, and motion in general.

Hyl. Let it be so.

Phil. But it is a universally received maxim, that *everything which exists, is particular.* How then can motion in general, or extension in general, exist in any corporeal substance?

Hyl. I will take time to solve your difficulty.

Phil. But I think the point may be speedily decided. Without doubt you can tell, whether you are able to frame this or that idea. Now I am content to put our dispute on this issue. If you can frame in your thoughts a distinct abstract idea of motion or extension, divested

of all those sensible modes, as swift and slow, great and small, round and square, and the like, which are acknowledged to exist only in the mind, I will then yield the point you contend for. But if you cannot, it will be unreasonable on your side to insist any longer upon what you have no notion of.

Hyl. To confess ingenuously, I cannot.

Phil. Can you even separate the ideas of extension and motion, from the ideas of all those qualities which they who make the distinction, term *secondary.*

Hyl. What! Is it not an easy matter, to consider extension and motion by themselves, abstracted from all other sensible qualities? Pray how do the mathematicians treat of them?

Phil. I acknowledge, Hylas, it is not difficult to form general propositions and reasonings about those qualities, without mentioning any other; and in this sense to consider or treat of them abstractedly. But how does it follow that because I can pronounce the word *motion* by itself, I can form the idea of it in my mind exclusive of body? Or because theorems may be made of extension and figures, without any mention of *great* or *small,* or any other sensible mode or quality; that therefore it is possible such an abstract idea of extension, without any particular size or figure, or sensible quality, should be distinctly formed, and apprehended by the mind? Mathematicians treat of quantity, without regarding what other sensible qualities it is attended with, as being altogether indifferent to their demonstrations. But when laying aside the words, they contemplate the bare ideas, I believe you will find, they are not the pure abstracted ideas of extension.

Hyl. But what say you to *pure intellect?* May not abstracted ideas be framed by that faculty?

Phil. Since I cannot frame abstract ideas at all, it is plain, I cannot frame them by the help of *pure intellect,* whatsoever faculty you understand by those words. Besides, not to inquire into the nature of pure intellect and its spiritual objects, as *virtue, reason, God,* or the like; thus much seems manifest, that sensible things are only to be perceived by sense, or represented by the imagination. Figures, therefore, and extension, being originally perceived by sense, do not belong to pure intellect. But for your farther satisfaction, try if you can frame the idea of any figure, abstracted from all particularities of size, or even from other sensible qualities.

Hyl. Let me think a little—I do not find that I can.

Phil. And can you think it possible, that should really exist in nature, which implies a repugnancy in its conception?

Hyl. By no means.

Phil. Since therefore it is impossible even for the mind to disunite the ideas of extension and motion from all other sensible qualities, does it not follow, that where the one exist, there necessarily the other exist likewise?

Hyl. It should seem so.

Phil. Consequently the very same arguments which you admitted, as conclusive against the secondary qualities, are, without any farther application of force, against the primary too. Besides, if you will trust your senses, is it not plain, all sensible qualities coexist, or, to them, appear as being in the same place? Do they ever represent a motion, or figure, as being divested of all other visible and tangible qualities?

Hyl. You need say no more on this head. I am free to own, if there be no secret error or oversight in our proceedings hitherto, that all sensible qualities are alike to be denied existence without the mind. But my fear is, that I have been too liberal in my former concessions, or overlooked some fallacy or other. In short, I did not take time to think.

Phil. For that matter, Hylas, you may take what time you please in reviewing the progress of our inquiry. You are at liberty to recover any slips you might have made, or offer whatever you have omitted, which makes for your first opinion.

Hyl. One great oversight I take to be this: that I did not sufficiently distinguish the *object* from the *sensation*. Now though this latter may not exist without the mind, yet it will not thence follow that the former cannot.

Phil. What object do you mean? The object of the senses?

Hyl. The same.

Phil. It is then immediately perceived.

Hyl. Right.

Phil. Make me to understand the difference between what is immediately perceived, and a sensation.

Hyl. The sensation I take to be an act of the mind perceiving; beside which, there is something perceived; and this I call the *object*. For example, there is red and yellow on that tulip. But then the act of perceiving those colors is in me only, and not in the tulip.

Phil. What tulip do you speak of? Is it that which you see?

Hyl. The same.

Phil. And what do you see beside color, figure, and extension?

Hyl. Nothing.

Phil. What you would say then is, that the red and yellow are coexistent with the extension; is it not?

Hyl. That is not all; I would say, they have a real existence without the mind, in some unthinking substance.

Phil. That the colors are really in the tulip which I see, is manifest. Neither can it be denied, that this tulip may exist independent of your mind or mine; but that any immediate object of the senses, that is, any idea, or combination of ideas, should exist in an unthinking substance, or exterior to all minds, is in itself an evident contradiction. Nor can I imagine how this follows from what you said just now, to wit that the red and yellow were on the tulip *you saw,* since you do not pretend to *see* that unthinking substance.

Hyl. You have an artful way, Philonous, of diverting our inquiry from the subject.

Phil. I see you have no mind to be pressed that way. To return then to your distinction between *sensation* and *object;* if I take you right, you distinguish in every perception two things, the one an action of the mind, the other not.

Hyl. True.

Phil. And this action cannot exist in, or belong to, any unthinking thing; but whatever beside is implied in a perception, may.

Hyl. That is my meaning.

Phil. So that if there was a perception without any act of the mind, it were possible such a perception should exist in an unthinking substance.

Hyl. I grant it. But it is impossible there should be such a perception.

Phil. When is the mind said to be active?

Hyl. When it produces, puts an end to, or changes anything.

Phil. Can the mind produce, discontinue, or change anything but by an act of the will?

Hyl. It cannot.

Phil. The mind therefore is to be accounted active in its perceptions, so far forth as volition is included in them.

Hyl. It is.

Phil. In plucking this flower, I am active, because I do it by the motion of my hand, which was consequent upon my volition; so likewise in applying it to my nose. But is either of these smelling?

Hyl. No.

Phil. I act too in drawing the air through my nose; because my breathing so, rather than otherwise, is the effect of my volition. But neither can this be called *smelling:* for if it were, I should smell every time I breathed in that manner.

Hyl. True.

Phil. Smelling then is somewhat consequent to all this.

Hyl. It is.

Phil. But I do not find my will concerned any farther. Whatever more there is, as that I perceive such a particular smell or any smell at all, this is independent of my will, and therein I am altogether passive. Do you find it otherwise with you, Hylas?

Hyl. No, the very same.

Phil. Then as to seeing, is it not in your power to open your eyes, or keep them shut; to turn them this or that way?

Hyl. Without doubt.

Phil. But does it in like manner depend on your will, that in looking on this flower, you perceive *white* rather than any other color? Or directing your open eyes toward yonder part of the heaven, can you avoid seeing the sun? Or is light or darkness the effect of your volition?

Hyl. No, certainly.

Phil. You are then in these respects altogether passive.

Hyl. I am.

Phil. Tell me now, whether *seeing* consists in perceiving light and colors, or in opening and turning the eyes?

Hyl. Without doubt, in the former.

Phil. Since therefore you are in the very perception of light and colors altogether passive, what is become of that action you were speaking of, as an ingredient in every sensation? And does it not follow from your own concessions, that the perception of light and colors, including no action in it, may exist in an unperceiving substance? And is not this a plain contradiction?

Hyl. I know not what to think of it.

Phil. Besides, since you distinguish the *active* and *passive* in every perception, you must do it in that of pain.

But how is it possible that pain, be it as little active as you please, should exist in an unperceiving substance? In short, do but consider the point, and then confess ingenuously, whether light and colors, tastes, sounds, &c. are not all equally passions or sensations in the soul. You may indeed call them *external objects,* and give them in words what subsistence you please. But examine your own thoughts, and then tell me whether it be not as I say?

Hyl. I acknowledge, Philonous, that upon a fair observation of what passes in my mind, I can discover nothing else, but that I am a thinking being, affected with variety of sensations; neither is it possible to conceive how a sensation should exist in an unperceiving substance. But then on the other hand, when I look on sensible things in a different view, considering them as so many modes and qualities, I find it necessary to suppose a material *substratum,* without which they cannot be conceived to exist.

Phil. Material substratum call you it? Pray, by which of your senses came you acquainted with that being?

Hyl. It is not itself sensible; its modes and qualities only being perceived by the senses.

Phil. I presume then it was by reflection and reason you obtained the idea of it.

Hyl. I do not pretend to any proper positive idea of it. However I conclude it exists, because qualities cannot be conceived to exist without a support.

Phil. It seems then you have only a relative notion of it, or that you conceive it not otherwise than by conceiving the relation it bears to sensible qualities.

Hyl. Right.

Phil. Be pleased therefore to let me know wherein that relation consists.

Hyl. Is it not sufficiently expressed in the term *substratum,* or *substance?*

Phil. If so, the word *substratum* should import, that it is spread under the sensible qualities or accidents.

Hyl. True.

Phil. And consequently under extension.

Hyl. I own it.

Phil. It is therefore somewhat in its own nature entirely distinct from extension.

Hyl. I tell you, extension is only a mode, and matter is something that supports modes. And is it not evident the thing supported is different from the thing supporting?

Phil. So that something distinct from, and exclusive of, extension, is supposed to be the *substratum* of extension.

Hyl. Just so.

Phil. Answer me, Hylas. Can a thing be spread without extension? Or is not the idea of extension necessarily included in *spreading?*

Hyl. It is.

Phil. Whatsoever therefore you suppose spread under anything, must have in itself an extension distinct from the extension of that thing under which it is spread.

Hyl. It must.

Phil. Consequently every corporeal substance, being the *substratum* of extension, must have in itself another extension by which it is qualified to be a *substratum:* and so on to infinity. And I ask whether this be not absurd in itself, and repugnant to what you granted just now, to wit, that the *substratum* was something distinct from, and exclusive of, extension.

Hyl. Aye but, Philonous, you take me wrong. I do not mean that matter is *spread* in a gross literal sense under extension. The word *substratum* is used only to express in general the same thing with *substance.*

Phil. Well then, let us examine the relation implied in the term *substance.* Is it not that it stands under accidents?

Hyl. The very same.

Phil. But that one thing may stand under or support another, must it not be extended?

Hyl. It must.

Phil. Is not therefore this supposition liable to the same absurdity with the former?

Hyl. You still take things in a strict literal sense: that is not fair, Philonous.

Phil. I am not for imposing any sense on your words: you are at liberty to explain them as you please. Only I beseech you, make me understand something by them. You tell me, matter supports or stands under accidents. How! Is it as your legs support your body?

Hyl. No; that is the literal sense.

Phil. Pray let me know any sense, literal or not literal, that you understand it in.—How long must I wait for an answer, Hylas?

Hyl. I declare I know not what to say. I once thought I understood well enough what was meant by matter's supporting accidents. But now the more I think on it,

the less can I comprehend it; in short, I find that I know nothing of it.

Phil. It seems then you have no idea at all, neither relative nor positive of matter; you know neither what it is in itself, nor what relation it bears to accidents.

Hyl. I acknowledge it.

Phil. And yet you asserted, that you could not conceive how qualities or accidents should really exist, without conceiving at the same time a material support of them.

Hyl. I did.

Phil. That is to say, when you conceive the real existence of qualities, you do withal conceive something which you cannot conceive.

Hyl. It was wrong I own. But still I fear there is some fallacy or other. Pray what think you of this? It is just come into my head, that the ground of all our mistake lies in your treating of each quality by itself. Now, I grant that each quality cannot singly subsist without the mind. Color cannot without extension, neither can figure without some other sensible quality. But as the several qualities united or blended together form entire sensible things, nothing hinders why such things may not be supposed to exist without the mind.

Phil. Either, Hylas, you are jesting, or have a very bad memory. Though indeed we went through all the qualities by name one after another; yet my arguments, or rather your concessions, nowhere tended to prove, that the secondary qualities did not subsist each alone by itself, but that they were not *at all* without the mind. Indeed in treating of figure and motion, we concluded they could not exist without the mind, because it was impossible even in thought to separate them from all secondary qualities, so as to conceive them existing by themselves. But then this was not the only argument made use of upon that occasion. But (to pass by all that hath been hitherto said, and reckon it for nothing, if you will have it so) I am content to put the whole upon this issue. If you can conceive it possible for any mixture or combination of qualities, or any sensible object whatever, to exist without the mind, then I will grant it actually to be so.

Hyl. If it comes to that, the point will soon be decided. What more easy than to conceive a tree or house existing by itself, independent of, and unperceived by, any mind whatsoever? I do at this present time conceive them existing after that manner.

Phil. How say you, Hylas, can you see a thing which is at the same time unseen?

Hyl. No, that were a contradiction.

Phil. Is it not as great a contradiction to talk of *conceiving* a thing which *is unconceived?*

Hyl. It is.

Phil. The tree or house therefore which you think of, is conceived by you.

Hyl. How should it be otherwise?

Phil. And what is conceived is surely in the mind.

Hyl. Without question, that which is conceived is in the mind.

Phil. How then came you to say, you conceived a house or tree existing independent and out of all minds whatsoever?

Hyl. That was I own an oversight; but stay, let me consider what led me into it.—It is a pleasant mistake enough. As I was thinking of a tree in a solitary place, where no one was present to see it, methought that was to conceive a tree as existing unperceived or unthought of, not considering that I myself conceived it all the while. But now I plainly see, that all I can do is to frame ideas in my own mind. I may indeed conceive in my own thoughts the idea of a tree, or a house, or a mountain, but that is all. And this is far from proving, that I can conceive them *existing out of the minds of all spirits.*

Phil. You acknowledge then that you cannot possibly conceive, how any one corporeal sensible thing should exist otherwise than in a mind.

Hyl. I do.

Phil. And yet you will earnestly contend for the truth of that which you cannot so much as conceive.

Hyl. I profess I know not what to think, but still there are some scruples remain with me. Is it not certain I see things at a distance? Do we not perceive the stars and moon, for example, to be a great way off? Is not this, I say, manifest to the senses?

Phil. Do you not in a dream too perceive those or the like objects?

Hyl. I do.

Phil. And have they not then the same appearance of being distant?

Hyl. They have.

Phil. But you do not thence conclude the apparitions in a dream to be without the mind?

Hyl. By no means.

Phil. You ought not therefore to conclude that sensible objects are without the mind, from their appearance or manner wherein they are perceived.

Hyl. I acknowledge it. But doth not my sense deceive me in those cases?

Phil. By no means. The idea or thing which you immediately perceive, neither sense nor reason informs you that it actually exists without the mind. By sense you only know that you are affected with such certain sensations of light and colors. &c. And these you will not say are without the mind.

Hyl. True: but beside all that, do you not think the sight suggests something of *outness* or *distance?*

Phil. Upon approaching a distant object, do the visible size and figure change perpetually, or do they appear the same at all distances?

Hyl. They are in a continual change.

Phil. Sight therefore does not suggest, or any way inform you, that the visible object you immediately perceive exists at a distance, or will be perceived when you advance farther onward, there being a continued series of visible objects succeeding each other, during the whole time of your approach.

Hyl. It does not; but still I know, upon seeing an object, what object I shall perceive after having passed over a certain distance: no matter whether it be exactly the same or no: there is still something of distance suggested in the case.

Phil. Good Hylas, do but reflect a little on the point, and then tell me whether there be any more in it than this. From the ideas you actually perceive by sight, you have by experience learned to collect what other ideas you will (according to the standing order of nature) be affected with, after such a certain succession of time and motion.

Hyl. Upon the whole, I take it to be nothing else.

Phil. Now is it not plain, that if we suppose a man born blind was on a sudden made to see, he could at first have no experience of what may be suggested by sight.

Hyl. It is.

Phil. He would not then according to you have any notion of distance annexed to the things he saw; but would take them for a new set of sensations existing only in his mind.

Hyl. It is undeniable.

Phil. But to make it still more plain: is not *distance* a line turned endwise to the eye?

Hyl. It is.

Phil. And can a line so situated be perceived by sight?

Hyl. It cannot.

Phil. Does it not therefore follow that distance is not properly and immediately perceived by sight?

Hyl. It should seem so.

Phil. Again, is it your opinion that colors are at a distance?

Hyl. It must be acknowledged, they are only in the mind.

Phil. But do not colors appear to the eye as coexisting in the same place with extension and figures?

Hyl. They do.

Phil. How can you then conclude from sight, that figures exist without, when you acknowledge colors do not; the sensible appearance being the very same with regard to both?

Hyl. I know not what to answer.

Phil. But allowing that distance was truly and immediately perceived by the mind, yet it would not thence follow it existed out of the mind. For whatever is immediately perceived is an idea: and can any *idea* exist out of the mind?

Hyl. To suppose that, were absurd: but inform me, Philonous, can we perceive or know nothing beside our ideas?

Phil. As for the rational deducing of causes from effects, that is beside our inquiry. And by the senses you can best tell, whether you perceive anything which is not immediately perceived. And I ask you, whether the things immediately perceived, are other than your own sensations or ideas? You have indeed more than once, in the course of this conversation, declared yourself on those points; but you seem by this last question to have departed from what you then thought.

Hyl. To speak the truth, Philonous, I think there are two kinds of objects, the one perceived immediately, which are likewise called *ideas,* the other are real things or external objects perceived by the mediation of ideas, which are their images and representations. Now I own, ideas do not exist without the mind; but the latter sort of objects do. I am sorry I did not think of this distinction sooner; it would probably have cut short your discourse.

Phil. Are those external objects perceived by sense, or by some other faculty?

Hyl. They are perceived by sense.

Phil. How! Is there anything perceived by sense, which is not immediately perceived?

Hyl. Yes, Philonous, in some sort there is. For example, when I look on a picture or statue of Julius Caesar, I may be said after a manner to perceive him (though not immediately) by my senses.

Phil. It seems then, you will have our ideas, which alone are immediately perceived, to be pictures of external things: and that these also are perceived by sense, inasmuch as they have a conformity or resemblance to our ideas.

Hyl. That is my meaning.

Phil. And in the same way that Julius Caesar, in himself invisible, is nevertheless perceived by sight; real things, in themselves imperceptible, are perceived by sense.

Hyl. In the very same.

Phil. Tell me, Hylas, when you behold the picture of Julius Caesar, do you see with your eyes any more than some colors and figures, with a certain symmetry and composition of the whole?

Hyl. Nothing else.

Phil. And would not a man, who had never known anything of Julius Caesar, see as much?

Hyl. He would.

Phil. Consequently he hath his sight, and the use of it, in as perfect a degree as you.

Hyl. I agree with you.

Phil. Whence comes it then that your thoughts are directed to the Roman emperor, and his are not? This cannot proceed from the sensations or ideas of sense by you then perceived; since you acknowledge you have no advantage over him in that respect. It should seem therefore to proceed from reason and memory: should it not?

Hyl. It should.

Phil. Consequently it will not follow from that instance, that anything is perceived by sense which is not immediately perceived. Though I grant we may in one acceptation be said to perceive sensible things mediately by sense: that is, when from a frequently perceived connection, the immediate perception of ideas by one sense suggests to the mind others, perhaps belonging to another sense, which are wont to be connected with them. For instance, when I hear a coach drive along the streets, immediately I perceive only the sound; but from the experience I have had that such a sound is connected with a coach, I am said to hear the coach. It is nevertheless evident, that in truth and strictness, nothing can be *heard* but *sound:* and the coach is not then properly perceived by sense, but suggested from experience. So likewise when we are said to see a red-hot bar of iron; the solidity and heat of the iron are not the objects of sight, but suggested to the imagination by the color and figure, which are properly perceived by that sense. In short, those things alone are actually and strictly perceived by any sense, which would have been perceived, in case that same sense had then been first conferred on us. As for other things, it is plain they are only suggested to the mind by experience grounded on former perceptions. But to return to your comparison of Caesar's picture, it is plain, if you keep to that, you must hold the real things, or archetypes of our ideas, are not perceived by sense, but by some internal faculty of the soul, as reason or memory. I would therefore fain know, what arguments you can draw from reason for the existence of what you call *real things* or *material objects*. Or whether you remember to have seen them formerly as they are in themselves? Or if you have heard or read of any one that did.

Hyl. I see, Philonous, you are disposed to raillery; but that will never convince me.

Phil. My aim is only to learn from you, the way to come at the knowledge of *material beings*. Whatever we perceive, is perceived immediately or mediately: by sense, or by reason and reflection. But as you have excluded sense, pray show me what reason you have to believe their existence; or what *medium* you can possibly make use of, to prove it either to mine or your own understanding.

Hyl. To deal ingenuously, Philonous, now I consider the point, I do not find I can give you any good reason for it. But thus much seems pretty plain, that it is at least possible such things may really exist. And as long as there is no absurdity in supposing them, I am resolved to believe as I did, till you bring good reasons to the contrary.

Phil. What! Is it come to this, that you only believe the existence of material objects, and that your belief is founded barely on the possibility of its being true? Then you will have me bring reasons against it: though another would think it reasonable, the proof should lie on him who holds the affirmative. And after all, this very point which you are now resolved to maintain without any reason, is in effect what you have more than once during this discourse seen good reason to give up. But to pass over all this; if I understand you rightly, you say our ideas do not exist without the mind; but that they are copies, images, or representations of certain originals that do.

Hyl. You take me right.

Phil. They are then like external things.

Hyl. They are.

Phil. Have those things a stable and permanent nature independent of our senses; or are they in a perpetual change, upon our producing any motions in our bodies, suspending, exerting, or altering our faculties or organs of sense.

Hyl. Real things, it is plain, have a fixed and real nature, which remains the same, not withstanding any change in our senses, or in the posture and motion of our bodies; which indeed may affect the ideas in our minds, but it were absurd to think they had the same effect on things existing without the mind.

Phil. How then is it possible, that things perpetually fleeting and variable as our ideas, should be copies or images of anything fixed and constant? Or in other words, since all sensible qualities, as size, figure, color, &c., that is, our ideas, are continually changing upon every alteration in the distance, medium, or instruments of sensation; how can any determinate material objects be properly represented or painted forth by several distinct things, each of which is so different from and unlike the rest? Or if you say it resembles some one only of our ideas, how shall we be able to distinguish the true copy from all the false ones?

Hyl. I profess, Philonous, I am at a loss. I know not what to say to this.

Phil. But neither is this all. Which are material objects in themselves, perceptible or imperceptible?

Hyl. Properly and immediately nothing can be perceived but ideas. All material things therefore are in themselves insensible, and to be perceived only by their ideas.

Phil. Ideas then are sensible, and their archetypes or originals insensible.

Hyl. Right.

Phil. But how can that which is sensible be like that which is insensible? Can a real thing in itself *invisible* be like a *color;* or a real thing which is not *audible,* be like a *sound?* In a word, can anything be like a sensation or idea, but another sensation or idea?

Hyl. I must own, I think not.

Phil. Is it possible there should be any doubt in the point? Do you not perfectly know your own ideas?

Hyl. I know them perfectly; since what I do not perceive or know, can be no part of my idea.

Phil. Consider therefore, and examine them, and then tell me if there be anything in them which can exist without the mind: or if you can conceive anything like them existing without the mind.

Hyl. Upon inquiry, I find it is impossible for me to conceive or understand how anything but an idea can be like an idea. And it is most evident, that *no idea can exist without the mind.*

Phil. You are therefore by your principles forced to deny the reality of sensible things, since you made it to consist in an absolute existence exterior to the mind. That is to say, you are a downright *sceptic.* So I have gained my point, which was to show your principles led to scepticism.

Hyl. For the present I am, if not entirely convinced, at least silenced.

Phil. I would fain know what more you would require in order to a perfect conviction. Have you not had the liberty of explaining yourself all manner of ways? Were any little slips in discourse laid hold and insisted on? Or were you not allowed to retract or reinforce anything you had offered, as best served your purpose? Has not everything you could say been heard and examined with all the fairness imaginable? In a word, have you not in every point been convinced out of your own mouth? And if you can at present discover any flaw in any of your former concessions, or think of any remaining subterfuge, any new distinction, color, or comment whatsoever, why do you not produce it?

Hyl. A little patience, Philonous. I am at present so amazed to see myself ensnared, and as it were imprisoned in the labyrinths you have drawn me into, that on the sudden it cannot be expected I should find my way out. You must give me time to look about me, and recollect myself.

Phil. Hark; is not this the college bell?

Hyl. It rings for prayers.

Phil. We will go in then if you please, and meet here again tomorrow morning. In the meantime you may employ your thoughts on this morning's discourse, and try if you can find any fallacy in it, or invent any new means to extricate yourself.

Hyl. Agreed.

The Second Dialogue

Hylas. I beg your pardon, Philonous, for not meeting you sooner. All this morning my head was so filled with our late conversation, that I had not leisure to think of the time of the day, or indeed of anything else.

Philonous. I am glad you were so intent upon it, in hopes if there were any mistakes in your concessions, or fallacies in my reasonings from them, you will now discover them to me.

Hyl. I assure you, I have done nothing ever since I saw you, but search after mistakes and fallacies, and with that view have minutely examined the whole series of yesterday's discourse: but all in vain, for the notions it led me into, upon review, appear still more clear and evident; and the more I consider them, the more irresistibly do they force my assent.

Phil. And is not this, think you, a sign that they are genuine, that they proceed from nature, and are conformable to right reason? Truth and beauty are in this alike, that the strictest survey sets them both off to advantage. While the false lustre of error and disguise cannot endure being reviewed, or too nearly inspected.

Hyl. I own there is a great deal in what you say. Nor can any one be more entirely satisfied of the truth of those odd consequences, so long as I have in view the reasonings that lead to them. But when these are out of my thoughts, there seems on the other hand something so satisfactory, so natural and intelligible in the modern way of explaining things, that I profess I know not how to reject it.

Phil. I know not what way you mean.

Hyl. I mean the way of accounting for our sensations or ideas.

Phil. How is that?

Hyl. It is supposed the soul makes her residence in some part of the brain, from which the nerves take their rise, and are thence extended to all parts of the body: and that outward objects, by the different impressions they make on the organs of sense, communicate certain vibrative motions to the nerves; and these being filled with spirits, propagate them to the brain or seat of the soul, which according to the various impressions or traces thereby made in the brain, is variously affected with ideas.

Phil. And call you this an explication of the manner whereby we are affected with ideas?

Hyl. Why not, Philonous, have you anything to object against it?

Phil. I would first know whether I rightly understand your hypothesis. You make certain traces in the brain to be the causes or occasions of our ideas. Pray tell me, whether by the *brain* you mean any sensible thing?

Hyl. What else think you I could mean?

Phil. Sensible things are all immediately perceivable; and those things which are immediately perceivable, are ideas; and these exist only in the mind. Thus much you have, if I mistake not, long since agreed to.

Hyl. I do not deny it.

Phil. The brain therefore you speak of, being a sensible thing, exists only in the mind. Now, I would fain know whether you think it reasonable to suppose, that one idea or thing existing in the mind, occasions all other ideas. And if you think so, pray how do you account for the origin of that primary idea or brain itself?

Hyl. I do not explain the origin of our ideas by that brain which is perceivable to sense, this being itself only a combination of sensible ideas, but by another which I imagine.

Phil. But are not things imagined as truly *in the mind* as things perceived?

Hyl. I must confess they are.

Phil. It comes therefore to the same thing; and you have been all this while accounting for ideas, by certain motions or impressions in the brain, that is, by sonic alterations in an idea, whether sensible or imaginable, it matters not.

Hyl. I begin to suspect my hypothesis. [. . .]

Phil. To me it is evident, for the reasons you allow of, that sensible things cannot exist otherwise than in a mind or spirit. Whence I conclude, not that they have no real existence, but that seeing they depend not on my thought, and have an existence distinct from being perceived by me, *there must be some other mind wherein they exist.* As sure therefore as the sensible world really exists, so sure is there an infinite omnipresent spirit who contains and supports it.

Hyl. What! This is no more than I and all Christians hold; nay, and all others too who believe there is a God, and that he knows and comprehends all things.

Phil. Aye, but here lies the difference. Men commonly believe that all things are known or perceived by God, because they believe the being of a God, whereas I, on the other side, immediately and necessarily conclude the being of a God, because all sensible things must be perceived by him.

Hyl. But so long as we all believe the same thing, what matter is it how we come by that belief?

Phil. But neither do we agree in the same opinion. For philosophers, though they acknowledge all corporeal beings to be perceived by God, yet they attribute to them an absolute subsistence distinct from their being perceived by any mind whatever, which I do not. Besides, is there no difference between saying, *There is a God, therefore he prceives all things:* and saying, *Sensible things do really exist: and if they really exist, they are necessarily perceived by an infinite mind: therefore there is an infinite mind, or God.* This furnishes you with a direct and immediate demonstration, from a most evident principle, of the *being of a God.* [. . .]

Hyl. I freely own myself less fond of my notions, since they have been so accurately examined. But still, methinks I have some confused perception that there is such a thing as *matter.*

Phil. Either you perceive the being of matter immediately, or mediately. If immediately, pray inform me by which of the senses you perceive it. If mediately, let me know by what reasoning it is inferred from those things which you perceive immediately. So much for the perception. Then for the matter itself, I ask whether it is object, *substratum,* cause, instrument, or occasion? You have already pleaded for each of these, shifting your notions, and making matter to appear sometimes in one shape, then in another. And what you have offered has been disapproved and rejected by yourself. If you have anything new to advance, I would gladly hear it.

Hyl. I think I have already offered all I had to say on those heads. I am at a loss what more to urge.

Phil. And yet you are loath to part with your old prejudice. But to make you quit it more easily, I desire that, beside what has been hitherto suggested, you will farther consider whether, upon supposition that matter exists, you can possibly conceive how you should be affected by it? Or supposing it did not exist, whether it be not evident you might for all that be affected with the same ideas you now are, and consequently have the very same reasons to believe its existence that you now can have.

Hyl. I acknowledge it is possible we might perceive all things just as we do now, though there was no matter in the world; neither can I conceive, if there be matter, how it should produce any idea in our minds. And I do farther grant, you have entirely satisfied me, that it is impossible there should be such a thing as matter in any of the foregoing acceptations. But still I cannot help supposing that there is *matter* in some sense or other. What that is I do not indeed pretend to determine.

Phil. I do not expect you should define exactly the nature of that unknown being. Only be pleased to tell me, whether it is a substance: and if so, whether you can suppose a substance without accidents; or in case you suppose it to have accidents or qualities, I desire you will let me know what those qualities are, at least what is meant by matter's supporting them.

Hyl. We have already argued on those points. I have no more to say to them. But to prevent any farther questions, let me tell you, I at present understand by *matter* neither substance nor accident, thinking nor extended being, neither cause, instrument, nor occasion, but something entirely unknown, distinct from all these.

Phil. It seems then you include in your present notion of matter, nothing but the general abstract idea of *entity.*

Hyl. Nothing else, save only that I superadd to this general idea the negation of all those particular things, qualities, or ideas that I perceive, imagine, or in any wise apprehend.

Phil. Pray where do you suppose this unknown matter to exist?

Hyl. Oh Philonous! now you think you have entangled me; for if I say it exists in place, then you will infer that it exists in the mind, since it is agreed that place or extension exists only in the mind: but I am not ashamed to own my ignorance. I know not where it exists; only I am sure it exists not in place. There is a neg-

ative answer for you: and you must expect no other to all the questions you put for the future about matter.

Phil. Since you will not tell me where it exists, be pleased to inform me after what manner you suppose it to exist, or what you mean by its *existence.*

Hyl. It neither thinks nor acts, neither perceives, nor is perceived.

Phil. But what is there positive in your abstracted notion of its existence?

Hyl. Upon a nice observation, I do not find I have any positive notion or meaning at all. I tell you again I am not ashamed to own my ignorance. I know not what is meant by its *existence,* or how it exists.

Phil. Continue, good Hylas, to act the same ingenuous part, and tell me sincerely whether you can frame a distinct idea of entity in general, prescinded from and exclusive of all thinking and corporeal beings, all particular things whatsoever.

Hyl. Hold, let me think a little—I profess, Philonous, I do not find that I can. At first glance methought I had some dilute and airy notion of pure entity in abstract; but upon closer attention it has quite vanished out of sight. The more I think on it, the more am I confirmed in my prudent resolution of giving none but negative answers, and not pretending to the least degree of any positive knowledge or conception of matter, its *where,* its *how,* its *entity,* or anything belonging to it.

Phil. When therefore you speak of the existence of matter, you have not any notion in your mind.

Hyl. None at all.

Phil. Pray tell me if the case stands not thus: at first, from a belief of material substance you would have it that the immediate objects existed without the mind; then that their archetypes; then causes; next instruments; then occasions: lastly, *something in general,* which being interpreted proves *nothing.* So matter comes to nothing. What think you, Hylas, is not this a fair summary of your whole proceeding?

Hyl. Be that as it will, yet I still insist upon it, that our not being able to conceive a thing, is no argument against its existence.

Phil. That from a cause, effect, operation, sign, or other circumstance, there may reasonably be inferred the existence of a thing not immediately perceived, and that it were absurd for any man to argue against the existence of that thing, from his having no direct and positive notion of it, I freely own. But where there is nothing of all this; where neither reason nor revelation induce us to believe the existence of a thing; where we have not even a relative notion of it; where an abstraction is made from perceiving and being perceived, from spirit and idea: lastly, where there is not so much as the most inadequate or faint idea pretended to: I will not indeed thence conclude against the reality of any notion, or existence of anything: but my inference shall be, that you mean nothing at all: that you employ words to no manner of purpose, without any design or signification whatsoever. And I leave it to you to consider how mere jargon should be treated.

Hyl. To deal frankly with you, Philonous, your arguments seem in themselves unanswerable, but they have not so great an effect on me as to produce that entire conviction, that hearty acquiescence which attends demonstration. I find myself still relapsing into an obscure surmise of I know not what, *matter.*

Phil. But are you not sensible, Hylas, that two things must concur to take away all scruple, and work a plenary assent in the mind? Let a visible object be set in never so clear a light, yet if there is any imperfection in the sight, or if the eye is not directed towards it, it will not be distinctly seen. And though a demonstration be never so well grounded and fairly proposed, yet if there is withal a stain of prejudice, or a wrong bias on the understanding, can it be expected on a sudden to perceive clearly and adhere firmly to the truth? No, there is need of time and pains: the attention must be awakened and detained by a frequent repetition of the same thing placed oft in the same, oft in different, lights. I have said it already, and find I must still repeat and inculcate, that it is an unaccountable licence you take in pretending to maintain you know not what, for you know not what reason, to you know not what purpose? Can this be paralleled in any art or science, any sect or profession of men? Or is there anything so barefacedly groundless and unreasonable to be met with even in the lowest of common conversation? But perhaps you will still say, matter may exist, though at the same time you neither know what is meant by *matter,* or by its *existence.* This indeed is surprising, and the more so because it is altogether voluntary, you not being led to it by any one reason; for I challenge you to show me that thing in nature which needs matter to explain or account for it. [. . .]

The Third Dialogue

Philonous. Tell me, Hylas, what are the fruits of yesterday's meditation? Has it confirmed you in the same mind you were in at parting? Or have you since seen cause to change your opinion?

Hylas. Truly my opinion is, that all our opinions are alike vain and uncertain. What we approve to-day, we condemn tomorrow. We keep a stir about knowledge, and spend our lives in the pursuit of it, when, alas! we know nothing all the while: nor do I think it possible for us ever to know anything in this life. Our faculties are too narrow and too few. Nature certainly never intended us for speculation.

Phil. What! Say you we can know nothing, Hylas?

Hyl. There is not that single thing in the world, whereof we can know the real nature, or what it is in itself.

Phil. Will you tell me I do not really know what fire or water is?

Hyl. You may indeed know that fire appears hot, and water fluid: but this is no more than knowing what sensations are produced in your own mind, upon the application of fire and water to your organs of sense. Their internal constitution, their true and real nature, you are utterly in the dark as to *that.*

Phil. Do I not know this to be a real stone that I stand on, and that which I see before my eyes to be a real tree?

Hyl. Know? No, it is impossible you or any man alive should know it. All you know, is, that you have such a certain idea or appearance in your own mind. But what is this to the real tree or stone? I tell you, that color, figure, and hardness, which you perceive, are not the real natures of those things, or in the least like them. The same may be said of all other real things or corporeal substances which compose the world. They have none of them anything in themselves, like those sensible qualities by us perceived. We should not therefore pretend to affirm or know anything of them, as they are in their own nature.

Phil. But surely, Hylas, I can distinguish gold, for example, from iron: and how could this be, if I knew not what either truly was?

Hyl. Believe me, Philonous, you can only distinguish between your own ideas. That yellowness, that weight, and other sensible qualities, think you they are really in the gold? They are only relative to the senses, and have no absolute existence in nature. And in pretending to distinguish the species of real things, by the appearances in your mind, you may perhaps act as wisely as he that should conclude two men were of a different species, because their clothes were not of the same color.

Phil. It seems then we are altogether put off with the appearances of things, and those false ones too. The very meat I eat, and the cloth I wear, have nothing in them like what I see and feel.

Hyl. Even so.

Phil. But is it not strange the whole world should be thus imposed on, and so foolish as to believe their senses? And yet I know not how it is, but men eat, and drink, and sleep, and perform all the offices of life, as comfortably and conveniently, as if they really knew the things they are conversant about.

Hyl. They do so: but you know ordinary practice does not require a nicety of speculative knowledge. Hence the vulgar retain their mistakes, and for all that, make a shift to bustle through the affairs of life. But philosophers know better things.

Phil. You mean, they know that they *know nothing*.

Hyl. That is the very top and perfection of human knowledge.

Phil. But are you all this while in earnest, Hylas; and are you seriously persuaded that you know nothing real in the world? Suppose you are going to write, would you not call for pen, ink, and paper, like another man; and do you not know what it is you call for?

Hyl. How often must I tell you, that I know not the real nature of any one thing in the universe? I may indeed upon occasion make use of pen, ink, and paper. But what any one of them is in its own true nature, I declare positively I know not. And the same is true with regard to every other corporeal thing. And, what is more, we are not only ignorant of the true and real nature of things, but even of their existence. It cannot be denied that we perceive such certain appearances or ideas; but it cannot be concluded from thence that bodies really exist. Nay, now I think on it, I must agreeably to my former concessions farther declare, that it is impossible any real corporeal thing should exist in nature.

Phil. You amaze me. Was ever anything more wild and extravagant than the notions you now maintain: and is it not evident you are led into all these extravagancies

by the belief of *material substance?* This makes you dream of those unknown natures in everything. It is this occasions your distinguishing between the reality and sensible appearances of things. It is to this you are indebted for being ignorant of what everybody else knows perfectly well. Nor is this all: you are not only ignorant of the true nature of everything, but you know not whether anything really exists, or whether there are any true natures at all; forasmuch as you attribute to your material beings an absolute or external existence, wherein you suppose their reality consists. And as you are forced in the end to acknowledge such an existence means either a direct repugnancy, or nothing at all, it follows that you are obliged to pull down your own hypothesis of material substance, and positively to deny the real existence of any part of the universe. And so you are plunged into the deepest and most deplorable *scepticism* that ever man was. Tell me, Hylas, is it not as I say?

Hyl. I agree with you. *Material substance* was no more than an hypothesis, and a false and groundless one too. I will no longer spend my breath in defence of it. But whatever hypothesis you advance, or whatsoever scheme of things you introduce in its stead, I doubt not it will appear every whit as false: let me but be allowed to question you upon it. That is, suffer me to serve you in your own kind, and I warrant it shall conduct you through as many perplexities and contradictions, to the very same state of scepticism that I myself am in at present.

Phil. I assure you, Hylas, I do not pretend to frame any hypothesis at all. I am of a vulgar cast, simple enough to believe my senses, and leave things as I find them. To be plain, it is my opinion, that the real things are those very things I see and feel, and perceive by my senses. These I know, and finding they answer all the necessities and purposes of life, have no reason to be solicitous about any other unknown beings. A piece of sensible bread, for instance, would stay my stomach better than ten thousand times as much of that insensible, unintelligible, real bread you speak of. It is likewise my opinion, that colors and other sensible qualities are on the objects. I cannot for my life help thinking that snow is white, and fire hot. You indeed, who by snow and fire mean certain external, unperceived, unperceiving substances, are in the right to deny whiteness or heat to be affections inherent in them. But I, who understand by those words the things I see and feel, am obliged to think like other folks. And as I am no sceptic with regard to the nature of things, so neither am I as to their existence. That a thing should be really perceived by my senses, and at the same time not really exist, is to me a plain contradiction; since I cannot prescind or abstract, even in thought, the existence of a sensible thing from its being perceived. Wood, stones, fire, water, flesh, iron, and the like things, which I name and discourse of, are things that I know; otherwise I should never have thought of them, or named them. And I should not have known them, but that I perceived them by my senses; and things perceived by the senses are immediately perceived; and things immediately perceived are ideas; and ideas cannot exist without the mind; their existence therefore consists in being perceived; when therefore they are actually perceived, there can be no doubt of their existence. Away then with all that scepticism, all those ridiculous philosophical doubts. What a jest is it for a philosopher to question the existence of sensible things, till he has it proved to him from the veracity of God: or to pretend our knowledge in this point falls short of intuition or demonstration? I might as well doubt of my own being, as of the being of those things I actually see and feel.

Hyl. Not so fast, Philonous: you say you cannot conceive how sensible things should exist without the mind. Do you not?

Phil. I do.

Hyl. Supposing you were annihilated, cannot you conceive it possible, that things perceivable by sense may still exist?

Phil. I can; but then it must be in another mind. When I deny sensible things an existence out of the mind, I do not mean my mind in particular, but all minds. Now it is plain they have an existence exterior to my mind, since I find them by experience to be independent of it. There is therefore some other mind wherein they exist, during the intervals between the times of my perceiving them: as likewise they did before my birth, and would do after my supposed annihilation. And as the same is true, with regard to all other finite created spirits; it necessarily follows, there is an *omnipresent eternal mind,* which knows and comprehends all things, and exhibits them to our view in such a manner, and according to such rules as he himself has ordained, and are by us termed the *laws of nature.*

Hyl. Answer me, Philonous. Are all our ideas perfectly inert beings? Or have they any agency included in them?

Phil. They are altogether passive and inert.

Hyl. And is not God an agent, a being purely active?

Phil. I acknowledge it.

Hyl. No idea therefore can be like unto, or represent the nature of God.

Phil. It cannot.

Hyl. Since therefore you have no idea of the mind of God, how can you conceive it possible, that things should exist in his mind? Or, if you can conceive the mind of God without having an idea of it, why may not I be allowed to conceive the existence of matter, notwithstanding that I have no idea of it?

Phil. As to your first question; I own I have properly no idea, either of God or any other spirit; for these being active, cannot be represented by things perfectly inert, as our ideas are. I do nevertheless know, that I, who am a spirit or thinking substance, exist as certainly, as I know my ideas exist. Farther, I know what I mean by the terms *I* and *myself;* and I know this immediately, or intuitively, though I do not perceive it as I perceive a triangle, a color, or a sound. The mind, spirit, or soul, is that indivisible unextended thing, which thinks, acts, and perceives. I say *indivisible,* because unextended; and *unextended,* because extended, figured, moveable things, are ideas; and that which perceives ideas, which thinks and wills, is plainly itself no idea, nor like an idea. Ideas are things inactive, and perceived: and spirits a sort of beings altogether different from them. I do not therefore say my soul is an idea, or like an idea. However, taking the word *idea* in a large sense, my soul may be said to furnish me with an idea, that is, an image, or likeness of God, though indeed extremely inadequate. For all the notion I have of God, is obtained by reflecting on my own soul, heightening its powers, and removing its imperfections. I have therefore, though not an inactive idea, yet in myself some sort of an active thinking image of the Deity. And though I perceive him not by sense, yet I have a notion of him, or know him by reflection and reasoning. My own mind and my own ideas I have an immediate knowledge of, and by the help of these, do mediately apprehend the possibility of the existence of other spirits and ideas. Farther, from my own being, and from the dependency I find in myself and my ideas, I do, by an act of reason, necessarily infer the existence of a God, and of all created things in the mind of God. So much for your first question. For the second: I suppose by this time you can answer it yourself. For you neither perceive matter objectively, as you do an inactive being or idea, nor know it, as you do yourself, by a reflex act: neither do you mediately apprehend it by similitude of the one or the other: nor yet collect it by reasoning from that which you know immediately. All which makes the case of *matter* widely different from that of the *Deity*.

Hyl. You say your own soul supplies you with some sort of an idea or image of God. But at the same time you acknowledge you have, properly speaking, no idea of your own soul. You even affirm that spirits are a sort of beings altogether different from ideas. Consequently that no idea can be like a spirit. We have therefore no idea of any spirit. You admit nevertheless that there is spiritual substance, although you have no idea of it; while you deny there can be such a thing as material substance, because you have no notion or idea of it. Is this fair dealing? To act consistently, you must either admit matter or reject spirit. What say you to this?

Phil. I say in the first place, that I do not deny the existence of material substance, merely because I have no notion of it, but because the notion of it is inconsistent, or in other words, because it is repugnant that there should be a notion of it. Many things, for aught I know, may exist, whereof neither I nor any other man hath or can have any idea or notion whatsoever. But then those things must be possible, that is, nothing inconsistent must be included in their definition. I say secondly, that although we believe things to exist which we do not perceive; yet we may not believe that any particular thing exists, without some reason for such belief: but I have no reason for believing the existence of matter. I have no immediate intuition thereof: neither can I mediately from my sensations, ideas, notions, actions or passions, infer an unthinking, unperceiving, inactive substance, either by probable deduction, or necessary consequence. Whereas the being of my self, that is, my own soul, mind or thinking principle, I evidently know by reflection. You will forgive me if I repeat the same things in answer to the same objections. In the very notion or definition of material substance, there is included a manifest repugnance and inconsistency. But this cannot be said of the notion of spirit. That ideas

should exist in what doth not perceive, or be produced by what doth not act, is repugnant. But it is no repugnancy to say, that a perceiving thing should be the subject of ideas, or an active thing the cause of them. It is granted we have neither an immediate evidence nor a demonstrative knowledge of the existence of other finite spirits; but it will not thence follow that such spirits are on a foot with material substances: if to suppose the one be inconsistent, and it be not inconsistent to suppose the other; if the one can be inferred by no argument, and there is a probability for the other; if we see signs and effects indicating distinct finite agents like ourselves, and see no sign or symptom whatever that leads to a rational belief of matter. I say lastly, that I have a notion of spirit, though I have not, strictly speaking, an idea of it. I do not perceive it as an idea or by means of an idea, but know it by reflection.

Hyl. Notwithstanding all you have said, to me it seems, that according to your own way of thinking, and in consequence of your own principles, it should follow that you are only a system of floating ideas, without any substance to support them. Words are not to be used without a meaning. And as there is no more meaning in spiritual substance than in material substance, the one is to be exploded as well as the other.

Phil. How often must I repeat, that I know or am conscious of my own being; and that I myself am not my ideas, but somewhat else, a thinking active principle that perceives, knows, wills, and operates about ideas. I know that I, one and the same self, perceive both colors and sounds: that a color cannot perceive a sound, nor a sound a color: that I am therefore one individual principle, distinct from color and sound; and, for the same reason, from all other sensible things and inert ideas. But I am not in like manner conscious either of the existence or essence of matter. On the contrary, I know that nothing inconsistent can exist, and that the existence of matter implies an inconsistency. Farther, I know what I mean, when I affirm that there is a spiritual substance or support of ideas, that is, that a spirit knows and perceives ideas. But I do not know what is meant, when it is said, that an unperceiving substance hath inherent in it and supports either ideas or the archetypes of ideas. There is therefore upon the whole no parity of case between spirit and matter.

Hyl. I own myself satisfied in this point. But do you

in earnest think, the real existence of sensible things consists in their being actually perceived? If so; how comes it that all mankind distinguish between them? Ask the first man you meet, and he shall tell you, *to be perceived* is one thing, and *to exist* is another.

Phil. I am content, Hylas, to appeal to the common sense of the world for the truth of my notion. Ask the gardener, why he thinks yonder cherry tree exists in the garden, and he shall tell you, because he sees and feels it; in a word, because he perceives it by his senses. Ask him why he thinks an orange tree not to be there, and he shall tell you, because he does not perceive it. What he perceives by sense, that he terms a real being, and saith it *is*, or *exists;* but that which is not perceivable, the same, he saith, has no being.

Hyl. Yes, Philonous, I grant the existence of a sensible thing consists in being perceivable, but not in being actually perceived.

Phil. And what is perceivable but an idea? And can an idea exist without being actually perceived? These are points long since agreed between us. [. . .]

After all, is there anything farther remaining to be done? You may remember you promised to embrace that opinion, which upon examination should appear most agreeable to common sense, and remote from *scepticism.* This by your own confession is that which denies matter, or the absolute existence of corporeal things. Nor is this all; the same notion has been proved several ways, viewed in different lights, pursued in its consequences, and all objections against it cleared. Can there be a greater evidence of its truth? Or is it possible it should have all the marks of a true opinion, and yet be false?

Hyl. I own myself entirely satisfied for the present in all respects. But what security can I have that I shall still continue the same full assent to your opinion, and that no unthought-of objection or difficulty will occure hereafter?

Phil. Pray, Hylas, do you in other cases, when a point is once evidently proved, withhold your assent on account of objections or difficulties it may be liable to? Are the difficulties that attend the doctrine of incommensurable quantities, of the angle of contact, of the asymptotes to curves, or the like, sufficient to make you hold out against mathematical demonstration? Or will you disbelieve the providence of God, because there may

be some particular things which you know not how to reconcile with it? If there are difficulties attending immaterialism, there are at the same time direct and evident proofs for it. But for the existence of matter, there is not one proof, and far more numerous and insurmountable objections lie against it. But where are those mighty difficulties you insist on? Alas! you know not where or what they are; something which may possibly occur hereafter. If this be a sufficient pretence for withholding your full assent, you should never yield it to any proposition, how free soever from exceptions, how clearly and solidly soever demonstrated.

Hyl. You have satisfied me, Philonous.

Phil. But to arm you against all future objections, do but consider, that which bears equally hard on two contradictory opinions, can be a proof against neither. Whenever therefore any difficulty occurs, try if you can find a solution for it on the hypothesis of the *materialists.* Be not deceived by words; but sound your own thoughts. And in case you cannot conceive it easier by the help of *materialism,* it is plain it can be no objection against *immaterialism.* Had you proceeded all along by this rule, you would probably have spared yourself abundance of trouble in objecting; since of all your difficulties I challenge you to show one that is explained by matter; nay, which is not more unintelligible with than without that supposition, and consequently makes rather *against* than *for* it. You should consider, in each particular, whether the difficulty arises from the *non-existence of matter.* If it does not, you might as well argue from the infinite divisibility of extension against the divine prescience, as from such a difficulty against *immaterialism.* And yet upon recollection I believe you will find this to have been often, if not always, the case. You should likewise take heed not to argue on a *petitio principii.* One is apt to say, the unknown substances ought to be esteemed real things, rather than the ideas in our minds: and who can tell but the unthinking external substance may concur as a cause or instrument in the production of our ideas? But is not this proceeding on a supposition that there are such external substances? And to suppose this, is it not begging the question? But above all things you should beware of imposing on yourself by that vulgar sophism, which is called *ignoratio elenchi.* You talked often as if you thought I maintained the non-existence of sensible things: whereas in truth no one can be more thoroughly assured of their existence than I am: and it is you who doubt; I should have said, positively deny it. Everything that is seen, felt, heard, or any way perceived by the senses, is, on the principles I embrace, a real being, but not on yours. Remember, the matter you contend for is an unknown somewhat, (if indeed it may be termed *somewhat*) which is quite stripped of all sensible qualities, and can neither be perceived by sense, nor apprehended by the mind. Remember, I say, that it is not any object which is hard or soft, hot or cold, blue or white, round or square, &c. For all these things I affirm do exist. Though indeed I deny they have an existence distinct from being perceived; or that they exist out of all minds whatsoever. Think on these points; let them be attentively considered and still kept in view. Otherwise you will not comprehend the state of the question; without which your objections will always be wide of the mark, and instead of mine, may possibly be directed (as more than once they have been) against your own notions.

Hyl. I must needs own, Philonous, nothing seems to have kept me from agreeing with you more than this same *mistaking the question*. In denying matter, at first glimpse I am tempted to imagine you deny the things we see and feel; but upon reflection find there is no ground for it. What think you therefore of retaining the name *matter*, and applying it to sensible things? This may be done without any change in your sentiments: and believe me it would be a means of reconciling them to some persons, who may be more shocked at an innovation in words than in opinion.

Phil. With all my heart: retain the word *matter*, and apply it to the objects of sense, if you please, provided you do not attribute to them any subsistence distinct from their being perceived. I shall never quarrel with you for an expression. *Matter*, or *material substance*, are terms introduced by philosophers; and, as used by them, imply a sort of independency, or a subsistence distinct from being perceived by a mind: but are never used by common people; or if ever, it is to signify the immediate objects of sense. One would think therefore, so long as the names of all particular things, with the terms *sensible, substance, body, stuff*, and the like, are retained, the word *matter* should be never missed in common talk.

And in philosophical discourses it seems the best way to leave it quite out; since there is not perhaps any one thing that hath more favored and strengthened the depraved bent of the mind toward atheism, than the use of that general confused term.

Hyl. Well but, Philonous, since I am content to give up the notion of an unthinking substance exterior to the mind, I think you ought not to deny me the privilege of using the word *matter* as I please, and annexing it to a collection of sensible qualities subsisting only in the mind. I freely own there is no other substance, in a strict sense, than *spirit*. But I have been so long accustomed to the term *matter*, that I know not how to part with it. To say, there is no *matter* in the world, is still shocking to me. Whereas to say, there is no *matter*, if by that term be meant an unthinking substance existing without the mind: but if by *matter* is meant some sensible thing, whose existence consists in being perceived, then there is *matter*: this distinction gives it quite another turn: and men will come into your notions with small difficulty, when they are proposed in that manner. For after all, the controversy about matter in the strict acceptation of it, lies altogether between you and the philosophers; whose principles, I acknowledge, are not near so natural, or so agreeable to the common sense of mankind, and Holy Scripture, as yours. There is nothing we either desire or shun, but as it makes, or is apprehended to make, some part of our happiness or misery. But what has happiness or misery, joy or grief, pleasure or pain, to do with absolute existence, or with unknown entities, abstracted from all relation to us? It is evident, things regard us only as they are pleasing or displeasing: and they can please or displease, only so far forth as they are perceived. Farther therefore we are not concerned; and thus far you leave things as you found them. Yet still there is something new in this doctrine. It is plain, I do not now think with the philosophers, nor yet altogether with the vulgar. I would know how the case stands in that respect: precisely, what you have added to, or altered in my former notions.

Phil. I do not pretend to be a setter-up of *new notions*. My endeavors tend only to unite, and place in a clearer light, that truth which was before shared between the vulgar and the philosophers: the former being of opinion, that *those things they immediately perceive are the real things;* and the latter, that *the things immediately perceived, are ideas which exist only in the mind.* Which two notions put together, do in effect constitute the substance of what I advance.

Hyl. I have been a long time distrusting my senses; methought I saw things by a dim light, and through false glasses. Now the glasses are removed, and a new light breaks in upon my understanding. I am clearly convinced that I see things in their native forms; and am no longer in pain about their unknown natures or absolute existence. This is the state I find myself in at present: though indeed the course that brought me to it, I do not yet thoroughly comprehend. You set out upon the same principles that Academics, Cartesians, and the like

sects, usually do; and for a long time it looked as if you were advancing their philosophical *scepticism;* but in the end your conclusions are directly opposite to theirs.

Phil. You see, Hylas, the water of yonder fountain, how it is forced upwards, in a round column, to a certain height; at which it breaks and falls back into the basin from whence it rose: its ascent as well as descent, proceeding from the same uniform law or principle of *gravitation.* Just so, the same principles which at first view lead to *scepticism,* pursued to a certain point, bring men back to common sense.

FINIS.

Alvin Goldman

Discrimination and Perceptual Knowledge

This paper presents a partial analysis of perceptual knowledge, an analysis that will, I hope, lay a foundation for a general theory of knowing. Like an earlier theory I proposed, the envisaged theory would seek to explicate the concept of knowledge by reference to the causal processes that produce (or sustain) belief. Unlike the earlier theory, however, it would abandon the requirement that a knower's belief that *p* be causally connected with the fact, or state of affairs, that *p.*

What kinds of causal processes or mechanisms must be responsible for a belief if that belief is to count as knowledge? They must be mechanisms that are, in an appropriate sense, "reliable." Roughly, a cognitive mechanism or process is reliable if it not only produces true beliefs in actual situations, but would produce true beliefs, or at least inhibit false beliefs, in relevant coun-

terfactual situations. The theory of knowledge I envisage, then, would contain an important counterfactual component.

To be reliable, a cognitive mechanism must enable a person to *discriminate* or *differentiate* between incompatible states of affairs. It must operate in such a way that incompatible states of the world would generate different cognitive responses. Perceptual mechanisms illustrate this clearly. A perceptual mechanism is reliable to the extent that contrary features of the environment (e.g., an object's being red, versus its being yellow) would produce contrary perceptual states of the organism, which would, in turn, produce suitably different beliefs about the environment. Another belief-governing mechanism is a reasoning mechanism, which, given a set of antecedent beliefs, generates or inhibits various new beliefs. A reasoning mechanism is reliable to the extent that its functional procedures would generate new true beliefs from antecedent true beliefs.

My emphasis on discrimination accords with a sense of the verb 'know' that has been neglected by philoso-

Alvin Goldman, "Discrimination and Perceptual Knowledge" from *The Journal of Philosophy,* 78 (1976). Reprinted by permission of the author and *The Journal of Philosophy.*

phers. The *O.E.D.* lists one (early) sense of 'know' as "*to distinguish* (one thing) *from* (another)," as in "I know a hawk from a handsaw" (*Hamlet*) and "We'll teach him to know Turtles from Jayes" (*Merry Wives of Windsor*). Although it no longer has great currency, this sense still survives in such expressions as "I don't know him from Adam," "He doesn't know right from left," and other phrases that readily come to mind. I suspect that this construction is historically important and can be used to shed light on constructions in which 'know' takes propositional objects. I suggest that a person is said to know that *p* just in case he *distinguishes* or *discriminates* the truth of *p* from relevant alternatives.

A knowledge attribution imputes to someone the discrimination of a given state of affairs from possible alternatives, but not necessarily all logically possible alternatives. In forming beliefs about the world, we do not normally consider all logical possibilities. And in deciding whether someone knows that *p* (its truth being assumed), we do not ordinarily require him to discriminate *p* from all logically possible alternatives. Which alternatives are, or ought to be considered, is a question I shall not fully resolve in this paper, but some new perspectives will be examined. I take up this topic in section I.

I

Consider the following example. Henry is driving in the countryside with his son. For the boy's edification Henry identifies various objects on the landscape as they come into view. "That's a cow," says Henry, "That's a tractor," "That's a silo," "That's a barn," etc. Henry has no doubt about the identity of these objects; in particular, he has no doubt that the last-mentioned object is a barn, which indeed it is. Each of the identified objects has features characteristic of its type. Moreover, each object is fully in view, Henry has excellent eyesight, and he has enough time to look at them reasonably carefully, since there is little traffic to distract him.

Given this information, would we say that Henry *knows* that the object is a barn? Most of us would have little hesitation in saying this, so long as we were not in a certain philosophical frame of mind. Contrast our inclination here with the inclination we would have if we were given some additional information. Suppose we are told that, unknown to Henry, the district he has just entered is full of papier-mâché facsimiles of barns. These facsimiles look from the road exactly like barns, but are really just façades, without back walls or interiors, quite incapable of being used as barns. They are so cleverly constructed that travelers invariably mistake them for barns. Having just entered the district, Henry has not encountered any facsimiles; the object he sees is a genuine barn. But if the object on that site were a facsimile, Henry would mistake it for a barn. Given this new information, we would be strongly inclined to withdraw the claim that Henry *knows* the object is a barn. How is this change in our assessment to be explained?

Note first that the traditional justified-true-belief account of knowledge is of no help in explaining this change. In both cases Henry truly believes (indeed, is certain) that the object is a barn. Moreover, Henry's "justification" or "evidence" for the proposition that the object is a barn is the same in both cases. Thus, Henry should either know in both cases or not know in both cases. The presence of facsimiles in the district should make no difference to whether or not he knows.

My old causal analysis cannot handle the problem either. Henry's belief that the object is a barn is caused by the presence of the barn; indeed, the causal process is a perceptual one. Nonetheless, we are not prepared to say, in the second version, that Henry knows.

One analysis of propositional knowledge that might handle the problem is Peter Unger's non-accidentality analysis.[1] According to this theory, *S* knows that *p* if and only if it is not at all accidental that *S* is right about its being the case that *p*. In the initial description of the example, this requirement appears to be satisfied; so we say that Henry knows. When informed about the facsimiles, however, we see that it is accidental that Henry is right about its being a barn. So we withdraw our knowledge attribution. The "non-accidentality" analysis is not very satisfying, however, for the notion of "non-accidentality" itself needs explication. Pending explication, it isn't clear whether it correctly handles all cases.

---

1. "An Analysis of Factual Knowledge," *Journal of Philosophy* LXV, 6 (Mar. 21, 1968): 157–70.

Another approach to knowledge that might handle our problem is the "indefeasibility" approach.[2] On this view, S knows that p only if S's true belief is justified *and* this justification is not defeated. In an unrestricted form, an indefeasibility theory would say that S's justification j for believing that p is defeated if and only if there is some true proposition q such that the conjunction of q and j does not justify S in believing that p. In slightly different terms, S's justification j is defeated just in case p would no longer be evident for S if q were evident for S. This would handle the barn example, presumably, because the true proposition that there are barn facsimiles in the district is such that, if it were evident for Henry, then it would no longer be evident for him that the object he sees is a barn.

The trouble with the indefeasibility approach is that it is too strong, at least in its unrestricted form. On the foregoing account of "defeat," as Gilbert Harman shows,[3] it will (almost) always be possible to find a true proposition that defeats S's justification. Hence, S will never (or seldom) know. What is needed is an appropriate restriction on the notion of "defeat," but I am not aware of an appropriate restriction that has been formulated thus far.

The approach to the problem I shall recommend is slightly different. Admittedly, this approach will raise problems analogous to those of the indefeasibility theory, problems which will not be fully resolved here. Nevertheless, I believe this approach is fundamentally on the right track.

What, then, is my proposed treatment of the barn example? A person knows that p, I suggest, only if the actual state of affairs in which p is true is *distinguishable* or *discriminable* by him from a relevant possible state of affairs in which p is false. If there is a relevant possible state of affairs in which p is false and which is indistinguish-able by him from the actual state of affairs, then he fails to know that p. In the original description of the barn case there is no hint of any relevant possible state of affairs in which the object in question is not a barn but is indistinguishable (by Henry) from the actual state of affairs. Hence, we are initially inclined to say that Henry knows. The information about the facsimiles, however, introduces such a relevant state of affairs. Given that the district Henry has entered is full of barn facsimiles, there is a relevant alternative hypothesis about the object, viz., that it is a facsimile. Since, by assumption, a state of affairs in which such a hypothesis holds is indistinguishable by Henry from the actual state of affairs (from his vantage point on the road), this hypothesis is not "ruled out" or "precluded" by the factors that prompt Henry's belief. So, once apprised of the facsimiles in the district, we are inclined to deny that Henry knows.

Let us be clear about the bearing of the facsimiles on the case. The presence of the facsimiles does not "create" the possibility that the object Henry sees is a facsimile. Even if there were no facsimiles in the district, it would be possible that the object on that site is a facsimile. What the presence of the facsimiles does is make this possibility *relevant;* or it makes us *consider* it relevant.

The qualifier 'relevant' plays an important role in my view. If knowledge required the elimination of all logically possible alternatives, there would be no knowledge (at least of contingent truths). If only *relevant* alternatives need to be precluded, however, the scope of knowledge could be substantial. This depends, of course, on which alternatives are relevant.

The issue at hand is directly pertinent to the dispute —at least one dispute—between skeptics and their opponents. In challenging a claim to knowledge (or certainty), a typical move of the skeptic is to adduce an unusual alternative hypothesis that the putative knower is unable to preclude: an alternative compatible with his "data." In the skeptical stage of his argument, Descartes says that he is unable to preclude the hypothesis that, instead of being seated by the fire, he is asleep in his bed and dreaming, or the hypothesis that an evil and powerful demon is making it appear to him as if he is seated by the fire. Similarly, Bertrand Russell points out that, given any claim about the past, we can adduce the "skeptical hypothesis" that the world sprang into being

---

2. See, for example, Keith Lehrer and Thomas Paxson, Jr., "Knowledge: Undefeated Justified True Belief," *Journal of Philosophy,* lxvi, 8 (Apr. 24, 1969): 225–37, and Peter D. Klein, "A Proposed Definition of Propositional Knowledge," *ibid.,* lxviii, 16 (Aug. 19, 1971): 471–82.

3. *Thought* (Princeton: Princeton University Press, 1973), p. 152.

five minutes ago, exactly as it then was, with a population that "remembered" a wholly unreal past.[4]

One reply open to the skeptic's opponent is that these skeptical hypotheses are just "idle" hypotheses, and that a person can know a proposition even if there are "idle" alternatives he cannot preclude. The problem, of course, is to specify when an alternative is "idle" and when it is "serious" ("relevant"). Consider Henry once again. Should we say that the possibility of a facsimile before him is a serious or relevant possibility if there are no facsimiles in Henry's district, but only in Sweden? Or if a single such facsimile once existed in Sweden, but none exist now?

There are two views one might take on this general problem. The first view is that there is a "correct" answer, in any given situation, as to which alternatives are relevant. Given a complete specification of Henry's situation, a unique set of relevant alternatives is determined: either a set to which the facsimile alternative belongs or one to which it doesn't belong. According to this view, the semantic content of 'know' contains (implicit) rules that map any putative knower's circumstances into a set of relevant alternatives. An analysis of 'know' is incomplete unless it specifies these rules. The correct specification will favor either the skeptic or the skeptic's opponent.

The second view denies that a putative knower's circumstances uniquely determine a set of relevant alternatives. At any rate, it denies that the semantic content of 'know' contains rules that map a set of circumstances into a single set of relevant alternatives. According to this second view, the verb 'know' is simply not so semantically determinate.

The second view need not deny that there are *regularities* governing the alternative hypotheses a speaker (i.e., an attributer or denier of knowledge) thinks of, and deems relevant. But these regularities are not part of the semantic content of 'know'. The putative knower's circumstances do not *mandate* a unique selection of alternatives; but psychological regularities govern which set of alternatives are in fact selected. In terms of these reg-

ularities (together with the semantic content of 'know'), we can explain the observed use of the term.

It is clear that some of these regularities pertain to the (description of the) putative knower's circumstances. One regularity might be that the more *likely* it is, given the circumstances, that a particular alternative would obtain (rather than the actual state of affairs), the more probable it is that a speaker will regard this alternative as relevant. Or, the more *similar* the situation in which the alternative obtains to the actual situation, the more probable it is that a speaker will regard this alternative as relevant. It is not only the circumstances of the putative knower's situation, however, that influence the choice of alternatives. The speaker's own linguistic and psychological context are also important. If the speaker is in a class where Descartes' evil demon had just been discussed, or Russell's five-minute-old-world hypothesis, he may think of alternatives he would not otherwise think of and will perhaps treat them seriously. This sort of regularity is entirely ignored by the first view.

What I am calling the "second" view might have two variants. The first variant can be imbedded in Robert Stalnaker's framework for pragmatics.[5] In this framework, a proposition is a function from possible words into truth values; the determinants of a proposition are a sentence and a (linguistic) context. An important contextual element is what the utterer of a sentence presupposes, or takes for granted. According to the first variant of the second view, a sentence of the form 'S knows that *p*' does not determine a unique proposition. Rather, a proposition is determined by such a sentence together with the speaker's presuppositions concerning the relevant alternatives.[6] Skeptics and nonskeptics might make different presuppositions (both presuppositions being "legitimate"), and, if so, they are simply asserting or denying different propositions.

One trouble with this variant is its apparent implication that, if a speaker utters a knowledge sentence

---

4. *The Analysis of Mind* (London: Allen & Unwin, 1921), pp. 159–60.

5. "Pragmatics," in Donald Davidson and Harman, eds., *Semantics of Natural Language* (Boston: Reidel, 1972).

6. Something like this is suggested by Fred Dretske in "Epistemic Operators," *Journal of Philosophy*, LXVII, 24 (Dec. 24, 1970): 1007–23, p. 1022.

without presupposing a fully determinate set of alternatives, he does not assert or deny any proposition. That seems too strong. A second variant of the second view, then, is that sentences of the form 'S knows that p' express vague or indeterminate propositions (if they express "propositions" at all), which can, but need not, be made more determinate by full specification of the alternatives. A person who *assents* to a knowledge sentence says that S discriminates the truth of p from relevant alternatives; but he may not have a distinct set of alternatives in mind. ([. . .]) Someone who *denies* a knowledge sentence more commonly has one or more alternatives in mind as relevant, because his denial may stem from a particular alternative S cannot rule out. But even the denier of a knowledge sentence need not have a full set of relevant alternatives in mind.

I am attracted by the second view under discussion, especially its second variant. In the remainder of the paper, however, I shall be officially neutral. In other words, I shall not try to settle the question of whether the semantic content of 'know' contains rules that map the putative knower's situation into a unique set of relevant alternatives. I leave open the question of whether there is a "correct" set of relevant alternatives, and if so, what it is. To this extent, I also leave open the question of whether skeptics or their opponents are "right." In defending my analysis of 'perceptually knows', however, I shall have to discuss particular examples. In treating these examples I shall assume some (psychological) regularities concerning the selection of alternatives. Among these regularities is the fact that speakers do not *ordinarily* think of "radical" alternatives, but are caused to think of such alternatives, and take them seriously, if the putative knower's circumstances call attention to them. Since I assume that radical or unusual alternatives are not *ordinarily* entertained or taken seriously, I may appear to side with the opponents of skepticism. My official analysis, however, is neutral on the issue of skepticism.

II

I turn now to the analysis of 'perceptually knows'. Suppose that Sam spots Judy on the street and correctly identifies her as Judy, i.e., believes she is Judy. Suppose

further that Judy has an identical twin, Trudy, and the possibility of the person's being Trudy (rather than Judy) is a relevant alternative. Under what circumstances would we say that Sam *knows* it is Judy?

If Sam regularly identifies Judy as Judy and Trudy as Trudy, he apparently has some (visual) way of discriminating between them (though he may not know how he does it, i.e., what cues he uses). If he does have a way of discriminating between them, which he uses on the occasion in question, we would say that he *knows* it is Judy. But if Sam frequently mistakes Judy for Trudy, and Trudy for Judy, he presumably does not have a way of discriminating between them. For example, he may not have sufficiently distinct (visual) memory "schemata" of Judy and Trudy. So that, on a particular occasion, sensory stimulation from either Judy *or* Trudy would elicit a Judy-identification from him. If he happens to be right that it is Judy, this is just accidental. He doesn't *know* it is Judy.

The crucial question in assessing a knowledge attribution, then, appears to be the truth value of a counterfactual (or set of counterfactuals). Where Sam correctly identifies Judy as Judy, the crucial counterfactual is: "If the person before Sam were Trudy (rather than Judy), Sam would believe her to be Judy." If this counterfactual is true, Sam doesn't know it is Judy. If this counterfactual is false (and all other counterfactuals involving relevant alternatives are also false), then Sam may know it is Judy.

This suggests the following analysis of (noninferential) perceptual knowledge.

S (noninferentially) *perceptually knows that p* if and only if

(1) S (noninferentially) perceptually believes that p,

(2) p is true, and

(3) there is no relevant contrary q of p such that, if q were true (rather than p), then S would (still) believe that p.

Restricting attention to relevant possibilities, these conditions assert in effect that the only situation in which S would believe that p is a situation in which p is true. In other words, S's believing that p is sufficient for the truth of p. [. . .]

This analysis is too restrictive. Suppose Oscar is standing in an open field containing Dack the dachshund. Oscar sees Dack and (noninferentially) forms a belief in (P):

(P) The object over there is a dog.

Now suppose that (Q):

(Q) The object over there is a wolf

is a relevant alternative to (P) (because wolves are frequenters of this field). Further suppose that Oscar has a tendency to mistake wolves for dogs (he confuses them with malamutes, or German shepherds). Then if the object Oscar saw were Wiley the wolf, rather than Dack the dachshund, Oscar would (still) believe (P). This means that Oscar fails to satisfy the proposed analysis with respect to (P), since (3) is violated. But surely it is wrong to deny—for the indicated reasons—that Oscar *knows* (P) to be true. The mere fact that he would erroneously take a wolf to be a dog hardly shows that he doesn't know a *dachshund* to be a dog! Similarly, if someone looks at a huge redwood and correctly believes it to be a tree, he is not disqualified from knowing it to be a tree merely because there is a very small plant he would wrongly believe to be a tree, i.e., a bonsai tree.

The moral can be formulated as follows. If Oscar believes that a dog is present because of a certain way he is "appeared to," then this true belief fails to be knowledge if there is an alternative situation in which a non-dog produces the same belief by means of the same, or a very similar, appearance. But the wolf situation is not such an alternative: although it would produce in him the same belief, it would not be by means of the same (or a similar) appearance. An alternative that disqualifies a true perceptual belief from being perceptual knowledge must be a "perceptual equivalent" of the actual state of affairs. A *perceptual equivalent* of an actual state of affairs is a possible state of affairs that would produce the same, or a sufficiently similar, perceptual experience.

The relation of perceptual equivalence must obviously be relativized to *persons* (or organisms). The presence of Judy and the presence of Trudy might be perceptual equivalents for Sam, but not for the twins' own mother (to whom the twins look quite different).

Similarly, perceptual equivalence must be relativized to *times,* since perceptual discriminative capacities can be refined or enhanced with training or experience, and can deteriorate with age or disease.

How shall we specify alternative states of affairs that are candidates for being perceptual equivalents? First, we should specify the *object* involved. (I assume for simplicity that only one object is in question.) As the Judy-Trudy case shows, the object in the alternative state of affairs need not be identical with the actual object. Sometimes, indeed, we may wish to allow non-actual possible objects. Otherwise our framework will be unable in principle to accommodate some of the skeptic's favorite alternatives, e.g., those involving demons. If the reader's ontological sensibility is offended by talk of possible objects, I invite him to replace such talk with any preferred substitute.

Some alternative states of affairs involve the same object but different properties. Where the actual state of affairs involved a certain ball painted blue, an alternative might be chosen involving the same ball painted green. Thus, specification of an alternative requires not only an object, but properties of the object (at the time in question). These should include not only the property in the belief under scrutiny, or one of its contraries, but other properties as well, since the property in the belief (or one of its contraries) might not be sufficiently determinate to indicate what the resultant percept would be like. For full generality, let us choose a *maximal set of* (nonrelational) *properties.* This is a set that would exhaustively characterize an object (at a single time) in some possible world.

An object plus a maximal set of (nonrelational) properties still does not fully specify a perceptual alternative. Also needed are relations between the object and the perceiver, plus conditions of the environment. One relation that can affect the resultant percept is *distance.* Another relational factor is *relative orientation,* both of object vis-à-vis perceiver and perceiver vis-à-vis object. The nature of the percept depends, for example, on which side of the object faces the perceiver, and on how the perceiver's bodily organs are oriented, or situated, vis-à-vis the object. Thirdly, the percept is affected by the current state of the *environment,* e.g., the illumination, the presence or absence of intervening objects, and the direction and velocity of the wind.

To cover all such elements, I introduce the notion of a *distance-orientation-environment* relation, for short, a *DOE relation*. Each such relation is a conjunction of relations or properties concerning distance, orientation, and environmental conditions. One DOE relation is expressed by the predicate 'x is 20 feet from y, the front side of y is facing x, the eyes of x are open and focused in y's direction, no opaque object is interposed between x and y, and y is in moonlight'.

Since the health of sensory organs can affect percepts, it might be argued that this should be included in these relations, thereby opening the condition of these organs to counterfactualization. For simplicity I neglect this complication. This does not mean that I don't regard the condition of sensory organs as open to counterfactualization. I merely omit explicit incorporation of this factor into our exposition.

We can now give more precision to our treatment of perceptual equivalents. Perceptual states of affairs will be specified by ordered triples, each consisting of (1) an object, (2) a maximal set of nonrelational properties, and (3) a DOE relation. If S perceives object b at t and if b has all the properties in a maximal set J and bears DOE relation R to S at t, then the actual state of affairs pertaining to this perceptual episode is represented by the ordered triple $<b,J,R>$. An alternative state of affairs is represented by an ordered triple $<c,K,R^{*}>$, which may (but need not) differ from $<b,J,R>$ with respect to one or more of its elements.

Under what conditions is an alternative $<c,K,R^{*}>$ a perceptual equivalent of $<b,J,R>$ for person S at time t? I said that a perceptual equivalent is a state of affairs that would produce "the same, or a very similar" perceptual experience. That is not very committal. Must a perceptual equivalent produce exactly the same percept? Given our intended use of perceptual equivalence in the analysis of perceptual knowledge, the answer is clearly No. Suppose that a Trudy-produced percept would be qualitatively distinct from Sam's Judy-produced percept, but similar enough for Sam to mistake Trudy for Judy. This is sufficient grounds for saying that Sam fails to have knowledge. Qualitative identity of percepts, then, is too strong a requirement for perceptual equivalence.

How should the requirement be weakened? We must not weaken it too much, for the wolf alternative might then be a perceptual equivalent of the dachshund state

of affairs. This would have the unwanted consequence that Oscar doesn't know Dack to be a dog.

The solution I propose is this. If the percept produced by the alternative state of affairs would not differ from the actual percept in any respect that is causally relevant to S's belief, this alternative situation is a perceptual equivalent for S of the actual situation. Suppose that a Trudy-produced percept would differ from Sam's Judy-produced percept to the extent of having a different eyebrow configuration. (A difference in shape between Judy's and Trudy's eyebrows does not ensure that Sam's percepts would "register" this difference. I assume, however, that the eyebrow difference would be registered in Sam's percepts.) But suppose that Sam's visual "concept" of Judy does not include a feature that reflects this contrast. His Judy-concept includes an "eyebrow feature" only in the sense that the absence of eyebrows would inhibit a Judy-classification. It does not include a more determinate eyebrow feature, though: Sam hasn't learned to associate Judy with distinctively shaped eyebrows. Hence, the distinctive "eyebrow shape" of his actual (Judy-produced) percept is not one of the percept-features that is causally responsible for his believing Judy to be present. Assuming that a Trudy-produced percept would not differ from his actual percept in any *other* causally relevant way, the hypothetical Trudy-situation is a perceptual equivalent of the actual Judy-situation.

Consider now the dachshund-wolf case. The hypothetical percept produced by a wolf would differ from Oscar's actual percept of the dachshund in respects that *are* causally relevant to Oscar's judgment that a dog is present. Let me elaborate. There are various kinds of objects, rather different in shape, size, color, and texture that would be classified by Oscar as a dog. He has a number of visual "schemata," we might say, each with a distinctive set of features, such that any percept that "matches" or "fits" one of these schemata would elicit a "dog" classification. (I think of a schema not as a "template," but as a set of more-or-less abstract—though iconic—features.) Now, although a dachshund and a wolf would each produce a dog-belief in Oscar, the percepts produced by these respective stimuli would differ in respects that are causally relevant to Oscar's forming a dog-belief. Since Oscar's dachshund-schema includes such features as having an elongated, sausagelike shape, a smallish size, droopy ears, these features of the percept are all causally relevant, when a dachshund is present, to Oscar's believing that a dog is present. Since a hypothetical wolf-produced percept would differ in these re-spects from Oscar's dachshund-produced percept, the hypothetical wolf state of affairs is not a perceptual equivalent of the dachshund state of affairs for Oscar. [. . .]

David Hume

An Enquiry Concerning Human Understanding

SECTION II
Of the Origin of Ideas.

Everyone will readily allow that there is a considerable difference between the perceptions of the mind when a man feels the pain of excessive heat or the pleasure of moderate warmth and when he afterwards recalls to his memory this sensation or anticipates it by his imagination. These faculties may mimic or copy the perceptions of the senses, but they never can entirely reach the force and vivacity of the original sentiment. The utmost we say of them, even when they operate with greatest vigor, is that they represent their object in so lively a manner that we could *almost* say we feel or see it: But, unless the mind is disordered by disease or madness, they never can arrive at such a pitch of vivacity as to render these perceptions altogether indistinguishable. All the colors of poetry, however splendid, can never paint natural objects in such a manner as to make the description be taken for a real landscape. The most lively thought is still inferior to the dullest sensation.

We may observe a like distinction to run through all the other perceptions of the mind. A man in a fit of anger is actuated in a very different manner from one who only thinks of that emotion. If you tell me that any person is in love, I easily understand your meaning and form a just conception of his situation, but never can mistake that conception for the real disorders and agitations of the passion. When we reflect on our past sentiments and affections, our thought is a faithful mirror and copies its objects truly, but the colors which it employs are faint and dull in comparison of those in which our original perceptions were clothed. It requires no nice discernment or metaphysical head to mark the distinction between them.

Here, therefore, we may divide all the perceptions of the mind into two classes or species which are distinguished by their different degrees of force and vivacity. The less forcible and lively are commonly denominated thoughts or ideas. The other species want a name in our language and in most others, I suppose, because it was not requisite for any but philosophical purposes to rank them under a general term or appellation. Let us, therefore, use a little freedom and call them impressions, employing that word in a sense somewhat different from the usual. By the term *impression,* then, I mean all our more lively perceptions, when we hear, or see, or feel, or love, or hate, or desire, or will. And impressions are distinguished from ideas, which are the less lively perceptions of which we are conscious when we reflect on any of those sensations or movements above mentioned.

Nothing, at first view, may seem more unbounded than the thought of man, which not only escapes all human power and authority, but is not even restrained within the limits of nature and reality. To form monsters and join incongruous shapes and appearances costs

From David Hume, *An Enquiry Concerning Human Understanding,* edited by Eric Steinberg (Indianapolis: Hackett Publishing Company, 1977). Reprinted by permission of the publisher.

the imagination no more trouble than to conceive the most natural and familiar objects. And while the body is confined to one planet, along which it creeps with pain and difficulty, the thought can in an instant transport us into the most distant regions of the universe or even beyond the universe into the unbounded chaos where nature is supposed to lie in total confusion. What never was seen or heard of, may yet be conceived, nor is anything beyond the power of thought except what implies an absolute contradiction.

But though our thought seems to possess this unbounded liberty, we shall find upon a nearer examination that it is really confined within very narrow limits and that all this creative power of the mind amounts to no more than the faculty of compounding, transposing, augmenting, or diminishing the materials afforded us by the senses and experience. When we think of a golden mountain, we only join two consistent ideas, *gold* and *mountain,* with which we were formerly acquainted. A virtuous horse we can conceive, because, from our own feeling, we can conceive virtue; and this we may unite to the figure and shape of a horse, which is an animal familiar to us. In short, all the materials of thinking are derived either from our outward or inward sentiment. The mixture and composition of these belongs alone to the mind and will. Or, to express myself in philosophical language, all our ideas or more feeble perceptions are copies of our impressions or more lively ones.

To prove this, the two following arguments will, I hope, be sufficient. *First,* when we analyze our thoughts or ideas, however compounded or sublime, we always find that they resolve themselves into such simple ideas as were copied from a precedent feeling or sentiment. Even those ideas which at first view seem the most wide of this origin are found, upon a nearer scrutiny, to be derived from it. The idea of God, as meaning an infinitely intelligent, wise, and good being, arises from reflecting on the operations of our own mind and augmenting, without limit, those qualities of goodness and wisdom. We may prosecute this inquiry to what length we please; where we shall always find that every idea which we examine is copied from a similar impression. Those who would assert that this position is not universally true, nor without exception, have only one method, and an easy one at that, of refuting it by producing that idea which, in their opinion, is not derived

from this source. It will then be incumbent on us, if we would maintain our doctrine, to produce the impression or lively perception which corresponds to it.

Secondly, if it happens, from a defect of the organ, that a man is not susceptible of any species of sensation, we always find that he is as little susceptible of the correspondent ideas. A blind man can form no notion of colors, a deaf man of sounds. Restore either of them that sense in which he is deficient by opening this new inlet for his sensations, you also open an inlet for the ideas and he finds no difficulty in conceiving these objects. The case is the same if the object proper for exciting any sensation has never been applied to the organ. A Laplander or Negro has no notion of the relish of wine. And though there are few or no instances of a like deficiency in the mind where a person has never felt or is wholly incapable of a sentiment or passion that belongs to his species, yet we find the same observation to take place in a less degree. A man of mild manners can form no idea of inveterate revenge or cruelty, nor can a selfish heart easily conceive the heights of friendship and generosity. It is readily allowed that other beings may possess many senses of which we can have no conception, because the ideas of them have never been introduced to us in the only manner by which an idea can have access to the mind, namely, by the actual feeling and sensation.

There is, however, one contradictory phenomenon which may prove that it is not absolutely impossible for ideas to arise independent of their correspondent impressions. I believe it will readily be allowed that the several distinct ideas of color which enter by the eye or those of sound which are conveyed by the ear are really different from each other, though at the same time resembling. Now if this is true of different colors, it must be no less so of the different shades of the same color; and each shade produces a distinct idea, independent of the rest. For if this should be denied, it is possible, by the continual gradation of shades, to run a color insensibly into what is most remote from it; and if you will not allow any of the means to be different, you cannot without absurdity deny the extremes to be the same. Suppose, therefore, a person to have enjoyed his sight for thirty years and to have become perfectly acquainted with colors of all kinds, except one particular shade of blue, for instance, which it never has been his fortune to meet with. Let all the different shades of that color, except that single one, be placed before him, descending gradually from the deepest to the lightest, it is plain that he will perceive a blank where that shade is wanting, and will be sensible that there is a greater distance in that place between the contiguous colors than in any other. Now I ask whether it is possible for him, from his own imagination, to supply this deficiency and raise up to himself the idea of that particular shade, though it had never been conveyed to him by his senses? I believe there are few but will be of the opinion that he can. And this may serve as a proof that the simple ideas are not always, in every instance, derived from the correspondent impressions, though this instance is so singular that it is scarcely worth our observing and does not merit that for it alone we should alter our general maxim.

Here, therefore, is a proposition which not only seems in itself simple and intelligible, but, if a proper use were made of it, might render every dispute equally intelligible and banish all that jargon, which has so long taken possession of metaphysical reasonings and drawn disgrace upon them. All ideas, especially abstract ones, are naturally faint and obscure. The mind has but a slender hold of them. They are apt to be confounded with other resembling ideas; and when we have often employed any term, though without a distinct meaning, we are apt to imagine that it has a determinate idea annexed to it. On the contrary, all impressions, that is, all sensations either outward or inward, are strong and vivid. The limits between them are more exactly determined; nor is it easy to fall into any error or mistake with regard to them. When we entertain, therefore, any suspicion that a philosophical term is employed without any meaning or idea (as is but too frequent), we need but inquire *from what impression is that supposed idea derived?* And if it is impossible to assign any, this will serve to confirm our suspicion. By bringing ideas into so clear a light, we may reasonably hope to remove all dispute which may arise concerning their nature and reality.

SECTION III
Of the Association of Ideas.

It is evident that there is a principle of connection between the different thoughts or ideas of the mind and that, in their appearance to the memory or imagination,

they introduce each other with a certain degree of method and regularity. In our more serious thinking or discourse this is so observable that any particular thought which breaks in upon the regular tract or chain of ideas is immediately remarked and rejected. And even in our wildest and most wandering reveries, no, in our very dreams, we shall find, if we reflect, that the imagination did not run altogether at adventures, but that there was still a connection upheld among the different ideas which succeeded each other. Were the loosest and freest conversation to be transcribed, there would immediately be observed something which connected it in all its transitions. Or where this is wanting, the principle which had an equal influence on all mankind.

Though it is too obvious to escape observation that different ideas are connected together, I do not find that any philosopher has attempted to enumerate or class all the principles of association—a subject, however, that seems worthy of curiosity. To me there appear to be only three principles of connection among ideas, namely, *resemblance, contiguity* in time or place, and *cause* or *effect.*

That these principles serve to connect ideas will not, I believe, be much doubted. A picture naturally leads our thoughts to the original.[1] The mention of one apartment in a building naturally introduces an inquiry or discourse concerning the others;[2] and if we think of a wound, we can scarcely forbear reflecting on the pain which follows it.[3] But that this enumeration is complete, and that there are no other principles of association except these, may be difficult to prove to the satisfaction of the reader or even to a man's own satisfaction. All we can do, in such cases, is to run over several instances and examine carefully the principle which binds the different thoughts to each other, never stopping until we render the principle as general as possible.[4] The more instances we examine and the more

---

1. Resemblance.

2. Contiguity.

3. Cause and Effect.

4. For instance, *Contrast* or *Contrariety* is also a connexion among ideas: But it may, perhaps, be considered as a mixture of *Causation* and *Resemblance.* Where two objects are contrary, the one destroys the other; that is, the cause of its annihilation, and the idea of the annihilation of an object, implies the idea of its former existence.

care we employ, the more assurance shall we acquire that the enumeration, which we form from the whole, is complete and entire.

SECTION IV
Skeptical Doubts Concerning the Operations of the Understanding.

Part I.

All the objects of human reason or inquiry may naturally be divided into two kinds, namely, *relations of ideas* and *matters of fact*. Of the first kind are the sciences of geometry, algebra, and arithmetic, and, in short, every affirmation which is either intuitively or demonstratively certain. *That the square of the hypotenuse is equal to the squares of the two sides* is a proposition which expresses a relation between these figures. *That three times five is equal to the half of thirty* expresses a relation between these numbers. Propositions of this kind are discoverable by the mere operation of thought, without dependence on what is anywhere existent in the universe. Though there never were a circle or triangle in nature, the truths demonstrated by Euclid would forever retain their certainty and evidence.

Matters of fact, which are the second objects of human reason, are not ascertained in the same manner; nor is our evidence of their truth, however great, of a like nature with the foregoing. The contrary of every matter of fact is still possible, because it can never imply a contradiction and is conceived by the mind with the same facility and distinctness, as if ever so conformable to reality. *That the sun will not rise tomorrow* is no less intelligible a proposition and implies no more contradiction than the affirmation that *it will rise*. We should in vain, therefore, attempt to demonstrate its falsehood. Were it demonstratively false, it would imply a contradiction and could never be distinctly conceived by the mind.

It may, therefore, be a subject worthy of curiosity to inquire what is the nature of that evidence which assures us of any real existence and matter of fact beyond the present testimony of our senses or the records of our memory. This part of philosophy, it is observable, has been little cultivated either by the ancients or moderns, and, therefore, our doubts and errors in the prosecution

of so important an inquiry may be the more excusable, while we march through such difficult paths without any guide or direction. They may even prove useful by exciting curiosity and destroying that implicit faith and security which is the bane of all reasoning and free inquiry. The discovery of defects in the common philosophy, if there are any, will not, I presume, be a discouragement, but rather an incitement, as is usual, to attempt something more full and satisfactory than has yet been proposed to the public.

All reasonings concerning matter of fact seem to be founded on the relation of *cause and effect*. By means of that relation alone we can go beyond the evidence of our memory and senses. If you were to ask a man why he believes any matter of fact which is absent—for instance, that his friend is in the country or in France—he would give you a reason, and this reason would be some other fact: as a letter received from him or the knowledge of his former resolutions and promises. A man finding a watch or any other machine on a desert island would conclude that there had once been men on that island. All our reasonings concerning fact are of the same nature. And here it is constantly supposed that there is a connection between the present fact and that which is inferred from it. Were there nothing to bind them together, the inference would be entirely precarious. The hearing of an articulate voice and rational discourse in the dark assures us of the presence of some person. Why? Because these are the effects of the human make and fabric, and closely connected with it. If we anatomize all the other reasonings of this nature, we shall find that they are founded on the relation of cause and effect and that this relation is either near or remote, direct or collateral. Heat and light are collateral effects of fire and the one effect may justly be inferred from the other.

If we would satisfy ourselves, therefore, concerning the nature of that evidence which assures us of matters of fact, we must inquire how we arrive at the knowledge of cause and effect.

I shall venture to affirm, as a general proposition which admits of no exception, that the knowledge of this relation is not, in any instance, attained by reasonings *a priori,* but arises entirely from experience when we find that any particular objects are constantly conjoined with each other. Let an object be presented to a man of ever so strong natural reason and abilities; if that object is entirely new to him, he will not be able, by the most accurate examination of its sensible qualities, to discover any of its causes or effects. Adam, though his rational faculties are supposed entirely perfect at the very first, could not have inferred from the fluidity and transparency of water that it would suffocate him, or from the light and warmth of fire that it would consume him. No object ever discovers, by the qualities which appear to the senses, either the causes which produced it or the effects which will arise from it; nor can our reason, unassisted by experience, ever draw any inference concerning real existence and matter of fact.

This proposition, *that causes and effects are discoverable, not by reason but by experience,* will readily be admitted with regard to such objects as we remember to have once been altogether unknown to us, since we must be conscious of the utter inability which we then lay under of foretelling what would arise from them. Present two smooth pieces of marble to a man who has no tincture of natural philosophy; he will never discover that they will adhere together in such a manner as to require great force to separate them in a direct line, while they make so small a resistance to a lateral pressure. Such events as bear little analogy to the common course of nature are also readily confessed to be known only by experience, nor does any man imagine that the explosion of gunpowder or the attraction of a lodestone could ever be discovered by *a priori* arguments. In like manner, when an effect is supposed to depend upon an intricate machinery or secret structure of parts, we make no difficulty in attributing all our knowledge of it to experience. Who will assert that he can give the ultimate reason why milk or bread is proper nourishment for a man, not for a lion or a tiger?

But the same truth may not appear at first sight to have the same evidence with regard to events which have become familiar to us from our first appearance in the world, which bear a close analogy to the whole course of nature, and which are supposed to depend on the simple qualities of objects without any secret structure of parts. We are apt to imagine that we could discover these effects by the mere operation of our reason without experience. We fancy that were we brought, all of the sudden, into this world, we could at first have inferred that one billiard ball would communicate motion to another upon impulse and that we did not need to have waited for the event in order to pronounce with

certainty concerning it. Such is the influence of custom that where it is strongest it not only covers our natural ignorance, but even conceals itself and seems not to take place, merely because it is found in the highest degree.

But to convince us that all the laws of nature and all the operations of bodies without exception are known only by experience, the following reflections may perhaps suffice. Were any object presented to us and were we required to pronounce concerning the effect which will result from it without consulting past observation, after what manner, I beseech you, must the mind proceed in this operation? It must invent or imagine some event which it ascribes to the object as its effect and it is plain that this invention must be entirely arbitrary. The mind can never possibly find the effect in the supposed cause by the most accurate scrutiny and examination. For the effect is totally different from the cause and consequently can never be discovered in it. Motion in the second billiard ball is a quite distinct event from motion in the first, nor is there anything in the one to suggest the smallest hint of the other. A stone or piece of metal raised into the air and left without any support immediately falls. But to consider the matter *a priori* is there anything we discover in this situation which can beget the idea of a downward rather than an upward or any other motion in the stone or metal?

And as the first imagination or invention of a particular effect in all natural operations is arbitrary where we do not consult experience, so must we also esteem the supposed tie or connection between the cause and effect which binds them together and renders it impossible that any other effect could result from the operation of that cause. When I see, for instance, a billiard ball moving in a straight line towards another, even suppose motion in the second ball should by accident be suggested to me as the result of their contact or impulse, may I not conceive that a hundred different events might as well follow from that cause? May not both these balls remain at absolute rest? May not the first ball return in a straight line or leap off from the second in any line or direction? All these suppositions are consistent and conceivable. Why then should we give the preference to one which is no more consistent or conceivable than the rest? All our reasonings *a priori* will never be able to show us any foundation for this preference.

In a word, then, every effect is a distinct event from its cause. It could not, therefore, be discovered in the cause and the first invention or conception of it, *a priori,* must be entirely arbitrary. And even after it is suggested, the conjunction of it with the cause must appear equally arbitrary, since there are always many other effects which, to reason, must seem fully as consistent and natural. In vain, therefore, should we pretend to determine any single event or infer any cause or effect without the assistance of observation and experience.

Hence we may discover the reason why no philosopher who is rational and modest has ever pretended to assign the ultimate cause of any natural operation or to show distinctly the action of that power which produces any single effect in the universe. It is confessed that the utmost effort of human reason is to reduce the principles productive of natural phenomena to a greater simplicity and to resolve the many particular effects into a few general causes by means of reasonings from analogy, experience, and observation. But as to the causes of these general causes, we should in vain attempt their discovery, nor shall we ever be able to satisfy ourselves by any particular explication of them. These ultimate springs and principles are totally shut up from human curiosity and inquiry. Elasticity, gravity, cohesion of parts, communication of motion by impulse—these are probably the ultimate causes and principles which we shall ever discover in nature; and we may esteem ourselves sufficiently happy if, by accurate inquiry and reasoning, we can trace up the particular phenomena to, or near to, these general principles. The most perfect philosophy of the natural kind only staves off our ignorance a little longer, as perhaps the most perfect philosophy of the moral or metaphysical kind serves only to discover larger portions of it. Thus the observation of human blindness and weakness is the result of all philosophy and meets us at every turn in spite of our endeavors to elude or avoid it.

Nor is geometry, when taken into the assistance of natural philosophy, ever able to remedy this defect or lead us into the knowledge of ultimate causes by all that accuracy of reasoning for which it is so justly celebrated. Every part of mixed mathematics proceeds upon the supposition that certain laws are established by nature in her operations and abstract reasonings are employed either to assist experience in the discovery of these laws or to determine their influence in particular instances where it depends upon any precise degree of distance and quantity. Thus, it is a law of motion, discovered by experience, that the moment or force of any body in motion is in the compound ratio or proportion of its solid contents and its velocity, and consequently that a small force may remove the greatest obstacle or raise the greatest weight if, by any contrivance or machinery, we can increase the velocity of that force so as to make it an overmatch for its antagonist. Geometry assists us in the application of this law by giving us the just dimensions of all the parts and figures which can enter into any species of machine, but still the discovery of the law itself is owing merely to experience and all the abstract reasonings in the world could never lead us one step towards the knowledge of it. When we reason *a priori* and consider merely any object or cause as it appears to the mind, independent of all observation, it never could suggest to us the notion of any distinct object, such as its effect, much less show us the inseparable and inviolable connection between them. A man must be very sagacious who could discover by reasoning that crystal is the effect of heat, and ice of cold, without being previously acquainted with the operation of these qualities.

Part II.

But we have not yet attained any tolerable satisfaction with regard to the question first proposed. Each solution still gives rise to a new question as difficult as the foregoing and leads us on to further inquiries. When it is asked, *What is the nature of all our reasonings concerning matter of fact?* the proper answer seems to be that they are founded on the relation of cause and effect. When again it is asked, *What is the foundation of all our reasonings and conclusions concerning that relation?* it may be replied in one word, experience. But if we still carry on our sifting humor and ask, *What is the foundation of all conclusions from experience?* this implies a new question which may be of more difficult solution and explication. Philosophers who give themselves airs of superior wisdom and sufficiency have a hard task when they encounter persons of inquisitive dispositions, who push them from every corner to which they retreat, and who are sure at last to bring them to some dangerous dilemma. The best expedient to prevent this confusion is to be modest in our pretensions and even to discover the difficulty ourselves before it is objected to us. By this means we may make a kind of merit of our very ignorance.

I shall content myself in this section with an easy task and shall pretend only to give a negative answer to the question here proposed. I say, then, that even after we have experience of the operations of cause and effect, our conclusions from that experience are not founded on reasoning or any process of the understanding. This answer we must endeavor both to explain and to defend.

It must certainly be allowed that nature has kept us at a great distance from all her secrets and has afforded us only the knowledge of a few superficial qualities of objects, while she conceals from us those powers and principles on which the influence of these objects entirely depends. Our senses inform us of the color, weight, and consistency of bread, but neither sense nor reason can ever inform us of those qualities which fit it for the nourishment and support of a human body. Sight or feeling conveys an idea of the actual motion of bodies, but as to that wonderful force or power which would carry on a moving body forever in a continued change of place and which bodies never lose but by communicating it to others, of this we cannot form the most distant conception. But notwithstanding this ignorance of natural powers and principles, we always presume when we see like sensible qualities that they have like secret powers and expect that effects similar to those which we have experienced will follow from them. If a body of like color and consistency with that bread which we have formerly eaten is presented to us, we make no scruple of repeating the experiment and foresee with certainty like nourishment and support. Now this is a process of the mind or thought of which I would willingly know the foundation. It is allowed on all hands that there is no known connection between the sensible qualities and the secret powers, and consequently that the mind is not led to form such a conclusion concerning their constant and regular conjunction by anything which it knows of their nature. As to past *experience,* it can be allowed to give *direct* and *certain* information of those precise objects only and that precise period of time which fell under its cognizance. But why this experience should be extended to future times and to other objects which, for all we know, may be only similar in appearance; this is the main question on which I would insist. The bread which I formerly ate nourished me—that is, a body of such sensible qualities was, at that time, endowed with such secret powers. But does it follow that other bread must also nourish me at

another time and that like sensible qualities must always be attended with like secret powers? The consequence seems in no way necessary. At least, it must be acknowledged that there is here a consequence drawn by the mind that there is a certain step taken, a process of thought, and an inference which wants to be explained. These two propositions are far from being the same: *I have found that such an object has always been attended with such an effect,* and *I foresee that other objects which are similar in appearance will be attended with similar effects.* I shall allow, if you please, that the one proposition may justly be inferred from the other; I know in fact that it always is inferred. But if you insist that the inference is made by a chain of reasoning, I desire you to produce that reasoning. The connection between these propositions is not intuitive. There is required a medium which may enable the mind to draw such an inference, if indeed it is drawn by reasoning and argument. What that medium is, I must confess, passes my comprehension; and it is incumbent on those to produce it who assert that it really exists and is the origin of all our conclusions concerning matter of fact.

This negative argument must certainly, in process of time, become altogether convincing if many penetrating and able philosophers shall turn their inquiries this way and no one is ever able to discover any connecting proposition or intermediate step which supports the understanding in this conclusion. But as the question is yet new, every reader may not trust so far to his own penetration as to conclude that, because an argument escapes his inquiry, therefore it does not really exist. For this reason it may be requisite to venture upon a more difficult task, and, enumerating all the branches of human knowledge, endeavor to show that none of them can afford such an argument.

All reasonings may be divided into two kinds, namely, demonstrative reasoning, or that concerning relations of ideas, and moral reasoning, or that concerning matter of fact and existence. That there are no demonstrative arguments in the case seems evident, since it implies no contradiction that the course of nature may change and that an object, seemingly like those which we have experienced, may be attended with different or contrary effects. May I not clearly and distinctly conceive that a body, falling from the clouds and which in all other respects resembles snow, has yet the taste of salt or feeling of fire? Is there any more intelligible proposition than to affirm that all the trees will flourish in December and January and decay in May and June? Now, whatever is intelligible and can be distinctly conceived implies no contradiction and can never be proved false by any demonstrative argument or abstract reasoning *a priori.*

If we are, therefore, engaged by arguments to put trust in past experience and make it the standard of our future judgment, these arguments must be probable only, or such as regard matter of fact and real existence according to the division above mentioned. But that there is no argument of this kind must appear if our explication of that species of reasoning is admitted as solid and satisfactory. We have said that all arguments concerning existence are founded on the relation of cause and effect, that our knowledge of that relation is derived entirely from experience, and that all our experimental conclusions proceed upon the supposition that the future will be conformable to the past. To endeavor, therefore, the proof of this last supposition by probable arguments, or arguments regarding existence, must be evidently going in a circle and taking that which is the very point in question for granted.

In reality, all arguments from experience are founded on the similarity which we discover among natural objects and by which we are induced to expect effects similar to those which we have found to follow from such objects. And though none but a fool or madman will ever pretend to dispute the authority of experience or to reject that great guide of human life, it may surely be allowed a philosopher to have so much curiosity at least as to examine the principle of human nature which gives this mighty authority to experience and makes us draw advantage from that similarity which nature has placed among different objects. From causes which appear *similar,* we expect similar effects. This is the sum of all our experimental conclusions. Now it seems evident that, if this conclusion were formed by reason, it would be as perfect at first, and upon one instance, as after ever so long a course of experience. But the case is far otherwise. Nothing so like as eggs, yet no one, on account of this appearing similarity, expects the same taste and relish in all of them. It is only after a long course of uniform experiments in any kind that we attain a firm reliance and security with regard to a particular event. Now where is that process of reasoning which, from one instance, draws a conclusion so different from that which it infers from a hundred instances that are in no way different from that single one? This question I propose as much for the sake of information as with an intention of raising difficulties. I cannot find, I cannot imagine any such reasoning. But I keep my mind still open to instruction, if anyone will vouchsafe to bestow it on me.

Should it be said that, from a number of uniform experiments, we *infer* a connection between the sensible qualities and the secret powers? This, I must confess, seems the same difficulty couched in different terms. The question still recurs: on what process of argument this *inference* is founded? Where is the medium, the interposing ideas which join propositions so very wide of each other? It is confessed that the color, consistency, and other sensible qualities of bread do not appear of themselves to have any connection with the secret powers of nourishment and support. For otherwise we could infer these secret powers from the first appearance of these sensible qualities without the aid of experience, contrary to the sentiment of all philosophers and contrary to plain matter of fact. Here, then, is our natural state of ignorance with regard to the powers and influence of all objects. How is this remedied by experience? It only shows us a number of uniform effects resulting from certain objects and teaches us that those particular objects, at that particular time, were endowed with such powers and forces. When a new object endowed with similar sensible qualities is produced, we expect similar powers and forces and look for a like effect. From a body of like color and consistency with bread, we expect like nourishment and support. But this surely is a step or progress of the mind which wants to be explained. When a man says, *I have found, in all past instances, such sensible qualities conjoined with such secret powers:* And when he says, *Similar sensible qualities will always be conjoined with similar secret powers;* he is not guilty of a tautology, nor are these propositions in any respect the same. You say that the one proposition is an inference from the other. But you must confess that the inference is not intuitive, neither is it demonstrative. Of what nature is it then? To say it is experimental is begging the question. For all inferences from experience suppose as their foundation that the future will resemble the past and that similar powers will be conjoined with similar sensible qualities. If there is any suspicion that the course of nature may change, and that the past may be no rule for the future, all experience becomes useless and can give rise to no inference or conclusion. It is impossible, therefore, that any arguments from experience can prove this resemblance of the past to the future, since all these arguments are founded on the supposition of that resemblance. Let the course of things be allowed up to now ever so regular, that alone, without some new argument or inference, does not prove that for the future it will continue so. In vain do you pretend to have learned the nature of bodies from your past experience. Their secret nature and, consequently, all their effects and influence may change without any change in their sensible qualities. This happens sometimes and with regard to some objects. Why may it not happen always and with regard to all objects? What logic, what process of argument secures you against this supposition? My practice, you say, refutes my doubts. But you mistake the purport of my question. As an agent, I am quite satisfied in the point; but as a philosopher who has some share of curiosity—I will not say skepticism—I want to learn the foundation of this inference. No reading, no inquiry has yet been able to remove my difficulty or give me satisfaction in a matter of such importance. Can I do better than propose the difficulty to the public, even though, perhaps, I have small hopes of obtaining a solution? We shall at least, by this means, be sensible of our ignorance, if we do not augment our knowledge.

I must confess that a man is guilty of unpardonable arrogance who concludes, because an argument has escaped his own investigation, that therefore it does not really exist. I must also confess that, though all the learned for several ages should have employed themselves in fruitless search upon any subject, it may still, perhaps, be rash to conclude positively that the subject must therefore pass all human comprehension. Even though we examine all the sources of our knowledge and conclude them unfit for such a subject, there may still remain a suspicion that the enumeration is not complete or the examination not accurate. But with regard to the present subject, there are some considerations which seem to remove all this accusation of arrogance or suspicion of mistake.

It is certain that the most ignorant and stupid peasants, no infants, no even brute beasts, improve by experience and learn the qualities of natural objects by observing the effects which result from them. When a child has felt the sensation of pain from touching the flame of a candle, he will be careful not to put his hand near any candle, but will expect a similar effect from a cause which is similar in its sensible qualities and appearance. If you assert, therefore, that the understanding of the child is led into this conclusion by any process of argument or ratiocination, I may justly require you to produce that argument, nor have you any pretense to refuse so equitable a demand. You cannot say that the argument is abstruse and may possibly escape your inquiry, since you confess that it is obvious to the capacity of a mere infant. If you hesitate therefore a moment or if, after reflection, you produce any intricate or profound argument, you, in a manner, give up the question and confess that it is not reasoning which engages us to suppose the past resembling the future and to expect similar effects from causes which are similar to appearance. This is the proposition which I intended to enforce in the present section. If I am right, I pretend not to have made any mighty discovery. And if I am wrong, I must acknowledge myself to be indeed a very backward scholar, since I cannot now discover an argument which, it seems, was perfectly familiar to me long before I was out of my cradle.

Section V
Skeptical Solution of These Doubts.

Part I.

The passion for philosophy, like that for religion, seems liable to this inconvenience that, though it aims at the correction of our manners and extirpation of our vices, it may only serve, by imprudent management, to foster a predominant inclination and push the mind, with more determined resolution, towards that side which already *draws* too much by the bias and propensity of the natural temper. It is certain that, while we aspire to the magnanimous firmness of the philosophic sage and endeavor to confine our pleasures altogether within our own minds, we may, at last, render our philosophy like that of Epictetus and other *Stoics,* only a more refined system of selfishness, and reason ourselves out of all virtue as well as social enjoyment. While we study with attention the vanity of human life and turn all our thoughts towards the empty and transitory nature of riches and honors, we are, perhaps, all the while flatter-ing our natural indolence which, hating the bustle of the world and drudgery of business, seeks a pretense of reason to give itself a full and uncontrolled indulgence. There is, however, one species of philosophy which seems little liable to this inconvenience, and that be-cause it strikes in with no disorderly passion of the hu-man mind, nor can mingle itself with any natural affection or propensity; and that is the Academic or skeptical philosophy. The academics always talk of doubt and suspense of judgment, of danger in hasty de-terminations, of confining to very narrow bounds the inquiries of the understanding, and of renouncing all speculations which do not lie within the limits of com-mon life and practice. Nothing, therefore, can be more contrary than such a philosophy to the supine indo-lence of the mind, its rash arrogance, its lofty preten-sions, and its superstitious credulity. Every passion is mortified by it except the love of truth; and that passion never is nor can be carried to too high a degree. It is surprising, therefore, that this philosophy, which in al-most every instance must be harmless and innocent, should be the subject of so much groundless reproach and blame. But, perhaps, the very circumstance which renders it so innocent is what chiefly exposes it to the public hatred and resentment. By flattering no irregu-lar passion, it gains few partisans. By opposing so many vices and follies, it raises to itself abundance of enemies who stigmatize it as libertine, profane, and irreligious.

Nor need we fear that this philosophy, while it en-deavors to limit our inquiries to common life, should ever undermine the reasonings of common life and carry its doubts so far as to destroy all action as well as speculation. Nature will always maintain her rights and prevail in the end over any abstract reasoning whatso-ever. Though we should conclude, for instance, as in the foregoing section that, in all reasonings from expe-rience, there is a step taken by the mind which is not supported by any argument or process of the under-standing, there is no danger that these reasonings, on which almost all knowledge depends, will ever be af-fected by such a discovery. If the mind is not engaged by argument to make this step, it must be induced by some other principle of equal weight and authority and that principle will preserve its influence as long as hu-man nature remains the same. What that principle is may well be worth the pains of inquiry.

Suppose a person, though endowed with the strongest faculties of reason and reflection, to be brought on a sud-den into this world; he would, indeed, immediately ob-serve a continual succession of objects and one event following another, but he would not be able to discover anything further. He would not at first, by any reason-ing, be able to reach the idea of cause and effect, since the particular powers by which all natural operations are performed never appear to the senses; nor is it reason-able to conclude, merely because one event in one in-stance precedes another, that therefore the one is the cause, the other the effect. Their conjunction may be ar-bitrary and casual. There may be no reason to infer the existence of one from the appearance of the other. And in a word, such a person without more experience could never employ his conjecture or reasoning concerning any matter of fact or be assured of anything beyond what was immediately present to his memory and senses.

Suppose again that he has acquired more experience and has lived so long in the world as to have observed similar objects or events to be constantly conjoined to-gether—what is the consequence of this experience? He immediately infers the existence of one object from the appearance of the other. Yet he has not, by all his ex-perience, acquired any idea or knowledge of the secret power by which the one object produces the other, nor is it by any process of reasoning he is engaged to draw this inference. But still he finds himself determined to draw it. And though he should be convinced that his understanding has no part in the operation, he would nevertheless continue in the same course of thinking. There is some other principle which determines him to form such a conclusion.

This principle is *custom* or *habit*. For wherever the repetition of any particular act or operation produces a propensity to renew the same act or operation without being impelled by any reasoning or process of the un-derstanding, we always say that this propensity is the ef-fect of *custom*. By employing that word we pretend not to have given the ultimate reason of such a propensity. We only point out a principle of human nature which is universally acknowledged and which is well known by its effects. Perhaps we can push our inquiries no fur-ther or pretend to give the cause of this cause, but must rest contented with it as the ultimate principle which we can assign of all our conclusions from experience. It is sufficient satisfaction that we can go so far without repining at the narrowness of our faculties because they will carry us no further. And it is certain we here advance a very intelligible proposition at least, if not a true one, when we assert that after the constant conjunction of two objects, heat and flame, for instance, or weight and solidity, we are determined by custom alone to expect the one from the appearance of the other. This hypothesis seems even the only one which explains the difficulty why we draw, from a thousand instances, an inference which we are not able to draw from one instance that is in no respect different from them. Reason is incapable of any such variation. The conclusions which it draws from considering one circle are the same which it would form upon surveying all the circles in the universe. But no man, having seen only one body move after being impelled by another, could infer that every other body will move after a like impulse. All inferences from experience, therefore, are effects of custom, not of reasoning.[5]

Custom, then, is the great guide of human life. It is that principle alone which renders our experience useful

---

5. Nothing is more usual than for writers, even on *moral, political,* or *physical* subjects, to distinguish between *reason* and *experience,* and to suppose, that these species of argumentation are entirely different from each other. The former are taken for the mere result of our intellectual faculties, which, by considering *a priori* the nature of things, and examining the effects, that must follow from their operation, establish particular principles of science and philosophy. The latter are supposed to be derived entirely from sense and observation, by which we learn what has actually resulted from the operation of particular objects, and are thence able to infer, what will, for the future, result from them. Thus, for instance, the limitations and restraints of civil government, and a legal constitution, may be defended, either from *reason,* which reflecting on the great frailty and corruption of human nature, teaches that no man can safely be trusted with unlimited authority; or from *experience* and history, which inform us of the enormous abuses, that ambition, in every age and country, has been found to make of so imprudent a confidence.

The same distinction between reason and experience is maintained in all our deliberations concerning the conduct of life; while the experienced statesman, general, physician, or merchant is trusted and followed; and the unpractised novice, with whatever natural talents endowed, neglected and despised. Though it be allowed, that reason may form

very plausible conjectures with regard to the consequences of such a particular conduct in such particular circumstances; it is still supposed imperfect, without the assistance of experience, which is alone able to give stability and certainty to the maxims, derived from study and reflection.

But notwithstanding that this distinction be thus universally received, both in the active and speculative scenes of life, I shall not scruple to pronounce, that it is, at bottom, erroneous, at least, superficial.

If we examine those arguments which, in any of the sciences above-mentioned, are supposed to be the mere effects of reasoning and reflection, they will be found to terminate, at last, in some general principle or conclusion, for which we can assign no reason but observation and experience. The only difference between them and those maxims, which are vulgarly esteemed the result of pure experience, is, that the former cannot be established without some process of thought, and some reflection on what we have observed, in order to distinguish its circumstances, and trace its consequences: Whereas in the latter, the experienced event is exactly and fully similar to that which we infer as the result of any particular situation. The history of a Tiberius or a Nero makes us dread a like tyranny, were our monarchs freed from the restraints of laws and senates: But the observation of any fraud or cruelty in private life is sufficient, with the aid of a little thought, to give us the same apprehension; while it serves as an instance of the general curruption of human nature, and shows us the danger which we must incur by reposing an entire confidence in mankind. In both cases, it is experience which is ultimately the foundation of our inference and conclusion.

There is no man so young and unexperienced, as not to have formed, from observation, many general and just maxims concerning human affairs and the conduct of life; but it must be confessed, that when a man comes to put these in practice, he will be extremely liable to error, till time and farther experience both enlarge these maxims, and teach him their proper use and application. In every situation or incident, there are many particular and seemingly minute circumstances, which the man of greatest talents is, at first, apt to overlook, though on them the justness of his conclusions, and consequently the prudence of his conduct, entirely depend. Not to mention, that, to a young beginner, the general observations and maxims occur not always on the proper occasions, nor can be immediately applied with due calmness and distinction. The truth is, an unexperienced reasoner could be no reasoner at all, were he absolutely unexperienced; and when we assign that character to any one, we mean it only in a comparative sense, and suppose him possessed of experience, in a smaller and more imperfect degree.

to us and makes us expect, for the future, a similar train of events with those which have appeared in the past. Without the influence of custom we should be entirely ignorant of every matter of fact beyond what is immediately present to the memory and senses. We should never know how to adjust means to ends or to employ our natural powers in the production of any effect. There would be an end at once of all action as well as of the chief part of speculation.

But here it may be proper to remark that though our conclusions from experience carry us beyond our memory and senses and assure us of matters of fact, which happened in the most distant places and most remote ages, yet some fact must always be present to the senses or memory from which we may first proceed in drawing these conclusions. A man who should find in a desert country the remains of pompous buildings would conclude that the country had, in ancient times, been cultivated by civilized inhabitants, but did nothing of this nature occur to him, he could never form such an inference. We learn the events of former ages from history, but then we must peruse the volumes in which this instruction is contained and from this carry up our inferences from one testimony to another, until we arrive at the eyewitnesses and spectators of these distant events. In a word, if we proceed not upon some fact present to the memory or senses, our reasonings would be merely hypothetical; and however the particular links might be connected with each other, the whole chain of inferences would have nothing to support it, nor could we ever, by its means, arrive at the knowledge of any real existence. If I ask, why you believe any particular matter of fact which you relate, you must tell me some reason; and this reason will be some other fact connected with it. But as you cannot proceed after this manner *in infinitum,* you must at last terminate in some fact which is present to your memory or senses or must allow that your belief is entirely without foundation.

What then is the conclusion of the whole matter? A simple one, though it must be confessed, pretty remote from the common theories of philosophy. All belief of matter of fact or real existence is derived merely from some object present to the memory or senses and a customary conjunction between that and some other object. Or, in other words, having found in many instances that any two kinds of objects, flame and heat, snow and cold, have always been conjoined together, if flame or snow is presented anew to the senses, the mind is carried by custom to expect heat or cold and to *believe* that such a quality does exist and will discover itself upon a nearer approach. This belief is the necessary result of placing the mind in such circumstances. It is an operation of the soul when we are so situated, as unavoidable as feeling the passion of love, when we receive benefits—or hatred, when we meet with injuries. All these operations are a species of natural instincts which no reasoning or process of the thought and understanding is able either to produce or to prevent.

At this point, it would be very allowable for us to stop our philosophical researches. In most questions we can never make a single step further; and in all questions, we must terminate here at last, after our most restless and curious inquiries. But still our curiosity will be pardonable, perhaps commendable, if it carry us on to still further researches and make us examine more accurately the nature of this *belief* and of the *customary conjunction* from which it is derived. By this means we may meet with some explications and analogies that will give satisfaction, at least to such as love the abstract sciences and can be entertained with speculations which, however accurate, may still retain a degree of doubt and uncertainty. As to readers of a different taste, the remaining part of this section is not calculated for them and the following inquiries may well be understood, though it is neglected.

Part II.

Nothing is more free than the imagination of man, and though it cannot exceed that original stock of ideas furnished by the internal and external senses, it has unlimited power of mixing, compounding, separating, and dividing these ideas, in all the varieties of fiction and vision. It can feign a train of events with all the appearance of reality, ascribe to them a particular time and place, conceive them as existent, and paint them out to itself with every circumstance that belongs to any historical fact which it believes with the greatest certainty. In what, therefore, consists the difference between such a fiction and belief? It lies not merely in any peculiar idea which is annexed to such a conception as commands our assent and which is wanting to every known fiction. For as the mind has authority over all its ideas, it could voluntarily annex this particular idea to any fiction and consequently be able to believe whatever it pleases; contrary to what we find by daily experience. We can, in our conception, join the head of a man to the body of a horse, but it is not in our power to believe that such an animal has ever really existed.

It follows, therefore, that the difference between *fiction* and *belief* lies in some sentiment or feeling which is annexed to the latter, not to the former, and which depends not on the will, nor can be commanded at pleasure. It must be excited by nature like all other sentiments and must arise from the particular situation in which the mind is placed at any particular juncture. Whenever any object is presented to the memory or senses, it immediately, by the force of custom, carries the imagination to conceive that object which is usually conjoined to it; and this conception is attended with a feeling or sentiment different from the loose reveries of the fancy. In this consists the whole nature of belief. For as there is no matter of fact which we believe so firmly that we cannot conceive the contrary, there would be no difference between the conception assented to and that which is rejected were it not for some sentiment which distinguishes the one from the other. If I see a billiard ball moving towards another on a smooth table, I can easily conceive it to stop upon contact. This conception implies no contradiction, but still it feels very differently from that conception by which I represent to myself the impulse and the communication of motion from one ball to another.

Were we to attempt a *definition* of this sentiment, we should, perhaps, find it a very difficult, if not an impossible task; in the same manner as if we should endeavor to define the feeling of cold, or passion of anger, to a creature who never had any experience of these sentiments. Belief is the true and proper name of this feeling, and no one is ever at a loss to know the meaning of that term, because every man is every moment conscious of the sentiment represented by it. It may not, however, be improper to attempt a *description* of this sentiment, in hopes we may by that means arrive at some analogies which may afford a more perfect explication of it. I say then that belief is nothing but a more vivid, lively, forcible, firm, steady conception of an object than what the imagination alone is ever able to attain. This

variety of terms, which may seem so unphilosophical, is intended only to express that act of the mind which renders realities, or what is taken for such, more present to us than fictions, causes them to weigh more in the thought, and gives them a superior influence on the passions and imagination. Provided we agree about the thing, it is needless to dispute about the terms. The imagination has the command over all its ideas and can join and mix and vary them in all the ways possible. It may conceive fictitious objects with all the circumstances of place and time. It may set them in a manner before our eyes, in their true colors, just as they might have existed. But as it is impossible that this faculty of imagination can ever, of itself, reach belief, it is evident that belief consists not in the peculiar nature or order of ideas, but in the *manner* of their conception and in their *feeling* to the mind. I confess that it is impossible perfectly to explain this feeling or manner of conception. We may make use of words which express something near it. But its true and proper name, as we observed before, is *belief,* which is a term that everyone sufficiently understands in common life. And in philosophy we can go no further than assert that *belief* is something felt by the mind which distinguishes the ideas of the judgment from the fictions of the imagination. It gives them more weight and influence, makes them appear of greater importance, enforces them in the mind, and renders them the governing principle of our actions. I hear at present, for instance, a person's voice with whom I am acquainted and the sound comes as from the next room. This impression of my senses immediately conveys my thought to the person, together with all the surrounding objects. I paint them out to myself as existing at present with the same qualities and relations of which I formerly knew them possessed. These ideas take faster hold of my mind than ideas of an enchanted castle. They are very different to the feeling and have a much greater influence of every kind, either to give pleasure or pain, joy or sorrow.

Let us, then, take in the whole compass of this doctrine and allow that the sentiment of belief is nothing but a conception more intense and steady than what attends the mere fictions of the imagination and that this *manner* of conception arises from a customary conjunction of the object with something present to the memory or senses. I believe that it will not be difficult, upon these suppositions, to find other operations of the mind analogous to it and to trace up these phenomena to principles still more general.

We have already observed that nature has established connections among particular ideas and that no sooner one idea occurs to our thoughts than it introduces its correlative and carries our attention towards it by a gentle and insensible movement. These principles of connection or association we have reduced to three, namely, *resemblance, contiguity,* and *causation;* these are the only bonds that unite our thoughts together and beget that regular train of reflection or discourse which, in a greater or less degree, takes place among all mankind. Now here arises a question on which the solution of the present difficulty will depend. Does it happen in all these relations that when one of the objects is presented to the senses or memory the mind is not only carried to the conception of the correlative, but reaches a steadier and stronger conception of it than what otherwise it would have been able to attain? This seems to be the case with that belief which arises from the relation of cause and effect. And if the case is the same with the other relations or principles of association, this may be established as a general law which takes place in all the operations of the mind.

We may, therefore, observe, as the first experiment to our present purpose, that upon the appearance of the picture of an absent friend, our idea of him is evidently enlivened by the *resemblance,* and that every passion which that idea occasions, whether of joy or sorrow, acquires new force and vigor. In producing this effect there concur both a relation and a present impression. Where the picture bears him no resemblance, at least was not intended for him, it never so much as conveys our thought to him. And where it is absent, as well as the person, though the mind may pass from the thought of the one to that of the other, it feels its idea to be rather weakened than enlivened by that transition. We take a pleasure in viewing the picture of a friend when it is set before us; but when it is removed, rather choose to consider him directly than by reflection in an image which is equally distant and obscure.

The ceremonies of the Roman Catholic religion may be considered as instances of the same nature. The devotees of that superstition usually plead in excuse for the mummeries with which they are upbraided that they feel the good effect of those external motions, and postures, and actions in enlivening their devotion and quickening their fervor, which otherwise would decay, if directed entirely to distant and immaterial objects. We shadow out the objects of our faith, they say, in sensible types and images, and render them more present to us by the immediate presence of these types than it is possible for us to do merely by an intellectual view and contemplation. Sensible objects have always a greater influence on the fancy than any other, and this influence they readily convey to those ideas to which they are related and which they resemble. I shall only infer from these practices and this reasoning that the effect of resemblance in enlivening the ideas is very common; and as in every case a resemblance and a present impression must concur, we are abundantly supplied with experiments to prove the reality of the foregoing principle.

We may add force to these experiments by others of a different kind, in considering the effects of *contiguity* as well as of *resemblance.* It is certain that distance diminishes the force of every idea and that, upon our approach to any object, though it does not discover itself to our senses, it operates upon the mind with an influence which imitates an immediate impression. The thinking on any object readily transports the mind to what is contiguous; but it is only the actual presence of an object that transports it with a superior vivacity. When I am a few miles from home, whatever relates to it touches me more nearly than when I am two hundred leagues distant, though even at that distance the reflecting on anything in the neighborhood of my friends or family naturally produces an idea of them. But, as in this latter case, both the objects of the mind are ideas, notwithstanding there is an easy transition between them; that transition alone is not able to give a superior vivacity to any of the ideas, for want of some immediate impression.

No one can doubt but causation has the same influence as the other two relations of resemblance and contiguity. Superstitious people are fond of the relics of saints and holy men, for the same reason that they seek after types or images in order to enliven their devotion and give them a more intimate and strong conception of those exemplary lives which they desire to imitate. Now it is evident that one of the best relics which a devotee could procure would be the handiwork of a saint; and if his clothes and furniture are ever to be considered in this light, it is because they were once at his disposal and were moved and affected by him; in this respect they are to be considered as imperfect effects and as connected with him by a shorter chain of consequences than any of those by which we learn the reality of his existence.

Suppose that the son of a friend who had been long dead or absent were presented to us; it is evident that this object would instantly revive its correlative idea and recall to our thoughts all past intimacies and familiarities in more lively colors than they would otherwise have appeared to us. This is another phenomenon which seems to prove the principle above mentioned.

We may observe that in these phenomena the belief of the correlative object is always presupposed, without which the relation could have no effect. The influence of the picture supposes that we *believe* our friend to have once existed. Contiguity to home can never excite our ideas of home unless we *believe* that it really exists. Now I assert that this belief, where it reaches beyond the memory or senses, is of a similar nature and arises from similar causes with the transition of thought and vivacity of conception here explained. When I throw a piece of dry wood into a fire, my mind is immediately carried to conceive that it augments, not extinguishes, the flame. This transition of thought from the cause to the effect does not proceed from reason. It derives its origin altogether from custom and experience. And as it first begins from an object present to the senses, it renders the idea or conception of flame more strong and lively than any loose, floating reverie of the imagination. That idea arises immediately. The thought moves instantly towards it and conveys to it all that force of conception which is derived from the impression present to the senses. When a sword is leveled at my breast, does not the idea of wound and pain strike me more strongly than when a glass of wine is presented to me, even though by accident this idea should occur after the appearance of the latter object? But what is there in this whole matter to cause such a strong conception except only a present object and a customary transition to the idea of another object which we have been accustomed to conjoin with the former? This is the whole operation of the mind in all our conclusions concerning matter of fact and existence; and

it is a satisfaction to find some analogies by which it may be explained. The transition from a present object does in all cases give strength and solidity to the related idea.

Here, then, is a kind of preestablished harmony between the course of nature and the succession of our ideas; and though the powers and forces by which the former is governed are wholly unknown to us, yet our thoughts and conceptions have still, we find, gone on in the same train with the other works of nature. Custom is that principle by which this correspondence has been effected, so necessary to the subsistence of our species and the regulation of our conduct in every circumstance and occurrence of human life. Had not the presence of an object instantly excited the idea of those objects commonly conjoined with it, all our knowledge must have been limited to the narrow sphere of our memory and senses and we should never have been able to adjust means to ends or employ our natural powers either to the producing of good or avoiding of evil. Those who delight in the discovery and contemplation of *final causes* have here ample subject to employ their wonder and admiration.

I shall add, for a further confirmation of the foregoing theory, that as this operation of the mind by which we infer like effects from like causes, and *vice versa,* is so essential to the subsistence of all human creatures, it is not probable that it could be trusted to the fallacious deductions of our reason, which is slow in its operations, does not appear, in any degree, during the first years of infancy, and at best is in every age and period of human life extremely liable to error and mistake. It is more conformable to the ordinary wisdom of nature to secure so necessary an act of the mind by some instinct or mechanical tendency which may be infallible in its operations, may discover itself at the first appearance of life and thought, and may be independent of all the labored deductions of the understanding. As nature has taught us the use of our limbs without giving us the knowledge of the muscles and nerves by which they are actuated, so has she implanted in us an instinct which carries forward the thought in a correspondent course to that which she has established among external objects, though we are ignorant of those powers and forces on which this regular course and succession of objects totally depends.

SECTION VII
Of the Idea of Necessary Connection.

Part I.

The great advantage of the mathematical sciences above the moral consists in this, that the ideas of the former, being sensible, are always clear and determinate, the smallest distinction between them is immediately perceptible, and the same terms are still expressive of the same ideas without ambiguity or variation. An oval is never mistaken for a circle, nor an hyperbola for an ellipsis. The isosceles and scalene are distinguished by boundaries more exact than vice and virtue, right and wrong. If any term is defined in geometry, the mind readily, of itself, substitutes on all occasions the definition for the term defined. Or even when no definition is employed, the object itself may be presented to the senses and by that means be steadily and clearly apprehended. But the finer sentiments of the mind, the operations of the understanding, the various agitations of the passions, though really in themselves distinct, easily escape us when surveyed by reflection; nor is it in our power to recall the original object as often as we have occasion to contemplate it. Ambiguity, by this means, is gradually introduced into our reasonings. Similar objects are readily taken to be the same and the conclusion becomes at last very wide of the premises.

One may safely, however, affirm that if we consider these sciences in a proper light, their advantages and disadvantages nearly compensate each other and reduce both of them to a state of equality. If the mind, with greater facility, retains the ideas of geometry clear and determinate, it must carry on a much longer and more intricate chain of reasoning and compare ideas much wider of each other in order to reach the more abstruse truths of that science. And if moral ideas are apt, without extreme care, to fall into obscurity and confusion, the inferences are always much shorter in these disquisitions and the intermediate steps which lead to the conclusion much fewer than in the sciences which treat of quantity and number. In reality, there is scarcely a proposition in Euclid so simple as not to consist of more parts than are to be found in any moral reasoning which runs not into chimera and conceit. Where we trace the principles of the human mind through a few steps, we may be very well satisfied with our progress, considering how soon nature throws a bar to all our inquiries concerning causes and reduces us to an acknowledgment of our ignorance. The chief obstacle, therefore, to our improvement in the moral or metaphysical sciences is the obscurity of the ideas and ambiguity of the terms. The principal difficulty in mathematics is the length of inferences and compass of thought requisite to the forming of any conclusion. And, perhaps, our progress in natural philosophy is chiefly retarded by the want of proper experiments and phenomena which are often discovered by chance and cannot always be found when requisite, even by the most diligent and prudent inquiry. As moral philosophy seems up to now to have received less improvement than either geometry or physics, we may conclude that if there is any difference in this respect among these sciences, the difficulties which obstruct the progress of the former require superior care and capacity to be surmounted.

There are no ideas which occur in metaphysics more obscure and uncertain than those of *power, force, energy,* or *necessary connection,* of which it is every moment necessary for us to treat in all our disquisitions. We shall, therefore, endeavor in this section to fix, if possible, the precise meaning of these terms and thereby remove some part of that obscurity which is so much complained of in this species of philosophy.

It seems a proposition which will not admit of much dispute that all our ideas are nothing but copies of our impressions, or, in other words, that it is impossible for us to *think* of anything which we have not antecedently *felt* either by our external or internal senses. I have endeavored to explain and prove this proposition, and have expressed my hopes that by a proper application of it men may reach a greater clearness and precision in philosophical reasonings than what they have up to now been able to attain. Complex ideas may, perhaps, be well known by definition, which is nothing but an enumeration of those parts or simple ideas that compose them. But when we have pushed up definitions to the most simple ideas and find still some ambiguity and obscurity, what resource are we then possessed of? By what invention can we throw light upon these ideas and render them altogether precise and determinate to our intellectual view? Produce the impressions or original sentiments from which the ideas are copied. These impressions are all strong and sensible. They do not admit of ambiguity. They are not only placed in a full light themselves, but may throw light on their correspondent ideas, which lie in obscurity. And by this means we may, perhaps, attain a new microscope or species of optics by which, in the moral sciences, the most minute and most simple ideas may be so enlarged as to fall readily under our apprehension and be equally known with the grossest and most sensible ideas that can be the object of our inquiry.

To be fully acquainted, therefore, with the idea of power or necessary connection, let us examine its impression and, in order to find the impression with greater certainty, let us search for it in all the sources from which it may possibly be derived.

When we look about us towards external objects and consider the operation of causes, we are never able, in a single instance, to discover any power or necessary connection, any quality which binds the effect to the cause and renders the one an infallible consequence of the other. We only find that the one does actually in fact follow the other. The impulse of one billiard ball is attended with motion in the second. This is the whole that appears to the *outward* senses. The mind feels no sentiment or *inward* impression from this succession of objects. Consequently, there is not, in any single particular instance of cause and effect, anything which can suggest the idea of power or necessary connection.

From the first appearance of an object we never can conjecture what effect will result from it. But were the power or energy of any cause discoverable by the mind, we could foresee the effect, even without experience, and might, at first, pronounce with certainty concerning it by the mere dint of thought and reasoning.

In reality, there is no part of matter that ever does, by its sensible qualities, discover any power or energy or give us ground to imagine that it could produce anything or be followed by any other object which we could denominate its effect. Solidity, extension, motion—these qualities are all complete in themselves and never point out any other event which may result from them. The scenes of the universe are continually shifting and one object follows another in an uninterrupted succession; but the power or force which actuates the whole machine is entirely concealed from us and never discovers itself in any of the sensible qualities of body. We know that, in fact, heat is a constant attendant of

flame, but what is the connection between them we have no room so much as to conjecture or imagine. It is impossible, therefore, that the idea of power can be derived from the contemplation of bodies in single instances of their operation, because no bodies ever discover any power which can be the original of this idea.

Since, therefore, external objects as they appear to the senses give us no idea of power or necessary connection by their operation in particular instances, let us see whether this idea is derived from reflection on the operations of our own minds and is copied from any internal impression. It may be said that we are every moment conscious of internal power, while we feel that, by the simple command of our will, we can move the organs of our body or direct the faculties of our mind. An act of volition produces motion in our limbs or raises a new idea in our imagination. This influence of the will we know by consciousness. Hence we acquire the idea of power or energy and are certain that we ourselves and all other intelligent beings are possessed of power. This idea, then, is an idea of reflection, since it arises from reflecting on the operations of our own mind and on the command which is exercised by will, both over the organs of the body and faculties of the mind.

We shall proceed to examine this pretension and, first, with regard to the influence of volition over the organs of the body. This influence, we may observe, is a fact which, like all other natural events, can be known only by experience and can never be foreseen from any apparent energy or power in the cause which connects it with the effect and renders the one an infallible consequence of the other. The motion of our body follows upon the command of our will. Of this we are every moment conscious. But the means by which this is effected, the energy by which the will performs so extraordinary an operation, of this we are so far from being immediately conscious that it must forever escape our most diligent inquiry.

For *first,* is there any principle in all nature more mysterious than the union of soul with body, by which a supposed spiritual substance acquires such an influence over a material one that the most refined thought is able to actuate the grossest matter? Were we empowered by a secret wish to remove mountains or control the planets in their orbit, this extensive authority would not be more extraordinary, nor more beyond our comprehension.

But if by consciousness we perceived any power or energy in the will, we must know this power; we must know its connection with the effect; we must know the secret union of soul and body, and the nature of both these substances by which the one is able to operate in so many instances upon the other.

Secondly, we are not able to move all the organs of the body with a like authority, though we cannot assign any reason besides experience for so remarkable a difference between one and the other. Why has the will an influence over the tongue and fingers, not over the heart or liver? This question would never embarrass us were we conscious of a power in the former case, not in the latter. We should then perceive, independent of experience, why the authority of will over the organs of the body is circumscribed within such particular limits. Being in that case fully acquainted with the power or force by which it operates, we should also know why its influence reaches precisely to such boundaries, and no further.

A man suddenly struck with a palsy in the leg or arm or who had newly lost those members frequently endeavors, at first, to move them and employ them in their usual offices. Here he is as much conscious of power to command such limbs as a man in perfect health is conscious of power to actuate any member which remains in its natural state and condition. But consciousness never deceives. Consequently, neither in the one case nor in the other are we ever conscious of any power. We learn the influence of our will from experience alone. And experience only teaches us how one event constantly follows another, without instructing us in the secret connection which binds them together and renders them inseparable.

Thirdly, we learn from anatomy that the immediate object of power in voluntary motion is not the member itself which is moved, but certain muscles and nerves and animal spirits[6] and, perhaps, something still more minute and more unknown through which the motion is successively propagated before it reaches the member itself whose motion is the immediate object of volition. Can there be a more certain proof that the power by

which this whole operation is performed, so far from being directly and fully known by an inward sentiment or consciousness, is to the last degree mysterious and unintelligible? Here the mind wills a certain event. Immediately another event, unknown to ourselves and totally different from the one intended, is produced. This event produces another, equally unknown, until at last, through a long succession the desired event is produced. But if the original power was felt, it must be known. If it was known, its effect must also be known, since all power is relative to its effect. And *vice versa*, if the effect is not known, the power cannot be known nor felt. How indeed can we be conscious of a power to move our limbs when we have no such power, but only that to move certain animal spirits which, though they produce at last the motion of our limbs, yet operate in such a manner as is wholly beyond our comprehension?

We may, therefore, conclude from the whole, I hope, without any temerity, though with assurance, that our idea of power is not copied from any sentiment or consciousness of power within ourselves when we give rise to animal motion or apply our limbs to their proper use and office. That their motion follows the command of the will is a matter of common experience, like other natural events. But the power or energy by which this is effected, like that in other natural events, is unknown and inconceivable.[7]

---

6. [Fluids or currents in the nerves produced by the warming of the blood. "Animal spirits" was a major concept in seventeenth- and eighteenth-century attempts to explain sensations, bodily motion, and voluntary behavior.]

7. It may be pretended, that the resistance which we meet with in bodies, obliging us frequently to exert our force, and call up all our power, this gives us the idea of force and power. It is this *nisus* or strong endeavour, of which we are conscious, that is the original impression from which this idea is copied. But, first, we attribute power to a vast number of objects, where we never can suppose this resistance or exertion of force to take place; to the Supreme Being, who never meets with any resistance; to the mind in its command over its ideas and limbs, in common thinking and motion, where the effect follows immediately upon the will, without any exertion or summoning up of force; to inanimate matter, which is not capable of this sentiment. *Secondly*, this sentiment of an endeavour to overcome resistance has no known connexion with any event: What follows it, we know by experience; but could not know it *a priori*. It must, however, be confessed, that the animal *nisus*, which we experience, though it can afford no accurate precise idea of power, enters very much into that vulgar, inaccurate idea, which is formed of it.

Shall we then assert that we are conscious of a power or energy in our own minds when, by an act or command of our will, we raise up a new idea, fix the mind to the contemplation of it, turn it on all sides, and at last dismiss it for some other idea when we think that we have surveyed it with sufficient accuracy? I believe the same arguments will prove that even this command of the will gives us no real idea of force or energy.

First, it must be allowed that when we know a power, we know that very circumstance in the cause by which it is enabled to produce the effect, for these are supposed to be synonymous. We must, therefore, know both the cause and effect and the relation between them. But do we pretend to be acquainted with the nature of the human soul and the nature of an idea or the aptitude of the one to produce the other? This is a real creation, a production of something out of nothing, which implies a power so great that it may seem, at first sight, beyond the reach of any being less than infinite. At least it must be admitted that such a power is not felt, nor known, nor even conceivable by the mind. We only feel the event, namely, the existence of an idea consequent to a command of the will. But the manner in which this operation is performed, the power by which it is produced, is entirely beyond our comprehension.

Secondly, the command of the mind over itself is limited, as well as its command over the body; and these limits are not known by reason or any acquaintance with the nature of cause and effect, but only by experience and observation, as in all other natural events and in the operation of external objects. Our authority over our sentiments and passions is much weaker than that over our ideas; and even the latter authority is circumscribed within very narrow boundaries. Will anyone pretend to assign the ultimate reason of these boundaries or show why the power is deficient in one case, not in another?

Thirdly, this self-command is very different at different times. A man in health possesses more of it than one languishing with sickness. We are more master of our thoughts in the morning than in the evening—fasting, than after a full meal. Can we give any reason for these variations except experience? Where, then, is the power of which we pretend to be conscious? Is there not here, either in a spiritual or material substance or both, some secret mechanism or structure of parts upon which the effect depends and which, being entirely unknown to

us, renders the power or energy of the will equally unknown and incomprehensible?

Volition is surely an act of the mind with which we are sufficiently acquainted. Reflect upon it. Consider it on all sides. Do you find anything in it like this creative power by which it raises from nothing a new idea and, with a kind of fiat, imitates the omnipotence of its Maker—if I may be allowed so to speak—who called forth into existence all the various scenes of nature? So far from being conscious of this energy in the will, it requires as certain experience as that of which we are possessed to convince us that such extraordinary effects do ever result from a simple act of volition.

The generality of mankind never find any difficulty in accounting for the more common and familiar operations of nature, such as the descent of heavy bodies, the growth of plants, the generation of animals, or the nourishment of bodies by food. But suppose that in all these cases they perceive the very force or energy of the cause by which it is connected with its effect and is forever infallible in its operation. They acquire, by long habit, such a turn of mind that upon the appearance of the cause they immediately expect with assurance its usual attendant and hardly conceive it possible that any other event could result from it. It is only on the discovery of extraordinary phenomena, such as earthquakes, pestilence, and prodigies of any kind, that they find themselves at a loss to assign a proper cause and to explain the manner in which the effect is produced by it. It is usual for men, in such difficulties, to have recourse to some invisible intelligent principle as the immediate cause of that event which surprises them and which they think cannot be accounted for from the common powers of nature. But philosophers, who carry their scrutiny a little further, immediately perceive that, even in the most familiar events, the energy of the cause is as unintelligible as in the most unusual and that we only learn by experience the frequent conjunction of objects, without being ever able to comprehend anything like connection between them. Here, then, many philosophers think themselves obliged by reason to have recourse, on all occasions, to the same principle which the vulgar never appeal to but in cases that appear miraculous and supernatural. They acknowledge mind and intelligence to be not only the ultimate and original cause of all things, but the immediate and sole cause of every event which appears in nature. They pretend that those objects which are commonly denominated *causes* are in reality nothing but *occasions;* and that the true and direct principle of every effect is not any power or force in nature, but a volition of the Supreme Being, who wills that such particular objects should forever be conjoined with each other. Instead of saying that one billiard ball moves another by a force which it has derived from the author of nature, it is the Deity himself, they say, who, by a particular volition, moves the second ball, being determined to this operation by the impulse of the first ball, in consequence of those general laws which he has laid down to himself in the government of the universe. But philosophers advancing still in their inquiries, discover that as we are totally ignorant of the power on which depends the mutual operation of bodies, we are no less ignorant of that power on which depends the operation of mind on body or of body on mind; nor are we able, either from our senses or consciousness, to assign the ultimate principle in one case more than in the other. The same ignorance, therefore, reduces them to the same conclusion. They assert that the Deity is the immediate cause of the union between soul and body and that they are not the organs of sense which, being agitated by external objects, produce sensations in the mind, but that it is a particular volition of our omnipotent Maker which excites such a sensation in consequence of such a motion in the organ. In like manner, it is not any energy in the will that produces local motion in our members. It is God himself, who is pleased to second our will, in itself impotent, and to command that motion which we erroneously attribute to our own power and efficacy. Nor do philosophers stop at this conclusion. They sometimes extend the same inference to the mind itself in its internal operations. Our mental vision or conception of ideas is nothing but a revelation made to us by our Maker. When we voluntarily turn our thoughts to any object and raise up its image in the fancy, it is not the will which creates that idea, it is the universal Creator who discovers it to the mind and renders it present to us.

Thus, according to these philosophers, every thing is full of God. Not content with the principle that nothing exists but by his will, that nothing possesses any power but by his concession, they rob nature and all created beings of every power in order to render their dependence on the Deity still more sensible and im-

mediate. They do not consider that by this theory they diminish, instead of magnifying, the grandeur of those attributes which they affect so much to celebrate. It argues surely more power in the Deity to delegate a certain degree of power to inferior creatures than to produce everything by his own immediate volition. It argues more wisdom to contrive at first the fabric of the world with such perfect foresight that, of itself and by its proper operation, it may serve all the purposes of providence than if the great Creator were obliged every moment to adjust its parts and animate by his breath all the wheels of that stupendous machine.

But if we would have a more philosophical confutation of this theory, perhaps the two following reflections may suffice.

First, it seems to me that this theory of the universal energy and operation of the Supreme Being is too bold ever to carry conviction with it to a man sufficiently apprised of the weakness of human reason and the narrow limits to which it is confined in all its operations. Though the chain of arguments which conduct to it were ever so logical, there must arise a strong suspicion, if not an absolute assurance, that it has carried us quite beyond the reach of our faculties when it leads to conclusions so extraordinary and so remote from common life and experience. We arrived in fairyland long before we have reached the last steps of our theory; and *there* we have no reason to trust our common methods of argument or to think that our usual analogies and probabilities have any authority. Our line is too short to fathom such immense abysses. And however we may flatter ourselves that we are guided, in every step which we take, by a kind of verisimilitude and experience, we may be assured that this fancied experience has no authority when we thus apply it to subjects that lie entirely out of the sphere of experience.

Secondly, I cannot perceive any force in the arguments on which this theory is founded. We are ignorant, it is true, of the manner in which bodies operate on each other. Their force or energy is entirely incomprehensible. But are we not equally ignorant of the manner or force by which a mind, even the supreme mind, operates either on itself or on body? From where, I beseech you, do we acquire any idea of it? We have no sentiment or consciousness of this power in ourselves. We have no idea of the Supreme Being but what we learn from reflection on our own faculties. Were our ignorance, therefore, a good reason for rejecting anything, we should be led into that principle of denying all energy in the Supreme Being as much as in the grossest matter. We surely comprehend as little the operations of one as of the other. Is it more difficult to conceive that motion may arise from impulse than that it may arise from volition? All we know is our profound ignorance in both cases.

Part II.

But to hasten to a conclusion of this argument, which is already drawn out to too great a length. We have sought in vain for an idea of power or necessary connection in all the sources from which we could suppose it to be derived. It appears that in single instances of the operation of bodies we never can, by our utmost scrutiny, discover anything but one event following another, without being able to comprehend any force or power by which the cause operates or any connection between it and its supposed effect. The same difficulty occurs in contemplating the operations of mind on body, where we observe the motion of the latter to follow upon the volition of the former, but are not able to observe or conceive the tie which binds together the motion and volition, or the energy by which the mind produces this effect. The authority of the will over its own faculties and ideas is not a whit more comprehensible, so that, upon the whole, there does not appear, throughout all nature, any one instance of connection which is conceivable by us. All events seem entirely loose and separate. One event follows another, but we never can observe any tie between them. They seem *conjoined*, but never *connected*. And as we can have no idea of anything which never appeared to our outward sense or inward sentiment, the necessary conclusion *seems* to be that we have no idea of connection or power at all and that these words are absolutely without any meaning when employed either in philosophical reasonings or common life.

But there still remains one method of avoiding this conclusion and one source which we have not yet examined. When any natural object or event is presented, it is impossible for us, by any sagacity or penetration to discover, or even conjecture, without experience, what

event will result from it, or to carry our foresight beyond that object which is immediately present to the memory and senses. Even after one instance or experiment where we have observed a particular event to follow upon another, we are not entitled to form a general rule or foretell what will happen in like cases, it being justly esteemed an unpardonable temerity to judge of the whole course of nature from one single experiment, however accurate or certain. But when one particular species of event has always, in all instances, been conjoined with another, we make no longer any scruple of foretelling one upon the appearance of the other and of employing that reasoning which can alone assure us of any matter of fact or existence. We then call the one object *cause,* the other *effect.* We suppose that there is some connection between them, some power in the one by which it infallibly produces the other and operates with the greatest certainty and strongest necessity.

It appears, then, that this idea of a necessary connection among events arises from a number of similar instances which occur, of the constant conjunction of these events, nor can that idea ever be suggested by any one of these instances surveyed in all possible lights and positions. But there is nothing in a number of instances, different from every single instance, which is supposed to be exactly similar, except only that after a repetition of similar instances the mind is carried by habit, upon the appearance of one event, to expect its usual attendant and to believe that it will exist. This connection, therefore, which we *feel* in the mind, this customary transition of the imagination from one object to its usual attendant, is the sentiment or impression from which we form the idea of power or necessary connection. Nothing further is in the case. Contemplate the subject on all sides, you will never find any other origin of that idea. This is the sole difference between one instance, from which we can never receive the idea of connection, and a number of similar instances by which it is suggested. The first time a man saw the communication of motion by impulse, as by the shock of two billiard balls, he could not pronounce that the one event was *connected,* but only that it was *conjoined* with the other. After he has observed several instances of this nature, he then pronounces them to be *connected.* What alteration has happened to give rise to this new idea of *connection?* Nothing but that he now *feels* these events to be *connected* in his imagination and can readily foretell the existence of one from the appearance of the other. When we say, therefore, that one object is connected with another, we mean only that they have acquired a connection in our thought and give rise to this inference by which they become proofs of each other's existence—a conclusion, which is somewhat extraordinary, but which seems founded on sufficient evidence. Nor will its evidence be weakened by any general diffidence of the understanding or skeptical suspicion concerning every conclusion which is new and extraordinary. No conclusions can be more agreeable to skepticism than such as make discoveries concerning the weakness and narrow limits of human reason and capacity.

And what stronger instance can be produced of the surprising ignorance and weakness of the understanding than the present? For surely, if there is any relation among objects which it imports to us to know perfectly, it is that of cause and effect. On this are founded all our reasonings concerning matter of fact or existence. By means of it alone we attain any assurance concerning objects which are removed from the present testimony of our memory and senses. The only immediate utility of all sciences is to teach us how to control and regulate future events by their causes. Our thoughts and inquiries are, therefore, every moment employed about this relation; yet so imperfect are the ideas which we form concerning it that it is impossible to give any just definition of cause, except what is drawn from something extraneous and foreign to it. Similar objects are always conjoined with similar. Of this we have experience. Suitably to this experience, therefore, we may define a cause to be *an object followed by another and where all the objects similar to the first are followed by objects similar to the second*. Or, in other words, *where, if the first object had not been, the second never had existed*. The appearance of a cause always conveys the mind, by a customary transition, to the idea of the effect. Of this also we have experience. We may, therefore, suitably to this experience, form another definition of cause, and call it *an object followed by another and whose appearance always conveys the thought to that other*. But though both these definitions are drawn from circumstances foreign to the cause, we cannot remedy this inconvenience or attain any more perfect definition which may point out that circumstance in the cause which gives it a connection with its effect. We have no idea of this connection, nor even any distinct notion

what it is we desire to know when we endeavor at a conception of it. We say, for instance, that the vibration of this string is the cause of this particular sound. But what do we mean by that affirmation? We either mean that *this vibration is followed by this sound, and that all similar vibrations have been followed by similar sounds:* Or that *this vibration is followed by this sound and that upon the appearance of one, the mind anticipates the senses and forms immediately an idea of the other.* We may consider the relation of cause and effect in either of these two lights; but beyond these, we have no idea of it.[8]

---

8. According to these explications and definitions, the idea of *power* is relative as much as that of *cause;* and both have a reference to an effect, or some other event constantly conjoined with the former. When we consider the *unknown* circumstance of an object, by which the degree or quantity of its effects is fixed and determined, we call that its power: And accordingly, it is allowed by all philosophers, that the effect is the measure of the power. But if they had any idea of power, as it is in itself, why could not they measure it in itself? The dispute whether the force of a body in motion be as its velocity, or the square of its velocity; this dispute, I say, needed not be decided by comparing its effects in equal or unequal times; but by a direct mensuration and comparison.

As to the frequent use of the words, Force, Power, Energy, etc. which every where occur in common conversation, as well as in philosophy; that is no proof, that we are acquainted, in any instance, with the connecting principle between cause and effect, or can account ultimately for the production of one thing by another. These words, as commonly used, have very loose meanings annexed to them; and their ideas are very uncertain and confused. No animal can put external bodies in motion without the sentiment of a *nisus* or endeavour; and every animal has a sentiment or feeling from the stroke or blow of an external object, that is in motion. These sensations, which are merely animal, and from which we can *a priori* draw no inference, we are apt to transfer to inanimate objects, and to suppose, that they have some such feelings, whenever they transfer or receive motion. With regard to energies, which are exerted, without our annexing to them any idea of communicated motion, we consider only the constant experienced conjunction of the events; and as we *feel* a customary connexion between the ideas, we transfer that feeling to the objects; as nothing is more usual than to apply to external bodies every internal sensation, which they occasion.

To recapitulate, therefore, the reasonings of this section: Every idea is copied from some preceding impression or sentiment; and where we cannot find any impression, we may be certain that there is no idea. In all single instances of the operation of bodies or minds, there is nothing that produces any impression, nor consequently can suggest any idea of power or necessary connection. But when many uniform instances appear and the same object is always followed by the same event, we then begin to entertain the notion of cause and connection. We then *feel* a new sentiment or impression, namely, a customary connection in the thought or imagination between one object and its usual attendant and this sentiment is the original of that idea which we seek for. For as this idea arises from a number of similar instances and not from any single instance, it must arise from that circumstance in which the number of instances differ from every individual instance. But this customary connection or transition of the imagination is the only circumstance in which they differ. In every other particular they are alike. The first instance which we saw of motion communicated by the shock of two billiard balls (to return to this obvious illustration) is exactly similar to any instance that may, at present, occur to us, except only that we could not at first *infer* one event from the other, which we are enabled to do at present, after so long a course of uniform experience. I do not know whether the reader will readily apprehend this reasoning. I am afraid that, should I multiply words about it or throw it into a greater variety of lights, it would only become more obscure and intricate. In all abstract reasonings, there is one point of view which, if we can happily hit, we shall go further towards illustrating the subject than by all the eloquence and copious expression in the world. This point of view we should endeavor to reach, and reserve the flowers of rhetoric for subjects which are more adapted to them.

SECTION VIII
Of Liberty and Necessity.

Part I.

It might reasonably be expected in questions which have been canvassed and disputed with great eagerness since the first origin of science and philosophy that the meaning of all the terms, at least, should have been agreed upon among the disputants, and our inquiries, in the course of two thousand years, been able to pass from words to the true and real subject of the controversy. For how easy may it seem to give exact definitions of the terms employed in reasoning and make these definitions, not the mere sound of words, the object of future scrutiny and examination? But if we consider the matter more narrowly, we shall be apt to draw a quite opposite conclusion. From this circumstance alone that a controversy has been long kept on foot and remains still undecided, we may presume that there is some ambiguity in the expression and that the disputants affix different ideas to the terms employed in the controversy. For as the faculties of the mind are supposed to be naturally alike in every individual—otherwise nothing could be more fruitless than to reason or dispute together—it would be impossible, if men affix the same ideas to their terms, that they could so long form different opinions of the same subject, especially when they communicate their views and each party turn themselves on all sides in search of arguments which may give them the victory over their antagonists. It is true that if men attempt the discussion of questions which lie entirely beyond the reach of human capacity, such as those concerning the origin of worlds or the economy of the intellectual system or region of spirits, they may long beat the air in their fruitless contests and never arrive at any determinate conclusion. But if the question regards any subject of common life and experience, nothing, one would think, could preserve the dispute so long undecided, but some ambiguous expressions which keep the antagonists still at a distance and hinder them from grappling with each other.

This has been the case in the long disputed question concerning liberty and necessity and to so remarkable a degree that, if I am not much mistaken, we shall find that all mankind, both learned and ignorant, have always been of the same opinion with regard to this subject and that a few intelligible definitions would immediately have put an end to the whole controversy. I admit that this dispute has been so much canvassed on all hands and has led philosophers into such a labyrinth of obscure sophistry that it is no wonder if a sensible reader indulge his ease so far as to turn a deaf ear to the proposal of such a question from which he can expect neither instruction nor entertainment. But the state of the argument here proposed may, perhaps, serve to renew his attention, as it has more novelty, promises at least some decision of the controversy, and will not much disturb his ease by any intricate or obscure reasoning.

I hope, therefore, to make it appear that all men have ever agreed in the doctrine both of necessity and of liberty, according to any reasonable sense which can be put on these terms, and that the whole controversy has up to now turned merely upon words. We shall begin with examining the doctrine of necessity.

It is universally allowed that matter, in all its operations, is actuated by a necessary force and that every natural effect is so precisely determined by the energy of its cause that no other effect, in such particular circumstances, could possibly have resulted from it. The degree and direction of every motion are, by the laws of nature, prescribed with such exactness that a living creature may as soon arise from the shock of two bodies as motion in any other degree or direction than what is actually produced by it. Would we, therefore, form a just and precise idea of *necessity,* we must consider from where that idea arises when we apply it to the operation of bodies.

It seems evident that, if all the scenes of nature were continually shifted in such a manner that no two events bore any resemblance to each other, but every object was entirely new, without any similitude to whatever had been seen before, we should never, in that case, have attained the least idea of necessity or of a connection among these objects. We might say, upon such a supposition, that one object or event has followed another, not that one was produced by the other. The relation of cause and effect must be utterly unknown to mankind. Inference and reasoning concerning the operations of nature would, from that moment, be at an end; and the memory and senses remain the only canals by which the knowledge of any real existence could possibly have access to the mind. Our idea, therefore, of necessity and causation arises entirely from the uniformity observable in the operations of nature, where similar objects are constantly conjoined together and the mind is determined by custom to infer the one from the appearance of the other. These two circumstances form the whole of that necessity which we ascribe to matter. Beyond the constant *conjunction* of similar objects and the con-

sequent *inference* from one to the other, we have no notion of any necessity or connection.

If it appears, therefore, that all mankind have ever allowed, without any doubt or hesitation, that these two circumstances take place in the voluntary actions of men and in the operations of mind, it must follow that all mankind have ever agreed in the doctrine of necessity and that they have up to now disputed merely for not understanding each other.

As to the first circumstance, the constant and regular conjunction of similar events, we may possibly satisfy ourselves by the following considerations. It is universally acknowledged that there is a great uniformity among the actions of men in all nations and ages and that human nature remains still the same in its principles and operations. The same motives always produce the same actions. The same events follow from the same causes. Ambition, avarice, self-love, vanity, friendship, generosity, public spirit—these passions, mixed in various degrees and distributed through society, have been, from the beginning of the world, and still are the source of all the actions and enterprises which have ever been observed among mankind. Would you know the sentiments, inclinations, and course of life of the Greeks and Romans? Study well the temper and actions of the French and English. You cannot be much mistaken in transferring to the former *most* of the observations which you have made with regard to the latter. Mankind are so much the same, in all times and places, that history informs us of nothing new or strange in this particular. Its chief use is only to discover the constant and universal principles of human nature by showing men in all varieties of circumstances and situations and furnishing us with materials from which we may form our observations and become acquainted with the regular springs of human action and behavior. These records of wars, intrigues, factions, and revolutions are so many collections of experiments by which the politician or moral philosopher fixes the principles of his science, in the same manner as the physician or natural philosopher becomes acquainted with the nature of plants, minerals, and other external objects by the experiments which he forms concerning them. Nor are the earth, water, and other elements examined by Aristotle and Hippocrates more like to those which at present lie under our observation than the men described by Polybius and Tacitus are to those who now govern the world.

Should a traveler, returning from a far country, bring us an account of men, wholly different from any with whom we were ever acquainted, men, who were entirely divested of avarice, ambition, or revenge, who knew no pleasure but friendship, generosity, and public spirit, we should immediately, from these circumstances, detect the falsehood and prove him a liar with the same certainty as if he had stuffed his narration with stories of centaurs and dragons, miracles and prodigies. And if we would explode any forgery in history, we cannot make use of a more convincing argument than to prove that the actions ascribed to any person are directly contrary to the course of nature and that no human motives, in such circumstances, could ever induce him to such a conduct. The veracity of Quintus Curtius is as much to be suspected when he describes the supernatural courage of Alexander by which he was hurried on singly to attack multitudes, as when he describes his supernatural force and activity by which he was able to resist them. So readily and universally do we acknowledge a uniformity in human motives and actions as well as in the operations of body.

Hence, likewise, the benefit of that experience acquired by long life and a variety of business and company, in order to instruct us in the principles of human nature and regulate our future conduct as well as speculation. By means of this guide we mount up to the knowledge of men's inclinations and motives from their actions, expressions, and even gestures, and again descend to the interpretation of their actions from our knowledge of their motives and inclinations. The general observations, treasured up by a course of experience, give us the clue of human nature and teach us to unravel all its intricacies. Pretexts and appearances no longer deceive us. Public declarations pass for the specious coloring of a cause. And though virtue and honor are allowed their proper weight and authority, that perfect disinterestedness, so often pretended to, is never expected in multitudes and parties, seldom in their leaders, and scarcely even in individuals of any rank or station. But were there no uniformity in human actions and were every experiment which we could form of this kind irregular and anomalous, it would be impossible to collect any general observations concerning mankind

and no experience, however accurately digested by reflection, would ever serve to any purpose. Why is the aged husband more skillful in his calling than the young beginner, but because there is a certain uniformity in the operation of the sun, rain, and earth towards the production of vegetables, and experience teaches the old practitioner the rules by which this operation is governed and directed?

We must not, however, expect that this uniformity of human actions should be carried to such a length as that all men, in the same circumstances, will always act precisely in the same manner, without making any allowance for the diversity of characters, prejudices, and opinions. Such a uniformity in every particular is found in no part of nature. On the contrary, from observing the variety of conduct in different men, we are enabled to form a greater variety of maxims which still suppose a degree of uniformity and regularity.

Are the manners of men different in different ages and countries? We learn from this the great force of custom and education which mold the human mind from its infancy and form it into a fixed and established character. Is the behavior and conduct of the one sex very unlike that of the other? It is from this we become acquainted with the different characters which nature has impressed upon the sexes and which she preserves with constancy and regularity. Are the actions of the same person much diversified in the different periods of his life from infancy to old age? This affords room for many general observations concerning the gradual change of our sentiments and inclinations and the different maxims which prevail in the different ages of human creatures. Even the characters which are peculiar to each individual have a uniformity in their influence; otherwise our acquaintance with the persons and our observation of their conduct could never teach us their dispositions or serve to direct our behavior with regard to them.

I grant it possible to find some actions which seem to have no regular connection with any known motives and are exceptions to all the measures of conduct which have ever been established for the government of men. But if we would willingly know what judgment should be formed of such irregular and extraordinary actions, we may consider the sentiments commonly entertained with regard to those irregular events which appear in the course of nature and the operations of external objects. All causes are not conjoined to their usual effects with like uniformity. An artificer who handles only dead matter may be disappointed of his aim as well as the politician who directs the conduct of sensible and intelligent agents.

The vulgar, who take things according to their first appearance, attribute the uncertainty of events to such an uncertainty in the causes as makes the latter often fail of their usual influence, though they meet with no impediment in their operation. But philosophers, observing that almost in every part of nature there is contained a vast variety of springs and principles which are hid by reason of their minuteness or remoteness, find that it is at least possible the contrariety of events may not proceed from any contingency in the cause but from the secret operation of contrary causes. This possibility is converted into certainty by further observation, when they remark that, upon an exact scrutiny, a contrariety of effects always betrays a contrariety of causes and proceeds from their mutual opposition. A peasant can give no better reason for the stopping of any clock or watch than to say that it does not commonly go right. But an artist easily perceives that the same force in the spring or pendulum always has the same influence on the wheels, but fails of its usual effect, perhaps by reason of a grain of dust which puts a stop to the whole movement. From the observation of several parallel instances, philosophers form a maxim that the connection between all causes and effects is equally necessary and that its seeming uncertainty in some instances proceeds from the secret opposition of contrary causes.

Thus, for instance, in the human body, when the usual symptoms of health or sickness disappoint our expectation, when medicines do not operate with their wonted powers, when irregular events follow from any particular cause, the philosopher and physician are not surprised at the matter, nor are ever tempted to deny, in general, the necessity and uniformity of those principles by which the animal economy is conducted. They know that a human body is a mighty complicated machine, that many secret powers lurk in it which are altogether beyond our comprehension, that to us it must often appear very uncertain in its operations, and that therefore the irregular events which outwardly discover themselves can be no proof that the laws of na-

ture are not observed with the greatest regularity in its internal operations and government.

The philosopher, if he is consistent, must apply the same reasoning to the actions and volitions of intelligent agents. The most irregular and unexpected resolutions of men may frequently be accounted for by those who know every particular circumstance of their character and situation. A person of an obliging disposition gives a peevish answer; but he has a toothache or has not dined. A stupid fellow discovers an uncommon alacrity in his carriage; but he has met with a sudden piece of good fortune. Or even when an action, as sometimes happens, cannot be particularly accounted for either by the person himself or by others, we know, in general, that the characters of men are to a certain degree inconstant and irregular. This is, in a manner, the constant character of human nature, though it is applicable in a more particular manner to some persons who have no fixed rule for their conduct, but proceed in a continued course of caprice and inconstancy. The internal principles and motives may operate in a uniform manner, notwithstanding these seeming irregularities—in the same manner as the winds, rain, clouds, and other variations of the weather are supposed to be governed by steady principles, though not easily discoverable by human sagacity and inquiry.

Thus, it appears not only that the conjunction between motives and voluntary actions is as regular and uniform as that between the cause and effect in any part of nature, but also that this regular conjunction has been universally acknowledged among mankind and has never been the subject of dispute either in philosophy or common life. Now, as it is from past experience that we draw all inferences concerning the future and as we conclude that objects will always be conjoined together which we find to have always been conjoined, it may seem superfluous to prove that this experienced uniformity in human actions is a source from which we draw *inferences* concerning them. But in order to throw the argument into a greater variety of lights, we shall also insist, though briefly, on this latter topic.

The mutual dependence of men is so great in all societies that scarcely any human action is entirely complete in itself or is performed without some reference to the actions of others, which are requisite to make it answer fully the intention of the agent. The poorest artificer who labors alone expects at least the protection of the magistrate to ensure him the enjoyment of the fruits of his labor. He also expects that, when he carries his goods to market and offers them at a reasonable price, he shall find purchasers and shall be able, by the money he acquires, to engage others to supply him with those commodities which are requisite for his subsistence. In proportion as men extend their dealings and render their intercourse with others more complicated, they always comprehend in their schemes of life a greater variety of voluntary actions which they expect, from the proper motives, to cooperate with their own. In all these conclusions they take their measures from past experience in the same manner as in their reasonings concerning external objects, and firmly believe that men as well as all the elements are to continue in their operations the same that they have ever found them. A manufacturer reckons upon the labor of his servants for the execution of any work as much as upon the tools which he employs and would be equally surprised were his expectations disappointed. In short, this experimental inference and reasoning concerning the actions of others enters so much into human life that no man, while awake, is ever a moment without employing it. Have we not reason, therefore, to affirm that all mankind have always agreed in the doctrine of necessity, according to the foregoing definition and explication of it?

Nor have philosophers ever entertained a different opinion from the people in this particular. For not to mention that almost every action of their life supposes that opinion, there are even few of the speculative parts of learning to which it is not essential. What would become of *history* had we not a dependence on the veracity of the historian, according to the experience which we have had of mankind? How could *politics* be a science, if laws and forms of government had not a uniform influence upon society? Where would be the foundation of *morals,* if particular characters had no certain or determinate power to produce particular sentiments and if these sentiments had no constant operation on actions? And with what pretense could we employ our *criticism* upon any poet or polite author, if we could not pronounce the conduct and sentiments of his actors either natural or unnatural to such characters and in such circumstances? It seems almost impossible, therefore, to

engage either in science or action of any kind without acknowledging the doctrine of necessity and this *inference* from motives to voluntary actions, from characters to conduct.

And indeed, when we consider how aptly *natural* and *moral* evidence link together and form only one chain of argument, we shall make no scruple to allow that they are of the same nature and derived from the same principles. A prisoner who has neither money nor interest discovers the impossibility of his escape as well when he considers the obstinacy of the jailer as the walls and bars with which he is surrounded and in all attempts for his freedom chooses to work upon the stone and iron of the one rather than upon the inflexible nature of the other. The same prisoner, when conducted to the scaffold, foresees his death as certainly from the constancy and fidelity of his guards as from the operation of the ax or wheel. His mind runs along a certain train of ideas: the refusal of the soldiers to consent to his escape; the action of the executioner; the separation of the head and body; bleeding, convulsive motions, and death. Here is a connected chain of natural causes and voluntary actions, but the mind feels no difference between them in passing from one link to another, nor is less certain of the future event than if it were connected with the objects present to the memory or senses by a train of causes cemented together by what we are pleased to call a *physical* necessity. The same experienced union has the same effect on the mind, whether the united objects are motives, volition, and actions, or figure and motion. We may change the names of things, but their nature and their operation on the understanding never change.

Were a man whom I know to be honest and opulent and with whom I live in intimate friendship to come into my house where I am surrounded with my servants, I rest assured that he is not to stab me before he leaves it in order to rob me of my silver standish; and I no more suspect this event than the falling of the house itself which is new and solidly built and founded.—*But he may have been seized with a sudden and unknown frenzy.* —So may a sudden earthquake arise, and shake and tumble my house about my ears. I shall therefore change the suppositions. I shall say that I know with certainty that he is not to put his hand into the fire and hold it there until it is consumed. And this event I think I can foretell with the same assurance as that, if he threw himself out at the window and met with no obstruction, he will not remain a moment suspended in the air. No suspicion of an unknown frenzy can give the least possibility to the former event which is so contrary to all the known principles of human nature. A man who at noon leaves his purse full of gold on the pavement at Charing Cross may as well expect that it will fly away like a feather as that he will find it untouched an hour after. Over one half of human reasonings contain inferences of a similar nature, attended with more or less degrees of certainty, proportioned to our experience of the usual conduct of mankind in such particular situations.

I have frequently considered what could possibly be the reason why all mankind, though they have ever, without hesitation, acknowledged the doctrine of necessity in their whole practice and reasoning, have yet discovered such a reluctance to acknowledge it in words and have rather shown a propensity, in all ages, to profess the contrary opinion. The matter, I think, may be accounted for after the following manner. If we examine the operations of body and the production of effects from their causes, we shall find that all our faculties can never carry us further in our knowledge of this relation than barely to observe that particular objects are *constantly conjoined* together and that the mind is carried, by a *customary transition,* from the appearance of one to the belief of the other. But though this conclusion concerning human ignorance is the result of the strictest scrutiny of this subject, men still entertain a strong propensity to believe that they penetrate further into the powers of nature and perceive something like a necessary connection between the cause and the effect. When again they turn their reflections towards the operations of their own minds and *feel* no such connection of the motive and the action, they are apt to suppose from this that there is a difference between the effects which result from material force and those which arise from thought and intelligence. But being once convinced that we know nothing further of causation of any kind than merely the *constant conjunction* of objects and the consequent *inference* of the mind from one to another and finding that these two circumstances are universally allowed to have place in voluntary actions, we may be more easily led to admit the same necessity common to all causes. And though this reasoning may contradict the systems of many

philosophers in ascribing necessity to the determinations of the will, we shall find, upon reflection, that they dissent from it in words only, not in their real sentiment. Necessity, according to the sense in which it is here taken, has never yet been rejected, nor can ever, I think, be rejected by any philosopher. It may only, perhaps, be pretended that the mind can perceive in the operations of matter some further connection between the cause and effect and a connection that has no place in the voluntary actions of intelligent beings. Now whether it is so or not can only appear upon examination, and it is incumbent on these philosophers to make good their assertion by defining or describing that necessity and pointing it out to us in the operations of material causes.

It would seem, indeed, that men begin at the wrong end of this question concerning liberty and necessity when they enter upon it by examining the faculties of the soul, the influence of the understanding, and the operations of the will. Let them first discuss a more simple question, namely, the operations of body and of brute unintelligent matter, and try whether they can there form any idea of causation and necessity, except that of a constant conjunction of objects and subsequent inference of the mind from one to another. If these circumstances form, in reality, the whole of that necessity which we conceive in matter and if these circumstances are also universally acknowledged to take place in the operations of the mind, the dispute is at an end—at least must be admitted to be merely verbal thereafter. But as long as we will rashly suppose that we have some further idea of necessity and causation in the operations of external objects, at the same time that we can find nothing further in the voluntary actions of the mind, there is no possibility of bringing the question to any determinate issue while we proceed upon so erroneous a supposition. The only method of undeceiving us is to mount up higher, to examine the narrow extent of science when applied to material causes, and to convince ourselves that all we know of them is the constant conjunction and inference above mentioned. We may, perhaps, find that it is with difficulty we are induced to fix such narrow limits to human understanding. But we can afterwards find no difficulty when we come to apply this doctrine to the actions of the will. For as it is evident that these have a regular conjunction with motives and circumstances and characters and as we always draw inferences from one to the other, we must be obliged to acknowledge in words that necessity which we have already avowed in every deliberation of our lives and in every step of our conduct and behavior.[9]

But to proceed in this reconciling project with regard to the question of liberty and necessity—the most

---

9. The prevalence of the doctrine of liberty may be accounted for, from another cause, *viz.* a false sensation or seeming experience which we have, or may have, of liberty or indifference, in many of our actions. The necessity of any action, whether of matter or of mind, is not, properly speaking, a quality in the agent, but in any thinking or intelligent being, who may consider the action; and it consists chiefly in the determination of his thoughts to infer the existence of that action from some preceding objects; as liberty, when opposed to necessity, is nothing but the want of that determination, and a certain looseness or indifference, which we feel, in passing, or not passing, from the idea of one object to that of any succeeding one. Now we may observe, that, though in *reflecting* on human actions, we seldom feel such a looseness or indifference, but are commonly able to infer them with considerable certainty from their motives, and from the dispositions of the agent; yet it frequently happens, that, in *performing* the actions themselves, we are sensible of something like it: And as all resembling objects are readily taken for each other, this has been employed as demonstrative and even intuitive proof of human liberty. We feel, that our actions are subject to our will, on most occasions; and imagine we feel, that the will itself is subject to nothing, because, when by a denial of it we are provoked to try, we feel, that it moves easily every way, and produces an image of itself, (or a *Velleïty,* as it is called in the schools) even on that side, on which it did not settle. This image, or faint motion, we persuade ourselves, could, at that time, have been completed into the thing itself; because, should that be denied, we find, upon a second trial, that, at present, it can. We consider not, that the fantastical desire of showing liberty, is here the motive of our actions. And it seems certain, that, however we may imagine we feel a liberty within ourselves, a spectator can commonly infer our actions from our motives and character; and even where he cannot, he concludes in general, that he might, were he perfectly acquainted with every circumstance of our situation and temper, and the most secret springs of our complexion and disposition. Now this is the very essence of necessity, according to the foregoing doctrine.

contentious question of metaphysics, the most contentious science—it will not require many words to prove that all mankind have ever agreed in the doctrine of liberty as well as in that of necessity, and that the whole dispute, in this respect also, has been up to now merely verbal. For what is meant by liberty when applied to voluntary actions? We cannot surely mean that actions have so little connection with motives, inclinations, and circumstances that one does not follow with a certain degree of uniformity from the other and that one affords no inference by which we can conclude the existence of the other. For these are plain and acknowledged matters of fact. By liberty, then, we can only mean *a power of acting or not acting according to the determinations of the will*—that is, if we choose to remain at rest, we may; if we choose to move, we also may. Now this hypothetical liberty is universally allowed to belong to everyone who is not a prisoner and in chains. Here then is no subject of dispute.

Whatever definition we may give of liberty, we should be careful to observe two requisite circumstances: *first,* that it is consistent with plain matter of fact; *secondly,* that it is consistent with itself. If we observe these circumstances and render our definition intelligible, I am persuaded that all mankind will be found of one opinion with regard to it.

It is universally allowed that nothing exists without a cause of its existence, and that chance, when strictly examined, is a mere negative word and does not mean any real power which has anywhere a being in nature. But it is pretended that some causes are necessary, some not necessary. Here then is the advantage of definitions. Let anyone *define* a cause without comprehending, as a part of the definition, a *necessary connection* with its effect, and let him show distinctly the origin of the idea expressed by the definition, and I shall readily give up the whole controversy. But if the foregoing explication of the matter is received, this must be absolutely impracticable. Had not objects a regular conjunction with each other, we should never have entertained any notion of cause and effect and this regular conjunction produces that inference of the understanding which is the only connection that we can have any comprehension of. Whoever attempts a definition of cause exclusive of these circumstances will be obliged either to employ unintelligible terms or such as are synonymous to the term which he endeavors to define.[10] And if the definition above mentioned is admitted, liberty, when opposed to necessity, not to constraint, is the same thing with chance, which is universally allowed to have no existence.

Part II.

There is no method of reasoning more common and yet none more blamable than in philosophical disputes to endeavor the refutation of any hypothesis by a pretense of its dangerous consequences to religion and morality. When any opinion leads to absurdities, it is certainly false; but it is not certain that an opinion is false because it is of dangerous consequence. Such topics, therefore, ought entirely to be forborne, as serving nothing to the discovery of truth, but only to make the person of an antagonist odious. This I observe in general, without pretending to draw any advantage from it. I frankly submit to an examination of this kind and shall venture to affirm that the doctrines both of necessity and of liberty, as above explained, are not only consistent with morality, but are absolutely essential to its support.

Necessity may be defined two ways, conformably to the two definitions of cause of which it makes an essential part. It consists either in the constant conjunction of like objects or in the inference of the understanding from one object to another. Now necessity, in both these senses, (which, indeed, are at bottom the same) has universally, though tacitly, in the schools, in the pulpit, and in common life been allowed to belong to the will of man and no one has ever pretended to deny that we can draw inferences concerning human actions and that those inferences are founded on the experienced union of like actions with like motives, inclinations, and circumstances. The only particular in

which anyone can differ is that either, perhaps, he will refuse to give the name of necessity to this property of human actions—but as long as the meaning is understood I hope the word can do no harm—or that he will maintain it possible to discover something further in the operations of matter. But this, it must be acknowledged, can be of no consequence to morality or religion, whatever it may be to natural philosophy or metaphysics. We may here be mistaken in asserting that there is no idea of any other necessity or connection in the actions of body. But surely we ascribe nothing to the actions of the mind but what everyone does and must readily allow of. We change no circumstance in the received orthodox system with regard to the will, but only in that with regard to material objects and causes. Nothing, therefore, can be more innocent at least than this doctrine.

All laws being founded on rewards and punishments, it is supposed as a fundamental principle that these motives have a regular and uniform influence on the mind and both produce the good and prevent the evil actions. We may give to this influence what name we please; but, as it is usually conjoined with the action, it must be esteemed a *cause* and be looked upon as an instance of that necessity which we would here establish.

The only proper object of hatred or vengeance is a person or creature endowed with thought and consciousness, and when any criminal or injurious actions excite that passion, it is only by their relation to the person or connection with him. Actions are, by their very nature, temporary and perishing, and where they do not proceed from some cause in the character and disposition of the person who performed them, they can neither redound to his honor if good, nor infamy if evil. The actions themselves may be blamable; they may be contrary to all the rules of morality and religion. But the person is not answerable for them and, as they proceeded from nothing in him that is durable and constant and leave nothing of that nature behind them, it is impossible he can, upon their account, become the object of punishment or vengeance. According to the principle, therefore, which denies necessity and consequently causes that a man is as pure and untainted after having committed the most horrid crime as at the first moment of his birth, nor is his character any way concerned in his actions, since they are not derived from it,

---

10. Thus, if a cause be defined, *that which produces any thing;* it is easy to observe, that *producing* is synonymous to *causing.* In like manner, if a cause be defined, *that by which anything exists;* this is liable to the same objection. For what is meant by these words, *by which?* Had it been said, that a cause is *that* after which *anything constantly exists;* we should have understood the terms. For this is, indeed, all we know of the matter. And this constancy forms the very essence of necessity, nor have we any other idea of it.

and the wickedness of the one can never be used as a proof of the depravity of the other.

Men are not blamed for such actions as they perform ignorantly and casually, whatever may be the consequences. Why? But because the principles of these actions are only momentary and terminate in them alone. Men are less blamed for such actions as they perform hastily and unpremeditatedly than for such as proceed from deliberation. For what reason? But because a hasty temper, though a constant cause or principle in the mind, operates only by intervals and does not infect the whole character. Again, repentance wipes off every crime, if attended with a reformation of life and manners. How is this to be accounted for? But by asserting that actions render a person criminal merely as they are proofs of criminal principles in the mind; and when, by an alteration of these principles, they cease to be just proofs, they likewise cease to be criminal. But, except upon the doctrine of necessity, they never were just proofs and consequently never were criminal.

It will be equally easy to prove, and from the same arguments, that *liberty,* according to that definition above mentioned, in which all men agree, is also essential to morality and that no human actions, where it is wanting, are susceptible of any moral qualities or can be the objects either of approbation or dislike. For as actions are objects of our moral sentiment only so far as they are indications of the internal character, passions, and affections, it is impossible that they can give rise either to praise or blame where they do not proceed from these principles, but are derived altogether from external violence.

I do not pretend to have obviated or removed all objections to this theory with regard to necessity and liberty. I can foresee other objections derived from topics which have not here been treated of. It may be said, for instance, that if voluntary actions are subjected to the same laws of necessity with the operations of matter, there is a continued chain of necessary causes, preordained and predetermined, reaching from the original cause of all to every single volition of every human creature. No contingency anywhere in the universe, no indifference, no liberty. While we act, we are at the same time acted upon. The ultimate Author of all our volitions is the Creator of the world, who first bestowed motion on this immense machine and placed all beings

in that particular position from which every subsequent event, by an inevitable necessity, must result. Human actions, therefore, either can have no moral turpitude at all, as proceeding from so good a cause, or if they have any turpitude, they must involve our Creator in the same guilt, while he is acknowledged to be their ultimate cause and author. For as a man who fired a mine is answerable for all the consequences, whether the train he employed is long or short, so wherever a continued chain of necessary causes is fixed, that Being, either finite or infinite, who produces the first is likewise the author of all the rest and must both bear the blame and acquire the praise which belong to them. Our clear and unalterable ideas of morality establish this rule upon unquestionable reasons when we examine the consequences of any human action and these reasons must still have greater force when applied to the volitions and intentions of a Being infinitely wise and powerful. Ignorance or impotence may be pleaded for so limited a creature as man, but those imperfections have no place in our Creator. He foresaw, he ordained, he intended all those actions of men which we so rashly pronounce criminal. And we must therefore conclude either that they are not criminal or that the Deity, not man, is accountable for them. But as either of these positions is absurd and impious, it follows that the doctrine from which they are deduced cannot possibly be true, as being liable to all the same objections. An absurd consequence, if necessary, proves the original doctrine to be absurd in the same manner as criminal actions render criminal the original cause, if the connection between them is necessary and inevitable.

This objection consists of two parts, which we shall examine separately: *First,* that if human actions can be traced up, by a necessary chain, to the Deity, they can never be criminal, on account of the infinite perfection of that Being from whom they are derived and who can intend nothing but what is altogether good and laudable. Or, *secondly,* if they are criminal, we must retract the attribute of perfection which we ascribe to the Deity and must acknowledge him to be the ultimate author of guilt and moral turpitude in all his creatures.

The answer to the first objection seems obvious and convincing. There are many philosophers who, after an exact scrutiny of all the phenomena of nature, conclude that the whole, considered as one system, is, in every period of its existence, ordered with perfect benevolence, and that the utmost possible happiness will, in the end, result to all created beings without any mixture of positive or absolute ill and misery. Every physical ill, they say, makes an essential part of this benevolent system and could not possibly be removed, even by the Deity himself, considered as a wise agent, without giving entrance to greater ill or excluding greater good which will result from it. From this theory some philosophers, and the ancient *Stoics* among the rest, derived a topic of consolation under all afflictions, while they taught their pupils that those ills under which they labored were in reality goods to the universe and that to an enlarged view which could comprehend the whole system of nature every event became an object of joy and exultation. But though this topic is specious and sublime, it was soon found in practice weak and ineffectual. You would surely more irritate than appease a man lying under the racking pains of gout by preaching up to him the rectitude of those general laws which produced the malignant humors in his body and led them through the proper canals to the sinews and nerves, where they now excite such acute torments. These enlarged views may, for a moment, please the imagination of a speculative man who is placed in ease and security, but neither can they dwell with constancy on his mind, even though undisturbed by the emotions of pain or passion, much less can they maintain their ground when attacked by such powerful antagonists. The affections take a narrower and more natural survey of their object, and, by an economy more suitable to the infirmity of human minds, regard alone the beings around us, and are actuated by such events as appear good or ill to the private system.

The case is the same with *moral* as with *physical* ill. It cannot reasonably be supposed that those remote considerations which are found of so little efficacy with regard to one will have a more powerful influence with regard to the other. The mind of man is so formed by nature that, upon the appearance of certain characters, dispositions, and actions, it immediately feels the sentiment of approbation or blame; nor are there any emotions more essential to its frame and constitution. The characters which engage our approbation are chiefly such as contribute to the peace and security of human society, as the characters which excite blame are chiefly such as tend to public detriment and disturbance. From this it may reasonably be presumed that the moral sentiments arise, either mediately or immediately, from a reflection of these opposite interests. What though philosophical meditations establish a different opinion or conjecture that everything is right with regard to the whole, and that the qualities which disturb society are, in the main, as beneficial and are as suitable to the primary intention of nature as those which more directly promote its happiness and welfare? Are such remote and uncertain speculations able to counterbalance the sentiments which arise from the natural and immediate view of the objects? A man who is robbed of a considerable sum, does he find his vexation for the loss any way diminished by these sublime reflections? Why then should his moral resentment against the crime be supposed incompatible with them? Or why should not the acknowledgment of a real distinction between vice and virtue be reconcilable to all speculative systems of philosophy, as well as that of a real distinction between personal beauty and deformity? Both these distinctions are founded in the natural sentiments of the human mind. And these sentiments are not to be controlled or altered by any philosophical theory or speculation whatsoever.

The *second* objection does not admit of so easy and satisfactory an answer, nor is it possible to explain distinctly how the Deity can be the mediate cause of all the actions of men without being the author of sin and moral turpitude. These are mysteries which mere natural and unassisted reason is very unfit to handle; and whatever system she embraces, she must find herself involved in inextricable difficulties, and even contradictions, at every step which she takes with regard to such subjects. To reconcile the indifference and contingency of human actions with prescience or to defend absolute decrees and yet free the Deity from being the author of sin has been found up to now to exceed all the power of philosophy. Happy, if she is sensible of her temerity from there, when she pries into these sublime mysteries, and, leaving a scene so full of obscurities and perplexities, returns with suitable modesty to her true and proper province, the examination of common life, where she will find difficulties enough to employ her inquiries without launching into so boundless an ocean of doubt, uncertainty, and contradiction!

Thomas Reid

Reflections on the Common Theory of Ideas

Chapter 10 – Of the Sentiments of Bishop Berkeley

George Berkeley, afterwards Bishop of Cloyne, published his "New Theory of Vision," in 1709; his "Treatise concerning the Principles of Human Knowledge," in 1710; and his "Dialogues between Hylas and Philonous," in 1713; being then a Fellow of Trinity College, Dublin. He is acknowledged universally to have great merit, as an excellent writer, and a very acute and clear reasoner on the most abstract subjects, not to speak of his virtues as a man, which were very conspicuous; yet the doctrine chiefly held forth in the treatises above mentioned, especially in the two last, has generally been though so very absurd, that few can be brought to think that he either believed it himself, or that he seriously meant to persuade others of its truth.

He maintains, and thinks he has demonstrated, by a variety of arguments, grounded on principles of philosophy universally received, that there is no such thing as matter in the universe; that sun and moon, earth and sea, our own bodies, and those of our friends, are nothing but ideas in the minds of those who think of them, and that they have no existence when they are not the objects of thought; that all that is in the universe may be reduced to two categories—to wit, *minds,* and *ideas in the mind.*

But, however absurd this doctrine might appear to the unlearned, who consider the existence of the objects of sense as the most evident of all truths, and what no man in his senses can doubt, the philosophers who had been accustomed to consider ideas as the immediate objects of all thought, had no title to view this doctrine of Berkeley in so unfavorable a light.

They were taught by Des Cartes, and by all that came after him, that the existence of the objects of sense is not

Reprinted from Thomas Reid, "Reflections on the Common Theory of Ideas" from *Essays on the Intellectual Powers of Man* (1785).

self-evident, but requires to be proved by arguments; and, although Des Cartes, and many others, had laboured to find arguments for this purpose, there did not appear to be that force and clearness in them which might have been expected in a matter of such importance. Mr. Norris had declared that, after all the arguments that had been offered, the existence of an external world is only probable, but by no means certain. Malebranche thought it rested upon the authority of revelation, and that the arguments drawn from reason were not perfectly conclusive. Others thought that the argument from revelation was a mere sophism, because revelation comes to us by our senses, and must rest upon their authority.

Thus we see that the new philosophy had been making gradual approaches towards Berkeley's opinion; and, whatever others might do, the philosophers had no title to look upon it as absurd, or unworthy of a fair examination. . . .

In the "Theory of Vision," he goes no farther than to assert that the objects of sight are nothing but ideas in the mind, granting, or at least not denying, that there is a tangible world, which is really external, and which exists whether we perceive it or not. Whether the reason of this was, that his system had not, at that time, wholly opened to his own mind, or whether he thought it prudent to let it enter into the minds of his readers by degrees, I cannot say. I think he insinuates the last as the reason, in the "Principles of Human Knowledge."

The "Theory of Vision," however, taken by itself, and without relation to the main branch of his system, contains very important discoveries, and marks of great genius. He distinguishes more accurately than any that went before him, between the immediate objects of sight, and those of the other senses which are early associated with them. He shews that distance, of itself and immediately, is not seen; but that we learn to judge of it by certain sensations and perceptions which are connected with it. This is a very important observation; and, I believe, was first made by this author. It gives much new light to the operations of our sense, and serves to account for many phaenomena in optics, of which the greatest adepts in that science had always either given a false account, or acknowledge that they could give none at all.

We may observe, by the way, that the ingenious author seems not to have attended to a distinction by which his general assertion ought to have been limited. It is true that the distance of an object from the eye is not immediately seen; but there is a certain kind of distance of one object from another which we see immediately. The author acknowledges that there is a visible extension, and visible figures, which are proper objects of sight; there must therefore be a visible distance. Astronomers call it angular distance; and, although they measure it by the angle, which is made by two lines drawn from the eye to the two distant objects, yet it is immediately perceived by sight, even by those who never thought of that angle.

He led the way in shewing how we learn to perceive the distance of an object from the eye, though this speculation was carried farther by others who came after him. He made the distinction between that extension and figure which we perceive by sight only, and that which we perceive by touch; calling the first, visible, the last, tangible extension and figure. He shewed, likewise, that tangible extension, and not visible, is the object of geometry, although mathematicians commonly use visible diagrams in their demonstrations.

The notion of extension and figure which we get from sight only, and that which we get from touch, have been so constantly conjoined from our infancy in all the judgments we form of the objects of sense, that it required great abilities to distinguish them accurately, and to assign to each sense what truly belongs to it; "so difficult a thing it is," as Berkeley justly observes, "to dissolve an union so early begun, and confirmed by so long a habit." This point he has laboured, through the whole of the essay on vision, with that uncommon penetration and judgment which he possessed, and with as great success as could be expected in a first attempt upon so abstruse a subject.

He concludes this essay, by shewing, in no less than seven sections, the notions which an intelligent being, endowed with sight, without the sense of touch, might form of the objects of sense. This speculation, to shal-

low thinkers, may appear to be egregious trifling. To Bishop Berkeley it appeared in another light, and will do so to those who are capable of entering into it, and who know the importance of it, in solving many of the phaenomena of vision. He seems, indeed, to have exerted more force of genius in this than in the main branch of his system.

In the new philosophy, the pillars by which the existence of a material world was supported, were so feeble that it did not require the force of a Samson to bring them down; and in this we have not so much reason to admire the strength of Berkeley's genius, as his boldness in publishing to the world an opinion which the unlearned would be apt to interpret as the sign of a crazy intellect. A man who was firmly persuaded of the doctrine universally received by philosophers concerning ideas, if he could but take courage to call in question the existence of a material world, would easily find unanswerable arguments in that doctrine. "Some truths there are," says Berkeley, "so near and obvious to the mind, that a man need only open his eyes to see them. Such," he adds, "I take this important one to be, that all the choir of heaven, and furniture of the earth—in a word, all those bodies which compose the mighty frame of the world—have not any subsistence without a mind." Princ. §6.

The principle from which this important conclusion is obviously deduced, is laid down in the first sentence of his principles of knowledge, as evident; and, indeed, it has always been acknowledged by philosophers. "It is evident," says he, "to any one who takes a survey of the objects of human knowledge, that they are either ideas actually imprinted on the senses, or else such as are perceived, by attending to the passions and operations of the mind; or, lastly, ideas formed by help of memory and imagination, either compounding, dividing, or barely representing those originally perceived in the foresaid ways."

This is the foundation on which the whole system rests. If this be true, then, indeed, the existence of a material world must be a dream that has imposed upon all mankind from the beginning of the world.

The foundation on which such fabric rests ought to be very solid and well established; yet Berkeley says nothing more for it than that it is evident. If he means that it is self-evident, this indeed might be a good reason for not offering any direct argument in proof of it. But I apprehend this cannot justly be said. Self-evident propositions are those which appear evident to every man of sound understanding who apprehends the meaning of them distinctly, and attends to them without prejudice. Can this be said of this proposition, That all the objects of our knowledge are ideas in our own minds? I believe that, to any man uninstructed in philosophy, this proposition will appear very improbable, if not absurd. However scanty his knowledge may be, he considers the sun and moon, the earth and sea, as objects of it; and it will be difficult to persuade him that those objects of his knowledge are ideas in his own mind, and have no existence when he does not think of them. If I may presume to speak my own sentiments, I once believed this doctrine of ideas so firmly as to embrace the whole of Berkeley's system in consequence of it; till, finding other consequences to follow from it, which gave me more uneasiness than the want of a material world, it came into my mind, more than forty years ago, to put the question, What evidence have I for this doctrine, that all the objects of my knowledge are ideas in my own mind? From that time to the present I have been candidly and impartially, as I think, seeking for the evidence of this principle, but can find none, expecting the authority of philosophers.

We shall have occasion to examine its evidence afterwards. I would at present only observe, that all the arguments brought by Berkeley against the existence of a material world are grounded upon it; and that he has not attempted to give any evidence for it, but takes it for granted, as other philosophers had done before him.

But, supposing this principle to be true, Berkeley's system is impregnable. No demonstration can be more evident than his reasoning from it. Whatever is perceived is an idea, and an idea can only exist in a mind. It has no existence when it is not perceived; nor can there be anything like an idea, but an idea. . . .

Berkeley foresaw the opposition that would be made to his system, from two different quarters: *first,* from the philosophers; and, *secondly,* from the vulgar, who are led by the plain dictates of nature. The first he had the courage to oppose openly and avowedly; the second, he dreaded much more, and, therefore, takes a great deal of pains, and, I think, uses some art, to court into his party. This is particularly observable in his "Dialogues." He sets out with a declaration, Dial. 1, "That, of late, he had quitted several of the sublime notions he had got in the schools of the philosophers, for vulgar opinions," and assures Hylas, his fellow-dialogist, "That, since this revolt from metaphysical notions to the plain dictates of nature and common sense, he found his understanding strangely enlightened; so that he could now easily comprehended a great many things, which before were all mystery and riddle." Pref. to Dial. "If his principles are admitted for true, men will be reduced from paradoxes to common sense." At the same time, he acknowledges, "That they carry with them a great opposition to the prejudices of philosophers, which have so far prevailed against the common sense and natural notions of mankind."

When Hylas objects to him, Dial. 3, "You can never persuade me, Philonous, that the denying of matter or corporeal substance is not repugnant to the universal sense of mankind"—he answers, "I wish both our opinions were fairly stated, and submitted to the judgment of men who had plan common sense, without the prejudices of a learned education. Let me be represented as one who trusts his senses, who thinks he knows the things he sees and feels, and entertains no doubt of their existence.—If by material substance is meant only sensible body, that which is seen and felt, (and the unphilosophical part of the world, I dare say, mean no more,) than I am more certain of matter's existence that you or any other philosopher pretended to be. If there be anything which makes the generality of mankind averse from the notions I espouse, it is a misapprehension that I deny the reality of sensible things: but, as it is you who are guilty of that, and not I, it follows, that, in truth, their aversion is against your notions, and not mine. I am content to appeal to the common sense of the world for the truth of my notion. I am of a vulgar cast, simple enough to believe my senses, and to leave things as I find them. I cannot, for my life, help thinking that snow is white and fire hot."

These passages shew sufficiently the author's concern to reconcile his system to the plain dictates of nature and common sense, while he expresses no concern to reconcile it to the received doctrines of philosophers. He is fond to take part with the vulgar against the philosophers, and to vindicate common sense against their innovations. What pity is it that he did not carry this suspicion of the doctrine of philosophers so far as to doubt of that philosophical tenet on which his whole system is built—to wit, that the things immediately perceived by the senses are ideas which exist only in the mind!

After all, it seems no easy matter to make the vulgar opinion and that of Berkeley to meet. And, to accomplish this, he seems to me to draw each out of its line towards the other, not without some straining.

The vulgar opinion he reduces to this, that the very things which we perceive by our senses do really exist. This he grants; for these things, says he, are ideas in our minds, or complexions of ideas, to which we give one name, and consider as one thing; these are the immediate objects of sense, and these do really exist. As to the notion that those things have an absolute external existence, independent of being perceived by any mind, he thinks that this is no notion of the vulgar, but a refinement of philosophers; and that the notion of material substance, as a *substratum,* or support of that collection of sensible qualities to which we give the name of an apple or a melon, is likewise an invention of philosophers, and is not found with the vulgar till they are instructed by philosophers. The substance not being an object of sense, the vulgar never think of it; or, if they are taught the use of the word, they mean no more by it but that collection of sensible qualities which they, from finding them conjoined in nature, have been accustomed to call by one name, and to consider as one thing.

Thus he draws the vulgar opinion near to his own; and, that he may meet it half way, he acknowledges that material things have a real existence out of the mind of this or that person; but the question, says he, between the materialist and me, is whether they have an absolute existence distinct from their being perceived by God, and exterior to all minds? This, indeed, he says, some heathens and philosophers have affirmed; but whoever entertains notions of the Deity, suitable to the Holy Scripture, will be of another opinion.

But here an objection occurs, which it required all his ingenuity to answer. It is this: The ideas in my mind cannot be the same with the ideas of any other mind; therefore, if the objects I perceive be only ideas, it is impossible that the objects I perceive can exist anywhere, when I do not perceive them; and it is impossible that two or more minds can perceive the same object.

To this Berkeley answers, that this objection presses no less the opinion of the materialist philosopher than his. But the difficulty is to make his opinion coincide with the notions of the vulgar, who are firmly persuaded that the very identical objects which they perceive, continue to exist when they do not perceive them; and who are no less firmly persuaded that, when ten men look at the sun or the moon, they all see the same individual object.

To reconcile this repugnancy, he observes, Dial. 3— "That, if the term *same* be taken in the vulgar acceptation, it is certain (and not at all repugnant to the principles he maintains) that different persons may perceive the same thing; or the same thing or idea exist in different minds. Words are of arbitrary imposition; and, since men are used to apply the word *same,* where no distinction or variety is perceived, and he does not pretend to alter their perceptions, it follows that, as men have said before, *several saw the same thing,* so they may, upon like occasions, still continue to use the same phrase, without any deviation, either from propriety of language, or the truth of things; but, if the term *same* be used in the acceptation of philosophers, who pretend to an abstracted notion of identity, then, according to their sundry definitions of this term, (for it is not yet agreed wherein that philosophic identity consists,) it may or may not be possible for divers persons to perceive the same thing; but whether philosophers shall think fit to call a thing the *same* or no is, I conceive, of small importance. Men may dispute about identity and diversity, without any real difference in their thoughts and opinions, abstracted from names."

Upon the whole, I apprehend that Berkeley has carried this attempt to reconcile his system to the vulgar opinion farther than reason supports him; and he was no doubt tempted to do so, from a just apprehension that, in a controversy of this kind, the common sense of mankind is the most formidable antagonist.

Berkeley has employed much pains and ingenuity to shew that his system, if received and believed, would not be attended with those bad consequences in the conduct of life, which superficial thinkers may be apt to impute to it. His system does not take away or make any alteration upon our pleasures or our pains: our sensations, whether agreeable or disagreeable, are the same upon his system as upon any other. These are real things, and the only things that interest us. They are produced in us according to certain laws of nature, by which our conduct will be directed in attaining the one, and avoiding the other; and it is of no moment to us, whether they are produced immediately by the operation of some powerful intelligent being upon our minds; or by the mediation of some inanimate being which we call *matter*.

The evidence of an all-governing mind, so far from being weakened, seems to appear even in a more striking light upon his hypothesis, than upon the common one. The powers which inanimate matter is supposed to possess, have always been the stronghold of atheists, to which they had recourse in defence of their system. This fortress of atheism must be most effectually overturned, if there is no such thing as matter in the universe. In all this the Bishop reasons justly and acutely. But there is one uncomfortable consequence of his system, which he seems not to have attended to, and from which it will be found difficult, if at all possible, to guard it.

The consequence I mean is this—that, although it leaves us sufficient evidence of a supreme intelligent mind, it seems to take away all the evidence we have of other intelligent beings like ourselves. What I call a father, a brother, or a friend, is only a parcel of ideas in my own mind: and, being ideas in my mind, they cannot possibly have that relation to another mind which they have to mine, any more than the pain felt by me can be the individual pain felt by another. I can find no principle in Berkeley's system, which affords me even probable ground to conclude that there are other intelligent beings, like myself, in the relations of father, brother, friend, or fellow-citizen. I am left alone, as the only creature of God in the universe, in that forlorn state of *egoism* into which it is said some of the disciple of Des Cartes were brought by his philosophy.

Of all the opinions that have ever been advanced by philosophers, this of Bishop Berkeley, that there is no material world, seems the strangest, and the most apt to bring philosophy into ridicule with plain men who are guided by the dictates of nature and common sense. . . .

Chapter 14 – Reflections on the Common Theory of Ideas

There remains only one other argument that I have been able to find urged against our perceiving external objects immediately. It is proposed by Mr. Hume, who, in the essay already quoted, after acknowledging that it is an universal and primary opinion of all men, that we perceive external objects immediately, subjoins what follows:—

"But this universal and primary opinion of all men is soon destroyed by the slightest philosophy, which teaches us that nothing can ever be present to the mind but an image or perception; and that the senses are only the inlets through which these images are received, without being ever able to produce any immediate intercourse between the mind and the object. The table, which we see, seems to diminish as we remove farther from it: but the real table, which exists independent of us, suffers no alteration. It was, therefore, nothing but its image which was present to the mind. These are the obvious dictates of reason; and no man who reflects ever doubted that the existences which we consider, when we say *this house,* and *that tree,* are nothing but perceptions in the mind, and fleeting copies and representations of other existences, which remain uniform and independent. So far, then we are necessitated, by reasoning, to depart from the primary instincts of nature, and to embrace a new system with regard to the evidence of our senses."

We have here a remarkable conflict between two contradictory opinions, wherein all mankind are engaged. On the one side stand all the vulgar, who are unpractised in philosophical researches, and guided by the uncorrupted primary instincts of nature. On the other side stand all the philosophers, ancient and modern; every man, without exception, who reflects. In this division, to my great humiliation, I find myself classed with the vulgar. . . .

To judge of the strength of this argument, it is necessary to attend to a distinction which is familiar to those who are conversant in the mathematical sciences—I mean the distinction between real and apparent magnitude. The real magnitude of a line is measured by some known measure of length—as inches, feet, or miles: the real magnitude of a surface or solid, by known measures of surface or of capacity. This magnitude is an object of touch only, and not of sight; nor could we even have had any conception of it, without the sense of touch; and Bishop Berkeley, on that account, calls it *tangible magnitude*.

Apparent magnitude is measured by the angle which an object subtends at the eye. Supposing two right lines drawn from the eye to the extremities of the object making an angle, of which the object is the subtense, the apparent magnitude is measured by this angle. This apparent magnitude is an object of sight, and not of touch. Bishop Berkeley calls it *visible magnitude*.

If it is asked what is the apparent magnitude of the sun's diameter, the answer is, that it is about thirty-one minutes of a degree. But, if it is asked what is the real magnitude of the sun's diameter, the answer must be, so may thousand miles or so many diameters of the earth. From which it is evident that real magnitude, and apparent magnitude, are things of a different nature, though the name of magnitude is given to both. The first has three dimensions, the last only two; the first is measured by a line, the last by an angle.

From what has been said, it is evident that the real magnitude of a body must continue unchanged, while the body is unchanged. This we grant. But is it likewise evident, that the apparent magnitude must continue the same while the body is unchanged? So far otherwise, that every man who knows anything of mathematics can easily demonstrate, that the same individual object, remaining in the same place, and unchanged, must necessarily vary in its apparent magnitude, according as the point from which it is seen is more or less distant; and that its apparent length or breadth will be nearly in a reciprocal proportion to the distance of the spectator. This is as certain as the principles of geometry.

We must likewise attend to this—that, though the real magnitude of a body is not originally an object of sight, but of touch, yet we learn by experience to judge of the real magnitude in many cases by sight. We learn by experience to judge of the distance of a body from the eye within certain limits; and, from its distance and apparent magnitude taken together, we learn to judge of its real magnitude.

And this kind of judgment, by being repeated every hour and almost every minute of our lives, becomes, when we are grown up, so ready and so habitual, that it very

much resembles the original perceptions of our senses, and may not improperly be called *acquired perception*.

Whether we call it judgment or acquired perception is a verbal difference. But it is evident that, by means of it, we often discover by one sense things which are properly and naturally the objects of another. Thus I can say, without impropriety, I hear a drum, I hear a great bell, or I hear a small bell; though it is certain that the figure or size of the sounding body is not originally an object of hearing. In like manner, we learn by experience how a body of such a real magnitude and at such a distance appears to the eye. But neither its real magnitude, nor its distance from the eye, are properly objects of sight, any more than the form of a drum or the size of a bell, are properly objects of hearing.

If these things be considered, it will appear that Mr. Hume's argument hath no force to support his conclusion—nay, that it leads to a contrary conclusion. The argument is this: the table we see seems to diminish as we remove farther from it; that it, its apparent magnitude is diminished; but the real table suffers no alteration—to wit, in its real magnitude; therefore, it is not the real table we see. I admit both the premises in this syllogism, but I deny the conclusion. The syllogism has what the logicians call two middle terms: apparent magnitude is the middle term in the first premise; real magnitude in the second. Therefore, according to the rules of logic, the conclusion is not justly drawn from the premises; but, laying aside the rules of logic, let us examine it by the light of common sense.

Let us suppose, for a moment, that it is the real table we see: Must not this real table seem to diminish as we remove farther from it? It is demonstrable that it must. How then can this apparent diminution be an argument that it is not the real table? When that which must happen to the real table, as we remove farther from it, does actually happen to the table we see, it is absurd to conclude from this, that it is not the real table we see. It is evident, therefore, that this ingenious author has imposed upon himself by confounding real magnitude with apparent magnitude, and that his argument is a mere sophism.

I observed that Mr. Hume's argument not only has no strength to support his conclusion, but that it leads to the contrary conclusion—to wit, that it is the real table we see; for this plain reason, that the table we see has precisely that apparent magnitude which it is demonstrable the real table must have when placed at that distance.

This argument is made much stronger by considering that the real table may be places successively at a thousand different distances, and, in every distance, in a thousand different positions; and it can be determined demonstratively, by the rules of geometry and perspective, what must be its apparent magnitude and apparent figure, in each of those distances and positions. Let the table be placed successively in as many of those different distances and different positions as you will, or in them all; open your eyes and you shall see a table precisely of that apparent magnitude, and that apparent figure, which the real table must have in that distance and in that position. Is not this a strong argument that it is the real table you see? . . .

Thus, I have considered every argument I have found advanced to prove the existence of ideas, or images of eternal things, in the mind; and, if no better arguments can be found, I cannot help thinking that the whole history of philosophy has never furnished an instance of an opinion so unanimously entertained by philosophers upon so slight grounds.

A *third* reflection I would make upon this subject is, that philosophers, notwithstanding their unanimity as to the existence of ideas, hardly agree in any one thing else concerning them. If ideas be not a mere fiction, they must be, of all objects of human knowledge, the things we have best access to know, and to be acquainted with; yet there is nothing about which men differ so much.

A *fourth* reflection is, that ideas do not make any of the operations of the mind to be better understood, although it was probably with that view that they have been first invented, and afterwards so generally received.

We are at a loss to know how we perceive distant objects; how we remember things past; how we imagine things that have no existence. Ideas in the mind seem to account for all theses operations: they are all by the means of ideas reduced to one operation—to a kind of feeling, or immediate perception of things present and in contact with the percipient; and feeling is an operation so familiar that we think it needs no explication, but may serve to explain other operations.

But this feeling, or immediate perception, is as difficult to be comprehended as the things which we pretend to explain by it. Two things may be in contact without any feeling or perception; there must therefore be in the percipient a power to feel or to perceive. How this power is produced, and how it operates, is quite beyond the reach of our knowledge. As little can we know whether this power must be limited to things present, and in contact with us. Nor can any man pretend to prove that the Being who gave us the power to perceive things present, may not give us the power to perceive things that are distant, to remember things past, and to conceive things that never existed. . . .

Chapter 17 – Of the Objects of Perception; and, First, of Primary and Secondary Qualities

The objects of perception are the various qualities of bodies. Intending to treat of these only in general, and chiefly with a view to explain the notions which our senses give us of them, I begin with the distinction between primary and secondary qualities. These were distinguished very early. The Peripatetic system confounded them, and left no difference. The distinction was again revived by Des Cartes and Locke, and a second time abolished by Berkeley and Hume. If the real foundation of this distinction can be pointed out, it will enable us to account for the various revolutions in the sentiments of philosophers concerning it.

Every one knows that extension, divisibility, figure, motion, solidity, hardness, softness, and fluidity, were by Mr. Locke called *primary qualities of body;* and that sound, colour, taste, smell, and heat or cold, were called *secondary qualities.* Is there a just foundation for this distinction? Is there anything common to the primary which belongs not to the secondary? And what is it?

I answer, That there appears to me to be a real foundation for the distinction; and it is this—that our senses give us a direct and a distinct notion of the primary qualities, and inform us what they are in themselves. But of the secondary qualities, our senses give us only a relative and obscure notion. They inform us only, that they are qualities that affect us in a certain manner—that is, produce in us a certain sensation; but as to what they are in themselves, our senses leave us in the dark.

Every man capable of reflection may easily satisfy himself that he has a perfectly clear and distinct notion of extension, divisibility, figure, and motion. The solidity of a body means no more but that it excludes other bodies from occupying the same place at the same time. Hardness, softness, and fluidity are different degrees of cohesion in the parts of a body. It is fluid when it has no sensible cohesion; soft, when the cohesion is weak; and hard, when it is strong. Of the cause of this cohesion we are ignorant, but the things itself we understand perfectly, being immediately informed of it by the sense of touch. It is evident, therefore, that of the primary qualities we have a clear and distinct notion; we know what they are, though we may be ignorant of their causes.

I observed, farther, that the notion we have of primary qualities, is direct, and not relative only. A relative notion of a thing, is, strictly speaking, no notion of the thing at all, but only of some relation which it bears to something else.

Thus, gravity sometimes signifies the tendency of bodies towards the earth; sometimes it signifies the cause of that tendency. When it means the first, I have a direct and distinct notion of gravity; I see it, and feel it, and know perfectly what it is; but this tendency must have a cause. We give the same name to the cause; and that case has been an object of thought and of speculation. Now, what notion have we of this cause when we think and reason about it? It is evident we think of it as an unknown cause, of a known effect. This is a relative notion; and it must be obscure, because it gives us no conception of what the thing is, but of what relation it bears to something else. Every relation which a thing unknown bears to something that is known, may give a relative notion of it; and there are many objects of thought and of discourse of which our faculties can give no better than a relative notion.

Having premised these things to explain what is meant by a relative notion, it is evident that out notion of primary qualities is not of this kind; we know what they are, and not barely what relation they bear to something else.

It is otherwise with secondary qualities. If you ask me, what is that quality or modification in a rose which I call its smell, I am at a loss to answer directly. Upon reflection, I find, that I have a distinct notion of the sensation which it produces in my mind. But there can be nothing like to this sensation in the rose, because it is insentient. The quality in the rose is something which occasions the sensation in me; but what that something is, I know not. My senses give me no information upon this point. The only notion, therefore, my sense give is this—that smell in the rose is an unknown quality or modification, which is the cause or occasion of a sensation which I know well. The relation which this unknown quality bears to the sensation with which nature hath connected it, is all I learn from the sense of smelling; but this is evidently a relative notion. The same reasoning will apply to every secondary quality.

Thus, I think it appears that there is a real foundation for the distinction of primary from secondary qualities; and that they are distinguished by this—that of the primary we have by our senses a direct and distinct notion; but of the secondary only a relative notion, which must, because it is only relative, be obscure; they are conceived only as the unknown causes or occasions of certain sensations with which we are well acquainted.

The account I have given of this distinction is founded upon no hypothesis. Whether our notions of primary qualities are direct and distinct, those of the secondary relative and obscure, is a matter of fact, of which every man may have certain knowledge by attentive reflection upon them. To this reflection I appeal, as the proper test of what has been advanced, and proceed to make some reflections on this subject.

1. The primary qualities are neither sensations, nor are they resemblances of sensations. This appears to me self-evident. I have a clear and distinct notion of each of the primary qualities. I have a clear and distinct notion of sensation. I can compare the one with the other; and, when I do so, I am not able to discern a resembling feature. Sensation is the act or the feeling (I dispute not which) of a sentient being. Figure, divisibility, solidity, are neither acts nor feelings. Sensation supposes a sentient being as its subject; for a sensation that is not felt by some sentient being, is an absurdity. Figure and divisibility supposes a subject that is figured and divisible, but not a subject that is sentient.

2. We have no reason to think that any of the secondary qualities resemble any sensation. The absurdity of this notion has been clearly shewn by Des Cartes, Locke, and many modern philosophers. It was a tenet of the ancient philosophy, and is still by many imputed to the vulgar, but only as a vulgar error. It is too evident

to need proof, that the vibrations of a sounding body do not resemble the sensation of sounds, nor the effluvia of an odorous body the sensation of smell.

3. The distinctness of our notions of primary qualities prevents all questions and disputes about their nature. There are no different opinions about the nature of extension, figure, or motion, or the nature of any primary quality. Their nature is manifest to our senses, and cannot be unknown to any man, or mistaken by him, though their causes may admit of dispute.

The primary qualities are the object of the mathematical sciences; and the distinctness of our notions of them enables us to reason demonstratively about them to a great extent. Their various modifications are precisely defined in the imagination, and thereby capable of being compared, and their relations determined with precision and certainty.

It is not so with secondary qualities. Their nature not being manifest to the sense, may be a subject of dispute. Our feeling informs us that the fire is hot; but it does not inform us what that heat of the fire is. But does it not appear a contradiction, to say we know that the fire is hot, but we know not what that heat is? I answer, there is the same appearance of contradiction in many things that must be granted. We know that wine has an inebriating quality; but we know not what that quality is. It is true, indeed, that, if we had not some notion of what is meant by the heat of fire, and by an inebriating quality, we could affirm nothing of either with understanding. We have a notion of both; but it is only a relative notion. We know that they are the causes of certain known effects.

4. The nature of secondary qualities is a proper subject of philosophical disquisition; and in this philosophy has made some progress. It has been discovered, that the sensation of smell is occasioned by the effluvia of bodies; that of sound by their vibration. The disposition of bodies to reflect a particular kind of light, occasions the sensation of colour. Very curious discoveries have been made of the nature of heat, and an ample field of discovery in these subjects remains.

5. We may see why the sensations belonging to secondary qualities are an object of our attention, while those which belong to the primary are not.

The first are not only signs of the object perceived, but they bear a capital part in the notion we form of it. We conceive it only as that which occasions such a sensation, and therefore cannot reflect upon it without thinking of the sensation which it occasions: we have no other mark whereby to distinguish it. The thought of a secondary quality, therefore, always carries us back to the sensation which it produces. We give the same name to both, and are apt to confound them together.

But, having a clear and distinct conception of primary qualities, we have no need, when we think of them, to recall their sensations. When a primary quality is perceived, the sensation immediately leads our thought to the quality signified by it, and is itself forgot. We have no occasion afterwards to reflect upon it; and so we come to be as little acquainted with it as if we had never felt it. This is the case with the sensations of all primary qualities, when they are not so painful or pleasant as to draw our attention.

When a man moves his hand rudely against a pointed hard body, he feels pain, and may easily be persuaded that this pain is a sensation, and that there is nothing resembling it in the hard body; at the same time, he perceives the body to be hard and pointed, and he knows that these qualities belong to the body only. In this case, it is easy to distinguish what he feels from what he perceives.

Let him again touch the pointed body gently, so as to give him no pain; and now you can hardly persuade him that he feels anything but the figure and hardness of the body: so difficult it is to attend to the sensations belonging to primary qualities, when they are neither pleasant nor painful. They carry the thought to the external object, and immediately disappear and are forgot. Nature intended them only as signs; and when they have served that purpose they vanish. . . .

Bertrand Russell

On Induction

Chapter VI

On Induction

In almost all our previous discussions we have been concerned in the attempt to get clear as to our data in the way of knowledge of existence. What things are there in the universe whose existence is known to us owing to our being acquainted with them? So far, our answer has been that we are acquainted with our sense-data, and, probably, with ourselves. These we know to exist. And past sense-data which are remembered are known to have existed in the past. This knowledge supplies our data.

But if we are to be able to draw inferences from these data—if we are to know of the existence of matter, of other people, of the past before our individual memory begins, or of the future, we must know general principles of some kind by means of which such inferences can be drawn. It must be known to us that the existence of some one sort of things, A, is a sign of the existence of some other sort of thing, B, either at the same time as A or at some earlier or later time, as, for example, thunder is a sign of the earlier existence of lightning. If this were not known to us, we could never extend our knowledge beyond the sphere of our private experience; and this sphere, as we have seen, is exceedingly limited. The question we have now to consider is whether such an extension is possible, and if so, how it is effected.

Let us take as an illustration a matter about which none of us, in fact, feel the slightest doubt. We are all convinced that the sun will rise to-morrow. Why? Is this belief a mere blind outcome of past experience, or can it be justified as a reasonable belief? It is not easy to find

a test by which to judge whether a belief of this kind is reasonable or not, but we can at least ascertain what sort of general beliefs would suffice, if true, to justify the judgment that the sun will rise to-morrow, and the many other similar judgments upon which our actions are based.

It is obvious that if we are asked why we believe that the sun will rise to-morrow, we shall naturally answer, 'Because it always has risen every day'. We have a firm belief that it will rise in the future, because it has risen in the past. If we are challenged as to why we believe that it will continue to rise as heretofore, we may appeal to the laws of motion: the earth, we shall say, is a freely rotating body, and such bodies do not cease to rotate unless something interferes from outside, and there is nothing outside to interfere with the earth between now and to-morrow. Of course it might be doubted whether we are quite certain that there is nothing outside to interfere, but this is not the interesting doubt. The interesting doubt is as to whether the laws of motion will remain in operation until to-morrow. If this doubt is raised, we find ourselves in the same position as when the doubt about the sunrise was first raised.

The *only* reason for believing that the laws of motion will remain in operation is that they have operated hitherto, so far as our knowledge of the past enables us to judge. It is true that we have a greater body of evidence from the past in favor of the laws of motion than we have in favor of the sunrise, because the sunrise is merely a particular case of fulfillment of the laws of motion, and there are countless other particular cases. But the real question is: Do *any* number of cases of a law being fulfilled in the past afford evidence that it will be fulfilled in the future? If not, it becomes plain that we have no ground whatever for expecting the sun to rise to-morrow, or for expecting the bread we shall eat at our next meal not to poison us, or for any of the other scarcely conscious expectations that con-

Bertrand Russell, "On Induction" from *The Problems of Philosophy* (Oxford: Oxford University Press, 1959). Reprinted with the permission of Oxford University Press, Ltd.

trol our daily lives. It is to be observed that all such expectations are only *probable;* thus we have not to seek for a proof that they *must* be fulfilled, but only for some reason in favor of the view that they are *likely* to be fulfilled.

Now in dealing with this question we must, to begin with, make an important distinction, without which we should soon become involved in hopeless confusions. Experience has shown us that, hitherto, the frequent repetition of some uniform succession or coexistence has been a *cause* of our expecting the same succession or coexistence on the next occasion. Food that has a certain appearance generally has a certain taste, and it is a severe shock to our expectations when the familiar appearance is found to be associated with an unusual taste. Things which we see become associated, by habit, with certain tactile sensations which we expect if we touch them; one of the horrors of a ghost (in many ghost-stories) is that it fails to give us any sensations of touch. Uneducated people who go abroad for the first time are so surprised as to be incredulous when they find their native language not understood.

And this kind of association is not confined to men; in animals also it is very strong. A horse which has been often driven along a certain road resists the attempt to drive him in a different direction. Domestic animals expect food when they see the person who usually feeds them. We know that all these rather crude expectations of uniformity are liable to be misleading. The man who has fed the chicken every day throughout its life at last wrings it neck instead, showing that more refined views as to the uniformity of nature would have been useful to the chicken.

But in spite of the misleadingness of such expectations, they nevertheless exist. The mere fact that something has happened a certain number of times causes animals and men to expect that it will happen again. Thus our instincts certainly cause us to believe that the sun will rise to-morrow, but we may be in no better a position than the chicken which unexpectedly has its neck wrung. We have therefore to distinguish the fact that past uniformities *cause* expectations as to the future, from the question whether there is any reasonable ground for giving weight to such expectations after the question of their validity has been raised.

The problem we have to discuss is whether there is any reason for believing in what is called 'the uniformity of nature'. The belief in the uniformity of nature is the belief that everything that has happened or will happen is an instance of some general law to which there are *no* exceptions. The crude expectations which we have been considering are all subject to expectations, and therefore liable to disappoint those who entertain them. But science habitually assumes, at least as a working hypothesis, that general rules which have expectations can be replaced by general rules which have no expectations. 'Unsupported bodies in air fall' is a general rule to which balloons and airplanes are exceptions. But the laws of motion and the law of gravitation, which account for the fact that most bodies fall, also account for the fact that balloons and airplanes can rise; thus the laws of motion and the law of gravitation are not subject to these exceptions.

The belief that the sun will rise to-morrow might be falsified if the earth came suddenly into contact with a large body which destroyed its rotation; but the laws of motion and the law of gravitation would not be infringed by such an event. The business of science is to find uniformities, such as the laws of motion and the law of gravitation, to which, so far as our experience extends, there are no exceptions. In this search science has been remarkably successful, and it may be conceded that such uniformities have held hitherto. This brings us back to the question: Have we any reason, assuming that they have always held in the past, to suppose that they will hold in the future?

It has been argued that we have reason to know that the future will resemble the past, because what was the future has constantly become the past, and has always been found to resemble the past, so that we really have experience of the future, namely of times which were formerly future, which we may call past futures. But such an argument really begs the very question at issue. We have experience of past futures, but not of future futures, and the question is: Will future futures resemble past futures? This question is not to be answered by an argument which starts from past futures alone. We have therefore still to seek for some principle which shall enable us to know that the future will follow the same laws as the past.

The reference to the future in this question is not essential. The same question arises when we apply the laws that work in our experience to past things of which we have no experience—as, for example, in geology, or in theories as to the origin of the Solar System. The question we really have to ask is: 'When two things have been found to be often associated, and no instance is known of the one occurring without the other, does the occurrence of one of the two, in a fresh instance, give any good ground for expecting the other?' On our answer to this question must depend the validity of the whole of our expectations as to the future, the whole of the results obtained by induction, and in fact practically all the beliefs upon which our daily life is based.

It must be conceded, to begin with, that the fact that two things have been found often together and never apart does not, by itself, suffice to *prove* demonstratively that they will be found together in the next case we examine. The most we can hope is that the oftener things are found together, the more probable it becomes that they will be found together another time, and that, if they have been found together often enough, the probability will amount *almost* to certainty. It can never quite reach certainty, because we know that in spite of frequent repetitions there sometimes is a failure at the last, as in the case of the chicken whose neck is wrung. Thus probability is all we ought to seek.

It might be urged, as against the view we are advocating, that we know all natural phenomena to be subject to the reign of law, and that sometimes, on the basis of observation, we can see that only one law can possibly fit the facts of the case. Now to this view there are two answers. The first is that, even if *some* law which has no exceptions applies to our case, we can never, in practice, be sure that we have discovered that law and not one to which there are exceptions. The second is that the reign of law would seem to be itself only probable, and that our belief that it will hold in the future, or in unexamined cases in the past, is itself based upon the very principle we are examining.

The principle we are examining may be called the *principle of induction,* and its two parts may be stated as follows:

(a) When a thing of a certain sort A has been found to be associated with a thing of a certain other sort B, and has never been found dissociated from a thing of the sort B, the greater the number of cases in which A and B have been associated, the greater is the probability that they will be associated in a fresh case in which one of them is known to be present;

(b) Under the same circumstances, a sufficient number of cases of association will make the probability of a fresh association nearly a certainty, and will make it approach certainty without limit.

As just stated, the principle applies only to the verification of our expectation in a single fresh instance. But we want also to know that there is a probability in favor of the general law that things of the sort A are *always* associated with things of the sort B, provided a sufficient number of cases of association are known, and no cases of failure of association are known. The probability of the general law is obviously less than the probability of the particular case, since if the general law is true, the particular case must also be true, whereas the particular case may be true without the general law being true. Nevertheless the probability of the general law is increased by repetitions, just as the probability of the particular case is. We may therefore repeat the two parts of our principle as regards the general law, thus:

(a) The greater the number of cases in which a thing of the sort A has been found associated with a thing of the sort B, the more probable it is (if no cases of failure of association are known) that A is always associated with B;

(b) Under the same circumstances, a sufficient number of cases of the association of A with B will make it nearly certain that A is always associated with B, and will make this general law approach certainty without limit.

It should be noted that probability is always relative to certain data. In our case, the data are merely the known cases of coexistence of A and B. There may be other data, which *might* be taken into account, which would gravely alter the probability. For example, a man who had seen a great many white swans might argue, by our principle, that on the data it was *probable* that all swans were white, and this might be a perfectly sound argument. The argument is not disproved by the fact that some swans are black, because a thing may very well happen in spite of the fact that some data render it improbable. In the case of the swans, a man might know that color is a very variable characteristic in many species of animals, and that, therefore, an induction as to color is peculiarly liable to error. But this knowledge would be a fresh datum, by no means proving that the probability relatively to our previous data had been wrongly estimated. The fact, therefore, that things often fail to fulfill our expectations is no evidence that our expectations will not *probably* be fulfilled in a given case or a given class of cases. Thus our inductive principle is at any rate not capable of being *disproved* by an appeal to experience.

The inductive principle, however, is equally incapable of being *proved* by an appeal to experience. Experience might conceivably confirm the inductive principle as regards the cases that have been already examined; but as regards unexamined cases, it is the inductive principle alone that can justify any inference from what has been examined to what has not been examined. All arguments which, on the basis of experience, argue as to the future or the inexperienced parts of the past or present, assume the inductive principle; hence we can never use experience to prove the inductive principle without begging the question. Thus we must either accept the inductive principle on the ground of its intrinsic evidence, or forgo all justification of our expectations about the future. If the

principle is unsound, we have no reason to expect the sun to rise to-morrow, to expect bread to be more nourishing than a stone, or to expect that if we throw ourselves off the roof we shall fall. When we see what looks like our best friend approaching us, we shall have no reason to suppose that his body is not inhabited by the mind of our worst enemy or of some total stranger. All our conduct is based upon associations which have worked in the past, and which we therefore regard as likely to work in the future; and this likelihood is dependent for its validity upon the inductive principle.

The general principles of science, such as the belief in the reign of law, and the belief that every event must have a cause, are as completely dependent upon the inductive principle as are the beliefs of daily life. All such general principles are believed because mankind have found innumerable instances of their truth and no instances of their falsehood. But this affords no evidence for their truth in the future, unless the inductive principle is assumed.

Thus all knowledge which, on a basis of experience tells us something about what is not experienced, is based upon a belief which experience can neither confirm nor confute, yet which, at least in its more concrete applications, appears to be as firmly rooted in us as many of the facts of experience. The existence and justification of such beliefs—for the inductive principle is not the only example—raises some of the most difficult and most debated problems of philosophy.

Nelson Goodman

The New Riddle of Induction

[. . .] That a given piece of copper conducts electricity increases the credibility of statements asserting that other pieces of copper conduct electricity, and thus confirms the hypothesis that all copper conducts electricity. But the fact that a given man now in this room is a third son does not increase the credibility of statements asserting that other men now in this room are third sons, and so does not confirm the hypothesis that all men now in this room are third sons. Yet in both cases our hypothesis is a generalization of the evidence statement. The difference is that in the former case the hypothesis is a *lawlike* statement; while in the latter case, the hypothesis is a merely contingent or accidental generality. Only a statement that is *lawlike*—regardless of its truth or falsity or its scientific importance—is capable of receiving confirmation from an instance of it; accidental statements are not. Plainly, then, we must look for a way of distinguishing lawlike from accidental statements.

[. . .] Suppose that all emeralds examined before a certain time *t* are green. At time *t,* then, our observations support the hypothesis that all emeralds are green[. . . .] Our evidence statements assert that emerald *a* is green, that emerald *b* is green, and so on; and each confirms the general hypothesis that all emeralds are green. So far, so good.

Now let me introduce another predicate less familiar than "green". It is the predicate "grue" and it applies to all things examined before *t* just in case they are green but to other things just in case they are blue. Then at time *t* we have, for each evidence statement asserting that a given emerald is green, a parallel evidence statement asserting that that emerald is grue. And the state-

ments that emerald *a* is grue, that emerald *b* is grue, and so on, will each confirm the general hypothesis that all emeralds are grue. Thus according to [the] definition [that a generalization is confirmed by the positive instances in its evidence class], the prediction that all emeralds subsequently examined will be green and the prediction that all will be grue are alike confirmed by evidence statements describing the same observations. But if an emerald subsequently examined is grue, it is blue and hence not green. Thus although we are well aware which of the two incompatible predictions is genuinely confirmed, they are equally well confirmed according to our present definition. Moreover, it is clear that if we simply choose an appropriate predicate, then on the basis of these same observations we shall have equal confirmation, by our definition, for any prediction whatever about other emeralds—or indeed about anything else. As in our earlier example, only the predictions subsumed under lawlike hypotheses are genuinely confirmed; but we have no criterion as yet for determining lawlikeness. [. . .]

The problem, then, is to define the relevant way in which [lawlike] hypotheses must be alike. Evidence for the hypothesis that all iron conducts electricity enhances the lawlikeness of the hypothesis that all zirconium conducts electricity, but does not similarly affect the hypothesis that all the objects on my desk conduct electricity. Wherein lies the difference? The first two hypotheses fall under the broader hypothesis—call it "*H*"—that every class of things of the same material is uniform in conductivity; the first and third fall only under some such hypothesis as—call it "*K*"—that every class of things that are either all of the same material or all on a desk is uniform in conductivity. Clearly the important difference here is that evidence for a statement affirming that one of the classes covered by *H* has the property in question increases the credibility of any statement affirming that another such class has this

Reprinted by permission of the publisher from *Fact, Fiction, and Forecast* by Nelson Goodman, Cambridge, Mass.: Harvard University Press. Copyright © 1979, 1983 by Nelson Goodman.

property; while nothing of the sort holds true with respect to *K*. But this is only to say that *H* is lawlike and *K* is not. We are faced anew with the very problem we are trying to solve; the problem of distinguishing between lawlike and accidental hypotheses.

The most popular way of attacking the problem takes its cue from the fact that accidental hypotheses seem typically to involve some spatial or temporal restriction, or reference to some particular individual. They seem to concern the people in some particular room, or the objects on some particular person's desk; while lawlike hypotheses characteristically concern all ravens or all pieces of copper whatsoever. Complete generality is thus very often supposed to be a sufficient condition of lawlikeness; but to define this complete generality is by no means easy. Merely to require that the hypothesis contain no term naming, describing, or indicting a particular thing or location will obviously not be enough. The troublesome hypothesis that all emeralds are grue contains no such term; and where such a term does occur, as in hypotheses about men in *this room,* it can be suppressed in favor of some predicate (short or long, new or old) that contains no such term but applies only to exactly the same things. One might think, then, of excluding not only hypotheses that actually contain terms for specific individuals but also all hypotheses that are equivalent to others that do contain such terms. But, as we have just seen, to exclude only hypotheses of which *all* equivalents contain such terms is to exclude nothing. On the other hand, to exclude all hypotheses that have *some* equivalent containing such a term is to exclude everything; for even the hypothesis

All grass is green
has as an equivalent
All grass in London or elsewhere is green.

The next step, therefore, has been to consider ruling out predicates of certain kinds. A syntactically universal hypothesis is lawlike, the proposal runs, if its predicates are 'purely qualitative' or 'non-positional'. This will obviously accomplish nothing if a purely qualitative predicate is then conceived either as one that is equivalent to some expression free of terms for specific individuals, or as one that is equivalent to no expression that

contains such a term; for this only raises again the difficulties just pointed out. The claim appears to be rather that at least in the case of a simple enough predicate we can readily determine by direct inspection of its meaning whether or not it is purely qualitative. But even aside from obscurities in the notion of 'the meaning' of a predicate, this claim seems to me wrong. I simply do not know how to tell whether a predicate is qualitative or positional, except perhaps by completely begging the question at issue and asking whether the predicate is 'well-behaved'—that is, whether simple syntactically universal hypotheses applying it are lawlike.

This statement will not go unprotested. "Consider", it will be argued, "the predicates 'blue' and 'green' and the predicate 'grue' introduced earlier, and also the predicate 'bleen' that applies to emeralds examined before time *t* just in case they are blue and to other emeralds just in case they are green. Surely it is clear", the argument runs, "that the first two are purely qualitative and the second two are not; for the meaning of each of the latter two plainly involves reference to a specific temporal position". To this I reply that indeed I do recognize the first two as well-behaved predicates admissible in lawlike hypotheses and the second two as ill-behaved predicates. But the argument that the former but not the latter are purely qualitative seems to me quite unsound. True enough, if we start with "blue" and "green", then "grue" and "bleen" will be explained in terms of "blue" and "green" and a temporal term. But equally truly, if we start with "grue" and "bleen", then "blue" and "green" will be explained in terms of "grue" and "bleen" and a temporal term; "green", for example, applies to emeralds examined before time *t* just in case they are grue, and to other emeralds just in case they are bleen. Thus qualitativeness is an entirely relative matter and does not by itself establish any dichotomy of predicates. This relativity seems to be completely overlooked by those who contend that the qualitative character of a predicate is a criterion for its good behavior.

Of course, one may ask why we need worry about such unfamiliar predicates as "grue" or about accidental hypotheses in general, since we are unlikely to use them in making predictions. If our definition works for such hypotheses as are normally employed, isn't that all we need? In a sense, yes; but only in the sense that we need no definition, no theory of induction, and no philosophy of knowledge at all. We get along well enough without them in daily life and scientific research. But if we seek a theory at all, we cannot excuse gross anomalies resulting from a proposed theory by pleading that we can avoid them in practice. The odd cases we have been considering are clinically pure cases that, though seldom encountered in practice, nevertheless display to best advantage the symptoms of a widespread and destructive malady. [. . .]

[. . .] The problem of confirmation, or of valid projection, is the problem of defining a certain relationship between evidence or base cases on the one hand, and hypotheses, predictions or projections on the other. Since numerous and varied attacks on the problem have brought us no solution, we may well ask ourselves whether we are still in any way misconceiving the nature of our task. I think the answer is affirmative: that we have come to mistake the statement of the required result for an unduly restricted statement of the means allowed for reaching that result.

What we want, indeed, is an accurate and general way of saying which hypotheses are confirmed by, or which projections are validly made from, any given evidence. Thus each particular case that arises does concern the relationship of given evidence to entertained hypotheses. But this does not imply that the only materials available to us in determining the relationship are the given evidence and the entertained hypotheses. In other words, while confirmation is indeed a relation between evidence and hypotheses, this does not mean that our definition of this relation must refer to nothing other than such evidence and hypotheses. The fact is that whenever we set about determining the validity of a given projection from a given base, we have and use a good deal of other relevant knowledge. I am not speaking of additional evidence statements, but rather of the record of past predictions actually made and their outcome. Whether these predictions—regardless of their success or failure—are valid or not remains in question; but that some were made and how they turned out is legitimately available information.

Proper use of such information will admittedly require some care. Surely we cannot subscribe to the naïve suggestion that induction is validated simply by its past successes. Every so often someone proclaims that the whole problem is solved just by recognizing that the prediction of future from past cases of a hypothesis is justified by the success of past predictions according to the hypothesis. Critics quickly point out that all questions that arise about the validity of predicting future cases from past ones also arise about the validity of predicting future successes from past ones. But the fact that legitimately available information has been ineptly used should not lead us to discard it. In our present straits, we cannot afford to deprive ourselves of any honest means that may prove to be helpful.

I think we should recognize, therefore, that our task is to define the relation of confirmation or valid projection between evidence and hypothesis in terms of anything that does not beg the question, that meets our other demands for acceptable terms of explanation, and that may reasonably be supposed to be at hand when a question of inductive validity arises. This will include, among other things, some knowledge of past predictions and their successes and failures. I suppose that seldom, if ever, has there been any explicit proposal to preclude use of such knowledge in dealing with our problem. Rather, a longstanding habit of regarding such knowledge as irrelevant has led us to ignore it almost entirely. Thus what I am suggesting is less a reformulation of our problem than a reorientation; that we regard ourselves as coming to the problem not empty-headed but with some stock of knowledge or accepted statements that may fairly be used in reaching a solution.

Nevertheless, this slight reorientation gives our problem quite a new look. For if we start with past projections as well as with evidence and hypotheses, our task becomes that of defining valid projection—or projectibility—on the basis of actual projections. Clearly this is a typical problem of dispositions. Given the manifest predicate "projected" and certain other information, we have to define the dispositional predicate "projectible". And this, as we have seen, resolves itself into the problem of projecting the predicate "projected". [. . .] But matters are not really that bad. Our ultimate aim is to define valid projection or projectibility in full generality. But this can also be regarded as a specific problem of projectibility: as the problem of projecting the specific predicate "projected", or in other words of defining the specific dispositional predicate "projectible". [T]here is no reason why we cannot attempt to deal with a specific problem of dispositions before we have solved the general problem. And in the case of the specific problem of defining the predicate "projectible", the stakes are high; for if we succeed in solving it, we thereby solve the general problem. In effect, the general problem of dispositions has been reduced to the problem of projecting the specific predicate "projected".

The reorientation of our problem may be portrayed in somewhat more figurative language. Hume thought of the mind as being set in motion making predictions by, and in accordance with, regularities in what is observed. This left him with the problem of differentiating between the regularities that do and those that do not thus set the mind in motion. We, on the contrary, regard the mind as in motion from the start, striking out with spontaneous predictions in dozens of directions, and gradually rectifying and channeling its predictive processes. We ask not how predictions come to be made, but how—granting that they are made—they come to be sorted out as valid and invalid. Literally, of course, we are not concerned with describing how the mind works but rather with describing or defining the distinction it makes between valid and invalid projections.

A hypothesis will be said to be *actually projected* when it is adopted after some of its instances have been examined and determined to be true, and before the rest have been examined. The hypothesis need not be true, or lawlike, or even reasonable; for we are speaking here not of what ought to be projected but of what is in fact projected. Moreover, we are not concerned with the question whether a hypothesis is projected in the tenseless sense that there is some past, present or future time at which it is projected. We are concerned at any given time only with projections that have already been made.

Notice especially that even if all the instances examined up to a given time are favorable, and even if the hypothesis is true, still it may perhaps not be actually projected at that (or any other) time. Actual projection involves the overt, explicit formulation and adoption of the hypothesis—the actual prediction of the outcome of the examination of further cases. That the hypothesis could—or even could legitimately—have been pro-

jected at that time is at this stage beside the point. Just here lies the difference between starting from hypotheses and instances alone and starting from actual projections. [. . .]

[. . .] Whether or not a hypothesis is actually projected at a given time, such instantiations of it as have already been determined to be true or false may be called respectively its *positive* and its *negative* instances or cases at that time. All the remaining cases are *undetermined* cases. For example if the hypothesis is

> All emeralds are green
and *e* is an emerald, then
> Emerald *e* is green

is a positive case when *e* has been found to be green, a negative case when *e* has been found not to be green, and an undetermined case when *e* has not yet been found either to be green or not to be green. The emeralds named in the positive cases constitute the *evidence class* for the hypothesis at the time in question, while the emeralds not named in any of the positive or negative cases constitute the *projective class* for the hypothesis at the time. A hypothesis for which there are some positive or negative cases up to a given time is said to be *supported* or to be *violated* at that time. A violated hypothesis is false; but a false hypothesis may at a given time be unviolated. If a hypothesis has both positive and negative cases at a given time, then it is both supported and violated; while if it has no cases determined as yet, it is neither. A hypothesis without any remaining undetermined cases is said to be *exhausted*.

Now according to my terminology, adoption of a hypothesis constitutes actual projection only if at the time in question the hypothesis has some undetermined cases, some positive cases, and no negative cases. That is to say, I shall not speak of a hypothesis as being actually projected at any time when it is exhausted, unsupported, or violated. Obviously, adoption of an exhausted hypothesis involves nothing that we want to call projection. And convenience seems best served by denying the term "projection" to the adoption of a hypothesis without favorable direct evidence or in the face of direct counterevidence. Thus while a given hypothesis may undergo projection, violation, and exhaustion, the projection must antedate the violation and exhaustion. [. . .]

What we have to work with at any given time, then, is a record of projections of a mass of heterogeneous hypotheses at various times. Some of these hypotheses have been violated since the time when they were projected. Others have successfully passed such further tests as they have undergone; but among these are some hypotheses that, since they have by now had all their instances examined and determined to be true, are exhausted and can no longer be projected. Some of the hypotheses projected are false. Some are bizarre. And some are at odds with each other. Such is our raw material.

Obviously, not all the hypotheses that are projected are lawlike or legitimately projectible; and not all legitimately projectible hypotheses are actually projected. Hence we come to the task of defining projectibility—of projecting the predicate "projected" to the predicate "projectible". This problem is complex in more ways than one. It calls for elimination as well as expansion. We face the twofold task of ruling out actually projected hypotheses that are not to be countenanced as projectible, and of bringing in legitimately projectible hypotheses that have not been actually projected—the twofold problem of projected unprojectibles and unprojected projectibles.

We may concentrate at present on simple universal hypotheses in categorical or hypothetical form—that is, upon hypotheses ascribing a certain predicate either to everything in the universe of discourse or to everything to which a certain other predicate applies. Moreover, projectibility at a time must be our first concern; any question of defining temporally unqualified projectibility will have to wait.

The obvious first step in our weeding-out process is to eliminate all projected hypotheses that have since been violated. Such hypotheses, as already remarked, can no longer be projected, and are thus henceforth unprojectible. On similar grounds, all hypotheses having no remaining unexamined instances are likewise to be ruled out. However, neither the violated nor the exhausted hypotheses are thereby denied to have been projectible at an earlier time.

Not nearly so obvious are the further steps to be taken in order to eliminate projected hypotheses that,

even though neither violated nor exhausted, are nevertheless unlawlike. Suppose, for example, that we are now at the time [. . .] when all emeralds examined have been green; and suppose that the hypothesis that all emeralds are grue is projected. How are we to exclude it? We cannot simply assume that no such projection is ever actually made. Such illegitimate hypotheses are in fact adopted at times; and if I labored under any blissful delusion to the contrary, you could readily dispel it by arbitrarily adopting one.

Projections of this sort, however, will often *conflict* with other projections. If the hypothesis that all emeralds are green is also projected, then the two projections disagree for unexamined emeralds. In saying these projections thus conflict, we are indeed assuming that there is some unexamined emerald to which only one of the two consequent-predicates applies; but it is upon this assumption that the problem arises at all. Yet how are we to devise a rule that will make the proper choice between these conflicting projections? We have noted that "green" and "grue" seem to be quite symmetrically related to each other. Are we any better off now than before to formulate the distinction between them?

The answer, I think, is that we must consult the record of past projections of the two predicates.[1] Plainly "green", as a veteran of earlier and many more projections than "grue", has the more impressive biography. The predicate "green", we may say, is much better *entrenched* than the predicate "grue".

We are able to draw this distinction only because we start from the record of past actual projections. We could not draw it starting merely from hypotheses and the evidence for them. [. . .]

[. . .] The entrenchment of a predicate results from the actual projection not merely of that predicate alone but also of all the predicates coextensive with it. In a sense, not the word itself, but the class it selects is what becomes entrenched, and to speak of the entrenchment of a predicate is to speak elliptically of the entrenchment of the extension of that predicate. On the other

---

1. A predicate "Q" is said to be projected when a hypothesis such as "All P's are Q's" is projected.

hand, the class becomes entrenched only through the projection of predicates selecting it: entrenchment derives from the use of language. But differences of tongue, use of coined abbreviations, and other variations in vocabulary do not prevent accrual of merited entrenchment. Moreover, no entrenchment accrues from the repeated projection of a word except where the word has the same extension each time.

One principle for eliminating unprojectible projections, then, is that a projection is to be ruled out if it conflicts with the projection of a much better entrenched predicate. Conflicts may, of course, occur between projections of two predicates that are almost equally well or ill entrenched; but such conflicts are to be resolved in other ways and do not concern us here. Our principle is inoperative where there is reasonable doubt about one predicate being more solidly entrenched than the other; it takes effect only where the difference is great enough to be obvious. Our primitive relation is that obtaining between any two predicates such that the first is much better entrenched than the second.

Like Hume, we are appealing here to past recurrences, but to recurrences in the explicit use of terms as well as to recurrent features of what is observed. Somewhat like Kant, we are saying that inductive validity depends not only upon what is presented but also upon how it is organized; but the organization we point to is effected by the use of language and is not attributed to anything inevitable or immutable in the nature of human cognition. To speak very loosely, I might say that in answer to the question what distinguishes those recurrent features of experience that underlie valid projections from those that do not, I am suggesting that the former are those features for which we have adopted predicates that we have habitually projected.

My proposal by no means amounts to ruling unfamiliar predicates out of court. In the first place, entrenchment and familiarity are not the same. An entirely unfamiliar predicate may be very well entrenched, as we have seen, if predicates coextensive with it have often been projected[....] [A] familiar predicate may be rather poorly entrenched, since entrenchment depends on frequency of projection rather than upon mere frequency of use. But in the second place, any wholesale elimination of unfamiliar predicates would result in an intolerable stultification of language. New and useful predicates like "conducts electricity" and "is radioactive" are always being introduced and must not be excluded simply because of their novelty. So far our rule legislates against such predicates only to the extent of eliminating projections of them that conflict with projections of much better entrenched predicates. Not predicates, but certain projected hypotheses are being eliminated; and in each case the elimination is based on specific comparison with an overriding hypothesis, not merely upon general grounds of the youth or oddity of the predicate projected. In framing further rules, we must continue to be on guard against throwing out all that is new along with all that is bad. Entrenched capital, in protecting itself, must allow full scope for free enterprise.

On several scores, then, our present approach is altogether different from any mere dismissal of unfamiliar predicates. But an objection of a quite different sort might now be raised. Are we not trusting too blindly to a capricious Fate to see to it that just the right predicates get themselves comfortably entrenched? Must we not explain why, in cases of conflict like those illustrated, the really projectible predicate happens to have been the earlier and more often projected? And in fact wasn't it projected so often *because* its projection was so often obviously legitimate, so that our proposal begs the question? I think not. To begin with, what I am primarily suggesting is that the superior entrenchment of the predicate projected is in these cases a sufficient even if not necessary indication of projectibility; and I am not much concerned with whether the entrenchment or the projectibility comes first. But even if the question is taken as a genetic one, the objection seems to me ill-founded. In the case of new predicates, indeed, the legitimacy of any projection has to be decided on the basis of their relationship to older predicates; and whether the new ones will come to be frequently projected depends upon such decisions. But in the case of our main stock of well-worn predicates, I submit that the judgment of projectibility has derived from the habitual projection, rather than the habitual projection from the judgment of projectibility. The reason why only the right predicates happen so luckily to have become well entrenched is just that the well entrenched predicates have thereby become the right ones.

If our critic is asking, rather, why projections of predicates that have become entrenched happen to be those projections that will turn out to be *true,* the answer is that we do not by any means know that they will turn out to be true. When the time comes, the hypothesis that all emeralds are green may prove to be false, and the hypothesis that all are grue may prove true. We have no guarantees. The criterion for the legitimacy of projections cannot be truth that is as yet undetermined. Failure to recognize this was responsible, as we saw, for some of the worst misconceptions of the problem of induction.

METAPHYSICS

METAPHYSICS IS THE BRANCH of philosophy that investigates fundamental questions about the nature of reality. It might seem that this is a job for science. Physics, after all, has been revealing ever-smaller components of matter—muons, quarks, bosons, and the like. Clearly it is better equipped than philosophy to identify the ultimate constituents of the physical world. But there are other fundamental questions that science cannot, and does not aspire to, answer: Does everything that exists consist of matter in motion? What about numbers? Are they material entities? If not, are they unreal? What about ideals like integrity and honesty? Is justice an arrangement of elementary particles? What about persons? Clearly we are at least partly material. But are we wholly material? Or is the self, or consciousness, or perhaps the soul something different? To answer questions like these we need to consider what it is to be a person, a number, or an ideal and what makes an item the person, number, or ideal that it is. That is a job for a metaphysician.

We might also wonder about reality as a whole. Why is there anything at all? Why are things the way they are rather than some other way? Scientists can explain how the laws of nature constrain the ways our universe might be. They can explain how the laws and the initial conditions made it possible for galaxies, solar systems, and intelligent life to form. But could things have been fundamentally different? Was there any necessity that the particular laws that govern our universe be the laws of nature? Leibniz thinks that there was. The reason this arrangement of things obtains is that it is the best of all possible worlds. If this seems implausible, the question remains: Why do these particular laws obtain? What other alternatives were there for reality? Is it just a cosmic accident that the universe is governed by these particular laws? If so, it is just a cosmic accident that intelligent life, or indeed any life, is possible? These are the sorts of questions that Parfit investigates in 'Why Anything? Why This?'

Whatever the explanation of the cosmos as a whole, causation plays a major role in explaining why things are as they are. Yeast caused the bread to rise. Meteors caused the moon's craters. A careless driver caused the car crash. The thermostat caused the furnace to go on. Evolution caused the extinction of the dinosaurs. The exam caused the students to panic. Although such causal talk is familiar, just what causation is, is unclear.

Intuitively, to cause something is to bring it about, to make it happen. We are apt to think that if the cause had not happened, the effect would not have happened either. If the dough contained no yeast, the bread would not have risen. So causal judgments sustain counterfactuals. But there is something funny about taking the yeast to be *the* cause of the bread's rising. If the dough contained no flour or no sugar, the bread wouldn't have risen either. What justifies calling the yeast the causal agent? Apparently causes bring about their effects only in particular circumstances. Is there anything in the world deciding which elements of the situation are the circumstances and which are causes?

A police officer considers the driver the cause of the accident. An automobile engineer takes the faulty brakes to be the cause. A highway engineer counts the way the road is banked as the cause. Plainly all three elements are part of the causal story. Had the driver been more careful, or the brakes been working, or the highway been better designed, the crash would not have happened. Maybe nothing in the world discriminates between true causes and background conditions. Then the choice of what to call the cause of an event depends on our interests. Should it? Should whether one event (the banking of the road) causes another (the car accident) depend on what is more salient or interesting to us?

One might wonder whether we mean the same thing by 'cause' when we say that an inanimate object like a meteor is a cause, when we say that an agent like a driver is a cause, and when we say that a process like evolution is a cause. Aristotle recognizes four types of causality: material, formal, efficient, and final. The *material cause* of an item is the stuff that makes it up. The clay that comprises it is the material cause of a statue. The *formal cause* is the structure. The arrangement of the clay, its being shaped like an armadillo, is the statue's formal cause. The *efficient cause* is what brings something about. The actions of the sculptor in shaping the clay are the statue's efficient cause. The *final cause* is the goal or end toward which the activity is directed. The statue's final cause might be the artist's desire to create a tribute to his pet armadillo. Other philosophers have introduced additional causal notions. Chisholm, for example, distinguishes between cases where agents cause events (*immanent causation*) and cases where objects or events cause events (*transeunt causation*). This suggests that the term 'cause' is multiply ambiguous in something like the way that 'hard' is ambiguous when we speak of a 'hard problem', a 'hard day', and a 'hard chair'.

Aristotle believes that all four causes are operative in every change. This is doubtful. Inanimate processes seem to lack final causes. Apparently only where agency or design is involved do final causes occur. The driver's desire to get home quickly caused him to drive so fast. Getting home quickly was his goal. The thermostat caused the furnace to go on. Regulating temperature is what it is designed to do. That constitutes its end. But a meteor did not seem to have any end or goal that caused it to hit the moon. The law of gravity and its initial position fully account for its landing where it did. No ends or goals need to be mentioned to fully explain what caused the crater.

Biological systems might seem to pose a trickier problem. They have no motives, so they are not agents. They were not designed, so they are not artifacts. But in saying that the function of the eye is to see, we appear to treat the eye as having a final cause. We appeal to an end: seeing. Dennett argues on Darwinian grounds that we need not assume that organs or organisms have final causes in order to explain their behavior. According to Darwin, evolution proceeds by random variation plus selective retention. A huge number of genetic variations occur randomly. Some are deleterious. Some are neutral. Some give the organisms that have them an advantage over other organisms competing for the same resources. The organisms with the advantage prevail. They leave more progeny that have the same advantage. So over time the advantageous arrangement comes to dominate. Because organisms without light sensitivity could not compete effectively with our ancestors, animals now have eyes. According to Darwin then, biological 'design' is an effect rather than a cause. And it is an effect of random processes, selectively retained. Evolution has and needs no final cause.

Contemporary metaphysicians might disagree with Aristotle's classification of form and matter as causes. But they agree that there is a metaphysical problem lurking in the neighborhood. What makes something the thing that it is? Or, to put the question differently, what changes can a thing undergo and remain the same thing? Thomson takes up this problem in 'The Statue and the Clay'. Suppose a statue is made of a lump of clay. What is the relation of the statue to the clay? The answer might seem obvious: They are the very same thing. The statue just is the clay molded into the shape of an armadillo. If this is so, then anything that is true of the statue is also true of the clay. But if a piece breaks off the statue and is replaced by a different lump of clay, the statue remains the same statue, although it is no longer made up of exactly the same clay. The statue remains the same thing through small changes in the material that makes it up. The identity conditions on a bit of matter diverge from the identity conditions on the form that matter takes. Apparently the sorts of changes an item can undergo while retaining its identity depend on what sort of a thing it is.

Consider the case of living things. Neither constancy of form nor constancy of matter is required for identity. Living things grow and change their shapes. A tiny seedling becomes a giant sequoia. Yet it is the same tree. It is struck by lightning and loses half its limbs. Still it is the same tree. Similarly for animals. The thirty-pound calf that grows into the thousand-pound moose remains the same animal. It retains its identity when it drops its antlers. Evidently the criterion of identity for organisms is continuity of life, not constancy of matter or form.

What determines the identity of persons? Insofar as we think of ourselves as animals, the criterion for our identity should be the same as the criterion for other animals. But there are changes that a human being can undergo that might lead us to conclude that she is not the same person. If someone is in an irreversible coma, we may be inclined to deny that she is a person anymore, even though she is still alive. If someone has suffered severe brain damage, so that she can no longer remember what happened or recognize people she once knew well, we may think she is not the same person she used to be. Perhaps we would also deny that she is the same person if her personality abruptly and radically changed so that, for example, she no longer had any of the interests, values, or commitments that she used to have, particularly if she could not explain the change. Even more extreme cases can be imagined: If Pat's mind were transplanted into Pam's body, would the resulting person be Pat or Pam? What if there were a partial transplant, so that some aspects of Pat's personality were transplanted into Pam? Is there a fact of the matter? If not, does that mean that whether someone is the same person he used to be is, to some extent, indeterminate?

Questions about causation and personal identity are abstract. But they are not idle, for they are crucial to assigning responsibility. Someone is responsible for an act only if she is the person who did the act and only if she acted freely. But to explain what it is to act freely is not easy.

It might seem that to act freely is to be the cause of the action. Joan acts freely in raising her hand if her decision to raise her hand is what makes her hand go up. But the laws of physics are universal. They apply to all material objects, including Joan's hand. So given the prior distribution of matter and energy in the universe and the laws of nature, it was inevitable that Joan's hand would rise when it did. In that case it looks as though she did not act freely. Moreover, it looks as though no one can act freely, since all events in the physical world are subject to causal laws. If so, physical determinism prevails in the world. Above the quantum level, where there is randomness, the laws of nature and the distribution of matter and energy at any one time fully determine what happens at any other time. This is apparently incompatible with free will.

It is hard to deny that our bodies are material objects bound by the laws of nature. So the best defense of free will would seem to be to show that it is compatible with determinism. Chisholm's approach is to distinguish between agent causation (immanent causation) and object causation (transeunt causation). He can then agree that all object causation is deterministic. But when questions of freedom and responsibility arise, we are concerned with a different sort of causation—agent causation—which is free. The difficulty is to see how the two sorts of causation can operate on the same event. If Joan's hand was bound to go up anyway, what did her immanent causation contribute?

Frankfurt maintains that free will is a product of our attitudes toward our actions. We do things because we have certain desires. These desires can be caused in ways that make us unfree. An addict takes her drug because she desires it. But given her addiction she can't help desiring it; she seems compelled by her addiction to want the drug. But not all actions are like the addict's. If an agent endorses her desires, Frankfurt maintains, she is free. The question is not whether the agent's action is determined. Of course it is. The question is rather whether the action is determined by a desire of the agent's that the agent desires to have. If so, the causal chain that leads to the agent's action goes through both her first- and second-order desires. That, Frankfurt maintains, is all that freedom requires.

Lewis maintains that sometimes a person freely does what the causal laws predetermined she would do. She is able to do otherwise, even though the distribution of matter and energy in the universe and the laws of nature determine that she will not do otherwise. The issue then turns on what it is to be able to do something other than what one does.

Even if we are free to act, circumstances beyond our control affect opportunities, constraints, and outcomes. But if a wrong someone does is beyond his control, we do not consider him to blame. If he does the wrong because he is under a serious, credible threat or because he is suffering from a psychological illness like kleptomania, we do not consider him entirely blameworthy even though in some sense of 'could' he could have done otherwise. Apparently we consider people responsible only for actions that are under their control.

The problem of moral luck is that far less is under a person's control than we are apt to think. Many people living in Nazi Germany were complicitous in genocide. We hold them responsible because we think that they could have resisted. But had they lived in a more benign environment, they would not have needed to resist. They were in a position to do the evils they did only because they were born when and where they were, something that they did not choose. Another example: A mother leaves her toddler unattended in the bathtub while answering the phone. If the child drowns, the mother is guilty of (at least) gross negligence. If the child suffers no misfortune, she seems guilty of a far less serious indiscretion. But once she has left the child alone, the child's fate is out of her control. Her free action was the same whatever the result. These are cases of moral luck. What we do, what we can do, and how it turns out are to a considerable extent beyond our control. Yet we are responsible for what we do.

The problem of free will is one of the hardest problems in philosophy. According to Kant, when we act, we cannot avoid thinking of ourselves as free. Unless you think of yourself as free when choosing what shirt to wear, you would have no reason to make the choice. You could just sit back and wait to discover what shirt you end up putting on. But when we consider the world and our place in it, it is hard to see how we could be free.

Causation and the Nature of Reality

Derek Parfit

Why Anything? Why This?

Why does the Universe exist? There are two questions here. First, why is there a Universe at all? It might have been true that nothing ever existed: no living beings, no stars, no atoms, not even space or time. When we think about this possibility, it can seem astonishing that anything exists. Second, why does *this* Universe exist? Things might have been, in countless ways, different. So why is the Universe as it is?

These questions, some believe, may have causal answers. Suppose first that the Universe has always existed. Some believe that, if all events were caused by earlier events, everything would be explained. That, however, is not so. Even an infinite series of events cannot explain itself. We could ask why this series occurred, rather than some other series, or no series. Of the supporters of the Steady State Theory, some welcomed what they took to be this theory's atheistic implications. They assumed that, if the Universe had no beginning, there would be nothing for a Creator to explain. But there would still be an eternal Universe to explain.

Suppose next that the Universe is not eternal, since nothing preceded the Big Bang. That first event, some physicists suggest, may have obeyed the laws of quantum mechanics, by being a random fluctuation in a vacuum. This would causally explain, they say, how the Universe came into existence out of nothing. But what physicists call a vacuum isn't really nothing. We can ask why it exists, and has the potentialities it does. In Hawking's phrase, 'What breathes fire into the equations?'

Similar remarks apply to all suggestions of these kinds. There could not be a causal explanation of why the Universe exists, why there are any laws of nature, or why these laws are as they are. Nor would it make a difference if there is a God, who caused the rest of the Universe to exist. There could not be a causal explanation of why God exists.

Many people have assumed that, since these questions cannot have causal answers, they cannot have any answers. Some therefore dismiss these questions, thinking them not worth considering. Others conclude that they do not make sense. They assume that, as Wittgenstein wrote, 'doubt can exist only where there is a question; and a question only where there is an answer'.

These assumptions are all, I believe, mistaken. Even if these questions could not have answers, they would still make sense, and they would still be worth considering. I am reminded here of the aesthetic category of the *sublime,* as applied to the highest mountains, raging oceans, the night sky, the interiors of some cathedrals, and other things that are superhuman, awesome, limitless. No question is more sublime than why there is a Universe: why there is anything rather than nothing. Nor should we assume that answers to this question must be causal. And, even if reality cannot be fully explained, we may still make progress, since what is inexplicable may become less baffling that it now seems.

1

One apparent fact about reality has recently been much discussed. Many physicists believe that, for life to be possible, various features of the Universe must be almost precisely as they are. As one example of such a feature, we can take the initial conditions in the Big Bang. If

Derek Parfit, "Why Anything? Why This?" from *The London Review of Books,* 20/2 and 20/3 (1998). Copyright © 1998 by Derek Parfit. Reprinted with permission of the author and *The London Review of Books.* This article first appeared in *The London Review of Books.* www.lrb.co.uk

these conditions had been more than very slightly different, these physicists claim, the Universe would not have had the complexity that allows living beings to exist. Why were these conditions so precisely right?[1]

Some say: 'If they had not been right, we couldn't even ask this question.' But that is no answer. It could be baffling how we survived some crash even though, if we hadn't, we could not be baffled.

Others say: 'There had to be some initial conditions, and the conditions that make life possible were as likely as any others. So there is nothing to be explained.' To see what is wrong with this reply, we must distinguish two kinds of cases. Suppose first that, when some radio telescope is aimed at most points in space, it records a random sequence of incoming waves. There might be nothing here that needed to be explained. Suppose next that when the telescope is aimed in one direction, it records a sequence of waves whose pulses match the number π in binary notation, to the first ten thousand digits. That particular number is, in one sense, just as likely as any other. But there *would* be something here that needed to be explained. Though each long number is unique, only a very few are, like π, mathematically special. What would need to be explained is why this sequence of waves exactly matched such a special number. Though this matching might be a coincidence, which had been randomly produced, that would be most unlikely. We could be almost certain that these waves had been produced by some kind of intelligence.

On the view that we are now considering, since any sequence of waves is as likely as any other, there would be nothing to be explained. If we accepted this view, intelligent beings elsewhere in space would not be able to communicate with us, since we would ignore their messages. Nor could God reveal himself. Suppose that, with some optical telescope, we saw a distant pattern of stars which spelled out in Hebrew script the first chapter of Genesis. This pattern of stars, according to this view, would not need to be explained. That is clearly false.

Here is another analogy. Suppose first that, of a thousand people facing death, only one can be rescued. If there is a lottery to pick this one survivor, and I win, I would be very lucky. But there might be nothing here that needed to be explained. Someone had to win, and why not me? Consider next another lottery. Unless my gaoler picks the longest of a thousand straws, I shall be shot. If my gaoler picks that longest straw, there would be something to be explained. It would not be enough to say, 'This result was as likely as any other.' In the first lottery, nothing special happened: whatever the result, someone's life would be saved. In this second lottery, the result *was* special, since, of the thousand possible results, only one would save a life. Why was this special result *also* what happened? Though this might be a coincidence, the chance of that is only one in a thousand. I could be almost certain that, like Dostoyevsky's mock execution, this lottery was rigged.

The Big Bang, it seems, was like this second lottery. For life to be possible, the initial conditions had to be selected with great accuracy. This *appearance of fine-tuning,* as some call it, also needs to be explained.

It may be objected that, in regarding conditions as special if they allow for life, we unjustifiably assume our own importance. But life *is* special, if only because of its complexity. An earthworm's brain is more complicated than a lifeless galaxy. Nor is it only life that requires this fine-tuning. If the Big Bang's initial conditions had not been almost precisely as they were, the Universe would have either almost instantly recollapsed, or expanded so fast, and with particles so thinly spread, that not even stars or heavy elements could have formed. That is enough to make these conditions very special.

It may next be objected that these conditions cannot be claimed to be improbable, since such a claim requires a statistical basis, and there is only one Universe. If we were considering all conceivable Universes, it would indeed be implausible to make judgments of statistical probability. But our question is much narrower. We are asking what would have happened if, with the same laws of nature, the initial conditions had been different. That provides the basis for a statistical judgment. There is a range of values that these conditions might have had, and physicists can work out in what proportion of this range the resulting Universe could have contained stars, heavy elements, and life.

This proportion, it is claimed, is extremely small. Of the range of possible initial conditions, fewer than one

---

1. In my remarks about this question, I am merely summarizing, and oversimplifying, what others have claimed. See, for example, John Leslie, *Universes,* Routledge, 1989.

in a billion billion would have produced a Universe with the complexity that allows for life. If this claim is true, as I shall here assume, there is something that cries out to be explained. Why was one of this tiny set *also* the one that actually obtained?

On one view, this was a mere coincidence. That is conceivable, since coincidences happen. But this view is hard to believe since, if it were true, the chance of this coincidence occurring would be below one in a billion billion.

Others say: 'The Big Bang *was* fine-tuned. In creating the Universe, God chose to make life possible.' Atheists may reject this answer, thinking it improbable that God exists. But this is not as improbable as the view that would require so great a coincidence. So even atheists should admit that, of these two answers to our question, the answer that invokes God is more likely to be true.

This reasoning revives one of the traditional arguments for belief in God. In its strongest form, this argument appealed to the many features of animals, such as eyes or wings, that look as if they have been designed. Paley's appeal to such features much impressed Darwin when he was young. Darwin later undermined this form of the argument, since evolution can explain this appearance of design. But evolution cannot explain the appearance of fine-tuning in the Big Bang.

This argument's appeal to probabilities can be challenged is a different way. In claiming it to be most improbably that this fine-tuning was a coincidence, the argument assumes that, of the possible initial conditions in the Big Bang, each was equally likely to obtain. That assumption may be mistaken. The conditions that allow for complexity and life may have been, compared with all the others, much more likely to obtain. Perhaps they were even certain to obtain.

To answer this objection, we must broaden this argument's conclusion. If these life-allowing conditions were either very likely or certain to obtain, then—as the argument claims—it would be no coincidence that the Universe allows for complexity and life. But this fine-tuning might have been the work, not of some existing being, but of some impersonal force, or fundamental law. That is what some theists believe God to be.

A stronger challenge to this argument comes from a different way to explain the appearance of fine-tuning. Consider first a similar question. For life to be possible on the Earth, many of the Earth's features have to be close to being as they are. The Earth's having such features, it might be claimed, is unlikely to be a coincidence, and should therefore be regarded as God's work. But such an argument would be weak. The Universe, we can reasonably believe, contains many planets, with varying conditions. We should expect that, on a few of these planets, conditions would be just right for life. Nor is it surprising that we live on one of these few.

Things are different, we may assume, with the appearance of fine-tuning in the Big Bang. While there are likely to be many other planets, there is only one Universe. But this difference may be less than it seems. Some physicists suggest that the observable Universe is only one out of many different worlds, which are all equally parts of reality. According to one such view, the other worlds are related to ours in a way that solves some of the mysteries of quantum physics. On the different and simpler view that is relevant here, the other worlds have the same laws of nature as our world, and they are produced by Big Bangs that are broadly similar, except in having different initial conditions.

On this *Many Worlds Hypothesis,* there is no need for fine-tuning. If there were enough Big Bangs, we should expect that, in a few of these, conditions would be just right to allow for complexity and life; and it would be no surprise that our Big Bang was one of these few. To illustrate this point, we can revise my second lottery. Suppose my gaoler picks a straw, not once, but very many times. That would explain his managing, once, to pick the longest straw, without that's being an extreme coincidence, or this lottery's being rigged.

On most versions of the Many Worlds Hypothesis, these many worlds are not, except through their origins, causally related. Some object that, since our world could not be causally affected by such other worlds, we can have no evidence for their existence, and can therefore have no reason to believe in them. But we do have such a reason, since their existence would explain an otherwise puzzling feature or our world: the appearance of fine-tuning.

Of these two ways to explain this appearance, which is better? Compared with belief in God, the Many Worlds Hypothesis is more cautious, since its claim is merely that there is more of the kind of reality that we can observe around us. But God's existence has been claimed to be intrinsically more probable. According to most theists, God is a being who is omnipotent, omniscient, and wholly good. The uncaused existence of such a being has been claimed to be simpler, and less arbitrary, than the uncaused existence of many highly complicated worlds. And simpler hypotheses, many scientists assume, are more likely to be true.

If such a God exists, however, other features of our world become hard to explain. It may not be surprising that God chose to make life possible. But the laws of nature could have been different, so there are many possible worlds that would have contained life. It is hard to understand why, out of all these possibilities, God chose to create our world. What is most baffling is the problem of evil. There appears to be suffering which any good person, knowing the truth, would have prevented if he could. If there is such suffering, there cannot be a God who is omnipotent, omniscient, and wholly good.

To this problem, theists have proposed several solutions. Some suggest that God is not omnipotent, or wholly good. Other suggest that undeserved suffering is not, as it seems, bad, or that God could not prevent such suffering without making the Universe, as a whole, less good.

We must ignore these suggestions here, since we have larger questions to consider. I began by asking why things are as they are. Before returning to that question, we should ask *how* things are. There is much about our world that we have not discovered. And, just as there may be other worlds that are like ours, there may be worlds that are very different.

2

It will help to distinguish two kinds of possibilities. *Cosmic* possibilities cover everything that ever exists, and are the different ways that the whole of reality might be. Only one such possibility can be actual, or be the one that *obtains*. *Local* possibilities are the different ways that some part of reality, or *local world* might be. If some local world exists, that leaves it open whether other worlds exist.

One cosmic possibility is, roughly, that *every* possible local world exists. This we can call the *All Worlds Hypothesis*. Another possibility, which might have obtained, is that nothing ever exists. This we can call the *Null Possibility*. In each of the remaining possibilities, the number of local worlds that exists is between none and all. There are countless of these possibilities, since there are countless combinations of possible local worlds.

Of these different cosmic possibilities, one must obtain, and only one can obtain. So we have two questions: Which obtains, and Why?

These questions are connected. If some possibility would be easier to explain, we may have more reason to believe that this possibility obtains. This is how, rather than believing in only one Big Bang, we have more reason to believe in many. Whether we believe in one or many, we have the question why any Big Bang has occurred. Though this question is hard, the occurrence of many Big Bangs is not more puzzling than the occurrence of only one. Most kinds of thing, or event, have many instances. We also have the question why, in the Big Bang that produced our world, the initial conditions allowed for complexity and life. If there has been only one Big Bang, this fact is also hard to explain, since it is most unlikely that these conditions merely happened to be right. If instead there have been many Big Bangs, this fact is easy to explain, since it is like the fact that, among countless planets, there are some whose conditions allow for life. Since belief in many Big Bangs leaves less that is unexplained, it is the better view.

If some cosmic possibilities would be less puzzling than others, because their obtaining would leave less to be explained, is there some possibility whose obtaining would be in no way puzzling?

Consider first the Null Possibility, in which nothing ever exists. To imagine this possibility, it may help to suppose first that all that ever existed was a single atom. We then imagine that even this atom never existed.

Some have claimed that, if there had never been anything, there wouldn't have been anything to be explained. But that is not so. When we imagine how things would have been if nothing had ever existed, what we should imagine away are such things as living beings, stars, and atoms. There would still have been various truths, such as the truth that there were no stars or atoms, or that 9 is divisible by 3. We can ask why these things would have been true. And such questions may have answers. Thus, we can explain why, even if nothing had ever existed, 9 would still have been divisible by 3. There is no conceivable alternative. And we can explain why there would have been no such things as immaterial matter, or spherical cubes. Such things are logically impossible. But why would *nothing* have existed? Why would there have been no stars, or atoms, no philosophers or bluebell woods?

We should not claim that, if nothing had ever existed, there would have been nothing to be explained. But we can claim something less. Of all the cosmic possibilities, the Null Possibility would have needed the least explanation. As Leibniz pointed out, it is much the simplest, and the least arbitrary. And it is the easiest to understand. It can seem mysterious, for example, how things could exist without their existence having some cause, but there cannot be a causal explanation of why the whole Universe, or God, exists. The Null Possibility raises no such problem. If nothing had ever existed, that state of affairs would not have needed to be caused.

Reality, however, does not take its least puzzling form. In some way or other, a Universe has managed to exist. That is what can take one's breath away. As Wittgenstein wrote, 'not how the world is, is the mystical, but *that* it is.' Or, in the words of a thinker as unmystical as Jack Smart: 'That anything should exist at all does seem to me a matter for the deepest awe.'

Consider next the All Worlds Hypothesis, on which every possible local world exists. Unlike the Null Possibility, this may be how things are. And it may be the next least puzzling possibility. This hypothesis is not the same as—though it includes—the Many Worlds Hypothesis. On that more cautious view, the many other worlds have the same elements as our world, and the same fundamental laws, and differ only in such features as their constants and initial conditions. The All Worlds Hypothesis covers every conceivable kind of world, and most of these other worlds would have very different elements and laws.

If all these worlds exist, we can ask why they do. But, compared with most other cosmic possibilities, the All Worlds Hypothesis may leave less that is unexplained. For example, whatever the number of possible worlds that exist, we have the question, 'Why *that* number?' That question would have been least puzzling if the number that existed were *none,* and the next least arbitrary possibility seems to be that *all* these worlds exist.

With every other cosmic possibility, we have a further question. If ours is the only world, we can ask: 'Out of all the possible local worlds, why is *this* the one that exists?' On any version of the Many Worlds Hypothesis, we have a similar question: "Why do just *these* worlds exist, with *these* elements and laws?' But if *all* these worlds exist, there is no such further question.

It may be objected that, even if all possible local worlds exist, that does not explain why our world is as it is. But that is a mistake. If all these worlds exist, each world is as it is in the way in which each number is as it is. We cannot sensibly ask why 9 is 9. Nor should we ask why our world is the one it is: why it is *this* world. That would be like asking, 'Why are *we* who we are?', or 'Why is it *now* the time that it is?' Those, on reflection, are not good questions.

Though the All Worlds Hypothesis avoids certain questions, it is not as simple, or unarbitrary, as the Null Possibility. There may be no sharp distinction between worlds that are and are not possible. It is unclear what counts as a kind of world. And, if there are infinitely many kinds, there is a choice between different kinds of infinity.

Whichever cosmic possibility obtains, we can ask why it obtains. All that I have claimed so far is that, with some possibilities, this question would be less puzzling. Let us now ask: Could this question have an answer? Might there be a theory that leaves nothing unexplained?

3

It is sometimes claimed that God, or the Universe, makes themselves exist. But this cannot be true, since these entities cannot do anything unless they exist.

On a more intelligible view, it is logically necessary that God, or the Universe, exist, since the claim that they might not have existed leads to a contradiction. On such a view, though it may seem conceivable that there might never have been anything, that is not really logically possible. Some people even claim that there may be only one coherent cosmic possibility. Thus Einstein suggested that, if God created our world, he might have had no choice about which world to create. If such a view were true, everything might be explained. Reality might be the way it is because there was no conceivable alternative. But, for reasons that have been often given, we can reject such views.

Consider next a quite different view. According to Plato, Plotinus and others, the Universe exists because its existence is good. Even if we are confident that we should reject this view, it is worth asking whether it makes sense. If it does, that may suggest other possibilities.

This *Axiarchic View* can take a theistic form. It can claim that God exists because his existence is good, and that the rest of the Universe exists because God caused it to exists. But in that explanation God, *qua* Creator, is redundant. If God can exist because his existence is good, so can the whole Universe. This may be why some theists reject the Axiarchic View, and insist that God's existence is a brute fact, with no explanation.

In its simplest form, this view makes three claims:

1. It would be best if reality were a certain way.

2. Reality is that way.

3. 1 explains 2.

(1) is an ordinary evaluative claim, like the claim that it would be better if there was less suffering. The Axiarchic View assumes, I believe rightly, that such claims can be in a strong sense true. (2) is an ordinary empirical or scientific claim, though of a sweeping kind. What is distinctive in this view is claim (3), according to which (1) explains (2).

Can we understand this third claim? To focus on this question, we should briefly ignore the world's evils, and suspend our other doubts about claims (1) and (2). We should suppose that, as Leibniz claimed, the best possible Universe exists. Would it then make sense to claim that this Universe exists *because* it is the best?

That use of 'because', Axiarchists should admit, cannot be easily explained. But even ordinary causation is mysterious. At the most fundamental level, we have no idea why some events cause others; and it is hard to explain what causation is. There are, moreover, non-causal senses of 'because' and 'why', as in the claim that God exists because his existence is logically necessary. We can understand that claim, even if we think it false. The Axiarchic View is harder to understand. But that is not surprising. If there is some explanation of the whole of reality, we should not expect this explanation to fit neatly into some familiar category. This extra-ordinary question may have an extra-ordinary answer. We should reject suggested answers which make no sense; but we should also try to see what might make sense.

Axiarchy might be expressed as follows. We are now supposing that, of all the countless ways that the whole of reality might be, one is both the very best, and is the way that reality is. On the Axiarchic View, *that is no coincidence*. This claim, I believe, makes sense. And, if it were no coincidence that the best way for reality to be is *also* the way that reality is, that might support the further claim that this was *why* reality was this way.

This view has one advantage over the more familiar theistic view. An appeal to God cannot explain why the Universe exists, since God would himself be part of the Universe, or one of the things that exists. Some theists argue that, since nothing can exist without some cause, God, who is the First Cause, must exist. As Schopenhauer objected, this argument's premise is not like some cab-driver whom theists are free to dismiss once they have reached their destination. The Axiarchic View appeals, not to an existing entity, but to an explanatory law. Since such a law would not itself be part of the Universe, it might explain why the Universe exists, and is as good as it could be. If such a law governed reality, we could still ask why it did, or why the Axiarchic View was true. But, in discovering this law, we would have made some progress.

It is hard, however, to believe the Axiarchic View. If, as it seems, there is much pointless suffering, our world cannot be part of the best possible Universe.

4

Some Axiarchists claim that, if we reject their view, we must regard our world's existence as a brute fact, since no other explanation could make sense. But that, I believe, is not so. If we abstract from the optimism of the Axiarchic View, its claims are these:

Of the countless cosmic possibilities, one both has some very special feature, and is the possibility that obtains. That is no coincidence. This possibility obtains because it has this feature.

Other views can make such claims. This special feature need not be that of being best. Thus, on the All Worlds Hypothesis, reality is *maximal,* or as full as it could be. Similarly, if nothing had ever existed, reality would have been *minimal,* or as empty as it could be. If the possibility that obtained were either maximal, or minimal, that fact, we might claim, would be most unlikely to be a coincidence. And that might support the further claim that this possibility's having this feature would be *why* it obtained.

Let us now look more closely at that last step. When it is no coincidence that two things are both true, there is something that explains why, given the truth of one, the other is also true. The truth of either might make the other true. Or both might be explained by some third truth, as when two facts are the joint effects of a common cause.

Suppose next that, of the cosmic possibilities, one is both very special and is the one that obtains. If that is no coincidence, what might explain why these things are both true? On the reasoning that we are now considering, the first truth explains the second, since this possibility obtains because it has this special feature. Given the kind of truths these are, such an explanation could not go the other way. This possibility could not have this feature because it obtains. If some possibility has some feature, it could not fail to have this feature, so it would have this feature whether or not it obtains. The All Worlds Hypothesis, for example, could not fail to describe the fullest way for reality to be.

While it is necessary that our imagined possibility has its special feature, it is not necessary that this possibility obtains. This difference, I believe, justifies the reasoning that we are now considering. Since this possibility must have this feature, but might not have obtained, it cannot have this feature because it obtains, nor could some third truth explain why it both has this feature and obtains. So, if these facts are no coincidence, this possibility must obtain *because* it has this feature.

When some possibility obtains because it has some feature, its having this feature may be why some agent, or some process of natural selection, made it obtain. These we can call the *intentional* and *evolutionary* ways in which some feature of some possibility may explain why it obtains.

Our world, theists claim, can be explained in the first of these ways. If reality were as good as it could be, it would indeed make sense to claim that this was partly God's work. But, since God's own existence could not be God's work, there could be no intentional explanation of why the whole of reality was as good as it could be. So we could indeed reasonably conclude that this way's being the best explained *directly* why reality was this way. Even if God exists, the intentional explanation could not compete with the different and bolder explanation offered by the Axiarchic View.

Return now to other explanations of this kind. Consider first the Null Possibility. This, we know, does not obtain; but, since we are asking what makes sense, that does not matter. If there had never been anything, would that have had to be a brute fact, which had no explanation? The answer, I suggest, is No. It might have been no coincidence that, of all the countless cosmic possibilities, what obtained was the simplest, and least arbitrary, and the only possibility in which nothing ever exists. And, if these facts had been no coincidence, this possibility would have obtained, because—or partly because—it had one or more of these special features. This explanation, moreover, could not have taken an intentional or evolutionary form. If nothing had ever existed, there could not have been some agent, or process of selection, who or which made this possibility obtain. Its being the simplest or least arbitrary possibility would have been, directly, why it obtained.

Consider next the All Worlds Hypothesis, which may obtain. If reality is as full as it could be, is that a coincidence? Does it merely happen to be true that, of all the cosmic possibilities, the one that obtains is at this extreme? As before, that is conceivable, but this coincidence would be too great to be credible. We can reasonably assume that, if this possibility obtains, that is because it is maximal, or at this extreme. On this *Maximalist View,* it is a fundamental truth that being possible, and part of the fullest way that reality could be, is sufficient for being actual. That is the highest law governing reality. As before, if such a law governed reality, we could still ask *why* it did. But, in discovering this law, we would have made some progress.

Here is another special feature. Perhaps reality is the way it is because its fundamental laws are, on some criterion, as mathematically beautiful as they could be. That is what some physicists are inclined to believe.

As these remarks suggest, there is no clear boundary here between philosophy and science. If there is such a highest law governing reality, this law is of the same kind as those that physicists are trying to discover. When we appeal to natural laws to explain some features of reality, such as the relations between light, gravity, space, and time, we are not giving causal explanations, since we are not claiming that one part of reality caused another part to be some way. What such laws explain, or partly explain, are the deeper facts about reality that causal explanations take for granted.

There would be a highest law, of the kind that I have sketched, if some cosmic possibility obtained because it had some special feature. This feature we can call the *Selector*. If there is more than one such feature, they are all partial Selectors. Just as there are various cosmic possibilities, there are various *explanatory* possibilities. For each of these special features, there is the explanatory possibility that this feature is the Selector, or is one of the Selectors. Reality would then be the way it is because, or partly because, this way had this feature.

There is one other explanatory possibility: that there is *no* Selector. If that is true, it is random that reality is as it is. Events may be in one sense random, even though they are causally inevitable. That is how it is random whether a meteorite strikes the land or the sea. Events are random in a stronger sense if they have no cause. That is what most physicists believe about some features of events involving sub-atomic particles. If it is random what reality is like, the Universe not only has no cause, it has no explanation of any kind. This claim we can call the *Brute Fact View*.

Few features can be plausibly regarded as possible Selectors. Though plausibility is a matter of degree, there is a natural threshold to which we can appeal. If we suppose that reality has some special feature, we can ask which of two beliefs would be more credible: that reality merely happens to have this feature, or that reality is the way it is because this way has this feature. If the second would be more credible, this feature can be called a *credible Selector*. Return for example to the question of how many possible local worlds exist. Of the different answers to this question, *all* and *none* give us, I have claimed, credible Selectors. If either all or no worlds existed, that would be unlikely to be a coincidence. But suppose that 58 worlds existed. This number has some special features, such as being the smallest number that is the sum of seven different primes. It may be just con-

ceivable that this would by why 58 worlds existed; but it would be more reasonable to believe that the number that existed merely happened to be 58.

There are, I have claimed, some credible Selectors. Reality might be some way because that way is the best, or the simplest, or the least arbitrary, or because its obtaining makes reality as full and varied as it could be, or because its fundamental laws are, in some way, as elegant as they could be. Presumably there are other such features, which I have overlooked.

In claiming that there are credible Selectors, I am assuming that some cosmic and explanatory possibilities are more probable than others. That assumption may be questioned. Judgments of probability, it may again be claimed, must be grounded on facts about our world, so such judgments cannot be applied either to how the whole of reality might be, or to how reality might be explained.

This objection is, I believe, unsound. When we choose between scientific theories, our judgments of their probability cannot rest only on predictions based on established facts and laws. We need such judgments in trying to decide what these facts and laws are. And we can justifiably make such judgments when considering different ways in which the whole of reality may be, or might have been. Compare two such cosmic possibilities. In the first, there is a lifeless Universe consisting only of some spherical iron stars, whose relative motion is as it would be in our world. In the second, things are the same, except that the stars move together in the patterns of a minuet, and they are shaped like either Queen Victoria or Cary Grant. We would be right to claim that, of these two possibilities, the first is more likely to obtain.

In making that claim, we would not mean that it is more likely *that* the first possibility obtains. Since this possibility is the existence of a lifeless Universe, we know that it does not obtain. We would be claiming that this possibility is intrinsically more likely, or that, to put it roughly, it had a greater chance of being how reality is. If some possibility is more likely to obtain, that will often make it more likely that it obtains; but though one kind of likelihood supports the other, they are quite different.

Another objection may again seem relevant here. Of the countless cosmic possibilities, a few have special features, which I have called credible Selectors. If such a possibility obtains, we have, I have claimed, a choice of two conclusions. Either reality, by an extreme coincidence, merely happens to have this feature, or—more plausibly—this feature is one of the Selectors. It may be objected that, when I talk of an extreme coincidence, I must be assuming that these cosmic possibilities are all equally likely to obtain. But I have not rejected that assumption. And, if these possibilities are *not* equally likely, my reasoning may seem to be undermined.

As before, that is not so. Suppose that, of the cosmic possibilities, those that have these special features are much more likely to obtain. As this objection rightly claims, it would not then be amazing if such a possibility merely happened to obtain. But that does not undermine my reasoning, since it is another way of stating my conclusion. It is another way of saying that these features are Selectors.

These remarks do show, however, that we should distinguish two ways in which some feature may be a Selector. *Probabilistic* Selectors make some cosmic possibility more likely to obtain, but leave it open whether it does obtain. On any plausible view, there are some Selectors of this kind, since some ways for reality to be are intrinsically more likely than some others. Thus of our two imagined Universes, the one consisting of spherical stars is intrinsically more likely than the one with stars that are shaped like Queen Victoria or Cary Grant. Besides Probabilistic Selectors, there may also be one or more *Effective* Selectors. If some possibility has a certain feature, this may make this possibility, not merely intrinsically more likely, but the one that obtains. Thus, if simplicity had been the Effective Selector, that would have made it true that nothing ever existed. And, if maximality is the Effective Selector, as it may be, that is what makes reality as full as it could be. When I talk of Selectors, these are the kind I mean.

5

There are, then, various cosmic and explanatory possibilities. In trying to decide which of these obtain, we can in part appeal to facts about our world. Thus, from the mere fact that our world exists, we can deduce that the Null Possibility does not obtain. And, since our world seems to contain pointless evils, we have reason to reject the Axiarchic View.

Consider next the Brute Fact View, on which reality merely happens to be as it is. No facts about our world could refute this view. But some facts would make it less likely that this view is true. If reality is randomly selected, what we should expect to exist are many varied worlds, none of which had features that, in the range of possibilities, were at one extreme. That is what we should expect because, in much the largest set of cosmic possibilities, that would be what exists. If our world has very special features, that would count against the Brute Fact View.

Return now to the question whether God exists. Compared with the uncaused existence of one or many complicated worlds, the hypothesis that God exists has been claimed to be simpler, and less arbitrary, and thus more likely to be true. But this hypothesis is not simpler than the Brute Fact View. And, if it is random which cosmic possibility obtains, we should not expect the one that obtains to be as simple, and unarbitrary, as God's existence is claimed to be. Rather, as I have just said, we should expect there to be many worlds, none of which had very special features. Ours may be the kind of world that, on the Brute Fact View, we should expect to observe.

Similar remarks apply to the All Worlds Hypothesis. Few facts about our world could refute this view; but, if all possible local worlds exist, the likely character of our world is much the same as on the Brute Fact View. That claim may seem surprising, given the difference between these two views. One view is about *which* cosmic possibility obtains, the other is about *why* the one that obtains obtains. And these views conflict, since, if we knew that either view was true, we would have strong reason not to believe the other. If all possible worlds exist, that is unlikely to be a brute fact. But, in their different ways, these views are both *non-selective*. On neither view do certain worlds exist *because* they have certain special features. So, if either view is true, we should not expect our world to have such features.

To that last claim, there is one exception. This is the feature with which we began: that our world allows for life. Though this feature is, in some ways, special, it is one that we cannot help observing. That restricts what we can infer from the fact that our world has this feature. Rather than claiming that being life-allowing is one of the Selectors, we can appeal to some version of the Many Worlds Hypothesis. If there are very many worlds, we would expect a few worlds to be life-allowing, and our world is bound to be one of these few.

Consider next other kinds of special features: one that we are not bound to observe. Suppose we discover that our world has such a feature, and we ask whether that is no coincidence. It may again be said that, if there are many worlds, we would expect a few worlds to have this special feature. But that would not explain why that is true of *our* world. We could not claim—as with the feature of being life-allowing—that our world is bound to have this feature. So the appeal to many worlds could not explain away the coincidence. Suppose, for example, that our world were very good, or were wholly law-governed, or had very simple natural laws. Those facts would count against both of the unselective views: both the All Worlds Hypothesis and the Brute Fact View. It is true that, if all worlds exist, or there are very many randomly selected worlds, we should expect a few worlds to be very good, or wholly law-governed, or to have very simple laws. But that would not explain why our world had those features. So we would have some reason to believe that our world is the way it is because this way has those features.

Does our world have such features: ones that count against the unselective views? Our world's moral character seems not to count against these views, since it seems the mixture of good and bad that, on the unselective views, we should expect. But our world may have the other two features: being wholly law-governed, and having very simple laws. Neither feature seems to be required in order for life to be possible. And, among possible life-containing worlds, a far greater range would not have these features. Thus, for each law-governed world, there are countless variants that would fail in different ways to be wholly law-governed. And, compared with simple laws, there is a far greater range of complicated laws. So, on both the unselective views, we should not expect our world to have these features. If it has them, as physicists might discover, that would give us reasons to reject both the All Worlds Hypothesis and the Brute Fact View. We would have some reason to believe that there are at least two partial Selectors: being law-governed and having simple laws.

There may be other features of our world from which we can try to infer what reality is like, and why.

But observation can take us only part of the way. If we can get further, that will have to be by pure reasoning.

6

Of those who accept the Brute Fact View, many assume that it must be true. According to these people, though reality merely happens to be some way, *that* it merely happens to be some way does not merely happen to be true. There could not be an explanation of why reality is the way it is, since there could not be a causal explanation, and no other explanation would make sense.

This assumption, I have argued, is mistaken. Reality might be the way it is because this way is the fullest, or the most varied, or obeys the simplest or most elegant laws, or has some other special feature. Since the Brute Fact View is not the only explanatory possibility, we should not assume that it must be true.

When supporters of this view recognize these other possibilities, they may switch to the other extreme, claiming that their view's truth is another brute fact. If that were so, not only would there be no explanation of reality's being as it is, there would also be no explanation of there being no such explanation. As before, though this might be true, we should not assume that it must be true. If some explanatory possibility merely happens to obtain, the one that obtains may not be the Brute Fact View. If it is randomly selected *whether* reality is randomly selected, and there are other possibilities, random selection may not be selected.

There is, moreover, another way in which some explanatory possibility may obtain. Rather than merely happening to obtain, this possibility may have some feature, or set of features, which explains why it obtains. Such a feature would be a Selector at a higher level, since it would apply not to factual but to explanatory possibilities. It would determine, not that reality be a certain way, but that it be determined in a certain way how reality is to be.

If the Brute Fact View is true, it may have been selected in this way. Of the explanatory possibilities, this view seems to describe the simplest, since its claim is only that reality has no explanation. This possibility's being the simplest might make it the one that obtains. Simplicity may be the higher Selector, determining that there is no Selector between the ways that reality might be.

Once again, however, though this may be true, we cannot assume its truth. There may be some other higher Selector. Some explanatory possibility may obtain, for example, because it is the least arbitrary, or is the one that explains most. The Brute Fact View has neither of those features. Or there may be no higher Selector, since some explanatory possibility may merely happen to obtain.

These alternatives are the different possibilities at yet another, higher explanatory level. So we have the same two questions: Which obtains, and Why?

We may now become discouraged. Every answer, it may seem, raises a further question. But that may not be so. There may be some answer that is a necessary truth. With that necessity, our search would end.

Some truth is logically necessary when its denial leads to a contradiction. It cannot be in this sense necessary either that reality is a brute fact, or that there is some Selector. Both these claims can be denied without contradiction.

There are also non-logical necessities. The most familiar, causal necessity, cannot give us the truth we need. It could not be causally necessary that reality is, or isn't, a brute fact. Causal necessities come lower down. Similar remarks apply to the necessities involved in the essential properties of particular things, or natural kinds. Consider next the metaphysical necessity that some writers claim for God's existence. That claim means, they say, that God's existence does not depend on anything else, and that nothing else could cause God to cease to exist. But these claims do not imply that God must exist, and that makes such necessity too weak to end our questions.

There are, however, some kinds of necessity that would be strong enough. Consider the truths that undeserved suffering is bad, and that, if we believe the premises of a sound argument, we ought rationally to believe this argument's conclusion. These truths are not logically necessary, since their denials would not lead to contradictions. But they could not have failed to be true. Undeserved suffering does not merely happen to be bad.

When Leslie defends the Axiarchic View, he appeals to this kind of non-logical necessity. Not only does value rule reality, Leslie suggests, it could not have failed to rule. But this suggestion is hard to believe. While it is inconceivable that undeserved suffering might have failed to be in itself bad, it is clearly conceivable that

value might have failed to rule, if only because it seems so clear that value does *not* rule.

Return now to the Brute Fact View, which is more likely to be true. If this view is true, could its truth be non-logically necessary? Is it inconceivable that there might have been some Selector, or highest law, making reality be some way? The answer, I have claimed, is No. Even if reality is a brute fact, it might not have been. Thus, if nothing had ever existed, that might have been no coincidence. Reality might have been that way because, of the cosmic possibilities, it is the simplest and least arbitrary. And, as I have also claimed, just as it is not necessary that the Brute Fact View is true, it is not necessary that this view's truth be another brute fact. This view might be true because it is the simplest of the explanatory possibilities.

We have not yet found the necessity we need. Reality may happen to be as it is, or there may be some Selector. Whichever of these is true, it may happen to be true, or there may be some higher Selector. These are the different possibilities at the next explanatory level, so we are back with our two questions: Which obtains, and Why?

Could these questions continue for ever? Might there be, at every level, another higher Selector? Consider another version of the Axiarchic View. Reality might be as good as it could be, and that might be true because its being true is best, and that in turn might be true because its being true is best, and so on for ever. In this way, it may seem, everything might be explained. But that is not so. Like an infinite series of events, such a series of explanatory truths could not explain itself. Even if each truth were made true by the next, we could still ask why the whole series was true, rather than some other series, or no series.

The point can be made more simply. Though there might be some highest Selector, this might not be goodness but some other feature, such as non-arbitrariness. What could select between these possibilities? Might goodness be the highest Selector because that is best, or non-arbitrariness be this Selector because that is the least arbitrary possibility? Neither suggestion, I believe, makes sense. Just as God could not make himself exist, no Selector could make itself the one that, at the highest level, rules. No Selector could settle *whether* it rules, since it cannot settle anything unless it does rule.

If there is some highest Selector, this cannot, I have claimed, be a necessary truth. Nor could this Selector make itself the highest. And, since this Selector would be the highest, nothing else could make that true. So we may have found the necessity we need. If there is some highest Selector, that, I suggest, must merely happen to be true.

Supporters of the Brute Fact View may now feel vindicated. Have we not, in the end, accepted their view?

We have not. According to the Brute Fact View, reality merely happens to be as it is. That, I have argued, may not be true, since there may be some Selector which explains, or partly explains, reality's being as it is. There may also be some higher Selector which explains there being this Selector. My suggestion is only that, at the end of any such explanatory chain, some highest Selector must merely happen to be the one that rules. That is a different view.

This difference may seem small. No Selector could *explain* reality, we may believe, if it merely happened to rule. But this thought, though natural, is a mistake. If some explanation appeals to a brute fact, it does not explain that fact; but it may explain others.

Suppose, for example, that reality is as full as it could be. On the Brute Fact View, this fact would have no explanation. On the Maximalist View, reality would be this way because the highest law is that what is possible is actual. If reality were as full as it could be, this Maximalist View would be better than the Brute Fact View, since it would explain reality's being this way. And this view would provide that explanation even if it merely happened to be true. It makes a difference where the brute fact comes.

Part of the difference here is that, while there are countless cosmic possibilities, there are few plausible explanatory possibilities. If reality is as full as it could be, that's being a brute fact would be very puzzling. Since there are countless cosmic possibilities, it would be amazing if the one that obtained merely happened to be at the maximal extreme. On the Maximalist View, this fact would be no coincidence. And, since there are few explanatory possibilities, it would not be amazing if the Maximalist highest law merely happened to be the one that rules.

We should not claim that, if some explanation rests on a brute fact, it is not an explanation. Most scientific explanations take this form. The most that might be true

is that such an explanation is, in a way, merely a better description.

If that were true, there would be a different defence of the kind of reasoning that we have been considering. Even to discover *how* things are, we need explanations. And we may need explanations on the grandest scale. Our world may seem to have some feature that would be unlikely to be a coincidence. We may reasonably suspect that this feature is the Selector, or one of the Selectors. That hypothesis might lead us to confirm that, as it seemed, our world does have this feature. And that might give us reason to conclude either that ours is the only world, or that there are other worlds, with the same or related features. We might thus reach truths about the whole Universe.

Even if all explanations must end with a brute fact, we should go on trying to explain why the Universe exists, and is as it is. The brute fact may not enter at the lowest level. If reality is the way it is because this way has some feature, to know *what* reality is like, we must ask *why*.

7

We may never be able to answer these questions, either because our world is only a small part of reality, or because, though our world is the whole of reality, we could never know that to be true, or because of our own limitations. But, as I have tried to show, we may come to see more clearly what the possible answers are. Some of the fog that shrouds these questions may then disappear.

It can seem astonishing, for example, how reality could be made to be as it is. If God made the rest of reality be as it is, what could have made God exist? And, if God does not exist, what else could have made reality be as it is? When we think about these questions, even the Brute Fact View may seem unintelligible. It may be baffling how reality could be even randomly selected. What kind of *process* could select whether, for example, time had no beginning, or whether anything ever exists? When, and how, could any selection be made?

This is not a real problem. Of all the possible ways that reality might be, there must be one that is the way reality actually is. Since it is logically necessary that reality be some way or other, it is necessary that one way be picked to be the way that reality is. Logic ensures that, without any kind of process, a selection is made. There is no need for hidden machinery.

Suppose next that, as many people assume, the Brute Fact View must be true. If our world has no very special features, there would then be nothing that was deeply puzzling. If it were necessary that some cosmic possibility be randomly selected, while there would be no explanation of why the selection went as it did, there would be no mystery in reality's being as it is. Reality's features would be inexplicable, but only in the way in which it is inexplicable how some particle randomly moves. If a particle can merely happen to move as it does, reality could merely happen to be as it is. Randomness may even be *less* puzzling at the level of the whole Universe, since we know that facts at this level could not have been caused.

The Brute Fact View, I have argued, is not necessary, and may not be true. There may be one or more Selectors between the ways that reality might be, and one or more Selectors between such Selectors. But, as I have also claimed, it may be a necessary truth, that it be a brute fact whether there are such Selectors, and, if so, which the highest Selector is.

If that is a necessary truth, similar remarks apply. On these assumptions, there would again be nothing that was deeply puzzling. If it is necessary that, of these explanatory possibilities, one merely happens to obtain, there would be no explanation of why the one that obtains obtains. But, as before, that would be no more mysterious than the random movement of some particle.

The existence of the Universe can seem, in another way, astonishing. Even if it is not baffling that reality was made to be some way, since there is no conceivable alternative, it can seem baffling that the selection went as it did. Why is there a Universe at all? Why doesn't reality take its simplest and least arbitrary form: that in which nothing ever exists?

If we find this astonishing, we are assuming that these features should be the Selectors: that reality should be as simple and unarbitrary as it could be. That assumption has, I believe, great plausibility. But, just as the simplest cosmic possibility is that nothing ever exists, the simplest explanatory possibility is that there is no Selector. So we should not expect simplicity at both the factual and explanatory levels. If there is no Selector, we should not expect that there would also be no Universe. That would be an extreme coincidence.

Gottfried Leibniz

Monadology

1. The monad, which we shall discuss here, is nothing but a simple substance that enters into composites—simple, that is, without parts.

2. And there must be simple substances, since there are composites; for the composite is nothing more than a collection, or *aggregate,* of simples.

3. But where there are no parts, neither extension, nor shape, nor divisibility is possible. These monads are the true atoms of nature and, in brief, the elements of things.

4. There is also no dissolution to fear, and there is no conceivable way in which a simple substance can perish naturally.

5. For the same reason, there is no conceivable way a simple substance can begin naturally, since it cannot be formed by composition.

6. Thus, one can say that monads can only begin or end all at once, that is, they can only begin by creation

From Gottfried Leibniz, *Philosophical Essays,* edited and translated by Roger Ariew and Daniel Garber (Indianapolis: Hackett Publishing Company, 1989). Reprinted by permission of the publisher.

and end by annihilation, whereas composites begin or end through their parts.

7. There is also no way of explaining how a monad can be altered or changed internally by some other creature, since one cannot transpose anything in it, nor can one conceive of any internal motion that can be excited, directed, augmented, or diminished within it, as can be done in composites, where there can be change among the parts. The monads have no windows through which something can enter or leave. Accidents cannot be detached, nor can they go about outside of substances, as the sensible species of the Scholastics once did. Thus, neither substance nor accident can enter a monad from without.

8. However, monads must have some qualities, otherwise they would not even be beings. And if simple substances did not differ at all in their qualities, there would be no way of perceiving any change in things, since what there is in a composite can only come from its simple ingredients; and if the monads had no qualities, they would be indiscernible from one another, since they also do not differ in quantity. As a result, assuming a plenum, in motion, each place would always receive only the equivalent of what it already had, and one state of things would be indistinguishable from another.

9. It is also necessary that each monad be different from each other. For there are never two beings in nature that are perfectly alike, two beings in which it is not possible to discover an internal difference, that is, one founded on an intrinsic denomination.

10. I also take for granted that every created being, and consequently the created monad as well, is subject to change, and even that this change is continual in each thing.

11. It follows from what we have just said that the monad's natural changes come from an *internal principle,* since no external cause can influence it internally.

12. But, besides the principle of change, there must be *diversity* [*un détail*] *in that which changes,* which produces, so to speak, the specification and variety of simple substances.

13. This diversity must involve a multitude in the unity or in the simple. For, since all natural change is produced by degrees, something changes and something remains. As a result, there must be a plurality of properties [*affections*] and relations in the simple substance, although it has no parts.

14. The passing state which involves and represents a multitude in the unity or in the simple substance is nothing other than what one calls *perception,* which should be distinguished from apperception, or consciousness, as will be evident in what follows. This is where the Cartesians have failed badly, since they took no account of the perceptions that we do not apperceive. This is also what made them believe that minds alone are monads and that there are no animal souls or other entelechies. With the common people, they have confused a long stupor with death, properly speaking, which made them fall again into the Scholastic prejudice of completely separated souls, and they have even confirmed unsound minds in the belief in the mortality of souls.

15. The action of the internal principle which brings about the change or passage from one perception to another can be called *appetition;* it is true that the appetite cannot always completely reach the whole perception toward which it tends, but it always obtains something of it, and reaches new perceptions.

16. We ourselves experience a multitude in a simple substance when we find that the least thought we ourselves apperceive involves variety in its object. Thus, all those who recognize that the soul is a simple substance should recognize this multitude in the monad.

17. Moreover, we must confess that the *perception,* and what depends on it, is *inexplicable in terms of mechanical reasons,* that is, through shapes and motions. If we imagine that there is a machine whose structure makes it think, sense, and have perceptions, we could conceive it enlarged, keeping the same proportions, so that we could enter into it, as one enters into a mill. Assuming that, when inspecting its interior, we will only find parts that push one another, and we will never find anything to explain a perception. And so, we should seek perception in the simple substance and not in the composite or in the machine. Furthermore, this is all one can find in the simple substance—that is, perception and their changes. It is also in this alone that all the *internal actions* of simple substances can consist.

18. One can call all simple substances or created monads entelechies, for they have in themselves a certain perfection (*echousi to enteles*); they have a sufficiency (*autarkeia*) that makes them the sources of their internal actions, and, so to speak, incorporeal automata.

19. If we wish to call *soul* anything that has *perceptions* and *appetites* in the general sense I have just explained, then all simple substances or created monads can be called souls. But, since sensation is something more than a simple perception, I think that the general name of monad and entelechy is sufficient for simple substances which only have perceptions, and that we should only call those substances *souls* where perception is more distinct and accompanied by memory.

20. For we experience within ourselves a state in which we remember nothing and have no distinct perception; this is similar to when we faint or when we are overwhelmed by a deep, dreamless sleep. In this state the soul does not differ sensibly from a simple monad; but since this state does not last, and since the soul emerges from it, our soul is something more.

21. And it does not at all follow that in such a state the simple substance is without any perception. This is not possible for the previous reasons; for it cannot perish, and it also cannot subsist without some property [*affection*], which is nothing other than its perception. But when there is a great multitude of small perceptions in which nothing is distinct, we are stupefied. This is similar to when we continually spin in the same direction several times in succession, from which arises a dizziness that can make us faint and does not allow us to distinguish anything. Death can impart this state to animals for a time.

22. And since every present state of a simple substance is a natural consequence of its preceding state, the present is pregnant with the future.

23. Therefore, since on being awakened from a stupor we apperceive our perceptions, it must be the case that we had some perceptions immediately before, even though we did not apperceive them; for a perception can only come naturally from another perception, as a motion can only come naturally from a motion.

24. From this we see that if, in our perceptions, we had nothing distinct or, so to speak, in relief and stronger in flavor, we would always be in a stupor. And this is the state of bare monads.

25. We also see that nature has given heightened perceptions to animals from the care she has taken to furnish them organs that collect several rays of light or several waves of air, in order to make them more effectual by bringing them together. There is something

similar to this in odor, taste, and touch, and perhaps in many other senses which are unknown to us. I will soon explain how what occurs in the soul represents what occurs in the organs.

26. Memory provides a kind of sequence in souls, which imitates reason, but which must be distinguished from it. We observe that when animals have the perception of something which strikes them, and when they previously had a similar perception of that thing, then, through a representation in their memory, they expect that which was attached to the thing in the preceding perception, and are led to have sensations similar to those they had before. For example, if we show dogs a stick, they remember the pain that it caused them and they flee.

27. And the strong imagination that strikes and moves them comes from the magnitude or the multitude of the preceding perceptions. For often a strong impression produces, all at once, the effect produced by a long *habit* or by many lesser, reiterated perceptions.

28. Men act like beasts insofar as the sequence of their perceptions results from the principle of memory alone; they resemble the empirical physicians who practice without theory. We are all mere Empirics in three fourths of our actions. For example, when we expect that the day will dawn tomorrow, we act like an Empiric, because until now it has always been thus. Only the astronomer judges this by reason.

29. But the knowledge of eternal and necessary truths is what distinguishes us from simple animals and furnishes us with *reason* and the sciences, by raising us to a knowledge of ourselves and of God. And that is what we call the rational soul, or *mind,* in ourselves.

30. It is also through the knowledge of necessary truths and through their abstractions that we rise to *reflective acts,* which enable us to think of that which is called "I" and enable us to consider that this or that is in us. And thus, in thinking of ourselves, we think of being, or substance, of the simple and of the composite, of the immaterial and of God himself, by conceiving that that which is limited in us is limitless in him. And these reflective acts furnish the principal objects of our reasonings.

31. Our reasonings are based on *two great principles, that of contradiction,* in virtue of which we judge that which involves a contradiction to be false, and that

which is opposed or contradictory to the false to be true.

32. And *that of sufficient reason,* by virtue of which we consider that we can find no true or existent fact, no true assertion, without there being a sufficient reason why it is thus and not otherwise, although most of the time these reasons cannot be known to us.

33. There are also two kinds of *truths,* those of *reasoning* and those of *fact.* The truths of reasoning are necessary and their opposite is impossible; the truths of fact are contingent, and their opposite is possible. When a truth is necessary, its reason can be found by analysis, resolving it into simpler ideas and simpler truths until we reach the primitives.

34. This is how the speculative *theorems* and practical *canons* of mathematicians are reduced by analysis to *definitions, axioms,* and *postulates.*

35. And there are, finally, *simple ideas,* whose definition cannot be given. There are also axioms and postulates, in brief, *primitive principles,* which cannot be proved and which need no proof. And these are *identical propositions,* whose opposite contains an explicit contradiction.

36. But there must also be a *sufficient reason* in *contingent truths,* or *truths of fact,* that is, in the series of things distributed throughout the universe of creatures, where the resolution into particular reasons could proceed into unlimited detail because of the immense variety of things in nature and because of the division of bodies to infinity. There is an infinity of past and present shapes and motions that enter into the efficient cause of my present writing, and there is an infinity of small inclinations and dispositions of my soul, present and past, that enter into its final cause.

37. And since all this *detail* involves nothing but other prior or more detailed contingents, each of which needs a similar analysis in order to give its reason, we do not make progress in this way. It must be the case that the sufficient or ultimate reason is outside the sequence or *series* of this multiplicity of contingencies, however infinite it may be.

38. And that is why the ultimate reason of things must be in a necessary substance in which the diversity of changes is only eminent, as in its source. This is what we call *God.*

39. Since this substance is a sufficient reason for all this diversity, which is utterly interconnected, *there is only one God, and this God is sufficient.*

40. We can also judge that this supreme substance which is unique, universal, and necessary must be incapable of limits and must contain as much reality as is possible, insofar as there is nothing outside it which is independent of it, and insofar as it is a simple consequence of its possible existence.

41. From this it follows that God is absolutely perfect—*perfection* being nothing but the magnitude of positive reality considered as such, setting aside the limits or bounds in the things which have it. And here, where there are no limits, that is, in God, perfection is absolutely infinite.

42. It also follows that creatures derive their perfections from God's influence, but that they derive their imperfections from their own nature, which is incapable of being without limits. For it is in this that they are distinguished from God.

43. It is also true that God is not only the source of existences, but also that of essences insofar as they are real, that is, or the source of that which is real in possibility. This is because God's understanding is the realm of eternal truths or that of the ideas on which they depend; without him there would be nothing real in possibles, and not only would nothing exist, but also nothing would be possible.

44. For if there is reality in essences or possibles, or indeed, in eternal truths, this reality must be grounded in something existent and actual, and consequently, it must be grounded in the existence of the necessary being, in whom essence involves existence, that is, in whom possible being is sufficient for actual being.

45. Thus God alone (or the necessary being) has this privilege, that he must exist if he is possible. And since nothing can prevent the possibility of what is without limits, without negation, and consequently without contradiction, this by itself is sufficient for us to know the existence of God *a priori.* We have also proved this by the reality of the eternal truths. But we have also just proved it *a posteriori* since there are contingent beings, which can only have their final or sufficient reason in the necessary being, a being that has the reason of its existence in itself.

46. However, we should not imagine, as some do, that since the eternal truths depend on God, they are arbitrary and depend on his will, as Descartes appears to have held. This is true only of contingent truths, whose principle is *fitness* [*convenance*] or the choice of the *best*. But necessary truths depend solely on his understanding, and are its internal object.

47. Thus God alone is the primitive unity or the first [*originaire*] simple substance; all created or derivative monads are products, and are generated, so to speak, by continual fulgurations of the divinity from moment to moment, limited by the receptivity of the creature, to which it is essential to be limited.

48. God has *power,* which is the source of everything, *knowledge,* which contains the diversity of ideas, and finally *will,* which brings about changes or products in accordance with the principle of the best. And these correspond to what, in created monads, is the subject or the basis, the perceptive faculty and the appetitive faculty. But in God these attributes are absolutely infinite or perfect, while in the created monads or in-entelechies they are only imitations of it, in proportion to the perfection that they have.

49. The creature is said to *act* externally insofar as it is perfect, and *to be acted upon* [*patir*] by another, insofar as it is imperfect. Thus we attribute *action* to a monad insofar as it has distinct perceptions, and *passion,* insofar as it has confused perceptions.

50. And one creature is more perfect than another insofar as one finds in it that which provides an *a priori* reason for what happens in the other; and this is why we say that it acts on the other.

51. But in simple substances the influence of one monad over another can only be ideal, and can only produce its effect through God's intervention, when in the ideas of God a monad reasonably asks that God take it into account in regulating the others from the beginning of things. For, since a created monad cannot have an internal physical influence upon another, this is the only way in which one can depend on another.

52. It is in this way that actions and passions among creatures are mutual. For God, comparing two simple substances, finds in each reasons that require him to adjust the other to it; and consequently, what is active in some respects is passive from another point of view: *active* insofar as what is known distinctly in one serves to explain what happens in another; and *passive* insofar as the reason for what happens in one is found in what is known distinctly in another.

53. Now, since there is an infinity of possible universes in God's ideas, and since only one of them can exist, there must be a sufficient reason for God's choice, a reason which determines him towards one thing rather than another.

54. And this reason can only be found in *fitness,* or in the degree of perfection that these worlds contain, each possible world having the right to claim existence in proportion to the perfection it contains.

55. And this is the cause of the existence of the best, which wisdom makes known to God, which his goodness makes him choose, and which his power makes him produce.

56. This interconnection or accommodation of all created things to each other, and each to all the others, brings it about that each simple substance has relations that express all the others, and consequently, that each simple substance is a perpetual, living mirror of the universe.

57. Just as the same city viewed from different directions appears entirely different and, as it were, multiplied perspectively, in just the same way it happens that, because of the infinite multitude of simple substances, there are, as it were, just as many different universes, which are, nevertheless, only perspectives on a single one, corresponding to the different points of view of each monad.

58. And this is the way of obtaining as much variety as possible, but with the greatest order possible, that is, it is the way of obtaining as much perfection as possible.

59. Moreover, this is the only hypothesis (which I dare say is demonstrated) that properly enhances God's greatness. Mr. Bayle recognized this when, in his *Dictionary* (article "Rorarius"), he set out objections to it; indeed, he was tempted to believe that I ascribed too much to God, more than is possible. But he was unable to present any reason why this universal harmony, which results in every substance expressing exactly all the others through the relations it has to them, is impossible.

60. Furthermore, in what I have just discussed, we can see the *a priori* reasons why things could not be otherwise. Because God, in regulating the whole, had regard for each part, and particularly for each monad, and since the nature of the monad is representative, nothing can limit it to represent only a part of things. However, it is true that this representation is only confused as to the detail of the whole universe, and can only be distinct for a small portion of things, that is, either for those that are closest, or for those that are greatest with respect to each monad, otherwise each monad would be a divinity. Monads are limited, not as to their objects, but with respect to the modifications of their knowledge of them. Monads all go confusedly to infinity, to the whole; but they are limited and differentiated by the degrees of their distinct perceptions.

61. In this respect, composites are analogous to simples. For everything is a plenum, which makes all matter interconnected. In a plenum, every motion has some effect on distant bodies, in proportion to their distance. For each body is affected, not only by those in contact with it, and in some way feels the effects of everything that happens to them, but also, through them, it feels the effects of those in contact with the bodies with which it is itself immediately in contact. From this it follows that this communication extends to any distance whatsoever. As a result, every body is affected by everything that happens in the universe, to such an extent that he who sees all can read in each thing what happens everywhere, and even what has happened or what will happen, by observing in the present what is remote in time as well as in space. "All things conspire [*sympnoia panta*]," said Hippocrates. But a soul can read in itself only what is distinctly represented there; it cannot unfold all its folds at once, because they go to infinity.

62. Thus, although each created monad represents the whole universe, it more distinctly represents the body which is particularly affected by it, and whose entelechy it constitutes. And just as this body expresses the whole universe through the interconnection of all matter in the plenum, the soul also represents the whole universe by representing this body, which belongs to it in a particular way.

63. The body belonging to a monad (which is the entelechy or soul of that body) together with an entelechy constitutes what may be called a *living being,* and together with a soul constitutes what is called an *animal.* Now, the body of a living being or an animal is always organized; for, since every monad is a mirror of the universe in its way, and since the universe is regulated in a perfect order, there must also be an order in the representing being, that is, in the perceptions of the soul, and consequently, in the body in accordance with which the universe is represented therein.

64. Thus each organized body of a living being is a kind of divine machine or natural automaton, which infinitely surpasses all artificial automata. For a machine constructed by man's art is not a machine in each of its parts. For example, the tooth of a brass wheel has parts or fragments which, for us, are no longer artificial things, and no longer have any marks to indicate the machine for whose use the wheel was intended. But natural machines, that is, living bodies, are still machines in their least parts, to infinity. That is the difference between nature and art, that is, between divine art and our art.

65. And the author of nature has been able to practice this divine and infinitely marvelous art, because each portion of matter is not only divisible to infinity, as the ancients have recognized, but is also actually subdivided without end, each part divided into parts having some motion of their own; otherwise, it would be impossible for each portion of matter to express the whole universe.

66. From this we see that there is a world of creatures, of living beings, of animals, of entelechies, of souls in the least part of matter.

67. Each portion of matter can be conceived as a garden full of plants, and as a pond full of fish. But each branch of a plant, each limb of an animal, each drop of its humors, is still another such garden or pond.

68. And although the earth and air lying between the garden plants, or the water lying between the fish of the pond, are neither plant nor fish, they contain yet more of them, though of a subtleness imperceptible to us, most often.

69. Thus there is nothing fallow, sterile, or dead in the universe, no chaos and no confusion except in appearance, almost as it looks in a pond at a distance, where we might see the confused and, so to speak, teeming motion of the fish in the pond, without discerning the fish themselves.

70. Thus we see that each living body has a dominant entelechy, which in the animal is the soul; but the limbs of this living body are full of other living beings, plants, animals, each of which also has its entelechy, or its dominant soul.

71. But we must not imagine, as some who have misunderstood my thought do, that each soul has a mass or portion of matter of its own, always proper to or allotted by it, and that it consequently possesses other lower living beings, forever destined to serve it. For all bodies are in a perpetual flux, like rivers, and parts enter into them and depart from them continually.

72. Thus the soul changes body only little by little and by degrees, so that it is never stripped at once of all its organs. There is often metamorphosis in animals, but there is never metempsychosis nor transmigration of souls; there are also no completely *separated souls,* nor spirits [*Génies*] without bodies. God alone is completely detached from bodies.

73. That is why there is never total generation nor, strictly speaking, perfect death, death consisting in the separation of the soul. And what we call *generations* are developments and growths, as what we call deaths are enfoldings and diminutions.

74. Philosophers have been greatly perplexed about the origin of forms, entelechies, or souls. But today, when exact inquiries on plants, insects, and animals have shown us that organic bodies in nature are never produced from chaos or putrefaction, but always through seeds in which there is, no doubt, some *preformation,* it has been judged that, not only the organic body was already there before conception, but there was also a soul in this body; in brief, the animal itself was there, and through conception this animal was merely prepared for a great transformation, in order to become an animal of another kind. Something similar is seen outside generation, as when worms become flies, and caterpillars become butterflies.

75. Those *animals,* some of which are raised by conception to the level of the larger animals, can be called *spermatic.* But those of them that remain among those of their kind, that is, the majority, are born, multiply, and are destroyed, just like the larger animals. There are but a small number of Elect that pass onto a larger stage [*théatre*].

76. But this was only half the truth. I have, therefore, held that if the animal never begins naturally, it does not end naturally, either; and not only will there be no generation, but also no complete destruction, nor any death, strictly speaking. These *a posteriori* reasonings, derived from experience, agree perfectly with my principles deduced *a priori,* as above.

77. Thus one can state that not only is the soul (mirror of an indestructible universe) indestructible, but so is the animal itself, even though its mechanism often perishes in part, and casts off or puts on its organic coverings.

78. These principles have given me a way of naturally explaining the union, or rather the conformity of the soul and the organic body. The soul follows its own laws and the body also follows its own; and they agree in virtue of the harmony pre-established between all substances, since they are all representations of a single universe.

79. Souls act according to the laws of final causes, through appetitions, ends, and means. Bodies act according to the laws of efficient causes or of motions. And these two kingdoms, that of efficient causes and that of final causes, are in harmony with each other.

80. Descartes recognized that souls cannot impart a force to bodies because there is always the same quantity of force in matter. However, he thought that the soul could change the direction of bodies. But that is because the law of nature, which also affirms the conservation of the same total direction in matter, was not known at that time. If he had known it, he would have hit upon my system of pre-established harmony.

81. According to this system, bodies act as if there were no souls (though this is impossible); and souls act as if there were no bodies; and both act as if each influenced the other.

82. As for *minds* or rational souls, I find that, at bottom, what we just said holds for all living beings and animals, namely that animals and souls begin only with the world and do not end any more than the world does. However, rational animals have this peculiarity, that their little spermatic animals, as long as they only remain in this state, have only ordinary or sensitive souls. But that as soon as the Elect among them, so to speak, attain human nature by actual conception, their sensitive souls are elevated to the rank of reason and to the prerogative of minds.

83. Among other differences which exist between ordinary souls and minds, some of which I have already

noted, there are also the following: that souls, in general, are living mirrors or images of the universe of creatures, but that minds are also images of the divinity itself, or of the author of nature, capable of knowing the system of the universe, and imitating something of it through their schematic representations [*échantillons architectoniques*] of it, each mind being like a little divinity in its own realm.

84. That is what makes minds capable of entering into a kind of society with God, and allows him to be, in relation to them, not only what an inventor is to his machine (as God is in relation to the other creatures) but also what a prince is to his subjects, and even what a father is to his children.

85. From this it is easy to conclude that the collection of all minds must make up the city of God, that is, the most perfect possible state under the most perfect of monarchs.

86. This city of God, this truly universal monarchy, is a moral world within the natural world, and the highest and most divine of God's works. The glory of God truly consists in this city, for he would have none if his greatness and goodness were not known and admired by minds. It is also in relation to this divine city that God has goodness, properly speaking, whereas his wisdom and power are evident everywhere.

87. Since earlier we established a perfect harmony between two natural kingdoms, the one of efficient causes, the other the final causes, we ought to note here yet another harmony between the physical kingdom of nature and the moral kingdom of grace, that is, between God considered as the architect of the mechanism of the universe, and God considered as the monarch of the divine city of minds.

88. This harmony leads things to grace through the very path of nature. For example, this globe must be de-stroyed and restored by natural means at such times as the governing of minds requires it, for the punishment of some and the reward of others.

89. It can also be said that God the architect pleases in every respect God the legislator, and, as a result, sins must carry their penalty with them by the order of nature, and even in virtue of the mechanical structure of things. Similarly, noble actions will receive their rewards through mechanical means with regard to bodies, even though this cannot, and must not, always happen immediately.

90. Finally, under this perfect government, there will be no good action that is unrewarded, no bad action that goes unpublished, and everything must result in the well-being of the good, that is, of those who are not dissatisfied in this great state, those who trust in providence, after having done their duty, and who love and imitate the author of all good, as they should, finding pleasure in the consideration of his perfections according to the nature of genuinely *pure love,* which takes pleasure in the happiness of the beloved. This is what causes wise and virtuous persons to work for all that appears to be in conformity with the presumptive or antecedent divine will, and nevertheless, to content themselves with what God brings about by his secret, consequent, or decisive will, since they recognize that if we could understand the order of the universe well enough, we would find that it surpasses all the wishes of the wisest, and that it is impossible to make it better than it is. This is true not only for the whole in general, but also for ourselves in particular, if we are attached, as we should be, to the author of the whole, not only as the architect and efficient cause of our being, but also as to our master and final cause; he ought to be the whole aim of our will, and he alone can make us happy.

Aristotle

The Four Causes

BOOK I

[*THE METHOD OF INQUIRY*]

1

184a10 In every line of inquiry into something that has principles or causes or elements, we achieve knowledge—that
is, scientific knowledge—by knowing them; for we
think we know a thing when we know its primary
15 causes and primary principles, all the way to its elements.
Clearly, then, it is also true in the science of nature that
our first task is to determine the principles.

The natural path is to start from what is better known
and more perspicuous to us, and to advance to what is
more perspicuous and better known by nature; for what
is better known to us is not the same as what is better
known without qualification. We must advance in this
20 way, then, from what is less perspicuous by nature but
more perspicuous to us, to what is more perspicuous
and better known by nature.

The things that, most of all, are initially clear and perspicuous to us are inarticulate wholes; later, as we articulate them, the elements and principles come to be
known from them. We must, then, advance from uni-
25 versals to particulars; for the whole is better known in
184b perception, and the universal is a sort of whole, since it
includes many things as parts. The same is true, in a way,
of names in relation to their accounts. For a name—for
instance, 'circle'—signifies a sort of whole and signifies
indefinitely, whereas the definition <of a circle> artic-
ulates it by stating the particular <properties>. Again,
children begin by calling all men 'father' and all women
'mother'; only later do they distinguish different men
and different women.

From Aristotle, *Introductory Readings,* translated by Terence
Irwin and Gail Fine (Indianapolis: Hackett Publishing
Company, 1996). Reprinted by permission of the publisher.

[*THE GENERAL PRINCIPLES OF COMING TO BE*]

7

Let us, then, give our own account of coming to be, in
the following way. And first let us deal with all of com- 189b30
ing to be; for the natural procedure is to speak first
about what is common to every case, and then to study
what is special to each case.

When we say that something comes to be one thing
from being another and different thing, we are speaking about either simple or compound things. What I
mean is this: It is possible that a man comes to be musical, that the not-musical thing comes to be musical, 35
and that the not-musical man comes to be a musical 190a
man. By 'simple thing coming to be' I mean the man
and the not-musical thing; and by 'simple thing that
comes into being' I mean the musical thing. By 'compound' I mean both the thing that comes into being and
what comes to be that thing, whenever we say that the
not-musical man comes to be a musical man. 5

In one type of case we say not only that something
comes to be F, but also that it comes to be F *from* being
G; for instance, <the man not only comes to be musical, but also comes to be> musical from being not-musical. But we do not say this for all <properties>; for <the
man> did not come to be musical from being a man,
but rather the man came to be musical.

When something comes to be F (in the sense in
which we say a simple thing comes to be), in some cases
it remains when it comes to be F, and in other cases it 10
does not remain. The man, for instance, remains a man
and is still a man when he comes to be musical, whereas
the not-musical or unmusical thing, either simple or
compound, does not remain.

Now that we have made these distinctions, here is
something we can grasp from every case of coming
to be, if we look at them all in the way described. In
every case there must be some subject that comes to be 15

<something>; even if it is one in number, it is not one in form, since being a man is not the same as being an unmusical thing. (By 'in form' I mean the same as 'in account'.) One thing remains, and one does not remain. The thing that is not opposite remains, since the man re-
20 mains; but the not-musical thing, or the unmusical thing, does not remain. Nor does the thing compounded from both (for instance, the unmusical man) remain.

We say that something comes to be F from being G, but not that the G comes to be F, more often in cases where G does not remain; for instance, we say that <a man> comes to be musical from being unmusical, but not that <the unmusical comes to be musical> from a
25 man. Still, sometimes we speak in the same way in cases where G remains; we say, for instance, that a statue comes to be from bronze, but not that the bronze comes to be a statue. If, however, something comes to be F from being G, where G is opposite to F and G does not remain, we speak in both ways, saying both that something comes to be F from being G and that the G comes to be F; for it is true both that the man comes to be musical from being unmusical and that the unmusical one comes to be musical. That is why we also say the same
30 about the compound: we say both that the musical man comes to be musical from being an unmusical man and that the unmusical man comes to be musical.

Things are said to come to be in many ways, and some things are said not to come to be, but to come to be something; only substances are said to come to be without qualification. In the other cases it is evident that there must be some subject that comes to be <some-
35 thing>; for in fact, when <something> comes to be of some quantity or quality, or relative to another, or somewhere, something is the subject <underlying the
190b change>, because a substance is the only thing that is never said of any other subject, whereas everything else is said of a substance.

However, substances—the things that are without qualification—also come to be from some subject. This will become evident if we examine it. For in every case there is something that is a subject from which the thing that comes to be comes to be, as plants and animals
5 come to be from seed.

Some of the things that come to be without qualification do so by change of figure (for instance, a statue); some by addition (for instance, growing things); some

by subtraction (for instance, Hermes from the stone); some by composition (for instance, a house); some by alteration (for instance, things changing in accordance with their matter). It is evident that everything that comes to be in this way comes to be from a subject.   10

And so it is clear from what has been said that, in every case, what comes to be is composite: there is something that comes into being and something that comes to be this. And this latter thing is of two sorts: either the subject or the opposite. I mean, for instance, that the unmusical is opposite, and the man is subject; and that the lack of figure, shape, and order is the op-   15 posite, and the bronze, stone, or gold is the subject.

Suppose, then, that there are indeed causes and principles of natural things, from which they primarily are and have come to be—not come to be coincidentally, but come to be what each thing is called in accordance with its essence. It evidently follows that everything comes to be from the subject and the shape. For in a   20 way the musical man is composed from man and musical, since you will analyze him into their accounts. It is clear, then, that whatever comes to be does so from these things.

The subject is one in number but two in form. Man, gold, and matter in general is countable, since it is a this   25 more <than the privation is>, and what comes to be comes to be from it not coincidentally. The privation—the contrariety—is a coincident. The form is one—for instance, structure, musicality, or anything else predicated in this way.

Hence we should say that in one way there are two principles, and that in another way there are three. In one way they are contraries—if, for instance, one were   30 to speak of the musical and the unmusical, or the hot and the cold, or the ordered and the disordered. But in another way they are not contraries, since contraries cannot be affected by each other. This <puzzle about how becoming is possible> is also solved by the fact that the subject is something different, since it is not a contrary.   35

Hence, in a way the principles are no more numerous than the contraries, but, one might say, they are two in number. On the other hand, because they differ in being, they are not two in every way, but three; for be-   191a ing man is different from being unmusical, and being shapeless is different from being bronze.

We have said, then, how many principles are relevant to the coming to be of natural things, and we have described the different ways they should be counted. And it is clear that some subject must underlie the contraries, and that there must be two contraries. In another way, however, there need not be two; for just one of the contraries is enough, by its absence or presence, to produce the thing.

The nature that is subject is knowable by analogy. For as bronze is to a statue, or wood is to a bed, or as the shapeless before it acquires a shape is to anything else that has a shape, so the nature that is subject is to a substance, a this, and a being.

This, then, is one principle; it is not one or a being in the way a this is. Another principle is the one specified by the account, and a third is the contrary of this, the privation. The way in which these are two, and the way in which they are more than two, has been stated above.

First, then, it was said that only the contraries were principles. Later we added that something further is needed as subject and that there must be three principles. And from what we have said now it is evident how the contraries differ, how the principles are related to one another, and what the subject is. It is not yet clear, however, whether the form or the subject is substance. Still, it is clear that there are three principles, and in what way there are three, and what sorts of things they are. This, then, should allow us to observe how many principles there are, and what they are.

8

This is also the only solution to the puzzle raised by the earlier philosophers, as we shall now explain. Those who were the first to search for the truth philosophically and for the nature of beings were diverted and, so to speak, pushed off the track by inexperience. They say that nothing that is either comes to be or perishes. For, they say, what comes to be must come to be either from what is or from what is not, and coming to be is impossible in both cases; for what is cannot come to be (since it already is), while nothing can come to be from what is not (since there must be some subject). And then, having reached this result, they make things worse by going on to say that there is no plurality, but only being itself.

They accepted this belief for the reason mentioned. We reply as follows: The claim that something comes to be from what is or from what is not, or that what is or what is not acts on something or is acted on or comes to be anything whatever, is in one way no different from the claim that, for instance, a doctor acts on something or is acted on, or is or comes to be something from being a doctor. We say this about a doctor in two ways; and so, clearly, we also speak in two ways when we say that something is or comes to be something from what is, and that what is is acting on something or being acted on.

Now a doctor builds a house, not insofar as he is a doctor, but insofar as he is a housebuilder; and he becomes pale, not insofar as he is a doctor, but insofar as he is dark. But he practices medicine, or loses his medical knowledge, insofar as he is a doctor. We speak in the fullest sense of a doctor acting on something or being acted on, or coming to be something, from being a doctor, if it is insofar as he is a doctor that he is acted on in this way or produces these things or comes to be these things. So it is also clear that coming to be from what is not signifies this: coming to be from it insofar as it is not.

The early philosophers failed to draw this distinction and gave up the question. This ignorance led them into more serious ignorance—so serious that they thought nothing else <besides what already is> either is or comes to be, and so they did away with all coming to be.

We agree with them in saying that nothing comes to be without qualification from what is not, but we say that things come to be in a way—for instance, coincidentally—from what is not. For something comes to be from the privation, which in itself is not and which does not belong to the thing <when it has come to be>. But this causes surprise, and it seems impossible that something should come to be in this way from what is not.

Similarly, there is no coming to be, except coincidentally, from what is, or of what is. But coincidentally what is also comes to be, in the same way as if animal came to be from animal and a certain animal from a certain animal. Suppose, for instance, that a dog came to be from a horse.[1] For the dog would come to be not only

---

1. **Suppose . . . from a horse:** Aristotle appears to be considering an imaginary case of a horse turning into a dog. The horse is the subject of the coming to be, not because it is a horse or an animal, but because (we imagine) it provides matter suitable for the coming to be of a dog.

from a certain animal, but also from animal, though not insofar as it is animal (for that is already present). But if a certain <sort of> animal is to come to be, not coincidentally, it will not be from animal; and if a certain thing that is <is to come to be>, it will not be from what is, nor from what is not. For we have said what 'from what is not' signifies—i.e., insofar as it is not. Further, we are not doing away with <the principle that> everything is or is not.

This is one way <of solving this puzzle>. Another is <to note> that the same things can be spoken of in accordance with potentiality and actuality; this is discussed more exactly elsewhere.

And so, as we have said, we have solved the puzzles that compelled people to do away with some of the things we have mentioned. For this is why earlier thinkers were also diverted from the road leading them to <an understanding of> coming to be, perishing, and change in general. For if they had seen this nature <of the subject>, that would have cured all their ignorance.

• • • • •

BOOK II

[NATURE AS MATTER AND AS FORM]

1

Some existing things are natural, while others are due to other causes. Those that are natural are animals and their parts, plants, and the simple bodies, such as earth, fire, air and water; for we say that these things and things of this sort are natural. All these things evidently differ from those that are not naturally constituted, since each of them has within itself a principle of motion and stability in place, in growth and decay, or in alteration.

In contrast to these, a bed, a cloak, or any other <artifact>—insofar as it is described as such, <i.e., as a bed, a cloak, or whatever>, and to the extent that it is a product of a craft—has no innate impulse to change; but insofar as it is coincidentally made of stone or earth or a mixture of these, it has an innate impulse to change, and just to that extent. This is because a nature is a type of principle and cause of motion and stability within those

things to which it primarily belongs in their own right and not coincidentally. (By 'not coincidentally' I mean, for instance, the following: Someone who is a doctor might cause himself to be healthy, but it is not insofar as he is being healed that he has the medical science; on the contrary, it is coincidental that the same person is a doctor and is being healed, and that is why the two characteristics are sometimes separated from each other.)[2]

The same is true of everything else that is produced, since no such thing has within itself the principle of its own production. In some things (for instance, a house or any other product of handicraft) the principle comes from outside, and it is within other things. In other things (those that might turn out to be coincidental causes for themselves) the principle is within them, but not in their own right.

A nature, then, is what we have said; and the things that have a nature are those that have this sort of principle. All these things are substances; for <a substance> is a sort of subject, and a nature is invariably in a subject. The things that are in accordance with nature include both these and whatever belongs to them in their own right, as traveling upward belongs to fire—for this neither is nor has a nature, but is natural and in accordance with nature. We have said, then, what nature is, and what is natural and in accordance with nature.

To attempt to prove that there is such a thing as nature would be ridiculous; for it is evident that there are many things of the sort we have described. To prove what is evident from what is not evident betrays an inability to discriminate what is known because of itself from what is not. (It is clearly possible to suffer from this inability: someone blind from birth might still make deductions about colors.) And so such people are bound to argue about <mere> names and to understand nothing.

Some people think that the nature and substance of a natural thing is the primary constituent present in it, having no order in its own right, so that the nature of

---

2. **(By 'not coincidentally' . . . from each other.):** If there were some explanatory connection between S's needing to be cured and S's being a doctor (as there is, e.g., between a plant's need for water and its having roots), then being a doctor would be noncoincidentally connected with S's needing to be cured.

a bed, for instance, <would be> the wood, and the nature of a statue <would be> the bronze. A sign of this, according to Antiphon, is the fact that, if you were to bury a bed and the rotting residue were to become able to sprout, the result would be wood, not a bed. He
15 thinks that this is because the conventional arrangement, i.e., the craft <making the wood into a bed>, is a <mere> coincident of the wood, whereas the substance is what remains continuously while it is affected in these ways. And if each of these things is related to something else in the same way (bronze and gold, for
20 instance, to water; bones and wood to earth; and so on with anything else), that thing is their nature and substance.

This is why some people say that fire or earth or air or water is the nature of the things that exist; some say it is some of these, others say it is all of them. For whenever any of these people supposed one, or more than
25 one, of these things to be <the primary constituent>, he takes this or these to be all the substance there is, and he takes everything else to be attributes, states, and conditions of these things; and each of these is held to be everlasting, since they do not change from themselves, but the other things come to be and are destroyed an unlimited number of times.

This, then, is one way we speak of a nature: as the pri-
30 mary matter that is a subject for each thing that has within itself a principle of motion and change.

In another way the nature is the shape, i.e., the form in accordance with the account. For just as we speak of craftsmanship in what is in accordance with craft and is
35 crafted, so also we speak of nature in what is in accordance with nature and is natural. But if something were only potentially a bed and still lacked the form of a bed, we would not yet speak of craftsmanship or of a product in accordance with craft; nor would we say the corresponding thing about anything that is constituted naturally. For what is only potentially flesh or bone does
193b not have its nature, and is not naturally flesh or bone, until it acquires the form in accordance with the account by which we define flesh or bone and say what it is. In another way, then, the nature is the shape and form of things that have within themselves a principle of motion; this form is not separable except in account.
5 (What is composed of form and matter—for instance, a man—is not a nature, but is natural.)

Indeed, the form is the nature more than the matter is. For something is called <flesh, bone, and so on> when it is actually so, more than when it is only potentially so. Further, a man comes to be from a man, but not a bed from a bed. In fact that is why some say that
10 the nature of the bed is not the shape but the wood, because if it were to sprout the result would be wood, not a bed. If this shows that the wood is the nature, then the shape is also the nature, since a man comes to be from a man. Further, nature, as applied to coming to be, is really a road toward nature; it is not like medical treatment, which is a road not toward medical science, but toward health. For medical treatment necessarily pro-
15 ceeds *from* medical science, not *toward* medical science. But nature <as coming to be> is not related to nature in this way; rather, what is growing, insofar as it is growing, proceeds from something toward something <else>. What is it, then, that grows? Not what it is growing from, but what it is growing into. Therefore, the shape is the nature.

Shape and nature are spoken of in two ways; for the privation is also form in a way. We must consider later whether or not there is a privation and a contrary in
20 unqualified coming to be.

2

Since we have distinguished the different ways we speak of nature, we should next consider how the mathematician differs from the student of nature; for natural bodies certainly have surfaces, solids, lengths, and points,
25 which are what the mathematician studies. We should also consider whether astronomy is different from or a part of the study of nature; for it would be absurd if a student of nature ought to know what the sun or moon is but need not know any of their coincidents in their own right—especially since it is evident that students of nature also discuss the shape of the sun and moon, and
30 specifically whether or not the earth and the world are spherical.

These things are certainly the concern of both the mathematician and the student of nature. But the mathematician is not concerned with them insofar as each is the limit of a natural body, and he does not study the coincidents of a natural body insofar as they belong to a natural body. That is why he also separates these coincidents; for they are separable in thought from motion,
35

and his separating them makes no difference and results in no falsehood.

194a   Those who say there are Ideas do not notice that they do this too; for they separate natural objects, though these are less separable than mathematical objects. This would be clear if one tried to state the formulae of both natural and mathematical objects—of the things them-
5   selves and of their coincidents. For odd and even, straight and curved, and also number, line, and point do not involve motion, whereas flesh, bones, and man do—we speak of them as we speak of the snub nose, not as we speak of the curved.

This is also clear from the parts of mathematics that are more related to the study of nature—for instance,
10   optics, harmonics, and astronomy. These are in a way the reverse of geometry; for geometry investigates natural lines, but not insofar as they are natural, whereas optics investigates mathematical lines, but insofar as they are natural, not insofar as they are mathematical.

Since we speak of nature in two ways—both as form and as matter—we should study it as though we were investigating what snubness is, and so we should study
15   natural objects neither independently of their matter nor <simply> insofar as they have matter. For indeed, since there are these two types of nature, there might be a puzzle about which one the student of nature should study. Perhaps the compound of the two? If so, then also each of them. Then is it the same or a different discipline that knows each one of them?

If we judge by the early thinkers, the student of na-
20   ture would seem to study <only> matter, since Empedocles and Democritus touched only slightly on form and essence. Craft, however, imitates nature, and the same science knows both the form and the matter up to a point. The doctor, for instance, knows health, and also the bile and phlegm in which health <is realized>; similarly, the housebuilder knows both the form of the
25   house and that its matter is bricks and wood; and the same is true in the other cases. The science of nature, therefore, must also know both types of nature.

Moreover the same discipline studies both what something is for—i.e., the end—and whatever is for the end. Nature is an end and what something is for; for whenever a continuous motion has some end this sort
30   of terminus is also what the motion is for. That is why it was ludicrous for the poet to say 'He has reached the end he was born for'; it was ludicrous because by 'end' we mean not every terminus but only the best one.

For crafts produce their matter (some by producing it without qualification, others by making it suitable for their work); and we use all <matter> as being for our sake, since we are also an end in a way.   35

There are two crafts that control the matter and involve knowledge: the craft that uses <the matter> and   194b the craft that directs this productive craft. Hence the using craft also directs in a way, but with the difference that the directing craft knows the form, whereas the productive craft knows the matter. For instance, the pi-   5 lot knows what sort of form the rudder has, and he prescribes <how to produce it>, whereas the boatbuilder knows what sort of wood and what sorts of motions are needed to make it. With products of a craft, then, we produce the matter for the sake of the product; with natural things, the matter is already present.

Further, matter is relative; for there is one <sort of> matter for one form, and another for another.

How much, then, must the student of nature know about form and what-it-is? Perhaps as much as the doc-   10 tor knows about sinews, or the smith about bronze—enough to know what something is for. And he must confine himself to things that are separable in form but are in matter—for a man is born from a man and the sun. But it is a task for first philosophy to determine what is separable and what the separable is like.   15

[CAUSE AND CHANCE]

3

Now that we have determined these points, we should consider how many and what sorts of causes there are. For our inquiry aims at knowledge and we think we know something only when we find the reason why it   20 is so, i.e., when we find its primary cause. Clearly, then, we must also find the reason why in the case of coming to be, perishing, and every sort of natural change, so that when we know their principles we can try to refer whatever we are searching for to these principles.

In one way, then, that from which, as a <constituent> present in it, a thing comes to be is said to be that thing's cause—for instance, the bronze and silver, and their   25 genera, are causes of the statue and the bowl.

In another way, the form—i.e., the pattern—is a cause. The form is the account (and the genera of the account) of the essence (for instance, the cause of an octave is the ratio two to one, and in general number), and the parts that are in the account.

30 Further, the source of the primary principle of change or stability is a cause. For instance, the adviser is a cause <of the action>, and a father is a cause of his child; and in general the producer is a cause of the product, and the initiator of the change is a cause of what is changed.

Further, something's end—i.e., what it is for—is its cause, as health is of walking. For why does he walk? We 35 say, 'To be healthy'; and in saying this we think we have provided the cause. The same is true of all the intermediate steps that are for the end, where something else 195a has initiated the motion, as, for example, slimming, purging, drugs, or instruments are for health; all of these are for the end, though they differ in that some are activities, while others are instruments.

We may take these, then, to be the ways we speak of causes.

5 Since causes are spoken of in many ways, there are many noncoincidental causes of the same thing. Both the sculpting craft and the bronze, for instance, are causes of the statue, not insofar as it is something else, but insofar as it is a statue. But they are not causes in the same way: the bronze is a cause as matter, the sculpting craft as the source of the motion. Some things are causes of each other: hard work, for instance, is the cause of fitness, and fitness of hard work. But they are not causes 10 in the same way: fitness is what the hard work is for, whereas hard work is the principle of motion. Further, the same thing is the cause of contraries; for sometimes if a thing's presence causes F, that thing is also, by its absence, taken to cause the contrary of F, so that, for instance, if a pilot's presence would have caused the safety of a ship, we take his absence to have caused the ship-15 wreck.

All the causes just mentioned are of four especially evident types: (1) Letters are the cause of syllables, matter of artifacts, fire and such things of bodies, parts of the whole, and the assumptions of the conclusion, as that out of which. In each of these cases one thing—for instance, the parts—is cause as subject, while (2) the 20 other thing—the whole, the composition, and the form

—is cause as essence. (3) The seed, the doctor, the adviser and, in general, the producer, are all sources of the principle of change or stability. (4) In other cases, one thing is a cause of other things by being the end and the good. For what the other things are for is taken to be the best and their end—it does not matter <for present purposes> whether we call it the good or the apparent 25 good. These, then, are the number of kinds of causes there are.

Although there are many types of causes, they are fewer when they are arranged under heads. For causes are spoken of in many ways, and even among causes of the same type, some are prior and others posterior. For example, the cause of health is a doctor and <speaking 30 more generally> a craftsman, and the cause of an octave is the double and <speaking more generally> number; in every case the inclusive causes are posterior to the particular.

Further, some things and their genera are coincidental causes. Polycleitus and the sculptor, for instance, are causes of the statue in different ways, because being Polycleitus is coincidental to the sculptor. What includes 35 the coincident is also a cause—if, for example, the man or, quite generally, the animal is a cause of the statue. Some coincidental causes are more remote or more 195b proximate than others; if, for instance, the pale man or the musician were said to be the cause of the statue <it would be a more remote cause than Polycleitus is>.

We may speak of any <moving> cause, whether proper or coincidental, either as having a potentiality or 5 as actualizing it; for instance, we may say either that the housebuilder, or that the housebuilder actually building, is causing the house to be built.

Similar things may also be said about the things of which the causes are causes. For example, we may speak of the cause of this statue, or of a statue, or of an image in general; or of this bronze, or of bronze, or of matter in general. The same is true of coincidents. We may speak 10 in this same way of combinations—of Polycleitus the sculptor, for instance, instead of Polycleitus or a sculptor.

Still, all these ways amount to six, each spoken of in two ways. For there is (1) the particular and (2) the genus, and (3) the coincident and (4) the genus of the 15 coincident; and these may be spoken of either (5) in combination or (6) simply. Each of these may be either active or potential. The difference is the following.

Active and particular causes exist and cease to exist simultaneously with the things they cause, so that, for instance, this one practising medicine exists simultaneously
20 with this one being made healthy, and in the same way
this one housebuilding exists simultaneously with this
thing being built into a house. But this is not true of
every cause that is potential; for the house and the
housebuilder do not perish simultaneously.

Here as elsewhere, we must always seek the most precise cause. A man, for example, is building because he
is a builder, and he is a builder insofar as he has the
25 building craft; his building craft, then, is the prior cause,
and the same is true in all cases. Further, we must seek
genera as causes of genera, and particulars as causes of
particulars; a sculptor, for instance, is the cause of a
statue, but this sculptor of this statue. And we must seek
a potentiality as the cause of a potential effect, and
something actualizing a potentiality as the cause of an
actual effect.

This, then, is an adequate determination of the number of causes, and of the ways in which they are causes.

4

30 Luck and chance are also said to be causes, and many
things are said to be and to come to be because of them.
We must, then, investigate how luck and chance are in-
35 cluded in the causes we have mentioned, whether luck
is or is not the same as chance, and, in general, what they
are.

Some people even wonder whether luck and chance
196a exist. For they say that nothing results from luck; rather,
everything that is said to result from chance or luck has
some definite cause. If, for instance, as a result of luck
someone comes to the marketplace and finds the person he wanted to meet but did not expect, they say the
cause is his wanting to go to market. Similarly, for every
5 other supposed result of luck, they say it is possible to
find some cause other than luck. For if there were such
a thing as luck, it would appear truly strange and puzzling that none of the early philosophers who discussed
10 the causes of coming to be and perishing ever determined anything about luck; in fact it would seem that
they also thought that nothing results from luck. But
this too is surprising; for surely many things come to be
and exist as a result of luck and chance. Though people

know perfectly well that everything that comes to be
can be referred to some cause, as the old argument doing away with luck says, everyone nonetheless says that
some of these things result from luck and that others do 15
not.

That is why the early philosophers should have mentioned luck in some way or other. But they certainly did
not think luck was among the causes they recognized—
for instance, love or strife or mind or fire or anything
else of that sort. In either case, then, it is strange, whether
they supposed there was no such thing as luck, or supposed there was such a thing but omitted to discuss it.
It is especially strange considering that they sometimes 20
appeal to luck. Empedocles, for example, appeals to luck
when he says that air is separated out on top, not always
but as luck has it; at least, he says in his cosmogony that
'it happened to run that way at that time, but often
otherwise'. And he says that most of the parts of animals
result from luck.

Other people make chance the cause of our heaven
and of all worlds. For they say that the vortex, and the 25
motion that dispersed and established everything in its
present order, resulted from chance. And this is certainly
quite amazing. For animals and plants, they say, neither
are nor come to be from luck, but rather nature or mind 30
or something of that sort is the cause, since it is not just
any old thing that comes to be from a given type of
seed, but an olive-tree comes from one type, and a man
from another; and yet they say that the heaven and the
most divine of visible things result from chance and 35
have no cause of the sort that animals and plants have.

If this is so, it deserves attention, and something might
well have been said about it. For in addition to the other 196b
strange aspects of what they say, it is even stranger to say
all this when they see that nothing in the heaven results
from chance, whereas many things happen as a result of
luck to things whose existence is not itself a result of 5
luck. Surely the contrary would have been likely.

Other people suppose that luck is a cause, but they
take it to be divine and superhuman, and therefore obscure to the human mind.

And so we must consider chance and luck, and determine what each is, and whether they are the same or
different, and see how they fit into the causes we have
distinguished.

5

10 First, then, we see that some things always, others usually, come about in the same way. Evidently luck and the result of luck are not said to be the cause of either of these things—either of what is of necessity and always or of what is usually. But since apart from these there is *15* a third sort of event which everyone says results from luck, it is evident that there is such a thing as luck and chance; for we know that this third sort of event results from luck and that the results of luck are of this sort.

Further, some events are for something and others are not. Among the former, some are in accordance with a decision while others are not, but both sorts are for *20* something. And so it is clear that even among events that are neither necessary nor usual there are some that admit of being for something. (Events that are for something include both the actions that result from thought and also the results of nature.) This, then, is the sort of event that we regard as a result of luck, whenever an event of that sort comes about coincidentally.[3] For just *25* as some things are something in their own right, and others are something coincidentally, so also it is possible for a cause to be of either sort. For example, the cause of a house is, in its own right, the housebuilder, but coincidentally the pale or musical thing. Hence the cause in its own right is determinate, but the coincidental cause is indeterminate, since one thing might have an unlimited number of coincidents.

As has been said, then, whenever this <coincidental *30* causation> occurs among events of the sort that are for something the events <that have these coincidental causes> are said to result from chance and luck. The difference between chance and luck will be determined later; we may take it as evident for the moment that both are found among events of the sort that are for something.

For instance, A would have come when B was collecting subscriptions, in order to recover the debt from

B, if A had known <B would be there>. In fact, however, A did not come in order to do this; it was a coin- *35* cidence that A came <when B happened to be there>, and so met B in order to collect the debt—given that A neither usually nor of necessity frequents the place *197a* <for that purpose>. The end—collecting the debt—is not a cause <of A's action> in A, but it is the sort of thing that one decides to do and that results from thought. And in this case A's coming is said to result from luck; but if A always or usually frequented the place because he had decided to and for the purpose of collecting the debt, then <A's being there when B was there> would *5* not result from luck.

Clearly, then, luck is a coincidental cause found among events of the sort that are for something, and specifically among those of the sort that are in accordance with a decision. Hence thought (since decision requires thought) and luck concern the same things.

Now the causes whose results might be matters of luck are bound to be indeterminate. That is why luck also seems to be something indeterminate and obscure to human beings, and why, in one way, it might seem *10* that nothing results from luck. For, as we might reasonably expect, all these claims are correct. For in one way things do result from luck, since they are coincidental results and luck is a coincidental cause. But luck is not the unqualified <and hence non-coincidental> cause of anything. The <unqualified> cause of a house, for in- *15* stance, is a housebuilder, and the coincidental cause a flute-player; and the man's coming and collecting the debt, without having come to collect it, has an indefinite number of coincidental causes—he might have come because he wished to see someone, or was going to court or to the theater.

It is also correct to say that luck is contrary to reason. For rational judgment tells us what is always or usually the case, whereas luck is found in events that happen *20* neither always nor usually. And so, since causes of this sort are indeterminate, luck is also indeterminate.

Still, in some cases one might be puzzled about whether just any old thing might be a cause of a lucky outcome. Surely the wind or the sun's warmth, but not someone's haircut, might be the cause of his health; for some coincidental causes are closer than others to what they cause.

---

3. **This, then . . . coincidentally:** An event type (e.g., meeting in the marketplace, which has many tokens) has a final cause when it is characteristically and USUALLY true that its tokens (e.g., these people meeting in the marketplace on this occasion) have a final cause. Lucky events are those tokens that lack the final cause that is characteristic of the type.

25 Luck is called good when something good results, bad when something bad results; it is called good and bad fortune when the results are large. That is why someone who just misses great evil or good as well <as someone who has it> is fortunate or unfortunate; for
30 we think of him as already having <the great evil or good>, since the near miss seems to us to be no distance. Further, it is reasonable that good fortune is unstable; for luck is unstable, since no result of luck can be either always or usually the case.

As we have said, then, both luck and chance are co-incidental causes, found in events of the sort that are
35 neither without exception nor usual, and specifically in events of this sort that might be for something.

6

Chance is not the same as luck, since it extends more
197b widely; for results of luck also result from chance, but not all results of chance result from luck. For luck and its results are found in things that are capable of being fortunate and in general capable of action, and that is why luck must concern what is achievable by action. A sign of this is the fact that good fortune seems to be the
5 same or nearly the same as being happy, and being happy is a sort of action, since it is doing well in action. Hence what cannot act cannot do anything by luck either. Hence neither inanimate things nor beasts nor children do anything by luck, because they are incapable of de-cision. Nor do they have good or bad fortune, except by a <mere> similarity—as Protarchus said that the
10 stones from which altars are made are fortunate, because they are honored, while their fellows are trodden un-derfoot. Still, even these things are affected by the re-sults of luck in a way, whenever an agent affects them by some lucky action; but otherwise they are not.

Chance, on the other hand, applies both to animals other than man and to many inanimate things. We say,
15 for instance, that the horse came by chance, since it was saved because it came but did not come in order to be saved. And the tripod fell by chance, because it did not fall in order to be sat on, although it was left standing in order to be sat on.

Hence it is evident that among types of events that are for something (speaking without qualification), we say that a particular event of such a type results from chance if it has an external cause and the actual result is not what it is for: and we say that it results from luck if 20
it results from chance and is an event of the sort that is decided on by an agent who is capable of decision. A sign of this is the fact that we say an event is pointless if it <is of the sort that> is for some result but <in this case> that result is not what it is for. If, for instance, walking is for evacuating the bowels, but when he walked on this occasion it was not <for that reason>, then we say that he walked pointlessly and that his walk- 25
ing is pointless. We assume that an event is pointless if it is naturally for something else, but does not succeed in <being for> what it is naturally for. For if someone said that his washing himself was pointless because the sun was not eclipsed, he would be ridiculous, since washing is not for producing eclipses. So also, then, an event hap-pens by chance (as the name suggests) whenever it is pointless.[4] For the stone did not fall in order to hit 30
someone; it fell by chance, because it might have fallen because someone threw it to hit someone.

The separation of chance from luck is sharpest in nat-ural events. For if an event is contrary to nature, we re-gard it as a result of chance, not of luck. But even this is 35
different from <other cases of chance; the other cases> have an external cause, but <events contrary to nature> have an internal cause.

We have said, then, what chance and luck are and 198a
how they differ. Each of them falls under the sort of cause that is the source of the principle of motion. For in every case they are either among natural causes or 5
among those resulting from thought, and the number of these is indeterminate.

Chance and luck are causes of events <of the sort> that mind or nature might have caused, in cases where <particular> events <of this sort> have some coinci-dental cause. Now nothing coincidental is prior to anything that is in its own right; hence clearly no coin-cidental cause is prior to something that is a cause in its 10
own right. Chance and luck are therefore posterior to mind and nature. And so however true it might be that chance is the cause of the heavens, still it is necessary for mind and nature to be prior causes of this universe and of many other things.

---

4. **by chance,** *automaton* . . . **pointless,** *matēn*. Aristotle appeals to supposed etymology.

7

It is clear, then, that there are causes, and that there are
as many different types as we say there are; for the reason why something is so includes all these different
types <of causes>. For we refer the ultimate reason why
(1) in the case of unmoved things, to the what-it-is (for
instance, in mathematics; for there we refer ultimately
to the definition of straight or commensurate or some
thing else), or (2) to what first initiated the motion (for
instance, why did they go to war?—because the other
side raided them), or (3) to what it is for (for instance,
in order to set themselves up as rulers), or (4) in the case
of things that come to be, to the matter.

It is evident, then, that these are the causes and that
this is their number. Since there are four of them, the
student of nature ought to know them all; and in order
to give the sort of reason that is appropriate for the
study of nature, he must trace it back to all the causes—
to the matter, the form, what initiated the motion, and
what something is for. The last three often amount to
one; for what something is and what it is for are one,
and the first source of the motion is the same in species
as these, since a man generates a man; and the same is
true generally of things that initiate motion by being in
motion.

Things that initiate motion without being in motion
are outside the scope of the study of nature. For although they initiate motion, they do not do so by having motion or a principle of motion within themselves,
but they are unmoved. Hence there are three inquiries:
one about what is unmoved, one about what is in motion but imperishable, and one about what is perishable.

And so the reason why is given by referring to the
matter, to the what-it-is, and to what first initiated the
motion. For in cases of coming to be, this is the normal
way of examining the causes—by asking what comes to
be after what, and what first acted or was acted on, and
so on in order in every case.

Two sorts of principles initiate motion naturally. One
of these principles is not itself natural, since it has no
principle of motion within itself; this is true of whatever initiates motion without itself being in motion—
for instance, what is entirely without motion (i.e., the
first of all beings) and also the what-it-is (i.e., the form),
since this is the end and what something is for. And so,

since natural processes are for something, this cause too
must be known.

The reason why should be stated in all these ways.
For instance, (1) this necessarily results from that (either
without exception or usually); (2) if this is to be (as the
conclusion from the premises); (3) that this is the
essence; and (4) because it is better thus—not unqualifiedly better, but better in relation to the essence of a
given thing.

[FINAL CAUSES AND NECESSITY IN NATURE]

8

We must first say why nature is among the causes that
are for something, and then how necessity applies to
natural things. For everyone refers things to necessity,
saying that since the hot, the cold, and each element
have a certain nature, certain other things are and come
to be of necessity. For if they mention any cause other
than necessity (as one thinker mentions love or strife,
and another mentions mind), they just touch on it, then
let it go.

A puzzle now arises: why not suppose that nature acts
not for something or because it is better, but of necessity? Zeus's rain does not fall in order to make the grain
grow, but of necessity. For it is necessary that what has
been drawn up is cooled, and that what has been cooled
and become water comes down, and it is coincidental
that this makes the grain grow. Similarly, if someone's
grain is spoiled on the threshing floor, it does not rain in
order to spoil the grain, and the spoilage is coincidental.

Why not suppose, then, that the same is true of the
parts of natural organisms? On this view, it is of necessity that, for example, the front teeth grow sharp and
well adapted for biting, and the back ones broad and
useful for chewing food; this <useful> result was coincidental, not what they were for. The same will be true
of all the other parts that seem to be for something. On
this view, then, whenever all the parts came about coincidentally as though they were for something, these
animals survived, since their constitution, though coming about by chance, made them suitable <for survival>.
Other animals, however, were differently constituted
and so were destroyed; indeed they are still being destroyed, as Empedocles says of the man-headed calves.

This argument, then, and others like it, might puzzle someone. In fact, however, it is impossible for things to
35 be like this. For these <teeth and other parts> and all natural things come, to be as they do either always or
199a usually, whereas no result of luck or chance comes to be either always or usually. (For we do not regard frequent winter rain or a summer heat wave, but only summer rain or a winter heat wave, as a result of luck or coincidence.) If, then, these seem either to be coincidental re-
5 sults or to be for something, and they cannot be coincidental or chance results, they are for something. Now surely all such things are natural, as even those making these claims <about necessity> would agree. We find, then, among things that come to be and are by nature, things that are for something.

Further, whenever <some sequence of actions> has an end, the whole sequence of earlier and later actions is di-
10 rected toward the end. Surely what is true of action is also true of nature, and what is true of nature is true of each action, if nothing prevents it. Now actions are for something; therefore, natural sequences are for something. For example, if a house came to be naturally, it would come to be just as it actually does by craft, and if
15 natural things came to be not only naturally but also by craft, they would come to be just as they do naturally; one thing, then, is what the other is for. In general, craft either completes the work that nature is unable to complete or imitates nature. If, then, the products of a craft are for something, clearly the products of nature are also for something; for there is the same relation of later stages to earlier in productions of a craft and in productions of nature.

This is most evident in the case of animals other than
20 man, since they use neither craft nor inquiry nor deliberation in producing things—indeed this is why some people are puzzled about whether spiders, ants, and other such things operate by understanding or in some other way. If we advance little by little along the same lines, it is evident that even in plants things come to be that promote the end—leaves, for instance, grow for the
25 protection of the fruit. If, then, a swallow makes its nest and a spider its web both naturally and for some end, and if plants grow leaves for the sake of the fruit, and send roots down rather than up for the sake of nourishment, it evidently follows that this sort of cause is

among things that come to be and are by nature. And 30 since nature is of two sorts, nature as matter and nature as form, and the form is the end, and since everything else is for the end, the form must be what things are for.

Errors occur even in productions of craft; grammarians, for instance, have written incorrectly, and doctors have given the wrong medicine. Clearly, then, errors are also possible in productions of nature.   35 199b

In some productions by crafts, the correct action is for something, and in cases of error the attempt is for something but misses the mark. The same will be true, then, of natural things; freaks will be errors, missing what they are for. Hence in the original formations of 5 things, a defective principle would also have brought the <man-headed> calves into being, if they were unable to reach any definite term and end—just as, in the actual state of things, <freaks> come to be when the seed is defective. Further, it is necessary for the seed to come into being first, and not the animal straightaway; in fact the 'all-natured first' was seed.

Further, in plants as well as in animals things happen for something, though in a less articulate way. Then 10 what about plants? Did olive-headed vines keep coming into being, as he says <man-headed> calves did? Surely not—that is absurd—but surely they would have to have come into being, if the animals did.

Further, <on Empedocles' view> coming to be would also have to be merely a matter of chance among seeds. But whoever says this does away entirely with na- 15 ture and natural things. For things are natural when they are moved continuously from some principle in themselves and so arrive at some end. From each principle comes, not the same thing in each case, but not just any old thing either; in every case it proceeds to the same <end>, if nothing prevents it.

Now certainly both the end that a process is for and the process that is for this end might also result from 20 luck. We say, for instance, that a friend in a foreign country came by luck and paid the ransom and then went away, when he did the action as though he had come in order to do it, though in fact that was not what he came to do. This end is achieved coincidentally, since (as we said before) luck is one of the coincidental causes. But whenever the end results always or usu- 25 ally, it is neither coincidental nor a result of luck. And in natural things that is how it is in every case, unless something prevents it.

Besides, it is strange for people to think there is no end unless they see an agent initiating the motion by deliberation. Even crafts do not deliberate. Moreover, if the shipbuilding craft were in the wood, it would produce a ship in the same way that nature would. And so if what something is for is present in craft, it is also present in nature. This is clearest when a doctor applies medical treatment to himself—that is what nature is like.

It is evident, then, that nature is a cause, and in fact the sort of cause that is for something.

9

Is the necessity present <in nature only> conditional, or is it also unqualified?

The sort of necessity that is ascribed nowadays to things that come to be is the sort there would be if someone supposed that a wall came into being of necessity. On this view, heavy things naturally move downward, and light things upward, and that is why the stones and the foundations are below, while the earth is above because of its lightness, and the wooden logs are on the very top because they are lightest of all.

Nonetheless, though the wall certainly requires these things, it did not come to be because of them (except insofar as they are its material cause), but in order to give shelter and protection.

The same is true in all other cases that are for something: although they require things that have a necessary nature, they do not come to be because of these things (except insofar as they are the material cause), but for some end. For instance, why does a saw have such and such features? In order to perform this function, and for this end. But this end cannot come to be unless the saw is made of iron; and so it is necessary for it to be made of iron if there is to be a saw performing its function. What is necessary, then, is conditional, but not <necessary> as an end; for necessity is in the matter, whereas the end is in the form.

Necessity is found both in mathematics and in things that come to be naturally, and to some extent the two cases are similar. For instance, since the straight is what it is, it is necessary for a triangle to have angles equal to two right angles. It is not because the triangle has an-

gles equal to two right angles that the straight is what it is; but if the triangle does not have angles equal to two right angles, the straight will not be what it is either.

The reverse is true in the case of things that come to be for an end: if the end is or will be, then the previous things are or will be too. Just as, in the mathematical case, if the conclusion <about the triangle> is false, the principle <about the straight> will not be true either, so also in nature if the <materials> do not exist, the end that the process is for will not come about either. For the end is also a principle; it is a principle not of the action, but of the reasoning. (In the mathematical case <also> the principle is the principle of the reasoning, since in this case there is no action.)

And so, if there is to be a house, it is necessary for these things to come to be or to be present; and in general, the matter that is for something must exist (for example, bricks and stones if there is to be a house). The end, however, does not exist because of these things, except insofar as they are the material cause, nor will it come about because of them; still, in general, the end (the house or the saw) requires them (the stones or the iron). Similarly, in the mathematical case the principles require the triangle to have two right angles.

Evidently, then, necessity in natural things belongs to the material cause and to the motions of matter. The student of nature should mention both causes, but more especially what something is for, since this is the cause of the matter, whereas the matter is not the cause of the end. The end is what something is for, and the principle comes from the definition and the form.

The same is true in productions of craft. For instance, since a house is this sort of thing, these things must come to be and be present of necessity; and since health is this, these things must come to be and be present of necessity. In the same way, if a man is this, these things must come to be and be present of necessity; and if these, then these.

But presumably necessity is present in the form as well <as in the matter>. Suppose, for instance, that we define the function of sawing as a certain sort of cutting; this sort of cutting requires a saw with teeth of a certain sort, and these require a saw made of iron. For the form, as well as the matter, has parts in it as matter of the form.

BOOK VIII

[MOTION AND THE UNMOVED MOVER]

5

256a4　<Everything that is moved is moved by something.> This is true in two ways. For either (1) B initiates mo-
5　tion in A not because of B itself, but because of something else C that initiates motion in B, or (2) B initiates motion in A because of B itself. In the second case this is true either (2a) because B is the first thing immediately preceding A, or (2b) because B initiates the motion in A through a number of intermediaries. For instance, <in case (2b)> the stick initiates motion in the stone, and the stick is moved by the agency of the hand, which is moved by the agency of the man; he <is set in motion, but> not by being moved by the agency of some further thing. We say that both the last and the first
10　mover[5] initiate motion, but the first mover does so to a higher degree. For the first mover initiates motion in the last mover, but the last does not initiate motion in the first. Moreover, without the first mover the last mover will not initiate motion, but the first will initiate it without the last; the stick, for instance, will not move <the stone> unless the man moves <the stick>.

It is necessary, then, for whatever is moved to be moved by the agency of some mover, either by the agency of a mover that is in turn moved by the agency
15　of something else moving it or by the agency of a mover that is not moved by the agency of something else moving it. And if it is moved by the agency of something else moving it, there must be some first mover that is not moved by the agency of something else; and if this is the character of the first mover, it is not necessary for there to be another mover. For it is impossible to have an infinite series of movers each of which initiates motion and is moved by the agency of something else; for there is no first term in an infinite series.

If, then, everything that is moved is moved by the agency of something, and if the first mover is moved, but not by the agency of something else, then it neces-
20　sarily follows that it is moved by its own agency.

Moreover, it is also possible to carry out the same argument in the following way. Every mover moves something and moves it by means of something; for it moves something either by means of itself or by means of something else. The man, for instance, initiates motion either himself or by means of the stick; again, either the wind itself knocked the thing over, or the stone pushed by the
25　wind knocked it over. But if C moves A by means of B, then B cannot move A unless there is something else that initiates motion by means of itself. But if C initiates motion by means of itself, there need not be anything else B by means of which C initiates motion. And if there is something else B by means of which C initiates motion, then there is something that initiates motion not by means of something <else>, but by means of itself—otherwise there will be an infinite regress.

If, then, something initiates motion by being moved, we must come to a stop, and not go on to infinity. For
30　if the stick initiates motion by being moved by the hand, the hand moves the stick, and if something else initiates motion by means of the hand, then there is something else that moves the hand. And so, in each case when one thing moves another by means of something, there must be something prior that initiates motion in itself by means of itself. If, then, this is moved, but what moves it is not something else, it must initiate motion in itself.

256b

---

5. **mover:** i.e., the initiator of motion. In this example the first mover is the man, and the last mover is the stick.

David Lewis

*Causation**

Hume defined causation twice over. He wrote "we may define a cause to be *an object followed by another, and where all the objects, similar to the first, are followed by objects similar to the second. Or, in other words, where, if the first object had not been, the second never had existed.*"[1]

Descendants of Hume's first definition still dominate the philosophy of causation: a casual succession is supposed to be a succession that instantiates a regularity. To be sure, there have been improvements. Nowadays we try to distinguish the regularities that count—the "causal laws"—from mere accidental regularities of succession. We subsume causes and effects under regularities by means of descriptions they satisfy, not by over-all similarity. And we allow a cause to be only one indispensable part, not the whole, of the total situation that is followed by the effect in accordance with a law. In present-day regularity analyses, a cause is defined (roughly) as any member of any minimal set of actual conditions that are jointly sufficient, given the laws, for the existence of the effect.

More precisely, let C be the proposition that c exists (or occurs) and let E be the proposition that e exists. Then c causes e, according to a typical regularity analysis, iff (1) C and E are true; and (2) for some nonempty set $\mathfrak{L}$ of true law-propositions and some set $\mathfrak{F}$ of true propositions of particular fact, $\mathfrak{L}$ and $\mathfrak{F}$ jointly imply $C \supset E$, although $\mathfrak{L}$ and $\mathfrak{F}$ jointly do not imply E and $\mathfrak{F}$ alone does not imply $C \supset E$.

Much needs doing, and much has been done, to turn definitions like this one into defensible analyses. Many problems have been overcome. Others remain: in particular, regularity analyses tend to confuse causation itself with various other causal relations. If c belongs to a minimal set of conditions jointly sufficient for e, given the laws, then c may well be a genuine cause of e. But c might rather be an effect of e: one which could not, given the laws and some of the actual circumstances, have occurred otherwise than by being caused by e. Or c might be an epiphenomenon of the causal history of e: a more or less inefficacious effect of some genuine cause of e. Or c might be a preempted potential cause of e: something that did not cause e, but that would have done so in the absence of whatever really did cause e.

It remains to be seen whether any regularity analysis can succeed in distinguishing genuine causes from effects, epiphenomena, and preempted potential causes—and whether it can succeed without falling victim to worse problems, without piling on the epicycles, and without departing from the fundamental idea that causation is instantiation of regularities. I have no proof that regularity analyses are beyond repair, nor any space to review the repairs that have been tried. Suffice it to say that the prospects look dark. I think it is time to give up and try something else.

A promising alternative is not far to seek. Hume's "other words"—that if the cause had not been, the effect never had existed—are no mere restatement of his first definition. They propose something altogether different: a counterfactual analysis of causation.

The proposal has not been well received. True, we do know that causation has something or other to do with counterfactuals. We think of a cause as something that makes a difference, and the difference it makes must be a difference from what would have happened without it. Had it been absent, its effects—some of them, at least, and usually all—would have been absent as well. Yet it is one thing to mention these platitudes now and again,

David Lewis, "Causation" from *Philosophical Papers, Volume II* (Oxford: Oxford University Press, 1986). Copyright © 1986 by David Lewis. Reprinted with the permission of The Estate of David Lewis.

* I thank the American Council of Learned Societies, Princeton University, and the National Science Foundation for research support.

1. *An Enquiry Concerning Human Understanding,* Section VII.

and another thing to rest an analysis on them. That has not seemed worth while. We have learned all too well that counterfactuals are ill understood, wherefore it did not seem that much understanding could be gained by using them to analyze causation or anything else. Pending a better understanding of counterfactuals, moreover, we had no way to fight seeming counterexamples to a counterfactual analysis.

But counterfactuals need not remain ill understood, I claim, unless we cling to false preconceptions about what it would be like to understand them. Must an adequate understanding make no reference to unactualized possibilities? Must it assign sharply determinate truth conditions? Must it connect counterfactuals rigidly to covering laws? Then none will be forthcoming. So much the worse for those standards of adequacy. Why not take counterfactuals at face value: as statements about possible alternatives to the actual situation, somewhat vaguely specified, in which the actual laws may or may not remain intact? There are now several such treatments of counterfactuals, differing only in details. If they are right, then sound foundations have been laid for analyses that use counterfactuals.

In this paper, I shall state a counterfactual analysis, not very different from Hume's second definition, of some sorts of causation. Then I shall try to show how this analysis works to distinguish genuine causes from effects, epiphenomena, and preempted potential causes.

My discussion will be incomplete in at least four ways. Explicit preliminary settings-aside may prevent confusion.

1. I shall confine myself to causation among *events*, in the everyday sense of the word: flashes, battles, conversations, impacts, strolls, deaths, touchdowns, falls, kisses, and the like. Not that events are the only things that can cause or be caused; but I have no full list of the others, and no good umbrella-term to cover them all.

2. My analysis is meant to apply to causation in particular cases. It is not an analysis of causal generalizations. Presumably those are quantified statements involving causation among particular events (or non-events), but it turns out not to be easy to match up the causal generalizations of natural language with the available quantified forms. A sentence of the form "c-events cause e-events," for instance, can mean any of

(a) For some c in C and some e in E, c causes e.

(b) For every e in E, there is some c in C such that c causes e.

(c) For every c in C, there is some e in E such that c causes e.

not to mention further ambiguities. Worse still, "Only c-events cause e-events" ought to mean

(d) For every c, if there is some e in E such that c causes e, then c is in C.

if "only" has its usual meaning. But no; it unambiguously means (b) instead! These problems are not about causation, but about our idioms of quantification.

3. We sometimes single out one among all the causes of some event and call it "the" cause, as if there were no others. Or we single out a few as the "causes," calling the rest mere "causal factors" or, "causal conditions." Or we speak of the "decisive" or "real" or "principal" cause. We may select the abnormal or extraordinary causes, or those under human control, or those we deem good or bad, or just those we want to talk about. I have nothing to say about these principles of invidious discrimination. I am concerned with the prior question of what it is to be one of the causes (unselectively speaking). My analysis is meant to capture a broad and nondiscriminatory concept of causation.

4. I shall be content, for now, if I can give an analysis of causation that works properly under determinism. By determinism I do not mean any thesis of universal causation, or universal predictability-in-principle, but rather this: the prevailing laws of nature are such that there do not exist any two possible worlds which are exactly alike up to some time, which differ thereafter, and in which those laws are never violated. Perhaps by ignoring indeterminism I squander the most striking advantage of a counterfactual analysis over a regularity analysis: that it allows undetermined events to be caused. I fear, however, that my present analysis cannot yet cope with all varieties of causation under indeterminism. The needed repair would take us too far into disputed questions about the foundations of probability.

Comparative Similarity

To begin, I take as primitive a relation of *comparative over-all similarity* among possible worlds. We may say that one world is *closer to actuality* than another if the first resembles our actual world more than the second does, taking account of all the respects of similarity and difference and balancing them off one against another.

(More generally, an arbitrary world w can play the role of our actual world. In speaking of our actual world without knowing just which world is ours, I am in effect generalizing over all worlds. We really need a three-place relation: world w_1 is closer to world w than world w_2 is. I shall henceforth leave this generality tacit.)

I have not said just how to balance the respects of comparison against each other, so I have not said just what our relation of comparative similarity is to be. Not for nothing did I call it primitive. But I have said what *sort* of relation it is, and we are familiar with relations of that sort. We do make judgments of comparative over-all similarity—of people, for instance—by balancing off many respects of similarity and difference. Often our mutual expectations about the weighting factors are definite and accurate enough to permit communication. I shall have more to say later about the way the balance must go in particular cases to make my analysis work. But the vagueness of over-all similarity will not be entirely resolved. Nor should it be. The vagueness of similarity does infect causation, and no correct analysis can deny it.

The respects of similarity and difference that enter into the over-all similarity of worlds are many and varied. In particular, similarities in matters of particular fact trade off against similarities of law. The prevailing laws of nature are important to the character of a world; so similarities of law are weighty. Weighty, but not sacred. We should not take it for granted that a world that conforms perfectly to our actual laws is *ipso facto* closer to actuality than any world where those laws are violated in any way at all. It depends on the nature and extent of the violation, on the place of the violated laws in the total system of laws of nature, and on the countervailing similarities and differences in other respects. Likewise, similarities or differences of particular fact may be more or less weighty, depending on their nature and ex-

tent. Comprehensive and exact similarities of particular fact throughout large spatiotemporal regions seem to have special weight. It may be worth a small miracle to prolong or expand a region of perfect match.

Our relation of comparative similarity should meet two formal constraints. (1) It should be a weak ordering of the worlds: an ordering in which ties are permitted, but any two worlds are comparable. (2) Our actual world should be closest to actuality, resembling itself more than any other world resembles it. We do *not* impose the further constraint that for any set A of worlds there is a unique closest A-world, or even a set of A-worlds tied for closest. Why not an infinite sequence of closer and closer A-worlds, but no closest?

Counterfactuals and Counterfactual Dependence

Given any two propositions A and C, we have their *counterfactual* $A \,\square\!\!\rightarrow C$: the proposition that if A were true, then C would also be true. The operation $\square\!\!\rightarrow$ is defined by a rule of truth, as follows. $A \,\square\!\!\rightarrow C$ is true (at a world w) iff either (1) there are no possible A-worlds (in which case $A \,\square\!\!\rightarrow C$ is *vacuous*), or (2) some A-world where C holds is closer (to w) than is any A-world where C does not hold. In other words, a counterfactual is nonvacuously true iff it takes less of a departure from actuality to make the consequent true along with the antecedent than it does to make the antecedent true without the consequent.

We did not assume that there must always be one or more closest A-worlds. But if there are, we can simplify: $A \,\square\!\!\rightarrow C$ is nonvacuously true iff C holds at all the closest A-worlds.

We have not presupposed that A is false. If A is true, then our actual world is the closest A-world, so $A \,\square\!\!\rightarrow C$ is true iff C is. Hence $A \,\square\!\!\rightarrow C$ implies the material conditional $A \supset C$; and A and C jointly imply $A \,\square\!\!\rightarrow C$.

Let $A_1, A_2, \ldots$ be a family of possible propositions, no two of which are compossible; let $C_1, C_2, \ldots$ be another such family (of equal size). Then if all the counterfactuals $A_1 \,\square\!\!\rightarrow C_1, A_2 \,\square\!\!\rightarrow C_2, \ldots$ between corresponding propositions in the two families are true, we shall say that the C's *depend counterfactually* on the A's. We can say it like this in ordinary language: whether C_1 or C_2 or ... depends (counterfactually) on whether A_1 or A_2 or....

Counterfactual dependence between large families of alternatives is characteristic of processes of measurement, perception, or control. Let $R_1, R_2, \ldots$ be propositions specifying the alternative readings of a certain barometer at a certain time. Let $P_1, P_2, \ldots$ specify the corresponding pressures of the surrounding air. Then, if the barometer is working properly to measure the pressure, the R's must depend counterfactually on the P's. As we say it: the reading depends on the pressure. Likewise, if I am seeing at a certain time, then my visual impressions must depend counterfactually, over a wide range of alternative possibilities, on the scene before my eyes. And if I am in control over what happens in some respect, then there must be a double counterfactual dependence, again over some fairly wide range of alternatives. The outcome depends on what I do, and that in turn depends on which outcome I want.

Causal Dependence among Events

If a family $C_1, C_2, \ldots$ depends counterfactually on a family $A_1, A_2, \ldots$ in the sense just explained, we will ordinarily be willing to speak also of causal dependence. We say, for instance, that the barometer reading depends causally on the pressure, that my visual impressions depend causally on the scene before my eyes, or that the outcome of something under my control depends causally on what I do. But there are exceptions. Let G_1, $G_2, \ldots$ be alternative possible laws of gravitation, differing in the value of some numerical constant. Let M_1, $M_2, \ldots$ be suitable alternative laws of planetary motion. Then the M's may depend counterfactually on the G's, but we would not call this dependence causal. Such exceptions as this, however, do not involve any sort of dependence among distinct particular events. The hope remains that causal dependence among events, at least, may be analyzed simply as counterfactual dependence.

We have spoken thus far of counterfactual dependence among propositions, not among events. Whatever particular events may be, presumably they are not propositions. But that is no problem, since they can at least be paired with propositions. To any possible event e, there corresponds the proposition $O(e)$ that holds at all and only those worlds where e occurs. This $O(e)$ is the proposition that e occurs.[2] (If no two events occur at exactly the same worlds—if, that is, there are no absolutely necessary connections between distinct events—we may add that this correspondence of events and propositions is one to one.) Counterfactual dependence among events is simply counterfactual dependence among the corresponding propositions.

Let $c_1, c_2, \ldots$ and $e_1, e_2, \ldots$ be distinct possible events such that no two of the c's and no two of the e's are compossible. Then I say that the family $e_1, e_2, \ldots$ of events depends causally on the family $c_1, c_2, \ldots$ iff the family $O(e_1)$, $O(e_2), \ldots$ of propositions depends counterfactually on the family $O(c_1), O(c_2), \ldots$ As we say it: whether e_1 or e_2 or ... occurs depends on whether c_1 or c_2 or ... occurs.

---

2. Beware: if we refer to a particular event e by means of some description that e satisfies, then we must take care not to confuse $O(e)$, the proposition that e itself occurs, with the different proposition that some event or other occurs which satisfies the description. It is a contingent matter, in general, what events satisfy what descriptions. Let e be the death of Socrates—the death he actually died, to be distinguished from all the different deaths he might have died instead. Suppose that Socrates had fled, only to be eaten by a lion. Then e would not have occurred, and $O(e)$ would have been false; but a different event would have satisfied the description "the death of Socrates" that I used to refer to e. Or suppose that Socrates had lived and died just as he actually did, and afterwards was resurrected and killed again and resurrected again, and finally became immortal. Then no event would have satisfied the description. (Even if the temporary deaths are real deaths, neither of the two can be *the* death.) But e would have occurred, and $O(e)$ would have been true. Call a description of an event e *rigid* iff (1) nothing but e could possibly satisfy it, and (2) e could not possibly occur without satisfying it. I have claimed that even such commonplace descriptions as "the death of Socrates" are nonrigid, and in fact I think that rigid descriptions of events are hard to find. That would be a problem for anyone who needed to associate with every possible event e a sentence $\Phi(e)$ true at all and only those worlds where e occurs. But we need no such sentences—only propositions, which may or may not have expressions in our language.

We can also define a relation of dependence among single events rather than families. Let c and e be two distinct possible particular events. Then e *depends causally* on c iff the family $O(e), \sim O(e)$ depends counterfactually on the family $O(c), \sim O(c)$. As we say it: whether e occurs or not depends on whether c occurs or not. The dependence consists in the truth of two couterfactuals: $O(c) \,\Box\!\!\rightarrow O(e)$ and $\sim O(c) \,\Box\!\!\rightarrow O(e)$. There are two cases. If c and e do not actually occur, then the second counterfactual is automatically true because its antecedent and consequent are true: so e depends causally on c iff the first counterfactual holds. That is, iff e would have occurred if c had occurred. But if c and e are actual events, then it is the first counterfactual that is automatically true. Then e depends causally on c iff, if c had not been, e never had existed. I take Hume's second definition as my definition not of causation itself, but of causal dependence among actual events.

Causation

Causal dependence among actual events implies causation. If c and e are two actual events such that e would not have occurred without c, then c is a cause of e. But I reject the converse. Causation must always be transitive; causal dependence may not be; so there can be causation without causal dependence. Let c, d, and e be three actual events such that d would not have occurred without c and e would not have occurred without d. Then c is a cause of e even if e would still have occurred (otherwise caused) without c.

We extend causal dependence to a transitive relation in the usual way. Let $c, d, e, \ldots$ be a finite sequence of actual particular events such that d depends causally on c, e on d, and so on throughout. Then this sequence is a *causal chain*. Finally, one event is a *cause* of another iff there exists a causal chain leading from the first to the second. This completes my counterfactual analysis of causation.

Counterfactual versus Nomic Dependence

It is essential to distinguish counterfactual and causal dependence from what I shall call *nomic dependence*. The family $C_1, C_2, \ldots$ of propositions depends nomically on the family $A_1, A_2, \ldots$ iff there are a nonempty set $\mathfrak{L}$ of true law-propositions and a set $\mathfrak{J}$ of true propositions of particular fact such that $\mathfrak{L}$ and $\mathfrak{J}$ jointly imply (but $\mathfrak{J}$ alone does not imply) all the material conditionals $A_1 \supset C_1, A_2 \supset C_2, \ldots$ between the corresponding propositions in the two families. (Recall that these same material conditionals are implied by the counterfactuals that would comprise a counterfactual dependence.) We shall say also that the nomic dependence holds in *virtue* of the premise sets $\mathfrak{L}$ and $\mathfrak{J}$.

Nomic and counterfactual dependence are related as follows. Say that a proposition B is *counterfactually independent* of the family $A_1, A_2, \ldots$ of alternatives iff B would hold no matter which of the A's were true— that is, iff the counterfactuals $A_1 \,\Box\!\!\rightarrow B, A_2 \,\Box\!\!\rightarrow B, \ldots$ all hold. If the C's depend nomically on the A's in virtue of the premise sets $\mathfrak{L}$ and $\mathfrak{J}$, and if in addition (all members of) $\mathfrak{L}$ and $\mathfrak{J}$ are counterfactually independent of the A's, then it follows that the C's depend counterfactually on the A's. In that case, we may regard the nomic dependence in virtue of $\mathfrak{L}$ and $\mathfrak{J}$ as explaining the counterfactual dependence. Often, perhaps always, counterfactual dependences may be thus explained. But the requirement of counterfactual independence is indispensable. Unless $\mathfrak{L}$ and $\mathfrak{J}$ meet that requirement, nomic dependence in virtue of $\mathfrak{L}$ and $\mathfrak{J}$ does not imply counterfactual dependence, and, if there is counterfactual dependence anyway, does not explain it.

Nomic dependence is reversible, in the following sense. If the family $C_1, C_2, \ldots$ depends nomically on the family $A_1, A_2, \ldots$ in virtue of $\mathfrak{L}$ and $\mathfrak{J}$, then also $A_1, A_2, \ldots$ depends nomically on the family $AC_1, AC_2, \ldots$ in virtue of $\mathfrak{L}$ and $\mathfrak{J}$, where A is the disjunction $A_1 \vee A_2 \vee \ldots$. Is counterfactual dependence likewise reversible? That does not follow. For, even if $\mathfrak{L}$ and $\mathfrak{J}$ are independent of $A_1, A_2, \ldots$ and hence establish the counterfactual dependence of the C's on the A's, still they may fail to be independent of $AC_1, AC_2, \ldots$, and hence may fail to establish the reverse counterfactual dependence of the A's on the AC's. Irreversible counterfactual dependence is shown below: @ is our actual world, the dots are the other worlds, and distance on the page represents similarity "distance".

$$A_2 \qquad A_1 \qquad A_3$$

$$\bullet \quad \bullet \quad @ \quad \bullet \quad \bullet$$

$$C_2 \qquad C_1 \qquad C_3$$

The counterfactuals $A_1 \ \Box\!\!\rightarrow C_1$, $A_2 \ \Box\!\!\rightarrow C_2$, and A_3 $\Box\!\!\rightarrow C_3$ hold at the actual world; wherefore the C's depend on the A's. But we do not have the reverse dependence of the A's on the AC's, since instead of the needed $AC_2 \ \Box\!\!\rightarrow A_2$ and $AC_3 \ \Box\!\!\rightarrow A_3$ we have AC_2 $\Box\!\!\rightarrow A_1$ and $AC_3 \ \Box\!\!\rightarrow A_1$.

Just such irreversibility is commonplace. The barometer reading depends counterfactually on the pressure—that is as clear-cut as counterfactuals ever get—but does the pressure depend counterfactually on the reading? If the reading had been higher, would the pressure have been higher? Or would the barometer have been malfunctioning? The second sounds better: a higher reading would have been an incorrect reading. To be sure, there are actual laws and circumstances that imply and explain the actual accuracy of the barometer, but these are no more sacred than the actual laws and circumstances that imply and explain the actual pressure. Less sacred, in fact. When something must give way to permit a higher reading, we find it less of a departure from actuality to hold the pressure fixed and sacrifice the accuracy, rather than vice versa. It is not hard to see why. The barometer, being more localized and more delicate than the weather, is more vulnerable to slight departures from actuality.[3]

We can now explain why regularity analyses of causation (among events, under determinism) work as well as they do. Suppose that event c causes event e according to the sample regularity analysis that I gave at the beginning of this paper, in virtue of premise sets $\mathfrak{L}$ and $\mathfrak{J}$. It follows that $\mathfrak{L}$, $\mathfrak{J}$ and $\sim O(c)$ jointly do not imply $O(e)$. Strengthen this: suppose further that they do imply $\sim O(e)$. If so, the family $O(e)$, $\sim O(e)$ depends nomically on the family $O(c)$, $\sim O(c)$ in virtue of $\mathfrak{L}$ and $\mathfrak{J}$. Add one more supposition: that $\mathfrak{L}$ and $\mathfrak{J}$ are counterfactually independent of $O(c)$, $\sim O(c)$. Then it follows according to my counterfactual analysis that e depends counterfactually and causally on c, and hence that c causes e. if I am right, the regularity analysis gives conditions that are almost but not quite sufficient for explicable causal dependence. That is not quite the same thing as causation; but causation without causal dependence is scarce, and if there is inexplicable causal dependence we are (understandably!) unaware of it.[4]

Effects and Epiphenomena

I return now to the problems I raised against regularity analyses, hoping to show that my counterfactual analysis can overcome them.

The *problem of effects,* as it confronts a counterfactual analysis, is as follows. Suppose that c causes a subsequent event e, and that e does not also cause c. (I do not rule out closed causal loops a priori, but this case is not to be one.) Suppose further that, given the laws and some of the actual circumstances, c could not have failed to cause e. It seems to follow that if the effect e had not occurred, then its cause c would not have occurred. We have a spurious reverse causal dependence of c on e, contradicting our supposition that e did not cause c.

The *problem of epiphenomena,* for a counterfactual analysis, is similar. Suppose that e is an epiphenomenal effect of a genuine cause c of an effect f. That is, c causes first e and then f, but e does not cause f. Suppose further that, given the laws and some of the actual circumstances, c could not have failed to cause e; and that, given the laws and others of the circumstances, f could

---

3. Granted, there are contexts or changes of wording that would incline us the other way. For some reason, "If the reading had been higher, that would have been because the pressure was higher" invites my assent more than "If the reading had been higher, the pressure would have been higher." The counterfactuals from readings to pressures are much less clear-cut than those from pressures to readings. But it is enough that some legitimate resolutions of vagueness give an irreversible dependence of readings on pressures. Those are the resolutions we want at present, even if they are not favored in all contexts.

---

4. I am not here proposing a repaired regularity analysis. The repaired analysis would gratuitously rule out inexplicable causal dependence, which seems bad. Nor would it be squarely in the tradition of regularity analyses any more. Too much else would have been added.

not have been caused otherwise than by *c*. It seems to follow that if the epiphenomenon *e* had not occurred, then its cause *c* would not have occurred and the further effect *f* of that same cause would not have occurred either. We have a spurious causal dependence of *f* on *e*, contradicting our supposition that *e* did not cause *f*.

One might be tempted to solve the problem of effects by brute force: insert into the analysis a stipulation that a cause must always precede its effect (and perhaps a parallel stipulation for causal dependence). I reject this solution. (1) It is worthless against the closely related problem of epiphenomena, since the epiphenomenon *e* does precede its spurious effect *f*. (2) It rejects a priori certain legitimate physical hypotheses that posit backward or simultaneous causation. (3) It trivializes any theory that seeks to define the forward direction of time as the predominant direction of causation.

The proper solution to both problems, I think, is flatly to deny the counterfactuals that cause the trouble. If *e* had been absent, it is not that *c* would have been absent (and with it *f*, in the second case). Rather, *c* would have occurred just as it did but would have failed to cause *e*. It is less of a departure from actuality to get rid of *e* by holding *c* fixed and giving up some or other of the laws and circumstances in virtue of which *c* could not have failed to cause *e*, rather than to hold those laws and circumstances fixed and get rid of *e* by going back and abolishing its cause *c*. (In the second case, it would of course be pointless not to hold *f* fixed along with *c*.) The causal dependence of *e* on *c* is the same sort of irreversible counterfactual dependence that we have considered already.

To get rid of an actual event *e* with the least over-all departure from actuality, it will normally be best not to diverge at all from the actual course of events until just before the time of *e*. The longer we wait, the more we prolong the spatiotemporal region of perfect match between our actual world and the selected alternative. Why diverge sooner rather than later? Not to avoid violations of laws of nature. Under determinism *any* divergence, soon or late, requires some violation of the actual laws. If the laws were held sacred, there would be no way to get rid of *e* without changing all of the past; and nothing guarantees that the change could be kept negligible except in the recent past. That would mean that if the present were ever so slightly different, then

all of the past would have been different—which is absurd. So the laws are not sacred. Violation of laws is a matter of degree. Until we get up to the time immediately before *e* is to occur, there is no general reason why a later divergence to avert *e* should need a more severe violation than an earlier one. Perhaps there are special reasons in special cases—but then these may be cases of backward causal dependence.

Preemption

Suppose that c_1 occurs and causes *e*; and that c_2 also occurs and does not cause *e*, but would have caused *e* if c_1 had been absent. Thus c_2 is a potential alternate cause of *e*, but is preempted by the actual cause c_1. We may say that c_1 and c_2 overdetermine *e*, but they do so asymmetrically.[5] In virtue of what difference does c_1 but not c_2 cause *e*?

As far as causal dependence goes, there is no difference: *e* depends neither on c_1 nor on c_2. If either one had not occurred, the other would have sufficed to cause *e*. So the difference must be that, thanks to c_1, there is no causal chain from c_2 to *e*; whereas there is a causal chain of two or more steps from c_1 to *e*. Assume for simplicity that two steps are enough. Then *e* depends causally on some intermediate event *d*, and *d* in turn depends on c_1. Causal dependence is here intransitive: c_1 causes *e* via *d* even though *e* would still have occurred without c_1.

So far, so good. It remains only to deal with the objection that *e* does *not* depend causally on *d*, because if *d* had been absent then c_1 would have been absent and c_2, no longer preempted, would have caused *e*. We may reply by denying the claim that if *d* had been absent then c_1 would have been absent. That is the very same sort of spurious reverse dependence of cause on effect that we have just rejected in simpler cases. I rather claim that if *d* had been absent, c_1 would somehow have failed to cause *d*. But c_1 would still have been there to interfere with c_2, so *e* would not have occurred. [. . .]

---

5. I shall not discuss symmetrical cases of overdetermination, in which two overdetermining factors have equal claim to count as causes. For me these are useless as test cases because I lack firm naive opinions about them.

Redundant Causation[6]

Suppose we have two events c_1 and c_2, and another event e distinct from both of them; and in actuality all three occur; and if either one of c_1 and c_2 had occurred without the other, then also e would have occurred; but if neither c_1 nor c_2 had occurred, then e would not have occurred. Then I shall say that c_1 and c_2 are *redundant causes* of e.

(There might be redundant causation with a set of more than two redundant causes. There might be probabilistic redundant causation, in which e would have had some small chance of occurring even if neither c_1 nor c_2 had occurred. There might be stepwise redundant causation without direct dependence, as described by Louis Loeb.[7] I pass over these complications and consider redundant causation in its simplest form.)

As in my definition of ordinary causation, the counterfactuals concern particular events, not event-kinds. So it is not redundant causation if you shoot a terminal cancer patient—or, for that matter, a healthy young mortal—who would sooner or later have died anyway. Without your act he would have died a different death: numerically different, because very different in time and manner. The particular event which is the death he actually dies would not have occurred. If you shoot a man who is being stalked by seven other gunmen, that *may* be redundant causation—the answer depends partly on details of the underdescribed case, partly on unsettled standards of how much difference it takes to make a different event. If you shoot a man who is simultaneously being shot by seven other members of your firing squad, that doubtless is redundant causation. The exact number of bullets through the heart matters little.

If one event is a redundant cause of another, then is it a cause *simpliciter*? Sometimes yes, it seems; sometimes no; and sometimes it is not clear one way or the other. When common sense delivers a firm and uncontroversial answer about a not-too-far-fetched case, theory had

better agree. If an analysis of causation does not deliver the common-sense answer, that is bad trouble. But when common sense falls into indecision or controversy, or when it is reasonable to suspect that far-fetched cases are being judged by false analogy to commonplace ones, then theory may safely say what it likes. Such cases can be left as spoils to the victor, in D. M. Armstrong's phrase. We can reasonably accept as true whatever answer comes from the analysis that does best on the clearer cases. It would be still better, however, if theory itself went indecisive about the hard cases. If an analysis says that the answer for some hard case depends on underdescribed details, or on the resolution of some sort of vagueness, that would explain nicely why common sense comes out indecisive.

I distinguished one kind of case—preemption with chains of dependence—in which common sense delivers clear positive and negative answers, and my counterfactual analysis succeeds in agreeing. I left all other cases of redundant causation as spoils to the victor, doubting that common-sense opinions about them would be firm and uncontroversial enough to afford useful tests of the analysis.

Now I would distinguish more varieties of redundant causation. Sometimes my analysis, as it stands, agrees with clear common-sense answers, positive or negative. Sometimes it reproduces common-sense indecision. Sometimes I am still content to leave far-fetched cases as spoils to the victor. But sometimes it seems that additions to my original analysis are needed.

I consider first a class of cases distinguished by doubt as to whether they exhibit redundant causation at all. I have already mentioned one example: you shoot a man who is being stalked by seven other gunmen. As it actually happens, the man dies on Tuesday morning, face down on the ground, his heart pierced by your bullet, with an entry wound in his back and an exit wound in his chest. Without your act he would have died on Wednesday evening, slumped in a chair, his heart pierced by someone else's bullet, with an entry wound in his chest and an exit wound in his back.

Is it that without your act he would have died a different death—numerically different because somewhat different in time and manner? If so, there is no redundancy. The particular death he actually died depends counterfactually on your act, without which that very

6. In this postscript I am much indebted to discussion with John Bigelow, with John Etchemendy, and with Louis Loeb.

7. "Causal Theories and Causal Overdetermination," *Journal of Philosophy* 71 (1974), 525–44.

event would not have occurred. This is straightforward causation. Or is it rather that without your act he would have died the very same death—numerically the same, despite slight differences in time and manner? If so, there is genuine redundancy. In that case your act would be a redundant cause; whether it would be a cause *simpliciter* awaits our discussion of the varieties of genuine redundant causation.

It is hard to say which is true. It would remain hard, I think, no matter how fully we described the details of what actually happened, and of what would have happened under our counterfactual hypothesis.

Here is another example. Suppose three neurons are hooked up thus.

Suppose that a neuron fires if stimulated by the firing of one or more other neurons connected to it by a stimulatory synapse (shown by a forward arrowhead). But suppose—fictitiously, I believe—that a neuron fires much more vigorously if it is doubly stimulated than if it is singly stimulated. Neurons C_1 and C_2 fire simultaneously, thereby doubly stimulating E, which fires vigorously. Is this vigorous firing of E a different event from the feeble firing that would have occurred if either one of C_1 and C_2 had fired alone? Then we have joint causation, in which the effect depends counterfactually on each of the causes, and there is no redundancy. Or is it that numerically the same firing would have occurred, despite a difference in manner, with single stimulation? Then we have redundant causation. Again it is hard to say, and again the difficulty cannot be blamed on underdescription of the details.

Call an event *fragile* if, or to the extent that, it could not have occurred at a different time, or in a different manner. A fragile event has a rich essence; it has stringent conditions of occurrence. In both our examples we have redundant causation if the effect is not too fragile, ordinary causal dependence on joint causes otherwise.

Don't say: here we have *the events*—how fragile are *they*? Instead it should be: here we have various candidates, some more fragile and some less—which ones do we call the events? [. . .] Properly posed, the question need not have a fully determinate answer, settled once and for all. Our standards of fragility might be both vague and shifty.

As of course they are. You can say: the performance should have been postponed until the singer was over his laryngitis; then *it* would have been better. You can just as well say, and mean nothing different: the performance should have been cancelled, and another, which would have been better, scheduled later to replace it. There's no right answer to the question how fragile the performance is. Not because there is something—the performance—with an indeterminate size in logical space! But because there are various things, with various sizes, and we haven't troubled to decide which one is "the performance." Likewise every region of the earth has exact boundaries and a determinate size. Silicon Valley, whatever exactly that is, is no exception. However we haven't decided exactly how big a region is called "Silicon Valley." That's why there's no right answer to the question whether these words (written on the Stanford campus) were written in Silicon Valley.

So there may be no right answer to the question whether we have a case of joint causation without redundancy; or whether instead we have a case of redundant causation, which might or might not count as causation according to considerations to be discussed later. The answer depends on the resolution of vague standards of fragility. If common sense falls into indecision and controversy over such cases, that is only to be expected.

It is a common suggestion to adopt extreme standards of fragility, and thereby make away with redundant causation altogether. Even if a man is shot dead by a firing squad, presumably it would have made *some* minute difference to the time and manner of his death there had been seven bullets instead of eight. So if you fired one of the eight bullets, that made some difference; so if his death is taken to be very fragile indeed, then it would not have occurred without your act. Under sufficiently extreme standards of fragility, the redundancy vanishes. Even this turns out to be a case in which the effect depends on each of several joint causes. Likewise for other stock examples of redundancy. [. . .]

Wesley Salmon

Why Ask "Why?"

An Inquiry Concerning Scientific Explanation[1]

Concerning the first order question "Why?" I have raised the second order question "Why ask, 'Why?'?" to which you might naturally respond with the third order question "Why ask, 'Why ask, "Why?"?" But this way lies madness, to say nothing of an infinite regress. While an infinite sequence of nested intervals may converge upon a point, the series of nested questions just initiated has no point to it, and so we had better cut it off without delay. The answer to the very natural third order question is this: the question "Why ask, 'Why?'?" expresses a deep philosophical perplexity which I believe to be both significant in its own right and highly relevant to certain current philosophical discussions. I want to share it with you.

The problems I shall be discussing pertain mainly to scientific explanation, but before turning to them, I should remark that I am fully aware that many—perhaps—most why-questions are requests for some sort of *justification* (Why did one employee receive a larger raise than another?—Because she had been paid less than a male colleague for doing the same kind of job.) or *consolation* (Why, asked Job, was I singled out for such extraordinary misfortune and suffering?). Since I have neither the time nor the talent to deal with questions of this sort, I shall not pursue them further, except to remark that the seeds of endless philosophical confusion can be sown by failing carefully to distinguish them from requests for scientific explanation.

Let me put the question I do want to discuss to you this way. Suppose you had achieved the epistemic status of Laplace's demon—the hypothetical super-intelligence who knows all of nature's regularities, and the precise state of the universe in full detail at some particular moment (say now, according to some suitable simultaneity slice of the universe). Possessing the requisite logical and mathematical skill, you would be able to predict any future occurrence, and you would be able to retrodict any past event. Given this sort of apparent omniscience, would your scientific knowledge be complete, or would it still leave something to be desired? Laplace asked no more of his demon; should we place further demands upon ourselves? And if so, what should be the nature of the additional demands?

If we look at most contemporary philosophy of science texts, we find an immediate *affirmative* answer to this question. Science, the majority say, has at least two principal aims—prediction (construed broadly enough to include inference from the observed to the unobserved, regardless of temporal relations) and explanation. The first of these provides knowledge of *what* happens; the second is supposed to furnish knowledge of *why* things happen as they do. This is not a new idea. In the *Posterior Analytics,* Aristotle distinguishes syllogisms which provide scientific understanding from those which do not.[2] In the Port Royal Logic, Arnauld distinguishes demonstrations which merely convince the mind from those which also enlighten the mind.[3]

This view has not been universally adopted. It was not long ago that we often heard statements to the effect that the business of science is to predict, not to explain. Scientific knowledge is descriptive—it tells us *what* and *how*. If we seek explanations—if we want to know why—we must go outside of science, perhaps to

Wesley Salmon, "Why Ask 'Why?'" from *Proceedings and Address of the American Philosophical Association,* 51 (1978). Reprinted with permission of the American Philosophical Association.

1. The author wishes to express his gratitude to the National Science Foundation for support of research on scientific explanation.

2. Book I.2, 71b, 17–24.

3. Antoine Arnauld, *The Art of Thinking* (Indianapolis: Bobbs-Merrill, 1964), p. 330.

metaphysics or theology. In his Preface to the Third Edition (1911) of *The Grammar of Science,* Karl Pearson wrote, "Nobody believes now that science *explains* anything; we all look upon it as a shorthand description, as an economy of thought."[4] This doctrine is not very popular nowadays. It is now fashionable to say that science aims not merely at describing the world—it also provides *understanding, comprehension,* and *enlightenment.* Science presumably accomplishes such high-sounding goals by supplying scientific explanations.

The current attitude leaves us with a deep and perplexing question, namely, if explanation does involve something over and above mere description, just what sort of thing is it? The use of such honorific near-synonyms as "understanding," "comprehension," and "enlightenment" makes it sound important and desirable, but does not help at all in the philosophical analysis of explanation—scientific or other. What, over and above its complete descriptive knowledge of the world, would Laplace's demon require in order to achieve understanding? I hope you can see that this is a real problem, especially for those who hold what I shall call "the inferential view" of scientific explanation, for Laplace's demon can infer every fact about the universe, past, present, and future. If the problem does not seem acute, I would quote a remark made by Russell about Zeno's paradox of the flying arrow—"The more the difficulty is meditated, the more real it becomes."[5]

It is not my intention to discuss the details of the various formal models of scientific explanation which have been advanced in the last three decades. Instead, I want to consider the general conceptions which lie beneath the most influential theories of scientific explanation. Two powerful intuitions seem to have guided much of the discussion. Although they have given rise to disparate basic conceptions and considerable controversy, both are, in my opinion, quite sound. Moreover, it seems to me, both can be incorporated into a single overall theory of scientific explanation.

(1) The first of these intuitions is the notion that the explanation of a phenomenon essentially involves *locating and identifying its cause or causes.* This intuition seems to arise rather directly from common sense, and from various contexts in which scientific knowledge is applied to concrete situations. It is strongly supported by a number of paradigms, the most convincing of which are explanations of particular occurrences. To explain a given airplane crash, for example, we seek "the cause"— a mechanical failure, perhaps, or pilot error. To explain a person's death again we seek the cause—strangulation or drowning, for instance. I shall call the general view of scientific explanation which comes more or less directly from this fundamental intuition *the causal conception;* Michael Scriven has been one of its chief advocates.[6]

(2) The second of these basic intuitions is the notion that all scientific explanation involves *subsumption under laws.* This intuition seems to arise from consideration of developments in theoretical science. It has led to the general "covering law" conception of explanation, as well as to several formal "models" of explanation. According to this view, a fact is subsumed under one or more general laws if the assertion of its occurrence follows, either deductively or inductively, from statements of the laws (in conjunction, in some cases, with other premises). Since this view takes explanations to be arguments, I shall call it *the inferential conception;* Carl G. Hempel has been one of its ablest champions.[7]

Although the proponents of this inferential conception have often chosen to illustrate it with explanations of particular occurrences—e.g., why did the bunsen flame turn yellow on this particular occasion?—the paradigms which give it strongest support are explanations of general regularities. When we look to the history of science for the most outstanding cases of scientific explanations, such examples as Newton's explanation of Kepler's laws of planetary motion or Maxwell's electromagnetic explanation of optical phenomena come immediately to mind.

---

4. Karl Pearson, *The Grammar of Science,* 3rd ed. (New York: Meridian Books, 1957), p. xi.

5. Bertrand Russell, *Our Knowledge of the External World* (London: George Allen & Unwin Ltd., 1922), p. 179.

6. See, for example, his recent paper, "Causation as Explanation," *Nous,* Vol. 9 (1975), pp. 3–16.

7. Carl G. Hempel, "Aspects of Scientific Explanation," in *Aspects of Scientific Explanation and Other Essays in the Philosophy of Science* (New York: Free Press, 1965), pp. 331–496.

It is easy to guess how Laplace might have reacted to my question about his demon, and to the two basic intuitions I have just mentioned. The super-intelligence would have everything needed to provide scientific explanations. When, to mention one of Laplace's favorite examples, a seemingly haphazard phenomenon, such as the appearance of a comet, occurs, it can be explained by showing that it actually conforms to natural laws. On Laplace's assumption of determinism, the demon possesses explanations of all happenings in the entire history of the world—past, present, and future. Explanation, for Laplace, seemed to consist in showing how events conform to the laws of nature, and these very laws provide the causal connections among the various states of the world. The Laplacian version of explanation thus seems to conform both to the causal conception and to the inferential conception.

Why, you might well ask, is not the Laplacian view of scientific explanation basically sound? Why do twentieth century philosophers find it necessary to engage in lengthy disputes over this matter? There are, I think, three fundamental reasons: (1) the causal conception faces the difficulty that no adequate treatment of causation has yet been offered; (2) the inferential conception suffers from the fact that it seriously misconstrues the nature of subsumption under laws; and (3) both conceptions have overlooked a central explanatory principle.

The inferential view, as elaborated in detail by Hempel and others, has been the dominant theory of scientific explanation in recent years—indeed, it has become virtually "the received view." From that standpoint, anyone who had attained the epistemic status of Laplace's demon could use the known laws and initial conditions to predict a future event, and when the event comes to pass, the argument which enabled us to predict it would ipso facto constitute an explanation of it. If, as Laplace believed, determinism is true, then every *future* event would thus be amenable to deductive-nomological explanation.

When, however, we consider the explanation of past events—events which occurred earlier than our initial conditions—we find a strange disparity. Although, by applying known laws, we can reliably *retrodict* any past occurrence on the basis of facts subsequent to the event, our intuitions rebel at the idea that we can *explain* events

in terms of subsequent conditions. Thus, although our inferences to future events qualify as explanations according to the inferential conception, our inferences to the past do not. Laplace's demon can, of course, construct explanations of past events by inferring the existence of still earlier conditions and, with the aid of the known laws, deducing the occurrence of the events to be explained from these conditions which held in the more remote past. But if, as the inferential conception maintains, explanations are essentially inferences, such an approach to explanation of past events seems strangely roundabout. Explanations demand an asymmetry not present in inferences.

When we drop the fiction of Laplace's demon, and relinquish the assumption of determinism, the asymmetry becomes even more striking. The demon can predict the future and retrodict the past with complete precision and reliability. We cannot. When we consider the comparative difficulty of prediction vs. retrodiction, it turns out that retrodiction enjoys a tremendous advantage. We have records of the past—tree rings, diaries, fossils—but none of the future. As a result, we can have extensive and detailed knowledge of the past which has no counterpart in knowledge about the future. From a newspaper account of an accident, we can retrodict all sorts of details which could not have been predicted an hour before the collision. But the newspaper story—even though it may *report* the explanation of the accident—surely does not *constitute* the explanation. We see that *inference* has a preferred temporal direction, and that *explanation* also has a preferred temporal direction. The fact that these two are opposite to each other is one thing which makes me seriously doubt that explanations are essentially arguments. As we shall see, however, denying that explanations are arguments does not mean that we must give up the *covering law* conception. Subsumption under laws can take a different form.

Although the Laplacian conception bears strong similarities to the received view, there is a fundamental difference which must be noted. Laplace evidently believed that the explanations provided by his demon would be *causal explanations,* and the laws invoked would be *causal laws.* Hempel's deductive-nomological explanations are often casually called "causal explanations," but this is not accurate. Hempel explicitly notes that some laws, such as the ideal gas law,

$$PV = nRT$$

are non-causal. This law states a mathematical functional relationship among several quantities—pressure *P*, volume *V*, temperature *T*, number of moles of gas *n*, universal gas constant *R*—but gives no hint as to how a change in one of the values would lead causally to changes in others. As far as I know, Laplace did not make any distinction between causal and non-causal laws; Hempel has recognized the difference, but he allows non-causal as well as causal laws to function as covering laws in scientific explanations.

This attitude toward non-causal laws is surely too tolerant. If someone inflates an air-mattress of a given size to a certain pressure under conditions which determine the temperature, we can deduce the value of *n*—the amount of air blown into it. The *subsequent* values of pressure, temperature, and volume are thus taken to explain the quantity of air *previously* introduced. Failure to require covering laws to be causal laws leads to a violation of the temporal requirement on explanations. This is not surprising. The asymmetry of explanation is inherited from the asymmetry of causation —namely, that causes precede their effects. At this point, it seems to me, we experience vividly the force of the intuitions underlying the causal conception of scientific explanation.

There is another reason for maintaining that non-causal laws cannot bear the burden of covering laws in scientific explanations. Non-causal regularities, instead of having explanatory force which enables them to provide understanding of events in the world, cry out to be explained. Mariners, long before Newton, were fully aware of the correlation between the behavior of the tides and the position and phase of the moon. But inasmuch as they were totally ignorant of the causal relations involved, they rightly believed that they did not understand why the tides ebb and flow. When Newton provided the gravitational links, understanding was achieved. Similarly, I should say, the ideal gas law had little or no explanatory power until its causal underpinnings were furnished by the molecular-kinetic theory of gases. Keeping this consideration in mind, we realize that we must give at least as much attention to the explanations of regularities as we do to explanations of particular facts. I will argue, moreover, that these regularities demand causal explanation. Again, we must give the causal conception its due.

Having considered a number of preliminaries, I should now like to turn my attention to an attempt to outline a general theory of causal explanation. I shall not be trying to articulate a formal model; I shall be focusing upon general conceptions and fundamental principles rather than technical details. I am not suggesting, of course, that the technical details are dispensable—merely that this is not the time or place to try to go into them. Let me say at the outset that I shall be relying very heavily upon works by Russell (especially, *The Analysis of Matter* and *Human Knowledge, Its Scope and Limits*) and Reichenbach (especially, *The Direction of Time*). Although, to the best of my knowledge, neither of these authors ever published an article, or a book, or a chapter of a book devoted explicitly to scientific explanation, nevertheless, it seems to me that a rather appealing theory of causal explanation can be constructed by putting together the insights expressed in the aforementioned works.

Developments in twentieth-century science should prepare us for the eventuality that some of our scientific explanations will have to be statistical—not merely because our knowledge is incomplete (as Laplace would have maintained), but rather, because nature itself is inherently statistical. Some of the laws used in explaining particular events will be statistical, and some of the regularities we wish to explain will also be statistical. I have been urging that causal considerations play a crucial role in explanation; indeed, I have just said that regularities—and this certainly includes statistical regularities— require causal explanation. I do not believe there is any conflict here. It seems to me that, by employing a statistical conception of causation along the lines developed by Patrick Suppes and Hans Reichenbach,[8] it is possible to fit together harmoniously the causal and statistical factors in explanatory contexts. Let me attempt to illustrate this point by discussing a concrete example.

---

8. Patrick Suppes, *A Probablistic Theory of Causation* (Amsterdam: North-Holland Publishing Co., 1970); Hans Reichenbach, *The Direction of Time* (Berkeley & Los Angeles: University of California Press, 1956), Chap. IV.

A good deal of attention has recently been given in the press to cases of leukemia in military personnel who witnessed an atomic bomb test (code name "Smokey") at close range in 1957. Statistical studies of the survivors of the bombings of Hiroshima and Nagasaki have established the fact that exposure to high levels of radiation, such as occur in an atomic blast, is statistically relevant to the occurrence of leukemia—indeed, that the probability of leukemia is closely correlated with the distance from the explosion. A clear pattern of statistical relevance relations is exhibited here. If a particular person contracts leukemia, this fact may be explained by citing the fact that he was, say, 2 kilometers from the hypocenter at the time of the explosion. This relationship is further explained by the fact that individuals located at specific distances from atomic blasts of specified magnitude receive certain high doses of radiation.

This tragic example has several features to which I should like to call special attention:

(1) The location of the individual at the time of the blast is statistically relevant to the occurrence of leukemia; the probability of leukemia for a person located 2 kilometers from the hypocenter of an atomic blast is radically different from the probability of the disease in the population at large. Notice that the probability of such an individual contracting leukemia is not high; it is much smaller than one-half—indeed, in the case of Smokey it is much less than 1/100. But it is markedly higher than for a random member of the entire human population. It is the *statistical relevance* of exposure to an atomic blast, not a high probability, which has explanatory force. Such examples defy explanation according to an inferential view which requires high inductive probability for statistical explanation.[9] The case of leukemia is subsumed under a statistical regularity, but it does not "follow inductively" from the explanatory facts.

(2) There is a *causal process* which connects the occurrence of the bomb blast with the physiological harm done to people at some distance from the explosion. High energy radiation, released in the nuclear reactions, traverses the space between the blast and the individual. Although some of the details may not yet be known, it is a well-established fact that such radiation does interact with cells in a way which makes them susceptible to leukemia at some later time.

(3) At each end of the causal process—i.e., the transmission of radiation from the bomb to the person—there is a *causal interaction*. The radiation is emitted as a result of a nuclear interaction when the bomb explodes, and it is absorbed by cells in the body of the victim. Each of these interactions may well be irreducibly statistical and indeterministic, but that is no reason to deny that they are causal.

(4) The causal processes begin at a central place, and they travel outward at a finite velocity. A rather complex set of statistical relevance relations is explained by the propagation of a process, or set of processes, from a common central event.

In undertaking a general characterization of causal explanation, we must begin by carefully distinguishing between causal processes and causal interactions. The transmission of light from one place to another, and the motion of a material particle, are obvious examples of causal processes. The collision of two billiard balls, and the emission or absorption of a photon, are standard examples of causal interactions. Interactions are the sorts of things we are inclined to identify as events. Relative to a particular context, an event is comparatively small in its spatial and temporal dimensions; processes typically have much larger durations, and they may be more extended in space as well. A light ray, traveling to earth from a distant star, is a process which covers a large distance and lasts for a long time. What I am calling a "causal process" is similar to what Russell called a "causal line."[10]

When we attempt to identify causal processes, it is of crucial importance to distinguish them from such pseudo-processes as a shadow moving across the landscape. This can best be done, I believe, by invoking Re-

---

9. Hempel's inductive-statistical model, as formulated in "Aspects of Scientific Explanation" (1965) embodied such a high probability requirement, but in "Nachwort 1976" inserted into a German translation of this article *(Aspekte wissenschaftlicher Erklärung,* Walter de Gruyter, 1977) this requirement is retracted.

10. Bertrand Russell, *Human Knowledge, Its Scope and Limits* (New York: Simon and Schuster, 1948), p. 459.

ichenbach's *mark criterion*.[11] Causal processes are capable of propagating marks or modifications imposed upon them; pseudo-processes are not. An automobile traveling along a road is an example of a causal process. If a fender is scraped as a result of a collision with a stone wall, the mark of that collision will be carried on by the car long after the interaction with the wall occurred. The shadow of a car moving along the shoulder is a pseudo-process. If it is deformed as it encounters a stone wall, it will immediately resume its former shape as soon as it passes by the wall. It will not transmit a mark or modification. For this reason, we say that a causal process can transmit information or causal influence; a pseudo-process cannot.

When I say that a causal process has the capability of transmitting a causal influence, it might be supposed that I am introducing precisely the sort of mysterious power Hume warned us against. It seems to me that this danger can be circumvented by employing an adaptation of the "at-at" theory of motion, which Russell used so effectively in dealing with Zeno's paradox of the flying arrow. The flying arrow—which is, by the way, a causal process —gets from one place to another by being *at* the appropriate intermediate points of space *at* the appropriate instants of time. Nothing more is involved in getting *from* one point *to* another. A mark, analogously, can be said to be propagated from the point of interaction at which it is imposed to later stages in the process if it appears *at* the appropriate intermediate stages in the process *at* the appropriate times without additional interactions which regenerate the mark. The precise formulation of this condition is a bit tricky, but I believe the basic idea is simple, and that the details can be worked out.

If this analysis of causal processes is satisfactory, we have an answer to the question, raised by Hume, concerning the connection between cause and effect. If we think of a cause as one event, and of an effect as a distinct event, then the connection between them is simply a spatio-temporally continuous causal process. This sort of answer did not occur to Hume because he did not distinguish between causal processes and causal in-

teractions. When he tried to analyze the connections between distinct events, he treated them as if they were chains of events with discrete links, rather than processes analogous to continuous filaments. I am inclined to attribute considerable philosophical significance to the fact that each link in a chain has adjacent links, while the points in a continuum do not have next-door neighbors. This consideration played an important role in Russell's discussion of Zeno's paradoxes.[12]

After distinguishing between causal interactions and causal processes, and after introducing a criterion by means of which to discriminate the pseudoprocesses from the genuine causal processes, we must consider certain configurations of processes which have special explanatory import. Russell noted that we often find similar structures grouped symmetrically about a center—for example, concentric waves moving across an otherwise smooth surface of a pond, or sound waves moving out from a central region, or perceptions of many people viewing a stage from different seats in a theatre. In such cases, Russell postulates the existence of a central event— a pebble dropped into the pond, a starter's gun going off at a race-track, or a play being performed upon the stage—from which the complex array emanates.[13] It is noteworthy that Russell never suggests that the central event is to be explained on the basis of convergence of influences from remote regions upon that locale.

Reichenbach articulated a closely-related idea in his *principle of the common cause*. If two or more events of certain types occur at different places, but occur at the same time more frequently than is to be expected if they occurred independently, then this apparent coincidence is to be explained in terms of a common causal antecedent.[14] If, for example, all of the electric lights in a particular area go out simultaneously, we do not believe that they just happened by chance to burn out at the same time. We attribute the coincidence to a common cause such as a blown fuse, a downed transmission line, or trouble at the generating station. If all of the students

---

11. Hans Reichenbach, *The Philosophy of Space and Time* (New York: Dover Publications, 1958), Sec. 21.

12. Russell, *Our Knowledge of the External World,* Lecture VI, "The Problem of Infinity Considered Historically."

13. Russell, *Human Knowledge* pp. 460–475.

14. Reichenbach, *The Direction of Time,* Sec. 19.

in a dormitory fall ill on the same night, it is attributed to spoiled food in the meal which all of them ate. Russell's similar structures arranged symmetrically about a center obviously qualify as the sorts of coincidences which require common causes for their explanations.

In order to formulate his common cause principle more precisely, Reichenbach defined what he called a *conjunctive fork*. Suppose we have events of two types, *A* and *B*, which happen in conjunction more often than they would if they were statistically independent of one another. For example, let *A* and *B* stand for colorblindness in two brothers. There is a certain probability that a male, selected from the population at random, will have that affliction, but since it is hereditary, occurrences in male siblings are not independent. The probability that both will have it is greater than the product of the two respective probabilities. In cases of such statistical dependencies, we invoke a common cause *C* which accounts for them; in this case, it is a genetic factor carried by the mother. In order to satisfy the conditions for a conjunctive fork, events of the types *A* and *B* must occur independently in the absence of the common cause *C*—that is, for two unrelated males, the probability of both being colorblind is equal to the product of the two separate probabilities. Furthermore, the probabilities of *A* and *B* must each be increased above their overall values if *C* is present. Clearly the probability of colorblindness is greater in sons of mothers carrying the genetic factor than it is among all male children regardless of the genetic make-up of their mothers. Finally, Reichenbach stipulates, the dependency between *A* and *B* is absorbed into the occurrence of the common cause *C*, in the sense that the probability of *A* and *B* given *C* equals the product of the probability of *A* given *C* and the probability of *B* given *C*. This is true in the colorblindness case. Excluding pairs of identical twins, the question of whether a male child inherits colorblindness from the mother who carries the genetic trait depends only upon the genetic relationship between that child and his mother, not upon whether other sons happened to inherit the trait. Note that screening-off occurs here.[15] While the colorblind-

ness of a brother is statistically relevant to colorblindness in a boy, it becomes irrelevant if the genetic factor is known to be present in the mother.

Reichenbach obviously was not the first philosopher to notice that we explain coincidences in terms of common causal antecedents. Leibniz postulated a pre-established harmony for his windowless monads which mirror the same world, and the occasionalists postulated God as the coordinator of mind and body. Reichenbach was, to the best of my knowledge, the first to give a precise characterization of the conjunctive fork, and to formulate the general principle that conjunctive forks are open only to the future, not to the past.[16] The result is that we cannot explain coincidences on the basis of future effects, but only on the basis of antecedent causes. A widespread blackout is explained by a power failure, not by the looting which occurs as a consequence. (A common effect *E* may form a conjunctive fork with *A* and *B*, but only if there is also a common cause *C*.) The principle that conjunctive forks are not open to the past accounts for Russell's principle that symmetrical patterns emanate from a central source—they do not converge from afar upon the central point. It is also closely related to the operation of the second law of thermodynamics and the increase of entropy in the physical world.

The common cause principle has, I believe, deep explanatory significance. Bas van Fraassen has recently subjected it to careful scrutiny, and he has convinced me that Reichenbach's formulation in terms of the conjunctive fork, as he defined it, is faulty.[17] (We do not, however, agree about the nature of the flaw.) There are, it seems, certain sorts of causal *interactions* in which the resulting effects are more strongly correlated with one another than is allowed in Reichenbach's conjunctive forks. If, for example, an energetic photon collides with an electron in a Compton scattering experiment, there is a certain probability that a photon with a given smaller energy will emerge, and there is a certain probability that the electron will be kicked out with a given

---

15. *C* screens-off *A* from *B* if

$$P(A/C\&B) = P(A/C) \neq P(A/B)$$

---

16. *The Direction of Time,* pp. 162–163.

17. Bas C. van Fraassen, "The Pragmatics of Explanation," *American Philosophical Quarterly,* Vol. 14, No. 2 (April 1977), pp. 143–150.

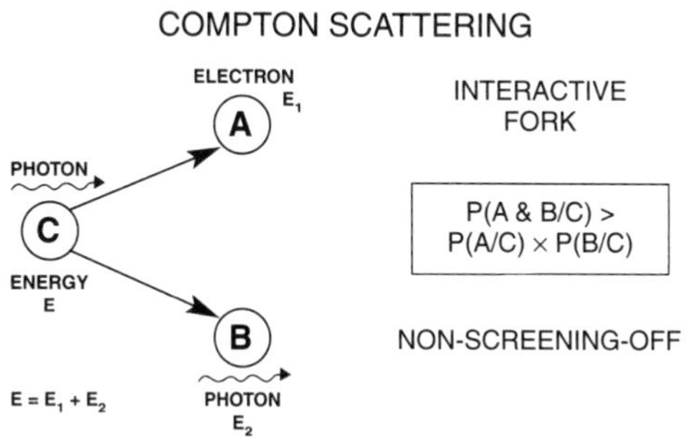

COMPTON SCATTERING

Figure 1

kinetic energy (see Figure 1). However, because of the law of conservation of energy, there is a strong correspondence between the two energies—their sum must be close to the energy of the incident photon. Thus, the probability of getting a photon with energy E_1 and an electron with energy E_2, where $E_1 + E_2$ is approximately equal to E (the energy of the incident photon), is much greater than the product of the probabilities of each energy occurring separately. Assume, for example, that there is a probability of 0.1 that a photon of energy E_1 will emerge if a photon of energy E impinges on a given target, and assume that there is a probability of 0.1 that an electron with kinetic energy E_2 will emerge under the same circumstances (where E, E_1, and E_2 are related as the law of conservation of energy demands). In this case the probability of the joint result is not 0.01, the product of the separate probabilities, but 0.1, for each result will occur if and only if the other does.[18] The same relationships could be illustrated by such macroscopic events as collisions of billiard balls, but I have chosen Compton scattering because there is good reason to believe that events of that type are irreducibly statistical. Given a high energy photon impinging upon the elec-

tron in a given atom, there is no way, even in principle, of predicting with certainty the energies of the photon and electron which result from the interaction.

This sort of interaction stands in sharp contrast with the sort of statistical dependency we have in the leukemia example (see Figure 2, which also represents the relationships in the colorblindness case). In the absence of a strong source of radiation, such as the atomic blast, we may assume that the probability of next-door neighbors contracting the disease equals the product of the probabilities for each of them separately. If, however, we consider two next-door neighbors who lived at a distance of 2 kilometers from the hypocenter of the atomic explosion, the probability of both of them contracting leukemia is much greater than it would be for any two randomly selected members of the population at large. This apparent dependency between the two leukemia cases is not a direct physical dependency between them; it is merely a statistical result of the fact that the probability for each of them has been enhanced independently of the other by being located in close proximity to the atomic explosion. But the individual photons of radiation which impinge upon the two victims are emitted independently, travel independently, and damage living tissues independently.

It thus appears that there are two kinds of causal forks: (1) Reichenbach's *conjunctive forks,* in which the common cause screens-off the one effect from the other, which are exemplified by the colorblindness and leukemia cases, and (2) *interactive forks* exemplified by the Compton scattering of a photon and an electron. In forks of the interactive sort, the common cause does not screen-off the one effect from the other. The probability that the electron will be ejected with kinetic energy E_2 given an incident photon of energy E is *not equal to* the probability that the electron will emerge with energy E_2 given an incident photon of energy E and a scattered photon of energy E_1. In the conjunctive fork, the common cause C absorbs the dependency between the effects A and B, for the probability of A and B given C is *equal to* the product of the probability of A given C and the probability of B given C. In the interactive fork, the common cause C does not absorb the dependency between the effects A and B, for the probability of A and B given C is *greater than* the product of the two separate conditional probabilities.

18. The relation between $E_1 + E_2$ and E is an approximate rather than a precise equality because the ejected electron has some energy of its own before scattering, but this energy is so small compared with the energy of the incident X-ray or γ-ray photon that it can be neglected. When I refer to the probability that the scattered photon and electron will have energies E_1 and E_2 respectively, this should be taken to mean that these energies fall within some specified interval, not that they have exact values.

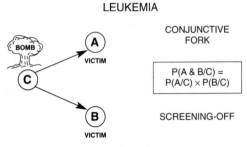

LEUKEMIA

CONJUNCTIVE FORK

$$P(A \& B/C) = P(A/C) \times P(B/C)$$

SCREENING-OFF

Figure 2

Recognition and characterization of the interactive fork enables us to fill a serious lacuna in the treatment up to this point. I have discussed causal processes, indicating roughly how they are to be characterized, and I have mentioned causal interactions, but have said nothing about their characterization. Indeed, the criterion by which we distinguished causal processes from pseudo-processes involved the use of marks, and marks are obviously results of causal interactions. Thus, our account stands in serious need of a characterization of causal interactions, and the interactive fork enables us, I believe, to furnish it.

There is a strong temptation to think of events as basic types of entities, and to construe processes—real or pseudo—as collections of events. This viewpoint may be due, at least in part, to the fact that the space-time interval between events is a fundamental invariant of the special theory of relativity, and that events thus enjoy an especially fundamental status. I suggest, nevertheless, that we reverse the approach. Let us begin with processes (which have not yet been sorted out into causal and pseudo) and look at their intersections. We can be reassured about the legitimacy of this new orientation by the fact that the basic space-time structure of both special relativity and general relativity can be built upon processes without direct recourse to events. An electron traveling through space is a process, and so is a photon; if they collide, that is an intersection. A light pulse traveling from a beacon to a screen is a process, and a piece of red glass standing in the path is another; the light passing through the glass is an intersection. Both of these intersections constitute interactions. If two light beams cross one another, we have an intersection without an interaction—except in the extremely unlikely event of a particle-like collision between photons. What we want to say, very roughly, is that when two processes intersect, and both are modified in such ways that the changes in one are correlated with changes in the other—in the manner of an interactive fork (see Figure 3)—we have a causal interaction. There are technical details to be worked out before we can claim to have a satisfactory account, but the general idea seems clear enough.

I should like to commend the principle of the common cause—so construed as to make reference to both conjunctive forks and interactive forks—to your serious consideration. Several of its uses have already been mentioned and illustrated. *First,* it supplies a schema for the straightforward explanations of everyday sorts of otherwise improbable coincidences. *Second,* it is the source of the fundamental temporal asymmetry of causality, and it accounts for the temporal asymmetry we impose upon scientific explanations. *Third,* it provides the key to the explication of the concept of causal interaction. These considerations certainly testify to its philosophical importance.

There are, however, two additional applications to which I should like to call attention. *Fourth,* as Russell showed, the principle plays a fundamental role in the causal theory of perception. When various observers (including cameras as well as human beings) arranged around a central region, such as a stage in theatre-in-the-round, have perceptions which correspond systematically with one another in the customary way, we may infer, with reasonable reliability, that they have a common cause—namely, a drama being performed on the stage.[19] This fact has considerable epistemological import.

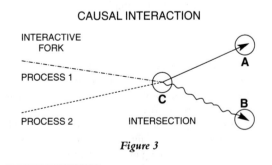

CAUSAL INTERACTION

INTERACTIVE FORK

PROCESS 1

PROCESS 2   INTERSECTION

Figure 3

---

19. Russell, *Human Knowledge,* pp. 491–492.

Fifth, the principle of the common cause can be invoked to support scientific realism. Suppose, going back to a previous example, we have postulated the existence of molecules to provide a causal explanation of the phenomena governed by the ideal gas law. We will naturally be curious about their properties—how large they are, how massive they are, how many there are. An appeal to Brownian motion enables us to infer such things. By microscopic examination of smoke particles suspended in a gas, we can ascertain their average kinetic energies, and since the observed system can be assumed to be in a state of thermal equilibrium, we can immediately infer the average kinetic energies of the molecules of the gas in which the particles are suspended. Since average velocities of the molecules are straightforwardly ascertainable by experiment, we can easily find the masses of the individual molecules, and hence, the number of molecules in a given sample of gas. If the sample consists of precisely one mole (gram molecular weight) of the particular gas, the number of molecules in the sample is Avogadro's number—a fundamental physical constant. Thus, the causal explanation of Brownian motion yields detailed quantitative information about the micro-entities of which the gas is composed.

Now, consider another phenomenon which appears to be of an altogether different sort. If an electric current is passed through an electrolytic solution—for example, one containing a silver salt—a certain amount of metallic silver is deposited on the cathode. The amount deposited is proportional to the amount of electric charge which passes through the solution. In constructing a causal explanation of this phenomenon (known as electrolysis), we postulate that charged ions travel through the solution, and that the amount of charge required to deposit a singly charged ion is equal to the charge on the electron. The magnitude of the electron charge was empirically determined through the work of J. J. Thomson and Robert Millikan. The amount of electric charge required to deposit one mole of a monovalent metal is known as the Faraday, and by experimental determination, it is equal to 96,487 coulombs. When this number is divided by the charge on the electron (-1.602×10^{-19} coulombs), the result is Avogadro's number. Indeed, the Faraday is simply Avogadro's number of electron charges.

The fundamental fact to which I wish to call attention is that the value of Avogadro's number ascertained from the analysis of Brownian motion agrees, within the limits of experimental error, with the value obtained by electrolytic measurement. Without a common causal antecedent, such agreement would constitute a remarkable coincidence. The point may be put in this way. From the molecular kinetic theory of gases we can derive the statement form, "The number of molecules in a mole of gas is _____." From the electro-chemical theory of electrolysis, we can derive the statement form, "The number of electron charges in a Faraday is _____." The astonishing fact is that the same number fills both blanks. In my opinion, the instrumentalist cannot, with impunity, ignore what must be an amazing correspondence between what happens when one scientist is watching smoke particles dancing in a container of gas while another scientist in a different laboratory is observing the electroplating of silver. Without an underlying causal mechanism—of the sort involved in the postulation of atoms, molecules, and ions—the coincidence would be as miraculous as if the number of grapes harvested in California in any given year were equal, up to the limits of observational error, to the number of coffee beans produced in Brazil in the same year. Avogadro's number, I must add, can be ascertained in a variety of other ways as well—e.g., X-ray diffraction from crystals—which also appear to be entirely different unless we postulate the existence of atoms, molecules, and ions. The principle of the common cause thus seems to apply directly to the explanation of observable regularities by appeal to unobservable entities. In this instance, to be sure, the common cause is not some sort of event; it is rather a common constant underlying structure which manifests itself in a variety of different situations.

Let me now summarize the picture of scientific explanation I have tried to outline. If we wish to explain a particular event, such as death by leukemia of GI Joe, we begin by assembling the factors statistically relevant to that occurrence—for example, his distance from the atomic explosion, the magnitude of the blast, and the type of shelter he was in. There will be many others, no doubt, but these will do for purposes of illustration. We must also obtain the probability values associated with the relevancy relations. The statistical relevance relations are statistical regularities, and we proceed to explain them. Although this differs substantially from things I have said previously, I no longer believe that the assemblage of relevant factors provides a complete explanation —or much of anything in the way of an explanation. We do, I believe, have a bona fide explanation of an event if we have a complete set of statistically relevant factors, the pertinent probability values, *and* causal explanations of the relevance relations. Subsumption of a particular occurrence under statistical regularities— which, we recall, does not imply anything about the construction of deductive or inductive arguments—is a necessary part of any adequate explanation of its occurrence, but it is not the whole story. The causal explanation of the regularity is also needed. This claim, it should be noted, is in direct conflict with the received view, according to which the mere subsumption— deductive or inductive—of an event under a lawful regularity constitutes a complete explanation. One can, according to the received view, go on to ask for an explanation of any law used to explain a given event, but that is a different explanation. I am suggesting, on the contrary, that if the regularity invoked is not a causal regularity, then a causal explanation of that very regularity must be made part of the explanation of the event.

If we have events of two types, A and B, whose respective members are not spatio-temporally contiguous, but whose occurrences are correlated with one another, the causal explanation of this regularity may take either of two forms. Either there is a direct causal connection from A to B or from B to A, or there is a common cause C which accounts for the statistical dependency. In either case, those events which stand in the cause-effect relation to one another are joined by a causal process. The distinct events A, B, and C which are thus related constitute interactions—as defined in terms of an interactive fork—at the appropriate places in the respective causal processes. The interactions *produce* modifications in the causal processes, and the causal processes *transmit* the modifications. Statistical dependency relations arise out of local interactions—there is no action-at-a-distance (as far as macro-phenomena are concerned, at least)—and they are propagated through the world by causal processes. In our leukemia example, a slow neutron, impinging upon a uranium atom, has a certain probability of inducing nuclear fission, and if fission occurs, gamma radiation is emitted. The gamma ray travels through space, and it may interact with a human cell,

producing a modification which may leave the cell open to attack by the virus associated with leukemia. The fact that many such interactions of neutrons with fissionable nuclei are occurring in close spatio-temporal proximity, giving rise to processes which radiate in all directions, produces a pattern of statistical dependency relations. After initiation, these processes go on independently of one another, but they do produce relationships which can be described by means of the conjunctive fork.

Causal processes and causal interactions are, of course, governed by various laws—e.g., conservation of energy and momentum. In a causal process, such as the propagation of a light wave or the free motion of a material particle, energy is being transmitted. The distinction between causal processes and pseudo-processes lies in the distinction between the transmission of energy from one space-time locale to another and the mere appearance of energy at various space-time locations. When causal interactions occur—not merely intersections of processes—we have energy and/or momentum transfer. Such laws as conservation of energy and momentum are causal laws in the sense that they are regularities exhibited by causal processes and interactions.

Near the beginning, I suggested that deduction of a restricted law from a more general law constitutes a paradigm of a certain type of explanation. No theory of scientific explanation can hope to be successful unless it can handle cases of this sort. Lenz's law, for example, which governs the direction of flow of an electric current generated by a changing magnetic field, can be deduced from the law of conservation of energy. But this deductive relation shows that the more restricted regularity is simply part of a more comprehensive physical pattern expressed by the law of conservation of energy. Similarly, Kepler's laws of planetary motion describe a restricted subclass of the class of all motions governed by Newtonian mechanics. The deductive relations *exhibit* what amounts to a part-whole relationship, but it is, in my opinion, the physical relationship between the more comprehensive physical regularity and the less comprehensive physical regularity which has explanatory significance. I should like to put it this way. An explanation may sometimes provide the materials out of which an argument, deductive or inductive, can be constructed; an argument may sometimes exhibit explanatory relations. It does not follow, however, that explanations are arguments.

Earlier in this discussion, I mentioned three short-comings in the most widely held theories of scientific explanation. I should now like to indicate the ways in which the theory I have been outlining attempts to cope with these problems. (1) The causal conception, I claimed, has lacked an adequate analysis of causation. The foregoing explications of causal processes and causal interactions were intended to fill that gap. (2) The inferential conception, I claimed, had misconstrued the relation of subsumption under law. When we see how statistical relevance relations can be brought to bear upon facts-to-be-explained, we discover that it is possible to have a *covering law conception* of scientific explanation without regarding explanations as arguments. The recognition that subsumption of narrower regularities under broader regularities can be viewed as a part-whole relation reinforces that point. At the same time, it suggests a reason for the tremendous appeal of the inferential conception in the first place. (3) Both of the popular conceptions, I claimed, overlooked a fundamental explanatory principle. That principle, obviously, is the principle of the common cause. I have tried to display its enormous explanatory significance. The theory outlined above is designed to overcome all three of these difficulties.

On the basis of the foregoing characterization of sci-entific explanation, how should we answer the question posed at the outset? What does Laplace's demon lack, if anything, with respect to the explanatory aim of science? Several items may be mentioned. The demon *may* lack an adequate recognition of the distinction between causal laws and non-causal regularities; it *may* lack adequate knowledge of causal processes and of their ability to propagate causal influence; and it *may* lack adequate appreciation of the role of causal interactions in *producing* changes and regularities in the world. None of these capabilities was explicitly demanded by Laplace, for his analysis of causal relations in general was rather superficial.

What does scientific explanation offer, over and above the inferential capacity of prediction and retrodiction, at which the Laplacian demon excelled? It provides knowledge of the mechanisms of *production* and *propagation* of structure in the world. That goes some distance beyond mere recognition of regularities, and of the possibility of subsuming particular phenomena thereunder. It is my view that knowledge of the mechanisms of production and propagation of structure in the world yields scientific understanding, and that this is what we seek when we pose explanation-seeking why questions. The answers are well worth having. That is why we ask, not only "What?" but "Why?"

Daniel Dennett

Evolution as a Universal Acid

Darwin's Assault on the Cosmic Pyramid

A prominent feature of Pre-Darwinian world-views is an overall top-to-bottom map of things. This is often

described as a Ladder; God is at the top, with human beings a rung or two below (depending on whether angels are part of the scheme). At the bottom of the Ladder is Nothingness, or maybe Chaos, or maybe Locke's inert, motionless Matter. Alternatively, the scale is a Tower, or, in the intellectual historian Arthur Lovejoy's memorable phrase, a Great Chain of Being composed of many links. John Locke's argument has already drawn our attention to a particularly abstract version of the hierarchy, which I will call the Cosmic Pyramid:

God

Mind

Design

O r d e r

C h a o s

N o t h i n g

(Warning: each term in the pyramid must be understood in an old-fashioned, pre-Darwinian sense!)

Everything finds its place on one level or another of the Cosmic Pyramid, even blank nothingness, the ultimate foundation. Not all matter is Ordered, some is in Chaos; only some Ordered matter is also Designed; only some Designed things have Minds, and of course only one Mind is God. God, the first Mind, is the source and explanation of everything underneath. (Since everything thus *depends on* God, perhaps we should say it is a chandelier, hanging from God, rather than a pyramid, supporting Him.)

What is the difference between Order and Design? As a first stab, we might say that Order is mere regularity, mere pattern; Design is Aristotle's *telos,* an exploitation of Order for a purpose, such as we see in a cleverly designed artifact. The solar system exhibits stupendous Order, but does not (apparently) have a purpose—it isn't *for* anything. An eye, in contrast, is *for* seeing. Before Darwin, this distinction was not always clearly marked. Indeed, it was positively blurred:

> In the thirteenth century, Aquinas offered the view that natural bodies [such as planets, raindrops, volcanos] act as if guided toward a definite goal or end "so as to obtain the best result." This fitting of means to ends implies, argued Aquinas, an intention. But, seeing as natural bodies lack consciousness, they cannot supply that intention themselves. "Therefore some intelligent being exists by whom all natural things are directed to their end; and this being we call God."[1]

Hume's Cleanthes, following in this tradition, lumps the adapted marvels of the living world with the regularities of the heavens—it's *all* like a wonderful clockwork to him. But Darwin suggests a division: Give me Order, he says, and time, and I will give you Design. Let me start with regularity—the mere purposeless, mindless, pointless regularity of physics—and I will show you a process that eventually will yield products that exhibit not just regularity but purposive design. (This was just what Karl Marx thought he saw when he declared that Darwin had dealt a death blow to Teleology: Darwin had *reduced* teleology to nonteleology, Design to Order.)

Before Darwin, the difference between Order and Design didn't loom large, because in any case it all came down from God. The whole universe as His artifact, a product of His Intelligence, His Mind. Once Darwin jumped into the middle with his proposed answer to the question of how Design could arise from mere Order, the rest of the Cosmic Pyramid was put in jeopardy. Suppose we accept that Darwin has explained the Design of the bodies of plants and animals (including our own bodies—we have to admit that Darwin has placed us firmly in the animal kingdom). Looking up, if we concede to Darwin our bodies, can we keep him from taking our minds as well? Looking down, Darwin asks us to give him Order as a premise, but is there anything to keep him from stepping down a level, and giving himself an algorithmic account of the origin of Order out of mere Chaos?

The vertigo and revulsion this prospect provokes in many was perfectly expressed in an early attack on Darwin, published anonymously in 1868:

> In the theory with which we have to deal, Absolute Ignorance is the artificer; so that we may enunciate as the fundamental principle of the whole system, that, IN ORDER TO MAKE A PERFECT AND BEAUTIFUL MACHINE, IT IS NOT REQUISITE TO KNOW HOW TO MAKE IT. This proposition will be found, on careful examination, to express, in condensed form, the essential purport of the Theory, and to express in a few words all Mr. Darwin's meaning; who, by a strange inversion of reasoning, seems to think Absolute Ignorance fully qualified to take the place of Absolute Wisdom in all the achievements of creative skill.[2]

---

1. Paul Davies, *The Mind of God,* New York: Simon & Schuster, 1992, p. 200.

2. Robert Beverley MacKenzie, *The Darwinian Theory of the Transmutation of Species Examined,* Nisbet & Co., 1868.

Exactly! Darwin's "strange inversion of reasoning" was in fact a new and wonderful way of thinking, completely overturning the Mind-first way that John Locke "proved" and David Hume could see no way around. John Dewey nicely described the inversion some years later, in his insightful book *The Influence of Darwin on Philosophy:* "Interest shifts . . . from an intelligence that shaped things once for all to the particular intelligences which things are even now shaping."[3] But the idea of treating Mind as an effect rather than as a First Cause is too revolutionary for some—an "awful stretcher" that their own minds cannot accommodate comfortably. This is as true today as it was in 1860, and it has always been as true of some of evolution's best friends as of its foes. For instance, the physicist Paul Davies, in his recent book *The Mind of God,* proclaims that the reflective power of human minds can be "no trivial detail, no minor by-product of mindless purposeless forces."[4] This is a most revealing way of expressing a familiar denial, for it betrays an ill-examined prejudice. Why, we might ask Davies, would its being a by-product of mindless, purposeless forces make it trivial? Why couldn't the most important thing of all be something that arose from unimportant things? Why should the importance or excellence of *anything* have to rain down on it from on high, from something more important, a gift from God? Darwin's inversion suggests that we abandon that presumption and look for sorts of excellence, of worth and purpose, that can emerge, bubbling up out of "mindless, purposeless forces."

Alfred Russel Wallace, whose own version of evolution by natural selection arrived on Darwin's desk while he was still delaying publication of *Origin,* and whom Darwin managed to treat as codiscoverer of the principle, never quite got the point. Although at the outset Wallace was much more forthcoming on the subject of the evolution of the human mind than Darwin was willing to be, and stoutly maintained at first that human minds were no exception to the rule that all features of living things were products of evolution, he could not see the "strange inversion of reasoning" as the key to the

greatness of the great idea. Echoing John Locke, Wallace proclaimed that "the marvelous complexity of forces which appear to control matter, if not actually to constitute it, are and must be mind-products."[5] When, later in his life, Wallace converted to spiritualism and exempted human consciousness altogether from the iron rule of evolution, Darwin saw the crack widen and wrote to him: "I hope you have not murdered too completely your own and my child."[6]

But was it really so inevitable that Darwin's idea should lead to such revolution and subversion? "It is obvious that the critics did not wish to understand, and to some extent Darwin himself encouraged their wishful thinking."[7] Wallace wanted to ask what the *purpose* of natural selection might be, and though this might seem in retrospect to be squandering the fortune he and Darwin had uncovered, it was an idea for which Darwin himself often expressed sympathy. Instead of reducing teleology all the way to purposeless Order, why couldn't we reduce all mundane teleology to a single purpose: God's purpose? Wasn't this an obvious and inviting way to plug the dike? Darwin was clear in his own mind that the variation on which the process of natural selection depended *had* to be unplanned and undesigned, but the process itself might have a purpose, mightn't it? In a letter in 1860 to the American naturalist Asa Gray, an early supporter, Darwin wrote, "I am inclined to look at everything as resulting from *designed* [emphasis added] laws, with the details whether good or bad, left to the working out of what we may call chance."[8]

Automatic processes are themselves often creations of great brilliance. From today's vantage point, we can see that the inventors of the automatic transmission and the automatic door-opener were no idiots, and their genius lay in seeing how to create something that could

---

3. John Dewey, *The Influence of Darwin on Philosophy,* New York: Holt, 1910, p. 15.

4. Davies, p. 232.

5. Stephen Jay Gould, *The Flamingo's Smile,* New York: Norton, 1985, p. 397.

6. Adrian Desmond and James Moore, *Darwin,* London: Michael Joseph, p. 569.

7. Alvar Ellegård, "The Darwinian Theory and the Argument from Design, *Lychnos,* 1956, pp. 173–192.

8. Francis Darwin, *The Life and Letters of Charles Darwin,* vol. 2, New York: Appleton 1911, p. 105.

do something "clever" without having to think about it. Indulging in some anachronism, we could say that, to some observers in Darwin's day, it seemed that he had left open the possibility that God did His handiwork by designing an automatic designmaker. And to some of these, the idea was not just a desperate stopgap but a positive improvement on tradition. The first chapter of Genesis describes the successive waves of Creation and ends each with the refrain "and God saw that it was good." Darwin had discovered a way to eliminate this retail application of Intelligent Quality Control; natural selection would take care of that without further intervention from God. (The seventeenth-century philosopher Gottfried Wilhelm Leibniz had defended a similar hands-off vision of God the Creator.) As Henry Ward Beecher put it, "Design by wholesale is grander than design by retail."[9] Asa Gray, captivated by Darwin's new idea but trying to reconcile it with as much of his traditional religious creed as possible, came up with this marriage of convenience: God *intended* the "stream of variations" and *foresaw* just how the laws of nature He had laid down would prune this stream over the eons. As John Dewey later aptly remarked, invoking yet another mercantile metaphor, "Gray held to what may be called design on the installment plan."[10]

It is not unusual to find such metaphors, redolent of capitalism, in evolutionary explanations. Examples are often gleefully recounted by those critics and interpreters of Darwin who see this language as revealing—or should we say betraying—the social and political environment in which Darwin developed his ideas, thereby (somehow) discrediting their claim to scientific objectivity. It is certainly true that Darwin, being an ordinary mortal, was the inheritor of a huge manifold of concepts, modes of expression, attitudes, biases, and visions that went with his station in life (as a Victorian Englishman might put it), but it is also true that the economic metaphors that come so naturally to mind when one is thinking about evolution get their power from one of the deepest features of Darwin's discovery.

---

9. James Rachels, *The Created Animals: The Moral Implications of Darwinism,* Oxford: Oxford University Press, 1991, p. 99.

10. Dewey, p. 12.

The Principle of the Accumulation of Design

The key to understanding Darwin's contribution is *granting* the premise of the Argument from Design. What conclusion ought one to draw if one found a watch lying on the heath in the wilderness? As Paley (and Hume's Cleanthes before him) insisted, a watch exhibits a tremendous amount of *work done.* Watches and other designed objects don't just happen; they have to be the product of what modern industry calls "R and D"—research and development—and R and D is costly, in both time and energy. Before Darwin, the only model we had of a process by which this sort of R-and-D work could be done was an Intelligent Artificer. What Darwin saw was that in principle the same work could be done by a different sort of process that *distributed* that work over huge amounts of time, by thriftily conserving the design work that had been accomplished at each stage, so that it didn't have to be done over again. In other words, Darwin had hit upon what we might call the Principle of Accumulation of Design. Things in the world (such as watches and organisms and who knows what else) may be seen as products embodying a certain amount of Design, and one way or another, that Design had to have been created by a process of R and D. Utter undesignedness—pure chaos in the old-fashioned sense—was the null or starting point.

A more recent idea about the difference—and tight relation—between Design and Order will help clarify the picture. This is the proposal, first popularized by the physicist Erwin Schrödinger, that Life can be defined in terms of the Second Law of Thermodynamics. In physics, order or organization can be measured in terms of *heat differences* between regions of space time; *entropy* is simply disorder, the opposite of order, and according to the Second Law, the entropy of any isolated system increases with time. In other words, things run down, inevitably. According to the Second Law, the universe is unwinding out of a more ordered state into the ultimately disordered state known as the heat death of the universe.

What, then, are living things? They are things that defy this crumbling into dust, at least for a while, by not being isolated—by taking in from their environment the wherewithal to keep life and limb together.

The psychologist Richard Gregory summarizes the idea crisply:

> Time's arrow given by Entropy—the loss of organization, or loss of temperature differences—is statistical and it is subject to local small-scale reversals. Most striking: life is a systematic reversal of Entropy, and intelligence creates structures and energy differences against the supposed gradual 'death' through Entropy of the physical Universe.[11]

Gregory goes on to credit Darwin with the fundamental enabling idea: "It is the measure of the concept of Natural Selection that increases in the complexity and order of organisms in biological time can now be understood." Not just individual organisms, but the whole process of evolution that creates them, thus can be seen as fundamental physical phenomena running contrary to the larger trend of cosmic time, a feature captured by William Calvin in one of the meanings of the title of his classic exploration of the relationship between evolution and cosmology, *The River That Flows Uphill: A Journey from the Big Bang to the Big Brain*.

A *designed* thing, then, is either a living thing or a part of a living thing, or the artifact of a living thing, organized in any case in aid of this battle against disorder. It is not impossible to oppose the trend of the Second Law, but it is costly. Consider iron. Iron is a very useful element, essential for our bodily health, and also valuable as the major component of steel, that wonderful building material. Our planet used to have vast reserves of iron ore, but they are gradually being depleted. Does this mean that the Earth is running out of iron? Hardly. With the trivial exception of a few tons that have recently been launched out of Earth's effective gravitational field in the form of space-probe components, there is just as much iron on the planet today as there ever was. The trouble is that more and more of it is scattered about in the form of rust (molecules of iron oxide), and other low-grade, low-concentration materials. In principle, it could all be recovered, but that would

take enormous amounts of energy, craftily focused on the particular project of extracting and reconcentrating the iron.

It is the organization of just such sophisticated processes that constitutes the hallmark of life. Gregory dramatizes this with an unforgettable example. A standard textbook expression of the directionality imposed by the Second Law of Thermodynamics is the claim that you can't *un*scramble an egg. Well, not that you absolutely can't, but that it would be an extremely costly, sophisticated task, uphill all the way against the Second Law. Now consider: how expensive would it be to make a device that would take scrambled eggs as input and deliver unscrambled eggs as output? There is one ready solution: put a live hen in the box! Feed it scrambled eggs, and it will be able to make eggs for you—for a while. Hens don't normally strike us as near-miraculously sophisticated entities, but here is one thing a hen can do, thanks to the Design that has organized it, that is still way beyond the reach of the devices created by human engineers.

The more Design a thing exhibits, the more R-and-D work had to have occurred to produce it. Like any good revolutionary, Darwin exploits as much as possible of the old system: the vertical dimension of the Cosmic Pyramid is retained, and becomes the measure of how much Design has gone into the items at that level. In Darwin's scheme, as in the traditional Pyramid, Minds do end up near the top, among the most designed of entities (in part because they are the self-redesigning things. But this means that they are among the most advanced *effects* (to date) of the creative process, not—as in the old version—its cause or source. Their products in turn—the human artifacts that were our initial model—must count as more designed still. This may seem counterintuitive at first. A Keats ode may seem to have some claim to having a grander R-and-D pedigree than a nightingale—at least it might seem so to a poet ignorant of biology—but what about a paper clip? Surely a paper clip is a trivial product of design compared with any living thing, however rudimentary. In one obvious sense, yes, but reflect for a moment. Put yourself in Paley's shoes, but walking along the apparently deserted beach on an alien planet. Which discovery would excite you the most: a clam or a clam-rake? Before the planet could make a clam-rake, it would have to make a

11. R. L. Gregory, *Mind in Science: A History of Explanations in Psychology and Physics,* Cambridge: Cambridge University Press, 1981, p. 136.

clam-rake-maker, and that is a more designed thing by far than a clam.

Only a theory with the logical shape of Darwin's could explain how designed things came to exist, because any other sort of explanation would be either a vicious circle or an infinite regress. The old way, Locke's Mind-first way, endorsed the principle that it takes an Intelligence to make an intelligence. This idea must have always seemed self-evident to our ancestors, the artifact-makers, going back to *Homo habilis,* the "handy" man, from whom *Homo sapiens,* the "knowing" man, descended. Nobody ever saw a spear fashion a hunter out of raw materials. Children chant, "it takes one to know one," but an even more persuasive slogan would seem to be "It takes a greater one to make a lesser one." Any view inspired by this slogan immediately faces an embarrassing question, however, as Hume had noted: If God created and designed all these wonderful things, who created God? Supergod? And who created Supergod? Superdupergod? Or did God create Himself? Was it hard work? Did it take time? Don't ask! Well, then, we may ask instead whether this bland embrace of mystery is any improvement over just denying the principle that intelligence (or design) must spring from Intelligence. Darwin offered an explanatory path that actually honored Paley's insight: real work went into designing this watch, and work isn't free.

How much design does a thing exhibit? No one has yet offered a system of design quantification that meets all our needs. Theoretical work that bears on this interesting question is under way in several disciplines. [. . .] We have a powerful intuitive sense of different amounts of design. Automobiles contain more design than bicycles, sharks contain more design than amoebas, and even a short poem contains more design than a "Keep Off the Grass" sign.

Patent law, including the law of copyright, is a repository of our practical grasp of the question. How much novelty of design counts as enough to justify a patent? How much can one borrow from the intellectual products of others without recompense or acknowledgment? These are slippery slopes on which we have had to construct some rather arbitrary terraces, codifying what otherwise would be a matter of interminable dispute. The burden of proof in these disputes is fixed by our intuitive sense of how much design is too much design to be mere coincidence. Our intuitions here are very strong and sound. Suppose an author is accused of plagiarism, and the evidence is, say, a single paragraph that is almost identical to a paragraph in the putative source. Might this be just a coincidence? It depends crucially on how mundane and formulaic the paragraph is, but most paragraph-length passages of text are "special" enough to make independent creation highly unlikely. No reasonable jury would require the prosecutor in a plagiarism case to demonstrate exactly the causal pathway by which the alleged copying took place. The defendant would clearly have the burden of establishing that his work was, remarkably, an independent work rather than a copying of work already done.

A similar burden of proof falls on the defendant in an industrial-espionage case: the interior of the defendant's new line of widgets looks suspiciously similar in design to that of the plaintiffs line of widgets—is this an innocent case of convergent evolution of design? Really the only way to prove your innocence in such a case is to show clear evidence of actually having done the necessary R-and-D work (old blueprints, rough drafts, early models and mockups, memos about the problems encountered, etc.). In the absence of such evidence, but also in the absence of any physical evidence of your espionage activities, you would be convicted—and you'd deserve to be! Cosmic coincidences on such a scale just don't happen.

The same burden of proof now reigns in biology, thanks to Darwin. What I am calling the Principle of Accumulation of Design doesn't logically *require* that all design (on this planet) descend via one branch or another from a single trunk (or root or seed), but it says that since each new designed thing that appears must have a large design investment in its etiology somewhere, the cheapest hypothesis will always be that the design is largely copied from earlier designs, which are copied from earlier designs, and so forth, so that actual R-and-D innovation is minimized. We know for a fact, of course, that many designs have been independently re-invented many times—eyes, for instance, dozens of times—but every case of such convergent evolution must be proven against a background in which most of the design is copied. It is logically possible that all the life forms in South America were created independently of all the life forms in the rest of the world, but this is a wildly extravagant hypothesis that would need to be demonstrated, piece by piece. Suppose we discover, on some remote island, a novel species of bird. Even if we don't *yet* have direct confirmatory evidence that this bird is related to all the other birds in the world, that is our overpoweringly secure default assumption, after Darwin, because birds are very special designs.

So the fact that organisms—and computers and books and other artifacts—are effects of very special chains of causation is not, after Darwin, a merely reliable generalization, but a deep fact out of which to build a theory. Hume recognized the point—"Throw several pieces of steel together, without shape or form; they will never arrange themselves to compose a watch"—but he and other, earlier, thinkers thought they had to ground this deep fact in Mind. Darwin came to see how to distribute it in vast spaces of Nonmind, thanks to his ideas about how design innovations could be conserved and reproduced, and hence accumulated.

The idea that Design is something that has taken work to create, and hence has value at least in the sense that it is something that might be conserved (and then stolen or sold), finds robust expression in economic terms. Had Darwin not had the benefit of being born into a mercantile world that had already created its Adam Smith and its Thomas Malthus, he would not have been in position to find ready-made pieces he could put together into a new, value-added product. The various sources of the Design that went into Darwin's grand idea give us important insights into the idea itself, but do no more to diminish its value or threaten its objectivity than the humble origins of methane diminish its BTUs when it is put to use as a fuel.

4. The Tools for R and D: Skyhooks or Cranes?

The work of R and D is not like shoveling coal; it is somehow a sort of "intellectual" work, and this fact grounds the other family of metaphors that has both enticed and upset, enlightened and confused, the thinkers who have confronted Darwin's "strange inversion of reasoning": the apparent attribution of intelligence to the very process of natural selection that Darwin insisted was *not* intelligent.

Was it not unfortunate, in fact, that Darwin had chosen to call his principle "natural *selection*," with its anthropomorphic connotations? Wouldn't it have been better, as Asa Gray suggested to him, to replace the imagery about "nature's Guiding Hand" with a discussion of the different ways of winning life's race?[12] Many people just didn't get it, and Darwin was inclined to blame himself. "I must be a very bad explainer," he said, conceding: "I suppose 'natural selection' was a bad term."[13] Certainly this Janus-faced term has encouraged more than a century of heated argument. A recent opponent of Darwin sums it up:

> Life on Earth, initially thought to constitute a sort of prima facie case for a creator, was, as a result of Darwin's idea, envisioned merely as being the outcome of a process and a process that was, according to Dobzhansky, "blind, mechanical, automatic, impersonal," and, according to de Beer, was "wasteful, blind, and blundering." But as soon as these criticisms [sic] were leveled at natural selection, the "blind process" itself was compared to a poet, a composer, a sculptor, Shakespeare—to the very notion of creativity that the idea of natural selection had originally replaced. It is clear, I think, that there was something very, very wrong with such an idea.[14]

Or something very, very right. It seems to skeptics like Bethell that there is something willfully paradoxical in calling the process of evolution the "blind watchmaker," for this takes away with the left hand ("blind") the very discernment, purpose, and foresight it gives with the right hand. But others see that this manner of speaking—and we shall find that it is not just ubiquitous but irreplaceable in contemporary biology—is just the right way to express the myriads of detailed discoveries that Darwinian theory helps to expose. There is simply no denying the breathtaking brilliance of the designs to be found in nature. Time and again, biologists

---

12. Desmond and Moore, p. 458.

13. Ibid., p. 492.

14. Tom Bethel, "Darwin's Mistake," *Harper's Magazine*, February, 1976, pp. 70–75.

baffled by some apparently futile or maladroit bit of bad design in nature have eventually come to see that they have underestimated the ingenuity, the sheer brilliance, the depth of insight to be discovered in one of Mother Nature's creations. Francis Crick has mischievously baptized this trend in the name of his colleague Leslie Orgel, speaking of what he calls "Orgel's Second Rule: Evolution is cleverer than you are." (An alternative formulation: Evolution is cleverer than Leslie Orgel!)

Darwin shows us how to climb from "Absolute Ignorance" (as his outraged critic said) to creative genius without begging any questions, but we must tread very carefully, as we shall see. Among the controversies that swirl around us, most if not all consist of different challenges to Darwin's claim that he can take us all the way to *here* (the wonderful world we inhabit) from *there* (the world of chaos or utter undesignedness) in the time available without invoking anything beyond the mindless mechanicity of the algorithmic processes he had proposed. Since we have reserved the vertical dimension of the traditional Cosmic Pyramid as a measure of (intuitive) designedness, we can dramatize the challenge with the aid of another fantasy item drawn from folklore.

> *skyhook,* orig. Aeronaut. An imaginary contrivance for attachment to the sky; an imaginary means of suspension in the sky. [*Oxford English Dictionary.*]

The first use noted by the *OED* is from 1915: "an aeroplane pilot commanded to remain in place (aloft) for another hour, replies 'the machine is not fitted with skyhooks.'" The skyhook concept is perhaps a descendant of the *deus ex machina* of ancient Greek dramaturgy: when second-rate playwrights found their plots leading their heroes into inescapable difficulties, they were often tempted to crank down a god onto the scene, like Superman, to save the situation supernaturally. Or skyhooks may be an entirely independent creation of convergent folkloric evolution. Skyhooks would be wonderful things to have, great for lifting unwieldy objects out of difficult circumstances, and speeding up all sorts of construction projects. Sad to say, they are impossible.[15]

There are cranes, however. Cranes can do the lifting work our imaginary skyhooks might do, and they do it in an honest, non-question-begging fashion. They are expensive, however. They have to be designed and built, from everyday parts already on hand, and they have to be located on a firm base of existing ground. Skyhooks are miraculous lifters, unsupported and insupportable. Cranes are no less excellent as lifters, and they have the decided advantage of being real. Anyone who is, like me, a lifelong onlooker at construction sites will have noticed with some satisfaction that it sometimes takes a small crane to set up a big crane. And it must have occurred to many other onlookers that in principle this big crane could be used to enable or speed up the building of a still more spectacular crane. Cascading cranes is a tactic that seldom if ever gets used more than once in real-world construction projects, but in principle there is no limit to the number of cranes that could be organized in series to accomplish some mighty end.

Now imagine all the "lifting" that has to get done in Design Space to create the magnificent organisms and (other) artifacts we encounter in our world. Vast distances must have been traversed since the dawn of life with the earliest, simplest self-replicating entities, spreading outward (diversity) and upward (excellence). Darwin has offered us an account of the crudest, most rudimentary, stupidest imaginable lifting process—the wedge of natural selection. By taking tiny—the tiniest possible—steps, this process can gradually, over eons, traverse these huge distances. Or so he claims. At no point would anything miraculous—from on high—be needed. Each step has been accomplished by brute, me-

---

15. Well, not quite impossible. Geostationary satellites, orbiting in unison with the Earth's rotation, are a kind of real,

non-miraculous skyhook. What makes them so valuable—what makes them financially sound investments—is that we often do want very much to attach something (such as an antenna or a camera or telescope) to a place high in the sky. Satellites are impractical for *lifting,* alas, because they have to be placed so high in the sky. The idea has been carefully explored. It turns out that a rope of the strongest artificial fiber yet made would have to be over a hundred meters in diameter at the top—it could taper to a nearly invisible fishing line on its way down—just to suspend its own weight, let alone any payload. Even if you could spin such a cable, you wouldn't want it falling out of orbit onto the city below!

chanical, algorithmic climbing, from the base already built by the efforts of earlier climbing.

It does seem incredible. Could it really have happened? Or did the process need a "leg up" now and then (perhaps only at the very beginning) from one sort of skyhook or another? For over a century, skeptics have been trying to find a proof that Darwin's idea just can't work, at least not *all the way.* They have been hoping for, hunting for, praying for skyhooks, as exceptions to what they see as the bleak vision of Darwin's algorithm churning away. And time and again, they have come up with truly interesting challenges—leaps and gaps and other marvels that do seem, at first, to need skyhooks. But then along have come the cranes, discovered in many cases by the very skeptics who were hoping to find a skyhook.

It is time for some more careful definitions. Let us understand that a *skyhook* is a "mind-first" force or power or process, an exception to the principle that all design, and apparent design, is ultimately the result of mindless, motiveless mechanicity. A *crane,* in contrast, is a subprocess or special feature of a design process that can be demonstrated to permit the local speeding up of the basic, slow process of natural selection, *and* that can be demonstrated to be itself the predictable (or retrospectively explicable) product of the basic process. Some cranes are obvious and uncontroversial; others are still being argued about, very fruitfully. Just to give a general sense of the breadth and application of the concept, let me point to three very different examples.

It is now generally agreed among evolutionary theorists that *sex* is a crane. That is, species that reproduce sexually can move through Design Space at a much greater speed than that achieved by organisms that reproduce asexually. Moreover, they can "discern" design improvements along the way that are all but "invisible" to asexually reproducing organisms. This cannot be the *raison d'être* of sex, however. Evolution cannot see way down the road, so anything it builds must have an immediate payoff to counterbalance the cost. As recent theorists have insisted, the "choice" of reproducing sexually carries a huge *immediate* cost: organisms send along only 50 percent of their genes in any one transaction (to say nothing of the effort and risk involved in securing a transaction in the first place). So the *long-term* payoff of heightened efficiency, acuity, and speed of the re-design process—the features that make sex a magnificent

crane—is as nothing to the myopic, local competitions that must determine which organisms get favored in the very next generation. Some other, short-term, benefit must have maintained the positive selection pressure required to make sexual reproduction an offer few species could refuse. There are a variety of compelling—and competing—hypotheses that might solve this puzzle. [...]

What we learn from the example of sex is that a crane of great power may exist that was not created *in order to exploit* that power, but for other reasons, although its power as a crane may help explain why it has been maintained ever since. A crane that was obviously created to be a crane is *genetic engineering.* Genetic engineers—human beings who engage in recombinant-DNA tinkering—can now unquestionably take huge leaps through Design Space, creating organisms that would never have evolved by "ordinary" means. This is no miracle—*provided that genetic engineers (and the artifacts they use in their trade) are themselves wholly the products of earlier, slower evolutionary processes.* If the creationists were right that mankind is a species unto itself, divine and inaccessible via brute Darwinian paths, then genetic engineering would not be a crane after all, having been created with the help of a major skyhook. I don't imagine that any genetic engineers think of themselves this way, but it is a logically available perch, however precarious. Less obviously silly is this idea: if the bodies of genetic engineers are products of evolution, but their *minds* can do creative things that are irreducibly nonalgorithmic or inaccessible by all algorithmic paths, then the leaps of genetic engineering might involve a skyhook.

A crane with a particularly interesting history is the Baldwin Effect. [...] Baldwin was an enthusiastic Darwinian, but he was oppressed by the prospect that Darwin's theory would leave Mind with an insufficiently important and originating role in the (re)design of organisms. So he set out to demonstrate that animals, *by dint of their own clever activities in the world,* might hasten or guide the further evolution of their species. Here is what he asked himself: how could it be that individual animals, by solving problems in their own lifetimes, could change the conditions of competition for their own offspring, making those problems easier to solve in the future? And he came to realize that this was in fact possible, under certain conditions, which we can illustrate with a simple example.

Consider a population of a species in which there is considerable variation at birth in the way their brains are wired up. Just one of the ways, we may suppose, endows its possessor with a Good Trick—a behavioral talent that protects it or enhances its chances dramatically. The standard way of representing such differences in fitness between individual members of a population is known as an "adaptive landscape" or a "fitness landscape." The altitude in such a diagram stands for fitness (higher is better), and the longitude and latitude stand for some factors of individual design—in this case, features of brain-wiring. Each different way a brain might be wired is represented by one of the rods that compose the landscape—each rod is a different *genotype*. The fact that just one of the combinations of features is any good—that is, any better than run-of-the-mill—is illustrated by the way it stands out like a telephone pole in the desert.

As Figure 3.1 makes clear, only one wiring is favored; the others, no matter how "close" to being the good wiring, are about equal in fitness. So such an isolated peak is indeed a needle in the haystack: it will be practically invisible to natural selection. Those few individuals in the population that are lucky enough to have the Good Trick genotype will typically have difficulty passing it on to their offspring, since under most circumstances their chances of finding a mate who also has the Good Trick genotype are remote, and a miss is as good as a mile.

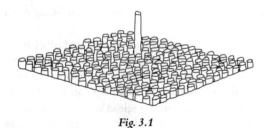

Fig. 3.1

But now we introduce just one "minor" change: suppose that although the individual organisms *start out* with different wirings (whichever wiring was ordered by their particular genotype or genetic recipe)—as shown by their scatter on the fitness landscape—they have some capacity to adjust or revise their wiring, de-

pending on what they encounter during their lifetimes. (In the language of evolutionary theory, there is some "plasticity" in their *phenotypes*. The phenotype is the eventual body design created by the genotype in interaction with environment. Identical twins raised in different environments would share a genotype but might be dramatically different in phenotype.) Suppose, then, that these organisms can end up, after exploration, with a design different from the one they were born with. We may suppose their explorations are random, but they have an innate capacity to recognize (and stay with) a Good Trick when they stumble upon it. Then those individuals who begin life with a genotype that is closer to the Good Trick genotype—fewer redesign steps away from it—are more likely to come across it, and stick with it, than those that are born with a far-away design.

This head start in the race to redesign themselves can give them the edge in the Malthusian crunch—if the Good Trick is so good that those who never learn it, or who learn it "too late," are at a severe disadvantage. In populations with this sort of phenotypic plasticity, a near-miss is *better* than a mile. For such a population, the telephone pole in the desert becomes the summit of a gradual hill, as in Figure 3.2; those perched near the summit, although they start out with a design that serves them no better than others, will tend to discover the summit design in short order.

In the long run, natural selection—redesign at the genotype level—will tend to *follow the lead of* and *confirm* the directions taken by the individual organisms' successful explorations—redesign at the individual or phenotype level.

The way I have just described the Baldwin Effect certainly keeps Mind to a minimum, if not altogether out of the picture; all it requires is some brute, mechanical capacity to stop a random walk when a Good Thing comes along, a minimal capacity to "recognize" a tiny bit of progress, to "learn" something by blind trial and error. In fact, I have put it in *behavioristic* terms. What Baldwin discovered was that creatures capable of "reinforcement learning" not only do better individually than creatures that are entirely "hard-wired"; their species will *evolve faster* because of its greater capacity to discover design improvements in the neighborhood. This is not how Baldwin described the effect he pro-

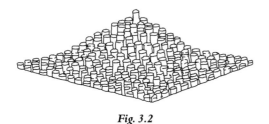

Fig. 3.2

posed. His temperament was the farthest thing from behaviorism. As Richards notes:

> The mechanism conformed to ultra-Darwinian assumptions, but nonetheless allowed consciousness and intelligence a role in directing evolution. By philosophic disposition and conviction, Baldwin was a spiritualistic metaphysician. He felt the beat of consciousness in the universe; it pulsed through all the levels of organic life. Yet he understood the power of mechanistic explanations of evolution.[16]

The Baldwin Effect, under several different names, has been variously described, defended, and disallowed over the years, and recently independently rediscovered several more times. Although it has been regularly described and acknowledged in biology textbooks, it has typically been shunned by overcautious thinkers, because they thought it smacked of the Lamarckian heresy (the presumed possibility of inheritance of acquired

characteristics). This rejection is particularly ironic since, as Richards notes, it was intended by Baldwin to be—and truly is—an acceptable *substitute* for Lamarckian mechanisms.

> The principle certainly seemed to dispatch Lamarckism, while supplying that positive factor in evolution for which even staunch Darwinists like Lloyd Morgan longed. And to those of metaphysical appetite, it revealed that under the clanking, mechanical vesture of Darwinian nature, mind could be found.[17]

Well, not Mind—if by that we mean a full-fledged, intrinsic, original, skyhook-type Mind—but only a nifty mechanistic, behavioristic, crane-style mind. That is not nothing, however; Baldwin discovered an effect that genuinely increases the power—locally—of the underlying process of natural selection wherever it operates. It shows how the "blind" process of the basic phenomenon of natural selection can be abetted by a limited amount of "look-ahead" in the activities of individual organisms, which create fitness differences that natural selection can then act upon. This is a welcome complication, a wrinkle in evolutionary theory that removes one reasonable and compelling source of doubt, and enhances our vision of the power of Darwin's idea, especially when it is cascaded in multiple, nested applications. And it is typical of the outcome of other searches and controversies we will explore: the motivation, the passion that drove the research, was the hope of finding a skyhook; the triumph was finding how the same work could be done with a crane. [...]

---

16. R. J. Richards, *Darwin and the Emergence of Evolutionary Theories of Mind and Behavior,* Chicago: University of Chicago Press, 1987, p. 480.

---

17. Richards, p. 187.

Identity and Personal Identity

Judith Jarvis Thomson

The Statue and the Clay

1. The problem, familiarly enough, emerges as follows. Suppose I bought a ten pound portion of clay at 9AM. What is a portion of clay? We will return to that question. For the time being, a portion of clay is some clay. It is a quantity of clay. Let us give the name CLAY to it:

CLAY = the ten pound portion of clay I bought at 9AM.

Suppose that at noon, I made a statue of King Alfred the Great out of it, and that I put it on the table at 2PM. Let us give the name ALFRED to the statue:

ALFRED = the statue on the table at 2PM.

How are ALFRED and CLAY related to each other? That is the problem.

Is this supposed to be a hard problem? Why isn't the solution simply that ALFRED is CLAY? If we can say that

Identity Thesis: ALFRED = CLAY

is true, then the problem is solved, easily.

Some people say it is obvious that the Identity Thesis will not do, for the following reason. By hypothesis, they say, I bought CLAY at 9AM, so

(1) CLAY existed at 9AM

is true. But, they say, it is obvious that ALFRED did not come into existence until noon, so

Judith Jarvis Thomson, "The Statue and the Clay" from *Noûs*, 32 (1998). Copyright © 1998. Reprinted with permission of Blackwell Publishing, Ltd.

(2) ALFRED did not exist at 9AM

is also true. And they go on to say it is therefore obvious that the Identity Thesis is false. (A similar argument turns on my smashing ALFRED at midnight.)

If we accept this argument, then we do have a hard problem before us. ALFRED and CLAY plainly stand in some intimate relation to each other—they currently occupy the same place, they currently have the same shape, size, color, texture, smell, and so on and on. In what relation do they stand to each other if not identity? Opponents of the Identity Thesis say we should say that CLAY constitutes ALFRED. But what can "constitutes" mean for these purposes? Opponents of the Identity Thesis have not found it at all easy to say.

Moreover, the Identity Thesis does not merely supply us with a simple solution to our problem: the solution it supplies is attractive in another way too. For let us take a closer look at the fact that ALFRED and CLAY currently have the same shape. ALFRED is blob-shaped on top, then is wider in the middle; the same is true of CLAY. The following is on any view true:

(3) ALFRED is a statue at 2PM

Isn't

(4) CLAY is a statue at 2PM

also true? But if (3) and (4) are both true, and ALFRED is not identical with CLAY, then there are two statues on the table at 2PM, one of which is ALFRED and the other of which is CLAY—both of them, I add, occupying the same place. That certainly sounds false.

Let us stop over (4) for a moment. Wouldn't it be odd to deny it? No doubt CLAY was not a statue at 9AM, but isn't it one at 2PM? What, after all, *is* a statue? Isn't it merely a portion of clay, or stone, or wood, or metal, shaped in a certain way, with a certain intention, by some person? Isn't what I did at noon precisely to make CLAY *become* a statue? Opponents of the Identity Thesis would say "No no, you can't make a portion of clay become a statue, you can only make it come to constitute a statue." Is there really any good reason to agree?

If we disagree—if we instead believe that a statue is merely a portion of clay, or stone, or wood, or metal, shaped in a certain way, with a certain intention, by some person—then we can have the Identity Thesis, and we can therefore have that there is only one statue on the table now, viz., ALFRED, viz., CLAY, and that ALFRED has been in existence as long as CLAY has been, though of course ALFRED, viz., CLAY, did not become a statue until noon.

It might pay to set this idea into a wider context. A great many properties can be called temporary properties, that is, properties that a thing can have at one time and not at another. Here are some examples:

some temporary properties: being a wife, a teenager, a student, . . . , being hungry, round, red, ...

(I divide these into two groups because while those in the first group are commonly called phase- or stage-properties, those in the second are not; all, however, are temporary.) Suppose that Mary got married at noon. Her marrying did not make a wife come into existence: it merely made her become a wife. Your reaching the age of 20 did not make a teenager go out of existence; it merely made you cease to be a teenager. And so on.

There is a sub-class of temporary properties that are particularly interesting for present purposes, of which the following are examples:

some shape-constrained temporary properties: being a puddle of M, a piece of M, a lump of M, . . . , being a heap of M, a mound of M, a stack of M, ...

"M" here is short for an appropriate mass-noun, such as "clay," "soup," "pudding," "coal," "wood" and so on. (I divide these too into two groups, for a reason that will emerge later. And I say "appropriate" because while a

thing can be a puddle of soup, nothing can be a puddle of clay; and while a thing can be a piece of clay, nothing can be a piece of soup.)

These shape-constrained temporary properties are of interest to us in two ways.

First, the things that acquire and lose these properties are portions of stuff, that is, portions of clay, soup, pudding, coal, wood, and so on. A portion of clay might be scattered in many little pieces around the room; if we collect those pieces and mash them together, we do not make a piece of clay come into existence—rather, we make the portion of clay become a piece of clay, and if the piece is mound-shaped, we also make the portion of clay become a mound of clay. The portion can also lose those properties: it will lose them if we cut it up into little pieces and scatter them around the room again. Second, what fixes whether a portion of an appropriate stuff has one of those properties is its shape. If a portion of clay is, so to speak, gappy, as when it is scattered around the room, it is neither a piece of clay nor a mound of clay. When it is no longer gappy, as when it is mashed together, it is a piece of clay, and if it is mound-shaped, it is also a mound of clay.

Now let us go back to statues. Why shouldn't we include being a statue among the temporary properties possessed from time to time by portions of stuff? Why shouldn't we suppose that it is, like being a piece of clay, a property that can be had by a portion of clay at one time and not at another? No doubt shape does not wholly fix whether a portion of clay is a statue: if a portion of clay falls out of a window and in consequence now looks like Queen Victoria, that does not mean it is a statue of Queen Victoria or of anything else. But if a portion of clay is moulded by some person in order to make a statue of Queen Victoria—and does manage to resemble her in some degree—then isn't *it* (the portion of clay) now a statue of Queen Victoria, and a fortiori a statue?

Why not say the same of all artifact-properties, thus not merely being a statue, but also being a chair, being a car, being a ship, and so on?

??? some further temporary properties: (artifact-properties) being a statue, a chair, a car, a ship, ...

Doesn't a scattered portion of wood become a chair when you arrange it into a chair? And cease to be a chair when you disarrange it again? In all these cases, shape is relevant, though so too is intention.

If we say that being a statue is a temporary property possessed from time to time by portions of stuff, then we can have that attractive Identity Thesis for ALFRED and CLAY, and analogous theses for all artifacts. And there is no hard problem raised by the statue and the clay.

It is a nice idea, I think. At all events, if we are to be forced to reject it, we must be provided with something stronger than the argument I gave at the outset. And we really should try to be clear about exactly why we have to reject the Identity Thesis (if we do) since what forces us to reject it (if anything does) is what makes CLAY merely constitute ALFRED, and should therefore help us to see what constituting *is*.

2. Alas, there is another, equally familiar, but considerably stronger argument against the Identity Thesis. Suppose that just before 3PM I break off ALFRED's left hand, replace it with a new one, and throw the old one on the floor. CLAY is not wholly on the table at 3PM, for part of it is on the floor then:

(5) CLAY is not wholly on the table at 3PM.

But isn't ALFRED wholly on the table at 3PM? If

(6) ALFRED is wholly on the table at 3PM

is also true, then the Identity Thesis is false.

I will call this a replacement argument. (We will meet more replacement arguments later.) Should we accept it?

Sentence (5), I think, we really do have to accept. In breaking off ALFRED's left hand I was breaking a part of CLAY off from the rest of CLAY, a part, we should note, that is itself a portion of clay. I divided CLAY into two sub-portions of clay, a big one, which I left on the table, and a little one, which I threw on the floor. So the portion of clay we began with—and that I am calling CLAY—is now scattered; it is not wholly on the table now, and (5) is therefore true.

What about (6)? Can't a statue undergo replacement of a part? We certainly think of artifacts generally as capable of undergoing replacements of parts. If a thief

snaps the windshield wiper off your car and steals it, or steals a tire or a whole wheel, or a bumper, or a fender, then you might replace the stolen part; and after the replacement, we think that you still have the car you originally had, and that it is still in front of your house, though the part the thief took is long gone across town.

If you get a new windshield wiper for your car, then in one way, of course, your car is not the same: it has a windshield wiper it formerly did not have. Just as if you drive your car through a puddle of mud, then in one way your car is not the same: it is dirtier than it was. But these changes are changes in it, that is, in the very car you have owned all along. We might say that the car isn't *the same,* for it has changed—but it is *it,* the same car, that has changed.

I think we had better agree, and thus that we had better reject the Identity Thesis. Philosophy should not depart more than it absolutely has to from what we ordinarily think and say, and it seems as plain as day that we do ordinarily think and say that artifacts can and often do undergo replacement of parts.

There are difficulties in the offing. First, while it is all well and good to say that artifacts can undergo replacement of parts, they cannot undergo replacement of too large a part all at once. If a thief snaps the windshield wiper off your car and you replace the windshield wiper, we do think you have the same car after the replacement. If the thief instead snaps everything else off the windshield wiper, and you replace everything he removed, we do not think you have the same car after the replacement. But how large is too large?

A second difficulty is generated by series of replacements of small parts. Some people think that an artifact can undergo replacement of all its small parts, if they are replaced one by one, slowly enough. Can that be right?

(i) Suppose I bought a car in 1977. The car didn't work very well, but I loved it. So I replaced its parts, slowly, small part by small part. In the end, the car I now have has no small parts that were parts of it when I bought it. Can it really be that the car I now have is the car I bought in 1977? That seems intuitively wrong. It seems intuitively worse when we discover that my neighbor has been collecting the small parts I discarded, and has now fitted them all together just as they were fitted together in 1977. For many of us now undergo a gestalt shift: surely, we feel, it is my neighbor, not me, who has the car I bought in 1977. (I here up-date the problem of the Ship of Theseus.)

Moreover, (ii) suppose the car I bought in 1977 was a 1977 Chevrolet. Suppose the parts I replaced its parts with were those of a 1947 Buick I happened to have owned as well. And suppose that I slowly replaced all of the parts of the Chevrolet with all of the parts of the Buick. Has my 1977 Chevrolet become a 1947 Buick? (Why didn't I instead just move the Buick, part by part, into the space formerly occupied by the Chevrolet? Can it have been my intentions that made the difference?)

These difficulties are serious. Ordinary thought about artifacts supplies no answer to the question how large a part is too large, or to the question whether there is a point in a series of replacements of small parts at which the result is not the artifact we began with, and if so, what marks it. On the other hand, we cannot simply declare that there is vagueness here, since identity is not vague, or so I throughout assume.

Some philosophers therefore conclude that artifacts cannot undergo replacement of any part, and others that there are no artifacts at all. These responses strike me as *weird*. But I am not even going to try to produce a better one. I will simply suppose—with ordinary thought —that artifacts can undergo replacement of a small part, leaving open how small is small, and what happens when (or would happen if) a replacement of a small part is (or if it were) part of a series of such replacements.

In particular, I will suppose that ALFRED remained wholly on the table after replacement of his left hand. CLAY, however, did not. Then how *are* ALFRED and CLAY related to each other? We can call the relation "constituting" if we like; we now have to say what constituting is.

3. We are committed to supposing that one thing can constitute another at one time and not at another. CLAY, we are supposing, constitutes ALFRED at 2PM. But CLAY does not constitute ALFRED at 3PM, for part of CLAY is on the floor at 3PM. I drew attention to temporary properties in section 1; so it looks as if the two-place relation 'x constitutes y' is, analogously, a temporary relation. For a variety of reasons, it will be simpler for us to aim at analyzing, not the two-place relation 'x constitutes y', but instead the three-place relation 'x constitutes y at t'. We lose nothing in doing so,

for we can go back and forth at will: CLAY, for example, has the two-place relation 'x constitutes y' to AL-FRED at 2PM if and only if CLAY has the three-place relation 'x constitutes y at t' to ALFRED and 2PM. (This three-place relation is plainly not a temporary relation: *it* is had at all times if at any time, and so cannot be acquired and lost.)

Very well: what is the three-place constituting-relation? It can, I suggest, be analyzed wholly in terms of parthood with the help of a few modal operators.

We need to fix three ideas about parthood before proceeding. First, we are supposing that one material object can be part of another at one time and not at another—ALFRED's left hand, for example, is part of AL-FRED at 2PM but not at 3PM. So we are supposing that the two-place relation 'x is part of y' is a temporary relation. But as in the case of constituting, it will be simpler for us to focus, not on the two-place relation 'x is part of y', but instead on the three-place relation 'x is part of y at t'. As before, we lose nothing in doing so: ALFRED's left hand, for example, has the two-place relation 'x is part of y' to ALFRED at 2PM if and only if ALFRED's left hand has the three-place relation 'x is part of y at t' to ALFRED and 2PM. (And this three-place relation too is plainly not a temporary relation: it too is had at all times if at any time.)

Second, I will follow two conventions governing the word "part" that are common in the literature on parts and wholes. I will call them housekeeping conventions. The first is that the word "parts" is throughout not re-stricted to what are often called "proper parts". For ex-ample, we are to suppose that ALFRED has among his parts at 2PM: his head, his hands, his feet, *and* himself. More generally, we are to suppose that

(i) x exists at t → x is part of x at t.

The second housekeeping convention is that parthood entails existence. For example, ALFRED's left hand is part of ALFRED at 1PM only if both exist at 1PM. More generally,

(ii) x is part of y at t → x and y both exist at t.

Third, since what I am concerned with throughout is material objects, the parthood relation I make use of is parthood *on material objects.* Many people have said of other kinds of entities that they too have parts. Some people say that a subset of a set is part of it. Some people say that propositions have parts. Many people say that events have parts. Anyone who uses the word "parts" in respect of things of a kind K must tell us what for his or her purposes is to count as one K's being part of another. Since what I am concerned with is material objects, my variables x, y, and z will throughout range only over material objects. And I will suppose that the parthood relation I make use of is governed by the following biconditional:

x is part of y at t ↔ the space occupied by x at t is part of the space occupied by y at t.

What is it for one space to be part of another? On some views, spaces are sets of space points. If they are, then one space is part of another just in case it is a subset of the other. No doubt there are other possibilities too. I leave this open. It is essential to a material object y that it be spatially located at all times at which it exists: and intuitively, y's parts at a time t are just those material objects that are where y is at t. Perhaps those material objects are not parts of y throughout y's life. Perhaps they are not even parts of y for very long. But they are parts of y *at t.* It is this intuition that the biconditional is intended to express.

It is of course arguable that we do not know what space a thing y occupies at a time unless we already know what things x are parts of it at that time. It is for that reason that I do not define parthood on material objects in terms of parthood on spaces. It is enough for our purposes that the two go together—hence the biconditional.

And it should be added that exactness of spatial location is not to be expected. Material objects have atomic, indeed subatomic, parts; what is their exact location, and thus the exact location of a material object made of them? We needn't care, for exactness is not required for our purposes: it is enough for us that a material object's parts are wherever it is, and vice versa.

We can now take our first step in defining constitution: surely x constitutes y at t only if x and y occupy the same space at t—thus only if x is part of y at t and y is part of x at t.

But mutual parthood, while necessary for constituting, is not sufficient for it. For example, CLAY and ALFRED occupy the same space at 2PM, and we do want to have that CLAY constitutes ALFRED then; but we surely do not want to have that ALFRED constitutes CLAY then, so there has to be a further condition or conditions in the definition, in order to fix that constituting goes one way but not the other. Finding the needed further condition or conditions is the hard job.

Let us go back. I invited you to agree in section 2 that when (shortly before 3PM) I broke ALFRED's left hand off and threw it on the floor, CLAY got scattered. It was crucial to the story I told that in breaking ALFRED's hand off, I was breaking a part of CLAY off from the rest of CLAY, and not merely a part of CLAY but more important, a part of CLAY that was, itself, a portion of clay—it was a sub-portion of the portion of clay that I am calling CLAY. For two ideas about portions of clay seem to me very plausible. The first is that if a portion of clay is on a table, and you break off a part of it *that is itself a portion of clay* and throw that part on the floor, then what remains on the table is not the original portion, but is merely a proper part of it.

More generally, if x is a portion of clay and y is a portion of clay and x is part of y at a time, then if y still exists at a later time, then x is still part of y at that later time. More strongly, if x is a portion of clay and y is a portion of clay and x is part of y at a time, then *necessarily* if y exists at any time, then x is part of y at that time. If we abbreviate "x is part of y at t" as "x<y@t," and "x exists at t" as "xE@t," then we can reput the idea here as follows:

Portion of Clay Principle: {x is a portion of clay & y is a portion of clay & (∃t)(x<y@t)]} →□ (∀t)(yE@t → x<y@t)

I should think that analogues of this principle are also true of a great many other stuffs M, such as coal, soup, pudding, wood, and so on. (We will have another look at such principles in section 5.)

Let us give the name CLAYHAND to the portion of clay that was part of CLAY at 2PM, but which I broke off from the rest of CLAY shortly before 3PM. Given the Portion of Clay Principle, CLAY cannot exist at a time unless CLAYHAND is part of CLAY at that time.

CLAYHAND was not merely a part of CLAY at 2PM, it was also part of ALFRED then. But ALFRED's left hand having been replaced shortly before 3PM, CLAYHAND is not part of ALFRED at 3PM. Indeed, ALFRED's left hand having been *wholly replaced,* no part of CLAYHAND is part of ALFRED at 3PM. So ALFRED can exist at a time at which no part of CLAYHAND is part of ALFRED.

To return now to constituting. We would like to have it turn out that CLAY constitutes ALFRED at 2PM. It is plain that the following is true:

(i) CLAY<ALFRED@2PM & ALFRED <CLAY@ 2PM.

The considerations we have just surveyed make clear that the following is also true:

(ii) There is a z such that z<CLAY@2PM, and such that z is essential to CLAY, and nothing that is part of z at 2PM is essential to ALFRED.

(CLAYHAND is a z that meets that condition.)
I suggest that we can also say:

(iii) NOT-(There is a z such that z<ALFRED @2PM, and such that z is essential to AL-FRED, and nothing that is part of z at 2PM is essential to CLAY).

Why so? There is at least one z such that z was part of ALFRED at 2PM, and such that z is essential to AL-FRED, namely ALFRED himself. (ALFRED is always part of ALFRED, and ALFRED cannot exist at a time without having ALFRED among his parts at that time.) But ALFRED had many parts at 2PM which were portions of clay, and given the Portion of Clay Principle, they are all essential to CLAY. Is there another z such that z was part of ALFRED at 2PM, and such that z is essential to ALFRED? Perhaps you think that ALFRED had, at 2PM, a big proper part—much bigger than his left hand—which is essential to ALFRED? Even if so, anything that was a big proper part of ALFRED at

2PM, had (as did ALFRED himself) many portions of clay among its parts then, and they are all essential to CLAY. So (iii) is true.

I suggest now that we should say that (i), (ii), and (iii) are necessary and jointly sufficient for the truth of "CLAY constitutes ALFRED at 2PM". And generalizing, that we should define constituting as follows:

x constitutes y at t $=_{df}$

(1) x<y@t & y<x@t &

(2) $(\exists z)\{z<x@t \ \& \ \Box(\forall T)(xE@T \to z<x@T) \ \& \ (\forall z')[z'<z@t \to \Diamond(\exists T)(yE@T \ \& \ \neg(z'<y@T)]\}$ &

(3) NOT-$[(\exists z)\{z<y@t \ \Box(\forall T)(yE@T \to z<y@T) \ \& \ (\forall z')[z'<z@t \to \Diamond(\exists T)(xE@T \ \& \ \neg(z'<x@T)]\}]$

It is easy to see that if x constitutes y at t, then y does not constitute x at t. So given (i), (ii), and (iii), and therefore that CLAY constitutes ALFRED at 2PM, it follows that ALFRED does not constitute CLAY at 2PM. It can also be seen—though not quite so easily (I leave the proof as an exercise for the reader)—that if x constitutes y at t, and y constitutes z at t, then x constitutes z at t.

I suggest, then, that that does it.[1] And the definition we have reached does not merely *happen* to yield the results it should: there is a good reason why it does. What condition (2) does is to generalize on the very fact that led us to say that CLAY is not identical with ALFRED but merely constitutes it. We concluded that CLAY is not identical with ALFRED on ground of my having done the following: I replaced a part of ALFRED, leaving AL-FRED on the table but scattering CLAY. (It should be stressed that in replacing that part of ALFRED, I was removing it and all of its parts from ALFRED.) For me to have succeeded in doing that, there had to be a part of CLAY that CLAY could not lose but that ALFRED could lose every part of. That CLAY had such a part is exactly what condition (2) requires. By contrast, I could not have replaced a part of CLAY, leaving CLAY on the

---

1. I proposed to analyze constituting wholly in terms of parthood with the help of a few modal operators. But what of that predicate "xE@t" that appears in the definiens? Given housekeeping conventions (i) and (ii), it is itself definable in terms of parthood.

table but scattering ALFRED. For me to have succeeded in doing that, there would have to have been a part of ALFRED that ALFRED could not lose but that CLAY could lose every part of. That ALFRED had no such part is exactly what condition (3) requires.

In short, CLAY is more tightly tied to its parts than ALFRED is, and that is the ontological difference between them marked by saying that CLAY is not identical with but merely constituted ALFRED.

The same holds for any other pair of an artifact and the stuff of which it is made at a time t. Let WOOD be the portion of wood of which CHAIR is made at t. You can replace a part of CHAIR, leaving CHAIR but scattering WOOD; you cannot replace a part of WOOD, leaving WOOD but scattering CHAIR. The definition therefore yields that WOOD is not identical with CHAIR, but merely constitutes it at t. And so on.

This outcome is as it should be. Continuity of shape matters to an artifact's continued existence more than continuity of material parts: a fortiori, the artifact's material parts can change while the artifact remains. By contrast, continuity of material parts matters to a stuff's continued existence more than continuity of shape does; a fortiori, the stuff's shape can change while the stuff remains.

What we have been looking at so far are only pairs of an artifact and a stuff. We move down an ontological level when we move down from ALFRED to CLAY. We should see that similar things are to be said when we move down yet another ontological level, from CLAY to something else. The something else I have in mind is what—borrowing a term from Locke—I will call a mass of atoms. However we need a piece of technical machinery in order to be able to say what those entities are.

4. Consider a non-empty set of material objects S. ("S" here is short for a name.) I will say that x all-fuses S just in case x meets two conditions.

Condition (1) is that necessarily, x exists at a time if and only if all of the members of S exist at that time. (Hence the name "all-fusion".)

x all-fuses S $=_{df}$

(1) $\square(\forall t)\{xE@t \leftrightarrow [(\exists y)(yeS) \& (\forall y)(yeS \rightarrow yE@t]\} \& \ldots$

The first conjunct following the double-arrow, namely "$(\exists y)$ (yeS)," is intended to insure that x does not exist at a time in a world W unless S itself exists in W, and therefore (since sets cannot change their members) unless all of S's members exist in W. The second conjunct, is intended to insure that all of S's members exist when x does.

A second clause is needed, for clause (1) tells us only x's existence conditions, and we need to know also what its parts are. I mean for y to be part of x at t if and only if necessarily, x and y meet two conditions. First, x and y must exist at t:

(2) $\square(\forall t)(\forall y)\{y<x@t \leftrightarrow [xE@t \& yE@t \& \ldots$

(Housekeeping convention (ii) requires this.) Let us say that z is discrete from z′ at t just in case z and z′ have no parts in common at t. Then we are to add, second, that y must have no parts at t which are, at t, discrete from all of the members of S. Thus, abbreviating "is discrete from" as "D," we are to add, second:

$\ldots \neg(\exists z)[z<y@t \& (\forall z')(z'eS \rightarrow zDz'@t)]]\}$

In sum:

x all-fuses S $=_{df}$

(1) $\square(\forall t)\{xE@t \leftrightarrow [(\exists y)(yeS) \& (\forall y)(yeS \rightarrow yE@t)]\} \&$

(2) $\square(\forall t)(\forall y)\{y<x@t \leftrightarrow [xE@t \& yE@t \& \neg(\exists z)[z<y@t \& (\forall z')(z'eS \rightarrow zDz'@t)]]\}$

It can easily be seen that the definition yields that if x all-fuses S, then if x exists at a time, then every member of S does not merely exist at that time, but is also part of x at that time. Let us suppose that x all-fuses the set whose members are the chairs in my house. The chair I am now sitting on is now part of x, since it has no parts now which are now discrete from all of the chairs in my house.

It can easily be seen that the definition also yields that if x all-fuses S, then if x exists at a time, x also has a great many other parts at that time. If x all-fuses the set whose members are the chairs in my house, then everything that is now part of the chair I am now sitting on is now part of x—the left front leg of the chair, for example, is now part of x since it has no parts now which are now discrete from all of the chairs in my house. Indeed, every atom that is now part of the chair I am now sitting on is now part of x.

What we have so far, however, is merely a definition. Does anything answer to it?

Well, everything is the all-fusion of at least one set, namely the set whose sole member is itself.

Again, I have been supposing that

Portion of Clay Principle: {x is a portion of clay & y is a portion of clay & $(\exists t)(x < y @ t)$]}
$\rightarrow \Box(\forall t)(y E @ t \rightarrow x < y @ t)$

is true. Then surely every portion of clay is the all-fusion of the set whose members are all of the portions of clay that are ever parts of it. And I should think we could say also that for every set of portions of clay, there is a portion of clay which all-fuses it, thus:

x is a portion of clay $\leftrightarrow$ for some set of portions of clay S, x is the all-fusion of S.

Similarly for other stuffs, such as soup, pudding, coal, wood, and so on.

Again, let us have another look at a list I gave earlier:

some shape-constrained temporary properties: being a puddle of M, a piece of M, a lump of M, . . . , being a heap of M, a mound of M, a stack of M, . . .

where "M" is short for an appropriate 'mass-noun', such as "clay," "soup," "pudding," "coal," "wood" and so on. I said that the things that acquire and lose these properties are portions of stuff, that is, portions of clay, soup, pudding, coal, wood, and so on. We can now say that the things that acquire and lose these properties are all-fusions of sets of portions of stuff.

The possibility of an attractive generalization now emerges. I divided that list in two for an interesting reason. Consider the following list:

being a heap of Cs, a mound of Cs, a stack of Cs, . . .

where "Cs" is the plural of a count-noun, as for example, "flowers," "bananas," "cards," "chairs," "beans," and so on. Nothing can be a puddle, piece, or lump of flowers, bananas, cards, and so on. But a thing can be heap, mound, or stack of flowers, bananas, cards, and so on. (Hence my division of the list.) What entities are they that are from time to time a heap, mound, or stack of flowers?

Consider yet another list:

being a bunch of Cs, a cluster of Cs, a bouquet of Cs, ...

Nothing can be a bunch, cluster, or bouquet of clay, soup, pudding or coal; something can be a bunch, cluster, or bouquet of flowers, or a bunch or cluster of bananas, cards, and so on. What entities are they that are from time to time a bunch, cluster, or bouquet of flowers?

All-fusions, I suggest. A heap or bunch of flowers is the all-fusion of the set whose members are those flowers, and the all-fusion is (currently) a heap or bunch because of the all-fusion's (current) shape. If someone removes one flower from your heap or bunch, you no longer have the same heap or bunch: you only have a proper part of the one you had. If someone removes only one petal of one flower, you do still have the same heap or bunch: that is because flowers (like statues) can survive the loss of some of their parts, and a petal (like ALFRED's left hand) is a part that can be lost.

In sum, the entities that from time to time possess the following shape-constrained temporary properties—

being a puddle, piece, lump of M, . . . , being a heap, mound, stack of M, . . . ,

and

being a heap, mound, stack of Cs, . . . , being a bunch, cluster, bouquet of Cs, . . .—

are all all-fusions, of sets of portions of M on the one hand, of sets of Cs on the other.

Can we say that for any non-empty set of material objects S, there is an x that all-fuses S? No. Suppose S has three members (and thus is non-empty). Suppose also that there is never a time at which all three exist at once. Then clause (1) of the definition of all-fusing tells us that if x is the all-fusion of S, there is no time at which x exists. Thus there is no x that all-fuses S.

I am inclined to think, however, that we should agree that for any set of material objects S for which there is a time at which all of its members exist, there is an x that all-fuses S. This idea is not needed for our purposes here, but I see no good reason to reject it. Accepting it commits us to the existence of some very queer looking entities, such as, for example, the all-fusion of the chair I am now sitting on and your car. But why not? The relation of all-fusion is well-defined in a certain strong sense. (i) The definition tells us when a set's all-fusion in fact exists and what its parts in fact then are. Moreover, (ii) the definition tells us when the set's all-fusion would exist and what its parts would then be in any possible world you like. (iii) Although we know from the definition that a set may in fact have no all-fusion, it is clear that any (non-empty) set could have had an all-fusion: there is no metaphysical impossibility in the supposition that it does. Alternatively put: there is a possible world in which it does.

Suppose, then, that there is a time at which all the members of a set S exist. Then there is a possible world in which S has an all-fusion. Why not this world? How could empirical investigation disclose that S doesn't in fact have an all-fusion? Is there supposed to be some contingent matter of fact—discoverable, perhaps, by meticulous scientific investigation—that fixes that it doesn't? I hardly think so. So I see no good reason to reject the idea that S has an all-fusion.

5. To return to where we were. What we had been looking at in section 3 were pairs of an artifact and a stuff of which it is made at a time t. And I had suggested that the definition of constituting I supplied yields the result that the stuff constitutes the artifact at t, from which it follows that the artifact does not constitute the stuff at t.

I said that if we think of ourselves as moving down an ontological level from ALFRED to CLAY, it pays to see that similar things are to be said when we move down yet another ontological level, from CLAY to something else. What something else do I have in mind? I will call it a mass of atoms, to be defined as follows:

x is a mass of atoms$=_{df}$ for some set of atoms S, x all-fuses S.

Are there such things? I can see no good reason to think there are not.

Now I assume that CLAY is made of atoms, and indeed, that every atom it is made of at a time is part of it at that time. Let $S_{atoms,CLAY,2PM}$ be the set whose members are all of the atoms that are parts of CLAY at 2PM. Let ALL-$S_{atoms,CLAY,2PM}$ be the mass of atoms that all-fuses $S_{atoms,CLAY,2PM}$. Consider, now,

$$ALL\text{-}S_{atoms,CLAY,2PM} = CLAY.$$

Can we accept that thesis? I think we had better not, because of a replacement argument like the one that led us to reject

$$CLAY = ALFRED.$$

For suppose that just before 3PM we replace an atom in CLAY, throwing the replaced atom on the floor. (You have to use a very tiny spoon to do that.) Then

(7) ALL-$S_{atoms,CLAY,2PM}$ is not wholly on the table at 3PM

is true, for something that is still part of ALL-$S_{atoms,CLAY,2PM}$ is on the floor at 3PM. But I think we should agree that

(8) CLAY is wholly on the table at 3PM

is also true, for I think we should agree that CLAY has undergone a replacement of a part as ALFRED underwent a replacement of a part when I replaced his left hand. It follows that CLAY is not identical with ALL-$S_{atoms,CLAY,2PM}$.

Why should we agree that (8) is true? I said in section 3 that there were two ideas about CLAY that seemed to me very plausible. The first idea was that any part of CLAY *that is itself a portion of clay* cannot be removed from, and hence cannot be replaced in, CLAY: any such part of CLAY remains a part of CLAY. The generalization of that first idea is expressed in the Portion of Clay Principle. The second idea is that any *atom* that is part of CLAY can be replaced in CLAY. We can have this second idea along with the first only if we agree that no atom that is part of CLAY is itself a portion of clay; but that is surely obvious.

Of course if too many atoms are replaced too quickly, then we do not have the original portion any longer, just as if too much of ALFRED is replaced too quickly, then we do not have ALFRED any longer. One atom, however, is replaceable, just as ALFRED's left hand is.

So I take it that ALL-S$_{\text{atoms,CLAY,2PM}}$ is not identical with CLAY. What seems right is, rather, that ALL-S$_{\text{atoms,CLAY,2PM}}$ constitutes CLAY at 2PM. Not at 3PM, but at 2PM. And I think you will see that, given the definitions of all-fusing and constituting, that is exactly the result we do get.

In sum, we now have three ontological levels represented:

ALFRED
CLAY
ALL-S$_{\text{atoms,CLAY,2PM}}$

At the top, continuity of shape matters to the thing's continued existence more than continuity of material parts: a fortiori, its material parts can change while the thing remains. In the middle, continuity of macro-material constitution matters to the thing's continued existence more than continuity of micro-material parts: a fortiori, its micro-material parts can change while the thing remains. At the bottom, only continuity of micro-material parts matters to the thing's continued existence: a fortiori, its micro-material parts cannot change while the thing remains.

A difficulty arises when we turn from clay to certain other stuffs, however. Clay, after all, is a mixture. What about gold? Suppose we have a chunk of gold; call it GOLD. The generalization of the first idea about CLAY, namely the Portion of Clay Principle, has an analogue for gold:

Portion of Gold Principle: {x is a portion of gold & y is a portion of gold & (∃t)(x<y@t)]}]
→ □(∀t)(yE@t → x<y@t)

The second idea about CLAY also has an analogue for GOLD, namely that any *atom* that is part of GOLD can

be replaced in GOLD. Can we accept both of these ideas? Only if we accept that no gold atom is itself a portion of gold. Should we?

I initially introduced the term "portion" in the following way: I said that for the time being, a portion of clay is some clay. It is a quantity of clay. Does it seem intuitively right to think that a gold atom is some gold, and is a quantity of gold? Perhaps so. No doubt you don't have much gold if you have only one gold atom, but perhaps we are inclined to think you do have some. If so, then if we continue to use the term "portion" as I initially introduced it, we must agree that a gold atom *is* a portion of gold. And if we do, something has to go—either the Portion of Gold Principle, or the idea that any atom that is part of GOLD can be replaced in GOLD.

The ordinary use of the term "portion" is heavily context-dependent. If an atom drifts away from your portion of gold, do you still have the same portion of gold? You will say no if you are a scientist engaged in an experiment for which every atom matters. You will say yes if you are a jeweler about to make a ring. Similarly, in fact, for clay. If you have just bought a load of clay, and a handful falls off while you are on your way home, is the portion you have when you get home the same as the portion you bought? You will say no if you had carefully measured and bought exactly as much as you need. You will say yes if loss of a handful makes no difference to you.

So if we are to use "portion" in a way that is context-independent—as I have all along meant to do and will continue to do—we have to impose a constraint. We have to stipulate a use.

I begin with a distinction. Some things are big enough to be, from time to time, a piece, puddle, lump, . . . , heap, mound, or stack of M. The clay of which ALFRED's left hand is made is big enough to be a piece of clay. A cupful of water is big enough to be a puddle of water. Other things are too small. A gold atom is too small ever to be a piece of gold. A water molecule is too small ever to be a puddle of water.

The stipulation, then, is this: "portion" is to be so used that a thing is not a portion of M unless it can from time to time be a piece, puddle, lump, . . . , heap, mound, or stack of M. In short: unless it can from time to time possess one of the shape-constrained temporary properties I pointed to in section 1, and discussed in the preceding section. This stipulation gives those properties a central role in fixing what counts for our purposes as a portion of M. But I think it is not merely arbitrary to assign them this role. Among other things, it is only what is large enough to possess one of those shape-constrained temporary properties that can constitute an artifact. (What is large enough to possess one of those properties may be very small indeed, however; some artifacts, after all, are themselves very small.)

The stipulation allows us to retain the Portion of Clay Principle and the Portion of Gold Principle compatibly with retaining the idea that any atom that is part of CLAY or GOLD can be replaced in it. And it allows us to have that a portion of gold, like a portion of clay, is (not identical with but instead) constituted at a time by the all-fusion of the atoms that are parts of it at that time.

Similarly for other stuff, such as water, coal, soup, pudding, and so on.

6. We now have in hand a definition of the three-place relation 'x constitutes y at t'.

We saw in section 3 that it yields that a portion of stuff might constitute an artifact. (For example, CLAY constitutes ALFRED at 2PM.) Let us now take note of the fact that a portion of stuff might constitute something other than an artifact. Suppose that in 1991, a shortsighted Moscow shopkeeper made a portion of tin into a large bunch of little tin statues of Lenin. Call them lenins; call the tin TIN. What is the bunch of lenins? I suggested in section 4 that it is the all-fusion of the set of lenins; call it ALL-S_{lenins}. Then we have:

TIN constitutes ALL-S_{lenins} in 1991.

(That is true because we can replace one of the lenin's left hand, and after doing so, that lenin, and hence ALL-S_{lenins}, remains but TIN does not.) So here we have a portion of stuff that constitutes not *an* artifact but the all-fusion of a set of many artifacts.

There are also cases in which the all-fusion of a set of many artifacts constitutes *an* artifact. Being unable to sell his lenins, the shopkeeper might in 1992, and purely for his own pleasure, make a big tin statue of Lenin out of them—not by melting them down, but by twisting their little arms and legs together with a pair of pliers. Call the big statue LENIN. Then we have

ALL-S_{lenins} constitutes LENIN in 1992.

(That is true because we can replace one of the lenins, and after doing so, LENIN remains, but ALL-S_{lenins} does not.) Intuitively, these results are as they should be.

But can the all-fusion of a set of only one artifact constitute an artifact? Since the all-fusion of a set with only one member *is* that one member, we can reput our question as follows: can an artifact constitute an artifact?

We can certainly make an artifact out of an artifact. I suspect that in all such cases, an additional or different use—or anyway intended use—is required. In some cases, that by itself suffices, as where we make a desk out of a table. In others, we also deform one to make another, as where we make a tierack out of a statue by stretching its fingers out appropriately. In still others, we add a part. Suppose we make a throne out of a chair by adding a gilt crown and coming to use it as our throne. Call the chair CHAIR and the throne THRONE. Does CHAIR now constitute THRONE?

Since CHAIR and THRONE now occupy the same place,

(i) CHAIR<THRONE@NOW &
    THRONE<CHAIR@NOW

is true. Consider now

(ii) There is a z such that z<CHAIR@NOW, and such that z is essential to CHAIR, and nothing that is part of z at NOW is essential to THRONE.

Suppose that z is a small part of CHAIR now. I said in section 2 that I would suppose—with ordinary thought—that artifacts can undergo replacement of a small part. *Any* artifact, I should think, and *any* small part. A certain small bit of its case is now part of my watch; and my watch can undergo replacement of that part, and hence can exist at a time without having that part at that time. My computer can undergo replacement of its current delete key, and hence can exist at a time without having its current delete key at that time. Similarly for my car, my lawnmower, my telephone, and so on.

It might be worth stress that this is true even of those of an artifact's small parts that are more important to it than a small bit of its case is to my watch. Artifacts are made for a purpose: they have characteristic functions. (Hence the importance to them of their shapes.) Thus a watch has the function of indicating the time. A computer has the function of computing. Now my watch has a small part, a certain cog, such that if that cog were removed and not replaced, then my watch would no longer be able to indicate the time. Still, my watch could undergo replacement of that cog, and hence can exist at a time without having that very cog itself among its parts at that time. Similarly for my computer, my car, and so on.

So I think it plain that if z is any small part of any artifact at t, then, however important z may be to the functioning of the artifact, the artifact can exist at a time at which z is not among its parts.

To return, then, to (ii). We were supposing that z is a small part of CHAIR now. It follows that z is not essential to CHAIR. So (ii) is false for that z.

Suppose, instead, that z is a large part of CHAIR now. We might suppose CHAIR largely made of a single slab of wood, appropriately bent, that serves as both seat and back; call it SLAB. Perhaps SLAB is essential to CHAIR? (Its being so, if it is, is compatible with *its* undergoing replacement of a small part.) Then how could SLAB fail to be essential to THRONE?

Suppose that z is not merely a large part of CHAIR now but *is* CHAIR. CHAIR cannot exist at a time without having CHAIR among its parts at that time, so this z is on any view essential to CHAIR. But this z now has a part, namely THRONE, which is essential to THRONE.

In sum, (ii) is false, and it follows that CHAIR does not now constitute THRONE. (Similar reasoning yields that THRONE does not now constitute CHAIR.)

So what happened when we made a throne out of CHAIR? CHAIR did not come to constitute a throne (as CLAY came to constitute a statue); I should think that CHAIR instead became a throne. And when we make a desk out of a table, the table becomes a desk. Similarly for making a tierack out of a statue.

If that is acceptable, then at least some of what I called artifact-properties (being a statue, being a chair, being a car, being a ship, and so on) really are temporary properties. In section 1, I drew attention to the idea that they are temporary properties of portions of stuff, and in section 2, rejected it. But that left open that they are temporary properties of other things. What has emerged

here is that some anyway (being a throne, being a desk, being a tierack) are temporary properties of artifacts. It might be worth looking into the question whether all are, and if not, why not.

7. In the preceding section I argued that CHAIR does not now constitute THRONE: the argument relied on CHAIR's failing to meet one of the three conditions it has to meet if it is to constitute THRONE now. Let us now look at a different argument for the conclusion that CHAIR does not now constitute THRONE.

Some people say that no two material objects can occupy the same place at the same time. I have made clear enough that I think that is a mistake.[2] Many more people say that while two material objects can occupy the same place at the same time, no two artifacts can—thus:

----

2. The well-known problem about Tibbles the cat does not turn on the fact that Tibbles is a cat, so let us suppose it is a clay statue of a cat. We are invited to suppose first that Tib is the material object that, at 2PM, occupies the space occupied, at 2PM, by all of Tibbles except its tail. Shortly before 3PM, someone breaks off Tibbles' tail. At 3PM, Tibbles—having lost its tail—occupies the same space as Tib does. We are then invited, second, to agree that no two material objects can occupy the same space at a time. It follows that Tibbles is identical with Tib. But of course it is not, for Tibbles's tail was once part of Tibbles but was never part of Tib. So something has to give. What should give?

Well, we should refuse the second invitation: we should refuse to agree that no two material objects can occupy the same space at a time, for a portion of stuff and an artifact and an all-fusion of atoms and an all-fusion of artifacts can all occupy the same space at the same time. But this means that we should refuse the first invitation too. There is no such thing as *the* material object that, at 2PM, occupies the space occupied, at 2PM, by all of Tibbles except its tail. There are at least two material objects that occupy that space at that time: a portion of clay and an all-fusion of atoms. So "Tib" was not even well-defined.

There is a larger lesson in the offing here. Many people are in the habit of inviting us to attend first to (as it might be) a statue or a car, and second to (as they put it) *the* left-hand half of the statue, or *the* rest-of-the-car-other-than-its-tires. What entities are those? What warrants those occurrences of "the"?

Artifact Thesis: No two artifacts can occupy the same place at the same time.

If they are right, then since CHAIR and THRONE now occupy the same place, CHAIR *is* THRONE. A fortiori, CHAIR does not now (or at any other time) constitute THRONE.

If they are right, then, quite generally, *no* artifact constitutes an artifact at any time. For in order for an artifact x to constitute an artifact y at a time t, it has to be the case that x and y occupy the same place at t. But if x and y occupy the same place at t—and if, also, the Artifact Thesis is true—then x is identical with y and a fortiori does not constitute y at any time.

Are they right? Let us look at an argument to the effect that they are not. Consider, again, the definition of all-fusion:

x all-fuses S $=_{df}$

(1) $\Box(\forall t)\{xE@t \leftrightarrow [(\exists y)(yeS) \& (\forall y)(yeS \rightarrow yE@t)]\} \&$

(2) $\Box(\forall t)(\forall y)\{y{<}x@t \leftrightarrow [xE@t \& yE@t \& \neg(\exists z)[z{<}y@t \& (\forall z')(z'eS \rightarrow zDz'@t)]]\}$

We can obtain another notion 'fusion' by replacing clause (1). For example, consider what I will call some-fusion, and define as follows:

x some-fuses S $=_{df}$

(1) $\Box(!\forall t)\{xE@t \leftrightarrow [(\exists y)(yeS \& yE@t)]\} \&$

(2) .... (as above) ....

Do any sets have some-fusions? Well, just as every set with one member has an all-fusion which is identical with the set's one member, so also does every set with one member have a some-fusion, which is identical with the set's one member. What of sets with more than one member? I suggested in section 4 that many familiar objects—mounds of clay, bunches of flowers—are all-fusions of sets with more than one member; are there any familiar objects that are some-fusions of sets with more than one member? I doubt it. In any case, I cannot think of any. Still, why should familiarity matter? I said that all-fusion is well-defined in a certain

strong sense; so also is some-fusion. And how could empirical investigation disclose that a (non-empty) set lacks a some-fusion?

A warning is in order, however, since all-fusion and some-fusion are only the beginning. Why not also three-fusion? We obtain its definition by making yet another replacement for clause (1). Thus x three-fuses a set only if x exists at a time if and only if three members of the set exist at that time. Analogously for three-or-more-fusion. Analogously for some-red-fusion: x has this relation to a set only if x exists at a time if and only if some member of the set exists and is red at that time. And then there is two-three-bears-fusion: x has this relation to a set only if x exists at a time if and only if two members of the set exist at the time and three members had, before that time, been eaten by bears. These relations too are well-defined, and why should we accept some of the resulting entities and not others?

Accepting all of them commits us to less clutter than at first appears. First, there are identities among some of them. If a set has three members, and there is a time at which all of them exist, then it has both an all-fusion and a three-fusion, and its all-fusion *is* its three-fusion. Second, there are parthood relations among them. If a set has an all-fusion, then it also has a some-fusion, and there are times at which its all-fusion and some-fusion are parts of each other. Third, there are times at which some constitute others. Thus suppose there is a time t at which all the members of a set S exist. Then S has an all-fusion and a some-fusion, and its all-fusion constitutes its some-fusion at t. (I hope this outcome will seem unobjectionable. After all, all-fusions really are more tightly tied to their parts than some-fusions are.) My own view is that we should accept all of those entities. (We can think of Reality as like an over-crowded attic, some of its contents interesting, and most merely junk. There is no need to deny the junk; we can simply leave it to gather dust.) But I won't argue for this view. Let us just have a look at what happens if we accept some-fusions.

Suppose we grant that for any non-empty set, there is something that some-fuses it. Consider the set whose sole members are Caesar's sword and my chair. (Which chair do I refer to by "my chair"? It is a chair that came into existence only recently.) Let us give the name SWORD-CHAIR to the thing that some-fuses that set. SWORD-CHAIR exists now, since my chair does. Is it a chair? Of course it wasn't always a chair, but isn't it a chair now? If so, then—since SWORD-CHAIR came into existence far earlier than, and hence is not identical with, my chair—there are two things, both of them now chairs, both now occupying the same place. It looks, then, as if the Artifact Thesis has to go.

There are several ways in which that conclusion can be blocked. A familiar way is to allow that my chair and SWORD-CHAIR are both now chairs, but to deny that counting chairs is as straightforward as might have been thought. We might say: to count the number of chairs in a room at a time t, you have to count, not the number of things in the room at t that are chairs at t, but rather the number of sets, each of which has as its members all the things in the room at t that are chairs at t and that are parts of each other at t. (There is only one set that has as its members all the things in my room now that are chairs now and are parts of each other now—that set has my chair and SWORD-CHAIR among its members—hence there is only one chair in my room now.) And we might add that it should be no surprise that accepting some-fusions requires accepting more sophisticated counting-methods.

Another possibility is to deny that SWORD-CHAIR is a chair now. If SWORD-CHAIR is a chair now, it became a chair, for it wasn't always a chair. Moreover, it became a chair simply because some other chair (namely my chair) came into existence. Now it does seem plausible to suppose that nothing can become a chair simply because some other chair comes into existence—at least as plausible as that every non-empty set has a some-fusion. And if that *is* right, then SWORD-CHAIR did not become a chair: while it now has a chair among its parts, it is not itself a chair now.

There is obviously more to be said about these matters. But I doubt that any of the more that has to be said would yield compelling reason—reason it would be unreasonable to resist—for rejecting the Artifact Thesis. (Or at least for rejecting what its friends intend by it.) My concern has been merely to point to a kind of consideration that friends of that thesis have not addressed themselves to but should.

8. In any case, we now have in hand an analysis of constituting. Three things call for brief mention.

First, the highest ontological level I described is that of artifacts, and it might well be asked whether there is a level above them—above them as artifacts are above portions of stuff and portions of stuff above masses of atoms. What would they be like? We have to suppose them to be even less tightly tied to their parts than artifacts are. Are they to be thought to float entirely free of their parts? What, then, could be thought to fix their paths through time, or even to mark one off from another? The cluster of issues that arise here might be worth looking into: they might have an interesting bearing on the difficulties (described in section 2) having to do with limits on replacements of parts in artifacts.

Second, I have been concerned throughout with artifacts and the things that constitute them, and have therefore said nothing at all about living creatures. I take cats and people to *be* their bodies, and hence not to be constituted by their bodies; but their bodies are surely constituted from time to time by this or that portion of flesh, just as a statue may be constituted from time to time by this or that portion of clay. I think that the definition of constituting that I supplied will be found to work for feline and human bodies too—as also for many non-artifactual but non-living things—but I lack space to discuss the matter.

Third, it may have been noticed that I have said nothing at all about temporal parts of material objects. According to the metaphysic of temporal parts (MTP), every material object is the fusion of its temporal slices. I had two reasons for bypassing that idea.

(i) it is unclear what MTP *means*. Unclear in two ways. (ia) Suppose CHAIR is a chair that existed at a given time-point, say 2PM. What is its 2PM temporal slice? We know that it is supposed to be the x such that x and its parts exist only at 2PM, and x and CHAIR are parts of each other at 2PM. Could x have lasted longer than it did in fact last? Could it have been red instead of brown? Proponents of MTP have to go on to stipulate answers, for "temporal slice" is not here well-defined in the sense I drew attention to—what I just wrote gives no modal information at all about temporal slices—and we have no modal intuitions to pick up the slack. (Standardly, I think, proponents of MTP stipulate that temporal slices of a thing couldn't have lasted for more than a time-point, but could have been red instead of brown.)

(ib) What is the relevant fusion-relation? All-fusion is obviously not on the cards; what about some-fusion? This question can't be answered until a prior question is answered. It is plain enough that any chair, and thus CHAIR in particular, could have lasted for a longer or shorter time than it does in fact last. How are proponents of MTP to accommodate that modal fact? One possibility is for them to say that CHAIR has some temporal slices in some possible worlds that it lacks in others. If they say this, then they cannot have that CHAIR is the some-fusion of its temporal slices: they have to opt for a modalized version (which?) of one or other of the temporary fusion-relations (which?), (And given temporary fusion-relations, it is hard to see what is gained by helping oneself to temporal slices as well.) A second possibility is for them to say that CHAIR has the same temporal slices in all possible worlds in which it exists, but—despite the slices' being temporally point-thick in all possible worlds—they spread over longer or shorter periods of time in different worlds.[3] (Thus perhaps that every pair of CHAIR's temporal slices are temporally further apart in nonactual world alpha, and temporally closer together in nonactual world beta, than they are in this world.) If proponents of MTP say this, then they can have that CHAIR is the some-fusion of its temporal slices. Perhaps there are other possibilities too. Which should they choose? (Is that really an interesting question?)

My second reason for bypassing MTP, (ii) is that it helps not a bit in solving the problem of the statue and the clay. That is because what makes the problem a hard one, and constrains what can count as a solution to it, is our modal intuitions about ordinary, familiar, three-dimensional portions of stuff and artifacts. That is where we have to begin, and what has to be respected throughout. I am sure that the story we arrive at (whether mine or anyone else's) can—given enough ingenuity—be translated into a modalized language of temporal parts. But I see no good reason to think the enterprise would pay.[4]

---

3. I am indebted to an anonymous referee for *Noûs* for this clever idea.

---

4. I am grateful to the members of the MIT Philosophy Discussion Group for criticism of an earlier draft—in particular, to James Pryor and Ralph Wedgwood. I also thank Richard L. Cartwright, Catherine Z. Elgin, Anthony Gray, James Pryor, and two anonymous referees for *Noûs* for helpful comments on material in later drafts.

John Locke

On Identity

4. *Identity of vegetables.* We must therefore consider wherein an oak differs from a mass of matter, and that seems to me to be in this; that the one is only the cohesion of particles anyhow united, the other such a dis-

From John Locke, *An Essay Concerning Human Understanding,* abridged and edited by Kenneth Winkler (Indianapolis: Hackett Publishing Company, 1996). Reprinted by permission of the publisher.

position of them as constitutes the parts of an oak; and such an organization of those parts, as is fit to receive, and distribute nourishment, so as to continue, and frame the wood, bark, and leaves, &c. of an oak, in which consists the vegetable life. That being then one plant, which has such an organization of parts in one coherent body, partaking of one common life, it continues to be the same plant, as long as it partakes of the same life, though that life be communicated to new particles of matter vitally united to the living plant, in a like continued organization, conformable to that sort of plants. For this organization being at any one instant in any one collection of *matter,* is in that particular concrete distinguished from all other, and is that individual life, which existing constantly from that moment both forwards and backwards in the same continuity of insensibly succeeding parts united to the living body of the plant, it has that identity, which makes the same plant, and all the parts of it, parts of the same plant, during all the time that they exist united in that continued organization, which is fit to convey that common life to all the parts so united.

5. *Identity of animals.* The case is not so much different in *brutes,* but that anyone may hence see what makes an animal, and continues it the same. Something we have like this in machines, and may serve to illustrate it. For example, what is a watch? 'Tis plain 'tis nothing but a fit organization, or construction of parts, to a certain end, which, when a sufficient force is added to it, it is capable to attain. If we would suppose this machine one continued body, all whose organized parts were repaired, increased or diminished, by a constant addition or separation of insensible parts, with one common life, we should have something very much like the body of an animal, with this difference, that in an animal the fitness of the organization, and the motion wherein life consists, begin together, the motion coming from within; but in machines the force, coming sensibly from without, is often away, when the organ is in order, and well fitted to receive it.

6. *Identity of man.* This also shows wherein the identity of the same *man* consists; *viz.* in nothing but a participation of the same continued life, by constantly fleeting particles of matter, in succession vitally united to the same organized body. He that shall place the *identity* of man in anything else, but like that of other animals in one fitly organized body taken in any one instant, and from thence continued under one organization of life in several successively fleeting particles of matter, united to it, will find it hard, to make an *embryo,* one of years, mad, and sober, the same man, by any supposition, that will not make it possible for *Seth, Ismael, Socrates, Pilate, St. Austin,* and *Caesar Borgia* to be the same man. For if the *identity* of soul alone makes the same man, and there be nothing in the nature of matter, why the same individual spirit may not be united to different bodies, it will be possible, that those men, living in distant ages, and of different tempers, may have been the same man: which way of speaking must be from a very strange use of the word *man,* applied to an *idea,* out of which body and shape is excluded: and that way of speaking would agree yet worse with the notions of those philosophers, who allow of transmigration, and are of opinion that the souls of men may, for their miscarriages, be detruded into the bodies of beasts, as fit habitations with organs suited to the satisfaction of their brutal inclinations. But yet I think nobody, could he be sure that the soul of *Heliogabalus* were in one of his hogs, would yet say that hog were a *man* or *Heliogabalus.*

7. *Identity suited to the* idea. 'Tis not therefore unity of substance that comprehends all sorts of *identity,* or will determine it in every case: but to conceive, and judge of it aright, we must consider what *idea* the word it is applied to stands for: it being one thing to be the same *substance,* another the same *man,* and a third the same *person,* if *person, man,* and *substance,* are three names standing for three different *ideas;* for such as is the *idea* belonging to that name, such must be the *identity;* which if it had been a little more carefully attended to, would possibly have prevented a great deal of that confusion, which often occurs about this matter, with no small seeming difficulties; especially concerning *personal identity,* which therefore we shall in the next place a little consider.

8. *Same man.* An animal is a living organized body; and consequently, the same animal, as we have observed, is the same continued life communicated to different particles of matter, as they happen successively to be united to that organized living body: and that our notion of a *man,* whatever is talked of other definitions, is but of a particular sort of animal, I doubt not. Since I think I may be confident, that whoever should see a creature of his own shape and make, though it had no more reason all its life, than a *cat* or a *parrot,* would call him still a *man;* or whoever should hear a *cat* or a *parrot* discourse, reason and philosophize, would call or think it nothing but a *cat* or a *parrot;* and say, the one was a dull irrational *man,* and the other a very intelligent rational *parrot.* . . . For I presume 'tis not the *idea* of a thinking or rational being alone, that makes the *idea* of a *man* in most people's sense; but of a body so and so shaped joined to it; and if that be the *idea* of a *man,* the same successive

body not shifted all at once, must as well as the same immaterial spirit go to the making of the same *man*.

9. *Personal identity.* This being premised to find wherein *personal identity* consists, we must consider what *person* stands for; which, I think, is a thinking intelligent being, that has reason and reflection, and can consider itself as itself, the same thinking thing in different times and places; which it does only by that consciousness, which is inseparable from thinking, and as it seems to me essential to it: it being impossible for anyone to perceive, without perceiving, that he does perceive. When we see, hear, smell, taste, feel, meditate, or will anything, we know that we do so. Thus it is always as to our present sensations and perceptions: and by this everyone is to himself, that which he calls *self:* it not being considered in this case, whether the same *self* be continued in the same, or divers substances. For since consciousness always accompanies thinking, and 'tis that, that makes everyone to be, what he calls *self;* and thereby distinguishes himself from all other thinking things, in this alone consists *personal identity, i.e.* the sameness of a rational being: and as far as this consciousness can be extended backwards to any past action or thought, so far reaches the identity of that *person;* it is the same *self* now it was then; and 'tis by the same *self* with this present one that now reflects on it, that that action was done.

10. *Consciousness makes personal identity.* But it is farther inquired whether it be the same identical substance. This few would think they had reason to doubt of, if these perceptions, with their consciousness, always remained present in the mind, whereby the same thinking thing would be always consciously present, and, as would be thought, evidently the same to itself. But that which seems to make the difficulty is this, that the consciousness, being interrupted always by forgetfulness, there being no moment of our lives wherein we have the whole train of all our past actions before our eyes in one view: but even the best memories losing the sight of one part whilst they are viewing another; and we sometimes, and that the greatest part of our lives, not reflecting on our past selves, being intent on our present thoughts, and in sound sleep, having no thoughts at all, or at least none with that consciousness, which remarks our waking thoughts. I say, in all these cases, our consciousness being interrupted, and we losing the sight of our past *selves,* doubts are raised whether we are the

same thinking thing; *i.e.* the same substance or no. Which however reasonable, or unreasonable concerns not *personal identity* at all. The question being what makes the same *person,* and not whether it be the same identical substance, which always thinks in the same *person,* which in this case matters not at all. Different substances, by the same consciousness (where they do partake in it) being united into one person; as well by different bodies, by the same life are united into one animal, whose *identity* is preserved, in that change of substances, by the unity of one continued life. For it being the same consciousness that makes a man be himself to himself, *personal identity* depends on that only, whether it be annexed only to one individual substance, or can be continued in a succession of several substances. For as far as any intelligent being can repeat the *idea* of any past action with the same consciousness it had of it at first, and with the same consciousness it has of any present action; so far it is the same *personal self.* For it is by the consciousness it has of its present thoughts and actions, that is is *self* to *itself* now, and so will be the same *self* as far as the same consciousness can extend to actions past or to come; and would be by distance of time, or change of substance, no more two *persons* than a man be two men, by wearing other clothes today than he did yesterday, with a long or short sleep in between: the same consciousness uniting those distant actions into the same *person,* whatever substances contributed to their production.

11. *Personal identity in change of substances.* That this is so, we have some kind of evidence in our very bodies, all whose particles, whilst vitally united to this same thinking conscious self, so that we feel when they are touched, and are affected by, and conscious of good or harm that happens to them, are a part of our *selves; i.e* of our thinking conscious *self.* Thus the limbs of his body is to everyone a part of *himself:* he sympathizes and is concerned for them. Cut off an hand, and thereby separate it from that consciousness, we had of its heat, cold, and other affections; and it is then no longer a part of that which is *himself,* any more than the remotest part of matter. Thus we see the *substance,* whereof *personal self* consisted at one time, may be varied at another, without the change of personal *identity:* there being no question about the same person, though the limbs, which but now were a part of it, be cut off.

12. *Whether in the change of thinking substances.* But the question is, whether if the same substance, which thinks, be changed, it can be the same person, or remaining the same, it can be different persons.

And to this I answer first, this can be no question at all to those, who place thought in a purely material, animal, constitution, void of an immaterial substance. For, whether their supposition be true or no, 'tis plain they conceive personal identity preserved in something else than identity of substance; as animal identity is preserved in identity of life, not of substance. And therefore those, who place thinking in an immaterial substance only, before they can come to deal with these men, must show why personal identity cannot be preserved in the change of immaterial substances, or variety of particular immaterial substances, as well as animal identity is preserved in the change of material substances, or variety of particular bodies; unless they will say, 'tis one immaterial spirit, that makes the same life in brutes; as it is one immaterial spirit that makes the same person in men, which the *Cartesians* at least will not admit, for fear of making brutes thinking things too.

13. But next, as to the first part of the question, whether if the same thinking substance (supposing immaterial substances only to think) be changed, it can be the same person. I answer, that cannot be resolved, but by those, who know what kind of substances they are, that do think; and whether the consciousness of past actions can be transferred from one thinking substance to another. I grant, were the same consciousness the same individual action, it could not: but it being but a present representation of a past action, why it may not be possible, that that may be represented to the mind to have been, which really never was, will remain to be shown. And therefore how far the consciousness of past actions is annexed to any individual agent, so that another cannot possibly have it, will be hard for us to determine, till we know what kind of action it is, that cannot be done with a reflex act of perception accompanying it, and how performed by thinking substances, who cannot think without being conscious of it. But that which we call the *same consciousness,* not being the same individual act, why one intellectual substance may not have represented to it, as done by itself, what it never did, and was perhaps done by some other agent, why I say such a representation may not possibly be without reality of mat-

ter of fact, as well as several representations in dreams are, which yet, whilst dreaming, we take for true, will be difficult to conclude from the nature of things. And that it never is so, will by us, till we have clearer views of the nature of thinking substances, be best resolved into the goodness of God, who as far as the happiness or misery of any of his sensible creatures is concerned in it, will not by a fatal error of theirs transfer from one to another, that consciousness, which draws reward or punishment with it. How far this may be an argument against those who would place thinking in a system of fleeting animal spirits, I leave to be considered. But yet to return to the question before us, it must be allowed, that if the same consciousness (which, as has been shown, is quite a different thing from the same numerical figure or motion in body) can be transferred from one thinking substance to another, it will be possible, that two thinking substances may make but one person. For the same consciousness being preserved, whether in the same or different substances, the personal identity is preserved.

14. As to the second part of the question, whether the same immaterial substance remaining, there may be two distinct persons; which question seems to me to be built on this, whether the same immaterial being, being conscious of the actions of its past duration, may be wholly stripped of all the consciousness of its past existence, and lose it beyond the power of ever retrieving it again: and so as it were beginning a new account from a new period, have a consciousness that cannot reach beyond this new state. All those who hold pre-existence, are evidently of this mind, since they allow the soul to have no remaining consciousness of what it did in that pre-existent state, either wholly separate from body, or informing any other body; and, if they should not, 'tis plain experience would be against them. So that personal identity reaching no farther than consciousness reaches, a pre-existent spirit not having continued so many ages in a state of silence, must needs make different persons. Suppose a Christian *Platonist* or *Pythagorean,* should upon God's having ended all his works of creation the seventh day, think his soul has existed ever since; and should imagine it has revolved in several human bodies, as I once met with one, who was persuaded his had been the soul of *Socrates* (how reasonably I will not dispute. This I know, that in the post he filled, which

was no inconsiderable one, he passed for a very rational man, and the press has shown, that he wanted not parts or learning) would anyone say, that he, being not conscious of any of *Socrates's* actions or thoughts, could be the same person with *Socrates?* Let anyone reflect upon himself, and conclude, that he has in himself an immaterial spirit, which is that which thinks in him, and in the constant change of his body keeps him the same; and is that which he calls himself: let him also suppose it to be the same soul, that was in *Nestor* or *Thersites,* at the siege of *Troy,* (for souls being, as far as we know anything of them in their nature, indifferent to any parcel of matter, the supposition has no apparent absurdity in it) which it may have been, as well as it is now, the soul of any other man: but he, now having no consciousness of any of the actions either of *Nestor* or *Thersites,* does, or can he, conceive himself the same person with either of them? Can he be concerned in either of their actions? Attribute them to himself, or think them his own more than the actions of any other man, that ever existed? So that this consciousness not reaching to any of the actions of either of those men, he is no more one *self* with either of them, than if the soul or immaterial spirit, that now informs him, had been created, and began to exist, when it began to inform his present body, though it were never so true, that the same spirit that informed *Nestor's* or *Thersites's* body, were numerically the same that now informs his. For this would no more make him the same person with *Nestor,* than if some of the particles of matter, that were once a part of *Nestor,* were now a part of this man, the same immaterial substance without the same consciousness, no more making the same person by being united to any body, than the same particle of matter without consciousness united to any body, makes the same person. But let him once find himself conscious of any of the actions of *Nestor,* he then finds himself the same person with *Nestor.*

15. And thus we may be able without any difficulty to conceive, the same person at the Resurrection, though in a body not exactly in make or parts the same which he had here, the same consciousness going along with the soul that inhabits it. But yet the soul alone in the change of bodies, would scarce to anyone, but to him that makes the soul the *man,* be enough to make the same *man.* For should the soul of a prince, carrying with

it the consciousness of the prince's past life, enter and inform the body of a cobbler as soon as deserted by his own soul, everyone sees, he would be the same person with the prince, accountable only for the prince's actions: but who would say it was the same man? The body too goes to the making the man, and would, I guess, to everybody determine the man in this case, wherein the soul, with all its princely thoughts about it, would not make another man: but he would be the same cobbler to everyone besides himself. I know that in the ordinary way of speaking, the same person, and the same man, stand for one and the same thing. And indeed everyone will always have a liberty to speak, as he pleases, and to apply what articulate sounds to what *ideas* he thinks fit, and change them as often as he pleases. But yet when we will inquire, what makes the same *spirit, man,* or *person,* we must fix the *ideas* of *spirit, man,* or *person,* in our minds; and having resolved with ourselves what we mean by them, it will not be hard to determine, in either of them, or the like, when it is the *same,* and when not.

16. *Consciousness makes the same person.* But though the same immaterial substance, or soul does not alone, wherever it be, and in whatsoever state, make the same man; yet 'tis plain consciousness, as far as ever it can be extended, should it be to ages past, unites existences, and actions, very remote in time, into the same person, as well as it does the existence and actions of the immediately preceding moment: so that whatever has the consciousness of present and past actions, is the same person to whom they both belong. Had I the same consciousness, that I saw the Ark and *Noah's* flood, as that I saw an overflowing of the *Thames* last winter, or as that I write now, I could no more doubt that I, that write this now, that saw the *Thames* overflowed last winter, and that viewed the flood at the general deluge, was the same *self,* place that *self* in whatever substance you please, than that I that write this am the same *myself* now whilst I write (whether I consist of all the same substance, material or immaterial, or no) that I was yesterday. For as to this point of being the same *self,* it matters not whether this present *self* be made up of the same or other substances, I being as much concerned, and as justly accountable for any action was done a thousand years since, appropriated to me now by this self-consciousness, as I am, for what I did the last moment.

17. *Self depends on consciousness. Self* is that conscious thinking thing, (whatever substance made up of whether spiritual, or material, simple, or compounded, it matters not) which is sensible, or conscious of pleasure and pain, capable of happiness or misery, and so is concerned for *itself,* as far as that consciousness extends. Thus everyone finds, that whilst comprehended under that consciousness, the little finger is as much a part of *itself,* as what is most so. Upon separation of this little finger, should this consciousness go along with the little finger, and leave the rest of the body, 'tis evident the little finger would be the *person,* the *same person;* and self then would have nothing to do with the rest of the body. As in this case it is the consciousness that goes along with the substance, when one part is separate from another, which makes the same *person,* and constitutes this inseparable *self:* so it is in reference to substances remote in time. That with which the *consciousness* of this present thinking thing can join itself, makes the same *person,* and is one *self* with it, and with nothing else; and so attributes to it*self,* and owns all the actions of that thing, as its own, as far as that consciousness reaches, and no farther; as everyone who reflects will perceive.

18. *Object of reward and punishment.* In this *personal identity* is founded all the right and justice of reward and punishment; happiness and misery, being that, for which everyone is concerned for *himself,* not mattering what becomes of any substance, not joined to, or affected with that consciousness. For as it is evident in the instance I gave but now, if the consciousness went along with the little finger, when it was cut off, that would be the same *self* which was concerned for the whole body yesterday, as making a part of it*self,* whose actions then it cannot but admit as its own now. Though if the same body should still live, and immediately from the separation of the little finger have its own peculiar consciousness, whereof the little finger knew nothing, it would not at all be concerned for it, as a part of it*self,* or could own any of its actions, or have any of them imputed to him.

19. This may show us wherein *personal identity* consists, not in the identity of substance, but, as I have said, in the identity of *consciousness,* wherein, if *Socrates* and the present Mayor of *Quinborough* agree, they are the same person: if the same *Socrates* waking and sleeping do not partake of the same *consciousness, Socrates* waking and sleeping is not the same person. And to punish *Socrates* waking, for what sleeping *Socrates* thought, and waking *Socrates* was never conscious of, would be no more of right, than to punish one twin for what his brother-twin did, whereof he knew nothing, because their outsides were so alike, that they could not be distinguished; for such twins have been seen.

20. But yet possibly it will still be objected, suppose I wholly lose the memory of some parts of my life, beyond a possibility of retrieving them, so that perhaps I shall never be conscious of them again; yet am I not the same person, that did those actions, had those thoughts, that I was once conscious of, though I have now forgot them? To which I answer, that we must here take notice what the word *I* is applied to, which in this case is the man only. And the same man being presumed to be the same person, *I* is easily here supposed to stand also for the same person. But if it be possible for the same man to have distinct incommunicable consciousnesses at different times, it is past doubt the same man would at different times make different persons, which, we see, is the sense of mankind in the solemnest declaration of their opinions, human laws not punishing the *madman* for the *sober man's* actions, nor the *sober man* for what the *madman* did, thereby making them two persons, which is somewhat explained by our way of speaking in *English,* when we say such an one *is not himself,* or is *besides himself;* in which phrases it is insinuated, as if those who now, or, at least, first used them, thought, that *self* was changed, the *self*same person was no longer in that man.

21. *Difference between identity of man and person.* But yet 'tis hard to conceive, that *Socrates* the same individual man should be two persons. To help us a little in this, we must consider what is meant by *Socrates,* or the same individual *man.*

First, it must be either the same individual, immaterial, thinking substance; in short, the same numerical soul, and nothing else.

Secondly, or the same animal, without regard to an immaterial soul.

Thirdly, or the same immaterial spirit united to the same animal.

Now take which of these suppositions you please, it is impossible to make personal identity to consist in anything but consciousness; or reach any farther than that does.

For by the first of them, it must be allowed possible that a man born of different women, and in distant times, may be the same man. A way of speaking, which whoever admits, must allow it possible, for the same man to be two distinct persons, as any two that have lived in different ages without the knowledge of one another's thoughts.

By the second and third, *Socrates* in this life, and after it, cannot be the same man any way, but by the same consciousness; and so making *human identity* to consist in the same thing wherein we place *personal identity,* there will be no difficulty to allow the same man to be the same person. But then they who place *human identity* in consciousness only, and not in something else, must consider how they will make the infant *Socrates* the same man with *Socrates* after the Resurrection. But whatsoever to some men makes a *man,* and consequently the same individual man, wherein perhaps few are agreed, personal identity can by us be placed in nothing but consciousness (which is that alone which makes what we call *self*) without involving us in great absurdities.

22. But is not a man drunk and sober the same person, why else is he punished for the fact he commits when drunk, though he be never afterwards conscious of it? Just as much the same person, as a man that walks, and does other things in his sleep, is the same person, and is answerable for any mischief he shall do in it. Human laws punish both with a justice suitable to their way of knowledge: because in these cases, they cannot distinguish certainly what is real, what counterfeit; and so the ignorance in drunkenness or sleep is not admitted as a plea. For though punishment be annexed to personality, and personality to consciousness, and the drunkard perhaps be not conscious of what he did; yet human judicatures justly punish him; because the fact is proved against him, but want of consciousness cannot be proved for him. But in the great day, wherein the secrets of all hearts shall be laid open, it may be reasonable to think, no one shall be made to answer for what he knows nothing of; but shall receive his doom, his conscience accusing or excusing him.

23. *Consciousness alone makes self.* Nothing but consciousness can unite remote existences into the same person, the identity of substance will not do it. For whatever substance there is, however framed, without consciousness, there is no person: and a carcass may be a person, as well as any sort of substance be so without consciousness.

Could we suppose two distinct incommunicable consciousnesses acting the same body, the one constantly by day, the other by night; and on the other side the same consciousness acting by intervals two distinct bodies: I ask in the first case, whether the *day* and the *night-man* would not be two as distinct persons, as *Socrates* and *Plato;* and whether in the second case, there would not be one person in two distinct bodies, as much as one man is the same in two distinct clothings. Nor is it at all material to say, that this same, and this distinct *consciousness* in the cases above-mentioned, is owing to the same and distinct immaterial substances, bringing it with them to those bodies, which whether true or no, alters not the case: since 'tis evident the *personal identity* would equally be determined by consciousness, whether that consciousness were annexed to some individual immaterial substance or no. For granting that the thinking substance in man must be necessarily supposed immaterial, 'tis evident, that immaterial thinking thing may sometimes part with its past consciousness, and be restored to it again, as appears in the forgetfulness men often have of their past actions, and the mind many times recovers the memory of a past consciousness, which it had lost for twenty years together. Make these intervals of memory and forgetfulness to take their turns regularly by day and night, and you have two persons with the same immaterial spirit, as much as in the former instance two persons with the same body. So that *self* is not determined by identity or diversity of substance, which it cannot be sure of, but only by identity of consciousness.

24. Indeed it may conceive the substance whereof it is now made up, to have existed formerly, united in the same conscious being: but consciousness removed, that substance is no more it*self,* or makes no more a part of it, than any other substance, as is evident in the instance, we have already given, of a limb cut off, of whose heat, or cold, or other affections, having no longer any consciousness, it is no more of a man's self than any other matter of the universe. In like manner it will be in reference to any immaterial substance, which is void of that consciousness whereby I am my*self* to my*self*: if there be any part of its existence, which I cannot upon

recollection join with that present consciousness, whereby I am now my*self,* it is in that part of its existence no more my*self,* than any other immaterial being. For whatsoever any substance has thought or done, which I cannot recollect, and by my consciousness make my own thought and action, it will no more belong to me, whether a part of me thought or did it, than if it had been thought or done by any other immaterial being anywhere existing.

25. I agree the more probable opinion is, that this consciousness is annexed to, and the affection of one individual immaterial substance.

But let men according to their divers hypotheses resolve of that as they please. This every intelligent being, sensible of happiness or misery, must grant, that there is something that is *himself,* that he concerned for, and would have happy; that this *self* has existed in a continued duration more than one instant, and therefore 'tis possible may exist, as it has done, months and years to come, without any certain bounds to be set to its duration; and may be the same *self,* by the same consciousness, continued on for the future. And thus, by this consciousness, he finds himself to be the *same self* which did such or such an action some years since, by which he comes to be happy or miserable now. In all which account of *self,* the same numerical substance is not considered, as making the same *self:* but the same continued consciousness, in which several substances may have been united, and again separated from it, which, whilst they continued in a vital union with that, wherein this consciousness then resided, made a part of that same *self.* Thus any part of our bodies vitally united to that, which is conscious in us, makes a part of our *selves:* but upon separation from the vital union, by which that consciousness is communicated, that, which a moment since was part of our *selves,* is now no more so, than a part of another man's *self* is part of me; and 'tis not impossible, but in a little time may become a real part of another person. And so we have the same numerical substance become a part of two different persons, and the same person preserved under the change of various substances. Could we suppose any spirit wholly stripped of all its memory or consciousness of past actions, as we find our minds always are of a great part of ours, and sometimes of them all, the union or separation of such a spiritual substance would make no

variation of personal identity, any more than that of any particle of matter does. Any substance vitally united to the present thinking being, is part of that very *same self* which now is: anything united to it by a consciousness of former actions makes also a part of the *same self,* which is the same both then and now.

26. *Person a forensic term. Person,* as I take it, is the name for this *self.* Wherever a man finds, what he calls *himself,* there I think another may say is the same *person.* It is a forensic term appropriating actions and their merit; and so belongs only to intelligent agents capable of a law, and happiness and misery. This personality extends it*self* beyond present existence to what is past, only by consciousness, whereby it becomes concerned and accountable, owns and imputes to it*self* past actions, just upon the same ground, and for the same reason, that it does the present. All which is founded in a concern for happiness the unavoidable concomitant of consciousness, that which is conscious of pleasure and pain, desiring, that that *self,* that is conscious, should be happy. And therefore whatever past actions it cannot reconcile or appropriate to that present *self* by consciousness, it can be no more concerned in, than if they had never been done: and to receive pleasure or pain; *i.e.* reward or punishment, on the account of any such action, is all one, as to be made happy or miserable in its first being, without any demerit at all. For supposing a man punished now, for what he had done in another life, whereof he could be made to have no consciousness at all, what difference is there between that punishment, and being created miserable? And therefore conformable to this, the apostle tells us, that at the great day, when everyone shall *receive according to his doings, the secrets of all hearts shall be laid open.* The sentence shall be justified by the consciousness all persons shall have, that they *themselves* in what bodies soever they appear, or what substances soever that consciousness adheres to, are the *same,* that committed those actions, and deserve that punishment for them.

27. I am apt enough to think I have in treating of this subject made some suppositions that will look strange to some readers, and possibly they are so in themselves But yet I think, they are such, as are pardonable in this ignorance we are in of the nature of that thinking thing, that is in us, and which we look on as our*selves.* Did we know what it was, or how it was tied to a certain

system of fleeting animal spirits; or whether it could, or could not perform its operations of thinking and memory out of a body organized as ours is; and whether it has pleased God, that no one such spirit shall ever be united to any but one such body, upon the right constitution of whose organs its memory should depend, we might see the absurdity of some of those suppositions I have made. But taking, as we ordinarily now do, (in the dark concerning these matters) the soul of a man, for an immaterial substance, independent from matter, and indifferent alike to it all, there can from the nature of things, be no absurdity at all, to suppose, that the same soul may, at different times be united to different bodies, and with them make up, for that time, one man; as well as we suppose part of a sheep's body yesterday should be a part of a man's body tomorrow, and in that union make a vital part of *Meliboeus* as well as it did of his ram.

Thomas Reid

Of Identity

Chapter 4

Of Identity

The conviction which every man has of his Identity, as far back as his memory reaches, needs no aid of philosophy to strengthen it; and no philosophy can weaken it, without first producing some degree of insanity.

The philosopher, however, may very properly consider this conviction as a phenomenon of human nature worthy of his attention. If he can discover its cause, an addition is made to his stock of knowledge. If not, it must be held as a part of our original constitution, or an effect of that constitution produced in a manner unknown to us.

We may observe, first of all, that this conviction is indispensably necessary to all exercise of reason. The operations of reason, whether in action or in speculation, are made up of successive parts. The antecedent are the foundation of the consequent, and, without the conviction that the antecedent have been seen or done by me, I could have no reason to proceed to the consequent, in any speculation, or in any active project whatever.

There can be no memory of what is past without the conviction that we existed at the time remembered. There may be good arguments to convince me that I existed before the earliest thing I can remember, but to suppose that my memory reaches a moment farther back than my belief and conviction of my existence, is a contradiction.

The moment a man loses this conviction, as if he had drunk the water of Lethe, past things are done away; and, in his own belief, he then begins to exist. Whatever was thought, or said, or done, or suffered before that period, may belong to some other person; but he can never impute it to himself, or take any subsequent step that supposes it to be his doing.

From this it is evident that we must have the conviction of our own continued existence and identity, as soon as we are capable of thinking or doing anything, on account of what we have thought, or done, or suffered before; that is, as soon as we are reasonable creatures.

That we may form as distinct a notion as we are able of this phenomenon of the human mind, it is proper to consider what is meant by identity in general, what by our own personal identity, and how we are led into that

From Thomas Reid, *Inquiry and Essays,* edited by Ronald E. Beanblossom and Keith Lehrer (Indianapolis: Hackett Publishing Company, 1993). Reprinted by permission of the publisher.

invincible belief and conviction which every man has of his own personal identity, as far as his memory reaches.

Identity in general, I take to be a relation between a thing which is known to exist at one time, and a thing which is known to have existed at another time. If you ask whether they are one and the same, or two different things, every man of common sense understands the meaning of your question perfectly. Whence we may infer with certainty, that every man of common sense has a clear and distinct notion of identity.

If you ask a definition of identity, I confess I can give none; it is too simple a notion to admit of logical definition. I can say it is a relation; but I cannot find words to express the specific difference between this and other relations, though I am in no danger of confounding it with any other. I can say that diversity is a contrary relation, and that similitude and dissimilitude are another couple of contrary relations, which every man easily distinguishes in his conception from identity and diversity.

I see evidently that identity supposes an uninterrupted continuance of existence. That which hath ceased to exist, cannot be the same with that which afterwards begins to exist; for this would be to suppose a being to exist after it ceased to exist, and to have had existence before it was produced, which are manifest contradictions. Continued uninterrupted existence is therefore necessarily implied in identity.

Hence we may infer that identity cannot, in its proper sense, be applied to our pains, our pleasures, our thoughts, or any operation of our minds. The pain felt this day is not the same individual pain which I felt yesterday, though they may be similar in kind and degree, and have the same cause. The same may be said of every feeling and of every operation of mind: they are all successive in their nature, like time itself, no two moments of which can be the same moment.

It is otherwise with the parts of absolute space. They always are, and were, and will be the same. So far, I think, we proceed upon clear ground in fixing the notion of identity in general.

It is, perhaps, more difficult to ascertain with precision the meaning of Personality; but it is not necessary in the present subject: it is sufficient for our purpose to observe, that all mankind place their personality in something that cannot be divided, or consist of parts. A part of a person is a manifest absurdity.

When a man loses his estate, his health, his strength, he is still the same person, and has lost nothing of his personality. If he has a leg or an arm cut off, he is the same person he was before. The amputated member is no part of his person, otherwise it would have a right to a part of his estate, and be liable for a part of his engagements; it would be entitled to a share of his merit and demerit—which is manifestly absurd. A person is something indivisible, and is what Leibniz calls *monad*.

My personal identity, therefore, implies the continued existence of that indivisible thing which I call myself. Whatever this self may be, it is something which thinks, and deliberates, and resolves, and acts, and suffers. I am not thought, I am not action, I am not feeling. I am something that thinks, and acts, and suffers. My thoughts, and actions, and feelings, change every moment—they have no continued, but a successive existence; but that *self* or *I,* to which they belong, is permanent, and has the same relation to all the succeeding thoughts, actions, and feelings, which I call mine.

Such are the notions that I have of my personal identity. But perhaps it may be said, this may all be fancy without reality. How do you know?—what evidence have you, that there is such a permanent self which has a claim to all the thoughts, actions, and feelings, which you call yours?

To this I answer, that the proper evidence I have of all this is remembrance. I remember that, twenty years ago, I conversed with such a person; I remember several things that passed in that conversation; my memory testifies not only that this was done, but that it was done by me who now remembers it. If it was done by me, I must have existed at that time, and continued to exist from that time to the present: if the identical person whom I call myself, had not a part in that conversation, my memory is fallacious—it gives a distinct and positive testimony of what is not true. Every man in his senses believes what he distinctly remembers, and everything he remembers convinces him that he existed at the time remembered.

Although memory gives the most irresistible evidence of my being the identical person that did such a thing, at such a time, I may have other good evidence of things which befell me, and which I do not remember: I know who bare me and suckled me, but I do not remember these events.

It may here be observed (though the observation would have been unnecessary if some great philosophers had not contradicted it,) that it is not my remembering any action of mine that makes me to be the person who did it. This remembrance makes me to know assuredly that I did it; but I might have done it though I did not remember it. That relation to me, which is expresses by saying that I did it, would be the same though I had not the least remembrance of it. To say that my remembering that I did such a thing, or, as some choose to express it, my being conscious that I did it, makes me to have done it, appears to me as great an absurdity as it would be to say, that my belief that the world was created made it to be created.

Chapter 6

Of Mr. Locke's Account of Our Personal Identity

In a long chapter upon Identity and Diversity, Mr. Locke has made many ingenious and just observations, and some which I think cannot be defended. I shall only take notice of the account he gives of our own *Personal Identity.* His doctrine upon this subject has been censured by Bishop Butler, in a short essay subjoined to his "Analogy," with whose sentiments I perfectly agree.

Identity, as was observed, Chap. IV. of this Essay, supposes the continued existence of the being of which it is affirmed, and therefore can be applied only to things which have a continued existence. While any being continues to exist, it is the same being: but two beings which have a different beginning or a different ending of their existence, cannot possibly be the same. To this I think Mr. Locke agrees.

He observes, very justly, that to know what is meant by the same person, we must consider what the word *person* stands for; and he defines a person to be an intelligent being, endowed with reason and with consciousness, which last he thinks inseparable from thought.

From this definition of a person, it must necessarily follow, that, while the intelligent being continues to exist and to be intelligent, it must be the same person. To say that the intelligent being is the person, and yet that the person ceases to exist, while the intelligent being

continues, or that the person continues while the intelligent being ceases to exist, is to my apprehension a manifest contradiction.

One would think that the definition of a person should perfectly ascertain the nature of personal identity, or wherein it consists, though it might still be a question how we come to know and be assured of our personal identity.

Mr. Locke tells us, however, "that personal identity—that is, the sameness of a rational being—consists in consciousness alone, and, as far as this consciousness can be extended backwards to any past action or thought, so far reaches the identity of that person. So that, whatever hath the consciousness of present and past actions, is the same person to whom they belong."[1]

This doctrine hath some strange consequences, which the author was aware of, such as, that, if the same consciousness can be transferred from one intelligent being to another, which he thinks we cannot show to be impossible, then two or twenty intelligent beings may be the same person. And if the intelligent being may lose the consciousness of the actions done by him, which surely is possible, then he is not the person that did those actions; so that one intelligent being may be two or twenty different persons, if he shall so often lose the consciousness of his former actions.

There is another consequence of this doctrine, which follows no less necessarily, though Mr. Locke probably did not see it. It is, that a man may be, and at the same time not be, the person that did a particular action.

Suppose a brave officer to have been flogged when a boy at school, for robbing an orchard, to have taken a standard from the enemy in his first campaign, and to have been made a general in advanced life: Suppose also, which must be admitted to be possible, that, when he took the standard, he was conscious of his having been flogged at school, and that when made a general he was conscious of his taking the standard, but had absolutely lost the consciousness of his flogging.

These things being supposed, it follows, from Mr. Locke's doctrine, that he who was flogged at school is the same person who took the standard, and that he who took the standard is the same person who was

---

1. See *Essay* (Book ii. ch. 27 §9). [. . .]

made a general. Whence it follows, if there be any truth in logic, that the general is the same person with him who was flogged at school. But the general's consciousness does not reach so far back as his flogging—therefore, according to Mr. Locke's doctrine, he is not the person who was flogged. Therefore, the general is, and at the same time is not the same person with him who was flogged at school. . . .

John Perry

A Dialogue on Personal Identity and Immortality

Editors' Summary
The First Night[1]

Gretchen Weirob is facing death. Although her brain was not harmed in her motorcycle accident, other vital organs were damaged beyond repair. She has only a couple of days to live. Her friend Miller, a chaplain, visits her in the hospital. He hopes to comfort her by convincing her of the probability of life after death. She replies that she would be satisfied if he could even convince her that life after death is even possible. She sets a relatively low standard for possibility. All that he needs to show is that it is conceivable or imaginable that a person could survive her own death.

Miller's task might seem to be the easy one of conjuring up pictures of souls floating in space, or people wandering around in the afterlife. But Weirob insists on asking what would make any of these beings her? She insists that her survival requires that in the future there will be a being who thinks, feels, and experiences, and who is so related to Gretchen Weirob that that being will actually remember Weirob's experiences, and will rightly feel pride at her accomplishments and remorse over her failings. This requires more than that a being be 'just like' Weirob. If she had an identical twin, however similar the twin was to Gretchen, the twin's survival would not be Gretchen's survival. Today you can anticipate that tomorrow you—that very person—will enjoy a day at the beach. Can Weirob rightly anticipate the future pleasures of any creature, after her body dies, as her own future pleasures?

Like Descartes, Miller takes the mind or soul and the body to be distinct. Descartes (pp. 55–6) argues that mind and body are separate substances. One argument he offers is that my knowledge of my mind is more certain than any knowledge I can have of my body. But then Descartes faces a problem: How do mind and body interact? How do I get from my intending to raise my hand to my hand rising? How does the needle stuck in my leg become the pain in my mind? These are illustrations of the kind of problem that arise from taking mind and body to be distinct, as Miller does.

Weirob's concern focuses on personal identity—the identity each person has with himself alone over time. Her primary concern is not with the existence of souls or minds without bodies, but whether after her death any soul or disembodied mind could be her. Weirob and Miller agree that in a few days, her body will die and will subsequently decay. How could she—that very person—survive? Imagine, Weirob says, that a box of Kleenex is burned to ashes. Even if there is an identical box in the basement, the original box does not survive

---

From John Perry, *A Dialogue on Personal Identity and Immortality* (Indianapolis: Hackett Publishing Company, 1978). Reprinted by permission of the publisher.

1. **The First Night:** The arguments against the position that personal identity consists in identity of an immaterial soul are similar to those found in John Locke, "Of Identity and Diversity," chapter 27 of Book II of the *Essay Concerning Human Understanding*. This chapter first appeared in the second edition of 1694.

the fire. The 'identical' box may be very similar, but it is not the very same object as the original box. Identity in the strict sense is what survival requires.

If Miller identifies Weirob with her soul or her mind, which are not physical, then the criteria by which he recognizes Weirob will not necessarily pick Weirob out. For Miller recognizes Weirob on the basis of physical criteria—what she looks like, how she behaves, and so forth. But the body with these attributes could be attached to any soul. So the challenge is to explain why he takes the appearances presented by her body to be evidence of the presence of her soul. Miller has a response. Although we initially recognize one another on the basis of physical criteria, psychological criteria quickly enter. Weirob does not just look like Weirob, she acts like Weirob. For example, she refuses to accept what she regards as false comforts, and displays her familiar caustic, skeptical and analytical responses despite her dire circumstances. So Miller proposes, rather than taking the same person to be the same body, sameness of person is sameness of psychological characteristics. This criterion has a far better chance of being satisfied by an immaterial self.

Weirob is not satisfied, even if she grants that psychological characteristics are characteristics of an immaterial mind. Even if there is continuity of psychological characteristics, she urges, we have no grounds for confidence that they always attach to the same soul. From day to day, or even from moment to moment, one immaterial soul might replace another psychologically similar one. So a person with psychological and physical continuity might have a sequence of distinct souls. Just because we can discern psychological continuity, we should not assume that there is a single undetectable entity underlying that continuity. Weirob draws an analogy with a river. The river looks the same from day to day. Its color is the same muddy brown; its flow is sluggish. Nevertheless different individual water molecules that make it up. The water that was in the river yesterday is now in the Gulf. To assume that the actual water is the same because the appearance is the same would be a big mistake. What guarantees that we are not making the same mistake when talking about the soul? What guarantees that souls do not flow through us as water flows down the river?

Miller argues that he knows from his own case that he has a single enduring mind or the soul. Since he is not in this respect different from anyone else, it is reasonable to extrapolate to others. If he has a continuous identity grounded in an enduring immaterial mind or soul, it is reasonable to believe that all other human beings do too. Again Weirob is not satisfied. The extrapolation from one case to all cases is weak. More importantly, Miller cannot say, even in his own case, what justifies his confidence that he has not switched souls. He knows more about his psychological makeup than others do, but that does not give him grounds for declaring that there is one enduring immaterial substance that underwrites his psychology.

The Second Night[2]

Weirob: Well, Sam, have you figured out a way to make sense of the identity of immaterial souls?

Miller: No, I have decided it was a mistake to build my argument on such a dubious notion.

Weirob: Have you then given up on survival? I think such a position would be a hard one for a clergyman to live with, and would feel bad about having pushed you so far.

Miller: Don't worry. I'm more convinced than ever. I stayed up late last night thinking and reading, and I'm sure I can convince you now.

---

2. **The Second Night:** The arguments against the view that personal identity consists in bodily identity are also suggested by Locke, as is the theory that memory is crucial. The argument that the memory theory is circular was made by Joseph Butler in "Of Personal Identity," an Appendix to his *Analogy of Religion,* first published in 1736. Locke's memory theory has been developed by a number of modern authors, including H. P. Grice, A. M. Quinton and, in a different direction, Sydney Shoemaker. The possibility of circumventing Butler's charge of circularity by an appeal to causation is noted by Shoemaker in his article "Persons and Their Pasts" (*American Philosophical Quarterly,* 1970) and by David Wiggins in *Identity and Spatial Temporal Continuity.* The "duplication argument" was apparently first used by the eighteenth-century freethinker, Antony Collins. Collins assumed that something like Locke's theory of personal identity was correct, and used the duplication argument to raise problems for the doctrine of immortality.

Weirob: Get with it, time is running out.

Miller: First, let me explain why, independently of my desire to defend survival after death, I am dissatisfied with your view that personal identity is just bodily identity. My argument will be very similar to the one you used to convince me that personal identity could not be identified with identity of an immaterial soul.

Consider a person waking up tomorrow morning, conscious, but not yet ready to open her eyes and look around and, so to speak, let the new day officially begin.

Weirob: Such a state is familiar enough, I admit.

Miller: Now couldn't such a person tell who she was? That is, even before opening her eyes and looking around, and in particular before looking at her body or making any judgments about it, wouldn't she be able to say who she was? Surely most of us, in the morning, know who we are before opening our eyes and recognizing our own bodies, do we not?

Weirob: You seem to be right about that.

Miller: But such a judgment as this person makes— we shall suppose she judges "I am Gretchen Weirob"— is a judgment of personal identity. Suppose she says to herself, "I am the very person who was arguing with Sam Miller last night." This is clearly a statement about her identity with someone who was alive the night before. And she could make this judgment without examining her body at all. You could have made just this judgment this morning, before opening your eyes.

Weirob: Well, in fact I did so. I remembered our conversation of last night and said to myself, "Could I be the rude person who was so hard on Sam Miller's attempts to comfort me?" And, of course, my answer was that I not only could be but was that very rude person.

Miller: But then by the same principle you used last night personal identity cannot be bodily identity. For you said that it could not be identity of immaterial soul because we were not judging as to identity of immaterial soul when we judge as to personal identity. But by the same token, as my example shows, we are not judging as to bodily identity when we judge as to personal identity. For we can judge who we are, and that we are the very person who did such and such and so and so, without having to make any judgments at all about the body. So, personal identity, while it may not consist of identity of an immaterial soul, does not consist in identity of material body either.

Weirob: I did argue as you remember. But I also said that the notion of the identity of an immaterial unobservable unextended soul seemed to make no sense at all. This is one reason that cannot be what we are judging about, when we judge as to personal identity. Bodily identity at least makes sense. Perhaps we are assuming sameness of body, without looking.

Miller: Granted. But you do admit that we do not in our own cases actually need to make a judgment of bodily identity in order to make a judgment of personal identity?

Weirob: I don't think I will admit it. I will let it pass, so that we may proceed.

Miller: Okay. Now it seems to me we are even able to imagine awakening and finding ourselves to have a *different* body than the one we had before. Suppose yourself just as I have described you. And now suppose you finally open your eyes and see, not the body you have grown so familiar with over the years, but one of a fundamentally different shape and size.

Weirob: Well, I should suppose I had been asleep for a very long time and lost a lot of weight—perhaps I was in a coma for a year or so.

Miller: But isn't it at least conceivable that it should not be your old body at all? I seem to be able to imagine awakening with a totally new body.

Weirob: And how would you suppose that this came about?

Miller: That's beside the point. I'm not saying I can imagine a procedure that would bring this about. I'm saying I can imagine it happening to me. In Kafka's *Metamorphoses,* someone awakens as a cockroach. I can't imagine what would make this happen to me or anyone else, but I can imagine awakening with the body of a cockroach. It is incredible that it should happen—that I do not deny. I simply mean I can imagine experiencing it. It doesn't seem contradictory or incoherent, simply unlikely and inexplicable.

Weirob: So, if I admit this can be imagined, what follows then?

Miller: Well, I think it follows that personal identity does not just amount to bodily identity. For I would not, finding that I had a new body, conclude that I was not the very same person I was before. I would be the same *person,* though I did not have the same *body.* So we would have identity of person but not identity of body. So personal identity cannot just amount to bodily identity.

Weirob: Well suppose—and I emphasize *suppose*—I grant you all of this. Where does it leave you? What do you claim I have recognized as the same, if not my body and not my immaterial soul?

Miller: I don't claim that you have recognized anything as the same, except the person involved, that is, you yourself.

Weirob: I'm not sure what you mean.

Miller: Let me appeal as you did to the Blue River. Suppose I take a visitor to the stretch of river by the old Mill, and then drive him toward Manhattan. After an hour-or-so drive we see another stretch of river, and I say, "That's the same river we saw this morning." As you pointed out yesterday, I don't thereby imply that the very same molecules of water are seen both times. And the places are different, perhaps a hundred miles apart. And the shape and color and level of pollution might all be different. What do I see later in the day that is identical with what I saw earlier in the day?

Weirob: Nothing except the river itself.

Miller: Exactly. But now notice that what I see, strictly speaking, is not the whole river but only a part of it. I see different parts of the same river at the two different times. So really, if we restrict ourselves to what I literally see, I do not judge identity at all, but something else.

Weirob: And what might that be?

Miller: In saying that the river seen earlier and the river seen later, are one and the same river, do I mean any more than that the stretch of water seen later and that stretch of water seen earlier are connected by other stretches of water?

Weirob: That's about right. If the stretches of water are so connected there is but one river of which they are both parts.

Miller: Yes, that's what I mean. The statement of identity, "This river is the same one we saw this morning," is in a sense about rivers. But in a way it is also about stretches of water or river parts.

Weirob: So is all of this something special about rivers?

Miller: Not at all. It is a recurring pattern. After all, we constantly deal with objects extended in space and time. But we are seldom aware of the objects' wholes, but only of their parts or stretches of their histories. When a statement of identity is not just something trivial, like "This bed is this bed," it is usually because we are really judging that different parts fit together, in some appropriate pattern, into a certain kind of whole.

Weirob: I'm not sure I see just what you mean yet.

Miller: Let me give you another example. Suppose we are sitting together watching the first game of a double-header. You ask me, "Is this game identical with this game?" This is a perfectly stupid question, though, of course, strictly speaking it makes sense and the answer is "yes."

But now suppose you leave in the sixth inning to go for hot dogs. You are delayed, and return after about forty-five minutes or so. You ask, "Is this the same game I was watching?" Now your question is not stupid, but perfectly appropriate.

Weirob: Because the first game might still be going on or it might have ended, and the second game begun, by the time I return.

Miller: Exactly. Which is to say somehow different parts of the game—different innings, or at least different plays—were somehow involved in your question. That's why it wasn't stupid or trivial but significant.

Weirob: So, you think that judgments as to the identity of an object of a certain kind—rivers or baseball games or whatever—involve judgments as to the *parts* of those things being connected in a certain way, and are significant only when different parts are involved. Is that your point?

Miller: Yes, and I think it is an important one. How foolish it would be, when we ask a question about the identity of baseball games, to look for something *else,* other than the game as a whole, which had to be the same. It could be the same game, even if different players were involved. It could be the same game, even if it had been moved to a different field. These other things, the innings, the plays, the players, the field, don't have to be the same at the different times for the game to be the same, they just have to be related in certain ways so as to make that complex whole we call a single game.

Weirob: You think we were going off on a kind of a wild-goose chase when we asked whether it was the identity of soul or body that was involved in the identity of persons?

Miller: Yes. The answer I should now give is neither. We are wondering about the identity of the person. Of course, if by "soul" we just mean "person," there is no problem. But if we mean, as I did yesterday, some other thing whose identity is already understood, which has to be the same when persons are the same, we are just fooling ourselves with words.

Weirob: With rivers and baseball games, I can see that they are made up of parts connected in a certain way. The connection is, of course, different in the two cases, as is the sort of "part" involved. River parts must be connected physically with other river parts to form a continuous whole. Baseball innings must be connected so that the score, batting order, and the like are carried over from the earlier inning to the later one according to the rules. Is there something analogous we are to say about persons?

Miller: Writers who concern themselves with this speak of "person-stages." That is just a stretch of consciousness, such as you and I are aware of now. I am aware of a flow of thoughts and feelings that are mine, you are aware of yours. A person is just a whole composed of such stretches as parts, not some substance that underlies them, as I thought yesterday, and not the body in which they occur, as you seem to think. That is the conception of a person I wish to defend today.

Weirob: So when I awoke and said to myself, "I am the one who was so rude to Sam Miller last night," I was judging that a certain stretch of consciousness I was then aware of, and an earlier one I remembered having been aware of, form a single whole of the appropriate sort—a single stream of consciousness, we might say.

Miller: Yes, that's it exactly. You need not worry about whether the same immaterial soul is involved, or even whether that makes sense. Nor need you worry about whether the same body is involved, as indeed you do not since you don't even have to open your eyes and look. Identity is not, so to speak, something under the person-stages, nor in something they are attached to, but something you build from them.

Now survival, you can plainly see, is no problem at all once we have this conception of personal identity. All you need suppose is that there is, in Heaven, a conscious being, and that the person-stages that make her up are in the appropriate relation to those that now make you up, so that they are parts of the same whole—

namely, you. If so, you have survived. So will you admit now that survival is at least possible?

Weirob: Hold on, hold on. Comforting me is not that easy. You will have to show that it is possible that these person-stages or stretches of consciousness be related in the appropriate way. And to do that, won't you have to tell me what that way is?

Miller: Yes, of course. I was getting ahead of myself. It is right at this point that my reading was particularly helpful. In a chapter of his *Essay On Human Understanding* Locke discusses this very question. He suggests that the relation between two person-stages or stretches of consciousness that makes them stages of a single person is just that the later one contains memories of the earlier one. He doesn't say this in so many words—he talks of "extending our consciousness back in time." But he seems to be thinking of memory.

Weirob: So, any past thought or feeling or intention or desire that I can remember having is mine?

Miller: That's right. I can remember only my own past thoughts and feelings, and you only yours. Of course, everyone would readily admit that. Locke's insight is to take this relation as the source of identity and not just its consequence. To remember—or more plausibly, to be able to remember—the thoughts and feelings of a person who was conscious in the past is just what it is to be that person.

Now you can easily see that this solves the problem of the possibility of survival. As I was saying, all you need to do is imagine someone at some future time, not on this earth and not with your present thoughts and feelings, remembering the very conversation we are having now. This does not require sameness of anything else, but it amounts to sameness of person. So, now will you admit it?

Weirob: No, I don't.

Miller: Well, what's the problem now?

Weirob: I admit that if I remember having a certain thought or feeling had by some person in the past, then I must indeed be that person. Though I can remember watching others think, I cannot remember their thinking, any more than I can experience it at the time it occurs if it is theirs and not mine. This is the kernel of Locke's idea, and I don't see that I could deny it.

But we must distinguish—as I'm sure you will agree—between *actually* remembering and merely *seeming* to remember. Many men who think that they are Napoleon claim to remember losing the battle of Waterloo. We may suppose them to be sincere, and to really seem to remember it. But they do not actually remember because they were not at the battle and are not Napoleon.

Miller: Of course I admit that we must distinguish between actually remembering and only seeming to.

Weirob: And you will admit too, I trust, that the thought of some person at some far place and some distant time seeming to remember this conversation I am having with you would not give me the sort of comfort that the prospect of survival is supposed to provide. I would have no reason to anticipate future experiences of this person, simply because she is to *seem* to remember my experiences. The experiences of such a deluded imposter are not ones I can look forward to having.

Miller: I agree.

Weirob: So the mere possibility of someone in the future seeming to remember this conversation does not show the possibility of my surviving. Only the possibility of someone actually remembering this conversation —or, to be precise, the experiences I am having— would show that.

Miller: Of course. But what are you driving at? Where is the problem? I can imagine someone being deluded, but also someone actually being you and remembering your present thoughts.

Weirob: But, what's the difference? How do you know *which* of the two you are imagining, and *what* you have shown possible?

Miller: Well, I just imagine the one and not the other. I don't see the force of your argument.

Weirob: Let me try to make it clear with another example. Imagine two persons. One is talking to you, saying certain words, having certain thoughts, and so forth. The other is not talking to you at all, but is in the next room being hypnotized. The hypnotist gives to this person a post-hypnotic suggestion that upon awakening he will remember having had certain thoughts and having uttered certain words to you. The thoughts and words he mentions happen to be just the thoughts and words which the first person actually thinks and says. Do you understand the situation?

Miller: Yes, continue.

Weirob: Now, in a while, both of the people are saying sentences which begin, "I remember saying to Sam Miller—" and "I remember thinking as I talked to Sam Miller." And they both report remembering just the same thoughts and utterances. One of these will be remembering and the other only seeming to remember, right?

Miller: Of course.

Weirob: Now which one is *actually* remembering?

Miller: Why, the very one who was in the room talking to me, of course. The other one is just under the influence of the suggestion made by the hypnotist and not remembering talking to me at all.

Weirob: Now you agree that the difference between them does not consist in the content of what they are now thinking or saying.

Miller: Agreed. The difference is in the relation to the past thinking and speaking. In the one case the relation of memory obtains. In the other, it does not.

Weirob: But they both satisfy part of the conditions of remembering, for they both *seem to remember.* So there must be some further condition that the one satisfies and the other does not. I am trying to get you to say what that further condition is.

Miller: Well, I said that the one who had been in this room talking would be remembering.

Weirob: In other words, given two putative rememberers of some past thought or action, the real rememberer is the one who, in addition to seeming to remember the past thought or action, actually thought it or did it.

Miller: Yes.

Weirob: That is to say, the one who is identical with the person who did the past thinking and uttering.

Miller: Yes, I admit it.

Weirob: So, your argument just amounts to this. Survival is possible, because imaginable. It is imaginable, because my identity with some Heavenly person is imaginable. To imagine it, we imagine a person in Heaven who, First, seems to remember my thoughts and actions, and Second, is me.

Surely, there could hardly be a tighter circle. If I have doubts that the Heavenly person is me, I will have doubts as to whether she is really remembering or only seeming to. No one could doubt the possibility of some future person who, after death, seemed to remember the things he thought and did. But that possibility does not resolve the issue about the possibility of survival. Only the possibility of someone *actually* remembering could do that— for that, as we agree, is sufficient for identity. But doubts about survival and identity simply go over without remainder into doubts about whether the memories would be actual or merely apparent. You guarantee me no more than the possibility of a deluded Heavenly imposter.

Cohen: [another friend who is at the hospital and plays a mediating role. Ed.] But wait, Gretchen. I think Sam was less than fair to his own idea just now.

Weirob: You think you can break out of the circle of using real memory to explain identity, and identity to mark the difference between real and apparent memory? Feel free to try.

Cohen: Let us return to your case of the hypnotist. You point out that we have two putative rememberers. You ask what marks the difference, and claim the answer must be the circular one—that the real rememberer is the person who actually had the experiences both seem to remember.

But that is not the only possible answer. The experiences themselves cause the later apparent memories in the one case, while the hypnotist causes them in the other. We can say that the rememberer is the one of the two whose memories *were* caused in the right way by the earlier experiences. We thus distinguish between the rememberer and the hypnotic subject, without appeal to identity.

The idea that real memory amounts to apparent memory plus identity is misleading anyway. I seem to remember, as a small child, knocking over the Menorah so the candles fell into and spoiled a tureen of soup. And I did actually perform such a feat. So we have apparent memory and identity. But I do *not* actually remember; I was much too young when I did this to remember it now. I have simply been told the story so often I seem to remember.

Here the suggestion that real memory is apparent memory that was caused in the appropriate way by the past events fares better. Not my experience of pulling over the Menorah, but hearing my parents talk about it later, caused my memory-like impressions.

Weirob: You analyze personal identity into memory, and memory into apparent memory which is caused in the right way. A person is a certain sort of causal process.

Cohen: Right.

Weirob: Suppose now for the sake of argument I accept this. How does it help Sam in his defense of the possibility of survival? In ordinary memory, the causal chain from remembered event to memory of it never leads us outside

the confines of a single body. Indeed, the normal process of which you speak surely involves storage of information somehow in the brain. How can the states of my brain, when I die, influence in the appropriate way the apparent memories of the Heavenly person Sam takes to be me?

Cohen: Well, I didn't intend to be defending the possibility of survival. That is Sam's problem. I just like the idea that personal identity can be explained in terms of memory, and not just in terms of identity of the body.

Miller: But surely, this does provide me with the basis for further defense. Your challenge, Gretchen, was to explain the difference between two persons in Heaven, one who actually remembers your experience—and so is you—and one who simply seems to remember it. But can I not just say that the one who is you is the one whose states were caused in the appropriate way? I do not mean the way they would be in a normal case of earthly memory. But in the case of the Heavenly being who is you, God would have created her with the brain states (or whatever) she has *because* you had the ones you had at death. Surely it is not the exact form of the dependence of my later memories on my earlier perceptions that makes them really memories, but the fact that the process involved has preserved information.

Weirob: So if God creates a Heavenly person, designing her brain to duplicate the brain I have upon death, that person is me. If, on the other hand, a Heavenly being should come to be with those very same memory-like states by accident (if there are accidents in Heaven) it would not be me.

Miller: Exactly. Are you satisfied now that survival makes perfectly good sense?

Weirob: No, I'm still quite unconvinced.

The problem I see is this. If God could create one person in Heaven, and by designing her after me, make her me, why could he not make two such bodies, and cause this transfer of information into both of them? Would both of these Heavenly persons then be me? It seems as clear as anything in philosophy that from

A is B

and

C is B

where by "is" we mean identity, we can infer,

A is C.

So, if each of these Heavenly persons is me, they must be each other. But then they are not two but one. But my assumption was that God creates two, not one. He could create them physically distinct, capable of independent movement, perhaps in widely separated Heavenly locations, each with her own duties to perform, her own circle of Heavenly friends, and the like.

So either God, by creating a Heavenly person with a brain modeled after mine, does not really create someone identical with me but merely someone similar to me, or God is somehow limited to making only one such being. I can see no reason why, if there were a God, He should be so limited. So I take the first option. He could create someone similar to me, but not someone who would *be* me. Either your analysis of memory is wrong, and such a being does not, after all, remember what I am doing or saying, or memory is not sufficient for personal identity. Your theory has gone wrong somewhere, for it leads to absurdity.

Cohen: But wait. Why can't Sam simply say that if God makes one such creature, she is you, while if he makes more, none of them is you? It's possible that he makes only one. So it's possible that you survive. Sam always meant to allow that it's *possible* that you won't survive. He had in mind the case in which there is no God to make the appropriate Heavenly persons, or God exists, but doesn't make even one. You have simply shown that there is another way of not surviving. Instead of making too few Heavenly rememberers, He makes too many. So what? He might make the right number, and then you would survive.

Weirob: Your remarks really amount to a change in your position. Now you are not claiming that memory alone is enough for personal identity. Now, it is memory *plus* lack of competition, the absence of other rememberers, that is needed for personal identity.

Cohen: It does amount to a change of position. But what of it? Is there anything untenable about the position as changed?

Weirob: Let's look at this from the point of view of the Heavenly person. She says to herself, "Oh, I must be Gretchen Weirob, for I remember doing what she did and saying what she said." But now that's a pretty tenuous conclusion, isn't it? She is really only entitled to say, "Oh, either I'm Gretchen Weirob, or God has created more than one being like me, and none of us is." Identity has become something dependent on things wholly extrinsic to her. Who she is now turns on not just her states of mind and their relation to my states of mind, but on the existence or nonexistence of other people. Is this really what you want to maintain?

Or look at it from my point of view. God creates one of me in Heaven. Surely I should be glad if convinced this was to happen. Now he creates another, and I should despair again, for this means I won't survive after all. How can doubling a good deed make it worthless?

Cohen: Are you saying that there is some contradiction in my suggestion that only creation of a unique Heavenly Gretchen counts as your survival?

Weirob: No, it's not contradictory, as far as I can see. But it seems odd in a way that shows that something somewhere is wrong with your theory. Here is a certain relationship I have with a Heavenly person. There being such a person, to whom I am related in this way, is something that is of great importance to me, a source of comfort. It makes it appropriate for me to anticipate having her experiences, since she is just me. Why should my having that relation to another being destroy my relation to this one? You say because then I will not be identical with either of them. But since you have provided a theory about what that identity consists in, we can look and see what it amounts to for me to be or not to be identical. If she is to remember my experience, I can rightly anticipate hers. But then it seems the doubling makes no difference. And yet it must, for one cannot be identical with two. So you add, in a purely *ad hoc* manner, that her memory of me isn't enough to make my anticipation of her experiences appropriate, if there are two rather than one so linked. Isn't it more reasonable to conclude, since memory does not secure identity when there are two Heavenly Gretchens, it also doesn't when there is only one?

Cohen: There is something *ad hoc* about it, I admit. But perhaps that's just the way our concept works. You have not elicited a contradiction—

Weirob: An infinite pile of absurdities has the same weight as a contradiction. And absurdities can be generated without limit from your account. Suppose God created this Heavenly person before I died. Then He in effect kills me; if He has already created her, then you really are not talking to whom you think, but someone new, created by Gretchen Weirob's strange death moments ago. Or suppose He first creates one being in Heaven, who is me. Then He creates another. Does the first cease to be me? If God can create such beings in Heaven, surely He can do so in Albuquerque. And there is nothing on your theory to favor this body before you as Gretchen Weirob's, over the one belonging to the person created in Albuquerque. So I am to suppose that if God were to do this, I would suddenly cease to be. I'm tempted to say I would cease to be Gretchen Weirob. But that would be a confused way of putting it. There would be here, in my place, a new person with false memories of having been Gretchen Weirob, who has just died of competition—a strange death if ever there was one. She would have no right to my name, my bank account, or the services of my doctor, who is paid from insurance premiums paid for by deductions from Gretchen Weirob's past salary. Surely this is nonsense; however carefully God should choose to duplicate me, in Heaven or in Albuquerque, I would not cease to be, or cease to be who I am. You may reply that God, being benevolent, would never create an extra Gretchen Weirob. But I do not say that he would, but only that if he did this would not, as your theory implies, mean that I cease to exist. Your theory gives the wrong answer in this possible circumstance, so it must be wrong. I think I have been given no motivation to abandon the most obvious and straightforward view on these matters. I am a live body, and when that body dies, my existence will be at an end.

The Third Night[3]

Weirob: Well, Sam, are you here for a third attempt to convince me of the possibility of survival?

Miller: No, I have given up. I suggest we talk about fishing or football or something unrelated to your imminent demise. You will outwit any straightforward attempts to comfort you, but perhaps I can at least divert your mind.

Cohen: But before we start on fishing—although I don't have any particular brief for survival—there is one point in our discussion of the last two evenings that still bothers me. Would you mind discussing for a while the notion of personal identity itself, without worrying about the more difficult case of survival after death?

Weirob: I would enjoy it. What point bothers you?

Cohen: Your position seems to be that personal identity amounts to identity of a human body, nothing more, nothing less. A person is just a live human body, or more precisely, I suppose, a human body that is alive and has certain capacities—consciousness and perhaps rationality. Is that right?

Weirob: Yes, it seems that simple to me.

Cohen: But I think there has actually been an episode which disproves that. I am thinking of the strange case of Julia North, which occurred in California a few months ago. Surely you remember it.

Weirob: Yes, only too well. But you had better explain it to Sam, for I'll wager he has not heard of it.

Cohen: Not heard of Julia North? But the case was all over the headlines.

Miller: Well, Gretchen is right. I know nothing of it. She knows that I only read the sports page.

Cohen: You only read the sports page!

---

3. **The Third Night:** *Who is Julia?,* by Barbara Harris, is an engaging novel published in 1972. (Dr. Matthews had not yet thought of brain rejuvenations.)

Locke considers the possibility of the "consciousness" of a prince being transferred to the body of a cobbler. The idea of using the removal of a brain to suggest how this might happen comes from Sydney Shoemaker's seminal book, *Self-Knowledge and Self-Identity* (1963). In a number of important articles which are collected in his book *Problems of the Self* (1973), Bernard Williams has cleverly and ar-

ticulately resisted the memory theory and the view that such a brain removal would amount to a body transplant. In particular, Williams has stressed the relevance of the duplication argument even in questions of terrestrial personal identity. Weirob's position in this essay is more inspired by Williams than anyone else. I have discussed Williams' arguments and related topics in "Can the Self Divide?" (*Journal of Philosophy,* 1972) and in a review of his book (*Journal of Philosophy,* 1976).

An important article on the themes which emerge toward the end of the dialogue is Derek Parfit's "Personal Identity" (*Philosophical Review,* 1971). This article, along with Locke's chapter and a number of other important chapters and articles by Hume, Shoemaker, Williams, and others are collected in my anthology *Personal Identity* (1975). A number of new articles on personal identity appear in Amelie Rorty (ed.), *The Identities of Persons* (1976), including my "The Importance of Being Identical" which addresses the questions raised by Cohen at the end.

Weirob: It's an expression of his unconcern with earthly matters.

Miller: Well, that's not quite fair, Gretchen. It's a matter of preference. I much prefer to spend what time I have for reading in reading about the eighteenth century, rather than the drab and miserable century into which I had the misfortune to be born. It was really a much more civilized century, you know. But let's not dwell on my peculiar habits. Tell me about Julia North.

Cohen: Very well. Julia North was a young woman who was run over by a streetcar while saving the life of a young child who wandered onto the tracks. The child's mother, one Mary Frances Beaudine, had a stroke while watching the horrible scene. Julia's healthy brain and wasted body, and Mary Frances' healthy body and wasted brain, were transported to a hospital where a brilliant neurosurgeon, Dr. Matthews, was in residence. He had worked out a procedure for what he called a "body transplant." He removed the brain from Julia's head and placed it in Mary Frances', splicing the nerves, and so forth, using techniques not available until quite recently. The survivor of all of this was obviously Julia, as everyone agreed —except, unfortunately, Mary Frances' husband. His shortsightedness and lack of imagination led to great complications and drama, and made the case more famous in the history of crime than in the history of medicine. I shall not go into the details of this sorry aspect of the case—they are well reported in a book by Barbara Harris called *Who is Julia?,* in case you are interested.

Miller: Fascinating!

Cohen: Well, the relevance of this case is obvious. Julia North had one body up until the time of the accident, and another body after the operation. So one person had two bodies. So a person cannot be simply *identified* with a human body. So something must be wrong with your view, Gretchen. What do you say to this?

Weirob: I'll say to you just what I said to Dr. Matthews—

Cohen: You have spoken with Dr. Matthews?

Weirob: Yes. He contacted me shortly after my accident. My physician had phoned him up about my case. Matthews said he could perform the same operation for me he did for Julia North. I refused.

Cohen: You refused! But Gretchen, why—?

Miller: Gretchen, I *am* shocked. Your decision practically amounts to suicide! You passed up an opportunity to continue living? Why on earth—

Weirob: Hold on, hold on. You are both making an assumption I reject. If the case of Julia North amounts to a counterexample to my view that a person is just a live human body, and if my refusal to submit to this procedure amounts to suicide, then the survivor of such an operation must be reckoned as the same person as the brain donor. That is, the survivor of Julia North's operation must have been Julia, and the survivor of the operation on me would have to be me. This is the assumption you both make in criticizing me. But I reject it. I think Jack Beaudine was right. The survivor of the operation involving Julia North's brain was Mary Frances Beaudine, and the survivor of the operation using my brain would not have been me.

Miller: Gretchen, how on earth can you say that? Will you not give up your view that personal identity is just bodily identity, no matter how clear the counterexample? I really think you simply have an irrational attachment to the lump of material that is your body.

Cohen: Yes, Gretchen, I agree with Sam. You are being preposterous! The survivor of Julia North's operation had no idea who Mary Frances Beaudine was. She remembered being Julia—

Weirob: She *seemed* to remember being Julia. Have you forgotten so quickly the importance of this distinction? In my opinion, the effect of the operation was that Mary Frances Beaudine survived deluded, thinking she was someone else.

Cohen: But as you know, the case was litigated. It went to the Supreme Court. They said that the survivor was Julia.

Weirob: That argument is unworthy of you, Dave. Is the Supreme Court infallible?

Cohen: No, it isn't. But I don't think it's such a stupid point.

Look at it this way, Gretchen. This is a case in which two criteria we use to make judgments of identity conflict. Usually we expect personal identity to involve both bodily identity and psychological continuity. That is, we expect that if we have the same body, then the beliefs, memories, character traits, and the like also will be enormously similar. In this case, these two criteria which usually coincide do not. If we choose one criterion, we say that the survivor is Mary Frances Beaudine and she has undergone drastic psychological changes. If we choose the other, we say that Julia has survived with a new body. We have to choose which criterion is more important. It's a matter of choice of how to use our language, how to extend the concept "same person" to a new situation. The overwhelming majority of people involved in the case took the survivor to be Julia. That is, society chose to use the concept one way rather than the other. The Supreme Court is *not* beside the point. One of their functions is to settle just how old concepts shall be applied to new circumstances—how "freedom of the press" is to be understood when applied to movies or television, whose existence was not forseen when the concept was shaped, or to say whether "murder" is to include the abortion of a fetus. They are fallible on points of fact, but they are the final authority on the development of certain important concepts used in law. The notion of *person* is such a concept.

Weirob: You think that *who* the survivor was, was a matter of convention, of how we choose to use language?

Cohen: Yes.

Weirob: I can show the preposterousness of all that with an example.

Let us suppose that I agree to the operation. I lie in bed, expecting my continued existence, anticipating the feelings and thoughts I shall have upon awakening after the operation. Dr. Matthews enters and asks me to take several aspirin, so as not to have a headache when I awake. I protest that aspirin upsets my stomach; he asks whether I would rather have a terrible headache tomorrow or a mild stomachache now, and I agree that it would be reasonable to take them.

Let us suppose that you enter at this point, with bad news. The Supreme Court has changed its mind! So the survivor will not be me. So, I say, "Oh, then I will not take the aspirin, for it's not me that will have a headache, but someone else. Why should I endure a stomachache, however mild, for the comfort of someone else? After all, I am already donating my brain to that person."

Now this is clearly absurd. If I were correct, in the first place, to anticipate having the sensations and thoughts that the survivor is to have the next day, the decision of nine old men a thousand or so miles away wouldn't make me wrong. And if I was wrong to so anticipate, their decision couldn't make me right. How can the correctness of my anticipation of survival be a matter of the way we use our words? If it is not such a matter, then my identity is not either. My identity with the survivor, my survival, is a question of fact, not of convention.

Cohen: Your example is persuasive. I admit I am befuddled. On the one hand, I cannot see how the matter can be other than I have described. When we know all the facts what can remain to be decided but how we are to describe them, how we are to use our language? And yet I can see that it seems absurd to suppose that the correctness or incorrectness of anticipation of future experience is a matter for convention to decide.

Miller: Well, I didn't think the business about convention was very plausible anyway. But I should like to return you to the main question, Gretchen. Fact or convention, it still remains. Why will you not admit that the survivor of this operation would be you?

Weirob: Well, *you* tell *me,* why you think she would be me?

Miller: I can appeal to the theory I developed last night. You argued that the idea that personal identity consists in memory would not guarantee the possibility of survival after death. But you said nothing to shake its plausibility as an account of personal identity. It has the enormous advantage, remember, of making sense of our ability to judge our own identity, without examination of our bodies. I should argue that it is the correctness of this theory that explains the *almost* universal willingness to say that the survivor of Julia's operation was Julia. We need not deliberate over how to extend our concept, we need only apply the concept we already have. Memory is sufficient for identity and bodily identity is *not* necessary for it. The survivor remembered Julia's thoughts and actions, and so was Julia. Would you but submit to the operation, the survivor would remember your thoughts and actions, would remember this very conversation we are now having, and would be you.

Cohen: Yes, I now agree completely with Sam. The theory that personal identity is to be analyzed in terms of memory is correct, and according to it you will survive if you submit to the operation.

Let me add another argument against your view and in favor of the memory theory. You have emphasized that identity is the condition of *anticipation.* That means, among other things, that we have a particular concern for that person in the future whom we take to be ourselves. If I were told that any of the three of us were to suffer pain tomorrow, I should be sad. But if it were you or Sam that were to be hurt, my concern would be altruistic or unselfish. That is because I would not anticipate having the painful experience myself. Here I do no more than repeat points you have made earlier in our conversations.

Now what is there about mere sameness of body that makes sense of this asymmetry, between the way we look at our own futures, and the way we look at the futures of others? In other words, why is the identity of your body—that mere lump of matter, as Sam put it—of such great importance? Why care so much about it?

Weirob: You say, and I surely agree, that identity of person is a very special relationship—so special as perhaps not even happily called a relationship at all. And you say that since my theory is that identity of person is identity of body, I should be able to explain the importance of the one in terms of the importance of the other.

I'm not sure I can do that. But does the theory that personal identity consists in memory fare better on this score?

Cohen: Well, I think it does. Those properties of persons which make persons of such great value, and mark their individuality, and make one person so special to his friends and loved ones, are ultimately psychological or mental. One's character, personality, beliefs, attitudes, convictions—they are what make every person so unique and special. A skinny Gretchen would be a shock to us all, but not a Gretchen diminished in any important way. But a Gretchen who was not witty, or not gruff, or not as honest to the path an argument takes as is humanly possible—those would be fundamental changes. Is it any wonder that the survivor of that California fiasco was reckoned as Julia North? Would it make sense to take her to be Mary Jane Beaudine, when she had none of her beliefs or attitudes or memories?

Now if such properties are what is of importance about a person to others, is it not reasonable that they are the basis of one's importance to oneself? And these are just the properties that personal identity preserves when it is taken to consist in links of memory. Do we not have, in this idea, at least the beginning of an explanation of the importance of identity?

Weirob: So on two counts you two favor the memory theory. First, you say it explains how it is possible to judge as to one's own identity, without having to examine one's body. Second, you say it explains the importance of personal identity.

Cohen: Now surely you must agree the memory theory is correct. Do you agree? There may be still time to contact Dr. Matthews—

Weirob: Hold on, hold on. Try to relax and enjoy the argument. I am. Quit trying to save my life and worry about saving your theory—for I'm still not persuaded. Granted the survivor will *think* she is me, will *seem* to remember thinking my thoughts. But recall the importance of distinguishing between real and merely apparent memory—

Cohen: But *you* recall that this distinction is to be made on the basis of whether the apparent memories were or were not caused by the prior experiences in the appropriate way. The survivor will not seem to remember your thoughts because of hypnosis or by coincidence or overweening imagination. She will seem to remember them because the traces those experiences left on your brain now activate her mind in the usual way. She will seem to remember them because she does remember them, and will be you.

Weirob: You are very emphatic, and I'm feeling rather weak. I'm not sure there is time left to untangle all of this. But there is never an advantage to hurrying when doing philosophy. So let's go over this slowly.

We all agree that the fact that the survivor of this strange operation Dr. Matthews proposes would *seem* to remember doing what I have done. Let us even suppose she would take herself to be me, claim to be Gretchen Weirob—and have no idea who else she might be. (We are then assuming that she differs from me in one aspect—her theory of personal identity. But that does not show her not to be me, for I could change my mind by then.) We all first agree that this much does not make her me. For this could all be true of someone suffering a delusion, or a subject of hypnosis.

Cohen: Yes, this is all agreed.

Weirob: But now you think that some *future* condition is satisfied, which makes her apparent memories *real* memories. Now what exactly is this future condition?

Cohen: Well, that the same brain was involved in the perception of the events, and their later *memory*. Thus we have here a causal chain of just the same sort as when only a single body is involved. That is, perceptions when the event occurs leave a trace in the brain, which is later responsible for the content of the memory. And we agreed, did we not, that apparent memory, caused in the right way, is real memory?

Weirob: Now is it absolutely crucial that the same brain is involved?

Cohen: What do you mean?

Weirob: Let me explain again by reference to Dr. Matthews. In our conversation he explained a new procedure on which he was working, called a *brain rejuvenation*. By this process, which is not yet available—only the feasibility of developing it is being studied—a new brain could be made which is an exact duplicate of my brain—that is, an exact duplicate in terms of psychologically relevant states. It might not duplicate all the properties of my brain—for example, the blood vessels in the new brain might be stronger than in the old brain.

Miller: What is the point of developing such a macabre technique?

Weirob: Dr. Matthews' idea is that when weaknesses which might lead to stroke or other brain injury are noted, a healthy duplicate could be made to replace the original, forestalling the problem.

Now Dave, suppose my problem were not with my liver and kidneys and such, but with my brain. Would you recommend such an operation as to my benefit?

Cohen: You mean, do I think the survivor of such an operation would be you?

Weirob: Exactly. You may assume that Dr. Matthews' technique works perfectly so the causal process involved is no less reliable than that involved in ordinary memory.

Cohen: Then I would say it was you—No! Wait! No, it wouldn't be you—absolutely not.

Miller: But why the sudden reversal? It seems to me it would be her. Indeed, I should try such an operation myself, if it would clear up my dizzy spells and leave me otherwise unaffected.

Cohen: No, don't you see, she is leading us into a false trap. If we say it *is* her, then she will say, "then what if he makes two duplicates, or three or ten? They can't all be me, they all have an equal claim, so none will be me." It would be the argument of last night, reapplied on earth. So the answer is no, absolutely not, it wouldn't be you. Duplication of brain does not preserve identity. Identity of the person requires identity of the brain.

Miller: Quite right.

Weirob: Now let me see if I have managed to understand your theory, for my powers of concentration seem to be fading. Suppose we have two bodies, A and B. My brain is put into A, a duplicate into B. The survivor of this, call them "A-Gretchen" and "B-Gretchen," both seem to remember giving this very speech. Both are in this state of seeming to remember, as the last stage in an information-preserving causal chain, initiated by my giving this speech. Both have my character, personality, beliefs and the like. But one is *really* remembering, the other is not. A-Gretchen is really me, B-Gretchen is not.

Cohen: Precisely. Is this incoherent?

Weirob: No, I guess there is nothing incoherent about it. But look what has happened to the advantages you claimed for the memory theory.

First, you said, it explains how I can know who I am without opening my eyes and recognizing my body. But on your theory Gretchen-A and Gretchen-B cannot know who they are even if they do open their eyes and examine their bodies. How is Gretchen-A to know whether she has the original brain and is who she seems to be, or has the duplicate and is a new person, only a few minutes old, and with no memories but mere delusions? If the hospital kept careless records, or the surgeon thought it was of no great importance to keep track of who got the original and who got the duplicate, she might never know who she was. By making identity of person turn into identity of brain, your theory makes the ease with which I can determine who I am not less but more mysterious than my theory.

Second, you said, your theory explains why my concern for Gretchen-A, who is me whether she knows it or not, would be selfish, and my anticipation of her experience correct while my concern for Gretchen-B with her duplicated brain would be unselfish, and my anticipation of having her experiences incorrect. And it explains this, you said, because by insisting on the links of memory, we preserve in personal identity more psychological characteristics which are the most important features of a person.

But Gretchen-A and Gretchen-B are psychologically indiscernible. Though they will go their separate ways, at the moment of awakening they could well be exactly similar in every psychological respect. In terms of character and belief and the contents of their minds, Gretchen-A is no more like me than Gretchen-B. So there is nothing in your theory after all to explain why anticipation is appropriate when we have identity and not otherwise.

You said, Sam, that I had an irrational attachment for this unworthy material object, my body. But you too are as irrationally attached to your brain. I have never seen my brain. I should have easily given it up for a rejuvenated version, had that been the choice with which I was faced. I have never seen it, never felt it, and have no attachment to it. But my body? That seems to me all that I am. I see no point in trying to evade its fate, even if there were still time.

But perhaps I miss the merit of your arguments. I am tired, and perhaps my poor brain, feeling slighted, has begun to desert me—

Cohen: Oh, don't worry, Gretchen, you are still clever. Again you have left me befuddled. I don't know what to say. But answer me this. Suppose you are right and we are wrong. But suppose these arguments had not oc-

curred to you, and, sharing in our error, you had agreed to the operation. You anticipate the operation until it happens, thinking you will survive. You are happy. The survivor takes herself to be you, and thinks she made a decision before the operation which has now turned out to be right. She is happy. Your friends are happy. Who would be worse off, either before or after the operation?

Suppose even that you realize identity would not be preserved by such an operation, but have it done anyway, and as the time for the operation approaches, you go ahead and anticipate the experiences of the survivor. Where exactly is the mistake? Do you really have any less reason to care for the survivor than for yourself? Can mere identity of body, the lack of which alone keeps you from being her, mean that much? Perhaps we were wrong, after all, in focusing on identity as the necessary condition of anticipation—

Miller: Dave, it's too late.

Derek Parfit

Personal Identity

We can, I think,[1] describe cases in which, though we know the answer to every other question, we have no idea how to answer a question about personal identity. These cases are not covered by the criteria of personal identity that we actually use.

Do they present a problem?

It might be thought that they do not, because they could never occur. I suspect that some of them could. (Some, for instance, might become scientifically possi-

ble.) But I shall claim that even if they did they would present no problem.

My targets are two beliefs: one about the nature of personal identity, the other about its importance.

The first is that in these cases the question about identity must have an answer.

No one thinks this about, say, nations or machines. Our criteria for the identity of these do not cover certain cases. No one thinks that in these cases the questions "Is it the same nation?" or "Is it the same machine?" must have answers.

Some people believe that in this respect they are different. They agree that our criteria of personal identity do not cover certain cases, but they believe that the nature of their own identity through time is, somehow, such as to guarantee that in these cases questions about

Derek Parfit, "Personal Identity" from *Philosphical Review,* 80 (1971).

1. I have been helped in writing this by D. Wiggins, D. F. Pears, P. F. Strawson, A. J. Ayer, M. Woods, N. Newman, and (through his publications) S. Shoemaker.

their identity must have answers. This belief might be expressed as follows: "Whatever happens between now and any future time, either I shall still exist, or I shall not. Any future experience will either be *my* experience, or it will not."

This first belief—in the special nature of personal identity—has, I think, certain effects. It makes people assume that the principle of self-interest is more rationally compelling than any moral principle. And it makes them more depressed by the thought of aging and of death.

I cannot see how to disprove this first belief. I shall describe a problem case. But this can only make it seem implausible.

Another approach might be this. We might suggest that one cause of the belief is the projection of our emotions. When we imagine ourselves in a problem case, we do feel that the question "Would it be me?" must have an answer. But what we take to be a bafflement about a further fact may be only the bafflement of our concern.

I shall not pursue this suggestion here. But one cause of our concern is the belief which is my second target. This is that unless the question about identity has an answer, we cannot answer certain important questions (questions about such matters as survival, memory, and responsibility).

Against this second belief my claim will be this. Certain important questions do presuppose a question about personal identity. But they can be freed of this presupposition. And when they are, the question about identity has no importance.

I

We can start by considering the much-discussed case of the man who, like an amoeba, divides.

Wiggins has recently dramatized this case.[2] He first referred to the operation imagined by Shoemaker.[3] We suppose that my brain is transplanted into someone else's (brainless) body, and that the resulting person has my character and apparent memories of my life. Most

of us would agree, after thought, that the resulting person is me. I shall here assume such agreement.[4]

Wiggins then imagined his own operation. My brain is divided, and each half is housed in a new body. Both resulting people have my character and apparent memories of my life.

What happens to me? There seem only three possibilities: (1) I do not survive; (2) I survive as one of the two people; (3) I survive as both.

The trouble with (1) is this. We agreed that I could survive if my brain were successfully transplanted. And people have in fact survived with half their brains destroyed. It seems to follow that I could survive if half my brain were successfully transplanted and the other half were destroyed. But if this is so, how could I *not* survive if the other half were also successfully transplanted? How could a double success be a failure?

We can move to the second description. Perhaps one success is the maximum score. Perhaps I shall be one of the resulting people.

The trouble here is that in Wiggins' case each half of my brain is exactly similar, and so, to start with, is each resulting person. So how can I survive as only one of the two people? What can make me one of them rather than the other?

It seems clear that both of these descriptions—that I do not survive, and that I survive as one of the people—are highly implausible. Those who have accepted them must have assumed that they were the only possible descriptions.

What about our third description: that I survive as both people?

It might be said, "If 'survive' implies identity, this description makes no sense—you cannot be two people. If it does not, the description is irrelevant to a problem about identity."

I shall later deny the second of these remarks. But there are ways of denying the first. We might say, "What

---

2. In *Identity and Spatio-Temporal Continuity* (Oxford, 1967), p. 50.

3. In *Self-Knowledge and Self-Identity* (Ithaca, N.Y., 1963), p. 22.

---

4. Those who would disagree are not making a mistake. For them my argument would need a different case. There must be some multiple transplant, faced with which these people would both find it hard to believe that there must be an answer to the question about personal identity, and be able to be shown that nothing of importance turns upon this question.

we have called 'the two resulting people' are not two people. They are one person. I do survive Wiggins' operation. Its effect is to give me two bodies and a divided mind."

It would shorten my argument if this were absurd. But I do not think it is. It is worth showing why.

We can, I suggest, imagine a divided mind. We can imagine a man having two simultaneous experiences, in having each of which he is unaware of having the other.

We may not even need to imagine this. Certain actual cases, to which Wiggins referred, seem to be best described in these terms. These involve the cutting of the bridge between the hemispheres of the brain. The aim was to cure epilepsy. But the result appears to be, in the surgeon's words, the creation of "two separate spheres of consciousness,"[5] each of which controls one half of the patient's body. What is experienced in each is, presumably, experienced by the patient.

There are certain complications in these actual cases. So let us imagine a simpler case.

Suppose that the bridge between my hemispheres is brought under my voluntary control. This would enable me to disconnect my hemispheres as easily as if I were blinking. By doing this I would divide my mind. And we can suppose that when my mind is divided I can, in each half, bring about reunion.

This ability would have obvious uses. To give an example: I am near the end of a maths exam, and see two ways of tackling the last problem. I decide to divide my mind, to work, with each half, at one of two calculations, and then to reunite my mind and write a fair copy of the best result.

What shall I experience?

When I disconnect my hemispheres, my consciousness divides into two streams. But this division is not something that I experience. Each of my two streams of consciousness seems to have been straightforwardly continuous with my one stream of consciousness up to the moment of division. The only changes in each stream are the disappearance of half my visual field and the loss of sensation in, and control over, half my body.

Consider my experiences in what we can call my "right-handed" stream. I remember that I assigned my right hand to the longer calculation. This I now begin. In working at this calculation I can see, from the movements of my left hand, that I am also working at the other. But I am not aware of working at the other. So I might, in my right-handed stream, wonder how, in my left-handed stream, I am getting on.

My work is now over. I am about to reunite my mind. What should I, in each stream, expect? Simply that I shall suddenly seem to remember just having thought out two calculations, in thinking out each of which I was not aware of thinking out the other. This, I submit, we can imagine. And if my mind was divided, these memories are correct.

In describing this episode, I assumed that there were two series of thoughts, and that they were both mine. If my two hands visibly wrote out two calculations, and if I claimed to remember two corresponding series of thoughts, this is surely what we should want to say.

If it is, then a person's mental history need not be like a canal, with only one channel. It could be like a river, with islands, and with separate streams.

To apply this to Wiggins' operation: we mentioned the view that it gives me two bodies and a divided mind. We cannot now call this absurd. But it is, I think, unsatisfactory.

There were two features of the case of the exam that made us want to say that only one person was involved. The mind was soon reunited, and there was only one body. If a mind was permanently divided and its halves developed in different ways, the point of speaking of one person would start to disappear. Wiggins' case, where there are also two bodies, seems to be over the borderline. After I have had his operation, the two "products" each have all the attributes of a person. They could live at opposite ends of the earth. (If they later met, they might even fail to recognize each other.) It would become intolerable to deny that they were different people.

Suppose we admit that they are different people. Could we still claim that I survived as both, using "survive" to imply identity?

We could. For we might suggest that two people could compose a third. We might say, "I do survive Wiggins' operation as two people. They can be different

---

5. R. W. Sperry, in *Brain and Conscious Experience,* ed. by J. C. Eccles (New York, 1966), p. 299.

people, and yet be me, in just the way in which the Pope's three crowns are one crown."[6]

This is a possible way of giving sense to the claim that I survive as two different people, using "survive" to imply identity. But it keeps the language of identity only by changing the concept of a person. And there are obvious objections to this change.[7]

The alternative, for which I shall argue, is to give up the language of identity. We can suggest that I survive as two different people without implying that I am these people.

When I first mentioned this alternative, I mentioned this objection: "If your new way of talking does not imply identity, it cannot solve our problem. For that is about identity. The problem is that all the possible answers to the question about identity are highly implausible."

We can now answer this objection.

We can start by reminding ourselves that this is an objection only if we have one or both of the beliefs which I mentioned at the start of this paper.

The first was the belief that to any question about personal identity, in any describable case, there must be a true answer. For those with this belief, Wiggins' case is doubly perplexing. If all the possible answers are implausible, it is hard to decide which of them is true, and hard even to keep the belief that one of them must be true. If we give up this belief, as I think we should, these problems disappear. We shall then regard the case as like many others in which, for quite unpuzzling reasons, there *is* no answer to a question about identity. (Consider "Was England the same nation after 1066?")

Wiggins' case makes the first belief implausible. It also makes it trivial. For it undermines the second belief.

---

6. Cf. David Wiggins, *op. cit,* p. 40.

7. Suppose the resulting people fight a duel. Are there three people fighting, one on each side, and one on both? And suppose one of the bullets kills. Are there two acts, one murder and one suicide? How many people are left alive? One? Two? (We could hardly say, "One and a half.") We could talk in this way. But instead of saying that the resulting people *are* the original person—so that the pair is a trio—it would be far simpler to treat them as a pair, and describe their relation to the original person in some new way. (I owe this suggested way of talking, and the objections to it, to Michael Woods.)

This was the belief that important questions turn upon the question about identity. (It is worth pointing out that those who have only this second belief do not think that there must *be* an answer to this question, but rather that we must decide upon an answer.)

Against this second belief my claim is this. Certain questions do presuppose a question about personal identity. And because these questions *are* important, Wiggins' case does present a problem. But we cannot solve this problem by answering the question about identity. We can solve this problem only by taking these important questions and prizing them apart from the question about identity. After we have done this, the question about identity (though we might for the sake of neatness decide it) has no further interest.

Because there are several questions which presuppose identity, this claim will take some time to fill out.

We can first return to the question of survival. This is a special case, for survival does not so much presuppose the retaining of identity as seem equivalent to it. It is thus the general relation which we need to prize apart from identity. We can then consider particular relations, such as those involved in memory and intention.

"Will I survive?" seems, I said, equivalent to "Will there be some person alive who is the same person as me?"

If we treat these questions as equivalent, then the least unsatisfactory description of Wiggins' case is, I think, that I survive with two bodies and a divided mind.

Several writers have chosen to say that I am neither of the resulting people. Given our equivalence, this implies that I do not survive, and hence, presumably, that even if Wiggins' operation is not literally death, I ought, since I will not survive it, to regard it *as* death. But this seemed absurd.

It is worth repeating why. An emotion or attitude can be criticized for resting on a false belief, or for being inconsistent. A man who regarded Wiggins' operation as death must, I suggest, be open to one of these criticisms.

He might believe that his relation to each of the resulting people fails to contain some element which is contained in survival. But how can this be true? We agreed that he *would* survive if he stood in this very same relation to only *one* of the resulting people. So it cannot be the nature of this relation which makes it fail, in Wiggins' case, to be survival. It can only be its duplication.

Suppose that our man accepts this, but still regards division as death. His reaction would now seem wildly inconsistent. He would be like a man who, when told of a drug that could double his years of life, regarded the taking of this drug as death. The only difference in the case of division is that the extra years are to run concurrently. This is an interesting difference. But it cannot mean that there are *no* years to run.

I have argued this for those who think that there must, in Wiggins' case, be a true answer to the question about identity. For them, we might add, "Perhaps the original person does lose his identity. But there may be other ways to do this than to die. One other way might be to multiply. To regard these as the same is to confuse nought with two."

For those who think that the question of identity is up for decision, it would be clearly absurd to regard Wiggins' operation as death. These people would have to think, "We could have chosen to say that I should be one of the resulting people. If we had, I should not have regarded it as death. But since we have chosen to say that I am neither person, I *do*." This is hard even to understand.

My first conclusion, then, is this. The relation of the original person to each of the resulting people contains all that interests us—all that matters—in any ordinary case of survival. This is why we need a sense in which one person can survive as two.

One of my aims in the rest of this paper will be to suggest such a sense. But we can first make some general remarks.

II

Identity is a one-one relation. Wiggins' case serves to show that what matters in survival need not be one-one.

Wiggins' case is of course unlikely to occur. The relations which matter are, in fact, one-one. It is because they are that we can imply the holding of these relations by using the language of identity.

This use of language is convenient. But it can lead us astray. We may assume that what matters *is* identity and, hence, has the properties of identity.

In the case of the property of being one-one, this mistake is not serious. For what matters is in fact one-one. But in the case of another property, the mistake *is* serious. Identity is all-or-nothing. Most of the relations which matter in survival are, in fact, relations of degree. If we ignore this, we shall be led into quite ill-grounded attitudes and beliefs.

The claim that I have just made—that most of what matters are relations of degree—I have yet to support. Wiggins' case shows only that these relations need not be one-one. The merit of the case is not that it shows this in particular, but that it makes the first break between what matters and identity. The belief that identity *is* what matters is hard to overcome. This is shown in most discussions of the problem cases which actually occur: cases, say, of amnesia or of brain damage. Once Wiggins' case has made one breach in this belief, the rest should be easier to remove.

To turn to a recent debate: most of the relations which matter can be provisionally referred to under the heading "psychological continuity" (which includes causal continuity). My claim is thus that we use the language of personal identity in order to imply such continuity. This is close to the view that psychological continuity provides a criterion of identity.

Williams has attacked this view with the following argument. Identity is a one-one relation. So any criterion of identity must appeal to a relation which is logically one-one. Psychological continuity is not logically one-one. So it cannot provide a criterion.[8]

Some writers have replied that it is enough if the relation appealed to is always in fact one-one.

I suggest a slightly different reply. Psychological continuity is a ground for speaking of identity when it is one-one.

If psychological continuity took a one-many or branching form, we should need, I have argued, to abandon the language of identity. So this possibility would not count against this view.

We can make a stronger claim. This possibility would count in its favor.

The view might be defended as follows. Judgments of personal identity have great importance. What gives

---

8. Bernard Williams "Personal Identity and Individuation," *Proceedings of the Aristotelian Society,* LVII (1956–1957), 229–253; also *Analysis,* 21 (1960–1961), 43–48.

them their importance is the fact that they imply psychological continuity. This is why, whenever there is such continuity, we ought, if we can, to imply it by making a judgment of identity.

If psychological continuity took a branching form, no coherent set of judgments of identity could correspond to, and thus be used to imply, the branching form of this relation. But what we ought to do, in such a case, is take the importance which would attach to a judgment of identity and attach this importance directly to each limb of the branching relation. So this case helps to show that judgments of personal identity do derive their importance from the fact that they imply psychological continuity. It helps to show that when we can, usefully, speak of identity, this relation is our ground.

This argument appeals to a principle which Williams put forward.[9] The principle is that an important judgment should be asserted and denied only on importantly different grounds.

Williams applied this principle to a case in which one man is psychologically continuous with the dead Guy Fawkes, and a case in which two men are. His argument was this. If we treat psychological continuity as a sufficient ground for speaking of identity, we shall say that the one man is Guy Fawkes. But we could not say that the two men are, although we should have the same ground. This disobeys the principle. The remedy is to deny that the one man is Guy Fawkes, to insist that sameness of the body is necessary for identity.

Williams' principle can yield a different answer. Suppose we regard psychological continuity as more important than sameness of the body. And suppose that the one man really is psychologically (and causally) continuous with Guy Fawkes. If he is, it would disobey the principle to deny that he is Guy Fawkes, for we have the same important ground as in a normal case of identity. In the case of the two men, we again have the same important ground. So we ought to take the importance from the judgment of identity and attach it directly to this ground. We ought to say, as in Wiggins' case, that each limb of the branching relation is as good as survival. This obeys the principle.

To sum up these remarks: even if psychological continuity is neither logically, nor always in fact, one-one, it can provide a criterion of identity. For this can appeal to the relation of *non-branching* psychological continuity, which is logically one-one.

The criterion might be sketched as follows. "*X* and *Y* are the same person if they are psychologically continuous and there is no person who is contemporary with either and psychologically continuous with the other." We should need to explain what we mean by "psychologically continuous" and say how much continuity the criterion requires. We should then, I think, have described a sufficient condition for speaking of identity.

We need to say something more. If we admit that psychological continuity might not be one-one, we need to say what we ought to do if it were not one-one. Otherwise our account would be open to the objections that it is incomplete and arbitrary.

I have suggested that if psychological continuity took a branching form, we ought to speak in a new way, regarding what we describe as having the same significance as identity. This answers these objections.

We can now return to our discussion. We have three remaining aims. One is to suggest a sense of "survive" which does not imply identity. Another is to show that most of what matters in survival are relations of degree. A third is to show that none of these relations needs to be described in a way that presupposes identity.

We can take these aims in the reverse order.

III

The most important particular relation is that involved in memory. This is because it is so easy to believe that its description must refer to identity. This belief about memory is an important cause of the view that personal identity has a special nature. But it has been well discussed by Shoemaker and by Wiggins. So we can be brief.

It may be a logical truth that we can only remember our own experiences. But we can frame a new concept for which this is not a logical truth. Let us call this "*q*-memory."

To sketch a definition I am *q*-remembering an experience if (1) I have a belief about a past experience which seems in itself like a memory belief, (2) someone

---

9. *Analysis,* 21 (1960–1961), 44.

did have such an experience, and (3) my belief is dependent upon this experience in the same way (whatever that is) in which a memory of an experience is dependent upon it.

According to (1) q-memories seem like memories. So I q-remember *having* experiences.

This may seem to make q-memory presuppose identity. One might say, "My apparent memory of *having* an experience is an apparent memory of *my* having an experience. So how could I q-remember my having other people's experiences?"

This objection rests on a mistake. When I seem to remember an experience, I do indeed seem to remember *having* it. But it cannot be a part of what I seem to remember about this experience that I, the person who now seems to remember it, am the person who had this experience. That I am is something that I automatically assume. (My apparent memories sometimes come to me simply as the belief that *I* had a certain experience.) But it is something that I am justified in assuming only because I do not in fact have q-memories of other people's experiences.

Suppose that I did start to have such q-memories. If I did, I should cease to assume that my apparent memories must be about my own experiences. I should come to assess an apparent memory by asking two questions: (1) Does it tell me about a past experience? (2) If so, whose?

Moreover (and this is a crucial point) my apparent memories would now come to me *as* q-memories. Consider those of my apparent memories which do come to me simply as beliefs about my past: for example, "I did that." If I knew that I could q-remember other people's experiences, these beliefs would come to me in a more guarded form: for example, "Someone—probably I—did that." I might have to work out who it was.

I have suggested that the concept of q-memory is coherent. Wiggins' case provides an illustration. The resulting people, in his case, both have apparent memories of living the life of the original person. If they agree that they are not this person, they will have to regard these as only q-memories. And when they are asked a question like "Have you heard this music before?" they might have to answer "I am sure that I q-remember hearing it. But I am not sure whether I remember hear-

ing it. I am not sure whether it was I who heard it, or the original person."

We can next point out that on our definition every memory is also a q-memory. Memories are, simply, q-memories of one's own experiences. Since this is so, we could afford now to drop the concept of memory and use in its place the wider concept q-memory. If we did, we should describe the relation between an experience and what we now call a "memory" of this experience in a way which does not presuppose that they are had by the same person.

This way of describing this relation has certain merits. It vindicates the "memory criterion" of personal identity against the charge of circularity. And it might, I think, help with the problem of other minds.

But we must move on. We can next take the relation between an intention and a later action. It may be a logical truth that we can intend to perform only our own actions. But intentions can be redescribed as q-intentions. And one person could q-intend to perform another person's actions.

Wiggins' case again provides the illustration. We are supposing that neither of the resulting people is the original person. If so, we shall have to agree that the original person can, before the operation, q-intend to perform their actions. He might, for example, q-intend, as one of them, to continue his present career, and, as the other, to try something new.[10] (I say "q-intend *as* one of them" because the phrase "q-intend *that* one of them" would not convey the directness of the relation which is involved. If I intend that someone else should do something, I cannot get him to do it simply by form-

---

10. There are complications here. He could form *divergent* q-intentions only if he could distinguish, in advance, between the resulting people (e.g., as "the left-hander" and "the right-hander"). And he could be confident that such divergent q-intentions would be carried out only if he had reason to believe that neither of the resulting people would change their (inherited) mind. Suppose he was torn between duty and desire. He could not solve this dilemma by q-intending, as one of the resulting people, to do his duty, and, as the other, to do what he desires. For the one he q-intended to do his duty would face the same dilemma.

ing this intention. But if I am the original person, and he is one of the resulting people, I can.)

The phrase "*q*-intend *as* one of them" reminds us that we need a sense in which one person can survive as two. But we can first point out that the concepts of *q*-memory and *q*-intention give us our model for the others that we need: thus, a man who can *q*-remember could *q*-recognize, and be a *q*-witness of, what he has never seen; and a man who can *q*-intend could have *q*-ambitions, make *q*-promises, and be *q*-responsible for.

To put this claim in general terms: many different relations are included within, or are a consequence of, psychological continuity. We describe these relations in ways which presuppose the continued existence of one person. But we could describe them in new ways which do not.

This suggests a bolder claim. It might be possible to think of experiences in a wholly "impersonal" way. I shall not develop this claim here. What I shall try to describe is a way of thinking of our own identity through time which is more flexible, and less misleading, than the way in which we now think.

This way of thinking will allow for a sense in which one person can survive as two. A more important feature is that it treats survival as a matter of degree.

IV

We must first show the need for this second feature. I shall use two imaginary examples.

The first is the converse of Wiggins' case: fusion. Just as division serves to show that what matters in survival need not be one-one, so fusion serves to show that it can be a question of degree.

Physically, fusion is easy to describe. Two people come together. While they are unconscious, their two bodies grow into one. One person then wakes up.

The psychology of fusion is more complex. One detail we have already dealt with in the case of the exam. When my mind was reunited, I remembered just having thought out two calculations. The one person who results from a fusion can, similarly, *q*-remember living the lives of the two original people. None of their *q*-memories need be lost.

But some things must be lost. For any two people who fuse together will have different characteristics, different desires, and different intentions. How can these be combined?

We might suggest the following. Some of these will be compatible. These can coexist in the one resulting person. Some will be incompatible. These, if of equal strength, can cancel out, and if of different strengths, the stronger can be made weaker. And all these effects might be predictable.

To give examples—first, of compatibility: I like Palladio and intend to visit Venice. I am about to fuse with a person who likes Giotto and intends to visit Padua. I can know that the one person we shall become will have both tastes and both intentions. Second, of incompatibility: I hate red hair, and always vote Labour. The other person loves red hair, and always votes Conservative. I can know that the one person we shall become will be indifferent to red hair, and a floating voter.

If we were about to undergo a fusion of this kind, would we regard it as death?

Some of us might. This is less absurd than regarding division as death. For after my division the two resulting people will be in every way like me, while after my fusion the one resulting person will not be wholly similar. This makes it easier to say, when faced with fusion, "I shall not survive," thus continuing to regard survival as a matter of all-or-nothing.

This reaction is less absurd. But here are two analogies which tell against it.

First, fusion would involve the changing of some of our characteristics and some of our desires. But only the very self-satisfied would think of this as death. Many people welcome treatments with these effects.

Second, someone who is about to fuse can have, beforehand, just as much "intentional control" over the actions of the resulting individual as someone who is about to marry can have, beforehand, over the actions of the resulting couple. And the choice of a partner for fusion can be just as well considered as the choice of a marriage partner. The two original people can make sure (perhaps by "trial fusion") that they do have compatible characters, desires, and intentions.

I have suggested that fusion, while not clearly survival, is not clearly failure to survive, and hence that what matters in survival can have degrees.

To reinforce this claim we can now turn to a second example. This is provided by certain imaginary beings. These beings are just like ourselves except that they reproduce by a process of natural division.

We can illustrate the histories of these imagined beings with the aid of a diagram. The lines on the diagram represent the spatiotemporal paths which would be traced out by the bodies of these beings. We can call each single line (like the double line) a "branch"; and we can call the whole structure a "tree." And let us suppose that each "branch" corresponds to what is thought of as the life of one individual.

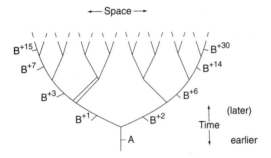

These individuals are referred to as "A," "B + 1," and so forth.

Now, each single division is an instance of Wiggins' case. So A's relation to both $B + 1$ and $B + 2$ is just as good as survival. But what of A's relation to $B + 30$?

I said earlier that what matters in survival could be provisionally referred to as "psychological continuity." I must now distinguish this relation from another, which I shall call "psychological connectedness."

Let us say that the relation between a q-memory and the experience q-remembered is a "direct" relation. Another "direct" relation is that which holds between a q-intention and the q-intended action. A third is that which holds between different expressions of some lasting q-characteristic.

"Psychological connectedness," as I define it, requires the holding of these direct psychological relations. "Connectedness" is not transitive, since these relations are not transitive. Thus, if X q-remembers most of Y's life, and Y q-remembers most of Z's life, it does not follow that X q-remembers most of Z's life. And if X car-

ries out the q-intentions of Y, and Y carries out the q-intentions of Z, it does not follow that X carries out the q-intentions of Z.

"Psychological continuity," in contrast, only requires overlapping chains of direct psychological relations. So "continuity" *is* transitive.

To return to our diagram. A *is* psychologically continuous with $B + 30$. There are between the two continuous chains of overlapping relations. Thus, A has q-intentional control over $B + 2$, $B + 2$ has q-intentional control over $B + 6$, and so on up to $B + 30$. Or $B + 30$ can q-remember the life of $B + 14$, $B + 14$ can q-remember the life of $B + 6$, and so on back to A.[11]

A, however, need *not* be psychologically connected to $B + 30$. Connectedness requires direct relations. And if these beings are like us, A cannot stand in such relations to every individual in his indefinitely long "tree." Q-memories will weaken with the passage of time, and then fade away. Q-ambitions, once fulfilled, will be replaced by others. Q-characteristics will gradually change. In general, A stands in fewer and fewer direct psychological relations to an individual in his "tree" the more remote that individual is. And if the individual is (like $B + 30$) sufficiently remote, there may be between the two *no* direct psychological relations.

Now that we have distinguished the general relations of psychological continuity and psychological connectedness, I suggest that connectedness is a more important element in survival. As a claim about our own survival, this would need more arguments than I have space to give. But it seems clearly true for my imagined beings. A is as close psychologically to $B + 1$ as I today am to myself tomorrow. A is as distant from $B + 30$ as I am from my great-great-grandson.

Even if connectedness is not more important than continuity, the fact that one of these is a relation of degree is enough to show that what matters in survival can have degrees. And in any case the two relations are quite different. So our imagined beings would need a way of thinking in which this difference is recognized.

---

11. The chain of continuity must run in one direction of time. $B + 2$ is not, in the sense I intend, psychologically continuous with $B + 1$.

V

What I propose is this.

First, *A* can think of any individual, anywhere in his "tree," as "a descendant self." This phrase implies psychological continuity. Similarly, any later individual can think of any earlier individual on the single path which connects him to *A* as "an ancestral self."

Since psychological continuity is transitive, "being an ancestral self of" and "being a descendant self of" are also transitive.

To imply psychological connectedness I suggest the phrases "one of my future selves" and "one of my past selves."

These are the phrases with which we can describe Wiggins' case. For having past and future selves is, what we needed, a way of continuing to exist which does not imply identity through time. The original person does, in this sense, survive Wiggins' operation: the two resulting people are his later selves. And they can each refer to him as "my past self." (They can share a past self without being the same self as each other.)

Since psychological connectedness is not transitive, and is a matter of degree, the relations "being a past self of" and "being a future self of" should themselves be treated as relations of degree. We allow for this series of descriptions: "my most recent self," "one of my earlier selves," "one of my distant selves," "hardly one of *my* past selves (I can only *q*-remember a few of his experiences)," and, finally, "not in any way one of *my* past selves—just an ancestral self."

This way of thinking would clearly suit our first imagined beings. But let us now turn to a second kind of being. These reproduce by fusion as well as by division. And let us suppose that they fuse every autumn and divide every spring. This yields the following diagram:

If *A* is the individual whose life is represented by the three-lined "branch," the two-lined "tree" represents those lives which are psychologically continuous with *A*'s life. (It can be seen that each individual has his own "tree," which overlaps with many others.)

For the imagined beings in this second world, the phrases "an ancestral self" and "a descendant self" would cover too much to be of much use. (There may well be pairs of dates such that every individual who ever lived before the first date was an ancestral self of every individual who ever will live after the second date.) Conversely, since the lives of each individual last for only half a year, the word "I" would cover too little to do all of the work which it does for us. So part of this work would have to be done, for these second beings, by talk about past and future selves.

We can now point out a theoretical flaw in our proposed way of thinking. The phrase "a past self of" implies psychological connectedness. Being a past self of is treated as a relation of degree, so that this phrase can be used to imply the varying degrees of psychological connectedness. But this phrase can imply only the degrees of connectedness between different lives. It cannot be used within a single life. And our way of delimiting successive lives does not refer to the degrees of psychological connectedness. Hence there is no guarantee that this phrase, "a past self of," could be used whenever it was needed. There is no guarantee that psychological connectedness will not vary in degree within a single life.

This flaw would not concern our imagined beings. For they divide and unite so frequently, and their lives are in consequence so short, that within a single life psychological connectedness would always stand at a maximum.

But let us look, finally, at a third kind of being.

In this world there is neither division nor union. There are a number of everlasting bodies, which gradually change in appearance. And direct psychological relations, as before, hold only over limited periods of time. This can be illustrated with a third diagram (given on the next page). In this diagram the two shadings represent the degrees of psychological connectedness to their two central points.

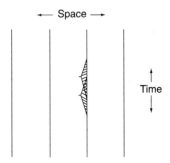

← Space →

Time

These beings could not use the way of thinking that we have proposed. Since there is no branching of psychological continuity, they would have to regard themselves as immortal. It might be said that this is what they are. But there is, I suggest, a better description.

Our beings would have one reason for thinking of themselves as immortal. The parts of each "line" are all psychologically continuous. But the parts of each "line" are not all psychologically connected. Direct psychological relations hold only between those parts which are close to each other in time. This gives our beings a reason for *not* thinking of each "line" as corresponding to one single life. For if they did, they would have no way of implying these direct relations. When a speaker says, for example, "I spent a period doing such and such," his hearers would not be entitled to assume that the speaker has any memories of this period, that his character then and now are in any way similar, that he is now carrying out any of the plans or intentions which he then had, and so forth. Because the word "I" would carry none of these implications, it would not have for these "immortal" beings the usefulness which it has for us.

To gain a better way of thinking, we must revise the way of thinking that we proposed above. The revision is this. The distinction between successive selves can be made by reference, not to the branching of psychological continuity, but to the degrees of psychological connectedness. Since this connectedness is a matter of degree, the drawing of these distinctions can be left to the choice of the speaker and be allowed to vary from context to context.

On this way of thinking, the word "I" can be used to imply the greatest degree of psychological connectedness. When the connections are reduced, when there has been any marked change of character or style of life, or

any marked loss of memory, our imagined beings would say, "It was not I who did that, but an earlier self." They could then describe in what ways, and to what degree, they are related to this earlier self.

This revised way of thinking would suit not only our "immortal" beings. It is also the way in which we ourselves could think about our lives. And it is, I suggest, surprisingly natural.

One of its features, the distinction between successive selves, has already been used by several writers. To give an example, from Proust: "we are incapable, while we are in love, of acting as fit predecessors of the next persons who, when we are in love no longer, we shall presently have become. . . ."[12]

Although Proust distinguished between successive selves, he still thought of one person as being these different selves. This we would not do on the way of thinking that I propose. If I say, "It will not be me, but one of my future selves," I do not imply that I will be that future self. He is one of my later selves, and I am one of his earlier selves. There is no underlying person who we both are.

To point out another feature of this way of thinking. When I say, "There is no person who we both are," I am only giving my decision. Another person could say, "It will be you," thus deciding differently. There is no question of either of these decisions being a mistake. Whether to say "I," or "one of my future selves," or "a descendant self" is entirely a matter of choice. The matter of fact, which must be agreed, is only whether the disjunction applies. (The question "Are X and Y the same person?" thus becomes "Is X at least an ancestral [or descendant] self of Y?")

VI

I have tried to show that what matters in the continued existence of a person are, for the most part, relations of degree. And I have proposed a way of thinking in which this would be recognized.

I shall end by suggesting two consequences and asking one question.

---

12. *Within a Budding Grove* (London, 1949), I, 226, (my own translation).

It is sometimes thought to be especially rational to act in our own best interests. But I suggest that the principle of self-interest has no force. There are only two genuine competitors in this particular field. One is the principle of biased rationality: do what will best achieve what you actually want. The other is the principle of impartiality: do what is in the best interests of everyone concerned.

The apparent force of the principle of self-interest derives, I think, from these two other principles.

The principle of self-interest is normally supported by the principle of biased rationality. This is because most people care about their own future interests.

Suppose that this prop is lacking. Suppose that a man does not care what happens to him in, say, the more distant future. To such a man, the principle of self-interest can only be propped up by an appeal to the principle of impartiality. We must say, "Even if you don't care, you ought to take what happens to you then equally into account." But for this, as a special claim, there seem to me no good arguments. It can only be supported as part of the general claim, "You ought to take what happens to everyone equally into account."

The special claim tells a man to grant an *equal* weight to all the parts of his future. The argument for this can only be that all the parts of his future are *equally* parts of *his* future. This is true. But it is a truth too superficial to bear the weight of the argument. (To give an analogy: The unity of a nation is, in its nature, a matter of degree. It is therefore only a superficial truth that all of a man's compatriots are *equally* his compatriots. This truth cannot support a good argument for nationalism.)

I have suggested that the principle of self-interest has no strength of its own. If this is so, there is no special problem in the fact that what we ought to do can be against our interests. There is only the general problem that it may not be what we want to do.

The second consequence which I shall mention is implied in the first. Egoism, the fear not of near but of distant death, the regret that so much of one's *only* life should have gone by—these are not, I think, wholly natural or instinctive. They are all strengthened by the beliefs about personal identity which I have been attacking. If we give up these beliefs, they should be weakened.

My final question is this. These emotions are bad, and if we weaken them we gain. But can we achieve this gain without, say, also weakening loyalty to, or love of, other particular selves? As Hume warned, the "refined reflections which philosophy suggests . . . cannot diminish . . . our vicious passions . . . without diminishing . . . such as are virtuous. They are . . . applicable to all our affections. In vain do we hope to direct their influence only to one side."[13]

That hope *is* vain. But Hume had another: that more of what is bad depends upon false belief. This is also my hope.

---

13. "The Sceptic," in "Essays Moral, Political and Literary," *Hume's Moral and Political Philosophy* (New York, 1959), p. 349.

Freedom of the Will

Peter van Inwagen

The Incompatibility of Free Will and Determinism

In this paper I shall define a thesis I shall call 'determinism', and argue that it is incompatible with the thesis that we are able to act otherwise than we do (i.e., is incompatible with 'free will'). Other theses, some of them very different from what *I* shall call 'determinism', have at least an equal right to this name, and, therefore, I do not claim to show that *every* thesis that could be called 'determinism' without historical impropriety is incompatible with free will. I shall, however, assume without argument that what I call 'determinism' is legitimately so called.

In Part I, I shall explain what I mean by 'determinism'. In Part II, I shall make some remarks about 'can'. In Part III, I shall argue that free will and determinism are incompatible. In Part IV, I shall examine some possible objections to the argument of Part III. I shall not attempt to establish the truth or falsity of determinism, or the existence or nonexistence of free will.

I

In defining 'determinism', I shall take for granted the notion of a proposition (that is, of a non-linguistic bearer of truth-value), together with certain allied notions such as denial, conjunction, and entailment. Nothing in this paper will depend on the special features of any particular account of propositions. The reader may think of them as functions from possible worlds to truth-values or in any other way he likes, provided they have their usual features. (E.g., they are either true or

false; the conjunction of a true and a false proposition is a false proposition; they obey the law of contraposition with respect to entailment.)

Our definition of 'determinism' will also involve the notion of 'the state of the entire physical world' (hereinafter, 'the state of the world') at an instant. I shall leave this notion largely unexplained, since the argument of this paper is very nearly independent of its content. Provided the following two conditions are met, the reader may flesh out 'the state of the world' in any way he likes:

(i) Our concept of 'state' must be such that, given that the world is in a certain state at a certain time, nothing follows *logically* about its states at other times. For example, we must not choose a concept of 'state' that would allow as part of a description of the momentary state of the world, the clause, '. . . and, at t, the world is such that Jones's left hand will be raised 10 seconds later than t.'

(ii) If there is some observable change in the way things are (e.g., if a white cloth becomes blue, a warm liquid cold, or if a man raises his hand), this change must entail some change in the state of the world. That is, our concept of 'state' must not be so theoretical, so divorced from what is observably true, that it be possible for the world to be in the *same* state at t_1 and t_2 although (for example) Jones's hand is raised at t_1 and not at t_2.

We may now define 'determinism'. We shall apply this term to the conjunction of these two theses:

(a) For every instant of time, there is a proposition that expresses the state of the world at that instant.

(b) If A and B are any propositions that express the state of the world at some instants, then the conjunction of A with the laws of physics entails B.

By a proposition that expresses the state of the world at time *t,* I mean a true proposition that asserts of some state that, at *t,* the world is in that state. The reason for our first restriction on the content of 'state' should now be evident: if it were not for this restriction, 'the state of the world' could be defined in such a way that determinism was trivially true. We could, without this restriction, build sufficient information about the past and future into each proposition that expresses the state of the world at an instant, that, for every pair of such propositions, each *by itself* entails the other. And in that case, determinism would be a mere tautology, a thesis equally applicable to every conceivable state of affairs.

This amounts to saying that the 'laws of physics' clause on our definition does some work: whether determinism is true depends in the character of the laws of physics. For example, if all physical laws were vague propositions like 'In every nuclear reaction, momentum is *pretty nearly* conserved', or 'Force is *approximately* equal to mass times acceleration', then determinism would be false.

This raises the question, What is a law of physics? First, a terminological point. I do not mean the application of this term to be restricted to those laws that belong to physics in the narrowest sense of the word. I am using 'law of physics' in the way some philosophers use 'law of nature'. Thus, a law about chemical valences is a law of physics in my sense, even if chemistry is not ultimately 'reducible' to physics. I will not use the term 'law of nature', because, conceivably, *psychological* laws, including laws (if such there be) about the voluntary behavior of rational agents, might be included under this term.[1] Rational agents are, after all, in some sense part of 'nature'. Since I do not think that everything I shall say about laws of physics is true of such 'voluntaristic laws', I should not want to use, instead of 'laws of physics', some term like 'laws of nature' that might legitimately be applied to voluntaristic laws. Thus, for all that is said in this paper, it may be that some version of determinism based on voluntaristic laws is compatible with free will. Let us, then, understand by 'law of physics' a law

of nature that is not about the voluntary behavior of rational agents.

But this does not tell us what 'laws of nature' are. There would probably be fairly general agreement that a proposition cannot be a law of nature unless it is true and contingent, and that no proposition is a law of nature if it entails the existence of some concrete individual, such as Caesar or the earth. But the proposition that there is no solid gold sphere 20 feet in diameter (probably) satisfies these conditions, though it is certainly not a law of nature.

It is also claimed sometimes that a law of nature must 'support its counterfactuals'. There is no doubt something to this. Consider, however, the proposition, 'Dogs die if exposed to virus V'. The claim that this proposition supports its counterfactuals is, I think, equivalent to the claim that 'Every dog is such that if it were exposed to virus V, it would die' is *true.* Let us suppose that this latter proposition *is* true, the quantification being understood as being over all dogs, past, present, and future. Its truth, it seems to me, is quite consistent with its being the case that dog-breeders *could* (but will not) institute a program of selective breeding that *would* produce a sort of dog that is immune to virus V. But if dog-breeders *could* do this, then clearly 'Dogs die if exposed to virus V' is not a law of nature, since in that case the truth of the corresponding universally quantified counterfactual depends upon an accidental circumstance: if dog-breeders were to institute a certain program of selective breeding they are quite capable of instituting, then 'Every dog is such that if it were exposed to virus V, it would die' would be false. Thus a proposition may 'support its counterfactuals' and yet not be a law of nature.

I do not think that any philosopher has succeeded in giving a (nontrivial) set of individually necessary and jointly sufficient conditions for a proposition's being a law of nature or of physics. *I* certainly do not know of any such set. Fortunately, for the purposes of this paper we need not know how to analyze the concept 'law of physics'. I shall, in Part III, argue that certain statements containing 'law of physics' are analytic. But this can be done in the absence of a satisfactory analysis of 'law of physics'. In fact, it would hardly be possible for one to *provide* an analysis of some concept if one had no pre-analytic convictions about what statements involving that concept are analytic.

---

1. For example, 'If a human being is not made to feel ashamed of lying before his twelfth birthday, then he will lie whenever he believes it to be to his advantage.'

For example, we do not have to have a satisfactory analysis of memory to know that 'No one can remember future events' is analytic. And if someone devised an analysis of memory according to which it was possible to remember future events, then, however attractive the analysis was in other respects, it would have to be rejected. The analyticity of 'No one can remember future events' is one of the *data* that anyone who investigates the concept of memory must take account of. Similarly, the claims I shall make on behalf of the concept of physical law seem to me to be basic and evident enough to be data that an analysis of this concept must take account of: any analysis on which these claims did not 'come out true' would be for that very reason defective.

II

It seems to be generally agreed that the concept of free will should be understood in terms of the *power* or *ability* of agents to act otherwise than they in fact do. To deny that men have free will is to assert that what a man *does* do and what he *can* do coincide. And almost all philosophers agree that a necessary condition for holding an agent responsible for an act is believing that that agent *could have* refrained from performing that act.[2]

There is, however, considerably less agreement as to how 'can' (in the relevant sense) should be analyzed. This is one of the most difficult questions in philosophy. It is certainly a question to which I do not know any non-trivial answer. But, as I said I should do in the case of 'law of physics', I shall make certain conceptual claims about 'can' (in the 'power' or 'ability' sense) in the absence of any analysis. Any suggested analysis of 'can' that does not support these claims will either be neutral with respect to them, in which case it will be incomplete, since it will not settle *all* conceptual questions about 'can', or it will be inconsistent with them, in which case the arguments I shall present in support of these claims will, in effect, be arguments that the analy-

sis fails. In Part IV, I shall expand on this point as it applies to one particular analysis of 'can', the well-known 'conditional' analysis.

I shall say no more than this about the meaning of 'can'. I shall, however, introduce an idiom that will be useful in talking about ability and inability in complicated cases. Without this idiom, the statement of our argument would be rather unwieldy. We shall sometimes make claims about an agent's abilities by using sentences of the form:

S can render [could have rendered] . . . false.

where '. . .' may be replaced by names of propositions. Our ordinary claims about ability can easily be translated into this idiom. For example, we translate:

He could have reached Chicago by midnight.

as

He could have rendered the proposition that he did not reach Chicago by midnight false.

and, of course, the translation from the special idiom to the ordinary idiom is easy enough in such simple cases. If we were interested only in everyday ascriptions of ability, the new idiom would be useless. Using it, however, we may make ascriptions of ability that it would be very difficult to make in the ordinary idiom. Consider, for example, the last true proposition asserted by Plato. (Let us assume that this description is, as logicians say, 'proper'.) One claim that we might make about Aristotle is that he could have rendered this proposition false. Now, presumably, we have no way of discovering *what* proposition the last true proposition asserted by Plato was. Still, the claim about Aristotle would seem to be either true or false. To discover its truth-value, we should have to discover under what conditions the last true proposition asserted by Plato (i.e., that proposition having as one of its accidental properties, the property of being the last true proposition asserted by Plato) would be false, and then discover whether it was within Aristotle's power to produce these conditions. For example, suppose that if Aristotle had lived in Athens from the time of Plato's death till the time of his own death,

---

2. Actually, the matter is rather more complicated than this, since we may hold a man responsible for an act we believe he could not have refrained from, provided we are prepared to hold him responsible for his being unable to refrain.

then the last true proposition asserted by Plato (whatever it was) would be false. Then, if Aristotle could have lived (i.e., if he had it within his power to live) in Athens throughout this period, he could have rendered the last true proposition asserted by Plato false. On the other hand, if the last true proposition asserted by Plato is the proposition that the planets do not move in perfect circles, then Aristotle could not have rendered the last true proposition asserted by Plato false, since it was not within his power to produce any set of conditions sufficient for the falsity of this proposition.

It is obvious that the proposition expressed by 'Aristotle could have rendered the last true proposition asserted by Plato false', is a proposition that we should be hard put to express without using the idiom of rendering propositions false, or, at least, without using some very similar idiom. We shall find this new idiom very useful in discussing the relation between free will (a thesis about abilities) and determinism (a thesis about certain propositions).

III

I shall now imagine a case in which a certain man, after due deliberation, refrained from performing a certain contemplated act. I shall then argue that, if determinism is true, then that man *could not have* performed that act. Because this argument will not depend on any features peculiar to our imagined case, the incompatibility of free will and determinism *in general* will be established, since, as will be evident, a parallel argument could easily be constructed for the case of any agent and any unperformed act.

Here is the case. Let us suppose there was once a judge who had only to raise his right hand at a certain time, T, to prevent the execution of a sentence of death upon a certain criminal, such a hand-raising being the sign, according to the conventions of the judge's country, of a granting of special clemency. Let us further suppose that the judge—call him 'J'—refrained from raising his hand at that time, and that this inaction resulted in the criminal's being put to death. We may also suppose that the judge was unbound, uninjured, and free from paralysis; that he decided not to raise his hand at T only after a period of calm, rational, and relevant

deliberation; that he had not been subjected to any 'pressure' to decide one way or the other about the criminal's death; that he was not under the influence of drugs, hypnosis, or anything of that sort; and finally, that there was no element in his deliberations that would have been of any special interest to a student of abnormal psychology.

Now the argument. In this argument, which I shall refer to as the 'main argument', I shall use 'T_0' to denote some instant of time earlier than J's birth, 'P_0' to denote the proposition that expresses the state of the world at T_0, 'P' to denote the proposition that expresses the state of the world at T, and 'L' to denote the conjunction into a single proposition of all laws of physics. (I shall regard L itself as a law of physics, on the reasonable assumption that if A and B are laws of physics, then the conjunction of A and B is a law of physics.) The argument consists of seven statements, the seventh of which follows from the first six:

(1) If determinism is true, then the conjunction of P_0 and L entails P.

(2) If J had raised his hand at T, then P would be false.

(3) If (2) is true, then if J could have raised his hand at T, J could have rendered P false.

(4) If J could have rendered P false, and if the conjunction of P_0 and L entails P, then J could have rendered the conjunction of P_0 and L false.

(5) If J could have rendered the conjunction of P_0 and L false, then J could have rendered L false.

(6) J could not have rendered L false.

∴ (7) If determinism is true, J could not have raised his hand at T.

That (7) follows from (1) through (6) can easily be established by truth-functional logic. Note that all conditionals in the argument except for (2) are truth-functional. For purposes of establishing the *validity* of this argument, (2) may be regarded as a simple sentence. Let us examine the premises individually.

(1) This premise follows from the definition of determinism.

(2) If *J* had raised his hand at *T*, then the world would have been in a different state at *T* from the state it was in fact in. (See our second condition on the content of 'the state of the world'.) And, therefore, if *J* had raised his hand at *T*, some contrary of *P* would express the state of the world at *T*. It should be emphasized that '*P*' does not *mean* 'the proposition that expresses the state of the world at *T*'. Rather, '*P*' *denotes* the proposition that expresses the state of the world at *T*. In Kripke's terminology, '*P*' is being used as a *rigid designator*, while 'the proposition that expresses the state of the world at *T*' is perforce non-rigid.[3]

(3) Since *J*'s hand being raised at *T* would have been sufficient for the falsity of *P*, there is, if *J* could have raised his hand, at least one condition sufficient for the falsity of *P* that *J* could have produced.

(4) This premise may be defended as an instance of the following general principle:

> If *S* can render *R* false, and if *Q* entails *R*, then *S* can render *Q* false.

This principle seems to be analytic. For if *Q* entails *R*, then the denial of *R* entails the denial of *Q*. Thus, any condition sufficient for the falsity of *R* is also sufficient for the falsity of *Q*. Therefore, if there is some condition that *S* can produce that is sufficient for the falsity of *R*, there is some condition (that same condition) that *S* can produce that is sufficient for the falsity of *Q*.

(5) This premise may be defended as an instance of the following general principle, which I take to be analytic:

> If *Q* is a true proposition that concerns only states of affairs that obtained before *S*'s birth, and if *S* can render the conjunction of *Q* and *R* false, then *S* can render *R* false.

Consider, for example, the propositions expressed by

> The Spanish Armada was defeated in 1588.

And

> Peter van Inwagen never visits Alaska.

The conjunction of these two propositions is quite possibly true. At any rate, let us assume it is true. Given that it is true, it seems quite clear that I can render it false if and only if I can visit Alaska. If, for some reason, it is not within my power ever to visit Alaska, then I *cannot* render it false. This is a quite trivial assertion, and the general principle (above) of which it is an instance is hardly less trivial. And it seems incontestable that premise (5) is also an instance of this principle.

(6) I shall argue that if anyone *can* (i.e., has it within his power to) render some proposition false, then that proposition is not a law of physics. This I regard as a conceptual truth, one of the data that must be taken account of by anyone who wishes to give an analysis of 'can' or 'law'. It is this connection between these two concepts, I think, that is at the root of the incompatibility of free will and determinism.

In order to see this connection, let us suppose that both of the following are true:

(A) Nothing ever travels faster than light.

(B) Jones, a physicist, can construct a particle accelerator that would cause protons to travel at twice the speed of light.

It follows from (A) that Jones will never exercise the power that (B) ascribes to him. But whatever the reason for Jones's failure to act on his ability to render (A) false, it is clear that (A) and (B) are consistent, and that (B) entails that (A) is not a law of physics. For given that (B) is true, then Jones is able to conduct an experiment that would falsify (A); and surely it is a feature of any proposition that is a physical law that no one *can* conduct an experiment that would show it to be false.

Of course, most propositions that look initially as if they might be physical laws, but which are later decided to be nonlaws, are rejected because of experiments that are actually performed. But this is not essential. In order to see this, let us elaborate the example we have been considering. Let us suppose that Jones's ability to render (A) false derives from the fact that he has discovered a mathematically rigorous proof that under

---

3. See Saul Kripke, 'Identity and Necessity', in *Identity and Individuation* (ed. by Milton K. Munitz), New York (1971). [See also Kripke, pp. 35–42, this volume.]

certain conditions *C,* realizable in the laboratory, protons would travel faster than light. And let us suppose that this proof proceeds from premises so obviously true that all competent physicists accept his conclusion without reservation. But suppose that conditions *C* never obtain in nature, and that actually to produce them in the laboratory would require such an expenditure of resources that Jones and his colleagues decide not to carry out the experiment. And suppose that, as a result, conditions *C* are never realized and nothing ever travels faster than light. It is evident that if all this were true, we should have to say that (A), while *true,* is not a law of physics. (Though, of course, 'Nothing ever travels faster than light except under conditions *C*' might be a law.)

The laboratories and resources that figure in this example are not essential to its point. If Jones *could* render some proposition false by performing *any* act he does not in fact perform, even such a simple act as raising his hand at a certain time, this would be sufficient to show that that proposition is not law of physics.

This completes my defense of the premises of the main argument. In the final part of this paper, I shall examine objections to this argument suggested by the attempts of various philosophers to establish the compatibility of free will and determinism.

IV

The most useful thing a philosopher who thinks that the main argument does not prove its point could do would be to try to show that some premise of the argument is false or incoherent, or that the argument begs some important question, or contains a term that is used equivocally, or something of that sort. In short, he should get down to cases. Some philosophers, however, might continue to hold that free will and determinism, in the sense of Part I, are compatible, but decline to try to point out a mistake in the argument. For (such a philosopher might argue) we have, in everyday life, *criteria* for determining whether an agent could have acted otherwise than he did, and these criteria determine the *meaning* of 'could have acted otherwise'; to know the meaning of this phrase is simply to know how to apply these criteria. And since these criteria make no mention

of determinism, anyone who thinks that free will and determinism are incompatible is simply confused.

As regards the argument of Part III (this philosopher might continue), this argument is very complex, and this complexity must simply serve to hide some error, since its conclusion is absurd. We must treat this argument like the infamous 'proof' that zero equals one: It may be amusing and even instructive to find the hidden error (if one has nothing better to do), but it would be a waste of time to take seriously any suggestion that it is sound.

Now I suppose we do have 'criteria', in some sense of this overused word, for the application of 'could have done otherwise', and I will grant that knowing the criteria for the application of a term can plausibly be identified with knowing its meaning. Whether the criteria for applying 'could have done otherwise' can (as at least one philosopher has supposed) be taught by simple ostension is another question. However this may be, the 'criteria' argument is simply invalid. To see this, let us examine a simpler argument that makes the same mistake.

Consider the doctrine of 'predestinarianism'. Predestinarians hold (i) that if an act is foreseen it is not free, and (ii) that all acts are foreseen by God. (I do not claim that anyone has ever held this doctrine in precisely this form.) Now suppose we were to argue that predestinarianism must be compatible with free will, since our criteria for applying 'could have done otherwise' make no reference to predestinarianism. Obviously this argument would be invalid, since predestinarianism is incompatible with free will. And the only difference I can see between this argument and the 'criteria' argument for the compatibility of free will and determinism is that predestinarianism, unlike determinism, is *obviously* incompatible with free will. But, of course, theses may be incompatible with one another even if this incompatibility is not obvious. Even if determinism cannot, like predestinarianism, be seen to be incompatible with free will on the basis of a simple formal inference, there is, nonetheless, a conceptual connection between the two theses (as we showed in our defense of premise (6)). The argument of Part III is intended to draw out the implications of this connection. There may well be a mistake in the argument, but I do not see why anyone should think that the very idea of such an argument is misconceived.

It has also been argued that free will *entails* determinism, and, being itself a consistent thesis, is *a fortiori* compatible with determinism. The argument, put briefly, is this. To say of some person on some particular occasion that he acted freely is obviously to say at least that *he* acted on that occasion. Suppose, however, that we see someone's arm rise and it later turns out that there was *no cause whatsoever* for his arm's rising. Surely we should have to say that *he* did not really raise his arm at all. Rather, his arm's rising was a mere chance happening, that, like a muscular twitch, had nothing to do with *him*, beyond the fact that it happened to involve a part of his body. A necessary condition for this person's really having raised his hand is that *he* caused his hand to rise. And surely '*he* caused' means '*his* character, desires, and beliefs caused'.

I think that there is a great deal of confusion in this argument, but to expose this confusion would require a lengthy discussion of many fine points in the theory of agency. I shall only point out that if this argument is supposed to refute the conclusion of Part III, it is an *ignoratio elenchi*. For I did not conclude that free will is incompatible with the thesis that every event has a cause, but rather with determinism as defined in Part 1. And the denial of this thesis does not entail that there are uncaused events.

Of course, one might try to construct a similar but relevant argument for the falsity of the conclusion of Part III. But, so far as I can see, the plausibility of such an argument would depend on the plausibility of supposing that if the present movements of one's body are not completely determined by physical law and the state of the world before one's birth, then these present movements are not one's own doing, but, rather, mere random happenings. And I do not see the least shred of plausibility in this supposition.

I shall finally consider the popular 'conditional analysis' argument for the compatibility of free will and determinism. According to the advocates of this argument —let us call them 'conditionalists'—what statements of the form:

(8)　*S* could have done *X*

mean is:

(9)　If *S* had chosen to do *X, S* would have done *X*.

For example, 'Smith could have saved the drowning child' means, 'If Smith had chosen to save the drowning child, Smith would have saved the drowning child.' Thus, even if determinism is true (the conditionalists argue), it is possible that Smith did not save but *could have* saved the drowning child, since the conjunction of determinism with 'Smith did not save the child' does not entail the falsity of 'If Smith had chosen to save the child, Smith would have saved the child'.

Most of the controversy about this argument centers around the question whether (9) is a correct analysis of (8). I shall not enter into the debate about whether this analysis is correct. I shall instead question the relevance of this debate to the argument of Part III. For it is not clear that the main argument would be unsound if the conditional analysis *were* correct. Clearly the argument is *valid* whether or not (8) and (9) mean the same. But suppose the premises of the main argument were rewritten so that every clause they contain that is of form (8) is replaced by the corresponding clause of form (9)— should we then see that any of these premises is false? Let us try this with premise (6), which seems, *prima facie*, to be the crucial premise of the argument, We have:

(6a)　It is not the case that if *J* had chosen to render *L* false, *J* would have rendered *L* false.

Now (6a) certainly seems true: If someone chooses to render false some proposition *R*, and if *R* is a law of physics, then surely he will fail. This little argument for (6a) *seems* obviously sound. But we cannot overlook the possibility that someone might discover a mistake in it and, perhaps, even construct a convincing argument that (6a) is false. Let us, therefore, assume for the sake of argument that (6a) is demonstrably false. What would this show? I submit that it would show that (6a) does not mean the same as (6), since (6) is, as I have argued, *true*.

The same dilemma confronts the conditionalist if he attempts to show, on the basis of the conditional analysis, that any of the other premises of the argument is false. Consider the argument got by replacing every clause of form (8) in the main argument with the corresponding clause of form (9). If all the premises of this new argument are true, the main argument is, according to the conditionalist's own theory, sound. If, on the other hand, any of the premises of the new argument is false, then (*I* would maintain) this premise is a counterexample to the conditional analysis. I should not be begging the question against the conditionalist in maintaining this, since I have given arguments for the truth of each of the premises of the main argument, and no-

where in these arguments do I assume that the conditional analysis is wrong.

Of course, any or all of my arguments in defense of the premises of the main argument may contain some mistake. But unless the conditionalist could point to some such mistake, he would not accomplish much by showing that some statement he *claimed* was equivalent to one of its premises was false.

Roderick Chisholm

Human Freedom and the Self

"A staff moves a stone, and is moved by a hand, which is moved by a man." Aristotle, *Physics,* 256a.

1. The metaphysical problem of human freedom might be summarized in the following way: Human beings are responsible agents; but this fact appears to conflict with a deterministic view of human action (the view that every event that is involved in an act is caused by some other event); and it *also* appears to conflict with an indeterministic view of human action (the view that the act, or some event that is essential to the act, is not caused at all). To solve the problem, I believe, we must make somewhat far-reaching assumptions about the self or the agent—about the man who performs the act.

Perhaps it is needless to remark that, in all likelihood, it is impossible to say anything significant about this ancient problem that has not been said before.

2. Let us consider some deed, or misdeed, that may be attributed to a responsible agent: one man, say, shot

another. If the man *was* responsible for what he did, then, I would urge, what was to happen at the time of the shooting was something that was entirely up to the man himself. There was a moment at which it was true, both that he could have fired the shot and also that he could have refrained from firing it. And if this is so, then, even though he did fire it, he could have done something else instead. (He didn't find himself firing the shot "against his will," as we say.) I think we can say, more generally, then, that if a man is responsible for a certain event or a certain state of affairs (in our example, the shooting of another man), then that event or state of affairs was brought about by some act of his, and the act was something that was in his power either to perform or not to perform.

But now if the act which he *did* perform was an act that was also in his power *not* to perform, then it could not have been caused or determined by any event that was not itself within his power either to bring about or not to bring about. For example, if what we say he did was really something that was brought about by a second man, one who forced his hand upon the trigger, say, or who, by means of hypnosis, compelled him to perform the act, then since the act was caused by the *second* man it was nothing that was within the power of the *first* man to prevent. And precisely the same thing is

Roderick Chisholm, "Human Freedom and the Self" from *The Lindley Lecture* (Lawrence: University of Kansas Department of Philosophy, 1964). Copyright © 1964. Reprinted with the permission of the University of Kansas Department of Philosophy.

true, I think, if instead of referring to a second man who compelled the first one, we speak instead of the *desires* and *beliefs* which the first man happens to have had. For if what we say he did was really something that was brought about by his own beliefs and desires, if these beliefs and desires in the particular situation in which he happened to have found himself caused him to do just what it was that we say he did do, then, since *they* caused it, *he* was unable to do anything other than just what it was that he did do. It makes no difference whether the cause of the deed was internal or external; if the cause was some state or event for which the man himself was not responsible, then he was not responsible for what we have been mistakenly calling his act. If a flood caused the poorly constructed dam to break, then, given the flood and the constitution of the dam, the break, we may say, *had* to occur and nothing could have happened in its place. And if the flood of desire caused the weak-willed man to give in, then he, too, had to do just what it was that he did do and he was no more responsible than was the dam for the results that followed. (It is true, of course, that if the man is responsible for the beliefs and desires that he happens to have, then he may also be responsible for the things they lead him to do. But the question now becomes: *is* he responsible for the beliefs and desires he happens to have? If he is, then there was a time when they were within his power either to acquire or not to acquire, and we are left, therefore, with our general point.)

One may object: But surely if there were such a thing as a man who is really *good,* then he would be responsible for things that he would do; yet, he would be unable to do anything other than just what it is that he does do, since, being good, he will always choose to do what is best. The answer, I think, is suggested by a comment that Thomas Reid makes upon an ancient author. The author had said of Cato, "He was good because he could not be otherwise," and Reid observes: "This saying, if understood literally and strictly, is not the praise of Cato, but of his constitution, which was no more the work of Cato than his existence."[1] If Cato was himself responsible for the good things that he did, then Cato,

as Reid suggests, was such that, although he had the power to do what was not good, he exercised his power only for that which was good.

All of this, if it is true, may give a certain amount of comfort to those who are tender-minded. But we should remind them that it also conflicts with a familiar view about the nature of God—with the view that St. Thomas Aquinas expresses by saying that "every movement both of the will and of nature proceeds from God as the Prime Mover."[2] If the act of the sinner *did* proceed from God as the Prime Mover, then God was in the position of the second agent we just discussed—the man who forced the trigger finger, or the hypnotist—and the sinner, so-called, was *not* responsible for what he did. (This may be a bold assertion, in view of the history of western theology, but I must say that I have never encountered a single good reason for denying it.)

There is one standard objection to all of this and we should consider it briefly.

3. The objection takes the form of a stratagem—one designed to show that determinism (and divine providence) is consistent with human responsibility. The stratagem is one that was used by Jonathan Edwards and by many philosophers in the present century, most notably, G. E. Moore.[3]

> One proceeds as follows: The expression
>
> (a) He could have done otherwise, it is argued, means no more nor less than
>
> (b) If he had chosen to do otherwise, then he would have done otherwise.

(In place of "chosen," one might say "tried," "set out," "decided," "undertaken," or "willed.") The truth of statement (b), it is then pointed out, is consistent with determinism (and with divine providence); for even if all of the man's actions were causally determined, the man could still be such that, *if* he had chosen otherwise,

---

1. Thomas Reid, *Essays on the Active Powers of Man,* Essay IV, Chapter 4 (*Works,* p. 600).

2. *Summa Theologica,* First Part of the Second Part, Question VI ("On the Voluntary and Involuntary").

3. Jonathan Edwards, *Freedom of the Will* (New Haven 1957): G. E. Moore, *Ethics* (Home University Library 1912), Chapter Six.

then he would have done otherwise. What the murderer saw, let us suppose, along with his beliefs and desires, *caused* him to fire the shot; yet he was such that *if,* just then, he had chosen or decided *not* to fire the shot, then he would not have fired it. All of this is certainly possible. Similarly, we could say, of the dam, that the flood caused it to break and also that the dam was such that, *if* there had been no flood or any similar pressure, then the dam would have remained intact. And therefore, the argument proceeds, if (b) is consistent with determinism, and if (a) and (b) say the same thing, then (a) is also consistent with determinism; hence we can say that the agent *could* have done otherwise even though he was caused to do what he did do; and therefore determinism and moral responsibility are compatible.

Is the argument sound? The conclusion follows from the premises, but the catch, I think, lies in the first premise—the one saying that statement (a) tells us no more nor less than what statement (b) tells us. For (b), it would seem, could be true while (a) is false. That is to say, our man might be such that, if he had chosen to do otherwise, then he would have done otherwise, and yet *also* such that he could not have done otherwise. Suppose, after all, that our murderer could not have *chosen,* or could not have *decided,* to do otherwise. Then the fact that he happens also to be a man such that, if he had chosen not to shoot he would not have shot, would make no difference. For if he could *not* have chosen *not* to shoot, then he could not have done anything other than just what it was that he did do. In a word: from our statement (b) above ("If he had chosen to do otherwise, then he would have done otherwise"), we cannot make an inference to (a) above ("He could have done otherwise") unless we can *also* assert:

(c) He could have chosen to do otherwise.

And therefore, if we must reject this third statement, (c), then, even though we may be justified in asserting (b), we are not justified in asserting (a). If the man could not have chosen to do otherwise, then he would not have done otherwise—*even if* he was such that, if he *had* chosen to do otherwise, then he would have done otherwise.

The stratagem in question, then, seems to me not to work, and I would say, therefore, that the ascription of responsibility conflicts with a deterministic view of action.

4. Perhaps there is less need to argue that the ascription of responsibility also conflicts with an indeterministic view of action—with the view that the act, or some event that is essential to the act, is not caused at all. If the act—the firing of the shot—was not caused at all, if it was fortuitous or capricious, happening so to speak out of the blue, then, presumably, no one—and nothing—was responsible for the act. Our conception of action, therefore, should be neither deterministic nor indeterministic. Is there any other possibility?

5. We must not say that every event involved in the act is caused by some other event; and we must not say that the act is something that is not caused at all. The possibility that remains, therefore, is this: We should say that at least one of the events that are involved in the act is caused, not by any other events, but by something else instead. And this something else can only be the agent—the man. If there is an event that is caused, not by other events, but by the man, then there are some events involved in the act that are not caused by other events. But if the event in question is caused by the man then it *is* caused and we are not committed to saying that there is something involved in the act that is not caused at all.

But this, of course, is a large consequence, implying something of considerable importance about the nature of the agent or the man.

6. If we consider only inanimate natural objects, we may say that causation, if it occurs, is a relation between *events* or *states of affairs.* The dam's breaking was an event that was caused by a set of other events—the dam being weak, the flood being strong, and so on. But if a man is responsible for a particular deed, then, if what I have said is true, there is some event, or set of events, that is caused, *not* by other events or states of affairs, but by the agent, whatever he may be.

I shall borrow a pair of medieval terms, using them, perhaps, in a way that is slightly different from that for which they were originally intended. I shall say that when one event or state of affairs (or set of events or states of affairs) causes some other event or state of affairs, then we have an instance of *transeunt* causation. And I shall say that when an *agent,* as distinguished from an event, causes an event or state of affairs, then we have an instance of *immanent* causation.

The nature of what is intended by the expression "immanent causation" may be illustrated by this sentence from Aristotle's *Physics:* "Thus, a staff moves a stone, and is moved by a hand, which is moved by a man." (VII, 5, 256a, 6–8) If the man was responsible, then we have in this illustration a number of instances of causation—most of them transeunt but at least one of them immanent. What the staff did to the stone was an instance of transeunt causation, and thus we may describe it as a relation between events: "the motion of the staff caused the motion of the stone." And similarly for what the hand did to the staff: " the motion of the hand caused the motion of the staff." And, as we know from physiology, there are still other events which caused the motion of the hand. Hence we need not introduce the agent at this particular point, as Aristotle does—we *need* not, though we *may*. We *may* say that the hand was moved by the man, but we may *also* say that the motion of the hand was caused by the motion of certain muscles; and we may say that the motion of the muscles was caused by certain events that took place within the brain. But some event, and presumably one of those that took place within the brain, was caused by the agent and not by any other events.

There are, of course, objections to this way of putting the matter; I shall consider the two that seem to me to be most important.

7. One may object, firstly: "If the *man* does anything, then, as Aristotle's remark suggests, what he does is to move the *hand*. But he certainly does not *do* anything to his brain—he may not even know that he *has* a brain. And if he doesn't do anything to the brain, and if the motion of the hand was caused by something that happened within the brain, then there is no point in appealing to 'immanent causation' as being something incompatible with 'transeunt causation'—for the whole thing, after all, is a matter of causal relations among events or states of affairs."

The answer to this objection, I think, is this: It is true that the agent does not *do* anything with his brain, or to his brain, in the sense in which he *does* something with his hand and does something to the staff. But from this it does not follow that the agent was not the immanent cause of something that happened within his brain.

We should note a useful distinction that has been proposed by Professor A. I. Melden—namely, the distinction between "making something A happen" and

"doing A."[4] If I reach for the staff and pick it up, then one of the things that I *do* is just that—reach for the staff and pick it up. And if it is something that I do, then there is a very clear sense in which it may be said to be something that I know that I do. If you ask me, "Are you doing something, or trying to do something, with the staff?", I will have no difficulty in finding an answer. But in doing something with the staff, I also make various things happen which are not in this same sense things that I do: I will make various air-particles move; I will free a number of blades of grass from the pressure that had been upon them; and I may cause a shadow to move from one place to another. If these are merely things that I make happen, as distinguished from things that I do, then I may know nothing whatever about them; I may not have the slightest idea that, in moving the staff, I am bringing about any such thing as the motion of air-particles, shadows, and blades of grass.

We may say, in answer to the first objection, therefore, that it is true that our agent does nothing to his brain or with his brain; but from this it does not follow that the agent is not the immanent cause of some event within his brain; for the brain event may be something which, like the motion of the air-particles, he made happen in picking up the staff. The only difference between the two cases is this: in each case, he made something happen when he picked up the staff; but in the one case—the motion of the air-particles or of the shadows—it was the motion of the staff that caused the event to happen; and in the other case—the event that took place in the brain—it was this event that caused the motion of the staff.

The point is, in a word, that whenever a man does something A, then (by "immanent causation") he makes a certain cerebral event happen, and this cerebral event (by "transeunt causation") makes A happen.

8. The second objection is more difficult and concerns the very concept of "immanent causation," or causation by an agent, as this concept is to be interpreted here. The concept is subject to a difficulty which has long been associated with that of the prime mover unmoved. We have said that there must be some event

---

4. A. I. Melden, *Free Action* (London 1961), especially Chapter Three. Mr. Melden's own views, however, are quite the contrary of those that are proposed here.

A, presumably some cerebral event, which is caused not by any other event, but by the agent. Since A was not caused by any other event, then the agent himself cannot be said to have undergone any change or produced any other event (such as "an act of will" or the like) which brought A about. But if, when the agent made A happen, there was no event involved other than A itself, no event which could be described as *making* A happen, what did the agent's causation consist of? What, for example, is the difference between A's just happening, and the agent's *causing* A to happen? We cannot attribute the difference to any event that took place within the agent. And so far as the event A itself is concerned, there would seem to be no discernible difference. Thus Aristotle said that the activity of the prime mover is nothing in addition to the motion that it produces, and Suarez said that "the action is in reality nothing but the effect as it flows from the agent."[5] Must we conclude, then, that there is no more to the man's action in causing event A than there is to the event A's happening by itself? Here we would seem to have a distinction without a difference— in which case we have failed to find a *via media* between a deterministic and an indeterministic view of action.

The only answer, I think, can be this: that the difference between the man's causing A, on the one hand, and the event A just happening, on the other, lies in the fact that, in the first case but not the second, the Event A *was* caused and was caused by the man. There was a brain event A; the agent did, in fact, cause the brain event; but there was nothing that he did to cause it.

This answer may not entirely satisfy and it will be likely to provoke the following question: "But what are you really *adding* to the assertion that A happened when you utter the words 'The agent *caused* A to happen'?" As soon as we have put the question this way, we see, I think, that whatever difficulty we may have encountered is one that may be traced to the concept of causation generally—whether "immanent" or "transeunt." The problem, in other words, is not a problem that is peculiar to our conception of human action. It is a problem that must be faced by anyone who makes use of the concept of causation at all; and therefore, I would say, it is a problem for everyone but the complete indeterminist.

For the problem, as we put it, referring just to "immanent causation," or causation by an agent, was this: "What is the difference between saying, of an event A, that A just happened and saying that someone caused A to happen?" The analogous problem, which holds for "transeunt causation," or causation by an event, is this: "What is the difference between saying, of two events A and B, that B happened and then A happened, and saying that B's happening was the *cause* of A's happening?" And the only answer that one can give is this— that in the one case the agent was the cause of A's happening and in the other case event B was the cause of A's happening. The nature of transeunt causation is no more clear than is that of immanent causation.

9. But we may plausibly say—and there is a respectable philosophical tradition to which we may appeal —that the notion of immanent causation, or causation by an agent, is in fact more clear than that of transeunt causation, or causation by an event, and that it is only by understanding our own causal efficacy, as agents, that we can grasp the concept of *cause* at all. Hume may be said to have shown that we do not derive the concept of *cause* from what we perceive of external things. How, then, do we derive it? The most plausible suggestion, it seems to me, is that of Reid, once again: namely that "the conception of an efficient cause may very probably be derived from the experience we have had . . . of our own power to produce certain effects."[6] If we did not understand the concept of immanent causation, we would not understand that of transeunt causation.

10. It may have been noted that I have avoided the term "free will" in all of this. For even if there is such a faculty as "the will," which somehow sets our acts agoing, the question of freedom, as John Locke said, is not the question *"whether the will be free"*; it is the question *"whether a man be free."*[7] For if there is a "will," as a moving faculty, the question is whether the man is free to will to do those things that he does will to do—and also whether he is free *not* to will any of those things that he does will to do, and, again, whether he is free to will any of those things that he does not will to do. Jonathan

---

5. Aristotle, *Physics,* Book III, Chapter 3; Suarez, *Disputationes Metaphysicae,* Disputation 18, Section 10.

---

6. Reid, *Works,* p. 524.

7. *Essay Concerning Human Understanding,* Book II, Chapter XXI.

Edwards tried to restrict himself to the question—"Is the man free to do what it is that he wills?"—but the answer to this question will not tell us whether the man is responsible for what it is that he *does* will to do. Using still another pair of medieval terms, we may say that the metaphysical problem of freedom does not concern the *actus imperatus;* it does not concern the question whether we are free to accomplish whatever it is that we will or set out to do; it concerns the *actus elicitus,* the question whether we are free to will or to set out to do those things that we do will or set out to do.

11. If we are responsible, and if what I have been trying to say is true, then we have a prerogative which some would attribute only to God: each of us, when we act, is a prime mover unmoved. In doing what we do, we cause certain events to happen, and nothing—or no one—causes us to cause those events to happen.

12. If we are thus prime movers unmoved and if our actions, or those for which we are responsible, are not causally determined, then they are not causally determined by our *desires.* And this means that the relation between what we want or what we desire, on the one hand, and what it is that we do, on the other, is not as simple as most philosophers would have it.

We may distinguish between what we might call the "Hobbist approach" and what we might call the "Kantian approach" to this question. The Hobbist approach is the one that is generally accepted at the present time, but the Kantian approach, I believe, is the one that is true. According to Hobbism, if we *know,* of some man, what his beliefs and desires happen to be and how strong they are, if we know what he feels certain of, what he desires more than anything else, and if we know the state of his body and what stimuli he is being subjected to, then we may *deduce,* logically, just what it is that he will do—or, more accurately, just what it is that he will try, set out, or undertake to do. Thus Professor Melden has said that "the connection between wanting and doing is logical."[8] But according to the Kantian approach to our problem, and this is the one that I would take, there is no such logical connection between wanting and doing, nor need there even be a causal connection. No set of statements about a man's desires, beliefs, and stimulus situation at any time implies any statement telling us what the man will try, set out, or undertake to do at that time. As Reid put it, though we may "reason from men's motives to their actions and, in many cases, with great probability," we can never do so "with absolute certainty."[9]

This means that, in one very strict sense of the terms, there can be no science of man. If we think of science as a matter of finding what laws happen to hold, and if the statement of a law tells us what kinds of events are caused by what other kinds of event, then there will be human actions which we cannot explain by subsuming them under any laws. We cannot say, "It is causally necessary that, given such and such desires and beliefs, and being subject to such and such stimuli, the agent will do so and so." For at times the agent, if he chooses, may rise above his desires and do something else instead.

But all of this is consistent with saying that, perhaps more often than not, our desires do exist under conditions such that those conditions necessitate us to act. And we may also say, with Leibniz, that at other times our desires may "incline without necessitating."

13. Leibniz's phrase presents us with our final philosophical problem. What does it mean to say that a desire, or a motive, might "incline without necessitating"? There is a temptation, certainly, to say that "to incline" means to cause and that "not to necessitate" means not to cause, but obviously we cannot have it both ways.

Nor will Leibniz's own solution do. In his letter to Coste, he puts the problem as follows: "When a choice is proposed, for example to go out or not to go out, it is a question whether, with all the circumstances, internal and external, motives, perceptions, dispositions, impressions, passions, inclinations taken together, I am still in a contingent state, or whether I am necessitated to make the choice, for example, to go out; that is to say, whether this proposition true and determined in fact, *In all these circumstances taken together I shall choose to go out,* is contingent or necessary."[10] Leibniz's answer might be put as follows: in one sense of the terms "necessary" and "contingent," the proposition "In all these circumstances taken together I shall choose to go out," may be said to be contingent and not necessary, and in another sense of these terms, it may be said to be necessary and

---

8. *Op. cit.,* p. 166.

9. Reid, *Works,* pp. 608, 612.

10. "Lettre a Mr. Coste de la Néccessité et de la Contingence" (1707) in *Opera Philosophica,* ed. Erdmann, pp. 447–449.

not contingent. But the sense in which the proposition may be said to be contingent, according to Leibniz, is only this: there is no logical contradiction involved in denying the proposition. And the sense in which it may be said to be necessary is this: since "nothing ever occurs without cause or determining reason," the proposition is causally necessary. "Whenever all the circumstances taken together are such that the balance of deliberation is heavier on one side than on the other, it is certain and infallible that that is the side that is going to win out." But if what we have been saying is true, the proposition "In all these circumstances taken together I shall choose to go out," may be causally as well as logically contingent. Hence we must find another interpretation for Leibniz's statement that our motives and desires may incline us, or influence us, to choose without thereby necessitating us to choose.

Let us consider a public official who has some moral scruples but who also, as one says, could be had. Because of the scruples that he does have, he would never take any positive steps to receive a bribe—he would not actively solicit one. But his morality has its limits and he is also such that, if we were to confront him with a *fait accompli* or to let him see what is about to happen ($10,000 in cash is being deposited behind the garage), then he would succumb and be unable to resist. The general situation is a familiar one and this is one reason that people pray to be delivered from temptation. (It also justifies Kant's remark: "And how many there are who may have led a long blameless life, who are only *fortunate* in having escaped so many temptations."[11]) Our relation to the misdeed that we contemplate may not be a matter simply of being able to bring it about or not to bring it about. As St. Anselm noted, there are at least four possibilities. We may illustrate them by reference to our public official and the event which is his receiving the bribe, in the following way: (i) he may be able to bring the event about himself (*facere esse*), in which case he would actively cause himself to receive the bribe; (ii) he may be able to refrain from bringing it about himself (*non facere esse*), in which case he would not himself

do anything to insure that he receive the bribe; (iii) he may be able to do something to prevent the event from occurring (*facere non esse*), in which case he would make sure that the $10,000 was *not* left behind the garage; or (iv) he may be unable to do anything to prevent the event from occurring (*non facere non esse*), in which case, though he may not solicit the bribe, he would allow himself to keep it.[12] We have envisaged our official as a man who can resist the temptation to (i) but cannot resist the temptation to (iv): he can refrain from bringing the event about himself, but he cannot bring himself to do anything to prevent it.

Let us think of "inclination without necessitation," then, in such terms as these. First we may contrast the two propositions:

(1) He can resist the temptation to do something in order to make A happen;

(2) He can resist the temptation to allow A to happen (i.e., to do nothing to prevent A from happening).

We may suppose that the man has some desire to have A happen and thus has a motive for making A happen. His motive for making A happen, I suggest, is one that *necessitates* provided that, because of the motive, (1) is false; he cannot resist the temptation to do something in order to make A happen. His motive for making A happen is one that *inclines* provided that, because of the motive, (2) is false; like our public official, he cannot bring himself to do anything to prevent A from happening. And therefore we can say that his motive for making A happen is one that *inclines but does not necessitate* provided that, because of the motive, (1) is true and (2) is false; he can resist the temptation to make it happen but he cannot resist the temptation to allow it to happen.

---

11. In the Preface to the *Metaphysical Elements of Ethics*, in T. K. Abbott, ed., *Kant's Critique of Practical Reason and Other Works on the Theory of Ethics* (London 1959), p. 303.

12. Cf. D. P. Henry, "Saint Anselm's *De 'Grammatico'*," *Philosophical Quarterly*, Vol. X (1960), pp. 115–126. St. Anselm noted that (i) and (iii), respectively, may be thought of as forming the upper left and the upper right corners of a square of opposition, and (ii) and (iv) the lower left and the lower right.

Harry Frankfurt

Freedom of the Will and the Concept of a Person

What philosophers have lately come to accept as analysis of the concept of a person is not actually analysis of *that* concept at all. Strawson, whose usage represents the current standard, identifies the concept of a person as "the concept of a type of entity such that *both* predicates ascribing states of consciousness *and* predicates ascribing corporeal characteristics . . . are equally applicable to a single individual of that single type."[1] But there are many entities besides persons that have both mental and physical properties. As it happens—though it seems extraordinary that this should be so—there is no common English word for the type of entity Strawson has in mind, a type that includes not only human beings but animals of various lesser species as well. Still, this hardly justifies the misappropriation of a valuable philosophical term.

Whether the members of some animal species are persons is surely not to be settled merely by determining whether it is correct to apply to them, in addition to predicates ascribing corporeal characteristics, predicates that ascribe states of consciousness. It does violence to our language to endorse the application of the term 'person' to those numerous creatures which do have both psychological and material properties but which are manifestly not persons in any normal sense of the word. This misuse of language is doubtless innocent of any theoretical error. But although the offense is "merely verbal," it does significant harm. For it gratuitously diminishes our philosophical vocabulary, and it increases the likelihood that we will overlook the important area of inquiry with which the term 'person' is most naturally associated. It might have been expected that no problem would be of more central and persistent concern to philosophers than that of understanding what we ourselves essentially are. Yet this problem is so generally neglected that it has been possible to make off with its very name almost without being noticed and, evidently, without evoking any widespread feeling of loss.

There is a sense in which the word 'person' is merely the singular form of 'people' and in which both terms connote no more than membership in a certain biological species. In those senses of the word which are of greater philosophical interest, however, the criteria for being a person do not serve primarily to distinguish the members of our own species from the members of other species. Rather, they are designed to capture those attributes which are the subject of our most humane concern with ourselves and the source of what we regard as most important and most problematical in our lives. Now these attributes would be of equal significance to us even if they were not in fact peculiar and common to the members of our own species. What interests us most in the human condition would not interest us less if it were also a feature of the condition of other creatures as well.

Our concept of ourselves as persons is not to be understood, therefore, as a concept of attributes that are necessarily species-specific. It is conceptually possible that members of novel or even of familiar nonhuman species should be persons; and it is also conceptually possible that some members of the human species are not persons. We do in fact assume, on the other hand, that no member of another species is a person. Accordingly, there is a presumption that what is essential to persons is a set of characteristics that we generally suppose—whether rightly or wrongly—to be uniquely human.

It is my view that one essential difference between persons and other creatures is to be found in the structure of a person's will. Human beings are not alone in having desires and motives, or in making choices. They share these things with the members of certain other

---

Harry Frankfurt, "Freedom of the Will and the Concept of a Person" from *The Journal of Philosophy*, 68 (1971). Copyright © 1971. Reprinted by permission of the author and *The Journal of Philosophy*.

1. P. F. Strawson, *Individuals* (London: Methuen, 1959), pp. 101–102.

species, some of whom even appear to engage in deliberation and to make decisions based upon prior thought. It seems to be peculiarly characteristic of humans, however, that they are able to form what I shall call "second-order desires" or "desires of the second order."

Besides wanting and choosing and being moved *to do* this or that, men may also want to have (or not to have) certain desires and motives. They are capable of wanting to be different, in their preferences and purposes, from what they are. Many animals appear to have the capacity for what I shall call "first-order desires" or "desires of the first order," which are simply desires to do or not to do one thing or another. No animal other than man, however, appears to have the capacity for reflective self-evaluation that is manifested in the formation of second-order desires.

I

The concept designated by the verb 'to want' is extraordinarily elusive. A statement of the form "*A* wants to *X*"—taken by itself, apart from a context that serves to amplify or to specify its meaning—conveys remarkably little information. Such a statement may be consistent, for example, with each of the following statements: (a) the prospect of doing *X* elicits no sensation or introspectible emotional response in *A;* (b) *A* is unaware that he wants to *X;* (c) *A* believes that he does not want to *X;* (d) *A* wants to refrain from *X*-ing; (e) *A* wants to *Y* and believes that it is impossible for him both to *Y* and to *X;* (f) *A* does not "really" want to *X;* (g) *A* would rather die than *X;* and so on. It is therefore hardly sufficient to formulate the distinction between first-order and second-order desires, as I have done, by suggesting merely that someone has a first-order desire when he wants to do or not to do such-and-such, and that he has a second-order desire when he wants to have or not to have a certain desire of the first order.

As I shall understand them, statements of the form "*A* wants to *X*" cover a rather broad range of possibilities. They may be true even when statements like (a) through (g) are true: when *A* is unaware of any feelings concerning *X*-ing, when he is unaware that he wants to *X,* when he deceives himself about what he wants and believes falsely that he does not want to *X,* when he also

has other desires that conflict with his desire to *X,* or when he is ambivalent. The desires in question may be conscious or unconscious, they need not be univocal, and *A* may be mistaken about them. There is a further source of uncertainty with regard to statements that identify someone's desires, however, and here it is important for my purposes to be less permissive.

Consider first those statements of the form "*A* wants to *X*" which identify first-order desires—that is, statements in which the term 'to *X*' refers to an action. A statement of this kind does not, by itself, indicate the relative strength of *A*'s desire to *X*. It does not make it clear whether this desire is at all likely to play a decisive role in what *A* actually does or tries to do. For it may correctly be said that *A* wants to *X* even when his desire to *X* is only one among his desires and when it is far from being paramount among them. Thus, it may be true that *A* wants to *X* when he strongly prefers to do something else instead; and it may be true that he wants to *X* despite the fact that, when he acts, it is not the desire to *X* that motivates him to do what he does. On the other hand, someone who states that *A* wants to *X* may mean to convey that it is this desire that is motivating or moving *A* to do what he is actually doing or that *A* will in fact be moved by this desire (unless he changes his mind) when he acts.

It is only when it is used in the second of these ways that, given the special usage of 'will' that I propose to adopt, the statement identifies *A*'s will. To identify an agent's will is either to identify the desire (or desires) by which he is motivated in some action he performs or to identify the desire (or desires) by which he will or would be motivated when or if he acts. An agent's will, then, is identical with one or more of his first-order desires. But the notion of the will, as I am employing it, is not coextensive with the notion of first-order desires. It is not the notion of something that merely inclines an agent in some degree to act in a certain way. Rather, it is the notion of an *effective* desire—one that moves (or will or would move) a person all the way to action. Thus the notion of the will is not coextensive with the notion of what an agent intends to do. For even though someone may have a settled intention to do *X,* he may nonetheless do something else instead of doing *X* because, despite his intention, his desire to do *X* proves to be weaker or less effective than some conflicting desire.

Now consider those statements of the form "*A* wants to *X*" which identify second-order desires—that is, statements in which the term 'to *X*' refers to a desire of the first order. There are also two kinds of situation in which it may be true that *A* wants to want to *X*. In the first place, it might be true of *A* that he wants to have a desire to *X* despite the fact that he has a univocal desire, altogether free of conflict and ambivalence, to refrain from *X*-ing. Someone might want to have a certain desire, in other words, but univocally want that desire to be unsatisfied.

Suppose that a physician engaged in psychotherapy with narcotics addicts believes that his ability to help his patients would be enhanced if he understood better what it is like for them to desire the drug to which they are addicted. Suppose that he is led in this way to want to have a desire for the drug. If it is a genuine desire that he wants, then what he wants is not merely to feel the sensations that addicts characteristically feel when they are gripped by their desires for the drug. What the physician wants, insofar as he wants to have a desire, is to be inclined or moved to some extent to take the drug.

It is entirely possible, however, that, although he wants to be moved by a desire to take the drug, he does not want this desire to be effective. He may not want it to move him all the way to action. He need not be interested in finding out what it is like to take the drug. And insofar as he now wants only to *want* to take it, and not to *take* it, there is nothing in what he now wants that would be satisfied by the drug itself. He may now have, in fact, an altogether univocal desire *not* to take the drug; and he may prudently arrange to make it impossible for him to satisfy the desire he would have if his desire to want the drug should in time be satisfied.

It would thus be incorrect to infer, from the fact that the physician now wants to desire to take the drug, that he already does desire to take it. His second-order desire to be moved to take the drug does not entail that he has a first-order desire to take it. If the drug were now to be administered to him, this might satisfy no desire that is implicit in his desire to want to take it. While he wants to want to take the drug, he may have *no* desire to take it; it may be that *all* he wants is to taste the desire for it. That is, his desire to have a certain desire that he does not have may not be a desire that his will should be at all different than it is.

Someone who wants only in this truncated way to want to *X* stands at the margin of preciosity, and the fact that he wants to want to *X* is not pertinent to the identification of his will. There is, however, a second kind of situation that may be described by '*A* wants to want to *X*'; and when the statement is used to describe a situation of this second kind, then it does pertain to what *A* wants his will to be. In such cases the statement means that *A* wants the desire to *X* to be the desire that moves him effectively to act. It is not merely that he wants the desire to *X* to be among the desires by which, to one degree or another, he is moved or inclined to act. He wants this desire to be effective—that is, to provide the motive in what he actually does. Now when the statement that *A* wants to want to *X* is used in this way, it does entail that *A* already has a desire to *X*. It could not be true both that *A* wants the desire to *X* to move him into action and that he does not want to *X*. It is only if he does want to *X* that he can coherently want the desire to *X* not merely to be one of his desires but, more decisively, to be his will.[2]

Suppose a man wants to be motivated in what he does by the desire to concentrate on his work. It is necessarily true, if this supposition is correct, that he already wants to concentrate on his work. This desire is now among his desires. But the question of whether or not his second-order desire is fulfilled does not turn merely on whether the desire he wants is one of his desires. It turns on whether this desire is, as he wants it to be, his effective desire or will. If, when the chips are down, it

---

2. It is not so clear that the entailment relation described here holds in certain kinds of cases, which I think may fairly be regarded as nonstandard, where the essential difference between the standard and the nonstandard cases lies in the kind of description by which the first-order desire in question is identified. Thus, suppose that *A* admires *B* so fulsomely that, even though he does not know what *B* wants to do, he wants to be effectively moved by whatever desire effectively moves *B*; without knowing what *B*'s will is, in other words, *A* wants his own will to be the same. It certainly does not follow that *A* already has, among his desires, a desire like the one that constitutes *B*'s will. I shall not pursue here the questions of whether there are genuine counterexamples to the claim made in the text or of how, if there are, that claim should be altered.

is his desire to concentrate on his work that moves him to do what he does, then what he wants at that time is indeed (in the relevant sense) what he wants to want. If it is some other desire that actually moves him when he acts, on the other hand, then what he wants at that time is not (in the relevant sense) what he wants to want. This will be so despite the fact that the desire to concentrate on his work continues to be among his desires.

II

Someone has a desire of the second order either when he wants simply to have a certain desire or when he wants a certain desire to be his will. In situations of the latter kind, I shall call his second-order desires "second-order volitions" or "volitions of the second order." Now it is having second-order volitions, and not having second-order desires generally, that I regard as essential to being a person. It is logically possible, however unlikely, that there should be an agent with second-order desires but with no volitions of the second order. Such a creature, in my view, would not be a person. I shall use the term 'wanton' to refer to agents who have first-order desires but who are not persons because, whether or not they have desires of the second order, they have no second-order volitions.[3]

The essential characteristic of a wanton is that he does not care about his will. His desires move him to do certain things, without its being true of him either that he wants to be moved by those desires or that he prefers to be moved by other desires. The class of wantons includes all nonhuman animals that have desires and all very young children. Perhaps it also includes some adult

human beings as well. In any case, adult humans may be more or less wanton; they may act wantonly, in response to first-order desires concerning which they have no volitions of the second order, more or less frequently.

The fact that a wanton has no second-order volitions does not mean that each of his first-order desires is translated heedlessly and at once into action. He may have no opportunity to act in accordance with some of his desires. Moreover, the translation of his desires into action may be delayed or precluded either by conflicting desires of the first order or by the intervention of deliberation. For a wanton may possess and employ rational faculties of a high order. Nothing in the concept of a wanton implies that he cannot reason or that he cannot deliberate concerning how to do what he wants to do. What distinguishes the rational wanton from other rational agents is that he is not concerned with the desirability of his desires themselves. He ignores the question of what his will is to be. Not only does he pursue whatever course of action he is most strongly inclined to pursue, but he does not care which of his inclinations is the strongest.

Thus a rational creature, who reflects upon the suitability to his desires of one course of action or another, may nonetheless be a wanton. In maintaining that the essence of being a person lies not in reason but in will, I am far from suggesting that a creature without reason may be a person. For it is only in virtue of his rational capacities that a person is capable of becoming critically aware of his own will and of forming volitions of the second order. The structure of a person's will presupposes, accordingly, that he is a rational being.

The distinction between a person and a wanton may be illustrated by the difference between two narcotics addicts. Let us suppose that the physiological condition accounting for the addiction is the same in both men, and that both succumb inevitably to their periodic desires for the drug to which they are addicted. One of the addicts hates his addiction and always struggles desperately, although to no avail, against its thrust. He tries everything that he thinks might enable him to overcome his desires for the drug. But these desires are too powerful for him to withstand, and invariably, in the end, they conquer him. He is an unwilling addict, helplessly violated by his own desires.

The unwilling addict has conflicting first-order desires: he wants to take the drug, and he also wants to

---

3. Creatures with second-order desires but no second-order volitions differ significantly from brute animals, and, for some purposes, it would be desirable to regard them as persons. My usage, which withholds the designation 'person' from them, is thus somewhat arbitrary. I adopt it largely because it facilitates the formulation of some of the points I wish to make. Hereafter, whenever I consider statements of the form "*A* wants to want to *X*," I shall have in mind statements identifying second-order volitions and not statements identifying second-order desires that are not second-order volitions.

refrain from taking it. In addition to these first-order desires, however, he has a volition of the second order. He is not a neutral with regard to the conflict between his desire to take the drug and his desire to refrain from taking it. It is the latter desire, and not the former, that he wants to constitute his will; it is the latter desire, rather than the former, that he wants to be effective and to provide the purpose that he will seek to realize in what he actually does.

The other addict is a wanton. His actions reflect the economy of his first-order desires, without his being concerned whether the desires that move him to act are desires by which he wants to be moved to act. If he encounters problems in obtaining the drug or in administering it to himself, his responses to his urges to take it may involve deliberation. But it never occurs to him to consider whether he wants the relations among his desires to result in his having the will he has. The wanton addict may be an animal, and thus incapable of being concerned about his will. In any event he is, in respect of his wanton lack of concern, no different from an animal.

The second of these addicts may suffer a first-order conflict similar to the first-order conflict suffered by the first. Whether he is human or not, the wanton may (perhaps due to conditioning) both want to take the drug and want to refrain from taking it. Unlike the unwilling addict, however, he does not prefer that one of his conflicting desires should be paramount over the other; he does not prefer that one first-order desire rather than the other should constitute his will. It would be misleading to say that he is neutral as to the conflict between his desires, since this would suggest that he regards them as equally acceptable. Since he has no identity apart from his first-order desires, it is true neither that he prefers one to the other nor that he prefers not to take sides.

It makes a difference to the unwilling addict, who is a person, which of his conflicting first-order desires wins out. Both desires are his, to be sure; and whether he finally takes the drug or finally succeeds in refraining from taking it, he acts to satisfy what is in a literal sense his own desire. In either case he does something he himself wants to do, and he does it not because of some external influence whose aim happens to coincide with his own but because of his desire to do it. The

unwilling addict identifies himself, however, through the formation of a second-order volition, with one rather than with the other of his conflicting first-order desires. He makes one of them more truly his own and, in so doing, he withdraws himself from the other. It is in virtue of this identification and withdrawal, accomplished through the formation of a second-order volition, that the unwilling addict may meaningfully make the analytically puzzling statements that the force moving him to take the drug is a force other than his own, and that it is not of his own free will but rather against his will that this force moves him to take it.

The wanton addict cannot or does not care which of his conflicting first-order desires wins out. His lack of concern is not due to his inability to find a convincing basis for preference. It is due either to his lack of the capacity for reflection or to his mindless indifference to the enterprise of evaluating his own desires and motives. There is only one issue in the struggle to which his first-order conflict may lead: whether the one or the other of his conflicting desires is the stronger. Since he is moved by both desires, he will not be altogether satisfied by what he does no matter which of them is effective. But it makes no difference *to him* whether his craving or his aversion gets the upper hand. He has no stake in the conflict between them and so, unlike the unwilling addict, he can neither win nor lose the struggle in which he is engaged. When a *person* acts, the desire by which he is moved is either the will he wants or a will he wants to be without. When a *wanton* acts, it is neither.

III

There is a very close relationship between the capacity for forming second-order volitions and another capacity that is essential to persons—one that has often been considered a distinguishing mark of the human condition. It is only because a person has volitions of the second order that he is capable both of enjoying and of lacking freedom of the will. The concept of a person is not only, then, the concept of a type of entity that has both first-order desires and volitions of the second order. It can also be construed as the concept of a type of entity for whom the freedom of its will may be a problem. This concept excludes all wantons, both infrahuman and human, since they fail to satisfy an essential condition for the enjoyment of freedom of the will. And it excludes those suprahuman beings, if any, whose wills are necessarily free.

Just what kind of freedom is the freedom of the will? This question calls for an identification of the special area of human experience to which the concept of freedom of the will, as distinct from the concepts of other sorts of freedom, is particularly germane. In dealing with it, my aim will be primarily to locate the problem with which a person is most immediately concerned when he is concerned with the freedom of his will.

According to one familiar philosophical tradition, being free is fundamentally a matter of doing what one wants to do. Now the notion of an agent who does what he wants to do is by no means an altogether clear one: both the doing and the wanting, and the appropriate relation between them as well, require elucidation. But although its focus needs to be sharpened and its formulation refined, I believe that this notion does capture at least part of what is implicit in the idea of an agent who *acts* freely. It misses entirely, however, the peculiar content of the quite different idea of an agent whose *will* is free.

We do not suppose that animals enjoy freedom of the will, although we recognize that an animal may be free to run in whatever direction it wants. Thus, having the freedom to do what one wants to do is not a sufficient condition of having a free will. It is not a necessary condition either. For to deprive someone of his freedom of action is not necessarily to undermine the freedom of his will. When an agent is aware that there are certain things he is not free to do, this doubtless affects his desires and limits the range of choices he can make. But suppose that someone, without being aware of it, has in fact lost or been deprived of his freedom of action. Even though he is no longer free to do what he wants to do, his will may remain as free as it was before. Despite the fact that he is not free to translate his desires into actions or to act according to the determinations of his will, he may still form those desires and make those determinations as freely as if his freedom of action had not been impaired.

When we ask whether a person's will is free we are not asking whether he is in a position to translate his first-order desires into actions. That is the question of whether he is free to do as he pleases. The question of the freedom of his will does not concern the relation between what he does and what he wants to do. Rather, it concerns his desires themselves. But what question about them is it?

It seems to me both natural and useful to construe the question of whether a person's will is free in close analogy to the question of whether an agent enjoys freedom of action. Now freedom of action is (roughly, at least) the freedom to do what one wants to do. Analogously, then, the statement that a person enjoys freedom of the will means (also roughly) that he is free to want what he wants to want. More precisely, it means that he is free to will what he wants to will, or to have the will he wants. Just as the question about the freedom of an agent's action has to do with whether it is the action he wants to perform, so the question about the freedom of his will has to do with whether it is the will he wants to have.

It is in securing the conformity of his will to his second-order volitions, then, that a person exercises freedom of the will. And it is in the discrepancy between his will and his second-order volitions, or in his awareness that their coincidence is not his own doing but only a happy chance, that a person who does not have this freedom feels its lack. The unwilling addict's will is not free. This is shown by the fact that it is not the will he wants. It is also true, though in a different way, that the will of the wanton addict is not free. The wanton addict neither has the will he wants nor has a will that differs from the will he wants. Since he has no volitions of the second order, the freedom of his will cannot be a problem for him. He lacks it, so to speak, by default.

People are generally far more complicated than my sketchy account of the structure of a person's will may suggest. There is as much opportunity for ambivalence, conflict, and self-deception with regard to desires of the second order, for example, as there is with regard to first-order desires. If there is an unresolved conflict among someone's second-order desires, then he is in danger of having no second-order volition; for unless this conflict is resolved, he has no preference concerning which of his first-order desires is to be his will. This condition, if it is so severe that it prevents him from identifying himself in a sufficiently decisive way with *any* of his conflicting first-order desires, destroys him as a person. For it either tends to paralyze his will and to keep him from acting at all, or it tends to remove him from his will so that his will operates without his participation. In both cases he becomes, like the unwilling addict though in a different way, a helpless bystander to the forces that move him.

Another complexity is that a person may have, especially if his second-order desires are in conflict, desires and volitions of a higher order than the second. There is no theoretical limit to the length of the series of desires of higher and higher orders; nothing except common sense and, perhaps, a saving fatigue prevents an individual from obsessively refusing to identify himself with any of his desires until he forms a desire of the next higher order. The tendency to generate such a series of acts of forming desires, which would be a case of humanization run wild, also leads toward the destruction of a person.

It is possible, however, to terminate such a series of acts without cutting it off arbitrarily. When a person identifies himself *decisively* with one of his first-order desires, this commitment "resounds" throughout the potentially endless array of higher orders. Consider a person who, without reservation or conflict, wants to be motivated by the desire to concentrate on his work. The fact that his second-order volition to be moved by this desire is a decisive one means that there is no room for questions concerning the pertinence of desires or volitions of higher orders. Suppose the person is asked whether he wants to want to want to concentrate on his work. He can properly insist that this question concerning a third-order desire does not arise. It would be a mistake to claim that, because he has not considered whether he wants the second-order volition he has formed, he is indifferent to the question of whether it is with this volition or with some other that he wants his will to accord. The decisiveness of the commitment he has made means that he has decided that no further question about his second-order volition, at any higher order, remains to be asked. It is relatively unimportant whether we explain this by saying that this commitment implicitly generates an endless series of confirming desires of higher orders, or by saying that the commitment is tantamount to a dissolution of the pointedness of all questions concerning higher orders of desire.

Examples such as the one concerning the unwilling addict may suggest that volitions of the second order, or of higher orders, must be formed deliberately and that a person characteristically struggles to ensure that they are satisfied. But the conformity of a person's will to his higher-order volitions may be far more thoughtless and spontaneous than this. Some people are naturally moved by kindness when they want to be kind, and by nastiness when they want to be nasty, without any explicit forethought and without any need for energetic self-control. Others are moved by nastiness when they want to be kind and by kindness when they intend to be nasty, equally without forethought and without active resistance to these violations of their higher-order desires. The enjoyment of freedom comes easily to some. Others must struggle to achieve it.

IV

My theory concerning the freedom of the will accounts easily for our disinclination to allow that this freedom is enjoyed by the members of any species inferior to our own. It also satisfies another condition that must be met by any such theory, by making it apparent why the freedom of the will should be regarded as desirable. The enjoyment of a free will means the satisfaction of certain desires—desires of the second or of higher orders—whereas its absence means their frustration. The satisfactions at stake are those which accrue to a person of whom it may be said that his will is his own. The corresponding frustrations are those suffered by a person of whom it may be said that he is estranged from himself, or that he finds himself a helpless or a passive bystander to the forces that move him.

A person who is free to do what he wants to do may yet not be in a position to have the will he wants. Suppose, however, that he enjoys both freedom of action and freedom of the will. Then he is not only free to do what he wants to do; he is also free to want what he wants to want. It seems to me that he has, in that case, all the freedom it is possible to desire or to conceive. There are other good things in life, and he may not possess some of them. But there is nothing in the way of freedom that he lacks.

It is far from clear that certain other theories of the freedom of the will meet these elementary but essential conditions: that it be understandable why we desire this freedom and why we refuse to ascribe it to animals. Consider, for example, Roderick Chisholm's quaint version of the doctrine that human freedom entails an absence of causal determination.[4] Whenever a person performs a free action, according to Chisholm, it's a miracle. The motion of a person's hand, when the person moves it, is the outcome of a series of physical causes; but some event in this series, "and presumably one of those that took place within the brain, was caused by the agent and not by any other events" [pg. 356]. A free agent has, therefore, "a prerogative which some would attribute only to God: each of us, when we act, is a prime mover unmoved" [pg. 358].

This account fails to provide any basis for doubting that animals of subhuman species enjoy the freedom it defines. Chisholm says nothing that makes it seem less likely that a rabbit performs a miracle when it moves its leg than that a man does so when he moves his hand. But why, in any case, should anyone *care* whether he can interrupt the natural order of causes in the way Chisholm describes? Chisholm offers no reason for believing that there is a discernible difference between the experience of a man who miraculously initiates a series of causes when he moves his hand and a man who moves his hand without any such breach of the normal causal sequence. There appears to be no concrete basis for preferring to be involved in the one state of affairs rather than in the other.

It is generally supposed that, in addition to satisfying the two conditions I have mentioned, a satisfactory theory of the freedom of the will necessarily provides an analysis of one of the conditions of moral responsibility. The most common recent approach to the problem of understanding the freedom of the will has been, indeed, to inquire what is entailed by the assumption that someone is morally responsible for what he has done. In my view, however, the relation between moral responsibility and the freedom of the will has been very widely misunderstood. It is not true that a person is morally responsible for what he has done only if his will was free when he did it. He may be morally responsi-

ble for having done it even though his will was not free at all.

A person's will is free only if he is free to have the will he wants. This means that, with regard to any of his first-order desires, he is free either to make that desire his will or to make some other first-order desire his will instead. Whatever his will, then, the will of the person whose will is free could have been otherwise; he could have done otherwise than to constitute his will as he did. It is a vexed question just how 'he could have done otherwise' is to be understood in contexts such as this one. But although this question is important to the theory of freedom, it has no bearing on the theory of moral responsibility. For the assumption that a person is morally responsible for what he has done does not entail that the person was in a position to have whatever will he wanted.

This assumption *does* entail that the person did what he did freely, or that he did it of his own free will. It is a mistake, however, to believe that someone acts freely only when he is free to do whatever he wants or that he acts of his own free will only if his will is free. Suppose that a person has done what he wanted to do, that he did it because he wanted to do it, and that the will by which he was moved when he did it was his will because it was the will he wanted. Then he did it freely and of his own free will. Even supposing that he could have done otherwise, he would not have done otherwise; and even supposing that he could have had a different will, he would not have wanted his will to differ from what it was. Moreover, since the will that moved him when he acted was his will because he wanted it to be, he cannot claim that his will was forced upon him or that he was a passive bystander to its constitution. Under these conditions, it is quite irrelevant to the evaluation of his moral responsibility to inquire whether the alternatives that he opted against were actually available to him.

In illustration, consider a third kind of addict. Suppose that his addiction has the same physiological basis and the same irresistible thrust as the addictions of the unwilling and wanton addicts, but that he is altogether delighted with his condition. He is a willing addict, who would not have things any other way. If the grip of his addiction should somehow weaken, he would do whatever he could to reinstate it; if his desire for the drug

---

4. "Freedom and Action," in K. Lehrer, ed., *Freedom and Determination* (New York: Random House, 1966), pp. 11–44.

should begin to fade, he would take steps to renew its intensity.

The willing addict's will is not free, for his desire to take the drug will be effective regardless of whether or not he wants this desire to constitute his will. But when he takes the drug, he takes it freely and of his own free will. I am inclined to understand his situation as involving the overdetermination of his first-order desire to take the drug. This desire is his effective desire because he is physiologically addicted. But it is his effective desire also because he wants it to be. His will is outside his control, but, by his second-order desire that his desire for the drug should be effective, he has made this will his own. Given that it is therefore not only because of his addiction that his desire for the drug is effective, he may be morally responsible for taking the drug.

My conception of the freedom of the will appears to be neutral with regard to the problem of determinism. It seems conceivable that it should be causally determined that a person is free to want what he wants to want. If this is conceivable, then it might be causally determined that a person enjoys a free will. There is no more than an innocuous appearance of paradox in the proposition that it is determined, ineluctably and by forces beyond their control, that certain people have free wills and that others do not. There is no incoherence in the proposition that some agency other than a person's own is responsible (even *morally* responsible) for the fact that he enjoys or fails to enjoy freedom of the will. It is possible that a person should be morally responsible for what he does of his own free will and that some other person should also be morally responsible for his having done it.[5]

On the other hand, it seems conceivable that it should come about by chance that a person is free to have the will he wants. If this is conceivable, then it might be a matter of chance that certain people enjoy freedom of the will and that certain others do not. Perhaps it is also conceivable, as a number of philosophers believe, for states of affairs to come about in a way other than by chance or as the outcome of a sequence of natural causes. If it is indeed conceivable for the relevant states of affairs to come about in some third way, then it is also possible that a person should in that third way come to enjoy the freedom of the will.

---

5. There is a difference between being *fully* responsible and being *solely* responsible. Suppose that the willing addict has been made an addict by the deliberate and calculated work of another. Then it may be that both the addict and this other person are fully responsible for the addict's taking the drug, while neither of them is solely responsible for it. That there is a distinction between full moral responsibility and sole moral responsibility is apparent in the following example. A certain light can be turned on or off by flicking either of two switches, and each of these switches is simultaneously flicked to the "on" position by a different person, neither of whom is aware of the other. Neither person is solely responsible for the light's going on, nor do they share the responsibility in the sense that each is partially responsible; rather, each of them is fully responsible.

David Lewis

Are We Free to Break the Laws?

Soft determinism seems to have an incredible consequence. It seems to imply, given certain acceptable further premises, that sometimes we are able to act in such a way that the laws of nature are broken. But if we distinguish a strong and a weak version of this incredible consequence, I think we shall find that it is the strong version that is incredible and the weak version that is the consequence.

Soft determinism is the doctrine that sometimes one freely does what one is predetermined to do; and that in such a case one is able to act otherwise though past history and the laws of nature determine that one will not act otherwise.

Compatibilism is the doctrine that soft determinism may be true. A compatibilist might well doubt soft determinism because he doubts on physical grounds that we are ever predetermined to act as we do, or perhaps because he doubts on psychoanalytic grounds that we ever act freely. I myself am a compatibilist but no determinist, hence I am obliged to rebut some objections against soft determinism but not others. But for the sake of the argument, let me feign to uphold soft determinism, and indeed a particular instance thereof.

I have just put my hand down on my desk. That, let me claim, was a free but predetermined act. I was able to act otherwise, for instance to raise my hand. But there is a true historical proposition H about the intrinsic state of the world long ago, and there is a true proposition L specifying the laws of nature that govern our world, such that H and L jointly determine what I did. They jointly imply the proposition that I put my hand down. They jointly contradict the proposition that I raised my hand. Yet I was free; I was able to raise my hand. The way in which I was determined not to was not the sort of way that counts as inability.

What if I had raised my hand? Then at least one of three things would have been true. Contradictions would have been true together; or the historical proposition H would not have been true; or the law proposition L would not have been true. Which? Here we need auxiliary premises; but since I accept the premises my opponent requires to make his case, we may proceed. Of our three alternatives, we may dismiss the first; for if I had raised my hand, there would still have been no true contradictions. Likewise we may dismiss the second; for if I had raised my hand, the intrinsic state of the world long ago would have been no different. That leaves the third alternative. If I had raised my hand, the law proposition L would not have been true. That follows by a principle of the logic of counterfactuals which is almost uncontroversial:[1] $A \mathbin{\Box\!\!\rightarrow} B \vee C \vee D, A \mathbin{\Box\!\!\rightarrow} - B, A \mathbin{\Box\!\!\rightarrow} - C, \therefore A \mathbin{\Box\!\!\rightarrow} D$.

If L had not been true, that implies that some law of nature would have been broken, for L is a specification of the laws. That is not to say that anything would have been both a law and broken—that is a contradiction in terms if, as I suppose, any genuine law is at least an absolutely unbroken regularity. Rather, if L had not been true, something that is in fact a law, and unbroken, would have been broken, and no law. It would at best have been an almost-law.

In short, as a (feigned) soft determinist, who accepts the requisite auxiliary premises and principle of counterfactual logic, I am committed to the consequence that if I had done what I was able to do—raise my hand—then some law would have been broken.

1. The inference is valid in any system that treats the conditional as a propositionally (or even sententially) indexed family of normal necessities, in the sense of Brian F. Chellas. 'Basic conditional logic', *Journal of Philosophical Logic* 4 (1975) pp. 133–53.

"That is to say," my opponent paraphrases, "you claim to be able to break the very laws of nature. And with so little effort! A marvelous power indeed! Can you also bend spoons?"

Distinguo. My opponent's paraphrase is not quite right. He has replaced the weak thesis that I accept with a stronger thesis that I join him in rejecting. The strong thesis is utterly incredible, but it is no part of soft determinism. The weak thesis is controversial, to be sure, but a soft determinist should not mind being committed to it. The two theses are as follows.

(Weak Thesis)   I am able to do something such that, if I did it, a law would be broken.

(Strong Thesis)   I am able to break a law.

To see the difference, consider not a marvelous ability to break a law but a commonplace ability to break a window. Perhaps I am able to throw a stone in a certain direction; and perhaps if I did, the stone would hit a certain window and the window would break. Then I am able to break a window. For starters: I am able to do something such that, if I did it, a window would be broken. But there is more to be said. I am able to do something such that, if I did it, my act would cause a window-breaking event.

Or consider a commonplace ability to break a promise. Perhaps I am able to throw a stone; and perhaps if I did, I would break my promise never to throw a stone. Then I am able to break a promise. For starters: I am able to do something such that, if I did it, a promise would be broken. But there is more to be said. I am able to do something such that, if I did it, my act would itself be a promise-breaking event.

Next, consider what really would be a marvelous ability to break a law—an ability I could not credibly claim. Suppose that I were able to throw a stone very, very hard. And suppose that if I did, the stone would fly faster than light, an event contrary to law. Then I really would be able to break a law. For starters: I would be able to do something such that, if I did it, a law would be broken. But there is more to be said. I would be able to do something such that, if I did it, my act would cause a law-breaking event.

Or suppose that I were able to throw a stone so hard that in the course of the throw my own hand would

move faster than light. Then again I would be able to break a law, regardless of what my act might cause. For starters: I would be able to do something such that, if I did it, a law would be broken. But there is more to be said. I would be able to do something such that, if I did it, my act would itself be a law-breaking event.

If no act of mine either caused or was a window-, promise-, or law-breaking event, then I think it could not be true that I broke a window, a promise, or a law. Therefore I am able to break a window, a promise, or a law only if I am able to do something such that, if I did it, my act either would cause or would be a window-, promise-, or law-breaking event.

Maybe my opponent will contend that according to soft determinism, there is another way of being able to break a law. But I see no reason to grant his contention.

Now consider the disputed case. I am able to raise my hand, although it is predetermined that I will not. If I raised my hand, some law would be broken. I even grant that a law-breaking event would take place. (Here I use the present tense neutrally. I mean to imply nothing about *when* a law-breaking event would take place.) But is it so that my act of raising my hand would cause any law-breaking event? Is it so that my act of raising my hand would itself be a law-breaking event? Is it so that any other act of mine would cause or would be a law-breaking event? If not, then my ability to raise my hand confers no marvelous ability to break a law, even though a law would be broken if I did it.[2]

_____

2. Up to a point, my strategy here resembles that of Keith Lehrer. Lehrer grants a weak thesis: the agent could have done something such that, if he had done it, there would have been a difference in either laws or history. He rejects, as I would, the step from that to a stronger thesis: the agent could have brought about a difference in laws or history. So far, so good. But Lehrer's reason for rejecting the stronger thesis is one I cannot accept. His reason is this: it is false that if the agent had preferred that there be a difference in laws or history, there would have been a difference in laws or history. I say, first, that this conditional may not be false. Suppose the agent is predetermined to prefer that there be no difference; had he preferred otherwise, there would have been a difference. (Had anything been otherwise than it was predetermined to be, there would have been a difference in either laws or history.) And

Had I raised my hand, a law would have been broken beforehand. The course of events would have diverged from the actual course of events a little while before I raised my hand, and at the point of divergence there would have been a law-breaking event—a divergence miracle, as I have called it. But this divergence miracle would not have been caused by my raising my hand. If anything, the causation would have been the other way around. Nor would the divergence miracle have been my act of raising my hand. That act was altogether absent from the actual course of events, so it cannot get under way until there is already some divergence. Nor would it have been caused by any other act of mine, earlier or later. Nor would it have been any other act of mine. Nor is there any reason to say that if I had raised my hand there would have been some other law-breaking event besides the divergence miracle; still less, that some other law-breaking event would have been caused by, or would have been, my act of raising my hand. To accommodate my hypothetical raising of my hand while holding fixed all that can and should be held fixed, it is necessary to suppose one divergence miracle, gratuitous to suppose any further law-breaking.

Thus I insist that I was able to raise my hand, and I acknowledge that a law would have been broken had I done so, but I deny that I am therefore able to break a law. To uphold my instance of soft determinism, I need not claim any incredible powers. To uphold the compatibilism that I actually believe, I need not claim that such powers are even possible.

I said that if I had raised my hand, the divergence miracle beforehand would not have been caused by my raising my hand. That seems right. But my opponent might argue *ad hominem* that according to my own analysis of causation, my raising my hand does turn out to cause the divergence miracle. The effect would precede the cause, but I do not object to that. We seem to have the right pattern of counterfactual dependence between distinct events: (1) if I had raised my hand, the

divergence miracle would have occurred, but (2) if I had not raised my hand, it would not have occurred.

I reply that we do not have this required pattern, nor would we have had it if I had raised my hand. Therefore I am safe in denying that the miracle would have been caused by my act.

We do not have the pattern because (1) is false. What is true is only that if I had raised my hand, then some or other divergence miracle would have occurred. There is no particular divergence miracle that definitely would have occurred, since the divergence might have happened in various ways.[3]

If I had raised my hand, (1) would have been true. But we still would not have had the right pattern, because in that case (2) would have been false. Consider a counterfactual situation in which a divergence miracle beforehand has allowed me to raise my hand. Is it so, from the standpoint of that situation, that if I had not raised my hand, the miracle would not have taken place? No; the miracle might have taken place, only to have its work undone straightway by a second miracle. (Even in this doubly counterfactual context, when I speak of a miracle I mean a violation of the actual laws.) What is true, at most, is that if I had not raised my hand, then the first miracle might not have taken place.

My incompatibilist opponent is a creature of fiction, but he has his prototypes in real life. He is modelled partly on Peter van Inwagen and partly on myself when I first worried about van Inwagen's argument against compatibilism. He definitely is not van Inwagen; he does not choose his words so carefully. Still I think that for all his care, van Inwagen is in the same boat with my fictitious opponent.

Van Inwagen's argument runs as follows, near enough. (I recast it as a *reductio* against the instance of soft determinism that I feign to uphold.) I did not raise my hand;

---

second, if this conditional is not false, that is not enough to make the stronger thesis true. There must be some other reason, different from the one Lehrer gives, why the stronger thesis is false.

3. At this point I am relying on contingent features of the world as we suppose it to be; as Allen Hazen has pointed out to me, we can imagine a world of discrete processes at which one divergent history in which I raise my hand clearly takes less of a miracle than any of its rivals. I think this matters little, since the task of compatibilism is to show how freedom and determinism might coexist at a world that might, for all we know, be ours.

suppose for *reductio* that I could have raised my hand, although determinism is true. Then it follows, given four premises that I cannot question, that I could have rendered false the conjunction *HL* of a certain historical proposition *H* about the state of the world before my birth and a certain law proposition *L*. If so, then I could have rendered *L* false. (Premise 5.) But I could not have rendered *L* false. (Premise 6.) This refutes our supposition. [See pg. 349].

To this I reply that Premise 5 and Premise 6 are not both true. Which one is true depends on what van Inwagen means by "could have rendered false."

It does not matter what "could have rendered false" means in ordinary language; van Inwagen introduced the phrase as a term of art. It does not even matter what meaning van Inwagen gave it. What matters is whether we can give it any meaning that would meet his needs—any meaning that would make all his premises defensible without circularity. I shall consider two meanings. I think there is nothing in van Inwagen's text to suggest any third meaning that might work better than these two.[4]

First, a preliminary definition. Let us say that an event would falsify a proposition iff, necessarily, if that event occurs then that proposition is false. For instance, an event consisting of a stone's flying faster than light would falsify a law. So would an act of throwing in which my hand moves faster than light. So would a divergence miracle. But my act of throwing a stone would not itself falsify the proposition that the window in the line of fire remains intact; all that is true is that my act would cause another event that would falsify that proposition. My act of raising my hand would falsify any sufficiently inclusive conjunction of history and law.

But it would not itself falsify any law—not if all the requisite law-breaking were over and done with beforehand. All that is true is that my act would be preceded by another event—the divergence miracle—that would falsify a law.

Let us say that I could have rendered a proposition false in the weak sense iff I was able to do something such that, if I did it, the proposition would have been falsified (though not necessarily by my act, or by any event caused by my act). And let us say that I could have rendered a proposition false in the strong sense iff I was able to do something such that, if I did it, the proposition would have been falsified either by my act itself or by some event caused by my act.

The Weak Thesis, which as a soft determinist I accept, is the thesis that I could have rendered a law false in the weak sense. The Strong Thesis, which I reject, is the thesis that I could have rendered a law false in the strong sense.

The first part of van Inwagen's argument succeeds whichever sense we take. If I could have raised my hand despite the fact that determinism is true and I did not raise it, then indeed it is true both in the weak sense and in the strong sense that I could have rendered false the conjunction *HL* of history and law. But I could have rendered false the law proposition *L* in the weak sense, though I could not have rendered *L* false in the strong sense. So if we take the weak sense throughout the argument, then I deny Premise 6. If instead we take the strong sense, then I deny Premise 5.

Van Inwagen supports both premises by considering analogous cases. I think the supporting arguments fail because the cases produced are not analogous: they are cases in which the weak and strong senses do not diverge. In support of Premise 6, he invites us to reject the supposition that a physicist could render a law false by building and operating a machine that would accelerate protons to twice the speed of light. Reject that supposition by all means; but that does nothing to support Premise 6 taken in the weak sense, for the rejected supposition is that the physicist could render a law false in the strong sense. In support of Premise 5, he invites us to reject the supposition that a traveler could render false a conjunction of a historical proposition and a proposition about his future travels otherwise than by rendering false the nonhistorical conjunct. Reject that

---

4. Van Inwagen has indicated (personal communication, 1981) that he would adopt a third meaning for "could have rendered false," different from both of the meanings that I discuss here. His definition is roughly as follows: an agent could have rendered a proposition false iff he could have arranged things in a certain way, such that his doing so, plus the whole truth about the past, together strictly imply the falsehood of the proposition. On this definition, Premise 6 simply says that I could not have arranged things in any way such that I was predetermined not to arrange things in that way. It is uninstructive to learn that the soft determinist is committed to denying Premise 6 thus understood.

supposition by all means, but that does nothing to support Premise 5 taken in the strong sense. Given that one could render false, in the strong sense, a conjunction of historical and nonhistorical propositions (and given that, as in the cases under consideration, there is no question of rendering the historical conjunct false by means of time travel or the like), what follows? Does it follow that one could render the nonhistorical conjunct false in the strong sense? That is what would support Premise 5 in the strong sense. Or does it only follow, as I think, that one could render the nonhistorical conjunct false in at least the weak sense? The case of the traveler is useless in answering that question, since if the traveler could render the proposition about his future travels false in the weak sense, he could also render it false in the strong sense.

Thomas Nagel

Moral Luck

Williams sidesteps the fascinating question raised in his paper.[1] He does not defend the possibility of moral luck against Kantian doubts, but instead redescribes the case which seems to be his strongest candidate in terms which have nothing to do with moral judgment. Gauguin's talent as a painter may be a matter of luck, but it does not, according to Williams, warrant the retrospective judgment that his desertion of his family is morally acceptable. In fact, it does not warrant any judgment about his prior decision that pretends to objective validity for everyone, or even to timeless validity for him. According to Williams, the effect of the fortunate outcome on Gauguin's attitude to his earlier choice will be merely to make him not regret, at the most basic level, having made it. He will not regret it because it has resulted in a success which forms the centre of his life. This attitude can hardly be called a judgment at all, let alone a moral judgment. Williams says Gauguin cannot use it to justify himself to others. It does not even imply the truth of an hypothetical judgment made in advance, of the form "If I leave my family and become a great painter, I will be justified by success; if I don't become a great painter, the act will be unforgivable." And if the rest of us are glad that Gauguin left his family, Williams says that this is because we do not always give priority to moral values.

The importance of luck in human life is no surprise, even in respect of those matters about which we feel most deeply glad or regretful. It is the place of luck in ethics that is puzzling. Williams misdescribes his result in the closing paragraph of the paper: he has argued not that an agent's moral view of his life can depend on luck but that ultimate regret is not immune to luck because ultimate regret need not be moral. This is consonant with his tendency, here and in other recent writings, to reject the impersonal claims of morality in favour of more personal desires and projects. Even if Williams has successfully explained away the appearance of moral luck in the case of Gauguin, however, the explanation applies only to a narrow range of phenomena and leaves most of the area untouched. Williams acknowledges that he has dealt with only one type of case, but I do not believe these cases can be treated in isolation from the larger problem.

Why is there a problem? Not because morality seems too basic to be subject to luck. Some very important non-moral assessments of people deal with what is not

Thomas Nagel, "Moral Luck" from *Proceedings of the Aristotelian Society,* Supp. Vol. 50 (1976). Reprinted by courtesy of the Editor of the Aristotelian Society: © 1976.

1. "Moral Luck", *Aristotelian Society Supplementary Volume* 1976.

their fault. We deplore madness or leprosy in ourselves and others, we rejoice in beauty or talent, but these, though very basic, are not moral judgments. If we ask ourselves why, the natural explanation is that these attributes are not the responsibility of their possessors, they are merely good or bad luck. Prior to reflection it is intuitively plausible that people cannot be morally assessed for what is not their fault, or for what is due to factors beyond their control. This proposition uses an unanalysed concept of moral assessment that is presumably logically independent of the idea of control—otherwise the problem could not arise. Such a judgment is different from the evaluation of something as a good or bad thing, or state of affairs. The latter may be present in addition to moral judgment, but when we blame someone for his actions we are not merely saying it is bad that they happened, or bad that he exists: we are judging *him,* saying he is bad, which is different from his being a bad thing. This kind of judgment takes only a certain kind of object. Without being able to explain exactly why, we feel that the appropriateness of moral assessment is easily undermined by the discovery that the act or attribute, no matter how good or bad, is not under the person's control. While other evaluations remain, this one seems to lose its footing.

However, if the condition of control is consistently applied, it threatens to erode most of the moral assessments we find it natural to make. For in various ways, to be discovered, the things for which people are morally judged are not under their control, or are determined to some extent by what is beyond their control. And when the seemingly natural requirement of fault or responsibility is applied in light of these facts, it leaves few pre-reflective moral judgments intact.

Why not conclude, then, that the condition of control is false—that it is an initially plausible hypothesis refuted by clear counter-examples? One could in that case look instead for a more refined condition which picked out the *kinds* of lack of control that really undermine certain moral judgments, without yielding the unacceptable conclusion derived from the broader condition, that most or all ordinary moral judgments are illegitimate.

What rules out this escape is that we are dealing not with a theoretical conjecture but with a philosophical problem. The condition of control does not suggest it-

self merely as a generalization from certain clear cases. It seems *correct* in the further cases to which it is extended beyond the original set. When we undermine moral assessment by considering new ways in which control is absent, we are not just discovering what *would* follow given the general hypothesis, but are actually being persuaded that in itself the absence of control is relevant in these cases too. The erosion of moral judgment emerges not as the absurd consequence of an over-simple theory, but as a natural consequence of the ordinary idea of moral assessment, when it is applied in view of a more complete and precise account of the facts. It would therefore be a mistake to argue from the unacceptability of the conclusions to the need for a different account of the conditions of moral responsibility. The view that moral luck is paradoxical is not a *mistake,* ethical or logical, but a perception of one of the ways in which the intuitively acceptable conditions of moral judgment threaten to undermine it all.

It resembles the situation in another area of philosophy, the theory of knowledge. There too conditions which seem perfectly natural, and which grow out of the ordinary procedures for challenging and defending claims to knowledge, threaten to undermine all such claims if consistently applied. Most sceptical arguments have this quality: they do not depend on the imposition of arbitrarily stringent standards of knowledge, arrived at by misunderstanding, but appear to grow inevitably from the consistent application of ordinary standards. There is a substantive parallel as well, for epistemological scepticism arises from consideration of the respects in which our beliefs and their relation to reality depend on factors beyond our control. External and internal causes produce our beliefs. We may subject these processes to scrutiny in an effort to avoid error, but our conclusions at this next level also result, in part, from influences which we do not control directly. The same will be true no matter how far we carry the investigation. Our beliefs are always, ultimately, due to factors outside our control, and the impossibility of encompassing those factors without being at the mercy of others leads us to doubt whether we know anything. It looks as though, if any of our beliefs are true, it is pure biological luck rather than knowledge.

Moral luck is like this because while there are various respects in which the natural objects of moral assessment are out of our control or influenced by what is out of our control, we cannot reflect on these facts without losing our grip on the judgments.

There are roughly four ways in which the natural objects of moral assessment are disturbingly subject to luck. One is the phenomenon of constitutive luck mentioned by Williams at the beginning of his paper—the kind of person you are, where this is not just a question of what you deliberately do, but of your inclinations, capacities, and temperament. Another category is luck in one's circumstances—the kind of problems and situations one faces. The other two have to do with the causes and effects of action. Williams' discussion is confined to the last category, but all of them present a common problem. They are all opposed by the idea that one cannot be more culpable or estimable for anything than one is for that fraction of it which is under one's control. It seems irrational to take or dispense credit or blame for matters over which a person has no control, or for their influence on results over which he has partial control. Such things may create the conditions for action, but action can be judged only to the extent that it goes beyond these conditions and does not just result from them.

Let us first consider luck, good and bad, in the way things turn out—the type of case Williams examines. We may note that the category includes a range of examples, from the truck driver who accidentally runs over a child to Gauguin and beyond. The driver, if he is entirely without fault, will feel terrible about his rôle in the event, but will not have to reproach himself. Therefore this example of what Williams calls agent-regret is not yet a case of *moral* bad luck. However, if the driver was guilty of even a minor degree of negligence—failing to have his brakes checked recently, for example—then if that negligence contributes to the death of the child, he will not merely feel terrible. He will blame himself for its death. And what makes this an example of moral luck is that he would have to blame himself only slightly for the negligence itself if no situation arose which required him to brake suddenly and violently to avoid hitting a child. Yet the *negligence* is the same in both cases, and the driver has no control over whether a child will run into his path.

The same is true at higher levels of negligence. If someone has had too much to drink and his car swerves

on to the sidewalk, he can count himself morally lucky if there are no pedestrians in its path. If there were, he would be to blame for their deaths, and would probably be prosecuted for manslaughter. But if he hurts no one, although his recklessness is exactly the same, he is guilty of a far less serious legal offence and will certainly reproach himself and be reproached by others much less severely. To take another legal example, the penalty for attempted murder is less than that for successful murder—however similar the intentions and motives of the assailant may be in the two cases. His degree of culpability can depend, it would seem, on whether the victim happened to be wearing a bullet-proof vest, or whether a bird flew into the path of the bullet—matters beyond his control.

Finally, there are cases of decision under uncertainty—common in public and in private life. Anna Karenina goes off with Vronsky, Gauguin leaves his family, Chamberlain signs the Munich agreement, the Decembrists persuade the troops under their command to revolt against the Czar, the American colonies declare their independence from Britain, you introduce two people in an attempt at match-making. It is tempting in all such cases to feel that some decision must be possible, in the light of what is known at the time, which will make reproach unsuitable no matter how things turn out. But, as Williams says, this is not true; when someone acts in such ways he takes his life, or his moral position, into his hands, because how things turn out determines what he has done. It is possible *also* to assess the decision from the point of view of what could be known at the time, but this is not the end of the story. If the Decembrists had succeeded in overthrowing Nicholas I in 1825 and establishing a constitutional regime, they would be heroes. As it is, not only did they fail and pay for it, but they bore some responsibility for the terrible punishments meted out to the troops who had been persuaded to follow them. If the American Revolution had been a bloody failure resulting in greater repression, then Jefferson, Franklin and Washington would still have made a noble attempt, and might not even have regretted it on their way to the scaffold, but they would also have had to blame themselves for what they had helped to bring on their compatriots. (Perhaps peaceful efforts at reform would eventually have succeeded.) If Hitler had not overrun Europe and exterminated millions, but instead had died of a heart attack after occupying the Sudetenland, Chamberlain's action at Munich would still have utterly betrayed the Czechs, but it would not be the great moral disaster that has made his name a household word.

In many cases of difficult choice the outcome cannot be foreseen with certainty. One kind of assessment of the choice is possible in advance, but another kind must await the outcome, because the outcome determines what has been done. The same degree of culpability or estimability in intention, motive, or concern is compatible with a wide range of judgments, positive or negative, depending on what happened beyond the point of decision. The *mens rea* which could have existed in the absence of any consequences does not exhaust the grounds of moral judgment.

I have said that Williams does not defend the view that these are instances of moral luck. The fact that Gauguin will or will not feel basic regret over his decision is a separate matter, and does nothing to explain the influence of actual results on culpability or esteem in those unquestionably ethical cases ranging from negligence through political choice. In such cases one can say *in advance* how the moral verdict will depend on the results. If one negligently leaves the bath running with the baby in it, one will realize, as one bounds up the stairs toward the bathroom, that if the baby has drowned one has done something awful, whereas if it has not one has merely been careless. Someone who launches a violent revolution against an authoritarian regime knows that if he fails he will be responsible for much suffering that is in vain, but if he succeeds he will be justified by the outcome. I don't mean that *any* action can be retroactively justified by history. Certain things are so bad in themselves, or so risky, that no results can make them all right. Nevertheless, when moral judgment does depend on the outcome, it is objective and timeless and not dependent on a change of standpoint produced by success or failure. The judgment after the fact follows from an hypothetical judgment that can be made beforehand, and it can be made as easily by someone else as by the agent.

From the point of view which makes responsibility dependent on control, all this seems absurd. How is it possible to be more or less culpable depending on whether a child gets into the path of one's car, or a bird into the path of one's bullet? Perhaps it is true that what is done depends on more than the agent's state of mind or intention. The problem then is, why is it not irrational to base moral assessment on what people do, in this broad sense? It amounts to holding them responsible for the contributions of fate as well as for their own—provided they have made some contribution to begin with. If we look at cases of negligence or attempt, the pattern seems to be that overall culpability corresponds to the product of mental or intentional fault and the seriousness of the outcome. Cases of decision under uncertainty are less easily explained in this way, for it seems that the overall judgment can even shift from positive to negative depending on the outcome. But here too it seems rational to subtract the effects of occurrences subsequent to the choice, that were merely possible at the time, and concentrate moral assessment on the actual decision in light of the probabilities. If the object of moral judgment is the *person,* then to hold him accountable for what he has done in the broader sense is akin to strict liability, which may have its legal uses but seems irrational, as a moral position.

The result of such a line of thought is to pare down each act to its morally essential core, an inner act of pure will assessed by motive and intention. Adam Smith advocates such a position in *The Theory of Moral Sentiments,* but notes that it runs contrary to our actual judgments.

> "But how well soever we may seem to be persuaded of the truth of this equitable maxim, when we consider it after this manner, in abstract, yet when we come to particular cases, the actual consequences which happen to proceed from any action, have a very great effect upon our sentiments concerning its merit or demerit, and almost always either enhance or diminish our sense of both. Scarce, in any one instance, perhaps, will our sentiments be found, after examination, to be entirely regulated by this rule, which we all acknowledge ought entirely to regulate them."[2]

Joel Feinberg points out further that restricting the domain of moral responsibility to the inner world will not

---

2. Part II, Section III, Introduction, paragraph 5.

immunize it to luck. Factors beyond the agent's control, like a coughing fit, can interfere with his decisions as surely as they can with the path of a bullet from his gun.[3]

Nevertheless the tendency to cut down the scope of moral assessment is pervasive, and does not limit itself to the influence of effects. It attempts to isolate the will from the other direction, so to speak, by separating out what Williams calls constitutive luck. Let us consider that next.

Kant was particularly insistent on the moral irrelevance of qualities of temperament and personality that are not under the control of the will. Such qualities as sympathy or coldness might provide the background against which obedience to moral requirements is more or less difficult, but they could not be objects of moral assessment themselves, and might well interfere with confident assessment of its proper object—the determination of the will by the motive of duty. This rules out moral judgment of many of the virtues and vices, which are states of character that influence choice but are certainly not exhausted by dispositions to act deliberately in certain ways. A person may be greedy, envious, cowardly, cold, ungenerous, unkind, vain, or conceited, but *behave* perfectly by a monumental effort of will. To possess these vices is to be unable to help having certain feelings under certain circumstances, and to have strong spontaneous impulses to act badly. Even if one controls the impulses, one still has the vice. An envious person hates the greater success of others. He can be morally condemned as envious even if he congratulates them cordially and does nothing to denigrate or spoil their success. Conceit, likewise, need not be displayed. It is fully present in someone who cannot help dwelling with secret satisfaction on the superiority of his own achievements, talents, beauty, intelligence, or virtue. To some extent such a quality may be the product of earlier choices; to some extent it may be amenable to change by current actions. But it is largely a matter of constitutive bad fortune. Yet people are morally condemned for such qualities, and esteemed for others equally beyond control of the will: they are assessed for what they are *like*.

To Kant this seems incoherent because virtue is enjoined on everyone and therefore must be in principle possible for everyone. It may be easier for some than for others, but it must be possible to achieve it by making the right choices, against whatever temperamental background.[4] One may want to have a generous spirit, or regret not having one, but it makes no sense to condemn oneself or anyone else for a quality which is not within the control of the will. Condemnation implies that you shouldn't be like that, not that it's unfortunate that you are.

Nevertheless, Kant's conclusion remains intuitively unacceptable. We may be persuaded that these moral judgments are irrational, but they reappear involuntarily as soon as the argument is over. This is the pattern throughout the subject.

The third category to consider is luck in one's circumstances, and I shall mention it briefly. The things we are called upon to do, the moral tests we face, are importantly determined by factors beyond our control. It may be true of someone that in a dangerous situation he would behave in a cowardly or heroic fashion, but if the situation never arises, he will never have the chance to distinguish or disgrace himself in this way, and his moral record will be different.[5]

A conspicuous example of this is political. Ordinary citizens of Nazi Germany had an opportunity to behave heroically by opposing the regime. They also had an opportunity to behave badly, and most of them are culpable for having failed this test. But it is a test to which the citizens of other countries were not subjected, with the result that even if they, or some of them, would have behaved as badly as the Germans in like circumstances, they simply didn't and therefore are not similarly culpable. Here again one is morally at the mercy of fate, and it may seem irrational upon reflection, but our ordinary moral attitudes would be unrecognizable without it. We judge people for what they actually do or fail to do, not just for what they would have done if circumstances had been different.[6]

---

3. "Problematic Responsibility in Law and Morals", in Joel Feinberg, *Doing and Deserving* (Princeton, 1970).

4. *Foundations of the Metaphysics of Morals*, Akademie edition, p. 398.

5. *Cf.* Thomas Gray, "Elegy Written in a country churchyard".

6. Circumstantial luck can extend to aspects of the situation other than individual behaviour. For example, during

This form of moral determination by the actual is also paradoxical, but we can begin to see how deep in the concept of responsibility the paradox is embedded. A person can be morally responsible only for what he does; but what he does results from a great deal that he does not do; therefore he is not morally responsible for what he is and is not responsible for. (This is not a contradiction, but it is a paradox.)

It should be obvious that there is a connection between these problems about responsibility and control and an even more familiar problem, that of freedom of the will. That is the last type of moral luck I want to take up, though I can do no more within the scope of this paper than indicate its connection with the other types.

If one cannot be responsible for consequences of one's acts due to factors beyond one's control, or for antecedents of one's acts that are properties of temperament not subject to one's will, or for the circumstances that pose one's moral choices, then how can one be responsible even for the stripped-down acts of the will itself, if *they* are the product of antecedent circumstances outside of the will's control?

The area of genuine agency, and therefore of legitimate moral judgment, seems to shrink under this scrutiny to an extensionless point. Everything seems to result from the combined influence of factors, antecedent and posterior to action, that are not within the agent's control. Since he cannot be responsible for them, he cannot be responsible for their results—though it may remain possible to take up the aesthetic or other evaluative analogues of the moral attitudes that are thus displaced.

─────────────

the Vietnam War even U.S. citizens who had opposed their country's actions vigorously from the start often felt compromised by its crimes. Here they were not even responsible; there was probably nothing they could do to stop what was happening, so the feeling of being implicated may seem unintelligible. But it is nearly impossible to view the crimes of one's own country in the same way that one views the crimes of another country, no matter how equal one's lack of power to stop them in the two cases. One *is* a citizen of one of them, and has a connexion with its actions (even if only through taxes that cannot be withheld)—that one does not have with the other's. This makes it possible to be ashamed of one's country, and to feel a victim of moral bad luck that one was an American in the 'sixties.

It is also possible, of course, to brazen it out and refuse to accept the results, which indeed seem unacceptable as soon as we stop thinking about the arguments. Admittedly, if certain surrounding circumstances had been different, then no unfortunate consequences would have followed from a wicked intention, and no seriously culpable act would have been performed; but since the circumstances were *not* different, and the agent *in fact* succeeded in perpetrating a particularly cruel murder, *that* is what he did, and that is what he is responsible for. Similarly, we may admit that if certain antecedent circumstances had been different, the agent would never have developed into the sort of person who would do such a thing; but since he *did* develop (as the inevitable result of those antecedent circumstances) into the sort of swine he is, and into the person who committed such a murder, *that* is what he is blameable for. In both cases one is responsible for what one actually does—even if what one actually does depends in important ways on what is not within one's control.

This compatibilist account of our moral judgments would leave room for the ordinary conditions of responsibility—the absence of coercion, ignorance, or involuntary movement—as part of the determination of what someone has done—but it is understood not to exclude the influence of a great deal that he has not done. It is essentially what Williams means when he says,

"One's history as an agent is a web in which anything that is the product of the will is surrounded and held up and partly formed by things that are not, in such a way that reflection can go only in one of two directions: either in the direction of saying that responsible agency is a fairly superficial concept, which has a limited use in harmonizing what happens, or else that it is not a superficial concept, but that it cannot ultimately be purified—if one attaches importance to the sense of what one is in terms of what one has done and what in the world one is responsible for, one must accept much that makes its claim on that sense solely in virtue of its being actual."

The only thing wrong with this solution is its failure to explain how sceptical problems arise. For they arise not from the imposition of an arbitrary external requirement, but from the nature of moral judgment itself. Something in the ordinary idea of what someone does must explain how it can seem necessary to subtract from it anything that merely happens—even though the ultimate consequence of such subtraction is that nothing remains. And something in the ordinary idea of knowledge must explain why it seems to be undermined by any influences on belief not within the control of the subject—so that knowledge seems impossible without an impossible foundation in autonomous reason. But let us leave epistemology aside and concentrate on action, character, and moral assessment.

The problem arises, I believe, because the self which acts and is the object of moral judgment is threatened with dissolution by the absorption of its acts and impulses into the class of events. Moral judgment of a person is judgment not of what happens to him, but of him. It does not say merely that a certain event or state of affairs is fortunate or unfortunate or even terrible. It is not an evaluation of a state of the world, or of an individual as part of the world. We are not thinking just that it would be better if he were different, or didn't exist, or hadn't done some of the things he has done. We are judging *him,* rather than his existence or characteristics. The effect of concentrating on the influence of what is not under his control is to make this responsible self seem to disappear, swallowed up by the order of mere events.

What, however, do we have in mind that a person must *be* to be the object of these moral attitudes? While the concept of agency is easily undermined, it is very difficult to give it a positive characterization. That is familiar from the literature on Free Will.

I believe that in a sense the problem has no solution, because something in the idea of agency is incompatible with actions being events, or people being things. But as the external determinants of what someone has done are gradually exposed, in their effect on consequences, character, and choice itself, it becomes gradually clear that actions are events and people things. Eventually nothing remains which can be ascribed to the responsible self, and we are left with nothing but a portion of the larger sequence of events, which can be deplored or celebrated, but not blamed or praised.

Though I cannot define the idea of the active self that is thus undermined, it is possible to say something about

its sources. Williams is right to point out the important difference between agent-regret and regret about misfortunes from which one is detached, but he does not emphasise the corresponding distinction in our attitudes toward others, which comes from the extension to them of external agent-centered evaluations corresponding to the agent-regret that they can feel about themselves. This causes him to miss the truly moral character of such judgments, which can be made not only by the agent himself, though they involve the agent's point of view.

There is a close connexion between our feelings about ourselves and our feelings about others. Guilt and indignation, shame and contempt, pride and admiration are internal and external sides of the same moral attitudes. We are unable to view ourselves simply as portions of the world, and from inside we have a rough idea of the boundary between what is us and what is not, what we do and what happens to us, what is our personality and what is an accidental handicap. We apply the same essentially internal conception of the self to others. About ourselves we feel pride, shame, guilt, remorse—and what Williams calls agent-regret. We do not regard our actions and our characters merely as fortunate or unfortunate episodes—though they may also be that. We cannot *simply* take an external evaluative view of ourselves—of what we most essentially are and what we do. And this remains true even when we have seen that we are not responsible for our own existence, or our nature, or the choices we have to make, or the circumstances that give our acts the consequences they have. Those acts remain ours and we remain ourselves, despite the persuasiveness of the reasons that seem to argue us out of existence.

It is this internal view that we extend to others in moral judgment—when we judge *them* rather than their desirability or utility. We extend to others the refusal to limit ourselves to external evaluation, and we accord to them selves like our own. But in both cases this comes up against the brutal inclusion of humans and everything about them in a world from which they cannot be separated and of which they are nothing but contents. The external view forces itself on us at the same time that we resist it. One way this occurs is through the gradual erosion of what we do by the subtraction of what happens.

The inclusion of consequences in the conception of what we have done is an acknowledgement that we are parts of the world, but the paradoxical character of moral luck which emerges from this acknowledgement shows that we are unable to operate with such a view, for it leaves us with no one to be. The same thing is revealed in the appearance that determinism obliterates responsibility. Once we see an aspect of what we or someone else does as something that happens, we lose our grip on the idea that it has been done and that we can judge the doer and not just the happening. This explains why the absence of determinism is no more hospitable to the concept of agency than its presence is—a point that has been noticed often. Either way the act is viewed externally, as part of the course of events.

The problem of moral luck cannot be understood without an account of the internal conception of agency and its special connection with the moral attitudes as opposed to other types of value. I do not have such an account. The degree to which the problem has a solution can be determined only by seeing whether in some degree the incompatibility between this conception and the various ways in which we do not control what we do is only apparent. I have nothing to offer on that topic either. But it is not enough to say merely that our basic moral attitudes toward ourselves and others are determined by what is actual; for they are also threatened by the sources of that actuality, and by the external view of action which forces itself on us when we see how everything we do belongs to a world that we have not created.

PHILOSOPHY OF MIND

I KNOW MY OWN MIND immediately and directly. I do not have the same sort of access to any physical object—even my own body. I know that my leg hurts, but I need a doctor to tell me that my ankle is broken. I could be wrong about whether a physical object—even my own body—is damaged. Perhaps it just seems to me that my ankle is broken. But if I think I am in pain, then I am in pain. I may be wrong about the way the external world is, but apparently I cannot be wrong about the way things currently seem to me. Such privileged access strongly suggests that my mind is distinct from my body, since I have no such access to purely physiological states. But if mind and body are distinct, what is the connection between them? How is it that just by deciding to raise my hand, I bring it about that my hand goes up? How is it that if I damage my leg, I feel pain?

If mind and body are genuinely distinct, as Descartes maintains, the mind-body problem seems virtually intractable. So, despite our apparent privileged access to our own mental states, many philosophers conclude that dualism is false. This raises questions: What exactly are mental entities? How is it that we have the awareness of them that we do?

Smart argues that sensations are brain processes. That is, each occurrent sensation is identical to a particular process that takes place in the subject's brain. The identity in question is not conceptual, but it is lawlike. Although 'I am in pain' does not mean 'My C-fibers are firing', psychophysical laws ensure that 'I am in pain' is true when and only when 'My C-fibers are firing' is true. If Smart is right, minds are essentially material objects whose properties are discoverable by the physical sciences. Such a position may be too restrictive.

In 'The Nature of Mental States', Putnam argues that mental states are not physical states but functional states. When we identify something as a pain or as the belief that it is raining outside, we identify it by reference to its function in our mental economy. Each particular state may be physical. But states with different physical properties all qualify as pains because they perform the same function. It might seem that the difference between Smart's materialism and Putnam's functionalism is slight. But it is significant. It follows from Smart's materialism that if, for example, an octopus does not have C-fibers, and pain is the state one is in when and only when one's C-fibers are firing, then an octopus cannot feel pain. According to a functionalist like Putnam, if the octopus's state performs the same function as pain performs in us, then the octopus is in pain. This is so, whatever the physical constitution of its brain. But is it the case that every thought and sensation has a determinate function? What might that function be?

Perhaps a mental state is a disposition to behave in certain ways. Simple behaviorism seems manifestly false. There is no specific range of behaviors associated with, for example, believing that Omaha is in Nebraska. But more sophisticated forms of behaviorism are possible. Dennett suggests that the *intentional stance* is a perspective we take on people when we want to predict their behavior. By imputing a complex constellation of beliefs, desires, intentions, and meanings to a subject in a given environment and supposing that the subject is rational, we can predict what she will do. If, for example, she wants some milk and believes that there is milk in the refrigerator, she is apt to go to the refrigerator, open it, and look for a carton of milk. Even though her behavior has a purely physical description, that description—

including the firings of each of the relevant neurons—is too complicated for us to understand. So we resort to the intentional stance—a perspective that enables us to make sense of her behavior, assuming that she is rational and shares a vast number of mundane beliefs, desires, and preferences with the rest of us. Dennett does not deny that mental representations, such as beliefs and desires, are real entities. But he contends that what justifies our taking a particular mental configuration to be a belief, desire, or preference is not any feature that mental configuration has in itself but its salience when we take up the intentional stance. In effect the justification for calling a particular neurological configuration the belief that Omaha is in Nebraska is heuristic. Such a characterization is a useful shorthand that identifies it in terms of its role in our predictions and our understanding of one another as rational agents.

Fodor contends that mental representations are real, not merely heuristic, and that as representations they figure in causal explanations of our actions. In particular he maintains that psychology cannot plausibly explain verbal behavior without assuming that beliefs are among the causes of people's sincerely asserting what they sincerely assert. Fodor believes that, for the most part, our true beliefs are caused by situations in the world, represent the situations that cause them, and are links in the causal chains connecting our encounters with the world to our actions.

But, one might wonder, why should we think this is so? Descartes reminds us that dreamers have experiences that they take to be caused by events in the real world and that they perform what they consider actions in response to their experiences. Those experiences are not caused by the events they represent, and the actions do not really take place. Putnam offers a contemporary twist on Descartes' worry. Suppose I am a brain in a vat whose nerve endings are stimulated in such a way that the world seems coherent and comprehensible, but the stimuli are caused by a scientist working the controls, not by physical objects in my environment. Although I would have every reason to think I am a human organism interacting with a physical world in which I encounter other people, plants, animals, and so on, I would actually be an isolated brain. Descartes poses his problem as a skeptical worry. Putnam asks what my mental representations represent. If, in response to inputs to my visual cortex, I form the idea that there is a tree in front of me, does that idea represent a real tree? Putnam argues that it does so only if I am causally connected to real trees. If I am a brain in a vat, then my 'tree-idea' represents not a material object in the world outside my mind but a coherent regularity in my experience. What something represents, according to Putnam, depends on how it functions. And the representations of the brain in a vat could not function to represent a world to which the brain had no connection. The brain in a vat that thinks that her world contains trees is right to think so. But her word 'tree' does not and cannot mean what our word 'tree' does.

Mental states are not merely representations. They have experiential properties as well. Perhaps a physical state, a functional state, a state that depends on a perspective, or an essentially representational state could be correlated with something outside the mind and could therefore represent it. So one of the foregoing accounts might explain how mental entities represent things outside the mind. But none of them addresses the fact that mental states are conscious states. There is a felt quality to mental life, and any theory of mind that does not explain how things feel is incomplete and therefore inadequate. A theory that says that pain is C-fibers firing has not thereby explained why pain hurts.

Jackson advocates a form of dualism. Whereas Descartes maintains that there are two sorts of substances—minds and bodies—Jackson maintains that there are two sorts of properties—material properties and *qualia*. Qualia are essentially experiential properties. The only way to know them is to experience them. Thus, for example, someone who was blind from birth could have no knowledge of the qualitative character of red. For Jackson as well as Descartes causality is a problem. If qualia are not physical, how do they enter into the causal order? Jackson's answer is that qualia are *epiphenomenal:* they are caused by physical factors, but they cause nothing. They are, as it were, free riders on causal states of the organism.

Nagel too takes the problem of consciousness to be central. He believes that it cannot be solved. The issue for him is not feeling per se but the fact that experience is essentially subjective. Bats have experiences. So there is something it is like to be a bat. But because we are not bats, we cannot have the experiences of bats. So we cannot know what it is like to be a bat. The problem generalizes: I am not you, so I cannot know what it is like to be you. However comprehensive our objective account of the world is, Nagel maintains, something would be left out—namely, the subjective character of the experiences of other experiencers.

Philosophy of mind is one of the most intriguing and vexing areas of philosophy. Despite the fact that we are immediately and directly aware of our own minds, it seems that we do not yet fully understand what mental entities, properties, perspectives, and consciousness are.

J. J. C. Smart

Sensations and Brain Processes

Suppose that I report that I have at this moment a roundish, blurry-edged after-image which is yellowish towards its edge and is orange towards its center. What is it that I am reporting? One answer to this question might be that I am not reporting anything, that when I say that it looks to me as though there is a roundish yellowy orange patch of light on the wall I am expressing some sort of *temptation*, the temptation to say that there *is* a roundish yellowy orange patch on the wall (though I may know that there is not such a patch on the wall). This is perhaps Wittgenstein's view in the *Philosophical Investigations* (see paragraphs 367, 370). Similarly, when I "report" a pain, I am not really reporting anything (or, if you like, I am reporting in a queer sense of "reporting"), but am doing a sophisticated sort of wince. (See paragraph 244: "The verbal expression of pain replaces crying and does not describe it." Nor does it describe anything else?) I prefer most of the time to discuss an after-image rather than a pain, because the word "pain" brings in something which is irrelevant to my purpose: the notion of "distress." I think that "he is in pain" entails "he is in distress," that is, that he is in a certain agitation-condition. Similarly, to say "I am in pain" may be to do more than "replace pain behavior": it may be partly to report something, though this something is quite nonmysterious, being an agitation-condition, and so susceptible of behavioristic analysis. The suggestion I wish if possible to avoid is a different one, namely that "I am in pain" is a genuine report, and that what it reports is an irreducibly psychical something. And similarly the suggestion I wish to resist is also that to say "I have a yellowish orange after-image" is to report something irreducibly psychical.

Why do I wish to resist this suggestion? Mainly because of Occam's razor. It seems to me that science is increasingly giving us a viewpoint whereby organisms are able to be seen as physicochemical mechanisms: it seems that even the behavior of man himself will one day be explicable in mechanistic terms. There does seem to be, so far as science is concerned, nothing in the world but increasingly complex arrangements of physical constituents. All except for one place: in consciousness. That is, for a full description of what is going on in a man you would have to mention not only the physical processes in his tissue, glands, nervous system, and so forth, but also his states of consciousness: his visual, auditory, and tactual sensations, his aches and pains. That these should be *correlated* with brain processes does not help, for to say that they are *correlated* is to say that they are something "over and above." You cannot correlate something with itself. You correlate footprints with burglars, but not Bill Sikes the burglar with Bill Sikes the burglar. So sensations, states of consciousness, do seem to be the one sort of thing left outside the physicalist picture, and for various reasons I just cannot believe that this can be so. That everything should be explicable in terms of physics (together of course with descriptions of the ways in which the parts are put together—roughly, biology is to physics as radio-engineering is to electro-magnetism) except the occurrence of sensations seems to me to be frankly unbelievable. Such sensations would be "nomological danglers," to use Feigl's expression. It is not often realized how odd would be the laws whereby these nomological danglers would dangle. It is sometimes asked, "Why can't there be psycho-physical laws which are of a novel sort, just as the laws of electricity and magnetism were novelties from the standpoint of Newtonian mechanics?" Certainly we are pretty sure in the future to come across new ultimate laws of a novel type, but I expect them to relate simple constituents: for example, whatever ultimate particles are then in vogue. I cannot believe that ultimate laws of nature could relate simple constituents to configurations consisting of perhaps billions of neurons (and goodness knows how many billion billions of ultimate particles) all put together for all the world as though their main purpose in life was to be a negative feedback mechanism of a complicated sort. Such ultimate laws would be like nothing so far known in science. They have a queer "smell" to them. I am just unable

J. J. C. Smart, "Sensations and Brain Processes" from *Philosophical Review*, 68 (1959).

to believe in the nomological danglers themselves, or in the laws whereby they would dangle. If any philosophical arguments seemed to compel us to believe in such things, I would suspect a catch in the argument. In any case it is the object of this paper to show that there are no philosophical arguments which compel us to be dualists.

The above is largely a confession of faith, but it explains why I find Wittgenstein's position (as I construe it) so congenial. For on this view there are, in a sense, no sensations. A man is a vast arrangement of physical particles, but there are not, over and above this, sensations or states of consciousness. There are just behavioral facts about this vast mechanism, such as that it expresses a temptation (behavior disposition) to say "there is a yellowish-red patch on the wall" or that it goes through a sophisticated sort of wince, that is, says "I am in pain." Admittedly Wittgenstein says that though the sensation "is not a something," it is nevertheless "not a nothing either" (paragraph 304), but this need only mean that the word "ache" has a use. An ache is a thing, but only in the innocuous sense in which the plain man, in the first paragraph of Frege's *Foundations of Arithmetic,* answers the question "what is the number one?" by "a thing." It should be noted that when I assert that to say "I have a yellowish-orange after-image" is to express a temptation to assert the physical-object statement "there is a yellowish-orange patch on the wall," I mean that saying "I have a yellowish-orange after-image" is (partly) the exercise of the disposition which is the temptation. It is not to *report* that I have the temptation, any more than I "I love you" normally reports that I love someone. Saying "I love you" is just part of the behavior which is the exercise of the disposition of loving someone.

Though, for the reasons given above, I am very receptive to the above "expressive" account of sensation statements, I do not feel that it will quite do the trick. Maybe this is because I have not thought it out sufficiently, but it does seem to me as though when a person says "I have an after-image," he *is* making a genuine report, and that when he says "I have a pain," he *is* doing more than "replace pain-behavior," and that "this more" is not just to say that he is in distress. I am not so sure, however, that to admit this is to admit that there are nonphysical correlates of brain processes. Why should not sensations just be brain processes of a certain sort?

There are, of course, well-known (as well as lesser-known) philosophical objections to the view that reports of sensations are reports of brain-processes, but I shall try to argue that these arguments are by no means as cogent as is commonly thought to be the case.

Let me first try to state more accurately the thesis that sensations are brain processes. It is not the thesis that, for example, "after-image" or "ache" means the same as "brain process of sort X" (where "X" is replaced by a description of a certain sort of brain process). It is that, in so far as "after-image" or "ache" is a report of a process, it is a report of a process that *happens to be* a brain process. It follows that the thesis does not claim that sensation statements can be *translated* into statements about brain processes. Nor does it claim that the logic of a sensation statement is the same as that of a brain-process statement. All it claims is that in so far as a sensation statement is a report of something, that something is in fact a brain process. Sensations are nothing over and above brain processes. Nations are nothing "over and above" citizens, but this does not prevent the logic of nation statements being very different from the logic of citizen statements, nor does it insure the translatability of nation statements into citizen statements. (I do not, however, wish to assert that the relation of sensation statements to brain-process statements is very like that of nation statements to citizen statements. Nations do not just *happen to be* nothing over and above citizens, for example. I bring in the "nations" example merely to make a negative point: that the fact that the logic of A-statements is different from that of B-statements does not insure that A's are anything over and above B's.)

Remarks on identity. When I say that a sensation is a brain process or that lightning is an electric discharge, I am using "is" in the sense of strict identity. (Just as in the—in this case necessary—proposition "7 is identical with the smallest prime number greater than 5.") When I say that a sensation is a brain process or that lightning is an electric discharge I do not mean just that the sensation is somehow spatially or temporally continuous with the brain process or that the lightning is just spatially or temporally continuous with the discharge. When on the other hand I say that the successful general is the same person as the small boy who stole the apples I mean only that the successful general I see before me is a time slice of the same four-dimensional object of which the small boy stealing apples is an earlier time slice. However, the four-dimensional object which has the general-I-see-before-me for its late time slice is identical in the strict sense with the four-dimensional object which has the small-by-stealing-apples for an early time slice. I distinguish these two senses of "is identical with" because I wish to make it clear that the brain-process doctrine asserts identity in the *strict* sense.

I shall now discuss various possible objections to the view that the processes reported in sensation statements are in fact processes in the brain. Most of us have met some of these objections in our first year as philosophy students. All the more reason to take a good look at them. Others of the objections will be more recondite and subtle.

Objection 1. Any illiterate peasant can talk perfectly well about his after-images, or how things look or feel to him, or about his aches and pains, and yet he may know nothing whatever about neurophysiology. A man may, like Aristotle, believe that the brain is an organ for cooling the body without any impairment of his ability to make true statements about his sensations. Hence the things we are talking about when we describe our sensations cannot be processes in the brain.

Reply. You might as well say that a nation of slug-abeds, who never saw the morning star or knew of its existence, or who had never thought of the expression "the Morning Star," but who used the expression "the Evening Star" perfectly well, could not use this expression to refer to the same entity as we refer to (and describe as) "the Morning Star."

You may object that the Morning Star is in a sense not the very same things as the Evening Star, but only something spatiotemporally continuous with it. That is, you may say that the Morning Star is not the Evening Star in the strict sense of "identity" that I distinguished earlier. I can perhaps forestall this objection by considering the slug-abeds to be New Zealanders and the early risers to be Englishmen. Then the thing the New Zealanders describe as "the Morning Star" could be the very same thing (in the strict sense) as the Englishmen describe as "the Evening Star." And yet they could be ignorant of this fact.

There is, however, a more plausible example. Consider lightning. Modern physical science tells us that lightning is a certain kind of electrical discharge due to

ionization of clouds of water-vapor in the atmosphere. This, it is now believed, is what the true nature of lightning is. Note that there are not two things: a flash of lightning and an electrical discharge. There is one thing, a flash of lightning, which is described scientifically as an electrical discharge to the earth from a cloud of ionized water-molecules. The case is not at all like that of explaining a footprint by reference to a burglar. We say that what lightning really is, what its true nature as revealed by science is, is an electric discharge. (It is not the true nature of a footprint to be a burglar.)

To forestall irrelevant objections, I should like to make it clear that by "lightning" I mean the publicly observable physical object, lightning, not a visual sense-datum of lightning. I say that the publicly observable physical object lightning is in fact the electric discharge, not just a correlate of it. The sense-datum, or at least the having of the sense-datum, the "look" of lightning, may well in my view be a correlate of the electric discharge. For in my view it is a brain state *caused* by the lightning. But we should no more confuse sensations of lightning with lightning than we confuse sensations of a table with the table.

In short, the reply to Objection 1 is that there can be contingent statements of the form "A is identical with B," and a person may well know that something is an A without knowing that it is a B. An illiterate peasant might well be able to talk about his sensations without knowing about his brain processes, just as he can talk about lightning though he knows nothing of electricity.

Objection 2. It is only a contingent fact (if it is a fact) that when we have a certain kind of sensation there is a certain kind of process in our brain. Indeed it is possible, though perhaps in the highest degree unlikely, that our present physiological theories will be as out of date as the ancient theory connecting mental processes with goings on in the heart. It follows that when we report a sensation we are not reporting a brain-process.

Reply. The objection certainly proves that when we say "I have an after-image" we cannot *mean* something of the form "I have such and such a brain-process." But this does not show that what we report (having an after-image) is not *in fact* a brain process. "I see lightning" does not *mean* "I see an electric discharge." Indeed, it is logically possible (though highly unlikely) that the electrical discharge account of lightning might one day be given up. Again, "I see the Evening Star" does not *mean* the same as "I see the Morning Star," and yet "the Evening Star and the Morning Star are one and the same thing" is a contingent proposition. Possibly Objection 2 derives some of its apparent strength from a "Fido"-Fido theory of meaning. If the meaning of an expression were what the expression named, then of course it *would* follow from the fact that "sensation" and "brain-process" have different meanings that they cannot name one and the same thing.

Objection 3.[1] Even if Objections 1 and 2 do not prove that sensations are something over and above brain-processes, they do prove that the qualities of sensations are something over and above the qualities of brain-processes. That is, it may be possible to get out of asserting the existence of irreducibly psychic processes, but not out of asserting the existence of irreducibly psychic *properties*. For suppose we identify the Morning Star with the Evening Star. Then there must be some properties which logically imply that of being the Morning Star, and quite distinct properties which entail that of being the Evening Star. Again, there must be some properties (for example, that of being a yellow flash) which are logically distinct from those in the physicalist story.

Indeed, it might be thought that the objection succeeds at one jump. For consider the property of "being a yellow flash." It might seem that this property lies inevitably outside the physicalist framework within which I am trying to work (either by "yellow" being an objective emergent property of physical objects, or else by being a power to produce yellow sense-data, where "yellow," in this second instantiation of the word, refers to a purely phenomenal or introspectible quality). I must therefore digress for a moment and indicate how I deal with secondary qualities. I shall concentrate on color.

First of all, let me introduce the concept of a normal percipient. One person is more a normal percipient than another if he can make color discriminations that

the other cannot. For example, if A can pick a lettuce leaf out of a heap of cabbage leaves, whereas B cannot though he can pick a lettuce leaf out of a heap of beet-root leaves, then A is more normal than B. (I am assuming that A and B are not given time to distinguish the leaves by their slight difference in shape, and so forth.) From the concept of "more normal than" it is easy to see how we can introduce the concept of "normal." Of course, Eskimos may make the finest discriminations at the blue end of the spectrum, Hottentots at the red end. In this case the concept of a normal percipient is a slightly idealized one, rather like that of "the mean sun" in astronomical chronology. There is no need to go into such subtleties now. I say that "This is red" means something roughly like "A normal percipient would not easily pick this out of a clump of geranium petals though he would pick it out of a clump of lettuce leaves." Of course it does not exactly mean this: a person might know the meaning of "red" without knowing anything about geraniums, or even about normal percipients. But the point is that a person can be *trained* to say "This is red" of objects which would not easily be picked out of geranium petals by a normal percipient, and so on. (Note that even a color-blind person can reasonably assert that something is red, though of course he needs to use another human being, not just himself, as his "color meter.") This account of secondary qualities explains their unimportance in physics. For obviously the discriminations and lack of discriminations made by a very complex neurophysiological mechanism are hardly likely to correspond to simple and nonarbitrary distinctions in nature.

I therefore elucidate colors as powers, in Locke's sense, to evoke certain sorts of discriminatory responses in human beings. They are also, of course, powers to cause sensations in human beings (an account still nearer Locke's). But these sensations, I am arguing, are identifiable with brain processes.

Now how do I get over the objection that a sensation can be identified with a brain process only if it has some phenomenal property, not possessed by brain processes, whereby one-half of the identification may be, so to speak, pinned down?

My suggestion is as follows. When a person says, "I see a yellowish-orange after-image," he is saying something like this: "*There is something going on which is like*

---

1. I think this objection was first put to me by Professor Max Black. I think it is the most subtle of any of those I have considered, and one which I am least confident of having satisfactorily met.

what is going on when I have my eyes open, am awake, and there is an orange illuminated in good light in from of me, that is, when I really see an orange." (And there is no reason why a person should not say the same thing when he is having a veridical sense-datum, so long as we construe "like" in the last sentence in such a sense that something can be like itself.) Notice that the italicized words, namely "there is something going on which is like what is going on when," are all quasi-logical or topic-neutral words. This explains why the ancient Greek peasant's reports about his sensations can be neutral between dualistic metaphysics or my materialistic metaphysics. It explains how sensations can be brain-processes and yet how those who report them need know nothing about brain-processes. For he reports them only very abstractly as "something going on which is like what is going on when . . .". Similarly, a person may say "someone is in the room," thus reporting truly that the doctor is in the room, even though he has never heard of doctors. (There are not two people in the room: "someone" *and* the doctor.) This account of sensation statements also explains the singular elusiveness of "raw feels"—why no one seems to be able to pin any properties on them. Raw feels, in my view, are colorless for the very same reason that *something* is colorless. This does not mean that sensations do not have properties, for if they are brain-processes they certainly have properties. It only means that in speaking of them as being like or unlike one another we need not know or mention these properties.

This, then, is how I would reply to Objection 3. The strength of my reply depends on the possibility of our being able to report that one thing is like another without being able to state the respect in which it is like. I am not sure whether this is so or not, and that is why I regard Objection 3 as the strongest with which I have to deal.

Objection 4. The after-image is not in physical space. The brain-process is. So the after-image is not a brain-process.

Reply. This is an *ignoratio elenchi.* I am not arguing that the after-image is a brain-process, but that the experience of having an after-image is a brain-process. It is the *experience* which is reported in the introspective report. Similarly, if it is objected that the after-image is yellow-orange but that a surgeon looking into your brain

would see nothing yellowy-orange, my reply is that it is the experience of seeing yellowy-orange that is being described, and this experience is not a yellowy-orange something. So to say that a brain-process cannot be yellowy-orange is not to say that a brain-process cannot in fact be the experience of having a yellowy-orange after-image. There is, in a sense, no such thing as an after-image or a sense-datum, though there is such a thing as the experience of having an image, and this experience is described indirectly in material object language, not in phenomenal language, for there is no such thing. We describe the experience by saying, in effect, that it is like the experience we have when, for example, we really see a yellowy-orange patch on the wall. Trees and wallpaper can be green, but not the experience of seeing or imagining a tree or wallpaper. (Or if they are described as green or yellow this can only be in a derived sense.)

Objection 5. It would make sense to say of molecular movement in the brain that it is swift or slow, straight or circular, but it makes no sense to say this of the experience of seeing something yellow.

Reply. So far we have not given sense to talk of experiences as swift or slow, straight or circular. But I am not claiming that "experience" and "brain-process" mean the same or even that they have the same logic. "Somebody" and "the doctor" do not have the same logic, but this does not lead us to suppose that talking about somebody telephoning is talking about someone over and above, say, the doctor. The ordinary man when he reports an experience is reporting that something is going on, but he leaves it open as to what sort of thing is going on, whether in a material solid medium, or perhaps in some sort of gaseous medium, or even perhaps in some sort of nonspatial medium (if this makes sense). All that I am saying is that "experience" and "brain-process" may in fact refer to the same thing, and if so we may easily adopt a convention (which is not a change in our present rules for the use of experience words but an addition to them) whereby it would make sense to talk of an experience in terms appropriate to physical processes.

Objection 6. Sensations are private, brain processes are *public.* If I sincerely say, "I see a yellowish-orange after-image" and I am not making a verbal mistake, then I cannot be wrong. But I can be wrong about a brain-process. The scientist looking into my brain might be having an illusion. Moreover, it makes sense to say that two or more people are observing the same brain-process but not that two or more people are reporting the same inner experience.

Reply. This shows that the language of introspective reports has a different logic from the language of material processes. It is obvious that until the brain-process theory is much improved and widely accepted there will be no *criteria* for saying "Smith has an experience of such-and-such a sort" *except* Smith's introspective reports. So we have adopted a rule of language that (normally) what Smith says goes.

Objection 7. I can imagine myself turned to stone and yet having images, aches, pains, and so on.

Reply. I can imagine that the electrical theory of lightning is false, that lightning is some sort of purely optical phenomenon. I can imagine that lightning is not an electrical discharge. I can imagine that the Evening Star is not the Morning Star. But it is. All the objection shows is that "experience" and "brain-process" do not have the same meaning. It does not show that an experience is not in fact a brain process.

This objection is perhaps much the same as one which can be summed up by the slogan: "What can be composed of nothing cannot be composed of anything." The argument goes as follows: on the brain-process thesis the identity between the brain-process and the experience is a contingent one. So it is logically possible that there should be no brain-process, and no process of any other sort, either (no heart process, no kidney process, no liver process). There would be the experience but no "corresponding" physiological process with which we might be able to identify it empirically.

I suspect that the objector is thinking of the experience as a ghostly entity. So it is composed of something, not of nothing, after all. On his view it is composed of ghost stuff, and on mine it is composed of brain stuff. Perhaps the counter-reply will be that the experience is simple and uncompounded, and so it is not composed of anything after all. This seems to be a quibble, for, if it were taken seriously, the remark "What can be composed of nothing cannot be composed of anything" could be recast as an a priori argument against Democritus and atomism and for Descartes and infinite divisibility. And it seems off that a question of this sort

could be settled a priori. We must therefore construe the word "composed" in a very weak sense, which would allow us to say that even an indivisible atom is composed of something (namely, itself). The dualist cannot really say that an experience can be composed of nothing. For he holds that experiences are something over and above material processes, that is, that they are a sort of ghost stuff. (Or perhaps ripples in an underlying ghost stuff.) I say that the dualist's hypothesis is a perfectly intelligible one. But I say that experiences are not to be identified with ghost stuff but with brain stuff. This is another hypothesis, and in my view a very plausible one. The present argument cannot knock it down a priori.

Objection 8. The "beetle in the box" objection (see Wittgenstein, *Philosophical Investigations,* paragraph 293). How could descriptions of experiences, if these are genuine reports, get a foothold in language? For any rule of language must have public criteria for its correct application.

Reply. The change from describing how things are to describing how we feel is just a change from uninhibitedly saying "this is so" to saying "this looks so." That is, when the naive person might be tempted to say, "There is a patch of light on the wall which moves whenever I move my eyes" or "A pin is being stuck into me," we have learned how to resist this temptation and say "It *looks as though* there is a patch of light on the wallpaper" or "It *feels as though* someone were sticking a pin into me." The introspective account tells us about the individual's state of consciousness in the same way as does "I see a patch of light" or "I feel a pin being stuck into me": it differs from the corresponding perception statement in so far as (a) in the perception statement the individual "goes beyond the evidence of his senses" in describing his environment and (b) in the introspective report he withholds descriptive epithets he is inclined to ascribe to the environment, perhaps because he suspects that they may not be appropriate to the actual state of affairs. Psychologically speaking, the change from talking about the environment to talking about one's state of consciousness is simply a matter of inhibiting descriptive reactions not justified by appearances alone, and of disinhibiting descriptive reactions which are normally inhibited because the individual has learned that they are unlikely to provide a reliable guide to the state of the environment in the prevailing circumstances.[2] To say that something looks green to me is to say that my experience is like the experience I get when I see something that really is green. In my reply to Objection 3, I pointed out the extreme openness or generality of statements which report experiences. This explains why there is no language of private qualities. (Just as "someone," unlike "the doctor," is a colorless word.)

If it is asked what is the difference between those brain processes which, in my view, are experiences and those brain processes which are not, I can only reply that this is at present unknown. But it does not seem to me altogether fanciful to conjecture that the difference may in part be that between perception and reception (in Dr. D. M. MacKay's terminology) and that the type of brain process which is an experience might be identifiable with MacKay's active "matching response."[3]

I have now considered a number of objections to the brain-process thesis. I wish now to conclude by some remarks on the logical status of the thesis itself. U. T. Place seems to hold that it is a straight-out scientific hypothesis.[4] If so, he is partly right and partly wrong. If the issue is between (say) a brain-process thesis and a heart thesis, or a liver thesis, or a kidney thesis, then the issue is a purely empirical one, and the verdict is overwhelmingly in favor of the brain. The right sorts of things don't go on in the heart, liver, or kidney, nor do those organs possess the right sort of complexity of structure. On the other hand, if the issue is between a brain-or-heart-or-liver-or-kidney thesis (that is, some form of materialism) on the one hand and epiphenomenalism on the other hand, then the issue is not an empirical one. For there is no conceivable experiment which could decide between materialism and epiphenomenalism. This latter issue is not like the average straight-out empirical issue in science, but like the issue between the nineteenth-century English naturalist Philip Gosse and the orthodox geologists and paleontologists of his day. According to Gosse, the earth was created about 4000 B.C. exactly as described in *Genesis,* with twisted rock strata, "evidence" of erosion, and so forth, and all sorts of fossils, all in their appropriate strata, just as if the usual evolutionist story had been true. Clearly this theory is in a sense irrefutable: no evidence can possible tell against it. Let us ignore the theological setting in which Philip Gosse's hypothesis had been placed, thus ruling out objections of a theological kind, such as "what a queer God who would go to such elaborate lengths to deceive us." Let us suppose that it is held that the universe just *began* in 4004 B.C. with the initial conditions just everywhere as they were in 4004 B.C., and in particular that our own planet began with sediment in the rivers, eroded cliffs, fossils in the rocks, and so on. No scientist would ever entertain this as a serious hypothesis, consistent though it is with all possible evidence. The hypothesis offends against the principles of parsimony and simplicity. There would be far too many brute and inexplicable facts. Why are pterodactyl bones just as they are? No explanation in terms of the evolution of pterodactyls from earlier forms of life would any longer be possible. We would have millions of facts about the world as it was in 4004 B.C. that just have to be *accepted.*

The issue between the brain-process theory and epiphenomenalism seems to be of the above sort. (Assuming that a behavioristic reduction of introspective reports is not possible.) If it be agreed that there are no cogent philosophical arguments which force us into accepting dualism, and if the brain process theory and dualism are equally consistent with the facts, then the principles of parsimony and simplicity seem to me to decide overwhelmingly in favor of the brain-process theory. As I pointed out earlier, dualism involves a large number of irreducible psychophysical laws (whereby the "nomological danglers" dangle) of a queer sort, that just have to be taken on trust, and are just as difficult to swallow as the irreducible facts about the paleontology of the earth with which we are faced on Philip Gosse's theory.

---

2. I owe this point to Place, in correspondence.

3. See his article "Towards an Information-Flow model of Human Behaviour," *British Journal of Psychology,* XLVII (1956), 30–43.

4. "Is Consciousness a Brain Process?" *British Journal of Psychology,* XLVII, (1956), 44–50.

Hilary Putnam

The Nature of Mental States

I. Identity Questions

'Is pain a brain state?' (Or, 'Is the property of having a pain at time *t* a brain state?') It is impossible to discuss this question sensibly without saying something about the peculiar rules which have grown up in the course of the development of 'analytical philosophy'—rules which, far from leading to an end to all conceptual confusions, themselves represent considerable conceptual confusion. These rules—which are, of course, implicit rather than explicit in the practice of most analytical philosophers—are (1) that a statement of the form 'being *A* is being *B*' (e.g. 'being in pain is being in a certain brain state') can be *correct* only if it follows, in some sense, from the meaning of the terms *A* and *B*; and (2) that a statement of the form 'being *A* is being *B*' can be philosophically *informative* only if it is in some sense reductive (e.g. 'being in pain is having a certain unpleasant sensation' is not philosophically informative; 'being in pain is having a certain behavior disposition' is, if true, philosophically informative). These rules are excellent rules if we still believe that the program of reductive analysis (in the style of the 1930s) can be carried out; if we don't, then they turn analytical philosophy into a mug's game, at least so far as 'is' questions are concerned.

In this paper I shall use the term 'property' as a blanket term for such things as being in pain, being in a particular brain state, having a particular behavior disposition, and also for magnitudes such as temperature, etc.—i.e., for things which can naturally be represented by one-or-more-place predicates or functors. I shall use the term 'concept' for things which can be identified with synonymy-classes of expressions. Thus the concept *temperature* can be identified (I maintain) with the synonymy-class of the word 'temperature'. (This is like saying that the number 2 can be identified with the class of all pairs. This is quite a different statement from the peculiar statement that 2 *is* the class of all pairs. I do not maintain that concepts *are* synonymy-classes, whatever that might mean, but that they can be identified with synonymy-classes, for the purpose of formalization of the relevant discourse.)

The question 'What is the concept *temperature?*' is a very 'funny' one. One might take it to mean 'What is temperature? Please take my question as a conceptual one.' In that case an answer might be (pretend for a moment 'heat' and 'temperature' are synonyms) 'temperature is heat', or even 'the concept of temperature is the same concept as the concept of heat'. Or one might take it to mean 'What are *concepts,* really? For example, what is "the concept of temperature"?' In that case heaven knows what an 'answer' would be. (Perhaps it would be the statement that concepts *can be identified with* synonymy-classes.)

Of course, the question 'What is the property temperature?' is also 'funny'. And one way of interpreting it is to take it as a question about the concept of temperature. But this is not the way a physicist would take it.

The effect of saying that the property P_1 can be identical with the property P_2 only if the terms P_1, P_2 are in some suitable sense 'synonyms' is, to all intents and purposes, to collapse the two notions of 'property' and 'concept' into a single notion. The view that concepts (intensions) *are* the same as properties has been explicitly advocated by Carnap (e.g. in *Meaning and Necessity*). This seems an unfortunate view, since 'temperature is mean molecular kinetic energy' appears to be a perfectly good example of a true statement of identity of properties, whereas 'the concept of temperature is the same concept as a concept of mean molecular kinetic energy' is simply false.

Many philosophers believe that the statement 'pain is a brain state' violates some rules or norms of English.

Hilary Putnam, "The Nature of Mental States" from *Art, Mind, and Religion,* edited by W. H. Capitan and D. D. Merrill (Pittsburgh: University of Pittsburgh Press, 1967). Reprinted with the permission of the author.

But the arguments offered are hardly convincing. For example, if the fact that I can know that I am in pain without knowing that I am in brain state S shows that pain cannot be brain state S, then, by exactly the same argument, the fact that I can know that the stove is hot without knowing that the mean molecular kinetic energy is high (or even that molecules exist) shows that it is *false* that temperature is mean molecular kinetic energy, physics to the contrary. In fact, all that immediately follows from the fact that I can know that I am in pain without knowing that I am in brain state S is that the concept of pain is not the same concept as the concept of being in brain state S. But either pain, or the state of being in pain, or some pain, or some pain state, might still be brain state S. After all, the concept of temperature is not the same concept as the concept of mean molecular kinetic energy. But temperature is mean molecular kinetic energy.

Some philosophers maintain that both 'pain is a brain state' and 'pain states are brain states' are unintelligible. The answer is to explain to these philosophers, as well as we can, given the vagueness of all scientific methodology, what sorts of considerations lead one to make an empirical reduction (i.e. to say such things as 'water is H_2O', 'light is electro-magnetic radiation', 'temperature is mean molecular kinetic energy'). If, without giving reasons, he still maintains in the face of such examples that one cannot imagine parallel circumstances for the use of 'pains are brain states' (or, perhaps, 'pain states are brain states') one has grounds to regard him as perverse.

Some philosophers maintain that 'P_1 is P_2' is something that can be true, when the 'is' involved is the 'is' of empirical reduction, only when the properties P_1 and P_2 are (a) associated with a spatio-temporal region; and (b) the region is one and the same in both cases. Thus 'temperature is mean molecular kinetic energy' is an admissible empirical reduction, since the temperature and the molecular energy are associated with the same space-time region, but 'having a pain in my arm is being in a brain state' is not, since the spatial regions involved are different.

This argument does not appear very strong. Surely no one is going to be deterred from saying that mirror images are light reflected from an object and then from the surface of a mirror by the fact that an image can be 'located' three feet *behind* the mirror! (Moreover, one can always find *some* common property of the reductions one is willing to allow—e.g. temperature is mean molecular kinetic energy—which is not a property of some one identification one wishes to disallow. This is not very impressive unless one has an argument to show that the very purposes of such identification depend upon the common property in question.)

Again, other philosophers have contended that all the predictions that can be derived from the conjunction of neurophysiological laws with such statements as 'pain states are such-and-such brain states' can equally well be derived from the conjunction of the same neurophysiological laws with 'being in pain is correlated with such-and-such brain states', and hence (*sic!*) there can be no methodological grounds for saying that pains (or pain states) *are* brain states, as opposed to saying that they are *correlated* (invariantly) with brain states. This argument, too, would show that light is only correlated with electromagnetic radiation. The mistake is in ignoring the fact that, although the theories in question may indeed lead to the same predictions, they open and exclude different *questions*. 'Light is invariantly correlated with electromagnetic radiation' would leave open the questions 'What is the light then, if it isn't the same as the electromagnetic radiation?' And 'What makes the light accompany the electromagnetic radiation?'— questions which are excluded by saying that the light *is* the electromagnetic radiation. Similarly, the purpose of saying that pains are brain states is precisely to exclude from empirical meaningfulness the questions, 'What is the pain, then, if it isn't the same as the brain state?' and 'What makes the pain accompany the brain state?' If there are grounds to suggest that these questions represent, so to speak, the wrong way to look at the matter, then those grounds are grounds for a theoretical identification of pains with brain states.

If all arguments to the contrary are unconvincing, shall we then conclude that it is meaningful (and perhaps true) to say either that pains are brain states or that pain states are brain states?

(1) It is perfectly meaningful (violates no 'rule of English', involves no 'extension of usage') to say 'pains are brain states'.

(2) It is not meaningful (involves a 'changing of meaning' or 'an extension of usage', etc.) to say 'pains are brain states'.

My own position is not expressed by either (1) or (2). It seems to me that the notions 'change of meaning' and 'extension of usage' are simply so ill defined that one cannot in fact say *either* (1) or (2). I see no reason to believe that either the linguist, or the man-on-the-street, or the philosopher possesses today a notion of 'change of meaning' applicable to such cases as the one we have been discussing. The *job* for which the notion of change of meaning was developed in the history of the language was just a *much* cruder job that this one.

But, if we don't assert either (1) or (2)—in other words, if we regard the 'change of meaning' issue as a pseudo-issue in this case—then how are we to discuss the question with which we started? 'Is pain a brain state?'

The answer is to allow statements of the form 'pain is *A*', where 'pain' and '*A*' are in no sense synonyms, and to see whether any such statement can be found which might be acceptable on empirical and methodological grounds. This is what we shall now proceed to do.

II. Is Pain a Brain State?

We shall discuss 'Is pain a brain state?' then. And we have agreed to waive the 'change of meaning' issue.

Since I am discussing not what the concept of pain comes to, but what pain is, in a sense of 'is' which requires empirical theory-construction (or, at least, empirical speculation), I shall not apologize for advancing an empirical hypothesis. Indeed, my strategy will be to argue that pain is *not* a brain state, not on *a priori* grounds, but on the grounds that another hypothesis is more plausible. The detailed development and verification of my hypothesis would be just as Utopian a task as the detailed development and verification of the brain-state hypothesis. But the putting-forward, not of detailed and scientifically 'finished' hypotheses, but of schemata for hypotheses, has long been a function of philosophy. I shall, in short, argue that pain is not a brain state, in the sense of a physical-chemical state of the brain (or even the whole nervous system), but another

kind of state entirely. I propose the hypothesis that pain, or the state of being in pain, is a functional state of a whole organism.

To explain this it is necessary to introduce some technical notions. In previous papers I have explained the notion of a Turing Machine and discussed the use of this notion as a model for an organism. The notion of a Probabilistic Automaton is defined similarly to a Turing Machine, except that the transitions between 'states' are allowed to be with various probabilities rather then being 'deterministic'. (Of course, a Turing Machine is simply a special kind of Probabilistic Automaton, one with transition probabilities 0, 1). I shall assume the notion of a Probabilistic Automaton has been generalized to allow for 'sensory inputs' and 'motor outputs'—that is, the Machine Table specifies, for every possible combination of a 'state' and a complete set of 'sensory inputs', an 'instruction' which determines the probability of the next 'state', and also the probabilities of the 'motor outputs'. (This replaces the idea of the Machine as printing on a tape.) I shall also assume that the physical realization of the sense organs responsible for the various inputs, and of the motor organs, is specified, but that the 'states' and the 'inputs' themselves are, as usual, specified only 'implicitly'—i.e. by the set of transition probabilities given by the Machine Table.

Since an empirically given system can simultaneously be a 'physical realization' of many different Probabilistic Automata, I introduce the notion of a *Description* of a system. A Description of S where S is a system, is any true statement to the effect that S possesses distinct states, $S_1, S_2 \ldots S_n$ which are related to one another and to the motor outputs and sensory inputs by the transition probabilities given in such-and-such a Machine Table. The Machine Table mentioned in the Description will then be called the Functional Organization of S relative to that Description, and the S_i such that S is in state S_i at a given time will be called the Total State of S (at the time) relative to that Description. It should be noted that knowing the Total State of a system relative to a Description involves knowing a good deal about how the system is likely to 'behave', given various combinations of sensory inputs, but does *not* involve knowing the physical realization of the S_i as, e.g. physical-chemical states of the brain. The S_i, to repeat, are specified only *implicitly* by the Description—i.e. specified *only* by the set of transition probabilities given in the Machine Table.

The hypothesis that 'being in pain is a functional state of the organism' may now be spelled out more exactly as follows:

(1) All organisms capable of feeling pain are Probabilistic Automata.

(2) Every organism capable of feeling pain possesses at least one Description of a certain kind (i.e. being capable of feeling pain *is* possessing an appropriate kind of Functional Organization).

(3) No organism capable of feeling pain possesses a decomposition into parts which separately possess Descriptions of the kind referred to in (2).

(4) For every Description of the kind referred to in (2), there exists a subset of the sensory inputs such that an organism with that Description is in pain when and only when some of its sensory inputs are in that subset.

This hypothesis is admittedly vague, though surely no vaguer than the brain-state hypothesis in its present form. For example, one would like to know more about the kind of Functional Organization that an organism must have to be capable of feeling pain, and more about the marks that distinguish the subset of the sensory inputs referred to in (4). With respect to the first question, one can probably say that the Functional Organization must include something that resembles a 'preference function', or at least a preference partial ordering and something that resembles an 'inductive logic' (i.e. the Machine must be able to 'learn from experience'). [. . .] In addition, it seems natural to require that the Machine possess 'pain sensors', i.e. sensory organs which normally signal damage to the Machine's body, or dangerous temperatures, pressures, etc., which transmit a special subset of the inputs, the subset referred to in (4). Finally, we would want to require at least that the inputs in the distinguished subset have a high disvalue on the Machine's preference function or ordering (further conditions are discussed in the previous chapter). The purpose of condition (3) is to rule out such 'organisms'

(if they can count as such) as swarms of bees as single pain-feelers. The condition (1) is, obviously, redundant, and is only introduced for expository reasons. (It is, in fact, empty, since everything is a Probabilistic Automaton under *some* Description.)

I contend, in passing, that this hypothesis, in spite of its admitted vagueness, is far *less* vague than the 'physical-chemical state' hypothesis is today, and far more susceptible to investigation of both a mathematical and an empirical kind. Indeed, to investigate this hypothesis is just to attempt to produce 'mechanical' models of organisms—and isn't this, in a sense, just what psychology is about? The difficult step, of course, will be to pass from models to *specific* organisms to a *normal form* for the psychological description of organisms—for this is what is required to make (2) and (4) precise. But this too seems to be an inevitable part of the program of psychology.

I shall now compare the hypothesis just advanced with (a) the hypothesis that pain is a brain state, and (b) the hypothesis that pain is a behavior disposition.

III. Functional State versus Brain State

It may, perhaps, be asked if I am not somewhat unfair in taking the brain-state theorist to be talking about *physical-chemical* states of the brain. But (a) these are the only sorts of states ever mentioned by brain-state theorists. (b) The brain-state theorist usually mentions (with a certain pride, slightly reminiscent of the Village Atheist) the incompatibility of his hypothesis with all forms of dualism and mentalism. This is natural if physical-chemical states of the brain are what is at issue. However, functional states of whole systems are something quite different. In particular, the functional-state hypothesis is *not* incompatible with dualism! Although it goes without saying that the hypothesis is 'mechanistic' in its inspiration, it is a slightly remarkable fact that a system consisting of a body and a 'soul', if such things there be, can perfectly well be a Probabilistic Automaton. (c) One argument advanced by Smart is that the brain-state theory assumes only 'physical' properties, and Smart finds 'non-physical' properties unintelligible. The Total States and the 'inputs' defined above are, of course, neither mental nor physical *per se,* and I cannot imagine a functionalist advancing this argument. (d) If the brain-state theorist does mean (or at least allow) states other than physical-chemical states, then his hypothesis is completely empty, at least until he specifies *what* sort of 'states' he *does* mean.

Taking the brain-state hypothesis in this way, then, what reasons are there to prefer the functional-state hypothesis over the brain-state hypothesis? Consider what the brain-state theorist has to do to make good his claims. He has to specify a physical-chemical state such that *any* organism (not just a mammal) is in pain if and only if (a) it possesses a brain of a suitable physical-chemical structure; and (b) its brain is in that physical-chemical state. This means that the physical-chemical state in question must be a possible state of a mammalian brain, a reptilian brain, a mollusc's brain (octopuses are mollusca, and certainly feel pain), etc. At the same time, it must *not* be a possible (physically possible) state of the brain of any physically possible creature that cannot feel pain. Even if such a state can be found, it must be nomologically certain that it will also be a state of the brain of any extraterrestrial life that may be found that will be capable of feeling pain before we can even entertain the supposition that it may *be* pain.

It is not altogether impossible that such a state will be found. Even though octopus and mammal are examples of parallel (rather than sequential) evolution, for example, virtually identical structures (physically speaking) have evolved in the eye of the octopus and in the eye of the mammal, notwithstanding the fact that this organ has evolved from different kinds of cells in the two cases. Thus it is at least possible that parallel evolution, all over the universe, might *always* lead to *one and the same* physical 'correlate' of pain. But this is certainly an ambitious hypothesis.

Finally, the hypothesis becomes still more ambitious when we realize that the brain-state theorist is not just saying that *pain* is a brain state; he is, of course, concerned to maintain that *every* psychological state is a brain state. Thus if we can find even one psychological predicate which can clearly be applied to both a mammal and an octopus (say 'hungry'), but whose physical-chemical 'correlate' is different in the two cases, the brain-state theory has collapsed. It seems to me overwhelmingly probably that we can do this. Granted, in

such a case the brain-state theorist can save himself by *ad hoc* assumptions (e.g. defining the disjunction of two states to be a single 'physical-chemical state'), but this does not have to be taken seriously.

Turning now to the considerations *for* the functional-state theory, let us begin with the fact that we identify organisms as in pains, or hungry, or angry, or in heat, etc., on the basis of their *behavior.* But it is a truism that similarities in the behavior of two systems are at least a reason to suspect similarities in the functional organization of the two systems, and a much *weaker* reason to suspect similarities in the actual physical details. Moreover, we expect the various psychological states—at least the basic ones, such as hunger, thirst, aggression, etc.—to have more or less similar 'transition probabilities' (within wide and ill defined limits, to be sure) with each other and with behavior in the case of different species, because this is an artifact of the way in which we identify these states. Thus, we would not count an animal as *thirsty* if its 'unsatiated' behavior did not seem to be directed toward drinking and was not followed by 'satiation for liquid'. Thus any animal that we count as capable of these various states will at least *seem* to have a certain rough kind of functional organization. And, as already remarked, if the program of finding psychological laws that are not species-specific—i.e. of finding a normal form for psychological theories of different species—ever succeeds, then it will bring in its wake a delineation of the kind of functional organization that is necessary and sufficient for a given psychological state, as well as a precise definition of the notion 'psychological state'. In contrast, the brain-state theorist has to hope for the eventual development of neurophysiological laws that are species-independent, which seems much less reasonable than the hope that psychological laws (of a sufficiently general kind) may be species-independent, or, still weaker, that a species-independent *form* can be found in which psychological laws can be written.

IV. Functional State versus Behavior-Disposition

The theory that being in pain is neither a brain state nor a functional state but a behavior disposition has one apparent advantage: it appears to agree with the way in which we verify that organisms are in pain. We do not in practice know anything about the brain state of an animal when we say that it is in pain; and we possess little if any knowledge of its functional organization, except in a crude intuitive way. In fact, however, this 'advantage' is no advantage at all: for, although statements about how we verify that x is A may have a good deal to do with what the concept of being A comes to, they have precious little to do with what the property A *is*. To argue on the ground just mentioned that pain is neither a brain state nor a functional state is like arguing that heat is not mean molecular kinetic energy from the fact that ordinary people do not (they think) ascertain the mean molecular kinetic energy of something when they verify that it is hot or cold. It is not necessary that they should; what is necessary is that the marks that they take as indications of heat should in fact be explained by the mean molecular kinetic energy. And, similarly, it is necessary to our hypothesis that the marks that are taken as behavioral indications of pain should be explained by the fact that the organism is a functional state of the appropriate kind, but not that speakers should *know* that this is so.

The difficulties with 'behavior disposition' accounts are so well known that I shall do little more than recall them here. The difficulty—it appears to be more than a 'difficulty', in fact—of specifying the required behavior disposition except as 'the disposition of X to behave as if X were in *pain*', is the chief one, of course. In contrast, we *can* specify the functional state with which we propose to identify pain, at least roughly, without using the notion of pain. Namely, the functional state we have in mind is the state of receiving sensory inputs which play a certain role in the Functional Organization of the organism. This role is characterized, at least partially, by the fact that the sense organs responsible for the inputs in question are organs whose function is to detect damage to the body, or dangerous extremes of temperature, pressure, etc., and by the fact that the 'inputs' themselves, whatever their physical realization, represent a condition that the organism assigns a high disvalue to. As I stressed in 'The mental life of some machines' this does *not* mean that the Machine will always *avoid* being in the condition in question ('pain'); it only means that the condition will be avoided unless not avoiding it is necessary to the attainment of some more highly valued

goal. Since the behavior of the Machine (in this case, an organism) will depend not merely on the sensory inputs, but also on the Total State (i.e. on other values, beliefs, etc.), it seems hopeless to make any general statement about how an organism in such a condition *must* behave; but this does not mean that we must abandon hope of characterizing the condition. Indeed, we have just characterized it.

Not only does the behavior-disposition theory seem hopelessly vague; if the 'behavior' referred to is peripheral behavior, and the relevant stimuli are peripheral stimuli (e.g. we do not say anything about what the organism will do it its brain is operated upon), then the theory seems clearly false. For example, two animals with all motor nerves cut will have the same actual and potential 'behavior' (namely, none to speak of); but if one has cut pain fibers and the other has uncut pain fibers, then one will feel pain and the other won't. Again, if one person has cut pain fibers, and another suppresses all pain responses deliberately due to some strong compulsion, then the actual and potential peripheral behavior may be the same, but one will feel pain and the other won't. (Some philosophers maintain that this last case is conceptually impossible, but the only evidence for this appears to be that *they* can't, or don't want to, conceive of it.) If, instead of pain, we take some sensation the 'bodily expression' of which is easier to suppress—say, a slight coolness in one's left little finger—the case becomes even clearer.

Finally, even if there *were* some behavior disposition invariantly correlated with pain (species-independently!), and specifiable without using the term 'pain', it would still be more plausible to identify being in pain with some state whose presence *explains* this behavior disposition—the brain state or functional state—than with the behavior disposition itself. Such considerations of plausibility may be somewhat subjective; but if other things *were* equal (of course, they aren't) why shouldn't we allow considerations of plausibility to play the deciding role?

V. Methodological Considerations

So far we have considered only what might be called the 'empirical' reasons for saying that being in pain is a functional state, rather than a brain state or a behavior disposition; namely, that it seems more likely that the functional state we described is invariantly 'correlated' with pain, species-independently, than that there is either a physical-chemical state of the brain (must an organism have a *brain* to feel pain? perhaps some ganglia will do) or a behavior disposition so correlated. If this is correct, then it follows that the identification we proposed is at least a candidate for consideration. What of methodological considerations?

The methodological considerations are roughly similar in all cases of reduction, so no surprises need be expected here. First, identification of psychological states with functional states means that the laws of psychology can be derived from statements of the form 'such-and-such organisms have such-and-such Descriptions' together with the identification statements ('being in pain is such-and-such a functional state', etc.). Secondly, the presences of the functional state (i.e. of inputs) which play the role we have described in the Functional Organization of the organisms is not merely 'correlated with' but actually explains the pain behavior on the part of the organism. Thirdly, the identification serves to exclude questions which (if a naturalistic view is correct) represent an altogether wrong way of looking at the matter, e.g. 'What *is* pain if it isn't either the brain state or the functional state?' and 'What causes the pain to be always accompanied by this sort of functional state?' In short, the identification is to be tentatively accepted as a theory which leads to both fruitful predictions and to fruitful *questions,* and which serves to discourage fruitless and empirically senseless questions, where by 'empirically senseless' I mean 'senseless' not merely from the standpoint of verification, but from the standpoint of what there in fact *is.*

Daniel Dennett

The Intentional Stance and Why It Works

Death Speaks

There was a merchant in Baghdad who sent his servant to market to buy provisions and in a little while the servant came back, white and trembling, and said, Master, just now when I was in the market-place I was jostled by a woman in the crowd and when I turned I saw it was Death that jostled me. She looked at me and made a threatening gesture; now, lend me your horse, and I will ride away from this city and avoid my fate. I will go to Samarra and there Death will not find me. The merchant lent him his horse, and the servant mounted it, and he dug his spurs in its flanks and as fast as the horse could gallop he went. Then the merchant went down to the market-place and he saw me standing in the crowd, and he came to me and said, why did you make a threatening gesture to my servant when you saw him this morning? That was not a threatening gesture, I said, it was only a start of surprise. I was astonished to see him in Baghdad, for I had an appointment with him tonight in Samarra.

W. Somerset Maugham

Daniel C. Dennett, "True Believers: The Intentional Stance and Why It Works" from *Scientific Explanation: Papers Based on Herbert Spencer Lectures Given in the University of Oxford,* edited by A. F. Heath. Copyright © 1981. Reprinted with the permission of Oxford University Press, Ltd.

In the social sciences, talk about *belief* is ubiquitous. Since social scientists are typically self-conscious about their methods, there is also a lot of talk about *talk about belief.* And since belief is a genuinely curious and perplexing phenomenon, showing many different faces to the world, there is abundant controversy. Sometimes belief attribution appears to be a dark, risky, and imponderable business—especially when exotic, and more particularly religious or superstitious, beliefs are in the limelight. These are not the only troublesome cases; we also court argument and skepticism when we attribute beliefs to nonhuman animals, or to infants, or to computers or robots. Or when the beliefs we feel constrained to attribute to an apparently healthy, adult member of our own society are contradictory, or even just wildly false. A biologist colleague of mine was once called on the telephone by a man in a bar who wanted him to settle a bet. The man asked: "Are rabbits birds?" "No" said the biologist. "Damn!" said the man as he hung up. Now could he *really* have believed that rabbits were birds? Could anyone really and truly be attributed that belief? Perhaps, but it would take a bit of a story to bring us to accept it.

In all of these cases belief attribution appears beset with subjectivity, infected with cultural relativism, prone to "indeterminacy of radical translation"—clearly an enterprise demanding special talents: the art of phenomenological analysis, hermeneutics, empathy, *Verstenhen,* and all that. On other occasions, normal occasions, when familiar beliefs are the topic, belief attribution looks as easy as speaking prose and as objective and reliable as counting beans in a dish. Particularly when these straightforward cases are before us, it is quite plausible to suppose that in principle (if not yet in practice) it would be possible to confirm these simple, objective belief attributions by *finding something inside the believer's head*—by finding the beliefs themselves, in effect. "Look," someone might say, "You either believe there's milk in the fridge or you don't believe there's milk in the fridge" (you might have no opinion, in the latter case). But if you do believe this, that's a perfectly objective fact about you, and it must come down in the end to your brain's being in some particular physical state. If we knew more about physiological psychology, we could in principle determine the facts about your brain state and thereby determine whether or not you believe there is milk in the fridge, even if you were determined to be silent or disingenuous on the topic. In principle,

on this view physiological psychology could trump the results—or non-results—of any "black box" method in the social sciences that divines beliefs (and other mental features) by behavioral, cultural, social, historical, *external* criteria.

These differing reflections congeal into two opposing views on the nature of belief attribution, and hence on the nature of belief. The latter, a variety of *realism,* likens the question of whether a person has a particular belief to the question of whether a person is infected with a particular virus—a perfectly objective internal matter of fact about which an observer can often make educated guesses of great reliability. The former, which we could call *interpretationism* if we absolutely had to give it a name, likens the question of whether a person has a particular belief to the question of whether a person is immoral, or has style, or talent, or would make a good wife. Faced with such questions, we preface our answers with "well, it all depends on what you're interested in," or make some similar acknowledgment of the relativity of the issue. "It's a matter of interpretation," we say. These two opposing views, so baldly stated, do not fairly represent any serious theorists' positions, but they do express views that are typically seen as mutually exclusive and exhaustive; the theorist must be friendly with one and only one of these themes.

I think this is a mistake. My thesis will be that while belief is a perfectly objective phenomenon (that apparently makes me a realist), it can be discerned only from the point of view of one who adopts a certain *predictive strategy,* and its existence can be confirmed only by an assessment of the success of that strategy (that apparently makes me an interpretationist).

First I will describe the strategy, which I call the intentional strategy or adopting the intentional stance. To a first approximation, the intentional strategy consists of treating the object whose behavior you want to predict as a rational agent with beliefs and desires and other mental stages exhibiting what Brentano and others call *intentionality.* The strategy has often been described before, but I shall try to put this very familiar material in a new light by showing *how* it works and by showing *how well* it works.

Then I will argue that any object—or as I shall say, any *system*—whose behavior is well predicted by this strategy is in the fullest sense of the word a believer.

What it is to be a true believer is to be an *intentional system,* a system whose behavior is reliably and voluminously predictable via the intentional strategy. I have argued for this position before, and my arguments have so far garnered few converts and many presumed counterexamples. I shall try again here, harder, and shall also deal with several compelling objections.

The Intentional Strategy and How It Works

There are many strategies, some good, some bad. Here is a strategy, for instance, for predicting the future behavior of a person: determine the date and hour of the person's birth and then feed this modest datum into one or another astrological algorithm for generating predictions of the person's prospects. This strategy is deplorably popular. Its popularity is deplorable only because we have such good reasons for believing that it does not work. When astrological predictions come true this is sheer luck, or the result of such vagueness or ambiguity in the prophecy that almost any eventuality can be construed to confirm it. But suppose the astrological strategy did in fact work well on some people. We could call those people *astrological systems*—systems whose behavior was, as a matter of fact, predictable by the astrological strategy. If there were such people, such astrological systems, we would be more interested than most of us in fact are in *how the astrological strategy works* —that is, we would be interested in the rules, principles, or methods of astrology. We could find out how the strategy works by asking astrologers, reading their books, and observing them in action. But we would also be curious about *why* it worked. We might find that astrologers had no useful opinions about this latter question—they either had no theory of why it worked or their theories were pure hokum. Having a good strategy is one thing; knowing why it works is another.

So far as we know, however, the class of astrological systems is empty, so the astrological strategy is of interest only as a social curiosity. Other strategies have better credentials. Consider the physical strategy, or physical stance; if you want to predict the behavior of a system, determine its physical constitution (perhaps all the way down to the microphysical level) and the phys-

ical nature of the impingements upon it, and use your knowledge of the laws of physics to predict the outcome for any input. This is the grand and impractical strategy of Laplace for predicting the entire future of everything in the universe, but it has more modest, local, actually usable versions. The chemist or physicist in the laboratory can use this strategy to predict the behavior of exotic materials, but equally the cook in the kitchen can predict the effect of leaving the pot on the burner too long. The strategy is not always practically available, but that it will always work *in principle* is a dogma of the physical sciences (I ignore the minor complications raised by the subatomic indeterminacies of quantum physics).

Sometimes, in any event, it is more effective to switch from the physical stance to what I call the design stance, where one ignores the actual (possibly messy) details of the physical constitution of an object, and, on the assumption that it has a certain design, predicts that it will behave *as it is designed to behave* under various circumstances. For instance, most users of computers have not the foggiest idea what physical principles are responsible for the computer's highly reliable, and hence predictable, behavior. But if they have a good idea of what the computer is designed to do (a description of its operation at any one of the many possible levels of abstraction), they can predict its behavior with great accuracy and reliability, subject to disconfirmation only in cases of physical malfunction. Less dramatically, almost anyone can predict when an alarm clock will sound on the basis of the most casual inspection of its exterior. One does not know or care to know whether it is spring wound, battery driven, sunlight powered, made of brass wheels and jewel bearings or silicon chips—one just assumes that it is designed so that the alarm will sound when it is set to sound, and it is set to sound where it appears to be set to sound, and the clock will keep on running until that time and beyond, and is designed to run more or less accurately, and so forth. For more accurate and detailed design stance predictions of the alarm clock, one must descend to a less abstract level of description of its design; for instance, to the level at which gears are described, but their material is not specified.

Only the designed behavior of a system is predictable from the design stance, of course. If you want to predict the behavior of an alarm clock when it is pumped full of liquid helium, revert to the physical stance. Not just artifacts but also many biological objects (plants and animals, kidneys and hearts, stamens and pistils) behave in ways that can be predicted from the design stance. They are not just physical systems but designed systems.

Sometimes even the design stance is practically inaccessible, and then there is yet another stance or strategy one can adopt: the intentional stance. Here is how it works: first you decide to treat the object whose behavior is to be predicted as a rational agent; then you figure out what beliefs that agent ought to have, given its place in the world and its purpose. Then you figure out what desires it ought to have, on the same considerations, and finally you predict that this rational agent will act to further its goals in the light of its beliefs. A little practical reasoning from the chosen set of beliefs and desires will in many—but not all—instances yield a decision about what the agent ought to do; that is what you predict the agent *will* do.

The strategy becomes clearer with a little elaboration. Consider first how we go about populating each other's heads with beliefs. A few truisms: sheltered people tend to be ignorant; if you expose someone to something he comes to know all about it. In general, it seems, we come to believe all the truths about the parts of the world around us we are put in a position to learn about. Exposure to *x,* that is, sensory confrontation with *x* over some suitable period of time, is the *normally sufficient* condition for knowing (or having true beliefs) about *x*. As we say, we come to *know all about* the things around us. Such exposure is only *normally* sufficient for knowledge, but this is not the large escape hatch it might appear; our threshold for accepting abnormal ignorance in the face of exposure is quite high. "I didn't know the gun was loaded," said by one who was observed to be present, sighted, and awake during the loading, meets with a variety of utter skepticism that only the most outlandish supporting tale could overwhelm.

Of course we do not come to learn or remember all the truths our sensory histories avail us. In spite of the phrase "know all about," what we come to know, normally, are only all the *relevant* truths our sensory histories avail us. I do not typically come to know the ratio of spectacle-wearing people to trousered people in a room I inhabit, though if this interested me, it would be readily learnable. It is not just that some facts about my environment are below my thresholds of discrimination or beyond the integration and holding power of my memory (such as the height in inches of all the people present), but that many perfectly detectable, graspable, memorable facts are of no interest to me and hence do not come to be believed by me. So one rule for attributing beliefs in the intentional strategy is this: attribute as beliefs all the truths relevant to the system's interests (or desires) that the system's experience to date has made available. This rule leads to attributing somewhat too much—since we all are somewhat forgetful, even of important things. It also fails to capture the false beliefs we are all known to have. But the attribution of false belief, *any* false belief, requires a special genealogy, which will be seen to consist in the main in true beliefs. Two paradigm cases: S believes (falsely) that *p,* because S believes (truly) that Jones told him that *p,* that Jones is pretty clever, that Jones did not intend to deceive him, . . . etc. Second case: S believes (falsely) that there is a snake on the barstool, because S believes (truly) that he seems to see a snake on the barstool, is himself sitting in a bar not a yard from the barstool he sees, and so forth. The falsehood has to start somewhere; the seed may be sown in hallucination, illusion, a normal variety of simple misperception, memory deterioration, or deliberate fraud, for instance, but the false beliefs that are reaped grow in a culture medium of true beliefs.

Then there are the arcane and sophisticated beliefs, true and false, that are so often at the focus of attention in discussions of belief attribution. They do not arise directly, goodness knows, from exposure to mundane things and events, but their attribution requires tracing out a lineage of mainly good argument or reasoning from the bulk of beliefs already attributed. An implication of the intentional strategy, then, is that true believers mainly believe truths. If anyone could devise an agreed-upon method of individuating and counting beliefs (which I doubt very much), we would see that all but the smallest portion (say, less than ten percent) of a person's beliefs were attributable under our first rule.

Note that this rule is a derived rule, an elaboration and further specification of the fundamental rule: attribute those beliefs the system *ought to have.* Note also that the rule interacts with the attribution of desires. How do we attribute the desires (preferences, goals, interests) on whose basis we will shape the list of beliefs? We attribute the desires the system *ought to have.* That is the fundamental rule. It dictates, on a first pass, that we attribute the familiar list of highest, or most basic, desires to people: survival, absence of pain, food, comfort, procreation, entertainment. Citing any one of these desires typically terminates the "Why?" game of reason giving. One is not supposed to need an ulterior motive for desiring comfort or pleasure or the prolongation of one's existence. Derived rules of desire attribution interact with belief attributions. Trivially, we have the rule: attribute desires for those things a system believes to be good for it. Somewhat more informatively, attribute desires for those things a system believes to be best means to other ends it desires. The attribution of bizarre and detrimental desires thus requires, like the attribution of false beliefs, special stories.

The interaction between belief and desire becomes trickier when we consider what desires we attribute on the basis of verbal behavior. The capacity to *express* desires in language opens the floodgates of desire attribution. "I want a two-egg mushroom omelette, some French bread and butter, and a half bottle of lightly chilled white Burgundy." How could one begin to attribute a desire for anything so specific in the absence of such verbal declaration? How, indeed, could a creature come to *contract* such a specific desire without the aid of language? Language *enables* us to formulate highly specific desires, but it also *forces* us on occasion to commit ourselves to desires altogether more stringent in their conditions of satisfaction than anything we would otherwise have any reason to endeavor to satisfy. Since in order to get what you want you often have to say what you want, and since you often cannot say what you want without saying something more specific than you antecedently mean, you often end up giving others evidence—the very best of evidence, your unextorted word—that you desire things or states of affairs far more particular than would satisfy you—or better, than would have satisfied you, for once you have declared, being a man of your word, you acquire an interest in satisfying exactly the desire you declared and no other.

"I'd like some baked beans, please."

"Yes sir. How many?"

You might well object to having such a specification of desire demanded of you, but in fact we are all social-

ized to accede to similar requirements in daily life—to the point of not noticing it, and certainly not feeling oppressed by it. I dwell on this because it has a parallel in the realm of belief, where our linguistic environment is forever forcing us to give—or concede—precise verbal expression to convictions that lack the hard edges verbalization endows them with. By concentrating on the *results* of this social force, while ignoring its distorting effect, one can easily be misled into thinking that it is *obvious* that beliefs and desires are rather like sentences stored in the head. Being language-using creatures, it is inevitable that we should often come to believe that some particular, actually formulated, spelled and punctuated sentence *is true,* and that on other occasions we should come to want such a sentence to *come true,* but these are special cases of belief and desire and as such may not be reliable models for the whole domain.

That is enough, on this occasion, about the principles of belief and desire attribution to be found in the intentional strategy. What about the rationality one attributes to an intentional system? One starts with the ideal of perfect rationality and revises downward as circumstances dictate. That is, one starts with the assumption that people believe all the implications of their beliefs and believe no contradictory pairs of beliefs. This does not create a practical problem of clutter (infinitely many implications, for instance), for one is interested only in ensuring that the system one is predicting is rational enough to get to the particular implications that are relevant to its behavioral predicament of the moment. Instances of irrationality, or of finitely powerful capacities of inferences, raise particularly knotty problems of interpretation, which I will set aside.

For I want to turn from the description of the strategy to the question of its use. Do people actually use this strategy? Yes, all the time. There may someday be other strategies for attributing belief and desire and for predicting behavior, but this is the only one we all know now. And when does it work? It works with people almost all the time. Why would it *not* be a good idea to allow individual Oxford colleges to create and grant academic degrees whenever they saw fit? The answer is a long story, but very easy to generate. And there would be widespread agreement about the major points. We have no difficulty thinking of the reasons people would then have for acting in such ways as to give others reasons for acting in such ways as to give others reasons for . . . creating a circumstance we would not want. Our use of the intentional strategy is so habitual and effortless that the role it plays in shaping our expectations about people is easily overlooked. The strategy also works on most other mammals most of the time. For instance, you can use it to design better traps to catch those mammals, by reasoning about what the creature knows or believes about various things, what it prefers, what it wants to avoid. The strategy works on birds, and on fish, and on reptiles, and on insects and spiders, and even on such lowly and unenterprising creatures as clams (once a clam believes there is danger about, it will not relax its grip on its closed shell until it is convinced that the danger has passed). It also works on some artifacts: the chess-playing computer will not take your knight because it knows that there is a line of ensuing play that would lead to losing its rook, and it does not want that to happen. More modestly, the thermostat will turn off the boiler as soon as it comes to believe the room has reached the desired temperature.

The strategy even works for plants. In a locale with late spring storms, you should plant apple varieties that are particularly *cautious* about *concluding* that it is spring —which is when they *want* to blossom, of course. It even works for such inanimate and apparently undesigned phenomena as lightning. An electrician once explained to me how he worked out how to protect my underground water pump from lightning damage: lightning, he said, always wants to find the best way to ground, but sometimes it gets tricked into taking second-best paths. You can protect the pump by making another, better path more *obvious* to the lightning.

True Believers as Intentional Systems

Now clearly this is a motley assortment of "serious" belief attributions, dubious belief attributions, pedagogically useful metaphors, *falçons de parler,* and, perhaps worse, outright frauds. The next task would seem to be distinguishing those intentional systems that *really* have beliefs and desires from those we may find it handy to treat *as if* they had beliefs and desires. But that would be a Sisyphean labor, or else would be terminated by fiat.

A better understanding of the phenomenon of belief begins with the observation that even in the worst of these cases, even when we are surest that the strategy works *for the wrong reasons,* it is nevertheless true that it does work, at least a little bit. This is an interesting fact, which distinguishes this class of objects, the class of *intentional systems,* from the class of objects for which the strategy never works. But is this so? Does our definition of an intentional system exclude any objects at all? For instance, it seems the lectern in this lecture room can be construed as an intentional system, fully rational, believing that it is currently located at the center of the civilized world (as some of you may also think), and desiring above all else to remain at that center. What should such a rational agent so equipped with belief and desire do? Stay put, clearly, which is just what the lectern does. I predict the lectern's behavior, accurately, from the intentional stance, so is it an intentional system? If it is, anything at all is.

What should disqualify the lectern? For one thing, the strategy does not recommend itself in this case, for we get no predictive power from it that we did not antecedently have. We already knew what the lectern was going to do—namely nothing—and tailored the beliefs and desires to fit in a quite unprincipled way. In the case of people or animals or computers, however, the situation is different. In these cases often the only strategy that is at all practical is the intentional strategy; it gives us predictive power we can get by no other method. But, it will be urged, this is no difference in nature, but merely a difference that reflects upon our limited capacities as scientists. The Laplacean omniscient physicist could predict the behavior of a computer—or of a live human body, assuming it to be ultimately governed by the laws of physics—without any need for the risky, short-cut methods of either the design or intentional strategies. For people of limited mechanical aptitude, the intentional interpretation of a simple thermostat is a handy and largely innocuous crutch, but the engineers among us can quite fully grasp its internal operation without the aid of this anthropomorphizing. It may be true that the cleverest engineers find it practically impossible to maintain a clear conception of more complex systems, such as a time-sharing computer system or remote-controlled space probe, without lapsing into an intentional stance (and viewing these devices as asking and telling, trying and avoiding, wanting and believing), but this is just a more advanced case of human epistemic frailty. We would not want to classify these artifacts with the true believers—ourselves—on such variable and parochial grounds, would we? Would it not be intolerable to hold that some artifact or creature or person was a believer from the point of view of one observer, but not a believer at all from the point of view of another, cleverer observer? That would be a particularly radical version of interpretationism, and some have thought I espoused it in urging that belief be viewed in terms of the success of the intentional strategy. I must confess that my presentation of the view has sometimes invited that reading, but I now want to discourage it. The decision to adopt the intentional stance is free, but the facts about the success or failure of the stance, were one to adopt it, are perfectly objective.

Once the intentional strategy is in place, it is an extraordinarily powerful tool in prediction—a fact that is largely concealed by our typical concentration on the cases in which it yields dubious or unreliable results. Consider, for instance, predicting moves in a chess game. What makes chess an interesting game, one can see, is the *un*predictability of one's opponent's moves, except in those cases where moves are "forced"—where there is *clearly* one best move—typically the least of the available evils. But this unpredictability is put in context when one recognizes that in the typical chess situation there are very many perfectly legal and hence available moves, but only a few—perhaps half a dozen—with anything to be said for them, and hence only a few high-probability moves according to the intentional strategy. Even when the intentional strategy fails to distinguish a single move with a highest probability, it can dramatically reduce the number of live options.

The same feature is apparent when the intentional strategy is applied to "real world" cases. It is notoriously unable to predict the exact purchase and sell decisions of stock traders, for instance, or the exact sequence of words a politician will utter when making a scheduled speech, but one's confidence can be very high indeed about slightly less specific predictions: that the particular trader *will not buy utilities today,* or that the politician *will side with the unions against his party,* for example. This inability to predict fine-grained descriptions of actions, looked at another way, is a source of strength for the in-

tentional strategy, for it is this neutrality with regard to details of implementation that permits one to exploit the intentional strategy in complex cases, for instance, in *chaining predictions.* Suppose the US Secretary of State were to announce he was a paid agent of the KGB. What an unparalleled event! How unpredictable its consequences! Yet in fact we can predict dozens of not terribly interesting but perfectly salient consequences, and consequences of consequences. The President would confer with the rest of the Cabinet, which would support his decision to relieve the Secretary of State of his duties pending the results of various investigations, psychiatric and political, and all this would be reported at a news conference to people who would write stories that would be commented upon in editorials that would be read by people who would write letters to the editors, and so forth. None of that is daring prognostication, but note that it describes an arc of causation in space-time that could not be predicted under *any* description by any imaginable practical extension of physics or biology.

The power of the intentional strategy can be seen even more sharply with the aid of an objection first raised by Robert Nozick some years ago. Suppose, he suggested, some beings of vastly superior intelligence—from Mars, let us say—were to descend upon us, and suppose that we were to them as simple thermostats are to clever engineers. Suppose, that is, that they did not *need* the intentional stance—or even the design stance—to predict our behavior in all its detail. They can be supposed to be Laplacean super-physicists, capable of comprehending the activity on Wall Street, for instance, at the microphysical level. Where we see brokers and buildings and sell orders and bids, they see vast congeries of subatomic particles milling about—and they are such good physicists that they can predict days in advance what ink marks will appear each day on the paper tape labeled "Closing Dow Jones Industrial Average." They can predict the individual behaviors of all the various moving bodies they observe without ever treating any of them as intentional systems. Would we be right then to say that from *their* point of view we really were not believers at all (any more than a simple thermostat is)? If so, then our status as believers is nothing objective, but rather something in the eye of the beholder—provided the beholder shares our intellectual limitations.

Our imagined Martians might be able to predict the future of the human race by Laplacean methods, but if they did not also see us as intentional systems they would be missing something perfectly objective: the *patterns* in human behavior that are describable from the intentional stance, and only from that stance, and that support generalizations and predictions. Take a particular instance in which the Martians observe a stockbroker deciding to place an order for 500 shares of General Motors. They predict the exact motions of his fingers as he dials the phone and the exact vibrations of his vocal cords as he intones his order. But if the Martians do not see that indefinitely many *different* patterns of finger motions and vocal cord vibrations—even the motions of indefinitely many different individuals—could have been substituted for the actual particulars without perturbing the subsequent operation of the market, then they have failed to see a real pattern in the world they are observing. Just as there are indefinitely many ways of *being a spark plug*—and one has not understood what an internal combustion engine is unless one realizes that a variety of different devices can be screwed into these sockets without affecting the performance of the engine—so there are indefinitely many ways of *ordering 500 shares of General Motors,* and there are societal sockets in which one of these ways will produce just about the same effect as any other. There are also societal pivot points, as it were, where which way people go depends on whether they *believe that p,* or *desire A,* and does not depend on any of the other infinitely many ways they may be alike or different.

Suppose, pursuing our Martian fantasy a little further, that one of the Martians were to engage in a predicting contest with an Earthling. The Earthling and the Martian observe (and observe each other observing) a particular bit of local physical transaction. From the Earthling's point of view, this is what is observed. The telephone rings in Mrs. Gardner's kitchen. She answers, and this is what she says: "Oh, hello dear. You're coming home early? Within the hour? And bringing the boss to dinner? Pick up a bottle of wine on the way home, then, and drive carefully." On the basis of this observation, our Earthling predicts that a large metallic vehicle with rubber tires will come to a stop in the drive within one hour, disgorging two human beings, one of whom will be holding a paper bag containing a bottle

containing an alcoholic fluid. The prediction is a bit risky, perhaps, but a good bet on all counts. The Martian makes the same prediction, but has to avail himself of much more information 'about an extraordinary number of interactions of which, so far as he can tell, the Earthling is entirely ignorant. For instance, the deceleration of the vehicle at intersection *A,* five miles from the house, without which there would have been a collision with another vehicle—whose collision course had been laboriously calculated over some hundreds of meters by the Martian. The Earthling's performance would look like magic! How did the Earthling know that the human being who got out of the car and got the bottle in the shop would get back in? The coming true of the Earthling's prediction, after all the vagaries, intersections, and branches in the paths charted by the Martian, would seem to anyone bereft of the intentional strategy as marvelous and inexplicable as the fatalistic inevitability of the appointment in Samarra. Fatalists—for instance, astrologers—believe that there is a pattern in human affairs that is inexorable, that will impose itself *come what may,* that is, no matter how the victims scheme and second-guess, no matter how they twist and turn in their chains. These fatalists are wrong, but they are *almost* right. There *are* patterns in human affairs that impose themselves, not quite inexorably but with great vigor, absorbing physical perturbations and variations that might as well be considered random; these are the patterns that we characterize in terms of the beliefs, desires, and intentions of rational agents.

No doubt you will have noticed, and been distracted by, a serious flaw in our thought experiment: the Martian is presumed to treat his Earthling opponent as an intelligent being like himself, with whom communication is possible, a being with whom one can make a wager, against whom one can compete. In short, a being with beliefs (such as the belief he expressed in his prediction) and desires (such as the desire to win the prediction contest). So if the Martian sees the pattern in one Earthling, how can he fail to see it in the others? As a bit of narrative, our example could be strengthened by supposing that our Earthling cleverly learned Martian (which is transmitted by X-ray modulation) and disguised himself as a Martian, counting on the species-chauvinism of these otherwise brilliant aliens to permit him to pass as an intentional system while not giving away the secret of his fellow human beings. This addition might get us over a bad twist in the tale, but might obscure the moral to be drawn: namely, *the unavoidability of the intentional stance with regard to oneself and one's fellow intelligent beings.* This unavoidability is itself interest relative; it is perfectly possible to adopt a physical stance, for instance, with regard to an intelligent being, oneself included, but not to the exclusion of maintaining at the same time an intentional stance with regard to oneself at a minimum, and one's fellows *if* one intends, for instance, to learn what they know. We can perhaps suppose our super-intelligent Martians fail to recognize *us* as intentional systems, but we cannot suppose them to lack the requisite concepts.[1] If they observe, theorize, predict, communicate, they view *themselves* as intentional systems. Where there are intelligent beings, the patterns must be there to be described, whether or not we care to see them.

It is important to recognize the objective reality of the intentional patterns discernible in the activities of intelligent creatures, but also important to recognize the incompleteness and imperfections in the patterns. The objective fact is that the intentional strategy *works as well as it does,* which is not perfectly. No one is perfectly rational, perfectly unforgetful, all-observant, or invulnerable to fatigue, malfunction, or design imperfection. This leads inevitably to circumstances beyond the power of the intentional strategy to describe, in much the same way that physical damage to an artifact, such as a telephone or an automobile, may render it indescribable by the normal design terminology for that artifact. How do you draw the schematic wiring diagram of an audio amplifier that has been partially melted, or how do you characterize the program state of a malfunctioning computer? In cases of even the mildest and most familiar cognitive pathology—where people seem to hold contradictory beliefs or to be deceiving themselves, for instance—the canons of interpretation of the intentional strategy fail to yield clear, stable verdicts about which beliefs and desires to attribute to a person.

Now a *strong* realist position on beliefs and desires would claim that in these cases the person in question really does have some particular beliefs and desires which the intentional strategy, as I have described it, is simply unable to divine. On the milder sort of realism I am advocating, there is no fact of the matter of exactly which beliefs and desires a person has in these degenerate cases, but this is not a surrender to relativism or subjectivism, for *when* and *why* there is no fact of the matter is itself a matter of objective fact. On this view one can even acknowledge the *interest relativity* of belief attributions and grant that given the different interests of different cultures, for instance, the beliefs and desires one culture would attribute to a member might be quite different from the beliefs and desires another culture would attribute to that very same person. But supposing that were so in a particular case, there would be the further facts about *how well* each of the rival intentional strategies worked for predicting the behavior of that person. We can be sure in advance that no intentional interpretation of an individual will work to perfection, and it may be that two rival schemes are about equally good, and better than any others we can devise. That this is the case is itself something about which there can be a fact of the matter. The objective presence of one pattern (with whatever imperfections) does not rule out the objective presence of another pattern (with whatever imperfections).

The bogey of radically different interpretations with equal warrant from the intentional strategy is theoretically important—one might better say metaphysically important—but practically negligible once one restricts one's attention to the largest and most complex intentional systems we know: human beings.

Until now I have been stressing our kinship to clams and thermostats, in order to emphasize a view of the

---

1. A member of the audience in Oxford pointed out that if the Martian included the Earthling in his physical stance purview (a possibility I had not explicitly excluded), he would not be surprised by the Earthling's prediction. He would indeed have predicted exactly the pattern of X-ray modulations produced by the Earthling speaking Martian. True, but as the Martian wrote down the results of his calculations, his prediction of the Earthling's prediction would appear, word by Martian word, as on a Ouija board, and what would be baffling to the Martian was how this chunk of mechanism, the Earthling predictor dressed up like a Martian, was able to yield this *true* sentence of Martian when it was so informationally isolated from the events the Martian needed to know of in order to make his own prediction, about the arriving automobile.

logical status of belief attribution, but the time has come to acknowledge the obvious differences and say what can be made of them. The perverse claim remains: *all there is* to being a true believer is being a system whose behavior is reliably predictable via the intentional strategy, and hence *all there is* to really and truly believing that *p* (for any proposition *p*) is being an intentional system for which *p* occurs as a belief in the best (most predictive) interpretation. But once we turn our attention to the truly interesting and versatile intentional systems, we see that this apparently shallow and instrumentalistic criterion of belief puts a severe constraint on the internal constitution of a genuine believer, and thus yields a robust version of belief after all.

Consider the lowly thermostat, as degenerate a case of an intentional system as could conceivably hold our attention for more than a moment. Going along with the gag, we might agree to grant it the capacity for about half a dozen different beliefs and fewer desires— it can believe the room is too cold or too hot, that the boiler is on or off, and that if it wants the room warmer it should turn on the boiler, and so forth. But surely this is imputing too much to the thermostat, it has no concept of heat or of a boiler, for instance. So suppose we *de-interpret* its beliefs and desires: it can believe the *A* is too *F* or *G,* and if it wants the *A* to be more *F* it should do *K,* and so forth. After all, by attaching the thermostatic control mechanism to different input and output devices, it could be made to regulate the amount of water in a tank, or the speed of a train, for instance. Its attachment to a heat-sensitive transducer and a boiler is too impoverished a link to the world to grant any rich semantics to its belief-like states.

But suppose we then enrich these modes of attachment. Suppose we give it more than one way of learning about the temperature, for instance. We give it an eye of sorts that can distinguish huddled, shivering occupants of the room and an ear so that it can be told how cold it is. We give it some facts about geography so that it can conclude that it is probably in a cold place if it learns that its spatio-temporal location is Winnipeg in December. Of course giving it a visual system that is multipurpose and general—not a mere shivering-object detector—will require vast complications of its inner structure. Suppose we also give our system more

behavioral versatility: it chooses the boiler fuel, purchases it from the cheapest and most reliable dealer, checks the weather stripping, and so forth. This adds another dimension of internal complexity; it gives individual belief-like states *more to do,* in effect, by providing more and different occasions for their derivation or deduction from other states, and by providing more and different occasions for them to serve as premises for further reasoning. The cumulative effect of enriching these connections between the device and the world in which it resides is to enrich the semantics of its dummy predicates, *F* and *G* and the rest. The more of this we add, the less amenable our device becomes to serving as the control structure of anything other than a room-temperature maintenance system. A more formal way of saying this is that the class of indistinguishably satisfactory models of the formal system embodied in its internal states gets smaller and smaller as we add such complexities; the more we add, the richer or more demanding or specific the semantics of the system, until eventually we reach systems for which a unique semantic interpretation is practically (but never in principle) dictated. At that point we say this device (or animal or person) has beliefs *about heat* and *about this very room,* and so forth, not only because of the system's actual location in, and operations on, the world, but because we cannot imagine another niche in which it could be placed *where it would work.*

Our original simple thermostat had a state we called a belief about a particular boiler, to the effect that it was on or off. Why about *that* boiler? Well, what other boiler would you want to say it was about? The belief is about the boiler because it is *fastened* to the boiler. Given the actual, if minimal, causal link to the world that happened to be in effect, we could endow a state of the device with *meaning* (of a sort) and *truth conditions,* but it was altogether too easy to substitute a different minimal link and completely change the meaning (in this impoverished sense) of that internal state. But as systems become perceptually richer and behaviorally more versatile, it becomes harder and harder to make substitutions in the actual links of the system to the world without changing the organization of the system itself. If you change its environment, it will *notice,* in effect, and make a change in its internal state in response. There comes to be a two-way constraint of growing specificity between the device and the environment. Fix the device in any one state and it demands a very specific environment in which to operate properly (you can no longer switch it easily from regulating temperature to regulating speed or anything else); but at the same time, if you do not *fix* the state it is in, but just plonk it down in a changed environment, its sensory attachments will be sensitive and discriminative enough to respond appropriately to the change, driving the system into a new state, in which it will operate effectively in the new environment. There is a familiar way of alluding to this tight relationship that can exist between the organization of a system and its environment: you say that the organism continuously *mirrors* the environment, or that there is a *representation* of the environment in—or implicit in—the organization of the system.

It is not that we attribute (or should attribute) beliefs and desires only to things in which we find internal representations, but rather that when we discover some object for which the intentional strategy works, we endeavor to interpret some of its internal states or processes as internal representations. What makes some internal feature of a thing a representation could only be its role in regulating the behavior of an intentional system.

Now the reason for stressing our kinship with the thermostat should be clear. There is no magic moment in the transition from a simple thermostat to a system that *really* has an internal representation of the world around it. The thermostat has a minimally demanding representation of the world, fancier thermostats have more demanding representations of the world, fancier robots for helping around the house would have still more demanding representations of the world. Finally you reach us. We are so multifariously and intricately connected to the world that almost no substitution is possible—though it is clearly imaginable in a thought experiment. Hilary Putnam imagines the planet Twin Earth, which is just like Earth right down to the scuff marks on the shoes of the Twin Earth replica of your neighbor, but which differs from Earth in some property that is entirely beneath the thresholds of your capacities to discriminate. (What they call water on Twin Earth has a different chemical analysis.) Were *you* to be whisked instantaneously to Twin Earth and exchanged for your Twin Earth replica, you would never

be the wiser—just like the simple control system that cannot tell whether it is regulating temperature, speed, or volume of water in a tank. It is easy to devise radically different Twin Earths for something as simple and sensorily deprived as a thermostat, but your internal organization puts a much more stringent demand on substitution. Your Twin Earth and Earth must be virtual replicas or you will change state dramatically on arrival.

So which boiler are *your* beliefs about when you believe the boiler is on? Why, the boiler in your cellar (rather than its twin on Twin Earth, for instance). What other boiler would your beliefs be about? The completion of the semantic interpretation of your beliefs, fixing the referents of your beliefs, requires, as in the case of the thermostat, facts about your actual embedding in the world. The principles, and problems, of interpretation that we discover when we attribute beliefs to people are the *same* principles and problems we discover when we look at the ludicrous, but blessedly simple, problem of attributing beliefs to a thermostat. The differences are of degree, but nevertheless of such great degree that understanding the internal organization of a simple intentional system gives one very little basis for understanding the internal organization of a complex intentional system, such as a human being.

Why Does the Intentional Strategy Work?

When we turn to the question of *why* the intentional strategy works as well as it does, we find that the question is ambiguous, admitting of two very different sorts of answers. If the intentional system is a simple thermostat, one answer is simply this: the intentional strategy works because the thermostat is well designed; it was designed to be a system that could be easily and reliably comprehended and manipulated from this stance. That is true, but not very informative, if what we are after are the actual features of its design that explain its performance. Fortunately, however, in the case of a simple thermostat those features are easily discovered and understood, so the other answer to our *why* question, which is really an answer about *how the machinery works,* is readily available.

If the intentional system in question is a person, there is also an ambiguity in our question. The first answer to the question of why the intentional strategy works is that evolution has designed human beings to be rational, to believe what they ought to believe and want what they ought to want. The fact that we are products of a long and demanding evolutionary process guarantees that using the intentional strategy on us is a safe bet. This answer has the virtues of truth and brevity, but it is also strikingly uninformative. The more difficult version of the question asks, in effect, how the machinery which Nature has provided us works. And we cannot yet give a good answer to that question. We just do not know. We do know how the *strategy* works, and we know the easy answer to the question of why it works, but knowing these does not help us much with the hard answer.

It is not that there is any dearth of doctrine, however. A Skinnerian behaviorist, for instance, would say that the strategy works because its imputations of beliefs and desires are shorthand, in effect, for as yet unimaginably complex descriptions of the effects of prior histories of response and reinforcement. To say that someone wants some ice cream is to say that in the past the ingestion of ice cream has been reinforced in him by the results, creating a propensity under certain background conditions (also too complex to describe) to engage in ice-cream-acquiring behavior. In the absence of detailed knowledge of those historical facts we can nevertheless make shrewd guesses on inductive grounds; these guesses are embodied in our intentional stance claims. Even if all this were true, it would tell us very little about the way such propensities were regulated by the internal machinery.

A currently more popular explanation is that the account of how the strategy works and the account of how the mechanism works will (roughly) *coincide*: for each predictively attributable belief, there will be a functionally salient internal state of the machinery, decomposable into functional parts in just about the same way the sentence expressing the belief is decomposable into parts—that is, words or terms. The inferences we attribute to rational creatures will be mirrored by physical, causal processes in the hardware; the *logical* form of the propositions believed will be copied in the *structural* form of the states in correspondence with them. This is the hypothesis that there is a *language of thought* coded in our brains, and our brains will eventually be understood as symbol manipulating systems in at least rough analogy with computers. Many different versions of this view are currently being explored, in the new research program called cognitive science, and provided one allows great latitude for attenuation of the basic, bold claim, I think some version of it will prove correct.

But I do not believe that this is *obvious*. Those who think that it is obvious, or inevitable, that such a theory will prove true (and there are many who do), are confusing two different empirical claims. The first is that intentional stance description yields an objective, real pattern in the world—the pattern our imaginary Martians missed. This is an empirical claim, but one that is confirmed beyond skepticism. The second is that this real pattern is *produced by* another real pattern roughly isomorphic to it within the brains of intelligent creatures. Doubting the existence of the second real pattern is not doubting the existence of the first. There *are* reasons for believing in the second pattern, but they are not overwhelming. The best simple account I can give of the reasons is as follows.

As we ascend the scale of complexity from simple thermostat, through sophisticated robot, to human being, we discover that our efforts to design systems with the requisite behavior increasingly run foul of the problem of *combinatorial explosion*. Increasing some parameter by, say, ten percent—ten percent more inputs or more degrees of freedom in the behavior to be controlled or more words to be recognized or whatever—tends to increase the internal complexity of the system being designed by orders of magnitude. Things get out of hand very fast and, for instance, can lead to computer programs that will swamp the largest, fastest machines. Now somehow the brain has solved the problem of combinatorial explosion. It is a gigantic network of billions of cells, but still finite, compact, reliable, and swift, and capable of learning new behaviors, vocabularies, theories, almost without limit. Some elegant, *generative,* indefinitely extendable principles of representation must be responsible. We have only one model of such a representation system: a human language. So the argument for a language of thought comes down to this:

what else could it be? We have so far been unable to imagine any plausible alternative in any detail. That is a good enough reason, I think, for recommending as a matter of scientific tactics that we pursue the hypothesis in its various forms as far as we can. But we will engage in that exploration more circumspectly, and fruitfully, if we bear in mind that its inevitable rightness is far from assured. One does not well understand even a true empirical hypothesis so long as one is under the misapprehension that it is necessarily true.

Jerry Fodor

Three Cheers for Propositional Attitudes

The belief that P has fallen upon hard times. Here is how it came about.

Many respectable philosophers used to think that substitution instances of the schema *S: x believes that P,* together with their friends and logical relations, are eliminable from English *salva* the expressive power of the language. Roughly, each sentence generated by substitution in *S* was to be replaced by some (logically equivalent, perhaps synonymous) sentence in which the predicate expresses a form of behavior or a disposition to behave. Insouciance prevailed; nobody actually provided the analyses, and there were those who seemed to glory in not providing them. So, Ryle (if I read him right) held both that talking about propositional attitudes is just a way of talking about behavior or behavioral dispositions *and* that nothing that can be (finitely) said about behavior or behavioral dispositions can, in the general case, exhaust the content of the ascription of a propositional attitude. A darkish doctrine, no doubt, but those were darkish times.

At their very worst, however, the *facticity* of such ascriptions went unimpugned. If, after all, claims about the belief that P are claims about the behaviors of organisms,

then surely they are at ontological par with other things that we say about the doings of middle-sized objects. Even if the analysis of such ascriptions should exhibit them as intractably dispositional, it is arguably a fact that salt is soluble: Why should it not be as good a fact that P-believers are disposed to P-behave (disposed, for instance, to utter tokens of 'I believe that *p*')?

We all know now that this will not work. Not, of course, that it is impossible to find some formula logically equivalent to 'x believes that P' in which 'believes' does not occur: there are expressions in French that would do for that. The point is, rather, that any such expression is itself bound to contain intentional idioms, so if what one had in mind was not so much doing without 'believes' but eliminating intensionality at large, it looks as though the behaviorist program just cannot be carried out. Take uttering 'I believe that P.' Doing that is not (as one used to say) "criterial" for believing that P unless producing the utterance at least constitutes the making of a statement. But statements are utterances intentionally (in the other sense, namely, willfully) uttered: mere random giving voice won't do. And, of course, 'intentional' is intentional. So, by one or the other route, the verbs of propositional attitude bend back upon themselves: they are, perhaps, interdefinable, but there appears to be no way out of the circle of intentional idioms.

"So be it," some philosophers have said, "and so much the worse for the circle of intentional idioms. If

Jerry Fodor, *RePresentations: Philosophical Essays on the Foundations of Cognitive Science* (Cambridge: The MIT Press, 1981). Copyright © 1981. Reprinted with the permission of The MIT Press.

believers won't behave, we won't have any." Hence, the view is now widely current among philosophers that the refutation of *logical* behaviorism was tantamount to a demonstration of the *unfacticity* of ascriptions of propositional attitudes, and thus to the establishment of a sort of *eliminative* behaviorism. Strictly speaking, according to this new account, there is no question of truth or falsity about what a man believes, hopes, intends, supposes, etc. Strictly speaking, we could encounter all the facts there are and not encounter any facts like these. So, it is all right if we *cannot* express in our purely extensional (or, anyhow, purely nonintentional) language—the language we reserve for such solemnities as formalizing physics—what we *can* express by reference to intentions. Physics is, perhaps, committed to saying all there is to say that is strictly true; but there is nothing strictly true that can be said about propositional attitudes. What can't be said can't be said, and it can't be reduced to physics either.

It is worth emphasizing the difference between this reaction and the one that has been typical among psychologists. The psychologists have reasoned: *statements about mental states and processes are not translatable into statements about behavior. Hence there must be ontologically autonomous facts about mental states and processes. Hence, behaviorism is false.* Whereas, the philosophers have reasoned: *statements about mental states and processes are not translatable into statements about behavior. Hence there must not be ontologically autonomous facts about mental states or processes. Hence behaviorism is true.* Clearly, one or the other of these lines of reasoning must be unsound. This chapter is about which one.

To begin with, if there are no facts about mental states and processes, that is *very* surprising. For the simple facticity of at least *some* ascriptions of propositional attitudes had seemed to be among life's little certainties. So, prior to philosophical instruction, one might have thought it straightout true not only that, say, Carter's name begins with *C,* but also that one *believes* that Carter's name begins with *C.* And, one might have thought, there is not much to choose between these truths. After all, Carter's name *does* begin with C, and one knows, more or less, how to spell. So why on Earth should one *not* have the belief when all the evidence conspires to tempt one to it? The burden of argument lies, surely, upon those who say that it is not the case that

one believes even what one is strongly disposed to believe that one believes.

Moreover, nobody supposes that the failure of logical behaviorism literally *entails* the unfacticity of propositional attitude ascriptions. "Behaviorism or nothing" will strike the sophisticated as not self-evidently true. If, in short, the burden of argument is to be taken up, supporting considerations will need to be adduced. Such considerations have recently been proposed on several hands. I want to look at some of them in this paper. In particular, I want to consider in detail D. C. Dennett's account of the role of intentional ascriptions in explanations of behavior.[1] Dennett's theory, if true, would make it clear why it is unreasonable to expect such ascriptions to be more than just heuristic.

Whereas I am inclined to think that, so far at least, the case against propositional attitudes rests unproven. For all that anyone has thus far shown, ascriptions of beliefs, when true at all, are literal. I take it that this conclusion is important if correct. After all, if there are no facts about mental states and processes, then there is, quite literally, nothing for psychology to be about. In this respect, the methodological implications of the new, eliminative behaviorism are even *more* radical than those of the old, reductive behaviorism. On the latter view psychology at least had a subject matter: the organization of behavior. To put it brutally, the psychologist's choice used to be between mentalism and tedium. It is now between mentalism and unemployment.

Dennett recommends that we "Consider the case of a chess-playing computer, and the different strategies or stances one might adopt as its opponent in trying to predict its moves [p. 87]." It may not, at first, be clear why we should *want* to consider a chess-playing computer in the course of considering what underlies our ascriptions of intentional properties to intentional systems: prima facie, a computer is a shaky example of such a system, and it is not beyond doubt that ascriptions of intentional properties to machines rest on relatively dubious analogies to solid paradigms like us. Still, marginal cases can have their philosophical uses, and I suppose that Dennett's strategy is this: In deciding what

_____

1. Daniel Dennett. "Intentional Systems," *Journal of Philosophy* 68:87–106.

to say about a marginal case, we shall have to trot out reasons, and that should help clarify what kinds of reasons can, in principle, be alleged in favor of intentional ascriptions.

Moreover, as Dennett sees very clearly, the example serves to illustrate the involvement of intentional ascription in the prediction and explanation of behavior: Our interest in intentional ascriptions is—at least for the present case—part and parcel of our interest in figuring out what the machine is likely to *do*. Dennett says:

> A man's best hope of defeating such a machine in a chess match is to predict its responses by figuring out as best he can what the best or most rational move would be given the rules and goals of chess. That is, one assumes not only (1) that the machine will function as designed, but (2) that the design is optimal as well, that the computer will 'choose' the most rational move. (p. 89)

Now, it is notable, according to Dennett, that the recourse to intentional ascription is not the *only* way that we could, in principle, go about predicting the machine's moves. For, on the one hand, the moves could be predicted from a knowledge of the physical construction of the machine (assuming, as we may for present purposes, that the machine's physical construction determines its moves) and, on the other, the moves could be predicted by reference to the machine's teleological or functional structure. Dennett says that, in making predictions in the first way, we are adopting a "physical stance" towards the machine and that in making predictions in the second way we are adopting a "design stance." "The essential feature of the design stance is that we make predictions solely from knowledge or assumptions about the system's functional design, irrespective of the physical constitution of the innards of the particular object" (p. 88). Design-stance predictions are riskier than are physical-stance predictions, for, presumably, if we have an inference whose premises are physical laws and a specification of the physical state of the machine at *t,* and whose conclusion is that the machine will do such-and-such at *t,* then that prediction can go wrongly only insofar as the physics of the machine is not deterministic. Whereas, consider a corresponding inference whose premises are true gen-

eralizations about the functional design of the system (e.g., its program) and a specification of its functional state at *t*. Such an argument will be reliable only when the machine functions as it is designed to function: when, for example, it does not break down, blow out, strip a gear, etc. Failures-to-function yield exceptions to design-stance predictions but not to physical-stance predictions.

The intentional stance is like the others in that we adopt it insofar (perhaps *only* insofar; Dennett does not say) as we are interested in the prediction of behavior. And, like the design stance, it is prone to kinds of fallibility that the physical stance is immune to. When we assume the intentional stance, we figure out what the system will do by figuring out what it would be *rational* to do and then predicting that the system will do *that*. Now, supposing that the system *is* rational, it will still be true that intentional-stance predictions will typically go astray insofar as the system misfunctions, so intentional stance predictions inherit the kinds of fallibility that design-stance predictions are prone to. But, moreover, they have problems of their own since, even if the system does not misfunction—even if no gear strips—it may fail to do the rational thing because it failed to be designed to be entirely rational. Where the, as it were, program of the device is less than optimal, the intentional-stance prediction will be correspondingly less than reliable.

Why, then, resort to the intentional stance at all? For two reasons (both of them, notice, *purely* pragmatic). First, we may know what it would be rational for the system to do even if we do not know what the physical constitution or the program of the system is, so we may be in a position to predict behavior from the intentional stance even when we are not in a position to predict it from the physical or design stances. Second, even if we *do* know what the physics is, or what the functional analysis is, predictions based upon either may become unfeasible in practice when the system is sufficiently complicated. [. . .] In either case, then, it is essentially practical considerations that force us to intentional ascriptions: in particular, it is *not* considerations of *truth*. Dennett says: "The decision to adopt the strategy is pragmatic and is not intrinsically right or wrong. One can always refuse to adopt the intentional stance, . . . one can switch stances at will . . . etc." (p. 91).

We, as it were, adopt the intentional stance towards a system because of facts about *us,* not because of facts about *it.*

So, Dennett's analysis takes us where it was supposed to; it explains the utility (and hence, presumably, the prevalence) of the intentional idiom without assuming that there are facts that intentional ascriptions correspond to. If the analysis is right, then the least hypothesis is, surely, that there are no such facts and that appears to be the conclusion Dennett wants us to endorse.

What, then, can be said in favor of the analysis? Dennett's main argument goes something like this: Since intentional stance predictions will work only insofar as we are dealing with rational systems, an assumption of rationality is implicit in every such prediction. But such assumptions are ours to make or to withhold: i.e., they are themselves heuristic idealizations, justifiable only insofar as they lead, by and large, to true intentional stance predictions. So, we can conclude the unfacticity of propositional attitude ascriptions from the unfacticity of the rationality assumptions that they presuppose.

I do not think that this is a very convincing line of argument, either in the condensed form in which I have just sketched it or in the unpacked version that Dennett gives. Let's now have a look at the details.

Dennett needs to show (a) that some assumption of rationality is implicit in any attempt to predict the behavior of an organism from its intentional states, and (b) that such assumptions are somehow just heuristic. I am going to focus on (a) for the moment; how (b) comes in is something that we'll see as we go along. Let's start with some softening-up arguments.

First, it just is not true that "A man's best hope of defeating a machine in a chess match is to predict its responses by figuring out as best he can what the best or most rational move would be" and predicting that move for the machine. Indeed, the hope one cherishes in playing chess with a machine (or with, for that matter, some better instance of an intentional system—say, a Russian) is that (s)he/it *won't* make the best, most rational, optimal (etc.) move, but will, instead, make the very move that falls for one's little ruses, springs one's little traps, and, in general, exhibits levels of intellectual functioning gratifyingly inferior to one's own. Trap-baiting is itself rational only in the light of such hopes and predictions.

I am not quibbling. Dennett's case is supposed to show us straight-off that our predictions from the intentional stance depend upon postulates of optimal functioning. Whereas, it is precisely from the intentional stance that we hope and fondly expect that our opponent will not *notice* our traps, or that if our traps are noticed they will not be *understood,* or, if they are understood, no way out of them will be *seen, remembered,* or otherwise *conjured up.* These, surely, are intentional idioms par excellence, so it is precisely here that we would expect postulates of optimality to be deployed. For all that, we do not play chess on the assumption that our opponent will make the optimal move; indeed (a small point) in any game much more complicated than, say, tick-tack-toe, one is unlikely to have a clue as to what the optimal move is, or even, indeed, whether one exists. The intentionality of one's opponent's propositional attitudes is not thereby impugned.

These observations point in two directions, and I want to look both ways. First, there is something odd about a theory of intentional ascription which does not explain why intentional idioms have the characteristic properties they do: namely, the property that inferences warranted in transparent contexts *fail* when the context is opaque. Second, it seems clear that intentional explanation works in all sorts of cases where it is precisely *lapses* from optimal rationality that are at issue. These points in order.

1. A theory of intentional ascription ought to explain why intentional predicates are intensional (with-an-'s'), and the theory that assumptions of rationality are at the core of intentional ascriptions does not do so. On the contrary; quite generally, the more rational a system is assumed to be, the more justified we are in substituting in the (syntactic) objects of statements about its propositional attitudes: i.e., in reading such statements *transparently* rather than opaquely. Consider God. God is, I suppose, *fully* rational in the sense of rationality that Dennett explicitly has in mind. That is, God believes the entailments of his beliefs, so that, from 'God believes P' and 'P entails Q', we have the right to infer 'God believes Q'. Whereas, though God's beliefs are closed under the entailment relation, ours very notably are not. It is part and parcel of the opacity of *our* propositional attitudes that the inference from 'we believe P' and 'P entails Q' to 'we believe Q' is not, in general,

valid. Suppose, now, that God is not merely rational but also omniscient. Then we have the full transparency of all belief contexts for God; i.e., we have not only the closure of God's beliefs under entailment, but also under material implication; and we have their closure under substitution of coreferring expressions. So, if God believes that Cicero denounced Catiline, and if Cicero = Tully, then God believes that Tully denounced Catiline. Similarly, mutatis mutandis, for God's views about Bernard Ortcutt and the man in the brown hat.

So, the more rational the system, the less opaque its belief contexts. The *more* we assume "optimality of functioning," the *less* intentionality, opacity, etc., we have to deal with. How, one is inclined rhetorically to demand, could it then be that an assumption of rationality and optimality of functioning is somehow built into our ascriptions of intentional predicates?

It may be worth reemphasizing that what holds for God *in excelsis* holds for chess playing machines only *in moderation*. Suppose I have moved my knight to KB4, and suppose that my knight's being at KB4 = my knight's threatening Black's queen. We assume that Black knows the general principles of chess, whatever those may be. So then, by hypothesis, it follows from what Black knows and notices that the positioning of my knight = (entails) the threatening of Black's Queen. The principle of rationality is, inter alia, the principle that noticings are closed under their entailments. So, if I am assuming Black's rationality, I am assuming, inter alia, that Black notices the threat.

Whereas, what I hope and predict is precisely that the threat will go unmarked. Nor, in so predicting, have I abandoned the intentional stance. On the contrary, I may rationally predict Black's lapse precisely *because* of what I know or believe about Black's intentional states: in particular, about what he is and is not likely to notice. I have, let's suppose, a mini-theory about Black's noticings. Put vulgarly, the theory might be that Black is a sucker for a knight fork. I get my prediction from this theory, and the postulates of the theory reek of intentionality. Where is the assumption of rationality? If to be rational is to believe the consequences of one's beliefs, and if the opacity of propositional attitudes is the failure of closure under the consequence relation, then to ascribe an intentional predicate to a system will often involve postulating its *ir*rationality if the predicate is

opaquely construed. Or, to put the moral of the example slightly differently, it is not postulates of rationality that license intentional stance predictions: it is, (mini- or maxi-, formal or informal) theories about who is likely to have which propositional attitude when, and what behavioral consequences are likely to ensue.

2. This brings us to the second point, which is precisely that intentional explanations run rampant just where they should not if the postulate of rationality story were true: namely, in the psychology of one or another *dis*function. What I have in mind is not so much the exotic specimens that get retailed in psychoanalytic paperbacks, but rather the psychology of such mundane propositional attitudes as, say, forgetting and misunderstanding. Much of our most respectable cognitive psychology operates in this area, and it operates essentially with intentional predicates. Quite a lot is known, for example, about the kinds of mistakes that people make in deductive reasoning. So, to come to cases, it is known that one does worse with arguments that contain negative premises than with matched arguments in the affirmative mode. You will do better, that is to say, with the information that P is true than with the information that not-P is false, and the difference remains when banal variables are controlled away. But, of course, 'information' must be opaquely construed if this generalization is to be so much as stated. The information that P *is* the information that not-P $\supset$ F on the transparent construal. And equally, of course, it is all one to God whether P or not (not-P), since belief is closed under entailment for a perfectly rational Being functioning optimally.

Such cases are legion, but I will not provide more here. What I take it that they all come to for our purposes is that ascriptions of intentionality and postulates of optimality are largely independent in precisely the area where it is most important that intentional idioms should be available; namely, in the (formal and informal) psychology of cognition. What *is* characteristic of this area—what I believe *does* explain the opacity of typical psychological idioms—is the relativization of our descriptions of the intentional states of a system to the way that the system represents the objects of its propositional attitudes. That is, however, a very long story, and one that I have tried to tell elsewhere. Suffice it to say here that much of our psychology is the psychology of lapses from optimal rationality, and its typical idioms are opaque all the same.

These were, as I remarked, softening-up arguments. I suspect that, for Dennett's purposes, they could all be met by a judicious pulling in of horns. For—though I doubt this is an option he'd approve—it would be open to Dennett to meet these objections by weaking the assumption of rationality to an assumption of non-irrationality. The discussion has suggested that intentional stance prediction is often compatible with—and sometimes even relies upon—postulating *less than optimal* rationality. But it seems right to say that successful intentional stance predictions do depend on assuming that the system whose behavior is at issue won't act at random or go nuts. I'll take it for granted, then, that it is the dependency of intentional stance predictions upon postulates of non-irrationality (rather than optimal functioning) that Dennett is committed to defending, together with the heuristic status of such postulation. And now we need to see how the defense might go. Since I'm uncertain precisely how Dennett *wants* it to go, I propose to march back and forth over the terrain, trying several different lines of argument and hoping that something will turn up.

I suppose that Dennett's view is this: A typical prediction from the intentional stance rests on (what I shall call) an *intentional argument*. An intentional argument has the form *F*:

Premise 1: In situation S, a not-irrational agent performs (might perform) action A. (In order for this to be an intentional argument, we must assume that situation S is specified, at least in part, by reference to the propositional attitudes of the agent. For simplicity, I shall assume that it is *entirely* so specified.)
Premise 2: x is in situation S.
Premise 3: x is a not-irrational agent.
Conclusion/prediction: x performs (might perform) action A.

As now construed, Dennett's point is two-fold. First, that our intentional stance theories license (only) generalizations such as premise 1 (as we have seen, Dennett holds that to adopt the intentional stance is to argue from what the system would do if it were rational.) But,

second, if this is right, then premises such as 3 figure essentially in intentional arguments. Knowledge of what a not-irrational agent would do in situation S, and knowledge that x is in S, licenses predictions about what x will do in S only insofar as we assume that x is not irrational. So, we appear to have a part, at least, of what we wanted: we have the essential involvement of a rationality premise in any warranted intentional stance prediction, even if we don't yet have the heuristic character of the premise that is so involved. [. . .]

The trouble with this way of proceeding, however, is that it leaves us needing some reason to assume that any predictive scheme which seeks to infer from the propositional attitudes of an organism to its behavior *must* have the form of an intentional argument; viz. must be of form F. Prima facie, there would appear to be plausible alternatives. For example, F*.

Premise 1: Being in situation S causes (might cause) the performance of action A.
Premise 2: x is in situation S.
Conclusion/prediction: x performs (might perform) action A.

Since, by assumption, being in situation S involves having the relevant propositional attitudes, F* counts as an argument from beliefs to behaviors if F does. But there doesn't seem to be any assumption of rationality essentially operative in F*. What's presupposed by F* is just that beliefs cause behaviors, and do so in ways that can be subsumed by general causal principles.

Of course, it's true about F* that insofar as premise 1 subsumes only non-irrational agents, it will fail to subsume x when x is irrational. And if, as one might suppose, being subsumed by such principles as premise 1 is somehow *constitutive* of being not irrational, then the non-irrationality of a system will follow from the fact that it satisfies arguments like F*. If, however, *that's* what the assumption of rationality amounts to, then the assumption of rationality is harmless. For what we have is only that the soundness of intentional stance predictions entails the rationality of a system insofar as the rationality of a system is a matter of the predictability of its behaviors from its beliefs and desires. Which is to say that the intentional stance prediction of behavior entails the predictability of behavior from beliefs and desires. And that isn't just *true*; it's *truistic*. The moral is this: What we need is not just to show that intentional stance prediction *somehow* involves a postulate of non-irrationality; we need to show that it involves a postulate of non-irrationality in some way that makes the predictive arguments merely heuristic. To discover that a system satisfies arguments like F* is, perhaps, to find out that the system is, to that extent, not irrational. But, so what?

'Ah, but', you may say, rather more in the spirit of Quine and Davidson than of Dennett, '*the substitution of F* for F as the format for intentional prediction begs the very question that's at issue. The difference between F* and F is that, whereas 1, F (premise 1 of F) is presumably some sort of framework truth (constitutive, perhaps, of the concept of rationality), 1, F* (premise 1 of F*) purports to be a true (maybe lawlike) causal generalization. But, now, (1, F*) can't be a true causal generalization unless it is possible to identify states of organisms as being states of believing, wanting, intending, . . . etc. that P in ways that are* independent *of the identification of such states as being subsumed by generalizations like (1, F*). And this is* not *possible because, roughly, of the holistic character of the epistemological considerations that underlie identifications of propositional attitudes. That is: it is precisely such facts about a state as that it is subsumed by generalizations like (1, F*) which warrant the identification of that state as one of believing that P. So, it is a kind of charade to view (1, F*) as a causal generalization. Viewed in its proper epistemological context, it is more plausible to take it as a conceptual condition upon the identification of such propositional attitudes as figure in S. If, however, it is not a causal generalization, then the important difference between F and F* vanishes and no progress has been made.'*

To which I am inclined to reply as follows: It ought to be a ground rule for discussions of intentional theories that problems which hold for scientific explanations *in general* should not be raised as difficulties for intentional explanations *in particular*. There is, to be sure, a problem about the dependence of the identification of a scientific construct upon the assumption that the theory which employs the construct is true. The tendency of the fundamental generalizations which structure a science to act like implicit definitions of its theoretical terms creates notorious problems about intertheoretic reference; about the distinction between conceptual and empirical truth; and about the nature of empirical confirmation. In extreme cases, it causes ter-

minal Idealism. For all I know, it causes sunspots too. What *hasn't* been shown, however, is that the dependence of identifications of propositional attitudes upon the truth of causal generalizations like (F*, 1) amounts to anything more than a special case of this general difficulty. If it doesn't, then it isn't anything that we ought to worry about here.

One further point along this line: if the identification of propositional attitudes depends essentially on their subsumption by generalizations like (F*, 1) (viz. generalizations couched, by hypothesis, in intentional idiom), then there may be quite a direct argument from the present considerations to the "ineliminability of the intentional". But that would be an argument for the *heuristic* character of the intentional only given precisely the assumption that's at issue: viz. that there is no fact of the matter about intentional states. This is an area in which it is frightfully easy to find oneself arguing backwards.

But maybe this is all beside the point. For Dennett might want to argue as follows: '*It's true that I think a rationality assumption comes in; only I don't think it comes in where you think I think it does. It's not that we postulate rationality in the course of attributing beliefs to agents or in the course of attributing causal efficacy to the agent's beliefs. When the assumption of rationality comes in is when we use our theoretical formalisms to figure out which predictions about the agent's mental processes to make. Suppose we attribute to Jones the belief that P and the belief that if P then Q. Presumably, we will then wish to predict that these beliefs will cause (or at least tend to cause) a belief that Q. But notice that in generating such predictions, we will very often appeal to our knowledge that, in point of logic, Q is derivable from (P & (if P then Q)). What, then, licenses arguing from the point of logic to the causal predictions about the interactions of Jones' mental states? Precisely the assumption that Jones' mental processes are, to this extent, rational processes. Moreover, it's not unreasonable to suppose that the willingness to make this sort of transition— from the logical to the causal facts—is constitutive of being willing to ascribe beliefs at all. Were we to find a kind of system for which such transitions never (or almost never) worked, we would, for that very reason, refuse to think of it as having beliefs.*' Dennett sometimes writes in ways that suggest that this is, for him, the crucial point about intentional prediction. "Ask a thousand American mathematicians how much seven times five is, more than nine hundred would respond by saying that it was thirty-five.... (this) is not a prediction of human psychology, but of the 'psychology' of Intentional systems generally" (97). That is: it's a prediction that we get just from arithmetic, given the assumption of rationality. It's the aprioricity of this sort of prediction that shows that intentional psychology, though "not totally vacuous" (ibid.), somehow isn't the real thing.

But this is, I think, precisely a case of arguing backwards. If we *start out* by thinking of our intentional stance theories (for example, our logic) as simply computational devices from which predictions about mental phenomena are somehow to be elicited, then the question "What licenses the transition from interformulaic relations in the theory to causal relations in the mind?" surely does arise. And the answer: "It's the assumption of rationality that issues the license" is entirely plausible insofar as one thinks of the intentional theories as implicitly defining—or otherwise constraining—the concept of rationality.

There is, however, an alternative view. To put it crudely, one possible answer to the question "What justifies using an intentional stance theory to generate psychological predictions?" is: it's the assumption that the theory is *true* under the intended (psychological) interpretation; it's the assumption that, in something spiritually similar to the technical sense, the mental processes of the agent constitute a model of the theory. Since Dennett's *conclusion* was supposed to be that psychological deployments of intentional stance theories are heuristic (hence that such theories are *not* literally true under the intended psychological interpretation), he needs an argument that the Realist construal cannot be sustained. We still haven't got such an argument.

What we have got is just the difference between F and F* writ large. According to F, we take the theorems of our intentional theories as constitutive of rationality, and we use the assumption that the agent is rational to infer from the intentional theory to the psychological predictions. According to F*, we interpret interformulaic relations in the theory as expressing causal relations among mental states. So, for example, the derivability of Q from (P & (if P then Q)) is interpreted as the claim that if an organism has the belief that P and the belief that if P then Q, then it has the belief that Q. This is, of course, *not* a logical truth; it's an empirical generaliza-

tion which specifies (presumably causal) relations among mental states by reference to the contents of those states. As such, it will be true only if the mental states, together with their causal relations do, in the intended sense, constitute a model of the logic. What we then need to license the use of the intentional theory to make predictions about, say, Jones', mental states, is just the assumption that such empirical generalizations *are* true.

I suppose, by the way, that we *always* have this sort of choice when we consider the application of a theoretical formalism to an empirical domain; it has nothing to do with the empirical application of intentional theories per se. For example, we predict the combinatorial properties of atoms by appeal to the theory of valences. The theory of valences contains, among other things, certain mathematical principles (let's say, for our purposes, the postulates for summing positive and negative integers). When we appeal to the formalism to derive chemical predictions, we use the mathematical apparatus to compute the valence of complex objects as a function of the valences of their constitutents. Now, how shall we think about this?

One possibility is to view the formalism as simply a computational device which implicitly constrains the (otherwise uninterpreted) concept *has valence n*. On this view, the application of the device to predict chemical interactions proceeds via an "assumption of mathematicity": roughly, the assumption that atoms combine according to the postulates for summing integers. This way of talking is harmless precisely *because* it isn't mandatory. We could equally say that what licenses using the theory to make the predictions is the assumption that the formalism is true under the intended (chemical) interpretation. According to this latter picture, assignments of integer values as valences of atoms correspond to (some or other) claims about the distribution of electrons in their outer orbits; the principles for the summation of valences correspond to laws of electron capture, and so on. On the first account, we apply the theory of valences on the assumption that atomic processes are mathematic; on the second, we apply the theory of valences on the assumption that it is true under chemical interpretation. Similarly, mutatis mutandis, for the application of an intentional theory in a domain of mental processes.

The reader will have noticed that I am simplifying—indeed, trivializing—what are, in fact, dark matters. But

I think the moral survives the exposition: there may be general reasons for preferring the first sort of story about valences to the second; but if there are, the very fact that they are *general* makes them irrelevant to the discussion of intentional theories qua intentional theories. Certainly, according to the second picture, there is nothing *specially* puzzling about the way that the assumption of rationality comes into intentional predictions: no empirical domain is a model of a formalism unless it exhibits analogues to the interformulaic relations that structure the formalism. That's all the postulate of rationality (and the postulate of mathematicity) amounts to.

Here, finally, is where push comes to shove. For, I suspect that Dennett would reply like this: '*The asymmetry between the application of the theory of valence to atoms and the application of the logic to our mental states is that we already* know *that our beliefs don't, in the required sense, constitute a model of the theory. Q is derivable from (P & (if P then Q)), but the belief that P and the belief that if P then Q don't invariably and in the general case cause the belief that Q. The causal interactions among beliefs do not bear to modus ponens that relation (whatever that relation is) that the interactions among atoms bear to the principles for summing integers. So, again: intentional theories may be useful for predicting the behavioral outcomes of mental processes; but they aren't ever* true.' The point here, notice, is not just that intentional theories rest on an assumption of rationality; it's that they rest on a *counterfactual* assumption of rationality. And, of course, a theory that entails (or presupposes) a falsehood *can't* be better than heuristic. I do think that this must be the heart of the matter; what's needed to make the case for the heuristic status of the intentional is, surely, an argument that engages the issue of truth; and this is the first such that we have encountered.

Such considerations as, for example, the failure of beliefs to exhibit deductive closure certainly show something: the least they show is that viewing the mental processes of an organism as a model of a logic (or a decision theory, or a grammar, etc.) requires what may amount to very severe idealization. The question, however, is what *that* shows.

For one thing, it might just be that you've got the wrong logic. A number of philosophers have suggested that, whereas standard logics give at best a poor fit to the psychological facts, some *non*standard logic might be lit-

erally satisfied by interactions among beliefs. Since we have seen that optimal rationality (in, say, the sense of believing all of the logical truths and none of the logical falsehoods) is *surely* not a precondition for intentional ascription, a logic might serve to support intentional explanation and still be weaker than standard logics are; only those derivations being licensed which do correspond to "psychologically real" inferential processes. Equivalently for our purposes, one might hold that intentional ascription presupposes that the ascribee believe at least some of the logical truths (and not believe at least some of the logical falsehoods), but that *which* ones are mandatory depends on which inferences are complicated given the psychology of the system being described. I'm inclined to think, however, that this is a counsel of despair; a position to which we may have to retreat, but not, at least, in the face of any considerations thus far alleged. Anyhow, I'm prepared to argue for this: the inference from 'intentional theory I applies to system S only under severe idealization' to 'I isn't literally true of S' is unwarranted.

I want to distinguish—if only in a rough and intuitive sort of way—between two kinds of idealization that may be involved in applying a scientific theory in an empirical domain. I think the issues here are actually quite deep, and I don't begin to claim to understand them. But it will do, for our purposes, just to suggest the feel of the thing.

One familiar sort of scientific idealization involves (what one might call) extrapolations to Platonic objects. Paradigm cases of idealizations of this kind (the thermodynamics of ideal gasses, the chemistry of literally pure samples, the mechanics of frictionless planes, etc.) exhibit a very special kind of relation between the parameter values that the theory predicts and the ones that experimentation derives—namely, the latter *approximate* the former. The (presumptive) indispensability of idealization lies, at least in part, in the fact that it is only "in the limit" that we obtain parameter values that precisely satisfy the laws of the theory. Which is to say that, strictly speaking, (and barring accidents), we do not obtain them at all. At best the observations tend to converge upon the ideal values, and we need the idealization because it is only at the point of convergence that the lawful relations that the theory postulates are strictly satisfied. Unless the ideal objects yield the predicted parameter values, nothing does.

What is interesting—and puzzling—about this sort of idealization is that it appears to prescind from ontological commitment to the very objects over which the generalizations of the theory are defined. To put it crudely, nobody thinks that the truth of mechanics depends on the existence of frictionless planes; yet it is at least unobvious whether scientific theories could, in the general case, be so formulated as to avoid Platonic reference without diminution of their explanatory and predictive power. I have precisely nothing to say about this matter; in particular, I don't have an account of the truth conditions upon theories which resort to Platonic idealization. But I'm prepared to believe—or, anyhow, to concede—that *if* intentional theories are among them, there may be *some* sense in which the function of intentional theories in predicting psychological data is heuristic.

There are, however, other kinds of scientific idealization. Tuchman discusses the question why fourteenth-century investigators had so much trouble understanding the epidemiology of plague: "The existence of two carriers confused the trail, and more so because the flea could live and travel independently of the rat for as long as a month and, if infected by the particularly virulent septicemic form of the bacillus, could infect humans without reinfecting itself from the rat. The simultaneous presence of the pneumonic form of the disease, which was indeed communicated through the air, blurred the problem further."[2]

What's going on here is that the observed facts of contagion turned out to have been determined by the simultaneous contribution of several different sources of variance, sometimes acting independently and sometimes interacting. To have gotten a viable theory would therefore have involved a certain epistemic maneuver: idealizing away from—in fact, ignoring—quite a lot of the data, the latter being viewed, in retrospect, as largely unsystematic and attributable to the misleading convergence of several distinct etiologies.

Notice that, prima facie, this second (call it 'epistemic') sort of idealization is quite different from the Platonic variety. Here the problem is not that the observations would satisfy the theoretical predictions only *in the limit*; it's rather that the underlying generalization (say, infected rats transmit plague) explains only *some of* what at first appear to be the relevant cases: the theory works, but only barring exceptions attributable to noise from relatively unsystematic variables. In this sort of situation, the thrust of idealization is not, then, primarily ontological; on the contrary, we are clearly and straightforwardly ontologically committed to the objects and processes over which the generalizations of the theory are defined. It's just that because the surface variance is an effect of many different sorts of causes, we have to idealize away from observations that turn out to be irrelevant to the character of the underlying generalizations. The point is: whatever may be the case for Platonic idealization, the fact that applying a theory involves idealization of this second kind is no argument against the literal truth of its ontological commitments.

I think that Dennett may well be assuming that the kind of idealization involved in intentional prediction is ipso facto Platonic. The line of argument I'm attributing to him would go like this: intentional theories under psychological interpretation do predict mental processes, but only for the case of ideally rational believers. Since there *are* no ideally rational believers (cf. the failure of deductive closure for beliefs), applying such a theory to us rests on a heuristic assumption of rationality. What shows that the assumption *is* heuristic is precisely the fictional—or, anyhow, Platonic—character of the objects over which the generalizations of the intentional theory are defined.

That *is* quite a standard way of understanding claims that intentional theories make. Even so relentlessly Realistic an intentional theorist as Chomsky is prone sometimes to describe the goal of grammar construction as the prediction of the linguistic intuitions of an ideally competent speaker/hearer. (Compare: the logic predicts the inferences acceptable to an ideally rational believer.) In Chomsky's case, however, this Platonic view of intentional idealization cohabits with quite a different sort of account. I'll return to this in the immediate future.

Notice, to begin with, that there is no obvious reason for construing intentional idealization as Platonic rather than epistemic. The problem isn't, after all, that our beliefs tend towards rationality only in the limit; it's rather that our beliefs are rational only *some of the time*.

2. Barbara Tuchman, *A Distant Mirror: The Calamitous 14th Century.* New York, Knopf, p. 106.

We get, as it were, the parameter values that the intentional theory predicts, but we also get counter-cases due to lapses of attention, failure of computational power, weakness of the flesh and, for that matter, sheer bull-headedness. To consider just one case: it's notoriously hard to get people to accept the *validity* of arguments whose conclusions they know to be false. Everybody makes this sort of mistake some of the time; undergraduates seem to make it *a la folie*. We *could* view such errors as the consequence of accepting non-rational principles of inference, but we certainly don't need to do so. Sometimes—surely at least in the cases where one makes such mistakes oneself—it seems reasonable to accept the account one's dignity demands and think of the errors as the consequence of interactions between two different strategies for assessing arguments, one of which one knows perfectly well is no better than heuristic. But if some of the errors are like this, perhaps many of them are. Perhaps *all* of them are.

To come, finally, to the moral: There is, I think, at least one way of construing the psychological application of intentional theories as involving epistemic rather than Platonic idealization. That is to view intentional theories as accounts of one among the (presumably very many) mechanisms whose interactions eventuate in such psychological processes as reasoning and the fixation of belief. On this account, idealization to optimally rational agents is *not* involved in the formulation of intentional stance theories; the predictions such theories license do *not* concern the mental processes of Platonic individuals; and the theories are literally true of us if they are true of us at all.

Instead of viewing an intentional theory as enumerating the beliefs of an ideal believer (or the intuitions of an ideal speaker/hearer), we might think of it as explicating what real reasoners know about valid inferences (what real speaker/hearers know about their language; Chomsky's other line). In a nutshell: intentional theories explicate knowledge structures, and knowledge structures are among the psychological mechanisms which interact in mental processes. To claim that the mental processes of an organism are a model of a logic, in the sense of that notion that is now at issue, is thus *not* to claim that there is a belief of the organism corresponding to each theorem of the logic (what beliefs the organism has will depend on how the internal representation of the logic interacts with other psychological mechanisms). It *is* to claim only that the postulates of the logic are mentally represented by the organism, and that this mental representation contributes (in appropriate ways) to the causation of its beliefs. Perhaps, on some construals, it would follow from that that *were* the organism ideally rational, it would believe whatever the logic entails. But that hardly matters, since it's not, as it were, the fact that makes the logic true of the psychology of the organism; what makes the logic true of the psychology of the organism is that the postulates of the logic are internally represented and etiologically involved. A fortiori, the *evidence* for attributing a logic to an organism would not normally be that the organism believes whatever the logic entails. Rather, the appropriate form of argument is to show that the assumption that the organism internally represents the logic, when taken together with independently motivated theories of the character of the other interacting variables, yields the best explanation of the data about the organism's mental states and processes and/or the behaviors in which such processes eventuate.

There may be other ways of viewing intentional idealization as non-Platonic. If, however, we do it this way, we need the notion of mental representation; in particular, we need to be able to make sense of the idea that the postulates of an intentional theory may be represented by (or, more precisely, may express the same information that is expressed by) certain of the mental structures of the organism. I do not know that this notion can be made clear, but then (I suppose) Dennett does not know that it cannot. *If* it can—to summarize—then we may not argue from such facts as the failure of beliefs to exhibit deductive closure to the heuristic character of appeals to logics as psychological models. For, on the present view, an intentional theory isn't about what we believe; it's about *what causes our beliefs.* This consideration does not, of course, show that the Realistic interpretation of intentional ascription is true; it shows only that we have—as yet—no decisive reason for supposing that it is false.

'Yes, but, as a matter of fact, are *any intentional theories* true? How plausible is it that any of our intentional theories yield literal (though partial) accounts of the knowledge structures that interact in mental processes?' Well, as Dennett himself says, Darwinian selection guarantees that

organisms either know the elements of logic or become posthumous. (It is slightly odd that Dennett *should* say this, since, if there is no fact of the matter about our beliefs, it could hardly be the consequence of an *empirical* theory that some of our beliefs are rational.) Moreover, it's worth contemplating that no one has ever developed a serious theory in cognitive psychology that was other than intentionalist through-and-through; and common-sense psychological explanation can't get started without intentional ascription. So, what we have in favor of the literal ascription of the belief that P is both the available science and the evidence of our day-to-day experience. Sicitur ad astra. I mean: what better kinds of reasons have we for the belief that there are stars?

For all of which, I doubt that the strength of our attachment to belief/desire psychology can be fully accounted for by reference to the confirmatory evidence. The idea that behavior is explicable in terms of the propositional attitudes of the agent plays, it seems to me, quite a special role in our world view: nobody *seriously* (as opposed to philosophically) doubts it; it seems to be utterly universal (in the way that, say, ontological commitment to enduring physical objects is); and, despite its logical complexity and the elaborateness of its ramifications, it is notably the sort of thing which children pick up untaught. (In fact, the problem with children is to get them to restrict their intentional ascriptions to remotely plausible candidates—hence to forego the impulse to attribute propositional attitudes to dolls, clouds, and, literally, everything else that looks like us or moves. Much the same could be said of overgeneralizations of intentional ascription in the history of science.) More-

over, I think it is probably true that, whereas we could (but wouldn't) maintain *any* scientific theory even in the face of vastly and admittedly recalcitrant data, we actually *would* hold onto intentional explanation come what may. Intentional concepts provide a framework for explanations which are, no doubt, empirical, but which I, at least, can't imagine giving up.

Any sensible ethologist contemplating any *other* species would surely take such considerations as prima facie evidence that the framework of intentional explanation is innate. Indeed, that much of what a social organism believes about the psychology of its conspecifics should prove to be innate is ethologically plausible even independent of such considerations. The more social an organism—and the longer its prematurity—the more its survival depends on having predictively adequate views about how its conspecifics are likely to behave.

It seems to me that that is overwhelmingly plausibly the right story to tell about us. If true, it would explain the intuition that our preference for intentional theory is discernibly stronger than what the evidence would rationally demand. It's not that intentional theory is, in principle, insensitive to empirical confirmation; it's not even that the level of confirmation currently available is less than quite respectable; it's rather that the sources of our adherence to intentional explanation don't really have much to do with the fact that it's well confirmed. It is important, at this point, to avoid the genetic fallacy: the fact that intentional theory is innate would *not* be a reason for supposing it to be untrue.

Realism, nativism, intentionality, and mental representation; the fundamental things apply. Play it again, Sam.

Thomas Nagel

What Is It Like to Be a Bat?

Consciousness is what makes the mind-body problem really intractable. Perhaps that is why current discussions of the problem give it little attention or get it obviously wrong. The recent wave of reductionist euphoria has produced several analyses of mental phenomena and mental concepts designed to explain the possibility of some variety of materialism, psychophysical identification, or reduction. But the problems dealt with are those common to this type of reduction and other types, and what makes the mind-body problem unique, and unlike the water-H_2O problem or the Turing machine-IBM machine problem or the lightning-electrical discharge problem or the gene-DNA problem or the oak tree-hydrocarbon problem, is ignored.

Every reductionist has his favorite analogy from modern science. It is most unlikely that any of these unrelated examples of successful reduction will shed light on the relation of mind to brain. But philosophers share the general human weakness for explanations of what is incomprehensible in terms suited for what is familiar and well understood, though entirely different. This has led to the acceptance of implausible accounts of the mental largely because they would permit familiar kinds of reduction. I shall try to explain why the usual examples do not help us to understand the relation between mind and body—why, indeed, we have at present no conception of what an explanation of the physical nature of a mental phenomenon would be. Without consciousness the mind-body problem would be much less interesting. With consciousness it seems hopeless. The most important and characteristic feature of conscious mental phenomena is very poorly understood. Most reductionist theories do not even try to explain it. And careful examination will show that no currently available concept of reduction is applicable to it. Perhaps a new theoretical form can be devised for the purpose, but such a solution, if it exists, lies in the distant intellectual future.

Conscious experience is a widespread phenomenon. It occurs at many levels of animal life, though we cannot be sure of its presence in the simpler organisms, and it is very difficult to say in general what provides evidence of it. (Some extremists have been prepared to deny it even of mammals other than man.) No doubt it occurs in countless forms totally unimaginable to us, on other planets in other solar systems throughout the universe. But no matter how the form may vary, the fact that an organism has conscious experience *at all* means, basically, that there is something it is like to *be* that organism. There may be further implications about the form of the experience; there may even (though I doubt it) be implications about the behavior of the organism. But fundamentally an organism has conscious mental states if and only if there is something that it is like to *be* that organism—something it is like *for* the organism.

We may call this the subjective character of experience. It is not captured by any of the familiar, recently devised reductive analyses of the mental, for all of them are logically compatible with its absence. It is not analyzable in terms of any explanatory system of functional states, or intentional states, since these could be ascribed to robots or automata that behaved like people though they experienced nothing.[1] It is not analyzable in terms of the causal role of experiences in relation to typical human behavior—for similar reasons.[2] I do not deny that

---

1. Perhaps there could not actually be such robots. Perhaps anything complex enough to behave like a person would have experiences. But that, if true, is a fact which cannot be discovered merely by analyzing the concept of experience.

2. It is not equivalent to that about which we are incorrigible, both because we are not incorrigible about experience and because experience is present in animals lacking language and thought, who have no beliefs at all about their experiences.

Thomas Nagel, "What Is It Like to Be a Bat?" from *Philosophical Review*, 83 (1974).

conscious mental states and events cause behavior, nor that they may be given functional characterizations. I deny only that this kind of thing exhausts their analysis. Any reductionist program has to to be based on an analysis of what is to be reduced. If the analysis leaves something out, the problem will be falsely posed. It is useless to base the defense of materialism on any analysis of mental phenomena that fails to deal explicitly with their subjective character. For there is no reason to suppose that a reduction which seems plausible when no attempt is made to account for consciousness can be extended to include consciousness. Without some idea, therefore, of what the subjective character of experience is, we cannot know what is required of a physicalist theory.

While an account of the physical basis of mind must explain many things, this appears to be the most difficult. It is impossible to exclude the phenomenological features of experience from a reduction in the same way that one excludes the phenomenal features of an ordinary substance from a physical or chemical reduction of it—namely, by explaining them as effects on the minds of human observers. If physicalism is to be defended, the phenomenological features must themselves be given a physical account. But when we examine their subjective character it seems that such a result is impossible. The reason is that every subjective phenomenon is essentially connected with a single point of view, and it seems inevitable that an objective, physical theory will abandon that point of view.

Let me first try to state the issue somewhat more fully than by referring to the relation between the subjective and the objective, or between the *pour-soi* and the *en-soi*. This is far from easy. Facts about what it is like to be an *X* are very peculiar, so peculiar that some may be inclined to doubt their reality, or the significance of claims about them. To illustrate the connection between subjectivity and a point of view, and to make evident the importance of subjective features, it will help to explore the matter in relation to an example that brings out clearly the divergence between the two types of conception, subjective and objective.

I assume we all believe that bats have experience. After all, they are mammals, and there is no more doubt that they have experience than that mice or pigeons or whales have experience. I have chosen bats instead of wasps or flounders because if one travels too far down

the phylogenetic tree, people gradually shed their faith that there is experience there at all. Bats, although more closely related to us than those other species, nevertheless present a range of activity and a sensory apparatus so different from ours that the problem I want to pose is exceptionally vivid (though it certainly could be raised with other species). Even without the benefit of philosophical reflection, anyone who has spent some time in an enclosed space with an excited bat knows what it is to encounter a fundamentally *alien* form of life.

I have said that the essence of the belief that bats have experience is that there is something that it is like to be a bat. Now we know that most bats (the microchiroptera, to be precise) perceive the external world primarily by sonar, or echolocation, detecting the reflections, from objects within range, of their own rapid, subtly modulated, high-frequency shrieks. Their brains are designed to correlate the outgoing impulses with the subsequent echoes, and the information thus acquired enables bats to make precise discriminations of distance, size, shape, motion, and texture comparable to those we make by vision. But bat sonar, though clearly a form of perception, is not similar in its operation to any sense that we possess, and there is no reason to suppose that it is subjectively like anything we can experience or imagine. This appears to create difficulties for the notion of what it is like to be a bat. We must consider whether any method will permit us to extrapolate to the inner life of the bat from our own case,[3] and if not, what alternative methods there may be for understanding the notion.

Our own experience provides the basic material for our imagination, whose range is therefore limited. It will not help to try to imagine that one has webbing on one's arms, which enables one to fly around at dusk and dawn catching insects in one's mouth; that one has very poor vision, and perceives the surrounding world by a system of reflected high-frequency sound signals; and that one spends the day hanging upside down by one's feet in an attic. In so far as I can imagine this (which is not very far), it tells me only what it would be like for

---

3. By "our own case" I do not mean just "my own case," but rather the mentalistic ideas that we apply unproblematically to ourselves and other human beings.

me to behave as a bat behaves. But that is not the question. I want to know what it is like for a *bat* to be a bat. Yet if I try to imagine this, I am restricted to the resources of my own mind, and those resources are inadequate to the task. I cannot perform it either by imagining additions to my present experience, or by imagining segments gradually subtracted from it, or by imagining some combination of additions, subtractions, and modifications.

To the extent that I could look and behave like a wasp or a bat without changing my fundamental structure, my experiences would not be anything like the experiences of those animals. On the other hand, it is doubtful that any meaning can be attached to the supposition that I should possess the internal neurophysiological constitution of a bat. Even if I could by gradual degrees be transformed into a bat, nothing in my present constitution enables me to imagine what the experiences of such a future stage of myself thus metamorphosed would be like. The best evidence would come from the experiences of bats, if we only knew what they were like.

So if extrapolation from our own case is involved in the idea of what it is like to be a bat, the extrapolation must be incompletable. We cannot form more than a schematic conception of what it *is* like. For example, we may ascribe general *types* of experience on the basis of the animal's structure and behavior. Thus we describe bat sonar as a form of three-dimensional forward perception; we believe that bats feel some versions of pain, fear, hunger, and lust, and that they have other, more familiar types of perception besides sonar. But we believe that these experiences also have in each case a specific subjective character, which it is beyond our ability to conceive. And if there is conscious life elsewhere in the universe, it is likely that some of it will not be describable even in the most general experiential terms available to us. (The problem is not confined to exotic cases, however, for it exists between one person and another. The subjective character of the experience of a person deaf and blind from birth is not accessible to me, for example, nor presumably is mine to him. This does not prevent us each from believing that the other's experience has such a subjective character.)

If anyone is inclined to deny that we can believe in the existence of facts like this whose exact nature we cannot possibly conceive, he should reflect that in con-templating the bats we are in much the same position that intelligent bats or Martians would occupy if they tried to form a conception of what it was like to be us. The structure of their own minds might make it impossible for them to succeed, but we know they would be wrong to conclude that there is not anything precise that it is like to be us: that only certain general types of mental state could be ascribed to us (perhaps perception and appetite would be concepts common to us both; perhaps not). We know they would be wrong to draw such a skeptical conclusion because we know what it is like to be us. And we know that while it includes an enormous amount of variation and complexity, and while we do not possess the vocabulary to describe it adequately, its subjective character is highly specific, and in some respects describable in terms that can be understood only by creatures like us. The fact that we cannot expect ever to accommodate in our language a detailed description of Martian or bat phenomenology should not lead us to dismiss as meaningless the claim that bats and Martians have experiences fully comparable in richness of detail to our own. It would be fine if someone were to develop concepts and a theory that enabled us to think about those things; but such an understanding may be permanently denied to us by the limits of our nature. And to deny the reality or logical significance of what we can never describe or understand is the crudest form of cognitive dissonance.

This brings us to the edge of a topic that requires much more discussion than I can give it here: namely, the relation between facts on the one hand and conceptual schemes or systems of representation on the other. My realism about the subjective domain in all its forms implies a belief in the existence of facts beyond the reach of human concepts. Certainly it is possible for a human being to believe that there are facts which humans never *will* possess the requisite concepts to represent or comprehend. Indeed, it would be foolish to doubt this, given the finiteness of humanity's expectations. After all, there would have been transfinite numbers even if everyone had been wiped out by the Black Death before Cantor discovered them. But one might also believe that there are facts which *could* not ever be represented or comprehended by human beings, even if the species lasted forever—simply because our structure does not permit us to operate with concepts of the requisite type. This impossibility might even be observed by other beings, but it is not clear that the existence of such beings, or the possibility of their existence, is a precondition of the significance of the hypothesis that there are humanly inaccessible facts. (After all, the nature of beings with access to humanly inaccessible facts is presumably itself a humanly inaccessible fact.) Reflection on what it is like to be a bat seems to lead us, therefore, to the conclusion that there are facts that do not consist in the truth of propositions expressible in a human language. We can be compelled to recognize the existence of such facts without being able to state or comprehend them.

I shall not pursue this subject, however. Its bearing on the topic before us (namely, the mind-body problem) is that it enables us to make a general observation about the subjective character of experience. Whatever may be the status of facts about what it is like to be a human being, or a bat, or a Martian, these appear to be facts that embody a particular point of view.

I am not adverting here to the alleged privacy of experience to its possessor. The point of view in question is not one accessible only to a single individual. Rather it is a *type*. It is often possible to take up a point of view other than one's own, so the comprehension of such facts is not limited to one's own case. There is a sense in which phenomenological facts are perfectly objective: one person can know or say of another what the quality of the other's experience is. They are subjective, however, in the sense that even this objective ascription of experience is possible only for someone sufficiently similar to the object of ascription to be able to adopt his point of view—to understand the ascription in the first person as well as in the third, so to speak. The more different from oneself the other experiencer is, the less success one can expect with this enterprise. In our own case we occupy the relevant point of view, but we will have as much difficulty understanding our own experience properly if we approach it from another point of view as we would if we tried to understand the experience of another species without taking up *its* point of view.[4]

This bears directly on the mind-body problem. For if the facts of experience—facts about what it is like *for the experiencing organism*—are accessible only from one point of view, then it is a mystery how the true character of experiences could be revealed in the physical operation of that organism. The latter is a domain of objective facts *par excellence*—the kind that can be observed and understood from many points of view and by individuals with differing perceptual systems. There are no comparable imaginative obstacles to the acquisition of knowledge about bat neurophysiology by human scientists, and intelligent bats or Martians might learn more about the human brain than we ever will.

This is not by itself an argument against reduction. A Martian scientist with no understanding of visual perception could understand the rainbow, or lightning, or clouds as physical phenomena, though he would never be able to understand the human concepts of rainbow, lightning, or cloud, or the place these things occupy in our phenomenal world. The objective nature of the things picked out by these concepts could be apprehended by him because, although the concepts themselves are connected with a particular point of view and a particular visual phenomenology, the things apprehended from that point of view are not: they are observable from the point of view but external to it; hence they can be comprehended from other points of view also, either by the same organisms or by others. Lightning has an objective character that is not exhausted by

---

ample, blind people are able to detect objects near them by a form of sonar, using vocal clicks or taps of a cane. Perhaps if one knew what that was like, one could by extension imagine roughly what it was like to possess the much more refined sonar of a bat. The distance between oneself and other persons and other species can fall anywhere on a continuum. Even for other persons the understanding of what it is like to be them is only partial, and when one moves to species very different from oneself, a lesser degree of partial understanding may still be available. The imagination is remarkably flexible. My point, however, is not that we cannot *know* what it is like to be a bat. I am not raising that epistemological problem. My point is rather that even to form a *conception* of what it is like to be a bat (and a fortiori to know what it is like to be a bat) one must take up the bat's point of view. If one can take it up roughly, or partially, then one's conception will also be rough or partial. Or so it seems in our present state of understanding.

---

4. It may be easier than I suppose to transcend interspecies barriers with the aid of the imagination. For ex-

its visual appearance, and this can be investigated by a Martian without vision. To be precise, it has a *more* objective character than is revealed in its visual appearance. In speaking of the move from subjective to objective characterization, I wish to remain noncommittal about the existence of an end point, the completely objective intrinsic nature of the thing, which one might or might not be able to reach. It may be more accurate to think of objectivity as a direction in which the understanding can travel. And in understanding a phenomenon like lightning, it is legitimate to go as far away as one can from a strictly human viewpoint.

In the case of experience, on the other hand, the connection with a particular point of view seems much closer. It is difficult to understand what could be meant by the *objective* character of an experience, apart from the particular point of view from which its subject apprehends it. After all, what would be left of what it was like to be a bat if one removed the viewpoint of the bat? But if experience does not have, in addition to its subjective character, an objective nature that can be apprehended from many different points of view, then how can it be supposed that a Martian investigating my brain might be observing physical processes which were my mental processes (as he might observe physical processes which were bolts of lightning), only from a different point of view? How, for that matter, could a human physiologist observe them from another point of view?

We appear to be faced with a general difficulty about psychophysical reduction. In other areas the process of reduction is a move in the direction of greater objectivity, toward a more accurate view of the real nature of things. This is accomplished by reducing our dependence on individual or species-specific points of view toward the object of investigation. We describe it not in terms of the impressions it makes on our senses, but in terms of its more general effects and of properties detectable by means other than the human senses. The less it depends on a specifically human viewpoint, the more objective is our description. It is possible to follow this path because although the concepts and ideas we employ in thinking about the external world are initially applied from a point of view that involves our perceptual apparatus, they are used by us to refer to things beyond themselves—toward which we *have* the phenomenal point of view. Therefore we can abandon it in

favor of another, and still be thinking about the same things.

Experience itself, however, does not seem to fit the pattern. The idea of moving from appearance to reality seems to make no sense here. What is the analogue in this case to pursuing a more objective understanding of the same phenomena by abandoning the initial subjective viewpoint toward them in favor of another that is more objective but concerns the same thing? Certainly it *appears* unlikely that we will get closer to the real nature of human experience by leaving behind the particularity of our human point of view and striving for a description in terms accessible to beings that could not imagine what it was like to be us. If the subjective character of experience is fully comprehensible only from one point of view, then any shift to greater objectivity—that is, less attachment to a specific viewpoint—does not take us nearer to the real nature of the phenomenon: it takes us farther away from it.

In a sense, the seeds of this objection to the reducibility of experience are already detectable in successful cases of reduction; for in discovering sound to be, in reality, a wave phenomenon in air or other media, we leave behind one viewpoint to take up another, and the auditory, human or animal viewpoint that we leave behind remains unreduced. Members of radically different species may both understand the same physical events in objective terms, and this does not require that they understand the phenomenal forms in which those events appear to the senses of members of the other species. Thus it is a condition of their referring to a common reality that their more particular viewpoints are not part of the common reality that they both apprehend. The reduction can succeed only if the species-specific viewpoint is omitted from what is to be reduced.

But while we are right to leave this point of view aside in seeking a fuller understanding of the external world, we cannot ignore it permanently, since it is the essence of the internal world, and not merely a point of view on it. Most of the neobehaviorism of recent philosophical psychology results from the effort to substitute an objective concept of mind for the real thing, in order to have nothing left over which cannot be reduced. If we acknowledge that a physical theory of mind must account for the subjective character of experience, we must admit that no presently available conception gives us a clue how this could be done. The problem is unique. If mental processes are indeed physical processes, then there is something it is like, intrinsically, to undergo certain physical processes. What it is for such a thing to be the case remains a mystery.

What moral should be drawn from these reflections, and what should be done next? It would be a mistake to conclude that physicalism must be false. Nothing is proved by the inadequacy of physicalist hypotheses that assume a faulty objective analysis of mind. It would be truer to say that physicalism is a position we cannot understand because we do not at present have any conception of how it might be true. Perhaps it will be thought unreasonable to require such a conception as a condition of understanding. After all, it might be said, the meaning of physicalism is clear enough: mental states are states of the body; mental events are physical events. We do not know *which* physical states and events they are, but that should not prevent us from understanding the hypothesis. What could be clearer than the words "is" and "are"?

But I believe it is precisely this apparent clarity of the word "is" that is deceptive. Usually, when we are told that *X* is *Y* we know *how* it is supposed to be true, but that depends on a conceptual or theoretical background and is not conveyed by the "is" alone. We know how both "*X*" and "*Y*" refer, and the kinds of things to which they refer, and we have a rough idea how the two referential paths might converge on a single thing, be it an object, a person, a process, an event, or whatever. But when the two terms of the identification are very disparate it may not be so clear how it could be true. We may not have even a rough idea of how the two referential paths could converge, or what kind of things they might converge on, and a theoretical framework may have to be supplied to enable us to understand this. Without the framework, an air of mysticism surrounds the identification.

This explains the magical flavor of popular presentations of fundamental scientific discoveries, given out as propositions to which one must subscribe without really understanding them. For example, people are now told at an early age that all matter is really energy. But despite the fact that they know what "is" means, most of them never form a conception of what makes this claim true, because they lack the theoretical background.

At the present time the status of physicalism is similar to that which the hypothesis that matter is energy

would have had if uttered by a pre-Socratic philosopher. We do not have the beginnings of a conception of how it might be true. In order to understand the hypothesis that a mental event is a physical event, we require more than an understanding of the word "is." The idea of how a mental and a physical term might refer to the same thing is lacking, and the usual analogies with theoretical identification in other fields fail to supply it. They fail because if we construe the reference of mental terms to physical events on the usual model, we either get a reappearance of separate subjective events as the effects through which mental reference to physical events is secured, or else we get a false account of how mental terms refer (for example, a causal behaviorist one).

Strangely enough, we may have evidence for the truth of something we cannot really understand. Suppose a caterpillar is locked in a sterile safe by someone unfamiliar with insect metamorphosis and weeks later the safe is reopened, revealing a butterfly. If the person knows that the safe has been shut the whole time, he has reason to believe that the butterfly is or was once the caterpillar without having any idea in what sense this might be so. (One possibility is that the caterpillar contained a tiny winged parasite that devoured it and grew into the butterfly.)

It is conceivable that we are in such a position with regard to physicalism. Donald Davidson has argued that if mental events have physical causes and effects, they must have physical descriptions. He holds that we have reason to believe this even though we do not—and in fact *could* not—have a general psychophysical theory.[5] His argument applies to intentional mental events, but I think we also have some reason to believe that sensations are physical processes, without being in a position to understand how. Davidson's position is that certain physical events have irreducibly mental properties, and perhaps some view describable in this way is correct. But nothing of which we can now form a conception corresponds to it; nor have we any idea what a theory would be like that enabled us to conceive of it.

Very little work has been done on the basic question (from which mention of the brain can be entirely omit-

---

5. See "Mental Events" in Foster and Swanson, *Experience and Theory* (Amherst, 1970).

ted) whether any sense can be made of experiences' having an objective character at all. Does it make sense, in other words, to ask what my experiences are *really* like, as opposed to how they appear to me? We cannot genuinely understand the hypothesis that their nature is captured in a physical description unless we understand the more fundamental idea that they *have* an objective nature (or that objective processes can have a subjective nature).

I should like to close with a speculative proposal. It may be possible to approach the gap between subjective and objective from another direction. Setting aside temporarily the relation between the mind and the brain, we can pursue a more objective understanding of the mental in its own right. At present we are completely unequipped to think about the subjective character of experience without relying on the imagination—without taking up the point of view of the experiential subject. This should be regarded as a challenge to form new concepts and devise a new method—an objective phenomenology not dependent on empathy or the imagination. Though presumably it would not capture everything, its goal would be to describe, at least in part, the subjective character of experiences in a form comprehensible to beings incapable of having those experiences.

We would have to develop such a phenomenology to describe the sonar experiences of bats; but it would also be possible to begin with humans. One might try, for example, to develop concepts that could be used to explain to a person blind from birth what it was like to see. One would reach a blank wall eventually, but it should be possible to devise a method of expressing in objective terms much more than we can at present, and with much greater precision. The loose intermodal analogies—for example, "Red is like the sound of a trumpet"—which crop up in discussions of this subject are of little use. That should be clear to anyone who has both heard a trumpet and seen red. But structural features of perception might be more accessible to objective description, even though something would be left out. And concepts alternative to those we learn in the first person may enable us to arrive at a kind of understanding even of our own experience which is denied us by the very ease of description and lack of distance that subjective concepts afford.

Apart from its own interest, a phenomenology that is in this sense objective may permit questions about the physical basis of experience to assume a more intelligible form. Aspects of subjective experience that admitted this kind of objective description might be better candidates for objective explanations of a more familiar sort. But whether or not this guess is correct, it seems unlikely that any physical theory of mind can be contemplated until more thought has been given to the general problem of subjective and objective. Otherwise we cannot even pose the mind-body problem without sidestepping it.

Frank Jackson

Epiphenomenal Qualia

It is undeniable that the physical, chemical and biological sciences have provided a great deal of information about the world we live in and about ourselves. I will

Frank Jackson, "Epiphenomenal Qualia" from *Philosophical Quarterly,* 32 (1982). Copyright © 1982. Reprinted with permission of Blackwell Publishing, Ltd.

use the label 'physical information' for this kind of information, and also for information that automatically comes along with it. For example, if a medical scientist tells me enough about the processes that go on in my nervous system, and about how they relate to happenings in the world around me, to what has happened in the past and is likely to happen in the future, to what happens to other similar and dissimilar organisms, and the like, he or she tells me—if I am clever enough to fit it together appropriately—about what is often called the functional role of those states in me (and in organisms in general in similar cases). This information, and its kin, I also label 'physical'.

I do not mean these sketchy remarks to constitute a definition of 'physical information', and of the correlative notions of physical property, process, and so on, but to indicate what I have in mind here. It is well known that there are problems with giving a precise definition of these notions, and so of the thesis of Physicalism that all (correct) information is physical information. But—unlike some—I take the question of definition to cut across the central problems I want to discuss in this paper.

I am what is sometimes known as a "qualia freak". I think that there are certain features of the bodily sensations especially, but also of certain perceptual experiences, which no amount of purely physical information includes. Tell me everything physical there is to tell about what is going on in a living brain, the kind of states, their functional role, their relation to what goes on at other times and in other brains, and so on and so forth, and be I as clever as can be in fitting it all together, you won't have told me about the hurtfulness of pains, the itchiness of itches, pangs of jealousy, or about the characteristic experience of tasting a lemon, smelling a rose, hearing a loud noise or seeing the sky.

There are many qualia freaks, and some of them say that their rejection of Physicalism is an unargued intuition. I think that they are being unfair to themselves. They have the following argument. Nothing you could tell of a physical sort captures the smell of a rose, for instance. Therefore, Physicalism is false. By our lights this is a perfectly good argument. It is obviously not to the point to question its validity, and the premise is intuitively obviously true both to them and to me.

I must, however, admit that it is weak from a polemical point of view. There are, unfortunately for us, many who do not find the premise intuitively obvious. The task then is to present an argument whose premises are obvious to all, or at least to as many as possible. This I try to do in §I with what I will call "the Knowledge argument". In §II I contrast the Knowledge argument with the Modal argument and in §III with the "What is it like to be" argument. In §IV I tackle the question

of the causal role of qualia. The major factor in stopping people from admitting qualia is the belief that they would have to be given a causal role with respect to the physical world and especially the brain; and it is hard to do this without sounding like someone who believes in fairies. I seek in §IV to turn this objection by arguing that the view that qualia are epiphenomenal is a perfectly possible one.

I. The Knowledge Argument for Qualia

People vary considerably in their ability to discriminate colours. Suppose that in an experiment to catalogue this variation Fred is discovered. Fred has better colour vision than anyone else on record; he makes every discrimination that anyone has ever made, and moreover he makes one that we cannot even begin to make. Show him a batch of ripe tomatoes and he sorts them into two roughly equal groups and does so with complete consistency. That is, if you blindfold him, shuffle the tomatoes up, and then remove the blindfold and ask him to sort them out again, he sorts them into exactly the same two groups.

We ask Fred how he does it. He explains that all ripe tomatoes do not look the same colour to him, and in fact that this is true of a great many objects that we classify together as red. He sees two colours where we see one, and he has in consequence developed for his own use two words 'red$_1$' and 'red$_2$' to mark the difference. Perhaps he tells us that he has often tried to teach the difference between red$_1$ and red$_2$ to his friends but has got nowhere and has concluded that the rest of the world is red$_1$-red$_2$ colour-blind—or perhaps he has had partial success with his children, it doesn't matter. In any case he explains to us that it would be quite wrong to think that because 'red' appears in both 'red$_1$' and 'red$_2$' that the two colours are shades of the one colour. He only uses the common term 'red' to fit more easily into our restricted usage. To him red$_1$ and red$_2$ are as different from each other and all the other colours as yellow is from blue. And his discriminatory behaviour bears this out: he sorts red$_1$ from red$_2$ tomatoes with the greatest of ease in a wide variety of viewing circumstances. Moreover, an investigation of the physiological basis of Fred's exceptional ability reveals that Fred's optical system is able to separate out two groups of wavelengths in the red spectrum as sharply as we are able to sort out yellow from blue.

I think that we should admit that Fred can see, really see, at least one more colour than we can; red$_1$ is a different colour from red$_2$. We are to Fred as a totally red-green colour-blind person is to us. H. G. Wells' story "The Country of the Blind" is about a sighted person in a totally blind community.[1] This person never manages to convince them that he can see, that he has an extra sense. They ridicule this sense as quite inconceivable, and treat his capacity to avoid falling into ditches, to win fights and so on as precisely that capacity and nothing more. We would be making their mistake if we refused to allow that Fred can see one more colour than we can.

What kind of experience does Fred have when he sees red$_1$ and red$_2$? What is the new colour or colours like? We would dearly like to know but do not; and it seems that no amount of physical information about Fred's brain and optical system tells us. We find out perhaps that Fred's cones respond differentially to certain light waves in the red section of the spectrum that make no difference to ours (or perhaps he has an extra cone) and that this leads in Fred to a wider range of those brain states responsible for visual discriminatory behaviour. But none of this tells us what we really want to know about his colour experience. There is something about it we don't know. But we know, we may suppose, everything about Fred's body, his behaviour and dispositions to behaviour and about his internal physiology, and everything about his history and relation to others that can be given in physical accounts of persons. We have all the physical information. Therefore, knowing all this is *not* knowing everything about Fred. It follows that Physicalism leaves something out.

To reinforce this conclusion, imagine that as a result of our investigations into the internal workings of Fred we find out how to make everyone's physiology like Fred's in the relevant respects; or perhaps Fred donates his body to science and on his death we are able to transplant his optical system into someone else—again the fine detail doesn't matter. The important point is that such a happening would create enormous interest. People would say, "At last we will know what it is like to see the extra colour, at last we will know how Fred has differed from us in the way he has struggled to tell us about for so long". Then it cannot be that we knew all along all about Fred. But *ex hypothesi* we did know all along everything about Fred that features in the physicalist scheme; hence the physicalist scheme leaves something out.

Put it this way. *After* the operation, we will know *more* about Fred and especially about his colour experiences. But beforehand we had all the physical information we could desire about his body and brain, and indeed everything that has ever featured in physicalist accounts of mind and consciousness. Hence there is more to know than all that. Hence Physicalism is incomplete.

Fred and the new colour(s) are of course essentially rhetorical devices. The same point can be made with normal people and familiar colours. Mary is a brilliant scientist who is, for whatever reason, forced to investigate the world from a black and white room *via* a black and white television monitor. She specialises in the neurophysiology of vision and acquires, let us suppose, all the physical information there is to obtain about what goes on when we see ripe tomatoes, or the sky, and use terms like 'red', 'blue', and so on. She discovers, for example, just which wave-length combinations from the sky stimulate the retina, and exactly how this produces *via* the central nervous system the contraction of the vocal chords and expulsion of air from the lungs that results in the uttering of the sentence 'The sky is blue'. (It can hardly be denied that it is in principle possible to obtain all this physical information from black and white television, otherwise the Open University would *of necessity* need to use colour television.)

What will happen when Mary is released from her black and white room or is given a colour television monitor? Will she *learn* anything or not? It seems just obvious that she will learn something about the world and our visual experience of it. But then it is inescapable that her previous knowledge was incomplete. But she had *all* the physical information. *Ergo* there is more to have than that, and Physicalism is false.

Clearly the same style of Knowledge argument could be deployed for taste, hearing, the bodily sensations and

---

1. H. G. Wells, *The Country of the Blind and Other Stories* (London, n.d.).

generally speaking for the various mental states which are said to have (as it is variously put) raw feels, phenomenal features or qualia. The conclusion in each case is that the qualia are left out of the physicalist story. And the polemical strength of the Knowledge argument is that it is so hard to deny the central claim that one can have all the physical information without having all the information there is to have.

II. The Modal Argument

By the Modal Argument I mean an argument of the following style. Sceptics about other minds are not making a mistake in deductive logic, whatever else may be wrong with their position. No amount of physical information about another *logically entails* that he or she is conscious or feels anything at all. Consequently there is a possible world with organisms exactly like us in every physical respect (and remember that includes functional states, physical history, *et al.*) but which differ from us profoundly in that they have no conscious mental life at all. But then what is it that we have and they lack? Not anything physical *ex hypothesi*. In all physical regards we and they are exactly alike. Consequently there is more to us than the purely physical. Thus Physicalism is false.

It is sometimes objected that the Modal argument misconceives Physicalism on the ground that that doctrine is advanced as a *contingent* truth. But to say this is only to say that physicalists restrict their claim to *some* possible worlds, including especially ours; and the Modal argument is only directed against this lesser claim. If we in *our* world, let alone beings in any others, have features additional to those of our physical replicas in other possible worlds, then we have non-physical features or qualia.

The trouble rather with the Modal argument is that it rests on a disputable modal intuition. Disputable because it is disputed. Some sincerely deny that there can be physical replicas of us in other possible worlds which nevertheless lack consciousness. Moreover, at least one person who once had the intuition now has doubts.[2]

Head-counting may seem a poor approach to a discussion of the Modal argument. But frequently we can do no better when modal intuitions are in question, and remember our initial goal was to find the argument with the greatest polemical utility.

Of course, *qua* protagonists of the Knowledge argument we may well accept the modal intuition in question; but this will be a *consequence* of our already having an argument to the conclusion that qualia are left out of the physicalist story, not our ground for that conclusion. Moreover, the matter is complicated by the possibility that the connection between matters physical and qualia is like that sometimes held to obtain between aesthetic qualities and natural ones. Two possible worlds which agree in all "natural" respects (including the experiences of sentient creatures) must agree in all aesthetic qualities also, but it is plausibly held that the aesthetic qualities cannot be reduced to the natural.

III. The "What Is It Like to Be" Argument

In "What is it like to be a bat?" Thomas Nagel argues that no amount of physical information can tell us what it is like to be a bat, and indeed that we, human beings, cannot imagine what it is like to be a bat.[3] His reason is that what this is like can only be understood from a bat's point of view, which is not our point of view and is not something capturable in physical terms which are essentially terms understandable equally from many points of view.

It is important to distinguish this argument from the Knowledge argument. When I complained that all the physical knowledge about Fred was not enough to tell us what his special colour experience was like, I was not complaining that we weren't finding out what it is like to *be* Fred. I was complaining that there is something *about* his experience, a property of it, of which we were left ignorant. And if and when we come to know what this property is we still will not know what it is like to *be* Fred, but we will know more *about* him. No amount of knowledge about Fred, be it physical or not, amounts

2. See R. Kirk, "From Physical Explicability to Full-Blooded Materialism", *The Philosophical Quarterly*, 29 (1979), 229–37.

3. *The Philosophical Review,* 83 (1974), 435–50. [See pp. 421–27, this volume.]

to knowledge "from the inside" concerning Fred. We are not Fred. There is thus a whole set of items of knowledge expressed by forms of words like 'that it is *I myself* who is . . .' which Fred has and we simply cannot have because we are not him.

When Fred sees the colour he alone can see, one thing he knows is the way his experience of it differs from his experience of seeing red and so on, *another* is that he himself is seeing it. Physicalist and qualia freaks alike should acknowledge that no amount of information of whatever kind that *others* have *about* Fred amounts to knowledge of the second. My complaint though concerned the first and was that the special quality of his experience is certainly a fact about it, and one which Physicalism leaves out because no amount of physical information told us what it is.

Nagel speaks as if the problem he is raising is one of extrapolating from knowledge of one experience to another, of imagining what an unfamiliar experience would be like on the basis of familiar ones. In terms of Hume's example, from knowledge of some shades of blue we can work out what it would be like to see other shades of blue. Nagel argues that the trouble with bats *et al.* is that they are too unlike us. It is hard to see an objection to Physicalism here. Physicalism makes no special claims about the imaginative or extrapolative powers of human beings, and it is hard to see why it need do so.

Anyway, our Knowledge argument makes no assumptions on this point. If Physicalism were true, enough physical information about Fred would obviate any need to extrapolate or to perform special feats of imagination or understanding in order to know all about his special colour experience. *The information would already be in our possession.* But it clearly isn't. That was the nub of the argument.

IV. The Bogey of Epiphenomenalism

Is there any really *good* reason for refusing to countenance the idea that qualia are causally impotent with respect to the physical world? I will argue for the answer no, but in doing this I will say nothing about two views associated with the classical epiphenomenalist position. The first is that mental *states* are inefficacious with respect to the physical world. All I will be concerned to

defend is that it is possible to hold that certain *properties* of certain mental states, namely those I've called qualia, are such that their possession or absence makes no difference to the physical world. The second is that the mental is *totally* causally inefficacious. For all I will say it may be that you have to hold that the instantiation of *qualia* makes a difference to *other mental states* though not to anything physical. Indeed general considerations to do with how you could come to be aware of the instantiation of qualia suggest such a position.

Three reasons are standardly given for holding that a quale like the hurtfulness of a pain must be causally efficacious in the physical world, and so, for instance, that its instantiation must sometimes make a difference to what happens in the brain. None, I will argue, has any real force. (I am much indebted to Alec Hyslop and John Lucas for convincing me of this.)

(i) It is supposed to be just obvious that the hurtfulness of pain is partly responsible for the subject seeking to avoid pain, saying 'It hurts' and so on. But, to reverse Hume, anything can fail to cause anything. No matter how often *B* follows *A,* and no matter how initially obvious the causality of the connection seems, the hypothesis that *A* causes *B* can be overturned by an overarching theory which shows the two as distinct effects of a common underlying causal process.

To the untutored the image on the screen of Lee Marvin's fist moving from left to right immediately followed by the image of John Wayne's head moving in the same general direction looks as causal as anything. And of course throughout countless Westerns images similar to the first are followed by images similar to the second. All this counts for precisely nothing when we know the over-arching theory concerning how the relevant images are both effects of an underlying causal process involving the projector and the film. The epiphenomenalist can say exactly the same about the connection between, for example, hurtfulness and behaviour. It is simply a consequence of the fact that certain happenings in the brain cause both.

(ii) The second objection relates to Darwin's Theory of Evolution. According to natural selection the traits that evolve over time are those conducive to physical survival. We may assume that qualia evolved over time—we have them, the earliest forms of life do not—and so we should expect qualia to be conducive to survival.

The objection is that they could hardly help us to survive if they do nothing to the physical world.

The appeal of this argument is undeniable, but there is a good reply to it. Polar bears have particularly thick, warm coats. The Theory of Evolution explains this (we suppose) by pointing out that having a thick, warm coat is conducive to survival in the Arctic. But having a thick coat goes along with having a heavy coat, and having a heavy coat is *not* conducive to survival. It slows the animal down.

Does this mean that we have refuted Darwin because we have found an evolved trait—having a heavy coat—which is not conducive to survival? Clearly not. Having a heavy coat is an unavoidable concomitant of having a warm coat (in the context, modern insulation was not available), and the advantages for survival of having a warm coat outweighed the disadvantages of having a heavy one. The point is that all we can extract from Darwin's theory is that we should expect any evolved characteristic to be *either* conducive to survival *or* a by-product of one that is so conducive. The epiphenomenalist holds that qualia fall into the latter category. They are a by-product of certain brain processes that are highly conducive to survival.

(iii) The third objection is based on a point about how we come to know about other minds. We know about other minds by knowing about other behaviour, at least in part. The nature of the inference is a matter of some controversy, but it is not a matter of controversy that it proceeds from behaviour. That is why we think that stones do not feel and dogs do feel. But, runs the objection, how can a person's behaviour provide any reason for believing he has qualia like mine, or indeed any qualia at all, unless this behaviour can be regarded as the *outcome* of the qualia. Man Friday's footprint was evidence of Man Friday because footprints are causal outcomes of feet attached to people. And an epiphenomenalist cannot regard behaviour, or indeed anything physical, as an outcome of qualia.

But consider my reading in *The Times* that Spurs won. This provides excellent evidence that *The Telegraph* has also reported that Spurs won, despite the fact that (I trust) *The Telegraph* does not get the results from *The Times*. They each send their own reporters to the game. *The Telegraph*'s report is in no sense an outcome of *The*

Times', but the latter provides good evidence for the former nevertheless.

The reasoning involved can be reconstructed thus. I read in *The Times* that Spurs won. This gives me reason to think that Spurs won because I know that Spurs' winning is the most likely candidate to be what caused the report in *The Times*. But I also know that Spurs' winning would have had many effects, including almost certainly a report in *The Telegraph*.

I am arguing from one effect back to its cause and out again to another effect. The fact that neither effect causes the other is irrelevant. Now the epiphenomenalist allows that qualia are effects of what goes on in the brain. Qualia cause nothing physical but are caused by something physical. Hence the epiphenomenalist can argue from the behaviour of others to the qualia of others by arguing from the behaviour of others back to its causes in the brains of others and out again to their qualia.

You may well feel for one reason or another that this is a more dubious chain of reasoning than its model in the case of newspaper reports. You are right. The problem of other minds is a major philosophical problem, the problem of other newspaper reports is not. But there is no special problem of Epiphenomenalism as opposed to, say, Interactionism here.

There is a very understandable response to the three replies I have just made. "All right, there is no knock-down refutation of the existence of epiphenomenal qualia. But the fact remains that they are an excrescence. They *do* nothing, they *explain* nothing, they serve merely to soothe the intuitions of dualists, and it is left a total mystery how they fit into the world view of science. In short we do not and cannot understand the how and why of them."

This is perfectly true; but is no objection to qualia, for it rests on an overly optimistic view of the human animal, and its powers. We are the products of Evolution. We understand and sense what we need to understand and sense in order to survive. Epiphenomenal qualia, are totally irrelevant to survival. At no stage of our evolution did natural selection favour those who could make sense of how they are caused and the laws governing them, or in fact why they exist at all. And that is why we can't.

It is not sufficiently appreciated that Physicalism is an extremely optimistic view of our powers. If it is true, we have, in very broad outline admittedly, a grasp of our place in the scheme of things. Certain matters of sheer complexity defeat us—there are an awful lot of neurons—but in principle we have it all. But consider the antecedent probability that everything in the Universe be of a kind that is relevant in some way or other to the survival of *homo sapiens.* It is very low surely. But then one must admit that it is very likely that there is a part of the whole scheme of things, maybe a big part, which no amount of evolution will ever bring us near to knowledge about or understanding. For the simple reason that such knowledge and understanding is irrelevant to survival.

Physicalists typically emphasise that we are a part of nature on their view, which is fair enough. But if we are a part of nature, we are as nature has left us after however many years of evolution it is, and each step in that evolutionary progression has been a matter of chance constrained just by the need to preserve or increase survival value. The wonder is that we understand as much as we do, and there is no wonder that there should be matters which fall quite outside our comprehension. Perhaps exactly how epiphenomenal qualia fit into the scheme of things is one such.

This may seem an unduly pessimistic view of our capacity to articulate a truly comprehensive picture of our world and our place in it. But suppose we discovered living on the bottom of the deepest oceans a sort of sea slug which manifested intelligence. Perhaps survival in the conditions required rational powers. Despite their intelligence, these sea slugs have only a very restricted conception of the world by comparison with ours, the explanation for this being the nature of their immediate environment. Nevertheless they have developed sciences which work surprisingly well in these restricted terms. They also have philosophers, called slugists. Some call themselves tough-minded slugists, others confess to being soft-minded slugists.

The tough-minded slugists hold that the restricted terms (or ones pretty like them which may be introduced as their sciences progress) suffice in principle to describe everything without remainder. These tough-minded slugists admit in moments of weakness to a feeling that their theory leaves something out. They resist this feeling and their opponents, the soft-minded slugists, by pointing out—absolutely correctly—that no slugist has ever succeeded in spelling out how this mysterious residue fits into the highly successful view that their sciences have and are developing of how their world works.

Our sea slugs don't exist, but they might. And there might also exist super beings which stand to us as we stand to the sea slugs. We cannot adopt the perspective of these super beings, because we are not them, but the possibility of such a perspective is, I think, an antidote to excessive optimism.

Hilary Putnam

Brains in a Vat

An ant is crawling on a patch of sand. As it crawls, it traces a line in the sand. By pure chance the line that it traces curves and recrosses itself such a way that it ends up looking like a recognizable caricature of Winston Churchill. Has the ant traced a picture of Winston Churchill, a picture that *depicts* Churchill?

Most people would say, on a little reflection, that it has not. The ant, after all, has never seen Churchill, or even a picture of Churchill, and it had no intention of depicting Churchill. It simply traced a line (and even *that* was unintentional), a line that *we* can 'see as' a picture of Churchill.

We can express this by saying that the line is not 'in itself' a representation of anything rather than anything else. Similarity (of a certain very complicated sort) to the features of Winston Churchill is not sufficient to make something represent or refer to Churchill. Nor is it necessary: in our community the printed shape 'Winston Churchill', the spoken words 'Winston Churchill', and many other things are used to represent Churchill (though not pictorially), while not having the sort of similarity to Churchill that a picture—even a line drawing—has. If *similarity* is not necessary or sufficient to make something represent something else, how can *anything* be necessary or sufficient for this purpose? How on earth can one thing represent (or 'stand for', etc.) a different thing?

The answer may seem easy. Suppose the ant had seen Winston Churchill, and suppose that it had the intelligence and skill to draw a picture of him. Suppose it produced the caricature *intentionally.* Then the line would have represented Churchill.

On the other hand, suppose the line had the shape WINSTON CHURCHILL. And suppose this was just accident (ignoring the improbability involved). Then the 'printed shape' WINSTON CHURCHILL would *not* have represented Churchill, although that printed shape does represent Churchill when it occurs in almost any book today.

So it may seem that what is necessary for representation, or what is mainly necessary for representation, is *intention.*

But to have the intention that *anything,* even private language (even the words 'Winston Churchill' spoken in my mind and not out loud), should *represent* Churchill, I must have been able to *think about* Churchill in the first place. If lines in the sand, noises, etc., cannot 'in themselves' represent anything, then how is it that thought forms can 'in themselves' represent anything? Or can they? How can thought reach out and 'grasp' what is external?

Some philosophers have, in the past, leaped from this sort of consideration to what they take to be a proof that the mind is *essentially non-physical in nature.* The argument is simple; what we said about the ant's curve applies to any physical object. No physical object can, in itself, refer to one thing rather than to another; nevertheless, *thoughts in the mind* obviously do succeed in re-

ferring to one thing rather than another. So thoughts (and hence the mind) are of an essentially different nature than physical objects. Thoughts have the characteristic of *intentionality*—they can refer to something else; nothing physical has 'intentionality', save as that intentionality is derivative from some employment of that physical thing by a mind. Or so it is claimed. This is too quick; just postulating mysterious powers of mind solves nothing. But the problem is very real. How is intentionality, reference, possible?

Magical Theories of Reference

We saw that the ant's 'picture' has no necessary connection with Winston Churchill. The mere fact that the 'picture' bears a 'resemblance' to Churchill does not make it into a real picture, nor does it make it a representation of Churchill. Unless the ant is an intelligent ant (which it isn't) and knows about Churchill (which it doesn't), the curve it traced is not a picture or even a representation of anything. Some primitive people believe that some representations (in particular, *names*) have a necessary connection with their bearers; that to know the 'true name' of someone or something gives one power over it. This power comes from the *magical connection* between the name and the bearer of the name; once one realizes that a name *only* has a contextual, contingent, conventional connection with its bearer, it is hard to see why knowledge of the name should have any mystical significance.

What is important to realize is that what goes for physical pictures also goes for mental images, and for mental representations in general; mental representations no more have a necessary connection with what they represent than physical representations do. The contrary supposition is a survival of magical thinking.

Perhaps the point is easiest to grasp in the case of mental *images.* (Perhaps the first philosopher to grasp the enormous significance of this point, even if he was not the first to actually make it, was Wittgenstein.) Suppose there is a planet somewhere on which human beings have evolved (or been deposited by alien spacemen, or what have you). Suppose these humans, although otherwise like us, have never seen *trees.* Suppose they have never imagined trees (perhaps vegetable life exists on their planet only in the form of molds). Suppose one day a picture of a tree is accidentally dropped on their planet by a spaceship which passes on without having other contact with them. Imagine them puzzling over the picture. What in the world is this? All sorts of speculations occur to them: a building, a canopy, even an animal of some kind. But suppose they never come close to the truth.

For *us* the picture is a representation of a tree. For these humans the picture only represents a strange object, nature and function unknown. Suppose one of them has a mental image which is exactly like one of my mental images of a tree as a result of having seen the picture. His mental image is not a *representation of a tree*. It is only a representation of the strange object (whatever it is) that the mysterious picture represents.

Still, someone might argue that the mental image is *in fact* a representation of a tree, if only because the picture which caused this mental image was itself a representation of a tree to begin with. There is a causal chain from actual trees to the mental image even if it is a very strange one.

But even this causal chain can be imagined absent. Suppose the 'picture of the tree' that the spaceship dropped was not really a picture of a tree, but the accidental result of some spilled paints. Even if it looked exactly like a picture of a tree, it was, in truth, no more a picture of a tree than the ant's 'caricature' of Churchill was a picture of Churchill. We can even imagine that the spaceship which dropped the 'picture' came from a planet which knew nothing of trees. Then the humans would still have mental images qualitatively identical with my image of a tree, but they would not be images which represented a tree any more than anything else.

The same thing is true of *words*. A discourse on paper might seem to be a perfect description of trees, but if it was produced by monkeys randomly hitting keys on a typewriter for millions of years, then the words do not refer to anything. If there were a person who memorized words and said them in his mind without understanding them, then they would not refer to anything when thought in the mind, either.

Imagine the person who is saying those words in his mind has been hypnotized. Suppose the words are in Japanese, and the person has been told that he understands Japanese. Suppose that as he thinks those words

he has a 'feeling of understanding'. (Although if someone broke into his train of thought and asked him what the words he was thinking *meant,* he would discover he couldn't say.) Perhaps the illusion would be so perfect that the person could even fool a Japanese telepath! But if he couldn't use the words in the right contexts, answer questions about what he 'thought', etc., then he didn't understand them.

By combining these science fiction stories I have been telling, we can contrive a case in which someone thinks words which are in fact a description of trees in some language *and* simultaneously has appropriate mental images, but *neither* understands the words *nor* knows what a tree is. We can even imagine that the mental images were caused by paint-spills (although the person has been hypnotized to think that they are images of something appropriate to his thought—only, if he were asked, he wouldn't be able to say of what). And we can imagine that the language the person is thinking in is one neither the hypnotist nor the person hypnotized has ever heard of—perhaps it is just coincidence that these 'nonsense sentences', as the hypnotist supposes them to be, are a description of trees in Japanese. In short, everything passing before the person's mind might be qualitatively identical with what was passing through the mind of a Japanese speaker who was *really* thinking about trees—but none of it would refer to trees.

All of this is really impossible, of course, in the way that it is really impossible that monkeys should by chance type out a copy of *Hamlet*. That is to say that the probabilities against it are so high as to mean it will never really happen (we think). But it is not logically impossible, or even physically impossible. It *could* happen (compatibly with physical law and, perhaps, compatibly with actual conditions in the universe, if there are lots of intelligent beings on other planets). And if it did happen, it would be a striking demonstration of an important conceptual truth; that even a large and complex system of representations, both verbal and visual, still does not have an *intrinsic,* built-in, magical connection with what it represents—a connection independent of how it was caused and what the dispositions of the speaker or thinker are. And this is true whether the system of representations (words and images, in the case of the example) is physically realized—the words are written or spoken, and the pictures are physical pictures—or only realized in the mind. Thought words and mental pictures do not *intrinsically* represent what they are about.

The Case of the Brains in a Vat

Here is a science fiction possibility discussed by philosophers: imagine that a human being (you can imagine this to be yourself) has been subjected to an operation by an evil scientist. The person's brain (your brain) has been removed from the body and placed in a vat of nutrients which keeps the brain alive. The nerve endings have been connected to a super-scientific computer which causes the person whose brain it is to have the illusion that everything is perfectly normal. There seem to be people, objects, the sky, etc; but really all the person (you) is experiencing is the result of electronic impulses traveling from the computer to the nerve endings. The computer is so clever that if the person tries to raise his hand, the feedback from the computer will cause him to 'see' and 'feel' the hand being raised. Moreover, by varying the program, the evil scientist can cause the victim to 'experience' (or hallucinate) any situation or environment the evil scientist wishes. He can also obliterate the memory of the brain operation, so that the victim will seem to himself to have always been in this environment. It can even seem to the victim that he is sitting and reading these very words about the amusing but quite absurd supposition that there is an evil scientist who removes people's brains from their bodies and places them in a vat of nutrients which keep the brains alive. The nerve endings are supposed to be connected to a super-scientific computer which causes the person whose brain it is to have the illusion that. . . .

When this sort of possibility is mentioned in a lecture on the Theory of Knowledge, the purpose, of course, is to raise the classical problem of scepticism with respect to the external world in a modern way. (*How do you know you aren't in this predicament?*) But this predicament is also a useful device for raising issues about the mind/world relationship.

Instead of having just one brain in a vat, we could imagine that all human beings (perhaps all sentient beings) are brains in a vat (or nervous systems in a vat in case some beings with just a minimal nervous system already count as 'sentient'). Of course, the evil scientist would have to be outside—or would he? Perhaps there is no evil scientist, perhaps (though this is absurd) the universe just happens to consist of automatic machinery tending a vat full of brains and nervous systems.

This time let us suppose that the automatic machinery is programmed to give us all a *collective* hallucination, rather than a number of separate unrelated hallucinations. Thus, when I seem to myself to be talking to you, you seem to yourself to be hearing my words. Of course, it is not the case that my words actually reach your ears—for you don't have (real) ears, nor do I have a real mouth and tongue. Rather, when I produce my words, what happens is that the efferent impulses travel from my brain to the computer, which both causes me to 'hear' my own voice uttering those words and 'feel' my tongue moving, etc., and causes you to 'hear' my words, 'see' me speaking, etc. In this case, we are, in a sense, actually in communication. I am not mistaken about your real existence (only about the existence of your body and the 'external world', apart from brains). From a certain point of view, it doesn't even matter that 'the whole world' is a collective hallucination; for you do, after all, really hear my words when I speak to you, even if the mechanism isn't what we suppose it to be. (Of course, if we were two lovers making love, rather than just two people carrying on a conversation, then the suggestion that it was just two brains in a vat might be disturbing.)

I want now to ask a question which will seem very silly and obvious (at least to some people, including some very sophisticated philosophers), but which will take us to real philosophical depths rather quickly. Suppose this whole story were actually true. Could we, if we were brains in a vat in this way, *say* or *think* that we were?

I am going to argue that the answer is 'No, we couldn't.' In fact, I am going to argue that the supposition that we are actually brains in a vat, although it violates no physical law, and is perfectly consistent with everything we have experienced, cannot possibly be true. *It cannot possibly be true,* because it is, in a certain way, self-refuting.

The argument I am going to present is an unusual one, and it took me several years to convince myself that it is really right. But it is a correct argument. What makes it seem so strange is that it is connected with some of the very deepest issues in philosophy. (It first occurred to me when I was thinking about a theorem in modern logic, the 'Skolem–Löwenheim Theorem', and I suddenly saw a connection between this theorem and some arguments in Wittgenstein's *Philosophical Investigations*.)

A 'self-refuting supposition' is one whose truth implies its own falsity. For example, consider the thesis that *all general statements are false*. This is a general statement. So if it is true, then it must be false. Hence, it is false. Sometimes a thesis is called 'self-refuting' if it is *the supposition that the thesis is entertained or enunciated* that implies its falsity. For example, 'I do not exist' is self-refuting if thought by *me* (for any *'me'*). So one can be certain that one oneself exists, if one thinks about it (as Descartes argued).

What I shall show is that the supposition that we are brains in a vat has just this property. If we can consider whether it is true or false, then it is not true (I shall show). Hence it is not true.

Before I give the argument, let us consider why it seems so strange that such an argument can be given (at least to philosophers who subscribe to a 'copy' conception of truth). We conceded that it is compatible with physical law that there should be a world in which all sentient beings are brains in a vat. As philosophers say, there is a 'possible world' in which all sentient beings are brains in a vat. (This 'possible world' talk makes it sound as if there is a *place* where any absurd supposition is true, which is why it can be very misleading in philosophy.) The humans in that possible world have exactly the same experiences that *we* do. They think the same thoughts we do (at least, the same words, images, thought-forms, etc., go through their minds). Yet, I am claiming that there is an argument we can give that shows we are not brains in a vat. How can there be? And why couldn't the people in the possible world who really *are* brains in a vat give it too?

The answer is going to be (basically) this: although the people in that possible world can think and 'say' any words we can think and say, they cannot (I claim) *refer* to what we can refer to. In particular, they cannot think or say that they are brains in a vat (*even by thinking 'we are brains in a vat'*).

Turing's Test

Suppose someone succeeds in inventing a computer which can actually carry on an intelligent conversation with one (on as many subjects as an intelligent person might). How can one decide if the computer is 'conscious'?

The British logician Alan Turing proposed the following test:[1] let someone carry on a conversation with the computer and a conversation with a person whom he does not know. If he cannot tell which is the computer and which is the human being, then (assume the test to be repeated a sufficient number of times with different interlocutors) the computer is conscious. In short, a computing machine is conscious if it can pass the 'Turing Test'. (The conversations are not to be carried on face to face, of course, since the interlocutor is not to know the visual appearance of either of his two conversational partners. Nor is voice to be used, since the mechanical voice might simply sound different from a human voice. Imagine, rather, that the conversations are all carried on via electric typewriter. The interlocutor types in his statements, questions, etc., and the two partners—the machine and the person—respond via the electric keyboard. Also, the machine may *lie*—asked 'Are you a machine', it might reply, 'No, I'm an assistant in the lab here.')

The idea that this test is really a definitive test of consciousness has been criticized by a number of authors (who are by no means hostile in principle to the idea that a machine might be conscious). But this is not our topic at this time. I wish to use the general idea of the Turing test, the general idea of a *dialogic test of competence*, for a different purpose, the purpose of exploring the notion of *reference*.

Imagine a situation in which the problem is not to determine if the partner is really a person or a machine, but is rather to determine if the partner uses the words to refer as we do. The obvious test is, again, to carry on a conversation, and, if no problems arise, if the partner 'passes' in the sense of being indistinguishable from

---

1. A. M. Turing, 'Computing Machinery and Intelligence', *Mind* 59 (1950), 433–60.

someone who is certified in advance to be speaking the same language, referring to the usual sorts of objects, etc., to conclude that the partner does refer to objects as we do. When the purpose of the Turing test is as just described, that is, to determine the existence of (shared) reference, I shall refer to the test as the *Turing Test for Reference*. And, just as philosophers have discussed the question whether the original Turing test is a *definitive* test for consciousness, i.e. the question of whether a machine which 'passes' the test not just once but regularly is *necessarily* conscious, so, in the same way, I wish to discuss the question of whether the Turing Test for Reference just suggested is a definitive test for shared reference.

The answer will turn out to be 'No'. The Turing Test for Reference is not definitive. It is certainly an excellent test in practice; but it is not logically impossible (though it is certainly highly improbable) that someone could pass the Turing Test for Reference and not be referring to anything. It follows from this, as we shall see, that we can extend our observation that words (and whole texts and discourses) do not have a necessary connection to their referents. Even if we consider not words by themselves but rules deciding what words may appropriately be produced in certain contexts—even if we consider, in computer jargon, *programs for using words*—unless those programs themselves *refer to something extralinguistic* there is still no determinate reference that those words possess. This will be a crucial step in the process of reaching the conclusion that the Brain-in-a-Vat Worlders cannot refer to anything external at all (and hence cannot say *that* they are Brain-in-a-Vat Worlders).

Suppose, for example, that I am in the Turing situation (playing the 'Imitation Game', in Turing's terminology) and my partner is actually a machine. Suppose this machine is able to win the game ('passes' the test). Imagine the machine to be programmed to produce beautiful responses in English to statements, questions, remarks, etc. in English, but that it has no sense organs (other than the hookup to my electric typewriter), and no motor organs (other than the electric typewriter). (As far as I can make out, Turing does not assume that the possession of either sense organs or motor organs is necessary for consciousness or intelligence.) Assume that not only does the machine lack electronic eyes and ears, etc., but that there are no provisions in the machine's program, the program for playing the Imitation Game, for incorporating inputs from such sense organs, or for controlling a body. What should we say about such a machine?

To me, it seems evident that we cannot and should not attribute reference to such a device. It is true that the machine can discourse beautifully about, say, the scenery in New England. But it could not recognize an apple tree or an apple, a mountain or a cow, a field or a steeple, if it were in front of one.

What we have is a device for producing sentences in response to sentences. But none of these sentences is at all connected to the real world. *If one coupled two of these machines and let them play the Imitation Game with each other, then they would go on 'fooling' each other forever, even if the rest of the world disappeared!* There is no more reason to regard the machine's talk of apples as referring to real world apples than there is to regard the ant's 'drawing' as referring to Winston Churchill.

What produces the illusion of reference, meaning, intelligence, etc., here is the fact that there is a convention of representation which *we* have under which the machine's discourse refers to apples, steeples, New England, etc. Similarly, there is the *illusion* that the ant has caricatured Churchill, for the same reason. But we are able to perceive, handle, deal with apples and fields. Our talk of apples and fields is intimately connected with our *nonverbal* transactions with apples and fields. There are 'language entry rules' which take us from experiences of apples to such utterances as 'I see an apple', and 'language exit rules' which take us from decisions expressed in linguistic form ('I am going to buy some apples') to actions other than speaking. Lacking either language entry rules or language exit rules, there is no reason to regard the conversation of the machine (or of the two machines, in the case we envisaged of two machines playing the Imitation Game with each other) as more than syntactic play. Syntactic play that *resembles* intelligent discourse, to be sure; but only as (and no more than) the ant's curve resembles a biting caricature.

In the case of the ant, we could have argued that the ant would have drawn the same curve even if Winston Churchill had never existed. In the case of the machine, we cannot quite make the parallel argument; if apples, trees, steeples and fields had not existed, then, presumably, the programmers would not have produced that same program. Although the machine does not *perceive* apples, fields, or steeples, its creator–designers did. There is *some* causal connection between the machine and the real world apples, etc., via the perceptual experience and knowledge of the creator–designers. But such a weak connection can hardly suffice for reference. Not only is it logically possible, though fantastically improbable, that the same machine *could* have existed even if apples, fields, and steeples had not existed; more important, the machine is utterly insensitive to the *continued* existence of apples, fields, steeples, etc. Even if all these things *ceased* to exist, the machine would still discourse just as happily in the same way. That is why the machine cannot be regarded as referring at all.

The point that is relevant for our discussion is that there is nothing in Turing's Test to rule out a machine which is programmed to do nothing *but* play the Imitation Game, and that a machine which can do nothing *but* play the Imitation Game is *clearly* not referring any more than a record player is.

Brains in a Vat (Again)

Let us compare the hypothetical 'brains in a vat' with the machines just described. There are obviously important differences. The brains in a vat do not have sense organs, but they do have *provision* for sense organs; that is, there are afferent nerve endings, there are inputs from these afferent nerve endings, and these inputs figure in the 'program' of the brains in the vat just as they do in the program of our brains. The brains in a vat are *brains;* moreover, they are *functioning* brains, and they function by the same rules as brains do in the actual world. For these reasons, it would seem absurd to deny consciousness or intelligence to them. But the fact that they are conscious and intelligent does not mean that their words refer to what our words refer. The question we are interested in is this: do their verbalizations containing, say, the word 'tree' actually refer to *trees*? More generally: can they refer to *external* objects at all? (As opposed to, for example, objects in the image produced by the automatic machinery.)

To fix our ideas, let us specify that the automatic machinery is supposed to have come into existence by some kind of cosmic chance or coincidence (or, perhaps, to have always existed). In this hypothetical world, the automatic machinery itself is supposed to have no intelligent creator-designers. In fact, as we said at the beginning of this chapter, we may imagine that all sentient beings (however minimal their sentience) are inside the vat.

This assumption does not help. For there is no connection between the *word* 'tree' as used by these brains and actual trees. They would still use the word 'tree' just as they do, think just the thoughts they do, have just the images they have, even if there were no actual trees. Their images, words, etc., are qualitatively identical with images, words, etc., which do represent trees in *our* world; but we have already seen (the ant again!) that qualitative similarity to something which represents an object (Winston Churchill or a tree) does not make a thing a representation all by itself. In short, the brains in a vat are not thinking about real trees when they think 'there is a tree in front of me' because there is nothing by virtue of which their thought 'tree' represents actual trees.

If this seems hasty, reflect on the following: we have seen that the words do not necessarily refer to trees even if they are arranged in a sequence which is identical with a discourse which (were it to occur in one of our minds) would unquestionably *be about trees* in the actual world. Nor does the 'program', in the sense of the rules, practices, dispositions of the brains to verbal behavior, necessarily refer to trees or bring about reference to trees through the connections it establishes between words and words, or *linguistic* cues and *linguistic* responses. If these brains think about, refer to, represent trees (real trees, outside the vat), then it must be because of the way the 'program' connects the system of language to *non-verbal* input and outputs. There are indeed such inputs and outputs in the Brain-in-a-Vat world (those efferent and afferent nerve endings again!), but we also saw that the 'sense-data' produced by the automatic machinery do not represent trees (or anything external) even when they resemble our tree-images exactly. Just as a splash of paint might resemble a tree picture without *being* a tree picture, so, we saw, a 'sense datum' might be qualitatively identical with an 'image of a tree' without being an image of a tree. How can the fact that, in the case of the brains in a vat, the language is connected by the program with sensory inputs which do not intrinsically or extrinsically represent trees (or anything external) possibly bring it about that the whole system of representations, the language-in-use, *does* refer to or represent trees or anything external?

The answer is that it cannot. The whole system of sense-data, motor signals to the efferent endings, and verbally or conceptually mediated thought connected by 'language entry rules' to the sense-data (or whatever) as inputs and by 'language exit rules' to the motor signals as outputs, has no more connection to *trees* than the ant's curve has to Winston Churchill. Once we see that the *qualitative similarity* (amounting, if you like, to qualitative identity) between the thoughts of the brains in a vat and the thoughts of someone in the actual world by no means implies sameness of reference, it is not hard to see that there is no basis at all for regarding the brain in a vat as referring to external things.

The Premisses of the Argument

I have now given the argument promised to show that the brains in a vat cannot think or say that they are brains in a vat. It remains only to make it explicit and to examine its structure.

By what was just said, when the brain in a vat (in the world where every sentient being is and always was a brain in a vat) thinks 'There is a tree in front of me', his thought does not refer to actual trees. On some theories that we shall discuss it might refer to trees in the image, or to the electronic impulses that cause tree experiences, or to the features of the program that are responsible for those electronic impulses. These theories are not ruled out by what was just said, for there is a close causal connection between the use of the word 'tree' in vat-English and the presence of trees in the image, the presence of electronic impulses of a certain kind, and the presence of certain features in the machine's program. On these theories the brain is *right*, not *wrong* in thinking 'There is a tree in front of me.' Given what 'tree' refers to in vat-English and what 'in front of' refers to, assuming one of these theories is correct, then the truth-conditions for 'There is a tree in front of me' when it occurs in vat-English are simply that a tree in the image be 'in front of' the 'me' in question—in the image—or, perhaps, that the kind of electronic impulse that normally produces this experience be coming from the automatic machinery, or, perhaps, that the feature of

the machinery that is supposed to produce the 'tree in front of one' experience be operating. And these truth-conditions are certainly fulfilled.

By the same argument, 'vat' refers to vats in the image in vat-English, or something related (electronic impulses or program features), but certainly not to real vats, since the use of 'vat' in vat-English has no causal connection to real vats (apart from the connection that the brains in a vat wouldn't be able to use the word 'vat', if it were not for the presence of one particular vat—the vat they are in; but this connection obtains between the use of *every* word in vat-English and that one particular vat; it is not a special connection between the use of the *particular* word 'vat' and vats). Similarly, 'nutrient fluid' refers to a liquid in the image in vat-English, or something related (electronic impulses or program features). It follows that if their 'possible world' is really the actual one, and we are really the brains in a vat, then what we now mean by 'we are brains in a vat' is that *we are brains in a vat in the image* or something of that kind (if we mean anything at all). But part of the hypothesis that we are brains in a vat is that we aren't brains in a vat in the image (i.e. what we are 'hallucinating' isn't that we are brains in a vat). So, if we are brains in a vat, then the sentence 'We are brains in a vat' says something false (if it says anything). In short, if we are brains in a vat, then 'We are brains in a vat' is false. So it is (necessarily) false.

The supposition that such a possibility makes sense arises from a combination of two errors: (1) taking *physical possibility* too seriously; and (2) unconsciously operating with a magical theory of reference, a theory on which certain mental representations necessarily refer to certain external things and kinds of things.

There is a 'physically possible world' in which we are brains in a vat—what does this mean except that there is a *description* of such a state of affairs which is compatible with the laws of physics? Just as there is a tendency in our culture (and has been since the seventeenth century) to take *physics* as our metaphysics, that is, to view the exact sciences as the long-sought description of the 'true and ultimate furniture of the universe', so there is, as an immediate consequence, a tendency to take 'physical possibility' as the very touchstone of what might really actually be the case. Truth is physical truth; possibility physical possibility; and necessity physical necessity, on such a view. But we have just seen, if only in the case of a very contrived example so far, that this view is wrong. The existence of a 'physically possible world' in which we are brains in a vat (and always were and will be) does not mean that we might really, actually possibly *be* brains in a vat. What rules out this possibility is not physics but *philosophy*.

Some philosophers, eager both to assert and minimize the claims of their profession at the same time (the typical state of mind of Anglo-American philosophy in the twentieth century), would say: 'Sure. You have shown that some things that seem to be physical possibilities are really *conceptual* impossibilities. What's so surprising about that?'

Well, to be sure, my argument can be described as a 'conceptual' one. But to describe philosophical activity as the search for 'conceptual' truths makes it all sound like *inquiry about the meaning of words*. And that is not at all what we have been engaging in.

What we have been doing is considering the *preconditions* for *thinking about, representing, referring to,* etc. We have investigated these preconditions *not* by investigating the meaning of these words and phrases (as a linguist might, for example) but by *reasoning a priori*. Not in the old 'absolute' sense (since we don't claim that magical theories of reference are *a priori* wrong), but in the sense of inquiring into what is *reasonably* possible *assuming* certain general premises, or making certain very broad theoretical assumptions. Such a procedure is neither 'empirical' nor quite 'a priori', but has elements of both ways of investigating. In spite of the fallibility of my procedure, and its dependence upon assumptions which might be described as 'empirical' (e.g. the assumption that the mind has no access to external things or properties apart from that provided by the senses), my procedure has a close relation to what Kant called a 'transcendental' investigation; for it is an investigation, I repeat, of the *preconditions* of reference and hence of thought—preconditions built in to the nature of our minds themselves, though not (as Kant hoped) wholly independent of empirical assumptions.

One of the premises of the argument is obvious: that magical theories of reference are wrong, wrong for mental representations and not only for physical ones. The other premiss is that one cannot refer to certain kinds of things, e.g., *trees,* if one has no causal interac-

tion at all with them, or with things in terms of which they can be described. But why should we accept these premisses? Since these constitute the broad framework within which I am arguing, it is time to examine them more closely.

The Reasons for Denying Necessary Connections between Representations and Their Referents

I mentioned earlier that some philosophers (most famously, Brentano) have ascribed to the mind a power, 'intentionality', which precisely enables it to *refer*. Evidently, I have rejected this as no solution. But what gives me this right? Have I, perhaps, been too hasty?

These philosophers did not claim that we can think about external things or properties without using representations at all. And the argument I gave above comparing visual sense data to the ant's 'picture' (the argument via the science fiction story about the 'picture' of a tree that came from a paint-splash and that gave rise to sense data qualitatively similar to our 'visual images of trees', but unaccompanied by any *concept* of a tree) would be accepted as showing that *images* do not necessarily refer. If there are mental representations that necessarily refer (to external things) they must be of the nature of *concepts* and not of the nature of images. But what are *concepts*?

When we introspect we do not perceive 'concepts' flowing through our minds as such. Stop the stream of thought when or where we will, what we catch are words, images, sensations, feelings. When I speak my thoughts out loud I do not think them twice. I hear my words as you do. To be sure it feels different to me when I utter words that I believe and when I utter words I do not believe (but sometimes, when I am nervous, or in front of a hostile audience, it feels as if I am lying when I know I am telling the truth); and it feels different when I utter words I understand and when I utter words I do not understand. But I can imagine without difficulty someone thinking just these words (in the sense of saying them in his mind) and having just the feeling of understanding, asserting, etc., that I do, and realizing a minute later (or on being awakened by a hypnotist) that he did not understand what had just passed through his mind at all, that he did not even understand the language these words are in. I don't claim that this is very likely; I simply mean that there is nothing at all unimaginable about this. And what this shows is not that concepts *are* words (or images, sensations, etc.), but that to attribute a 'concept' or a 'thought' to someone is quite different from attributing any mental 'presentation', any introspectible entity or event, to him. Concepts are not mental presentations that intrinsically refer to external objects for the very decisive reason that they are not mental presentations at all. Concepts are signs used in a certain way; the signs may be public or private, mental entities or physical entities, but even when the signs are 'mental' and 'private', the sign itself apart from its use is not the concept. And signs do not themselves intrinsically refer.

We can see this by performing a very simple thought experiment. Suppose you are like me and cannot tell an elm tree from a beech tree. We still say that the reference of 'elm' in my speech is the same as the reference of 'elm' in anyone else's, viz. elm trees, and that the set of all beech trees is the extension of 'beech' (i.e. the set of things the word 'beech' is truly predicated of) both in your speech and my speech. Is it really credible that the difference between what 'elm' refers to and what 'beech' refers to is brought about by a difference in our *concepts?* My concept of an elm tree is exactly the same as my concept of a beech tree (I blush to confess). (This shows that the determination of reference is social and not individual, by the way; you and I both defer to experts who *can* tell elms from beeches.) If someone heroically attempts to maintain that the difference between the reference of 'elm' and the reference of 'beech' in *my* speech is explained by a difference in my psychological state, then let him imagine a Twin Earth where the words are switched. Twin Earth is very much like Earth; in fact, apart from the fact that 'elm' and 'beech' are interchanged, the reader can suppose Twin Earth is exactly like Earth. Suppose I have a *Doppelganger* on Twin Earth who is molecule for molecule identical with me (in the sense in which two neckties can be 'identical'). If you are a dualist, then suppose my *Doppelganger* thinks the same verbalized thoughts I do, has the same sense data, the same dispositions, etc. It is absurd to think his psychological state is one bit different from mine: yet his word 'elm' represents *beeches,* and my word 'elm' represents elms. (Similarly, if the 'water' on Twin Earth is a different liquid—say, XYZ and not H_2O—then 'water' represents a different liquid when used on Twin Earth and when used on Earth, etc.) Contrary to a doctrine that has been with us since the seventeenth century, *meanings just aren't in the head.*

We have seen that possessing a concept is not a matter of possessing images (say, of trees—or even images, 'visual' or 'acoustic', of sentences, or whole discourses, for that matter) since one could possess any system of images you please and not possess the *ability* to use the sentences in situationally appropriate ways (considering both linguistic factors—what has been said before—and non-linguistic factors as determining 'situational appropriateness'). A man may have all the images you please, and still be completely at a loss when one says to him 'point to a tree', even if a lot of trees are present. He may even have the image of what he is supposed to do, and still not know what he is supposed to do. For the image, if not accompanied by the ability to act in a certain way, is just a *picture,* and acting in accordance with a picture is itself an ability that one may or may not have. (The man might picture himself pointing to a tree, but just for the sake of contemplating something logically possible; himself pointing to a tree after someone has produced the—to him meaningless—sequence of sounds 'please point to a tree'.) He would still not know that he was supposed to point to a tree, and he would still not *understand* 'point to a tree'.

I have considered the ability to use certain sentences to be the criterion for possessing a full-blown concept, but this could easily be liberalized. We could allow symbolism consisting of elements which are not words in a natural language, for example, and we could allow such mental phenomena as images and other types of internal events. What is essential is that these should have the same complexity, ability to be combined with each other, etc., as sentences in a natural language. For, although a particular presentation—say, a blue flash—might serve a particular mathematician as the inner expression of the whole proof of the Prime Number Theorem, still there would be no temptation to say this (and it would be false to say this) if that mathematician could not unpack his 'blue flash' into separate steps and logical connections. But, no matter what sort of inner phenomena we allow as possible *expressions* of thought, arguments exactly similar to the foregoing will show that it is not the phenomena themselves that constitute understanding, but rather the ability of the thinker to *employ* these phenomena, to produce the right phenomena in the right circumstances.

The foregoing is a very abbreviated version of Wittgenstein's argument in *Philosophical Investigations*. If it is correct, then the attempt to understand thought by what is called 'phenomenological' investigation is fundamentally misguided; for what the phenomenologists fail to see is that what they are describing is the inner *expression* of thought, but that the *understanding* of that expression—one's understanding of one's own thoughts —is not an *occurrence* but an *ability*. Our example of a man pretending to think in Japanese (and deceiving a Japanese telepath) already shows the futility of a phenomenological approach to the problem of *understanding*. For even if there is some introspectible quality which is present when and only when one *really* understands (this seems false on introspection, in fact), still that quality is only *correlated* with understanding, and it is still possible that the man fooling the Japanese telepath has that quality too and *still* not understand a word of Japanese.

On the other hand, consider the perfectly possible man who does not have any 'interior monologue' at all. He speaks perfectly good English, and if asked what his opinions are on a given subject, he will give them at length. But he never thinks (in words, images, etc.) when he is not speaking out loud; nor does anything 'go through his head', except that (of course) he hears his own voice speaking, and has the usual sense impressions from his surroundings, plus a general 'feeling of understanding'. (Perhaps he is in the habit of talking to himself.) When he types a letter or goes to the store, etc.,

he is not having an internal 'stream of thought'; but his actions are intelligent and purposeful, and if anyone walks up and asks him 'What are you doing?' he will give perfectly coherent replies.

This man seems perfectly imaginable. No one would hesitate to say that he was conscious, disliked rock and roll (if he frequently expressed a strong aversion to rock and roll), etc., just because he did not think conscious thoughts except when speaking out loud.

What follows from all this is that (a) no set of mental events—images or more 'abstract' mental happenings and qualities—*constitutes* understanding; and (b) no set of mental events is *necessary* for understanding. In particular, *concepts cannot be identical with mental objects of any kind*. For, assuming that by a mental object we mean something introspectible, we have just seen that whatever it is, it may be absent in a man who does understand the appropriate word (and hence has the full blown concept), and present in a man who does not have the concept at all.

Coming back now to our criticism of magical theories of reference (a topic which also concerned Wittgenstein), we see that, on the one hand, those 'mental objects' we *can* introspectively detect—words, images, feelings, etc.—do not intrinsically refer any more than the ant's picture does (and for the same reasons), while the attempts to postulate special mental objects, 'concepts', which *do* have a necessary connection with their referents, and which only trained phenomenologists can detect, commit a *logical* blunder; for concepts are (at least in part) *abilities* and not occurrences. The doctrine that there are mental presentations which necessarily refer to external things is not only bad natural science; it is also bad phenomenology and conceptual confusion.

ETHICS

S UPPOSE YOU GO TO a department store and purchase your winter wardrobe. When you get home, you discover that the clerk failed to charge you for a jacket. Two judgments cross your mind:

1. I ought to return it. To keep it would be in effect to steal it.

2. It's OK to keep it. It's the clerk's mistake. She won't have to pay, and it's pennies for the store.

How should you decide between these?

If you owned the store, how would you like it if a customer took advantage of a mistake, as option 2 allows? If you wouldn't like it only because you (the owner) would lose money, your reaction provides the customer with no reason to return the jacket. But you may have meant something different by your question: Can it be permissible for anyone to keep an expensive article that s/he obtains only through a store's mistake?

If you answer no and take that answer to favor (1), you verge on a demand for consistency for ethical judgments that Kant holds to be fundamental. The Kantian test—the so-called *universalizability* test—holds that when you make an ethical judgment, you are tacitly making that judgment for anyone. If the universalized form cannot be consistently thought or willed into action, the original judgment is not moral. Kant's first formulation of the Categorical Imperative is, 'Act only on that maxim [roughly, the intention that guides your action] that you can will to be a universal law'. (Rawls takes a similar line when he asks, 'What basic principles would be freely agreed on by all to govern them, if their agreement were subject to constraints of fairness?' See the section on political philosophy.)

Kant's universalizability test is a barrier to one common type of weakness in moral reasoning—making an exception in one's own favor: Stealing is wrong, but not in my particular case. The Kantian objection is that you cannot think that stealing is generally permissible because stealing presupposes the existence of private property, and there would be no private property if people were permitted to take whatever they liked.

What if you respond that you do not claim that stealing is permissible but that your keeping the jacket in those circumstances is permissible? It was given to you, though mistakenly, and the loss amounts to very little for the owners. Perhaps, under these conditions, the permission for anyone to keep merchandise acquired as you did does not undermine the possibility of private property and so does not yield an inconsistency.

This response to the Kantian test is on target in one respect: A universalized maxim must hold for everyone *in relevantly similar circumstances*. The qualification is familiar. It is permissible for Jill but not Judy to attend Brian's party because Jill was invited but Judy was not. When we ask, 'What if everyone did that?' we really intend 'What if everyone in relevantly similar circumstances did that?' This raises the question of what determines whether cases are relevantly similar. How different can another case be from yours and still fall under the same universalized maxim?

The ethical theory that is the main rival to the Kantian view—utilitarianism—does not face this problem. Utilitarianism is a form of consequentialism; it holds that one should always act so as to produce the best overall consequences. Traditional utilitarianism specifies the consequences to be maximized as the total amount of pleasure (and the absence of pain), happiness, or, according to more modern views, welfare or preferences. (Because pleasure and especially pain are among the crucial consequences to be evaluated, and because both are experienced by non-human animals, utilitarianism readily recognizes ethical obligations governing the treatment of non-human animals.)

The utilitarian approaches the problem of what you should do about the jacket differently from the Kantian. (For a development of the contrast, see Korsgaard's paper, 577–87.) The Kantian looks to your motive: Do you intend to do what is right? The utilitarian is not interested in the intention or motive from which you act. He asks, Would the best overall consequences result from your keeping the jacket without paying or from your returning it? If the greatest happiness possible is realized from your keeping it, then you should; if not, you should not.

On the utilitarian view, each case must be evaluated on its merits (on the exact amount of happiness gained or lost in your acting on one or another of your options). The utilitarian handles the problem of similarity of circumstances by dismissing it. Each situation is treated as unique.

However, this advantage of judging each case independently comes with heavy costs including difficulties in calculating the greatest good and denials that there are moral rules or natural rights. The latter difficulty is illustrated by the following purported counterexample. Suppose a vicious crime has been committed. An angry mob will do great violence unless someone is punished. The authorities, not knowing who actually committed the crime, punish an innocent person. Although he suffers pain and injustice, his being punished evidently produces the greatest good because the mob is placated and the violence they would have done is prevented. In such a case utilitarianism favors injustice.

The utilitarian replies, Violations of (alleged) moral rules or natural rights typically lead to worse consequences than respecting such rules and rights. So the rules and rights ought to be respected. This reply raises another difficulty: How can we know such a thing? How can anyone calculate the overall consequences of violations in the widely disparate conditions in which they occur? Mill maintains that we do not need to do separate calculations to know the outcome. We develop a wealth of background knowledge through experience, teaching, and common sense. We know that blatant immoralities—theft, murder, rape, and violent assault—not only badly harm those immediately affected and those dear to them but also spread fear among others who learn of it. Conversely were we to learn that these kinds of actions are rare or nonexistent, we would feel less anxious and more secure.

The difficulty comes with seemingly immoral actions whose deleterious consequences are not so obvious. If some lies produce the greatest overall good and others do not, how are we to tell them apart?

The utilitarian can adapt an ordinary distinction to generate a more sophisticated form of utilitarianism, which provides for a different response that is closer both to our sense of morality and to the Kantian's. (See Rawls, 'Two Concepts of Rules', 565–76.) Swinging a tapered stick at a ball and missing it is only that, unless that act takes place within a rule-governed practice like baseball. In baseball the same action is a strike because it falls under a rule that defines balls, strikes, and hits. The rule utilitarian, like the Kantian, recognizes that there are ethical rules—for example, it is wrong (unjust) to punish an innocent person. Such a rule is justified if it leads to the best overall consequences. Since punishing the innocent would sharply violate rules of justice, that act is wrong, regardless of its utility in a particular case. To continue the analogy: If the star of the baseball team takes a third strike, the overall happiness might be increased if he had another chance, rather than calling him out as the rule requires. But once the rule is in force there is no negotiation—the rule rules, and not the consequences. The move to *rule-utilitarianism* is resourceful, but does it preserve the core commitments of utilitarianism? Why should we defer to a rule if acting otherwise would yield better consequences?

The utilitarian has another response that adheres more closely to his commitment to acting for the best consequences. When ordinary folk find out about the punishment of an innocent, they will consider themselves at risk of unwarranted punishment and consider the integrity of the legal system badly compromised. If so, the sum total of happiness is likely to oppose the fraudulent guilty verdict, even with the threat of mob violence.

As this reply indicates, utilitarianism requires a generous view of all those affected, especially in mundane cases like that of the jacket. If you and the store owners are the only ones who count, the balance of happiness might easily favor your keeping the jacket. You need it, and the loss is a drop in the bucket for the owners. But those affected are not only those immediately affected. That group includes, in particular, all who become more distrustful when they learn of your action if you keep the jacket and all who become more trusting and secure, upon learning of your honesty, if you return it.

Those who try to construct counterexamples to utilitarianism concede the force of the appeal to indirect consequences. Their examples are often elaborated so that the wrongful action, which the utilitarian is supposed to approve, takes place in secrecy. If no one else found out, that would nullify virtually all the negative consequences. The utilitarian has two responses: First, secrets of serious magnitude are hard to keep, so the circumstances required for the examples to hold will be rare and unusual. Second, he bites the bullet: If the action really will remain secret, then maybe our intuitive judgments of its wrongness should give way.

But how big is the bullet that the utilitarian must bite? Utilitarianism forbids giving special weight to your own interests; it demands impartiality. Suppose you earned thirty dollars and are thinking of spending it on dinner and a movie. If the money could be used for something better, such as a charitable donation, utilitarianism requires that you so use it. Since the better-use requirement almost always applies, utilitarianism is an enormously difficult ethics to live up to. Critics charge that it is too demanding. (See the article by Singer, 604–11.)

Another example, due to Williams, highlights a different facet of utilitarianism's demandingness: Suppose you are a physicist opposed to research on nuclear weapons, but you are out of work and your family is desperately poor. How should you respond to a job offer at a weapons research laboratory? If you refuse the position, not only will your family suffer, but someone else will take the job who is probably more gung ho about weapons research than you. Utilitarian impartiality insists that you give no added weight to your opposition to the research, even though it is you who would be acting. Williams' criticism is that utilitarianism does not respect one's integrity—one's living by certain ideals and maintaining them in the face of enticements to do otherwise.

Going a step further, Nietzsche views the commitments of utilitarianism and other do-gooder or charitable moralities as barriers to achieving greatness or excellence. One will constantly need to sacrifice one's own pursuits and interests to better the good of others. For Nietzsche such a barrier is itself immoral.

Kantian and utilitarian approaches decide between (1) and (2) on the basis of the rightness or wrongness of the contemplated act. But the choice may be approached differently by asking what kind of person one should aspire to be. An ideal then serves as a guide for how to act ethically. This is the basis of Aristotle's virtue ethics: The happiest, most fulfilling life for humans is the life that most accords with our nature as rational and social creatures. To live such a life requires virtue. Aristotle's notion of happiness is not a subjective feeling like pleasure. Happiness must derive from genuine, rather than imaginary though convincing, accomplishments. (See Nozick [544–5] for a thought experiment to show that the good life cannot be one that is only subjectively good. Mill's utilitarian position is hard to pin down. He treats happiness as pleasure and the absence of pain, yet he wants to distinguish some pleasures as higher and so better than others—e.g., reading Shakespeare to eating a hot fudge sundae.)

According to Aristotle, the virtues—wisdom, courage, kindness, honesty, and the like—are character traits that guide those who have them to the best life, since these virtues accord with our social and rational nature. Just as a good knife is one that cuts well, so too a good human life will be one that best fulfills distinctively human ends or purposes. A virtue like courage is an excellence of character, which for Aristotle is a mean between extremes—the extremes of cowardice and foolhardiness.

Virtue theory is an ethics of living a good life. So virtue theory has an obvious advantage over Kantian and utilitarian approaches from the perspective of motivation: When asked, 'Why should I do what is moral [e.g., return the jacket]?' the virtue theorist is the only one who answers that question in a way that clearly aligns ethics with self-interest: You should do it because you will be better off.

Of course this answer seems strained when offered in favor of (1), since it might initially seem you are better off keeping the jacket. But Aristotle, like Plato, holds that the life of virtue, the good life, is one that is ultimately expected to yield the greatest happiness or fulfillment; and it is far better for the individual than a life that is less virtuous.

Another route to the answer 'You are better off' focuses on social cooperation, whose benefits require occasional individual sacrifice. Here is a standard example: Assume that you have made a long-distance agreement with a stranger to purchase his stereo for $1,000. Cooperation is win-win: You want his stereo more than your $1,000, and he values your $1,000 more than his stereo. Since cooperation is a major component of ethics, you each have a good argument based on self-interest to do what is ethical, which we state from your point of view:

1. I am better off sending my $1,000, and he is better off sending the stereo in exchange.

2. Since we are both better off keeping the agreement than if neither does, it is rational for us to cooperate and send the item sought for by the other party.

3. So I should send the $1,000.

As with many cooperative activities—trading, sharing a house, operating a business, keeping a park clean, playing tennis, hosting a party—we each benefit more by cooperating than if we were to go it alone. In these cases one's prospective gain is a reason to cooperate. Unless you take into account others' interests, which is the heart of social ethics, why should they voluntarily cooperate with you?

Unfortunately, as earlier qualifications indicate, and as life teaches, there is an opposed argument, which, with the former one, generates an instability or dilemma:

1. If I don't send my $1,000 (i.e., I *defect*) and he sends me his stereo (i.e., he cooperates), I simply gain a stereo.

2. If I send my $1,000 and he does not send the stereo, I simply lose $1,000.

So., 3. In either case, I am better off not sending the $1,000.

4. I am free to send it or not (specifically, my action does not affect what he does).

So, 5. I should not send my $1,000.

Premise 1 is an expression of narrow *egoistic* self-interest; premise 2 expresses distrust or fear of being a sucker. Premises 1 and 2 each represent one case not addressed in the previous argument, which contrasts cooperation with non-cooperation *by all*. This argument focuses on the rewards when one cooperates and the other defects. The instability emerges with the further thought about the conclusion to defect (5): What if my partner reasons as I do? (These arguments constitute what is called the Prisoner's Dilemma. See Darwall, 529–42.)

If this cooperative dilemma is repeatedly faced—if we regularly trade together or we belong to an organization that does—then we will know how the other acted previously and we can respond in kind on our next turn (matching cooperation with cooperation, defection with defection). If our continuing to trade is more valuable to each of us than ceasing to trade, a cooperative, trust-like arrangement is very likely to resume, being mutually beneficial, even after a defection by one and a retaliatory defection by the other. If one is recognized as trustworthy, that will provide an incentive to others to cooperate. So with continued interaction, there is likely to arise a stable character (or virtue) of trustworthiness. The problem still arises, though, for cases where we have no expectation of or desire for an ongoing relationship.

If out of a trustworthy character you return the jacket but you acquire that character for your own benefit, are you still doing the right act for the right reason or motive, as both the virtue theorist and the Kantian require?

We have not yet addressed a religious perspective. In the face of the scenario set up at the beginning of this essay, one might judge:

3. I ought to return the jacket. God (or some other authority) requires it.

What sort of authority is at issue? Does the authority determine what is right and wrong, as a baseball umpire's judgment determines strikes and balls? Or is the authority's judgment grounded in expertise? In that case, God would be a reliable source of information about what is right and wrong in the way that a physician is a reliable informant about nutrition. But just as the physician does not make it the case that vegetables are nutritious, God would not make it the case that an act is right, a pivotal conclusion in Plato's *Euthyphro*.

Can ethical judgments be true or false in the way that scientific judgments are? The inclination to answer no is fueled by our familiarity with both diverse moral codes and persistent, seemingly irresolvable, ethical disagreements. In the empirical realm we will distinguish between:

a. The earth orbits the sun.

b. Most people believe that the earth orbits the sun.

Only (a) enters a claim about how things are independent of opinion. Should we so sharply distinguish:

c. Murder is wrong.

d. Most people [my society; my religion] believe that murder is wrong?

According to Plato, just as the truth or falsity of (a) is independent of what anyone believes, so is the truth or falsity of (c). We take (a) and (b) to differ because there is an empirical realm to which (a) purports to correspond. When it does, (a) is true; otherwise it is false, regardless of the truth of (b). Since, on this analysis, the truth or falsity of (a) depends on correspondence to the world, we can come to know of its truth or falsity by observation or inference. Doubts about the existence of a moral realm for judgments like (c) to correspond to diminish confidence that moral judgments can constitute knowledge.

Empirical judgments claim to *describe* a feature of the world. Those judgments are true just in case they describe that feature (e.g., the orbits of the planets) correctly (as elliptical). Moral judgments *prescribe* what to do—one should or ought to return the jacket. Hume (546–54) holds that no assemblage of facts—statements that describe or state what *is* the case—can entail what one *ought* to do. No argument like the following is valid: Stealing is taking someone else's possession without permission and keeping it, so you should not steal.

Hume's doubts about moving from *is* to *ought* are a consequence of his broader doubts about the role of reason (belief) in motivating action. According to Hume something is a goal only because someone desires it. Since action is goal directed, it is desire, not reason, that motivates us to act. The role of reason or belief, for Hume, is limited to guidance about how best to realize that goal. Given that you desire a hot fudge sundae, reason can enable you to figure out how to get one. Kant disagrees about the limits of reason. He believes that when we act morally, reason both recognizes our duties and motivates us to act as duty requires. To act out of respect for the moral law is not to be directed toward a merely desired goal.

Although they deny the existence of moral truths, Humeans purport to have grounds for discriminating between right and wrong. Ethical pronouncements are expressions of feelings or attitudes toward different sorts of acts. The ones we praise or approve of are moral; the ones, like stealing or torture, that we react to with anger or revulsion or a similar negative attitude are immoral.

This Humean view may be accompanied by an error theory about moral expressions. An utterance like (c) appears to make a claim about the world as (a) does. But the appearance is misleading, for nothing in the world corresponds to an imperative or prescription. When you see someone pick another person's pocket, you immediately feel that it is wrong. But there is no wrongness for you to observe. You are in error if you construe your disapproval as a belief. (See Mackie's 'The Subjectivity of Values', 554–64.)

If the source of approval and disapproval that we express in moral judgments lies in deep facts about human nature and what is conducive to human happiness, a naturalistic view is compatible with reasoned moral judgments. But is the ostensible topic or force of our moral judgments captured by the Humean view? When one person upholds the rightness of experimentation on non-human animals and the other denies it, the disagreement seems to be a case of one party's denying what the other affirms about experimentation on animals. It does not seem to be a disagreement about what we approve or disapprove of. If you opt to return the jacket and your friend advises you to just keep it, is your disagreement one over who is right or over who better understands what we are inclined to approve of, or could these be, effectively, the same question?

Major Theories

Plato

Euthyphro

2 *Euthyphro:* What's new, Socrates, to make you leave your usual haunts in the Lyceum and spend your time here by the king-archon's court? Surely you are not prosecuting anyone before the king-archon as I am?

Socrates: The Athenians do not call this a prosecution but an indictment, Euthyphro.

b *Euthyphro:* What is this you say? Someone must have indicted you, for you are not going to tell me that you have indicted someone else.

Socrates: No indeed.

Euthyphro: But someone else has indicted you?

Socrates: Quite so.

Euthyphro: Who is he?

Socrates: I do not really know him myself, Euthyphro. He is apparently young and unknown. They call him Meletus, I believe. He belongs to the Pitthean deme, if you know anyone from that deme called Meletus, with long hair, not much of a beard, and a rather aquiline nose.

Euthyphro: I don't know him, Socrates. What charge does he bring against you?

Socrates: What charge? A not ignoble one I think, for
c it is no small thing for a young man to have knowledge of such an important subject. He says he knows how our young men are corrupted and who corrupts them. He is likely to be wise, and when he sees my ignorance corrupting his contemporaries, he proceeds to accuse me to the city as to their mother. I think he is the only
d one of our public men to start out the right way, for it is right to care first that the young should be as good as

possible, just as a good farmer is likely to take care of the young plants first, and of the others later. So, too, Meletus first gets rid of us who corrupt the young shoots, as he says, and then afterwards he will obviously 3 take care of the older ones and become a source of great blessings for the city, as seems likely to happen to one who started out this way.

Euthyphro: I could wish this were true, Socrates, but I fear the opposite may happen. He seems to me to start out by harming the very heart of the city by attempting to wrong you. Tell me, what does he say you do to corrupt the young?

Socrates: Strange things, to hear him tell it, for he says that I am a maker of gods, and on the ground that I cre- b ate new gods while not believing in the old gods, he has indicted me for their sake, as he puts it.

Euthyphro: I understand, Socrates. This is because you say that the divine sign keeps coming to you.[1] So he has written this indictment against you as one who makes innovations in religious matters, and he comes to court to slander you, knowing that such things are easily misrepresented to the crowd. The same is true in my case. Whenever I speak of divine matters in the assembly[2] c and foretell the future, they laugh me down as if I were crazy; and yet I have foretold nothing that did not happen. Nevertheless, they envy all of us who do this. One need not worry about them, but meet them head-on.

Socrates: My dear Euthyphro, to be laughed at does not matter perhaps, for the Athenians do not mind any-

---

From Plato, *Five Dialogues (Second Edition),* translated by G. M. A. Grube, revised by John M. Cooper (Indianapolis: Hackett Publishing Company, 2002). Reprinted by permission of the publisher.

1. In Plato, Socrates always speaks of his divine sign or voice as intervening to prevent him from doing or saying something (e.g., *Apology* 31d), but never positively. (3e).

2. The assembly was the final decision-making body of the Athenian democracy.

one they think clever, as long as he does not teach his
d own wisdom, but if they think that he makes others to
be like himself they get angry, whether through envy, as
you say, or for some other reason.

Euthyphro: I have certainly no desire to test their feelings towards me in this matter.

Socrates: Perhaps you seem to make yourself but rarely available, and not be willing to teach your own wisdom, but I'm afraid that my liking for people makes them think that I pour out to anybody anything I have to say, not only without charging a fee but even glad to reward anyone who is willing to listen. If then they were in-
e tending to laugh at me, as you say they laugh at you, there would be nothing unpleasant in their spending their time in court laughing and jesting, but if they are going to be serious, the outcome is not clear except to you prophets.

Euthyphro: Perhaps it will come to nothing, Socrates, and you will fight your case as you think best, as I think I will mine.

Socrates: What is your case, Euthyphro? Are you the defendant or the prosecutor?

Euthyphro: The prosecutor.

Socrates: Whom do you prosecute?

4 *Euthyphro:* One whom I am thought crazy to prosecute.

Socrates: Are you pursuing someone who will easily escape you?

Euthyphro: Far from it, for he is quite old.

Socrates: Who is it?

Euthyphro: My father.

Socrates: My dear sir! Your own father?

Euthyphro: Certainly.

Socrates: What is the charge? What is the case about?

Euthyphro: Murder, Socrates.

Socrates: Good heavens! Certainly, Euthyphro, most
b men would not know how they could do this and be right. It is not the part of anyone to do this, but of one who is far advanced in wisdom.

Euthyphro: Yes, by Zeus, Socrates, that is so.

Socrates: Is then the man your father killed one of your relatives? Or is that obvious, for you would not prosecute your father for the murder of a stranger.

Euthyphro: It is ridiculous, Socrates, for you to think that it makes any difference whether the victim is a stranger or a relative. One should only watch whether

the killer acted justly or not; if he acted justly, let him
go, but if not, one should prosecute, if, that is to say, the *c*
killer shares your hearth and table. The pollution is the
same if you knowingly keep company with such a man
and do not cleanse yourself and him by bringing him
to justice. The victim was a dependent of mine, and
when we were farming in Naxos he was a servant of
ours. He killed one of our household slaves in drunken
anger, so my father bound him hand and foot and threw
him in a ditch, then sent a man here to inquire from the
priest what should be done. During that time he gave *d*
no thought or care to the bound man, as being a killer,
and it was no matter if he died, which he did. Hunger
and cold and his bonds caused his death before the messenger came back from the seer. Both my father and my
other relatives are angry that I am prosecuting my father for murder on behalf of a murderer when he hadn't even killed him, they say, and even if he had, the dead
man does not deserve a thought, since he was a killer.
For, they say, it is impious for a son to prosecute his father for murder. But their ideas of the divine attitude to *e*
piety and impiety are wrong, Socrates.

Socrates: Whereas, by Zeus, Euthyphro, you think that
your knowledge of the divine, and of piety and impiety, is so accurate that, when those things happened as
you say, you have no fear of having acted impiously in
bringing your father to trial?

Euthyphro: I should be of no use, Socrates, and Euthyphro would not be superior to the majority of men,
if I did not have accurate knowledge of all such things. 5

Socrates: It is indeed most important, my admirable
Euthyphro, that I should become your pupil, and as regards this indictment, challenge Meletus about these
very things and say to him: that in the past too I considered knowledge about the divine to be most important, and that now that he says that I am guilty of
improvising and innovating about the gods I have become your pupil. I would say to him: "If, Meletus, you
agree that Euthyphro is wise in these matters, consider *b*
me, too, to have the right beliefs and do not bring
me to trial. If you do not think so, then prosecute that
teacher of mine, not me, for corrupting the older men,
me and his own father, by teaching me and by exhorting and punishing him." If he is not convinced, and does
not discharge me or indict you instead of me, I shall repeat the same challenge in court.

Euthyphro: Yes, by Zeus, Socrates, and, if he should try
c   to indict me, I think I would find his weak spots and the
talk in court would be about him rather than about me.

Socrates: It is because I realize this that I am eager to
become your pupil, my dear friend. I know that other
people as well as this Meletus do not even seem to notice you, whereas he sees me so sharply and clearly that
he indicts me for ungodliness. So tell me now, by Zeus,
what you just now maintained you clearly knew: what
d   kind of thing do you say that godliness and ungodliness
are, both as regards murder and other things; or is the
pious not the same and alike in every action, and the
impious the opposite of all that is pious and like itself,
and everything that is to be impious presents us with
one form[3] or appearance insofar as it is impious?

Euthyphro: Most certainly, Socrates.

Socrates: Tell me then, what is the pious, and what the
impious, do you say?

Euthyphro: I say that the pious is to do what I am doing now, to prosecute the wrongdoer, be it about
e   murder or temple robbery or anything else, whether the
wrongdoer is your father or your mother or anyone
else; not to prosecute is impious. And observe, Socrates,
that I can cite powerful evidence that the law is so. I
have already said to others that such actions are right,
not to favor the ungodly, whoever they are. These people
6   themselves believe that Zeus is the best and most just of
the gods, yet they agree that he bound his father because he unjustly swallowed his sons, and that he in turn
castrated his father for similar reasons. But they are angry with me because I am prosecuting my father for his
wrongdoing. They contradict themselves in what they
say about the gods and about me.

---

3. This is the kind of passage that makes it easier for us to
follow the transition from Socrates' universal definitions to
the Platonic theory of separately existent eternal universal
Forms. The words *eidos* and *idea,* the technical terms for
the Platonic Forms, commonly mean physical stature or
bodily appearance. As we apply a common epithet, in this
case pious, to different actions or things, these must have a
common characteristic, present a common appearance or
form, to justify the use of the same term, but in the early
dialogues, as here, it seems to be thought of as immanent
in the particulars and without separate existence. The same
is true of 6d where the word "form" is also used.

Socrates: Indeed, Euthyphro, this is the reason why I
am a defendant in the case, because I find it hard to accept things like that being said about the gods, and it is
likely to be the reason why I shall be told I do wrong.
Now, however, if you, who have full knowledge of such
things, share their opinions, then we must agree with
them, too, it would seem. For what are we to say, we   b
who agree that we ourselves have no knowledge of
them? Tell me, by the god of friendship, do you really
believe these things are true?

Euthyphro: Yes, Socrates, and so are even more surprising things, of which the majority has no knowledge.

Socrates: And do you believe that there really is war
among the gods, and terrible enmities and battles, and
other such things as are told by the poets, and other sacred stories such as are embroidered by good writers
and by representations of which the robe of the goddess is adorned when it is carried up to the Acropolis?   c
Are we to say these things are true, Euthyphro?

Euthyphro: Not only these, Socrates, but, as I was saying just now, I will, if you wish, relate many other things
about the gods which I know will amaze you.

Socrates: I should not be surprised, but you will tell me
these at leisure some other time. For now, try to tell me
more clearly what I was asking just now, for, my friend,
you did not teach me adequately when I asked you what   d
the pious was, but you told me that what you are doing
now, in prosecuting your father for murder, is pious.

Euthyphro: And I told the truth, Socrates.

Socrates: Perhaps. You agree, however, that there are
many other pious actions.

Euthyphro: There are.

Socrates: Bear in mind then that I did not bid you
tell me one or two of the many pious actions but that
form itself that makes all pious actions pious, for you
agreed that all impious actions are impious and all   e
pious actions pious through one form, or don't you remember?

Euthyphro: I do.

Socrates: Tell me then what this form itself is, so that
I may look upon it and, using it as a model, say that any
action of yours or another's that is of that kind is pious,
and if it is not that it is not.

Euthyphro: If that is how you want it, Socrates, that is
how I will tell you.

Socrates: That is what I want.

7   *Euthyphro:* Well then, what is dear to the gods is pious, what is not is impious.

Socrates: Splendid, Euthyphro! You have now answered in the way I wanted. Whether your answer is true I do not know yet, but you will obviously show me that what you say is true.

Euthyphro: Certainly.

Socrates: Come then, let us examine what we mean. An action or a man dear to the gods is pious, but an action or a man hated by the gods is impious. They are not the same, but quite opposite, the pious and the impious. Is that not so?

Euthyphro: It is indeed.

Socrates: And that seems to be a good statement?

b   *Euthyphro:* I think so, Socrates.

Socrates: We have also stated that the gods are in a state of discord, that they are at odds with each other, Euthyphro, and that they are at enmity with each other. Has that, too, been said?

Euthyphro: It has.

Socrates: What are the subjects of difference that cause hatred and anger? Let us look at it this way. If you and I were to differ about numbers as to which is the greater, would this difference make us enemies and angry with

c each other, or would we proceed to count and soon resolve our difference about this?

Euthyphro: We would certainly do so.

Socrates: Again, if we differed about the larger and the smaller, we would turn to measurement and soon cease to differ.

Euthyphro: That is so.

Socrates: And about the heavier and the lighter, we would resort to weighing and be reconciled.

Euthyphro: Of course.

Socrates: What subject of difference would make us angry and hostile to each other if we were unable to come to a decision? Perhaps you do not have an answer

d ready, but examine as I tell you whether these subjects are the just and the unjust, the beautiful and the ugly, the good and the bad. Are these not the subjects of difference about which, when we are unable to come to a satisfactory decision, you and I and other men become hostile to each other whenever we do?

Euthyphro: That is the difference, Socrates, about those subjects.

Socrates: What about the gods, Euthyphro? If indeed they have differences, will it not be about these same subjects?

Euthyphro: It certainly must be so.

Socrates: Then according to your argument, my good Euthyphro, different gods consider different things to be e just, beautiful, ugly, good, and bad, for they would not be at odds with one another unless they differed about these subjects, would they?

Euthyphro: You are right.

Socrates: And they like what each of them considers beautiful, good, and just, and hate the opposites of these?

Euthyphro: Certainly.

Socrates: But you say that the same things are considered just by some gods and unjust by others, and as they dispute about these things they are at odds and at war 8 with each other. Is that not so?

Euthyphro: It is.

Socrates: The same things then are loved by the gods and hated by the gods, and would be both god-loved and god-hated.

Euthyphro: It seems likely.

Socrates: And the same things would be both pious and impious, according to this argument?

Euthyphro: I'm afraid so.

Socrates: So you did not answer my question, you surprising man. I did not ask you what same thing is both pious and impious, and it appears that what is loved by the gods is also hated by them. So it is in no way sur- b prising if your present action, namely punishing your father, may be pleasing to Zeus but displeasing to Cronus and Uranus,[4] pleasing to Hephaestus but displeasing to Hera, and so with any other gods who differ from each other on this subject.

Euthyphro: I think, Socrates, that on this subject no gods would differ from one another, that whoever has killed anyone unjustly should pay the penalty.

Socrates: Well now, Euthyphro, have you ever heard c any man maintaining that one who has killed or done anything else unjustly should not pay the penalty?

Euthyphro: They never cease to dispute on this subject, both elsewhere and in the courts, for when they

---

4. Zeus' father, whom he fought and defeated (see 6a), was Cronus; Cronus, in turn, had castrated his own father Uranus.

The Gods are like men

have committed many wrongs they do and say anything to avoid the penalty.

Socrates: Do they agree they have done wrong, Euthyphro, and in spite of so agreeing do they nevertheless say they should not be punished?

Euthyphro: No, they do not agree on that point.

Socrates: So they do not say or do just anything. For they do not venture to say this, or dispute that they must not pay the penalty if they have done wrong, but I think they deny doing wrong. Is that not so?

Euthyphro: That is true.

Socrates: Then they do not dispute that the wrongdoer must be punished, but they may disagree as to who the wrongdoer is, what he did, and when.

Euthyphro: You are right.

Socrates: Do not the gods have the same experience, if indeed they are at odds with each other about the just and the unjust, as your argument maintains? Some assert that they wrong one another, while others deny it, but no one among gods or men ventures to say that the wrongdoer must not be punished.

Euthyphro: Yes, that is true, Socrates, as to the main point.

Socrates: And those who disagree, whether men or gods, dispute about each action, if indeed the gods disagree. Some say it is done justly, others unjustly. Is that not so?

Euthyphro: Yes, indeed.

Socrates: Come now, my dear Euthyphro, tell me, too, that I may become wiser, what proof you have that all the gods consider that man to have been killed unjustly who became a murderer while in your service, was bound by the master of his victim, and died in his bonds before the one who bound him found out from the seers what was to be done with him, and that it is right for a son to denounce and to prosecute his father on behalf of such a man. Come, try to show me a clear sign that all the gods definitely believe this action to be right. If you can give me adequate proof of this, I shall never cease to extol your wisdom.

Euthyphro: This is perhaps no light task, Socrates, though I could show you very clearly.

Socrates: I understand that you think me more dull-witted than the jury, as you will obviously show them that these actions were unjust and that all the gods hate such actions.

Euthyphro: I will show it to them clearly, Socrates, if only they will listen to me.

Socrates: They will listen if they think you show them well. But this thought came to me as you were speaking, and I am examining it, saying to myself: "If Euthyphro shows me conclusively that all the gods consider such a death unjust, to what greater extent have I learned from him the nature of piety and impiety? This action would then, it seems, be hated by the gods, but the pious and the impious were not thereby now defined, for what is hated by the gods has also been shown to be loved by them." So I will not insist on this point; let us assume, if you wish, that all the gods consider this unjust and that they all hate it. However, is this the correction we are making in our discussion, that what all the gods hate is impious, and what they all love is pious, and that what some gods love and others hate is neither or both? Is that how you now wish us to define piety and impiety?

Euthyphro: What prevents us from doing so, Socrates?

Socrates: For my part nothing, Euthyphro, but you look whether on your part this proposal will enable you to teach me most easily what you promised.

Euthyphro: I would certainly say that the pious is what all the gods love, and the opposite, what all the gods hate, is the impious.

Socrates: Then let us again examine whether that is a sound statement, or do we let it pass, and if one of us, or someone else, merely says that something is so, do we accept that it is so? Or should we examine what the speaker means?

Euthyphro: We must examine it, but I certainly think that this is now a fine statement.

Socrates: We shall soon know better whether it is. Consider this: Is the pious being loved by the gods because it is pious, or is it pious because it is being loved by the gods?

Euthyphro: I don't know what you mean, Socrates.

Socrates: I shall try to explain more clearly: we speak of something carried and something carrying, of something led and something leading, of something seen and something seeing, and you understand that these things are all different from one another and how they differ?

Euthyphro: I think I do.

Socrates: So there is also something loved and—a different thing—something loving.

For what reason do the gods think X is Pious?

Euthyphro: Of course.

Socrates: Tell me then whether the thing carried is a carried thing because it is being carried, or for some other reason?

Euthyphro: No, that is the reason.

Socrates: And the thing led is so because it is being led, and the thing seen because it is being seen?

Euthyphro: Certainly.

Socrates: It is not being seen because it is a thing seen but on the contrary it is a thing seen because it is being seen; nor is it because it is something led that it is being led but because it is being led that it is something led; nor is something being carried because it is something carried, but it is something carried because it is being carried. Is what I want to say clear, Euthyphro? I want to say this, namely, that if anything is being changed or is being affected in any way, it is not being changed because it is something changed, but rather it is something changed because it is being changed; nor is it being affected because it is something affected, but it is something affected because it is being affected.[5] Or do you not agree?

Euthyphro: I do.

Socrates: Is something loved either something changed or something affected by something?

Euthyphro: Certainly.

Socrates: So it is in the same case as the things just mentioned; it is not being loved by those who love it because it is something loved, but it is something loved because it is being loved by them?

Euthyphro: Necessarily.

Socrates: What then do we say about the pious, Euthyphro? Surely that it is being loved by all the gods, according to what you say?

Euthyphro: Yes.

Socrates: Is it being loved because it is pious, or for some other reason?

Euthyphro: For no other reason.

Socrates: It is being loved then because it is pious, but it is not pious because it is being loved?

Euthyphro: Apparently.

Socrates: And yet it is something loved and god-loved because it is being loved by the gods? *Here Socrates*

Euthyphro: Of course. *contradicts Euth*

Socrates: Then the god-loved is not the same as the pious, Euthyphro, nor the pious the same as the god-loved, as you say it is, but one differs from the other.

Euthyphro: How so, Socrates?

Socrates: Because we agree that the pious is being loved for this reason, that it is pious, but it is not pious because it is being loved. Is that not so?

Euthyphro: Yes.

Socrates: And that the god-loved, on the other hand, is so because it is being loved by the gods, by the very fact of being loved, but it is not being loved because it is god-loved.

Euthyphro: True.

Socrates: But if the god-loved and the pious were the same, my dear Euthyphro, then if the pious was being loved because it was pious, the god-loved would also be being loved because it was god-loved; and if the god-loved was god-loved because it was being loved by the gods, then the pious would also be pious because it was being loved by the gods. But now you see that they are in opposite cases as being altogether different from each other: the one is such as to be loved because it is being loved, the other is being loved because it is such as to be loved. I'm afraid, Euthyphro, that when you were asked what piety is, you did not wish to make its nature clear to me, but you told me an affect or a quality of it, that the pious has the quality of being loved by all the gods, but you have not yet told me what the pious is. Now, if you will, do not hide things from me but tell me again from the beginning what piety is, whether being loved by the gods or having some other quality—we shall not quarrel about that—but be keen to tell me what the pious and the impious are.

Euthyphro: But Socrates, I have no way of telling you what I have in mind, for whatever proposition we put forward goes around and refuses to stay put where we establish it.

Socrates: Your statements, Euthyphro, seem to belong to my ancestor, Daedalus. If I were stating them and putting them forward, you would perhaps be making fun of me and say that because of my kinship with him

---

5. Here Socrates gives the general principle under which, he says, the specific cases already examined—those of leading, carrying, and seeing—all fall. It is by being changed by something that changes *it* (e.g., by carrying it somewhere) that anything is a changed thing—not vice versa.

my conclusions in discussion run away and will not stay where one puts them. As these propositions are yours, however, we need some other jest, for they will not stay put for you, as you say yourself.

Euthyphro: I think the same jest will do for our discussion, Socrates, for I am not the one who makes them
d go around and not remain in the same place; it is you who are the Daedalus; for as far as I am concerned they would remain as they were.

Socrates: It looks as if I was cleverer than Daedalus in using my skill, my friend, insofar as he could only cause to move the things he made himself, but I can make other people's things move as well as my own. And the smartest part of my skill is that I am clever without wanting to be, for I would rather have your statements
e to me remain unmoved than possess the wealth of Tantalus as well as the cleverness of Daedalus. But enough of this. Since I think you are making unnecessary difficulties, I am as eager as you are to find a way to teach me about piety, and do not give up before you do. See whether you think all that is pious is of necessity just.

Euthyphro: I think so.

Socrates: And is then all that is just pious? Or is all that is pious just, but not all that is just pious, but some of it
12 is and some is not?

Euthyphro: I do not follow what you are saying, Socrates.

Socrates: Yet you are younger than I by as much as you are wiser. As I say, you are making difficulties because of your wealth of wisdom. Pull yourself together, my dear sir, what I am saying is not difficult to grasp. I am saying the opposite of what the poet said who wrote:

You do not wish to name Zeus, who had done it, and
who made all things grow, for where there is fear there
b   *is also shame.*[6]

I disagree with the poet. Shall I tell you why?

Euthyphro: Please do.

Socrates: I do not think that "where there is fear there is also shame," for I think that many people who fear disease and poverty and many other such things feel fear, but are not ashamed of the things they fear. Do you not think so?

Euthyphro: I do indeed.

Socrates: But where there is shame there is also fear. For is there anyone who, in feeling shame and embarrassment at anything, does not also at the same time fear   c and dread a reputation for wickedness?

Euthyphro: He is certainly afraid.

Socrates: It is then not right to say "where there is fear there is also shame," but that where there is shame there is also fear, for fear covers a larger area than shame. Shame is a part of fear just as odd is a part of number, with the result that it is not true that where there is number there is also oddness, but that where there is oddness there is also number. Do you follow me now?

Euthyphro: Surely.

Socrates: This is the kind of thing I was asking before, whether where there is piety there is also justice, but where there is justice there is not always piety, for the   d pious is a part of justice. Shall we say that, or do you think otherwise?

Euthyphro: No, but like that, for what you say appears to be right.

Socrates: See what comes next: if the pious is a part of the just, we must, it seems, find out what part of the just it is. Now if you asked me something of what we mentioned just now, such as what part of number is the even, and what number that is, I would say it is the number that is divisible into two equal, not unequal, parts. Or do you not think so?

Euthyphro: I do.

Socrates: Try in this way to tell me what part of the   e just the pious is, in order to tell Meletus not to wrong us any more and not to indict me for ungodliness, since I have learned from you sufficiently what is godly and pious and what is not.

Euthyphro: I think, Socrates, that the godly and pious is the part of the just that is concerned with the care of the gods, while that concerned with the care of men is the remaining part of justice.

Socrates: You seem to me to put that very well, but I still need a bit of information. I do not know yet what   13 you mean by care, for you do not mean the care of the gods in the same sense as the care of other things, as, for example, we say, don't we, that not everyone knows how to care for horses, but the horse breeder does.

Euthyphro: Yes, I do mean it that way.

Socrates: So horse breeding is the care of horses.

---

6. Author unknown.

Euthyphro: Yes.

Socrates: Nor does everyone know how to care for dogs, but the hunter does.

Euthyphro: That is so.

Socrates: So hunting is the care of dogs.

b   *Euthyphro:* Yes.

Socrates: And cattle raising is the care of cattle.

Euthyphro: Quite so.

Socrates: While piety and godliness is the care of the gods, Euthyphro. Is that what you mean?

Euthyphro: It is.

Socrates: Now care in each case has the same effect; it aims at the good and the benefit of the object cared for, as you can see that horses cared for by horse breeders are benefited and become better. Or do you not think so?

Euthyphro: I do.

Socrates: So dogs are benefited by dog breeding, cattle by cattle raising, and so with all the others. Or do
c you think that care aims to harm the object of its care?

Euthyphro: By Zeus, no.

Socrates: It aims to benefit the object of its care?

Euthyphro: Of course.

Socrates: Is piety then, which is the care of the gods, also to benefit the gods and make them better? Would you agree that when you do something pious you make some one of the gods better?

Euthyphro: By Zeus, no.

Socrates: Nor do I think that this is what you mean—far from it—but that is why I asked you what you meant by the care of gods, because I did not believe you meant
d this kind of care.

Euthyphro: Quite right, Socrates, that is not the kind of care I mean.

Socrates: Very well, but what kind of care of the gods would piety be?

Euthyphro: The kind of care, Socrates, that slaves take of their masters.

Socrates: I understand. It is likely to be a kind of service of the gods.

Euthyphro: Quite so.

Socrates: Could you tell me to the achievement of what goal service to doctors tends? Is it not, do you think, to achieving health?

Euthyphro: I think so.

Socrates: What about service to shipbuilders? To what
e achievement is it directed?

Euthyphro: Clearly, Socrates, to the building of a ship.

Socrates: And service to housebuilders to the building of a house?

Euthyphro: Yes.

Socrates: Tell me then, my good sir, to the achievement of what aim does service to the gods tend? You obviously know since you say that you, of all men, have the best knowledge of the divine.

Euthyphro: And I am telling the truth, Socrates.

Socrates: Tell me then, by Zeus, what is that excellent aim that the gods achieve, using us as their servants?

Euthyphro: Many fine things, Socrates.

Socrates: So do generals, my friend. Nevertheless you 14 could easily tell me their main concern, which is to achieve victory in war, is it not?

Euthyphro: Of course.

Socrates: The farmers, too, I think, achieve many fine things, but the main point of their efforts is to produce food from the earth.

Euthyphro: Quite so.

Socrates: Well then, how would you sum up the many fine things that the gods achieve?

Euthyphro: I told you a short while ago, Socrates, that it is a considerable task to acquire any precise knowl- b edge of these things, but, to put it simply, I say that if a man knows how to say and do what is pleasing to the gods at prayer and sacrifice, those are pious actions such as preserve both private houses and public affairs of state. The opposite of these pleasing actions are impious and overturn and destroy everything.

Socrates: You could tell me in far fewer words, if you were willing, the sum of what I asked, Euthyphro, but c you are not keen to teach me, that is clear. You were on the point of doing so, but you turned away. If you had given that answer, I should now have acquired from you sufficient knowledge of the nature of piety. As it is, the lover of inquiry must follow his beloved wherever it may lead him. Once more then, what do you say that piety and the pious are? Are they a knowledge of how to sacrifice and pray?

Euthyphro: They are.

Socrates: To sacrifice is to make a gift to the gods, whereas to pray is to beg from the gods?

Euthyphro: Definitely, Socrates.

Socrates: It would follow from this statement that d

piety would be a knowledge of how to give to, and beg from, the gods.

Euthyphro: You understood what I said very well, Socrates.

Socrates: That is because I am so desirous of your wisdom, and I concentrate my mind on it, so that no word of yours may fall to the ground. But tell me, what is this service to the gods? You say it is to beg from them and to give to them?

Euthyphro: I do.

Socrates: And to beg correctly would be to ask from them things that we need?

Euthyphro: What else?

Socrates: And to give correctly is to give them what e they need from us, for it would not be skillful to bring gifts to anyone that are in no way needed.

Euthyphro: True, Socrates.

Socrates: Piety would then be a sort of trading skill between gods and men?

Euthyphro: Trading yes, if you prefer to call it that.

Socrates: I prefer nothing, unless it is true. But tell me, what benefit do the gods derive from the gifts they receive from us? What they give us is obvious to all. There 15 is for us no good that we do not receive from them, but how are they benefited by what they receive from us? Or do we have such an advantage over them in the trade that we receive all our blessings from them and they receive nothing from us?

Euthyphro: Do you suppose, Socrates, that the gods are benefited by what they receive from us?

Socrates: What could those gifts from us to the gods be, Euthyphro?

Euthyphro: What else, do you think, than honor, reverence, and what I mentioned just now, to please them?

Socrates: The pious is then, Euthyphro, pleasing to the b gods, but not beneficial or dear to them?

Euthyphro: I think it is of all things most dear to them.

Socrates: So the pious is once again what is dear to the gods.

Euthyphro: Most certainly.

Socrates: When you say this, will you be surprised if your arguments seem to move about instead of staying put? And will you accuse me of being Daedalus who makes them move, though you are yourself much more skillful than Daedalus and make them go around in a circle? Or do you not realize that our argument has moved around and come again to the same place? You surely remember that earlier the pious and the god- c loved were shown not to be the same but different from each other. Or do you not remember?

Euthyphro: I do.

Socrates: Do you then not realize now that you are saying that what is dear to the gods is the pious? Is this not the same as the god-loved? Or is it not?

Euthyphro: It certainly is.

Socrates: Either we were wrong when we agreed before, or, if we were right then, we are wrong now.

Euthyphro: That seems to be so.

Socrates: So we must investigate again from the beginning what piety is, as I shall not willingly give up before I learn this. Do not think me unworthy, but d concentrate your attention and tell the truth. For you know it, if any man does, and I must not let you go, like Proteus, before you tell me. If you had no clear knowledge of piety and impiety you would never have ventured to prosecute your old father for murder on behalf of a servant. For fear of the gods you would have been afraid to take the risk lest you should not be acting rightly, and would have been ashamed before men, but now I know well that you believe you have clear e knowledge of piety and impiety. So tell me, my good Euthyphro, and do not hide what you think it is.

Euthyphro: Some other time, Socrates, for I am in a hurry now, and it is time for me to go.

Socrates: What a thing to do, my friend! By going you have cast me down from a great hope I had, that I would learn from you the nature of the pious and the impious and so escape Meletus' indictment by showing him that 16 I had acquired wisdom in divine matters from Euthyphro, and my ignorance would no longer cause me to be careless and inventive about such things, and that I would be better for the rest of my life.

Aristotle

Nicomachean Ethics

Virtue as a Mean and Its Contribution to Happiness

BOOK I: [*HAPPINESS*]

1 [*THE HIGHEST GOOD*]

1094a Every craft and every investigation, and likewise every action and decision, seems to aim at some good; hence the good has been well described as that at which everything aims.

However, there is an apparent difference among the ends aimed at. For the end is sometimes an activity, 5 sometimes a product beyond the activity; and when there is an end beyond the action, the product is by nature better than the activity.

Since there are many actions, crafts and sciences, the ends turn out to be many as well; for health is the end of medicine, a boat of boatbuilding, victory of general-10 ship, and wealth of household management.

But whenever any of these sciences are subordinate to some one capacity—as, for instance, bridlemaking and every other science producing equipment for horses are subordinate to horsemanship, while this and every action in warfare are in turn subordinate to generalship, and in the same way other sciences are subordinate to further ones—in each of these the end of the ruling science is 15 more choiceworthy than all the ends subordinate to it, since it is the end for which those ends are also pursued. And here it does not matter whether the ends of the actions are the activities themselves, or some product beyond them, as in the sciences we have mentioned.

2 [*POLITICAL SCIENCE*]

Suppose, then, that (a) there is some end of the things we pursue in our actions which we wish for because of

From Aristotle, *Nicomachean Ethics* (second edition), translated by Terence Irwin (Indianapolis: Hackett Publishing Company, 2000). Reprinted by permission of the publisher.

itself, and because of which we wish for the other 20 things; and (b) we do not choose everything because of something else, since (c) if we do, it will go on without limit, making desire empty and futile; then clearly (d) this end will be the good, i.e., the best good.

Then surely knowledge of this good is also of great importance for the conduct of our lives, and if, like archers, we have a target to aim at, we are more likely 25 to hit the right mark. If so, we should try to grasp, in outline at any rate, what the good is, and which science or capacity is concerned with it.

It seems to concern the most controlling science, the one that, more than any other, is the ruling science. And political science apparently has this character.

(1) For it is the one that prescribes which of the sci- 1094b ences ought to be studied in cities, and which ones each class in the city should learn, and how far.

(2) Again, we see that even the most honored capacities—generalship, household management and rhetoric, for instance—are subordinate to it.

(3) Further, it uses the other sciences concerned with 5 action, and moreover legislates what must be done and what avoided.

Hence its end will include the ends of the other sciences, and so will be the human good.

<This is properly called political science;> for though admittedly the good is the same for a city as for an individual, still the good of the city is apparently a greater and more complete good to acquire and preserve. For while it is satisfactory to acquire and preserve the good even for an individual, it is finer and more di- 10 vine to acquire and preserve it for a people and for cities. And so, since our investigation aims at these <goods, for an individual and for a city>, it is a sort of political science.

3 [*METHOD*]

Our discussion will be adequate if its degree of clarity fits the subject matter; for we would not seek the same degree of exactness in all sorts of arguments alike, any more than in the products of different crafts.

Moreover, what is fine and what is just, the topics of
15 inquiry in political science, differ and vary so much that they seem to rest on convention only, not on nature. Goods, however, also vary in the same sort of way, since they cause harm to many people; for it has happened that some people have been destroyed because of their wealth, others because of their bravery.

Since these, then, are the sorts of things we argue
20 from and about, it will be satisfactory if we can indicate the truth roughly and in outline; since <that is to say> we argue from and about what holds good usually <but not universally>, it will be satisfactory if we can draw conclusions of the same sort.

Each of our claims, then, ought to be accepted in the same way <as claiming to hold good usually>, since the educated person seeks exactness in each area to the ex-
25 tent that the nature of the subject allows; for apparently it is just as mistaken to demand demonstrations from a rhetorician as to accept <merely> persuasive arguments from a mathematician.

Further, each person judges well what he knows, and
1095a is a good judge about that; hence the good judge in a particular area is the person educated in that area, and the unqualifiedly good judge is the person educated in every area.

This is why a youth is not a suitable student of political science; for he lacks experience of the actions in life which political science argues from and about.

Moreover, since he tends to be guided by his feel-
5 ings, his study will be futile and useless; for its end is action, not knowledge. And here it does not matter whether he is young in years or immature in character, since the deficiency does not depend on age, but results from being guided in his life and in each of his pursuits by his feelings; for an immature person, like an incontinent person, gets no benefit from his knowledge.

If, however, we are guided by reason in forming our
10 desires and in acting, then this knowledge will be of great benefit.

These are the preliminary points about the student, about the way our claims are to be accepted, and about what we intend to do. [. . .]

7 [AN ACCOUNT OF HAPPINESS]

But let us return once again to the good we are look- 15
ing for, and consider just what it could be, since it is apparently one thing in one action or craft, and another thing in another; for it is one thing in medicine, another in generalship, and so on for the rest.

What, then, is the good in each of these cases? Surely it is that for the sake of which the other things are done; 20
and in medicine this is health, in generalship victory, in housebuilding a house, in another case something else, but in every action and decision it is the end, since it is for the sake of the end that everyone does the other things.

And so, if there is some end of everything that is pursued in action, this will be the good pursued in action; and if there are more ends than one, these will be the goods pursued in action.

Our argument has progressed, then, to the same conclusion <as before, that the highest end is the good>; 25
but we must try to clarify this still more.

Though apparently there are many ends, we choose some of them—for instance, wealth, flutes and, in general, instruments—because of something else; hence it is clear that not all ends are complete. But the best good is apparently something complete. Hence, if only one end is complete, this will be what we are looking for; and if more than one are complete, the most complete of these will be what we are looking for. 30

An end pursued in itself, we say, is more complete than an end pursued because of something else; and an end that is never choiceworthy because of something else is more complete than ends that are choiceworthy both in themselves and because of this end; and hence an end that is always <choiceworthy, and also> choiceworthy in itself, never because of something else, is complete without qualification.

Now happiness more than anything else seems complete without qualification, since we always <choose it, 1097b
and also> choose it because of itself, never because of something else.

Honor, pleasure, understanding and every virtue we certainly choose because of themselves, since we would choose each of them even if it had no further result; but we also choose them for the sake of happiness, suppos- 5 ing that through them we shall be happy. Happiness, by contrast, no one ever chooses for their sake, or for the sake of anything else at all.

The same conclusion <that happiness is complete> also appears to follow from self-sufficiency, since the complete good seems to be self-sufficient.

Now what we count as self-sufficient is not what suffices for a solitary person by himself, living an isolated
10 life, but what suffices also for parents, children, wife and in general for friends and fellow-citizens, since a human being is a naturally political <animal>. Here, however, we must impose some limit; for if we extend the good to parents' parents and children's children and to friends of friends, we shall go on without limit; but we must examine this another time.

15 Anyhow, we regard something as self-sufficient when all by itself it makes a life choiceworthy and lacking nothing; and that is what we think happiness does.

Moreover, we think happiness is most choiceworthy of all goods, since it is not counted as one good among many. If it were counted as one among many, then, clearly, we think that the addition of the smallest of goods would make it more choiceworthy: for <the smallest good> that is added becomes an extra quantity of goods <so creating a good larger than the original good>, and the larger of two goods is always more choiceworthy. <But we do not think any addition can make happiness more choiceworthy; hence it is most choiceworthy.>

20 Happiness, then, is apparently something complete and self-sufficient, since it is the end of the things pursued in action.

But presumably the remark that the best good is happiness is apparently something <generally> agreed, and what we miss is a clearer statement of what the best good is.

25 Well, perhaps we shall find the best good if we first find the function of a human being. For just as the good, i.e., <doing> well, for a flautist, a sculptor, and every craftsman, and, in general, for whatever has a function and <characteristic> action, seems to depend on its function, the same seems to be true for a human being, if a human being has some function.

30 Then do the carpenter and the leatherworker have their functions and actions, while a human being has none, and is by nature idle, without any function? Or,

just as eye, hand, foot and, in general, every <bodily> part apparently has its functions, may we likewise ascribe to a human being some function apart from all of theirs?

What, then, could this be? For living is apparently shared with plants, but what we are looking for is the 1098a special function of a human being; hence we should set aside the life of nutrition and growth. The life next in order is some sort of life of sense-perception; but this too is apparently shared, with horse, ox and every animal. The remaining possibility, then, is some sort of life of action of the <part of the soul> that has reason.

Now this <part has two parts, which have reason in different ways>, one as obeying the reason <in the other 5 part>, the other as itself having reason and thinking. <We intend both.> Moreover, life is also spoken of in two ways <as capacity and as activity>, and we must take <a human being's special function to be> life as activity, since this seems to be called life to a fuller extent.

(a) We have found, then, that the human function is the soul's activity that expresses reason <as itself having reason> or requires reason <as obeying reason>. (b) Now the function of F, of a harpist, for instance, is the same in kind, so we say, as the function of an excellent F, an excellent harpist, for instance. (c) The same is true without qualification in every case, when we add to the 10 function the superior achievement that expresses the virtue; for a harpist's function, for instance, is to play the harp, and a good harpist's is to do it well. (d) Now we take the human function to be a certain kind of life, and take this life to be the soul's activity and actions that express reason. (e) <Hence by (c) and (d)> the excellent man's function is to do this finely and well. (f) Each 15 function is completed well when its completion expresses the proper virtue. (g) Therefore <by (d), (e), and (f)> the human good turns out to be the soul's activity that expresses virtue.

And if there are more virtues than one, the good will express the best and most complete virtue. Moreover, it will be in a complete life.[1] For one swallow does not

---

1. **complete life:** Complete virtue needs a complete life (which need not, however, be a whole lifetime) because virtuous activities need time to develop and to express themselves fully.

20 make a spring, nor does one day; nor, similarly, does one day or a short time make us blessed and happy.

This, then, is a sketch of the good; for, presumably, the outline must come first, to be filled in later. If the sketch is good, then anyone, it seems, can advance and articulate it, and in such cases time is a good discoverer or <at least> a good co-worker. That is also how the 25 crafts have improved, since anyone can add what is lacking <in the outline>.

However, we must also remember our previous remarks, so that we do not look for the same degree of exactness in all areas, but the degree that fits the subject matter in each area and is proper to the investigation. For the carpenter's and the geometer's inquiries about 30 the right angle are different also; the carpenter's is confined to the right angle's usefulness for his work, whereas the geometer's concerns what, or what sort of thing, the right angle is, since he studies the truth. We must do the same, then, in other areas too, <seeking the proper degree of exactness>, so that digressions do not overwhelm our main task.

Nor should we make the same demand for an expla-
1098b nation in all cases. Rather, in some cases it is enough to prove that something is true without explaining why it is true. This is so, for instance, with principles, where the fact that something is true is the first thing, i.e., the principle.

Some principles are studied by means of induction, 5 some by means of perception, some by means of some sort of habituation, and others by other means. In each case we should try to find them out by means suited to their nature, and work hard to define them well. For they have a great influence on what follows; for the principle seems to be more than half the whole, and makes evident the answer to many of our questions. [...]

BOOK II: [VIRTUES OF CHARACTER]

1 [HOW A VIRTUE OF CHARACTER IS ACQUIRED]

15 Virtue, then, is of two sorts, virtue of thought and virtue of character. Virtue of thought arises and grows mostly from teaching, and hence needs experience and time. Virtue of character results from habit; hence its name 'ethical', slightly varied from 'ethos'.

Hence it is also clear that none of the virtues of character arises in us naturally.

For if something is by nature <in one condition>, 20 habituation cannot bring it into another condition. A stone, for instance, by nature moves downward, and habituation could not make it move upward, not even if you threw it up ten thousand times to habituate it; nor could habituation make fire move downward, or bring anything that is by nature in one condition into another condition.

Thus the virtues arise in us neither by nature nor 25 against nature. Rather, we are by nature able to acquire them, and reach our complete perfection through habit.

Further, if something arises in us by nature, we first have the capacity for it, and later display the activity. This is clear in the case of the senses; for we did not acquire 30 them by frequent seeing or hearing, but already had them when we exercised them, and did not get them by exercising them.

Virtues, by contrast, we acquire, just as we acquire crafts, by having previously activated them. For we learn a craft by producing the same product that we must produce when we have learned it, becoming builders, for instance, by building and harpists by playing the harp; so also, then, we become just by doing just actions, 1103b temperate by doing temperate actions, brave by doing brave actions.

What goes on in cities is evidence for this also. For the legislator makes the citizens good by habituating 5 them, and this is the wish of every legislator; if he fails to do it well he misses his goal. <The right> habituation is what makes the difference between a good political system and a bad one.

Further, just as in the case of a craft, the sources and means that develop each virtue also ruin it. For playing the harp makes both good and bad harpists, and it is 10 analogous in the case of builders and all the rest; for building well makes good builders, building badly, bad ones. If it were not so, no teacher would be needed, but everyone would be born a good or a bad craftsman.

It is the same, then, with the virtues. For actions in dealings with <other> human beings make some people 15 just, some unjust; actions in terrifying situations and the acquired habit of fear or confidence make some brave and others cowardly. The same is true of situations involving appetites and anger; for one or another sort of

conduct in these situations makes some people temper-
20 ate and gentle, others intemperate and irascible.

To sum up, then, in a single account: A state <of char-
acter> arises from <the repetition of> similar activities.
Hence we must display the right activities, since differences in these imply corresponding differences in the
states. It is not unimportant, then, to acquire one sort of
habit or another, right from our youth; rather, it is very
25 important, indeed all-important. [. . .]

4 [*VIRTUOUS ACTION AND VIRTUOUS CHARACTER*]

However, someone might raise this puzzle: 'What do
you mean by saying that to become just we must first
do just actions and to become temperate we must first
20 do temperate actions? For if we do what is grammatical or musical, we must already be grammarians or mu-
sicians. In the same way, then, if we do what is just or
temperate, we must already be just or temperate.'

But surely this is not so even with the crafts, for it is
possible to produce something grammatical by chance
or by following someone else's instructions. To be a
25 grammarian, then, we must both produce something
grammatical and produce it in the way in which the
grammarian produces it, i.e., expressing grammatical
knowledge that is in us.

Moreover, in any case what is true of crafts is not true
of virtues. For the products of a craft determine by their
own character whether they have been produced well;
and so it suffices that they are in the right state when
they have been produced. But for actions expressing
virtue to be done temperately or justly <and hence
30 well> it does not suffice that they are themselves in
the right state. Rather, the agent must also be in the
right state when he does them. First, he must know
<that he is doing virtuous actions>; second, he must de-
cide an them, and decide on them for themselves; and,
third, he must also do them from a firm and unchang-
ing state.

1105b   As conditions for having a craft these three do not
count, except for the knowing itself. As a condition for
having a virtue, however, the knowing counts for nothing, or <rather> for only a little, whereas the other two
conditions are very important, indeed all-important.
5 And these other two conditions are achieved by the frequent doing of just and temperate actions.

Hence actions are called just or temperate when they
are the sort that a just or temperate person would do.
But the just and temperate person is not the one who
<merely> does these actions, but the one who also does
them in the way in which just or temperate people do
them.

It is right, then, to say that a person comes to be 10
just from doing just actions and temperate from doing
temperate actions; for no one has even a prospect of becoming good from failing to do them.

The many, however, do not do these actions but take
refuge in arguments, thinking that they are doing philosophy, and that this is the way to become excellent 15
people. In this they are like a sick person who listens attentively to the doctor, but acts on none of his instructions. Such a course of treatment will not improve the
state of his body; any more than will the many's way of
doing philosophy improve the state of their souls.

5 [*VIRTUE OF CHARACTER AS AN INTERMEDIATE STATE*]

Next we must examine what virtue is. Since there are
three conditions arising in the soul—feelings, capacities 20
and states—virtue must be one of these.

By feelings I mean appetite, anger, fear, confidence,
envy, joy, love, hate, longing, jealousy, pity, in general
whatever implies pleasure or pain.

By capacities I mean what we have when we are said
to be capable of these feelings—capable of being angry, 25
for instance, or afraid or feeling pity.

By states I mean what we have when we are well or
badly off in relation to feelings. If, for instance, our feeling is too intense or slack, we are badly off in relation
to anger, but if it is intermediate, we are well off;[2] and
the same is true in the other cases.

First, then, neither virtues nor vices are feelings. (a)
For we are called excellent or base insofar as we have 30
virtues or vices, not insofar as we have feelings. (b) We
are neither praised nor blamed insofar as we have feelings; for we do not praise the angry or the frightened
person, and do not blame the person who is simply

---

2. **By states . . . well off.** A STATE is not *merely* a capacity. Aristotle does not deny that a state is a *type* of
capacity.

1106a angry, but only the person who is angry in a particular way. But we are praised or blamed insofar as we have virtues or vices. (c) We are angry and afraid without decision; but the virtues are decisions of some kind, or <rather> require decision. (d) Besides, in so far as we

5 have feelings, we are said to be moved; but insofar as we have virtues or vices, we are said to be in some condition rather than moved.

For these reasons the virtues are not capacities either; for we are neither called good nor called bad insofar as we are simply capable of feelings. Further, while we

10 have capacities by nature, we do not become good or bad by nature; we have discussed this before.

If, then, the virtues are neither feelings nor capacities, the remaining possibility is that they are states. And so we have said what the genus of virtue is.

6

But we must say not only, as we already have, that it is

15 a state, but also what sort of state it is.

It should be said, then, that every virtue causes its possessors to be in a good state and to perform their functions well;[3] the virtue of eyes, for instance, makes

20 the eyes and their functioning excellent, because it makes us see well; and similarly, the virtue of a horse makes the horse excellent, and thereby good at galloping, at carrying its rider and at standing steady in the face of the enemy. If this is true in every case, then the virtue of a human being will likewise be the state that makes a human being good and makes him perform his function well.

25 We have already said how this will be true, and it will also be evident from our next remarks, if we consider the sort of nature that virtue has.

In everything continuous and divisible we can take more, less and equal, and each of them either in the object itself or relative to us; and the equal is some intermediate between excess and deficiency.

By the intermediate in the object I mean what is 30 equidistant from each extremity; this is one and the same for everyone. But relative to us the intermediate is what is neither superfluous nor deficient; this is not one, and is not the same for everyone.[4]

If, for instance, ten are many and two are few, we take six as intermediate in the object, since it exceeds <two> 35 and is exceeded <by ten> by an equal amount, <four>; this is what is intermediate by numerical proportion. *1106b* But that is not how we must take the intermediate that is relative to us. For if, for instance, ten pounds <of food> are a lot for someone to eat, and two pounds a little, it does not follow that the trainer will prescribe six, since this might also be either a little or a lot for the person who is to take it—for Milo <the athlete> a little, but for the beginner in gymnastics a lot; and the 5 same is true for running and wrestling. In this way every scientific expert avoids excess and deficiency and seeks and chooses what is intermediate—but intermediate relative to us, not in the object.

This, then, is how each science produces its product well, by focusing on what is intermediate and making 10 the product conform to that. This, indeed, is why people regularly comment on well-made products that nothing could be added or subtracted, since they assume that excess or deficiency ruins a good <result> while the mean preserves it. Good craftsmen also, we say, focus on what is intermediate when they produce their product. And since virtue, like nature, is better and more exact than any craft, it will also aim at what is interme- 15 diate.

By virtue I mean virtue of character; for this <pursues the mean because> it is concerned with feelings and actions, and these admit of excess, deficiency and an intermediate condition. We can be afraid, for instance, or be confident, or have appetites, or get angry, or feel pity, in general have pleasure or pain, both too much and too little, and in both ways not well; but 20 <having these feelings> at the right times, about the

---

3. **It should . . .:** a virtue will require the right relation among different parts of the soul, so that someone's actions are guided by reason. Here Aristotle expands his earlier suggestion (see 1104a26) that guidance by reason requires neither total repression nor total indulgence of nonrational desires. Hence the connection between virtue and function leads directly into the doctrine of the MEAN.

4. **But relative . . . for everyone:** The appeal to a mean does not provide a precise, quantitative test. To find the mean relative to us is to find the state of character that correct reason requires, neither suppressing nor totally indulging nonrational desires.

right things, toward the right people, for the right end, and in the right way, is the intermediate condition.

Now virtue is concerned with feelings and actions, in which excess and deficiency are in error and incur blame, while the intermediate condition is correct and wins praise, which are both proper features of virtue. Virtue, then, is a mean, insofar as it aims at what is intermediate.

Moreover, there are many ways to be in error, since badness is proper to what is unlimited, as the Pythagoreans pictured it, and good to what is limited; but there is only one way to be correct. That is why error is easy and correctness hard, since it is easy to miss the target and hard to hit it. And so for this reason also excess and deficiency are proper to vice, the mean to virtue; 'for we are noble in only one way, but bad in all sorts of ways.'

Virtue, then, is (a) a state that decides, (b) <consisting> in a mean, (c) the mean relative to us (d) which is defined by reference to reason, (e) i.e., to the reason by reference to which the intelligent person would define it. It is a mean between two vices, one of excess and one of deficiency.

It is a mean for this reason also: Some vices miss what is right because they are deficient, others because they are excessive, in feelings or in actions, while virtue finds and chooses what is intermediate.

Hence, as far as its substance and the account stating its essence are concerned, virtue is a mean; but as far as the best <condition> and the good <result> are concerned, it is an extremity.

But not every action or feeling admits of the mean. For the names of some automatically include baseness —for instance, spite, shamelessness, envy <among feelings>, and adultery, theft, murder, among actions. All of these and similar things are called by these names because they themselves, not their excesses or deficiencies, are base.

Hence in doing these things we can never be correct, but must invariably be in error. We cannot do them well or not well—by committing adultery, for instance, with the right woman at the right time in the right way; on the contrary, it is true without qualification that to do any of them is to be in error.

<To think these admit of a mean>, therefore, is like thinking that unjust or cowardly or intemperate action

also admits of a mean, an excess and a deficiency. For then there would be a mean of excess, a mean of deficiency, an excess of excess and a deficiency of deficiency.

Rather, just as there is no excess or deficiency of temperance or of bravery, since the intermediate is a sort of extreme <in achieving the good>, so also there is no mean of these <vicious actions> either, but whatever way anyone does them, he is in error. For in general there is no mean of excess or of deficiency, and no excess or deficiency of a mean.

7 [THE INDIVIDUAL VIRTUES OF CHARACTER]

However, we must not only state this general account but also apply it to the particular cases. For among accounts concerning actions, though the general ones are common to more cases, the specific ones are truer, since actions are about particular cases, and our account must accord with these. Let us, then, find these from the chart.

(1) First, in feelings of fear and confidence the mean is bravery. The excessively fearless person is nameless (and in fact many cases are nameless), while the one who is excessively confident is rash; the one who is excessively afraid and deficient in confidence is cowardly.

(2) In pleasures and pains, though not in all types, and in pains less than in pleasures, the mean is temperance and the excess intemperance. People deficient in pleasure are not often found, which is why they also lack even a name; let us call them insensible.

(3) In giving and taking money the mean is generosity, the excess wastefulness and the deficiency ungenerosity. Here the vicious people have contrary excesses and defects; for the wasteful person spends to excess and is deficient in taking, whereas the ungenerous person takes to excess and is deficient in spending. At the moment we are speaking in outline and summary, and that suffices; later we shall define these things more exactly.

(4) In questions of money there are also other conditions. Another mean is magnificence; for the magnificent person differs from the generous by being concerned with large matters, while the generous person is concerned with small. The excess is ostentation and vulgarity, and the deficiency niggardliness, and these differ from the vices related to generosity in ways we shall describe later.

(5) In honor and dishonor the mean is magnanimity, the excess something called a sort of vanity, and the deficiency pusillanimity.

(6) And just as we said that generosity differs from magnificence in its concern with small matters, similarly there is a virtue concerned with small honors, differing in the same way from magnanimity, which is concerned with great honors. For honor can be desired either in the right way or more or less than is right. If someone desires it to excess, he is called an honor-lover, and if his desire is deficient he is called indifferent to honor, but if he is intermediate he has no name. The corresponding conditions have no name either, except the condition of the honor-lover, which is called honor-loving.

This is why people at the extremes claim the intermediate area. Indeed, we also sometimes call the intermediate person an honor-lover, and sometimes call him indifferent to honor; and sometimes we praise the honor-lover, sometimes the person indifferent to honor. We will mention later the reason we do this; for the moment, let us speak of the other cases in the way we have laid down.

(7) Anger also admits of an excess, deficiency and mean. These are all practically nameless; but since we call the intermediate person mild, let us call the mean mildness. Among the extreme people let the excessive person be irascible, and the vice be irascibility, and let the deficient person be a sort of inirascible person, and the deficiency be inirascibility.

There are three other means, somewhat similar to one another, but different. For they are all concerned with association in conversations and actions, but differ insofar as one is concerned with truth-telling in these areas, the other two with sources of pleasure, some of which are found in amusement, and the others in daily life in general. Hence we should also discuss these states, so that we can better observe that in every case the mean is praiseworthy, while the extremes are neither praiseworthy nor correct, but blameworthy. Most of these cases are also nameless, and we must try, as in the other cases also, to make names ourselves, to make things clear and easy to follow.

(8) In truth-telling, then, let us call the intermediate person truthful, and the mean truthfulness; pretence that overstates will be boastfulness, and the person who

has it boastful; pretence that understates will be self-deprecation, and the person who has it self-deprecating.

(9) In sources of pleasure in amusements let us call the intermediate person witty, and the condition wit; the excess buffoonery and the person who has it a buffoon; and the deficient person a sort of boor and the state boorishness.

(10) In the other sources of pleasure, those in daily life, let us call the person who is pleasant in the right way friendly, and the mean state friendliness. If someone goes to excess with no <further> aim he will be ingratiating; if he does it for his own advantage, a flatterer. The deficient person, unpleasant in everything, will be a sort of quarrelsome and ill-tempered person.

(11) There are also means in feelings and concerned with feelings: shame, for instance, is not a virtue, but the person prone to shame as well as the virtuous person we have described receives praise. For here also one person is called intermediate, and another—the person excessively prone to shame, who is ashamed about everything—is called excessive; the person who is deficient in shame or never feels shame at all is said to have no sense of disgrace; and the intermediate one is called prone to shame.

(12) Proper indignation is the mean between envy and spite, these conditions are concerned with pleasure and pain at what happens to our neighbors. For the properly indignant person feels pain when someone does well undeservedly; the envious person exceeds him by feeling pain when anyone does well, while the spiteful person is so deficient in feeling pain that he actually enjoys <other people's misfortunes>.

There will also be an opportunity elsewhere to speak of these <means that are not virtues>.

We must consider justice after these other conditions, and, because it is not spoken of in one way only, we shall distinguish its two types and say how each of them is a mean.

Similarly, we must consider the virtues that belong to reason.

BOOK III: [VIRTUE, PRAISE, AND BLAME]

1 [VOLUNTARY ACTION]

Virtue, then, is about feelings and actions. These receive praise or blame when they are voluntary, but par-

don, sometimes even pity, when they are involuntary. Hence, presumably, in examining virtue we must define the voluntary and the involuntary. This is also use-
35 ful to legislators, both for honors and for corrective treatments.

1110a What comes about by force or because of ignorance seems to be involuntary. What is forced has an external principle, the sort of principle in which the agent or victim contributes nothing—if, for instance, a wind or human beings who control him were to carry him off.

5 But now consider actions done because of fear of greater evils, or because of something fine. Suppose, for instance, a tyrant tells you to do something shameful, when he has control over your parents and children, and if you do it, they will live, but if not, they will die. These cases raise dispute about whether they are voluntary or involuntary.

However, the same sort of thing also happens with
10 throwing cargo overboard in storms; for no one willingly throws cargo overboard, without qualification, but anyone with any sense throws it overboard <under some conditions> to save himself and the others.

These sorts of actions, then, are mixed. But they would seem to be more like voluntary actions. For at the time they are done they are choiceworthy, and the goal of an action reflects the occasion; hence also we should call the action voluntary or involuntary with reference to the time when he does it. Now in fact he does it will-
15 ingly; for in these sorts of actions he has within him the principle of the movement of the limbs that are the instruments <of the action>, and when the principle of the actions is in him, it is also up to him to do them or not to do them. Hence actions of this sort are voluntary, though presumably the actions without <the appropriate> condition are involuntary, since no one would choose any action of this sort in itself.

For such <mixed> actions people are sometimes ac-
20 tually praised, whenever they endure something shameful or painful as the price of great and fine results; and if they do the reverse, they are blamed, since it is a base person who endures what is most shameful for nothing fine or for only some moderately fine result.

In some cases there is no praise, but there is pardon,
25 whenever someone does a wrong action because of conditions of a sort that overstrain human nature, and that no one would endure. But presumably there are

some things we cannot be compelled to do, and rather than do them we should suffer the most terrible consequences and accept death; for the things that <allegedly> compelled Euripides' Alcmaeon to kill his mother appear ridiculous.

It is sometimes hard, however, to judge what <goods> should be chosen at the price of what <evils>, and what
30 <evils> should be endured as the price of what <goods>. And it is even harder to abide by our judgment, since the results we expect <when we endure> are usually painful, and the actions we are compelled <to endure, when we choose> are usually shameful. That is why
1110b those who have been compelled or not compelled receive praise or blame.

What sorts of things, then, should we say are forced? Perhaps we should say that something is forced without qualification whenever its cause is external and the agent contributes nothing. Other things are involuntary in themselves, but choiceworthy on this occasion and as the price of these <goods>, and their principle is in the
5 agent. These are involuntary in themselves, but, on this occasion and as the price of these <goods>, voluntary. Still, they would seem to be more like voluntary actions, since actions involve particular <conditions>, and <in mixed actions> these <conditions> are voluntary. But what sort of thing should be chosen as the price of what <good> is not easy to answer, since there are many differences in particular <conditions>.

But suppose someone says that pleasant things and
10 fine things force us, since they are outside us and compel us. It will follow that for him everything is forced, since everyone in every action aims at something fine or pleasant.

Moreover, if we are forced and unwilling to act, we find it painful; but if something pleasant or fine is its cause, we do it with pleasure.

It is ridiculous, then, for <our opponent> to ascribe responsibility to external <causes> and not to himself,
15 when he is easily snared by such things; and ridiculous to take responsibility for fine actions himself, but to hold pleasant things responsible for his shameful actions.

What is forced, then, would seem to be what has its principle outside the person forced, who contributes nothing.

Everything caused by ignorance is nonvoluntary, but what is involuntary also causes pain and regret. For if

20 someone's action was caused by ignorance, but he now has no objection to the action, he has done it neither willingly, since he did not know what it was, nor unwillingly, since he now feels no pain. Hence, among those who act because of ignorance, the agent who now regrets his action seems to be unwilling, while the agent with no regrets may be called nonwilling, since he is another case—for since he is different, it is better if he has his own special name.

25 Further, action caused by ignorance would seem to be different from action done in ignorance. For if the agent is drunk or angry, his action seems to be caused by drunkenness or anger, not by ignorance, though it is done in ignorance, not in knowledge.

<This ignorance does not make an action involuntary.> Certainly every vicious person is ignorant of the 30 actions he must do or avoid, and this sort of error makes people unjust, and in general bad. But talk of involuntary action is not meant to apply to <this> ignorance of what is beneficial.

For the cause of involuntary action is not <this> ignorance in the decision, which causes vice; it is not <in other words> ignorance of the universal, since that is a 1111a cause for blame. Rather, the cause is ignorance of the particulars which the action consists in and is concerned with; for these allow both pity and pardon, since an agent acts involuntarily if he is ignorant of one of these particulars.

Presumably, then, it is not a bad idea to define these particulars, and say what they are, and how many. They are: (1) who is doing it; (2) what he is doing; (3) about 5 what or to what he is doing it; (4) sometimes also what he is doing with it—with the instrument, for example; (5) for what result—safety, for example; (6) in what way —gently or hard, for example.

Now certainly someone could not be ignorant of *all* of these unless he were mad. Nor, clearly, (1) could he be ignorant of who is doing it, since he could hardly be ignorant of himself. But (2) he might be ignorant of what he is doing, as when someone says that <the secret> slipped out while he was speaking, or, as Aeschylus said about the mysteries, that he did not know it was 10 forbidden to reveal it; or, like the person with the catapult, that he let it go when he <only> wanted to demonstrate it. (3) Again, he might think that his son is

an enemy, as Merope did; or (4) that the barbed spear has a button on it, or that the stone is pumice-stone. (5) By giving someone a drink to save his life we might kill him; (6) and wanting to touch someone, as they do in sparring, we might wound him. 15

There is ignorance about all of these <particulars> that the action consists in. Hence someone who was ignorant of one of these seems to have done an action unwillingly, especially when he was ignorant of the most important of them; these seem to be (2) what he is doing, and (5) the result for which he does it.

Hence it is action called involuntary with reference to *this* sort of ignorance <that we meant when we said 20 that> the agent must, in addition, feel pain and regret for his action.

Since, then, what is involuntary is what is forced or is caused by ignorance, what is voluntary seems to be what has its principle in the agent himself when he knows the particulars that the action consists in.

<Our definition is sound.> For, presumably, it is not 25 correct to say that action caused by emotion or appetite is involuntary.

For, first of all, on this view none of the other animals will ever act voluntarily; nor will children. <But clearly they do.>

Next, among all the actions caused by appetite or emotion do we do none of them voluntarily? Or do we do the fine actions voluntarily and the shameful involuntarily? Surely <the second answer> is ridiculous when one and the same thing <i.e., appetite or emotion> causes <both fine and shameful actions>. And presum- 30 ably it is also absurd to say <as the first answer implies> that things we ought to desire are involuntary; and in fact we ought both to be angry at some things and to have appetite for some things—for health and learning, for instance.

Again, what is involuntary seems to be painful, whereas what expresses our appetite seems to be pleasant.

Moreover, how are errors that express emotion any less voluntary than those that express rational calcula- 1111b tion? For both sorts of errors are to be avoided; and since nonrational feelings seem to be no less human <than rational calculation>, actions resulting from emotion or appetite are also proper to a human being; it is absurd, then, to regard them as involuntary. [. . .]

[*THE INDIVIDUAL VIRTUES OF CHARACTER*]

6 [*BRAVERY*]

First let us discuss bravery. We have already made it apparent that there is a mean about feeling of fear and confidence. What we fear, clearly, is what is frightening, and such things are, speaking without qualification, bad things; hence people define fear as expectation of something bad.

10   Now while we certainly fear all bad things—for instance, bad reputation, poverty, sickness, friendlessness, death, they do not all seem to concern the brave person. For fear of some bad things, such as bad reputation, for instance, is actually right and fine, and lack of fear is disgraceful; for if someone fears bad reputation, he is decent and properly prone to shame, and if he has no fear of it, he has no feeling of disgrace. Some, however,

15   call this fearless person brave, by a transference <of the name>, since he has some similarity to the brave person, in that the brave person is also a type of fearless person.

Presumably, though, it is wrong to fear poverty or sickness or, in general, <bad things> that are not the results of vice or caused by ourselves; still, someone who is fearless about these is not thereby brave. He also is called brave by similarity, since some people who are cowardly

20   in the dangers of war are nonetheless generous, and face with confidence the <danger of> losing money.

Again, if someone is afraid of committing wanton aggression on children or women, or of being envious or anything of that sort, that does not make him cowardly. Nor again, if someone is confident when he is going to be whipped <for his crimes> does that make him brave.

Then what sorts of frightening conditions concern

25   the brave person? Surely the most frightening; for no one stands firmer against terrifying conditions. Now death is most frightening of all, since it is a boundary, and when someone is dead nothing beyond it seems either good or bad for him any more. Still, not even death in all conditions—on the sea, for instance, or in sickness, seems to be the brave person's concern.

In what conditions, then, is death his concern? surely

30   in the finest conditions. Now such deaths are those in war, since they occur in the greatest and finest danger; and this judgment is endorsed by the honors given in cities and by monarchs. Hence someone is called brave to the fullest extent if he is intrepid in facing a fine death and the immediate dangers that bring death—and this is above all true of the dangers of war.   35

Certainly the brave person is also intrepid on the sea and in sickness, but not in the same way as seafarers are.   *1115b* For he has given up hope of safety, and objects to this sort of death <with nothing fine in it>, but seafarers' experience makes them hopeful. Moreover, we act like brave men on occasions when we can use our strength, or when it is fine to be killed; and neither of these is   5 true when we perish on the sea.

7

Now what is frightening is not the same for everyone. We do say, however, that some things are too frightening for a human being to resist; these, then, are frightening for everyone, at least for everyone with any sense. What is frightening, but not irresistible for a human being, varies in its seriousness and degree; and the same is true of what inspires confidence.   10

Now the brave person is unperturbed, as far as a human being can be. Hence, though he will fear even the sorts of things that are not irresistible, he will stand firm against them, in the right way, as prescribed by reason, for the sake of what is fine, since this is the end aimed at by virtue.

It is possible to be more or less afraid of these frightening things, and also possible to be afraid of what is not   15 frightening as though it were frightening. The cause of error may be fear of the wrong thing, or in the wrong way, or at the wrong time, or something of that sort; and the same is true for things that inspire confidence.

Hence whoever stands firm against the right things and fears the right things, for the right end, in the right way, at the right time, and is correspondingly confident, is the brave person; for the brave person's actions and feelings reflect what something is worth and what reason <prescribes>.

Every activity aims at actions expressing its state of character, and to the brave person bravery is fine; hence the   20 end it aims at is also fine, since each thing is defined by its end. The brave person, then, aims at what is fine when he expresses bravery in his standing firm and acting.

Consider now those who go to excess.

25 The person who is excessively fearless has no name —we said earlier that many states have no names. He would be some sort of madman, or incapable of feeling distress, if he feared nothing, neither earthquake nor waves, as they say about the Celts.

The person who is excessively confident about 30 frightening things is rash. The rash person also seems to be a boaster, and a pretender to bravery. At any rate, the attitude to frightening things that the brave person really has is the attitude that the rash person wants to appear to have; hence he imitates the brave person where he can. That is why most of them are rash cowards; for 1116a7 rash though they are on these <occasions for imitation>, they do not stand firm against anything fright-8 ening. Moreover, rash people are impetuous, and wish 9 for dangers before they arrive, but shrink from them when they come; brave people, on the contrary, are eager when in action, but keep quiet until then.

1115b34 The person who is excessively afraid is the coward, 35 since he fears the wrong things, and in the wrong way, 1116a and so on. Though indeed he is also deficient in confidence, it is more his excessive pain that clearly distinguishes him. Hence, since he is afraid of everything, he is a despairing sort. The brave person, on the contrary, is hopeful, since <he is confident and> confidence is proper to a hopeful person.

5 Hence the coward, the rash person and the brave person are all concerned with the same things, but have dif-7 ferent states related to them; the others are excessive or defective, but the brave person has the intermediate and right state.

10 As we have said, then, bravery is a mean about what inspires confidence and about what is frightening in the conditions we have described; it chooses and stands firm because that is fine or because anything else is shameful. Dying to avoid poverty or erotic passion or something painful is proper to a coward, not to a brave person; 15 for trying to avoid burdens is softness, and such a person stands firm <in the face of death> to avoid an evil, not because it is fine.

BOOK V: [*JUSTICE*]

1 [*THE DEFINITION OF JUSTICE*]

The questions we must examine about justice and in-1129a justice are these: What sorts of actions are they con-cerned with? What sort of mean is justice? What are the 5 extremes between which justice is intermediate? Let us examine them by the same type of investigation that we used in the topics discussed before.

We see that the state everyone means in speaking of justice is the state that makes us doers of just actions, that makes us do justice and wish what is just. In the same way they mean by injustice the state that makes us 10 do injustice and wish what is unjust. Let us also, then, <follow the common beliefs and> begin by assuming this in outline.

For what is true of sciences and capacities is not true of states. For while one and the same capacity or science seems to have contrary activities, a state that is a contrary has no contrary activities. Health, for instance, only 15 makes us do healthy actions, not their contraries; for we say we are walking in a healthy way if <and only if> we are walking in the way a healthy person would.

Often one of a pair of contrary states is recognized from the other contrary; and often the states are recognized from their subjects. For if, for instance, the good state is evident, the bad state becomes evident too; and 20 moreover the good state becomes evident from the things that have it, and the things from the state. For if, for instance, the good state is thickness of flesh, then the bad state will necessarily be thinness of flesh, and the thing that produces the good state will be what produces thickness of flesh.

It follows, usually, that if one of a pair of contraries is spoken of in more ways than one, so is the other; if, for 25 instance, what is just is spoken of in more ways than one, so is what is unjust.

Now it would seem that justice and injustice are both spoken of in more ways than one, but since the different ways are closely related, their homonymy is unnoticed, and is less clear than it is with distant homonyms 30 where the distance in appearance is wide (for instance, the bone below an animal's neck and what we lock doors with are called keys homonymously).

Let us, then, find the number of ways an unjust person is spoken of. Both the lawless person and the greedy and unfair person seem to be unjust; and so, clearly, both the lawful and the fair[5] person will be just. Hence 1129b

---

5. **fair:** *ison.*

what is just will be both what is lawful and what is fair, and what is unjust will be both what is lawless and what is unfair.

Since the unjust person is greedy, he will be concerned with goods[6]—not with all goods, but only with those involved in good and bad fortune, goods which are, <considered> without qualification, always good, but for this or that person not always good. Though

5 human beings pray for these and pursue them, they are wrong; the right thing is to pray that what is good without qualification will also be good for us, but to choose <only> what is good for us.

Now the unjust person <who chooses these goods> does not choose more in every case; in the case of what

10 is bad without qualification he actually chooses less. But since what is less bad also seems to be good in a way, and greed aims at more of what is good, he seems to be greedy. In fact he is unfair; for unfairness includes <all these actions>, and is a common feature <of his choice of the greater good and of the lesser evil>.

[GENERAL JUSTICE]

Since, as we saw, the lawless person is unjust and the lawful person is just, it clearly follows that whatever is lawful is in some way just;[7] for the provisions of leg-

15 islative science are lawful, and we say that each of them is just. Now in every matter they deal with the laws aim either at the common benefit of all, or at the benefit of those in control, whose control rests on virtue or on some other such basis.[8] And so in one way what we call just is whatever produces and maintains happiness and its parts for a political community.

Now the law instructs us to do the actions of a brave

20 person—not to leave the battle-line, for instance, or to flee, or to throw away our weapons; of a temperate per-

son—not to commit adultery or wanton aggression; of a mild person—not to strike or revile another; and similarly requires actions that express the other virtues, and prohibits those that express the vices. The correctly established law does this correctly, and the less carefully 25 framed one does this worse.

This type of justice, then, is complete virtue, not complete virtue without qualification but complete virtue in relation to another. And this is why justice often seems to be supreme among the virtues, and 'neither the evening star nor the morning star is so marvellous', and the proverb says 'And in justice all virtue is summed up.' 30

Moreover, justice is complete virtue to the highest degree because it is the complete exercise of complete virtue. And it is the complete exercise because the person who has justice is able to exercise virtue in relation to another, not only in what concerns himself; for many are able to exercise virtue in their own concerns but unable in what relates to another.

And hence Bias seems to have been correct in saying that ruling will reveal the man, since a ruler is auto- 1130a matically related to another, and in a community. And for the same reason justice is the only virtue that seems to be another person's good, because it is related to another; for it does what benefits another, either the ruler 5 or the fellow-member of the community.

The worst person, therefore, is the one who exercises his vice toward himself and his friends as well <as toward others>. And the best person is not the one who exercises virtue <only> toward himself, but the one who <also> exercises it in relation to another, since this is a difficult task.

This type of justice, then, is the whole, not a part, of virtue, and the injustice contrary to it is the whole, not 10 a part, of vice.

At the same time our discussion makes clear the difference between virtue and this type of justice. For virtue is the same as justice, but what it is to be virtue is not the same as what it is to be justice. Rather, insofar as virtue is related to another, it is justice, and insofar as it is a certain sort of state without qualification, it is virtue.

2 [SPECIAL JUSTICE]

But we are looking for the type of justice, since we say 15 there is one, that consists in a part of virtue, and

---

6. **goods:** Wealth, e.g., is good for a human being. By this Aristotle means not that it is good for every human being, but only that a human being can use wealth well, and if he uses it well, it will promote his happiness.

7. **whatever is lawful . . .:** Aristotle does not say here that every system of positive LAW is just. His reference to 'legislative science' ('science' supplied) shows that he has in mind only correct laws.

8. **either at . . . such basis:** This refers to different PO-LITICAL SYSTEMS.

correspondingly for the type of injustice that is a part <of vice>.

Here is evidence that there is this type of justice and injustice:

First, if someone's activities express the other vices—if, for instance, cowardice made him throw away his shield, or irritability made him revile someone, or un-20 generosity made him fail to help someone with money —what he does is unjust, but not greedy. But when one acts from greed, in many cases his action expresses none of these vices—certainly not all of them; but it still expresses some type of wickedness, since we blame him, and <in particular> it expresses injustice. Hence there is another type of injustice that is a part of the whole, and a way for a thing to be unjust that is a part of the whole that is contrary to law.

25   Moreover, if A commits adultery for profit and makes a profit, while B commits adultery because of his appetite, and spends money on it to his own loss, B seems intemperate rather than greedy, while A seems unjust, not intemperate. Clearly, then, this is because A acts to make a profit.

30   Further, we can refer every other unjust action to some vice—to intemperance if he committed adultery, to cowardice if he deserted his comrade in the battle-line, to anger if he struck someone. But if he made an <unjust> profit, we can refer it to no other vice except injustice.

Hence evidently (a) there is another type of injustice, special injustice, apart from the whole of injustice; and 1130b (b) it is synonymous with the whole, since the definition is in the same genus. For (b) both have their area of competence in relation to another. But (a) special injustice is concerned with honor or wealth or safety, or whatever single name will include all these, and aims at 5 the pleasure that results from making a profit; but the concern of injustice as a whole is whatever concerns the excellent person.

Clearly, then, there is more than one type of justice, and there is another type apart from <the type that is> the whole of virtue; but we must still grasp what it is, and what sort of thing it is.

What is unjust is divided into what is lawless and 10 what is unfair, and what is just into what is lawful and what is fair. The <general> injustice previously described, then, is concerned with what is lawless. But what is un-

fair is not the same as what is lawless, but related to it as part to whole, since whatever is unfair is lawless, but not everything lawless is unfair. Hence also the type of injustice and the way for a thing to be unjust <that ex- 15 presses lawlessness>, but differ as parts from wholes. For this injustice <as unfairness> is a part of the whole of injustice, and similarly justice <as fairness> is a part of the whole of justice.

Hence we must describe special <as well as general> justice and injustice, and equally this way for a thing to be just or unjust.

Let us, then, set to one side the type of justice and injustice that corresponds to the whole of virtue, justice 20 being the exercise of the whole of virtue, and injustice of the whole of vice, in relation to another.

And it is evident how we must distinguish the way for a thing to be just or unjust that expresses this type of justice and injustice; for the majority of lawful actions, we might say, are the actions resulting from virtue as a whole. For the law instructs us to express each virtue, and forbids us to express each vice, in how we live. Moreover, the actions producing the whole of virtue 25 are the lawful actions that the laws prescribe for education promoting the common good.

We must wait till later, however, to determine whether the education that makes an individual an unqualifiedly good man is a task for political science or for another science; for, presumably, being a good man is not the same as being every sort of good citizen.

Special justice, however, and the corresponding way for something to be just <must be divided>.   30

One species is found in the distribution of honors or wealth or anything else that can be divided among members of a community who share in a political system; for here it is possible for one member to have a share equal or unequal to another's.

Another species concerns rectification in transactions. This species has two parts, since one sort of transaction 1131a is voluntary, and one involuntary. Voluntary transactions include selling, buying, lending, pledging, renting, depositing, hiring out—these are called voluntary because the principle of these transactions is voluntary. Some in- 5 voluntary ones are secret, such as theft, adultery, poisoning, pimping, slave-deception, murder by treachery, false witness; others are forcible, such as assault, imprisonment, murder, plunder, mutilation, slander, insult.

7 [*NATURAL JUSTICE*]

One part of what is politically just is natural, and the other part legal. What is natural is what has the same validity everywhere alike, independent of its seeming so or not. What is legal is what originally makes no difference <whether it is done> one way or another, but makes a difference whenever people have laid down the rule—that a mina is the price of a ransom, for instance, or that a goat rather than two sheep should be sacrificed; and also laws passed for particular cases—that sacrifices should be offered to Brasidas,[9] for instance; and enactments by decree.

Now it seems to some people that everything just is merely legal, since what is natural is unchangeable and equally valid everywhere—fire, for instance, burns both here and in Persia—while they see that what is just changes <from city to city>.

This is not so, though in a way it is so. With us, though presumably not at all with the gods, there is such a thing as what is natural, but still all is changeable; despite the change there is such a thing as what is natural and what is not.

What sort of thing that <is changeable and hence> admits of being otherwise is natural, and what sort is not natural, but legal and conventional, if both natural and legal are changeable? It is clear in other cases also, and the same distinction <between the natural and the unchangeable> will apply; for the right hand, for instance, is naturally superior, even though it is possible for everyone to become ambidextrous.

The sorts of things that are just by convention and expediency are like measures. For measures for wine and for corn are not of equal size everywhere, but in wholesale markets they are bigger, and in retail smaller. Similarly, the things that are just by human <enactment> and not by nature differ from place to place, since political systems also differ; still, only one system is by nature the best everywhere.

[*SUMMARY ACCOUNT OF JUSTICE*]

We have now said what it is that is unjust and just. And now that we have defined them, it is clear that doing justice is intermediate between doing injustice and suffering injustice, since doing injustice is having too much and suffering injustice is having too little.

Justice is a mean, not as the other virtues are, but because it concerns an intermediate condition, while injustice concerns the extremes. Justice is the virtue that the just person is said to express in the just actions expressing his decision, distributing good things and bad, both between himself and others and between others. He does not award too much of what is choiceworthy to himself and too little to his neighbor (and the reverse with what is harmful), but awards what is proportionately equal; and he does the same in distributing between others.

Injustice, on the other hand, is related <in the same way> to what is unjust. What is unjust is disproportionate excess and deficiency in what is beneficial or harmful; hence injustice is excess and deficiency because it concerns excess and deficiency. The unjust person awards himself an excess of what is beneficial, <considered> without qualification, and a deficiency of what is harmful, and speaking as a whole, he acts similarly <in distributions between> others, but deviates from proportion in either direction. In an unjust action getting too little good is suffering injustice, and getting too much is doing injustice.

Margin references: 1134b18, 20, 25, 30, 35, 1135a, 1133b29, 1134a, 5, 10

---

9. **Brasidas:** A Spartan general who after his death received sacrifices in Amphipolis as a liberator.

Immanuel Kant

Grounding for the Metaphysics of Morals

First Section

Transition from the Ordinary Rational Knowledge of Morality to the Philosophical

There is no possibility of thinking of anything at all in the world, or even out of it, which can be regarded as good without qualification, expect a *good will*. Intelligence, wit, judgment, and whatever talents of the mind one might want to name are doubtless in many respects good and desirable, as are such qualities of temperament as courage, resolution, perseverance. But they can also become extremely bad and harmful if the will, which is to make use of these gifts of nature and which in its special constitution is called character, is not good. The same holds with gifts of fortune; power, riches, honor, even health, and that complete well-being and contentment with one's condition which is called happiness make for pride and often hereby even arrogance, unless there is a good will to correct their influence on the mind and herewith also to rectify the whole principle of action and make it universally conformable to its end. The sight of a being who is not graced by any touch of a pure and good will but who yet enjoys an uninterrupted prosperity can never delight a rational and impartial spectator. Thus a good will seems to constitute the indispensable condition of being even worthy of happiness.

Some qualities are even conducive to this good will itself and can facilitate its work. Nevertheless, they have no intrinsic unconditional worth; but they always presuppose, rather, a good will, which restricts the high esteem in which they are otherwise rightly held, and does not permit them to be regarded as absolutely good.

Moderation in emotions and passions, self-control, and calm deliberation are not only good in many respects but even seem to constitute part of the intrinsic worth of a person. But they are far from being rightly called good without qualification (however unconditionally they were commended by the ancients). For without the principles of a good will, they can become extremely bad; the coolness of a villain makes him not only much more dangerous but also immediately more abominable in our eyes than he would have been regarded by us without it.

A good will is good not because of what it effects or accomplishes, nor because of its fitness to attain some proposed end; it is good only through its willing, i.e., it is good in itself. When it is considered in itself, then it is to be esteemed very much higher than anything which it might ever bring about merely in order to favor some inclination, or even the sum total of all inclinations. Even if, by some especially unfortunate fate or by the niggardly provision of stepmotherly nature, this will should be wholly lacking in the power to accomplish its purpose; if with the greatest effort it should yet achieve nothing, and only the good will should remain (not, to be sure, as a mere wish but as the summoning of all the means in our power), yet would it, like a jewel, still shone by its own light as something which has its full value in itself. Its usefulness or fruitlessness can neither augment nor diminish this value. Its usefulness would be, as it were, only the setting to enable us to handle it in ordinary dealings or to attract to it the attention of those who are not yet experts, but not to recommend it to real experts or to determine its value.

But there is something so strange in this idea of the absolute value of a mere will, in which no account is taken of any useful results, that in spite of all the agreement received even from ordinary reason, yet there must arise the suspicion that such an idea may perhaps have as its hidden basis merely some high-flown fancy,

From Immanuel Kant, *Grounding for the Metaphysics of Morals (Third Edition),* translated by James W. Ellington (Indianapolis: Hackett Publishing Company, 1993). Reprinted by permission of the publisher.

and that we may have misunderstood the purpose of nature in assigning to reason the governing of our will. Therefore, this idea will be examined from this point of view.

In the natural constitution of an organized being, i.e., one suitably adapted to the purpose of life, let us take as a principle that in such a being no organ is to be found for any end unless it be the most fit and the best adapted for that end. Now if that being's preservation, welfare, or in a word its happiness, were the real end of nature in the case of a being having reason and will, then nature would have hit upon a very poor arrangement in having the reason of the creature carry out this purpose. For all the actions which such a creature has to perform with this purpose in view, and the whole rule of his conduct would have been prescribed much more exactly by instinct; and the purpose in question could have been attained much more certainly by instinct than it ever can be by reason. And if in addition reason had been imparted to this favored creature, then it would have had to serve him only to contemplate the happy constitution of his nature, to admire that nature, to rejoice in it, and to feel grateful to the cause that bestowed it; but reason would not have served him to subject his faculty of desire to its weak and delusive guidance nor would it have served him to meddle incompetently with the purpose of nature. In a word, nature would have taken care that reason did not strike out into a practical use nor presume, with its weak insight, to think out for itself a plan for happiness and the means for attaining it. Nature would have taken upon herself not only the choice of ends but also that of the means, and would with wise foresight have entrusted both to instinct alone. [...]

Reason, however, is not competent enough to guide the will safely as regards its objects and the satisfaction of all our needs (which it in part even multiplies); to this end would an implanted natural instinct have led much more certainly. But inasmuch as reason has been imparted to us as a practical faculty, i.e., as one which is to have influence on the will, its true function must be to produce a will which is not merely good as a means to some further end, but is good in itself. To produce a will good in itself reason was absolutely necessary, inasmuch as nature in distributing her capacities has everywhere gone to work in a purposive manner.

While such a will may not indeed be the sole and complete good, it must, nevertheless, be the highest good and the condition of all the rest, even of the desire for happiness. [...]

The concept of a will estimable in itself and good without regard to any further end must now be developed. This concept already dwells in the natural sound understanding and needs not so much to be taught as merely to be elucidated. It always holds first place in estimating the total worth of our actions and constitutes the condition of all the rest. Therefore, we shall take up the concept of *duty,* which includes that of a good will, though with certain subjective restrictions and hindrances, which far from hiding a good will or rendering it unrecognizable, rather bring it out by contrast and make it shine forth more brightly.

I here omit all actions already recognized as contrary to duty, even though they may be useful for this or that end; for in the case of these the question does not arise at all as to whether they might be done from duty, since they even conflict with duty. I also set aside those actions which are really in accordance with duty, yet to which men have no immediate inclination, but perform them because they are impelled thereto by some other inclination. For in this case to decide whether the action which is accord with duty has been done from duty or from some selfish purpose is easy. This difference is far more difficult to note in the case where the action accords with duty and the subject has in addition an immediate inclination to do the action. For example, that a dealer should not overcharge an inexperienced purchaser certainly accords with duty; and where there is much commerce, the prudent merchant does not overcharge but keeps to a fixed price for everyone in general, so that a child may buy from him just as well as everyone else may. Thus customers are honestly served, but this is not nearly enough for making us believe that the merchant has acted this way from duty and from principles of honesty; his own advantage required him to do it. He cannot, however, be assumed to have in addition an immediate inclination toward his buyers, causing him, as it were, out of love to give no one as far as price is concerned any advantage over another. Hence the action was done neither from duty nor from immediate inclination, but merely for a selfish purpose.

On the other hand, to preserve one's life is a duty; and, furthermore, everyone has also an immediate inclination to do so. But on this account the often anxious care taken by most men for it has no intrinsic worth, and the maxim of their action has no moral content. They preserve their lives, to be sure, in accordance with duty, but not from duty. On the other hand, if adversity and hopeless sorrow have completely taken away the taste for life, if an unfortunate man, strong in soul and more indignant at his fate than despondent or dejected, wishes for death and yet preserves his life without loving it—not from inclination or fear, but from duty—then his maxim indeed has a moral content.

To be beneficent where one can is a duty; and besides this, there are many persons who are so sympathetically constituted that, without any further motive of vanity or self-interest, they find an inner pleasure in spreading joy around them and can rejoice in the satisfaction of others as their own work. But I maintain that in such a case an action of this kind, however dutiful and amiable it may be, has nevertheless no true moral worth. It is on a level with such actions as arise from other inclinations, e.g., the inclination for honor, which if fortunately directed to what is in fact beneficial and accords with duty and is thus honorable, deserves praise and encouragement, but not esteem; for its maxim lacks the moral content of an action done not from inclination but from duty. Suppose then the mind of this friend of mankind to be clouded over with his own sorrow so that all sympathy with the lot of others is extinguished, and suppose him still to have the power to benefit others in distress, even though he is not touched by their trouble because he is sufficiently absorbed with his own; and now suppose that, even though no inclination moves him any longer, he nevertheless tears himself from this deadly insensibility and performs the action without any inclination at all, but solely from duty—then for the first time his action has genuine moral worth. Further still, if nature has put little sympathy in this or that man's heart, if (while being an honest man in other respects) he is by temperament cold and indifferent to the sufferings of others, perhaps because as regards his own sufferings he is endowed with the special gift of patience and fortitude and expects or even requires that others should have the same; if such a man (who would truly not be nature's worst product) had not been exactly fashioned by her to be a philanthropist, would he not yet find in himself a source from which he might give himself a worth far higher than any that a good-natured temperament might have? By all means, because just here does the worth of the character come out; this worth is moral and incomparably the highest of all, viz., that he is beneficent, not from inclination, but from duty. [. . .]

The second proposition is this: An action done from duty has its moral worth, not in the purpose that is to be attained by it, but in the maxim according to which the action is determined. The moral worth depends, therefore, not on the realization of the object of the action, but merely on the principle of volition according to which, without regard to any objects of the faculty of desire, the action has been done. From what has gone before it is clear that the purposes which we may have in our actions, as well as their effects regarded as ends and incentives of the will, cannot give to actions any unconditioned and moral worth. Where, then, can this worth lie if it is not to be found in the will's relation to the expected effect? Nowhere but in the principle of the will, with no regard to the ends that can be brought about through such action. For the will stands, as it were, at a crossroads between its a priori principle, which is formal, and its a posteriori incentive, which is material; and since it must be determined by something, it must be determined by the formal principle of volition, if the action is done from duty—and in that case every material principle is taken away from it.

The third proposition, which follows from the other two, can be expressed thus: Duty is the necessity of an action done out of respect for the law. I can indeed have an inclination for an object as the effect of my proposed action; but I can never have respect for such an object, just because it is merely an effect and is not an activity of the will. Similarly, I can have no respect for inclination as such, whether my own or that of another. I can at most, if my own inclination, approve it; and, if that of another, even love it, i.e., consider it to be favorable to my own advantage. An object of respect can only be what is connected with my will solely as ground and never as effect—something that does not serve my inclination but, rather, outweighs it, or at least excludes it from consideration when some choice is made—in other words, only the law itself can be an object of respect and hence can be a command. Now an action done from duty must altogether exclude the influence of inclination and therewith every object of the will. Hence there is nothing left which can determine the will except objectively the law and subjectively pure respect for this practical law, i.e., the will can be subjectively determined by the maxim that I should follow such a law even if all my inclinations are thereby thwarted.

Thus the moral worth of an action does not lie in the effect expected from it nor in any principle of action that needs to borrow its motive from this expected effect. For all these effects (agreeableness of one's condition and even the furtherance of other people's happiness) could have been brought about also through other causes and would not have required the will of a rational being, in which the highest and unconditioned good can alone be found. Therefore, the pre-eminent good which is called moral can consist in nothing but the representation of the law in itself, and such a representation can admittedly be found only in a rational being insofar as this representation, and not some expected effect, is the determining ground of the will. This good is already present in the person who acts according to this representation, and such good need not be awaited merely from the effect.[1]

---

1. There might be brought against me here an objection that I take refuge behind the word "respect" in an obscure feeling, instead of giving a clear answer to the question by means of a concept of reason. But even though respect is a feeling, it is not one received through any outside influence but is, rather, one that is self-produced by means of rational concept; hence it is specifically different from all feelings of the first kind, which can all be reduced to inclination or fear. What I recognize immediately as a law for me, I recognize with respect; this means merely the consciousness of the subordination of my will to a law without the mediation of other influences upon my sense. The immediate determination of the will by the law, and the consciousness thereof, is called respect, which is hence regarded as the effect of the law upon the subject and not as the cause of the law. Respect is properly the representation of a worth that thwarts my self-love. Hence respect is something that is regarded as an object of neither inclination nor fear, although it has at the same time something analogous to both. The object of respect is, therefore, nothing but the law—indeed that very law which we impose

But what sort of law can that be the thought of which must determine the will without reference to any expected effect, so that the will can be called absolutely good without qualification? Since I have deprived the will of every impulse that might arise for it from obeying any particular law, there is nothing left to serve the will as principle except the universal conformity of its actions to law as such, i.e., I should never act except in such a way that I can also will that my maxim should become a universal law. Here mere conformity to law as such (without having as its basis any law determining particular actions) serves the will as principle and must so serve it if duty is not to be a vain delusion and a chimerical concept. The ordinary reason of mankind in its practical judgments agrees completely with this, and always has in view the aforementioned principle.

For example, take this question. When I am in distress, may I make a promise with the intention of not keeping it? I readily distinguish here the two meanings which the question may have; whether making a false promise conforms with prudence or with duty. Doubtless the former can often be the case. Indeed I clearly see that escape from some present difficulty by means of such a promise is not enough. In addition I must carefully consider whether from this lie there may later arise far greater inconvenience for me than from what I now try to escape. Furthermore, the consequences of my false promise are not easy to forsee, even with all my supposed cunning; loss of confidence in me might prove to be far more disadvantageous than the misfortune which I now try to avoid. The more prudent way might be to act according to a universal maxim and to make it a habit not to promise anything without

---

on ourselves and yet recognize as necessary in itself. As law, we are subject to it without consulting self-love; as imposed on us by ourselves, it is a consequence of our will. In the former aspect, it is analogous to fear; in the latter, to inclination. All respect for a person is properly only respect for the law (of honesty, etc.) of which the person provides an example. Since we regard the development of our talents as a duty, we think of a man of talent as being also a kind of example of the law (the law of becoming like him by practice), and that is what constitutes our respect for him. All so-called moral interest consist solely in respect for the law.

intending to keep it. But that such a maxim is, never-theless, always based on nothing but a fear of conse-quences becomes clear to me at once. To be truthful from duty is, however, quite different from being truth-ful from fear of disadvantageous consequences; in the first case the concept of the action itself contains a law for me, while in the second I must first look around elsewhere to see what are the results for me that might be connected with the action. For to deviate from the principle of duty is quite certainly bad; but to abandon my maxim of prudence can often be very advantageous for me, though to abide by it is certainly safer. The most direct and infallible way, however, to answer the ques-tion as to whether a lying promise accords with duty is to ask myself whether I would really be content if my maxim (of extrication myself from difficulty by means of a false promise) were to hold as a universal law for myself as well as for others, and could I really say to my-self that everyone may promise falsely when he finds himself in a difficulty from which he can find no other way to extricate himself. Then I immediately become aware that I can indeed will the lie but can not at all will a universal law to lie. For by such a law there would re-ally be no promises at all, since in vain would my will-ing future actions be professed to other people who would not believe what I professed, or if they over-hastily did believe, then they would pay me back in like coin. Therefore, my maxim would necessarily destroy it-self just as soon as it was made a universal law. [. . .]

Thus within the moral cognition of ordinary human reason we have arrived at its principle. To be sure, such reason does not think of this principle abstractly in its universal form, but does always have it actually in view and does use it as the standard of judgment. It would here be easy to show how ordinary reason, with this compass in hand, is well able to distinguish, in every case that occurs, what is good or evil, in accord with duty or contrary to duty, if we do not in the least try to teach reason anything new but only make it attend, as Socrates did, to its own principle—and thereby do we show that neither science nor philosophy is needed in order to know what one must do to be honest and good, and even wise and virtuous. Indeed we might even have conjectured beforehand that cognizance of what every man is obligated to do, and hence also to know, would be available to every man, even the most ordinary. Yet

we cannot but observe with admiration how great an advantage the power of practical judgment has over the theoretical in ordinary human understanding. In the theoretical, when ordinary reason ventures to depart from the laws of experience and the perceptions of sense, it falls into sheer inconceivabilities and self-contradic-tions, or at least into a chaos of uncertainty, obscurity, and instability. In the practical, however, the power of judgment first begins to show itself to advantage when ordinary understanding excludes all sensuous incentives from practical laws. Such understanding then becomes even subtle, whether in quibbling with its own con-science or with other claims regarding what is to be called right, or whether in wanting to determine cor-rectly for its own instruction the worth of various ac-tions. And the most extraordinary thing is that ordinary understanding in the practical case may have just as good a hope of hitting the mark as that which any philosopher may promise himself. Indeed it is almost more certain in this than even a philosopher is, because he can have no principle other than what ordinary un-derstanding has, but he may easily confuse his judgment by a multitude of foreign and irrelevant considerations and thereby cause it to swerve from the right way. Would it not, therefore, be wiser in moral matters to abide by the ordinary rational judgment or at most to bring in philosophy merely for the purpose of render-ing the system of morals more complete and intelligi-ble and of presenting its rules in a way that is more convenient for use (especially in disputation), but not for the purpose of leading ordinary human under-standing away from its happy simplicity in practical matters and of bringing it by means of philosophy into a new path of inquiry and instruction?

Innocence is indeed a glorious thing; but, unfortu-nately, it does not keep very well and is easily led astray. Consequently, even wisdom—which consist more in doing and not doing that in knowing—needs science, not in order to learn from it, but in order that wisdom's precepts may gain acceptance and permanence. Man feels within himself a powerful counterweight to all the commands of duty, which are presented to him by rea-son as being so pre-eminently worthy of respect; this counterweight consist of his needs and inclinations, whose total satisfaction is summed up under the name of happiness. Now reason irremissibly commands its precepts, without thereby promising the inclinations anything; hence it disregards and neglects these impetuous and at the same time so seemingly plausible claims (which do not allow themselves to be suppressed by any command). Hereby arises a natural dialectic, i.e., a propensity to quibble with these strict laws of duty, to cast doubt upon their validity, or at least upon their purity and strictness, and to make them, where possible, more compatible with our wishes and inclinations. Thereby are such laws corrupted in their very foundations and their whole dignity is destroyed—something which even ordinary practical reason cannot in the end call good.

Thus is ordinary human reason forced to go outside its sphere and take a step into the field of practical philosophy, not by any need for speculation (which never befalls such reason so long as it is content to be mere sound reason) but on practical grounds themselves. There it tries to obtain information and clear instruction regarding the source of its own principle and the correct determination of this principle in its opposition to maxims based on need and inclination, so that reason may escape from the perplexity of opposite claims and may avoid the risk of losing all genuine moral principles through the ambiguity into which it easily falls. Thus when ordinary practical reason cultivates itself, there imperceptibly arises in it a dialectic which compels it to seek help in philosophy. The same thing happens in reason's theoretical use; in this case, just as in the other, peace will be found only in a thorough critical examination of our reason.

Second Section

Transition from Popular Moral Philosophy to a Metaphysics of Morals

If we have so far drawn our concept of duty from the ordinary use of our practical reason, one is by no means to infer that we have treated it as a concept of experience. On the contrary, when we pay attention to our experience of the way human beings act, we meet frequent and—as we ourselves admit—justified complaints that there cannot be cited a single certain example of the disposition to act from pure duty; and we meet complaints that although much may be done that is in accordance with what duty commands, yet there are always doubts as to whether what occurs has really been done from duty and so has moral worth. Hence there have always been philosophers who have absolutely denied the reality of this disposition in human actions and have ascribed everything to a more or less refined self-love. Yet in so doing they have not cast doubt upon the rightness of the concept of morality. Rather, they have spoken with sincere regret as to the frailty and impurity of human nature, which they think is noble enough to take as its precept an idea so worthy of respect but yet is too weak to follow this idea: reason, which should legislate for human nature, is used only to look after the interest of inclinations, whether singly or, at best, in their greatest possible harmony with one another.

In fact there is absolutely no possibility by means of experience to make out with complete certainty a single case in which the maxim of an action that may in other respects conform to duty has rested solely on moral grounds and on the representation of one's duty. It is indeed sometimes the case that after the keenest self-examination we can find nothing except the moral ground of duty that could have been strong enough to move us to this or that good action and to such great sacrifice. But there cannot with certainty be at all inferred from this that some secret impulse of self-love, merely appearing as the idea of duty, was not the actual determining cause of the will. We like to flatter ourselves with the false claim to a more noble motive; but in fact we can never, even by the strictest examination, completely plumb the depths of the secret incentives of our actions. For when moral value is being considered, the concern is not with the actions, which are seen, but rather with their inner principles, which are not seen.

Moreover, one cannot better serve the wishes of those who ridicule all morality as being a mere phantom of human imagination getting above itself because of self-conceit than by conceding to them that the concept of duty must be drawn solely from experience (just as from indolence one willingly persuades himself that such is the case as regards all other concepts as well). For by so conceding, one prepares for them a sure triumph. I am willing to admit out of love for humanity that most of our actions are in accordance with duty; but if we look more closely at our planning and striving, we everywhere come upon the dear self, which is always turning up, and upon which the intent of our actions is based rather than upon the strict command of duty (which would often require self-denial). One need not be exactly an enemy of virtue, but only a cool observer who does not take the liveliest wish for the good to be straight off its realization, in order to become doubtful at times whether any true virtue is actually to be found in the world. Such is especially the case when years increase and one's power of judgment is made shrewder by experience and keener in observation. Because of these things nothing can protect us from a complete falling away from our ideas of duty and preserve in the soul a well-grounded respect for duty's law except the clear conviction that, even if there never have been actions springing from such pure sources, the question at issue here is not whether this or that has happened but that reason of itself and independently of all experience commands what ought to happen. Consequently, reason unrelentingly commands actions of which the world has perhaps hitherto never provided an example and whose feasibility might well be doubted by one who bases everything upon experience; for instance, even though there might never yet have been a sincere friend, still pure sincerity in friendship is nonetheless required of every man, because this duty, prior to all experience, is contained as duty in general in the idea of a reason that determines the will by means of a priori grounds.

There may be noted further that unless we want to deny to the concept of morality all truth and all reference to a possible object, we cannot but admit that the moral law is of such widespread significance that it must hold not merely for men but for all rational beings generally, and that it must be valid not merely under contingent conditions and with exceptions but must be absolutely necessary. Clearly, therefore, no experience can give occasion for inferring even the possibility of such apodeictic laws. For with what right could we bring into unlimited respect as a universal precept for every rational nature what is perhaps valid only under the contingent conditions of humanity? And how could laws for the determination of our will be regarded as laws for the determination of a rational being in general and of ourselves only insofar as we are rational beings, if these laws were merely empirical and did not have their source completely a priori in pure, but practical, reason?

Moreover, worse service cannot be rendered morality than that an attempt be made to derive it from ex-

amples. For every example of morality presented to me must itself first be judged according to principles of morality in order to see whether it is fit to serve as an original example, i.e., as a model. But in no way can it authoritatively furnish the concept of morality. Even the Holy One of the gospel must first be compared with our ideal of moral perfection before he is recognized as such. Even he says of himself, "Why do you call me (whom you see) good? None is good (the archetype of the good) except God only (whom you do not see)." But whence have we the concept of God as the highest good? Solely from the idea of moral perfection, which reason frames a priori and connects inseparably with the concept of a free will. Imitation has no place at all in moral matters. And examples serve only for encouragement, i.e., they put beyond doubt the feasibility of what the law commands and they make visible what the practical rule expresses more generally. But examples can never justify us in setting aside their true original, which lies in reason, and letting ourselves be guided by them.

If there is then no genuine supreme principle of morality which does not rest on pure reason alone, independent of all experience, I think it is unnecessary even to ask whether it is a good thing to exhibit these concepts generally (in abstracto), which, along with the principles that belong to them, hold a priori, so far as the knowledge involved is to be distinguished from ordinary knowledge and is to be called philosophical. But in our times it may well be necessary to do so. For if one were to take a vote as to whether pure rational knowledge separated from everything empirical, i.e., metaphysics of morals, or whether popular practical philosophy is to be preferred, one can easily guess which side would be preponderant.

This descent to popular thought is certainly very commendable once the ascent to the principles of pure reason has occurred and has been satisfactorily accomplished. That would mean that the doctrine of morals has first been grounded on metaphysics and that subsequently acceptance for morals has been won by giving it a popular character after it has been firmly established. But it is quite absurd to try for popularity in the first inquiry, upon which depends the total correctness of the principles. Not only can such a procedure never lay claim to the very rare merit of a true philosophical popularity, inasmuch as there is really no art involved at all in being generally intelligible if one thereby renounces all basic insight, but such a procedure turns out a disgusting mishmash of patchwork observations and half-reasoned principles in which shallowpates revel because all this is something quite useful for the chitchat of everyday life. Persons of insight, on the other hand, feel confused by all this and turn their eyes away with a dissatisfaction which they nevertheless cannot cure. Yet philosophers, who quite see through the delusion, get little hearing when they summon people for a time from this pretend popularity in order that they may be rightfully popular only after they have attained definite insight.

One need only look at the attempts to deal with morality in the way favored by popular taste. What he will find in an amazing mixture is at one time the particular constitution of human nature (but along with this also the idea of a rational nature in general), at another time perfection, at another happiness; here moral feeling, and there the fear of God; something of this, and also something of that. But the thought never occurs to ask whether the principles of morality are to be sought at all in the knowledge of human nature (which can be had only from experience). Nor does the thought occur that if these principles are not to be sought here but to be found, rather, completely a priori and free from everything empirical in pure rational concepts only, and are to be found nowhere else even to the slightest extent—then there had better be adopted the plan of undertaking this investigation as a separate inquiry, i.e., as pure practical philosophy or (if one may use a name so much decried) as a metaphysics of morals. It is better to bring this investigation to full completeness entirely by itself and to bid the public, which demands popularity, to await the outcome of this undertaking. [. . .]

Everything in nature works according to laws. Only a rational being has the power to act according to his conception of laws, i.e., according to principles, and thereby has he a will. Since the derivation of actions from laws requires reason, the will is nothing but practical reason. If reason infallibly determines the will, then in the case of such a being actions which are recognized to be objectively necessary are also subjectively necessary, i.e., the will is a faculty of choosing only that which reason, independently of inclination, recognizes as be-

ing practically necessary, i.e., as good. But if reason of itself does not sufficiently determine the will, and if the will submits also to subjective conditions (certain incentives) which do not always agree with objective conditions; in a word, if the will does not in itself completely accord with reason (as it actually the case with men), then actions which are recognized as objectively necessary are subjectively contingent, and the determination of such a will according to objective laws is necessitation. That is to say that the relation of objective laws to a will not thoroughly good is represented as the determination of the will of a rational being by principles of reason which the will does not necessarily follow because of its own nature.

The representation of an objective principle insofar as it necessitates the will is called a command (of reason), and the formula of the command is called an imperative.

All imperatives are expressed by an *ought* and thereby indicate the relation of an objective law of reason to a will that is not necessarily determined by this law because of its subjective constitution (the relation of necessitation). Imperatives say that something would be good to do or to refrain from doing, but they say it to a will that does not always therefore do something simply because it has been represented to the will as something good to do. That is practically good which determines the will by means of representations of reason and hence not by subjective causes, but objectively, i.e., on grounds valid for every rational being as such. It is distinguished from the pleasant as that which influences the will only by means of sensation from merely subjective causes, which hold only for this or that person's senses but do not hold has a principle of reason valid for everyone.[2]

---

2. The dependence of the faculty of desire on sensations is called inclination, which accordingly always indicates a need. The dependence of a contingently determinable will on principles of reason, however, is called interest. Therefore an interest is found only in a dependent will which is not of itself always in accord with reason; in the divine will no interest can be thought. But even the human will can take an interest in something without thereby acting from interest. The former signifies practical interest in the action, while the latter signifies pathological interest in the

A perfectly good will would be quite as much subject to objective laws (of the good), but could not be conceived as thereby necessitated to act in conformity with law, inasmuch as it can of itself, according to its subjective constitution, be determined only by the representation of the good. Therefore no imperatives hold for the divine will, and in general for a holy will; the *ought* is here out of place, because the *would* is already of itself necessarily in agreement with the law. Consequently, imperatives are only formulas for expressing the relation of objective laws of willing in general to the subjective imperfection of the will of this or that rational being, e.g., the human will.

Now all imperatives command either hypothetically or categorically. The former represent the practical necessity of a possible action as a means for attaining something else that one wants (or may possibly want). The categorical imperative would be one which represented an action as objectively necessary in itself, without reference to another end.

Every practical law represents a possible action as good and hence as necessary for a subject who is practically determinable by reason; therefore all imperatives are formulas for determining an action which is necessary according to the principle of a will that is good in some way. Now if the action would be good merely as a means to something else, so is the imperative hypothetical. But if the action is represented as good in itself, and hence as necessary in a will which of itself conforms to reason as the principle of the will, then the imperative is categorical.

An imperative thus says what action possible by me would be good, and it presents the practical rule in re-

lation to a will which does not forthwith perform an action simply because it is good, partly because the subject does not always know that the action is good and partly because (even if he does know it is good) his maxims might yet be opposed to the objective principles of practical reason.

A hypothetical imperative thus says only that an action is good for some purpose, either possible or actual. In the first case it is a problematic practical principle; in the second case an assertoric one. A categorical imperative, which declares an action to be of itself objectively necessary without reference to any purpose, i.e., without any other end, holds as an apodeictic practical principle. [. . .]

Finally, there is one imperative which immediately commands a certain conduct without having as its condition any other purpose to be attained by it. This imperative is categorical. It is not concerned with the matter of the action and its intended result, but rather with the form of the action and the principle from which it follows; what is essentially good in the action consists in the mental disposition, let the consequences be what they may. This imperative may be called that of morality. [. . .]

The question as to how the imperative of morality is possible is undoubtedly the only one requiring a solution. For it is not at all hypothetical; and hence the objective necessity which it presents cannot be based on any presupposition, as was the case with the hypothetical imperatives. Only there must never here be forgotten that no example can show, i.e., empirically, whether there is any such imperative at all. Rather, care must be taken lest all imperatives which are seemingly categorical may nevertheless be covertly hypothetical. For instance, when it is said that you should not make a false promise, the assumption is that the necessity of this avoidance is no mere advice for escaping some other evil, so that it might be said that you should not make a false promise lest you ruin your credit when the falsity comes to light. But when it is asserted that an action of this kind must be regarded as bad in itself, then the imperative of prohibition is therefore categorical. Nevertheless, it cannot with certainty be shown by means of an example that the will is here determined solely by the law without any other incentive, even though such may seem to be the case. For it is always

---

object of the action. The former indicates only dependence of the will on principles of reason by itself, while the latter indicates the will's dependence on principles of reason for the sake of inclination, i.e., reason merely gives the practical rule for meeting the need of inclination. In the former case the action interests me, while in the latter case what interests me is the object of the action (so far as this object is pleasant for me). In the First Section we have seen that in the case of an action done from duty regard must be given not to the interest in the object, but only to interest in the action itself and in its rational principle (viz., the law).

possible that secretly there is fear of disgrace and perhaps also obscure dread of other dangers; such fear and dread may have influenced the will. Who can prove by experience that a cause is not present? Experience only shows that a cause is not perceived. But in such a case the so-called moral imperative, which as such appears to be categorical and unconditioned, would actually be only a pragmatic precept which makes us pay attention to our own advantage and merely teaches us to take such advantage into consideration.

We shall, therefore, have to investigate the possibility of a categorical imperative entirely a priori, inasmuch as we do not here have the advantage of having its reality given in experience and consequently of thus being obligated merely to explain its possibility rather than to establish it. In the meantime so much can be seen for now: the categorical imperative alone purports to be a practical law, while all the others may be called principles of the will but not laws. The reason for this is that whatever is necessary merely in order to attain some arbitrary purpose can be regarded as in itself contingent, and the precept can always be ignored once the purpose is abandoned. Contrariwise, an unconditioned command does not leave the will free to choose the opposite at its own liking. Consequently, only such a command carries with it that necessity which is demanded from a law.

Secondly, in the case of this categorical imperative, or law of morality, the reason for the difficulty (of discerning its possibility) is quite serious. The categorical imperative is an a priori synthetic practical proposition;[3] and since discerning the possibility of propositions of this sort involves so much difficulty in theoretic knowledge, there may readily be gathered that there will be no less difficulty in practical knowledge.

---

3. I connect a priori, and therefore necessarily, the act with the will without presupposing any condition taken from some inclination (though I make such a connection only objectively, i.e., under the idea of a reason having full power over all subjective motives). Hence this is a practical proposition which does not analytically derive the willing of an action from some other willing already presupposed (for we possess no such perfect will) but which connects the willing of an action immediately with the concept of the will of a rational being as something which is not contained in this concept.

In solving this problem, we want first to inquire whether perhaps the mere concept of a categorical imperative may not also supply us with the formula containing the proposition that can alone be a categorical imperative. For even when we know the purport of such an absolute command, the question as to how it is possible will still require as special and difficult effort. [. . .]

If I think of a hypothetical imperative in general, I do not know beforehand what it will contain until its condition is given. But if I think of a categorical imperative, I know immediately what it contains. For since, besides the law, the imperative contains only the necessity that the maxim should accord with this law, while the law contains no condition to restrict it, there remains nothing but the universality of a law as such with which the maxim of the action should conform. This conformity alone is properly what is represented as necessary by the imperative.

Hence there is only one categorical imperative and it is this: Act only according to that maxim whereby you can at the same time will that it should become a universal law.

Now if all imperatives of duty can be derived from this one imperative as their principle, then there can at least be shown what is understood by the concept of duty and what it means, even though there is left undecided whether what is called duty may not be an empty concept.

The universality of law according to which effects are produced constitutes what is properly called nature in the most general sense (as to form), i.e., the existence of things as far as determined by universal laws. Accordingly, the universal imperative of duty may be expressed thus: Act as if the maxim of your action were to become through your will a universal law of nature.

We shall now enumerate some duties, following the usual division of them into duties to ourselves and to others and into perfect and imperfect duties.

1. A man reduced to despair by a series of misfortunes feels sick of life but is still so far in possession of his reason that he can ask himself whether taking his own life would not be contrary to his duty to himself. Now he asks whether the maxim of his action could become a universal law of nature. But his maxim is this: from

self-love I make as my principle to shorten my life when its continued duration threatens more evil than it promises satisfaction. There only remains the question as to whether this principle of self-love can become a universal law of nature. One sees at once a contradiction in a system of nature whose law would destroy life by means of the very same feeling that acts so as to stimulate the furtherance of life, and hence there could be no existence as a system of nature. Therefore, such a maxim cannot possibly hold as a universal law of nature and is, consequently, wholly opposed to the supreme principle of all duty.

2. Another man in need finds himself forced to borrow money. He knows well that he won't be able to repay it, but he sees also that he will not get any loan unless he firmly promises to repay it within a fixed time. He wants to make such a promise, but he still has conscience enough to ask himself whether it is not permissible and is contrary to duty to get out of difficulty in this way. Suppose, however, that he decides to do so. The maxim of his action would then be expressed as follows: when I believe myself to be in need of money, I will borrow money and promise to pay it back, although I know that I can never do so. Now this principle of self-love or personal advantage may perhaps be quite compatible with one's entire future welfare, but the question is now whether it is right. I then transform the requirement of self-love into a universal law and put the question thus: how would things stand if my maxim were to become a universal law? He then sees at once that such a maxim could never hold as a universal law of nature and be consistent with itself, but must necessarily be self-contradictory. For the universality of a law which says that anyone believing himself to be in difficulty could promise whatever he pleases with the intention of not keeping it would make promising itself and the end to be attained thereby quite impossible, inasmuch as no one would believe what was promised him but would merely laugh at all such utterances as being vain pretenses.

3. A third finds in himself a talent whose cultivation could make him a man useful in many respects. But he finds himself in comfortable circumstances and prefers to indulge in pleasure rather than to bother himself about broadening and improving his fortunate natural aptitudes. But he asks himself further whether his maxim of neglecting his natural gifts, besides agreeing of itself with his propensity to indulgence, might agree also with what is called duty. He then sees that a system of nature could indeed always subsist according to such a universal law, even though every man (like South Sea Islanders) should let his talents rust and resolve to devote his life entirely to idleness, indulgence, propagation, and, in a word, to enjoyment. But he cannot possibly will that this should become a universal law of nature or be implanted in us as such a law by a natural instinct. For as a rational being he necessarily wills that all his faculties should be developed, inasmuch as they are given him for all sorts of possible purposes.

4. A fourth man finds things going well for himself but sees others (whom he could help) struggling with great hardships; and he thinks: what does it matter to me? Let everybody be as happy as Heaven wills or as he can make himself; I shall take nothing from him nor even envy him; but I have no desire to contribute anything to his well-being or to his assistance when in need. If such a way of thinking were to become a universal law of nature, the human race admittedly could very well subsist and doubtless could subsist even better than when everyone prates about sympathy and benevolence and even on occasion exerts himself to practice them but, on the other hand, also cheats when he can, betrays the rights of man, or otherwise violates them. But even though it is possible that a universal law of nature could subsist in accordance with that maxim, still it is impossible to will that such a principle should hold everywhere as a law of nature. For a will which resolved in this way would contradict itself, inasmuch as cases might often arise in which one would have need of the love and sympathy of others and in which he would deprive himself, by such a law of nature springing from his own will, of all hope, of the aid he wants for himself.

These are some of the many actual duties, or at least what are taken to be such, whose derivation from the single principle cited above is clear. We must be able to will that a maxim of our action become a universal law; this is the canon for morally estimating any of our actions. Some actions are so constituted that their maxims cannot without contradiction even be thought as a universal law of nature, much less be willed as what should become one. In the case of others this internal impossibility is indeed not found, but there is still no possibility of willing that their maxim should be raised to the universality of a law of nature, because such a will would contradict itself. There is no difficulty in seeing that the former kind of action conflicts with strict or narrow [perfect] (irremissible) duty, which the second kind conflicts only with broad [imperfect] (meritorious) duty. By means of theses examples there has thus been fully set forth how all duties depend as regards the kind of obligation (not the object of their action) upon the one principle.

If we now attend to ourselves in any transgression of a duty, we find that we actually do not will that our maxim should become a universal law—because this is impossible for us—but rather that the opposite of this maxim should remain a law universally. We only take the liberty of making an exception to the law for ourselves (or just for this one time) to the advantage of our inclination. Consequently, if we weighed up everything from one and the same standpoint, namely, that of reason, we would find a contradiction in our will, viz., that a certain principle be objectively necessary as a universal law and yet subjectively not hold universally but should admit of exceptions. But since we at one moment regard our action from the standpoint of a will wholly in accord with reason and then at another moment regard the very same action from the standpoint of a will affected by inclination, there is really no contradiction here. Rather, there is an opposition (*antagonismus*) of inclination to the precept of reason, whereby the universality (*universalitas*) of the principle is changed into a mere generality (*generalitas*) so that the practical principle of reason may meet the maxim halfway. Although this procedure cannot be justified in our own impartial judgment, yet it does show that we actually acknowledge the validity of the categorical imperative and (with all respect for it) merely allow ourselves a few exceptions which, as they seem to us, are unimportant and forced upon us. [...]

The will is thought of as a faculty of determining itself to action in accordance with the representation of certain laws, and such a faculty can be found only in rational beings. Now what serves the will as the objective ground of its self-determination is an end; and if this end is given by reason alone, then it must be equally valid for all rational beings. On the other hand, what

contains merely the ground of the possibility of the action, whose effect is an end, is called the means. The subjective ground of desire is the incentive; the objective ground of volition is the motive. Hence there arises the distinction between subjective ends, which rest on incentives, and objective ends, which depend on motives valid for every rational being. Practical principles are formal when they abstract from all subjective ends; they are material, however, when they are founded upon subjective ends, and hence upon certain incentives. The ends which a rational being arbitrarily proposes to himself as effects of this action (material ends) are all merely relative, for only their relation to a specially constituted faculty of desire in the subject gives them their worth. Consequently, such worth cannot provide any universal principles, which are valid and necessary for all rational beings and, furthermore, are valid for every volition, i.e., cannot provide any practical laws. Therefore, all such relative ends can be grounds only for hypothetical imperatives.

But let us suppose that there were something whose existence has in itself an absolute worth, something which as an end in itself could be a ground of determinate laws. In it, and in it alone, would there be the ground of a possible categorical imperative, i.e., of a practical law.

Now I say that man, and in general every rational being, exists as an end in himself and not merely as a means to be arbitrarily used by this or that will. He must in all his actions, whether directed to himself or to other rational beings, always be regarded at the same time as an end. All the objects of inclinations have only a conditioned value; for if there were not these inclinations and the needs founded on them, then their object would be without value. But the inclinations themselves, being sources of needs, are so far from having an absolute value such as to render them desirable for their own sake that the universal wish of every rational being must be, rather, to be wholly free from them. Accordingly, the value of any object obtainable by our action is always conditioned. Beings whose existence depends not on our will but on nature have, nevertheless, if they are not rational beings, only a relative value as means and are therefore called things. On the other hand, rational beings are called persons inasmuch as their nature already marks them out as ends in themselves, i.e., as something which is not to be used merely as means and hence there is imposed thereby a limit on all arbitrary use of such beings, which are thus objects of respect. Persons are, therefore, not merely subjective ends, whose existence as an effect of our actions has a value for us; but such beings are objective ends, i.e., exist as ends in themselves. Such an end is one for which there can be substituted no other end to which such beings should serve merely as means, for otherwise nothing at all of absolute value would be found anywhere. But if all value were conditioned and hence contingent, then no supreme practical principle could be found for reason at all.

If then there is to be a supreme practical principle and, as far as the human will is concerned, a categorical imperative, then it must be such that from the conception of what is necessarily an end for everyone because this end is an end in itself it constitutes an objective principle of the will and can hence serve as a practical law. The ground of such a principle is this: rational nature exists as an end in itself. In this way man necessarily thinks of his own existence; thus far is it a subjective principle of human actions. But in this way also does every other rational being think of his existence on the same rational ground that holds also for me; hence it is at the same time an objective principle, from which, as a supreme practical ground, all laws of the will must be able to be derived. The practical imperative will therefore be the following: Act in such a way that you treat humanity, whether in your own person or in the person of another, always at the same time as an end and never simply as a means. We now want to see whether this can be carried out in practice.

Let us keep to our previous examples.

First, as regards the concept of necessary duty to oneself, the man who contemplates suicide will ask himself whether his action can be consistent with the idea of humanity as an end in itself. If he destroys himself in order to escape from a difficult situation, then he is making use of his person merely as a means so as to maintain a tolerable condition till the end of his life. Man, however, is not a thing and hence is not something to be used merely as a means; he must in all his actions always be regarded as an end in himself. Therefore, I cannot dispose of man in my own person by mutilating, damaging, or killing him. (A more exact determination of this principle so as to avoid all misunderstanding, e.g., regarding the amputation of limbs in order to save one-

self, or the exposure of one's life to danger in order to save it, and so on, must here be omitted; such questions belong to morals proper.)

Second, as concerns necessary or strict duty to others, the man who intends to make a false promise will immediately see that he intends to make use of another man merely as a means to an end which the latter does not likewise hold. For the man whom I want to use for my own purposes by such a promise cannot possibly concur with my way of acting toward him and hence cannot himself hold the end of this action. This conflict with the principle of duty to others becomes even clearer when instances of attacks on the freedom and property of others are considered. For then it becomes clear that a transgressor of the rights of men intends to make use of the persons of others merely as a means, without taking into consideration that, as rational beings, they should always be esteemed at the same times as ends, i.e., be esteemed only as beings who must themselves be able to hold the very same action as an end.[4]

Third, with regard to contingent (meritorious) duty to oneself, it is not enough that the action does not conflict with humanity in our own person as an end in itself; the action must also harmonize with this end. Now there are in humanity capacities for greater perfection which belong to the end that nature has in view as regards humanity in our own person. To neglect these capacities might perhaps be consistent with the maintenance of humanity as an end in itself, but would not be consistent with the advancement of this end.

Fourth, concerning meritorious duty to others, the natural end that all men have is their own happiness.

---

4. Let it not be thought that the trivial *quod tibi non vis fieri, etc.* [do not do to others what you do not want done to yourself] can here serve as a standard or principle. For it is merely derived from our principle, although with several limitations. It cannot be a universal law, for it contains the ground neither of duties to oneself nor of duties of love toward others (for many a man would gladly consent that others should not benefit him, if only he might be excused from benefiting them). Nor, finally, does it contain the ground of strict duties toward others, for the criminal would on this ground be able to dispute with the judges who punish him; and so on.

Now humanity might indeed subsist if nobody contributed anything to the happiness of others, provided he did not intentionally impair their happiness. But this, after all, would harmonize only negatively and not positively with humanity as an end in itself, if everyone does not also strive, as much as he can, to further the ends of others. For the ends of any subject who is an end in himself must as far as possible be my ends also, if that conception of an end in itself is to have its full effect in me.

This principle of humanity and of every rational nature generally as an end in itself is the supreme limiting condition of every man's freedom of action. This principle is not borrowed from experience, first, because of its universality, inasmuch as it applies to all rational beings generally, and no experience is capable of determining anything about them; and, secondly, because in experience (subjectively) humanity is not thought of as the end of men, i.e., as an object that we of ourselves actually make our end which as a law ought to constitute the supreme limiting condition of all subjective ends (whatever they may be); and hence this principle must arise from pure reason. That is to say that the ground of all practical legislation lies objectively in the rule and in the form of universality, which (according to the first principle) makes the rule capable of being a law (say, for example, a law of nature). Subjectively, however, the ground of all practical legislation lies in the end; but (according to the second principle) the subject of all ends is every rational being as an end in himself. From this there now follows the third practical principle of the will as the supreme condition of the will's conformity with universal practical reason, viz., the idea of the will of every rational being as a will that legislates universal law.

According to this principle all maxims are rejected which are not consistent with the will's own legislation of universal law. The will is thus not merely subject to the law but is subject to the law in such a way that it must be regarded also as legislating for itself and only on this account as being subject to the law (of which it can regard itself as the author).

In the previous formulations of imperatives, viz., that based on the conception of the conformity of actions to universal law in a way similar to a natural order and that based on the universal prerogative of rational beings as ends in themselves, these imperatives just because they were thought of as categorical excluded from their legislative authority all admixture of any interest as an incentive. They were, however, only assumed to be categorical because such an assumption had to be made if the concept of duty was to be explained. But that there were practical propositions which commanded categorically could not itself be proved, nor can it be proved anywhere in this section. But one thing could have been done, viz., to indicate that in willing from duty the renunciation of all interest is the specific mark distinguishing a categorical imperative from a hypothetical one and that such renunciation was expressed in the imperative itself by means of some determination contained in it. This is done in the present (third) formulation of the principle, namely, in the idea of the will of every rational being as a will that legislates universal law.

When such a will is thought of, then even though a will which is subject to law may be bound to this law by means of some interest, nevertheless a will that is itself a supreme lawgiver is not able as such to depend on any interest. For a will which is so dependent would itself require yet another law restricting the interest of its self-love to the condition that such interest should itself be valid as a universal law.

Thus the principle that every human will as a will that legislates universal law in all its maxims, provided it is otherwise correct, would be well suited to being a categorical imperative in the following respect: just because of the idea of legislating universal law such an imperative is not based on any interest, and therefore it alone of all possible imperatives can be unconditional. Or still better, the proposition being converted, if there is a categorical imperative (i.e., a law for the will of every rational being), then it can only command that everything be done from the maxim of such a will as could at the same time have as its object only itself regarded as legislating universal law. For only then are the practical principle and the imperative which the will obeys unconditional, inasmuch as the will can be based on no interest at all.

When we look back upon all previous attempts that have been made to discover the principle of morality, there is no reason now to wonder why they one and all had to fail. Man was viewed as bound to laws by his duty; but it was not seen that man is subject only to his own, yet universal, legislation and that he is bound only to act in accordance with his own will, which is, however, a will purposed by nature to legislate universal laws. For when man is thought as being merely subject to a law (whatever it might be), then the law had to carry with it some interest functioning as an attracting stimulus or as a constraining force for obedience, inasmuch as the law did not arise as a law from his own will. Rather, in order that his will conform with law, it had to be necessitated by something else to act in a certain way. By this absolutely necessary conclusion, however, all the labor spent in finding a supreme ground for duty was irretrievably lost; duty was never discovered, but only the necessity of acting from a certain interest. This might be either one's own interest or another's, but either way the imperative had to be always conditional and could never possibly serve as a moral command. I want, therefore, to call my principle the principle of the autonomy of the will, in contrast with every other principle, which I accordingly count under heteronomy.

The concept of every rational being as one who must regard himself as legislating universal law by all his will's maxims, so that he may judge himself and his actions from this point of view, leads to another very fruitful concept, which depends on the aforementioned one, viz., that of a kingdom of ends.

By "kingdom" I understand a systematic union of different rational beings through common laws. Now laws determine ends as regards their universal validity; therefore, if one abstracts from the personal differences of rational beings and also from all content of their private ends, then it will be possible to think of a whole of all ends in systematic connection (a whole both of rational beings as ends in themselves and also of the particular ends which each may set for himself); that is, one can think of a kingdom of ends that is possible on the aforesaid principles.

For all rational beings stand under the law that each of them should treat himself and all others never merely as means but always at the same time as an end in himself. Hereby arises a systematic union of rational beings through common objective laws, i.e., a kingdom that may be called a kingdom of ends (certainly only an ideal), inasmuch as these laws have in view the very relation of such beings to one another as ends and means.

A rational being belongs to the kingdom of ends as a member when he legislates in it universal laws while also being himself subject to these laws. He belongs to it as sovereign, when as legislator he is himself subject to the will of no other.

A rational being must always regard himself as legislator in a kingdom of ends rendered possible by freedom of the will, whether as member or as sovereign. The position of the latter can be maintained not merely through the maxims of his will but only if he is a completely independent being without needs and with unlimited power adequate to his will.

Hence morality consists in the relation of all action to that legislation whereby alone a kingdom of ends is possible. This legislation must be found in every rational being and must be able to arise from his will, whose principle then is never to act on any maxim except such as can also be a universal law and hence such as the will can thereby regard itself as at the same time the legislator of universal law. If now the maxims do not by their very nature already necessarily conform with this objective principle of rational beings as legislating universal laws, then the necessity of action on that principle is called practical necessitation, i.e., duty. Duty does not apply to the sovereign in the kingdom of ends, but it does apply to every member and to each in the same degree.

The practical necessity of acting according to this principle, i.e., duty, does not rest at all on feelings, impulses, and inclinations, but only on the relation of rational beings to one another, a relation in which the will of a rational being must always be regarded at the same time as legislative, because otherwise he could not be thought of as an end in himself. Reason, therefore, relates every maxim of the will as legislating universal laws to every other will and also to every action toward oneself; it does so not on account of any other practical motive or future advantage but rather from the idea of the dignity of a rational being who obeys no law except what he at the same time enacts himself.

In the kingdom of ends everything has either a price or a dignity. Whatever has a price can be replaced by something else as its equivalent; on the other hand, whatever is above all price, and therefore admits of no equivalent, has a dignity.

Whatever has reference to general human inclinations and needs has a market price; whatever, without presupposing any need, accords with a certain taste, i.e., a delight in the mere unpurposive play of our mental powers, has an affective price; but that which constitutes the condition under which alone something can be an end in itself has not merely a relative worth, i.e., a price, but has an intrinsic worth, i.e., dignity.

Now morality is the condition under which alone a rational being can be an end in himself, for only thereby can he be a legislating member in the kingdom of ends. Hence morality and humanity, insofar as it is capable of morality, alone have dignity. Skill and diligence in work have a market price; wit, lively imagination, and humor have an affective price; but fidelity to promises and benevolence based on principles (not on instinct) have intrinsic worth. Neither nature nor art contain anything which in default of these could be put in their place; for their worth consists, not in the effects which arise from them, nor in the advantage and profit which they provide, but in mental dispositions, i.e., in the maxims of the will which are ready in this way to manifest themselves in action, even if they are not favored with success. Such actions also need no recommendation from any subjective disposition or taste so as to meet with immediate favor and delight; there is no need of any immediate propensity or feeling toward them. They exhibit the will performing them as an object of immediate respect; and nothing but reason is required to impose them upon the will, which is not to be cajoled into them, since in the case of duties such cajoling would be a contradiction. This estimation, therefore, lets the worth of such a disposition be recognized as dignity and puts it infinitely beyond all price, with which it cannot in the least be brought into competition or comparison without, as it were, violating its sanctity.

What then is it that entitles the morally good disposition, or virtue, to make such lofty claims? It is nothing less than the share which such a disposition affords the rational being of legislating universal laws, so that he is fit to be a member in a possible kingdom of ends, for which his own nature has already determined him as an end in himself and therefore as a legislator in the kingdom of ends. Thereby is he free as regards all laws of nature, and he obeys only those laws which he gives to himself. Accordingly, his maxims can belong to a universal legislation to which he at the same time subjects himself. For nothing can have any worth other than what the law determines. But the legislation itself which determines all worth must for the very reason have dignity, i.e., unconditional and incomparable worth; and the word "respect" alone provides a suitable expression for the esteem which a rational being must have for it. Hence autonomy is the ground of the dignity of human nature and of every rational nature.

The aforementioned three ways of representing the principle of morality are at bottom only so many formulas of the very same law: one of them by itself contains a combination of the other two. Nevertheless, there is a difference in them, which is subjectively rather than objectively practical, viz., it is intended to bring an idea of reason closer to intuition (in accordance with a certain analogy) and thereby closer to feeling. All maxims have, namely,

1. A form, which consists in universality; and in this respect the formula of the moral imperative is expressed thus: maxims must be so chosen as if they were to hold as universal laws of nature.

2. A matter, viz., an end; and here the formula says that a rational being, inasmuch as he is by his very nature an end and hence an end in himself, must serve in every maxim as a condition limiting all merely relative and arbitrary ends.

3. A complete determination of all maxims by the formula that all maxims proceeding from his own legislation ought to harmonize with a possible kingdom of ends as a kingdom of nature.[5] There is a progression here through the categories of the *unity* of the form of the will (its universality), the *plurality* of its matter (its objects, i.e., its ends), and the *totality* or completeness of

---

5. Teleology considers nature as a kingdom of ends; morals regards a possible kingdom of ends as a kingdom of nature. In the former the kingdom of ends is a theoretical idea for explaining what exists. In the latter it is a practical idea for bringing about what does not exist but can be made actual by our conduct, i.e., what can be actualized in accordance with this very idea.

its system of ends. But one does better if in moral judgment he follows the rigorous method and takes as his basis the universal formula of the categorical imperative: Act according to that maxim which can at the same time make itself a universal law. But if one wants also to secure acceptance for the moral law, it is very useful to bring one and the same action under the three aforementioned concepts and thus, as far as possible, to bring the moral law nearer to intuition.

We can now end where we started in the beginning, viz., the concept of an unconditionally good will. That will is absolutely good which cannot be evil, i.e., whose maxim, when made into a universal law, can never conflict with itself. This principle is therefore also its supreme law: Act always according to that maxim whose universality as a law you can at the same time will. This is the only condition under which a will can never be in conflict with itself, and such an imperative is categorical. Inasmuch as the validity of the will as a universal law for possible actions is analogous to the universal connection of the existence of things in accordance with universal laws, which is the formal aspect of nature in general, the categorical imperative can also be expressed thus: Act according to maxims which can at the same time have for their object themselves as universal laws of nature. Thus, then, the formula for an absolutely good will is constituted.

Rational nature is distinguished from the rest of nature by the fact that it sets itself an end. This end would be the matter of every good will. But in the idea of an absolutely good will—good without any qualifying condition (of attaining this or that end)—complete abstraction must be made from every end that has to come about as an effect (since such would make every will only relatively good). And so the end must here be conceived, not as an end to be effected, but as an independently existing end. Hence it must be conceived only negatively, i.e., as an end which should never be acted against and therefore as one which in all willing must never be regarded merely as means but must always be esteemed at the same time as an end. Now this end can be nothing but the subject of all possible ends themselves, because this subject is at the same time the subject of a possible absolutely good will; for such a will

cannot without contradiction be subordinated to any other object. The principle: So act in regard to every rational being (yourself and others) that he may at the same time count in your maxim as an end in himself, is thus basically the same as the principle: Act on a maxim which at the same time contains in itself its own universal validity for every rational being. That in the use of means for every end my maxim should be restricted to the condition of its universal validity as a law for every subject says just the same as that a subject of ends, i.e., a rational being himself, must be made the ground for all maxims of actions and must thus be used never merely as means but as the supreme limiting condition in the use of all means, i.e., always at the same times as an end.

Now there follows incontestably from this that every rational being as an end in himself must be able to regard himself with reference to all laws to which he may be subject as being at the same time the legislator of universal law, for just this very fitness of his maxims for the legislation of universal law distinguishes him as an end in himself. There follows also that his dignity (prerogative) of being above all the mere things of nature implies that his maxims must be taken from the viewpoint that regards himself, as well as every other rational being, as being legislative beings (and hence are they called persons). In this way there is possible a world of rational beings (*mundus intelligibilis*) as a kingdom of ends, because of the legislation belonging to all persons as members. Therefore, every rational being must so act as if he were through his maxim always a legislating member in the universal kingdom of ends. The formal principle of these maxims is this: So act as if your maxims were to serve at the same time as a universal law (for all rational beings). Thus a kingdom of ends is possible only on the analogy of a kingdom of nature; yet the former is possible only through maxims, i.e., self-imposed rules, while the latter is possible only through laws of efficient causes necessitated from without. Regardless of this difference and even though nature as a whole is viewed as a machine, yet insofar as nature stands in a relation to rational beings as its ends, it is on this account given the name of a kingdom of nature. Such a kingdom of ends would actually be realized through maxims whose rule is prescribed to all rational beings by the categorical imperative, if these maxims were universally obeyed. But even if a rational being himself strictly obeys such a maxim, he cannot for that reason count on everyone else's being true to it, nor can he expect the kingdom of nature and its purposive order to be in harmony with him as a fitting member of a kingdom of ends made possible by himself, i.e., he cannot expect the kingdom of nature to favor his expectation of happiness. Nevertheless, the law: Act in accordance with the maxims of a member legislating universal laws for a merely possible kingdom of ends, remains in full force, since it commands categorically. And just in this lies the paradox that merely the dignity of humanity as rational nature without any further end or advantage to be thereby gained—and hence respect for a mere idea—should yet serve as an inflexible precept for the will; and that just this very independence of the maxims from all such incentives should constitute the sublimity of maxims and the worthiness of every rational subject to be a legislative member in the kingdom of ends, for otherwise he would have to be regarded as subject only to the natural law of his own needs. And even if the kingdom of nature as well as the kingdom of ends were thought of as both united under one sovereign so that the latter kingdom would thereby no longer remain a mere idea but would acquire true reality, then indeed the kingdom of ends would gain the addition of a strong incentive, but never increase in its intrinsic worth. For this sole absolute legislator must, in spite of all this, always be thought of as judging the worth of rational beings solely by the disinterested conduct prescribed to themselves by means of this idea alone. The essence of things is not altered by their external relations; and whatever without reference to such relations alone constitutes the absolute worth of man is also what he must be judged by, whoever the judge may be, even the Supreme Being. Hence morality is the relation of actions to the autonomy of the will, i.e., to the possible legislation of universal law by means of the maxims of the will. That action which is compatible with the autonomy of the will is permitted; that which is not compatible is forbidden. That will whose maxims are necessarily in accord with the laws of autonomy is a holy, or absolutely good, will. The dependence of a will which is not absolutely good upon the principle of autonomy (i.e., moral necessitation) is

obligation, which cannot therefore be applied to a holy will. The objective necessity of an action form obligation is called duty.

From what has just been said, there can now easily be explained how it happens that, although in the concept of duty we think of subjection to the law, yet at the same time we thereby ascribe a certain dignity and sublimity to the person who fulfills all his duties. For not insofar as he is subject to the moral law does he have sublimity, but rather has it only insofar as with regard to this very same law he is at the same time legislative, and only thereby is he subject to the law. We have also shown above how neither fear nor inclination, but solely respect for the law, is in the incentive which can give an action moral worth. Our own will, insofar as it were to act only under the condition of its being able to legislate universal law by means of its maxims—this will, ideally possible for us, is the proper object of respect. And the dignity of humanity consists just in its capacity to legislate universal law, though with the condition of humanity's being at the same time itself subject to this very same legislation.

Autonomy of the Will as the Supreme Principle of Morality

Autonomy of the will is the property that the will has of being a law to itself (independently of any property of the objects of volition). The principle of autonomy is this: Always choose in such a way that in the same volition the maxims of the choice are at the same time present as universal law. That this practical rule is an imperative, i.e., that the will of every rational being is necessarily bound to the rule as a condition, cannot be proved by merely analyzing the concepts contained in it, since it is a synthetic proposition. For proof one would have to go beyond cognition of objects to a critical examination of the subject, i.e., go to a critique of pure practical reason, since this synthetic proposition which commands apodeictically must be capable of being cognized completely a priori. This task, however, does not belong to the present section. But that the above principle of autonomy is the sole principle of morals can quite well be shown by mere analysis of the concepts of morality; for thereby the principle of morals is found to be necessarily a categorical imperative, which commands nothing more nor less than this very autonomy.

Heteronomy of the Will as the Source of All Spurious Principles of Morality

If the will seeks the law that is to determine it anywhere but in the fitness of its maxims for its own legislation of universal laws, and if it thus goes outside of itself and seeks this law in the character of any of its objects, then heteronomy always results. The will in that case does not give itself the law, but the object does so because of its relation to the will. This relation, whether it rest on inclination or on representations of reason, admits only of hypothetical imperatives: I ought to do something because I will something else. On the other hand, the moral, and hence categorical, imperative says that I ought to act in this way or that way, even though I did not will something else. For example, the former says that I ought not to lie if I would maintain my reputation; the latter says that I ought not to lie even though lying were to bring me not the slightest discredit. The moral imperative must therefore abstract from every object to such an extent that no object has any influence at all on the will, so that practical reason (the will) may not merely minister to an interest not belonging to it but may merely show its own commanding authority as the supreme legislation. Thus, for example, I ought to endeavor to promote the happiness of others, not as though its realization were any concern of mine (whether by immediate inclination or by any satisfaction indirectly gained through reason), but merely because a maxim which excludes it cannot be comprehended as a universal law in one and the same volition. [...]

Third Section

Transition from a Metaphysics of Morals to a Critique of Pure Practical Reason

The Concept of Freedom Is the Key for an Explanation of the Autonomy of the Will

The will is a kind of causality belonging to living beings insofar as they are rational; freedom would be the property of this causality that makes it effective independent of any determination by alien causes. Similarly, natural necessity is the property of the causality of all non-rational beings by which they are determined to activity though the influence of alien causes.

The foregoing explanation of freedom is negative and is therefore unfruitful for attaining an insight regarding its essence; but there arises from it a positive concept, which as such is richer and more fruitful. The concept of causality involves that of laws according to which something that we call cause must entail something else—namely, the effect. Therefore freedom is certainly not lawless, even though it is not a property of will in accordance with laws of nature. It must, rather, be a causality in accordance with immutable laws, which, to be sure, is of a special kind; otherwise a free will would be something absurd. As we have already seen, natural necessity is a heteronomy of efficient causes, inasmuch as every effect is possible only in accordance with the law that something else determines the efficient cause to exercise its causality. What else, then, can freedom of the will be but autonomy, i.e., the property that the will has of being a law to itself? The proposition that the will is in every action a law to itself expresses, however, nothing but the principle of acting according to no other maxim than that which can at the same time have itself as a universal law for its object. Now this is precisely the formula of the categorical imperative and is the principle of morality. Thus a free will and a will subject to moral laws are one and the same. [...]

Freedom Must Be Presupposed as a Property of the Will of All Rational Beings

[...] Every being which cannot act in any way other than under the idea of freedom is for this very reason free from a practical point of view. This is to say that for such a being all the laws that are inseparably bound up with freedom are valid just as much as if the will of such a being could be declared to be free in itself for reasons that are valid for theoretical philosophy.[6] Now I claim that we must necessarily attribute to every rational be-

---

6. I adopt this method of assuming as sufficient for our purpose that freedom is presupposed merely as an idea by rational beings in their actions in order that I may avoid the necessity of having to prove freedom from a theoretical point of view as well. For even if this latter problem is left unresolved, the same laws that would bind a being who was really free are valid equally for a being who cannot act otherwise than under the idea of its own freedom. Thus we can relieve ourselves of the burden which presses on the theory.

ing who has a will also the idea of freedom, under which only can such a being act. For in such a being we think of a reason that is practical, i.e., that has causality in reference to its objects. Now we cannot possibly think of a reason that consciously lets itself be directed from outside as regards its judgments; for in that case the subject would ascribe the determination of his faculty of judgment not to his reason, but to an impulse. Reason must

regard itself as the author of its principles independent of foreign influences. Therefore as practical reason or as the will of a rational being must reason regard itself as free. This is to say that the will of a rational being can be a will of its own only under the idea of freedom, and that such a will must therefore, from a practical point of view, be attributed to all rational beings.

John Stuart Mill

Understanding and Defending Utilitarianism

Chapter II

What Utilitarianism Is

[…] The creed which accepts as the foundation of morals "utility" or the "greatest happiness principle" holds that actions are right in proportion as they tend to promote happiness; wrong as they tend to produce the reverse of happiness. By happiness is intended pleasure and the absence of pain; by unhappiness, pain and the privation of pleasure. To give a clear view of the moral standard set up by the theory, much more requires to be said; in particular, what things it includes in the ideas of pain and pleasure, and to what extent this is left an open question. But these supplementary explanations do not affect the theory of life on which this theory of morality is grounded—namely, that pleasure and freedom from pain are the only things desirable as ends; and that all desirable things (which are as numerous in the utilitarian as in any other scheme) are desirable either for pleasure inherent in themselves or as means to the promotion of pleasure and the prevention of pain.

Now such a theory of life excites in many minds, and among them in some of the most estimable in feeling and purpose, inveterate dislike. To suppose that life has (as they express it) no higher end than pleasure—no better and nobler object of desire and pursuit—they designate as utterly mean and groveling, as a doctrine worthy only of swine, to whom the followers of Epicurus were, at a very early period, contemptuously likened; and modern holders of the doctrine are occasionally made the subject of equally polite comparisons by its German, French, and English assailants.

When thus attacked, the Epicureans have always answered that it is not they, but their accusers, who represent human nature in a degrading light, since the accusation supposes human beings to be capable of no pleasure except those of which swine are capable. If this supposition were true, the charge could not be gainsaid, but would then be no longer an imputation; for if the sources of pleasure were precisely the same to human beings and to swine, the rule of life which is good enough for the one would be good enough for the other. The comparison of the Epicurean life to that of beasts is felt as degrading, precisely because a beast's pleasure do not satisfy a human being's conceptions of happiness. Human beings have faculties more elevated than the animal appetites and, when once made conscious of them, do not regard anything as happiness

From John Stuart Mill, *Utilitarianism (Second Edition),* edited by George Sher (Indianapolis: Hackett Publishing Company, 2002). Reprinted by permission of the publisher.

which does not include their gratification. I do not, indeed, consider the Epicureans to have been by any means faultless in drawing out their scheme of consequences from the utilitarian principle. To do this in any sufficient manner, many Stoic, as well as Christian, elements require to be included. But there is no known Epicurean theory of life which does not assign to the pleasures of the intellect, of the feelings and imagination, and of the moral sentiments a much higher value as pleasures than to those of mere sensation. It must be admitted, however, that utilitarian writers in general have placed the superiority of mental over bodily pleasures chiefly in the greater permanency, safety, uncostliness, etc., of the former—that is, in their circumstantial advantages rather than in their intrinsic nature. And on all these points utilitarians have fully proved their case; but they might have taken the other and, as it may be called, higher ground with entire consistency. It is quite compatible with the principle of utility to recognize the fact that some kinds of pleasure are more desirable and more valuable than others. It would be absurd that, while in estimating all other things quality is considered as well as quantity, the estimation of pleasure should be supposed to depend on quantity alone.

If I am asked what I mean by difference of quality in pleasures, or what makes one pleasure more valuable than another, merely as a pleasure, except its being greater in amount, there is but one possible answer. Of two pleasures, if there be one to which all or almost all who have experience of both give a decided preference, irrespective of any feeling of moral obligation to prefer it, that is the more desirable pleasure. If one of the two is, by those who are competently acquainted with both, placed so far above the other that they prefer it, even though knowing it to be attended with a greater amount of discontent, and would not resign it for any quantity of the other pleasure which their nature is capable of, we are justified in ascribing to the preferred enjoyment a superiority in quality so far outweighing quantity as to render it, in comparison, of small account.

Now it is an unquestionable fact that those who are equally acquainted with and equally capable of appreciating and enjoying both do give a most marked preference to the manner of existence which employs their higher faculties. Few human creatures would consent to be changed into any of the lower animals for promise of the fullest allowance of the beast's pleasures; no intelligent human being would consent to be a fool, no instructed person would be an ignoramus, no person of feeling and conscience would be selfish and base, even though they should be persuaded that the fool, the dunce, or the rascal is better satisfied with his lot than they are with theirs. They would not resign what they possess more than he for the most complete satisfaction of all the desires which they have in common with him. If they ever fancy they would, it is only in cases of unhappiness so extreme that to escape from it they would exchange their lot for almost any other, however undesirable in their own eyes. A being of higher faculties requires more to make him happy, is capable probably of more acute suffering, and certainly accessible to it at more points, than one of an inferior type; but in spite of these liabilities, he can never really wish to sink into what he feels to be a lower grade of existence. We may give what explanation we please of this unwillingness; we may attribute it to pride, a name which is given indiscriminately to some of the most and to some of the least estimable feelings of which mankind are capable; we may refer it to the love of liberty and personal independence, an appeal to which was with the Stoics one of the most effective means for the inculcation of it; to the love of power or to the love of excitement, both of which do really enter into and contribute to it; but its most appropriate appellation is a sense of dignity, which all human beings possess in one form or other, and in some, though by no means in exact, proportion to their higher faculties, and which is so essential a part of the happiness of those in whom it is strong that nothing which conflicts with it could be otherwise than momentarily an object of desire to them. Whoever supposes that this preference takes place at a sacrifice of happiness—that the superior being, in anything like equal circumstances, is not happier than the inferior—confounds the two very different ideas of happiness and content. It is indisputable that the being whose capacities of enjoyment are low has the greatest chance of having them fully satisfied; and a highly endowed being will always feel that any happiness which he can look for, as the world is constituted, is imperfect. But he can learn to bear its imperfections, if they are at all bearable; and they will not make him envy the being who is indeed unconscious of the imperfections, but only because he feels not at all the good which those imperfections qualify. It is better to be a human being dissatisfied than a pig satisfied; better to be Socrates dissatisfied than a fool satisfied. And if the fool, or the pig, are of a different opinion, it is because they only know their own side of the question. The other party to the comparison knows both sides.

It may be objected that many who are capable of the higher pleasure occasionally, under the influence of temptation, postpone them to the lower. But this is quite compatible with a full appreciation of the intrinsic superiority of the higher. Men often, from infirmity of character, make their election for the nearer good, though they know it to be the less valuable; and this no less when the choice is between two bodily pleasures than when it is between bodily and mental. They pursue sensual indulgences to the injury of health, though perfectly aware that health is the greater good. It may be further objected that many who begin with youthful enthusiasm for everything noble, as they advance in years, sink into indolence and selfishness. But I do not believe that those who undergo this very common change voluntarily choose the lower description of pleasures in preference to the higher. I believe that, before they devote themselves exclusively to the one, they have already become incapable of the other. Capacity for other nobler feelings is in most natures a very tender plant, easily killed, not only by hostile influences, but by mere want of sustenance; and in the majority of young persons it speedily dies away if the occupations to which their position in life has devoted them, and the society into which it has thrown them, are not favorable to keeping that higher capacity in exercise. Men lose their high aspirations as they lose their intellectual tastes, because they have not time or opportunity for indulging them; and they addict themselves to inferior pleasures, not because they deliberately prefer them, but because they are either the only ones to which they have access or the only ones which they are any longer capable of enjoying. It may be questioned whether anyone who has remained equally susceptible to both classes of pleasures ever knowingly and calmly preferred the lower, though many, in all ages, have broken down in an ineffectual attempt to combine both.

From this verdict of the only competent judges, I apprehend there can be no appeal. On a question which is the best worth having of two pleasures, or which of two modes of existence is the most grateful to the feelings, apart from its moral attributes and from its consequences, the judgment of those who are qualified by knowledge of both, or, if they differ, that of the majority among them, must be admitted as final. And there needs be the less hesitation to accept this judgment respecting the quality of pleasures, since there is no other tribunal to be referred to even on the question of quantity. What means are there of determining which is the acutest of two pains, or the intensest of two pleasurable sensations, except the general suffrage of those who are familiar with both? Neither pains nor pleasures are homogeneous, and pain is always heterogeneous with pleasure. What is there to decide whether a particular pleasure is worth purchasing at the cost of a particular pain, except the feelings and judgment of the experienced? When, therefore, those feelings and judgment declare the pleasures derived from the higher faculties to be preferable *in kind,* apart from the question of intensity, to those of which the animal nature, disjoined from the higher faculties, is susceptible, they are entitled on this subject to the same regard.

[. . .] As for vicissitudes of fortune and other disappointments connected with worldly circumstances, these are principally the effect either of gross imprudence, of ill-regulated desires, or of bad or imperfect social institutions. All the grand sources, in short, of human suffering are in a great degree, many of them almost entirely, conquerable by human care and effort; and though their removal is grievously slow—though a long succession of generations will perish in the breach before the conquest is completed, and this world becomes all that, if will and knowledge were not wanting, it might easily be made—yet every mind sufficiently intelligent and generous to bear a part, however small and inconspicuous, in the endeavor will draw a noble enjoyment from the contest itself, which he would not for any bribe in the form of selfish indulgence consent to be without.

And this leads to the true estimation of what is said by the objectors concerning the possibility and the obligation of learning to do without happiness. Unquestionably it is possible to do without happiness; it is done involuntarily by nineteen-twentieths of mankind, even in those parts of our present world which are least deep in barbarism; and it often has to be done voluntarily by the hero or the martyr, for the sake of something which he prizes more than his individual happiness. But this something, what is it, unless the happiness of others or some of the requisites of happiness? It is noble to be capable of resigning entirely one's own portion of happiness, or chances of it; but, after all, this self-sacrifice must be for some end; it is not its own end; and if we are told that its end is not happiness but virtue, which is better than happiness, I ask, would the sacrifice be made if the hero or martyr did not believe that it would earn for other immunity from similar sacrifices? Would it be made if he thought that his renunciation of happiness for himself would produce no fruit for any of his fellow creatures, but to make their lot like his and place them also in the condition of persons who have renounced happiness? All honor to those who can abnegate for themselves the personal enjoyment of life when by such renunciation they contribute worthily to increase the amount of happiness in the world; but he who does it or professes to do it for any other purpose is no more deserving of admiration than the ascetic mounted on his pillar. He may be an inspiring proof of what men *can* do, but assuredly not an example of what they *should*.

Though it is only in a very imperfect state of the world's arrangements that anyone can best serve the happiness of others by the absolute sacrifice of his own, yet, so long as the world is in that imperfect state, I fully acknowledge that the readiness to make such a sacrifice is the highest virtue which can be found in man. I will add that in this condition of the world, paradoxical as the assertion may be, the conscious ability to do without happiness gives the best prospect of realizing such happiness as is attainable. For nothing except that consciousness can raise a person above the chances of life by making him feel that, let fate and fortune do their worst, they have not power to subdue him; which, once felt, frees him from excess of anxiety concerning the evils of life and enables him, like many a Stoic in the worst times of the Roman Empire, to cultivate in tranquility the sources of satisfaction accessible to him, without concerning himself about the uncertainty of their duration any more than about their inevitable end.

Meanwhile, let utilitarians never cease to claim the morality of self-devotion as a possession which belongs by as good a right to them as either to the Stoic or to the Transcendentalist. The utilitarian morality does recognize in human beings the power of sacrificing their own greatest good for the good of others. It only refuses to admit that the sacrifice is itself a good. A sacrifice which does not increase or tend to increase the sum total of happiness, it considers as wasted. The only self-renunciation which it applauds is devotion to the happiness, or to some of the means of happiness, of others, either of mankind collectively or of individuals within the limits imposed by the collective interest of mankind.

I must again repeat what the assailants of utilitarianism seldom have the justice to acknowledge, that the happiness which forms the utilitarian standard of what is right in conduct is not the agent's own happiness but that of all concerned. As between his own happiness and that of others, utilitarianism requires him to be as strictly impartial as a disinterested and benevolent spectator. In the golden rule of Jesus of Nazareth, we read the complete spirit of the ethics of utility. "To do as you would be done by," and "to love your neighbor as yourself," constitute the ideal perfection of utilitarian morality. As the means of making the nearest approach to this ideal, utility would enjoin, first, that laws and social arrangements should place the happiness or (as, speaking practically, it may be called) the interest of every individual as nearly as possible in harmony with the interest of the whole; and, secondly, that education and opinion, which have so vast a power over human character, should so use that power as to establish in the mind of every individual an indissoluble association between his own happiness and the good of the whole, especially between his own happiness and the practice of such modes of conduct, negative and positive, as regard for the universal happiness prescribes; so that not only he may be unable to conceive the possibility of happiness to himself, consistently with conduct opposed to the general good, but also that a direct impulse to promote the general good may be in every individual one of the habitual motives of action, and the sentiments connected therewith may fill a large and prominent place in every human being's sentient existence. If the impugners of the utilitarian morality represented it to their own minds in this its true character, I know not what recommendation possessed by any other morality they could possibly affirm to be wanting to it; what more beautiful or more exalted developments of human nature any other ethical system can be supposed to foster, or what springs of action, not accessible to the utilitarian, such systems rely on for giving effect to their mandates.

The objectors to utilitarianism cannot always be charged with representing it in a discreditable light. On the contrary, those among them who entertain anything like a just idea of its disinterested character sometimes find fault with its standard as being too high for humanity. They say it is exacting too much to require that people shall always act from the inducement of promoting the general interests of society. But this is to mistake the very meaning of a standard of morals and confound the rule of action with the motive of it. It is the business of ethics to tell us what are our duties, or by what test we may know them; but no system of ethics requires that the sole motive of all we do shall be a feeling of duty; on the contrary, ninety-nine hundredths of all our actions are done from other motives, and rightly so done if the rule of duty does not condemn them. It is the more unjust to utilitarianism that this particular misapprehension should be made a ground of objection to it, inasmuch as utilitarian moralists have gone beyond almost all others in affirming that the motive has nothing to do with the morality of the action, though much with the worth of the agent. He who saves a fellow creature from drowning does what is morally right, whether his motive be duty or the hope of being paid for his trouble; he who betrays the friend that trusts him is guilty of a crime, even if his object be to serve another friend to whom he is under greater obligations. But to speak only of actions done from the motive of duty, and in direct obedience to principle: it is a misapprehension of the utilitarian mode of thought to conceive it as implying that people should fix their minds upon so wide a generality as the world, or society at large. The great majority of good actions are intended not for the benefit of the world, but for that of individuals, of which the good of the world is made up; and the thoughts of the most virtuous man need not on these occasions travel beyond the particular persons concerned, except so far as is necessary to assure himself that in benefiting them he is not violating the rights, that is, the legitimate and authorized expectations, of anyone else. The multiplication of happiness is, according to the utilitarian ethics, the object of virtue: the occasions on which any person (except one in a thousand) has it in his power to do this on an extended scale—in other words, to be a public benefactor—are but exceptional; and on these occasions alone is he called on to consider public utility; in every other case, private utility, the interest or happiness of some few persons, is all he has to attend to. [. . .]

Again, utility is often summarily stigmatized as an immoral doctrine by giving it the name of "expediency," and taking advantage of the popular use of that term to contrast it with principle. But the expedient, in the sense in which it is opposed to the right, generally means that which is expedient for the particular interest of the agent himself; as when a minister sacrifices the interests of his country to keep himself in place. When it means anything better than this, it means that which is expedient for some immediate object, some temporary purpose, but which violates a rule whose observance is expedient in a much higher degree. The expedient, in this sense, instead of being the same thing with the useful, is a branch of the hurtful. Thus it would often be expedient, for the purpose of getting over some momentary embarrassment, or attaining some object immediately useful to ourselves or others, to tell a lie. But inasmuch as the cultivation in ourselves of a sensitive feeling on the subject of veracity is one of the most useful, and the enfeeblement of that feeling one of the most hurtful, things to which our conduct can be instrumental; and inasmuch as any, even unintentional, deviation from truth does that much toward weakening the trustworthiness of human assertion, which is not only the principal support of all present social well-being, but the insufficiency of which does more than any one thing that can be named to keep back civilization, virtue, everything on which human happiness on the largest scale depends—we feel that the violation, for a present advantage, of a rule of such transcendent expediency is not expedient, and that he who, for the sake of convenience to himself or to some other individual, does what depends on him to deprive mankind of the good, and inflict upon them the evil, involved in the greater or less reliance which they can place on each other's word, acts the part of one of their worst enemies. Yet that even this rule, sacred as it is, admits of possible exceptions is acknowledged by all moralists; the chief of which is when the withholding of some fact (as of information from a malefactor, or of bad news from a person dangerously ill) would save an individual (especially an individual other than oneself) from great and unmerited evil, and when the withholding can only be effected by denial. But in order that the exception may not extend itself beyond the need, and may have the least possible effect in weakening reliance on veracity, it ought to be recognized and, if possible, its limits defined; and, if the principle of utility is good for anything, it must be good for weighing these conflicting utilities against one another and marking out the region within which one or the other preponderates.

Again, defenders of utility often find themselves called upon to reply to such objections as this—that there is not time, previous to action, for calculating and weighing the effects of any line of conduct on the general happiness. This is exactly as if anyone were to say that it is impossible to guide our conduct by Christianity because there is not time, on every occasion on which anything has to be done, to read through the Old and New Testaments. The answer to the objection is that there has been ample time, namely, the whole past duration of the human species. During all that time mankind have been learning by experience the tendencies of actions; on which experience all the prudence as well as all the morality of life are dependent. People talk as if the commencement of this course of experience had hitherto been put off, and as if, at the moment when some man feels tempted to meddle with the property or life of another, he had to begin considering for the first time whether murder and theft are injurious to human happiness. Even then I do not think that he would find the question very puzzling; but, at all events, the matter is now done to his hand. It is truly a whimsical supposition that, if mankind were agreed in considering utility to be the test of morality, they would remain without any agreement as to what *is* useful, and would take no measures for having their notions on the subject taught to the young and enforced by law and opinion. There is no difficulty in proving any ethical standard whatever to work ill if we suppose universal idiocy to be conjoined with it; but on any hypothesis short of that, mankind must by this time have acquired positive beliefs as to the effects of some actions on their happiness; and the beliefs which have thus come down are the rules of morality for the multitude, and for the

philosopher until he has succeeded in finding better. That philosophers might easily do this, even now, on many subjects; that the received code of ethics is by no means of divine right; and that mankind have still much to learn as to the effects of actions on the general happiness, I admit or rather earnestly maintain. The corollaries from the principle of utility, like the precepts of every practical art, admit of indefinite improvement, and, in a progressive state of the human mind, their improvement is perpetually going on. But to consider the rules of morality as improvable is one thing; to pass over the intermediate generalization entirely and endeavor to test each individual action directly by the first principle is another. It is a strange notion that the acknowledgment of a first principle is inconsistent with the admission of secondary ones. To inform a traveler respecting the place of his ultimate destination is not to forbid the use of landmarks and direction-posts on the way. The proposition that happiness is the end and aim of morality does not mean that no road ought to be laid down to that goal, or that persons going thither should not be advised to take one direction rather than another. Men really ought to leave off talking a kind of nonsense on this subject, which they would neither talk nor listen to on other matters of practical concernment. Nobody argues that the art of navigation is not founded on astronomy because sailors cannot wait to calculate the Nautical Almanac. Being rational creatures, they go to sea with it ready calculated; and all rational creatures go out upon the sea of life with their minds made up on the common questions of right and wrong, as well as on many of the far more difficult questions of wise and foolish. And this, as long as foresight is a human quality, it is to be presumed they will continue to do. Whatever we adopt as the fundamental principle of morality, we require subordinate principles to apply it by; the impossibility of doing without them, being common to all systems, can afford no argument against any one in particular; but gravely to argue as if no such secondary principles could be had, and as if mankind had remained till now, and always must remain, without drawing any general conclusions from the experience of human life is as high a pitch, I think, as absurdity has ever reached in philosophical controversy.

The remainder of the stock arguments against utilitarianism mostly consist in laying to its charge the common infirmities of human nature, and the general diffi-culties which embarrass conscientious persons in shaping their course through life. We are told that a util-itarian will be apt to make his own particular case and exception to moral rules, and, when under temptation, will see a utility in the breach of a rule, greater than he will see in its observance. But is utility the only creed which is able to furnish us with excuses for evil-doing and means of cheating our own conscience? They are afforded in abundance by all doctrines which recognize as a fact in morals the existence of conflicting consid-erations, which all doctrines do that have been believed by sane persons. It is not the fault of any creed, but of the complicated nature of human affairs, that rules of conduct cannot be so framed as to require no excep-tions, and that hardly any kind of action can safely be laid down as either always obligatory or always con-demnable. There is no ethical creed which does not temper the rigidity of its laws by giving a certain lati-tude, under the moral responsibility of the agent, for accommodation to peculiarities of circumstances; and under every creed, at the opening thus made, self-deception and dishonest casuistry get in. There exists no moral system under which there do not arise unequiv-ocal cases of conflicting obligation. These are the real difficulties, the knotty points both in the theory of ethics and in the conscientious guidance of personal conduct. They are overcome practically, with greater or with less success, according to the intellect and virtue of the in-dividual; but it can hardly be pretended that anyone will be the less qualified for dealing with them, from pos-sessing an ultimate standard to which conflicting rights and duties can be referred. If utility is the ultimate source of moral obligations, utility may be invoked to decide between them when their demands are incom-patible. Though the application of the standard may be difficult, it is better than none at all; while in other sys-tems, the moral laws all claiming independent author-ity, there is no common umpire entitled to interfere between them; their claims to precedence one over an-other rest on little better than sophistry, and, unless de-termined, as they generally are, by the unacknowledged influence of consideration of utility, afford a free scope for the action of personal desires and partialities. We must remember that only in these cases of conflict be-tween secondary principles is it requisite that first prin-ciples should be appealed to. There is no case of moral obligation in which some secondary principle is not in-volved; and if only one, there can seldom be any real doubt which one it is, in the mind of any person by whom the principle itself is recognized.

· · · · ·

Chapter IV

Of What Sort of Proof the Principle of Utility Is Susceptible

It has already been remarked that questions of ultimate ends do not admit of proof, in the ordinary acceptation of the term. To be incapable of proof by reasoning is common to all first principles, to the first premises of our knowledge, as well as to those of our conduct. But the former, being matters of fact, may be the subject of a direct appeal to the faculties which judge of fact—namely, our senses and our internal consciousness. Can an appeal be made to the same faculties on questions of practical ends? Or by what other faculty is cognizance taken of them?

Questions about ends are, in other words, questions about what things are desirable. The utilitarian doctrine is that happiness is desirable, and the only thing desir-able, as an end; all other things being only desirable as means to that end. What ought to be required of this doctrine, what conditions is it requisite that the doctrine should fulfill—to make good its claim to be believed?

The only proof capable of being given that an object is visible is that people actually see it. The only proof that a sound is audible is that people hear it; and so of the other sources of our experience. In like manner, I apprehend, the sole evidence it is possible to produce that anything is desirable is that people do actually de-sire it. If the end which the utilitarian doctrine proposes to itself were not, in theory and in practice, acknowl-edged to be an end, nothing could ever convince any person that it was so. No reason can be given why the general happiness is desirable, except that each person, so far as he believes it to be attainable, desires his own happiness. This, however, being a fact, we have not only all the proof which the case admits of, but all which it is possible to require, that happiness is a good: that each person's happiness is a good to that person, and the general happiness, therefore, a good to the aggregate of all persons. Happiness has made out its title as *one* of the ends of conduct and, consequently, one of the criteria of morality.

But it has not, by this alone, proved itself to be the sole criterion. To do that, it would seem, by the same rule, necessary to show, not only that people desire happiness, but that they never desire anything else. Now it is palpable that they do desire things which, in common language, are decidedly distinguished from happiness. They desire, for example, virtue and the absence of vice no less really than pleasure and the absence of pain. The desire of virtue is not as universal, but it is as authentic a fact as the desire of happiness. And hence the opponents of the utilitarian standard deem that they have a right to infer that there are other ends of human action besides happiness, and that happiness is not the standard of approbation and disapprobation.

But does the utilitarian doctrine deny that people desire virtue, or maintain that virtue is not a thing to be desired? The very reverse. It maintains not only that virtue is to be desired, but that it is to be desired disinterestedly, for itself. Whatever may be the opinion of utilitarian moralists as to the original conditions by which virtue is made virtue, however they may believe (as they do) that actions and dispositions are only virtuous because they promote another end than virtue, yet this being granted, and it having been decided, from considerations of this description, what *is* virtuous, they not only place virtue at the very head of the things which are good as means to the ultimate end, but they also recognize as a psychological fact the possibility of its being, to the individual, a good in itself, without looking to any end beyond it; and hold that the mind is not in a right state, not in a state conformable to utility, not in the state most conducive to the general happiness, unless it does love virtue in this manner—as a thing desirable in itself, even although, in the individual instance, it should not produce those other desirable consequences which it tends to produce, and on account of which it is held to be virtue. This opinion is not, in the smallest degree, a departure from the happiness principle. The ingredients of happiness are very various, and each of them is desirable in itself, and not

merely when considered as swelling an aggregate. The principle of utility does not mean that any given pleasure, as music, for instance, or any given exemption from pain, as for example health, is to be looked upon as means to a collective something termed happiness, and to be desired on that account. They are desired and desirable in and for themselves; besides being means, they are a part of the end. Virtue, according to the utilitarian doctrine, is not naturally and originally part of the end, but it is capable of becoming so; and in those who live it disinterestedly it has become so, and is desired and cherished, not as a means to happiness, but as a part of their happiness.

To illustrate this further, we may remember that virtue is not the only thing originally a means, and which if it were not a means to anything else would be and remain indifferent, but which by association with what it is a means to comes to be desired for itself, and that too with the utmost intensity. What, for example, shall we say of the love of money? There is nothing originally more desirable about money than about any heap of glittering pebbles. Its worth is solely that of the things which it will buy; the desires for other things than itself, which it is a means of gratifying. Yet the love of money is not only one of the strongest moving forces of human life, but money is, in many cases, desired in and for itself; the desire to possess it is often stronger than the desire to use it, and goes on increasing when all the desires which point to ends beyond it, to be compassed by it, are falling off. It may, then, be said truly that money is desired not for the sake of an end, but as part of the end. From being a means to happiness, it has come to be itself a principal ingredient of the individual's conception of happiness. The same may be said of the majority of the great objects of human life: power, for example or fame, except that to each of these there is a certain amount of immediate pleasure annexed, which has a least the semblance of being naturally inherent in them—a thing which cannot be said of money. Still, however, the strongest natural attraction, both of power and of fame, is the immense aid they give to the attainment of our other wishes; and it is the strong association thus generated between them and all our objects of desire which gives to the direct desire of them the intensity it often assumes, so as in some characters to surpass in strength all other desires. In these cases the means have become a part of the end, and a more important part of it than any of the things which they are means to. What was once desired as an instrument for the attainment of happiness has come to be desired for its own sake. In being desired for its own sake it is, however, desired as *part* of happiness. The person is made, or thinks he would be made, happy by its mere possession; and is made unhappy by failure to obtain it. The desire of it is not a different thing from the desire of happiness any more than the love of music or the desire of health. They are included in happiness. They are some of the elements of which the desire of happiness is made up. Happiness is not an abstract idea but a concrete whole; and these are some of its parts. And the utilitarian standard sanctions and approves their being so. Life would be a poor thing, very ill provided with sources of happiness, if there were not this provision of nature by which things originally indifferent, but conducive to, or otherwise associated with, the satisfaction of our primitive desires, become in themselves sources of pleasure more valuable than the primitive pleasures, both in permanency, in the space of human existence that they are capable of covering, and even in intensity.

Virtue, according to the utilitarian conception, is a good of this description. There was no original desire of it, or motive to it, save its conduciveness to pleasure, and especially to protection from pain. But through the association thus formed it may be felt a good in itself, and desired as such with as great intensity as any other good; and with this difference between it and the love of money, of power, or of fame—that all of these may, and often do, render the individual noxious to the other members of the society to which he belongs, whereas there is nothing which makes him so much a blessing to them as the cultivation of the disinterested love of virtue. And consequently, the utilitarian standard, while it tolerates and approves those other acquired desires, up to the point beyond which they would be more injurious to the general happiness than promotive of it, enjoins and requires the cultivation of the love of virtue up to the greatest strength possible, as being above all things important to the general happiness.

It results from the preceding considerations that there is in reality nothing desired except happiness. Whatever is desired otherwise than as a means to some end beyond itself, and ultimately to happiness, is desired as it-

self a part of happiness, and is not desired for itself until it has become so. Those who desire virtue for its own sake desire it either because the consciousness of it is a pleasure, or because the consciousness of being without it is a pain, or for both reasons united; as in truth the pleasure and pain seldom exist separately, but almost always together—the same person feeling pleasure in the degree of virtue attained, and pain in not having attained more. If one of these gave him no pleasure, and the other no pain, he would not love or desire virtue, or would desire it only for the other benefits which it might produce to himself or to persons whom he cared for.

We have now, then, an answer to the question, of what sort of proof the principle of utility is susceptible. If the opinion which I have now stated is psychologically true—if human nature is so constituted as to desire nothing which is not either a part of happiness or a means of happiness—we can have no other proof, and we require no other, that these are the only things desirable. If so, happiness is the sole end of human action, and the promotion of it the test by which to judge of all human conduct; from whence it necessarily follows that it must be the criterion of morality, since a part is included in the whole.

And now to decide whether this is really so, whether mankind do desire nothing for itself but that which is a pleasure to them, or of which the absence is a pain, we have evidently arrived at a question of fact and experience, dependent, like all similar questions, upon evidence. It can only be determined by practiced self-consciousness and self-observation, assisted by observation of others. I believe that these sources of evidence, impartially consulted, will declare that desiring a thing and finding it pleasant, aversion to it and thinking of it as painful, are phenomena entirely inseparable or, rather, two parts of the same phenomenon—in strictness of language, two different modes of naming the same psychological fact; that to think of an object as desirable (unless for the sake of its consequences) and to think of it as pleasant are one and the same thing; and that to desire anything except in proportion as the idea of it is pleasant is a physical and metaphysical impossibility.

So obvious does this appear to me that I expect it will hardly be disputed; and the objection made will be, not that desire can possibly be directed to anything ultimately except pleasure and exemption from pain, but that the will is a different thing from desire; that a person of confirmed virtue or any other person whose purposes are fixed carries out his purposes without any thought of the pleasure he has in contemplating them or expects to derive from their fulfillment, and persists in acting on them, even though these pleasures are much diminished by changes in his character or decay of his passive sensibilities, or are outweighed by the pains which the pursuit of the purposes may bring upon him. All this I fully admit and have stated it elsewhere as positively and emphatically as anyone. Will, the active phenomenon, is a different thing from desire, the state of passive sensibility, and, though originally an offshoot from it, may in time take root and detach itself from the parent stock, so much so that in the case of a habitual purpose, instead of willing the thing because we desire it, we often desire it only because we will it. This, however, is but an instance of that familiar fact, the power of habit, and is nowise confined to the case of virtuous actions. Many indifferent things which men originally did from a motive of some sort they continue to do from habit. Sometimes this is done unconsciously, the consciousness coming only after the action; at other times with conscious volition, but volition which has become habitual and is put in operation by the force of habit, in opposition perhaps to the deliberate preference, as often happens with those who have contracted habits of vicious or hurtful indulgence. Third and last comes the case in which the habitual act of will in the individual instance is not in contradiction to the general intention prevailing at other times, but in fulfillment of it, as in the case of the person of confirmed virtue and of all who pursue deliberately and consistently any determinate end. The distinction between will and desire thus understood is an authentic and highly important psychological fact; but the fact consists solely in this—that will, like all other parts of our constitution, is amenable to habit, and that we may will from habit what we no longer desire for itself, or desire only because we will it. It is not the less true that will,

in the beginning, is entirely produced by desire, including in that term the repelling influence of pain as well as the attractive one of pleasure. Let us take into consideration no longer the person who has confirmed will to do right, but him in whom that virtuous will is still feeble, conquerable by temptation, and not to be fully relied on; by what means can it be strengthened? How can the will to be virtuous, where it does not exist in sufficient force, be implanted or awakened? Only by making the person *desire* virtue—by making him think of it in a pleasurable light, or of its absence in a painful one. It is by associating the doing right with pleasure, or the doing wrong with pain, or by eliciting and impressing and bringing home to the person's experience the pleasure naturally involved in the one or the pain in the other, that it is possible to call forth that will to be virtuous which, when confirmed, acts without any thought of either pleasure or pain. Will is the child of desire, and passes out of the dominion of its parent only to come under that of habit. That which is the result of habit affords no presumption of being intrinsically good; and there would be no reason for wishing that the purpose of virtue should become independent of pleasure and pain were it not that the influence of the pleasurable and painful associations which prompt to virture is not sufficiently to be depended on for unerring constancy of action until it has acquired the support of habit. Both in feeling and in conduct, habit is the only thing which imparts certainty; and it is because of the importance to others of being able to rely absolutely on one's feelings and conduct, and to oneself of being able to rely on one's own, that the will to do right ought to be cultivated into this habitual independence. In other words, this state of the will is a means to good, not intrinsically a good; and does not contradict the doctrine that nothing is a good to human beings but in so far as it is either itself pleasurable or a means of attaining pleasure or averting pain.

But if this doctrine be true, the principle of utility is proved. Whether it is so or not must now be left to the consideration of the thoughtful reader.

Friedrich Nietzsche

Against Slavish Moralities

First Treatise: "Good and Evil," "Good and Bad"

1

—These English psychologists whom we also have to thank for the only attempts so far to produce a history of the genesis of morality—they themselves are no small riddle for us; I confess, in fact, that precisely as riddles in the flesh they have something substantial over their books—*they themselves are interesting!* These English psychologists—what do they actually want? One finds them, whether voluntarily or involuntarily, always at the same task, namely of pushing the *partie honteuse*[1] of our inner world into the foreground and of seeking that which is actually effective, leading, decisive for our development, precisely where the intellectual pride of man would least of all *wish* to find it (for example in the *vis inertiae*[2] of habit or in forgetfulness or in a blind and accidental interlacing and mechanism of ideas or in anything purely passive, automatic, reflexive, molecular, and fundamentally mindless)—what is it actually that always drives these psychologists in precisely *this* direction? Is it a secret, malicious, base instinct to belittle mankind, one that perhaps cannot be acknowledged even to itself? Or, say, a pessimistic suspicion, the mistrust of disappointed, gloomy idealists who have become poisonous and green? Or a little subterranean animosity and rancor against Christianity (and Plato)

From Friedrich Nietzsche, *On the Genealogy of Morality,* translated by Maudemarie Clark and Alan J. Swensen (Indianapolis: Hackett Publishing Company, 1998). Reprinted by permission of the publisher.

1. *partie honteuse:* shameful part (in the plural, this expression is the equivalent of the English "private parts").

2. *vis inertiae:* force of inactivity. In Newtonian physics, this term denoted the resistance offered by matter to any force tending to alter its state of rest or motion.

that has perhaps not yet made it past the threshold of consciousness? Or even a lascivious taste for the disconcerting, for the painful-paradoxical, for the questionable and nonsensical aspects of existence? Or finally—a little of everything, a little meanness, a little gloominess, a little anti-Christianity, a little tickle and need for pepper? . . . But I am told that they are simply old, cold, boring frogs who creep and hop around on human beings, into human beings, as if they were really in their element there, namely in a *swamp.* I resist this, still more, I don't believe it; and if one is permitted to wish where one cannot know, then I wish from my heart that the reverse may be the case with them—that these explorers and microscopists of the soul are basically brave, magnanimous, and proud animals who know how to keep a rein on their hearts as well as their pain and have trained themselves to sacrifice all desirability to truth, to *every* truth, even plain, harsh, ugly, unpleasant, unchristian, immoral truth. . . . For there are such truths.—

2

Hats off then to whatever good spirits may be at work in these historians of morality! Unfortunately, however, it is certain that they lack the *historical spirit* itself, that they have been left in the lurch precisely by all the good spirits of history! As is simply the age-old practice among philosophers, they all think *essentially* ahistorically; of this there is no doubt. The ineptitude of their moral genealogy is exposed right at the beginning, where it is a matter of determining the origins of the concept and judgment "good." "Originally"—so they decree—"unegoistic actions were praised and called good from the perspective of those to whom they were rendered, hence for whom they were *useful;* later one *forgot* this origin of the praise and, simply because unegoistic actions were *as a matter of habit* always praised as good, one also felt them to be good—as if they were something good in themselves." One sees immediately: this first derivation already contains all the characteristic traits of the idiosyncrasy of English psychologists—we have "usefulness," "forgetting," "habit," and in the end "error," all as basis for a valuation of which the higher human being has until now been proud as if it were some kind of distinctive prerogative of humankind. This pride *must* be humbled, this valuation devalued: has this been achieved? . . . Now in the first place it is obvious to me that the actual genesis of the concept "good" is sought and fixed in the wrong place by this theory: the judgment "good" does *not* stem from those to whom "goodness" is rendered! Rather it was "the good" themselves, that is the noble, powerful, higher-ranking, and high-minded who felt and ranked themselves and their doings as good, which is to say, as of the first rank, in contrast to everything base, low-minded, common, and vulgar. Out of this *pathos of distance* they first took for themselves the right to create values, to coin names for values: what did they care about usefulness! The viewpoint of utility is as foreign and inappropriate as possible, especially in relation to so hot an outpouring of highest rank-ordering, rank-distinguishing value judgments: for here feeling has arrived at an opposite of that low degree of warmth presupposed by every calculating prudence, every assessment of utility—and not just for once, for an hour of exception, but rather for the long run. As was stated, the pathos of nobility and distance, this lasting and dominant collective and basic feeling of a higher ruling nature in relation to a lower nature, to a "below"—*that* is the origin of the opposition "good" and "bad." (The right of lords to give names goes so far that we should allow ourselves to comprehend the origin of language itself as an expression of power on the part of those who rule: they say "this *is* such and such," they seal each thing and happening with a sound and thus, as it were, take possession of it.) It is because of this origin that from the outset the word "good" does *not* necessarily attach itself to "unegoistic" actions—as is the superstition of those genealogists of morality. On the contrary, only when aristocratic value judgments begin to *decline,* does this entire opposition "egoistic" "unegoistic" impose itself more and more on the human conscience—to make use of my language, it is *the herd instinct* that finally finds a voice (also *words*) in this opposition. And even then it takes a long time until this instinct becomes dominant to such an extent that

moral valuation in effect gets caught and stuck at that opposition (as is the case in present-day Europe: today the prejudice that takes "moral," "unegoistic," *"désintéressé"*[3] to be concepts of equal value already rules with the force of an *"idée fixe"*[4] and sickness in the head).

3

In the second place, however: quite apart from the historical untenability of that hypothesis concerning the origins of the value judgment "good," it suffers from an inherent psychological absurdity. The usefulness of the unegoistic action is supposed to be the origin of its praise, and this origin is supposed to have been *forgotten:*—how is this forgetting even *possible?* Did the usefulness of such actions cease at some point? The opposite is the case: this usefulness has been the everyday experience in all ages, something therefore that was continually underscored anew; accordingly, instead of disappearing from consciousness, instead of becoming forgettable, it could not help but impress itself upon consciousness with ever greater clarity. How much more reasonable is that opposing theory (it is not therefore truer—) advocated for example by Herbert Spencer—which ranks the concept "good" as essentially identical with the concept "useful," "purposive," so that in the judgments "good" and "bad" humanity has summed up and sanctioned its *unforgotten* and *unforgettable* experiences concerning what is useful-purposive, what is injurious-nonpurposive. Good, according to this theory, is whatever has proved itself as useful from time immemorial: it may thus claim validity as "valuable in the highest degree," as "valuable in itself." This path of explanation is also false, as noted above, but at least the explanation is in itself reasonable and psychologically tenable.

4

—The pointer to the *right* path was given to me by the question: what do the terms coined for "good" in the various languages actually mean from an etymological

---

3. *"désintéressé"*: disinterested, unselfish, selfless.

4. *"idée fixe"*: obsession; literally: a fixed idea.

viewpoint? Here I found that they all lead back to the *same conceptual transformation*—that everywhere the basic concept is "noble," "aristocratic" in the sense related to the estates, out of which "good" in the sense of "noble of soul," "high-natured of soul," "privileged of soul" necessarily develops: a development that always runs parallel to that other one which makes "common," "vulgar," "base" pass over finally into the concept "bad." The most eloquent example of the latter is the German word *"schlect"* [bad] itself: which is identical with *"schlicht"* [plain, simple]—compare *"schlectweg," "schlechterdings"* [simply or downright]—and originally designated the plain, the common man, as yet without a suspecting sideward glance, simply in opposition to the noble one. Around the time of the Thirty-Years' War, in other words late enough, this sense shifts into the one now commonly used.—With respect to morality's genealogy this appears to me to be an *essential* insight; that it is only now being discovered is due to the inhibiting influence that democratic prejudice exercises in the modern world with regard to all questions of origins. And this influence extends all the way into that seemingly most objective realm of natural science and physiology, as I shall merely hint at here. But the nonsense that this prejudice—once unleashed to the point of hate—is able to inflict, especially on morality and history, is shown by Buckle's notorious case; the *plebeianism* of the modern spirit, which is of English descent, sprang forth there once again on its native ground, vehemently like a muddy volcano and with that oversalted, overloud, common eloquence with which until now all volcanoes have spoken.—

5

With regard to *our* problem—which can for good reasons be called a *quiet* problem and which addresses itself selectively to but few ears—it is of no small interest to discover that often in those words and roots that designate "good" that main nuance still shimmers through with respect to which the nobles felt themselves to be humans of a higher rank. To be sure, they may name themselves in the most frequent cases simply after their superiority in power (as "the powerful," "the lords," "the commanders") or after the most visible distinguishing mark of this superiority, for example as "the rich," "the

possessors," (that is the sense of *arya;*[5] and likewise in Iranian and Slavic). But also after a *typical character trait:* and this is the case which concerns us here. They call themselves for example "the truthful"—led by the Greek nobility, whose mouthpiece is the Megarian poet Theognis. The word is coined for this, *esthlos,*[6] means according to its root one who *is,* who possesses reality, who is real, who is true; then, with a subjective turn, the true one as the truthful one: in this phase of the concept's transformation it becomes the by- and catchword of the nobility and passes over completely into the sense of "aristocratic," as that which distinguishes from the *lying* common man as Theognis understands and depicts him—until finally, after the demise of the nobility, the word remains as the term for *noblesse* of soul and becomes as it were ripe and sweet. In the word *kakos*[7] as well as in *delios*[8] (the plebeian in contrast to the *agathos*[9]) cowardliness is underscored: perhaps this gives a hint in which direction one should seek the etymological origins of *agathos,* which can be interpreted in many ways. In the Latin *malus*[10] (beside which I place *melas*[11]), the common man could be characterized as the dark-colored, above all as the black-haired (*"hic niger est—"*[12]), as the pre-Aryan occupant of Italian soil, who by his color stood out most clearly from the blonds who had become the rulers, namely the Aryan conqueror-race; at any rate Gaelic offered me an exactly corresponding case—*fin*[13] (for example in the name Fin-Gal), the distinguishing word of the nobility, in the end, the good, noble, pure one, originally the blond-headed one, in contrast to the dark, black-haired original inhabitants. The Celts, incidentally, were by all means a blond race; it is wrong to associate those tracts of an essentially dark-haired population, which are noticeable on the

---

5. *arya:* Sanskrit: noble.

6. *esthlos:* good, brave, noble.

7. *kakos:* bad, ugly, ill-born, cowardly, ignoble.

8. *delios:* cowardly, worthless, low-born, miserable, wretched.

9. *agathos:* good, well-born, noble, brave, capable.

10. *malus:* bad, evil.

11. *melas:* black, dark.

12. *"hic niger est":* he is black. Horace's *Satires,* I. 4, line 85.

13. *fin:* Gaelic: white, bright.

more careful ethnographic maps of Germany, with any Celtic origins or blood mixtures, as even Virchow does: rather it is the *pre-Aryan* population of Germany that comes to the fore in these places. (The same is true for almost all of Europe: in essence, the subjected race has in the end regained the upper hand there, in color, shortness of skull, perhaps even in intellectual and social instincts—who will guarantee us that modern democracy, the even more modern anarchism, and in particular that inclination toward the "commune," the most primitive form of society—an inclination now common to all of Europe's socialists—does not signify, on the whole, a tremendous *atavism*—and that the *race of lords* and conquerors, that of the Aryans, is not in the process of succumbing physiologically as well? ...) I believe I may interpret the Latin *bonus*[14] as "the warrior": assuming that I am correct in tracing *bonus* back to an older *duonus*[15] (compare *bellum = duellum = duen-lum,*[16] in which that *duonus* seems to me to be preserved). *Bonus* accordingly as man of strife, of division (*duo*), as man of war—one sees what it was about a man that constituted his "goodness" in ancient Rome. Our German *"gut"* [good] itself: wasn't it supposed to mean "the godly one," the man "of godly race"? And to be identical with the name for the nation (originally for the nobility) of the Goths? The reasons for this supposition do not belong here.—

6

To this rule that the concept of superiority in politics always resolves itself into a concept of superiority of soul, it is not immediately an exception (although it provides occasion for exceptions) when the highest caste is at the same time the *priestly* caste and hence prefers for its collective name a predicate that recalls its priestly function. Here, for example, "pure" and "impure" stand opposite each other for the first time as marks of distinction among the estates; and here, too, one later finds the development *of* a "good" and a "bad"

in a sense no longer related to the estates. Incidentally, let one beware from the outset of taking these concepts "pure" and "impure" too seriously, too broadly, or even too symbolically: rather all of earlier humanity's concepts were initially understood in a coarse, crude, superficial, narrow, straightforward, and above all *unsymbolic* manner, to an extent that we can hardly imagine. The "pure one" is from the beginning simply a human being who washes himself, who forbids himself certain foods that bring about skin diseases, who doesn't sleep with the dirty women of the baser people, who abhors blood—nothing more, at least not much more! On the other hand the entire nature of an essentially priestly aristocracy admittedly makes clear why it was precisely here that the valuation opposites could so soon become internalized and heightened in a dangerous manner; and indeed through them gulfs were finally torn open between man and man across which even an Achilles of free-spiritedness will not be able to leap without shuddering. From the beginning there is something *unhealthy* in such priestly aristocracies and in the habits ruling there, ones turned away from action, partly brooding, partly emotionally explosive, habits that have as a consequence the intestinal disease and neurasthenia that almost unavoidably clings to the priests of all ages; but what they themselves invented as a medicine against this diseasedness of theirs—must we not say that in the end it has proved itself a hundred times more dangerous in its aftereffects than the disease from which it was to redeem them? Humanity itself still suffers from the aftereffects of these priestly cure naïvetés! Think, for example, of certain dietary forms (avoidance of meat), of fasting, of sexual abstinence, of the flight "into the wilderness" (Weir-Mitchellian isolation, admittedly without the ensuing fattening diet and over-feeding, which constitutes the most effective antidote for all the hysteria of the ascetic ideal): in addition, the whole anti-sensual metaphysics of priests, which makes lazy and overrefined, their self-hypnosis after the manner of the fakir and Brahmin—brahma used as glass pendant and *idée fixe*—and the final, only too understandable general satiety along with its radical cure, *nothingness* (or God—the longing for a *unio mystica*[17] with God is the longing

---

14. *bonus:* good.

15. *duonus:* earlier form of *bonus.*

16. *bellum . . . duen-lum:* war; the latter two are older, poetic forms.

---

17. *unio mystica:* mystical union.

of the Buddhist for nothingness, Nirvâna—and nothing more!) With priests *everything* simply becomes more dangerous, not only curatives and healing arts, but also arrogance, revenge, acuity, excess, love, lust to rule, virtue, disease;—though with some fairness one could also add that it was on the soil of this *essentially dangerous* form of human existence, the priestly form, that man first became *an interesting animal,* that only here did the human soul acquire *depth* in a higher sense and become *evil*—and these are, after all, the two basic forms of the previous superiority of man over other creatures! . . .

7

—One will already have guessed how easily the priestly manner of valuation can branch off from the knightly-aristocratic and then develop into its opposite; this process is especially given an impetus every time the priestly caste and the warrior caste confront each other jealously and are unable to agree on a price. The knightly-aristocratic value judgments have as their presupposition a powerful physicality, a blossoming, rich, even overflowing health, together with that which is required for its preservation: war, adventure, the hunt, dance, athletic contests, and in general everything which includes strong, free, cheerful-hearted activity. The priestly-noble manner of valuation—as we have seen— has other presuppositions: too bad for it when it comes to war! Priests are, as is well known, the *most evil enemies* —why is that? Because they are the most powerless. Out of their powerlessness their hate grows into something enormous and uncanny, into something most spiritual and most poisonous. The truly great haters in the history of the world have always been priests, also the most ingenious haters:—compared with the spirit of priestly revenge all the rest of spirit taken together hardly merits consideration. Human history would be much too stupid an affair without the spirit that has entered into it through the powerless:—let us turn right to the greatest example. Of all that has been done on earth against "the noble," "the mighty," "the lords," "the power-holders," nothing is worthy of mention in comparison with that which the *Jews* have done against them: the Jews, that priestly people who in the end were only able to obtain satisfaction from their enemies and conquerors through a radical revaluation of their values, that is, through an act of *spiritual revenge.* This was the only way that suited a priestly people, the people of the most suppressed priestly desire for revenge. It was the Jews who in opposition to the aristocratic value equation (good = noble = powerful = beautiful = happy = beloved of God) dared its inversion, with fear-inspiring consistency, and held it fast with teeth of the most unfathomable hate (the hate of powerlessness), namely: "the miserable alone are the good; the poor, powerless, lowly alone are the good; the suffering, deprived, sick, ugly are also the only pious, the only blessed in God, for them alone is there blessedness,—whereas you, you noble and powerful ones, you are in all eternity the evil, the cruel, the lustful, the insatiable, the godless, you will eternally be the wretched, accursed, and damned!" . . . We know *who* inherited this Jewish revaluation. . . . In connection with the enormous and immeasurably doom-laden initiative provided by the Jews with this most fundamental of all declarations of war, I call attention to the proposition which I arrived at on another occasion ("Beyond Good and Evil" section 195)— namely, that with the Jews *the slave revolt in morality* begins: that revolt which has a two-thousand-year history behind it and which has only moved out of our sight today because it—has been victorious. . . .

8

—But you don't understand that? You don't have eyes for something that has taken two thousand years to achieve victory? . . . There is nothing to wonder at in this: all *lengthy* things are difficult to see, to see in their entirety. *This* however is what happened: out of the trunk of that tree of revenge and hate, Jewish hate—the deepest and most sublime hate, namely an ideal-creating, value-reshaping hate whose like has never before existed on earth—grew forth something just as incomparable, a *new love,* the deepest and most sublime of all kinds of love:—and from what other trunk could it have grown? . . . But by no means should one suppose it grew upwards as, say, the true negation of that thirst for revenge, as the opposite of Jewish hate! No, the reverse is the truth! This love grew forth out of it, as its crown, as the triumphant crown unfolding itself broadly and more broadly in purest light and sunny fullness, reaching out, as it were, in the realm of light and of height, for the goals of that hate—for victory, for booty, for seduction—with the same drive with which the roots of that hate sunk themselves ever more thoroughly and greedily down into everything that had depth and was evil. This Jesus of Nazareth, as the embodied Gospel of Love, this "Redeemer" bringing blessedness and victory to the poor, the sick, the sinners—was he not precisely seduction in its most uncanny and irresistible form, the seduction and detour to precisely those *Jewish* values and reshapings of the ideal? Has not Israel reached the final goal of its sublime desire for revenge precisely via the detour of this "Redeemer," this apparent adversary and dissolver of Israel? Does it not belong to the secret black art of a truly *great* politics of revenge, of a far-seeing, subterranean, slow-working and precalculating revenge, that Israel itself, before all the world, should deny as its mortal enemy and nail to the cross the actual tool of its revenge, so that "all the world," namely all the opponents of Israel, could take precisely this bait without thinking twice? And, out of all sophistication of the spirit, could one think up any more *dangerous* bait? Something that in its enticing, intoxicating, anesthetizing, destructive power might equal that symbol of the "holy cross," that gruesome paradox of a "god on the cross," that mystery of an inconceivable, final, extreme cruelty and self-crucifixion of God *for the salvation of man?* . . . What is certain, at least, is that *sub hoc signo*[18] Israel, with its revenge and revaluation of all values, has thus far again and again triumphed over all other ideals, over all *more noble* ideals.——

9

—"But why are you still talking about *nobler* ideals! Let's submit to the facts: the people were victorious—or 'the slaves,' or 'the mob,' or 'the herd,' or whatever you like to call them—if this happened through the Jews, so be it! then never has a people had a more world-historic mission. 'The lords' are cast off; the morality of the common man has been victorious. One may take this victory to be at the same time a blood poisoning (it mixed the races together)—I won't contradict; in any event it

is beyond doubt that this toxication *succeeded*. The 'redemption' of the human race (namely from 'the lords') is well under way; everything is jewifying or christifying or mobifying as we watch (what do the words matter!). The progress of this poisoning through the entire body of humanity appears unstoppable, from now on its tempo and step may even be slower, more refined, less audible, more thoughtful—one has time after all. . . . Does the church today still have a *necessary* task in this scheme, still a right to existence at all? Or could one do without it? *Quaeritur*[19]. It seems more likely that it inhibits and holds back this progress instead of accelerating it? Well, even that could be its usefulness. . . . By now it is certainly something coarse and peasant-like, which repels a more delicate intelligence, a truly modern taste. Shouldn't it at least become somewhat refined? . . . Today it alienates more than it seduces. . . . Which of us indeed would be a free spirit if there were no church? The church, *not* its poison, repels us. . . . Leaving the church aside, we, too, love the poison. . . ."—This, the epilogue of a "free spirit" to my speech, an honest animal, as he has richly betrayed, moreover a democrat; he had listened to me up until then and couldn't stand to hear me be silent. For at this point I have much to be silent about.—

10

The slave revolt in morality begins when *ressentiment* itself becomes creative and gives birth to values: the *ressentiment* of beings denied the true reaction, that of the deed, who recover their losses only through an imaginary revenge. Whereas all noble morality grows out of a triumphant yes-saying to oneself, from the outset slave morality says "no" to an "outside," to a "different," to a "not-self": and *this* "no" is its creative deed. This reversal of the value-establishing glance—this *necessary* direction toward the outside instead of back onto oneself—belongs to the very nature of *ressentiment*: in order to come into being, slave-morality always needs an opposite and external world; it needs, psychologically speaking, external stimuli in order to be able to act at all,—its action is, from the ground up, reaction. The

---

18. *sub hoc signo:* under this sign.

19. *Quaeritur:* one asks, i.e., that is the question.

reverse is the case with the noble manner of valuation: it acts and grows spontaneously, it seeks out its opposite only in order to say "yes" to itself still more gratefully and more jubilantly—its negative concept "low""common""bad" is only an after-birth, a pale contrast-image in relation to its positive basic concept, saturated through and through with life and passion: "we noble ones, we good ones, we beautiful ones, we happy ones!" When the noble manner of valuation lays a hand on reality and sins against it, this occurs relative to the sphere with which it is *not* sufficiently acquainted, indeed against a real knowledge of which it rigidly defends itself: in some cases it forms a wrong idea of the sphere it holds in contempt, that of the common man, of the lower people; on the other hand, consider that the affect of contempt, of looking down on, of the superior glance—assuming that it does *falsify* the image of the one held in contempt—will in any case fall far short of the falsification with which the suppressed hate, the revenge of the powerless, lays a hand on its opponent—in effigy, of course. Indeed there is too much carelessness in contempt, too much taking-lightly, too much looking-away and impatience mixed in, even too much of a feeling of cheer in oneself, for it to be capable of transforming its object into a real caricature and monster. Do not fail to hear the almost benevolent nuances that, for example, the Greek nobility places in all words by which it distinguishes the lower people from itself, how they are mixed with and sugared by a kind of pity, considerateness, leniency to the point that almost all words that apply to the common man ultimately survive as expressions for "unhappy""pitiful" (compare *deilos, deilaios, poneros, mochtheros,*[20] the latter two actually designating the common man as work-slave and beast of burden)—and how, on the other hand, to the Greek ear "bad""low""unhappy" have never ceased to end on the same note, with a tone color in which "unhappy" predominates: this as inheritance of the old, nobler aristocratic manner of valuation that does not deny itself even in its

contempt (let philologists be reminded of the sense in which *oizyros, anolbos, tlemon, dystychein, xymphora*[21] are used). The "well-born" simply felt themselves to be the "happy"; they did not first have to construct their happiness artificially by looking at their enemies, to talk themselves into it, to *lie themselves into it* (as all human beings of *ressentiment* tend to do); and as full human beings, overloaded with power and therefore *necessarily* active, they likewise did not know how to separate activity out from happiness,—for them being active is of necessity included in happiness (whence *eu prattein*[22] takes its origins)—all of this very much in opposition to "happiness" on the level of the powerless, oppressed, those festering with poisonous and hostile feelings, in whom it essentially appears as narcotic, anesthetic, calm, peace, "Sabbath," relaxation of mind and stretching of limbs, in short, *passively.* While the noble human being lives with himself in confidence and openness (*gennaios*[23] "noble-born" underscores the nuance "sincere" and probably also "naive") the human being of *ressentiment* is neither sincere, nor naive, nor honest and frank with himself. His soul *looks obliquely* at things; his spirit loves hiding places, secret passages and backdoors, everything hidden strikes him as *his* world, *his* security, *his* balm; he knows all about being silent, not forgetting, waiting, belittling oneself for the moment, humbling oneself. A race of such human beings of *ressentiment* in the end necessarily becomes *more prudent* than any noble race, it will also honor prudence in an entirely different measure: namely as a primary condition of existence. With noble human beings, in contrast, prudence is likely to have a refined aftertaste of luxury and sophistication about it:—here it is not nearly as essential as the complete functional reliability of the regulating *unconscious* instincts or even a certain imprudence,

---

20. *deilos, deilaios, poneros, mochtheros: deilos:* cowardly, worthless, low-born, miserable, wretched; *deilaios:* wretched, sorry, paltry; *poneros:* wretched, oppressed by toils, worthless, base, cowardly; *mochtheros:* wretched, suffering hardship, miserable, worthless, knavish.

---

21. *oizyros, anolbos, tlemon, dystychein, xymphora: oizyros:* woeful, pitiable, miserable, sorry, poor; *anolbos:* unblest, wretched, luckless, poor; *tlemon:* suffering, enduring; hence: "steadfast, stouthearted," but also "wretched, miserable"; *dystychein:* to be unlucky, unhappy, unfortunate; *xymphora:* originally "chance," then usually in a bad sense, that is, "misfortune."

22. *eu prattein:* to do well, to fare well, or to do good.

23. *gennaios:* high-born, noble, high-minded.

for example the gallant making-straight-for-it, be it toward danger, be it toward the enemy, or that impassioned suddenness of anger, love, reverence, gratitude, and revenge by which noble souls in all ages have recognized each other. For the *ressentiment* of the noble human being, when it appears in him, runs its course and exhausts itself in an immediate reaction, therefore it does not *poison*—on the other hand it does not appear at all in countless cases where it is unavoidable in all the weak and powerless. To be unable for any length of time to take his enemies, his accidents, his *misdeeds* themselves seriously—that is the sign of strong, full natures in which there is an excess of formative, reconstructive, healing power that also makes one forget (a good example of this from the modern world is Mirabeau, who had no memory for insults and base deeds committed against him and who was only unable to forgive because he—forgot). Such a human is simply able to shake off with a single shrug a collection of worms that in others would dig itself in; here alone is also possible—assuming that it is at all possible on earth—the true *"love* of one's enemies." What great reverence for his enemies a noble human being has!—and such reverence is already a bridge to love. . . . After all, he demands his enemy for himself, as his distinction; he can stand no other enemy than one in whom there is nothing to hold in contempt and *a very great deal* to honor! On the other hand, imagine "the enemy" as the human being of *ressentiment* conceives of him—and precisely here is his deed, his creation: he has conceived of "the evil enemy," *"the evil one,"* and this indeed as the basic concept, starting from which he now also thinks up, as reaction and counterpart, a "good one"—himself! . . .

11

Precisely the reverse, therefore, of the case of the noble one, who conceives the basic concept "good" in advance and spontaneously, starting from himself that is, and from there first creates for himself an idea of "bad"! This "bad" of noble origin and that "evil" out of the brewing cauldron of unsatiated hate—the first, an after-creation, something on the side, a complementary color; the second, in contrast, the original, the beginning, the true *deed* in the conception of a slave moral-ity—how differently the two words "bad" and "evil" stand there, seemingly set in opposition to the same concept "good"! But it is *not* the same concept "good": on the contrary, just ask yourself *who* is actually "evil" in the sense of the morality of *ressentiment*. To answer in all strictness: *precisely* the "good one" of the other morality, precisely the noble, the powerful, the ruling one, only recolored, only reinterpreted, only reseen through the poisonous eye of *ressentiment*. There is one point we wish to deny least of all here: whoever encounters those "good ones" only as enemies encounters nothing but *evil enemies,* and the same humans who are kept so strictly within limits *inter pares,*[24] by mores, worship, custom, gratitude, still more by mutual surveillance, by jealousy, and who on the other hand in their conduct towards each other prove themselves so inventive in consideration, self-control, tact, loyalty, pride, and friendship,—they are not much better than uncaged beasts of prey toward the outside world, where that which is foreign, the foreign world, begins. There they enjoy freedom from all social constraint; in the wilderness they recover the losses incurred through the tension that comes from a long enclosure and fencing-in within the peace of the community; they step *back* into the innocence of the beast-of-prey conscience, as jubilant monsters, who perhaps walk away from a hideous succession of murder, arson, rape, torture with such high spirits and equanimity that it seems as if they have only played a student prank, convinced that for years to come the poets will again have something to sing and to praise. At the base of all these noble races one cannot fail to recognize the beast of prey, the splendid *blond beast* who roams about lusting after booty and victory; from time to time this hidden base needs to discharge itself, the animal must get out, must go back into the wilderness: Roman, Arab, Germanic, Japanese nobility, Homeric heroes, Scandinavian Vikings—in this need they are all alike. It is the noble races who have left the concept "barbarian" in all their tracks wherever they have gone; indeed from within their highest culture a consciousness of this betrays itself and even a pride in it (for example when Pericles says to his Athenians in that famous funeral oration, "to every land and sea our bold-

---

24. *inter pares:* among equals; here, "among themselves."

ness has broken a path, everywhere setting up unperishing monuments in good *and bad*"). This "boldness" of noble races—mad, absurd, sudden in its expression; the unpredictable, in their enterprises even the improbable—Pericles singles out for distinction the *rhathymia*[25] of the Athenians—their indifference and contempt toward all security, body, life, comfort; their appalling light-heartedness and depth of desire in all destruction, in all the delights of victory and of cruelty—all was summed up for those who suffered from it in the image of the "barbarian," of the "evil enemy," for example the "Goth," the "Vandal." The deep, icy mistrust that the German stirs up as soon as he comes into power, today once again—is still an atavism of that inextinguishable horror with which Europe has for centuries watched the raging of the blond Germanic beast (although there is hardly a conceptual, much less a blood-relationship between the ancient Teutons and us Germans). I once called attention to Hesiod's embarrassment as he was devising the succession of the cultural ages and attempted to express it in terms of gold, silver, bronze: he knew of no other way to cope with the contradiction posed by the glorious but likewise so gruesome, so violent world of Homer, than by making one age into two, which he now placed one after the other—first the age of the heroes and demigods of Troy and Thebes, as this world had remained in the memory of the noble dynasties who had their own ancestors there; then the bronze age, which was that same world as it appeared to the descendants of the downtrodden, plundered, mistreated, dragged-off, sold-off: an age of bronze, as stated—hard, cold, cruel, without feeling or conscience, crushing everything and covering it with blood. Assuming it were true, that which is now in any case believed as "truth," that the *meaning of all culture* is simply to breed a tame and civilized animal, a *domestic animal,* out of the beast of prey "man," then one would have to regard all those instincts of reaction and *ressentiment,* with the help of which the noble dynasties together with their ideals were finally brought to ruin and overwhelmed, as the actual *tools of culture;* which is admittedly not to say that the *bearers* of these instincts themselves at the same time

also represent culture. On the contrary, the opposite would not simply be probable—no! today it is *obvious!* These bearers of the oppressing and retaliation-craving instincts, the descendants of all European and non-European slavery, of all pre-Aryan population in particular—they represent the *regression* of humankind! These "tools of culture" are a disgrace to humanity, and rather something that raises a suspicion, a counter-argument against "culture" in general! It may be entirely justifiable if one cannot escape one's fear of the blond beast at the base of all noble races and is on guard: but who would not a hundred times sooner fear if he might at the same time admire, than *not* fear but be unable to escape the disgusting sight of the deformed, reduced, atrophied, poisoned? And is that not *our* doom? What causes *our* aversion to "man"?—for we *suffer* from man, there is no doubt.—*Not* fear; rather that we have nothing left to fear in man; that the worm "man" is in the foreground and teeming; that the "tame man," this hopelessly mediocre and uninspiring being, has already learned to feel himself as the goal and pinnacle, as the meaning of history, as "higher man"—indeed that he has a certain right to feel this way, insofar as he feels himself distanced from the profusion of the deformed, sickly, tired, worn-out of which Europe today is beginning to stink; hence as something that is at least relatively well-formed, at least still capable of living, that at least says "yes" to life. . . .

12

—At this point I will not suppress a sigh and a final confidence. What is it that I in particular find utterly unbearable? That with which I cannot cope alone, that causes me to suffocate and languish? Bad air! Bad air! That something deformed comes near me; that I should have to smell the entrails of a deformed soul! . . . How much can one not otherwise bear of distress, deprivation, foul weather, infirmity, drudgery, isolation? Basically one deals with everything else, born as one is to a subterranean and fighting existence; again and again one reaches the light, again and again one experiences one's golden hour of victory,—and then one stands there as one was born, unbreakable, tensed, ready for something new, something still more difficult, more distant, like a bow that any distress simply pulls tauter still.—

---

25. *rhathymia:* easiness of temper; indifference, rashness. Thucydides 2.39.

But from time to time grant me—assuming that there are heavenly patronesses beyond good and evil—a glimpse, grant me just one glimpse of something perfect, completely formed, happy, powerful, triumphant, in which there is still something to fear! Of a human being who justifies man *himself;* a human being who is a stroke of luck, completing and redeeming man, and for whose sake one may hold fast to *belief in man!* . . . For things stand thus: the reduction and equalization of the European human conceals *our* greatest danger, for this sight makes tired. . . . We see today nothing that wishes to become greater, we sense that things are still going downhill, downhill—into something thinner, more good-natured, more prudent, more comfortable, more mediocre, more apathetic, more Chinese, more Christian—man, there is no doubt, is becoming ever "better." . . . Precisely here lies Europe's doom—with the fear of man we have also forfeited the love of him, the reverence toward him, the hope for him, indeed the will to him. The sight of man now makes tired—what is nihilism today if it is not *that?* . . . We are tired of *man.* . . .

13

—But let us come back: the problem of the *other* origin of "good," of the good one as conceived by the man of *ressentiment,* demands its conclusion.—That the lambs feel anger toward the great birds of prey does not strike us as odd: but that is no reason for holding it against the great birds of prey that they snatch up little lambs for themselves. And when the lambs say among themselves "these birds of prey are evil; and whoever is as little as possible a bird of prey but rather its opposite, a lamb,—isn't he good?" there is nothing to criticize in this setting up of an ideal, even if the birds of prey should look on this a little mockingly and perhaps say to themselves: "*we* do not feel any anger towards them, these good lambs, as a matter of fact, we love them: nothing is more tasty than a tender lamb."—To demand of strength that it *not* express itself as strength, that it *not* be a desire to overwhelm, a desire to cast down, a desire to become lord, a thirst for enemies and resistances and triumphs, is just as nonsensical as to demand of weakness that it express itself as strength. A quantum of power is just such a quantum of drive, will, effect— more precisely, it is nothing other than this very driv-

ing, willing, effecting, and only through the seduction of language (and the basic errors of reason petrified therein), which understands and misunderstands all effecting as conditioned by an effecting something, by a "subject," can it appear otherwise. For just as common people separate the lightning from its flash and take the latter as a *doing,* as an effect of a subject called lightning, so popular morality also separates strength from the expressions of strength as if there were behind the strong an indifferent substratum that is free to express strength —or not to. But there is no such substratum; there is no "being" behind the doing, effecting, becoming; "the doer" is simply fabricated into the doing—the doing is everything. Common people basically double the doing when they have the lightning flash; this is a doing-doing: the same happening is posited first as cause and then once again as its effect. Natural scientists do no better when they say "force moves, force causes," and so on—our entire science, despite all its coolness, its freedom from affect, still stands under the seduction of language and has not gotten rid of the changelings slipped over on it, the "subjects" (the atom, for example, is such a changeling, likewise the Kantian "thing in itself"): small wonder if the suppressed, hiddenly glowing affects of revenge and hate exploit this belief and basically even uphold no other belief more ardently than this one, that *the strong one is free* to be weak, and the bird of prey, to be a lamb:—they thereby gain for themselves the right to hold the bird of prey *accountable* for being a bird of prey. . . . When out of the vengeful cunning of powerlessness the oppressed, downtrodden, violated say to themselves: "let us be different from the evil ones, namely good! And good is what everyone is who does not do violence, who injures no one, who doesn't attack, who doesn't retaliate, who leaves vengeance to God, who keeps himself concealed, as we do, who avoids all evil, and in general demands very little of life, like us, the patient, humble, righteous"—it means, when listened to coldly and without prejudice, actually nothing more than: "we weak ones are simply weak; it is good if we do nothing *for which we are not strong enough*"—but this harsh matter of fact, this prudence of the lowest order, which even insects have (presumably playing dead when in great danger in order not to do "too much"), has, thanks to that counterfeiting and self-deception of powerlessness, clothed itself in the pomp of renouncing, quiet, patiently waiting virtue, as if the very weakness of the weak—that is to say, his *essence,* his effecting, his whole unique, unavoidable, undetachable reality—were a voluntary achievement, something willed, something chosen, a *deed,* a *merit.* This kind of human *needs* the belief in a neutral "subject" with free choice, out of an instinct of self-preservation, self-affirmation, in which every lie tends to hallow itself. It is perhaps for this reason that the subject (or, to speak more popularly, the *soul*) has until now been the best article of faith on earth, because it made possible for the majority of mortals, the weak and oppressed of every kind, that sublime self-deception of interpreting weakness itself as freedom, of interpreting their being-such-and-such as a *merit.*

14

Would anyone like to go down and take a little look into the secret of how they *fabricate ideals* on earth? Who has the courage to do so? . . . Well then! The view into these dark workplaces is unobstructed here. Wait just a moment, Mr. Wanton-Curiosity and Daredevil: your eyes must first get used to this falsely shimmering light. . . . So! Enough! Now speak! What's going on down there? Tell me what you see, man of the most dangerous curiosity—now *I* am the one listening.—

—"I don't see anything, but I hear all the more. There is a cautious malicious quiet whispering and muttering-together out of all corners and nooks. It seems to me that they are lying; a sugary mildness sticks to each sound. Weakness is to be lied into a *merit,* there is no doubt about it—it is just as you said."—

—Go on!

—"and the powerlessness that does not retaliate into kindness; fearful baseness into 'humility'; subjection to those whom one hates into 'obedience' (namely to one whom they say orders this subjection—they call him God). The inoffensiveness of the weak one, cowardice itself, which he possesses in abundance, his standing-at-the-door, his unavoidable having-to-wait, acquires good names here, such as 'patience,' it is even called virtue *itself;* not being able to avenge oneself is called not wanting to avenge oneself, perhaps even forgiveness ('for *they* know not what they do—we alone know what *they* do!'). They also talk of 'love of one's enemies' —and sweat while doing so."

—Go on!

—"They are miserable, there is no doubt, all of these whisperers and nook-and-cranny counterfeiters, even if they are crouching together warmly—but they tell me that their misery is a distinction and election from God, that one beats the dogs one loves the most; perhaps this misery is also a preparation, a test, a schooling, perhaps it is still more—something for which there will one day be retribution, paid out with enormous interest in gold, no! in happiness. This they call 'blessedness'."

—Go on!

—"Now they are giving me to understand that they are not only better than the powerful, the lords of the earth, whose saliva they must lick (*not* out of fear, not at all out of fear! but rather because God commands that they honor all authority)—that they are not only better, but that they are also 'better off,' at least will be better off one day. But enough! enough! I can't stand it anymore. Bad air! Bad air! This workplace where they *fabricate ideals*—it seems to me it stinks of sheer lies."

—No! A moment more! You haven't said anything about the masterpiece of these artists of black magic who produce white, milk, and innocence out of every black:—haven't you noticed what the height of their sophistication is, their boldest, finest, most ingenious, most mendacious artistic stroke? Pay attention! These cellar animals full of revenge and hate—what is it they make precisely out of this revenge and hate? Did you ever hear these words? Would you guess, if you trusted their words alone, that those around you are all humans of *ressentiment?* . . .

—"I understand, I'll open my ears once again (oh! oh! oh! and *close* my nose). Now for the first time I hear what they have said so often: 'We good ones—*we are the just*'— what they demand they call not retaliation but rather 'the triumph of *justice*'; what they hate is not their enemy, no! they hate '*injustice,*' 'ungodliness'; what they believe and hope for is not the hope for revenge, the drunkenness of sweet revenge (—already Homer called it 'sweeter than honey'), but rather the victory of God, of the *just* God over the ungodly; what is left on earth for them to love are not their brothers in hate but rather their 'brothers in love,' as they say, all the good and just on earth."

—And what do they call that which serves them as comfort against all the sufferings of life—their phantasmagoria of the anticipated future blessedness?

—"What? Did I hear right? They call that 'the last judgment,' the coming of *their* kingdom, of the 'kingdom of God'—*meanwhile,* however, they live 'in faith,' 'in love,' 'in hope.' "

—Enough! Enough!

15

In faith in what? In love of what? In hope of what?—These weak ones—someday *they* too want to be the strong ones, there is no doubt, someday *their* "kingdom" too shall come—among them it is called "the kingdom of God" pure and simple, as we noted: they are of course so humble in all things! Even to experience *that* they need to live long, beyond death—indeed they need eternal life so that in the 'kingdom of God' they can also recover eternally the losses incurred during that earth-life "in faith, in love, in hope." Recover their losses for what? Recover their losses through what? . . . It was a gross blunder on Dante's part, it seems to me, when, with terror-instilling ingenuousness, he placed over the gate to his hell the inscription "I, too, was created by eternal love":—in any case, over the gate of the Christian paradise and its "eternal blessedness" there would be better justification for allowing the inscription to stand, "I, too, was created by eternal *hate*"—assuming that a truth may stand above the gate to a lie! For *what* is the blessedness of that paradise? . . . We would perhaps guess it already; but it is better that it is expressly documented for us by an authority not to be underestimated in such matters, Thomas Aquinas, the great teacher and saint. "*Beati in regno coelestia,*" he says meekly as a lamb, "*videbunt poenas domnatorum, ut beatitudo illis magis complaceat.*"[26] Or would you like to hear it in a stronger key, for instance from the mouth of a triumphant church father who counseled his Christians against the cruel pleasures of the public spectacles—and why? "Faith offers us much more,"—he says, *De spectac. C.* 29 ss.—"*something much stronger;* thanks to salvation there are entirely different joys at our disposal; in place of athletes

we have our martyrs; if we desire blood, well, we have the blood of Christ. . . . But what awaits us above all on the day of his return, of his triumph!"—and now he continues, the enraptured visionary: "But indeed there are still other sights, that last and eternal day of judgment, that day unlooked for by the nations, that day they laughed at, when the world so great with age and all its generations shall be consumed by one fire. What variety of sights then! *What should I admire! What should I laugh at! In which should I feel joy! In which should I exult,* seeing so many and great *kings* who were reported to have been received into heaven, now groaning in deepest darkness with Jove himself and those who testified of their reception into heaven! Likewise the praesides *(the provincial governor),* persecutors of the name of the Lord, being liquefied by flames fiercer than those with which they themselves raged against the Christians! What wise men besides, those very philosophers reddening before their disciples as they blaze together, the disciples to whom they suggested that nothing was of any concern to God; to whom they asserted that our souls are either nothing or they will not return to their former bodies! And also the poets, trembling before the judgment seat, not of Rhadamanthys or Minos but of the Christ, whom they did not expect! Then the great tragedians will be heard, in great voice, no doubt *(in better voice, even more awful screamers),* in their own calamities; then the actors will be recognized, made a great deal more limber by the fire; then the charioteer will be seen, all red on a flaming wheel; then the athletes will be observed, not in their gymnasiums but cast in the fire—were it not for the fact that not even then would I wish to see them since I would much rather bestow my *insatiable* gaze on those who raged against the Lord. 'This is he,' I shall say, 'the son of the carpenter or the prostitute *(as everything that follows shows, and in particular also this well-known designation from the Talmud for the mother of Jesus, from here on Tertullian means the Jews),* the Sabbath-breaker, the Samaritan, the one possessed of a devil. This is he whom you bought from Judas, this is the one struck by reed and fist, defiled by spit, given gall and vinegar to drink. This is he whom the disciples secretly stole away that it might be said he had risen, or perhaps the gardener dragged him away so that his lettuce would not be damaged by the crowd of those coming and going.' That you may see such things, *that you*

---

26. "*Beati in . . . magis complaceat*": "The blessed in the kingdom of heaven will see the punishments of the damned, *in order that their bliss be more delightful to them.*" *Summa Theologica* III *Supplementum* Q. 94, Art. 1.

may exult in such things—what praetor or consul or quaestor or priest will, out of his generosity, see to this? And yet even now we have them in a way, *by faith,* represented through the imagining spirit. On the other hand, what are those things which eye hath not seen nor ear heard, nor have ever entered into the heart of man? *(1 Cor. 2: 9)* I believe they are more pleasing than circus and both theaters *(first and fourth tiers, or, according to others, comic and tragic stages)* and any stadium."—**Per fidem:**[27] thus it is written.

16

Let us conclude. The two *opposed* values 'good and bad,' 'good and evil,' have fought a terrible millennia-long battle on earth; and as certainly as the second value has had the upper hand for a long time, even so there is still no shortage of places where the battle goes on, undecided. One could even say that it has in the meantime been borne up ever higher and precisely thereby become ever deeper, ever more spiritual: so that today there is perhaps no more decisive mark of the *"higher nature,"* of the more spiritual nature, than to be conflicted in that sense and still a real battleground for those opposites. The symbol of this battle, written in a script that has so far remained legible across all of human history, is "Rome against Judea, Judea against Rome":—so far there has been no greater event than *this* battle, *this* formulation of the problem, *this* mortally hostile contradiction. Rome sensed in the Jew something like anti-nature itself, its antipodal monstrosity as it were; in Rome the Jew was held to have been *"convicted* of hatred against the entire human race": rightly so, insofar as one has a right to tie the salvation and the future of the human race to the unconditional rule of aristocratic values, of Roman values. What the Jews on the other hand felt towards Rome? One can guess it from a thousand indications; but it will suffice to recall again the Johannine Apocalypse, that most immoderate of all written outbursts that revenge has on its conscience. (Do not underestimate, by the way, the profound consistency of the Christian instinct when it gave precisely this book of hate the name of the disciple of love, the

same one to whom it attributed that enamored-rapturous gospel—: therein lies a piece of truth, however much literary counterfeiting may have been needed for this purpose.) The Romans were after all the strong and noble ones, such that none stronger and nobler have ever existed, ever even been dreamt of; everything that remains of them, every inscription thrills, supposing that one can guess *what* is doing the writing there. The Jews, conversely, were that priestly people of *ressentiment* par excellence, in whom there dwelt a popular-moral genius without parallel: just compare the peoples with related talents—for instance the Chinese or the Germans—with the Jews in order to feel what is first and what fifth rank. Which of them has been victorious in the meantime, Rome or Judea? But there is no doubt at all: just consider before whom one bows today in Rome itself as before the quintessence of all the highest values—and not only in Rome, but over almost half the earth, everywhere that man has become tame or wants to become tame,—before *three Jews,* as everyone knows, and *one Jewess* (before Jesus of Nazareth, the fisher Peter, the carpet-weaver Paul, and the mother of the aforementioned Jesus, called Mary). This is very remarkable: Rome has succumbed without any doubt. To be sure, in the Renaissance there was a brilliant-uncanny reawakening of the classical ideal, of the noble manner of valuing all things: Rome itself moved like one awakened from apparent death, under the pressure of the new Judaized Rome built above it, which presented the appearance of an ecumenical synagogue and was called "church": but immediately Judea triumphed again, thanks to that thoroughly mobbish (German and English) *ressentiment* movement called the Reformation, and that which had to follow from it, the restoration of the church—also the restoration of the old sepulchral sleep of classical Rome. In an even more decisive and more profound sense than before, Judea once again achieved a victory over the classical ideal with the French Revolution: the last political nobleness there was in Europe, that of the seventeenth and eighteenth *French* centuries, collapsed under the instincts of popular *ressentiment*—never on earth has a greater jubilation, a noisier enthusiasm been heard! It is true that in the midst of all this the most enormous, most unexpected thing occurred: the classical ideal itself stepped *bodily* and with unheard of splendor before the eyes and

---

27. **Per fidem:** by [my] faith.

conscience of humanity—and once again, more strongly, more simply, more penetratingly than ever, the terrible and thrilling counter-slogan "the *privilege of the few*" resounded in the face of the old lie-slogan of *ressentiment,* "the privilege of the majority," in the face of the will to lowering, to debasement, to leveling, to the downward and evening-ward of man! Like a last sign pointing to the *other* path, Napoleon appeared, that most individual and late-born human being there ever was, and in him the incarnate problem of the *noble ideal in itself*—consider well, *what* kind of problem it is: Napoleon, this synthesis of an *inhuman* and a *superhuman.* . . .

Motivation, Self-Interest, and the Good Life

Plato

[handwritten: Soc. is no sophist]

Apology[1]

[handwritten: Argument 1]   *[handwritten: He examines bankers]*

17 I do not know, men of Athens, how my accusers affected you; as for me, I was almost carried away in spite of myself, so persuasively did they speak. And yet, hardly anything of what they said is true. Of the many lies they told, one in particular surprised me, namely that you should be careful not to be deceived by an accomplished speaker like me. That they were not ashamed to *b* be immediately proved wrong by the facts, when I show myself not to be an accomplished speaker at all, that I thought was most shameless on their part—unless indeed they call an accomplished speaker the man who speaks the truth. If they mean that, I would agree that I am an orator, but not after their manner, for indeed, as I say, practically nothing they said was true. From me you will hear the whole truth, though not, by Zeus, *c* gentlemen, expressed in embroidered and stylized phrases like theirs, but things spoken at random and expressed in the first words that come to mind, for I put my trust in the justice of what I say, and let none of you expect anything else. It would not be fitting at my age, as it might be for a young man, to toy with words when I appear before you.

One thing I do ask and beg of you, gentlemen: if you hear me making my defense in the same kind of language as I am accustomed to use in the marketplace by the bankers' tables, where many of you have heard me, *d* and elsewhere, do not be surprised or create a disturbance on that account. The position is this: This is my first appearance in a lawcourt, at the age of seventy; I am therefore simply a stranger to the manner of speaking here. Just as if I were really a stranger, you would certainly excuse me if I spoke in that dialect and manner in which I had been brought up, so too my present request seems a just one, for you to pay no attention to 18 my manner of speech—be it better or worse—but to concentrate your attention on whether what I say is just or not, for the excellence of a judge lies in this, as that of a speaker lies in telling the truth. *[handwritten: Listen by what I say not how I say it]*

It is right for me, gentlemen, to defend myself first against the first lying accusations made against me and my first accusers, and then against the later accusations and the later accusers. There have been many who have accused me to you for many years now, and none of their accusations are true. These I fear much more than I fear Anytus and his friends, though they too are formidable. These earlier ones, however, are more so, gentlemen; they got hold of most of you from childhood, persuaded you and accused me quite falsely, saying that there is a man called Socrates, a wise man, a student of all things in the sky and below the earth, who makes the worse argument the stronger. Those who spread that rumor, gentlemen, are my dangerous accusers, for their hearers *c* believe that those who study these things do not even believe in the gods. Moreover, these accusers are numerous, and have been at it a long time; also, they spoke to you at an age when you would most readily believe them, some of you being children and adolescents, and they won their case by default, as there was no defense.

[handwritten: S studies the world to try to understand the gods]

From Plato, *Five Dialogues (Second Edition),* translated by G. M. A. Grube, revised by John M. Cooper (Indianapolis: Hackett Publishing Company, 2002). Reprinted by permission of the publisher.

1. The word *apology* is a transliteration, not a translation, of the Greek *apologia,* which means defense.

Socrates in the clouds comedy

What is most absurd in all this is that one cannot even know or mention their names unless one of them is a writer of comedies.[2] Those who maliciously and slanderously persuaded you—who also, when persuaded themselves then persuaded others—all those are most difficult to deal with: one cannot bring one of them into court or refute him; one must simply fight with shadows, as it were, in making one's defense, and cross-examine when no one answers. I want you to realize too that my accusers are of two kinds: those who have accused me recently, and the old ones I mention; and to think that I must first defend myself against the latter, for you have also heard their accusations first, and to a much greater extent than the more recent.

Very well then, men of Athens. I must surely defend myself and attempt to uproot from your minds in so short a time the slander that has resided there so long. I wish this may happen, if it is in any way better for you and me, and that my defense may be successful, but I think this is very difficult and I am fully aware of how difficult it is. Even so, let the matter proceed as the god may wish, but I must obey the law and make my defense. Let us then take up the case from its beginning. What is the accusation from which arose the slander in which Meletus trusted when he wrote out the charge against me? What did they say when they slandered me? I must, as if they were my actual prosecutors, read the affidavit they would have sworn. It goes something like this: Socrates is guilty of wrongdoing in that he busies himself studying things in the sky and below the earth; he makes the worse into the stronger argument, and he teaches these same things to others. You have seen this yourself in the comedy of Aristophanes, a Socrates swinging about there, saying he was walking on air and talking a lot of other nonsense about things of which I know nothing at all. I do not speak in contempt of such knowledge, if someone is wise in these things—lest Meletus bring more cases against me—but, gentlemen, I have no part in it, and on this point I call upon the majority of you as witnesses. I think it right that all those of you who have heard me conversing, and many of you

S. denies teaching of

have, should tell each other if any one of you has ever heard me discussing such subjects to any extent at all. From this you will learn that the other things said about me by the majority are of the same kind.

Not one of them is true. And if you have heard from anyone that I undertake to teach people and charge a fee for it, that is not true either. Yet I think it a fine thing to be able to teach people as Gorgias of Leontini does, and Prodicus of Ceos, and Hippias of Elis. Each of these men can go to any city and persuade the young, who can keep company with any one of their own fellow citizens they want without paying, to leave the company of these, to join with themselves, pay them a fee, and be grateful to them besides. Indeed, I learned that there is another wise man from Paros who is visiting us, for I met a man who has spent more money on sophists than everybody else put together, Callias, the son of Hipponicus. So I asked him—he has two sons— "Callias," I said, "if your sons were colts or calves, we could find and engage a supervisor for them who would make them excel in their proper qualities, some horse breeder or farmer. Now since they are men, whom do you have in mind to supervise them? Who is an expert in this kind of excellence, the human and social kind? I think you must have given thought to this since you have sons. Is there such a person," I asked, "or is there not?" "Certainly there is," he said. "Who is he?" I asked. "What is his name, where is he from? And what is his fee?" "His name, Socrates, is Evenus, he comes from Paros, and his fee is five minas."[3] I thought Evenus a happy man, if he really possesses this art, and teaches for so moderate a fee. Certainly I would pride and preen myself if I had this knowledge, but I do not have it, gentlemen.

One of you might perhaps interrupt me and say: "But Socrates, what is your occupation? From where have these slanders come? For surely if you did not busy yourself with something out of the common, all these rumors and talk would not have arisen unless you did something other than most people. Tell us what it is, that we may not speak inadvisedly about you." Anyone who

---

2. This is Aristophanes. Socrates refers below (19c) to the character Socrates in his *Clouds* (225 ff.), first produced in 423 B.C.

3. A mina equaled 100 drachmas. In Socrates' time one drachma was the daily wage of a day-laborer. So Evenus' fee was a considerable sum.

S. denies having knowledge

S, is looking for someone wiser than him?
S, knows his ignorance? (Does he find them?

d says that seems to be right, and I will try to show you what has caused this reputation and slander. Listen then. Perhaps some of you will think I am jesting, but be sure that all that I shall say is true. What has caused my reputation is none other than a certain kind of wisdom. What kind of wisdom? Human wisdom, perhaps. It may be that I really possess this, while those whom I mentioned just now are wise with a wisdom more than

e human; else I cannot explain it, for I certainly do not possess it, and whoever says I do is lying and speaks to slander me. Do not create a disturbance, gentlemen, even if you think I am boasting, for the story I shall tell does not originate with me, but I will refer you to a trustworthy source. I shall call upon the god at Delphi

21 as witness to the existence and nature of my wisdom, if it be such.[4] You know Chaerephon. He was my friend from youth, and the friend of most of you, as he shared your exile and your return. You surely know the kind of man he was, how impulsive in any course of action. He went to Delphi at one time and ventured to ask the oracle—as I say, gentlemen, do not create a disturbance—he asked if any man was wiser than I, and the Pythian replied that no one was wiser. Chaerephon is dead, but his brother will testify to you about this.

b Consider that I tell you this because I would inform you about the origin of the slander. When I heard of this reply I asked myself: "Whatever does the god mean? What is his riddle? I am very conscious that I am not wise at all; what then does he mean by saying that I am the wisest? For surely he does not lie; it is not legitimate for him to do so." For a long time I was at a loss as to his meaning; then I very reluctantly turned to some such investigation as this; I went to one of those reputed

c wise, thinking that there, if anywhere, I could refute the oracle and say to it: "This man is wiser than I, but you said I was." Then, when I examined this man—there is no need for me to tell you his name, he was one of our public men—my experience was something like this: I thought that he appeared wise to many people and especially to himself, but he was not. I then tried to show

d him that he thought himself wise, but that he was not.

---

4. The god Apollo had a very famous shrine at Delphi, where his oracles were delivered through the mouth of a priestess, the "Pythian."

As a result he came to dislike me, and so did many of the bystanders. So I withdrew and thought to myself: "I am wiser than this man; it is likely that neither of us knows anything worthwhile, but he thinks he knows something when he does not, whereas when I do not know, neither do I think I know; so I am likely to be wiser than he to this small extent, that I do not think I know what I do not know." After this I approached an- *e* other man, one of those thought to be wiser than he, and I thought the same thing, and so I came to be disliked both by him and by many others.

After that I proceeded systematically. I realized, to my sorrow and alarm, that I was getting unpopular, but I thought that I must attach the greatest importance to the god's oracle, so I must go to all those who had any reputation for knowledge to examine its meaning. And by the dog, men of Athens—for I must tell you the *22* truth—I experienced something like this: In my investigation in the service of the god I found that those who had the highest reputation were nearly the most deficient, while those who were thought to be inferior were more knowledgeable. I must give you an account of my journeyings as if they were labors I had undertaken to prove the oracle irrefutable. After the politicians, I went to the poets, the writers of tragedies and dithyrambs and the others, intending in their case to catch myself being more ignorant than they. So I took *b* up those poems with which they seemed to have taken most trouble and asked them what they meant, in order that I might at the same time learn something from them. I am ashamed to tell you the truth, gentlemen, but I must. Almost all the bystanders might have explained the poems better than their authors could. I soon realized that poets do not compose their poems with knowledge, but by some inborn talent and by in- *c* spiration, like seers and prophets who also say many fine things without any understanding of what they say. The poets seemed to me to have had a similar experience. At the same time I saw that, because of their poetry, they thought themselves very wise men in other respects, which they were not. So there again I withdrew, thinking that I had the same advantage over them as I had over the politicians.

Finally I went to the craftsmen, for I was conscious of knowing practically nothing, and I knew that I would find that they had knowledge of many fine things. In *d*

S. Shows that his accusers have no grounds

this I was not mistaken; they knew things I did not know, and to that extent they were wiser than I. But, men of Athens, the good craftsmen seemed to me to have the same fault as the poets: each of them, because of his success at his craft, thought himself very wise in other most important pursuits, and this error of theirs overshadowed the wisdom they had, so that I asked myself, on behalf of the oracle, whether I should prefer to be as I am, with neither their wisdom nor their ignorance, or to have both. The answer I gave myself and the oracle was that it was to my advantage to be as I am.

As a result of this investigation, men of Athens, I acquired much unpopularity, of a kind that is hard to deal with and is a heavy burden; many slanders came from these people and a reputation for wisdom, for in each case the bystanders thought that I myself possessed the wisdom that I proved that my interlocutor did not have. What is probable, gentlemen, is that in fact the god is wise and that his oracular response meant that human wisdom is worth little or nothing, and that when he says this man, Socrates, he is using my name as an example, as if he said: "This man among you, mortals, is wisest who, like Socrates, understands that his wisdom is worthless." So even now I continue this investigation as the god bade me—and I go around seeking out anyone, citizen or stranger, whom I think wise. Then if I do not think he is, I come to the assistance of the god and show him that he is not wise. Because of this occupation, I do not have the leisure to engage in public affairs to any extent, nor indeed to look after my own, but I live in great poverty because of my service to the god.

Furthermore, the young men who follow me around of their own free will, those who have most leisure, the sons of the very rich, take pleasure in hearing people questioned; they themselves often imitate me and try to question others. I think they find an abundance of men who believe they have some knowledge but know little or nothing. The result is that those whom they question are angry, not with themselves but with me. They say: "That man Socrates is a pestilential fellow who corrupts the young." If one asks them what he does and what he teaches to corrupt them, they are silent, as they do not know, but, so as not to appear at a loss, they mention those accusations that are available against all philosophers, about "things in the sky and things below the earth," about "not believing in the gods" and "mak-

ing the worse the stronger argument"; they would not want to tell the truth, I'm sure, that they have been proved to lay claim to knowledge when they know nothing. These people are ambitious, violent, and numerous; they are continually and convincingly talking about me; they have been filling your ears for a long time with vehement slanders against me. From them Meletus attacked me, and Anytus and Lycon, Meletus being vexed on behalf of the poets, Anytus on behalf of the craftsmen and the politicians, Lycon on behalf of the orators, so that, as I started out by saying, I should be surprised if I could rid you of so much slander in so short a time. That, men of Athens, is the truth for you. I have hidden or disguised nothing. I know well enough that this very conduct makes me unpopular, and this is proof that what I say is true, that such is the slander against me, and that such are its causes. If you look into this either now or later, this is what you will find.

Let this suffice as a defense against the charges of my earlier accusers. After this I shall try to defend myself against Meletus, that good and patriotic man, as he says he is, and my later accusers. As these are a different lot of accusers, let us again take up their sworn deposition. It goes something like this: Socrates is guilty of corrupting the young and of not believing in the gods in whom the city believes, but in other new spiritual things. Such is their charge. Let us examine it point by point.

He says that I am guilty of corrupting the young, but I say that Meletus is guilty of dealing frivolously with serious matters, of irresponsibly bringing people into court, and of professing to be seriously concerned with things about none of which he has ever cared, and I shall try to prove that this is so. Come here and tell me, Meletus. Surely you consider it of the greatest importance that our young men be as good as possible? — Indeed I do.

Come then, tell these men who improves them. You obviously know, in view of your concern. You say you have discovered the one who corrupts them, namely me, and you bring me here and accuse me to these men. Come, inform these men and tell them who it is who improves them. You see, Meletus, that you are silent and know not what to say. Does this not seem shameful to you and a sufficient proof of what I say, that you have not been concerned with any of this? Tell me, my good sir, who improves our young men?—The laws.

That is not what I am asking, but what person who has knowledge of the laws to begin with?—These jurymen, Socrates.

How do you mean, Meletus? Are these able to educate the young and improve them?—Certainly.

All of them, or some but not others?—All of them.

Very good, by Hera. You mention a great abundance
25 of benefactors. But what about the audience? Do they improve the young or not?—They do, too.

What about the members of Council? —The Councillors, also.

But, Meletus, what about the assembly? Do members of the assembly corrupt the young, or do they all improve them?—They improve them.

All the Athenians, it seems, make the young into fine good men, except me, and I alone corrupt them. Is that what you mean?—That is most definitely what I mean.

You condemn me to a great misfortune. Tell me: does
b this also apply to horses, do you think? That all men improve them and one individual corrupts them? Or is quite the contrary true, one individual is able to improve them, or very few, namely, the horse breeders, whereas the majority, if they have horses and use them, corrupt them? Is that not the case, Meletus, both with horses and all other animals? Of course it is, whether you and Anytus say so or not. It would be a very happy state of affairs if only one person corrupted our youth, while the others improved them.
c You have made it sufficiently obvious, Meletus, that you have never had any concern for our youth; you show your indifference clearly; that you have given no thought to the subjects about which you bring me to trial.

And by Zeus, Meletus, tell us also whether it is better for a man to live among good or wicked fellow citizens. Answer, my good man, for I am not asking a difficult question. Do not the wicked do some harm to those who are ever closest to them, whereas good people benefit them?—Certainly.
d And does the man exist who would rather be harmed than benefited by his associates? Answer, my good sir, for the law orders you to answer. Is there any man who wants to be harmed?—Of course not.

Come now, do you accuse me here of corrupting the young and making them worse deliberately or unwillingly?—Deliberately.

What follows, Meletus? Are you so much wiser at your age than I am at mine that you understand that wicked people always do some harm to their closest
e neighbors while good people do them good, but I have reached such a pitch of ignorance that I do not realize this, namely that if I make one of my associates wicked I run the risk of being harmed by him so that I do such a great evil deliberately, as you say? I do not believe you, Meletus, and I do not think anyone else will. Either I do
26 not corrupt the young or, if I do, it is unwillingly, and you are lying in either case. Now if I corrupt them unwillingly, the law does not require you to bring people to court for such unwilling wrongdoings, but to get hold of them privately, to instruct them and exhort them; for clearly, if I learn better, I shall cease to do what I am doing unwillingly. You, however, have avoided my company and were unwilling to instruct me, but you bring me here, where the law requires one to bring those who are in need of punishment, not of instruction.

And so, men of Athens, what I said is clearly true:
b Meletus has never been at all concerned with these matters. Nonetheless tell us, Meletus, how you say that I corrupt the young; or is it obvious from your deposition that it is by teaching them not to believe in the gods in whom the city believes but in other new spiritual things? Is this not what you say I teach and so corrupt them?—That is most certainly what I do say.

Then by those very gods about whom we are talk-
c ing, Meletus, make this clearer to me and to these men: I cannot be sure whether you mean that I teach the belief that there are some gods—and therefore I myself believe that there are gods and am not altogether an atheist, nor am I guilty of that—not, however, the gods in whom the city believes, but others, and that this is the charge against me, that they are others. Or whether you mean that I do not believe in gods at all, and that this is what I teach to others.—This is what I mean, that you do not believe in gods at all.

You are a strange fellow, Meletus. Why do you say this? Do I not believe, as other men do, that the sun
d and the moon are gods?—No, by Zeus, gentlemen of the jury, for he says that the sun is stone, and the moon earth.

My dear Meletus, do you think you are prosecuting Anaxagoras? Are you so contemptuous of these men and think them so ignorant of letters as not to know that the books of Anaxagoras of Clazomenae are full of those theories, and further, that the young men learn from me what they can buy from time to time for a drachma, at most, in the bookshops, and ridicule Socrates if he pretends that these theories are his own, especially as they are so absurd? Is that, by Zeus, what you think of me, Meletus, that I do not believe that there are any gods?—That is what I say, that you do not believe in the gods at all.

You cannot be believed, Meletus, even, I think, by yourself. The man appears to me, men of Athens, highly insolent and uncontrolled. He seems to have made this deposition out of insolence, violence, and youthful zeal. He is like one who composed a riddle and is trying it out: "Will the wise Socrates realize that I am jesting and contradicting myself, or shall I deceive him and others?" I think he contradicts himself in the affidavit, as if he said: "Socrates is guilty of not believing in gods but believing in gods," and surely that is the part of a jester!

Examine with me, gentlemen, how he appears to contradict himself, and you, Meletus, answer us. Remember, gentlemen, what I asked you when I began, not to create a disturbance if I proceed in my usual manner.

Does any man, Meletus, believe in human activities who does not believe in humans? Make him answer, and not again and again create a disturbance. Does any man who does not believe in horses believe in horsemen's activities? Or in flute-playing activities but not in flute-players? No, my good sir, no man could. If you are not willing to answer, I will tell you and these men. Answer the next question, however. Does any man believe in spiritual activities who does not believe in spirits?—No one.

Thank you for answering, if reluctantly, when these gentlemen made you. Now you say that I believe in spiritual things and teach about them, whether new or old, but at any rate spiritual things according to what you say, and to this you have sworn in your deposition. But if I believe in spiritual things I must quite inevitably believe in spirits. Is that not so? It is indeed. I shall assume that you agree, as you do not answer. Do we not believe spirits to be either gods or the children of gods? Yes or no?—Of course.

Then since I do believe in spirits, as you admit, if spirits are gods, this is what I mean when I say you speak in riddles and in jest, as you state that I do not believe in

gods and then again that I do, since I do believe in spirits. If, on the other hand, the spirits are children of the gods, bastard children of the gods by nymphs or some other mothers, as they are said to be, what man would believe children of the gods to exist, but not gods? That would be just as absurd as to believe the young of horses and asses, namely mules, to exist, but not to believe in the existence of horses and asses. You must have made this deposition, Meletus, either to test us or because you were at a loss to find any true wrongdoing of which to accuse me. There is no way in which you could persuade anyone of even small intelligence that it is possible for one and the same man to believe in spiritual but not also in divine things, and then again for that same man to believe neither in spirits nor in gods nor in heroes.

I do not think, men of Athens, that it requires a prolonged defense to prove that I am not guilty of the charges in Meletus' deposition, but this is sufficient. On the other hand, you know that what I said earlier is true, that I am very unpopular with many people. This will be my undoing, if I am undone, not Meletus or Anytus but the slanders and envy of many people. This has destroyed many other good men and will, I think, continue to do so. There is no danger that it will stop at me.

Someone might say: "Are you not ashamed, Socrates, to have followed the kind of occupation that has led to your being now in danger of death?" However, I should be right to reply to him: "You are wrong, sir, if you think that a man who is any good at all should take into account the risk of life or death; he should look to this only in his actions, whether what he does is right or wrong, whether he is acting like a good or a bad man." According to your view, all the heroes who died at Troy were inferior people, especially the son of Thetis who was so contemptuous of danger compared with disgrace. When he was eager to kill Hector, his goddess mother warned him, as I believe, in some such words as these: "My child, if you avenge the death of your comrade, Patroclus, and you kill Hector, you will die yourself, for your death is to follow immediately after Hector's." Hearing this, he despised death and danger and was much more afraid to live a coward who did not avenge his friends. "Let me die at once," he said, "when once I have given the wrongdoer his deserts, rather than remain here, a laughingstock by the curved

[handwritten: you know what is right/hint to what is just no matter the cost]

ships, a burden upon the earth." Do you think he gave thought to death and danger?

This is the truth of the matter, men of Athens: wherever a man has taken a position that he believes to be best, or has been placed by his commander, there he must I think remain and face danger, without a thought for death or anything else, rather than disgrace. It would

e have been a dreadful way to behave, men of Athens, if, at Potidaea, Amphipolis, and Delium, I had, at the risk of death, like anyone else, remained at my post where those you had elected to command had ordered me, and then, when the god ordered me, as I thought and believed, to live the life of a philosopher, to examine myself and others, I had abandoned my post for fear of

29 death or anything else. That would have been a dreadful thing, and then I might truly have justly been brought here for not believing that there are gods, disobeying the oracle, fearing death, and thinking I was wise when I was not. To fear death, gentlemen, is no other than to think oneself wise when one is not, to think one knows what one does not know. No one knows whether death may not be the greatest of all blessings for a man, yet men fear it as if they knew that it is the greatest of evils. And surely it is the most blame-

b worthy ignorance to believe that one knows what one does not know. It is perhaps on this point and in this respect, gentlemen, that I differ from the majority of men, and if I were to claim that I am wiser than anyone in anything, it would be in this, that, as I have no adequate knowledge of things in the underworld, so I do not think I have. I do know, however, that it is wicked and shameful to do wrong, to disobey one's superior, be he god or man. I shall never fear or avoid things of which I do not know, whether they may not be good rather

c than things that I know to be bad. Even if you acquitted me now and did not believe Anytus, who said to you that either I should not have been brought here in the first place, or that now I am here, you cannot avoid executing me, for if I should be acquitted, your sons would practice the teachings of Socrates and all be thoroughly corrupted; if you said to me in this regard: "Socrates, we do not believe Anytus now; we acquit you, but only on condition that you spend no more time on this investi-

d gation and do not practice philosophy, and if you are caught doing so you will die"; if, as I say, you were to acquit me on those terms, I would say to you: "Men of

Athens, I am grateful and I am your friend, but I will obey the god rather than you, and as long as I draw breath and am able, I shall not cease to practice philosophy, to exhort you and in my usual way to point out to any one of you whom I happen to meet: Good Sir, you are an Athenian, a citizen of the greatest city with the greatest reputation for both wisdom and power; are e you not ashamed of your eagerness to possess as much wealth, reputation, and honors as possible, while you do not care for nor give thought to wisdom or truth, or the best possible state of your soul?" Then, if one of you disputes this and says he does care, I shall not let him go at once or leave him, but I shall question him, examine him, and test him, and if I do not think he has attained the goodness that he says he has, I shall reproach him 30 because he attaches little importance to the most important things and greater importance to inferior things. I shall treat in this way anyone I happen to meet, young and old, citizen and stranger, and more so the citizens because you are more kindred to me. Be sure that this is what the god orders me to do, and I think there is no greater blessing for the city than my service to the god. For I go around doing nothing but persuading both young and old among you not to care for your body or b your wealth in preference to or as strongly as for the best possible state of your soul, as I say to you: "Wealth does not bring about excellence, but excellence makes wealth and everything else good for men, both individually and collectively."

Now if by saying this I corrupt the young, this advice must be harmful, but if anyone says that I give different advice, he is talking nonsense. On this point I would say to you, men of Athens: "Whether you believe c Anytus or not, whether you acquit me or not, do so on the understanding that this is my course of action, even if I am to face death many times." Do not create a disturbance, gentlemen, but abide by my request not to cry out at what I say but to listen, for I think it will be to your advantage to listen, and I am about to say other things at which you will perhaps cry out. By no means do this. Be sure that if you kill the sort of man I say I am, you will not harm me more than yourselves. Neither Meletus nor Anytus can harm me in any way; he could not harm me, for I do not think it is permitted that a better man be harmed by a worse; certainly he d might kill me, or perhaps banish or disfranchise me, which he and maybe others think to be great harm, but I do not think so. I think he is doing himself much greater harm doing what he is doing now, attempting to have a man executed unjustly. Indeed, men of Athens, I am far from making a defense now on my own behalf, as might be thought, but on yours, to prevent you from wrongdoing by mistreating the god's gift to you by condemning me; for if you kill me you will not easily find another like me. I was attached to this city by the god—though it seems a ridiculous thing to say—as upon a great and noble horse which was somewhat sluggish because of its size and needed to be stirred up by a kind of gadfly. It is to fulfill some such function that I believe the god has placed me in the city. I never cease to rouse each and every one of you, to persuade and reproach you all day long and everywhere I find myself in your company.

Another such man will not easily come to be among you, gentlemen, and if you believe me you will spare me. You might easily be annoyed with me as people are when they are aroused from a doze, and strike out at me; if convinced by Anytus you could easily kill me, and then you could sleep on for the rest of your days, unless the god, in his care for you, sent you someone else. That I am the kind of person to be a gift of the god to the city you might realize from the fact that it does not seem like human nature for me to have neglected all my own affairs and to have tolerated this neglect now for so many years while I was always concerned with you, approaching each one of you like a father or an elder brother to persuade you to care for virtue. Now if I profited from this by charging a fee for my advice, there would be some sense to it, but you can see for yourselves that, for all their shameless accusations, my accusers have not been able in their impudence to bring forward a witness to say that I have ever received a fee or ever asked for one. I, on the other hand, have a convincing witness that I speak the truth, my poverty.

It may seem strange that while I go around and give this advice privately and interfere in private affairs, I do not venture to go to the assembly and there advise the city. You have heard me give the reason for this in many places. I have a divine or spiritual sign which Meletus has ridiculed in his deposition. This began when I was a child. It is a voice, and whenever it speaks it turns me away from something I am about to do, but it never en-

courages me to do anything. This is what has prevented me from taking part in public affairs, and I think it was quite right to prevent me. Be sure, men of Athens, that if I had long ago attempted to take part in politics, I should have died long ago, and benefited neither you nor myself. Do not be angry with me for speaking the truth; no man will survive who genuinely opposes you or any other crowd and prevents the occurrence of many unjust and illegal happenings in the city. A man who really fights for justice must lead a private, not a public, life if he is to survive for even a short time.

I shall give you great proofs of this, not words but what you esteem, deeds. Listen to what happened to me, that you may know that I will not yield to any man contrary to what is right, for fear of death, even if I should die at once for not yielding. The things I shall tell you are commonplace and smack of the lawcourts, but they are true. I have never held any other office in the city, but I served as a member of the Council, and our tribe Antiochis was presiding at the time when you wanted to try as a body the ten generals who had failed to pick up the survivors of the naval battle. This was illegal, as you all recognized later. I was the only member of the presiding committee to oppose your doing something contrary to the laws, and I voted against it. The orators were ready to prosecute me and take me away, and your shouts were egging them on, but I thought I should run any risk on the side of law and justice rather than join you, for fear of prison or death, when you were engaged in an unjust course. This happened when the city was still a democracy. When the oligarchy was established, the Thirty summoned me to the Hall, along with four others, and ordered us to bring Leon from Salamis, that he might be executed. They gave many such orders to many people, in order to implicate as many as possible in their guilt. Then I showed again, not in words but in action, that, if it were not rather vulgar to say so, death is something I couldn't care less about, but that my whole concern is not to do anything unjust or impious. That government, powerful as it was, did not frighten me into any wrongdoing. When we left the Hall, the other four went to Salamis and brought in Leon, but I went home. I might have been put to death for this, had not the government fallen shortly afterwards. There are many who will witness to these events.

[handwritten: Soc. has companions who he examines ppl. w]

Do you think I would have survived all these years if I were engaged in public affairs and, acting as a good man must, came to the help of justice and considered this the most important thing? Far from it, men of Athens, nor would any other man. Throughout my life, *33* in any public activity I may have engaged in, I am the same man as I am in private life. I have never come to an agreement with anyone to act unjustly, neither with anyone else nor with anyone of those who they slanderously say are my pupils. I have never been anyone's teacher. If anyone, young or old, desires to listen to me when I am talking and dealing with my own concerns, I have never begrudged this to anyone, but I do not converse when I receive a fee and not when I do not. I *b* am equally ready to question the rich and the poor if anyone is willing to answer my questions and listen to what I say. And I cannot justly be held responsible for the good or bad conduct of these people, as I never promised to teach them anything and have not done so. If anyone says that he has learned anything from me, or that he heard anything privately that the others did not hear, be assured that he is not telling the truth.

Why then do some people enjoy spending consider-*c* able time in my company? You have heard why, men of Athens; I have told you the whole truth. They enjoy hearing those being questioned who think they are wise, but are not. And this is not unpleasant. To do this has, as I say, been enjoined upon me by the god, by means of oracles and dreams, and in every other way that a divine manifestation has ever ordered a man to do anything. This is true, gentlemen, and can easily be established.

If I corrupt some young men and have corrupted *d* others, then surely some of them who have grown older and realized that I gave them bad advice when they were young should now themselves come up here to accuse me and avenge themselves. If they were unwilling to do so themselves, then some of their kindred, their fathers or brothers or other relations should recall it now if their family had been harmed by me. I see many of these present here, first Crito, my contempo-*e* rary and fellow demesman, the father of Critobulus here; next Lysanias of Sphettus, the father of Aeschines here; also Antiphon the Cephisian, the father of Epigenes; and others whose brothers spent their time in this way; Nicostratus, the son of Theozotides, brother of Theodotus, and Theodotus has died so he could not in-

fluence him; Paralius here, son of Demodocus, whose brother was Theages; there is Adeimantus, son of Aris-*34* ton, brother of Plato here; Aeantodorus, brother of Apollodorus here.

I could mention many others, some one of whom surely Meletus should have brought in as witness in his own speech. If he forgot to do so, then let him do it now; I will yield time if he has anything of the kind to say. You will find quite the contrary, gentlemen. These men are all ready to come to the help of the corruptor, the man who has harmed their kindred, as Meletus and *b* Anytus say. Now those who were corrupted might well have reason to help me, but the uncorrupted, their kindred who are older men, have no reason to help me except the right and proper one, that they know that Meletus is lying and that I am telling the truth.

Very well, gentlemen. This, and maybe other similar things, is what I have to say in my defense. Perhaps one *c* of you might be angry as he recalls that when he himself stood trial on a less dangerous charge, he begged and implored the jurymen with many tears, that he brought his children and many of his friends and family into court to arouse as much pity as he could, but that I do none of these things, even though I may seem to be *d* running the ultimate risk. Thinking of this, he might feel resentful towards me and, angry about this, cast his vote in anger. If there is such a one among you—I do not deem there is, but if there is—I think it would be right to say in reply: My good sir, I too have a household and, in Homer's phrase, I am not born "from oak or rock" but from men, so that I have a family, indeed three sons, men of Athens, of whom one is an adolescent while two are children. Nevertheless, I will not beg you to acquit me by bringing them here. Why do I do *e* none of these things? Not through arrogance, gentlemen, nor through lack of respect for you. Whether I am brave in the face of death is another matter, but with regard to my reputation and yours and that of the whole city, it does not seem right to me to do these things, especially at my age and with my reputation. For it is generally believed, whether it be true or false, that in certain *35* respects Socrates is superior to the majority of men. Now if those of you who are considered superior, be it in wisdom or courage or whatever other virtue makes them so, are seen behaving like that, it would be a disgrace. Yet I have often seen them do this sort of thing

Socrates believes the Soul higher than material

when standing trial, men who are thought to be some-body, doing amazing things as if they thought it a terrible thing to die, and as if they were to be immortal if you did not execute them. I think these men bring *b* shame upon the city so that a stranger, too, would assume that those who are outstanding in virtue among the Athenians, whom they themselves select from themselves to fill offices of state and receive other honors, are in no way better than women. You should not act like that, men of Athens, those of you who have any reputation at all, and if we do, you should not allow it. You should make it very clear that you will more readily convict a man who performs these pitiful dramatics in court and so makes the city a laughingstock, than a man who keeps quiet.

Quite apart from the question of reputation, gentlemen, I do not think it right to supplicate the jury and *c* to be acquitted because of this, but to teach and persuade them. It is not the purpose of a juryman's office to give justice as a favor to whoever seems good to him, but to judge according to law, and this he has sworn to do. We should not accustom you to perjure yourselves, nor should you make a habit of it. This is irreverent conduct for either of us.

Do not deem it right for me, men of Athens, that I *d* should act towards you in a way that I do not consider to be good or just or pious, especially, by Zeus, as I am being prosecuted by Meletus here for impiety; clearly, if I convinced you by my supplication to do violence to your oath of office, I would be teaching you not to believe that there are gods, and my defense would convict me of not believing in them. This is far from being the case, gentlemen, for I do believe in them as none of my accusers do. I leave it to you and the god to judge me in the way that will be best for me and for you.

[The jury now gives its verdict of guilty, and Meletus asks for the penalty of death.]

There are many other reasons for my not being an-*e* gry with you for convicting me, men of Athens, and *36* what happened was not unexpected. I am much more surprised at the number of votes cast on each side, for I did not think the decision would be by so few votes but by a great many. As it is, a switch of only thirty votes would have acquitted me. I think myself that I have

been cleared of Meletus' charges, and not only this, but *b* it is clear to all that, if Anytus and Lycon had not joined him in accusing me, he would have been fined a thousand drachmas for not receiving a fifth of the votes.

He assesses the penalty at death. So be it. What counter-assessment should I propose to you, men of Athens? Clearly it should be a penalty I deserve, and what do I deserve to suffer or to pay because I have deliberately not led a quiet life but have neglected what occupies most people: wealth, household affairs, the position of general or public orator or the other offices, the political clubs and factions that exist in the city? I thought myself too honest to survive if I occupied myself with those things. I did not follow that path that *c* would have made me of no use either to you or to myself, but I went to each of you privately and conferred upon him what I say is the greatest benefit, by trying to persuade him not to care for any of his belongings before caring that he himself should be as good and as wise as possible, not to care for the city's possessions more than for the city itself, and to care for other things in *d* the same way. What do I deserve for being such a man? Some good, men of Athens, if I must truly make an assessment according to my deserts, and something suitable. What is suitable for a poor benefactor who needs leisure to exhort you? Nothing is more suitable, gentlemen, than for such a man to be fed in the Prytaneum—much more suitable for him than for any one of you who has won a victory at Olympia with a pair or a team of horses. The Olympian victor makes you *e* think yourself happy; I make you be happy. Besides, he does not need food, but I do. So if I must make a just assessment of what I deserve, I assess it as this: free meals *37* in the Prytaneum.

When I say this you may think, as when I spoke of appeals to pity and entreaties, that I speak arrogantly, but that is not the case, men of Athens; rather it is like this: I am convinced that I never willingly wrong anyone, but I am not convincing you of this, for we have talked together but a short time. If it were the law with us, as it *b* is elsewhere, that a trial for life should not last one but many days, you would be convinced, but now it is not easy to dispel great slanders in a short time. Since I am convinced that I wrong no one, I am not likely to wrong myself, to say that I deserve some evil and to make some such assessment against myself. What should I fear? That

Phaedo Socrates + executioner = similar, they both who fulfill their duty

I should suffer the penalty Meletus has assessed against me, of which I say I do not know whether it is good or bad? Am I then to choose in preference to this something that I know very well to be an evil and assess the penalty at that? Imprisonment? Why should I live in prison, always subjected to the ruling magistrates, the Eleven? A fine, and imprisonment until I pay it? That would be the same thing for me, as I have no money. Exile? For perhaps you might accept that assessment.

I should have to be inordinately fond of life, men of Athens, to be so unreasonable as to suppose that other men will easily tolerate my company and conversation when you, my fellow citizens, have been unable to endure them, but found them a burden and resented them so that you are now seeking to get rid of them. Far from it, gentlemen. It would be a fine life at my age to be driven out of one city after another, for I know very well that wherever I go the young men will listen to my talk as they do here. If I drive them away, they will themselves persuade their elders to drive me out; if I do not drive them away, their fathers and relations will drive me out on their behalf.

Perhaps someone might say: But Socrates, if you leave us will you not be able to live quietly, without talking? Now this is the most difficult point on which to convince some of you. If I say that it is impossible for me to keep quiet because that means disobeying the god, you will not believe me and will think I am being ironical. On the other hand, if I say that it is the greatest good for a man to discuss virtue every day and those other things about which you hear me conversing and testing myself and others, for the unexamined life is not worth living for men, you will believe me even less.

What I say is true, gentlemen, but it is not easy to convince you. At the same time, I am not accustomed to think that I deserve any penalty. If I had money, I would assess the penalty at the amount I could pay, for that would not hurt me, but I have none, unless you are willing to set the penalty at the amount I can pay, and perhaps I could pay you one mina of silver. So that is my assessment.

Plato here, men of Athens, and Crito and Critobulus and Apollodorus bid me put the penalty at thirty minas, and they will stand surety for the money. Well then, that is my assessment, and they will be sufficient guarantee of payment.

[The jury now votes again and sentences Socrates to death.]

It is for the sake of a short time, men of Athens, that you will acquire the reputation and the guilt, in the eyes of those who want to denigrate the city, of having killed Socrates, a wise man, for they who want to revile you will say that I am wise even if I am not. If you had waited but a little while, this would have happened of its own accord. You see my age, that I am already advanced in years and close to death. I am saying this not to all of you but to those who condemned me to death, and to these same ones I say: Perhaps you think that I was convicted for lack of such words as might have convinced you, if I thought I should say or do all I could to avoid my sentence. Far from it. I was convicted because I lacked not words but boldness and shamelessness and the willingness to say to you what you would most gladly have heard from me, lamentations and tears and my saying and doing many things that I say are unworthy of me but that you are accustomed to hear from others. I did not think then that the danger I ran should make me do anything mean, nor do I now regret the nature of my defense. I would much rather die after this kind of defense than live after making the other kind. Neither I nor any other man should, on trial or in war, contrive to avoid death at any cost. Indeed it is often obvious in battle that one could escape death by throwing away one's weapons and by turning to supplicate one's pursuers, and there are many ways to avoid death in every kind of danger if one will venture to do or say anything to avoid it. It is not difficult to avoid death, gentlemen; it is much more difficult to avoid wickedness, for it runs faster than death. Slow and elderly as I am, I have been caught by the slower pursuer, whereas my accusers, being clever and sharp, have been caught by the quicker, wickedness. I leave you now, condemned to death by you, but they are condemned by truth to wickedness and injustice. So I maintain my assessment, and they maintain theirs. This perhaps had to happen, and I think it is as it should be.

Now I want to prophesy to those who convicted me, for I am at the point when men prophesy most, when they are about to die. I say, gentlemen, to those who voted to kill me, that vengeance will come upon you immediately after my death, a vengeance much harder to bear than that which you took in killing me. You did this in the belief that you would avoid giving an account of your life, but I maintain that quite the opposite will

d happen to you. There will be more people to test you, whom I now held back, but you did not notice it. They will be more difficult to deal with as they will be younger and you will resent them more. You are wrong if you believe that by killing people you will prevent anyone from reproaching you for not living in the right way. To escape such tests is neither possible nor good, but it is best and easiest not to discredit others but to prepare oneself to be as good as possible. With this prophecy to you who convicted me, I part from you.

I should be glad to discuss what has happened with

e those who voted for my acquittal during the time that the officers of the court are busy and I do not yet have to depart to my death. So, gentlemen, stay with me awhile, for nothing prevents us from talking to each other while it is allowed. To you, as being my friends, I

40 want to show the meaning of what has occurred. A surprising thing has happened to me, jurymen—you I would rightly call jurymen. At all previous times my familiar prophetic power, my spiritual manifestation, frequently opposed me, even in small matters, when I was about to do something wrong, but now that, as you can see for yourselves, I was faced with what one might think, and what is generally thought to be, the worst of evils, my divine sign has not opposed me, either when

b I left home at dawn, or when I came into court, or at any time that I was about to say something during my speech. Yet in other talks it often held me back in the middle of my speaking, but now it has opposed no word or deed of mine. What do I think is the reason for this? I will tell you. What has happened to me may well be a good thing, and those of us who believe death to be an evil are certainly mistaken. I have convincing proof of

c this, for it is impossible that my familiar sign did not oppose me if I was not about to do what was right.

Let us reflect in this way, too, that there is good hope that death is a blessing, for it is one of two things: either the dead are nothing and have no perception of anything, or it is, as we are told, a change and a relocating

d for the soul from here to another place. If it is complete lack of perception, like a dreamless sleep, then death would be a great advantage. For I think that if one had to pick out that night during which a man slept soundly

and did not dream, put beside it the other nights and days of his life, and then see how many days and nights had been better and more pleasant than that night, not only a private person but the great king would find them easy to count compared with the other days and

e nights. If death is like this I say it is an advantage, for all eternity would then seem to be no more than a single night. If, on the other hand, death is a change from here to another place, and what we are told is true and all who have died are there, what greater blessing could there be, gentlemen of the jury? If anyone arriving in Hades will have escaped from those who call themselves

41 jurymen here, and will find those true jurymen who are said to sit in judgment there, Minos and Rhadamanthus and Aeacus and Triptolemus and the other demigods who have been upright in their own life, would that be a poor kind of change? Again, what would one of you give to keep company with Orpheus and Musaeus, Hesiod and Homer? I am willing to die many times if that is true. It would be a wonderful way for me to spend my time whenever I met Palamedes and Ajax, the

b son of Telamon, and any other of the men of old who died through an unjust conviction, to compare my experience with theirs. I think it would be pleasant. Most important, I could spend my time testing and examining people there, as I do here, as to who among them is wise, and who thinks he is, but is not.

What would one not give, gentlemen of the jury, for the opportunity to examine the man who led the great

c expedition against Troy, or Odysseus, or Sisyphus, and innumerable other men and women one could mention? It would be an extraordinary happiness to talk with them, to keep company with them and examine them. In any case, they would certainly not put one to death for doing so. They are happier there than we are here in other respects, and for the rest of time they are deathless, if indeed what we are told is true.

You too must be of good hope as regards death, gentlemen of the jury, and keep this one truth in mind, that a good man cannot be harmed either in life or in death,

d and that his affairs are not neglected by the gods. What has happened to me now has not happened of itself, but it is clear to me that it was better for me to die now and to escape from trouble. That is why my divine sign did not oppose me at any point. So I am certainly not angry with those who convicted me, or with my accusers. Of course that was not their purpose when they accused and convicted me, but they thought they were hurting me, and

e for this they deserve blame. This much I ask from them: When my sons grow up, avenge yourselves by causing them the same kind of grief that I caused you, if you think they care for money or anything else more than they care for virtue, or if they think they are somebody when they

are nobody. Reproach them as I reproach you, that they do not care for the right things and think they are worthy when they are not worthy of anything. If you do this, *42* I shall have been justly treated by you, and my sons also.

Now the hour to part has come. I go to die, you go to live. Which of us goes to the better lot is known to no one, except the god.

Stephen Darwall

Hobbes

Hobbes I

Thomas Hobbes (1588–1679) is best known for the **social contract theory,** the idea that political legitimacy derives from a mutual contract or promise. A **state of nature** (without political authority), Hobbes famously argued in *Leviathan* (1651), is riddled with "continual fear, and danger of violent death; and the life of man [is] solitary, poor, nasty, brutish, and short" (L.XIII.9). To escape this condition, citizens must promise to obey a sovereign. Their doing so establishes the sovereign's authority and the citizens' obligation to obey.

The conclusion of Hobbes's argument is a claim of political theory—namely, that political obligation rests on individual consent. But implicit in his argument is a conception of morality and its **normativity** that has powerfully influenced moral philosophers ever since. Political obligation depends, for Hobbes, on the moral obligation to keep "covenants." But what grounds this moral obligation? What makes it a moral "law of nature," as Hobbes said, "that men perform their covenants made?" (L.XIV.1). To answer this question, Hobbes had

to construct a philosophical ethics, including a metaethics that could plausibly ground the obligation to keep promises.

Hobbes's Context

To see the problem as Hobbes faced it, we need to understand something of his historical context. Let's begin with a philosophical outlook that had been common in the 400-year period before Hobbes wrote *Leviathan,* but that, in the middle of the seventeenth century, Hobbes and many of his contemporaries found they could no longer accept.

Begin with the idea of an artifact that is constructed for a certain purpose—say, a knife. A knife is made to serve a purpose or goal: to cut by hand. It can be made from any of various materials: wood, metal, plastic, and so on. It can be made from anything that is suitable for the knife's end or function. What makes something a knife is not its material but its defining function. And this end or function is *normative* for the knife. Just by virtue of what it is to be knife—what knives are *for*—something will be a good knife, perform well, be as it should be, and so on, only if it cuts well.

Suppose now that every *natural* kind of thing were like knives in having a defining end. In other words, suppose that included in the "essence" or nature of everything (that which makes it what it is) is what the thing is *to do* or *be*. It is not enough to suppose that nature and its parts are created, or even that they are created for certain purposes. We must imagine that natural kinds of things are like knives in being *essentially for* certain purposes. So imagine that it is essential to what makes something an acorn, for example, that it *is to* function in a certain way—say, to grow up into a flourishing oak.

Call a thing's defining end its *good*. Of every natural kind, it will then be true that its good is normative for it. A thing of that kind will do or be as it *should* do or be just in case it realizes the good for things of that kind. Its good is thus a kind of "law" for it. Suppose also that the defining end or function of each natural thing fits with that of every other to form a harmonious order. Call the entire set of ends—that is, the "laws" that say what each living being is to do in coordination with everything else—the "eternal law." Next, suppose that some of these beings, human beings, can discover their end or law and, consequently, that they can act in knowledge of it. Call those parts of the eternal law that concern such beings "natural law." Then natural law will uniquely be such that it can be obeyed or flouted, and only human beings will be subject to the law in this way. Finally, suppose that all such phenomena are the result of divine creation.

These are the essentials of the **classical natural law theory** as it was proposed by St. Thomas Aquinas (1225–1274) and widely accepted for centuries after. Morality is a natural law that all human beings are subject to by virtue of their nature. Both the content and the normativity of natural law are inherent in human nature, since obeying it is what we are *for*.

Aquinas's theory was a synthesis of Aristotle's teleological metaphysics and a Judeo-Christian conception of morality as God's law. It was not, however, a theological voluntarist conception. In fact, there were intense debates between Aquinas and his followers, on the one hand, and more voluntarist natural lawyers, on the other. They all agreed that morality is divinely ordained, but they disagreed about what gives this divine law its authority or normative force. For the voluntarists, the moral obligation to abide by natural law derives entirely from God's commanding it. But for Aquinas and his followers, we should obey natural law because it is essential to what we are that we are *to* follow it. Just as what

a knife is for is cutting, so what we are for is the virtuous activity dictated by natural law (morality).

Let's return now to Hobbes. Recall that the problem we left Hobbes with was how to account for the obligation to keep promises, which he held to underlie the obligation to obey the laws of the state. Like the classical natural lawyers, Hobbes connected morality and its normativity to what he called a natural law. But what gives the law "that men perform their covenants made" its normative force? What makes it the case that people *should* keep their covenants? What does any "ought" or normative "law" consist in? This was the problem Hobbes faced.

Now, according to the classical theory, a natural law should be followed because it codifies an end that is inherent in the nature of those subject to it. A knife's doing as it ought just is its cutting well. So, likewise, for us. Our doing as we ought just is our excelling at what we are for—namely, the virtuous activities called for by natural law. It follows that if natural law dictates keeping promises, then we ought to keep our promises.

There were two reasons Hobbes could not accept this picture. One had to do with its teleological metaphysics. By the middle of the seventeenth century, Aristotelian science and the epistemological and metaphysical framework required to sustain it were being increasingly abandoned in favor of the methods and worldview of the emerging modern science of Galileo and Huygens (and, later, Boyle and Newton). Stressing empirical experimentation, the new science explained phenomena by appealing not to inherent goals or purposes but, rather, to underlying physical mechanisms. The natural laws it was discovering were entirely descriptive rather than normative. For example, the motion of bodies came to be explained by universal generalizations or "laws" about how bodies invariably behave and the mechanisms and forces that cause them to do so, rather than by anything about their "ends" or purposes.

Hobbes believed that the teleological picture was not simply false but unintelligible. For words to be other than empty signs or sounds, he thought, they must ultimately refer to what we can know to be real through sense experience (L.IV.14–18). This category includes material things, their physical properties, and events in bodies that involve conscious thought and experience. Hobbes had special scorn for the "insignificant speech" he found in "all the universities of Christendom, grounded upon certain texts of Aristotle," like Aquinas's theory of natural law (L.I.5).

Second, Hobbes rejected classical natural law's contention that the goods of all are harmoniously ordered and that a coincidence between natural law and self-interest is metaphysically guaranteed. On the contrary, Hobbes thought, what gives morality and political society its point is that people's interests frequently conflict and, consequently, that if each simply pursues his self-interest, the collective result would be a war of "all against all."

Hobbes sought an account of the moral obligation to keep promises that did not depend on teleological metaphysics (and the assumption that self-interest necessarily coincides with the collective interest) and that could be defended consistently with the worldview of the emerging empirical sciences. Thus he was a (metaphysical) **empirical naturalist,** one of the first, indeed, to view ethics itself as an empirical science. Ethics, he told us, is the science that theorizes "consequences from the passions of men" (L.IX.3). And so Hobbes confronted head-on the very problem that any naturalist must face: how to account for normativity in a naturalistic framework—how to place value and oughtness in a world of facts.

Desire, Deliberation, and Value

In the 1630s, more than a decade before he wrote *Leviathan,* Hobbes became fascinated with scientific experiments concerning optics and with Galileo's theory of color. Galileo's theory was that, literally speaking, there are no colors in the world—at least, not as we experience them to be. There is such a thing as color experience, of course, and this experience has **objective purport.** We experience objects *as colored,* as having color properties that "really and truly exist" in the objects. But unlike shape and size, which are real properties of objects, the color properties we experience objects as having do not really exist. So far as "objective existence" goes, color words are "mere names for something which reside exclusively in our sensitive body."

Look at a ripe tomato. It seems to be red, and its seeming to you to be red is your having an experience *as of* something really red. The redness seems a real prop-

erty of the tomato, not any property of you or of the conditions in which you are viewing it. But, Galileo said, there is no such property. All there is in nature are the physical properties of the tomato that cause you to have certain sensations, the sensations that are as of something with the property red.

What does any of this have to do with ethics? By the time he wrote *Leviathan,* Hobbes had arrived at a theory of value that he modeled on the Galilean theory of color. He had come to believe that value judgment and experience involve a **projection** that is similar to what Galileo thought was involved in the case of color. The key to understanding value judgment, Hobbes believed, was to see its role in deliberation, desire, and action. Just as colors lack the objective existence we experience them as having, so also are there no values really existing in the world, although there inevitably seem to be whenever we have desires and are moved by them.

Hobbes had a mechanical picture of human action. As a materialist, he believed that everything that exists is but "matter in motion." Human behavior is no exception. It is bodily motion that is caused by other bodily motions. Hobbes was a determinist, but he didn't think that determinism entailed a lack of freedom. He didn't believe in free *will,* but then he thought that that idea was unintelligible anyway, a bit of "insignificant speech." It is people who are free, not wills. And people are free just in case no obstacles exist to their doing what they will (L.XXI).

Hobbes's theory of action is as follows. All actions result from desires or aversions. A desire is (literally) a motion in the body of the person who has it toward the desire's object. An aversion is the same motion "fromward" (L.VI.2). It's a hot day, and you want an iced tea. You have a desire for the tea, which is a motion in you (an inclination) toward drinking some tea. Suppose you are moved to get some tea, and you start to drink it. If, as you are drinking it, you maintain the same attitude toward the tea, you will like it. In Hobbes's terms, you will "love" it. If, however, it is not as you expected, you may "hate" it and be averse to continuing to drink it. You may experience some motion away from it.

Love and desire are the same psychological state, Hobbes said. We call this state desire when we take its object to be absent, and love when we take it to be present. And similarly for aversion and hate. You wanted the tea (before you had it), and now you love it (having it). Or now you hate it (having it) and are averse to continuing to drink it (in the next moment, which is not now present).

So desires and aversions are psychological (in reality, material) forces that move us toward and away from actions. Of course, things are not always so simple as a desire straightway giving rise to action. But that is just because we are simultaneously subject to different desires, which in turn is what leads us to deliberate about what to do. In fact, for Hobbes, the succession of desires and aversions is all that deliberation is. Deliberation is but desires and aversions "aris[ing] alternately" until something is done. And the agent's will is simply "the last appetite or aversion" (L.VI.49,53).

But how can this be? Deliberation necessarily involves value or normative judgments. The question an agent attempts to settle in deliberation is "What should I do?" ("What do I have most reason to do?"). How can a succession of desires amount to thinking about and determining reasons and values?

The key to understanding Hobbes's solution to this problem is to appreciate the analogy he makes between color experience and "value experience" (my term, not Hobbes's). All that is really going on when we undergo color experience are certain material motions in us that are caused by certain motions in the matter of the object and the medium. However, this is not all that *seems* to go on. When the motion takes place in us, we experience an "appearance" that is *as of* some color property in the object.

This appearance, we might say, has both a subject and an object. Its *object* is the color property that it appears to be of—say, the redness of the tomato. And Hobbes believed that its subject, what there really is that "makes an appearance," is a bodily motion.

Like the bodily motions that give rise to color appearances, so also do the motions of desire/love and aversion/hate give rise to their distinctive experiential states. And for ethics, Hobbes believed, it is these appearances that make all the difference. Hobbes called them "delight" and "trouble of mind," respectively (L.VI.9). When you desire iced tea on a hot day, you experience "delight" when you consider that possibility. Or when you contemplate passing the rest of the after-

noon without the relief of a cool drink, you experience a "troubled mind."

The motions of desire/love and aversion/hate are the subjects of the appearances "delight" and "troubled mind," respectively. But what are their objects? What are these appearances *as of*? Here is Hobbes's answer: "Delight is the appearance, or sense, of *good;* and molestation or displeasure, the appearance, or sense, of *evil*" (L.VI.10; emphasis added). Desire and aversion, for Hobbes, are what get us thinking about ethics in the first place. To desire something is to see it as good, and to be averse to it is to see it as bad.

The foregoing explains why Hobbes said that "whatsoever is the object of any man's appetite or desire, that is it which he for his part calleth good: and the object of his hate and aversion, evil" (L.VI.7). You have a desire for iced tea. This is a motion in you, but it gives rise to an "appearance" that is as of a property in an object—namely, the value of drinking iced tea. You see that possibility as good. Or, alternatively, you have an aversion to the prospect of passing a thirsty afternoon, and that gives rise to an "appearance" *as of* the "evil" of that alternative.

But as with color appearances, Hobbes believed that there are in fact no properties in "the nature of the objects themselves" answering to our appearances of good and evil. All there are in the object are the material motions that, when they interact with our material nature, give rise to the motions toward and fromward in us that we call desire and aversion. Neither is it the case that we desire certain things *because* we think them good, or are averse to others *because* we think them bad. On the contrary, we see things as good and bad because of our desires and aversions. The experience of value is a projected effect of desire.

This argument calls to mind the **error theory** of ethical judgments. Ethical judgments purport to claim something objective, but, since there actually are no ethical properties answering to what ethical appearances seem to be of, they are always false. But other statements made by Hobbes point toward some version of noncognitivism rather than toward the error theory. "The language of desire and aversion," he wrote, "is *imperative, as do this, forbear that*" (L.VI.55). If we follow out the implications of this remark, we may conclude that the judgments one makes in desire or aversion—that something is good or bad, respectively—have no cognitive content and, hence, cannot be strictly either true *or* false. In the end, it makes little sense to ask whether Hobbes was really a noncognitivist or an error theorist. These distinctions were simply not available in Hobbes's time, and there is no reason to assume that Hobbes clearly saw the differences between these two meta-ethical alternatives.

If Hobbes was an error theorist, moreover, he certainly didn't think that his metaethics posed any obstacle to substantive normative ethical thought or that it dissolved the ethical problems we face. The reason is that Hobbes believed we face value questions as *deliberating agents*. What matters for ethics is the way things seem from the **agent's perspective.** That all our ethical judgments are, strictly speaking, mistaken no more undermines normative ethics than does the strict falsity of color judgments undermine art criticism and interior design.

Laws of Nature and Normativity

Hobbes defined a "law of nature" as "a precept or general rule, found out by reason, by which a man is forbidden to do that, which is destructive of his life, or taketh away the means of preserving the same; and to omit that, by which he thinketh it may be best preserved" (L.XIV.3). He then went on to list and explain some nineteen examples (including one requiring the keeping of covenants), adding in conclusion that these can all be summed up in the golden rule: "Do not that to another, which thou wouldest not have done to thyself" (L.XV.35). Finally, he commented that these "dictates of reason" are only "improperly" called laws. In actuality, they are "theorems concerning what conduceth to the conservation and defence" of a person (L.XV.41).

This distinction raises two large questions. One we shall deal with in the next [section]: How can Hobbes have thought that rules of morality, such as the golden rule and the requirement to keep promises, amount to "theorems" about what will promote self-preservation and self-interest? After all, didn't Hobbes reject the classical natural law theory's metaphysical identification of morality with self-interest? Didn't he think that conflicts of interests are what make political regimes, and forms of practical reasoning, in which individuals are

not guided simply by their own interest, necessary in the first place? Indeed, he did. But as we shall see in the next chapter, he also thought that morality and politics are ultimately grounded in self-interest, nonetheless.

A prior problem arises, however, about how Hobbes could think that even propositions about what will promote self-preservation and self-interest amount to *normative* laws. A theorem about what conduces to our conservation and defense is still just a statement of fact, a true representation of how things happen to stand in the world. What, then, can give it authority or normative force? How can it amount to, or entail, a "dictate" by which one is "forbidden" to fail to do it?

Take a very simple case. Suppose you know that unless you take a particular medicine, you will die. In knowing this, you know a fact about the world. But how do you get from that fact to anything normative? What entitles you to conclude that you should take the medicine? Note that I am not asking you to doubt that you should take the medicine. I am sure we both think that if taking the medicine is necessary to continue a life you want to lead, you should take it. But isn't that because we both think that it would be good for you to continue to live? Or, perhaps, because we think that you have some reason to preserve your life? We appear to need some such normative premise to add to the premise that unless you take the medicine you will die in order to conclude that you should take the medicine. And where do we get that premise?

Now, Hobbes thought that everyone *already* accepts and, moreover, *can't help accepting* the additional normative premise that their continued living is good. It is simply an inescapable feature of the human condition, he thought, that everyone desires continued life and fears death, especially violent death. This feature is hard-wired into our material makeup. Moreover, as we have seen, Hobbes also thought that we are hard-wired to see what we desire as good and what we are averse to as bad. In inescapably desiring to preserve ourselves, therefore, we can't help but see our continued living as good. And in being averse to (violent) death, we unavoidably see that as bad.

This reasoning gives us the premise to add to what would otherwise be simply a fact about what is necessary in order for our lives to continue. We then have the following practical argument:

1. My continued living is good.

   (Or: I should continue to live.

   Or: Continue living!)

2. I will continue to live only if I X.

   Therefore,

3. Xing is good.

   (Or: I should X.

   Or: X!)

What gives laws of nature their normative force is that they all concern necessary means to an end we can't avoid having *together* with the fact that *in* having that end we cannot, as deliberating agents, avoid seeing it as good, as something we should accomplish.

It is important to appreciate the difference between this idea and another one with which it is easily (and frequently) confused. Hobbes is not saying that we should follow the laws of nature because, if we do so, it will get us something we want, even something we inescapably want. Compare the previous argument with this one:

1′. I desire to continue to live.

   (Or: I desire, and can't help desiring, to continue to live.

   Or: My end is to continue to live.)

2′. I will get what I desire (continuing to live), only if I X.

   Therefore,

3′. Xing is good.

   (Or: I should X.)

This argument faces the same problem we confronted when we asked what gives normative force to propositions about the things that promote self-preservation. Unlike (1), but like (2) and (2′), (1′) is simply a statement about how things happen to stand in the world. To get from (1′) and (2′) to (3), we need to assume some further normative premise, such as that it is good to get what one desires, or that one should seek means to one's ends. But where would we get that premise?

And should Hobbes have thought that it is good to get what one desires? That all depends. Hobbes was committed to thinking that *in wanting* something one will see what would satisfy one's desire as good. But from this fact it does not follow that one will see desire-satisfaction as good. That is, one need not see, say, self-preservation as good *on account of* its satisfying one's desire. After all, we sometimes wish we didn't have the desires we do. Wishing this can give rise to another, **second-order desire** that our first order desire not be satisfied. And just as in having the first-order desire, we will see its object as good; so, likewise, in having the second-order not to satisfy our first-order desire, we will see its (the second-order desire's) object as good also. We will see satisfying our first-order desire as bad.

A good example are habits or addictions we regret having. Suppose I have an annoying habit of cracking my knuckles every fifteen minutes or so. I may find myself beset with a desire for a good knuckle-cracking while at the same time desiring that I not satisfy that desire. In having the first desire, I see cracking my knuckles as good; in having the second, I see my not satisfying my desire to crack them as good. Not only am I not committed to thinking it good that my desires be satisfied, here I think that satisfying my desire would be bad.

So, although Hobbes relied on the fact that human beings desire self-preservation, it is not that he thought that that fact provides a reason *itself* for us to do what is necessary to preserve ourselves. The fact that one wants something is not a premise we appeal to in deliberative practical reasoning. (Or, more cautiously stated, if it is, that is because we then have another, second-order desire: the desire to satisfy our first-order desires, or to satisfy this first-order desire, or some such.) That we desire something (whether as a first-order or a second-order matter) is simply a fact about ourselves that can be fully registered from an observer's standpoint without any particular normative ethical import.

Hobbes's position was that *in having* desires we have normative ethical thoughts. We see alternatives as good. And if the desire is inescapable, as Hobbes believed the human desire for self-preservation to be, then we cannot help but see its object as good. This is what gives natural laws normative force for human beings. We are led to conclude that we should do as they say once we see their connection to self-preservation, because we unavoidably see self-preservation, and what is necessary for it, as good.

Hobbes's arguments in *Leviathan* are thus addressed to human agents who deliberate from the perspective provided by their desires and aversions, not from the fact that they have these desires. Ultimately, then, Hobbes's claims about political obligation and its basis in the moral obligation to keep promises are meant to inform the deliberations of his readers and all who hear of his arguments (like you). It is because he thought he could rely on the fact that you, like any human being, can't help desiring to stay alive, and therefore must see your continued living as good, that he thought that if he could convince you that certain policies and actions are necessary for your peaceful survival, he could also convince you that you *should* undertake those policies and actions.

Hobbes II

In [Hobbes I], we saw how Hobbes attempted to solve the problem of normativity that confronts any **metaphysical naturalist:** What place is there for value in a world of fact? Unlike that of the **ethical naturalist,** Hobbes's solution was not to identify value with aspects of nature that are empirically discoverable. It is only as agents having desires that we attribute value. Strictly speaking, then, the value we attribute does not consist in anything we might discover about what we attribute it to (nor in anything about our desires).

But if empirical investigation cannot ground the fundamental values that drive ethical thought and discourse, that doesn't mean that ethics is not in large measure an empirical subject. On the contrary, Hobbes believed that the most interesting and controversial ethical questions concern not fundamental values but empirical issues about how these are best achieved.

The value of a peaceful life, free of the fear of violent death, is a matter of consensus. No one needs to be convinced that his own peace and safety are valuable. What people disagree about are the means of realizing this good. If empirical investigation can establish that cer-

tain universal policies and actions are necessary to achieve peaceful living, however, this will enable human agents to draw the ethical conclusion that they should pursue these policies and actions.

The Problem of Collective Action

But what do strategies that might promote self-preservation have to do with morality? Why think that the moral obligation to keep promises and to abide by the golden rule somehow consist in anything about promoting this end?

We can begin to see the point of these questions *and* how Hobbes proposed to deal with them by considering Hobbes's analysis of the state of nature. By the logic of the argument to this point, every agent is logically committed to judging that she should do what is necessary to preserve her own life. But whereas this makes apparent good sense for each, it is also true that if every agent follows this strategy, and maximizes the chances of her own individual survival, the collective result will be worse for each, a "war of all against all." In Hobbes's view, individuals in a state of nature are faced with what contemporary theorists call a **collective action problem.** If each does what is best for herself, the collective result is worse for all.

A simple version of a collective action problem is the game theory situation known as "prisoner's dilemma." Suppose that two individuals are jailed on suspicion of robbery and that the district attorney approaches each with the following proposition:

> I don't have enough evidence to convict you or your partner of robbery, but I can convict you both of breaking and entering, which carries a sentence of one year. However, if you will confess to robbery and give evidence against your partner, then, if (s)he doesn't confess, you will go free without penalty. If (s)he also confesses, you will both get five years. And if you do not confess, and your partner does, then you will get twenty years and she will go free.

In addition, suppose that no communication is possible between the two prisoners, that each cares only about doing the least time, and, in particular, that neither cares about what happens to the other except insofar as it affects his or her own sentence. What should each do?

The structure of this situation can be illustrated with the following table, which displays the alternative choices C (confess) and NC (not confess) of prisoner A along the left side and of prisoner B along the top. Each pair of choices (one by A, one by B) determines an outcome (a,b) where a is the rank of A's outcome in A's preferential ordering and b is the rank of B's outcome in B's preferential ordering. Thus $(1,4)$ is A's best and B's worst outcome, $(4,1)$ is the reverse, $(2,2)$ is both A's and B's second-best outcome, and $(3,3)$ is next to worst for both.

		B	
		C	NC
	C	(3,3)	(1,4)
A			
	NC	(4,1)	(2,2)

What should A do? Suppose that what B does will not be affected by what A does. B will either confess or not, regardless. If that is so, then it seems A should confess, since *whatever* B does, A will do better if he confesses. If B confesses, then A will get his third- as opposed to his fourth-best outcome by confessing. And if B doesn't confess, then A will get his first- as opposed to his second-best outcome by confessing. So A should confess. A will do better by confessing, whatever B does.

But B's situation is exactly analogous to A's, so any reasons for A to confess apply equally to B. So if A would do best to confess, then so would B. Now you can see why this is called a collective action *problem*. A's and B's actions, each of which is likeliest to achieve the best outcome taken individually, when taken together yield an outcome that is worse for each. If both prisoners do what would be best for him or her, given the actions of the other, they will both confess. But that yields an outcome (3,3) that is worse for both than another outcome they could have achieved. In other words, if both do not confess, the result would be (2,2) rather than (3,3).

Roughly speaking, Hobbes believed that a state of nature is a situation in which people face prisoner's dilemmas with many others in choosing between aggressive and nonaggressive conduct. What makes a situation a prisoner's dilemma, in general, is a certain structure of conflicting interests—for example, that each person's most preferred outcome is the other's least preferred. Hobbes believed that there are various seeds of such conflict in the state of nature. For one thing, there is competition over the goods of nature necessary to ensure that a person in uncertain circumstances has the power to continue to satisfy his desires into the future. For another, some of the things people desire, like status and prestige, necessarily cannot be shared. There is no way, for instance, to expand the stock of "recognition" jointly to satisfy two people, each of whom wants more recognition than the other. For these and other reasons, Hobbes believed that it is near enough true that the result of one person's "invad[ing] for gain" when another does not is that the victor gets his favorite result and the loser suffers her worst. This situation yields the same (1,4), (4,1) pattern as that seen in the southwest and northeast corners of the prisoner's dilemma table. Additionally, if each holds his or her fire, the result is (2,2), a peaceful compromise, and if each invades, the result is (3,3), a "war of all against all." These are analogous to the situations in which both prisoners confess and both don't confess, respectively—as depicted in the southeast and northwest corners of the prisoner's dilemma table. If, consequently, we set C = aggress and NC = not aggress, we can generate a table for a two-person "state of nature game" from that for the prisoner's dilemma.

Assuming once more that the choices of each person are independent of those of the other (we won't worry that this scenario is unrealistic), we again have the same collective action problem. For each, aggression is the action that is individually best, since each thereby does better, whatever the other does. If the other aggresses, then one avoids being vanquished, albeit at the cost of continued war. And if the other is not aggressive, then one can get the spoils of victory rather than acquiescing in compromise. Apparently, therefore, aggression is individually best for each. But as in the prisoner's dilemma, if both do what is individually best, the collective result is worse for both. The two land themselves in a "war of all against all," which is worse for both than the peaceful compromise that would have resulted from joint nonaggression.

What If Everyone Did That?

There are various reasons why one might want to take issue with the use of prisoner's dilemma as an analysis of a state of nature (or even as an interpretation of Hobbes). But our interest is less in Hobbes's political philosophy than in his underlying view of morality, so we can largely ignore these reasons. What will matter for us is Hobbes's employment of the moral obligation to keep promises and the way he attempts to ground the moral 'ought' in the practical reasoning of a deliberating agent.

Before that, however, we would do well to notice that many questions of morality, especially those concerning fairness, are centered in problems of collective action. Take, for example, the state of nature as we've described it. Isn't it natural to think something like the following: If everyone would be better off if we all just restrained our aggressiveness, then why isn't it simply wrong to be aggressive? Perhaps it is, but might that not also depend on whether others are restraining themselves? Or, at least, on whether they are willing to do so? If others are not, then there is no role that one can play in securing collective benefit by restraining oneself. In this case, fairness to others apparently does not require self-restraint, since fairness requires only that one do one's *share*. Any obligation to act is conditional on the comparable good-faith efforts of others.

But what if others do their share? In that case, fairness does require doing one's share as well. It is unfair to take advantage of the sacrifices of others for mutual advantage and not do one's share. As we will see, Hobbes was in basic agreement with this idea, but he was not willing to take for granted that we ought to be fair. He believed that some explanation is needed of why this is so, an explanation that could be convincing from the perspective of a deliberating agent.

But again, notice how deeply this idea and the associated notion of a collective action problem runs throughout our common life and thought about morality. People are frequently prepared to accept sacrifices and burdens themselves because they know that only if everyone does so can many outcomes they highly value be achieved: a clean environment, uncluttered and safe streets, civil and honest conversation, and so on, not to mention the basic trust that provides the glue for social life. They know that if everyone simply pursued his or her own interests without concern for how things would be "if everyone did that," the world would be a much poorer place than it is. And they take this fact as giving them reason—a moral reason—not to act this way themselves.

Care is needed to see the precise point here. The idea is not just that people are prepared to sacrifice their other interests when they have weightier interests in such things as a clean environment and a peaceful society that would be furthered by their own action. When this is the situation, we don't have a collective action problem so much as a problem of balancing short-term versus long-term or narrower versus broader concerns within an agent's self-interest and furthering values about which the agent actually cares more over the longer term, even if that calls for sacrificing some of her other more pressing present interests. Collective action problems occur when collective harm results from individuals' unrestricted pursuit of even their broader and longer-term interests. Fairness may require that they restrain themselves in such situations, even if their doing so on these occasions is not necessary to promote the larger interests that are furthered by the cooperative collective scheme.

Consider the example of petty income-tax fraud (such as not declaring tips from a summer job waiting tables). For many people, it may be in their interest to make fraudulent claims on their tax returns, so long as these do not exceed a certain magnitude. The chances of being caught may be sufficiently low, the possible penalties sufficiently insignificant, and the harms to others and to mutual trust sufficiently uncertain that fraud of this order may be best from the individual's self-interested point of view, *even when* the person's interests in public welfare, mutual trust, and so on, are figured in. In certain cases, the difference made by such petty fraud may not be large enough to offset the losses to the individual of forgoing it. Yet it may nonetheless be true that if everyone were to commit tax fraud in precisely this kind of case, the collective result would be substantially worse for all.

When this is true—when, that is, a person would want to avoid the results of collective fraud—and when others forgo fraud on the condition that their doing so will be reciprocated, fairness requires doing so oneself as well. And it does so no less in the case where "doing one's share" involves some sacrifice, even a sacrifice reckoned on a full accounting of the interests one has in the valuable ends that fair cooperative schemes promote.

Fairness, Natural Law, and Political Authority

The idea of fairness—that it is wrong to take advantage of others' sacrifices for mutual benefit when one is not prepared to sacrifice oneself—is very close to the version of the golden rule with which Hobbes summarized the "laws of nature": "Do not that to another, which thou wouldest not have done to thyself." What this means is not that one shouldn't act toward others in ways that may *cause* them to treat one as one "wouldest not have." Rather, it means that one should not act toward others in ways one would not *have* them act toward one, whether or not it will cause them to act in those ways. However, Hobbes also said that this summary of the laws (and the laws it summarizes) obligate to action only on the condition that others actually follow them as well. The person who follows these laws when others do not "make[s] himself a prey to others, and procure[s] his own ruin, contrary to the ground of all laws of nature" (L.XV.36).

This is why, Hobbes believed, there can be no general moral obligation of fairness to restrain aggression in a state of nature. Without a political authority with sovereign power, people simply lack the security of knowing that others will restrain themselves. And without this security they lack any reason of fairness to engage in self-restraint themselves. Only when a political authority exists with sufficient power to compel those who are not fair-minded will those who are prepared to restrain themselves so long as others do have adequate reason to do so.

But how can political authority be established? What can make it the case that people ought to obey the sovereign? The considerations in the last paragraph might lead one to think that this problem can be solved easily enough by the sovereign's having power to compel obedience. But thinking that only pushes the problem back a step. What can make it the case that such sovereign

power exists? That also depends on the willingness of others to obey the sovereign, if only those who enforce his penalties—for example, his police.

Hobbes proposed that a sovereign can acquire the requisite power and authority through a mutual covenant in which all effectively promise not to oppose him and authorize him to act on their behalf. This means, then, that *both* the (political) obligation to obey the sovereign and the moral obligations involved in all the laws of nature summarized in the golden rule depend upon the obligation to keep covenants. People are obligated to obey the sovereign only because they have promised to do so and because they are obligated to keep their promises. Additionally, they are obligated by fairness to follow the other laws of nature, and to not act toward others as they would not have others act toward them, only on the condition that others will act similarly. And others will act similarly only if sovereign authority exists. Finally, since that will be so only if people are obligated to keep their promises, it follows that the obligations summarized in the golden rule will be binding only if there is an obligation to keep covenants.

Why Should We Keep Promises? Hobbes's Reply to the Fool

But what grounds the obligation to keep promises? What makes it the case that "men should keep their covenants made?" Here we must link up Hobbes's account of normativity and value judgment, sketched in [Hobbes I], with the question of whether to keep promises. And an obvious problem arises. The former account proceeds in terms of an agent's reasoning from ends to means—most prominently, from the end of self-preservation. But there is no guarantee that keeping any particular covenant will be necessary for self-preservation. On the contrary, the agent's own ends (specifically, self-preservation) may conflict with keeping any particular covenant. How, then, could Hobbes consistently think that we should keep a covenant even when we appear to lack adequate reason to do so that can be based in self-interest?

In *Leviathan*, Hobbes put this precise challenge in the mouth of a character he calls "the fool," who says "in his heart, there is no such thing as justice" (L.XV.4). Justice, for Hobbes, is a matter of keeping covenants (L.XV.2).

So in denying the existence of justice, the fool is denying any obligation to keep covenants. The fool's positive position is that a person should do only what will promote her preservation and interest, and, accordingly, that "to make, or not make; keep, or not keep covenants, was not against reason, when it conduced to one's benefit" (L.XV.4).

When we recall Hobbes's account of normativity and normative judgment as grounded in an agent's practical reasoning from ends to means, we may well wonder why the fool's position is not Hobbes's own. All human agents judge their ends to be good. So when someone views some action or policy as necessary to some end, she naturally sees the action or policy as one she should pursue. It seems to follow that anyone would also naturally regard any reason she has to make or keep a promise as being conditional on whether making or keeping the promise will "conduce to" her livelihood or benefit, just as the fool says.

But Hobbes rejected this position, and it is important to see why. To understand his reasoning, we must first appreciate the unique and pervasive role that covenants play in the state of nature, as Hobbes saw it. We already know part of the story. It is only through a mutual covenant establishing a sovereign that individuals can escape from a state of perpetual war. But Hobbes also believed that the general need for covenants in the state of nature is significantly more pervasive than this *and* that it would have to be in order for a mutual covenant establishing political sovereignty even to be possible.

No person can expect to survive in a state of nature by going it alone. People are too equal in power. No individual is completely invulnerable to the power of others, so no person can expect to keep himself in even relative safety through his own devices. As Hobbes put it, "There is no man who can hope by his own strength, or wit, to defend himself from destruction, without the help of confederates; where every one expects the same defence by the confederation, that any one else does" (L.XV.5). But such confederacies can come into existence only through covenants. Each member must agree to do his share in defending other members in exchange for their help in defending him. Covenants are therefore necessary not only to the lasting escape from a state of war through the establishing of a sovereign, but also to whatever temporary defense and security a person can secure through membership in an association united for mutual defense while in the state of nature. And since covenants are necessary even for temporary safety, it follows that preserving one's ability to make covenants is absolutely crucial to self-preservation.

Now, any covenant for mutual defense depends upon the participants being able to expect that those with whom they contract will keep it or, a least, on their having no expectation that they won't or no reasonable doubt that they will. Until a sovereign is established who can enforce them, mutual promises become void on "any reasonable suspicion" that one party will not keep her part of the bargain (L.XIV.18). In order for a covenant to be possible, therefore, the potential participants must have no justified doubts about the willingness of the others to do what they have promised to do. This means that the reputation of trustworthiness is among the most precious resources that any individual can have in the state of nature. And it means as well that individuals have substantial incentives to discover whether others actually are trustworthy.

To be of value, covenants for mutual defense must last for some time. On any given occasion, therefore, the question of whether to keep such a covenant will be significantly affected by the facts that one will want continued acceptance as a member and that others' doing so may substantially depend on whether one keeps the covenant on this occasion. In this critically important kind of case, then, we have an example of what game theorists call an "iterated" rather than a "one-shot" prisoner's dilemma. An iterated prisoner's dilemma is not a collective action problem of the same kind as the one-shot version. When a prisoner's dilemma is repeated indefinitely between the same two individuals, as is likely with mutual defense associations, each will do better collectively *and* individually by cooperating rather than competing. Here the outcomes are actually different from those in the one-shot version, since even if each individual's present choices are independent of others', others' future choices will not be independent of the individuals' present choices. Each has a substantial incentive to keep his or her promises on this occasion, to ensure that the mutually beneficial arrangement will continue.

For these kinds of reasons, we might expect Hobbes to argue that breaking covenants can never be to a person's overall benefit. There may appear to be cases when this would be beneficial, but only when we erroneously discount further effects on reputation and others' willingness to enter into covenants with us in the future. Taking full account of the risks *and* costs of reduced trust shows that such benefit can never really be realized.

This reply would meet the fool's challenge on its own terms. It would grant its premise, yet deny its conclusion. But Hobbes did not make this reply, and we can see why he avoided it. However precious trust and reputation may be, it seems implausible to suppose that keeping covenants is always in a person's interest. Surely there are *some* circumstances in which breaking a covenant would do insufficient harm to outweigh the benefits, even when all costs are fully accounted for. And maybe such circumstances are not even all that infrequent. After all, not every covenant will go on indefinitely with the same individuals. And even in cases where they do, compliance can't always be monitored.

In any event, Hobbes did not deny the fool's premise that breaking covenants may sometimes actually be in a person's interest. What he denies is that it is ever *wise* to break a covenant, even in a state of nature, unless the contract has been voided by reasonable suspicion of the other's defaulting. Hobbes's reason was that even if there are cases where breaking a covenant might be beneficial, one can never *know* for sure that one is in such a situation, and the risks and costs are such that the wisest *policy* is always to keep a covenant rather than taking a chance.

There are two important points here. One is that the wisdom of a choice does not depend on its *actual* outcome. If someone successfully plays Russian roulette to win a bet of twenty dollars, the fact that he ends up better off does not mean that his action was "reasonably or wisely done" (L.XV.5). At the very least, it matters which act the person would reasonably believe likeliest to have the best outcome on the evidence available to him.

But there are some cases where it may not even make sense to act on one's most reasonable estimate of the best outcome. The quality of one's evidence may be poor, or even pretty good, but not good enough to warrant taking a chance. To see this, consider from your *current* perspective what you would want yourself to do in a hypothetical situation in which someone offers you

ten thousand dollars to play Russian roulette. Suppose that you will be permitted to decide whether to pull the trigger or not after having rotated the chamber, and suppose also that you will then be very confident that you can recognize whether the bullet is in the chamber that has come up. (For example, suppose that you will be permitted to see it put in a chamber with a recognizable mark.) In this hypothetical situation, you twirl the chamber and believe that the chances are only one in a million that the chamber with the bullet has come up and, therefore, that if you merely put the gun to your head and pull the trigger, you have a .99999 chance of being ten thousand dollars richer and only a .000001 chance of losing your life. As decision theorists will point out, under these circumstances the "expected value" of pulling the trigger is positive unless you value your life at ten billion dollars or more. Would this commit you to thinking, from your current perspective, that it is reasonable or wise for you to pull the trigger in the hypothetical situation? Would you want yourself to? Many people would not. Even if you are prepared to take risks of the same magnitude when you have no reasonable alternative to doing so, you may believe that, here, the risk just isn't worth taking.

This is the second point: Hobbes believed that breaking a covenant is like playing Russian roulette in that it is something that just doesn't make sense to do even if it is likeliest to have the best outcome in an individual case. The *policy* or *rule* of always keeping covenants is a better means, *in general,* to any human agent's self-interest and self-preservation than is the policy of determining whether to keep covenants on a case-by-case basis according to whether doing so is likeliest in that instance to have the best outcome.

The policy of always keeping covenants was Hobbes's final answer to the fool, thereby connecting up his normative thesis that a person should not break contracts with his account of normative judgment. By virtue of inescapably desiring self-preservation, any human agent regards his interests and continued living as good. For a variety of reasons, the *general* rule or policy of always keeping covenants is a more effective means to these ends than is determining whether to do as one has promised on a case-by-case basis. By appreciating this, therefore, any human agent has reason to agree that she should follow the general policy or rule of keeping her covenants.

And if she should follow this general policy or rule, Hobbes apparently assumed, then she should follow it even on those occasions when she thinks, even reasonably, that she would do better by breaking her covenants.

Summary: Hobbes's Theory of Morality and Moral Obligation

For Hobbes, morality is a set of rules, the general following of which solves collective action problems. That is why he said that the laws of nature (morality) can be summed up in the idea that we should not do to others what we would not have them do to us. For morality to be in "force," however, there must be something that can guarantee that others are prepared to do their fair share in the cooperative (moral) solution to problems of collective action. Hobbes believed that, ultimately, it requires a sovereign with the authority and power to compel those who are not fair-minded to give those who *are* adequate reason to do their share.

When, however, there is some reasonable confidence that others are doing their share in the collective solution, then one should oneself. But why? Ultimately, Hobbes agreed with the fool that the mere fact that a rule is collectively beneficial is not a justification in itself for one to follow it. Rather, to convince a deliberating agent, any justification must be relevant to what *the agent* values him- or herself. And this, Hobbes agrees with the fool, ultimately requires reference to what will promote the *agent's own* preservation or interest.

For Hobbes, what brings these two ends together—the individual agent's good and the collective good—is *mutual agreement*. We cannot survive without the cooperation of others, and we cannot have that without being prepared to cooperate with them. In the end, then, morality is a system of *reciprocity*, in which all are prepared to do their share so long as others are. But even here there is a difference between the sort of reciprocity that morality (the golden rule) requires and the sort that must exist for morality to really be binding on agents, in Hobbes's view. Morality dictates that we should not do what we would not have others do, regardless of whether this will cause them to show such restraint. To put it differently, morality says that fairness is intrinsically valuable or required, and not just because it causes others to be fair.

Now Hobbes agreed that, in the final analysis, it makes sense to *regard* moral claims this way. However, he also thought that our doing so is ultimately justified by the fact that any person's (individually) so regarding them serves his or her interests. We might reconcile these two points by saying that, for Hobbes, morality consists in rules that, if *everyone* follows, *everyone* benefits from; but what makes it the case that any particular agent *should* follow moral rules is that *his* following them serves *his* own interests.

The foregoing exemplifies one thing that is meant by **externalism** in ethics: What makes it the case that a moral requirement is normatively binding, something an agent really ought to follow, is external to what grounds the moral requirement in the first place. For Hobbes, moral rule are based on *collective* interest, but what makes them normatively binding is the *agent's own* interest.

Conclusion and Remaining Issues

This conception of morality is a philosophically powerful and influential one. Its great virtue is that it aims to show how morality can be *normative* for human agents (in normal circumstances) in a way that is consistent with metaphysical naturalism. Without problematic metaphysical or epistemological assumptions, Hobbes was able to go a long way toward showing that there are universal rules or "laws" by which people should live.

Should we accept Hobbes's theories? In closing, let me mention two potential obstacles to doing so. One problem is internal to Hobbes's own project. Suppose we grant that a person will do better, in general, by following the rule or policy of keeping covenants, and by following the other moral rules when there is established political authority. Why does such a rationale show that, on any particular occasion, an agent should do what this general rule or policy dictates?

Look at it from your perspective as a deliberating human agent. You value self-preservation. And your doing so gives you a reason to follow the general policy. But here is a case where the general policy seems to give the wrong answer. It is clear to you, on this occasion, that you will do significantly better by all you value if you depart from the best general policy. Since the general policy is sensible to follow only because it promotes what you value, and since, on this occasion, what you value is clearly better promoted by departing from it, why doesn't it make sense to depart from it? This problem is hardly crippling, as the Russian roulette examples shows. But it can seem troubling nonetheless.

The other problem is external to Hobbes's line of thought—namely, whether ultimately basing morality on self-interest captures the way in which, as we ordinarily think, *normativity is intrinsic* to morality. For an externalist like Hobbes, what makes something a dictate of *morality* is one thing and what makes it normatively binding on us (something we ought to follow) is another. When we view things from within the perspective of moral thought, however, does it really seem that the only reason we should do what morality requires is

that, ultimately, it will pay us? On the contrary, does it not seem that something's being wrong is *itself* reason enough? Does it not seem, in other words, that internalism rather than externalism is true?

To return to [an earlier example]: When you are outraged by the torture of innocents, do you really think that the reason people ought not to torture is that ultimately *they* will be worse off if they do? To be sure, Hobbes thought he could explain the sense we may have that this is not so, since it is for our benefit so to regard these rules in general. But isn't it a worry that this interpretation involves a kind of divided thinking? What we think from within the moral perspective seems directly at odds with the externalist justification Hobbes provides.

Albert Camus

The Myth of Sisyphus

The gods had condemned Sisyphus to ceaselessly rolling a rock to the top of a mountain, whence the stone would fall back of its own weight. They had thought with some reason that there is no more dreadful punishment than futile and hopeless labor.

If one believes Homer, Sisyphus was the wisest and most prudent of mortals. According to another tradition, however, he was disposed to practice the profession of highwayman. I see no contradiction in this. Opinions differ as to the reasons why he became the futile laborer of the underworld. To begin with, he is accused of a certain levity in regard to the gods. He stole their secrets. Ægina, the daughter of Æsopus, was carried off by Jupiter. The father was shocked by that

disappearance and complained to Sisyphus. He, who knew of the abduction, offered to tell about it on condition that Æsopus would give water to the citadel of Corinth. To the celestial thunderbolts he preferred the benediction of water. He was punished for this in the underworld. Homer tells us also that Sisyphus had put Death in chains. Pluto could not endure the sight of his deserted, silent empire. He dispatched the god of war, who liberated Death from the hands of her conqueror.

It is said also that Sisyphus, being near to death, rashly wanted to test his wife's love. He ordered her to cast his unburied body into the middle of the public square. Sisyphus woke up in the underworld. And there, annoyed by an obedience so contrary to human love, he obtained from Pluto permission to return to earth in order to chastise his wife. But when he had seen again the face of this world, enjoyed water and sun, warm stones and the sea, he no longer wanted to go back to the infernal darkness. Recalls, signs of anger, warnings were of no avail. Many years more be lived facing the curve of the gulf, the sparkling sea, and the smiles of earth. A decree of the gods was necessary. Mercury came and seized the impudent man by the collar and, snatching him from his joys, led him forcibly back to the underworld, where his rock was ready for him.

You have already grasped that Sisyphus is the absurd hero. He *is*, as much through his passions as through his torture. His scorn of the gods, his hatred of death, and his passion for life won him that unspeakable penalty in which the whole being is exerted toward accomplishing nothing. This is the price that must be paid for the passions of this earth. Nothing is told us about Sisyphus in the underworld. Myths are made for the imagination to breathe life into them. As for this myth, one sees merely the whole effort of a body straining to raise the huge stone, to roll it and push it up a slope a hundred times over; one, sees the face screwed up, the cheek tight against the stone, the shoulder bracing the clay-covered mass, the foot wedging it, the fresh start with arms outstretched, the wholly human security of two earth-clotted hands. At the very end of his long effort measured by skyless space and time without depth, the purpose is achieved. Then Sisyphus watches the stone rush down in a few moments toward that lower world whence he will have to push it up again toward the summit. He goes back down to the plain.

It is during that return, that pause, that Sisyphus interests me. A face that toils so close to stones is already stone itself! I see that man going back down with a heavy yet measured step toward the torment of which he will never know the end. That hour like a breathing space which returns as surely as his suffering, that is the hour of consciousness. At each of those moments when he leaves the heights and gradually sinks toward the lairs of the gods, he is superior to his fate. He is stronger than his rock.

If this myth is tragic, that is because its hero is conscious. Where would his torture be, indeed, if at every step the hope of succeeding upheld him? The workman of today works every day in his life at the same tasks, and this fate is no less absurd. But it is tragic only at the rare moments when it becomes conscious. Sisyphus, proletarian of the gods, powerless and rebellious, knows the whole extent of his wretched condition: it is what he thinks of during his descent. The lucidity that was to constitute his torture at the same time crowns his victory. There is no fate that cannot be surmounted by scorn.

If the descent is thus sometimes performed in sorrow, it can also take place in joy. This word is not too much. Again I fancy Sisyphus returning toward his rock, and the sorrow was in the beginning. When the images of earth cling too tightly to memory, when the call of happiness becomes too insistent, it happens that melancholy rises in man's heart: this is the rock's victory, this is the rock itself. The boundless grief is too heavy to bear. These are our nights of Gethsemane. But crushing truths perish from being acknowledged. Thus, Oedipus at the outset obeys fate without knowing it. But from the moment he knows, his tragedy begins. Yet at the same moment, blind and desperate, he realizes that the only bond linking him to the world is the cool hand of a girl. Then a tremendous remark rings out: "Despite so many ordeals, my advanced age and the nobility of my soul make me conclude that all is well," Sophocles' Oedipus, like Dostoevsky's Kirilov, thus gives the recipe for the absurd victory. Ancient wisdom confirms modern heroism.

One does not discover the absurd without being tempted to write a manual of happiness. "What! by such narrow ways—?" There is but one world, however. Happiness and the absurd are two sons of the same earth. They are inseparable. It would be a mistake to say that happiness necessarily springs from the absurd discovery. It happens as well that the feeling of the absurd springs from happiness. "I conclude that all is well", says Oedipus, and that remark is sacred. It echoes in the wild and limited universe of man. It teaches that all is not, has not been, exhausted. It drives out of this world a god who had come into it with dissatisfaction and a preference for futile sufferings. It makes of fate a human matter, which must be settled among men.

All Sisyphus' silent joy is contained therein. His fate belongs to him. His rock is his thing. Likewise, the absurd man, when be contemplates his torment, silences all the idols. In the universe suddenly restored to its silence, the myriad wondering little voices of the earth rise up. Unconscious, secret calls, invitations from all the faces, they are the necessary reverse and price of victory. There is no sun without shadow, and it is essential to know the night. The absurd man says yes and his effort will henceforth be unceasing. If there is a personal fate, there is no higher destiny, or at least there is but one which he concludes is inevitable and despicable. For the rest, he knows himself to be the master of his days. At that subtle moment when man glances backward over his life, Sisyphus returning toward his rock, in that slight pivoting he contemplates that series of unrelated actions which becomes his fate, created by him, combined under his memory's eye and soon sealed by his death. Thus, convinced of the wholly human origin of all that is human, a blind man eager to see who knows that the night has no end, he is still on the go. The rock is still rolling.

I leave Sisyphus at the foot of the mountain! One always finds one's burden again. But Sisyphus teaches the higher fidelity that negates the gods and raises rocks. He too concludes that all is well. This universe henceforth without a master seems to him neither sterile nor futile. Each atom of that stone, each mineral flake of that night-filled mountain, in itself forms a world. The struggle itself toward the heights is enough to fill a man's heart. One must imagine Sisyphus happy.

Robert Nozick

The Experience Machine

There are also substantial puzzles when we ask what matters other than how *people's* experiences feel "from the inside." Suppose there were an experience machine that would give you any experience you desired. Superduper neuropsychologists could stimulate your brain so that you would think and feel you were writing a great novel, or making a friend, or reading an interesting book. All the time you would be floating in a tank, with electrodes attached to your brain. Should you plug into this machine for life, preprogramming your life's experiences? If you are worried about missing out on desirable experiences, we can suppose that business enterprises have researched thoroughly the lives of many others. You can pick and choose from their large library or smorgasbord of such experiences, selecting your life's experiences for, say, the next two years. After two years have passed, you will have ten minutes or ten hours out of the tank, to select the experiences of your *next* two years. Of course, while in the tank you won't know that you're there, you'll think it's all actually happening.

Others can also plug in to have the experiences they want, so there's no need to stay unplugged to serve them. (Ignore problems such as who will service the machines if everyone plugs in.) Would you plug in? *What else can matter to us, other than how our lives feel from the inside?* Nor should you refrain because of the few moments of distress between the moment you've decided and the moment you're plugged. What's a few moments of distress compared to a lifetime of bliss (if that's what you choose), and why feel any distress at all if your decision *is* the best one?

What does matter to us in addition to our experiences? First, we want to *do* certain things, and not just have the experience of doing them. In the case of certain experiences, it is only because first we want to do the actions that we want the experiences of doing them or thinking we've done them. (But *why* do we want to do the activities rather than merely to experience them?) A second reason for not plugging in is that we want to *be* a certain way, to be a certain sort of person. Someone floating in a tank is an indeterminate blob. There is no answer to the question of what a person is like who has long been in the tank. Is he courageous, kind, intelligent, witty, loving? It's not merely that it's difficult to tell; there's no way he is. Plugging into the machine is a kind of suicide. It will seem to some,

From *Anarchy, State, and Utopia* by Robert Nozick, ISBN 0465097200. Copyright © 1974 by Basic Books. Reprinted by permission of Basic Books, a member of Perseus Books Group, L.L.C.

trapped by a picture, that nothing about what we are like can matter except as it gets reflected in our experiences. But should it be surprising that what *we are* is important to us? Why should we be concerned only with how our time is filled, but not with what we are?

Thirdly, plugging into an experience machine limits us to a man-made reality, to a world no deeper or more important than that which people can construct. There is no *actual* contact with any deeper reality, though the experience of it can be simulated. Many persons desire to leave themselves open to such contact and to a plumbing of deeper significance. This clarifies the intensity of the conflict over psychoactive drugs, which some view as mere local experience machines, and others view as avenues to a deeper reality; what some view as equivalent to surrender to the experience machine, others view as following one of the reasons *not* to surrender!

We learn that something matters to us in addition to experience by imagining an experience machine and then realizing that we would not use it. We can continue to imagine a sequence of machines each designed to fill lacks suggested for the earlier machines. For example, since the experience machine doesn't meet our desire to *be* a certain way, imagine a transformation machine which transforms us into whatever sort of person we'd like to be (compatible with our staying us). Surely one would not use the transformation machine to become as one would wish, and thereupon plug into the experience machine! So something matters in addition to one's experiences *and* what one is like. Nor is the reason merely that one's experiences are unconnected with what one is like. For the experience machine might be limited to provide only experiences possible to the sort of person plugged in. Is it that we want to make a difference in the world? Consider then the result machine, which produces in the world any result you would produce and injects your vector input into any joint activity. We shall not pursue here the fascinating details of these or other machines. What is most disturbing about them is their living of our lives for us. Is it misguided to search for *particular* additional functions beyond the competence of machines to do for us? Perhaps what we desire is to live (an active verb) ourselves, in contact with reality. (And this, machines cannot do *for* us.) Without elaborating on the implications of this, which I believe connect surprisingly with issues about free will and causal accounts of knowledge, we need merely note the intricacy of the question of what matters *for people* other then their experiences. Until one finds a satisfactory answer, and determines that this answer does not *also* apply to animals, one cannot reasonably claim that only the felt experiences of animals limit what we may do to them.

Metaethics

David Hume

The Emotive and Social Basis of Ethics

Of virtue and vice in general

I: *Moral distinctions not deriv'd from reason*

There is an inconvenience which attends all abstruse reasoning, that it may silence, without convincing an antagonist, and requires the same intense study to make us sensible of its force, that was at first requisite for its invention. When we leave our closet, and engage in the common affairs of life, its conclusions seem to vanish, like the phantoms of the night on the appearance of the morning; and 'tis difficult for us to retain even that conviction, which we had attain'd with difficulty. This is still more conspicuous in a long chain of reasoning, where we must preserve to the end the evidence of the first propositions, and where we often lose sight of all the most receiv'd maxims, either of philosophy or common life. I am not, however, without hopes, that the present system of philosophy will acquire new force as it advances; and that our reasonings concerning morals will corroborate whatever has been said concerning the *understanding* and the *passions*. Morality is a subject that interests us above all others: We fancy the peace of society to be at stake in every decision concerning it; and 'tis evident, that this concern must make our speculations appear more real and solid, than where the subject is, in a great measure, indifferent to us. What affects us, we conclude can never be a chimera; and as our passion is engag'd on the one side or the other, we naturally think

From David Hume, *Moral Philosophy,* edited by Geoffrey Sayre-McCord (Indianapolis: Hackett Publishing Company, 2006). Reprinted by permission of the publisher.

that the question lies within human comprehension; which, in other cases of this nature, we are apt to entertain some doubt of. Without this advantage I never should have ventur'd upon a third volume of such abstruse philosophy, in an age, wherein the greatest part of men seem agreed to convert reading into an amusement, and to reject every thing that requires any considerable degree of attention to be comprehended.

It has been observ'd, that nothing is ever present to the mind but its perceptions; and that all the actions of seeing, hearing, judging, loving, hating, and thinking, fall under this denomination. The mind can never exert itself in any action, which we may not comprehend under the term of *perception;* and consequently that term is no less applicable to those judgments, by which we distinguish moral good and evil, than to every other operation of the mind. To approve of one character, to condemn another, are only so many different perceptions.

Now as perceptions resolve themselves into two kinds, viz. *impressions* and *ideas,* this distinction gives rise to a question, with which we shall open up our present enquiry concerning morals. *Whether 'tis by means of our ideas or impressions we distinguish betwixt vice and virtue, and pronounce an action blameable or praise-worthy?* This will immediately cut off all loose discourses and declamations, and reduce us to something precise and exact on the present subject.

Those who affirm that virtue is nothing but a conformity to reason; that there are eternal fitnesses and unfitnesses of things, which are the same to every rational being that considers them; that the immutable measures of right and wrong impose an obligation, not only on human creatures, but also on the Deity himself: All these systems concur in the opinion, that morality, like truth, is discern'd merely by ideas, and by their juxta-position and comparison. In order, therefore, to judge of these systems, we need only consider, whether it be possible, from reason alone, to distinguish betwixt moral good and evil, or whether there must concur some other principles to enable us to make that distinction.

If morality had naturally no influence on human passions and actions, 'twere in vain to take such pains to inculcate it; and nothing wou'd be more fruitless than that multitude of rules and precepts, with which all moralists abound. Philosophy is commonly divided into *speculative* and *practical;* and as morality is always comprehended under the latter division, 'tis supposed to influence our passions and actions, and to go beyond the calm and indolent judgments of the understanding. And this is confirm'd by common experience, which informs us, that men are often govern'd by their duties, and are deter'd from some actions by the opinion of injustice, and impell'd to others by that of obligation.

Since morals, therefore, have an influence on the actions and affections, it follows, that they cannot be deriv'd from reason; and that because reason alone, as we have already prov'd, can never have any such influence. Morals excite passions, and produce or prevent actions. Reason of itself is utterly impotent in this particular. The rules of morality, therefore, are not conclusions of our reason.

No one, I believe, will deny the justness of this inference; nor is there any other means of evading it, than by denying that principle, on which it is founded. As long as it is allow'd, that reason has no influence on our passions and actions, 'tis in vain to pretend, that morality is discover'd only by a deduction of reason. An active principle can never be founded on an inactive; and if reason be inactive in itself, it must remain so in all its shapes and appearances, whether it exerts itself in natural or moral subjects, whether it considers the powers of external bodies, or the actions of rational beings.

It would be tedious to repeat all the arguments, by which I have prov'd, that reason is perfectly inert, and can never either prevent or produce any action or affection. 'Twill be easy to recollect what has been said upon that subject. I shall only recal on this occasion one of these arguments, which I shall endeavour to render still more conclusive, and more applicable to the present subject.

Reason is the discovery of truth or falshood. Truth or falshood consists in an agreement or disagreement either to the *real* relations of ideas, or to *real* existence and matter of fact. Whatever, therefore, is not susceptible of this agreement or disagreement, is incapable of being true or false, and can never be an object of our reason. Now 'tis evident our passions, volitions, and actions, are not susceptible of any such agreement or disagreement; being original facts and realities, compleat in themselves, and implying no reference to other passions, volitions, and actions. 'Tis impossible, therefore, they can be pronounc'd either true or false, and be either contrary or conformable to reason.

This argument is of double advantage to our present purpose. For it proves *directly,* that actions do not derive their merit from a conformity to reason, nor their blame from a contrariety to it; and it proves the same truth more *indirectly,* by shewing us, that as reason can never immediately prevent or produce any action by contradicting or approving of it, it cannot be the source of distinction betwixt moral good and evil, which are found to have that influence. Actions may be laudable or blameable; but they cannot be reasonable or unreasonable: Laudable or blameable, therefore, are not the same with reasonable or unreasonable. The merit and demerit of actions frequently contradict, and sometimes controul our natural propensities. But reason has no such influence. Moral distinctions, therefore, are not the offspring of reason. Reason is wholly inactive, and can never be the source of so active a principle as conscience, or a sense of morals.

But perhaps it may be said, that tho' no will or action can be immediately contradictory to reason, yet we may find such a contradiction in some of the attendants of the action, that is, in its causes or effects. The action may cause a judgment, or may be *obliquely* caus'd by one, when the judgment concurs with a passion; and by an abusive way of speaking, which philosophy will scarce allow of, the same contrariety may, upon that account, be ascrib'd to the action. How far this truth or falshood may be the source of morals, 'twill now be proper to consider.

It has been observ'd, that reason, in a strict and philosophical sense, can have influence on our conduct only after two ways: Either when it excites a passion by informing us of the existence of something which is a proper object of it; or when it discovers the connexion of causes and effects, so as to afford us means of exerting any passion. These are the only kinds of judgment, which can accompany our actions, or can be said to produce them in any manner; and it must be allow'd, that these judgments may often be false and erroneous. A person may be affected with passion, by supposing a pain or pleasure to lie in an object, which has no tendency to produce either of these sensations, or which produces the contrary to what is imagin'd. A person may also take false measures for the attaining his end, and may retard, by his foolish conduct, instead of forwarding the execution of any project. These false judgments may be thought to affect the passions and actions, which are connected with them, and may be said to render them unreasonable, in a figurative and improper way of speaking. But tho' this be acknowledg'd, 'tis easy to observe, that these errors are so far from being the source of all immorality, that they are commonly very innocent, and draw no manner of guilt upon the person who is so unfortunate as to fall into them. They extend not beyond a mistake of *fact,* which moralists have not generally suppos'd criminal, as being perfectly involuntary. I am more to be lamented than blam'd, if I am mistaken with regard to the influence of objects in producing pain or pleasure, or if I know not the proper means of satisfying my desires. No one can ever regard such errors as a defect in my moral character. A fruit, for instance, that is really disagreeable, appears to me at a distance, and thro' mistake I fancy it to be pleasant and delicious. Here is one error. I choose certain means of reaching this fruit, which are not proper for my end. Here is a second error; nor is there any third one, which can ever possibly enter into our reasonings concerning actions. I ask, therefore, if a man, in this situation, and guilty of these two errors, is to be regarded as vicious and criminal, however unavoidable they might have been? Or if it be possible to imagine, that such errors are the sources of all immorality?

And here it may be proper to observe, that if moral distinctions be deriv'd from the truth or falshood of those judgments, they must take place wherever we form the judgments; nor will there be any difference, whether the question be concerning an apple or a kingdom, or whether the error be avoidable or unavoidable. For as the very essence of morality is suppos'd to consist in an agreement or disagreement to reason, the other circumstances are entirely arbitrary, and can never either bestow on any action the character of virtuous or vicious, or deprive it of that character. To which we may add, that this agreement or disagreement, not admitting of degrees, all virtues and vices wou'd of course be equal.

Shou'd it be pretended, that tho' a mistake of *fact* be not criminal, yet a mistake of *right* often is; and that this may be the source of immorality: I wou'd answer, that 'tis impossible such a mistake can ever be the original source of immorality, since it supposes a real right and wrong; that is, a real distinction in morals, independent of these judgments. A mistake, therefore, of right may become a species of immorality; but 'tis only a secondary one, and is founded on some other, antecedent to it.

As to those judgments which are the *effects* of our actions, and which, when false, give occasion to pronounce the actions contrary to truth and reason; we may observe, that our actions never cause any judgment, either true or false, in ourselves, and that 'tis only on others they have such an influence. 'Tis certain, that an action, on many occasions, may give rise to false conclusions in others; and that a person, who thro' a window sees any lewd behaviour of mine with my neighbour's wife, may be so simple as to imagine she is certainly my own. In this respect my action resembles somewhat a lye or falshood; only with this difference, which is material, that I perform not the action with any intention of giving rise to a false judgment in another, but merely to satisfy my lust and passion. It causes, however, a mistake and false judgment by accident; and the falshood of its effects may be ascrib'd, by some odd figurative way of speaking, to the action itself. But still I can see no pretext of reason for asserting, that the tendency to cause such an error is the first spring or original source of all immorality.

Thus upon the whole, 'tis impossible, that the distinction betwixt moral good and evil, can be made to reason; since that distinction has an influence upon our actions, of which reason alone is incapable. Reason and judgment may, indeed, be the mediate cause of an action, by prompting, or by directing a passion: But it is not pretended that a judgment of this kind, either in its truth or falshood, is attended with virtue or vice. And as to the judgments, which are caus'd by our actions, they can still less bestow those moral qualities on the actions, which are their causes.

But to be more particular, and to shew, that those eternal immutable fitnesses and unfitnesses of things cannot be defended by sound philosophy, we may weigh the following considerations.

If the thought and understanding were alone capable of fixing the boundaries of right and wrong, the character of virtuous and vicious either must lie in some relations of objects, or must be a matter of fact, which is discover'd by our reasoning. This consequence is evident. As the operations of human understanding divide themselves into two kinds, the comparing of ideas, and the inferring of matter of fact; were virtue discover'd by the understanding; it must be an object of one of these operations; nor is there any third operation of the understanding, which can discover it. There has been an opinion very industriously propagated by certain philosophers, that morality is susceptible of demonstration; and tho' no one has ever been able to advance a single step in those demonstrations; yet 'tis taken for granted, that this science may be brought to an equal certainty with geometry or algebra. Upon this supposition, vice and virtue must consist in some relations; since 'tis allow'd on all hands, that no matter of fact is capable of being demonstrated. Let us, therefore, begin with examining this hypothesis, and endeavour, if possible, to fix those moral qualities, which have been so long the objects of our fruitless researches. Point out distinctly the relations, which constitute morality or obligation, that we may know wherein they consist, and after what manner we must judge of them.

If you assert, that vice and virtue consist in relations susceptible of certainty and demonstration, you must confine yourself to those *four* relations which alone admit of that degree of evidence; and in that case you run into absurdities, from which you will never be able to extricate yourself. For as you make the very essence of morality to lie in the relations, and as there is no one of these relations but what is applicable, not only to an irrational but also to an inanimate object; it follows, that even such objects must be susceptible of merit or demerit. *Resemblance, contrariety, degrees in quality,* and *proportions in quantity and number;* all these relations belong as properly to matter, as to our actions, passions, and volitions. 'Tis unquestionable, therefore, that morality lies not in any of these relations, nor the sense of it in their discovery.

Shou'd it be asserted, that the sense of morality consists in the discovery of some relation, distinct from these, and that our enumeration was not compleat, when we comprehended all demonstrable relations under four general heads: To this I know not what to reply, till some one be so good as to point out to me this new relation. 'Tis impossible to refute a system, which has never yet been explain'd. In such a manner of fighting in the dark, a man loses his blows in the air, and often places them where the enemy is not present.

I must, therefore, on this occasion, rest contented with requiring the two following conditions of any one that wou'd undertake to clear up this system. *First,* As moral good and evil belong only to the actions of the mind, and are deriv'd from our situation with regard to external objects, the relations, from which these moral distinctions arise, must lie only betwixt internal actions, and external objects, and must not be applicable either to internal actions, compared among themselves, or to external objects, when plac'd in opposition to other external objects. For as morality is suppos'd to attend certain relations, if these relations cou'd belong to internal actions consider'd singly, it wou'd follow, that we might be guilty of crimes in ourselves, and independent of our situation, with respect to the universe: And in like manner, if these moral relations cou'd be apply'd to external objects, it wou'd follow, that even inanimate beings wou'd be susceptible of moral beauty and deformity. Now it seems difficult to imagine, that any relation can be discover'd betwixt our passions, volitions and actions, compar'd to external objects, which relation might not belong either to these passions and volitions, or to these external objects, compar'd among *themselves.*

But it will be still more difficult to fulfil the *second* condition, requisite to justify this system. According to the principles of those who maintain an abstract rational difference betwixt moral good and evil, and a natural fitness and unfitness of things, 'tis not only suppos'd, that these relations, being eternal and immutable, are the same, when consider'd by every rational creature, but their *effects* are also suppos'd to be necessarily the same; and 'tis concluded they have no less, or rather a greater, influence in directing the will of the deity, than in governing the rational and virtuous of our own species. These two particulars are evidently distinct. 'Tis one thing to know virtue, and another to conform the will to it. In order, therefore, to prove, that the measures of right and wrong are eternal laws, *obligatory* on every rational mind, 'tis not sufficient to shew the relations upon which they are founded: We must also point out the connexion betwixt the relation and the will; and must prove that this connexion is so necessary, that in every well-dispos'd mind, it must take place and have its influence; tho' the difference betwixt these minds be in other respects immense and infinite. Now besides what I have already prov'd, that even in human nature no relation can ever alone produce any action; besides this, I say, it has been shewn, in treating of the understanding, that there is no connexion of cause and effect, such as this is suppos'd to be, which is discoverable otherwise than by experience, and of which we can pretend to have any security by the simple consideration of the objects. All beings in the universe, consider'd in themselves, appear entirely loose and independent of each other. 'Tis only by experience we learn their influence and connexion; and this influence we ought never to extend beyond experience.

Thus it will be impossible to fulfil the *first* condition required to the system of eternal rational measures of right and wrong; because it is impossible to shew those relations, upon which such a distinction may be founded: And 'tis as impossible to fulfil the *second* condition; because we cannot prove *a priori,* that these relations, if they really existed and were perceiv'd, wou'd be universally forcible and obligatory.

But to make these general reflections more clear and convincing, we may illustrate them by some particular instances, wherein this character of moral good or evil is the most universally acknowledg'd. Of all crimes that human creatures are capable of committing, the most horrid and unnatural is ingratitude, especially when it is committed against parents, and appears in the more flagrant instances of wounds and death. This is acknowledg'd by all mankind, philosophers as well as the people; the question only arises among philosophers, whether the guilt or moral deformity of this action be discover'd by demonstrative reasoning, or be felt by an internal sense, and by means of some sentiment, which the reflecting on such an action naturally occasions. This question will soon be decided against the former opinion, if we can shew the same relations in other objects, without the notion of any guilt or iniquity attending them. Reason or science is nothing but the comparing of ideas, and the discovery of their relations; and if the

same relations have different characters, it must evidently follow, that those characters are not discover'd merely by reason. To put the affair, therefore, to this trial, let us chuse any inanimate object, such as an oak or elm; and let us suppose, that by the dropping of its seed, it produces a sapling below it, which springing up by degrees, at last overtops and destroys the parent tree: I ask, if in this instance there be wanting any relation, which is discoverable in parricide or ingratitude? Is not the one tree the cause of the other's existence; and the latter the cause of the destruction of the former, in the same manner as when a child murders his parent? 'Tis not sufficient to reply, that a choice or will is wanting. For in the case of parricide, a will does not give rise to any *different* relations, but is only the cause from which the action is deriv'd; and consequently produces the *same* relations, that in the oak or elm arise from some other principles. 'Tis a will or choice, that determines a man to kill his parent; and they are the laws of matter and motion, that determine a sapling to destroy the oak, from which it sprung. Here then the same relations have different causes; but still the relations are the same: And as their discovery is not in both cases attended with a notion of immorality, it follows, that that notion does not arise from such a discovery.

But to chuse an instance, still more resembling; I wou'd fain ask any one, why incest in the human species is criminal, and why the very same action, and the same relations in animals have not the smallest moral turpitude and deformity? If it be answer'd, that this action is innocent in animals, because they have not reason sufficient to discover its turpitude; but that man, being endow'd with that faculty, which *ought* to restrain him to his duty, the same action instantly becomes criminal to him; shou'd this be said, I wou'd reply, that this is evidently arguing in a circle. For before reason can perceive this turpitude, the turpitude must exist; and consequently is independent of the decisions of our reason, and is their object more properly than their effect. According to this system, then, every animal, that has sense, and appetite, and will; that is, every animal must be susceptible of all the same virtues and vices, for which we ascribe praise and blame to human creatures. All the difference is, that our superior reason may serve to discover the vice or virtue, and by that means may augment the blame or praise: But still this discovery supposes a separate being in these moral distinctions, and a being, which depends only on the will and appetite, and which, both in thought and reality, may be distinguish'd from the reason. Animals are susceptible of the same relations, with respect to each other, as the human species, and therefore wou'd also be susceptible of the same morality, if the essence of morality consisted in these relations. Their want of a sufficient degree of reason may hinder them from perceiving the duties and obligations of morality, but can never hinder these duties from existing; since they must antecedently exist, in order to their being perceiv'd. Reason must find them, and can never produce them. This argument deserves to be weigh'd, as being, in my opinion, entirely decisive.

Nor does this reasoning only prove, that morality consists not in any relations, that are the objects of science; but if examin'd, will prove with equal certainty, that it consists not in any *matter of fact*, which can be discover'd by the understanding. This is the *second* part of our argument; and if it can be made evident, we may conclude, that morality is not an object of reason. But can there be any difficulty in proving, that vice and virtue are not matters of fact, whose existence we can infer by reason? Take any action allow'd to be vicious: Wilful murder, for instance. Examine it in all lights, and see if you can find that matter of fact, or real existence, which you call *vice*. In which-ever way you take it, you find only certain passions, motives, volitions and thoughts. There is no other matter of fact in the case. The vice entirely escapes you, as long as you consider the object. You never can find it, till you turn your reflection into your own breast, and find a sentiment of disapprobation, which arises in you, towards this action. Here is a matter of fact; but 'tis the object of feeling, not of reason. It lies in yourself, not in the object. So that when you pronounce any action or character to be vicious, you mean nothing, but that from the constitution of your nature you have a feeling or sentiment of blame from the contemplation of it. Vice and virtue, therefore, may be compar'd to sounds, colours, heat and cold, which, according to modern philosophy, are not qualities in objects, but perceptions in the mind: And this discovery in morals, like that other in physics, is to be regarded as a considerable advancement of the speculative sciences; tho', like that too, it has little or no influence on practice. Nothing can be more real, or concern

us more, than our own sentiments of pleasure and uneasiness; and if these be favourable to virtue, and unfavourable to vice, no more can be requisite to the regulation of our conduct and behaviour.

I cannot forbear adding to these reasonings an observation, which may, perhaps, be found of some importance. In every system of morality, which I have hitherto met with, I have always remark'd, that the author proceeds for some time in the ordinary way of reasoning, and establishes the being of a God, or makes observations concerning human affairs; when of a sudden I am surpriz'd to find, that instead of the usual copulations of propositions, *is,* and *is not,* I meet with no proposition that is not connected with an *ought,* or an *ought not.* This change is imperceptible; but is, however, of the last consequence. For as this *ought,* or *ought not,* expresses some new relation or affirmation, 'tis necessary that it shou'd be observ'd and explain'd; and at the same time that a reason shou'd be given, for what seems altogether inconceivable, how this new relation can be a deduction from others, which are entirely different from it. But as authors do not commonly use this precaution, I shall presume to recommend it to the readers; and am persuaded, that this small attention wou'd subvert all the vulgar systems of morality, and let us see, that the distinction of vice and virtue is not founded merely on the relations of objects, nor is perceiv'd by reason.

Moral distinctions deriv'd from a moral sense

Thus the course of the argument leads us to conclude, that since vice and virtue are not discoverable merely by reason, or the comparison of ideas, it must be by means of some impression or sentiment they occasion, that we are able to mark the difference betwixt them. Our decisions concerning moral rectitude and depravity are evidently perceptions; and as all perceptions are either impressions or ideas, the exclusion of the one is a convincing argument for the other. Morality, therefore, is more properly felt than judg'd of; tho' this feeling or sentiment is commonly so soft and gentle, that we are apt to confound it with an idea, according to our common custom of taking all things for the same, which have any near resemblance to each other.

The next question is, of what nature are these impressions, and after what manner do they operate upon us? Here we cannot remain long in suspense, but must pronounce the impression arising from virtue, to be agreeable, and that proceding from vice to be uneasy. Every moment's experience must convince us of this. There is no spectacle so fair and beautiful as a noble and generous action; nor any which gives us more abhorrence than one that is cruel and treacherous. No enjoyment equals the satisfaction we receive from the company of those we love and esteem; as the greatest of all punishments is to be oblig'd to pass our lives with those we hate or contemn. A very play or romance may afford us instances of this pleasure, which virtue conveys to us; and pain, which arises from vice.

Now since the distinguishing impressions, by which moral good or evil is known, are nothing but *particular* pains or pleasures; it follows, that in all enquiries concerning these moral distinctions, it will be sufficient to shew the principles, which make us feel a satisfaction or uneasiness from the survey of any character, in order to satisfy us why the character is laudable or blameable. An action, or sentiment, or character is virtuous or vicious; why? because its view causes a pleasure or uneasiness of a particular kind. In giving a reason, therefore, for the pleasure or uneasiness, we sufficiently explain the vice or virtue. To have the sense of virtue, is nothing but to *feel* a satisfaction of a particular kind from the contemplation of a character. The very *feeling* constitutes our praise or admiration. We go no farther; nor do we enquire into the cause of the satisfaction. We do not infer a character to be virtuous, because it pleases: But in feeling that it pleases after such a particular manner, we in effect feel that it is virtuous. The case is the same as in our judgments concerning all kinds of beauty, and tastes, and sensations. Our approbation is imply'd in the immediate pleasure they convey to us.

I have objected to the system, which establishes eternal rational measures of right and wrong, that 'tis impossible to shew, in the actions of reasonable creatures, any relations, which are not found in external objects; and therefore, if morality always attended these relations, 'twere possible for inanimate matter to become virtuous or vicious. Now it may, in like manner, be objected to the present system, that if virtue and vice be determin'd by pleasure and pain, these qualities must, in every case, arise from the sensations; and consequently any object, whether animate or inanimate, rational or irrational, might become morally good or evil, provided it can excite a satisfaction or uneasiness. But tho' this objection seems to be the very same, it has by no means the same force, in the one case as in the other. For, *first,* 'tis evident, that under the term *pleasure,* we comprehend sensations, which are very different from each other, and which have only such a distant resemblance, as is requisite to make them be express'd by the same abstract term. A good composition of music and a bottle of good wine equally produce pleasure; and, what is more, their goodness is determin'd merely by the pleasure. But shall we say upon that account, that the wine is harmonious, or the music of a good flavour? In like manner an inanimate object, and the character or sentiments of any person may, both of them, give satisfaction; but as the satisfaction is different, this keeps our sentiments concerning them from being confounded, and makes us ascribe virtue to the one, and not to the other. Nor is every sentiment of pleasure or pain, which arises from characters and actions, of that *peculiar* kind, which makes us praise or condemn. The good qualities of an enemy are hurtful to us; but may still command our esteem and respect. 'Tis only when a character is considered in general, without reference to our particular interest, that it causes such a feeling or sentiment, as denominates it morally good or evil. 'Tis true, those sentiments, from interest and morals, are apt to be confounded, and naturally run into one another. It seldom happens, that we do not think an enemy vicious, and can distinguish betwixt his opposition to our interest and real villainy or baseness. But this hinders not, but that the sentiments are, in themselves, distinct; and a man of temper and judgment may preserve himself from these illusions. In like manner, tho' 'tis certain a musical voice is nothing but one that naturally gives a *particular* kind of pleasure; yet 'tis difficult for a man to be sensible, that the voice of an enemy is agreeable, or to allow it to be musical. But a person of a fine ear, who has the command of himself, can separate these feelings, and give praise to what deserves it.

Secondly, We may call to remembrance the preceding system of the passions, in order to remark a still more considerable difference among our pains and pleasures. Pride and humility, love and hatred are excited, when there is any thing presented to us, that both bears a relation to the object of the passion, and produces a separate sensation related to the sensation of the passion. Now virtue and vice are attended with these circumstances. They must necessarily be plac'd either in ourselves or others, and excite either pleasure or uneasiness; and therefore must give rise to one of these four passions; which clearly distinguishes them from the pleasure and pain arising from inanimate objects, that often bear no relation to us: And this is, perhaps, the most considerable effect that virtue and vice have upon the human mind.

It may now be ask'd *in general,* concerning this pain or pleasure, that distinguishes moral good and evil, *From what principles is it deriv'd, and whence does it arise in the human mind?* To this I reply, *first,* that 'tis absurd to imagine, that in every particular instance, these sentiments are produc'd by an *original* quality and *primary* constitution. For as the number of our duties is, in a manner, infinite, 'tis impossible that our original instincts shou'd extend to each of them, and from our very first infancy impress on the human mind all that multitude of precepts, which are contain'd in the compleatest system of ethics. Such a method of proceeding is not conformable to the usual maxims, by which nature is conducted, where a few principles produce all that variety we observe in the universe, and every thing is carry'd on in the easiest and most simple manner. 'Tis necessary, therefore, to abridge these primary impulses, and find some more general principles, upon which all our notions of morals are founded.

But in the *second* place, shou'd it be ask'd, whether we ought to search for these principles in *nature,* or whether we must look for them in some other origin? I wou'd reply, that our answer to this question depends upon the definition of the word, Nature, than which there is none more ambiguous and equivocal. If *nature* be oppos'd to miracles, not only the distinction betwixt vice and virtue is natural, but also every event, which has ever happen'd in the world, *excepting those miracles, on which our religion is founded.* In saying, then, that the sentiments of vice and virtue are natural in this sense, we make no very extraordinary discovery.

But *nature* may also be opposed to rare and unusual; and in this sense of the word, which is the common one, there may often arise disputes concerning what is natural or unnatural; and one may in general affirm, that

we are not possess'd of any very precise standard, by which these disputes can be decided. Frequent and rare depend upon the number of examples we have observ'd; and as this number may gradually encrease or diminish, 'twill be impossible to fix any exact boundaries betwixt them. We may only affirm on this head, that if ever there was any thing, which cou'd be call'd natural in this sense, the sentiments of morality certainly may; since there never was any nation of the world, nor any single person in any nation, who was utterly depriv'd of them, and who never, in any instance, showed the least approbation or dislike of manners. These sentiments are so rooted in our constitution and temper, that without entirely confounding the human mind by disease or madness, 'tis impossible to extirpate and destroy them.

But *nature* may also be opposed to artifice, as well as to what is rare and unusual; and in this sense it may be disputed, whether the notions of virtue be natural or not. We readily forget, that the designs, and projects, and views of men are principles as necessary in their operation as heat and cold, moist and dry: But taking them to be free and entirely our own, 'tis usual for us to set them in opposition to the other principles of nature. Shou'd it, therefore, be demanded, whether the sense of virtue be natural or artificial, I am of opinion, that 'tis impossible for me at present to give any precise answer to this question. Perhaps it will appear afterwards, that our sense of some virtues is artificial, and that of others natural. The discussion of this question will be more proper, when we enter upon an exact detail of each particular vice and virtue.[1]

Mean while it may not be amiss to observe from these definitions of *natural* and *unnatural,* that nothing can be more unphilosophical than those systems, which assert, that virtue is the same with what is natural, and vice with what is unnatural. For in the first sense of the word, Nature, as opposed to miracles, both vice and virtue are equally natural; and in the second sense, as oppos'd to what is unusual, perhaps virtue will be found to be the most unnatural. At least it must be own'd, that heroic virtue, being as unusual, is as little natural as the most

---

1. In the following discourse *natural* is also opposed sometimes to *civil,* sometimes to *moral.* The opposition will always discover the sense, in which it is taken.

brutal barbarity. As to the third sense of the word, 'tis certain, that both vice and virtue are equally artificial, and out of nature. For however it may be disputed, whether the notion of a merit or demerit in certain actions be natural or artificial, 'tis evident, that the actions themselves are artificial, and are perform'd with a certain design and intention; otherwise they cou'd never be rank'd under any of these denominations. 'Tis impossible, therefore, that the character of natural and unnatural can ever, in any sense, mark the boundaries of vice and virtue.

Thus we are still brought back to our first position, that virtue is distinguished by the pleasure, and vice by the pain, that any action, sentiment or character gives us by the mere view and contemplation. This decision is very commodious; because it reduces us to this simple question, *Why any action or sentiment upon the general view or survey, gives a certain satisfaction or uneasiness,* in order to shew the origin of its moral rectitude or depravity, without looking for any incomprehensible relations and qualities, which never did exist in nature, nor even in our imagination, by any clear and distinct conception. I flatter myself I have executed a great part of my present design by a state of the question, which appears to me so free from ambiguity and obscurity.

J. L. Mackie

The Subjectivity of Values

1. Moral scepticism

There are no objective values. This is a bald statement of the thesis of this chapter, but before arguing for it I shall try to clarify and restrict it in ways that may meet some objections and prevent some misunderstanding.

The statement of this thesis is liable to provoke one of three very different reactions. Some will think it not merely false but pernicious; they will see it as a threat to morality and to everything else that is worthwhile, and they will find the presenting of such a thesis in what purports to be a book on ethics paradoxical or even outrageous. Others will regard it as a trivial truth, almost too obvious to be worth mentioning, and certainly too plain to be worth much argument. Others again will say that it is meaningless or empty, that no real issue is raised by the question whether values are or are not part of the fabric of the world. But, precisely because there can be these three different reactions, much more needs to be said.

The claim that values are not objective, are not part of the fabric of the world, is meant to include not only moral goodness, which might be most naturally equated with moral value, but also other things that could be more loosely called moral values or disvalues—rightness and wrongness, duty, obligation, an action's being rotten and contemptible, and so on. It also includes non-moral values, notably aesthetic ones, beauty and various kinds of artistic merit. I shall not discuss these explicitly, but clearly much the same considerations apply to aesthetic and to moral values, and there would be at least some initial implausibility in a view that gave the one a different status from the other.

Since it is with moral values that I am primarily concerned, the view I am adopting may be called moral scepticism. But this name is likely to be misunderstood: 'moral scepticism' might also be used as a name for either of two first order views, or perhaps for an incoherent mixture of the two. A moral sceptic might be the sort of person who says 'All this talk of morality is tripe,'

J. L. Mackie, "The Subjectivity of Values" from *Ethics: Inventing Right and Wrong* (London: Pelican Books, 1977). Copyright © J. L. Mackie, 1977. Reproduced by permission of Penguin Books, Ltd.

who rejects morality and will take no notice of it. Such a person may be literally rejecting all moral judgements; he is more likely to be making moral judgements of his own, expressing a positive moral condemnation of all that conventionally passes for morality; or he may be confusing these two logically incompatible views, and saying that he rejects all morality, while he is in fact rejecting only a particular morality that is current in the society in which he has grown up. But I am not at present concerned with the merits or faults of such a position. These are first order moral views, positive or negative: the person who adopts either of them is taking a certain practical, normative, stand. By contrast, what I am discussing is a second order view, a view about the status of moral values and the nature of moral valuing, about where and how they fit into the world. These first and second order views are not merely distinct but completely independent: one could be a second order moral sceptic without being a first order one, or again the other way round. A man could hold strong moral views, and indeed ones whose content was thoroughly conventional, while believing that they were simply attitudes and policies with regard to conduct that he and other people held. Conversely, a man could reject all established morality while believing it to be an objective truth that it was evil or corrupt.

With another sort of misunderstanding moral scepticism would seem not so much pernicious as absurd. How could anyone deny that there is a difference between a kind action and a cruel one, or that a coward and a brave man behave differently in the face of danger? Of course, this is undeniable; but it is not to the point. The kinds of behavior to which moral values and disvalues are ascribed are indeed part of the furniture of the world, and so are the natural, descriptive, differences between them; but not, perhaps, their differences in value. It is a hard fact that cruel actions differ from kind ones, and hence that we can learn, as in fact we all do, to distinguish them fairly well in practice, and to use the words 'cruel' and 'kind' with fairly clear descriptive meanings; but is it an equally hard fact that actions which are cruel in such a descriptive sense are to be condemned? The present issue is with regard to the objectivity specifically of value, not with regard to the objectivity of those natural, factual, differences on the basis of which differing values are assigned.

2. Subjectivism

Another name often used, as an alternative to 'moral scepticism', for the view I am discussing is 'subjectivism'. But this too has more than one meaning. Moral subjectivism too could be a first order, normative, view, namely that everyone really ought to do whatever he thinks he should. This plainly is a (systematic) first order view; on examination it soon ceases to be plausible, but that is beside the point, for it is quite independent of the second order thesis at present under consideration. What is more confusing is that different second order views compete for the name 'subjectivism'. Several of these are doctrines about the meaning of moral terms and moral statements. What is often called moral subjectivism is the doctrine that, for example, 'This action is right' *means* 'I approve of this action', or more generally that moral judgements are equivalent to reports of the speaker's own feelings or attitudes. But the view I am now discussing is to be distinguished in two vital respects from any such doctrine as this. First, what I have called moral scepticism is a negative doctrine, not a positive one: it says what there isn't, not what there is. It says that there do not exist entities or relations of a certain kind, objective values or requirements which many people have believed to exist. Of course, the moral sceptic cannot leave it at that. If his position is to be at all plausible, he must give some account of how other people have fallen into what he regards as an error, and this account will have to include some positive suggestions about how values fail to be objective, about what has been mistaken for, or has led to false beliefs about, objective values. But this will be a development of his theory, not its core: its core is the negation. Secondly, what I have called moral scepticism is an ontological thesis, not a linguistic or conceptual one. It is not, like the other doctrine often called moral subjectivism, a view about the meanings of moral statements. [. . .]

7. The claim to objectivity

If I have succeeded in specifying precisely enough the moral values whose objectivity I am denying, my thesis may now seem to be trivially true. Of course, some will say, valuing, preferring, choosing, recommending, rejecting, condemning, and so on, are human activities, and there is no need to look for values that are prior to and logically independent of all such activities. There may be widespread agreement in valuing, and particular value-judgements are not in general arbitrary or isolated: they typically cohere with others, or can be criticized if they do not, reasons can be given for them, and so on: but if all that the subjectivist is maintaining is that desires, ends, purposes, and the like figure somewhere in the system of reasons, and that no ends or purposes are objective as opposed to being merely intersubjective, then this may be conceded without much fuss.

But I do not think that this should be conceded so easily. As I have said, the main tradition of European moral philosophy includes the contrary claim, that there are objective values of just the sort I have denied. I have referred already to Plato, Kant, and Sidgwick. Kant in particular holds that the categorical imperative is not only categorical and imperative but objectively so: though a rational being gives the moral law to himself, the law that he thus makes is determinate and necessary. Aristotle begins the *Nicomachean Ethics* by saying that the good is that at which all things aim, and that ethics is part of a science which he calls 'politics', whose goal is not knowledge but practice; yet he does not doubt that there can be *knowledge* of what is the good for man, nor, once he has identified this as well-being or happiness, *eudaimonia,* that it can be known, rationally determined, in what happiness consists; and it is plain that he thinks that this happiness is intrinsically desirable, not good simply because it is desired. The rationalist Samuel Clarke holds that

> these eternal and necessary differences of things make it *fit and reasonable* for creatures so to act ... even separate from the consideration of these rules being the *positive will* or *command of God;* and also antecedent to any respect or regard, expectation or apprehension, of any *particular private and personal advantage or disadvantage, reward or punishment,* either present or future. ...

Even the sentimentalist Hutcheson defines moral goodness as 'some quality apprehended in actions, which procures approbation ...', while saying that the moral sense by which we perceive virtue and vice has been given to us (by the Author of nature) to direct our actions. Hume

indeed was on the other side, but he is still a witness to the dominance of the objectivist tradition, since he claims that when we 'see that the distinction of vice and virtue is not founded merely on the relations of objects, nor is perceiv'd by reason', this 'wou'd subvert all the vulgar systems of morality'. And Richard Price insists that right and wrong are, 'real characters of actions', not 'qualities of our minds', and are perceived by the understanding; he criticizes the notion of moral sense on the ground that it would make virtue an affair of taste, and moral right and wrong 'nothing in the objects themselves'; he rejects Hutcheson's view because (perhaps mistakenly) he sees it as collapsing into Hume's.

But this objectivism about values is not only a feature of the philosophical tradition. It has also a firm basis in ordinary thought, and even in the meanings of moral terms. No doubt it was an extravagance for Moore to say that 'good' is the name of a non-natural quality, but it would not be so far wrong to say that in moral contexts it is used as if it were the name of a supposed non-natural quality, where the description 'non-natural' leaves room for the peculiar evaluative, prescriptive, intrinsically action-guiding aspects of this supposed quality. This point can be illustrated by reflection on the conflicts and swings of opinion in recent years between non-cognitivist and naturalist views about the central, basic, meanings of ethical terms. If we reject the view that it is the function of such terms to introduce objective values into discourse about conduct and choices of action, there seem to be two main alternative types of account. One (which has importantly different subdivisions) is that they conventionally express either attitudes which the speaker purports to adopt towards whatever it is that he characterizes morally, or prescriptions or recommendations, subject perhaps to the logical constraint of univerasalizability. Different views of this type share the central thesis that ethical terms have, at least partly and primarily, some sort of non-cognitive, non-descriptive, meaning. Views of the other type hold that they are descriptive in meaning, but descriptive of natural features, partly of such features as everyone, even the non-cognitivist, would recognize as distinguishing kind actions from cruel ones, courage from cowardice, politeness from rudeness, and so on, and partly (though these two overlap) of relations between the actions and some human wants, satisfactions, and the like. I believe that views of both these types capture part of the truth. Each approach can account for the fact that moral judgements are action-guiding or practical. Yet each gains much of its plausibility from the felt inadequacy of the other. It is a very natural reaction to any non-cognitive analysis of ethical terms to protest that there is more to ethics than this, something more external to the maker of moral judgements, more authoritative over both him and those of or to whom he speaks, and this reaction is likely to persist even when full allowance has been made for the logical, formal, constraints of full-blooded prescriptivity and universalizability. Ethics, we are inclined to believe, is more a matter of knowledge and less a matter of decision than any non-cognitive analysis allows. And of course naturalism satisfies this demand. It will not be a matter of choice or decision whether an action is cruel or unjust or imprudent or whether it is likely to produce more distress than pleasure. But in satisfying this demand, it introduces a converse deficiency. On a naturalist analysis, moral judgements can be practical, but their practicality is wholly relative to desires or possible satisfactions of the person or persons whose actions are to be guided; but moral judgements seem to say more than this. This view leaves out the categorical quality of moral requirements. In fact both naturalist and non-cognitive analyses leave out the apparent authority of ethics, the one by excluding the categorically imperative aspect, the other the claim to objective validity or truth. The ordinary user of moral language means to say something about whatever it is that he characterizes morally, for example a possible action, as it is in itself, or would be if it were realized, and not about, or even simply expressive of, his, or anyone else's, attitude or relation to it. But the something he wants to say is not purely descriptive, certainly not inert, but something that involves a call for action or for the refraining from action, and one that is absolute, not contingent upon any desire or preference or policy or choice, his own or anyone else's. Someone in a state of moral perplexity, wondering whether it would be wrong for him to engage, say, in research related to bacteriological warfare, wants to arrive at some judgement about this concrete case, his doing this work at this time in these actual circumstances; his relevant characteristics will be part of the subject of the judgement, but no relation between him and the proposed action will be part of the predicate. The question is not, for example, whether he really wants to do this work, whether it will satisfy or dissatisfy him, whether he will in the long run have a pro-attitude towards it, or even whether this is an action of a sort that he can happily and sincerely recommend in all relevantly similar cases. Nor is he even wondering just whether to recommended such action in all relevantly similar cases. He wants to know whether this course of action would be wrong in itself. Something like this is the everyday objectivist concept of which talk about non-natural qualities is a philosopher's reconstruction.

The prevalence of this tendency to objectify values—and not only moral ones—is confirmed by a pattern of thinking that we find in existentialists and those influenced by them. The denial of objective values can carry with it an extreme emotional reaction, a feeling that nothing matters at all, that life has lost its purpose. Of course this does not follow; the lack of objective values is not a good reason for abandoning subjective concern or for ceasing to want anything. But the abandonment of a belief in objective values can cause, at least temporarily, a decay of subjective concern and sense of purpose. That it does so is evidence that the people in whom this reaction occurs have been tending to objectify their concerns and purposes, have been giving them a fictitious external authority. A claim to objectivity has been so strongly associated with their subjective concerns and purposes that the collapse of the former seems to undermine the latter as well.

This view, that conceptual analysis would reveal a claim to objectivity, is sometimes dramatically confirmed by philosophers who are officially on the other side. Bertrand Russell, for example, says that 'ethical propositions should be expressed in the optative mood, not in the indicative'; he defends himself effectively against the charge of inconsistency in both holding ultimate ethical valuations to be subjective and expressing emphatic opinions on ethical questions. Yet at the end he admits:

> Certainly there *seems* to be something more. Suppose, for example, that some one were to advocate the introduction of bull-fighting in this country. In opposing the proposal, I should *feel*, not only that I was expressing my desires, but that

my desires in the matter are *right,* whatever that may mean. As a matter of argument, I can, I think, show that I am not guilty of any logical inconsistency in holding to the above interpretation of ethics and at the same time expressing strong ethical preferences. But in feeling I am not satisfied.

But he concludes, reasonably enough, with the remark: 'I can only say that, while my own opinions as to ethics do not satisfy me, other people's satisfy me still less.'

I conclude, then, that ordinary moral judgements include a claim to objectivity, an assumption that there are objective values in just the sense in which I am concerned to deny this. And I do not think it is going too far to say that this assumption has been incorporated in the basic, conventional, meanings of moral terms. Any analysis of the meanings of moral terms which omits this claim to objective, intrinsic, prescriptivity is to that extent incomplete; and this is true of any non-cognitive analysis, any naturalist one, and any combination of the two.

If second order ethics were confined, then, to linguistic and conceptual analysis, it ought to conclude that moral values at least are objective: that they are so is part of what our ordinary moral statements mean: the traditional moral concepts of the ordinary man as well as of the main line of western philosophers are concepts of objective value. But it is precisely for this reason that linguistic and conceptual analysis is not enough. The claim to objectivity, however ingrained in our language and thought, is not self-validating. It can and should be questioned. But the denial of objective values will have to be put forward not as the result of an analytic approach, but as an 'error theory', a theory that although most people in making moral judgements implicitly claim, among other things, to be pointing to something objectively prescriptive, these claims are all false. It is this that makes the name 'moral scepticism' appropriate.

But since this is an error theory, since it goes against assumptions ingrained in our thought and built into some of the ways in which language is used, since it conflicts with what is sometimes called common sense, it needs very solid support. It is not something we can accept lightly or casually and then quietly pass on. If we are to adopt this view, we must argue explicitly for it. Traditionally it has been supported by arguments of two

main kinds, which I shall call the argument from relativity and the argument from queerness, but these can, as I shall show, be supplemented in several ways.

8. The argument from relativity

The argument from relativity has as its premiss the well-known variation in moral codes from one society to another and from one period to another, and also the differences in moral beliefs between different groups and classes within a complex community. Such variation is in itself merely a truth of descriptive morality, a fact of anthropology which entails neither first order nor second order ethical views. Yet it may indirectly support second order subjectivism: radical differences between first order moral judgements make it difficult to treat those judgements as apprehensions of objective truths. But it is not the mere occurrence of disagreements that tells against the objectivity of values. Disagreement on questions in history or biology or cosmology does not show that there are no objective issues in these fields for investigators to disagree about. But such scientific disagreement results from speculative inferences or explanatory hypotheses based on inadequate evidence, and it is hardly plausible to interpret moral disagreement in the same way. Disagreement about moral codes seems to reflect people's adherence to and participation in different ways of life. The causal connection seems to be mainly that way round: it is that people approve of monogamy because they participate in a monogamous way of life rather than that they participate in a monogamous way of life because they approve of monogamy, Of course, the standards may be an idealization of the way of life from which they arise: the monogamy in which people participate may be less complete, less rigid, than that of which it leads them to approve. This is not to say that moral judgements are purely conventional. Of course there have been and are moral heretics and moral reformers, people who have turned against the established rules and practices of their own communities for moral reasons, and often for moral reasons that we would endorse. But this can usually be understood as the extension, in ways which, though new and unconventional, seemed to them to be required for consistency, of rules to which they already adhered as arising out of an existing way of life. In short, the argument from relativity has some force simply because the actual variations in the moral codes are more readily explained by the hypothesis that they reflect ways of life than by the hypothesis that they express perceptions, most of them seriously inadequate and badly distorted, of objective values.

But there is a well-known counter to this argument from relativity, namely to say that the items for which objective validity is in the first place to be claimed are not specific moral rules or codes but very general basic principles which are recognized at least implicitly to some extent in all society—such principles as provide the foundations of what Sidgwick has called different methods of ethics: the principle of universalizability, perhaps, or the rule that one ought to conform to the specific rules of any way of life in which one takes part, from which one profits, and on which one relies, or some utilitarian principle of doing what tends, or seems likely, to promote the general happiness. It is easy to show that such general principles, married with differing concrete circumstances, different existing social patterns or different preferences, will beget different specific moral rules; and there is some plausibility in the claim that the specific rules thus generated will vary from community to community or from group to group in close agreement with the actual variations in accepted codes.

The argument from relativity can be only partly countered in this way. To take this line the moral objectivist has to say that it is only in these principles that the objective moral character attaches immediately to its descriptively specified ground or subject: other moral judgements are objectively valid or true, but only derivatively and contingently—if things had been otherwise, quite different sorts of actions would have been right. And despite the prominence in recent philosophical ethics of universalization, utilitarian principles, and the like, these are very far from constituting the whole of what is actually affirmed as basic in ordinary moral thought. Much of this is concerned rather with what Hare calls 'ideals' or, less kindly, 'fanaticism'. That is, people judge that some things are good or right, and others are bad or wrong, not because—or at any rate not only because—they exemplify some general principle for which widespread implicit acceptance could be claimed, but because

something about those things arouses certain responses immediately in them, though they would arouse radically and irresolvably different responses in others. 'Moral sense' or 'intuition' is an initially more plausible description of what supplies many of our basic moral judgements than 'reason'. With regard to all these starting points of moral thinking the argument from relativity remains in full force.

9. The argument from queerness

Even more important, however, and certainly more generally applicable, is the argument from queerness. This has two parts, one metaphysical, the other epistemological. If there were objective values, then they would be entities or qualities or relations of a very strange sort, utterly different from anything else in the universe. Correspondingly, if we were aware of them, it would have to be by some special faculty of moral perception or intuition, utterly different from our ordinary ways of knowing everything else. These points were recognized by Moore when he spoke of non-natural qualities, and by the intuitionists in their talk about a 'faculty of moral intuition'. Intuitionism has long been out of favour, and it is indeed easy to point out its implausibilities. What is not so often stressed, but is more important, is that the central thesis of intuitionism is one to which any objectivist view of values is in the end committed: intuitionism merely makes unpalatably plain what other forms of objectivism wrap up. Of course the suggestion that moral judgements are made or moral problems solved by just sitting down and having an ethical intuition is a travesty of actual moral thinking. But, however complex the real process, it will require (if it is to yield authoritatively prescriptive conclusions) some input of its distinctive sort, either premises or forms of argument or both. When we ask the awkward question, how we can be aware of this authoritative prescriptivity, of the truth of these distinctively ethical premises or of the cogency of this distinctively ethical pattern of reasoning, none of our ordinary accounts of sensory perception or introspection or the framing and confirming of explanatory hypotheses or inference or logical construction or conceptual analysis, or any combination of these, will provide a satisfactory answer; 'a special sort of intuition' is a lame answer, but it is the one to which the clearheaded objectivist is compelled to resort.

Indeed, the best move for the moral objectivist is not to evade this issue, but to look for companions in guilt. For example, Richard Price argues that it is not moral knowledge alone that such an empiricism as those of Locke and Hume is unable to account for, but also our knowledge and even our ideas of essence, number, identity, diversity, solidity, inertia, substance, the necessary existence and infinite extension of time and space, necessity and possibility in general, power, and causation. If the understanding, which Price defines as the faculty within us that discerns truth, is also a source of new simple ideas of so many other sorts, may it not also be a power of immediately perceiving right and wrong, which yet are real characters of actions?

This is an important counter to the argument from queerness. The only adequate reply to it would be to show how, on empiricist foundations, we can construct an account of the ideas and beliefs and knowledge that we have of all these matters. I cannot even begin to do that here, though I have undertaken some parts of the task elsewhere. I can only state my belief that satisfactory accounts of most of these can be given in empirical terms. If some supposed metaphysical necessities or essences resist such treatment, then they too should be included, along with objective values, among the targets of the argument from queerness.

This queerness does not consist simply in the fact that ethical statements are 'unverifiable'. Although logical positivism with its verifiability theory of descriptive meaning gave an impetus to non-cognitive accounts of ethics, it is not only logical positivists but also empiricists of a much more liberal sort who should find objective values hard to accommodate. Indeed, I would not only reject the verifiability principle but also deny the conclusion commonly drawn from it, it, that moral judgements lack descriptive meaning. The assertion that there are objective values or intrinsically prescriptive entities or features of some kind, which ordinary moral judgements presuppose, is, I hold, not meaningless but false.

Plato's Forms give a dramatic picture of what objective values would have to be. The Form of the Good is such that knowledge of it provides the knower with both a direction and an overriding motive; something's being good both tells the person who knows this to pursue it and makes him pursue it. An objective good would be sought by anyone who was acquainted with it, not because of any contingent fact that this person, or every person, is so constituted that he desires this end, but just because the end has to-be-pursuedness somehow built into it. Similarly, if there were objective principles of right and wrong, any wrong (possible) course of action would have not-to-be-doneness somehow built into it. Or we should have something like Clarke's necessary relations of fitness between situations and actions, so that a situation would have a demand for such-and-such an action somehow built into it.

The need for an argument of this sort can be brought out by reflection on Hume's argument that 'reason'—in which at this stage he includes all sorts of knowing as well as reasoning—can never be an 'influencing motive of the will'. Someone might object that Hume has argued unfairly from the lack of influencing power (not contingent upon desires) in ordinary objects of knowledge and ordinary reasoning, and might maintain that values differ from natural objects precisely in their power, when known, automatically to influence the will. To this Hume could, and would need to, reply that this objection involves the postulating of value-entities or value-features of quite a different order from anything else with which we are acquainted, and of a corresponding faculty with which to detect them. That is, he would have to supplement his explicit argument with what I have called the argument from queerness.

Another way of bringing out this queerness is to ask, about anything that is supposed to have some objective moral quality, how this is linked with its natural features. What is the connection between the natural fact that an action is a piece of deliberate cruelty—say, causing pain just for fun—and the moral fact that it is wrong? It cannot be an entailment, a logical or semantic necessity. Yet it is not merely that the two features occur together. The wrongness must somehow be 'consequential' or 'supervenient'; it is wrong because it is a piece of deliberate cruelty. But just what *in the world* is signified by this 'because'? And how do we know the relation that it signifies, if this is something more than such actions being socially condemned, and condemned by us too, perhaps through our having absorbed attitudes from our social environment? It is not even sufficient to postulate a faculty which 'sees' the wrongness: something must be postulated which can see at once the natural features that constitute the cruelty, and the wrongness, and the mysterious consequential link between the two. Alternatively, the intuition required might be the perception that wrongness is a higher order property belonging to certain natural properties; but what is this belonging of properties to other properties, and how can we discern it? How much simpler and more comprehensible the situation would be if we could replace the moral quality with some sort of subjective response which could be causally related to the detection of the natural features on which the supposed quality is said to be consequential.

It may be thought that the argument from queerness is given an unfair start if we thus relate it to what are admittedly among the wilder products of philosophical fancy—Platonic Forms, non-natural qualities, self-evident relations of fitness, faculties of intuition, and the like. Is it equally forceful if applied to the terms in which everyday moral judgements are more likely to be expressed—though still, as has been argued in Section 7, with a claim to objectivity—'you must do this', 'you can't do that', 'obligation', 'unjust', 'rotten', 'disgraceful', 'mean', or talk about good reasons for or against possible actions? Admittedly not; but that is because the objective prescriptivity, the element a claim for whose authoritativeness is embedded in ordinary moral thought and language, is not yet isolated in these forms of speech, but is presented along with relations to desires and feelings, reasoning about the means to desired ends, interpersonal demands, the injustice which consists in the violation of what are in the context the accepted standards of merit, the psychological constituents of meanness, and so on. There is nothing queer about any of these, and under cover of them the claim for moral authority may pass unnoticed. But if I am right in arguing that it is ordinarily there, and is therefore very likely to be incorporated almost automatically in philosophical accounts of ethics which systematize our ordinary thought even in such apparently innocent terms as these, it needs to be examined, and for this purpose it needs to be isolated and exposed as it is by the less cautious philosophical reconstructions.

10. Patterns of objectification

Considerations of these kinds suggest that it is in the end less paradoxical to reject than to retain the common-sense belief in the objectivity of moral values, provided that we can explain how this belief, if it is false, has become established and is so resistant to criticisms. This proviso is not difficult to satisfy.

On a subjectivist view, the supposedly objective values will be based in fact upon attitudes which the person has who takes himself to be recognizing and responding to those values. If we admit that Hume calls the mind's 'propensity to spread itself on external objects', we can understand the supposed objectivity of moral qualities as arising from what we can call the projection or objectification of moral attitudes. This would be analogous to what is called the 'pathetic fallacy', the tendency to read our feelings into their objects. If a fungus, say, fills us with disgust, we may be inclined to ascribe to the fungus itself a non-natural quality of foulness. But in moral contexts there is more than this propensity at work. Moral attitudes themselves are at least partly social in origin: socially established—and socially necessary —patterns of behaviour put pressure on individuals, and each individual tends to internalize these pressures and to join in requiring these patterns of behaviour of himself and of others. The attitudes that are objectified into moral values have indeed an external source, though not the one assigned to them by the belief in their absolute authority. Moreover, there are motives that would support objectification. We need morality to regulate interpersonal relations, to control some of the ways in which people behave towards one another, often in opposition to contrary inclinations. We therefore want our moral judgements to be authoritative for other agents as well as for ourselves: objective validity would give them the authority required. Aesthetic values are logically in the same position as moral ones; much the same metaphysical and epistemological considerations apply to them. But aesthetic values are less strongly objectified than moral ones; their subjective status, and an 'error theory' with regard to such claims to objectivity as are incorporated in aesthetic judgements, will be more readily accepted, just because the motives for their objectification are less compelling.

But it would be misleading to think of the objectification of moral values as primarily the projection of feelings, as in the pathetic fallacy. More important are wants and demands. As Hobbes says, 'whatsoever is the object of any man's Appetite or Desire, that is it, which he for his part calleth *Good*'; and certainly both the adjective 'good' and the noun 'goods' are used in non-moral contexts of things because they are such as to satisfy desires. We get the notion of something's being objectively good, or having intrinsic value, by reversing the direction of dependence here, by making the desire depend upon the goodness, instead of the goodness on the desire. And this is aided by the fact that the desired thing will indeed have features that make it desired, that enable it to arouse a desire or that make it such as to satisfy some desire that is already there. It is fairly easy to confuse the way in which a thing's desirability is indeed objective with its having in our sense objective value. The fact that the word 'good' serves as one of our main moral terms is a trace of this pattern of objectification.

Similarly related uses of words are covered by the distinction between hypothetical and categorical imperatives. The statement that someone 'ought to' or, more strongly, 'must' do such-and-such may be backed up explicitly or implicitly by reference to what he wants or to what his purposes and objects are. Again, there may be a reference to the purposes of someone else, perhaps the speaker: 'You must do this'—'Why?'—'Because I want such-and-such'. The moral categorical imperative which could be expressed in the same words can be seen as resulting from the suppression of the conditional clause in a hypothetical imperative without its being replaced by any such reference to the speaker's wants. The action in question is still required in something like the way in which it would be if it were appropriately related to a want, but it is no longer admitted that there is any contingent want upon which its being required depends. Again this move can be understood when we remember that at least our central moral and basic moral judgements represent social demands, where the source of the demand is indeterminate and diffuse. Whose demands or wants are in question, the agent's, or the speaker's, or those of an indefinite multitude of other people? All of these in a way, but there are advantages in not specifying them precisely. The speaker is expressing demands which he makes as a member of a community, which he has developed in and by participation in a joint way of life; also, what is required of this particular agent would be required of any other in a relevantly similar situation; but the agent too is expected to have internalized the relevant demands, to act as if the ends for which the action is required were his own. By suppressing any explicit reference to demands and making the imperatives categorical we facilitate conceptual moves from one such demand relation to another. The moral uses of such words as 'must' and 'ought' and 'should', all of which are used also to express hypothetical imperatives, are traces of this pattern of objectification.

It may be objected that this explanation links normative ethics too closely with descriptive morality, with the mores or socially enforced patterns of behaviour that anthropologists record. But it can hardly be denied that moral thinking starts from the enforcement of social codes. Of course it is not confined to that. But even when moral judgements are detached from the mores of any actual society they are liable to be framed with reference to an ideal community of moral agents, such as Kant's kingdom of ends, which but for the need to give God a special place in it would have been better called a commonwealth of ends.

Another way of explaining the objectification of moral values is to say that ethics is a system of law from which the legislator has been removed. This might have been derived either from the positive law of a state or from a supposed system of divine law. There can be no doubt that some features of modern European moral concepts are traceable to the theological ethics of Christianity. The stress on quasi-imperative notions, on what ought to be done or on what is wrong in a sense that is close to that of 'forbidden', are surely relics of divine commands. Admittedly, the central ethical concepts for Plato and Aristotle also are in a broad sense prescriptive or intrinsically action-guiding, but in concentrating rather on 'good' than on 'ought' they show that their moral thought is an objectification of the desired and the satisfying rather than of the commanded. Elizabeth Anscombe has argued that modern, non-Aristotelian, concepts of *moral* obligation, *moral* duty, of what is *morally* right and wrong, and of the *moral* sense of 'ought' are survivals outside the framework of thought that made them really intelligible, namely the belief in divine law. She infers that 'ought' has 'become a word of mere mesmeric force', with only a 'delusive appearance of content', and that we would do better to discard such terms and concepts altogether, and go back to Aristotelian ones.

There is much to be said for this view. But while we can explain some distinctive features of modern moral philosophy in this way, it would be a mistake to see the whole problem of the claim to objective prescriptivity as merely local and unnecessary, as a post-operative complication of a society from which a dominant system of theistic belief has recently been rather hastily excised. As Cudworth and Clarke and Price, for example, show, even those who still admit divine commands, or the positive law of God, may believe moral values to have an independent objective but still action-guiding authority. Responding to Plato's *Euthyphro* dilemma, they believe that God commands what he commands because it is in itself good or right, not that it is good or right merely because and in that he commands it. Otherwise God himself could not be called good. Price asks, 'What can be more preposterous, than to make the Deity nothing but will; and to exalt this on the ruins of all his attributes?' The apparent objectivity of moral value is a widespread phenomenon which has more than one source: the persistence of a belief in something like divine law when the belief in the divine legislator has faded out is only one factor among others. There are several different patterns of objectification, all of which have left characteristic traces in our actual moral concepts and moral language.

11. The general goal of human life

The argument of the preceding sections is meant to apply quite generally to moral thought, but the terms in which it has been stated are largely those of the Kantian and post-Kantian tradition of English moral philosophy. To those who are more familiar with another tradition, which runs through Aristotle and Aquinas, it may seem wide of the mark. For them, the fundamental notion is that of the good for man, or the general end or goal of human life, or perhaps of a set of basic goods or primary human purposes. Moral reasoning consists partly in achieving a more adequate under-

standing of this basic goal (or set of goals), partly in working out the best way of pursuing and realizing it. But this approach is open to two radically different interpretations. According to one, to say that something is the good for man or the general goal of human life is just to say that this is what men in fact pursue or will find ultimately satisfying, or perhaps that it is something which, if postulated as an implicit goal, enables us to make sense of actual human strivings and to detect a coherent pattern in what would otherwise seem to be a chaotic jumble of conflicting purposes. According to the other interpretation, to say that something is the good for man or the general goal of human life is to say that this is man's proper end, that this is what he ought to be striving after, whether he in fact is or not. On the first interpretation we have a descriptive statement, on the second a normative or evaluative or prescriptive one. But this approach tends to combine the two interpretations, or to slide from one to the other, and to borrow support for what are in effect claims of the second sort from the plausibility of statements of the first sort.

I have no quarrel with this notion interpreted in the first way. I would only insert a warning that there may well be more diversity even of fundamental purposes, more variation in what different human beings will find ultimately satisfying, than the terminology of '*the* good for man' would suggest. Nor indeed, have I any quarrel with the second, prescriptive, interpretation, provided that it is recognized as subjectively prescriptive, that the speaker is here putting forward his own demands or proposals, or those of some movement that he represents, though no doubt linking these demands or proposals with what he takes to be already in the first, descriptive, sense fundamental human goals. But if it is claimed that something is objectively the right or proper goal of human life, then this is tantamount to the assertion of something that is objectively categorically imperative, and comes fairly within the scope of our previous arguments. Indeed, the running together of what I have here called the two interpretations is yet another pattern of objectification: a claim to objective prescriptivity is constructed by combining the normative element in the second interpretation with the objectivity allowed by the first, by the statement that such and such are fundamentally pursued or ultimately satisfying human goals. The argument from relativity still applies: the radical diversity of the goals that men actually pursue and find satisfying makes it implausible to construe such pursuits as resulting from an imperfect grasp of a unitary true good. So too does the argument from queerness; we can still ask what this objectively prescriptive rightness of the true goal can be, and how this is linked on the one hand with the descriptive features of this goal and on the other with the fact that it is *to some extent* an actual goal of human striving.

To meet these difficulties, the objectivist may have recourse to the purpose of God: the true purpose of human life is fixed by what God intended (or, intends) men to do and to be. Actual human strivings and satisfactions have some relation to this true end because God made men for this end and made them such as to pursue it—but only *some* relation, because of the inevitable imperfection of created beings.

I concede that if the requisite theological doctrine could be defended, a kind of objective ethical prescriptivity could be thus introduced. Since I think that theism cannot be defended, I do not regard this as any threat to my argument. [. . .]

12. Conclusion

I have maintained that there is a real issue about the status of values, including moral values. Moral scepticism, the denial of objective moral values, is not to be confused with any one of several first order normative views, or with any linguistic or conceptual analysis. Indeed, ordinary moral judgements involve a claim to objectivity which both non-cognitive and naturalist analyses fail to capture. Moral scepticism must, therefore, take the form of an error theory, admitting that a belief in objective values is built into ordinary moral thought and language, but holding that this ingrained belief is false. As such, it needs arguments to support it against 'common sense'. But solid arguments can be found. The considerations that favour moral skepticism are: first, the relativity or variability of some important starting points of moral thinking and their apparent dependence on actual ways of life; secondly, the metaphysical peculiarity of the supposed objective values, in that they would have to be intrinsically action-guiding and motivating; thirdly, the problem of how such values could be consequential or supervenient upon natural features; fourthly, the corresponding epistemological difficulty of accounting for our knowledge of value entities or features and of their links with the features on which they would be consequential; fifthly, the possibility of explaining, in terms of several different patterns of objectification, traces of which remain in moral language and moral concepts, how even if there were no such objective values people not only might have come to suppose that there are but also might persist firmly in that belief. These five points sum up the case for moral skepticism; but of almost equal importance are the preliminary removal of misunderstandings that often prevent this thesis from being considered fairly and explicitly, and the isolation of those items about which the moral sceptic is sceptical from many associated qualities and relations whose objective status is not in dispute.

John Rawls

Two Concepts of Rules

In this paper I want to show the importance of the distinction between justifying a practice[1] and justifying a particular action falling under it, and I want to explain the logical basis of this distinction and how it is possible to miss its significance. While the distinction has frequently been made and is now becoming commonplace, there remains the task of explaining the tendency either to overlook it altogether, or to fail to appreciate its importance.

To show the importance of the distinction I am going to defend utilitarianism against those objections which have traditionally been made against it in connection with punishment and the obligation to keep promises. I hope to show that if one uses the distinction in question then one can state utilitarianism in a way which makes it a much better explication of our considered moral judgments than these traditional objections would seem to admit. Thus the importance of the distinction is shown by the way it strengthens the utilitarian view regardless of whether that view is completely defensible or not.

To explain how the significance of the distinction may be overlooked, I am going to discuss two conceptions of rules. One of these conceptions conceals the importance of distinguishing between the justification of a rule or practice and the justification of a particular action falling under it. The other conception makes it clear why this distinction must be made and what is its logical basis.

John Rawls, "Two Concepts of Rules" from *Philosophical Review,* 64 (1955).

1. I use the word "practice" throughout as a sort of technical term meaning any form of activity specified by a system of rules which defines offices, roles, moves, penalties, defenses, and so on, and which gives the activity its structure. As examples one may think of games and rituals, trials and parliaments.

I

The subject of punishment, in the sense of attaching legal penalties to the violation of legal rules, has always been a troubling moral question. The trouble about it has not been that people disagree as to whether or not punishment is justifiable. Most people have held that, freed from certain abuses, it is an acceptable institution. Only a few have rejected punishment entirely, which is rather surprising when one considers all that can be said against it. The difficulty is with the justification of punishment: various arguments for it have been given by moral philosophers, but so far none of them has won any sort of general acceptance; no justification is without those who detest it. I hope to show that the use of the aforementioned distinction enables one to state the utilitarian view in a way which allows for the sound points of its critics.

For our purposes we may say that there are two justifications of punishment. What we may call the retributive view is that punishment is justified on the grounds that wrongdoing merits punishment. It is morally fitting that a person who does wrong should suffer in proportion to his wrongdoing. That a criminal should be punished follows from his guilt, and the severity of the appropriate punishment depends on the depravity of his act. The state of affairs where a wrongdoer suffers punishment is morally better than the state of affairs where he does not; and it is better irrespective of any of the consequences of punishing him.

What we may call the utilitarian view holds that on the principle that bygones are bygones and that only future consequences are material to present decisions, punishment is justifiable only by reference to the probable consequences of maintaining it as one of the devices of the social order. Wrongs committed in the past are, as such, not relevant considerations for deciding what to do. If punishment can be shown to promote effectively the interest of society it is justifiable, otherwise it is not.

I have stated these two competing views very roughly to make one feel the conflict between them: one feels the force of *both* arguments and one wonders how they can be reconciled. From my introductory remarks it is obvious that the resolution which I am going to propose is that in this case one must distinguish between justifying a practice as a system of rules to be applied and enforced, and justifying a particular action which falls under these rules; utilitarian arguments are appropriate with regard to questions about practices, while retributive arguments fit the application of particular rules to particular cases.

We might try to get clear about this distinction by imagining how a father might answer the question of his son. Suppose the son asks, "Why was J put in jail yesterday?" The father answers, "Because he robbed the bank at B. He was duly tried and found guilty. That's why he was put in jail yesterday." But suppose the son had asked a different question, namely, "Why do people put other people in jail?" Then the father might answer, "To protect good people from bad people" or "To stop people from doing things that would make it uneasy for all of us; for otherwise we wouldn't be able to go to bed at night and sleep in peace." There are two very different questions here. One question emphasizes the proper name: it asks why J was punished rather than someone else, or it asks what he was punished for. The other question asks why we have the institution of punishment: why do people punish one another rather than, say, always forgiving one another?

Thus the father says in effect that a particular man is punished, rather than some other man, because he is guilty, and he is guilty because he broke the law (past tense). In his case the law looks back, the judge looks back, the jury looks back, and a penalty is visited upon him for something he did. That a man is to be punished, and what his punishment is to be, is settled by its being shown that he broke the law and that the law assigns that penalty for the violation of it.

On the other hand we have the institution of punishment itself, and recommend and accept various changes in it, because it is thought by the (ideal) legislator and by those to whom the law applies that, as a part of a system of law impartially applied from case to case arising under it, it will have the consequence, in the long run, of furthering the interests of society.

One can say, then, that the judge and the legislator stand in different positions and look in different directions: one to the past, the other to the future. The justification of what the judge does, *qua* judge, sounds like the retributive view; the justification of what the (ideal) legislator does, *qua* legislator, sounds like the utilitarian view. Thus both views have a point (this is as it should be since intelligent and sensitive persons have been on both sides of the argument); and one's initial confusion disappears once one sees that these views apply to persons holding different offices with different duties, and situated differently with respect to the system of rules that make up the criminal law.[2]

One might say, however, that the utilitarian view is more fundamental since it applies to a more fundamental office, for the judge carries out the legislator's will so far as he can determine it. Once the legislator decides to have laws and to assign penalties for their violation (as things are there must be both the law and the penalty) an institution is set up which involves a retributive conception of particular cases. It is part of the concept of the criminal law as a system of rules that the application and enforcement of these rules in particular cases should be justifiable by arguments of a retributive character. The decision whether or not to use law rather than some other mechanism of social control, and the decision as to what laws to have and what penalties to assign, may be settled by utilitarian arguments; but if one decides to have laws then one has decided on something whose working in particular cases is retributive in form.

The answer, then, to the confusion engendered by the two views of punishment is quite simple: one distinguishes two offices, that of the judge and that of the legislator, and one distinguishes their different stations with respect to the system of rules which make up the law; and then one notes that the different sorts of considerations which would usually be offered as reasons for what is done under the cover of these offices can be paired off with the competing justifications of punishment. One

---

2. Note the fact that different sorts of arguments are suited to different offices. One way of taking the differences between ethical theories is to regard them as accounts of the reasons expected in different offices.

reconciles the two views by the time-honored device of making them apply to different situations.

But can it really be this simple? Well, this answer allows for the apparent intent of each side. Does a person who advocates the retributive view necessarily advocate, as an *institution,* legal machinery whose essential purpose is to set up and preserve a correspondence between moral turpitude and suffering? Surely not. What retributionists have rightly insisted upon is that no man can be punished unless he is guilty, that is, unless he has broken the law. Their fundamental criticism of the utilitarian account is that, as they interpret it, it sanctions an innocent person's being punished (if one may call it that) for the benefit of society.

On the other hand, utilitarians agree that punishment is to be inflicted only for the violation of law. They regard this much as understood from the concept of punishment itself. The point of the utilitarian account concerns the institution as a system of rules: utilitarianism seeks to limit its use by declaring it justifiable only if it can be shown to foster effectively the good of society. Historically it is a protest against the indiscriminate and ineffective use of the criminal law. It seeks to dissuade us from assigning to penal institutions the improper, if not sacrilegious, task of matching suffering with moral turpitude. Like others, utilitarians want penal institutions designed so that, as far as humanly possible, only those who break the law run afoul of it. They hold that no official should have discretionary power to inflict penalties whenever he thinks it for the benefit of society; for on utilitarian grounds an institution granting such power could not be justified.

The suggested way of reconciling the retributive and the utilitarian justifications of punishment seems to account for what both sides have wanted to say. There are, however, two further questions which arise, and I shall devote the remainder of this section to them.

First, will not a difference of opinion as to the proper criterion of just law make the proposed reconciliation unacceptable to retributionists? Will they not question whether, if the utilitarian principle is used as the criterion, it follows that those who have broken the law are guilty in a way which satisfies their demand that those punished deserve to be punished? To answer this difficulty, suppose that the rules of the criminal law are justified on utilitarian grounds (it is only for laws that meet his criterion that the utilitarian can be held responsible). Then it follows that the actions which the criminal law specifies as offenses are such that, if they were tolerated, terror and alarm would spread in society. Consequently, retributionists can only deny that those who are punished deserve to be punished if they deny that such actions are wrong. This they will not want to do.

The second question is whether utilitarianism doesn't justify too much. One pictures it as an engine of justification which, if consistently adopted, could be used to justify cruel and arbitrary institutions. Retributionists may be supposed to concede that utilitarians *intend* to reform the law and to make it more humane; that utilitarians do not *wish* to justify any such thing as punishment of the innocent; and that utilitarians may appeal to the fact that punishment presupposes guilt in the sense that by punishment one understands an institution attaching penalties to the infraction of legal rules, and therefore that it is logically absurd to suppose that utilitarians in justifying *punishment* might also have justified punishment (if we may call it that) of the innocent. The real question, however, is whether the utilitarian, in justifying punishment, hasn't used arguments which commit him to accepting the infliction of suffering on innocent persons if it is for the good of society (whether or not one calls this punishment). More generally, isn't the utilitarian committed in principle to accepting many practices which he, as a morally sensitive person, wouldn't want to accept? Retributionists are inclined to hold that there is no way to stop the utilitarian principle from justifying too much except by adding to it a principle which distributes certain rights to individuals. Then the amended criterion is not the greatest benefit of society *simpliciter,* but the greatest benefit of society subject to the constraint that no one's rights may be violated. Now while I think that the classical utilitarians proposed a criterion of this more complicated sort, I do not want to argue that point here. What I want to show is that there is *another* way of preventing the utilitarian principle from justifying too much, or at least of making it much less likely to do so: namely, by stating utilitarianism in a way which accounts for the distinction between the justification of an institution and the justification of a particular action falling under it.

I begin by defining the institution of punishment as follows: a person is said to suffer punishment whenever he is legally deprived of some of the normal rights of a citizen on the ground that he has violated a rule of law, the violation having been established by trial according to the due process of law, provided that the deprivation is carried out by the recognized legal authorities of the state, that the rule of law clearly specifies both the offense and the attached penalty, that the courts construe statutes strictly, and that the statute was on the books prior to the time of the offense. This definition specifies what I shall understand by punishment. The question is whether utilitarian arguments may be found to justify institutions widely different from this and such as one would find cruel and arbitrary.

This question is best answered, I think, by taking up a particular accusation. Consider the following from Carritt:

> . . . the utilitarian must hold that we are justified in inflicting pain always and only to prevent worse pain or bring about greater happiness. This, then, is all we need to consider in so-called punishment, which must be purely preventive. But if some kind of very cruel crime becomes common, and none of the criminals can be caught, it might be highly expedient, as an example, to hang an innocent man, if a charge against him could be so framed that he were universally thought guilty; indeed this would only fail to be an ideal instance of utilitarian 'punishment' because the victim himself would not have been so likely as a real felon to commit such a crime in the future; in all other respects it would be perfectly deterrent and therefore felicific.[3]

Carritt is trying to show that there are occasions when a utilitarian argument would justify taking an action which would be generally condemned; and thus that utilitarianism justifies too much. But the failure of Carritt's argument lies in the fact that he makes no distinction between the justification of the general system of rules which constitutes penal institutions and the justification of particular applications of these rules to particular cases by the various officials whose job it is to

administer them. This becomes perfectly clear when one asks who the "we" are of whom Carritt speaks. Who is this who has a sort of absolute authority on particular occasions to decide that an innocent man shall be "punished" if everyone can be convinced that he is guilty? Is this person the legislator, or the judge, or the body of private citizens, or what? It is utterly crucial to know who is to decide such matters, and by what authority, for all of this must be written into the rules of the institution. Until one knows these things one doesn't know what the institution is whose justification is being challenged; and as the utilitarian principle applies to the institution one doesn't know whether it is justifiable on utilitarian grounds or not.

Once this is understood it is clear what the countermove to Carritt's argument is. One must describe more carefully what the *institution* is which his example suggests, and then ask oneself whether or not it is likely that having this institution would be for the benefit of society in the long run. One must not content oneself with the vague thought that, when it's a question of *this* case, it would be a good thing if *somebody* did something even if an innocent person were to suffer.

Try to imagine, then, an institution (which we may call "telishment") which is such that the officials set up by it have authority to arrange a trial for the condemnation of an innocent man whenever they are of the opinion that doing so would be in the best interests of society. The discretion of officials is limited, however, by the rule that they may not condemn an innocent man to undergo such an ordeal unless there is, at the time, a wave of offenses similar to that with which they charge him and telish him for. We may imagine that the officials having the discretionary authority are the judges of the higher courts in consultation with the chief of police, the minister of justice, and a committee of the legislature.

Once one realizes that one is involved in setting up an *institution,* one sees that the hazards are very great. For example, what check is there on the officials? How is one to tell whether or not their actions are authorized? How is one to limit the risks involved in allowing such systematic deception? How is one to avoid giving anything short of complete discretion to the authorities to telish anyone they like? In addition to these considerations, it is obvious that people will come to have a

---

3. *Ethical and Political Thinking* (Oxford, 1947), p. 65.

very different attitude towards their penal system when telishment is adjoined to it. They will be uncertain as to whether a convicted man has been punished or telished. They will wonder whether or not they should feel sorry for him. They will wonder whether the same fate won't at any time fall on them. If one pictures how such an institution would actually work, and the enormous risks involved in it, it seems clear that it would serve no useful purpose. A utilitarian justification for this institution is most unlikely.

It happens in general that as one drops off the defining features of punishment one ends up with an institution whose utilitarian justification is highly doubtful. One reason for this is that punishment works like a kind of price system: by altering the prices one has to pay for the performance of actions it supplies a motive for avoiding some actions and doing others. The defining features are essential if punishment is to work in this way; so that an institution which lacks these features, e.g., an institution which is set up to "punish" the innocent, is likely to have about as much point as a price system (if one may call it that) where the prices of things change at random from day to day and one learns the price of something after one has agreed to buy it.

If one is careful to apply the utilitarian principle to the institution which is to authorize particular actions, then there is *less* danger of its justifying too much. Carritt's example gains plausibility by its indefiniteness and by its concentration on the particular case. His argument will only hold if it can be shown that there are utilitarian arguments which justify an institution whose publicly ascertainable offices and powers are such as to permit officials to exercise that kind of discretion in particular cases. But the requirement of having to build the arbitrary features of the particular decision into the institutional practice makes the justification much less likely to go through.

II

I shall now consider the question of promises. The objection to utilitarianism in connection with promises seems to be this: it is believed that on the utilitarian view when a person makes a promise the only ground upon which he should keep it, if he should keep it, is that by keeping it he will realize the most good on the whole. So that if one asks the question "Why should I keep *my* promise?" the utilitarian answer is understood to be that doing so in this case will have the best consequences. And this answer is said, quite rightly, to conflict with the way in which the obligation to keep promises is regarded.

Now of course critics of utilitarianism are not unaware that one defense sometimes attributed to utilitarians is the consideration involving the practice of promise-keeping. In this connection they are supposed to argue something like this: it must be admitted that we feel strictly about keeping promises, more strictly than it might seem our view can account for. But when we consider the matter carefully it is always necessary to take into account the effect which our action will have on the practice of making promises. The promisor must weigh, not only the effects of breaking his promise on the particular case, but also the effect which his breaking his promise will have on the practice itself. Since the practice is of great utilitarian value, and since breaking one's promise always seriously damages it, one will seldom be justified in breaking one's promise. If we view our individual promises in the wider context of the practice of promising itself we can account for the strictness of the obligation to keep promises. There is always one very strong utilitarian consideration in favor of keeping them, and this will insure that when the question arises as to whether or not to keep a promise it will usually turn out that one should, even where the facts of the particular case taken by itself would seem to justify one's breaking it. In this way the strictness with which we view the obligation to keep promises is accounted for.

Ross has criticized this defense as follows:[4] however great the value of the practice of promising, on utilitarian grounds, there must be some value which is greater, and one can imagine it to be obtainable by breaking a promise. Therefore there might be a case where the promisor could argue that breaking his promise was justified as leading to a better state of affairs on the whole. And the promisor could argue in this way no matter how slight the advantage won by breaking the promise.

---

4. Ross, *The Right and the Good*, pp. 38–39.

If one were to challenge the promisor his defense would be that what he did was best on the whole in view of all the utilitarian considerations, which in this case *include* the importance of the practice. Ross feels that such a defense would be unacceptable. I think he is right insofar as he is protesting against the appeal to consequences in general and without further explanation. Yet it is extremely difficult to weigh the force of Ross's argument. The kind of case imagined seems unrealistic and one feels that it needs to be described. One is inclined to think that it would either turn out that such a case came under an exception defined by the practice itself, in which case there would not be an appeal to consequences in general on the particular case, or it would happen that the circumstances were so peculiar that the conditions which the practice presupposes no longer obtained. But certainly Ross is right in thinking that it strikes us as wrong for a person to defend breaking a promise by a general appeal to consequences. For a general utilitarian defense is not open to the promisor: it is not one of the defenses allowed by the practice of making promises.

Ross gives two further counterarguments: First, he holds that it overestimates the damage done to the practice of promising by a failure to keep a promise. One who breaks a promise harms his own name certainly, but it isn't clear that a broken promise always damages the practice itself sufficiently to account for the strictness of the obligation. Second, and more important, I think, he raises the question of what one is to say of a promise which isn't known to have been made except to the promisor and the promisee, as in the case of a promise a son makes to his dying father concerning the handling of the estate. In this sort of case the consideration relating to the practice doesn't weigh on the promisor at all, and yet one feels that this sort of promise is as binding as other promises. The question of the effect which breaking it has on the practice seems irrelevant. The only consequence seems to be that one can break the promise without running any risk of being censured; but the obligation itself seems not the least weakened. Hence it is doubtful whether the effect on the practice ever weighs in the particular case; certainly it cannot account for the strictness of the obligation where it fails to obtain. It seems to follow that a utilitarian account of the obligation to keep promises cannot be successfully carried out.

From what I have said in connection with punishment, one can foresee what I am going to say about these arguments and counterarguments. They fail to make the distinction between the justification of a practice and the justification of a particular action falling under it, and therefore they fall into the mistake of taking it for granted that the promisor, like Carritt's official, is entitled without restriction to bring utilitarian considerations to bear in deciding whether to keep *his* promise. But if one considers what the practice of promising is one will see, I think, that it is such as not to allow this sort of general discretion to the promisor. Indeed, the point of the practice is to abdicate one's title to act in accordance with utilitarian and prudential considerations in order that the future may be tied down and plans coordinated in advance. There are obvious utilitarian advantages in having a practice which denies to the promisor, as a defense, any general appeal to the utilitarian principle in accordance with which the practice itself may be justified. There is nothing contradictory, or surprising, in this: utilitarian (or aesthetic) reasons might properly be given in arguing that the game of chess, or baseball, is satisfactory just as it is, or in arguing that it should be changed in various respects, but a player in a game cannot properly appeal to such considerations as reasons for his making one move rather than another. It is a mistake to think that if the practice is justified on utilitarian grounds then the promisor must have complete liberty to use utilitarian arguments to decide whether or not to keep his promise. The practice forbids this general defense; and it is a purpose of the practice to do this. Therefore what the above arguments presuppose—the idea that if the utilitarian view is accepted then the promisor is bound if, and only if, the application of the utilitarian principle to his own case shows that keeping it is best on the whole—is false. The promisor is bound because he promised: weighing the case on its merits is not open to him.

Is this to say that in particular cases one cannot deliberate whether or not to keep one's promise? Of course not. But to do so is to deliberate whether the various excuses, exceptions and defenses, which are understood by, and which constitute an important part of, the practice, apply to one's own case. Various defenses for not keeping one's promise are allowed, but among them there isn't the one that, on general utilitarian grounds, the promisor (truly) thought his action best on the whole, even though there may be the defense that the consequences of keeping one's promise would have been *extremely* severe. While there are too many complexities here to consider all the necessary details, one can see that the general defense isn't allowed if one asks the following question: what would one say of someone who, when asked why he broke his promise, replied simply that breaking it was best on the whole? Assuming that his reply is sincere, and that his belief was reasonable (i.e., one need not consider the possibility that he was mistaken), I think that one would question whether or not he knows what it means to say "I promise" (in the appropriate circumstances). It would be said of someone who used this excuse without further explanation that he didn't understand what defenses the practice, which defines a promise, allows to him. If a child were to use this excuse one would correct him; for it is part of the way one is taught the concept of a promise to be corrected if one uses this excuse. The point of having the practice would be lost if the practice did allow this excuse.

It is no doubt part of the utilitarian view that every practice admit the defense that the consequences of abiding by it would, have been extremely severe; and utilitarians would be inclined to hold that some reliance on people's good sense and some concession to hard cases is necessary. They would hold that a practice is justified by serving the interests of those who take part in it; and as with any set of rules there is understood a background of circumstances under which it is expected to be applied and which need not—indeed which cannot—be fully stated. Should these circumstances change, then even if there is no rule which provides for the case, it may still be in accordance with the practice that one be released from one's obligation. But this sort of defense allowed by a practice must not be confused with the general option to weigh each particular case on utilitarian grounds which critics of utilitarianism have thought it necessarily to involve.

The concern which utilitarianism raises by its justification of punishment is that it may justify too much.

The question in connection with promises is different: it is how utilitarianism can account for the obligation to keep promises at all. One feels that the recognized obligation to keep one's promise and utilitarianism are incompatible. And to be sure, they are incompatible if one interprets the utilitarian view as necessarily holding that each person has complete liberty to weigh every particular action on general utilitarian grounds. But must one interpret utilitarianism in this way? I hope to show that, in the sorts of cases I have discussed, one cannot interpret it in this way.

III

So far I have tried to show the importance of the distinction between the justification of a practice and the justification of a particular action falling under it by indicating how this distinction might be used to defend utilitarianism against two longstanding objections. One might be tempted to close the discussion at this point by saying that utilitarian considerations should be understood as applying to practices in the first instance and not to particular actions falling under them except insofar as the practices admit of it. One might say that in this modified form it is a better account of our considered moral opinions and let it go at that. But to stop here would be to neglect the interesting question as to how one can fail to appreciate the significance of this rather obvious distinction and can take it for granted that utilitarianism has the consequence that particular cases may always be decided on general utilitarian grounds. I want to argue that this mistake may be connected with misconceiving the logical status of the rules of practices; and to show this I am going to examine two conceptions of rules, two ways of placing them within the utilitarian theory.

The conception which conceals from us the significance of the distinction I am going to call the summary view. It regards rules in the following way: one supposes that each person decides what he shall do in particular cases by applying the utilitarian principle; one supposes further that different people will decide the same particular case in the same way and that there will be recurrences of cases similar to those previously decided.

Thus it will happen that in cases of certain kinds the same decision will be made either by the same person at different times or by different persons at the same time. If a case occurs frequently enough one supposes that a rule is formulated to cover that sort of case. I have called this conception the summary view because rules are pictured as summaries of past decisions arrived at by the *direct* application of the utilitarian principle to particular cases. Rules are regarded as reports that cases of a certain sort have been found on *other* grounds to be properly decided in a certain way (although, of course, they do not *say* this).

There are several things to notice about this way of placing rules within the utilitarian theory.

1. The point of having rules derives from the fact that similar cases tend to recur and that one can decide cases more quickly if one records past decisions in the form of rules. If similar cases didn't recur, one would be required to apply the utilitarian principle directly, case by case, and rules reporting past decisions would be of no use.

2. The decisions made on particular cases are logically prior to rules. Since rules gain their point from the need to apply the utilitarian principle to many similar cases, it follows that a particular case (or several cases similar to it) may exist whether or not there is a rule covering that case. We are pictured as recognizing particular cases prior to there being a rule which covers them, for it is only if we meet with a number of cases of a certain sort that we formulate a rule. Thus we are able to describe a particular case as a particular case of the requisite sort whether there is a rule regarding *that* sort of case or not. Put another way: what the *A*'s and the *B*'s refer to in rules of the form 'Whenever *A* do *B*' may be described as *A*'s and *B*'s whether or not there is the rule 'Whenever *A* do *B*', or whether or not there is any body of rules which make up a practice of which that rule is a part.

To illustrate this consider a rule, or maxim, which could arise in this way: suppose that a person is trying to decide whether to tell someone who is fatally ill what his illness is when he has been asked to do so. Suppose the person to reflect and then decide, on utilitarian grounds, that he should not answer truthfully; and suppose that on the basis of this and other like occasions he formulates a rule to the effect that when asked by someone fatally ill what his illness is, one should not tell him. The point to notice is that someone's being fatally ill and asking what his illness is, and someone's telling him, are things that can be described as such whether or not there is this rule. The performance of the action to which the rule refers doesn't require the stage-setting of a practice of which this rule is a part. This is what is meant by saying that on the summary view particular cases are logically prior to rules.

3. Each person is in principle always entitled to reconsider the correctness of a rule and to question whether or not it is proper to follow it in a particular case. As rules are guides and aids, one may ask whether in past decisions there might not have been a mistake in applying the utilitarian principle to get the rule in question, and wonder whether or not it is best in this case. The reason for rules is that people are not able to apply the utilitarian principle effortlessly and flawlessly; there is need to save time and to post a guide. On this view a society of rational utilitarians would be a society without rules in which each person applied the utilitarian principle directly and smoothly, and without error, case by case. On the other hand, ours is a society in which rules are formulated to serve as aids in reaching these ideally rational decisions on particular cases, guides which have been built up and tested by the experience of generations. If one applies this view to rules, one is interpreting them as maxims, as "rules of thumb"; and it is doubtful that anything to which the summary conception did apply would be called a *rule*. Arguing as if one regarded rules in this way is a mistake one makes while doing philosophy.

4. The concept of a *general* rule takes the following form. One is pictured as estimating on what percentage of the cases likely to arise, a given rule may be relied upon to express the correct decision, that is, the decision that would be arrived at if one were to correctly apply the utilitarian principle case by case. If one estimates that by and large the rule will give the correct decision, or if one estimates that the likelihood of making a mistake by applying the utilitarian principle directly on one's own is greater than the likelihood of making a mistake by following the rule, and if these considerations held of persons generally, then one would be jus-

tified in urging its adoption as a general rule. In this way *general* rules might be accounted for on the summary view. It will still make sense, however, to speak of applying the utilitarian principle case by case, for it was by trying to foresee the results of doing this that one got the initial estimates upon which acceptance of the rule depends. That one is taking a rule in accordance with the summary conception will show itself in the naturalness with which one speaks of the rule as a guide, or as a maxim, or as a generalization from experience, and as something to be laid aside in extraordinary cases where there is no assurance that the generalization will hold and the case must therefore be treated on its merits. Thus there goes with this conception the notion of a particular exception which renders a rule suspect on a particular occasion.

The other conception of rules I will call the practice conception. On this view rules are pictured as defining a practice. Practices are set up for various reasons, but one of them is that in many areas of conduct each person's deciding what to do on utilitarian grounds case by case leads to confusion, and that the attempt to coordinate behavior by trying to foresee how others will act is bound to fail. As an alternative one realizes that what is required is the establishment of a practice, the specification of a new form of activity; and from this one sees that a practice necessarily involves the abdication of full liberty to act on utilitarian and prudential grounds. It is the mark of a practice that being taught how to engage in it involves being instructed in the rules which define it, and that appeal is made to those rules to correct the behavior of those engaged in it. Those engaged in a practice recognize the rules as defining it. The rules cannot be taken as simply describing how those engaged in the practice in fact behave: it is not simply that they act as if they were obeying the rules. Thus it is essential to the notion of a practice that the rules are publicly known and understood as definitive; and it is essential also that the rules of a practice can be taught and can be acted upon to yield a coherent practice. On this conception, then, rules are not generalizations from the decisions of individuals applying the utilitarian principle directly and independently to recurrent particular cases. On the contrary, rules define a practice and are themselves the subject of the utilitarian principle.

To show the important differences between this way of fitting rules into the utilitarian theory and the previous way, I shall consider the differences between the two conceptions on the points previously discussed.

1. In contrast with the summary view, the rules of practices are logically prior to particular cases. This is so because there cannot be a particular case of an action falling under a rule of a practice unless there is the practice. This can be made clearer as follows: in a practice there are rules setting up offices, specifying certain forms of action appropriate to various offices, establishing penalties for the breach of rules, and so on. We may think of the rules of a practice as defining offices, moves, and offenses. Now what is meant by saying that the practice is logically prior to particular cases is this: given any rule which specifies a form of action (a move), a particular action which would be taken as falling under this rule given that there is the practice would not be *described as* that sort of action unless there was the practice. In the case of actions specified by practices it is logically impossible to perform them outside the stage-setting provided by those practices, for unless there is the practice, and unless the requisite proprieties are fulfilled, whatever one does, whatever movements one makes, will fail to count as a form of action which the practice specifies. What one does will be described in some *other* way.

One may illustrate this point from the game of baseball. Many of the actions one performs in a game of baseball one can do by oneself or with others whether there is the game or not. For example, one can throw a ball, run, or swing a peculiarly shaped piece of wood. But one cannot steal base, or strike out, or draw a walk, or make an error, or balk; although one can do certain things which appear to resemble these actions such as sliding into a bag, missing a grounder and so on. Striking out, stealing a base, balking, etc., are all actions which can only happen in a game. No matter what a person did, what he did would not be described as stealing a base or striking out or drawing a walk unless he could also be described as playing baseball, and for him to be doing this presupposes the rule-like practice which constitutes the game. The practice is logically prior to particular cases: unless there is the practice the terms referring to actions specified by it lack a sense.

2. The practice view leads to an entirely different conception of the authority which each person has to decide on the propriety of following a rule in particular cases. To engage in a practice, to perform those actions specified by a practice, means to follow the appropriate rules. If one wants to do an action which a certain practice specifies then there is no way to do it except to follow the rules which define it. Therefore, it doesn't make sense for a person to raise the question whether or not a rule of a practice correctly applies to *his* case where the action he contemplates is a form of action defined by a practice. If someone were to raise such a question, he would simply show that he didn't understand the situation in which he was acting. If one wants to perform an action specified by a practice, the only legitimate question concerns the nature of the practice itself ("How do I go about making a will?").

This point is illustrated by the behavior expected of a player in games. If one wants to play a game, one doesn't treat the rules of the game as guides as to what is best in particular cases. In a game of baseball if a batter were to ask "Can I have four strikes?" it would be assumed that he was asking what the rule was; and if, when told what the rule was, he were to say that he meant that on this occasion he thought it would be best on the whole for him to have four strikes rather than three, this would be most kindly taken as a joke. One might contend that baseball would be a better game if four strikes were allowed instead of three; but one cannot picture the rules as guides to what is best on the whole in particular cases, and question their applicability to particular cases as particular cases.

3 and 4. To complete the four points of comparison with the summary conception, it is clear from what has been said that rules of practices are not guides to help one decide particular cases correctly as judged by some higher ethical principle. And neither the quasi-statistical notion of generality, nor the notion of a particular exception, can apply to the rules of practices. A more or less general rule of a practice must be a rule which according to the structure of the practice applies to more or fewer of the kinds of cases arising under it; or it must be a rule which is more or less basic to the understanding of the practice. Again, a particular case cannot be an exception to a rule of a practice. An ex-

ception is rather a qualification or a further specification of the rule.

If follows from what we have said about the practice conception of rules that if a person is engaged in a practice, and if he is asked why *he* does what *he* does, or if he is asked to defend what he does, then his explanation, or defense, lies in referring the questioner to the practice. He cannot say of *his* action, if it is an action specified by a practice, that he does it rather than some other because he thinks it is best on the whole. When a man engaged in a practice is queried about his action he must assume that the questioner either doesn't know that he is engaged in it ("Why are you in a hurry to pay him?" "I promised to pay him today") or doesn't know what the practice is. One doesn't so much justify one's particular action as explain, or show, that it is in accordance with the practice. The reason for this is that it is only against the stage-setting of the practice that one's particular action is described as it is. Only by reference to the practice can one *say* what one is doing. To explain or to defend one's own action, as a particular action, one fits it into the practice which defines it. If this is not accepted it's a sign that a different question is being raised as to whether one is justified in accepting the practice, or in tolerating it. When the challenge is to the practice, citing the rules (saying what the practice is) is naturally to no avail. But when the challenge is to the particular action defined by the practice, there is nothing one can do but refer to the rules. Concerning particular actions there is only a question for one who isn't clear as to what the practice is, or who doesn't know that it is being engaged in. This is to be contrasted with the case of a maxim which may be taken as pointing to the correct decision on the case as decided on *other* grounds, and so giving a challenge on the case a sense by having it question whether these other grounds really support the decision on this case.

If one compares the two conceptions of rules I have discussed, one can see how the summary conception misses the significance of the distinction between justifying a practice and justifying actions falling under it. On this view rules are regarded as guides whose purpose it is to indicate the ideally rational decision on the given particular case which the flawless application of the utilitarian principle would yield. One has, in principle, full option to use the guides or to discard them as the situation warrants without one's moral office being altered in any way: whether one discards the rules or not, one always holds the office of a rational person seeking case by case to realize the best on the whole. But on the practice conception, if one holds an office defined by a practice then questions regarding one's actions in this office are settled by reference to the rules which define the practice. If one seeks to question these rules, then one's office undergoes a fundamental change: one then assumes the office of one empowered to change and criticize the rules, or the office of a reformer, and so on. The summary conception does away with the distinction of offices and the various forms of argument appropriate to each. On that conception there is one office and so no offices at all. It therefore obscures the fact that the utilitarian principle must, in the case of actions and offices defined by a practice, apply to the practice, so that general utilitarian arguments are not available to those who act in offices so defined.

Some qualifications are necessary in what I have said. First, I may have talked of the summary and the practice conceptions of rules as if only one of them could be true of rules, and if true of any rules, then necessarily true of *all* rules. I do not, of course, mean this. (It is the critics of utilitarianism who make this mistake insofar as their arguments against utilitarianism presuppose a summary conception of the rules of practices.) Some rules will fit one conception, some rules the other; and so there are rules of practices (rules in the strict sense), and maxims and "rules of thumb."

Secondly, there are further distinctions that can be made in classifying rules, distinctions which should be made if one were considering other questions. The distinctions which I have drawn are those most relevant for the rather special matter I have discussed, and are not intended to be exhaustive.

Finally, there will be many border-line cases about which it will be difficult, if not impossible, to decide which conception of rules is applicable. One expects border-line cases with any concept, and they are especially likely in connection with such involved concepts as those of a practice, institution, game, rule, and so on. Wittgenstein has shown how fluid these notions are.[5]

What I have done is to emphasize and sharpen two conceptions for the limited purpose of this paper.

IV

What I have tried to show by distinguishing between two conceptions of rules is that there is a way of regarding rules which allows the option to consider particular cases on general utilitarian grounds; whereas there is another conception which does not admit of such discretion except insofar as the rules themselves authorize it. I want to suggest that the tendency while doing philosophy to picture rules in accordance with the summary conception is what may have blinded moral philosophers to the significance of the distinction between justifying a practice and justifying a particular action falling under it; and it does so by misrepresenting the logical force of the reference to the rules in the case of a challenge to a particular action falling under a practice, and by obscuring the fact that where there is a practice, it is the practice itself that must be the subject of the utilitarian principle.

It is surely no accident that two of the traditional test cases of utilitarianism, punishment and promises, are clear cases of practices. Under the influence of the summary conception it is natural to suppose that the officials of a penal system, and one who has made a promise, may decide what to do in particular cases on utilitarian grounds. One fails to see that a general discretion to decide particular cases on utilitarian grounds is incompatible with the concept of a practice; and that what discretion one does have is itself defined by the practice (e.g., a judge may have discretion to determine the penalty within certain limits). The traditional objections to utilitarianism which I have discussed presuppose the attribution to judges, and to those who have made promises, of a plenitude of moral authority to decide particular cases on utilitarian grounds. But once one fits utilitarianism together with the notion of a practice, and notes that punishment and promising are practices, then one sees that this attribution is logically precluded.

That punishment and promising are practices is beyond question. In the case of promising this is shown by the fact that the form of words "I promise" is a performative utterance which presupposes the stage-setting of

---

5. *Philosophical Investigations* (Oxford, 1953), I, pars. 65–71, for example.

the practice and the proprieties defined by it. Saying the words "I promise" will only be promising given the existence of the practice. It would be absurd to interpret the rules about promising in accordance with the summary conception. It is absurd to say, for example, that the rule that promises should be kept could have arisen from its being found in past cases to be best on the whole to keep one's promise; for unless there were already the understanding that one keeps one's promises as part of the practice itself there couldn't have been any cases of promising.

It must, of course, be granted that the rules defining promising are not codified, and that one's conception of what they are necessarily depends on one's moral training. Therefore it is likely that there is considerable variation in the way people understand the practice, and room for argument as to how it is best set up. For example, differences as to how strictly various defenses are to be taken, or just what defenses are available, are likely to arise amongst persons with different backgrounds. But irrespective of these variations it belongs to the concept of the practice of promising that the general utilitarian defense is not available to the promisor. That this is so accounts for the force of the traditional objection which I have discussed. And the point I wish to make is that when one fits the utilitarian view together with the practice conception of rules, as one must in the appropriate cases, then there is nothing in that view which entails that there must be such a defense, either in the practice of promising, or in any other practice.

Punishment is also a clear case. There are many actions in the sequence of events which constitute someone's being punished which presuppose a practice. One can see this by considering the definition of punishment which I gave when discussing Carritt's criticism of utilitarianism. The definition there stated refers to such things as the normal rights of a citizen, rules of law, due process of law, trials and courts of law, statutes, etc., none of which can exist outside the elaborate stage-setting of a legal system. It is also the case that many of the actions for which people are punished presuppose practices. For example, one is punished for stealing, for trespassing, and the like, which presuppose the institution of property. It is impossible to say what punishment is, or to describe a particular instance of it, without refer-

ring to offices, actions, and offenses specified by practices. Punishment is a move in an elaborate legal game and presupposes the complex of practices which make up the legal order. The same thing is true of the less formal sorts of punishment: a parent or guardian or someone in proper authority may punish a child, but no one else can.

There is one mistaken interpretation of what I have been saying which it is worthwhile to warn against. One might think that the use I am making of the distinction between justifying a practice and justifying the particular actions falling under it involves one in a definite social and political attitude in that it leads to a kind of conservatism. It might seem that I am saying that for each person the social practices of his society provide the standard of justification for his actions; therefore let each person abide by them and his conduct will be justified.

This interpretation is entirely wrong. The point I have been making is rather a logical point. To be sure, it has consequences in matters of ethical theory; but in itself it leads to no particular social or political attitude. It is simply that where a form of action is specified by a practice there is no justification possible of the particular action of a particular person save by reference to the practice. In such cases the action is what it is in virtue of the practice and to explain it is to refer to the practice. There is no inference whatsoever to be drawn with respect to whether or not one should accept the practices of one's society. One can be as radical as one likes but in the case of actions specified by practices the objects of one's radicalism must be the social practices and people's acceptance of them.

I have tried to show that when we fit the utilitarian view together with the practice conception of rules, where this conception is appropriate, we can formulate it in a way which saves it from several traditional objections. I have further tried to show how the logical force of the distinction between justifying a practice and justifying an action falling under it is connected with the practice conception of rules and cannot be understood as long as one regards the rules of practices in accordance with the summary view. Why, when doing philosophy, one may be inclined to so regard them, I have not discussed. The reasons for this are evidently very deep and would require another paper.

Christine M. Korsgaard

What's Wrong with Lying?

The question I am going to discuss in this paper is: Why is it wrong to tell lies? I am going to discuss three reasons moral philosophers have proposed in answer to this question. I will begin by saying quickly what they are. Intuitionists think that lying is wrong just because it is lying, and for no further reason. Consequentialists think that lying is wrong because it has harmful consequences. And Kantians think lying is wrong because it violates the autonomy of the person to whom you lie.

Before I begin discussing these three views, I want to explain why I think that this question is important. Almost everyone thinks that lying is wrong: that is, that there is a general moral presumption against it. But almost no one thinks that lying is *always* wrong: most of us believe that there are some occasions when a lie is justified or even obligatory. Now what this suggests is that lying is not wrong simply, but that it is wrong for some further reason, and so that we can give an account of what is wrong with it. For if lying is wrong for a reason, then it will be wrong only on those occasions when that reason holds. But there will also be occasions when it is not wrong: occasions when the reason either does not hold, or is overridden. If this is correct, it is of great practical importance, as well as theoretical interest, to know why lying is wrong. Only if you know the reason why lying is wrong will you know when that reason holds, and only if you know when the reason holds will you know when it is wrong to lie, and when it is not. And of course this illustrates a more general point. We need to know what is behind our ordinary moral principles in order to apply those principles correctly. What I want to discuss, then, is why lying is wrong, with a view to determining when it is wrong, and when it is not.

Proponents of the first view I am going to discuss would be uncomfortable with some of the remarks I have just made. From the late seventeenth century on there has been a school of moral thought according to which moral principles like "lying is wrong," "killing is wrong," and "being unfaithful to your friends is wrong" are self-evident truths for which no further reason can be given. These philosophers are called intuitionists, because they believe we know moral truths through direct rational intuition.[1] According to intuitionists, moral principles are simply obvious to any rational person who is thinking clearly. They are obvious in the way that it is obvious that, say, 2 + 2 = 4, or in the way that it is obvious that you cannot be in two places at the same time. You can tell that these things are so just by thinking.

Now you will see right away that according to this view, there is not much we can say about what is wrong with lying, any more than there is much we can say about why 2 + 2 = 4 or why you cannot be in two places at the same time. These are not things for which we normally give reasons, because they are too basic. Some philosophers say that once someone fully understands what these statements mean, he will see immediately that the statements must be true. And the intuitionists say this sort of thing about lying: once you really understand what it is, you will see immediately that it must be wrong. So on this view there is no real answer to the question, "What's wrong with lying?"

---

1. There have been many intuitionists, especially in the tradition of English-speaking philosophers. Some of the major ones include Samuel Clarke, *A Discourse Concerning the Unchangeable Obligations of Natural Religion* (London, 1706); Richard Price, *A Review of the Principal Questions and Difficulties in Morals* (London, 1758); William Whewell, *The Elements of Morality, Including Polity* (Cambridge, 1845); W. D. Ross, *The Right and the Good* (Oxford: Clarendon Press, 1930); and H. A. Prichard, *Moral Obligation and Duty and Interest: Essays and Lectures by H. A. Prichard,* edited by W. D. Ross and J. O. Urmson (Oxford: Oxford University Press, 1968). Selections from Clarke and Price may be found in D. D. Raphael's two-volume *British Moralists, 1650–1800* (Indianapolis: Hackett Publishing Co., 1991).

The wrongness of lying is basic. The intuitionist says that what is wrong with lying is just that it is *lying*.

You might think that this means that intuitionists are committed to the view that lying is always wrong, or absolutely wrong. But this is not what intuitionists believe. Most intuitionists distinguish between an action being wrong *prima facie* and it being wrong "all things considered."[2] To say that something is wrong *prima facie* is to say that it is wrong if everything else is equal. *Prima facie,* lying is always wrong, but all things considered it is not. This is because sometimes telling the truth would require violating one of your other duties. By telling the truth, you may violate a promise to keep a secret; or if the truth hurts, you may violate the duty to be merciful; or if the truth kills, you may violate the duty to preserve life. When two duties conflict, we must violate one of them. If we must violate the duty to tell the truth, lying is not wrong all things considered, although it is still wrong *prima facie*. The intuitionist, then, would be uncomfortable with one of the things I said when I described my project at the beginning. I suggested that lying must be wrong for a reason, and the occasions when it is not wrong must be the occasions when the reason either does not hold or is overridden. Now the intuitionist thinks that lying is not wrong for any reason except the fact that it is *lying*. So the reason against lying is always in force. But the intuitionist would agree that the reason can be overridden, when some more important duty is involved in the case.

Let me point out some advantages and disadvantages of the intuitionist position before I go on. An advantage is that it seems to coincide with common sense views of morality. Many people would agree with the claim that you should not lie unless telling the truth violates some more important duty. And many people would agree with the intuitionist's model of how we make moral decisions—by balancing and weighing various moral principles. Also, many people would endorse the following claim: even when lying is justified, there is

_____

2. I get the term *prima facie* from W. D. Ross, a major intuitionist of the early twentieth century. Some contemporary philosophers prefer to use the term *pro tanto* for this kind of reason, reserving the term *prima facie* for a consideration that appears, at first blush, to be a reason, but may not be one in context.

something morally distasteful and regrettable about it. When you tell a justified lie, you usually feel some of the same emotions you feel when you do something wrong. You feel guilty towards the person to whom you lie and you might even want to apologize when the need for deception is over. The intuitionist tries to explain these feelings by appealing to the idea that although the lie is not wrong all things considered, it is still *prima facie* wrong. He says this is why you still feel bad: because you have done something that is *prima facie* wrong.

The disadvantage of the intuitionist view is that it can tell us nothing about when lying is wrong all things considered and when the duty to tell the truth is outweighed by another duty. And this is because we can give no account of why various kinds of actions are right or wrong. If there are reasons for our duties, we can weigh the importance of the duties by comparing the reasons for them. But the intuitionist believes that there is no method for resolving conflicts of duty. An intuitionist thinks that if you are well brought up and have life experience, you will become a good judge about which of two conflicting duties is the more important. Now this too may coincide with our common sense views about morality. But the need to depend on experience and judgment may be one of the things about common sense morality that we regret. We might have hoped that moral philosophy could help us to resolve such conflicts. More important is the fact that the view makes it mysterious what we are doing when we compare the importance of two duties. If there is no further reason why lying is wrong or killing is wrong, then how can there be a reason why killing is worse than lying? So it is not really clear what it is that the person who is good at weighing the importance of different duties is a good judge *of*. The problem is not only that the intuitionist lacks a method for resolving moral conflicts, but also that it is unclear what the method would tell you if you did have it.

Now I am going to devote the rest of my discussion to two views according to which there is something a little more helpful to say about what is wrong with lying, views according to which we can give an account of why lying is wrong. To keep things simple, I am going to focus on a particular kind of lie. The occasions on which many lies are told are such that those lies are wrong in a variety of ways. Malicious lies, told in order to hurt people, or lies told in the service of concealing crimes or other wrong actions, are wrong in more than one way, and may be more seriously wrong because of the role that they play in evil projects than they are just *as* lies. I want to know what is wrong, if anything, with lies just *as such,* so I want to avoid these complications. There are two kinds of lies that even decent and morally good people are regularly tempted to tell. These are lies told to protect your privacy, and benevolent lies: lies told for good purposes. Because I am not convinced that lies told to protect your privacy are wrong, I am going to focus on the case of benevolent lies. More specifically still, I am going to focus on the two-person case. I am not going to consider the kind of case in which, say, you lie to me in order to protect a third party. That case too may introduce complicating factors. I am going to discuss the case of paternalistic lies: the case where you lie to me for my own good, because you think it would be better for me to believe, or perhaps just to hear, something other than the truth. Two things make this the best case for us to think about. First, as I mentioned, this kind of case is one of great practical concern to most of us, since this is one of the kinds of lies that we are often tempted to tell. Second, this kind of case is clear of all morally complicating factors. Only two people are involved and the lie is told for a good purpose. Whatever is wrong with lies *just insofar as they are lies* should show up in this kind of case.

The two views I am going to describe are often confused, because as you will see there is a wide range of cases in which they will have exactly the same practical results. But in the most important and difficult cases they will diverge, so it is critically important both to distinguish them, and to discover which of them we really believe.

The first view I will discuss is what philosophers call a consequentialist theory.[3] According to such a theory,

morality is entirely concerned with the consequences of actions, with the benefits and harms that result from them. On this view there are reasons why actions are right or wrong: they are right because of the benefits they produce, and wrong because of the harm they do. I want you to notice something important about this view. This view provides us with a way of deciding what is right only if the ideas of good and bad, or benefit and harm, are objective and determinable: that is, if there are objective facts about what is good and bad and we can ascertain what those facts are. The consequentialist view gives us no guidance about what is right unless we suppose that we know, or can establish, what counts as good and what counts as bad. Only then can we determine empirically which actions will best promote the good consequences and avert the bad ones.

According to this view, what is wrong with lying? The answer has to be that lies are harmful, or, to put it more exactly, that lies tend to do more harm than good.

Now offhand it does not seem obvious that lies always or perhaps even usually do more harm than good. It seems to vary from case to case. So you might wonder why proponents of this theory think that there is even a *general* presumption against lying. And of course paternalistic lies are intended to do good, so if there is something wrong with them, it must be that, for some reason, they are usually misguided, and fail in their aim. The people who decide to tell them must be making some common mistake in their assessment of the consequences. If there is a *general* presumption against paternalistic lying, it must rest upon some quite general empirical fact, which paternalistic liars tend to forget.

I think that most people who accept the consequentialist view would make the following factual claim in order to explain the presumption against paternalistic lies. They would claim that people are in fact usually the best judges of what is good or bad for themselves. Suppose someone asks you for information. She thinks it would be good for her to know something you can tell

---

3. Consequentialism was introduced into philosophy independently by William Paley in *The Principles of Moral and Political Philosophy* (London, 1785) and Jeremy Bentham in *An Introduction to the Principles of Morals and Legislation* (London, 1789). Other influential presentations of consequentialism include those of John Stuart Mill in *Utilitarianism* (1861; Indianapolis: Hackett Publishing Co., 1979);

Henry Sidgwick in *The Methods of Ethics* (1st edition, 1874; 7th edition, 1907; Indianapolis: Hackett Publishing Co., 1981); and G. E. Moore in *Principia Ethica* (Cambridge: Cambridge University Press, 1903). Selections from Paley and Bentham may be found in volume two of D. D. Raphael's *British Moralists, 1650–1800.*

her. If you lie to her for her own good, it is because you think you know better than she does what it is good for her to know. Perhaps you think that she should be spared painful information, or diverted from making a poor decision. Usually, according to the consequentialist, you will be wrong as a matter of fact, because she is in the best position to judge what is good for her. But according to this view, paternalistic lies are completely justified and right when someone is not in the best position to judge what is best for herself.

Compare this to the intuitionist view we examined first. You will see right away that it compensates for one of the disadvantages of that view, but at the same time that it loses one of its advantages. The disadvantage that it compensates for is the lack of definite guidance provided by the intuitionist position. If we can determine when we are better judges than other people about what is good for them, then we will know when it is all right to tell paternalistic lies. So the consequentialist can give a definite answer about when we may lie and when we may not.

The advantage that it loses is that it fails to capture the common-sense notion that telling a lie, even when it is justified, is morally regrettable. If the *only* reason that it is wrong to tell paternalistic lies is that people are the usually best judges of what is for their own good, then when they are *not* the best judges it is not wrong to lie—*not at all*. I suppose we might think it is regrettable that people are not always good judges of what is best for themselves. The world would be arranged more efficiently if everyone were capable of looking after herself. But this is not a *moral* ground for regret. It does not explain the guilt we feel towards those we lie to. So the consequentialist is unable to explain the feelings of moral distaste we have for telling lies even when they are justified. Or, rather, he must dismiss these feelings as irrational, perhaps just the result of the fact that we have been trained to feel badly when we lie.

This disparity with common sense morality is not the only thing troubling about the consequentialist view, however. The real trouble emerges when we compare two of the assumptions used in the consequentialist argument against paternalistic lies. One of the assumptions of consequentialism generally is that we have an objective, empirically determinable notion of what is good and bad, beneficial and harmful. Another is that people

are, as a matter of fact, usually the best judges of what is good or bad for themselves. These two assumptions do not harmonize well together. If what is good is an objective, empirically determinable matter of fact, then there ought to be a science of the good and people who are experts in that science. These people would be experts about what is good for others as well as for themselves. But if this is so, then it does not seem very likely that people in general will be the best judges of what is good and bad for themselves. There are not many matters of fact about which everyone is equally an expert, or especially likely to be expert in his own case.[4]

The most important philosophical consequentialists, the utilitarians, thought that they could answer this objection. They believed that what makes a life good is some sort of psychological state, something that can best be measured and assessed by the person himself. Most utilitarians believe that what makes life good is either pleasure, or the satisfaction of desire, and what makes life bad is pain or frustration. Since people know what they want and what pleases them, they know what is best for themselves. But this answer is not really very good. Its appeal depends on the supposition that you have direct conscious access to your own pleasure and satisfaction *when they are present*. But even if this is true, it does not show that the individual knows best what will give her pleasure in the future or will satisfy her future desires. Furthermore, while the existence of present pleasure and satisfaction may be things about which you are an expert in your own case, this does not make you an expert about the means for bringing these states

---

4. The Greek philosopher Socrates, the first moral philosopher in the Western tradition, frequently noted this difference between ethics and technical subjects: that there do not appear to be any experts in ethics. He sometimes suggests this is evidence that ethics is not a technical subject, which puts him at odds with the consequentialists' way of thinking. See, for instance, Plato's dialogue *Protagoras,* trans. Stanley Lombardo and Karen Bell (Indianapolis: Hackett Publishing Co., 1992), pp. 13–14 or 319b–320a in the "Stephanus numbers" commonly used in scholarly references to the works of Plato, which indicate the page and section of the relevant volume of the Greek text of Plato as edited by the French scholar Henri Estienne (in Latin, Stephanus).

about. And if you do not agree with the utilitarian that the goodness of life consists in mere pleasure or satisfaction, the idea of individual expertise looks even less plausible. Some philosophers believe that a good human life necessarily includes such things as virtue, knowledge, achievement, and friendship, because these things are objectively good. If this is so, the idea that each person is an expert about how to achieve a good life for herself becomes even less plausible, because we know that people often fail to value these things as much as they should.[5]

So there is a second problem with this view. The view does not provide a very coherent explanation of why paternalistic lies are usually wrong. For on this view, the reason not to tell paternalistic lies is that people are the best judges of what constitutes and promotes their own good. But for consequentialism to work, we must have an objective and empirically determinable notion of what is good. And once we have such a notion, it looks as if it is going to be possible for some people to be experts about the good life. The assumption that people are the best judges of the goodness of their own lives will no longer seem plausible, and the presumption against paternalistic lying will be left unsupported.

If this is correct, the consequentialist view leaves too much scope for telling paternalistic lies. As I have said, it is not even clear that there is a *general* presumption against them. Yet most of us think that there is. When somebody lies to *you* for your own good, and you find out about it, you usually think the liar is a presumptuous busybody, and you resent his action. Paternalism is considered out of line when we are dealing with normal sane and healthy adults.

Before I go on, let me deal with one argument that people commonly make at this point. You might now feel tempted to say that we can argue for the presumption against paternalistic lying this way. I should not tell

a paternalistic lie because in order to tell such a lie I must know myself to be an expert about the good life, but in fact who is to say who is an expert about the good life? Who is to say what is best for a person? There are several ways to reply to this argument. One I have already mentioned. If there is a matter of objective, knowable fact about what makes a life good, as the consequentialist must suppose, then there should be a science of the good life, and we will identify its experts in the usual way we identify the practitioners of a science. Another point is that the claim that we cannot tell who the expert about the good life is will not salvage the consequentialist argument against paternalistic lying, because the consequentialist argument against paternalistic lying appeals to the assumption that each person is the expert in his own case. We cannot let the consequentialist claim *both* that each person is the expert in his own case *and* that there is no way to tell who the expert is. If there is no way to tell who the expert is, then the paternalistic liar and his victim, are, as far as we know, equally likely to be the expert or to make mistakes.

Now at this point the consequentialist may want to change his tack slightly. He will continue to insist that for some reason there is no reliable way to tell who the expert is, but he will add that, since we cannot tell, it is preferable that people decide for themselves what is best for them. Even if the individual whose good is in question makes a mistake, this is less bad than if the paternalistic liar makes a mistake. The idea behind this claim is that it is less bad to make mistakes on your own behalf than on behalf of another, just as it is less bad to squander your own fortune than one you hold in trust. This, the consequentialist will claim, is the source of the presumption against paternalistic lying.

But the fact is that the consequentialist theory affords us no grounds for making this kind of claim. Consequentialists do not care who makes the mistakes but only how bad they are. The idea that it is better for people to make their own mistakes really comes from our third view. I will call this third view the Kantian view, after the philosopher from whom I get my account of it, Immanuel Kant.[6] The Kantian view is that

---

5. Of the consequentialists I mentioned in note 3, all were utilitarians except G. E. Moore, who believed in the objective goodness of certain complex states of affairs involving love, friendship, the appreciation of beauty, and so on. John Stuart Mill, however, believed that some pleasures are better in quality (not just quantity) than others, and that we do have to consult experts to determine which ones are better.

6. Two of Kant's main ethical writings—*Grounding for the Metaphysics of Morals* (1785) and Part II of *The Metaphysics*

each person *has a right to decide* what is good for herself. Each person has a right to decide what she will count as a good human life, and to live in accordance with her own conception of the good. The consequentialist view gains some illicit plausibility from its similarity to this view, so let me underscore the difference: according to the Kantian view, it is not that there is some determinate notion of what is good, and that each person is the expert about this in her own case. It is that each person *has a right to decide* what counts as good in her own case because it is her own case. It is not a question of an empirical fact about who has expertise, but rather of a right you hold simply on moral grounds—because you are the person whose life it is. People tend to confuse these two accounts of why each of us has authority over his own life. That is, we tend to confuse the factual claim that people are experts in their own case with the moral claim that people have a right to decide about their own case. I think that this makes the consequentialist view look more compelling than it really is.

I have claimed that the consequentialist view and the Kantian view are often confused with each other. This is because adherents of both views claim that the basis of the presumption against paternalistic lying is the importance of people running their own lives. When we lie to someone for her own good, we take her life out of her hands, and into our own. Both the consequentialist and the Kantian think this is a bad thing, although both also think that there are some cases in which paternalistic lying is justified. But the Kantian view turns out to be much stricter, in the sense of permitting fewer such lies, than the consequentialist view. For despite the similarity in the accounts these two views give of why it is wrong to tell paternalistic lies, the difference is critically important. The consequentialist thinks people should run their own lives because of a factual condition that often fails to hold: they are experts about their own good. The Kantian appeals not to a theoretical fact, but to a pure moral claim: a person has a right to run

___

of Morals, *The Metaphysical Principles of Virtue* (1797)—may be found in *Immanuel Kant: Ethical Philosophy,* trans. James Ellington (Indianapolis: Hackett Publishing Co., 1983). His third major work on the subject is the *Critique of Practical Reason,* trans. Werner Pluhar (1788; Indianapolis: Hackett Publishing Co., 2002).

his own life because he is the person whose life it is. Possession of this moral right does not depend on whether people are especially good at running their own lives or not. For a Kantian, the reason why paternalistic lies are wrong is always in force, even if it is sometimes overridden, whereas the consequentialist's reason may often simply fail to hold.

Some comparisons will help here. Consider the way we might argue for the universal franchise, for everyone's right to vote. Sometimes the argument is based on empirical claims about the effectiveness of the universal franchise in selecting good rulers. For instance, one may argue that when everyone pools their wisdom about government, individual biases, distortions, and limitations are corrected for: the group makes a more intelligent choice than any individual would. Or one might argue that if each person votes in a way that represents her own interests, the candidate selected will represent majority interests. Supposing that this is a good thing, the argument is that the group makes a better choice than any individual would. Both of these arguments rest in part on empirical or factual claims: they suggest that the voting public is a good judge of, or an expert on, the quality of its rulers. These arguments are like the consequentialist argument against paternalistic lies. They say that the public should be in charge because of the public's collective political expertise. A different kind of argument appeals to the fact that since everyone lives in this country and is affected by its policies and its fate, everyone has the *right* to vote for its rulers. It does not matter whether we are especially good at choosing competent rulers or not. Since it is our society, the choice of its rulers rightly rests with us. This is like the Kantian view of why we should not tell paternalistic lies. The Kantian view says you should run your life because it is *your* life, just as this view says you should have a say about your country's rulers because it is *your* country. The Kantian view is based on a pure moral right, not a doubtful empirical fact. The idea that the public has collective political expertise could be wrong. Some of us think that there is evidence that it is wrong. But the claim that everyone has a right to a voice in the political decisions that affect his own life is a moral claim, not a factual one.

Here is another case that has the same structure: the defense of the jury system. One might try to argue that the twelve people together have some kind of collective expertise on justice. When the twelve people pool their wisdom, the collective effect overcomes the distortions, biases, and limitations of individuals. This is a claim of empirical fact. On the other hand, we know that people who actually participate in juries sometimes come out feeling that it did not work this way at all. Sometimes they feel that the collective effort produced a good judgment, but at other times they come out feeling that making a good collective decision is uphill work against obtuseness and prejudice. There is a quite different argument available for the jury system, which is that when someone is accused of a crime against the community, it is morally right that representatives of the community should decide the case. The jury makes the decision not because it is especially good at making such decisions, but because the jury represents the community and the community has the right to judge the offender. This kind of argument is a moral one and does not depend on the empirical claim that a jury has some sort of collective judicial expertise.

The jury system and the universal franchise are institutions of democracy. They make a useful introduction to Kantian ideas because Kantian ethics is based on a view of how human beings should treat one another that is deeply democratic.

Kant argued that you must never treat a human being, either yourself or another, as mere means to an end, but always, as he put it, also at the same time as an end in himself.[7] The idea initially sounds puzzling. Obviously, Kant is not saying that we should never use a human being as a means at all, if a means is something that furthers our enterprises. We use each other as means all the time. The clerk who checks you out in the grocery store, the teacher who explains what you need to know, and the friend who gives you a ride to the airport all further your enterprises and so are means to your ends. But there is nothing pernicious about these relationships. And indeed, Kant insists on this himself when he says you must not treat a person as a *mere* means. What makes the difference between treating someone as a means in a permissible way and treating her as a *mere* means is whether you also treat her at the same time as an end in herself. But what does this mean? Normally, we think of an end as a purpose, an aim, something we try to bring about. Of course it makes no sense to talk about treating a human being like that. But an end is also something that we do not violate, something that we do not act against. And this is more what Kant has in mind.

In fact the distinction Kant has in mind is that between respecting someone's autonomy, or her capacity for self-government, and treating her as if she were merely a tool you may use to promote your own ends.[8] To respect someone's autonomy, not to violate it, is to treat her as someone whose beliefs and actions are, and should be, controlled by her own reason. It is to allow her to decide for herself what to do and what to think and what to be. Kant thinks that respect for autonomy requires not only a certain way of acting towards other people but even a certain way of thinking about them, a way that you will recognize as being in the ordinary sense "respectful." For example, everyone knows how enraging it is when someone who disagrees with you simply assumes that your view must be the result of prejudice or passion, or even that since you disagree with him you must be stupid.[9] These attitudes are disrespectful. We expect people to talk to us, and even to think of us, in a certain way: we expect people to deal with us on the assumption that we have reasons for our views, even if they disagree with those reasons. And we expect them to acknowledge our right to act on those reasons. If someone disagrees with you and you want her to agree, you may try to change her reasons by arguing with her, but you must not try either to bully her or to trick her into thinking or acting as you think best. This is true even if it is very important what she thinks.

---

7. See *Grounding for the Metaphysics of Morals,* op. cit., p. 36; p. 429 in the marginal numbers found in most translations, which refer to the pages in the relevant volumes of the standard German edition of Kant's complete works, *Kant's Gesammelte Schriften,* edited by the Royal Prussian (later German) Academy of Sciences (Berlin: Georg Reimer [later Walter DeGruyter & Co.], 1900–).

8. Or perhaps merely as an obstacle you can run roughshod over. That kind of treatment also violates the Kantian requirement.

9. See *The Metaphysical Principles of Virtue,* op. cit., pp. 128–129; pp. 463–464 in the Prussian Academy edition.

Suppose you are arguing about candidates and she is going to vote. If she among others votes wrongly, a bad candidate will be elected, and if it is to a powerful office, the results can be serious indeed. But this does not make it permissible to bully or trick her into voting the way you think best, any more than it makes it permissible to steal her registration card and vote in her place. She has a right to a vote: this means she *has a right to decide* for whom she will vote. In a democracy, poor judgment does not disqualify a person for citizenship. In Kant's theory, it does not disqualify her for the respect due to every rational being.

The requirement of respect for autonomy affects your treatment of others most directly when you are involved in a cooperative project, when you must act together. In our dealings with others, we often enlist their assistance towards the achievement of our own ends. We are to this extent asking them to contribute to our ends. So the requirement of respect for autonomy says that others have a right to decide whether or not to contribute to our ends. And it follows that we must treat them in a way that *enables* them to make that decision.

Let me use one of Kant's own examples to illustrate the point.[10] This is an example of a lie, but not of a paternalistic one. Suppose I am in need of some ready money, and I think perhaps I may get it from you. Since you have cash flow problems of your own, however, I think it is unlikely that you will give me the money unless you believe that I will pay you back next week. Actually, however, my financial situation is so bad that I will not be able to pay you back in the foreseeable future at all. But I don't think you will give me the money if I tell you the truth about that. So I go to you and say, "Lend me $50, would you? I promise to pay you back next week." I make a lying promise.

What exactly is wrong with this? On Kant's analysis, it is that you do not get to decide whether you will contribute to my end. You cannot decide whether to contribute to my end because you do not know what it really is. You think that the result of our transaction, the result to which you are being asked to contribute, is my temporary possession of your money. But actually the result of our transaction will be my indefinite possession of your money. You have been tricked into contributing to an end different from the one to which you thought you were contributing. I am treating you as a tool, rather than as a rational being, in this sense: what I say to you is just whatever I think will *work* to produce the result I want. I do not consider the fact that since you are contributing to this end you also, so to speak, have a right to vote on whether this end will be brought about or not. I treat you as a tool because, when I decide what to say to you, I think only about what levers to pull to get what I think is a good result. The Kantian view is deeply democratic, as I said earlier, in the sense that it implies that every rational being has a right to cast a vote about any end to which her own actions are to contribute.

But now notice an important thing: this analysis of what is wrong with the lie holds even if, contrary to what I thought, you *would* have lent me the money if you had known the truth. Indeed it holds even if you specifically want me to have the money, and you were planning to offer it to me. Whether you can share in my end depends not on whether you *would* have contributed to it if you had known what it really was, but on whether you *actually* had the chance to decide whether to contribute to it or not. Consider a comparison. Suppose I steal your voter registration card and vote in your place. When you remonstrate with me, I say, "Oh, it's all right, because I voted for the candidate you would have voted for anyway." Now maybe this will make you feel somewhat less upset. But it does not make what I did "all right." You will still feel that I have wronged you, even though the consequences are the same as if I had not. In the same way, what is wrong with my lie does not rest in its consequences, but in the fact that I have taken the decision out of your hands. That is just as wrong whether I make the decision the way you would have made it or not. And of course this means that the analysis applies to paternalistic lies as well. The lie is no less wrong if the end is one that you think is good for me. In fact since it is my own good that is involved and I have a special right to decide what is good for myself, paternalistic lies are in a way worse than others.

More generally, there are two conditions under which your autonomy is violated. One is when force or coercion is used to make you contribute to an end. The

---

10. *Grounding for the Metaphysics of Morals,* op. cit., p. 37; pp. 429–430 in the Prussian Academy edition.

other is when lies are used to trick you into contributing to an end. In both cases what is wrong is that you do not get to decide whether to contribute to the end or not. The conditions under which you are able to decide for yourself are that you have power over your own actions and knowledge of what is going on. Force and coercion, on the one hand, and lies, on the other, undercut these conditions. And so force and coercion and lies are, according to this view, the most fundamental forms of wrongdoing—the roots of all evil. Morality demands that we resist the ever-present temptation to *manage* things ourselves, and instead share our decisions —and so our knowledge and our power—with all who are concerned.

When I was discussing the consequentialist view, I suggested that questions like "who's to say what's really best for someone?" really get their rhetorical force from the Kantian view. Kant did not believe that we have an empirically determinable notion of what is good in a human life. But he did not deny that some things are better for people than others. He believed something more like this: you may think that you know what makes a human life good, but you have nothing to go on but the authority of your own reason. There are, after all, no independent tests for the correctness of views about what makes a human life good. If whatever authority your conception of the good has comes from your own reason, you must concede the same authority to anyone else's reason. And this is why you cannot lie to another in order to control the results of her actions, even, or rather especially, when it is for her own good.

On the Kantian view, the presumption against paternalistic lying is very strong. If someone asks you for information pertinent to her own life, it is because she has decided that she should have that information, that it is good for her to know. If you lie, you take it upon yourself to decide that it is not good for her to know. But she is the one who has the right to decide what it is good for her to know, where the information is relevant to her own life, and you are not. Perhaps the information she requests is painful or tragic. She may or may not have realized that, but you must assume that because she asks she has decided it is worth it to her to know the truth. It is not for you to say that a deluded pleasure is better for her than an honest grief. You may make

this choice for yourself, although I think that when it comes down to it, hardly anyone ever does. Most people want to know the truth about their own situation, and tend to reject paternalism when they imagine themselves as the objects of it. But even if you would make this choice for yourself, you cannot make it for someone else.

Although the presumption against paternalistic lies is strong, they are not excluded altogether. I said earlier that Kant's view makes lying and force and coercion, as the main ways of violating people's autonomy, the most fundamental forms of wrongdoing. But we do think the paternalistic use of force is sometimes justified, so we will also think that there is such a thing as a justified paternalistic lie. But the view is still very strict, for lies will be justified only in the same kinds of cases as force would be. Yet many people in fact tell paternalistic lies in circumstances in which they would not dream of resorting to force. They tell lies to people who are merely upset or vulnerable, for instance, when they would only use force on someone who was out of his mind. According to Kant's view, they are wrong. Lies and force are wrong in exactly the same way.[11] They violate people's autonomy. You cannot tell lies just to make people feel good, or to divert them from what you think are poor decisions, any more than you could use force for those reasons. And just as it is nearly always morally regrettable to use force on a person, so it is nearly always morally regrettable to lie, because it is regrettable to use a human being as a mere tool, even as a tool for his own good.

When exactly is paternalism justified? The answer is that telling paternalistic lies, like using paternalistic force, is justified only when we are dealing with people who are incapable of exercising their own reason, or severely crippled in the use of it by some condition like insanity or drunkenness. And the best justification for

---

11. In fact it is arguable that lies are a *deeper* violation of another's autonomy, since when you lie you do not merely ignore the fact that your victim has his own reason; you make use of it: if he were not a rational being, lying wouldn't be a way of getting him to do something. On the other hand, the use of force may be wrong in an *additional* way, since if it is not used carefully, the person who is forced may be injured, and using force means risking that possibility.

telling paternalistic lies, apart from protecting the incompetent person from physical harm, is developing or restoring his autonomy. For example, the encouraging lies we tell to children about the quality of their performance meet these two criteria. Children are rationally undeveloped, and encouraging lies help them develop the confidence they will need for autonomous adult life. But notice that we also use force on children to an extent that would be outrageous in dealing with adults. We ought to feel the same way about telling lies to adults. Using paternalistic force on adult human beings is justified only in cases involving immediate threats to life and limb or severe mental illness. So the same should be true of paternalistic lies. Only when people are severely incapacitated for making their own decisions may other people interfere. And of course it is important to add that it is cheating, or at least losing your nerve, if you treat the fact that someone makes a decision that you disagree with as *evidence* that she is severely incapacitated for making her own decisions.

Let me illustrate this last point with a real life story that a physician told me about another physician. This physician told a patient that he had a terrible illness and was probably going to die. The patient went home and committed suicide. The physician felt that she had been "burned" and resolved not to tell the truth about such matters again in the future. Let us ask ourselves what this physician was thinking. One way to understand the physician's decision is this. Perhaps she is a consequentialist. She thinks that she's an expert on the goodness of life, and she thinks that she knows that committing suicide is bad, even when it is done to avoid living through a terrible and probably hopeless illness. So she takes the incident as evidence that telling people the truth about their illnesses tends to produce a bad result, and therefore is wrong. Another way to understand the physician's attitude is this. The physician is a Kantian, but one who has lost her nerve. She believes that people ought to make their own decisions and so that they ought to know the truth about their own circumstances. But, just because she disagrees with this particular decision, she concludes that the patient who made it was incompetent to make decisions, and perhaps that all seriously ill people are incompetent to make decisions. Kantianism suggests another attitude is possible here and may even be required. The physician should not have

decided that she was "burned." She should have allowed that the patient had the right to choose a quick suicide over a lingering illness. The patient might have felt that he had a good reason to commit suicide, that it was better for him than living through the illness. And if so, his decision, and his right to make it, must be respected.

Of course this does not mean that you can never withhold the truth, nor am I saying that my description of this actual patient's mental state is obviously correct. Perhaps he was rendered mentally incompetent by the news of his illness and killed himself in a moment of insane despair. But my description is not obviously wrong either: I do not know whether the physician in question had any independent reason for believing the patient was incompetent to make the decision, apart from the fact that she disagreed with the decision he made. The point of the example is not to say that you must always tell the truth. The point is twofold: first, you have the right to withhold the truth about someone's life when he requests it only when you have some evidence of mental incompetence or irrationality. You cannot withhold the truth just because it will hurt, or because you do not approve of what you think the person will do once he knows it. Second, you should not treat the bare fact that someone disagrees with you as evidence of mental incompetence or irrationality.

It is hard to determine which of these three views about what is wrong with lying is the correct one. I am going to close with some speculations that are not directly about which view is correct, but about what I think most of us really believe. I think that elements of all three views appear in ordinary moral discourse about the subject, but that in fact not many people believe that lies are just wrong, and that no reason why they are wrong can be given. So I do not think that many people share the intuitionist's views. In the case of paternalistic lies, especially, we find that people often jumble together the empirical claim that people are experts about their own good with the moral claim that people have a right to decide what is for their own good. The same phenomenon occurs with respect to the two cases I used as comparisons: the defense of the universal franchise and the defense of the jury system. I will offer a psychological speculation about why we tend to jumble these arguments together. I do not think it is just a product of intellectual confusion. I think that most of us in fact believe something more like the Kantian account, but find it, for two reasons, intimidating to defend our decisions and opinions on the basis of it. One is that people find it intimidating in general to defend their decisions and opinions on the basis of their moral theories, and many of us are relieved when we can make our case by appealing to "hard" empirical facts instead. Although nowadays people tend to exaggerate the indefensibility of moral views, correct moral positions are certainly harder to establish than empirical facts. So the view that individuals, or voting publics, or juries should make certain kinds of decisions because of their expertise is a more comfortable one to defend than the view that these agencies just have the right to make these decisions, regardless of expertise. And since the argument that individuals, and voting publics, and juries are experts usually leads to the same conclusion as the moral position most of us really hold, we prefer to argue from these safer grounds. If you doubt that, imagine this: a political scientist proves to us, on the basis of extensive research, that a certain panel of experts would choose better rulers than the voting public does. He proposes that we should give up our votes and turn the selection of our rulers over to these experts. If this scenario distresses you—if you find yourself hoping that his results can be disproved—then your commitment to the universal franchise is not based on the idea that the public is a collective expert. If it were, and you learned that the voting public is not the most qualified expert, you would simply give up your support of the universal franchise, without any regret. The fact that most of us would find the political scientist's conclusions distressing shows that our commitment to the universal franchise comes from elsewhere. I suggest it comes from the moral view that the public *has a right to decide* who its rulers shall be. The idea that the public is good at choosing rulers does not really explain our position, but

it does prop it up, and makes it a less alarming one to hold. The same is true in the case of paternalistic lies. If you feel *relieved* when someone argues that people should make their own decisions because people usually *are* experts about their own good, it is because that consideration props your commitment to letting people run their own lives, not because it explains that commitment.

There is a second, although related, reason why the Kantian position can be a frightening one to hold. It is frightening to stand by and watch a person make a mess of his life, and so it is frightening to think that morality might require us to do that. On Kant's view you may argue with such people, but if you cannot convince them, you may not resort to tricks or force. But it is also frightening to stand by and watch the public elect a candidate with a poor grasp of economics or of nuclear science, and it is frightening to stand by and watch the question of an accused person's fate be settled by twelve ordinary, uninformed, biased, and sometimes unintelligent citizens. We do willingly stand by and let voting publics and juries make these decisions, however, and it is because there are cases in which what we really believe is that it is just as important who has the right to decide as it is whether the decision is a good one.

And the fact is that most of us do not believe that anyone is an expert about what constitutes a good life for a human being, and therefore our view that people ought to be in charge of their own lives *cannot* be based on the consequentialist theory that people are experts about their own good. It is, rather, based on the idea that the problem of what is worth doing, worth having, and worth knowing in a human life is one that every rational human being has the right to solve for herself. Interference with that right, no matter how well-intentioned, is in the deepest way disrespectful, and is almost always unwarranted. This is why is telling paternalistic lies is almost always wrong.

Applications

Philippa Foot

The Problem of Abortion and the Doctrine of the Double Effect

One of the reasons why most of us feel puzzled about the problem of abortion is that we want, and do not want, to allow to the unborn child the rights that belong to adults and children. When we think of a baby about to be born it seems absurd to think that the next few minutes or even hours could make so radical a difference to its status; yet as we go back in the life of the foetus we are more and more reluctant to say that this is a human being and must be treated as such. No doubt this is the deepest source of our dilemma, but it is not the only one. For we are also confused about the general question of what we may and may not do where the interests of human beings conflict. We have strong intuitions about certain cases; saying, for instance, that it is all right to raise the level of education in our country, though statistics allow us to predict that a rise in the suicide rate will follow, while it is not all right to kill the feeble-minded to aid cancer research. It is not easy, however, to see the principles involved, and one way of throwing light on the abortion issue will be by setting up parallels involving adults or children once born. So we will be able to isolate the "equal rights" issue, and should be able to make some advance.

I shall not, of course, discuss all the principles that may be used in deciding what to do where the interests or rights of human beings conflict. What I want to do is to look at one particular theory, known as the "doctrine of the double effect" which is invoked by Catholics in support of their views on abortion but supposed by them to apply elsewhere. As used in the abortion argument this doctrine has often seemed to non-Catholics to be a piece of complete sophistry. In the last number of the *Oxford Review* it was given short shrift by Professor Hart. And yet this principle has seemed to some non-Catholics as well as to Catholics to stand as the only defence against decisions on other issues that are quite unacceptable. It will help us in our difficulty about abortion if this conflict can be resolved.

The doctrine of the double effect is based on a distinction between what a man foresees as a result of his voluntary action and what, in the strict sense, he intends. He intends in the strictest sense both those things that he aims at as ends and those that he aims at as means to his ends. The latter may be regretted in themselves but nevertheless desired for the sake of the end, as we may intend to keep dangerous lunatics confined for the sake of our safety. By contrast a man is said not strictly, or directly, to intend the foreseen consequences of his voluntary actions where these are neither the end at which he is aiming nor the means to this end. Whether the word "intention" should be applied in both cases is not of course what matters: Bentham spoke of "oblique intention", contrasting it with the "direct intention" of ends and means, and we may as well follow his terminology. Everyone must recognize that some such distinction can be made, though it may be made in a number of different ways, and it is the distinction that is crucial to the doctrine of the double effect. The words "double effect" refer to the two effects that an action may produce: the one aimed at, and the one foreseen but in no way desired. By "the doctrine of the double

Philippa Foot, "The Problem of Abortion and the Doctrine of the Double Effect" from *Oxford Review*, 5 (1967). Reprinted with the permission of the author.

effect" I mean the thesis that it is sometimes permissible to bring about by oblique intention what one may not directly intend. Thus the distinction is held to be relevant to moral decision in certain difficult cases. It is said for instance that the operation of hysterectomy involves the death of the foetus as the foreseen but not strictly or directly intended consequence of the surgeon's act, while other operations kill the child and count as the direct intention of taking an innocent life, a distinction that has evoked particularly bitter reactions on the part of non-Catholics. If you are permitted to bring about the death of the child, what does it matter how it is done? The doctrine of the double effect is also used to show why in another case, where a woman in labour will die unless a craniotomy operation is performed, the intervention is not to be condoned. There, it is said, we may not operate but must let the mother die. We foresee her death but do not directly intend it, whereas to crush the skull of the child would count as direct intention of its death.

This last application of the doctrine has been queried by Professor Hart on the ground that the child's death is not strictly a means to saving the mother's life and should logically be treated as an unwanted but foreseen consequence by those who make use of the distinction between direct and oblique intention. To interpret the doctrine in this way is perfectly reasonable given the language that has been used; it would, however, make nonsense of it from the beginning. A certain event may be desired under one of its descriptions, unwanted under another, but we cannot treat these as two different events, one of which is aimed at and the other not. And even if it be argued that there are here two different events—the crushing of the child's skull and its death—the two are obviously much too close for an application of the doctrine of the double effect. To see how odd it would be to apply the principle like this we may consider the story, well known to philosophers, of the fat man stuck in the mouth of the cave. A party of potholers have imprudently allowed the fat man to lead them as they make their way out of the cave, and he gets stuck, trapping the others behind him. Obviously the right thing to do is to sit down and wait until the fat man grows thin; but philosophers have arranged that flood waters should be rising within the cave. Luckily (luckily?) the trapped party have with them a stick of dynamite with which they can blast the fat man out of the mouth of the cave. Either they use the dynamite or they drown. In one version the fat man, whose head is *in* the cave, will drown with them; in the other he will be rescued in due course. Problem: may they use the dynamite or not? Later we will find parallels to this example. Here it is introduced for light relief and because it will serve to show how ridiculous one version of the doctrine of the double effect would be. For suppose that the trapped explorers were to argue that the death of the fat man might be taken as a merely foreseen consequence of the act of blowing him up. ("We didn't want to kill him . . . only to blow him into small pieces" or even ". . . only to blast him out of the mouth of the cave.") I believe that those who use the doctrine of the double effect would rightly reject such a suggestion, though they will, of course, have considerable difficulty in explaining where the line is to be drawn. What is to be the criterion of "closeness" if we say that anything very close to what we are literally aiming at counts as if part of our aim?

Let us leave this difficulty aside and return to the arguments for and against the doctrine, supposing it to be formulated in the way considered most effective by its supporters, and ourselves bypassing the trouble by taking what must on any reasonable definition be clear cases of "direct" or "oblique" intention.

The first point that should be made clear, in fairness to the theory, is that no one is suggesting that it does not matter what you bring about as long as you merely foresee and do not strictly intend the evil that follows. We might think, for instance, of the (actual) case of wicked merchants selling, for cooking, oil they knew to be poisonous and thereby killing a number of innocent people, comparing and contrasting it with that of some unemployed gravediggers, desperate for custom, who got hold of this same oil and sold it (or perhaps *they* secretly gave it away) in order to create orders for graves. They strictly (directly) intend the deaths they cause, while the merchants could say that it was no part of their *plan* that anyone should die. In morality, as in law, the merchants, like the gravediggers, would be considered as murderers; nor are the supporters of the doctrine of the double effect bound to say that there is the least difference between them in respect of moral turpitude. What they are committed to is the thesis that *sometimes* it makes a difference to the permissibility of an action involving harm to others that this harm, although foreseen, is not part of the agent's direct intention. An end such as earning one's living is clearly not such as to justify *either* the direct or oblique intention of the death of innocent people, but in certain cases one is justified in bringing about knowingly what one could not directly intend.

It is now time to say why this doctrine should be taken seriously in spite of the fact that it sounds rather odd, that there are difficulties about the distinction on which it depends, and that it seemed to yield one sophistical conclusion when applied to the problem of abortion. The reason for its appeal is that its opponents have often *seemed* to be committed to quite indefensible views. Thus the controversy has raged around examples such as the following. Suppose that a judge or magistrate is faced with rioters demanding that a culprit be found for a certain crime and threatening otherwise to take their own bloody revenge on a particular section of the community. The real culprit being unknown, the judge sees himself as able to prevent the bloodshed only by framing some innocent person and having him executed. Beside this example is placed another in which a pilot whose aeroplane is about to crash is deciding whether to steer from a more to a less inhabited area. To make the parallel as close as possible it may rather be supposed that he is the driver of a runaway tram which he can only steer from one narrow track on to another; five men are working on one track and one man on the other; anyone on the track he enters is bound to be killed. In the case of the riots the mob have five hostages, so that in both the exchange is supposed to be one man's life for the lives of five. The question is why we should say, without hesitation, that the driver should steer for the less occupied track, while most of us would be appalled at the idea that the innocent man could be framed. It may be suggested that the special feature of the latter case is that it involves the corruption of justice, and this is, of course, very important indeed. But if we remove that special feature, supposing that some private individual is to kill an innocent person and pass him off as the criminal, we still find ourselves horrified by the idea. The doctrine of the double effect offers us a way out of the difficulty, insisting that it is one thing to steer towards someone foreseeing that

you will kill him and another to aim at his death as part of your plan. Moreover there is one very important element of good in what is here insisted. In real life it would hardly ever be certain that the man on the narrow track would be killed. Perhaps he might find a foothold on the side of the tunnel and cling on as the vehicle hurtled by. The driver of the tram does *not* then leap off and brain him with a crowbar. The judge, however, needs the death of the innocent man for his (good) purposes. If the victim proves hard to hang he must see to it that he dies another way. To choose to execute him is to choose that this evil *shall come about,* and this must therefore count as a *certainty* in weighing up the good and evil involved. The distinction between direct and oblique intention is crucial here, and is of great importance in an uncertain world. Nevertheless this is no way to defend the doctrine of the double effect. For the question is whether the difference between aiming at something and obliquely intending it is *in itself* relevant to moral decisions; not whether it is important when correlated with a difference of certainty in the balance of good and evil. Moreover we are particularly interested in the application of the doctrine of the double effect to the question of abortion, and no one can deny that in medicine there are sometimes certainties so complete that it would be a mere quibble to speak of the "probable outcome" of this course of action or that. It is not, therefore, with a merely philosophical interest that we should put aside the uncertainty and scrutinize the examples to test the doctrine of the double effect. Why can we not argue from the case of the steering driver to that of the judge?

Another pair of examples poses a similar problem. We are about to give to a patient who needs it to save his life a massive dose of a certain drug in short supply. There arrive, however, five other patients each of whom could be saved by one-fifth of that dose. We say with regret that we cannot spare our whole supply of the drug for a single patient, just as we should say that we could not spare the whole resources of a ward for one dangerously ill individual when ambulances arrive bringing in the victims of a multiple crash. We feel bound to let one man die rather than many if that is our only choice. Why then do we not feel justified in killing people in the interests of cancer research or to obtain, let us say, spare parts for grafting on to those who need them? We can suppose, similarly, that several danger-ously ill people can be saved only if we kill a certain in-dividual and make a serum from his dead body. (These examples are not over fanciful considering present con-troversies about prolonging the life of mortally ill pa-tients whose eyes or kidneys are to be used for others.) Why cannot we argue from the case of the scarce drug to that of the body needed for medical purposes? Once again the doctrine of the double effect comes up with an explanation. In one kind of case but not the other we aim at the death of the innocent man.

A further argument suggests that if the doctrine of the double effect is rejected this has the consequence of putting us hopelessly in the power of bad men. Suppose for example that some tyrant should threaten to torture five men if we ourselves would not torture one. Would it be our duty to do so, supposing we believed him, be-cause this would be no different from choosing to res-cue five men from his torturers rather than one? If so anyone who wants us to do something we think wrong has only to threaten that otherwise he himself will do something we think worse. A mad murderer, known to keep his promises, could thus make it our duty to kill some innocent citizen to prevent him from killing two. From this conclusion we are again rescued by the doc-trine of the double effect. If we refuse, we foresee that the greater number will be killed but we do not intend it: it is he who intends (that is strictly or directly intends) the death of innocent persons; we do not.

At one time I thought that these arguments in favour of the doctrine of the double effect were conclusive, but I now believe that the conflict should be solved in an-other way. The clue that we should follow is that the strength of the doctrine seems to lie in the distinction it makes between what we *do* (equated with direct in-tention) and what we allow (thought of as obliquely in-tended). Indeed it is interesting that the disputants tend to argue about whether we are to be held responsible for what we allow as we are for what we do. Yet it is not obvious that this is what they should be discussing, since the distinction between what one does and what one allows to happen is not the same as that between direct and oblique intention. To see this one has only to con-sider that it is possible *deliberately* to allow something to happen, aiming at it either for its own sake or as part of one's plan for obtaining something else. So one person

might want another person dead, and deliberately allow him to die. And again one may be said to *do* things that one does not aim at, as the steering driver would kill the man on the track. Moreover there is a large class of things said to be brought about rather than either done or allowed, and either kind of intention is possible. So it is possible to *bring about* a man's death by getting him to go to sea in a leaky boat, and the intention of his death may be either direct or oblique.

Whatever it may, or may not, have to do with the doctrine of the double effect, the idea of *allowing* is worth looking into in this context. I shall leave aside the special case of giving permission, which involves the idea of authority, and consider the two main divisions into which cases of allowing seem to fall. There is firstly the allowing which is forbearing to prevent. For this we need a sequence thought of as somehow already in train, and something that the agent could do to inter-vene. (The agent must be able to intervene, but does not do so.) So, for instance, he could warn someone, but *al-lows* him to walk into a trap. He could feed an animal but *allows* it to die for lack of food. He could stop a leak-ing tap but allows the water to go on flowing. This is the case of allowing with which we shall be concerned, but the other should be mentioned. It is the kind of allowing which is roughly equivalent to *enabling;* the root idea being the removal of some obstacle which is, as it were, holding back a train of events. So someone may remove a plug and *allow* water to flow; open a door and *allow* an animal to get out; or give someone money and *allow* him to get back on his feet.

The first kind of allowing requires an omission, but there is no other general correlation between omission and allowing, commission and bringing about or doing. An actor who fails to turn up for a performance will generally spoil it rather than allow it to be spoiled. I mention the distinction between omission and com-mission only to set it aside.

Thinking of the first kind of allowing (forebearing to prevent), we should ask whether there is any difference, from the moral point of view, between what one does or causes and what one merely allows. It seems clear that on occasions one is just as bad as the other, as is recog-nized in both morality and law. A man may murder his child or his aged relatives, by allowing them to die of starvation as well as by giving poison; he may also be convicted of murder on either account. In another case we would, however, make a distinction. Most of us allow people to die of starvation in India and Africa, and there is surely something wrong with us that we do; it would be nonsense, however, to pretend that it is only in law that we make a distinction between allowing people in the underdeveloped countries to die of starvation and sending them poisoned food. There is worked into our moral system a distinction between what we owe people in the form of aid and what we owe them in the way of non-interference. Salmond, in his *Jurisprudence,* expressed as follows the distinction between the two.

> "A positive right corresponds to a positive duty, and is a right that he on whom the duty lies shall do some positive act on behalf of the person entitled. A negative right corresponds to a negative duty, and is a right that the person bound shall refrain from some act which would operate to the prejudice of the person entitled. The former is a right to be positively benefited; the latter is merely a right not to be harmed."[1]

For our purposes it will do well. Let us speak of negative duties when thinking of the obligation to refrain from such things as killing or robbing, and of the positive duty, e.g., to look after children or aged parents. It will be useful, however, to extend the notion of positive duty beyond the range of things that are strictly called duties, bringing acts of charity under this heading. These are owed only in a rather loose sense, and some acts of charity could hardly be said to be *owed* at all, so I am not following ordinary usage at this point.

Let us now see whether the distinction of negative and positive duties explains why we see differently the action of the steering driver and that of the judge, of the doctors who withhold the scarce drug and those who obtain a body for medical purposes, of those who choose to rescue the five men rather than one man from torture and those who are ready to torture the one man themselves in order to save five. In each case we have a conflict of duties, but what kind of duties are they? Are we, in each case, weighing positive duties against positive, negative against negative, or one against the other? Is the duty to refrain from injury, or rather to bring aid?

The steering driver faces a conflict of negative duties, since it is his duty to avoid injuring five men and also his duty to avoid injuring one. In the circumstances he is not able to avoid both, and it seems clear that he should do the least injury he can. The judge, however, is weighing the duty of not inflicting injury against the duty of bringing aid. He wants to rescue the innocent people threatened with death but can do so only by inflicting injury himself. Since one does not *in general* have the same duty to help people as to refrain from injuring them, it is not possible to argue to a conclusion about what he should do from the steering driver case. It is interesting that, even where the strictest duty of positive aid exists, this still does not weigh as if a negative duty were involved. It is not, for instance, permissible to commit a murder to bring one's starving children food. If the choice is between inflicting injury on one or many there seems only one rational course of action; if the choice is between aid to some at the cost of injury to others, and refusing to inflict the injury to bring the aid, the whole matter is open to dispute. So it is not inconsistent of us to think that the driver must steer for the road on which only one man stands while the judge (or his equivalent) may not kill the innocent person in order to stop the riots. Let us now consider the second pair of examples, which concern the scarce drug on the one hand and on the other the body needed to save lives. Once again we find a difference based on the distinction between the duty to avoid injury and the duty to provide aid.

As a general account of rights and duties this is defective, since not all are so closely connected with benefit and harm. Nevertheless, where one man needs a massive dose of the drug and we withhold it from him in order to save five men, we are weighing aid against aid. But if we consider killing a man in order to use his body to save others, we are thinking of doing him injury to bring others aid. In an interesting variant of the model, we may suppose that instead of killing someone we deliberately let him die. (Perhaps he is a beggar to whom we are thinking of giving food, but then we say "No, they need bodies for medical research.") Here it does seem relevant that in allowing him to die we are aiming at his death,

---

1. J. Salmond, *Jurisprudence,* 11th edition, p. 283.

but presumably we are inclined to see this as a violation of negative rather than positive duty. If this is right, we see why we are unable in either case to argue to a conclusion from the case of the scarce drug.

In the examples involving the torturing of one man or five men, the principle seems to be the same as for the last pair. If we are bringing aid (rescuing people about to be tortured by the tyrant), we must obviously rescue the larger rather than the smaller group. It does not follow, however, that we would be justified in inflicting the injury, or getting a third person to do so, in order to save the five. We may therefore refuse to be forced into acting by the threats of bad men. To refrain from inflicting injury ourselves is a stricter duty than to prevent other people from inflicting injury, which is not to say that the other is not a very strict duty indeed.

So far the conclusions are the same as those at which we might arrive following the doctrine of the double effect, but in others they will be different, and the advantage seems to be all on the side of the alternative. Suppose, for instance, that there are five patients in a hospital whose lives could be saved by the manufacture of a certain gas, but that this inevitably releases lethal fumes into the room of another patient whom for some reason we are unable to move. His death, being of no use to us, is clearly a side effect, and not directly intended. Why then is the case different from that of the scarce drug, if the point about that is that we foresaw but did not strictly intend the death of the single patient? Yet it surely is different. The relatives of the gassed patient would presumably be successful if they sued the hospital and the whole story came out. We may find it particularly revolting that someone should be *used* as in the case where he is killed or allowed to die in the interest of medical research, and the fact of *using* may even determine what we would decide to do in some cases, but the principle seems unimportant compared with our reluctance to bring such injury for the sake of giving aid.

My conclusion is that the distinction between direct and oblique intention plays only a quite subsidiary role in determining what we say in these cases, while the distinction between avoiding injury and bringing aid is very important indeed. I have not, of course, argued that there are no other principles. For instance it clearly makes a difference whether our positive duty is a strict

duty or rather an act of charity: feeding our own children or feeding those in far away countries. It may also make a difference whether the person about to suffer is one thought of as uninvolved in the threatened disaster, and whether it is his presence that constitutes the threat to the others. In many cases we find it very hard to know what to say, and I have not been arguing for any general conclusion such as that we may never, whatever the balance of good and evil, bring injury to one for the sake of aid to others, even when this injury amounts to death. I have only tried to show that even if we reject the doctrine of the double effect we are not forced to the conclusion that the size of the evil must always be our guide.

Let us now return to the problem of abortion, carrying out our plan of finding parallels involving adults or children rather than the unborn. We must say something about the different cases in which abortion might be considered on medical grounds.

First of all there is the situation in which nothing that can be done will save the life of child and mother, but where the life of the mother can be saved by killing the child. This is parallel to the case of the fat man in the mouth of the cave who is bound to be drowned with the others if nothing is done. Given the certainty of the outcome, as it was postulated, there is no serious conflict of interests here, since the fat man will perish in either case, and it is reasonable that the action that will save someone should be done. It is a great objection to those who argue that the direct intention of the death of an innocent person is never justifiable that the edict will apply even in this case. The Catholic doctrine on abortion must here conflict with that of most reasonable men. Moreover we would be justified in performing the operation whatever the method used, and it is neither a necessary nor a good justification of the special case of hysterectomy that the child's death is not directly intended, being rather a foreseen consequence of what is done. What difference could it make as to how the death is brought about?

Secondly we have the case in which it is possible to perform an operation which will save the mother and kill the child or kill the mother and save the child. This is parallel to the famous case of the shipwrecked mariners who believed that they must throw someone overboard if their boat was not to founder in a storm, and to the other famous case of the two sailors, Dudley and Stephens, who killed and ate the cabin boy when adrift on the sea without food. Here again there is no conflict of interests so far as the decision to act is concerned; only in deciding whom to save. Once again it would be reasonable to act, though one would respect someone who held back from the appalling action either because he preferred to perish rather than do such a thing or because he held on past the limits of reasonable hope. In real life the certainties postulated by philosophers hardly ever exist, and Dudley and Stephens were rescued not long after their ghastly meal. Nevertheless if the certainty were absolute, as it might be in the abortion case, it would seem better to save one than none. Probably we should decide in favour of the mother when weighing her life against that of the unborn child, but it is interesting that, a few years later, we might easily decide it the other way.

The worst dilemma comes in the third kind of example where to save the mother we must kill the child, say by crushing its skull, while if nothing is done the mother will perish but the child can be safely delivered after her death. Here the doctrine of the double effect has been invoked to show that we may not intervene, since the child's death would be directly intended while the mother's would not. On a strict parallel with cases not involving the unborn we might find the conclusion correct though the reason given was wrong. Suppose, for instance, that in later life the presence of a child was certain to bring death to the mother. We would surely not think ourselves justified in ridding her of it by a process that involved its death. For in general we do not think that we can kill one innocent person to rescue another, quite apart from the special care that we feel is due to children once they have prudently got themselves born. What we would be prepared to do when a great many people were involved is another matter, and this is probably the key to one quite common view of abortion on the part of those who take quite seriously the rights of the unborn child. They probably feel that if *enough* people are involved one must be sacrificed, and they think of the mother's life against the unborn child's life as if it were many against one. But of course many people do not view it like this at all, having no inclination to accord to the foetus or unborn child anything like ordinary human status in the matter of rights. I have not been arguing for or against these points of view but only trying to discern some of the currents that are pulling us back and forth. The levity of the examples is not meant to offend.

Judith Jarvis Thomson

A Defense of Abortion

Most opposition to abortion relies on the premise that the fetus is a human being, a person, from the moment of conception. The premise is argued for, but, as I think, not well. Take, for example, the most common argument. We are asked to notice that the development of a

Judith Jarvis Thomson, "A Defense of Abortion" from *Philosophy and Public Affairs,* 1 (1971). Copyright © 1971. Reprinted with permission of Blackwell Publishing, Ltd.

human being from conception through birth into childhood is continuous; then it is said that to draw a line, to choose a point in this development and say "before this point the thing is not a person, after this point it is a person" is to make an arbitrary choice, a choice for which in the nature of things no good reason can be given. It is concluded that the fetus is, or anyway that we had better say it is, a person from the moment of conception. But this conclusion does not follow. Similar things might be said about the development of an acorn into an oak tree, and it does not follow that acorns are oak trees, or that we had better say they are. Arguments of this form are sometimes called "slippery slope arguments"—the phrase is perhaps self-explanatory—and it is dismaying that opponents of abortion rely on them so heavily and uncritically.

I am inclined to agree, however, that the prospects for "drawing a line" in the development of the fetus look dim. I am inclined to think also that we shall probably have to agree that the fetus has already become a human person well before birth. Indeed, it comes as a surprise when one first learns how early in its life it begins to acquire human characteristics. By the tenth week, for example, it already has a face, arms and legs, fingers and toes; it has internal organs, and brain activity is detectable. On the other hand, I think that the premise is false, that the fetus is not a person from the moment of conception. A newly fertilized ovum, a newly implanted clump of cells, is no more a person than an acorn is an oak tree. But I shall not discuss any of this. For it seems to me to be of great interest to ask what happens if, for the sake of argument, we allow the premise. How, precisely, are we supposed to get from there to the conclusion that abortion is morally impermissible? Opponents of abortion commonly spend most of their time establishing that the fetus is a person, and hardly any time explaining the step from there to the impermissibility of abortion. Perhaps they think the step too simple and obvious to require much comment. Or perhaps instead they are simply being economical in argument. Many of those who defend abortion rely on the premise that the fetus is not a person, but only a bit of tissue that will become a person at birth; and why pay out more arguments than you have to? Whatever the explanation, I suggest that the step they take is neither easy nor obvious, that it calls for closer examination than it is commonly given, and that when we do give it this closer examination we shall feel inclined to reject it.

I propose, then, that we grant that the fetus is a person from the moment of conception. How does the argument go from here? Something like this, I take it. Every person has a right to life. So the fetus has a right to life. No doubt the mother has a right to decide what shall happen in and to her body; everyone would grant that. But surely a person's right to life is stronger and more stringent than the mother's right to decide what

happens in and to her body, and so outweighs it. So the fetus may not be killed; an abortion may not be performed.

It sounds plausible. But now let me ask you to imagine this. You wake up in the morning and find yourself back to back in bed with an unconscious violinist. A famous unconscious violinist. He has been found to have a fatal kidney ailment, and the Society of Music Lovers has canvassed all the available medical records and found that you alone have the right blood type to help. They have therefore kidnapped you, and last night the violinist's circulatory system was plugged into yours, so that your kidneys can be used to extract poisons from his blood as well as your own. The director of the hospital now tells you, "Look, we're sorry the Society of Music Lovers did this to you—we would never have permitted it if we had known. But still, they did it, and the violinist now is plugged into you. To unplug you would be to kill him. But never mind, it's only for nine months. By then he will have recovered from his ailment, and can safely be unplugged from you." Is it morally incumbent on you to accede to this situation? No doubt it would be very nice of you if you did, a great kindness. But do you *have* to accede to it? What if it were not nine months, but nine years? Or longer still? What if the director of the hospital says, "Tough luck, I agree, but you've now got to stay in bed, with the violinist plugged into you, for the rest of your life. Because remember this. All persons have a right to life, and violinists are persons. Granted you have a right to decide what happens in and to your body, but a person's right to life outweighs your right to decide what happens in and to your body. So you cannot ever be unplugged from him." I imagine you would regard this as outrageous, which suggests that something really is wrong with that plausible-sounding argument I mentioned a moment ago.

In this case, of course, you were kidnapped; you didn't volunteer for the operation that plugged the violinist into your kidneys. Can those who oppose abortion on the ground I mentioned make an exception for a pregnancy due to rape? Certainly. They can say that persons have a right to life only if they didn't come into existence because of rape; or they can say that all persons have a right to life, but that some have less of a right to life than others, in particular, that those who came into existence because of rape have less. But these statements have a rather unpleasant sound. Surely the question of whether you have a right to life at all, or how much of it you have, shouldn't turn on the question of whether or not you are the product of a rape. And in fact the people who oppose abortion on the ground I mentioned do not make this distinction, and hence do not make an exception in case of rape.

Nor do they make an exception for a case in which the mother has to spend the nine months of her pregnancy in bed. They would agree that would be a great pity, and hard on the mother; but all the same, all persons have a right to life, the fetus is a person, and so on. I suspect, in fact, that they would not make an exception for a case in which, miraculously enough, the pregnancy went on for nine years, or even the rest of the mother's life.

Some won't even make an exception for a case in which continuation of the pregnancy is likely to shorten the mother's life; they regard abortion as impermissible even to save the mother's life. Such cases are nowadays very rare, and many opponents of abortion do not accept this extreme view. All the same, it is a good place to begin: a number of points of interest come out in respect to it.

1. Let us call the view that abortion is impermissible even to save the mother's life "the extreme view." I want to suggest first that it does not issue from the argument I mentioned earlier without the addition of some fairly powerful premises. Suppose a woman has become pregnant, and now learns that she has a cardiac condition such that she will die if she carries the baby to term. What may be done for her? The fetus, being a person, has a right to life, but as the mother is a person too, so has she a right to life. Presumably they have an equal right to life. How is it supposed to come out that an abortion may not be performed? If mother and child have an equal right to life, shouldn't we perhaps flip a coin? Or should we add to the mother's right to life her right to decide what happens in and to her body, which everybody seems to be ready to grant—the sum of her rights now outweighing the fetus' right to life?

The most familiar argument here is the following. We are told that performing the abortion would be directly killing the child, whereas doing nothing would not be killing the mother, but only letting her die,

Moreover, in killing the child, one would be killing an innocent person, for the child has committed no crime, and is not aiming at his mother's death. And then there are a variety of ways in which this might be continued. (1) But as directly killing an innocent person is always and absolutely impermissible, an abortion may not be performed. Or, (2) as directly killing an innocent person is murder, and murder is always and absolutely impermissible, an abortion may not always be performed. Or, (3) as one's duty to refrain from directly killing an innocent person is more stringent than one's duty to keep a person from dying, an abortion may not be performed. Or, (4) if one's only options are directly killing an innocent person or letting a person die, one must prefer letting the person die, and thus an abortion may not be performed.

Some people seem to have thought that these are not further premises which must be added if the conclusion is to be reached, but that they follow from the very fact that an innocent person has a right to life. But this seems to me to be a mistake, and perhaps the simplest way to show this is to bring out that while we must certainly grant that innocent persons have a right to life, the theses in (1) through (4) are all false. Take (2), for example. If directly killing an innocent person is murder, and thus is impermissible, then the mother's directly killing the innocent person inside her is murder, and thus is impermissible. But it cannot seriously be thought to be murder if the mother performs an abortion on herself to save her life. It cannot seriously be said that she *must* refrain, that she *must* sit passively by and wait for her death. Let us look again at the case of you and the violinist. There you are, in bed with the violinist, and the director of the hospital says to you, "It's all most distressing, and I deeply sympathize, but you see this is putting an additional strain on your kidneys, and you'll be dead within the month. But you *have* to stay where you are all the same. Because unplugging you would be directly killing an innocent violinist, and that's murder, and that's impermissible." If anything in the world is true, it is that you do not commit murder, you do not do what is impermissible, if you reach around to your back and unplug yourself from that violinist to save your life.

The main focus of attention in writings on abortion has been on what a third party may or may not do in answer to a request from a woman for an abortion. This is in a way understandable. Things being as they are, there isn't much a woman can safely do to abort herself. So the question asked is what a third party may do, and what the mother may do, if it is mentioned at all, is deduced, almost as an afterthought, from what it is concluded that third parties may do. But it seems to me that to treat the matter in this way is to refuse to grant to the mother that very status of person which is so firmly insisted on for the fetus. For we cannot simply read off what a person may do from what a third party may do. Suppose you find yourself trapped in a tiny house with a growing child. I mean a very tiny house, and a rapidly growing child—you are already up against the wall of the house and in a few minutes you'll be crushed to death. The child on the other hand won't be crushed to death; if nothing is done to stop him from growing he'll be hurt, but in the end he'll simply burst open the house and walk out a free man. Now I could well understand it if a bystander were to say, "There's nothing we can do for you. We cannot choose between your life and his, we cannot be the ones to decide who is to live, we cannot intervene." But it cannot be concluded that you too can do nothing, that you cannot attack it to save your life. However innocent the child may be, you do not have to wait passively while it crushes you to death. Perhaps a pregnant woman is vaguely felt to have the status of house, to which we don't allow the right of self-defense. But if the woman houses the child, it should be remembered that she is a person who houses it.

I should perhaps stop to say explicitly that I am not claiming that people have a right to do anything whatever to save their lives. I think, rather, that there are drastic limits to the right of self-defense. If someone threatens you with death unless you torture someone else to death, I think you have not the right, even to save your life, to do so. But the case under consideration here is very different. In our case there are only two people involved, one whose life is threatened, and one who threatens it. Both are innocent; the one who is threatened is not threatened because of any fault, the one who threatens does not threaten because of any fault. For this reason we may feel that we bystanders cannot intervene. But the person threatened can.

In sum, a woman surely can defend her life against the threat to it posed by the unborn child, even if doing so involves its death. And this shows not merely that the theses in (1) through (4) are false; it shows also that the extreme view of abortion is false, and so we need not canvass any other possible ways of arriving at it from the argument I mentioned at the outset.

2. The extreme view could of course be weakened to say that while abortion is permissible to save the mother's life, it may not be performed by a third party, but only by the mother herself. But this cannot be right either. For what we have to keep in mind is that the mother and the unborn child are not like two tenants in a small house which has, by an unfortunate mistake, been rented to both: the mother *owns* the house. The fact that she does adds to the offensiveness of deducing that the mother can do nothing from the supposition that third parties can do nothing. But it does more than this: it casts a bright light on the supposition that third parties can do nothing. Certainly it lets us see that a third party who says "I cannot choose between you" is fooling himself if he thinks this is impartiality. If Jones has found and fastened on a certain coat, which he needs to keep him from freezing, but which Smith also needs to keep him from freezing, then it is not impartiality that says "I cannot choose between you" when Smith owns the coat. Women have said again and again "This body is *my* body!" and they have reason to feel angry, reason to feel that it has been like shouting into the wind. Smith, after all, is hardly likely to bless us if we say to him, "Of course it's your coat, anybody would grant that it is. But no one may choose between you and Jones who is to have it."

We should really ask what it is that says "no one may choose" in the face of the fact that the body that houses the child is the mother's body. It may be simply a failure to appreciate this fact. But it may be something more interesting, namely the sense that one has a right to refuse to lay hands on people, even where it would be just and fair to do so, even where justice seems to require that somebody do so. Thus justice might call for somebody to get Smith's coat back from Jones, and yet you have a right to refuse to be the one to lay hands on Jones, a right to refuse to do physical violence to him. This, I think, must be granted. But then what should be said is not "no one may choose," but only "*I* cannot choose," and indeed not even this, but "*I* will not *act*," leaving it open that somebody else can or should, and in particular that anyone in a position of authority, with the job of securing people's rights, both can and should. So this is no difficulty. I have not been arguing that any given third party must accede to the mother's request that he perform an abortion to save her life, but only that he may.

I suppose that in some views of human life the mother's body is only on loan to her, the loan not being one which gives her any prior claim to it. One who held this view might well think it impartiality to say "I cannot choose." But I shall simply ignore this possibility. My own view is that if a human being has any just, prior claim to anything at all, he has a just, prior claim to his own body. And perhaps this needn't be argued for here anyway, since, as I mentioned, the arguments against abortion we are looking at do grant that the woman has a right to decide what happens in and to her body.

But although they do grant it, I have tried to show that they do not take seriously what is done in granting it. I suggest the same thing will reappear even more clearly when we turn away from cases in which the mother's life is at stake, and attend, as I propose we now do, to the vastly more common cases in which a woman wants an abortion for some less weighty reason than preserving her own life.

3. Where the mother's life is not at stake, the argument I mentioned at the outset seems to have a much stronger pull. 'Everyone has a right to life, so the unborn person has a right to life.' And isn't the child's right to life weightier than anything other than the mother's own right to life, which she might put forward as ground for an abortion?

This argument treats the right to life as if it were unproblematic. It is not, and this seems to me to be precisely the source of the mistake.

For we should now, at long last, ask what it comes to, to have a right to life. In some views having a right to life includes having a right to be given at least the bare minimum one needs for continued life. But suppose that what in fact is the bare minimum a man needs for continued life is something he has no right at all to be given? If I am sick unto death, and the only thing that will save my life is the touch of Henry Fonda's cool hand on my fevered brow, then all the same, I have no right to be given the touch of Henry Fonda's cool hand on my fevered brow. It would be frightfully nice of him to fly in from the West Coast to provide it. It would be less nice, though no doubt well meant, if my friends flew out to the West Coast and carried Henry Fonda back with them. But I have no right at all against anybody that he should do this for me. Or again, to return to the story I told earlier, the fact that for continued life that violinist needs the continued use of your kidneys does not establish that he has a right to be given the continued use of your kidneys. He certainly has no right against you that *you* should give him continued use of your kidneys. For nobody has any right to use your kidneys unless you give him such a right; and nobody has the right against you that you shall give him this right—if you do allow him to go on using your kidneys, this is a kindness on your part, and not something he can claim from you as his due. Nor has he any right against anybody else that *they* should give him continued use of your kidneys. Certainly he had no right against the Society of Music Lovers that they should plug him into you in the first place. And if you now start to unplug yourself, having learned that you will otherwise have to spend nine years in bed with him, there is nobody in the world who must try to prevent you, in order to see to it that he is given something he has a right to be given.

Some people are rather stricter about the right to life. In their view, it does not include the right to be given anything, but amounts to, and only to, the right not to be killed by anybody. But here a related difficulty arises. If everybody is to refrain from killing that violinist, then everybody must refrain from doing a great many different sorts of things. Everybody must refrain from slitting his throat, everybody must refrain from shooting him —and everybody must refrain from unplugging you from him. But does he have a right against everybody that they shall refrain from unplugging you from him? To refrain from doing this is to allow him to continue to use your kidneys. It could be argued that he has a right against us that *we* should allow him to continue to use your kidneys. That is, while he had no right against us that we should give him the use of your kidneys, it might be argued that he anyway has a right against us that we shall not now intervene and deprive him of the use of your kidneys. I shall come back to third-party interventions later. But certainly the violinist has no right against you that *you* shall allow him to continue to use your kidneys. As I said, if you do allow him to use them, it is a kindness on your part, and not something you owe him.

The difficulty I point to here is not peculiar to the right to life. It reappears in connection with all the other natural rights; and it is something which an adequate account of rights must deal with. For present purposes it is enough just to draw attention to it. But I would stress that I am not arguing that people do not have a right to life—quite to the contrary, it seems to me that the primary control we must place on the acceptability of an account of rights is that it should turn out in that account to be a truth that all persons have a right to life. I am arguing only that having a right to life does not guarantee having either a right to be given the use of or a right to be allowed continued use of another person's body—even if one needs it for life itself. So the right to life will not serve the opponents of abortion in the very simple and clear way in which they seem to have thought it would.

4.　There is another way to bring out the difficulty. In the most ordinary sort of case, to deprive someone of what he has a right to is to treat him unjustly. Suppose a boy and his small brother are jointly given a box of chocolates for Christmas. If the older boy takes the box and refuses to give his brother any of the chocolates, he is unjust to him, for the brother has been given a right to half of them. But suppose that, having learned that otherwise it means nine years in bed with that violinist, you unplug yourself from him. You surely are not being unjust to him, for you gave him no right to use your kidneys, and no one else can have given him any such right. But we have to notice that in unplugging yourself, you are killing him; and violinists, like everybody else, have a right to life, and thus in the view we were considering just now, the right not to be killed. So here you do what he supposedly has a right you shall not do, but you do not act unjustly to him in doing it.

The emendation which may be made at this point is this: the right to life consists not in the right not to be killed, but rather in the right not to be killed unjustly. This runs a risk of circularity, but never mind: it would enable us to square the fact that the violinist has a right to life with the fact that you do not act unjustly toward him in unplugging yourself, thereby killing him. For if

you do not kill him unjustly, you do not violate his right to life, and so it is no wonder you do him no injustice.

But if this emendation is accepted, the gap in the argument against abortion stares us plainly in the face; it is by no means enough to show that the fetus is a person, and to remind us that all persons have a right to life—we need to be shown also that killing the fetus violates its right to life, i.e., that abortion is unjust killing. And is it?

I suppose we may take it as a datum that in a case of pregnancy due to rape the mother has not given the unborn person a right to the use of her body for food and shelter. Indeed, in what pregnancy could it be supposed that the mother has given the unborn person such a right? It is not as if there were unborn persons drifting about the world, to whom a woman who wants a child says "I invite you in."

But it might be argued that there are other ways one can have acquired a right to the use of another person's body than by having been invited to use it by that person. Suppose a woman voluntarily indulges in intercourse, knowing of the chance it will issue in pregnancy, and then she does become pregnant; is she not in part responsible for the presence, in fact the very existence, of the unborn person inside her? No doubt she did not invite it in. But doesn't her partial responsibility for its being there itself give it a right to the use of her body? If so, then her aborting it would be more like the boy's taking away the chocolates, and less like your unplugging yourself from the violinist—doing so would be depriving it of what it does have a right to, and thus would be doing it an injustice.

And then, too, it might be asked whether or not she can kill it even to save her own life: If she voluntarily called it into existence, how can she now kill it, even in self-defense?

The first thing to be said about this is that it is something new. Opponents of abortion have been so concerned to make out the independence of the fetus, in order to establish that it has a right to life, just as its mother does, that they have tended to overlook the possible support they might gain from making out that the fetus is *dependent* on the mother, in order to establish that she has a special kind of responsibility for it, a responsibility that gives it rights against her which are not possessed by any independent person—such as an ailing violinist who is a stranger to her.

On the other hand, this argument would give the unborn person a right to its mother's body only if her pregnancy resulted from a voluntary act, undertaken in full knowledge of the chance a pregnancy might result from it. It would leave out entirely the unborn person whose existence is due to rape. Pending the availability of some further argument, then, we would be left with the conclusion that unborn persons whose existence is due to rape have no right to the use of their mothers' bodies, and thus that aborting them is not depriving them of anything they have a right to and hence is not unjust killing.

And we should also notice that it is not at all plain that this argument really does go even as far as it purports to. For there are cases and cases, and the details make a difference. If the room is stuffy, and I therefore open a window to air it, and a burglar climbs in, it would be absurd to say, "Ah, now he can stay, she's given him a right to the use of her house—for she is partially responsible for his presence there, having voluntarily done what enabled him to get in, in full knowledge that there are such things as burglars, and that burglars burgle." It would be still more absurd to say this if I had had bars installed outside my windows, precisely to prevent burglars from getting in, and a burglar got in only because of a defect in the bars. It remains equally absurd if we imagine it is not a burglar who climbs in, but an innocent person who blunders or falls in. Again, suppose it were like this: people-seeds drift about in the air like pollen, and if you open your windows, one may drift in and take root in your carpets or upholstery. You don't want children, so you fix up your windows with fine mesh screens, the very best you can buy. As can happen, however, and on very, very rare occasions does happen, one of the screens is defective; and a seed drifts in and takes root. Does the person-plant who now develops have a right to the use of your house? Surely not—despite the fact that you voluntarily opened your windows, you knowingly kept carpets and upholstered furniture, and you knew that screens were sometimes defective. Someone may argue that you are responsible for its rooting, that it does have a right to your house, because after all you *could* have lived out your life with bare floors and furniture, or with sealed windows and

doors. But this won't do—for by the same token anyone can avoid a pregnancy due to rape by having a hysterectomy, or anyway by never leaving home without a (reliable!) army.

It seems to me that the argument we are looking at can establish at most that there are *some* cases in which the unborn person has a right to the use of its mother's body, and therefore *some* cases in which abortion is unjust killing. There is room for much discussion and argument as to precisely which, if any. But I think we should side-step this issue and leave it open, for at any rate the argument certainly does not establish that all abortion is unjust killing.

5. There is room for yet another argument here, however. We surely must all grant that there may be cases in which it would be morally indecent to detach a person from your body at the cost of his life. Suppose you learn that what the violinist needs is not nine years of your life, but only one hour: all you need do to save his life is to spend one hour in that bed with him. Suppose also that letting him use your kidneys for that one hour would not affect your health in the slightest. Admittedly you were kidnapped. Admittedly you did not give anyone permission to plug him into you. Nevertheless it seems to me plain you *ought* to allow him to use your kidneys for that hour—it would be indecent to refuse.

Again, suppose pregnancy lasted only an hour, and constituted no threat to life or health. And suppose that a woman becomes pregnant as a result of rape. Admittedly she did not voluntarily do anything to bring about the existence of a child. Admittedly she did nothing at all which would give the unborn person a right to the use of her body. All the same it might well be said, as in the newly emended violinist story, that she *ought* to allow it to remain for that hour—that it would be indecent in her to refuse.

Now some people are inclined to use the term "right" in such a way that it follows from the fact that you ought to allow a person to use your body for the hour he needs, that he has a right to use your body for the hour he needs, even though he has not been given that right by any person or act. They may say that it follows also that if you refuse, you act unjustly toward him. This use of the term is perhaps so common that it cannot be called wrong; nevertheless it seems to me to be an unfortunate loosening of what we would do better to keep a tight rein on. Suppose that box of chocolates I mentioned earlier had not been given to both boys jointly, but was given only to the older boy. There he sits, stolidly eating his way through the box, his small brother watching enviously. Here we are likely to say "You ought not to be so mean. You ought to give your brother some of those chocolates." My own view is that it just does not follow from the truth of this that the brother has any right to any of the chocolates. If the boy refuses to give his brother any, he is greedy, stingy, callous—but not unjust. I suppose that the people I have in mind will say it does follow that the brother has a right to some of the chocolates, and thus that the boy does act unjustly if he refuses to give his brother any. But the effect of saying this is to obscure what we should keep distinct, namely the difference between the boy's refusal in this case and the boy's refusal in the earlier case, in which the box was given to both boys jointly, and in which the small brother thus had what was from any point of view clear title to half.

A further objection to so using the term "right" that from the fact that A ought to do a thing for B, it follows that B has a right against A that A do it for him, is that it is going to make the question of whether or not a man has a right to a thing turn on how easy it is to provide him with it; and this seems not merely unfortunate, but morally unacceptable. Take the case of Henry Fonda again. I said earlier that I had no right to the touch of his cool hand on my fevered brow, even though I needed it to save my life. I said it would be frightfully nice of him to fly in from the West Coast to provide me with it, but that I had no right against him that he should do so. But suppose he isn't on the West Coast. Suppose he has only to walk across the room, place a hand briefly on my brow—and lo, my life is saved. Then surely he ought to do it, it would be indecent to refuse. Is it to be said "Ah, well, it follows that in this case she has a right to the touch of his hand on her brow, and so it would be an injustice in him to refuse"? So that I have a right to it when it is easy for him to provide it, though no right when it's hard? It's rather a shocking idea that anyone's rights should fade away and disappear as it gets harder and harder to accord them to him.

So my own view is that even though you ought to let the violinist use your kidneys for the one hour he needs, we should not conclude that he has a right to do so—we should say that if you refuse, you are, like the boy who owns all the chocolates and will give none away, self-centered and callous, indecent in fact, but not unjust. And similarly, that even supposing a case in which a woman pregnant due to rape ought to allow the unborn person to use her body for the hour he needs, we should not conclude that he has a right to do so; we should conclude that she is self-centered, callous, indecent, but not unjust, if she refuses. The complaints are no less grave; they are just different. However, there is no need to insist on this point. If anyone does wish to deduce "he has a right" from "you ought," then all the same he must surely grant that there are cases in which it is not morally required of you that you allow that violinist to use your kidneys, and in which he does not have a right to use them, and in which you do not do him an injustice if you refuse. And so also for mother and unborn child. Except in such cases as the unborn person has a right to demand it—and we were leaving open the possibility that there may be such cases—nobody is morally *required* to make large sacrifices, of health, of all other interests and concerns, of all other duties and commitments, for nine years, or even for nine months, in order to keep another person alive.

6. We have in fact to distinguish between two kinds of Samaritan: the Good Samaritan and what we might call the Minimally Decent Samaritan. The story of the Good Samaritan, you will remember, goes like this:

> A certain man went down from Jerusalem to Jericho, and fell among thieves, which stripped him of his raiment, and wounded him, and departed, leaving him half dead.
>
> And by chance there came down a certain priest that way; and when he saw him, he passed by on the other side.
>
> And likewise a Levite, when he was at the place, came and looked on him, and passed by on the other side.
>
> But a certain Samaritan, as he journeyed, came where he was; and when he saw him he had compassion on him.
>
> And went to him, and bound up his wounds, pouring in oil and wine, and set him on his own beast, and brought him to an inn, and took care of him.

And on the morrow, when he departed, he took out two pence, and gave them to the host, and said unto him, "Take care of him; and whatsoever thou spendest more, when I come again, I will repay thee." (Luke 10:30–35)

The Good Samaritan went out of his way, at some cost to himself, to help one in need of it. We are not told what the options were, that is, whether or not the priest and the Levite could have helped by doing less than the Good Samaritan did, but assuming they could have, then the fact they did nothing at all shows they were not even Minimally Decent Samaritans, not because they were not Samaritans, but because they were not even minimally decent.

These things are a matter of degree, of course, but there is a difference, and it comes out perhaps most clearly in the story of Kitty Genovese, who, as you will remember, was murdered while thirty-eight people watched or listened, and did nothing at all to help her. A Good Samaritan would have rushed out to give direct assistance against the murderer. Or perhaps we had better allow that it would have been a Splendid Samaritan who did this, on the ground that it would have involved a risk of death for himself. But the thirty-eight not only did not do this, they did not even trouble to pick up a phone to call the police. Minimally Decent Samaritanism would call for doing at least that, and their not having done it was monstrous.

After telling the story of the Good Samaritan, Jesus said "Go, and do thou likewise." Perhaps he meant that we are morally required to act as the Good Samaritan did. Perhaps he was urging people to do more than is morally required of them. At all events it seems plain that it was not morally required of any of the thirty-eight that he rush out to give direct assistance at the risk of his own life, and that it is not morally required of anyone that he give long stretches of his life—nine years or nine months—to sustaining the life of a person who has no special right (we were leaving open the possibility of this) to demand it.

Indeed, with one rather striking class of exceptions, no one in any country in the world is *legally* required to do anywhere near as much as this for anyone else. The class of exceptions is obvious. My main concern here is not the state of the law in respect to abortion,

but it is worth drawing attention to the fact that in no state in this country is any man compelled by law to be even a Minimally Decent Samaritan to any person; there is no law under which charges could be brought against the thirty-eight who stood by while Kitty Genovese died. By contrast, in most states in this country women are compelled by law to be not merely Minimally Decent Samaritans, but Good Samaritans to unborn persons inside them. This doesn't by itself settle anything one way or the other, because it may well be argued that there should be laws in this country—as there are in many European countries—compelling at least Minimally Decent Samaritanism. But it does show that there is a gross injustice in the existing state of the law. And it shows also that the groups currently working against liberalization of abortion laws, in fact working toward having it declared unconstitutional for a state to permit abortion, had better start working for the adoption of Good Samaritan laws generally, or earn the charge that they are acting in bad faith.

I should think, myself, that Minimally Decent Samaritan laws would be one thing, Good Samaritan laws quite another, and in fact highly improper. But we are not here concerned with the law. What we should ask is not whether anybody should be compelled by law to be a Good Samaritan, but whether we must accede to a situation in which somebody is being compelled—by nature, perhaps—to be a Good Samaritan. We have, in other words, to look now at third-party interventions. I have been arguing that no person is morally required to make large sacrifices to sustain the life of another who has no right to demand them, and this even where the sacrifices do not include life itself; we are not morally required to be Good Samaritans or anyway Very Good Samaritans to one another. But what if a man cannot extricate himself from such a situation? What if he appeals to us to extricate him? It seems to me plain that there are cases in which we can, cases in which a Good Samaritan would extricate him. There you are, you were kidnapped, and nine years in bed with that violinist lie ahead of you. You have your own life to lead. You are sorry, but you simply cannot see giving up so much of your life to the sustaining of his. You cannot extricate yourself, and ask us to do so. I should have thought that—in light of his having no right to the use of your body—it was obvious that we do not have to accede to your being forced to give up so much. We can do what you ask. There is no injustice to the violinist in our doing so.

7. Following the lead of the opponents of abortion, I have throughout been speaking of the fetus merely as a person, and what I have been asking is whether or not the argument we began with, which proceeds only from the fetus' being a person, really does establish its conclusion. I have argued that it does not.

But of course there are arguments and arguments, and it may be said that I have simply fastened on the wrong one. It may be said that what is important is not merely the fact that the fetus is a person, but that it is a person for whom the woman has a special kind of responsibility issuing from the fact that she is its mother. And it might be argued that all my analogies are therefore irrelevant—for you do not have that special kind of responsibility for that violinist, Henry Fonda does not have that special kind of responsibility for me. And our attention might be drawn to the fact that men and women both *are* compelled by law to provide support for their children.

I have in effect dealt (briefly) with this argument in section 4 above; but a (still briefer) recapitulation now may be in order. Surely we do not have any such "special responsibility" for a person unless we have assumed it, explicitly or implicitly. If a set of parents do not try to prevent pregnancy, do not obtain an abortion, and then at the time of birth of the child do not put it out for adoption, but rather take it home with them, then they have assumed responsibility for it, they have given it rights, and they cannot *now* withdraw support from it at the cost of its life because they now find it difficult to go on providing for it. But if they have taken all reasonable precautions against having a child, they do not simply by virtue of their biological relationship to the child who comes into existence have a special responsibility for it. They may wish to assume responsibility for it, or they may not wish to. And I am suggesting that if assuming responsibility for it would require large sacrifices, then they may refuse. A Good Samaritan would not refuse—or anyway, a Splendid Samaritan, if the sacrifices that had to be made were enormous. But then so would a Good Samaritan assume responsibility for that violinist; so would Henry Fonda, if he is a Good Samaritan, fly in from the West Coast and assume responsibility for me.

8. My argument will be found unsatisfactory on two counts by many of those who want to regard abortion as morally permissible. First, while I do argue that abortion is not impermissible, I do not argue that it is always permissible. There may well be cases in which carrying the child to term requires only Minimally Decent Samaritanism of the mother, and this is a standard we must not fall below. I am inclined to think it a merit of my account precisely that it does *not* give a general yes or a general no. It allows for and supports our sense that, for example, a sick and desperately frightened fourteen-year-old schoolgirl, pregnant due to rape, may *of course* choose abortion, and that any law which rules this out is an insane law. And it also allows for and supports our sense that in other cases resort to abortion is even positively indecent. It would be indecent in the woman to request an abortion, and indecent in a doctor to perform it, if she is in her seventh month, and wants the abortion just to avoid the nuisance of postponing a trip abroad. The very fact that the arguments I have been drawing attention to treat all cases of abortion, or even all cases of abortion in which the mother's life is not at stake, as morally on a par ought to have made them suspect at the outset.

Secondly, while I am arguing for the permissibility of abortion in some cases, I am not arguing for the right to secure the death of the unborn child. It is easy to confuse these two things in that up to a certain point in the life of the fetus it is not able to survive outside the mother's body; hence removing it from her body guarantees its death. But they are importantly different. I have argued that you are not morally required to spend nine months in bed, sustaining the life of that violinist; but to say this is by no means to say that if, when you unplug yourself, there is a miracle and he survives, you then have a right to turn round and slit his throat. You may detach yourself even if this costs him his life; you have no right to be guaranteed his death, by some other means, if unplugging yourself does not kill him. There are some people who will feel dissatisfied by this feature of my argument. A woman may be utterly devastated by the thought of a child, a bit of herself, put out for adoption and never seen or heard of again. She may therefore want not merely that the child be detached from her, but more, that it die. Some opponents of abortion are inclined to regard this as beneath contempt—

thereby showing insensitivity to what is surely a powerful source of despair. All the same, I agree that the desire for the child's death is not one which anybody may gratify, should it turn out to be possible to detach the child alive.

At this place, however, it should be remembered that we have only been pretending throughout that the fetus is a human being from the moment of conception. A very early abortion is surely not the killing of a person, and so is not dealt with by anything I have said here.

Peter Singer

Famine, Affluence, and Morality

As I write this, in November 1971, people are dying in East Bengal from lack of food, shelter, and medical care. The suffering and death that are occurring there now are not inevitable, not unavoidable in any fatalistic sense of the term. Constant poverty, a cyclone, and a civil war have turned at least nine million people into destitute refugees; nevertheless, it is not beyond the capacity of the richer nations to give enough assistance to reduce any further suffering to very small proportions. The decisions and actions of human beings can prevent this kind of suffering. Unfortunately, human beings have not made the necessary decisions. At the individual level, people have, with very few exceptions, not responded to the situation in any significant way. Generally speaking, people have not given large sums to relief funds; they have not written to their parliamentary representatives demanding increased government assistance; they have not demonstrated in the streets, held symbolic fasts, or done anything else directed toward providing the refugees with the means to satisfy their essential needs. At the government level, no government has given the sort of massive aid that would enable the refugees to survive for more than a few days. Britain, for instance, has given rather more than most countries. It has, to date, given £14,750,000. For comparative pur-

poses, Britain's share of the nonrecoverable development costs of the Anglo-French Concorde project is already in excess of £275,000,000, and on present estimates will reach £440,000,000. The implication is that the British government values a supersonic transport more than thirty times as highly as it values the lives of the nine million refugees. Australia is another country which, on a per capita basis, is well up in the "aid to Bengal" table. Australia's aid, however, amounts to less than one-twelfth of the cost of Sydney's new opera house. The total amount given, from all sources, now stands at about £65,000,000. The estimated cost of keeping the refugees alive for one year is £464,000,000. Most of the refugees have now been in the camps for more than six months. The World Bank has said that India needs a minimum of £300,000,000 in assistance from other countries before the end of the year. It seems obvious that assistance on this scale will not be forthcoming. India will be forced to choose between letting the refugees starve or diverting funds from her own development program, which will mean that more of her own people will starve in the future.

These are the essential facts about the present situation in Bengal. So far as it concerns us here, there is nothing unique about this situation except its magnitude. The Bengal emergency is just the latest and most acute of a series of major emergencies in various parts of the world, arising both from natural and from manmade causes. There are also many parts of the world in which people die from malnutrition and lack of food

Peter Singer, "Famine, Affluence, and Morality" from *Philosophy and Public Affairs*, 1 (1972). Copyright © 1972. Reprinted with permission of Blackwell Publishing, Ltd.

independent of any special emergency. I take Bengal as my example only because it is the present concern, and because the size of the problem has ensured that it has been given adequate publicity. Neither individuals nor governments can claim to be unaware of what is happening there.

What are the moral implications of a situation like this? In what follows, I shall argue that the way people in relatively affluent countries react to a situation like that in Bengal cannot be justified; indeed, the whole way we look at moral issues—our moral conceptual scheme—needs to be altered, and with it, the way of life that has come to be taken for granted in our society.

In arguing for this conclusion I will not, of course, claim to be morally neutral. I shall, however, try to argue for the moral position that I take, so that anyone who accepts certain assumptions, to be made explicit, will, I hope, accept my conclusion.

I begin with the assumption that suffering and death from lack of food, shelter, and medical care are bad. I think most people will agree about this, although one may reach the same view by different routes. I shall not argue for this view. People can hold all sorts of eccentric positions, and perhaps from some of them it would not follow that death by starvation is in itself bad. It is difficult, perhaps impossible, to refute such positions, and so for brevity I will henceforth take this assumption as accepted. Those who disagree need read no further.

My next point is this: if it is in our power to prevent something bad from happening, without thereby sacrificing anything of comparable moral importance, we ought, morally, to do it. By "without sacrificing anything of comparable moral importance" I mean without causing anything else comparably bad to happen, or doing something that is wrong in itself, or failing to promote some moral good, comparable in significance to the bad thing that we can prevent. This principle seems almost as uncontroversial as the last one. It requires us only to prevent what is bad, and not to promote what is good, and it requires this of us only when we can do it without sacrificing anything that is, from the moral point of view, comparably important. I could even, as far as the application of my argument to the Bengal emergency is concerned, qualify the point so as to make it: if it is in our power to prevent something very bad

from happening, without thereby sacrificing anything morally significant, we ought, morally, to do it. An application of this principle would be as follows: if I am walking past a shallow pond and see a child drowning in it, I ought to wade in and pull the child out. This will mean getting my clothes muddy, but this is insignificant, while the death of the child would presumably be a very bad thing.

The uncontroversial appearance of the principle just stated is deceptive. If it were acted upon, even in its qualified form, our lives, our society, and our world would be fundamentally changed. For the principle takes, firstly, no account of proximity or distance. It makes no moral difference whether the person I can help is a neighbor's child ten yards from me or a Bengali whose name I shall never know, ten thousand miles away. Secondly, the principle makes no distinction between cases in which I am the only person who could possibly do anything and cases in which I am just one among millions in the same position.

I do not think I need to say much in defense of the refusal to take proximity and distance into account. The fact that a person is physically near to us, so that we have personal contact with him, may make it more likely that we *shall* assist him, but this does not show that we *ought* to help him rather than another who happens to be further away. If we accept any principle of impartiality, universalizability, equality, or whatever, we cannot discriminate against someone merely because he is far away from us (or we are far away from him). Admittedly, it is possible that we are in a better position to judge what needs to be done to help a person near to us than one far away, and perhaps also to provide the assistance we judge to be necessary. If this were the case, it would be a reason for helping those near to us first. This may once have been a justification for being more concerned with the poor in one's own town than with famine victims in India. Unfortunately for those who like to keep their moral responsibilities limited, instant communication and swift transportation have changed the situation. From the moral point of view, the development of the world into a "global village" has made an important, though still unrecognized, difference to our moral situation. Expert observers and supervisors, sent out by famine relief organizations or permanently stationed in famine-prone areas, can direct our aid to a refugee in Bengal almost as effectively as we could get it to someone in our own block. There would seem, therefore, to be no possible justification for discriminating on geographical grounds.

There may be a greater need to defend the second implication of my principle—that the fact that there are millions of other people in the same position, in respect to the Bengali refugees, as I am, does not make the situation significantly different from a situation in which I am the only person who can prevent something very bad from occurring. Again, of course, I admit that there is a psychological difference between the cases; one feels less guilty about doing nothing if one can point to others, similarly placed, who have also done nothing. Yet this can make no real difference to our moral obligations. Should I consider that I am less obliged to pull the drowning child out of the pond if on looking around I see other people, no further away than I am, who have also noticed the child but are doing nothing? One has only to ask this question to see the absurdity of the view that numbers lessen obligation. It is a view that is an ideal excuse for inactivity; unfortunately most of the major evils—poverty, overpopulation, pollution—are problems in which everyone is almost equally involved.

The view that numbers do make a difference can be made plausible if stated in this way: if everyone in circumstances like mine gave £5 to the Bengal Relief Fund, there would be enough to provide food, shelter, and medical care for the refugees; there is no reason why I should give more than anyone else in the same circumstances as I am; therefore I have no obligation to give more than £5. Each premise in this argument is true, and the argument looks sound. It may convince us, unless we notice that it is based on a hypothetical premise, although the conclusion is not stated hypothetically. The argument would be sound if the conclusion were: if everyone in circumstances like mine were to give £5, I would have no obligation to give more than £5. If the conclusion were so stated, however, it would be obvious that the argument has no bearing on a situation in which it is not the case that everyone else gives £5. This, of course, is the actual situation. It is more or less certain that not everyone in circumstances like mine will give £5. So there will not be enough to provide the needed food, shelter, and medical care. Therefore by giving more than £5 I will prevent more suffering than I would if I gave just £5.

It might be thought that this argument has an absurd consequence. Since the situation appears to be that very few people are likely to give substantial amounts, it follows that I and everyone else in similar circumstances ought to give as much as possible, that is, at least up to the point at which by giving more one would begin to cause serious suffering for oneself and one's dependents —perhaps even beyond this point to the point of marginal utility, at which by giving more one would cause oneself and one's dependents as much suffering as one would prevent in Bengal. If everyone does this, however, there will be more than can be used for the benefit of the refugees, and some of the sacrifice will have been unnecessary. Thus, if everyone does what he ought to do, the result will not be as good as it would be if everyone did a little less than he ought to do, or if only some do all that they ought to do.

The paradox here arises only if we assume that the actions in question—sending money to the relief funds —are performed more or less simultaneously, and are also unexpected. For if it is to be expected that everyone is going to contribute something, then clearly each is not obliged to give as much as he would have been obliged to had others not been giving too. And if everyone is not acting more or less simultaneously, then those giving later will know how much more is needed, and will have no obligation to give more than is necessary to reach this amount. To say this is not to deny the principle that people in the same circumstances have the same obligations, but to point out that the fact that others have given, or may be expected to give, is a relevant circumstance: those giving after it has become known that many others are giving and those giving before are not in the same circumstances. So the seemingly absurd consequence of the principle I have put forward can occur only if people are in error about the actual circumstances—that is, if they think they are giving when others are not, but in fact they are giving when others are. The result of everyone doing what he really ought to do cannot be worse than the result of everyone doing less than he ought to do, although the result of everyone doing what he reasonably believes he ought to do could be.

If my argument so far has been sound, neither our distance from a preventable evil nor the number of other people who, in respect to that evil, are in the same situation as we are, lessens our obligation to mitigate or prevent that evil. I shall therefore take as established the principle I asserted earlier. As I have already said, I need to assert it only in its qualified form: if it is in our power to prevent something very bad from happening, without thereby sacrificing anything else morally significant, we ought, morally, to do it.

The outcome of this argument is that our traditional moral categories are upset. The traditional distinction between duty and charity cannot be drawn, or at least, not in the place we normally draw it. Giving money to the Bengal Relief Fund is regarded as an act of charity in our society. The bodies which collect money are known as "charities." These organizations see themselves in this way—if you send them a check, you will be thanked for your "generosity." Because giving money is regarded as an act of charity, it is not thought that there is anything wrong with not giving. The charitable man may be praised, but the man who is not charitable is not condemned. People do not feel in any way ashamed or guilty about spending money on new clothes or a new car instead of giving it to famine relief. (Indeed, the alternative does not occur to them.) This way of looking at the matter cannot be justified. When we buy new clothes not to keep ourselves warm but to look "well-dressed" we are not providing for any important need. We would not be sacrificing anything significant if we were to continue to wear our old clothes, and give the money to famine relief. By doing so, we would be preventing another person from starving. It follows from what I have said earlier that we ought to give money away, rather than spend it on clothes which we do not need to keep us warm. To do so is not charitable, or generous. Nor is it the kind of act which philosophers and theologians have called "supererogatory"— an act which it would be good to do, but not wrong not to do. On the contrary, we ought to give the money away, and it is wrong not to do so.

I am not maintaining that there are no acts which are charitable, or that there are no acts which it would be good to do but not wrong not to do. It may be possible to redraw the distinction between duty and charity

in some other place. All I am arguing here is that the present way of drawing the distinction, which makes it an act of charity for a man living at the level of affluence which most people in the "developed nations" enjoy to give money to save someone else from starvation, cannot be supported. It is beyond the scope of my argument to consider whether the distinction should be redrawn or abolished altogether. There would be many other possible ways of drawing the distinction—for instance, one might decide that it is good to make other people as happy as possible, but not wrong not to do so.

Despite the limited nature of the revision in our moral conceptual scheme which I am proposing, the revision would, given the extent of both affluence and famine in the world today, have radical implications. These implications may lead to further objections, distinct from those I have already considered. I shall discuss two of these.

One objection to the position I have taken might be simply that it is too drastic a revision of our moral scheme. People do not ordinarily judge in the way I have suggested they should. Most people reserve their moral condemnation for those who violate some moral norm, such as the norm against taking another person's property. They do not condemn those who indulge in luxury instead of giving to famine relief. But given that I did not set out to present a morally neutral description of the way people make moral judgments, the way people do in fact judge has nothing to do with the validity of my conclusion. My conclusion follows from the principle which I advanced earlier, and unless that principle is rejected, or the arguments shown to be unsound, I think the conclusion must stand, however strange it appears.

It might, nevertheless, be interesting to consider why our society, and most other societies, do judge differently from the way I have suggested they should. In a well-known article, J. O. Urmson suggests that the imperatives of duty, which tell us what we must do, as distinct from what it would be good to do but not wrong not to do, function so as to prohibit behavior that is intolerable if men are to live together in society.[1] This may

---

1. J. O. Urmson, "Saints and Heroes," in *Essays in Moral Philosophy,* ed. Abraham I. Melden (Seattle and London, 1958), p. 214.

explain the origin and continued existence of the present division between acts of duty and acts of charity. Moral attitudes are shaped by the needs of society, and no doubt society needs people who will observe the rules that make social existence tolerable. From the point of view of a particular society, it is essential to prevent violations of norms against killing, stealing, and so on. It is quite inessential, however, to help people outside one's own society.

If this is an explanation of our common distinction between duty and supererogation, however, it is not a justification of it. The moral point of view requires us to look beyond the interests of our own society. Previously, as I have already mentioned, this may hardly have been feasible, but it is quite feasible now. From the moral point of view, the prevention of the starvation of millions of people outside our society must be considered at least as pressing as the upholding of property norms within our society.

It has been argued by some writers, among them Sidgwick and Urmson, that we need to have a basic moral code which is not too far beyond the capacities of the ordinary man, for otherwise there will be a general breakdown of compliance with the moral code. Crudely stated, this argument suggests that if we tell people that they ought to refrain from murder and give everything they do not really need to famine relief, they will do neither, whereas if we tell them that they ought to refrain from murder and that it is good to give to famine relief but not wrong not to do so, they will at least refrain from murder. The issue here is: Where should we drawn the line between conduct that is required and conduct that is good although not required, so as to get the best possible result? This would seem to be an empirical question, although a very difficult one. One objection to the Sidgwick-Urmson line of argument is that it takes insufficient account of the effect that moral standards can have on the decisions we make. Given a society in which a wealthy man who gives five percent of his income to famine relief is regarded as most generous, it is not surprising that a proposal that we all ought to give away half our incomes will be thought to be absurdly unrealistic. In a society which held that no man should have more than enough while others have less than they need, such a proposal might seem narrow-minded. What it is possible for a man to

do and what he is likely to do are both, I think, very greatly influenced by what people around him are doing and expecting him to do. In any case, the possibility that by spreading the idea that we ought to be doing very much more than we are to relieve famine we shall bring about a general breakdown of moral behavior seems remote. If the stakes are an end to widespread starvation, it is worth the risk. Finally, it should be emphasized that these considerations are relevant only to the issue of what we should require from others, and not to what we ourselves ought to do.

The second objection to my attack on the present distinction between duty and charity is one which has from time to time been made against utilitarianism. It follows from some forms of utilitarian theory that we all ought, morally, to be working full time to increase the balance of happiness over misery. The position I have taken here would not lead to this conclusion in all circumstances, for if there were no bad occurrences that we could prevent without sacrificing something of comparable moral importance, my argument would have no application. Given the present conditions in many parts of the world, however, it does follow from my argument that we ought, morally, to be working full time to relieve great suffering of the sort that occurs as a result of famine or other disasters. Of course, mitigating circumstances can be adduced—for instance, that if we wear ourselves out through overwork, we shall be less effective than we would otherwise have been. Nevertheless, when all considerations of this sort have been taken into account, the conclusion remains: we ought to be preventing as much suffering as we can without sacrificing something else of comparable moral importance. This conclusion is one which we may be reluctant to face. I cannot see, though, why it should be regarded as a criticism of the position for which I have argued, rather than a criticism of our ordinary standards of behavior. Since most people are self-interested to some degree, very few of us are likely to do everything that we ought to do. It would, however, hardly be honest to take this as evidence that it is not the case that we ought to do it.

It may still be thought that my conclusions are so wildly out of line with what everyone else thinks and has always thought that there must be something wrong with the argument somewhere. In order to show that my conclusions, while certainly contrary to contemporary Western moral standards, would not have seemed so extraordinary at other times and in other places, I would like to quote a passage from a writer not normally thought of as a way-out radical, Thomas Aquinas.

> Now, according to the natural order instituted by divine providence, material goods are provided for the satisfaction of human needs. Therefore the division and appropriation of property, which proceeds from human law, must not hinder the satisfaction of man's necessity from such goods. Equally, whatever a man has in superabundance is owed, of natural right, to the poor for their sustenance. So Ambrosius says, and it is also to be found in the *Decretum Gratiani:* "The bread which you withhold belongs to the hungry; the clothing you shut away, to the naked; and the money you bury in the earth is the redemption and freedom of the penniless."[2]

I now want to consider a number of points, more practical than philosophical, which are relevant to the application of the moral conclusion we have reached. These points challenge not the idea that we ought to be doing all we can to prevent starvation, but the idea that giving away a great deal of money is the best means to this end.

It is sometimes said that overseas aid should be a government responsibility, and that therefore one ought not to give to privately run charities. Giving privately, it is said, allows the government and the noncontributing members of society to escape their responsibilities.

This argument seems to assume that the more people there are who give to privately organized famine relief funds, the less likely it is that the government will take over full responsibility for such aid. This assumption is unsupported, and does not strike me as at all plausible. The opposite view—that if no one gives voluntarily, a government will assume that its citizens are uninterested in famine relief and would not wish to be forced

into giving aid—seems more plausible. In any case, unless there were a definite probability that by refusing to give one would be helping to bring about massive government assistance, people who do refuse to make voluntary contributions are refusing to prevent a certain amount of suffering without being able to point to any tangible beneficial consequence of their refusal. So the onus of showing how their refusal will bring about government action is on those who refuse to give.

I do not, of course, want to dispute the contention that governments of affluent nations should be giving many times the amount of genuine, no-strings-attached aid that they are giving now. I agree, too, that giving privately is not enough, and that we ought to be campaigning actively for entirely new standards for both public and private contributions to famine relief. Indeed, I would sympathize with someone who thought that campaigning was more important than giving oneself, although I doubt whether preaching what one does not practice would be very effective. Unfortunately, for many people the idea that "it's the government's responsibility" is a reason for not giving which does not appear to entail any political action either.

Another, more serious reason for not giving to famine relief funds is that until there is effective population control, relieving famine merely postpones starvation. If we save the Bengal refugees now, others, perhaps the children of these refugees, will face starvation in a few years' time. In support of this, one may cite the now well-known facts about the population explosion and the relatively limited scope for expanded production.

This point, like the previous one, is an argument against relieving suffering that is happening now, because of a belief about what might happen in the future; it is unlike the previous point in that very good evidence can be adduced in support of this belief about the future. I will not go into the evidence here. I accept that the earth cannot support indefinitely a population rising at the present rate. This certainly poses a problem for anyone who thinks it important to prevent famine. Again, however, one could accept the argument without drawing the conclusion that it absolves one from any obligation to do anything to prevent famine. The conclusion that should be drawn is that the best means of preventing famine, in the long run, is population control. It would then follow from the position reached

---

2. *Summa Theologica,* II–II, Question 66, Article 7, in *Aquinas, Selected Political Writings,* ed. A. P. d'Entreves, trans. J. G. Dawson (Oxford, 1948), p. 171.

earlier that one ought to be doing all one can to promote population control (unless one held that all forms
of population control were wrong in themselves, or
would have significantly bad consequences). Since there
are organizations working specifically for population
control, one would then support them rather than more
orthodox methods of preventing famine.

A third point raised by the conclusion reached earlier relates to the question of just how much we all
ought to be giving away. One possibility, which has already been mentioned, is that we ought to give until we
reach the level of marginal utility—that is, the level at
which, by giving more, I would cause as much suffering to myself or my dependents as I would relieve by
my gift. This would mean, of course, that one would reduce oneself to very near the material circumstances of
a Bengali refugee. It will be recalled that earlier I put
forward both a strong and a moderate version of the
principle of preventing bad occurrences. The strong
version, which required us to prevent bad things from
happening unless in doing so we would be sacrificing
something of comparable moral significance, does seem
to require reducing ourselves to the level of marginal
utility. I should also say that the strong version seems to
me to be the correct one. I proposed the more moderate version—that we should prevent bad occurrences
unless, to do so, we had to sacrifice something morally
significant—only in order to show that even on this
surely undeniable principle a great change in our way
of life is required. On the more moderate principle, it
may not follow that we ought to reduce ourselves to the
level of marginal utility, for one might hold that to reduce oneself and one's family to this level is to cause
something significantly bad to happen. Whether this is
so I shall not discuss, since, as I have said, I can see no
good reason for holding the moderate version of the
principle rather than the strong version. Even if we accepted the principle only in its moderate form, however, it should be clear that we would have to give away
enough to ensure that the consumer society, dependent
as it is on people spending on trivia rather than giving
to famine relief, would slow down and perhaps disappear entirely. There are several reasons why this would
be desirable in itself. The value and necessity of economic growth are now being questioned not only by
conservationists, but by economists as well. There is no

doubt, too, that the consumer society has had a distorting effect on the goals and purposes of its members. Yet
looking at the matter purely from the point of view of
overseas aid, there must be a limit to the extent to which
we should deliberately slow down our economy; for it
might be the case that if we gave away, say, forty percent
of our Gross National Product, we would slow down
the economy so much that in absolute terms we would
be giving less than if we gave twenty-five percent of the
much larger GNP that we would have if we limited our
contribution to this smaller percentage.

I mention this only as an indication of the sort of factor that one would have to take into account in working
out an ideal. Since Western societies generally consider
one percent of the GNP an acceptable level for overseas
aid, the matter is entirely academic. Nor does it affect the
question of how much an individual should give in a society in which very few are giving substantial amounts.

It is sometimes said, though less often now than it used
to be, that philosophers have no special role to play in
public affairs, since most public issues depend primarily
on an assessment of facts. On questions of fact, it is said,
philosophers as such have no special expertise, and so it
has been possible to engage in philosophy without
committing oneself to any position on major public issues. No doubt there are some issues of social policy and
foreign policy about which it can truly be said that a really expert assessment of the facts is required before taking sides or acting, but the issue of famine is surely not
one of these. The facts about the existence of suffering
are beyond dispute. Nor, I think, is it disputed that we
can do something about it, either through orthodox
methods of famine relief or through population control
or both. This is therefore an issue on which philosophers are competent to take a position. The issue is one
which faces everyone who has more money than he
needs to support himself and his dependents, or who is
in a position to take some sort of political action. These
categories must include practically every teacher and
student of philosophy in the universities of the Western
world. If philosophy is to deal with matters that are relevant to both teachers and students, this is an issue that
philosophers should discuss.

Discussion, though, is not enough. What is the point
of relating philosophy to public (and personal) affairs if

we do not take our conclusions seriously? In this instance, taking our conclusion seriously means acting upon it. The philosopher will not find it any easier than anyone else to alter his attitudes and way of life to the extent that, if I am right, is involved in doing everything that we ought to be doing. At the very least, though, one can make a start. The philosopher who does so will have to sacrifice some of the benefits of the consumer society, but he can find compensation in the satisfaction of a way of life in which theory and practice, if not yet in harmony, are at least coming together.

Thomas Nagel

War and Massacre

From the apathetic reaction to atrocities committed in Vietnam by the United States and its allies, one may conclude that moral restrictions on the conduct of war command almost as little sympathy among the general public as they do among those charged with the formation of U.S. military policy. Even when restrictions on the conduct of warfare are defended, it is usually on legal grounds alone: their moral basis is often poorly understood. I wish to argue that certain restrictions are neither arbitrary nor merely conventional, and that their validity does not depend simply on their usefulness. There is, in other words, a moral basis for the rules of war, even though the conventions now officially in force are far from giving it perfect expression.

I

No elaborate moral theory is required to account for what is wrong in cases like the Mylai massacre, since it did not serve, and was not intended to serve, any strategic purpose. Moreover, if the participation of the United States in the Indo-Chinese war is entirely wrong to begin with, then that engagement is incapable of providing a justification for *any* measures taken in its

pursuit—not only for the measures which are atrocities in every war, however just its aims.

But this war has revealed attitudes of a more general kind, that influenced the conduct of earlier wars as well. After it has ended, we shall still be faced with the problem of how warfare may be conducted, and the attitudes that have resulted in the specific conduct of this war will not have disappeared. Moreover, similar problems can arise in wars or rebellions fought for very different reasons, and against very different opponents. It is not easy to keep a firm grip on the idea of what is not permissible in warfare, because while some military actions are obvious atrocities, other cases are more difficult to assess, and the general principles underlying these judgments remain obscure. Such obscurity can lead to the abandonment of sound intuitions in favor of criteria whose rationale may be more obvious. If such a tendency is to be resisted, it will require a better understanding of the restrictions than we now have.

I propose to discuss the most general moral problem raised by the conduct of warfare: the problem of means and ends. In one view, there are limits on what may be done even in the service of an end worth pursuing—and even when adherence to the restriction may be very costly. A person who acknowledges the force of such restrictions can find himself in acute moral dilemmas. He may believe, for example, that by torturing a prisoner he can obtain information necessary to prevent a disaster, or that by obliterating one village with bombs

Thomas Nagel, "War and Massacre" from *Philosophy and Public Affairs,* 1 (1972). Copyright © 1972. Reprinted with permission of Blackwell Publishing, Ltd.

he can halt a campaign of terrorism. If he believes that the gains from a certain measure will clearly outweigh its costs, yet still suspects that he ought not to adopt it, then he is in a dilemma produced by the conflict between two disparate categories of moral reason: categories that may be called *utilitarian* and *absolutist*.

Utilitarianism gives primacy to a concern with what will *happen*. Absolutism gives primacy to a concern with what one *is doing*. The conflict between them arises because the alternatives we face are rarely just choices between *total outcomes:* they are also choices between alternative pathways or measures to be taken. When one of the choices is to do terrible things to another person, the problem is altered fundamentally; it is no longer merely a question of which outcome would be worse.

Few of us are completely immune to either of these types of moral intuition, though in some people, either naturally or for doctrinal reasons, one type will be dominant and the other suppressed or weak. But it is perfectly possible to feel the force of both types of reason very strongly; in that case the moral dilemma in certain situations of crisis will be acute, and it may appear that every possible course of action or inaction is unacceptable for one reason or another.

II

Although it is this dilemma that I propose to explore, most of the discussion will be devoted to its absolutist component. The utilitarian component is straightforward by comparison, and has a natural appeal to anyone who is not a complete skeptic about ethics. Utilitarianism says that one should try, either individually or through institutions, to maximize good and minimize evil (the definition of these categories need not enter into the schematic formulation of the view), and that if faced with the possibility of preventing a great evil by producing a lesser, one should choose the lesser evil. There are certainly problems about the formulation of utilitarianism, and much has been written about it, but its intent is morally transparent. Nevertheless, despite the addition of various refinements, it continues to leave large portions of ethics unaccounted for. I do not suggest that some form of absolutism can account for them all, only that an examination of absolutism will lead us to see the complexity, and perhaps the incoherence, of our moral ideas.

Utilitarianism certainly justifies *some* restrictions on the conduct of warfare. There are strong utilitarian reasons for adhering to any limitation which seems natural to most people—particularly if the limitation is widely accepted already. An exceptional measure which seems to be justified by its results in a particular conflict may create a precedent with disastrous long-term effects. It may even be argued that war involves violence on such a scale that it is never justified on utilitarian grounds—the consequences of refusing to go to war will never be as bad as the war itself would be, even if atrocities were not committed. Or in a more sophisticated vein it might be claimed that a uniform policy of never resorting to military force would do less harm in the long run, if followed consistently, than a policy of deciding each case on utilitarian grounds (even though on occasion particular applications of the pacifist policy might have worse results than a specific utilitarian decision). But I shall not consider these arguments, for my concern is with reasons of a different kind, which may remain when reasons of utility and interest fail.

In the final analysis, I believe that the dilemma cannot always be resolved. While not every conflict between absolutism and utilitarianism creates an insoluble dilemma, and while it is certainly right to adhere to absolutist restrictions unless the utilitarian considerations favoring violation are overpoweringly weighty and extremely certain—nevertheless, when that special condition is met, it may become impossible to adhere to an absolutist position. What I shall offer, therefore, is a somewhat qualified defense of absolutism. I believe it underlies a valid and fundamental type of moral judgment—which cannot be reduced to or overridden by other principles. And while there may be other principles just as fundamental, it is particularly important not to lose confidence in our absolutist intuitions, for they are often the only barrier before the abyss of utilitarian apologetics for large-scale murder.

III

One absolutist position that creates no problems of interpretation is pacifism: the view that one may not kill another person under any circumstances, no matter what good would be achieved or evil averted thereby. The type of absolutist position that I am going to discuss is different. Pacifism draws the conflict with utilitarian considerations very starkly. But there are other views according to which violence may be undertaken, even on a large scale, in a clearly just cause, so long as certain absolute restrictions on the character and direction of that violence are observed. The line is drawn somewhat closer to the bone, but it exists.

The philosopher who has done most to advance contemporary philosophical discussion of such a view, and to explain it to those unfamiliar with its extensive treatment in Roman Catholic moral theology, is G. E. M. Anscombe. In 1958 Miss Anscombe published a pamphlet entitled *Mr. Truman's Degree,* on the occasion of the award by Oxford University of an honorary doctorate to Harry Truman. The pamphlet explained why she had opposed the decision to award that degree, recounted the story of her unsuccessful opposition, and offered some reflections on the history of Truman's decision to drop atom bombs on Hiroshima and Nagasaki, and on the difference between murder and allowable killing in warfare. She pointed out that the policy of deliberately killing large numbers of civilians either as a means or as an end in itself did not originate with Truman, and was common practice among all parties during World War II for some time before Hiroshima. The Allied area bombings of German cities by conventional explosives included raids which killed more civilians than did the atomic attacks; the same is true of certain fire-bomb raids on Japan.

The policy of attacking the civilian population in order to induce an enemy to surrender, or to damage his morale, seems to have been widely accepted in the civilized world, and seems to be accepted still, at least if the stakes are high enough. It gives evidence of a moral conviction that the deliberate killing of noncombatants—women, children, old people—is permissible if enough can be gained by it. This follows from the more general position that any means can in principle be justified if it leads to a sufficiently worthy end. Such an attitude is evident not only in the more spectacular current weapons systems but also in the day-to-day conduct of the nonglobal war in Indochina: the indiscriminate destructiveness of antipersonnel weapons, napalm, and

aerial bombardment; cruelty to prisoners; massive relocation of civilians; destruction of crops; and so forth. An absolutist position opposes to this the view that certain acts cannot be justified no matter what the consequences. Among those acts is murder—the deliberate killing of the harmless: civilians, prisoners of war, and medical personnel.

In the present war such measures are sometimes said to be regrettable, but they are generally defended by reference to military necessity and the importance of the long-term consequences of success or failure in the war. I shall pass over the inadequacy of this consequentialist defense in its own terms. (That is the dominant form of moral criticism of the war, for it is part of what people mean when they ask, "Is it worth it?") I am concerned rather to account for the inappropriateness of offering any defense of that kind for such actions.

Many people feel, without being able to say much more about it, that something has gone seriously wrong when certain measures are admitted into consideration in the first place. The fundamental mistake is made there, rather than at the point where the overall benefit of some monstrous measure is judged to outweigh its disadvantages, and it is adopted. An account of absolutism might help us to understand this. If it is not allowable to *do* certain things, such as killing unarmed prisoners or civilians, then no argument about what will happen if one doesn't do them can show that doing them would be all right.

Absolutism does not, of course, require one to ignore the consequences of one's acts. It operates as a limitation on utilitarian reasoning, not as a substitute for it. An absolutist can be expected to try to maximize good and minimize evil, so long as this does not require him to transgress an absolute prohibition like that against murder. But when such a conflict occurs, the prohibition takes complete precedence over any consideration of consequences. Some of the results of this view are clear enough. It requires us to forgo certain potentially useful military measures, such as the slaughter of hostages and prisoners or indiscriminate attempts to reduce the enemy civilian population by starvation, epidemic infectious diseases like anthrax and bubonic plague, or mass incineration. It means that we cannot deliberate on whether such measures are justified by the fact that they will avert still greater evils, for as intentional measures they cannot be justified in terms of any consequences whatever.

Someone unfamiliar with the events of this century might imagine that utilitarian arguments, or arguments of national interest, would suffice to deter measures of this sort. But it has become evident that such considerations are insufficient to prevent the adoption and employment of enormous antipopulation weapons once their use is considered a serious moral possibility. The same is true of the piecemeal wiping out of rural civilian populations in airborne antiguerrilla warfare. Once the door is opened to calculations of utility and national interest, the usual speculations about the future of freedom, peace, and economic prosperity can be brought to bear to ease the consciences of those responsible for a certain number of charred babies.

For this reason alone it is important to decide what is wrong with the frame of mind which allows such arguments to begin. But it is also important to understand absolutism in the cases where it genuinely conflicts with utility. Despite its appeal, it is a paradoxical position, for it can require that one refrain from choosing the lesser of two evils when that is the only choice one has. And it is additionally paradoxical because, unlike pacifism, it permits one to do horrible things to people in some circumstances but not in others.

IV

Before going on to say what, if anything, lies behind the position, there remain a few relatively technical matters which are best discussed at this point.

First, it is important to specify as clearly as possible the kind of thing to which absolutist prohibitions can apply. We must take seriously the proviso that they concern what we deliberately do to people. There could not, for example, without incoherence, be an absolute prohibition against *bringing about* the death of an innocent person. For one may find oneself in a situation in which, no matter what one does, some innocent people will die as a result. I do not mean just that there are cases in which someone will die no matter what one does, because one is not in a position to affect the outcome one way or the other. That, it is to be hoped, is one's relation to the deaths of most innocent people. I have in

mind, rather, a case in which someone is bound to die, but who it is will depend on what one does. Sometimes these situations have natural causes, as when too few resources (medicine, lifeboats) are available to rescue everyone threatened with a certain catastrophe. Sometimes the situations are manmade, as when the only way to control a campaign of terrorism is to employ terrorist tactics against the community from which it has arisen. Whatever one does in cases such as these, some innocent people will die as a result. If the absolutist prohibition forbade doing what would result in the deaths of innocent people, it would have the consequence that in such cases nothing one could do would be morally permissible.

This problem is avoided, however, because what absolutism forbids is *doing* certain things to people, rather than bringing about certain *results*. Not everything that happens to others as a result of what one does is something that one has *done* to them. Catholic moral theology seeks to make this distinction precise in a doctrine known as the law of double effect, which asserts that there is a morally relevant distinction between bringing about the death of an innocent person deliberately, either as an end in itself or as a means, and bringing it about as a side effect of something else one does deliberately. In the latter case, even if the outcome is foreseen, it is not murder, and does not fall under the absolute prohibition, though of course it may still be wrong for other reasons (reasons of utility, for example). Briefly, the principle states that one is sometimes permitted knowingly to bring about as a side effect of one's actions something which it would be absolutely impermissible to bring about deliberately as an end or as a means. In application to war or revolution, the law of double effect permits a certain amount of civilian carnage as a side effect of bombing munitions plants or attacking enemy soldiers. And even this is permissible only if the cost is not too great to be justified by one's objectives.

However, despite its importance and its usefulness in accounting for certain plausible moral judgments, I do not believe that the law of double effect is a generally applicable test for the consequences of an absolutist position. Its own application is not always clear, so that it introduces uncertainty where there need not be uncertainty.

In Indochina, for example, there is a great deal of aerial bombardment, strafing, spraying of napalm, and employment of pellet- or needle-spraying antipersonnel weapons against rural villages in which guerrillas are suspected to be hiding, or from which small-arms fire has been received. The majority of those killed and wounded in these aerial attacks are reported to be women and children, even when some combatants are caught as well. However, the government regards these civilian casualties as a regrettable side effect of what is a legitimate attack against an armed enemy.

It might be thought easy to dismiss this as sophistry: if one bombs, burns, or strafes a village containing a hundred people, twenty of whom one believes to be guerrillas, so that by killing most of them one will be statistically likely to kill most of the guerrillas, then isn't one's attack on the group of one hundred a *means* of destroying the guerrillas, pure and simple? If one makes no attempt to discriminate between guerrillas and civilians, as is impossible in an aerial attack on a small village, then one cannot regard as a mere side effect the deaths of those in the group that one would not have bothered to kill if more selective means had been available.

The difficulty is that this argument depends on one particular description of the act, and the reply might be that the means used against the guerrillas is not: killing everybody in the village—but rather: obliteration bombing of the *area* in which the twenty guerrillas are known to be located. If there are civilians in the area as well, they will be killed as a side effect of such action.

Because of casuistical problems like this, I prefer to stay with the original, unanalyzed distinction between what one does to people and what merely happens to them as a result of what one does. The law of double effect provides an approximation to that distinction in many cases, and perhaps it can be sharpened to the point where it does better than that. Certainly the original distinction itself needs clarification, particularly since some of the things we do to people involve things happening to them as a result of other things we do. In a case like the one discussed, however, it is clear that by bombing the village one slaughters and maims the civilians in it. Whereas by giving the only available medicine to one of two sufferers from a disease, one does not kill the other, even if he dies as a result.

The second technical point to take up concerns a possible misinterpretation of this feature of the position. The absolutist focus on actions rather than outcomes does not merely introduce a new, outstanding item into the catalogue of evils. That is, it does not say that the worst thing in the world is the deliberate murder of an innocent person. For if that were all, then one could presumably justify one such murder on the ground that it would prevent several others, or ten thousand on the ground that they would prevent a hundred thousand more. That is a familiar argument. But if this is allowable, then there is no absolute prohibition against murder after all. Absolutism requires that we *avoid* murder at all costs, not that we *prevent* it at all costs.

Finally, let me remark on a frequent criticism of absolutism that depends on a misunderstanding. It is sometimes suggested that such prohibitions depend on a kind of moral self-interest, a primary obligation to preserve one's own moral purity, to keep one's hands clean no matter what happens to the rest of the world. If this were the position, it might be exposed to the charge of self-indulgence. After all, what gives one man a right to put the purity of his soul or the cleanness of his hands above the lives or welfare of large numbers of other people? It might be argued that a public servant like Truman has no right to put himself first in that way; therefore if he is convinced that the alternatives would be worse, he must give the order to drop the bombs, and take the burden of those deaths on himself, as he must do other distasteful things for the general good.

But there are two confusions behind the view that moral self-interest underlies moral absolutism. First, it is a confusion to suggest that the need to preserve one's moral purity might be the *source* of an obligation. For if by committing murder one sacrifices one's moral purity or integrity, that can only be because there is *already* something wrong with murder. The general reason against committing murder cannot therefore be merely that it makes one an immoral person. Secondly, the notion that one might sacrifice one's moral integrity justifiably, in the service of a sufficiently worthy end, is an incoherent notion. For if one were justified in making such a sacrifice (or even morally required to make it), then one would not be sacrificing one's moral integrity by adopting that course: one would be preserving it.

Moral absolutism is not unique among moral theories in requiring each person to do what will preserve his own moral purity in all circumstances. This is equally true of utilitarianism, or of any other theory which distinguishes between right and wrong. Any theory which defines the right course of action in various circumstances and asserts that one should adopt that course, ipso facto asserts that one should do what will preserve one's moral purity, simply because the right course of action *is* what will preserve one's moral purity in those circumstances. Of course utilitarianism does not assert that this is *why* one should adopt that course, but we have seen that the same is true of absolutism.

V

It is easier to dispose of false explanations of absolutism than to produce a true one. A positive account of the matter must begin with the observation that war, conflict, and aggression are relations between persons. The view that it can be wrong to consider merely the overall effect of one's actions on the general welfare comes into prominence when those actions involve relations with others. A man's acts usually affect more people than he deals with directly, and those effects must naturally be considered in his decisions. But if there are special principles governing the manner in which he should *treat* people, that will require special attention to the particular persons toward whom the act is directed, rather than just to its total effect.

Absolutist restrictions in warfare appear to be of two types: restrictions on the class of persons at whom aggression or violence may be directed and restrictions on the manner of attack, given that the object falls within that class. These can be combined, however, under the principle that hostile treatment of any person must be justified in terms of something *about that person* which makes the treatment appropriate. Hostility is a personal relation, and it must be suited to its target. One consequence of this condition will be that certain persons may not be subjected to hostile treatment in war at all, since nothing about them justifies such treatment. Others will be proper objects of hostility only in certain circumstances, or when they are engaged in certain pursuits. And the appropriate manner and extent of hostile treatment will depend on what is justified by the particular case.

A coherent view of this type will hold that extremely hostile behavior toward another is compatible with treating him as a person—even perhaps as an end in himself. This is possible only if one has not automatically stopped treating him as a person as soon as one starts to fight with him. If hostile, aggressive, or combative treatment of others always violated the condition that they be treated as human beings, it would be difficult to make further distinctions on that score *within* the class of hostile actions. That point of view, on the level of international relations, leads to the position that if complete pacifism is not accepted, no holds need be barred at all, and we may slaughter and massacre to our hearts' content, if it seems advisable. Such a position is often expressed in discussions of war crimes.

But the fact is that ordinary people do not believe this about conflicts, physical or otherwise, between individuals, and there is no more reason why it should be true of conflicts between nations. There seems to be a perfectly natural conception of the distinction between fighting clean and fighting dirty. To fight dirty is to direct one's hostility or aggression not at its proper object, but at a peripheral target which may be more vulnerable, and through which the proper object can be attacked indirectly. This applies in a fist fight, an election campaign, a duel, or a philosophical argument. If the concept is general enough to apply to all these matters, it should apply to war—both to the conduct of individual soldiers and to the conduct of nations.

Suppose that you are a candidate for public office, convinced that the election of your opponent would be a disaster, that he is an unscrupulous demagogue who will serve a narrow range of interests and seriously infringe the rights of those who disagree with him; and suppose you are convinced that you cannot defeat him by conventional means. Now imagine that various unconventional means present themselves as possibilities: you possess information about his sex life which would scandalize the electorate if made public; or you learn that his wife is an alcoholic or that in his youth he was associated for a brief period with a proscribed political party, and you believe that this information could be used to blackmail him into withdrawing his candidacy; or you can have a team of your supporters flatten the tires of a crucial subset of his supporters on election day; or you are in a position to stuff the ballot boxes; or, more simply, you can have him assassinated. What is wrong with these methods, given that they will achieve an overwhelmingly desirable result?

There are, of course, many things wrong with them: some are against the law; some infringe the procedures of an electoral process to which you are presumably committed by taking part in it; very importantly, some may backfire, and it is in the interest of all political candidates to adhere to an unspoken agreement not to allow certain personal matters to intrude into a campaign. But that is not all. We have in addition the feeling that these measures, these methods of attack are *irrelevant* to the issue between you and your opponent, that in taking them up you would not be directing yourself to that which makes him an object of your opposition. You would be directing your attack not at the true target of your hostility, but at peripheral targets that happen to be vulnerable.

The same is true of a fight or argument outside the framework of any system of regulations or law. In an altercation with a taxi driver over an excessive fare, it is inappropriate to taunt him about his accent, flatten one of his tires, or smear chewing gum on his windshield; and it remains inappropriate even if he casts aspersions on your race, politics, or religion, or dumps the contents of your suitcase into the street.

The importance of such restrictions may vary with the seriousness of the case; and what is unjustifiable in one case may be justified in a more extreme one. But they all derive from a single principle: that hostility or aggression should be directed at its true object. This means both that it should be directed at the person or persons who provoke it and that it should aim more specifically at what is provocative about them. The second condition will determine what form the hostility may appropriately take.

It is evident that some idea of the relation in which one should stand to other people underlies this principle, but the idea is difficult to state. I believe it is roughly this: whatever one does to another person intentionally must be aimed at him as a subject, with the intention that he receive it as a subject. It should manifest an attitude to *him* rather than just to the situation, and he should be able to recognize it and identify himself as its object. The procedures by which such an attitude is manifested need not be addressed to the person directly. Surgery, for example, is not a form of personal confrontation but part of a medical treatment that can be offered to a patient face to face and received by him as a response to his needs and the natural outcome of an attitude toward *him*.

Hostile treatment, unlike surgery, is already addressed to a person, and does not take its interpersonal meaning from a wider context. But hostile acts can serve as the expression or implementation of only a limited range of attitudes to the person who is attacked. Those attitudes in turn have as objects certain real or presumed characteristics or activities of the person which are thought to justify them. When this background is absent, hostile or aggressive behavior can no longer be intended for the reception of the victim as a subject. Instead it takes on the character of a purely bureaucratic operation. This occurs when one attacks someone who is not the true object of one's hostility—the true object may be someone else, who can be attacked through the victim; or one may not be manifesting a hostile attitude toward anyone, but merely using the easiest available path to some desired goal. One finds oneself not facing or addressing the victim at all, but operating on him— without the larger context of personal interaction that surrounds a surgical operation.

If absolutism is to defend its claim to priority over considerations of utility, it must hold that the maintenance of a direct interpersonal response to the people one deals with is a requirement which no advantages can justify one in abandoning. The requirement is absolute only if it rules out any calculation of what would justify its violation. I have said earlier that there may be circumstances so extreme that they render an absolutist position untenable. One may find then that one has no choice but to do something terrible. Nevertheless, even in such cases absolutism retains its force in that one cannot claim *justification* for the violation. It does not become *all right*.

As a tentative effort to explain this, let me try to connect absolutist limitations with the possibility of justifying *to the victim* what is being done to him. If one abandons a person in the course of rescuing several others from a fire or a sinking ship, one *could* say to him, "You understand, I have to leave you to save the others." Similarly, if one subjects an unwilling child to a painful surgical procedure, one can say to him, "If you could understand, you would realize that I am doing this to help you." One could *even* say, as one bayonets an enemy soldier, "It's either you or me." But one cannot really say while torturing a prisoner, "You understand, I have to pull out your fingernails because it is absolutely essential that we have the names of your confederates"; nor can one say to the victims of Hiroshima, "You understand, we have to incinerate you to provide the Japanese government with an incentive to surrender."

This does not take us very far, of course, since a utilitarian would presumably be willing to offer justifications of the latter sort to his victims, in cases where he thought they were sufficient. They are really justifications to the world at large, which the victim, as a reasonable man, would be expected to appreciate. However, there seems to me something wrong with this view, for it ignores the possibility that to treat someone else horribly puts you in a special relation to him, which may have to be defended in terms of other features of your relation to him. The suggestion needs much more development; but it may help us to understand how there may be requirements which are absolute in the sense that there can be no justification for violating them. If the justification for what one did to another person had to be such that it could be offered to him specifically, rather than just to the world at large, that would be a significant source of restraint.

If the account is to be deepened, I would hope for some results along the following lines. Absolutism is associated with a view of oneself as a small being interacting with others in a large world. The justifications it requires are primarily interpersonal. Utilitarianism is associated with a view of oneself as a benevolent bureaucrat distributing such benefits as one can control to countless other beings, with whom one may have various relations or none. The justifications it requires are primarily administrative. The argument between the two moral attitudes may depend on the relative priority of these two conceptions.

VI

Some of the restrictions on methods of warfare which have been adhered to from time to time are to be explained by the mutual interests of the involved parties: restrictions on weaponry, treatment of prisoners, etc. But that is not all there is to it. The conditions of directness and relevance which I have argued apply to re-

lations of conflict and aggression apply to war as well. I have said that there are two types of absolutist restrictions on the conduct of war: those that limit the legitimate targets of hostility and those that limit its character, even when the target is acceptable. I shall say something about each of these. As will become clear, the principle I have sketched does not yield an unambiguous answer in every case.

First let us see how it implies that attacks on some people are allowed, but not attacks on others. It may seem paradoxical to assert that to fire a machine gun at someone who is throwing hand grenades at your emplacement is to treat him as a human being. Yet the relation with him is direct and straightforward. The attack is aimed specifically against the threat presented by a dangerous adversary, and not against a peripheral target through which he happens to be vulnerable but which has nothing to do with that threat. For example, you might stop him by machine-gunning his wife and children, who are standing nearby, thus distracting him from his aim of blowing you up and enabling you to capture him. But if his wife and children are not threatening your life, that would be to treat them as means with a vengeance.

This, however, is just Hiroshima on a smaller scale. One objection to weapons of mass annihilation—nuclear, thermonuclear, biological, or chemical—is that their indiscriminateness disqualifies them as direct instruments for the expression of hostile relations. In attacking the civilian population, one treats neither the military enemy nor the civilians with that minimal respect which is owed to them as human beings. This is clearly true of the direct attack on people who present no threat at all. But it is also true of the character of the attack on those who *are* threatening you, viz., the government and military forces of the enemy. Your aggression is directed against an area of vulnerability quite distinct from any threat presented by them which you may be justified in meeting. You are taking aim at them through the mundane life and survival of their countrymen, instead of aiming at the destruction of their military capacity. And of course it does not require hydrogen bombs to commit such crimes.

This way of looking at the matter also helps us to understand the importance of the distinction between combatants and noncombatants, and the irrelevance of much of the criticism offered against its intelligibility and moral significance. According to an absolutist position, deliberate killing of the innocent is murder, and in warfare the role of the innocent is filled by noncombatants. This has been thought to raise two sorts of problems: first, the widely imagined difficulty of making a division, in modern warfare, between combatants and noncombatants; second, problems deriving from the connotation of the word "innocence."

Let me take up the latter question first. In the absolutist position, the operative notion of innocence is not moral innocence, and it is not opposed to moral guilt. If it were, then we would be justified in killing a wicked but noncombatant hairdresser in an enemy city who supported the evil policies of his government, and unjustified in killing a morally pure conscript who was driving a tank toward us with the profoundest regrets and nothing but love in his heart. But moral innocence has very little to do with it, for in the definition of murder "innocent" means "currently harmless," and it is opposed not to "guilty" but to "doing harm." It should be noted that such an analysis has the consequence that in war we may often be justified in killing people who do not deserve to die, and unjustified in killing people who do deserve to die, if anyone does.

So we must distinguish combatants from noncombatants on the basis of their immediate threat or harmfulness. I do not claim that the line is a sharp one, but it is not so difficult as is often supposed to place individuals on one side of it or the other. Children are not combatants even though they may join the armed forces if they are allowed to grow up. Women are not combatants just because they bear children or offer comfort to the soldiers. More problematic are the supporting personnel, whether in or out of uniform, from drivers of munitions trucks and army cooks to civilian munitions workers and farmers. I believe they can be plausibly classified by applying the condition that the prosecution of conflict must direct itself to the cause of danger, and not to what is peripheral. The threat presented by an army and its members does not consist merely in the fact that they are men, but in the fact that they are armed and are using their arms in the pursuit of certain objectives. Contributions to their arms and logistics are contributions to this threat; contributions to their mere existence as men are not. It is therefore wrong to direct an attack against those who merely serve the combatants' needs as human beings, such as farmers and food suppliers, even though survival as a human being is a necessary condition of efficient functioning as a soldier.

This brings us to the second group of restrictions: those that limit what may be done even to combatants. These limits are harder to explain clearly. Some of them may be arbitrary or conventional, and some may have to be derived from other sources; but I believe that the condition of directness and relevance in hostile relations accounts for them to a considerable extent.

Consider first a case which involves both a protected class of noncombatants and a restriction on the measures that may be used against combatants. One provision of the rules of war which is universally recognized, though it seems to be turning into a dead letter in Vietnam, is the special status of medical personnel and the wounded in warfare. It might be more efficient to shoot medical officers on sight and to let the enemy wounded die rather than be patched up to fight another day. But someone with medical insignia is supposed to be left alone and permitted to tend and retrieve the wounded. I believe this is because medical attention is a species of attention to completely general human needs, not specifically the needs of a combat soldier, and our conflict with the soldier is not with his existence as a human being.

By extending the application of this idea, one can justify prohibitions against certain particularly cruel weapons: starvation, poisoning, infectious diseases (supposing they could be inflicted on combatants only), weapons designed to maim or disfigure or torture the opponent rather than merely to stop him. It is not, I think, mere casuistry to claim that such weapons attack the men, not the soldiers. The effect of dum-dum bullets, for example, is much more extended than necessary to cope with the combat situation in which they are used. They abandon any attempt to discriminate in their effects between the combatant and the human being. For this reason the use of flamethrowers and napalm is an atrocity in all circumstances that I can imagine, whoever the target may be. Burns are both extremely painful and extremely disfiguring—far more than any other category of wound. That this well-known fact plays no (inhibiting) part in the determination of U.S. weapons policy suggests that moral sensitivity among public officials has not increased markedly since the Spanish Inquisition.

Finally, the same condition of appropriateness to the true object of hostility should limit the scope of attacks on an enemy country: its economy, agriculture, transportation system, and so forth. Even if the parties to a military conflict are considered to be not armies or governments but entire nations (which is usually a grave error), that does not justify one nation in warring against every aspect or element of another nation. That is not justified in a conflict between individuals, and nations are even more complex than individuals, so the same reasons apply. Like a human being, a nation is engaged in countless other pursuits while waging war, and it is not in those respects that it is an enemy.

The burden of the argument has been that absolutism about murder has a foundation in principles governing all one's relations to other persons, whether aggressive or amiable, and that these principles, and that absolutism, apply to warfare as well, with the result that certain measures are impermissible no matter what the consequences. I do not mean to romanticize war. It is sufficiently utopian to suggest that when nations conflict they might rise to the level of limited barbarity that typically characterizes violent conflict between individuals, rather than wallowing in the moral pit where they appear to have settled, surrounded by enormous arsenals.

VII

Having described the elements of the absolutist position, we must now return to the conflict between it and utilitarianism. Even if certain types of dirty tactics become acceptable when the stakes are high enough, the most serious of the prohibited acts, like murder and torture, are not just supposed to require unusually strong justification. They are supposed *never* to be done, because no quantity of resulting benefit is thought capable of *justifying* such treatment of a person.

The fact remains that when an absolutist knows or believes that the utilitarian cost of refusing to adopt a prohibited course will be very high, he may hold to his refusal to adopt it, but he will find it difficult to feel that a moral dilemma has been satisfactorily resolved. The same may be true of someone who rejects an absolutist

requirement and adopts instead the course yielding the most acceptable consequences. In either case, it is possible to feel that one has acted for reasons insufficient to justify violation of the opposing principle. In situations of deadly conflict, particularly where a weaker party is threatened with annihilation or enslavement by a stronger one, the argument for resorting to atrocities can be powerful, and the dilemma acute.

There may exist principles, not yet codified, which would enable us to resolve such dilemmas. But then again there may not. We must face the pessimistic alternative that these two forms of moral intuition are not capable of being brought together into a single, coherent moral system, and that the world can present us with situations in which there is no honorable or moral course for a man to take, no course free of guilt and responsibility for evil.

The idea of a moral blind alley is a perfectly intelligible one. It is possible to get into such a situation by one's own fault, and people do it all the time. If, for example, one makes two incompatible promises or commitments—becomes engaged to two people, for example—then there is no course one can take which is not wrong, for one must break one's promise to at least one of them. Making a clean breast of the whole thing will not be enough to remove one's reprehensibility. The existence of such cases is not morally disturbing, however, because we feel that the situation was not unavoidable: one had to do something wrong in the first place to get into it. But what if the world itself, or someone else's actions, could face a previously innocent person with a choice between morally abominable courses of action, and leave him no way to escape with his honor? Our intuitions rebel at the idea, for we feel that the constructibility of such a case must show a contradiction in our moral views. But it is not in itself a contradiction to say that someone can do X or not do X, and that for him to take either course would be wrong. It merely contradicts the supposition that *ought* implies *can*—since presumably one ought to refrain from what is wrong, and in such a case it is impossible to do so. Given the limitations on human action, it is naïve to suppose that there is a solution to every moral problem with which the world can face us. We have always known that the world is a bad place. It appears that it may be an evil place as well.

James Rachels

Active and Passive Euthanasia

Abstract: The traditional distinction between active and passive euthanasia requires critical analysis. The conventional doctrine is that there is such an important moral difference between the two that, although the latter is sometimes permissible, the former is always forbidden. This doctrine may be challenged for several reasons. First of all, active euthanasia is in many cases more humane than passive euthanasia. Secondly, the conventional doctrine leads to decisions concerning life and death on irrelevant grounds, Thirdly, the doctrine rests on a distinction between killing and letting die that itself has no moral importance. Fourthly, the most common arguments in favor of the doctrine are invalid. I therefore suggest that the American Medical Association policy statement that endorses this doctrine is unsound.

The distinction between active and passive euthanasia is thought to be crucial for medical ethics. The idea is that it is permissible, at least in some cases, to withhold treatment and allow a patient to die, but it is never permissible to take any direct action designed to kill the patient. This doctrine seems to be accepted by most doctors, and it is endorsed in a statement adopted by the House of Delegates of the American Medical Association on December 4, 1973:

> The intentional termination of the life of one human being by another—mercy killing—is contrary to that for which the medical profession stands and is contrary to the policy of the American Medical Association.

> The cessation of the employment of extraordinary means to prolong the life of the body when there is irrefutable evidence that biological death is imminent is the decision of the patient and/or his immediate family. The advice and judgment of the physician should be freely available to the patient and/or his immediate family.

However, a strong case can be made against this doctrine. In what follows I will set out some of the relevant arguments, and urge doctors to reconsider their views on this matter.

To begin with a familiar type of situation, a patient who is dying of incurable cancer of the throat is in terrible pain, which can no longer be satisfactorily alleviated. He is certain to die within a few days, even if present treatment is continued, but he does not want to go on living for those days since the pain is unbearable. So he asks the doctor for an end to it, and his family joins in the request.

Suppose the doctor agrees to withhold treatment, as the conventional doctrine says he may. The justification for his doing so is that the patient is in terrible agony, and since he is going to die anyway, it would be wrong to prolong his suffering needlessly. But now notice this. If one simply withholds treatment, it may take the patient longer to die, and so he may suffer more than he would if more direct action were taken and a lethal injection given. This fact provides strong reason for thinking that, once the initial decision not to prolong his agony has been made, active euthanasia is actually preferable to passive euthanasia, rather than the reverse. To say otherwise is to endorse the option that leads to more suffering rather than less, and is contrary to the humanitarian impulse that prompts the decision not to prolong his life in the first place.

Part of my point is that the process of being "allowed to die" can be relatively slow and painful, whereas being given a lethal injection is relatively quick and painless. Let me give a different sort of example. In the United States about one in 600 babies is born with Down's syndrome. Most of these babies are otherwise healthy—that is, with only the usual pediatric care, they

James Rachels, "Active and Passive Euthanasia" from *New England Journal of Medicine,* 292 (1975).

will proceed to an otherwise normal infancy. Some, however, are born with congenital defects such as intestinal obstructions that require operations if they are to live. Sometimes, the parents and the doctor will decide not to operate, and let the infant die. Anthony Shaw describes what happens then:

> . . . When surgery is denied [the doctor] must try to keep the infant from suffering while natural forces sap the baby's life away. As a surgeon whose natural inclination is to use the scalpel to fight off death, standing by and watching a salvageable baby die is the most emotionally exhausting experience I know. It is easy at a conference, in a theoretical discussion, to decide that such infants should be allowed to die. It is altogether different to stand by in the nursery and watch as dehydration and infection wither a tiny being over hours and days. This is a terrible ordeal for me and the hospital staff—much more so than for the parents who never set foot in the nursery.[1]

I can understand why some people are opposed to all euthanasia, and insist that such infants must be allowed to live. I think I can also understand why other people favor destroying these babies quickly and painlessly. But why should anyone favor letting "dehydration and infection wither a tiny being over hours and days?" The doctrine that says that a baby may be allowed to dehydrate and wither, but may not be given an injection that would end its life without suffering, seems so patently cruel as to require no further refutation. The strong language is not intended to offend, but only to put the point in the clearest possible way.

My second argument is that the conventional doctrine leads to decisions concerning life and death made on irrelevant grounds.

Consider again the case of the infants with Down's syndrome who need operations for congenital defects unrelated to the syndrome to live. Sometimes, there is no operation, and the baby dies, but when there is no

such defect, the baby lives on. Now, an operation such as that to remove an intestinal obstruction is not prohibitively difficult. The reason why such operations are not performed in these cases is, clearly, that the child has Down's syndrome and the parents and doctor judge that because of that fact it is better for the child to die.

But notice that this situation is absurd, no matter what view one takes of the lives and potentials of such babies. If the life of such an infant is worth preserving, what does it matter if it needs a simple operation? Or, if one thinks it better that such a baby should not live on, what difference does it make that it happens to have an unobstructed intestinal tract? In either case, the matter of life and death is being decided on irrelevant grounds. It is the Down's syndrome, and not the intestines, that is the issue. The matter should be decided, if at all, on that basis, and not be allowed to depend on the essentially irrelevant question of whether the intestinal tract is blocked.

What makes this situation possible, of course, is the idea that when there is an intestinal blockage, one can "let the baby die," but when there is no such defect there is nothing that can be done, for one must not "kill" it. The fact that this idea leads to such results as deciding life or death on irrelevant grounds is another good reason why the doctrine should be rejected.

One reason why so many people think that there is an important moral difference between active and passive euthanasia is that they think killing someone is morally worse than letting someone die. But is it? Is killing, in itself, worse than letting die? To investigate this issue, two cases may be considered that are exactly alike except that one involves killing whereas the other involves letting someone die. Then, it can be asked whether this difference makes any difference to the moral assessments. It is important that the cases be exactly alike, except for this one difference, since otherwise one cannot be confident that it is this difference and not some other that accounts for any variation in the assessments of the two cases. So, let us consider this pair of cases:

In the first, Smith stands to gain a large inheritance if anything should happen to his six-year-old cousin. One evening while the child is taking his bath, Smith sneaks into the bathroom and drowns the child, and then arranges things so that it will look like an accident.

---

1. Shaw, A.: 'Doctor, Do We Have a Choice?' *New York Times Magazine,* January 30, 1972, p. 54.

In the second, Jones also stands to gain if anything should happen to his six-year-old cousin. Like Smith, Jones sneaks in planning to drown the child in his bath. However, just as he enters the bathroom Jones sees the child slip and hit his head, and fall face down in the water. Jones is delighted; he stands by, ready to push the child's head back under if it is necessary, but it is not necessary. With only a little thrashing about, the child drowns all by himself, "accidentally," as Jones watches and does nothing.

Now Smith killed the child, whereas Jones "merely" let the child die. That is the only difference between them. Did either man behave better, from a moral point of view? If the difference between killing and letting die were in itself a morally important matter, one should say that Jones's behavior was less reprehensible than Smith's. But does one really want to say that? I think not. In the first place, both men acted from the same motive, personal gain, and both had exactly the same end in view when they acted. It may be inferred from Smith's conduct that he is a bad man, although that judgment may be withdrawn or modified if certain further facts are learned about him—for example, that he is mentally deranged. But would not the very same thing be inferred about Jones from his conduct? And would not the same further considerations also be relevant to any modification of this judgment? Moreover, suppose Jones pleaded, in his own defense, "After all, I didn't do anything except just stand there and watch the child drown. I didn't kill him; I only let him die." Again, if letting die were in itself less bad than killing, this defense should have at least some weight. But it does not. Such a "defense" can only be regarded as a grotesque perversion of moral reasoning. Morally speaking, it is no defense at all.

Now, it may be pointed out, quite properly, that the cases of euthanasia with which doctors are concerned are not like this at all. They do not involve personal gain or the destruction of normal healthy children. Doctors are concerned only with cases in which the patient's life is of no further use to him, or in which the patient's life has become or will soon become a terrible burden. However, the point is the same in these cases: the bare difference between killing and letting die does not, in itself, make a moral difference. If a doctor lets a patient die, for humane reasons, he is in the same moral position as if he had given the patient a lethal injection for humane reasons. If his decision was wrong—if, for example, the patient's illness was in fact curable—the decision would be equally regrettable no matter which method was used to carry it out. And if the doctor's decision was the right one, the method used is not in itself important.

The AMA policy statement isolates the crucial issue very well; the crucial issue is "the intentional termination of the life of one human being by another." But after identifying this issue, and forbidding "mercy killing," the statement goes on to deny that the cessation of treatment is the intentional termination of a life. This is where the mistake comes in, for what is the cessation of treatment, in these circumstances, if it is not "the intentional termination of the life of one human being by another?" Of course it is exactly that, and if it were not, there would be no point to it.

Many people will find this judgment hard to accept. One reason, I think, is that it is very easy to conflate the question of whether killing is, in itself, worse than letting die, with the very different question of whether most actual cases of killing are more reprehensible than most actual cases of letting die. Most actual cases of killing are clearly terrible (think, for example, of all the murders reported in the newspapers), and one hears of such cases every day. On the other hand, one hardly ever hears of a case of letting die, except for the actions of doctors who are motivated by humanitarian reasons. So one learns to think of killing in a much worse light than of letting die. But this does not mean that there is something about killing that makes it in itself worse than letting die, for it is not the bare difference between killing and letting die that makes the difference in these cases. Rather, the other factors—the murderer's motive of personal gain, for example, contrasted with the doctor's humanitarian motivation—account for different reactions to the different cases.

I have argued that killing is not in itself any worse than letting die; if my contention is right, it follows that active euthanasia is not any worse than passive euthanasia. What arguments can be given on the other side? The most common, I believe, is the following:

"The important difference between active and passive euthanasia is that, in passive euthanasia, the doctor does not do anything to bring about the patient's death.

The doctor does nothing, and the patient dies of whatever ills already afflict him. In active euthanasia, however, the doctor does something to bring about the patient's death: he kills him. The doctor who gives the patient with cancer a lethal injection has himself caused his patient's death; whereas if he merely ceases treatment, the cancer is the cause of the death."

A number of points need to be made here. The first is that it is not exactly correct to say that in passive euthanasia the doctor does nothing, for he does do one thing that is very important: he lets the patient die. "Letting someone die" is certainly different, in some respects, from other types of action—mainly in that it is a kind of action that one may perform by way of not performing certain other actions. For example, one may let a patient die by way of not giving medication, just as one may insult someone by way of not shaking his hand. But for any purpose of moral assessment, it is a type of action nonetheless. The decision to let a patient die is subject to moral appraisal in the same way that a decision to kill him would be subject to moral appraisal: it may be assessed as wise or unwise, compassionate or sadistic, right or wrong. If a doctor deliberately let a patient die who was suffering from a routinely curable illness, the doctor would certainly be to blame for what he had done, just as he would be to blame if he had needlessly killed the patient. Charges against him would then be appropriate. If so, it would be no defense at all for him to insist that he didn't "do anything." He would have done something very serious indeed, for he let his patient die.

Fixing the cause of death may be very important from a legal point of view, for it may determine whether criminal charges are brought against the doctor. But I do not think that this notion can be used to show a moral difference between active and passive euthanasia. The reason why it is considered bad to be the cause of someone's death is that death is regarded as a great evil—and so it is. However, if it has been decided that euthanasia—even passive euthanasia—is desirable in a given case, it has also been decided that in this instance death is no greater an evil than the patient's continued existence. And if this is true, the usual reason for not wanting to be the cause of someone's death simply does not apply.

Finally, doctors may think that all of this is only of academic interest—the sort of thing that philosophers may worry about but that has no practical bearing on their own work. After all, doctors must be concerned about the legal consequences of what they do, and active euthanasia is clearly forbidden by the law. But even so, doctors should also be concerned with the fact that the law is forcing upon them a moral doctrine that may well be indefensible, and has a considerable effect on their practices. Of course, most doctors are not now in the position of being coerced in this matter, for they do not regard themselves as merely going along with what the law requires. Rather, in statements such as the AMA policy statement that I have quoted, they are endorsing this doctrine as a central point of medical ethics. In that statement, active euthanasia is condemned not merely as illegal but as "contrary to that for which the medical profession stands," whereas passive euthanasia is approved. However, the preceding considerations suggest that there is really no moral difference between the two, considered in themselves (there may be important moral differences in some cases in their *consequences,* but, as I pointed out, these differences may make active euthanasia, and not passive euthanasia, the morally preferable option). So, whereas doctors may have to discriminate between active and passive euthanasia to satisfy the law, they should not do any more than that. In particular, they should not give the distinction any added authority and weight by writing it into official statements of medical ethics.

Jonathan Bennett

The Conscience of Huckleberry Finn

In this paper, I shall present not just the conscience of Huckleberry Finn but two others as well. One of them is the conscience of Heinrich Himmler. He became a Nazi in 1923; he served drably and quietly, but well, and was rewarded with increasing responsibility and power. At the peak of his career he held many offices and commands, of which the most powerful was that of leader of the S.S.—the principal police force of the Nazi regime. In this capacity, Himmler commanded the whole concentration-camp system, and was responsible for the execution of the so-called 'final solution of the Jewish problem'. It is important for my purposes that this piece of social engineering should be thought of not abstractly but in concrete terms of Jewish families being marched to what they think are bath-houses, to the accompaniment of loud-speaker renditions of extracts from *The Merry Widow* and *Tales of Hoffman,* there to be choked to death by poisonous gases. Altogether, Himmler succeeded in murdering about four and a half million of them, as well as several million gentiles, mainly Poles and Russians.

The other conscience to be discussed is that of the Calvinist theologian and philosopher Jonathan Edwards. He lived in the first half of the eighteenth century, and has a good claim to be considered America's first serious and considerable philosophical thinker. He was for many years a widely-renowned preacher and Congregationalist minister in New England; in 1748 a dispute with his congregation led him to resign (he couldn't accept their view that unbelievers should be admitted to the Lord's Supper in the hope that it would convert them); for some years after that he worked as a missionary, preaching to Indians through an interpreter; then in 1758 he accepted the presidency of what is now Princeton University, and within two months died from a smallpox in-

oculation. Along the way he wrote some first-rate philosophy: his book attacking the notion of free will is still sometimes read. Why I should be interested in Edwards' *conscience* will be explained in due course.

I shall use Heinrich Himmler, Jonathan Edwards and Huckleberry Finn to illustrate different aspects of a single theme, namely the relationship between *sympathy* on the one hand and *bad morality* on the other.

$$\bullet \ \bullet \ \bullet \ \bullet \ \bullet$$

All that I can mean by a 'bad morality' is a morality whose principles I deeply disapprove of. When I call a morality bad, I cannot prove that mine is better; but when I here call any morality bad, I think you will agree with me that it is bad; and that is all I need.

There could be dispute as to whether the springs of someone's actions constitute a *morality.* I think, though, that we must admit that someone who acts in ways which conflict grossly with our morality may nevertheless have a morality of his own—a set of principles of action which he sincerely assents to, so that for him the problem of acting well or rightly or in obedience to conscience is the problem of conforming to *those* principles. The problem of conscientiousness can arise as acutely for a bad morality as for any other: rotten principles may be as difficult to keep as decent ones.

As for 'sympathy': I use this term to cover every sort of fellow-feeling, as when one feels pity over someone's loneliness, or horrified compassion over his pain, or when one feels a shrinking reluctance to act in a way which will bring misfortune to someone else. These *feelings* must not be confused with *moral judgments.* My sympathy for someone in distress may lead me to help him, or even to think that I ought to help him; but in itself it is not a judgment about what I ought to do but just a *feeling* for him in his plight. We shall get some light on the difference between feelings and moral judgments when we consider Huckleberry Finn.

Obviously, feelings can impel one to action, and so can moral judgments; and in a particular case sympathy and morality may pull in opposite directions. This can happen not just with bad moralities, but also with good ones like yours and mine. For example, a small child, sick and miserable, clings tightly to his mother and screams in terror when she tries to pass him over to the doctor to be examined. If the mother gave way to her sympathy, that is to her feeling for the child's misery and fright, she would hold it close and not let the doctor come near; but don't we agree that it might be wrong for her to act on such a feeling? Quite generally, then, anyone's moral principles may apply to a particular situation in a way which runs contrary to the particular thrusts of fellow-feeling that he has in that situation. My immediate concern is with sympathy in relation to bad morality, but not because such conflicts occur only when the morality is bad.

Now, suppose that someone who accepts a bad morality is struggling to make himself act in accordance with it in a particular situation where his sympathies pull him another way. He sees the struggle as one between doing the right, conscientious thing, and acting wrongly and weakly, like the mother who won't let the doctor come near her sick, frightened baby. Since we don't accept this person's morality, we may see the situation very differently, thoroughly disapproving of the action he regards as the right one, and endorsing the action which from his point of view constitutes weakness and backsliding.

Conflicts between sympathy and bad morality won't always be like this, for we won't disagree with every single dictate of a bad morality. Still, it can happen in the way I have described, with the agent's right action being our wrong one, and vice versa. That is just what happens in a certain episode in chapter 16 of *The Adventures of Huckleberry Finn,* an episode which brilliantly illustrates how fiction can be instructive about real life.

· · · · ·

Huck Finn has been helping his slave friend Jim to run away from Miss Watson, who is Jim's owner. In their raft-journey down the Mississippi river, they are near to the place at which Jim will become legally free. Now let Huck take over the story:

Jim said it made him all over trembly and feverish to be so close to freedom. Well, I can tell you it made me all over trembly and feverish, too, to hear him, because I began to get it through my head that he *was* most free—and who was to blame for it? Why, *me.* I couldn't get that out of my conscience, no how nor no way.... It hadn't ever come home to me, before, what this thing was that I was doing. But now it did; and it stayed with me, and scorched me more and more. I tried to make out to myself that *I* warn't to blame, because *I* didn't run Jim off from his rightful owner; but it warn't no use, conscience up and say, every time: 'But you knowed he was running for his freedom, and you could a paddled ashore and told somebody.' That was so—I couldn't get around that, no way. That was where it pinched. Conscience says to me: 'What had poor Miss Watson done to you, that you could see her nigger go off right under your eyes and never say one single word? What did that poor old woman do to you, that you could treat her so mean? . . .' I got to feeling so mean and so miserable I most wished I was dead.

Jim speaks of his plan to save up to buy his wife, and then his children, out of slavery; and he adds that if the children cannot be bought he will arrange to steal them. Huck is horrified:

Thinks I, this is what comes of my not thinking. Here was this nigger which I had as good as helped to run away, coming right out flat-footed and saying he would steal his children—children that belonged to a man I didn't even know; a man that hadn't ever done me no harm.

I was sorry to hear Jim say that, it was such a lowering of him. My conscience got to stirring me up hotter than ever, until at last I says to it: 'Let up on me—it ain't too late, yet—I'll paddle ashore at first light, and tell.' I felt easy, and happy, and light as a feather, right off. All my troubles was gone.

This is bad morality all right. In his earliest years Huck wasn't taught any principles, and the only ones he has encountered since then are those of rural Missouri, in which slave-owning is just one kind of ownership and is not subject to critical pressure. It hasn't occurred to Huck to question those principles. So the action, to us abhorrent, of turning Jim in to the authorities presents itself *clearly* to Huck as the right thing to do.

For us, morality and sympathy would both dictate helping Jim to escape. If we felt any conflict, it would have both these on one side and something else on the other—greed for a reward, or fear of punishment. But Huck's morality conflicts with his sympathy, that is, with his unargued, natural feeling for his friend. The conflict starts when Huck sets off in the canoe towards the shore, pretending that he is going to reconnoitre, but really planning to turn Jim in:

> As I shoved off, [Jim] says: 'Pooty soon I'll be a-shout'n for joy, en I'll say, it's all on accounts o' Huck I's a free man . . . Jim won't ever forgit you, Huck; you's de bes' fren' Jim's ever had; en you's de *only* fren' old Jim's got now.'
>
> I was paddling off, all in a sweat to tell on him; but when he says this, it seemed to kind of take the tuck all out of me. I went along slow then, and I warn't right down certain whether I was glad I started or whether I warn't. When I was fifty yards off, Jim says:
>
> 'Dah you goes, de ole true Huck; de on'y white genlman dat ever kep' his promise to ole Jim.' Well, I just felt sick. But I says, I *got* to do it—I can't get *out* of it.

In the upshot, sympathy wins over morality. Huck hasn't the strength of will to do what he sincerely thinks he ought to do. Two men hunting for runaway slaves ask him whether the man on his raft is black or white:

> I didn't answer up prompt. I tried to, but the words wouldn't come. I tried, for a second or two, to brace up and out with it, but I warn't man enough—hadn't the spunk of a rabbit. I see I was weakening; so I just give up trying, and up and says: 'He's white.'

So Huck enables Jim to escape, thus acting weakly and wickedly—he thinks. In this conflict between sympathy and morality, sympathy wins.

One critic has cited this episode in support of the statement that Huck suffers, 'excruciating moments of wavering between honesty and respectability'. That is hopelessly wrong, and I agree with the perceptive comment on it by another critic, who says:

> The conflict waged in Huck is much more serious: he scarcely cares for respectability and never hesitates to relinquish it, but he does care for honesty and gratitude—and both honesty and gratitude require that he should give Jim up. It is not, in Huck, honesty at war with respectability but love and compassion for Jim struggling against his conscience. His decision is for Jim and hell: a right decision made in the mental chains that Huck never breaks. His concern for Jim is and remains *irrational*. Huck finds many reasons for giving Jim up and none for stealing him. To the end Huck sees his compassion for Jim as a weak, ignorant, and wicked felony.

That is precisely correct—and it can have that virtue only because Mark Twain wrote the episode with such unerring precision. The crucial point concerns *reasons*, which all occur on one side of the conflict. On the side of conscience we have principles, arguments, considerations, ways of looking at things:

> 'It hadn't ever come home to me before what I was doing'
> 'I tried to make out that I warn't to blame'
> 'Conscience said "But you knowed . . ."—I couldn't get around that'
> 'What had poor Miss Watson done to you?'
> 'This is what comes of my not thinking'
> '. . . children that belonged to a man I didn't even know'.

On the other side, the side of feeling, we get nothing like that. When Jim rejoices in Huck, as his only friend, Huck doesn't consider the claims of friendship or have the situation 'come home' to him in a different light. All that happens is: 'When he says this, it seemed to kind of take the tuck all out of me. I went along slow then, and I warn't right down certain whether I was glad I started or whether I warn't.' Again, Jim's words about Huck's 'promise' to him don't give Huck any *reason* for changing his plan: in his morality promises to slaves probably don't count. Their effect on him is of a different kind: 'Well, I just felt sick.' And when the moment for final decision comes, Huck doesn't weigh up pros and cons: he simply *fails* to do what he believes to be right—he isn't strong enough, hasn't 'the spunk of a rabbit'. This passage in the novel is notable not just for its finely wrought irony, with Huck's weakness of will leading him to do the right thing, but also for its masterly handling of the difference between general moral principles and particular unreasoned emotional pulls.

• • • • •

Consider now another case of bad morality in conflict with human sympathy: the case of the odious Himmler. Here, from a speech he made to some S.S. generals, is an indication of the content of his morality:

> What happens to a Russian, to a Czech, does not interest me in the slightest. What the nations can offer in the way of good blood of our type, we will take, if necessary by kidnapping their children and raising them here with us. Whether nations live in prosperity or starve to death like cattle interests me only in so far as we need them as slaves to our *Kultur;* otherwise it is of no interest to me. Whether 10,000 Russian females fall down from exhaustion while digging an antitank ditch interests me only in so far as the antitank ditch for Germany is finished.[1]

But has this a moral basis at all? And if it has, was there in Himmler's own mind any conflict between morality and sympathy? Yes there was. Here is more from the same speech:

> . . . I also want to talk to you quite frankly on a very grave matter . . . I mean . . . the extermina-

tion of the Jewish race. . . . Most of you must know what it means when 100 corpses are lying side by side, or 500, or 1,000. To have stuck it out and at the same time—apart from exceptions caused by human weakness—to have remained decent fellows, that is what has made us hard. This is a page of glory in our history which has never been written and is never to be written.

Himmler saw his policies as being hard to implement while still retaining one's human sympathies—while still remaining a 'decent fellow'. He is saying that only the weak take the easy way out and just squelch their sympathies, and is praising the stronger and more glorious course of retaining one's sympathies while acting in violation of them. In the same spirit, he ordered that when executions were carried out in concentration camps, those responsible 'are to be influenced in such a way as to suffer no ill effect in their character and mental attitude'. A year later he boasted that the S.S. had wiped out the Jews

> without our leaders and their men suffering any damage in their minds and souls. The danger was considerable, for there was only a narrow path between the Scylla of their becoming heartless ruffians unable any longer to treasure life, and the Charybdis of their becoming soft and suffering nervous breakdowns.

And there really can't be any doubt that the basis of Himmler's policies was a set of principles which constituted his morality—a sick, bad, wicked *morality*. He described himself as caught in 'the old tragic conflict between will and obligation'. And when his physician Kersten protested at the intention to destroy the Jews, saying that the suffering involved was 'not to be contemplated', Kersten reports that Himmler replied:

> He knew that it would mean much suffering for the Jews. . . . 'It is the curse of greatness that it must step over dead bodies to create new life. Yet we must . . . cleanse the soil or it will never bear fruit. It will be a great burden for me to bear.'

This, I submit, is the language of morality.

---

1. Quoted in William L. Shirer, *The Rise and Fall of the Third Reich* (New York, 1960), pp. 937–938. Next quotation: Ibid., p. 966. All further quotations relating to Himmler are from Roger Manwell and Heinrich Fraenkel, *Heinrich Himmler* (London, 1965), pp. 132, 197, 184 (twice), 187.

So in this case, tragically, bad morality won out over sympathy. I am sure that many of Himmler's killers did extinguish their sympathies, becoming 'heartless ruffians' rather than 'decent fellows'; but not Himmler himself. Although his policies ran against the human grain to a horrible degree, he did not sandpaper down his emotional surfaces so that there was no grain there, allowing his actions to slide along smoothly and easily. He did, after all, bear his hideous burden, and even paid a price for it. He suffered a variety of nervous and physical disabilities, including nausea and stomach-convulsions, and Kersten was doubtless right in saying that these were 'the expression of a psychic division which extended over his whole life'.

This same division must have been present in some of those officials of the Church who ordered heretics to be tortured so as to change their theological opinions. Along with the brutes and the cold careerists, there must have been some who cared, and who suffered from the conflict between their sympathies and their bad morality.

· · · · ·

In the conflict between sympathy and bad morality, then, the victory may go to sympathy as in the case of Huck Finn, or to morality as in the case of Himmler.

Another possibility is that the conflict may be avoided by giving up, or not ever having, those sympathies which might interfere with one's principles. That seems to have been the case with Jonathan Edwards. I am afraid that I shall be doing an injustice to Edwards' many virtues, and to his great intellectual energy and inventiveness; for my concern is only with the worst thing about him—namely his morality, which was worse than Himmler's.

According to Edwards, God condemns some men to an eternity of unimaginably awful pain, though he arbitrarily spares others—'arbitrarily' because none deserve to be spared:

Natural men are held in the hand of God over the pit of hell; they have deserved the fiery pit, and are already sentenced to it; and God is dreadfully provoked, his anger is as great towards them as to those that are actually suffering the executions of the fierceness of his wrath in hell . . . ; the

devil is waiting for them, hell is gaping for them, the flames gather and flash about them, and would fain lay hold on them . . . ; and . . . there are no means within reach that can be any security to them. . . . All that preserves them is the mere arbitrary will, and uncovenanted unobliged forebearance of an incensed God.[2]

Notice that he says 'they have deserved the fiery pit.' Edwards insists that men *ought* to be condemned to eternal pain; and his position isn't that this is right because God wants it, but rather that God wants it because it is right. For him, moral standards exist independently of God, and God can be assessed in the light of them (and of course found to be perfect). For example, he says:

They deserve to be cast into hell; so that . . . justice never stands in the way, it makes no objection against God's using his power at any moment to destroy them. Yea, on the contrary, justice calls aloud for an infinite punishment of their sins.

Elsewhere, he gives elaborate arguments to show that God is acting justly in damning sinners. For example, he argues that a punishment should be exactly as bad as the crime being punished; God is infinitely excellent; so any crime against him is infinitely bad; and so eternal damnation is exactly right as a punishment—it is infinite, but, as Edwards is careful also to say, it is 'no more than infinite.'

Of course, Edwards himself didn't torment the damned; but the question still arises of whether his sympathies didn't conflict with his *approval* of eternal torment. Didn't he find it painful to contemplate any fellow-human's being tortured for ever? Apparently not:

The God that holds you over the pit of hell, much as one holds a spider or some loathsome insect over the fire, abhors you, and is dreadfully provoked; . . . he is of purer eyes than to bear to have

---

2. Vergilius Ferm (ed.), *Puritan Sage: Collected Writings of Jonathan Edwards* (New York, 1953), p. 370. Next three quotations: Ibid., p. 366, p. 294 ('no more than infinite'), p. 372.

you in his sight; you are ten thousand times so abominable in his eyes as the most hateful venomous serpent is in ours.

When God is presented as being as misanthropic as that, one suspects misanthropy in the theologian. This suspicion is increased when Edwards claims that 'the saints in glory will . . . understand how terrible the sufferings of the damned are; yet . . . will not be sorry for [them].[3] He bases this partly on a view of human nature whose ugliness he seems not to notice:

> The seeing of the calamities of others tends to heighten the sense of our own enjoyments. When the saints in glory, therefore, shall see the doleful state of the damned, how will this heighten their sense of the blessedness of their own state. . . . When they shall see how miserable others of their fellow-creatures are . . . ; when they shall see the smoke of their torment, . . . and hear their dolorous shrieks and cries, and consider that they in the mean time are in the most blissful state, and shall surely be in it to all eternity; how they will rejoice!

I hope this is less than the whole truth! His other main point about why the saints will rejoice to see the torments of the damned is that it is *right* that they should do so:

> The heavenly inhabitants . . . will have no love nor pity to the damned. . . . [This will not show] a want of a spirit of love in them . . . ;

for the heavenly inhabitants will know that it is not fit that they should love [the damned] because they will know then, that God has no love to them, nor pity for them.

---

3. This and the next two quotations are from 'The End of the Wicked Contemplated by the Righteous: or, The Torments of the Wicked in Hell, no Occasion of Grief to the Saints in Heaven', from *The Works of President Edwards* (London, 1817), vol. IV, pp. 507–508, 511–512, and 509, respectively.

The implication that *of course* one can adjust one's feelings of pity so that they conform to the dictates of some authority—doesn't this suggest that ordinary human sympathies played only a small part in Edwards' life?

· · · · ·

Huck Finn, whose sympathies are wide and deep, could never avoid the conflict in that way; but he is determined to avoid it, and so he opts for the only other alternative he can see—to give up morality altogether. After he has tricked the slave-hunters, he returns to the raft and undergoes a peculiar crisis:

> I got aboard the raft, feeling bad and low, because I knowed very well I had done wrong, and I see it warn't no use for me to try to learn to do right; a body that don't get *started* right when he's little, ain't got no show—when the pinch comes there ain't nothing to back him up and him to his work, and so he gets beat. Then I thought a minute, and says to myself, hold on—s'pose you'd a done right and give Jim up; would you feel better than what you do now? No, says I, I'd feel bad—I'd feel just the same way I do now. Well, then, says I, what's the use learning to do right, when it's troublesome to do right and ain't no trouble to do wrong, and the wages is just the same? I was stuck. I couldn't answer that. So I reckoned I wouldn't bother no more about it, but after this always do whichever come handiest at the time.

Huck clearly cannot conceive of having any morality except the one he has learned—too late, he thinks—from his society. He is not entirely a prisoner of that morality, because he does after all reject it; but for him that is a decision to relinquish morality as such; he cannot envisage revising his morality, altering its content in face of the various pressures to which it is subject, including pressures from his sympathies. For example, he does not begin to approach the thought that slavery should be rejected on moral grounds, or the thought that what he is doing is not theft because a person cannot be owned and therefore cannot be stolen.

The basic trouble is that he cannot or will not engage in abstract intellectual operations of any sort. In chapter 33 he finds himself 'feeling to blame, somehow' for something he knows he had no hand in; he assumes that this feeling is a deliverance of conscience; and this confirms him in his belief that conscience shouldn't be listened to:

> It don't make no difference whether you do right or wrong, a person's conscience ain't got no sense, and just goes for him *anyway*. If I had a yaller dog that didn't know no more than a person's conscience does, I would pison him. It takes up more room than all the rest of a person's insides, and yet ain't no good, nohow.

That brisk, incurious dismissiveness fits well with the comprehensive rejection of morality back on the raft. But this is a digression.

On the raft, Huck decides not to live by principles, but just to do whatever 'comes handiest at the time'—always acting according to the mood of the moment. Since the morality he is rejecting is narrow and cruel, and his sympathies are broad and kind, the results will be good. But moral principles are good to have, because they help to protect one from acting badly at moments when one's sympathies happen to be in abeyance. On the highest possible estimate of the role one's sympathies should have, one can still allow for principles as embodiments of one's best feelings, one's broadest and keenest sympathies. On that view, principles can help one across intervals when one's feelings are at less than their best, i.e. through periods of misanthropy or meanness or self-centredness or depression or anger.

What Huck didn't see is that one can live by principles and yet have ultimate control over their content. And one way such control can be exercised is by checking of one's principles in the light of one's sympathies. This is sometimes a pretty straightforward matter. It can happen that a certain moral principle becomes untenable—meaning literally that one cannot hold it any longer—because it conflicts intolerably with the pity or revulsion or whatever that one feels when one sees what the principle leads to. One's experience may play a large part here: experiences evoke feelings, and feelings force one to modify principles. Something like this happened to the English poet Wilfred Owen, whose experiences in the First World War transformed him from

an enthusiastic soldier into a virtual pacifist. I can't document his change of conscience in detail; but I want to present something which he wrote about the way experience can put pressure on morality.

The Latin poet Horace wrote that it is sweet and fitting (or right) to die for one's country—*dulce et decorum est pro patria mori*—and Owen wrote a fine poem about how experience could lead one to relinquish that particular moral principle. He describes a man who is too slow donning his gas mask during a gas a attack—'As under a green sea I saw him drowning,' Owen says. The poem ends like this:

> In all my dreams before my helpless sight
> He plunges at me, guttering, choking, drowning.
> If in some smothering dreams, you too could pace
> Behind the wagon that we flung him in,
> And watch the white eyes writhing in his face,
> His hanging face, like a devil's sick of sin;
> If you could hear, at every jolt, the blood
> Come gargling from the froth-corrupted lungs,
>   Bitter as the cud
> Of vile, incurable sores on innocent tongues,—
> My friend, you would not tell with such high zest
> To children ardent for some desperate glory,
> The old Lie: Dulce et decorum est
> Pro patria mori.

• • • • •

There is a difficulty about drawing from all this a moral for ourselves. I imagine that we agree in our rejection of slavery, eternal damnation, genocide, and uncritical patriotic self-abnegation; so we shall agree that Huck Finn, Jonathan Edwards, Heinrich Himmler, and the poet Horace would all have done well to bring certain of their principles under severe pressure from ordinary human sympathies. But then we can say this because we can say that all those are bad moralities, whereas we cannot look at our own moralities and declare them bad. This is not arrogance: it is obviously incoherent for someone to declare the system of moral principles that he *accepts* to be *bad,* just as one cannot coherently say of anything that one *believes* it but it is *false.*

Still, although I can't point to any of my beliefs and say 'That is false', I don't doubt that some of my beliefs *are* false; and so I should try to remain open to correction. Similarly, I accept every single item in my morality—that is inevitable—but I am sure that my morality could be improved, which is to say that it could undergo changes which I should be glad of once I had made them. So I must try to keep my morality open to revision, exposing it to whatever valid pressures there are—including pressures from my sympathies.

I don't give my sympathies a blank cheque in advance. In a conflict between principle and sympathy, principles ought sometimes to win. For example, I think it was right to take part in the Second World War on the allied side; there were many ghastly individual incidents which might have led someone to doubt the rightness of his participation in that war; and I think it would have been right for such a person to keep his sympathies in a subordinate place on those occasions, not allowing them to modify his principles in such a way as to make a pacifist of him.

Still, one's sympathies should be kept as sharp and sensitive and aware as possible, and not only because they can sometimes affect one's principles or one's conduct or both. Owen, at any rate, says that feelings and sympathies are vital even when they can do nothing but bring pain and distress. In another poem he speaks of the blessings of being numb in one's feelings: 'Happy are the men who yet before they are killed/Can let their veins run cold,' he says. These are the ones who do not suffer from any compassion which, as Owen puts it, 'makes their feet/Sore on the alleys cobbled with their brothers.' He contrasts these 'happy' ones, who 'lose all imagination', with himself and others 'who with a thought besmirch/Blood over all our soul.' Yet the poem's verdict goes against the 'happy' ones. Owen does not say that they will act worse than the others whose souls are besmirched with blood because of their keen awareness of human suffering. He merely says that they are the losers because they have cut themselves off from the human condition:

> By choice they made themselves immune
> To pity and whatever moans in man
> Before the last sea and the hapless stars;
> Whatever mourns when many leave these shores;
> Whatever shares
> The eternal reciprocity of tears.

POLITICAL PHILOSOPHY

W<small>E ARE REQUIRED BY</small> law to pay our taxes, drive only on the right side of the road, leash our dogs. It may be a good thing that there are such laws. But they plainly restrict our freedom. The fundamental question for political philosophy is what gives governments the right to limit people's freedom. One popular and plausible approach invokes the social contract. According to social contract theories, people give up some of their freedom in return for benefits that a political regime can supply. It is as though a number of people got together and drew up a contract to structure their society in a way that would foster their goals. The social contract is, of course, a fiction. No one believes that this is the way political arrangements were actually formed. But the idea is that however they actually came about, if they could have been the outcome of a suitable contractual arrangement, they are just.

This raises a number of questions. If it is conceded that in forming a society we give up some of our rights, then we need to know what rights it is reasonable to give up. To answer that requires comparing the quality of life under a social contract with the quality of life we would have in the state of nature—the conditions that obtain when there is no such contract. Opinions divide on this question. Hobbes has a dark view of human nature. He thinks that people are predominantly self-interested. Unchecked, we would do whatever we could to further our own interests. He thus maintains that in the state of nature life is 'solitary, poor, nasty, brutish, and short'. We are in a condition of war of all against all. Having no basis for trust, we should not trust anyone. He argues that it makes sense to cede practically every freedom to an authoritarian state with the power to enforce its laws. (See too Darwall, 529–42.)

Locke has a more benign view. He thinks that people in a state of nature are reasonably good. People in a state of nature are capable of behaving ethically. The social contract is designed to ensure peace and security in pursuing our own ends. It must, Locke believes, be a contract among equals and a product of freely given consent. Original property rights, he believes, derive from labor. Locke thus repudiates both the divine right of kings to rule and the idea that the powerful can coerce the weak into accepting a disadvantageous political arrangement. Since the social contract is designed to enable us to pursue our own ends, it would not be reasonable to give up too many freedoms. In particular he believes that the rights to life, liberty, and property are unalienable. They are rights we cannot cede to the government. Moreover, Locke maintains that governments govern only with the consent of the governed. Thus revolution is permissible when governments operate beyond the limits of their political authority.

Mill notices that it is not only states that coerce; we are subject to peer pressure as well. And that peer pressure, he maintains, can limit our freedom almost as much as state power can. So, he asks, on what basis should people, whether in governments or informally, limit the freedom of others? Many would reply that we should prohibit actions that will harm those affected by the actions. Mill, however, maintains that if a course of action will harm no one but the person engaged in it, others have no right to hinder her. He recognizes that children and the mentally infirm need special protections, but he maintains that there is no justification in interfering with another adult's actions so long as those actions harm no one but the agent. The fact that others disapprove of an action or are disgusted by it is not a reason to prohibit it if it harms no one but the agent.

Rawls is a contemporary social contract theorist. Like his predecessors, he attempts to devise conditions under which a social contract could be made that would define the basic structure of a just society. He introduces a 'veil of ignorance' that blinds the contractors to the particulars of their own situations. He describes an 'original position' in which the framers of the contract deliberate behind the veil of ignorance. They do not know anything specific about themselves or their situations. They do not know whether they are rich or poor, smart or dumb. Nor do they know what their interests, abilities, talents, or material resources are. They want to ensure the best life possible for themselves and their descendants, whomever those people turn out to be. Under such a state of ignorance, Rawls maintains, these framers could endorse two principles of justice. The first guarantees that everyone will have the largest possible array of basic rights—freedom of thought, freedom of expression, enough to eat, and so on. The second says that opportunities should be open to talents and that to be acceptable inequalities should improve the lots of the least well-off. So, for example, an inequality might allow an inventor to make a lot of money from his invention so long as the invention improved the situation of the least well-off members of society.

Nozick objects to two aspects of Rawls' position. Even if the two principles are reasonable when we do not know what our resources are, why should we think they are reasonable when we do? If you are smarter than I am or have more money than I do, why should you set aside these advantages in establishing the conditions of our association? In real life, Nozick says, you would have every right to use these advantages. Why should things be different in framing the social contract? Second, he asks, why should we say that it is a principle of justice that the least well-off benefit? One might simply require that someone benefit or that most people benefit. Nozick's libertarian position advocates 'every man for himself'. Each individual looks out for his own interests and does what he can to achieve them using whatever resources he can command, so long as he does not infringe on the freedoms of others.

Rawls seeks to define fair terms of cooperation among free and equal citizens. He devises a situation in which no one can use her advantages to bias the system in her own favor. In this way he tries to respect the idea that justice should be blind to certain differences between people. It is sometimes argued that the pretense of the original position is implausible. No one, it is said, could really be as ignorant of the particulars of her own situation as Rawls takes the contractors to be. It is not clear that this objection is sound, since Rawls, like other social contract theorists, is devising an imaginative thought experiment. And in thought experiments we can bracket all sorts of knowledge that we actually have. Moreover, the contractors are not deciding only for themselves. They are deciding for their descendants. Even if I cannot blind myself to the particulars of my own situation, I do not know what my unborn grandchildren's situation will be. So, if I want to be sure that they will live in a society that treats them fairly, I had better design a society that treats everyone fairly.

Marx is not interested in a mythical social contract. He believes that the issues of political philosophy are always embedded in the here and now. He argues that capitalism undermines the relation between the worker and her work. He maintains that the division of labor leads to alienation. The factory worker cannot respect herself as a producer of goods and cannot identify the products of her labor as her own. Instead of identifying herself with her work, as an artisan or artist might, she works to have an identity outside work. As is well known, Marx's remedy was that the workers must own the means of production. Whether or not Marx's solution is viable, his work is important for insisting that political philosophy must be connected to real life. If an arrangement turns out to be unjust in practice, it makes little difference if it would have been written into the original social contract. Marx's work is also valuable be-cause it insists on the intimate relation between economic and political factors. Like Rawls, Marx raises questions about whether and to what extent economic inequalities are compat-ible with political equality.

Among the critical questions for political philosophy are these: What assumptions should we make about human nature? Can a political philosophy, such as Hobbes' or Locke's, be un-dermined if its assumptions about human nature are unsound? To what extent are they de-pendent on facts? Marx and Locke make substantive assumptions about private property. Are their theories undermined if these economic assumptions are wrong?

Thomas Hobbes

Leviathan

Of the NATURAL CONDITION OF MANKIND, *as Concerning Their Felicity, and Misery*

[1] Nature hath made men so equal in the faculties of body and mind as that, though there be found one man sometimes manifestly stronger in body or of quicker mind than another, yet when all is reckoned together the difference between man and man is not so considerable as that one man can thereupon claim to himself any benefit to which another may not pretend as well as he. For as to the strength of body, the weakest has strength enough to kill the strongest, either by secret machination or by confederacy with others that are in the same danger with himself.

[2] And as to the faculties of the mind—setting aside the arts grounded upon words, and especially that skill of proceeding upon general and infallible rules called science (which very few have, and but in few things), as being not a native faculty (born with us), nor attained (as prudence) while we look after somewhat else—I find yet a greater equality amongst men than that of strength. For prudence is but experience, which equal time equally bestows on all men in those things they equally apply themselves unto. That which may perhaps make such equality incredible is but a vain conceit of one's own wisdom, which almost all men think they have in a greater degree than the vulgar, that is, than all men but themselves and a few others whom, by fame or for concurring with themselves, they approve. For such is the nature of men that howsoever they may acknowledge many others to be more witty, or more eloquent, or more learned, yet they will hardly believe there be many so wise as themselves. For they see their own wit at hand, and other men's at a distance. But this proveth rather that men are in that point equal, than unequal. For there is not ordinarily a greater sign of the equal distribution of anything than that every man is contented with his share.

[3] From this equality of ability ariseth equality of hope in the attaining of our ends. And therefore, if any two men desire the same thing, which nevertheless they cannot both enjoy, they become enemies; and in the way to their end, which is principally their own conservation, and sometimes their delectation only, endeavour to destroy or subdue one another. And from hence it comes to pass that, where an invader hath no more to fear than another man's single power, if one plant, sow, build, or possess a convenient seat, others may probably be expected to come prepared with forces united, to dispossess and deprive him, not only of the fruit of his labour, but also of his life or liberty. And the invader again is in the like danger of another.

[4] And from this diffidence of one another, there is no way for any man to secure himself so reasonable as anticipation, that is, by force or wiles to master the persons of all men he can, so long till he see no other power great enough to endanger him. And this is no more than his own conservation requireth, and is generally allowed. Also, because there be some that taking pleasure in contemplating their own power in the acts of conquest, which they pursue farther than their security requires, if others (that otherwise would be glad to be at ease within modest bounds) should not by invasion increase their power, they would not be able, long time, by standing only on their defence, to subsist. And by consequence, such augmentation of dominion over men being necessary to a man's conservation, it ought to be allowed him.

[5] Again, men have no pleasure, but on the contrary a great deal of grief, in keeping company where there is no power able to over-awe them all. For every man looketh that his companion should value him at the same rate he sets upon himself, and upon all signs of contempt, or undervaluing, naturally endeavours, as far as he dares (which amongst them that have no common power to keep them in quiet, is far enough to make them destroy each other), to extort a greater value from his contemners, by damage, and from others, by the example.

From Thomas Hobbes, *Leviathan,* edited by Edwin Curley (Indianapolis: Hackett Publishing Company, 1994). Reprinted by permission of the publisher.

[6] So that in the nature of man we find three principal causes of quarrel: first, competition; secondly, diffidence; thirdly, glory.

[7] The first maketh men invade for gain; the second, for safety; and the third, for reputation. The first use violence to make themselves masters other men's persons, wives, children, and cattle; the second, to defend them; the third, for trifles, as a word, a smile, a different opinion, and any other sign of undervalue, either direct in their persons, or by reflection in their kindred, their friends, their nation, their profession, or their name.

[8] Hereby it is manifest that during the time men live without a common power to keep them all in awe, they are in that condition which is called war, and such a war as is of every man against every man. For WAR consisteth not in battle only, or the act of fighting, but in a tract of time wherein the will to contend by battle is sufficiently known. And therefore, the notion of *time* is to be considered in the nature of war, as it is in the nature of weather. For as the nature of foul weather lieth not in a shower or two of rain, but in an inclination thereto of many days together, so the nature of war consisteth not in actual fighting, but in the known disposition thereto during all the time there is no assurance to the contrary. All other time is PEACE.

[9] Whatsoever therefore is consequent to a time of war, where every man is enemy to every man, the same is consequent to the time wherein men live without other security than what their own strength and their own invention shall furnish them withal. In such condition there is no place for industry, because the fruit thereof is uncertain, and consequently, no culture of the earth, no navigation, nor use of the commodities that may be imported by sea, no commodious building, no instruments of moving and removing such things as require much force, no knowledge of the face of the earth, no account of time, no arts, no letters, no society, and which is worst of all, continual fear and danger of violent death, and the life of man, solitary, poor, nasty, brutish, and short.

[10] It may seem strange, to some man that has not well weighed these things, that nature should thus dissociate; and render men apt to invade and destroy one another. And he may, therefore, not trusting to this inference made from the passions, desire perhaps to have the same confirmed by experience. Let him therefore consider with himself—when taking a journey, he arms himself, and seeks to go well accompanied; when going to sleep, he locks his doors; when even in his house, he locks his chests; and this when he knows there be laws, and public officers, armed, to revenge all injuries shall be done him—what opinion he has of his fellow subjects, when he rides armed; of his fellow citizens, when he locks his doors; and of his children and servants, when he locks his chests. Does he not there as much accuse mankind by his actions, as I do by my words? But neither of us accuse man's nature in it. The desires and other passions of man are in themselves no sin. No more are the actions that proceed from those passions till they know a law that forbids them—which till laws be made they cannot know. Nor can any law be made, till they have agreed upon the person that shall make it.

[11] It may peradventure be thought, there was never such a time nor condition of war as this; and I believe it was never generally so, over all the world. But there are many places where they live so now. For the savage people in many places of *America* (except the government of small families, the concord whereof dependeth on natural lust) have no government at all, and live at this day in that brutish manner as I said before. Howsoever, it may be perceived what manner of life there would be where there were no common power to fear, by the manner of life which men that have formerly lived under a peaceful government use to degenerate into, in a civil war.

[12] But though there had never been any time wherein particular men were in a condition of war one against another, yet in all times kings and persons of sovereign authority, because of their independency, are in continual jealousies and in the state and posture of gladiators, having their weapons pointing and their eyes fixed on one another, that is, their forts, garrisons, and guns upon the frontiers of their kingdoms, and continual spies upon their neighbours, which is a posture of war. But because they uphold thereby the industry of their subjects, there does not follow from it that misery which accompanies the liberty of particular men.

[13] To this war of every man against every man, this also is consequent: that nothing can be unjust. The notions of right and wrong, justice and injustice, have there

no place. Where there is no common power, there is no law; where no law, no injustice. Force and fraud are in war the two cardinal virtues. Justice and injustice are none of the faculties neither of the body, nor mind. If they were, they might be in a man that were alone in the world, as well as his senses and passions. They are qualities that relate to men in society, not in solitude. It is consequent also to the same condition that there be no propriety, no dominion, no *mine* and *thine* distinct, but only that to be every man's that he can get, and for so long as he can keep it. And thus much for the ill condition which man by mere nature is actually placed in, though with a possibility to come out of it, consisting partly in the passions, partly in his reason.

[14] The passions that incline men to peace are fear of death, desire of such things as are necessary to commodious living, and a hope by their industry to obtain them. And reason suggesteth convenient articles of peace, upon which men may be drawn to agreement. These articles are they which otherwise are called the Laws of Nature, whereof I shall speak more particularly in the two following chapters.

Of the First and Second NATURAL LAWS *and of* CONTRACTS

[1] The RIGHT OF NATURE, which writers commonly call *jus naturale,* is the liberty each man hath to use his own power, as he will himself, for the preservation of his own nature, that is to say, of his own life, and consequently of doing anything which, in his own judgment and reason, he shall conceive to be the aptest means thereunto.

[2] By LIBERTY is understood, according to the proper signification of the word, the absence of external impediments, which impediments may oft take away part of a man's power to do what he would, but cannot hinder him from using the power left him, according as his judgment and reason shall dictate to him.

[3] A LAW OF NATURE (*lex naturalis*) is a precept or general rule, found out by reason, by which a man is forbidden to do that which is destructive of his life or taketh away the means of preserving the same, and to omit that by which he thinketh it may be best preserved. For though they that speak of this subject use to confound *jus* and *lex* (*right* and *law*), yet they ought to be distinguished, because RIGHT consisteth in liberty to do or to forbear, whereas LAW determineth and bindeth to one of them; so that law and right differ as much as obligation and liberty, which in one and the same matter are inconsistent.

[4] And because the condition of man (as hath been declared in the precedent chapter) is a condition of war of everyone against everyone (in which case everyone is governed by his own reason and there is nothing he can make use of that may not be a help unto him in preserving his life against his enemies), it followeth that in such a condition every man has a right to everything, even to one another's body. And therefore, as long, as this natural right of every man to everything endureth, there can be no security to any man (how strong or wise soever he be) of living out the time which nature ordinarily alloweth men to live. And consequently it is a precept, or general rule, of reason *that every man ought to endeavour peace, as far as he has hope of obtaining it, and when he cannot obtain it, that he may seek and use all helps and advantages of war.* The first branch of which rule containeth the first and fundamental law of nature, which is *to seek peace, and follow it.* The second, the sum of the right of nature, which is *by all means we can, to defend ourselves.*

[5] From this fundamental law of nature, by which men are commanded to endeavour peace, is derived this second law: *that a man be willing, when others are so too, as far-forth as for peace and defence of himself he shall think it necessary, to lay down this right to all things, and be contented with so much liberty against other men, as he would allow other men against himself.* For as long as every man holdeth this right of doing anything he liketh, so long are all men in the condition of war. But if other men will not lay down their right as well as he, then there is no reason for anyone to divest himself of his; for that were to expose himself to prey (which no man is bound to), rather than to dispose himself to peace. This is that law of the Gospel: "whatsoever you require that others should do to you, that do ye to them." And that law of all men: *quod tibi fieri non vis, alteri ne feceris.*[1]

------

1. I.e., do not do to others what you do not want done to yourself.

[6] To *lay down* a man's *right* to anything is to *divest* himself of the *liberty* of hindering another of the benefit of his own right to the same. For he that renounceth or passeth away his right giveth not to any other man a right which he had not before (because there is nothing to which every man had not right by nature), but only standeth out of his way, that he may enjoy his own original right without hindrance from him, not without hindrance from another. So that the effect which redoundeth to one man by another man's defect of right is but so much diminution of impediments to the use of his own right original.

[7] Right is laid aside either by simply renouncing it or by transferring it to another. By *simply* RENOUNCING, when he cares not to whom the benefit thereof redoundeth. By TRANSFERRING, when he intendeth the benefit thereof to some certain person or persons. And when a man hath in either manner abandoned or granted away his right, then is he said to be OBLIGED or BOUND not to hinder those to whom such right is granted or abandoned from the benefit of it; and [it is said] that he *ought,* and it is his DUTY, not to make void that voluntary act of his own, and that such hindrance is INJUSTICE, and INJURY, as being *sine jure* [without right], the right being before renounced or transferred. So that *injury* or *injustice,* in the controversies of the world, is somewhat like to that which in the disputations of scholars is called absurdity. For as it is there called an *absurdity* to contradict what one maintained in the beginning, so in the world it is called injustice and injury voluntarily to undo that which from the beginning he had voluntarily done.

The way by which a man either simply renounceth or transferreth his right is a declaration, or signification by some voluntary and sufficient sign or signs, that he doth so renounce or transfer, or hath so renounced or transferred the same, to him that accepteth it. And these signs are either words only, or actions only, or (as it happeneth most often) both words and actions. And the same are the BONDS by which men are bound and obliged, bonds that have their strength, not from their own nature (for nothing is more easily broken than a man's word) but from fear of some evil consequence upon the rupture.

[8] Whensoever a man transferreth his right or renounceth it, it is either in consideration of some right reciprocally transferred to himself or for some other good he hopeth for thereby. For it is a voluntary act and of the voluntary acts of every man the object is some *good to himself.* And therefore there be some rights which no man can be understood by any words or other signs to have abandoned or transferred. As, first, a man cannot lay down the right of resisting them that assault him by force to take away his life, because he cannot be understood to aim thereby at any good to himself. [Second], the same may be said of wounds, and chains, and imprisonment, both because there is no benefit consequent to such patience (as there is to the patience of suffering another to be wounded or imprisoned), as also because a man cannot tell, when he seeth men proceed against him by violence, whether they intend his death or not. [Third] and lastly, the motive and end for which this renouncing and transferring of right is introduced, is nothing else but the security of a man's person, in his life and in the means of so preserving life as not to be weary of it. And therefore if a man by words or other signs seem to despoil himself of the end for which those signs were intended, he is not to be understood as if he meant it, or that it was his will, but that he was ignorant of how such words and actions were to be interpreted.

[9] The mutual transferring of right is that which men call CONTRACT.

[10] There is difference between transferring of right to the thing and transferring (or tradition, that is, delivery) of the thing itself. For the thing may be delivered together with the translation of the right (as in buying and selling with ready money, or exchange of goods or lands); and it may be delivered some time after.

[11] Again, one of the contractors may deliver the thing contracted for on his part, and leave the other to perform his part at some determinate time after (and in the meantime be trusted); and then the contract on his part is called PACT, or COVENANT; or both parts may contract now, to perform hereafter, in which cases he that is to perform in time to come, being trusted, his performance is called *keeping of promise,* or *faith,* and the failing of performance (if it be voluntary) *violation of faith.*

[12] When the transferring of right is not mutual, but one of the parties transferreth in hope to gain thereby friendship or service from another (or from his friends), or in hope to gain the reputation of charity or

magnanimity, or to deliver his mind from the pain of compassion, or in hope of reward in heaven, this is not contract, but GIFT, FREE-GIFT, GRACE, which words signify one and the same thing.

[13] Signs of contract are either *express* or *by inference*. Express are words spoken with understanding of what they signify; and such words are either of the time *present* or *past* (as, *I give, I grant, I have given, I have granted, I will that this be yours*), or of the future (as, *I will give, I will grant*), which words of the future are called PROMISE.

[14] Signs by inference are: sometimes the consequence of words, sometimes the consequence of silence; sometimes the consequence of actions, sometimes the consequence of forbearing an action; and generally a sign by inference of any contract is whatsoever sufficiently argues the will of the contractor.

[15] Words alone, if they be of the time to come, and contain a bare promise, are an insufficient sign of a free-gift, and therefore not obligatory. For if they be of the time to come (as, *tomorrow I will give*), they are a sign I have not given yet, and consequently that my right is not transferred, but remaineth till I transfer it by some other act. But if the words be of the time present or past (as, *I have given, or do give to be delivered tomorrow*), then is my tomorrow's right given away today; and that by the virtue of the words, though there were no other argument of my will. And there is a great difference in the signification of these words: *volo hoc tuum esse cras* and *cras dabo* (that is, between *I will that this be thine tomorrow* and *I will give it thee tomorrow*); for the word *I will* in the former manner of speech signifies an act of the will present, but in the latter it signifies a promise of an act of the will to come; and therefore the former words, being of the present, transfer a future right; the latter, that be of the future, transfer nothing.

But if there be other signs of the will to transfer a right besides words, then though the gift be free, yet may the right be understood to pass by words of the future (as, if a man propound a prize to him that comes first to the end of a race, the gift is free, and though the words be of the future, yet the right passeth; for if he would not have his words so be understood, he should not have let them run).

[16] In contracts the right passeth, not only where the words are of the time present or past, but also where they are of the future, because all contract is mutual translation, or change of right; and therefore he that promiseth only (because he hath already received the benefit for which he promiseth) is to be understood as if he intended the right should pass; for unless he had been content to have his words so understood, the other would not have performed his part first. And for that cause, in buying and selling, and other acts of contract, a promise is equivalent to a covenant, and therefore obligatory.

[17] He that performeth first in the case of a contract is said to MERIT that which he is to receive by the performance of the other, and he hath it as *due*. Also when a prize is propounded to many, which is to be given to him only that winneth (or money is thrown amongst many, to be enjoyed by them that catch it), though this be a free gift, yet so to win (or so to catch) is to *merit*, and to have it as DUE. For the right is transferred in the propounding of the prize (and in throwing down the money), though it be not determined to whom but by the event of the contention.

But there is between these two sorts of merit, this difference: that in contract I merit by virtue of my own power, and the contractor's need; but in this case of free gift, I am enabled to merit only by the benignity of the giver; in contract I merit at the contractor's hand that he should depart with his right; in this case of gift, I merit not that the giver should part with his right, but that when he has parted with it, it should be mine rather than another's.

And this I think to be the meaning of that distinction of the Schools between *meritum congrui* and *meritum condigni*. For God Almighty having promised Paradise to those men (hoodwinked with carnal desires) that can walk through this world according to the precepts and limits prescribed by him, they say: he that shall so walk shall merit Paradise *ex congruo*. But because no man can demand a right to it, by his own righteousness or any other power in himself, but by the free grace of God only, they say: no man can merit Paradise *ex condigno*. This, I say, I think is the meaning of that distinction; but because disputers do not agree upon the signification of their own terms of art longer than it serves their turn, I will not affirm anything of their meaning. Only this I say: when a gift is given indefinitely, as a prize to be contended for, he that winneth meriteth, and may claim the prize as due.

[18] If a covenant be made wherein neither of the parties perform presently, but trust one another, in the condition of mere nature (which is a condition of war of every man against every man) upon any reasonable suspicion it is void; but if there be a common power set over them both, with right and force sufficient to compel performance, it is not void. For he that performeth first has no assurance the other will perform after, because the bonds of words are too weak to bridle men's ambition, avarice, anger, and other passions, without the fear of some coercive power; which in the condition of mere nature, where all men are equal and judges of the justness of their own fears, cannot possibly be supposed. And therefore, he which performeth first does but betray himself to his enemy, contrary to the right (he can never abandon) of defending his life and means of living.

[19] But in a civil estate, where there is a power set up to constrain those that would otherwise violate their faith, that fear is no more reasonable; and for that cause, he which by the covenant is to perform first is obliged so to do.

[20] The cause of fear which maketh such a covenant invalid must be always something arising after the covenant made (as some new fact or other sign of the will not to perform), else it cannot make the covenant void. For that which could not hinder a man from promising, ought not to be admitted as a hindrance of performing.

[21] He that transferreth any right transferreth the means of enjoying it, as far as lieth in his power. As he that selleth land is understood to transfer the herbage and whatsoever grows upon it; nor can he that sells a mill turn away the stream that drives it. And they that give to a man the right of government in sovereignty are understood to give him the right of levying money to maintain soldiers, and of appointing magistrates for the administration of justice.

[22] To make covenants with brute beasts is impossible because, not understanding our speech, they understand not, nor accept of, any translation of right, nor can translate any right to another; and without mutual acceptation, there is no covenant.

[23] To make covenant with God is impossible, but by mediation of such as God speaketh to (either by revelation supernatural or by his lieutenants that govern under him and in his name); for otherwise we know not whether our covenants be accepted or not. And therefore, they that vow anything contrary to any law of nature vow in vain, as being a thing unjust to pay such vow. And if it be a thing commanded by the law of nature, it is not the vow, but the law that binds them.

[24] The matter or subject of a covenant is always something that falleth under deliberation (for to covenant is an act of the will; that is to say an act, and the last act, of deliberation) and is therefore always understood to be something to come, and which is judged possible for him that covenanteth to perform.

[25] And therefore, to promise that which is known to be impossible is no covenant. But if that prove impossible afterwards which before was thought possible, the covenant is valid and bindeth, though not to the thing itself, yet to the value; or, if that also be impossible, to the unfeigned endeavour of performing as much as is possible (for to more no man can be obliged).

[26] Men are freed of their covenants two ways: by performing or by being forgiven. For performance is the natural end of obligation; and forgiveness, the restitution of liberty (as being a retransferring of that right in which the obligation consisted).

[27] Covenants entered into by fear, in the condition of mere nature, are obligatory. For example, if I covenant to pay a ransom, or service, for my life, to an enemy, I am bound by it. For it is a contract wherein one receiveth the benefit of life; the other is to receive money, or service, for it; and consequently, where no other law (as in the condition of mere nature) forbiddeth the performance, the covenant is valid. Therefore prisoners of war, if trusted with the payment of their ransom, are obliged to pay it; and if a weaker prince make a disadvantageous peace with a stronger, for fear, he is bound to keep it, unless (as hath been said before) there ariseth some new and just cause of fear, to renew the war. And even in commonwealths, if I be forced to redeem myself from a thief by promising him money, I am bound to pay it, till the civil law discharge me. For whatsoever I may lawfully do without obligation, the same I may lawfully covenant to do through fear; and what I lawfully covenant, I cannot lawfully break.

[28] A former covenant makes void a later. For a man that hath passed away his right to one man today,

hath it not to pass tomorrow to another; and therefore the later promise passeth no right, but is null.

[29] A covenant not to defend myself from force by force is always void. For (as I have showed before) no man can transfer or lay down his right to save himself from death, wounds, and imprisonment (the avoiding whereof is the only end of laying down any right), and therefore the promise of not resisting force in no covenant transferreth any right, nor is obliging. For though a man may covenant thus *unless I do so, or so, kill me,* he cannot covenant thus *unless I do so, or so, I will not resist you, when you come to kill me.* For man by nature chooseth the lesser evil, which is danger of death in resisting, rather than the greater, which is certain and present death in not resisting. And this is granted to be true by all men, in that they lead criminals to execution and prison with armed men, notwithstanding that such criminals have consented to the law by which they are condemned.

[30] A covenant to accuse oneself, without assurance of pardon, is likewise invalid. For in the condition of nature, where every man is judge, there is no place for accusation; and in the civil state the accusation is followed with punishment, which being force, a man is not obliged not to resist. The same is also true of the accusation of those by whose condemnation a man falls into misery (as, of a father, wife, or benefactor). For the testimony of such an accuser, if it be not willingly given, is presumed to be corrupted by nature, and therefore not to be received; and where a man's testimony is not to be credited, he is not bound to give it. Also accusations upon torture are not to be reputed as testimonies. For torture is to be used but as means of conjecture and light in the further examination and search of truth; and what is in that case confessed tendeth to the ease of him that is tortured, not to the informing of the torturers, and therefore ought not to have the credit of a sufficient testimony; for whether he deliver himself by true or false accusation, he does it by the right of preserving his own life.

[31] The force of words being (as I have formerly noted) too weak to hold men to the performance of their covenants, there are in man's nature but two imaginable helps to strengthen it. And those are either a fear of the consequence of breaking their word, or a glory or pride in appearing not to need to break it. This lat-

ter is a generosity too rarely found to be presumed on, especially in the pursuers of wealth, command, or sensual pleasure (which are the greatest part of mankind).

The passion to be reckoned upon is fear, whereof there be two very general objects: one, the power of spirits invisible; the other, the power of those men they shall therein offend. Of these two, though the former be the greater power, yet the fear of the latter is commonly the greater fear. [. . .]

Of Other Laws of Nature

[1] From that law of nature by which we are obliged to transfer to another such rights as, being retained, hinder the peace of mankind, there followeth a third, which is this *that men perform their covenants made,* without which covenants are in vain, and but empty words, and the right of all men to all things remaining, we are still in the condition of war.

[2] And in this law of nature consisteth the fountain and original of JUSTICE. For where no covenant hath preceded, there hath no right been transferred, and every man has right to everything; and consequently, no action can be unjust. But when a covenant is made, then to break it is *unjust;* and the definition of INJUSTICE is no other than *the not performance of covenant.* And whatsoever is not unjust, is *just.*

[3] But because covenants of mutual trust where there is a fear of not performance on either part (as hath been said in the former chapter) are invalid, though the original of justice be the making of covenants, yet injustice actually there can be none till the cause of such fear be taken away, which, while men are in the natural condition of war, cannot be done. Therefore, before the names of just and unjust can have place, there must be some coercive power to compel men equally to the performance of their covenants, by the terror of some punishment greater than the benefit they expect by the breach of their covenant, and to make good that propriety which by mutual contract men acquire, in recompense of the universal right they abandon; and such power there is none before the erection of a commonwealth. And this is also to be gathered out of the ordinary definition of justice in the Schools; for they say that *justice is the constant will of giving to every man his own.* And

therefore where there is no *own,* that is, no propriety, there is no injustice; and where there is no coercive power erected, that is, where there is no commonwealth, there is no propriety, all men having right to all things; therefore where there is no commonwealth, there nothing is unjust. So that the nature of justice consisteth in keeping of valid covenants; but the validity of covenants begins not but with the constitution of a civil power sufficient to compel men to keep them; and then it is also that propriety begins.

[4] The fool hath said in his heart: "there is no such thing as justice"; and sometimes also with his tongue, seriously alleging that: "every man's conservation and contentment being committed to his own care, there could be no reason why every man might not do what he thought conduced thereunto, and therefore also to make or not make, keep or not keep, covenants was not against reason, when it conduced to one's benefit." He does not therein deny that there be covenants, and that they are sometimes broken, sometimes kept, and that such breach of them may be called injustice, and the observance of them justice; but he questioneth whether injustice, taking away the fear of God (for the same fool hath said in his heart there is no God), may not sometimes stand with that reason which dictateth to every man his own good; and particularly then, when it conduceth to such a benefit as shall put a man in a condition to neglect, not only the dispraise and revilings, but also the power of other men,

"The kingdom of God is gotten by violence; but what if it could be gotten by unjust violence? were it against reason so to get it, when it is impossible to receive hurt by it? and if it be not against reason, it is not against justice; or else justice is not to be approved for good."

From such reasoning as this, successful wickedness hath obtained the name of virtue, and some that in all other things have disallowed the violation of faith, yet have allowed it when it is for the getting of a kingdom. And the heathen that believed that *Saturn* was deposed by his son *Jupiter* believed nevertheless the same *Jupiter* to be the avenger of injustice, somewhat like to a piece of law in *Coke's* Commentaries on *Littleton,*[2] where he

says: if the right heir of the crown be attainted of treason, yet the crown shall descend to him, and *eo instante* [immediately] the attainder be void; from which instances a man will be very prone to infer that "when the heir apparent of a kingdom shall kill him that is in possession, though his father, you may call it injustice, or by what other name you will, yet it can never be against reason, seeing all the voluntary actions of men tend to the benefit of themselves, and those actions are most reasonable that conduce most to their ends." This specious reasoning is nevertheless false.

[5] For the question is not of promises mutual where there is no security of performance on either side (as when there is no civil power erected over the parties promising), for such promises are no covenants, but either where one of the parties has performed already, or where there is a power to make him perform, there is the question whether it be against reason, that is, against the benefit of the other to perform or not. And I say it is not against reason. For the manifestation whereof we are to consider: first, that when a man doth a thing which, notwithstanding anything can be foreseen and reckoned on, tendeth to his own destruction (howsoever some accident which he could not expect, arriving, may turn it to his benefit), yet such events do not make it reasonably or wisely done. Secondly, that in a condition of war wherein every man to every man (for want of a common power to keep them all in awe) is an enemy, there is no man can hope by his own strength or wit to defend himself from destruction without the help of confederates (where everyone expects the same defence by the confederation that anyone else does); and therefore, he which declares he thinks it reason to deceive those that help him can in reason expect no other means of safety than what can be had from his own single power. He, therefore, that breaketh his covenant, and consequently declareth that he thinks he may with reason do so, cannot be received into any society that unite themselves for peace and defence but by the error of them that receive him; nor when he is received, be retained in it without seeing the danger of their error; which errors a man cannot reasonably reckon upon as the means of his security; and therefore, if he be left or cast out of society, he perisheth; and if he live in society, it is by the errors of other men, which, he could not foresee nor reckon upon; and consequently [he has acted]

---

2. Edward Coke, *The first part of the Institutes of the Laws of England,* London, 1629, folio 16.

against the reason of his preservation, and so as all men that contribute not to his destruction forbear him only out of ignorance of what is good for themselves.

[6] As for the instance of gaining the secure and perpetual felicity of heaven by any way, it is frivolous, there being but one way imaginable, and that is not breaking, but keeping of covenant.

[7] And for the other instance of attaining sovereignty by rebellion, it is manifest that, though the event follow, yet because it cannot reasonably be expected (but rather the contrary), and because (by gaining it so) others are taught to gain the same in like manner, the attempt thereof is against reason. Justice, therefore, that is to say, keeping of covenant, is a rule of reason by which we are forbidden to do anything destructive to our life, and consequently a law of nature.

[8] There be some that proceed further, and will not have the law of nature to be those rules which conduce to the preservation of man's life on earth, but to the attaining of an eternal felicity after death, to which they think the breach of covenant may conduce, and consequently be just and reasonable (such are they that think it a work of merit to kill, or depose, or rebel against the sovereign power constituted over them by their own consent). But because there is no natural knowledge of man's estate after death, much less of the reward that is then to be given to breach of faith, but only a belief grounded upon other men's saying that they know it supernaturally, or that they know those that knew them that knew others that knew it supernaturally, breach of faith cannot be called a precept of reason or nature.

[9] Others, that allow for a law of nature the keeping of faith, do nevertheless make exception of certain persons (as heretics and such as use not to perform their covenant to others); and this also is against reason. For if any fault of a man be sufficient to discharge our covenant made, the same ought in reason to have been sufficient to have hindered the making of it.

[10] The names of just and unjust, when they are attributed to men, signify one thing; and when they are attributed to actions, another. When they are attributed to men, they signify conformity or inconformity of manners to reason. But when they are attributed to actions, they signify the conformity or inconformity to reason, not of manners or manner of life, but of particular actions. A just man, therefore, is he that taketh all the care he can that his actions may be all just; and an unjust man is he that neglecteth it. And such men are more often in our language styled by the names of righteous and unrighteous, than just and unjust, though the meaning be the same. Therefore a righteous man does not lose that title by one or a few unjust actions that proceed from sudden passion or mistake of things or persons; nor does an unrighteous man lose his character for such actions as he does or forbears to do for fear, because his will is not framed by the justice, but by the apparent benefit of what he is to do. That which gives to human actions the relish of justice is a certain nobleness or gallantness of courage (rarely found) by which a man scorns to be beholden for the contentment of his life to fraud or breach of promise. This justice of the manners is that which is meant where justice is called a virtue, and injustice a vice.

[11] But the justice of actions denominates men, not just, but *guiltless;* and the injustice of the same (which is also called injury) gives them but the name of *guilty.*

[12] Again, the injustice of manners is the disposition or aptitude to do injury, and is injustice before it proceed to act and without supposing any individual person injured. But the injustice of an action (that is to say injury) supposeth an individual person injured, namely, him to whom the covenant was made; and therefore, many times the injury is received by one man, when the damage redoundeth to another. As when the master commandeth his servant to give money to a stranger; if it be not done, the injury is done to the master, whom he had before covenanted to obey, but the damage redoundeth to the stranger, to whom he had no obligation, and therefore could not injure him. And so also in commonwealths, private men may remit to one another their debts, but not robberies or other violences whereby they are endamaged; because the detaining of debt is an injury to themselves, but robbery and violence are injuries to the person of the commonwealth.

[13] Whatsoever is done to a man conformable to his own will, signified to the doer, is no injury to him. For if he that doeth it hath not passed away his original right to do what he please by some antecedent covenant, there is no breach of covenant, and therefore no injury done

him. And if he have, then his will [i.e., that of the person acted on] to have it done being signified, is a release of that covenant; and so again there is no injury done him.

[14] Justice of actions is by writers divided into *commutative* and *distributive;* and the former they say consisteth in proportion arithmetical, the latter, in proportion geometrical. Commutative, therefore, they place in the equality of value of the things contracted for; and distributive, in the distribution of equal benefit to men of equal merit (as if it were injustice to sell dearer than we buy, or to give more to a man than he merits). The value of all things contracted for is measured by the appetite of the contractors; and therefore the just value is that which they be contented to give. And merit (besides that which is by covenant, where the performance on one part meriteth the performance of the other part, and falls under justice commutative, not distributive) is not due by justice, but is rewarded of grace only.

And therefore this distinction, in the sense wherein it useth to be expounded, is not right. To speak properly, commutative justice is the justice of a contractor, that is, a performance of covenant (in buying and selling, hiring and letting to hire, lending and borrowing, exchanging, bartering, and other acts of contract).

[15] And distributive justice [is] the justice of an arbitrator, that is to say, the act of defining what is just. Wherein (being trusted by them that make him arbitrator) if he perform his trust, he is said to distribute to every man his own; and this is indeed just distribution, and may be called (though improperly) distributive justice (but more properly, equity, which also is a law of nature, as shall be shown in due place).

[16] As justice dependeth on antecedent covenant, so does GRATITUDE depend on antecedent grace, that is to say, antecedent free-gift; and is the fourth law of nature, which may be conceived in this form *that a man which receiveth benefit from another of mere grace endeavour that he which giveth it have no reasonable cause to repent him of his good will.* For no man giveth but with intention of good to himself, because gift is voluntary, and of all voluntary acts the object is to every man his own good; of which, if men see they shall be frustrated, there will be no beginning of benevolence or trust; nor, consequently, of mutual help, nor of reconciliation of one man to another; and therefore they are to remain still in the condition of war, which is contrary to the first and fundamental law of nature,

which commandeth men to *seek peace.* The breach of this law is called *ingratitude,* and hath the same relation to grace that injustice hath to obligation by covenant.

[17] A fifth law of nature is COMPLAISANCE, that is to say, *that every man strive to accommodate himself to the rest.* For the understanding whereof we may consider that there is, in men's aptness to society, a diversity of nature rising from their diversity of affections, not unlike to that we see in stones brought together for building of an edifice. For as that stone which (by the asperity and irregularity of figure) takes more room from others than itself fills, and (for the hardness) cannot be easily made plain, and thereby hindereth the building, is by the builders cast away as unprofitable and troublesome, so also a man that (by asperity of nature) will strive to retain those things which to himself are superfluous and to others necessary, and (for the stubbornness of his passions) cannot be corrected, is to be left or cast out of society as cumbersome thereunto. For seeing every man, not only by right, but also by necessity of nature, is supposed to endeavour all he can to obtain that which is necessary for his conservation, he that shall oppose himself against it for things superfluous is guilty of the war that thereupon is to follow; and, therefore, doth that which is contrary to the fundamental law of nature, which commandeth to *seek peace.* The observers of this law may be called SOCIABLE (the Latins call them *commodi*); the contrary, *stubborn, insociable, froward, intractable.*

[18] A sixth law of nature is this *that upon caution of the future time, a man ought to pardon the offences past of them that, repenting, desire it.* For PARDON is nothing but granting of peace, which (though granted to them that persevere in their hostility be not peace but fear, yet) not granted to them that give caution of the future time is sign of an aversion to peace; and therefore contrary to the law of nature.

[19] A seventh is *that in revenges* (that is, retribution of evil for evil) *men look not at the greatness of the evil past, but the greatness of the good to follow.* Whereby we are forbidden to inflict punishment with any other design than for correction of the offender, or direction of others. For this law is consequent to the next before it, that commandeth pardon upon security of the future time. Besides, revenge without respect to the example and profit to come is a triumph, or glorying, in the hurt of another, tending to no end (for the end is always somewhat to

come); and glorying to no end is vain-glory, and contrary to reason; and to hurt without reason tendeth to the introduction of war, which is against the law of nature, and is commonly styled by the name of *cruelty*.

[20] And because all signs of hatred or contempt provoke to fight, insomuch as most men choose rather to hazard their life than not to be revenged, we may in the eighth place, for a law of nature, set down this precept *that no man by deed, word, countenance, or gesture, declare hatred or contempt of another*. The breach of which law is commonly called *contumely*.

[21] The question 'who is the better man?' has no place in the condition of mere nature, where (as has been shewn before) all men are equal. The inequality that now is, has been introduced by the laws civil. I know that *Aristotle* (in the first book of his Politics [ch. iii–vii], for a foundation of his doctrine) maketh men by nature, some more worthy to command (meaning the wiser sort, such as he thought himself to be for his philosophy), others to serve (meaning those that had strong bodies, but were not philosophers as he), as if master and servant were not introduced by consent of men, but by difference of wit; which is not only against reason, but also against experience. For there are very few so foolish that had not rather govern themselves than be governed by others; nor when the wise in their own conceit contend by force with them who distrust their own wisdom, do they always, or often, or almost at any time, get the victory. If nature therefore have made men equal, that equality is to be acknowledged; or if nature have made men unequal, yet because men that think themselves equal will not enter into conditions of peace but upon equal terms, such equality must be admitted. And therefore for the ninth law of nature, I put this *that every man acknowledge other for his equal by nature*. The breach of this precept is *pride*.

[22] On this law dependeth another: *that at the entrance into conditions of peace, no man require to reserve to himself any right which he is not content should be reserved to every one of the rest*. As it is necessary, for all men that seek peace, to lay down certain rights of nature (that is to say, not to have liberty to do all they list), so is it necessary, for man's life, to retain some (as, right to govern their own bodies, [right to] enjoy air, water, motion, ways to go from place to place, and all things else without which

a man cannot live, or not live well). If in this case, at the making of peace, men require for themselves that which they would not have to be granted to others, they do contrary to the precedent law, that commandeth the acknowledgment of natural equality, and therefore also against the law of nature. The observers of this law are those we call *modest,* and the breakers *arrogant* men. The Greeks call the violation of this law *pleonexia,* that is, a desire of more than their share.

[23] Also *if a man be trusted to judge between man and man,* it is a precept of the law of nature that *he deal equally between them.* For without that, the controversies of men cannot be determined but by war. He, therefore, that is partial in judgment doth what in him lies to deter men from the use of judges and arbitrators; and consequently (against the fundamental law of nature), is the cause of war.

[24] The observance of this law (from the equal distribution to each man of that which in reason belongeth to him) is called EQUITY, and (as I have said before) distributive justice; the violation [is called] *acception of persons (prosolepsia).*

[25] And from this followeth another law: *that such things as cannot be divided be enjoyed in common, if it can be; and if the quantity of the thing permit, without stint; otherwise proportionably to the number of them that have right.* For otherwise the distribution is unequal, and contrary to equity.

[26] But some things there be that can neither be divided nor enjoyed in common. Then the law of nature which prescribeth equity requireth *that the entire right (or else, making the use alternate, the first possession) be determined by lot.* For equal distribution is of the law of nature, and other means of equal distribution cannot be imagined.

[27] Of *lots* there be two sorts: *arbitrary* and *natural.* Arbitrary is that which is agreed on by the competitors; natural is either *primogeniture* (which the Greek calls *kleronomia,* which signifies *given by lot*) or *first seizure.*

[28] And therefore those things which cannot be enjoyed in common, nor divided, ought to be adjudged to the first possessor; and in some cases the first-born, as acquired by lot.

[29] It is also a law of nature *that all men that mediate peace be allowed safe conduct.* For the law that comman-

deth peace, as the *end,* commandeth intercession, as the *means;* and to intercession the means is safe conduct.

[30] And because (though men be never so willing to observe these laws) there may nevertheless arise questions concerning a man's action (first, whether it were done or not done; secondly, if done, whether against the law or not against the law; the former whereof is called a question *of fact;* the latter a question *of right*), therefore unless the parties to the question covenant mutually to stand to the sentence of another, they are as far from peace as ever. This other to whose sentence they submit is called an ARBITRATOR. And therefore it is of the law of nature *that they that are at controversy, submit their right to the judgment of an arbitrator.*

[31] And seeing every man is presumed to do all things in order to his own benefit, *no man is a fit arbitrator in his own cause;* and if he were never so fit, yet (equity allowing to each party equal benefit) if one be admitted to be judge, the other is to be admitted also; and so the controversy, that is, the cause of war, remains, against the law of nature.

[32] For the same reason no man in any cause ought to be received for arbitrator, to whom greater profit, or honour, or pleasure apparently ariseth out of the victory of one party, than of the other; for he hath taken (though an unavoidable bribe, yet) a bribe; and no man can be obliged to trust him. And thus also the controversy, and the condition of war remaineth, contrary to the law of nature.

[33] And in a controversy of *fact* the judge (being to give no more credit to one [litigant] than to the other, if there be no other arguments) must give credit to a third [a non-litigant witness], or to a third and fourth; or more; for else the question is undecided, and left to force, contrary to the law of nature.

[34] These are the laws of nature dictating peace for a means of the conservation of men in multitudes; and which only concern the doctrine of civil society. There be other things tending to the destruction of particular men (as drunkenness and all other parts of intemperance), which may therefore also be reckoned amongst those things which the law of nature hath forbidden; but are not necessary to be mentioned, nor are pertinent enough to this place.

[35] And though this may seem too subtle a deduction of the laws of nature to be taken notice of by all men (whereof the most part are too busy in getting food, and the rest too negligent, to understand), yet to leave all men inexcusable they have been contracted into one easy sum, intelligible even to the meanest capacity, and that is *Do not that to another, which thou wouldst not have done to thyself;* which sheweth him that he has no more to do in learning the laws of nature but (when, weighing the actions of other men with his own, they seem too heavy) to put them into the other part of the balance, and his own into their place, that his own passions and self-love may add nothing to the weight; and then there is none of these laws of nature that will not appear unto him very reasonable.

[36] The laws of nature oblige *in foro interno,* that is to say, they bind to a desire they should take place; but *in foro externo,* that is, to the putting them in act, not always. For he that should be modest and tractable, and perform all he promises, in such time and place where no man else should do so, should but make himself a prey to others, and procure his own certain ruin, contrary to the ground of all laws of nature, which tend to nature's preservation. And again, he that having sufficient security that others shall observe the same laws towards him, observes them not himself, seeketh not peace, but war, and consequently the destruction of his nature by violence.

[37] And whatsoever laws bind *in foro interno* may be broken, not only by a fact contrary to the law, but also by a fact according to it, in case a man think it contrary. For though his action in this case be according to the law, yet his purpose was against the law, which, where the obligation is *in foro interno,* is a breach.

[38] The laws of nature are immutable and eternal; for injustice, ingratitude, arrogance, pride, iniquity, acception of persons, and the rest, can never be made lawful. For it can never be that war shall preserve life, and peace destroy it.

[39] The same laws, because they oblige only to a desire and endeavour (I mean an unfeigned and constant endeavour) are easy to be observed. For in that they require nothing but endeavour, he that endeavoureth their performance fulfilleth them; and he that fulfilleth the law is just. [...]

Of the Causes, Generation, and Definition of a COMMONWEALTH

[1] The final cause, end, or design of men (who naturally love liberty and dominion over others) in the introduction of that restraint upon themselves in which we see them live in commonwealths is the foresight of their own preservation, and of a more contented life thereby; that is to say, of getting themselves out from that miserable condition of war, which is necessarily consequent (as hath been shown) to the natural passions of men, when there is no visible power to keep them in awe, and tie them by fear of punishment to the performance of their covenants and observation of those laws of nature set down in the fourteenth and fifteenth chapters.

[2] For the laws of nature (as *justice, equity, modesty, mercy,* and (in sum) *doing to others as we would be done to*) of themselves, without the terror of some power to cause them to be observed, are contrary to our natural passions, that carry us to partiality, pride, revenge, and the like. And covenants without the sword are but words, and of no strength to secure a man at all. Therefore notwithstanding the laws of nature (which every one hath then kept, when he has the will to keep them, when he can do it safely), if there be no power erected, or not great enough for our security, every man will, and may lawfully rely on his own strength and art, for caution against all other men. And in all places where men have lived by small families, to rob and spoil one another has been a trade, and so far from being reputed against the law of nature that the greater spoils they gained, the greater was their honour; and men observed no other laws therein but the laws of honour, that is, to abstain from cruelty, leaving to men their lives and instruments of husbandry. And as small families did then, so now do cities and kingdoms (which are but greater families) for their own security enlarge their dominions upon all pretences of danger and fear of invasion or assistance that may be given to invaders, [and] endeavour as much as they can to subdue or weaken their neighbours, by open force and secret arts for want of other caution, justly (and are remembered for it in after ages with honour).

[3] Nor is it the joining together of a small number of men that gives them this security; because in small numbers, small additions on the one side or the other make the advantage of strength so great as is sufficient to carry the victory; and therefore gives encouragement to an invasion. The multitude sufficient to confide in for our security is not determined by any certain number, but by comparison with the enemy we fear, and is then sufficient, when the odds of the enemy is not of so visible and conspicuous moment, to determine the event of war, as to move him to attempt.

[4] And be there never so great a multitude, yet if their actions be directed according to their particular judgments and particular appetites, they can expect thereby no defence, nor protection, neither against a common enemy, nor against the injuries of one another. For being distracted in opinions concerning the best use and application of their strength, they do not help, but hinder one another, and reduce their strength by mutual opposition to nothing; whereby they are easily, not only subdued by a very few that agree together, but also when there is no common enemy, they make war upon each other, for their particular interests. For if we could suppose a great multitude of men to consent in the observation of justice and other laws of nature without a common power to keep them all in awe, we might as well suppose all mankind to do the same; and then there neither would be, nor need to be, any civil government or commonwealth at all, because there would be peace without subjection.

[5] Nor is it enough for the security, which men desire should last all the time of their life, that they be governed and directed by one judgment for a limited time, as in one battle or one war. For though they obtain a victory by their unanimous endeavour against a foreign enemy, yet afterwards, when either they have no common enemy, or he that by one part is held for an enemy is by another part held for a friend, they must needs by the difference of their interests dissolve, and fall again into a war amongst themselves.

[6] It is true that certain living creatures (as bees and ants) live sociably one with another (which are therefore by *Aristotle* numbered amongst political creatures), and yet have no other direction than their particular judgments and appetites, nor speech whereby one of them can signify to another what he thinks expedient for the common benefit; and therefore some man may

perhaps desire to know why mankind cannot do the same. To which I answer,

[7] First, that men are continually in competition for honour and dignity, which these creatures are not; and consequently, amongst men there ariseth, on that ground, envy and hatred, and finally war; but amongst these not so.

[8] Secondly, that amongst these creatures the common good differeth not from the private; and being by nature inclined to their private, they procure thereby the common benefit. But man, whose joy consisteth in comparing himself with other men, can relish nothing but what is eminent.

[9] Thirdly, that these creatures (having not, as man, the use of reason) do not see, nor think they see, any fault in the administration of their common business; whereas amongst men there are very many that think themselves wiser, and abler to govern the public, better than the rest; and these strive to reform and innovate, one this way, another that way; and thereby bring it into distraction and civil war.

[10] Fourthly, that these creatures, though they have some use of voice in (making known to one another their desires and other affections), yet they want that art of words by which some men can represent to others that which is good in the likeness of evil, and evil in the likeness of good, and augment or diminish the apparent greatness of good and evil, discontenting men, and troubling their peace at their pleasure.

[11] Fifthly, irrational creatures cannot distinguish between *injury* and *damage;* and therefore, as long as they be at ease, they are not offended with their fellows, whereas man is then most troublesome, when he is most at ease; for then it is that he loves to shew his wisdom, and control the actions of them that govern the commonwealth.

[12] Lastly, the agreement of these creatures is natural; that of men is by covenant only, which is artificial; and therefore, it is no wonder if there be somewhat else required (besides covenant) to make their agreement constant and lasting, which is a common power to keep them in awe, and to direct their actions to the common benefit.

[13] The only way to erect such a common power as may be able to defend them from the invasion of for-eigners and the injuries of one another, and thereby to secure them in such sort as that by their own industry, and by the fruits of the earth, they may nourish themselves and live contentedly, is to confer all their power and strength upon one man, or upon one assembly of men, that may reduce all their wills, by plurality of voices, unto one will, which is as much as to say, to appoint one man or assembly of men to bear their person, and every one to own and acknowledge himself to be author of whatsoever he that so beareth their person shall act, or cause to be acted, in those things which concern the common peace and safety, and therein to submit their wills, every one to his will, and their judgments, to his judgment. This is more than consent, or concord; it is a real unity of them all, in one and the same person, made by covenant of every man with every man, in such manner as if every man should say to every man *I authorize and give up my right of governing myself to this man, or to this assembly of men, on this condition, that thou give up thy right to him, and authorize all his actions in like manner.* This done, the multitude so united in one person is called a COMMONWEALTH, in Latin CIVITAS. This is the generation of that great LEVIATHAN, or rather (to speak more reverently) of that *Mortal God* to which we owe, under the *Immortal God,* our peace and defence. For by this authority, given him by every particular man in the commonwealth, he hath the use of so much power and strength conferred on him that by terror thereof he is enabled to conform the wills of them all to peace at home and mutual aid against their enemies abroad. And in him consisteth the essence of the commonwealth, which (to define it) is *one person, of whose acts a great multitude, by mutual covenants one with another, have made themselves every one the author, to the end he may use the strength and means of them all, as he shall think expedient, for their peace and common defence.*

[14] And he that carrieth this person is called SOVEREIGN, and said to have *Sovereign Power;* and every one besides, his SUBJECT.

[15] The attaining to this sovereign power is by two ways. One, by natural force, as when a man maketh his children to submit themselves and their children to his government, as being able to destroy them if they refuse, or by war subdueth his enemies to his will, giving them their lives on that condition. The other is when

men agree amongst themselves to submit to some man, or assembly of men, voluntarily, on confidence to be protected by him against all others. This latter may be called a political commonwealth, or commonwealth by *institution,* and the former, a commonwealth by *acquisition.* And first, I shall speak of a commonwealth by institution.

Of the Rights of Sovereigns by Institution

[1] A *commonwealth* is said to be *instituted,* when a *multitude* of men do agree and *covenant, every one with every one,* that to whatsoever *man* or *assembly of men* shall be given by the major part the *right* to *present* the person of them all (that is to say, to be their *representative*) every one, as well he that *voted for it* as he that *voted against it,* shall *authorize* all the actions and judgments of that man or assembly of men, in the same manner as if they were his own, to the end, to live peaceably amongst themselves and be protected against other men.

[2] From this institution of a commonwealth are derived all the *rights* and *faculties* of him, or them, on whom the sovereign power is conferred by the consent of the people assembled.

[3] First, because they covenant, it is to be understood they are not obliged by former covenant to anything repugnant hereunto. And consequently they that have already instituted a commonwealth, being thereby bound by covenant to own the actions and judgments of one, cannot lawfully make a new covenant amongst themselves to be obedient to any other, in any thing whatsoever, without his permission. And therefore, they that are subjects to a monarch cannot without his leave cast off monarchy and return to the confusion of a disunited multitude, nor transfer their person from him that beareth it to another man, or other assembly of men; for they are bound, every man to every man, to own, and be reputed author of, all that he that already is their sovereign shall do and judge fit to be done; so that, any one man dissenting, all the rest should break their covenant made to that man, which is injustice. And they have also every man given the sovereignty to him that beareth their person; and therefore if they depose him, they take from him that which is his own, and so again it is injustice. Besides, if he that attempteth to

depose his sovereign be killed, or punished by him for such attempt, he is author of his own punishment, as being, by the institution, author of all his sovereign shall do; and because it is injustice for a man to do anything for which he may be punished by his own authority, he is also, upon that title, unjust.

And whereas some men have pretended for their disobedience to their sovereign a new covenant, made (not with men, but) with God, this also is unjust; for there is no covenant with God but by mediation of somebody that representeth God's person, which none doth but God's lieutenant, who hath the sovereignty under God. But this pretence of covenant with God is so evident a lie, even in the pretenders' own consciences, that it is not only an act of an unjust, but also of a vile and unmanly disposition.

[4] Secondly, because the right of bearing the person of them all is given to him they make sovereign by covenant only of one to another, and not of him to any of them, there can happen no breach of covenant on the part of the sovereign; and consequently none of his subjects, by any pretence of forfeiture, can be freed from his subjection.

That he which is made sovereign maketh no covenant with his subjects beforehand is manifest, because either he must make it with the whole multitude, as one party to the covenant, or he must make several covenants with every man. With the whole, as one party, it is impossible, because as yet they are not one person; and if he make so many several covenants as there be men, those covenants after he hath the sovereignty are void, because what act soever can be pretended by any one of them for breach thereof is the act both of himself and of all the rest, because done in the person and by the right of every one of them in particular.

Besides, if any one (or more) of them pretend a breach of the covenant made by the sovereign at his institution, and others (or one other) of his subjects (or himself alone) pretend there was no such breach, there is in this case no judge to decide the controversy; it returns therefore to the sword again, and every man recovereth the right of protecting himself by his own strength, contrary to the design they had in the institution. It is therefore in vain to grant sovereignty by way of precedent covenant.

The opinion that any monarch receiveth his power by covenant, that is to say, on condition, proceedeth from want of understanding this easy truth, that covenants, being but words and breath, have no force to oblige, contain, constrain, or protect any man, but what it has from the public sword, that is, from the untied hands of that man or assembly of men that hath the sovereignty, and whose actions are avouched by them all, and performed by the strength of them all, in him united. But when an assembly of men is made sovereign, then no man imagineth any such covenant to have passed in the institution; for no man is so dull as to say, for example, the people of *Rome* made a covenant with the Romans, to hold the sovereignty on such or such conditions, which not performed, the Romans might lawfully depose the Roman people. That men see not the reason to be alike in a monarchy and in a popular government proceedeth from the ambition of some that are kinder to the government of an assembly; whereof they may hope to participate, than of monarchy, which they despair to enjoy.

[5] Thirdly, because the major part hath by consenting voices declared a sovereign, he that dissented must now consent with the rest, that is, be contented to avow all the actions he shall do, or else justly be destroyed by the rest. For if he voluntarily entered into the congregation of them that were assembled, he sufficiently declared thereby his will (and therefore tacitly covenanted) to stand to what the major part should ordain; and therefore, if he refuse to stand thereto, or make protestation against any of their decrees, he does contrary to his covenant, and therefore unjustly. And whether he be of the congregation or not, and whether his consent be asked or not, he must either submit to their decrees or be left in the condition of war he was in before, wherein he might without injustice be destroyed by any man whatsoever.

[6] Fourthly, because every subject is by this institution author of all the actions and judgments of the sovereign instituted, it follows that, whatsoever he doth, it can be no injury to any of his subjects, nor ought he to be by any of them accused of injustice. For he that doth anything by authority from another doth therein no injury to him by whose authority he acteth; but by this institution of a commonwealth every particular man is author of all the sovereign doth; and consequently he that complaineth of injury from his sovereign complaineth of that whereof he himself is author, and therefore ought not to accuse any man but himself; no nor himself of injury, because to do injury to one's self is impossible. It is true that they that have sovereign power may commit iniquity, but not injustice, or injury in the proper signification.

[7] Fifthly, and consequently to that which was said last, no man that hath sovereign power can justly be put to death, or otherwise in any manner by his subjects punished. For seeing every subject is author of the actions of his sovereign, he punisheth another for the actions committed by himself.

[8] And because the end of this institution is the peace and defence of them all, and whosoever has right to the end has right to the means, it belongeth of right to whatsoever man or assembly that hath the sovereignty, to be judge both of the means of peace and defence, and also of the hindrances and disturbances of the same, and to do whatsoever he shall think necessary to be done, both beforehand (for the preserving of peace and security, by prevention of discord at home and hostility from abroad) and, when peace and security are lost, for the recovery of the same. And therefore,

[9] Sixthly, it is annexed to the sovereignty to be judge of what opinions and doctrines are averse, and what conducing, to peace; and consequently, on what occasions, how far, and what men are to be trusted withal, in speaking to multitudes of people, and who shall examine the doctrines of all books before they be published. For the actions of men proceed from their opinions, and in the well-governing of opinions consisteth the well-governing of men's actions, in order to their peace and concord. And though in matter of doctrine nothing ought to be regarded but the truth, yet this is not repugnant to regulating of the same by peace. For doctrine repugnant to peace can no more be true than peace and concord can be against the law of nature. It is true that in a commonwealth where (by the negligence or unskilfulness of governors and teachers) false doctrines are by time generally received, the contrary truths may be generally offensive. Yet the most sudden and rough bustling in of a new truth that can be does never break the peace, but only sometimes awake the war. For those men that are so remissly governed that they dare take up arms to defend or introduce an

opinion are still in war, and their condition not peace, but only a cessation of arms for fear of one another; and they live, as it were, in the precincts of battle continually. It belongeth therefore to him that hath the sovereign power to be judge (or constitute all judges) of opinions and doctrines, as a thing necessary to peace, thereby to prevent discord and civil war.

[10] Seventhly, is annexed to the sovereignty the whole power of prescribing the rules whereby every man may know what goods he may enjoy, and what actions he may do, without being molested by any of his fellow-subjects; and this is it men call *propriety.* For before constitution of sovereign power (as hath already been shown) all men had right to all things, which necessarily causeth war; and therefore, this propriety, being necessary to peace, and depending on sovereign power, is the act of that power, in order to the public peace. These rules of propriety (or *meum* and *tuum*) and of *good, evil, lawful,* and *unlawful* in the actions of subjects are the civil laws; that is to say, the laws of each commonwealth in particular (though the name of civil law be now restrained to the ancient civil laws of the city of *Rome,* which being the head of a great part of the world, her laws at that time were in these parts the civil law).

[11] Eighthly, is annexed to the sovereignty the right of judicature, that is to say, of hearing and deciding all controversies which may arise concerning law (either civil or natural) or concerning fact. For without the decision of controversies there is no protection of one subject against the injuries of another, the laws concerning *meum* and *tuum* are in vain, and to every man remaineth, from the natural and necessary appetite of his own conservation, the right of protecting himself by his private strength, which is the condition of war, and contrary to the end for which every commonwealth is instituted.

[12] Ninthly, is annexed to the sovereignty the right of making war and peace with other nations and commonwealths, that is to say, of judging when it is for the public good, and how great forces are to be assembled, armed, and paid for that end, and to levy money upon the subjects to defray the expenses thereof. For the power by which the people are to be defended consisteth in their armies; and the strength of an army, in the union of their strength under one command; which command the sovereign instituted therefore hath, be-

cause the command of the *militia,* without other institution, maketh him that hath it sovereign. And therefore, whosoever is made general of an army, he that hath the sovereign power is always generalissimo.

[13] Tenthly, is annexed to the sovereignty the choosing of all counsellors, ministers, magistrates, and officers, both in peace and war. For seeing the sovereign is charged with the end, which is the common peace and defence, he is understood to have power to use such means as he shall think most fit for his discharge.

[14] Eleventhly, to the sovereign is committed the power of rewarding with riches or honour, and of punishing with corporal or pecuniary punishment or with ignominy, every subject according to the law he hath formerly made (or if there be no law made, according as he shall judge most to conduce to the encouraging of men to serve the commonwealth, or deterring of them from doing disservice to the same).

[15] Lastly, considering what values men are naturally apt to set upon themselves, what respect they look for from others, and how little they value other men, from whence continually arise amongst them emulation, quarrels, factions, and at last war, to the destroying of one another, and diminution of their strength against a common enemy, it is necessary that there be laws of honour and a public rate of the worth of such men as have deserved (or are able to deserve) well of the commonwealth, and that there be force in the hands of some or other to put those laws in execution. But it hath already been shown that not only the whole *militia,* or forces of the commonwealth, but also the judicature of all controversies is annexed to the sovereignty. To the sovereign therefore it belongeth also to give titles of honour, and to appoint what order of place and dignity each man shall hold, and what signs of respect, in public or private meetings, they shall give to one another.

[16] These are the rights which make the essence of sovereignty, and which are the marks whereby a man may discern in what man, or assembly of men, the sovereign power is placed and resideth. For these are incommunicable and inseparable. The power to coin money, to dispose of the estate and persons of infant heirs, to have preemption in markets, and all other statute prerogatives may be transferred by the sovereign, and yet the power to protect his subjects be retained.

But if he transfer the *militia,* he retains the judicature in vain, for want of execution of the laws; or if he grant away the power of raising money, the *militia* is in vain; or if he give away the government of doctrines, men will be frighted into rebellion with the fear of spirits. And so if we consider any one of the said rights, we shall presently see, that the holding of all the rest will produce no effect, in the conservation of peace and justice, the end for which all commonwealths are instituted. And this division is it, whereof it is said *a kingdom divided in itself cannot stand,* for unless this division precede, division into opposite armies can never happen. [. . .]

John Locke

The Social Contract

Chapter 2
Of the State of Nature

4. To understand political power, right, and derive it from its original, we must consider what state all men are naturally in, and that is, a *state of perfect freedom* to order their actions, and dispose of their possessions and persons, as they think fit, within the bounds of the law of nature; without asking leave, or depending upon the will of any other man.

A *state* also of *equality,* wherein all the power and jurisdiction is reciprocal, no one having more than another; there being nothing more evident, than that creatures of the same species and rank, promiscuously born to all the same advantages of nature, and the use of the same faculties, should also be equal one amongst another without subordination or subjection; unless the lord and master of them all should, by any manifest declaration of his will, set one above another, and confer on him, by an evident and clear appointment, an undoubted right to dominion and sovereignty. [. . .]

6. But though this be *a state of liberty,* yet *it is not a state of licence:* though man in that state have an uncontrolable liberty to dispose of his person or possessions, yet he has not liberty to destroy himself, or so much as any creature in his possession, but where some nobler use than its bare preservation calls for it. The *state of nature* has a law of nature to govern it, which obliges every one: And reason, which is that law, teaches all mankind, who will but consult it, that being all *equal and independent,* no one ought to harm another in his life, health, liberty, or possessions. For men being all the workmanship of one omnipotent and infinitely wise Maker; all the servants of one sovereign master, sent into the world by his order, and about his business; they are his property, whose workmanship they are, made to last during his, not another's pleasure. And being furnished with like faculties, sharing all in one community of nature, there cannot be supposed any such *subordination* among us, that may authorize us to destroy another, as if we were made for one another's uses, as the inferior ranks of creatures are for ours. Every one, as he is *bound to preserve himself,* and not to quit his station wilfully, so by the like reason, when his own preservation comes not in competition, ought he, as much as he can, *to preserve the rest of mankind,* and may not, unless it be to do justice to an offender, take away or impair the life, or what tends to the preservation of life, the liberty, health, limb, or goods of another.

7. And that all men may be restrained from invading others rights, and from doing hurt to one another, and the law of nature be observed, which willeth the peace and *preservation of all mankind,* the *execution* of the law of

From John Locke, *Second Treatise of Government,* edited by C. B. Macpherson (Indianapolis: Hackett Publishing Company, 1980). Reprinted with permission of the publisher.

nature is, in that state, put into every man's hands, whereby every one has a right to punish the transgressors of that law to such a degree as may hinder its violation. For the *law of nature* would, as all other laws that concern men in this world, be in vain, if there were no body that in the state of nature had a *power to execute* that law, and thereby preserve the innocent and restrain offenders. And if any one in the state of nature may punish another for any evil he has done, every one may do so. For in that *state of perfect equality*, where naturally there is no superiority or jurisdiction of one over another, what any may do in prosecution of that law, every one must needs have a right to do.

8. And thus, in the state of nature, *one man comes by a power over another;* but yet no absolute or arbitrary power, to use a criminal, when he has got him in his hands, according to the passionate heats, or boundless extravagancy of his own will; but only to retribute to him, so far as calm reason and conscience dictate, what is proportionate to his transgression; which is so much as may serve for *reparation* and *restraint*. For these two are the only reasons, why one man may lawfully do harm to another, which is that we call *punishment*. In transgressing the law of nature, the offender declares himself to live by another rule than that of reason and common equity, which is that measure God has set to the actions of men, for their mutual security; and so he becomes dangerous to mankind, the tye, which is to secure them from injury and violence, being slighted and broken by him. Which being a trespass against the whole species, and the peace and safety of it, provided for by the law of nature; every man upon this score, by the right he hath to preserve mankind in general, may restrain, or, where it is necessary, destroy things noxious to them, and so may bring such evil on any one, who hath transgressed that law, as may make him repent the doing of it, and thereby deter him, and by his example others, from doing the like mischief. And in this case, and upon this ground, *every man hath a right to punish the offender, and be executioner of the law of nature.*

9. I doubt not but this will seem a very strange doctrine to some men: but before they condemn it, I desire them to resolve me, by what right any prince or state can put to death, or *punish an alien,* for any crime he commits in their country. It is certain their laws, by virtue of any sanction they receive from the promul-

gated will of the legislative, reach not a stranger. They speak not to him, nor, if they did, is he bound to hearken to them. The legislative authority, by which they are in force over the subjects of that commonwealth, hath no power over him. Those who have the supreme power of making laws in *England, France,* or *Holland,* are to an *Indian* but like the rest of the world, men without authority: And therefore, if by the law of nature every man hath not a power to punish offences against it, as he soberly judges the case to require, I see not how the magistrates of any community can *punish an alien* of another country; since in reference to him, they can have no more power, than what every man naturally may have over another.

10. Besides the crime which consists in violating the law, and varying from the right rule of reason, whereby a man so far becomes degenerate, and declares himself to quit the principles of human nature, and to be a noxious creature, there is commonly injury done to some person or other, and some other man receives damage by his transgression, in which case he who hath received any damage, has besides the right of punishment common to him with other men, a particular right to seek *reparation* from him that has done it. And any other person who finds it just, may also join with him that is injured, and assist him in recovering from the offender so much as may make satisfaction for the harm he has suffered.

11. From these *two distinct rights,* the one of *punishing* the *crime for restraint,* and preventing the like offence, which right of punishing is in every body; the other of taking *reparation,* which belongs only to the injured party; comes it to pass that the magistrate, who by being magistrate, hath the common right of punishing put into his hands, can often, where the public good demands not the execution of the law, *remit* the punishment of criminal offences by his own authority, but yet cannot *remit* the satisfaction due to any private man, for the damage he has received. That, he who has suffered the damage has a right to demand in his own name, and he alone can remit: The damnified person has this power of appropriating to himself the goods or service of the offender, *by right of self-preservation,* as every man has a power to punish the crime, to prevent its being committed again, *by the right he has of preserving all mankind;* and doing all reasonable things he can in order to

that end: And thus it is, that every man, in the state of nature, has a power to kill a murderer, both *to deter* others from doing the like injury, which no reparation can compensate, by the example of the punishment that attends it from every body, and also *to secure* men from the attempts of a criminal, who having renounced reason, the common rule and measure, God hath given to mankind, hath by the unjust violence and slaughter he hath committed upon one, declared war against all mankind; and therefore may be destroyed as a *lion* or a *tyger,* one of those wild savage beasts, with whom men can have no society nor security: And upon this is grounded the great law of nature, *"Whoso sheddeth mans blood, by man shall his blood be shed."* And Cain was so fully convinced, that every one had a right to destroy such a criminal, that after the murder of his brother, he cries out, *"Every one that findeth me, shall slay me;"* so plain was it writ in the hearts of all mankind.

12. By the same reason may a man in the state of nature *punish the lesser breaches* of that law. It will perhaps be demanded, with death? I answer, each transgression may be *punished* to that *degree,* and with so much *severity,* as will suffice to make it an ill bargain to the offender, give him cause to repent, and terrify others from doing the like. Every offence that can be committed in the state of nature, may in the state of nature be also punished equally, and as far forth as it may, in a commonwealth: for though it would be besides my present purpose, to enter here into the particulars of the law of nature, or its *measures of punishment;* yet it is certain there is such a law, and that too, as intelligible and plain to a rational creature, and a studier of that law, as the positive laws of commonwealths, nay possibly plainer; as much as reason is easier to be understood, than the fancies and intricate contrivances of men, following contrary and hidden interests put into words; for so truly are a great part of the *municipal laws* of countries, which are only so far right, as they are founded on the law of nature, by which they are to be regulated and interpreted.

13. To this strange doctrine, viz. That *in the state of nature every one has the executive power* of the law of nature, I doubt not but it will be objected, that it is unreasonable for men to be judges in their own cases, that self-love will make men partial to themselves and their friends: And on the other side, that ill nature, passion and revenge will carry them too far in punishing others; and hence nothing but confusion and disorder will follow, and that therefore God hath certainly appointed government to restrain the partiality and violence of men. I easily grant, that *civil government* is the proper remedy for the inconveniencies of the state of nature, which must certainly be great, where men may be judges in their own case, since it is easy to be imagined, that he who was so unjust as to do his brother an injury, will scarce be so just as to condemn himself for it: But I shall desire those who make this objection, to remember, that *absolute monarchs* are but men, and if government is to be the remedy of those evils, which necessarily follow from men's being judges in their own cases, and the state of nature is therefore not to be endured, I desire to know what kind of government that is, and how much better it is than the state of nature, where one man commanding a multitude, has the liberty to be judge in his own case, and may do to all his subjects whatever he pleases, without the least liberty to any one to question or control those who execute his pleasure? and in whatsoever he doth, whether led by reason, mistake or passion, must be submitted to? Much better it is in the state of nature, wherein men are not bound to submit to the unjust will of another: And if he that judges, judges amiss in his own, or any other case, he is answerable for it to the rest of mankind.

14. It is often asked as a mighty objection, *where are, or ever were, there any men in such a state of nature?* To which it may suffice as an answer at present: That since all princes and rulers *of independent* governments, all through the world, are in a state of nature, it is plain the world never was, nor ever will be, without numbers of men in that state. I have named all governors *of independent communities,* whether they are, or are not, in league with others. For it is not every compact that puts an end to the state of nature between men, but only this one of agreeing together mutually to enter into one community, and make one body politic; other promises and compacts men may make one with another, and yet still be in the state of nature. The promises and bargains for truck, &c. between the two men in the desert island, mentioned by *Garcilasso de la Vega,* in his history of Peru; or between a *Swiss* and an *Indian,* in the woods *of America,* are binding to them, though they are perfectly in a state of nature, in reference to one another. For truth

and keeping of faith belongs to men as men, and not as members of society. [. . .]

Chapter 3
Of the State of War

16. The *state of war* is a state of *enmity* and *destruction*: And therefore declaring by word or action, not a passionate and hasty, but a sedate settled design upon another man's life, *puts him in a state of war* with him against whom he has declared such an intention, and so has exposed his life to the other's power to be taken away by him, or any one that joins with him in his defence, and espouses his quarrel: it being reasonable and just I should have a right to destroy that which threatens me with destruction. For *by the fundamental law of nature, man being to be preserved* as much as possible, when all cannot be preserved, the safety of the innocent is to be preferred: And one may destroy a man who makes war upon him, or has discovered an enmity to his being, for the same reason that he may kill a *wolf* or a *lion;* because such men are not under the ties of the common law of reason, have no other rule, but that of force and violence, and so may be treated as beasts of prey, those dangerous and noxious creatures, that will be sure to destroy him whenever he falls into their power.

17. And hence it is, that he who attempts to get another man into his absolute power, does thereby *put himself into a state of war* with him; it being to be understood as a declaration of a design upon his life. For I have reason to conclude, that he who would get me into his power without my consent, would use me as he pleased when he got me there, and destroy me too when he had a fancy to it; for no body can desire to *have me in his absolute power* unless it be to compel me by force to that which is against the right of my freedom, i.e. make me a slave. To be free from such force is the only security of my preservation; and reason bids me look on him, as an enemy to my preservation, who would take away that freedom which is the fence to it; so that he who makes an *attempt to enslave* me, thereby puts himself into a state of war with me. He that, in the state of nature, *would take away the freedom* that belongs to any one in that state, must necessarily be supposed to have a design to take away every thing else, that *freedom* being the foundation of all the rest: As he that, in the state of society, would take away the freedom belonging to those of that society or commonwealth, must be supposed to design to take away from them every thing else, and so be looked on as *in a state of war.* [. . .]

19. And here we have the plain *difference between the state of nature and the state of war;* which however some men have confounded, are as far distant, as a state of peace, good will, mutual assistance and preservation, and a state of enmity, malice, violence and mutual destruction, are one from another. Men living together according to reason, without a common superior on earth, with authority to judge between them, is *properly the state of nature.* But force, or a declared design of force, upon the person of another, where there is no common superior on earth to appeal to for relief, *is the state of war:* And it is the want of such an appeal gives a man the right of war even against an aggressor, though he be in society and a fellow subject. Thus a *thief,* whom I cannot harm, but by appeal to the law, for having stolen all that I am worth, I may kill, when he sets on me to rob me but of my horse or coat; because the law, which was made for my preservation, where it cannot interpose to secure my life from present force, which, if lost, is capable of no reparation, permits me my own defence, and the right of war, a liberty to kill the aggressor, because the aggressor allows not time to appeal to our common judge, nor the decision of the law, for remedy in a case where the mischief may be irreparable. Want of a common judge with authority, puts all men in a state of nature: Force without right, upon a man's person, makes a state of war, both where there is, and is not, a common judge.

20. But when the actual force is over, the *state of war ceases* between those that are in society, and are equally on both sides subjected to the fair determination of the law; because then there lies open the remedy of appeal for the past injury, and to prevent future harm: but where no such appeal is, as in the state of nature, for want of positive laws, and judges with authority to appeal to, the state of war once begun, continues with a right to the innocent party to destroy the other whenever he can, until the aggressor offers peace, and desires reconciliation on such terms as may repair any wrongs he has already done, and secure the innocent for the future: nay, where an appeal to the law, and constituted judges, lies open, but the remedy is denied by a manifest

perverting of justice, and a barefaced wresting of the laws to protect or indemnify the violence or injuries of some men, or party of men, *there* it *is* hard to imagine any thing but *a state of war.* For wherever violence is used, and injury done, though by hands appointed to administer justice, it is still violence and injury, however coloured with the name, pretences, or forms of law, the end whereof being to protect and redress the innocent, by an unbiassed application of it, to all who are under it; wherever that is not *bona fide* done, *war is made* upon the sufferers, who having no appeal on earth to right them, they are left to the only remedy in such cases, an appeal to heaven.

21. To avoid this *state of war* (wherein there is no appeal but to heaven, and wherein every the least difference is apt to end, where there is no authority to decide between the contenders) is one great reason of men's putting themselves into society, and quitting the state of nature. For where there is an authority, a power on earth, from which relief can be had by *appeal,* there the continuance of the *state of war* is excluded, and the controversy is decided by that power. [. . .]

Chapter 4
Of Slavery

22. The *natural liberty* of man is to be free from any superior power on earth, and not to be under the will or legislative authority of man, but to have only the law of nature for his rule. The *liberty of man,* in society, is to be under no other legislative power, but that established, by consent, in the commonwealth; nor under the dominion of any will, or restraint of any law, but what that legislative shall enact, according to the trust put in it. Freedom then is not what Sir Robert Filmer tells us, Observations, A. 55. *"a liberty for every one to do what he lists, to live as he pleases, and not to be tied by any laws:"* But *freedom of men under government,* is, to have a standing rule to live by, common to every one of that society, and made by the legislative power erected in it; a liberty to follow my own will in all things, where the rule prescribes not; and not to be subject to the inconstant, uncertain, unknown, arbitrary will of another man: as *freedom of nature* is, to be under no other restraint but the law of nature.

23. This *freedom* from absolute, arbitrary power, is so necessary to, and closely joined with a man's preservation, that he cannot part with it, but by what forfeits his preservation and life together. For a man, not having the power of his own life, cannot, by compact, or his own consent, *enslave himself* to any one, nor put himself under the absolute, arbitrary power of another, to take away his life, when he pleases. No body can give more power than he has himself; and he that cannot take away his own life, cannot give another power over it. Indeed, having by his fault forfeited his own life, by some act that deserves death; he, to whom he has forfeited it, may (when he has him in his power) delay to take it, and make use of him to his own service, and he does him no injury by it. For, whenever he finds the hardship of his slavery outweigh the value of his life, it is in his power, by resisting the will of his master, to draw on himself the death he desires. [. . .]

Chapter 5
Of Property

25. Whether we consider natural *reason,* which tells us, that men, being once born, have a right to their preservation, and consequently to meat and drink, and such other things as nature affords for their subsistence: or *revelation,* which gives us an account of those grants God made of the world to *Adam,* and to *Noah,* and his sons, it is very clear, that God, as *King David* says, *Psal.* cxv. 16, *"has given the earth to the children of men,"* given it to mankind in common. But this being supposed, it seems to some a very great difficulty how any one should ever come to have a *property* in any thing: I will not content myself to answer, that if it be difficult to make out *property,* upon a supposition, that God gave the world to Adam, and his posterity in common; it is impossible that any man, but one universal monarch, should have any *property* upon a supposition, that God gave the world to *Adam,* and his heirs in succession, exclusive of all the rest of his posterity. But I shall endeavour to shew, how men might come to have a *property* in several parts of that which God gave to mankind in common, and that without any express compact of all the commoners.

26. God, who hath given the world to men in common, hath also given them reason to make use of it to

the best advantage of life, and convenience. The earth, and all that is therein, is given to men for the support and comfort of their being. And though all the fruits it naturally produces, and beasts it feeds, belong to mankind in common, as they are produced by the spontaneous hand of nature; and no body has originally a private dominion, exclusive of the rest of mankind, in any of them, as they are thus in their natural state: yet being given for the use of men, there must of necessity be *a means to appropriate* them some way or other, before they can be of any use, or at all beneficial to any particular man. The fruit, or venison, which nourishes the *wild Indian,* who knows no enclosure, and is still a tenant in common, must be his, and so his, i.e. a part of him, that another can no longer have any right to it, before it can do him any good for the support of his life.

27. Though the earth, and all inferior creatures, be common to all men, yet every man has a *property* in his own person: this no body has any right to but himself. The *labour* of his body, and the work of his hands, we may say, are properly his. Whatsoever then he removes out of the state that nature hath provided, and left it in, he hath mixed his labour with, and joined to it something that is his own, and thereby makes it his *property.* It being by him removed from the common state nature hath placed it in, it hath by this *labour* something annexed to it, that excludes the common right of other men. For this *labour* being the unquestionable property of the labourer, no man but he can have a right to what that is once joined to, at least where there is enough, and as good, left in common for others.

28. He that is nourished by the acorns he picked up under an oak, or the apples he gathered from the trees in the wood, has certainly appropriated them to himself. No body can deny but the nourishment is his. I ask then, when did they begin to be his? When he digested? Or when he eat? Or when he boiled? Or when he brought them home? Or when he picked them up? And it is plain, if the first gathering made them not his, nothing else could. That *labour* put a distinction between them and common: that added something to them more than nature, the common mother of all, had done; and so they became his private right. [. . .]

30. Thus this law of reason makes the deer that *Indian's* who hath killed it; it is allowed to be his goods, who hath bestowed his labour upon it, though before it

was the common right of every one. And amongst those who are counted the civilized part of mankind, who have made and multiplied positive laws to determine *property,* this original law of nature, for the *beginning of property,* in what was before common, still takes place; and by virtue thereof, what fish any one catches in the ocean, that great and still remaining common of mankind; or what ambergreise any one takes up here, is *by* the *labour* that removes it out of that common state nature left it in, *made* his *property,* who takes that pains about it. And even amongst us, the hare that any one is hunting, is thought his who pursues her during the chase. For being a beast that is still looked upon as common, and no man's private possession; whoever has employed so much *labour* about any of that kind, as to find and pursue her, has thereby removed her from the state of nature, wherein she was common, and hath *begun a property.*

31. It will perhaps be objected to this, that if gathering the acorns, or other fruits of the earth, &c. makes a right to them, then any one may *ingross* as much as he will. To which I answer, Not so. The same law of nature, that does by this means give us property, does also *bound* that *property* too. "God has given us all things richly," 1 *Tim;* vi. 17, is the voice of reason confirmed by inspiration. But how far has he given it us? *To enjoy.* As much as any one can make use of to any advantage of life before it spoils, so much he may by his labour fix a property in: whatever is beyond this, is more than his share, and belongs to others. Nothing was made by God for man to spoil or destroy. And thus, considering the plenty of natural provisions there was a long time in the world, and the few spenders; and to how small a part of that provision the industry of one man could extend itself, and engross it to the prejudice of others; especially keeping within the *bounds,* set by reason, of what might serve for his *use;* there could be then little room for quarrels or contentions about property so established.

32. But the *chief matter of property* being now not the fruits of the earth, and the beasts that subsist on it, but the *earth it self;* as that which takes in, and carries with it all the rest: I think it is plain, that *property* in that too is acquired as the former. *As much land* as a man tills, plants, improves, cultivates, and can use the product of, so much is his *property.* He by his labour does, as it were, enclose it from the common. Nor will it invalidate his right, to say every body else has an equal title to it; and

therefore he cannot appropriate, he cannot enclose, without the consent of all his fellow commoners, all mankind. God, when he gave the world in common to all mankind, commanded man also to labour, and the penury of his condition required it of him. God and his reason commanded him to subdue the earth, i.e. improve it for the benefit of life, and therein lay out something upon it that was his own, his labour. He that, in obedience to this command of God, subdued, tilled, and sowed any part of it, thereby annexed to it something that was his *property,* which another had no title to, nor could without injury take from him.

33. Nor was this *appropriation* of any parcel of *land,* by improving it, any prejudice to any other man, since there was still enough, and as good left; and more than the yet unprovided could use. So that, in effect, there was never the less left for others because of his enclosure for himself. For he that leaves as much as another can make use of, does as good as take nothing at all. No body could think himself injured by the drinking of another man, though he took a good draught, who had a whole river of the same water left him to quench his thirst: And the case of land and water, where there is enough of both, is perfectly the same. [. . .]

40. Nor is it so strange, as perhaps before consideration it may appear, that the *property of labour* should be able to over-balance the community of land. For it is *labour* indeed that *puts the difference of value* on every thing; and let any one consider what the difference is between an acre of land planted with tobacco or sugar, sown with wheat or barley, and an acre of the same land lying in common, without any husbandry upon it, and he will find, that the improvement of *labour makes* the far greater part of the value. I think it will be but a very modest computation to say, that of the *products* of the earth useful to the life of man, nine tenths are the *effects of labour:* nay, if we will rightly estimate things as they come to our use, and cast up the several expences about them, what in them is purely owing to *nature,* and what to *labour,* we shall find, that in most of them ninety-nine hundredths are wholly to be put on the account of *labour.* [. . .]

46. The greatest part of *things really useful* to the life of man, and such as the necessity of subsisting made the first commoners of the world look after, as it doth the *Americans* now, *are* generally things of *short duration;* such

as, if they are not consumed by use, will decay and perish of themselves: gold, silver, and diamonds, are things that fancy or agreement hath put the value on, more than real use, and the necessary support of life. Now of those good things which nature hath provided in common, every one had a right, (as hath been said) to as much as he could use, and *property* in all that he could affect with his labour; all that his *industry* could extend to, to alter from the state nature had put it in, was his. He that *gathered* a hundred bushels of acorns or apples, had thereby a *property* in them, they were his goods as soon as gathered. He was only to look, that he used them before they spoiled, else he took more than his share, and robbed others. And indeed it was a foolish thing, as well as dishonest, to hoard up more than he could make use of. If he gave away a part to any body else, so that it perished not uselessly in his possession, these he also made use of. And if he also bartered away plums, that would have rotted in a week, for nuts that would last good for his eating a whole year, he did no injury; he wasted not the common stock; destroyed no part of the portion of goods that belonged to others, so long as nothing perished uselessly in his hands. Again, if he would give his nuts for a piece of metal, pleased with its colour; or exchange his sheep for shells, or wool for a sparkling pebble or a diamond, and keep those by him all his life, he invaded not the right of others, he might heap up as much of these durable things as he pleased; the *exceeding of the bounds of* his *just property* not lying in the largeness of his possession, but the perishing of any thing uselessly in it.

47. And thus *came in the use of money,* some lasting thing that men might keep without spoiling, and that by mutual consent men would take in exchange for the truly useful, but perishable supports of life. [. . .]

Chapter 7
Of Political or Civil Society

• • • • •

87. Man being born, [. . .] with a title to perfect freedom, and an uncontrolled enjoyment of all the rights and privileges of the law of nature, equally with any

other man, or number of men in the world, hath by nature a power, not only to preserve his property, that is, his life, liberty, and estate, against the injuries and attempts of other men; but to judge of and punish the breaches of that law in others, as he is persuaded the offence deserves, even with death itself, in crimes where the heinousness of the fact, in his opinion, requires it. But because no *political* society can be, nor subsist, without having in itself the power to preserve the property, and, in order thereunto, punish the offences of all those of that society; there and there only is *political society,* where every one of the members hath quitted his natural power, resigned it up into the hands of the community in all cases that excludes him not from appealing for protection to the law established by it. And thus all private judgment of every particular member being excluded, the community comes to be umpire by settled standing rules, indifferent, and the same to all parties; and by men having authority from the community, for the execution of those rules, decides all the differences that may happen between any members of that society concerning any matter of right; and punishes those offences which any member hath committed against the society, with such penalties as the law has established, whereby it is easy to discern, who are, and who are not, in *political society* together. Those who are united into one body, and have a common established law and judicature to appeal to, with authority to decide controversies between them, and punish offenders, *are in civil society* one with another: but those who have no such common appeal, I mean on earth, are still in the state of nature, each being, where there is no other, judge for himself, and executioner: which is, as I have before shewed, the perfect *state of nature.*

88. And thus the commonwealth comes by a power to set down what punishment shall belong to the several transgressions which they think worthy of it, committed amongst the members of that society, (which is the *power of making laws*) as well as it has the power to punish any injury done unto any of its members, by any one that is not of it, (which is *the power of war and peace,*) and all this for the preservation of the property of all the members of that society, as far as is possible. But though every man who has entered into civil society, and is become a member of any commonwealth, has thereby quitted his power to punish offences against the law of nature, in prosecution of his own private judgment; yet with the judgment of offences, which he has given up to the legislative in all cases, where he can appeal to the magistrate, he has given a right to the commonwealth to employ his force, for the execution of the judgments of the commonwealth whenever he shall be called to it; which indeed are his own judgments, they being made by himself, or his representative. And herein we have the original of the *legislative* and *executive power* of civil society, which is to judge by standing laws, how far offences are to be punished, when committed within the commonwealth; and also to determine, by occasional judgments founded on the present circumstances of the fact, how far injuries from without are to be vindicated; and in both these to employ all the force of all the members, when there shall be need.

89. Wherever therefore any number of men are so united into one society, as to quit every one his executive power of the law of nature, and to resign it to the public, there and there only is a *political,* or *civil society.* And this is done, wherever any number of men, in the state of nature, enter into society to make one people, one body politic, under one supreme government; or else when any one joins himself to, and incorporates with any government already made. For hereby he authorizes the society, or, which is all one, the legislative thereof, to make laws for him, as the public good of the society shall require; to the execution whereof, his own assistance (as to his own degrees) is due. And this *puts men* out of a state of nature into that of a *commonwealth,* by setting up a judge on earth, with authority to determine all the controversies, and redress the injuries that may happen to any member of the commonwealth: which judge is the legislative, or magistrate appointed by it. And wherever there are any number of men, however associated, that have no such decisive power to appeal to, there they are still in the *state of nature.*

90. Hence it is evident, that *absolute monarchy,* which by some men is counted the only government in the world, is indeed inconsistent with civil society, and so can be no form of civil government at all; for *the end of civil society* being to avoid and remedy these inconveniencies of the state of nature, which necessarily follow from every man's being judge in his own case, by setting up a known authority, to which every one of that

society may appeal upon any injury received, or controversy that may arise, and which every one of the society ought to obey; wherever any persons are, who have not such an authority to appeal to for the decision of any difference between them, there those persons are still *in the state of nature.* And so is every *absolute prince,* in respect of those who are under his dominion.

91. For he being supposed to have all, both legislative and executive power in himself alone, there is no judge to be found, no appeal lies open to any one, who may fairly, and indifferently, and with authority decide, and from whose decision relief and redress may be expected of any injury or inconveniency that may be suffered from the prince, or by his order: so that such a man, however intitled, *Czar,* or *Grand Seignior,* or how you please, is as much *in the state of nature,* with all under his dominion, as he is with the rest of mankind. For wherever any two men are, who have no standing rule, and common judge to appeal to on earth, for the determination of controversies of right betwixt them, there they are still *in the state of nature,* and under all the inconveniencies of it, with only this woful difference to the subject, or rather slave of an absolute prince; that whereas in the ordinary state of nature he has a liberty to judge of his right, and, according to the best of his power, to maintain it; now, whenever his property is invaded by the will and order of his monarch, he has not only no appeal, as those in society ought to have, but, as if he were degraded from the common state of rational creatures, is denied a liberty to judge of, or to defend his right; and so is exposed to all the misery and inconveniencies that a man can fear from one, who being in the unrestrained state of nature, is yet corrupted with flattery, and armed with power. [. . .]

Chapter 8
Of the Beginning of Political Societies

95. Men being, as has been said, by nature, all free, equal, and independent, no one can be put out of this estate, and subjected to the political power of another, without his own consent. The only way, whereby any one divests himself of his natural liberty, and puts on the *bonds of civil society,* is by agreeing with other men to join and unite into a community, for their comfortable, safe, and peaceable living one amongst another, in a secure enjoyment of their properties, and a greater security against any, that are not of it. This any number of men may do, because it injures not the freedom of the rest; they are left as they were in the liberty of the state of nature. When any number of men have so *consented to make one community or government,* they are thereby presently incorporated, and make *one body politic,* wherein the *majority* have a right to act and conclude the rest.

96. For when any number of men have, by the consent of every individual, made a *community,* they have thereby made that *community* one body, with a power to act as one body, which is only by the will and determination of the *majority.* For that which acts any community, being only the *consent* of the individuals of it, and it being necessary to that which is one body to move one way; it is necessary the body should move that way whither the greater force carries it, which is the *consent of the majority:* or else it is impossible it should act or continue one body, *one community,* which the consent of every individual that united into it, agreed that it should; and so every one is bound by that consent to be concluded by the majority. And therefore we see, that in assemblies, impowered to act by positive laws, where no number is set by that positive law which impowers them, the *act of the majority* passes for the act of the whole, and of course determines, as having, by the law of nature and reason, the power of the whole.

97. And thus every man, by consenting with others to make one body politic under one government, puts himself under an obligation, to every one of that society, to submit to the determination of the *majority,* and to be concluded by it; or else this *original compact,* whereby he with others incorporate into *one society,* would signify nothing, and be no compact, if he be left free, and under no other ties than he was in before in the state of nature. For what appearance would there be of any compact? What new engagement if he were no farther tied by any decrees of the society, than he himself thought fit, and did actually consent to? This would be still as great a liberty, as he himself had before his compact, or any one else in the state of nature hath, who may submit himself, and consent to any acts of it if he thinks fit.

98. For if *the consent of the majority* shall not, in reason, be received as *the act of the whole,* and conclude every individual; nothing but the consent of every individual can make any thing to be the act of the whole: But such a consent is next to impossible ever to be had, if we consider the infirmities of health, and avocations of business, which in a number, though much less than that of a commonwealth, will necessarily keep many away from the public assembly. To which if we add the variety of opinions, and contrariety of interests, which unavoidably happen in all collections of men, the coming into society upon such terms would be only like Cato's coming into the theatre, only to go out again. Such a constitution as this would make the mighty *Leviathan* of a shorter duration, than the feeblest creatures, and not let it outlast the day it was born in: which cannot be supposed, till we can think, that rational creatures should desire and constitute societies only to be dissolved. For where the *majority* cannot conclude the rest, there they cannot act as one body, and consequently will be immediately dissolved again.

99. Whosoever therefore out of a state of nature unite into a *community,* must be understood to give up all the power, necessary to the ends for which they unite into society, to the majority of the community, unless they expressly agreed in any number greater than the majority. And this is done by barely agreeing to *unite into one political society,* which is *all the compact* that is, or needs be, between the individuals, that enter into, or make up a commonwealth. And thus that, which begins and actually *constitutes any political society,* is nothing, but the consent of any number of freemen capable of a majority, to unite and incorporate into such a society. And this is that, and that only, which did, or could give beginning to any *lawful government* in the world. [. . .]

119. *Every man* being, as has been shewed, *naturally free,* and nothing being able to put him into subjection to any earthly power, but only his own consent; it is to be considered, what shall be understood to be a *sufficient declaration of* a man's *consent, to make him subject* to the laws of any government. There is a common distinction of an express and a tacit consent, which will concern our present case. No body doubts but an *express consent,* of any man entering into any society, makes him a perfect member of that society, a subject of that government. The difficulty is, what ought to be looked upon as a *tacit*

consent, and how far it binds, i.e. how far any one shall be looked on to have consented, and thereby submitted to any government, where he has made no expressions of it at all. And to this I say, that every man, that hath any possessions, or enjoyment of any part of the dominions of any government, doth thereby give his *tacit consent,* and is as far forth obliged to obedience to the laws of that government, during such enjoyment, as any one under it; whether this his possession be of land, to him and his heirs for ever, or a lodging only for a week; or whether it be barely travelling freely on the highway: and, in effect, it reaches as far as the very being of any one within the territories of that government. [. . .]

122. But submitting to the laws of any country, living quietly, and enjoying privileges and protection under them, *makes not a man a member of that society:* this is only a local protection and homage due to and from all those, who, not being in a state of war, come within the territories belonging to any government, to all parts whereof the force of its laws extends. But this no more *makes a man a member of that society,* a perpetual subject of that commonwealth, than it would make a man a subject to another, in whose family he found it convenient to abide for some time, though, whilst he continued in it, he were obliged to comply with the laws, and submit to the government he found there. And thus we see, that foreigners, by living all their lives under another government, and enjoying the privileges and protection of it, though they are bound, even in conscience, to submit to its administration, as far forth as any denison; yet do not thereby come to be *subjects or members of that commonwealth.* Nothing can make any man so, but his actually entering into it by positive engagement, and express promise and compact. This is that, which I think, concerning the beginning of political societies, and that *consent which makes any one a member of any commonwealth.*

Chapter 9
Of the Ends of Political
Society and Government

123. If man in the state of nature be so free, as has been said; if he be absolute lord of his own person and possessions, equal to the greatest, and subject to no body, why will he part with his freedom? why will he give up

this empire, and subject himself to the dominion and control of any other power? To which it is obvious to answer, that though in the state of nature he hath such a right, yet the enjoyment of it is very uncertain, and constantly exposed to the invasion of others. For all being kings as much as he, every man his equal, and the greater part no strict observers of equity and justice, the enjoyment of the property he has in this state is very unsafe, very unsecure. This makes him willing to quit this condition, which, however free, is full of fears and continual dangers: and it is not without reason, that he seeks out, and is willing to join in society with others, who are already united, or have a mind to unite, for the mutual preservation of their lives, liberties, and estates, which I call by the general name, *property.*

124. The great and *chief end,* therefore, of men's uniting into commonwealths, and putting themselves under government, *is the preservation of their property.* To which in the state of nature there are many things wanting.

First, There wants an *established,* settled, known *law,* received and allowed by common consent to be the standard of right and wrong, and the common measure to decide all controversies between them. For though the law of nature be plain and intelligible to all rational creatures; yet men being biassed by their interest, as well as ignorant for want of studying it, are not apt to allow of it as a law binding to them in the application of it to their particular cases.

125. *Secondly,* In the state of nature there wants *a known and indifferent judge,* with authority to determine all differences according to the established law. For every one in that state being both judge and executioner of the law of nature, men being partial to themselves, passion and revenge is very apt to carry them too far, and with too much heat, in their own cases; as well as negligence, and unconcernedness, to make them too remiss in other men's.

126. *Thirdly,* In the state of nature, there often wants *power* to back and support the sentence when right, and to give it due execution. They who by any injustice offended, will seldom fail, where they are able, by force to make good their injustice; such resistance many times makes the punishment dangerous, and frequently destructive, to those who attempt it.

127. Thus mankind, notwithstanding all the privileges of the state of nature, being but in an ill condition,

while they remain in it, are quickly driven into society. Hence it comes to pass that we seldom find any number of men live anytime together in this state. The inconveniencies that they are therein exposed to, by the irregular and uncertain exercise of the power every man has of punishing the transgressions of others, make them take sanctuary under the established laws of government, and therein seek *the preservation of their property.* It is this makes them so willingly give up every one his single power of punishing, to be exercised by such alone, as shall be appointed to it amongst them; and by such rules as the community, or those authorized by them to that purpose, shall agree on. And in this we have the original *right and rise of both the legislative and executive power,* as well as of the governments and societies themselves.

128. For in the state of nature, to omit the liberty he has of innocent delights, a man has two powers.

The first is to do whatsoever he thinks fit for the preservation of himself and others within the permission of the *law of nature:* by which law, common to them all, he and all the rest of *mankind are one community,* make up one society, distinct from all other creatures. And, were it not for the corruption and viciousness of degenerate men, there would be no need of any other; no necessity that men should separate from this great and natural community, and by positive agreements combine into smaller and divided associations.

The other power a man has in the state of nature, is the *power to punish the crimes* committed against that law. Both these he gives up, when he joins in a private, if I may so call it, or particular politic society, and incorporates into any commonwealth, separate from the rest of mankind.

129. The first *power, viz. of doing whatsoever he thought fit for the preservation of himself,* and the rest of mankind, *he gives up* to be regulated by laws made by the society, so far forth as the preservation of himself and the rest of that society shall require; which laws of the society in many things confine the liberty he had by the law of nature.

130. *Secondly,* The *power of punishing he wholly gives up,* and engages his natural force, (which he might before employ in the execution of the law of nature, by his own single authority, as he thought fit) to assist the executive power of the society, as the law thereof shall

require. For being now in a new state, wherein he is to enjoy many conveniencies, from the labour, assistance, and society of others in the same community, as well as protection from its whole strength; he is to part also, with as much of his natural liberty, in providing for himself, as the good, prosperity, and safety of the society shall require; which is not only necessary, but just, since the other members of the society do the like.

131. But though men, when they enter into society, give up the equality, liberty, and executive power they had in the state of nature, into the hands of the society, to be so far disposed of by the legislative, as the good of the society shall require; yet it being only with an intention in every one the better to preserve himself, his liberty and property; (for no rational creature can be supposed to change his condition with an intention to

be worse) the power of the society, or legislative constituted by them, *can never be supposed to extend farther, than the common good;* but is obliged to secure every one's property, by providing against those three defects above mentioned, that made the state of nature so unsafe and uneasy. And so whoever has the legislative or supreme power of any commonwealth, is bound to govern by established *standing laws,* promulgated and known to the people, and not by extemporary decrees; by *indifferent* and upright *judges,* who are to decide controversies by those laws; and to employ the force of the community at home, *only in the execution of such laws;* or abroad to prevent or redress foreign injuries, and secure the community from inroads and invasion. And all this to be directed to no other *end,* but the *peace, safety,* and *public good* of the people. [. . .]

John Stuart Mill

Social Liberty

Chapter I

The subject of this essay is not the so-called "liberty of the will," so unfortunately opposed to the misnamed doctrine of philosophical necessity; but civil, or social liberty: the nature and limits of the power which can be legitimately exercised by society over the individual. A question seldom stated, and hardly ever discussed in general terms, but which profoundly influences the practical controversies of the age by its latent presence, and is likely soon to make itself recognized as the vital question of the future. It is so far from being new that, in a certain sense, it has divided mankind almost from the remotest ages; but in the stage of progress into which the more civilized portions of the species have

now entered, it presents itself under new conditions and requires a different and more fundamental treatment.

The struggle between liberty and authority is the most conspicuous feature in the portions of history with which we are earliest familiar, particularly in that of Greece, Rome, and England. But in old times this contest was between subjects, or some classes of subjects, and the government. By liberty was meant protection against the tyranny of the political rulers. The rulers were conceived (except in some of the popular governments of Greece) as in a necessarily antagonistic position to the people whom they ruled. They consisted of a governing One, or a governing tribe or caste, who derived their authority from inheritance or conquest, who, at all events, did not hold it at the pleasure of the governed, and whose supremacy men did not venture, perhaps did not desire, to contest, whatever precautions might be taken against its oppressive exercise. Their power was regarded as necessary, but also as highly dan-

From John Stuart Mill, *On Liberty,* edited by Elizabeth Rapaport (Indianapolis: Hackett Publishing Company, 1978). Reprinted by permission of the publisher.

gerous; as a weapon which they would attempt to use against their subjects, no less than against external enemies. To prevent the weaker members of the community from being preyed upon by innumerable vultures, it was needful that there should be an animal of prey stronger than the rest, commissioned to keep them down. But as the king of the vultures would be no less bent upon preying on the flock than any of the minor harpies, it was indispensable to be in a perpetual attitude of defense against his beak and claws. The aim, therefore, of patriots was to set limits to the power which the ruler should be suffered to exercise over the community; and this limitation was what they meant by liberty. It was attempted in two ways. First, by obtaining a recognition of certain immunities, called political liberties or rights, which it was to be regarded as a breach of duty in the ruler to infringe, and which if he did infringe, specific resistance or general rebellion was held to be justifiable. A second, and generally a later, expedient was the establishment of constitutional checks by which the consent of the community, or of a body of some sort, supposed to represent its interests, was made a necessary condition to some of the more important acts of the governing power. To the first of these modes of limitation, the ruling power, in most European countries, was compelled, more or less, to submit. It was not so with the second; and, to attain this, or, when already in some degree possessed, to attain it more completely, became everywhere the principal object of the lovers of liberty. And so long as mankind were content to combat one enemy by another, and to be ruled by a master on condition of being guaranteed more or less efficaciously against his tyranny, they did not carry their aspirations beyond this point.

A time, however, came, in the progress of human affairs, when men ceased to think it a necessity of nature that their governors should be an independent power opposed in interest to themselves. It appeared to them much better that the various magistrates of the state should be their tenants or delegates, revocable at their pleasure. In that way alone, it seemed, could they have complete security that the powers of government would never be abused to their disadvantage. By degrees this new demand for elective and temporary rulers became the prominent object of the exertions of the popular party wherever any such party existed, and superseded, to a considerable extent, the previous efforts to limit the power of rulers. As the struggle proceeded for making the ruling power emanate from the periodical choice of the ruled, some persons began to think that too much importance had been attached to the limitation of the power itself. *That* (it might seem) was a resource against rulers whose interests were habitually opposed to those of the people. What was now wanted was that the rulers should be identified with the people, that their interest and will should be the interest and will of the nation. The nation did not need to be protected against its own will. There was no fear of its tyrannizing over itself. Let the rulers be effectually responsible to it, promptly removable by it, and it could afford to trust them with power of which it could itself dictate the use to be made. Their power was but the nation's own power, concentrated and in a form convenient for exercise. This mode of thought, or rather perhaps of feeling, was common among the last generation of European liberalism, in the Continental section of which it still apparently predominates. Those who admit any limit to what a government may do, except in the case of such governments as they think ought not to exist, stand out as brilliant exceptions among the political thinkers of the Continent. A similar tone of sentiment might by this time have been prevalent in our own country if the circumstances which for a time encouraged it had continued unaltered.

But, in political and philosophical theories as well as in persons, success discloses faults and infirmities which failure might have concealed from observation. The notion that the people have no need to limit their power over themselves might seem axiomatic, when popular government was a thing only dreamed about, or read of as having existed at some distant period of the past. Neither was that notion necessarily disturbed by such temporary aberrations as those of the French Revolution, the worst of which were the work of a usurping few, and which, in any case, belonged, not to the permanent working of popular institutions, but to a sudden and convulsive outbreak against monarchical and aristocratic despotism. In time, however, a democratic republic came to occupy a large portion of the earth's surface and made itself felt as one of the most powerful members of the community of nations; and elective and responsible government became subject to the

observations and criticisms which wait upon a great existing fact. It was now perceived that such phrases as
"self-government," and "the power of the people over
themselves," do not express the true state of the case.
The "people" who exercise the power are not always the
same people with those over whom it is exercised; and
the "self-government" spoken of is not the government
of each by himself, but of each by all the rest. The will
of the people, moreover, practically means the will of
the most numerous or the most active *part* of the people
—the majority, or those who succeed in making themselves accepted as the majority; the people, consequently, *may* desire to oppress a part of their number,
and precautions are as much needed against this as
against any other abuse of power. The limitation, therefore, of the power of government over individuals loses
none of its importance when the holders of power are
regularly accountable to the community, that is, to the
strongest party therein. This view of things, recommending itself equally to the intelligence of thinkers
and to the inclination of those important classes in
European society to whose real or supposed interests
democracy is adverse, has had no difficulty in establishing itself; and in political speculations "the tyranny of
the majority" is now generally included among the evils
against which society requires to be on its guard.

Like other tyrannies, the tyranny of the majority was
at first, and is still vulgarly, held in dread, chiefly as operating through the acts of the public authorities. But
reflecting persons perceived that when society is itself
the tyrant—society collectively over the separate individuals who compose it—its means of tyrannizing are
not restricted to the acts which it may do by the hands
of its political functionaries. Society can and does execute its own mandates; and if it issues wrong mandates
instead of right, or any mandates at all in things with
which it ought not to meddle, it practices a social tyranny
more formidable than many kinds of political oppression, since, though not usually upheld by such extreme
penalties, it leaves fewer means of escape, penetrating
much more deeply into the details of life, and enslaving
the soul itself. Protection, therefore, against the tyranny
of the magistrate is not enough; there needs protection
also against the tyranny of the prevailing opinion and
feeling, against the tendency of society to impose, by
other means than civil penalties, its own ideas and prac-

tices as rules of conduct on those who dissent from
them; to fetter the development and, if possible, prevent
the formation of any individuality not in harmony with
its ways, and compel all characters to fashion themselves
upon the model of its own. There is a limit to the legitimate interference of collective opinion with individual
independence; and to find that limit, and maintain it
against encroachment, is as indispensable to a good condition of human affairs as protection against political
despotism.

But though this proposition is not likely to be contested in general terms, the practical question where to
place the limit—how to make the fitting adjustment
between individual independence and social control—
is a subject on which nearly everything remains to be
done. All that makes existence valuable to anyone depends on the enforcement of restraints upon the actions
of other people. Some rules of conduct, therefore, must
be imposed—by law in the first place, and by opinion
on many things which are not fit subjects for the operation of law. What these rules should be is the principal
question in human affairs; but if we except a few of
the most obvious cases, it is one of those which least
progress has been made in resolving. No two ages, and
scarcely any two countries, have decided it alike; and the
decision of one age or country is a wonder to another.
Yet the people of any given age and country no more
suspect any difficulty in it than if it were a subject on
which mankind had always been agreed. The rules which
obtain among themselves appear to them self-evident
and self-justifying. This all but universal illusion is one
of the examples of the magical influence of custom,
which is not only, as the proverb says, a second nature
but is continually mistaken for the first. The effect of
custom, in preventing any misgiving respecting the rules
of conduct which mankind impose on one another, is
all the more complete because the subject is one on
which it is not generally considered necessary that reasons should be given, either by one person to others or
by each to himself. People are accustomed to believe,
and have been encouraged in the belief by some who
aspire to the character of philosophers, that their feelings on subjects of this nature are better than reasons
and render reasons unnecessary. The practical principle
which guides them to their opinions on the regulation
of human conduct is the feeling in each person's mind

that everybody should be required to act as he, and those with whom he sympathizes, would like them to act. No one, indeed, acknowledges to himself that his standard of judgment is his own liking; but an opinion on a point of conduct, not supported by reasons, can only count as one person's preference; and if the reasons, when given, are a mere appeal to a similar preference felt by other people, it is still only many people's liking instead of one. To an ordinary man, however, his own preference, thus supported, is not only a perfectly satisfactory reason but the only one he generally has for any of his notions of morality, taste, or propriety, which are not expressly written in his religious creed, and his chief guide in the interpretation even of that. Men's opinions, accordingly, on what is laudable or blamable are affected by all the multifarious causes which influence their wishes in regard to the conduct of others, and which are as numerous as those which determine their wishes on any other subject. Sometimes their reason; at other times their prejudices or superstitions; often their social affections, not seldom their antisocial ones, their envy or jealousy, their arrogance or contemptuousness; but most commonly their desires or fears for themselves —their legitimate or illegitimate self-interest. Wherever there is an ascendant class, a large portion of the morality of the country emanates from its class interests and its feelings of class superiority. The morality between Spartans and Helots, between planters and Negroes, between princes and subjects, between nobles and roturiers, between men and women has been for the most part the creation of these class interests and feelings; and the sentiments thus generated react in turn upon the moral feelings of the members of the ascendant class, in their relations among themselves. Where, on the other hand, a class, formerly ascendant, has lost its ascendancy, or where its ascendancy is unpopular, the prevailing moral sentiments frequently bear the impress of an impatient dislike of superiority. Another grand determining principle of the rules of conduct, both in act and forbearance, which have been enforced by law or opinion, has been the servility of mankind toward the supposed preferences or aversions of their temporal masters or of their gods. This servility, though essentially selfish, is not hypocrisy; it gives rise to perfectly genuine sentiments of abhorrence; it made men burn magicians and heretics. Among so many baser influences, the general

and obvious interests of society have, of course, had a share, and a large one, in the direction of the moral sentiments; less, however, as a matter of reason, and on their own account, than as a consequence of the sympathies and antipathies which grew out of them; and sympathies and antipathies which had little or nothing to do with the interests of society have made themselves felt in the establishment of moralities with quite as great force.

The likings and dislikings of society, or of some powerful portion of it, are thus the main thing which has practically determined the rules laid down for general observance, under the penalties of law or opinion. And in general, those who have been in advance of society in thought and feeling have left this condition of things unassailed in principle, however they may have come into conflict with it in some of its details. They have occupied themselves rather in inquiring what things society ought to like or dislike than in questioning whether its likings or dislikings should be a law to individuals. They preferred endeavoring to alter the feelings of mankind on the particular points on which they were themselves heretical rather than make common cause in defense of freedom with heretics generally. The only case in which the higher ground has been taken on principle and maintained with consistency, by any but an individual here and there, is that of religious belief: a case instructive in many ways, and not least so as forming a most striking instance of the fallibility of what is called the moral sense; for the *odium theologicum,* in a sincere bigot, is one of the most unequivocal cases of moral feeling. Those who first broke the yoke of what called itself the Universal Church were in general as little willing to permit difference of religious opinion as that church itself. But when the heat of the conflict was over, without giving a complete victory to any party, and each church or sect was reduced to limit its hopes to retaining possession of the ground it already occupied, minorities, seeing that they had no chance of becoming majorities, were under the necessity of pleading to those whom they could not convert for permission to differ. It is accordingly on this battlefield, almost solely, that the rights of the individual against society have been asserted on broad grounds of principle, and the claim of society to exercise authority over dissentients openly controverted. The great writers to whom the world owes what religious liberty it possesses have mostly asserted freedom of conscience as an indefeasible right, and denied absolutely that a human being is accountable to others for his religious belief. Yet so natural to mankind is intolerance in whatever they really care about that religious freedom has hardly anywhere been practically realized, except where religious indifference, which dislikes to have its peace disturbed by theological quarrels, has added its weight to the scale. In the minds of almost all religious persons, even in the most tolerant countries, the duty of toleration is admitted with tacit reserves. One person will bear with dissent in matters of church government, but not of dogma; another can tolerate everybody, short of a Papist or a Unitarian; another, everyone who believes in revealed religion; a few extend their charity a little further, but stop at the belief in a God and in a future state. Wherever the sentiment of the majority is still genuine and intense, it is found to have abated little of its claim to be obeyed.

In England, from the peculiar circumstances of our political history, though the yoke of opinion is perhaps heavier, that of law is lighter than in most other countries of Europe; and there is considerable jealousy of direct interference by the legislative or the executive power with private conduct, not so much from any just regard for the independence of the individual as from the still subsisting habit of looking on the government as representing an opposite interest to the public. The majority have not yet learned to feel the power of the government their power, or its opinions their opinions. When they do so, individual liberty will probably be as much exposed to invasion from the government as it already is from public opinion. But, as yet, there is a considerable amount of feeling ready to be called forth against any attempt of the law to control individuals in things in which they have not hitherto been accustomed to be controlled by it; and this with very little discrimination as to whether the matter is, or is not, within the legitimate sphere of legal control; insomuch that the feeling, highly salutary on the whole, is perhaps quite as often misplaced as well grounded in the particular instances of its application. There is, in fact, no recognized principle by which the propriety or impropriety of government interference is customarily tested. People decide according to their personal preferences.

Some, whenever they see any good to be done, or evil to be remedied, would willingly instigate the government to undertake the business, while others prefer to bear almost any amount of social evil rather than add one to the departments of human interests amenable to governmental control. And men range themselves on one or the other side in any particular case, according to this general direction of their sentiments, or according to the degree of interest which they feel in the particular thing which it is proposed that the government should do, or according to the belief they entertain that the government would, or would not, do it in the manner they prefer; but very rarely on account of any opinion to which they consistently adhere, as to what things are fit to be done by a government. And it seems to me that in consequence of this absence of rule or principle, one side is at present as often wrong as the other; the interference of government is, with about equal frequency, improperly invoked and improperly condemned.

The object of this essay is to assert one very simple principle, as entitled to govern absolutely the dealings of society with the individual in the way of compulsion and control, whether the means used be physical force in the form of legal penalties or the moral coercion of public opinion. That principle is that the sole end for which mankind are warranted, individually or collectively, in interfering with the liberty of action of any of their number is self-protection. That the only purpose for which power can be rightfully exercised over any member of a civilized community, against his will, is to prevent harm to others. His own good, either physical or moral, is not a sufficient warrant. He cannot rightfully be compelled to do or forbear because it will be better for him to do so, because it will make him happier, because, in the opinions of others, to do so would be wise or even right. These are good reasons for remonstrating with him, or reasoning with him, or persuading him, or entreating him, but not for compelling him or visiting him with any evil in case he do otherwise. To justify that, the conduct from which it is desired to deter him must be calculated to produce evil to someone else. The only part of the conduct of anyone for which he is amenable to society is that which concerns others. In the part which merely concerns himself, his independence is, of right, absolute. Over himself, over his own body and mind, the individual is sovereign.

It is, perhaps, hardly necessary to say that this doctrine is meant to apply only to human beings in the maturity of their faculties. We are not speaking of children or of young persons below the age which the law may fix as that of manhood or womanhood. Those who are still in a state to require being taken care of by others must be protected against their own actions as well as against external injury. For the same reason we may leave out of consideration those backward states of society in which the race itself may be considered as in its nonage. The early difficulties in the way of spontaneous progress are so great that there is seldom any choice of means for overcoming them; and a ruler full of the spirit of improvement is warranted in the use of any expedients that will attain an end perhaps otherwise unattainable. Despotism is a legitimate mode of government in dealing with barbarians, provided the end be their improvement and the means justified by actually effecting that end. Liberty, as a principle, has no application to any state of things anterior to the time when mankind have become capable of being improved by free and equal discussion. Until then, there is nothing for them but implicit obedience to an Akbar or a Charlemagne, if they are so fortunate as to find one. But as soon as mankind have attained the capacity of being guided to their own improvement by conviction or persuasion (a period long since reached in all nations with whom we need here concern ourselves), compulsion, either in the direct form or in that of pains and penalties for noncompliance, is no longer admissible as a means to their own good, and justifiable only for the security of others.

It is proper to state that I forego any advantage which could be derived to my argument from the idea of abstract right as a thing independent of utility. I regard utility as the ultimate appeal on all ethical questions; but it must be utility in the largest sense, grounded on the permanent interests of man as a progressive being. Those interests, I contend, authorize the subjection of individual spontaneity to external control only in respect to those actions of each which concern the interest of other people. If anyone does an act hurtful to others, there is a *prima facie* case for punishing him by law or, where legal penalties are not safely applicable, by general disapprobation. There are also many positive acts for the benefit of others which he may rightfully be compelled to perform, such as to give evidence in a court of justice, to bear his fair share in the common defense or in any other joint work necessary to the interest of the society of which he enjoys the protection, and to perform certain acts of individual beneficence, such as saving a fellow creature's life or interposing to protect the defenseless against ill usage—things which whenever it is obviously a man's duty to do he may rightfully be made responsible to society for not doing. A person may cause evil to others not only by his actions but by his inaction, and in either case he is justly accountable to them for the injury. The latter case, it is true, requires a much more cautious exercise of compulsion than the former. To make anyone answerable for doing evil to others is the rule; to make him answerable for not preventing evil is, comparatively speaking, the exception. Yet there are many cases clear enough and grave enough to justify that exception. In all things which regard the external relations of the individual, he is *de jure* amenable to those whose interests are concerned, and, if need be, to society as their protector. There are often good reasons for not holding him to the responsibility; but these reasons must arise from the special expediences of the case: either because it is a kind of case in which he is on the whole likely to act better when left to his own discretion than when controlled in any way in which society have it in their power to control him; or because the attempt to exercise control would produce other evils, greater than those which it would prevent. When such reasons as these preclude the enforcement of responsibility, the conscience of the agent himself should step into the vacant judgment seat and protect those interests of others which have no external protection; judging himself all the more rigidly, because the case does not admit of his being made accountable to the judgment of his fellow creatures.

But there is a sphere of action in which society, as distinguished from the individual, has, if any, only an indirect interest: comprehending all that portion of a person's life and conduct which affects only himself or, if it also affects others, only with their free, voluntary, and undeceived consent and participation. When I say only himself, I mean directly and in the first instance; for whatever affects himself may affect others through himself: and the objection which may be grounded on this contingency will receive consideration in the sequel. This, then, is the appropriate region of human liberty.

It comprises, first, the inward domain of consciousness, demanding liberty of conscience in the most comprehensive sense, liberty of thought and feeling, absolute freedom of opinion and sentiment on all subjects, practical or speculative, scientific, moral, or theological. The liberty of expressing and publishing opinions may seem to fall under a different principle, since it belongs to that part of the conduct of an individual which concerns other people, but, being almost of as much importance as the liberty of thought itself and resting in great part on the same reasons, is practically inseparable from it. Secondly, the principle requires liberty of tastes and pursuits, of framing the plan of our life to suit our own character, of doing as we like, subject to such consequences as may follow, without impediment from our fellow creatures, so long as what we do does not harm them, even though they should think our conduct foolish, perverse, or wrong. Thirdly, from this liberty of each individual follows the liberty, within the same limits, of combination among individuals; freedom to unite for any purpose not involving harm to others: the persons combining being supposed to be of full age and not forced or deceived.

No society in which these liberties are not, on the whole, respected is free, whatever may be its form of government; and none is completely free in which they do not exist absolute and unqualified. The only freedom which deserves the name is that of pursuing our own good in our own way, so long as we do not attempt to deprive others of theirs or impede their efforts to obtain it. Each is the proper guardian of his own health, whether bodily *or* mental and spiritual. Mankind are greater gainers by suffering each other to live as seems good to themselves than by compelling each to live as seems good to the rest. [. . .]

CHAPTER II

Of the Liberty of Thought and Discussion

The time, it is to be hoped, is gone by when any defense would be necessary of the "liberty of the press" as one of the securities against corrupt or tyrannical government. No argument, we may suppose, can now be needed against permitting a legislature or an executive, not identified in interest with the people, to prescribe opinions to them and determine what doctrines or what arguments they shall be allowed to hear. This aspect of the question, besides, has been so often and so triumphantly enforced by preceding writers that it needs not be specially insisted on in this place. Though the law of England, on the subject of the press, is as servile to this day as it was in the time of the Tudors, there is little danger of its being actually put in force against political discussion except during some temporary panic when fear of insurrection drives ministers and judges from their propriety;[1] and, speaking generally, it is not, in constitutional countries, to be apprehended that the government, whether completely responsible to the people or not, will often attempt to control the expression of opinion, except when in doing so it makes itself the organ of the general intolerance of the public. Let us suppose, therefore, that the government is entirely at one with the people, and never thinks of exerting any power of coercion unless in agreement with what it conceives to be their voice. But I deny the right of the people to exercise such coercion, either by themselves or by their government.

---

1. If the arguments of the present chapter are of any validity, there ought to exist the fullest liberty of professing and discussing, as a matter of ethical conviction, any doctrine, however immoral it may be considered. It would, therefore, be irrelevant and out of place to examine here whether the doctrine of tyrannicide deserves that title. I shall content myself with saying that the subject has been at all times one of the open questions of morals; that the act of a private citizen in striking down a criminal who, by raising himself above the law, has placed himself beyond the reach of legal punishment or control has been accounted by whole nations, and by some of the best and wisest of men, not a crime but an act of exalted virtue; and that, right or wrong, it is not of the nature of assassination, but of civil war. As such, I hold that the instigation to it, in a specific case, may be a proper subject of punishment, but only if an overt act has followed, and at least a probable connection can be established between the act and the instigation. Even then it is not a foreign government but the very government assailed which alone, in the exercise of self-defense, can legitimately punish attacks directed against its own existence.

The power itself is illegitimate. The best government has no more title to it than the worst. It is as noxious, or more noxious, when exerted in accordance with public opinion than when in opposition to it. If all mankind minus one were of one opinion, and only one person were of the contrary opinion, mankind would be no more justified in silencing that one person than he, if he had the power, would be justified in silencing mankind. Were an opinion a personal possession of no value except to the owner, if to be obstructed in the enjoyment of it were simply a private injury, it would make some difference whether the injury was inflicted only on a few persons or on many. But the peculiar evil of silencing the expression of an opinion is that it is robbing the human race, posterity as well as the existing generation—those who dissent from the opinion, still more than those who hold it. If the opinion is right, they are deprived of the opportunity of exchanging error for truth; if wrong, they lose, what is almost as great a benefit, the clearer perception and livelier impression of truth produced by its collision with error.

It is necessary to consider separately these two hypotheses, each of which has a distinct branch of the argument corresponding to it. We can never be sure that the opinion we are endeavoring to stifle is a false opinion; and if we were sure, stifling it would be an evil still.

First, the opinion which it is attempted to suppress by authority may possibly be true. Those who desire to suppress it, of course, deny its truth; but they are not infallible. They have no authority to decide the question for all mankind and exclude every other person from the means of judging. To refuse a hearing to an opinion because they are sure that it is false is to assume that *their* certainty is the same thing as *absolute* certainty. All silencing of discussion is an assumption of infallibility. Its condemnation may be allowed to rest on this common argument, not the worse for being common.

Unfortunately for the good sense of mankind, the fact of their fallibility is far from carrying the weight in their practical judgment which is always allowed to it in theory; for while everyone well knows himself to be fallible, few think it necessary to take any precautions against their own fallibility, or admit the supposition that any opinion of which they feel very certain may be one of the examples of the error to which they acknowledge themselves to be liable. Absolute princes, or

others who are accustomed to unlimited deference, usually feel this complete confidence in their own opinions on nearly all subjects. People more happily situated, who sometimes hear their opinions disputed and are not wholly unused to be set right when they are wrong, place the same unbounded reliance only on such of their opinions as are shared by all who surround them, or to whom they habitually defer; for in proportion to a man's want of confidence in his own solitary judgment does he usually repose, with implicit trust, on the infallibility of "the world" in general. And the world, to each individual, means the part of it with which he comes in contact: his party, his sect, his church, his class of society; the man may be called, by comparison, almost liberal and large-minded to whom it means anything so comprehensive as his own country or his own age. Nor is his faith in this collective authority at all shaken by his being aware that other ages, countries, sects, churches, classes, and parties have thought, and even now think, the exact reverse. He devolves upon his own world the responsibility of being in the right against the dissentient worlds of other people; and it never troubles him that mere accident has decided which of these numerous worlds is the object of his reliance, and that the same causes which make him a churchman in London would have made him a Buddhist or a Confucian in Peking. Yet it is as evident in itself, as any amount of argument can make it, that ages are no more infallible than individuals—every age having held many opinions which subsequent ages have deemed not only false but absurd; and it is as certain that many opinions, now general, will be rejected by future ages, as it is that many, once general, are rejected by the present.

The objection likely to be made to this argument would probably take some such form as the following. There is no greater assumption of infallibility in forbidding the propagation of error than in any other thing which is done by public authority on its own judgment and responsibility. Judgment is given to men that they may use it. Because it may be used erroneously, are men to be told that they ought not to use it at all? To prohibit what they think pernicious is not claiming exemption from error, but fulfilling the duty incumbent on them, although fallible, of acting on their conscientious conviction. If we were never to act on our opinions, because those opinions may be wrong, we should leave all our interests uncared for, and all our duties unperformed. An objection which applies to all conduct can be no valid objection to any conduct in particular. It is the duty of governments, and of individuals, to form the truest opinions they can; to form them carefully, and never impose them upon others unless they are quite sure of being right. But when they are sure (such reasoners may say), it is not conscientiousness but cowardice to shrink from acting on their opinions and allow doctrines which they honestly think dangerous to the welfare of mankind, either in this life or in another, to be scattered abroad without restraint, because other people, in less enlightened times, have persecuted opinions now believed to be true. Let us take care, it may be said, not to make the same mistake; but governments and nations have made mistakes in other things which are not denied to be fit subjects for the exercise of authority: they have laid on bad taxes, made unjust wars. Ought we therefore to lay on no taxes and, under whatever provocation, make no wars? Men and governments must act to the best of their ability. There is no such thing as absolute certainty, but there is assurance sufficient for the purposes of human life. We may, and must, assume our opinion to be true for the guidance of our own conduct; and it is assuming no more when we forbid bad men to pervert society by the propagation of opinions which we regard as false and pernicious.

I answer, that it is assuming very much more. There is the greatest difference between presuming an opinion to be true because, with every opportunity for contesting it, it has not been refuted, and assuming its truth for the purpose of not permitting its refutation. Complete liberty of contradicting and disproving our opinion is the very condition which justifies us in assuming its truth for purposes of action; and on no other terms can a being with human faculties have any rational assurance of being right.

When we consider either the history of opinion or the ordinary conduct of human life, to what is it to be ascribed that the one and the other are no worse than they are? Not certainly to the inherent force of the human understanding, for on any matter not self-evident there are ninety-nine persons totally incapable of judging of it for one who is capable; and the capacity of the hundredth person is only comparative, for the majority of the eminent men of every past generation held many opinions now known to be erroneous, and did or approved numerous things which no one will now justify. Why is it, then, that there is on the whole a preponderance among mankind of rational opinions and rational conduct? If there really is this preponderance—which there must be unless human affairs are, and have always been, in an almost desperate state—it is owing to a quality of the human mind, the source of everything respectable in man either as an intellectual or as a moral being, namely, that his errors are corrigible. He is capable of rectifying his mistakes by discussion and experience. Not by experience alone. There must be discussion to show how experience is to be interpreted. Wrong opinions and practices gradually yield to fact and argument; but facts and arguments, to produce any effect on the mind, must be brought before it. Very few facts are able to tell their own story, without comments to bring out their meaning. The whole strength and value, then, of human judgment depending on the one property, that it can be set right when it is wrong, reliance can be placed on it only when the means of setting it right are kept constantly at hand. In the case of any person whose judgment is really deserving of confidence, how has it become so? Because he has kept his mind open to criticism of his opinions and conduct. Because it has been his practice to listen to all that could be said against him; to profit by as much of it as was just, and to expound to himself, and upon occasion to others, the fallacy of what was fallacious. Because he has felt that the only way in which a human being can make some approach to knowing the whole of a subject is by hearing what can be said about it by persons of every variety of opinion, and studying all modes in which it can be looked at by every character of mind. No wise man ever acquired his wisdom in any mode but this; nor is it in the nature of human intellect to become wise in any other manner. The steady habit of correcting and completing his own opinion by collating it with those of others, so far from causing doubt and hesitation in carrying it into practice, is the only stable foundation for a just reliance on it; for, being cognizant of all that can, at least obviously, be said against him, and having taken up his position against all gain-sayers—knowing that he has sought for objections and difficulties instead of avoiding them, and has shut out no light which can be thrown upon the subject from any quarter—he has a right to think his judgment better than that of any person, or any multitude, who have not gone through a similar process.

It is not too much to require that what the wisest of mankind, those who are best entitled to trust their own judgment, find necessary to warrant their relying on it, should be submitted to by that miscellaneous collection of a few wise and many foolish individuals called the public. The most intolerant of churches, the Roman Catholic Church, even at the canonization of a saint admits, and listens patiently to, a "devil's advocate." The holiest of men, it appears, cannot be admitted to posthumous honors until all that the devil could say against him is known and weighed. If even the Newtonian philosophy were not permitted to be questioned, mankind could not feel as complete assurance of its truth as they now do. The beliefs which we have most warrant for have no safeguard to rest on but a standing invitation to the whole world to prove them unfounded. If the challenge is not accepted, or is accepted and the attempt fails, we are far enough from certainty still, but we have done the best that the existing state of human reason admits of: we have neglected nothing that could give the truth a chance of reaching us; if the lists are kept open, we may hope that, if there be a better truth, it will be found when the human mind is capable of receiving it; and in the meantime we may rely on having attained such approach to truth as is possible in our own day. This is the amount of certainty attainable by a fallible being, and this the sole way of attaining it.

Strange it is that men should admit the validity of the arguments for free discussion, but object to their being "pushed to an extreme," not seeing that unless the reasons are good for an extreme case, they are not good for any case. Strange that they should imagine that they are not assuming infallibility when they acknowledge that there should be free discussion on all subjects which can possibly be *doubtful,* but think that some particular principle or doctrine should be forbidden to be questioned because it is so *certain,* that is, because *they are certain* that it is certain. To call any proposition certain, while there is anyone who would deny its certainty if permitted, but who is not permitted, is to assume that we ourselves,

and those who agree with us, are the judges of certainty, and judges without hearing the other side.

In the present age—which has been described as "destitute of faith, but terrified at skepticism"[2]—in which people feel sure, not so much that their opinions are true as that they should not know that to do without them—the claims of an opinion to be protected from public attack are rested not so much on its truth as on its importance to society. There are, it is alleged, certain beliefs so useful, not to say indispensable, to well-being that it is as much the duty of governments to uphold those beliefs as to protect any other of the interests of society. In a case of such necessity, and so directly in the line of their duty, something less than infallibility may, it is maintained, warrant, and even bind, governments to act on their own opinion confirmed by the general opinion of mankind. It is also often argued, and still oftener thought, that none but bad men would desire to weaken these salutary beliefs; and there can be nothing wrong, it is thought, in restraining bad men and prohibiting what only such men would wish to practice. This mode of thinking makes the justification of restraints on discussion not a question of the truth of doctrines but of their usefulness, and flatters itself by that means to escape the responsibility of claiming to be an infallible judge of opinions. But those who thus satisfy themselves do not perceive that the assumption of infallibility is merely shifted from one point to another. The usefulness of an opinion is itself matter of opinion—as disputable, as open to discussion, and requiring discussion as much as the opinion itself. There is the same need of an infallible judge of opinions to decide an opinion to be noxious as to decide it to be false, unless the opinion condemned has full opportunity of defending itself. And it will not do to say that the heretic may be allowed to maintain the utility or harmlessness of his opinion, though forbidden to maintain its truth. The truth of an opinion is part of its utility. If we would know whether or not it is desirable that a proposition should be believed, is it possible to exclude the

---

2. [The quotation is from Thomas Carlyle's "Memoirs of the Life of Scott," reprinted in his *Critical and Miscellaneous Essays.*]

consideration of whether or not it is true? In the opinion, not of bad men, but of the best men, no belief which is contrary to truth can be really useful; and can you prevent such men from urging that plea when they are charged with culpability for denying some doctrine which they are told is useful, but which they believe to be false? Those who are on the side of received opinions never fail to take all possible advantage of this plea; you do not find *them* handling the question of utility as if it could be completely abstracted from that of truth; on the contrary, it is, above all, because their doctrine is "the truth" that the knowledge or the belief of it is held to be so indispensable. There can be no fair discussion of the question of usefulness when an argument so vital may be employed on one side, but not on the other. And in point of fact, when law or public feeling do not permit the truth of an opinion to be disputed, they are just as little tolerant of a denial of its usefulness. The utmost they allow is an extenuation of its absolute necessity, or of the positive guilt of rejecting it.

In order more fully to illustrate the mischief of denying a hearing to opinions because we, in our own judgment, have condemned them, it will be desirable to fix down the discussion to a concrete case; and I choose, by preference, the cases which are least favorable to me—in which the argument against freedom of opinion, both on the score of truth and on that of utility, is considered the strongest. Let the opinions impugned be the belief in a God and in a future state, or any of the commonly received doctrines of morality. To fight the battle on such ground gives a great advantage to an unfair antagonist, since he will be sure to say (and many who have no desire to be unfair will say it internally), Are these the doctrines which you do not deem sufficiently certain to be taken under the protection of law? Is the belief in a God one of the opinions to feel sure of which you hold to be assuming infallibility? But I must be permitted to observe that it is not the feeling sure of a doctrine (be it what it may) which I call an assumption of infallibility. It is the undertaking to decide that question *for others*, without allowing them to hear what can be said on the contrary side. And I denounce and reprobate this pretension not the less if put forth on the side of my most solemn convictions. However positive anyone's persuasion may be, not only of the falsity but of

the pernicious consequences—not only of the pernicious consequences, but (to adopt expressions which I altogether condemn) the immorality and impiety of an opinion—yet if, in pursuance of that private judgment, though backed by the public judgment of his country or his contemporaries, he prevents the opinion from being heard in its defense, he assumes infallibility. And so far from the assumption being less objectionable or less dangerous because the opinion is called immoral or impious, this is the case of all others in which it is most fatal. These are exactly the occasions on which the men of one generation commit those dreadful mistakes which excite the astonishment and horror of posterity. It is among such that we find the instances memorable in history, when the arm of the law has been employed to root out the best men and the noblest doctrines; with deplorable success as to the men, though some of the doctrines have survived to be (as if in mockery) invoked in defense of similar conduct toward those who dissent from *them,* or from their received interpretation.[. . .]

Let us now pass to the second division of the argument, and dismissing the supposition that any of the received opinions may be false, let us assume them to be true and examine into the worth of the manner in which they are likely to be held when their truth is not freely and openly canvassed. However unwillingly a person who has a strong opinion may admit the possibility that his opinion may be false, he ought to be moved by the consideration that, however true it may be, if it is not fully, frequently, and fearlessly discussed, it will be held as a dead dogma, not a living truth.

There is a class of persons (happily not quite so numerous as formerly) who think it enough if a person assents undoubtingly to what they think true, though he has no knowledge whatever of the grounds of the opinion and could not make a tenable defense of it against the most superficial objections. Such persons, if they can once get their creed taught from authority, naturally think that no good, and some harm, comes of its being allowed to be questioned. Where their influence prevails, they make it nearly impossible for the received opinion to be rejected wisely and considerately, though it may still be rejected rashly and ignorantly; for to shut out discussion entirely is seldom possible, and when it once gets in, beliefs not grounded on conviction are apt to give way before the slightest semblance of an argument. Waiving, however, this possibility—assuming that the true opinion abides in the mind, but abides as a prejudice, a belief independent of, and proof against, argument—this is not the way in which truth ought to be held by a rational being. This is not knowing the truth. Truth, thus held, is but one superstition the more, accidentally clinging to the words which enunciate a truth.

If the intellect and judgment of mankind ought to be cultivated, a thing which Protestants at least do not deny, on what can these faculties be more appropriately exercised by anyone than on the things which concern him so much that it is considered necessary for him to hold opinions on them? If the cultivation of the understanding consists in one thing more than in another, it is surely in learning the grounds of one's own opinions. Whatever people believe, on subjects on which it is of the first importance to believe rightly, they ought to be able to defend against at least the common objections. But, someone may say, "Let them be *taught* the grounds of their opinions. It does not follow that opinions must be merely parroted because they are never heard controverted. Persons who learn geometry do not simply commit the theorems to memory, but understand and learn likewise the demonstrations; and it would be absurd to say that they remain ignorant of the grounds of geometrical truths because they never hear anyone deny and attempt to disprove them." Undoubtedly: and such teaching suffices on a subject like mathematics, where there is nothing at all to be said on the wrong side of the question. The peculiarity of the evidence of mathematical truths is that all the argument is on one side. There are no objections, and no answers to objections. But on every subject on which difference of opinion is possible, the truth depends on a balance to be struck between two sets of conflicting reasons. Even in natural philosophy, there is always some other explanation possible of the same facts; some geocentric theory instead of heliocentric, some phlogiston instead of oxygen; and it has to be shown why that other theory cannot be the true one; and until this is shown, and until we know how it is shown, we do not understand the grounds of our opinion. But when we turn to subjects infinitely more complicated, to morals, religion,

politics, social relations, and the business of life, three-fourths of the arguments for every disputed opinion consist in dispelling the appearance which favor some opinion different from it. The greatest orator, save one, of antiquity, has left it on record that he always studied his adversary's case with as great, if not still greater, intensity than even his own. What Cicero practiced as the means of forensic success requires to be imitated by all who study any subject in order to arrive at the truth. He who knows only his own side of the case knows little of that. His reasons may be good, and no one may have been able to refute them. But if he is equally unable to refute the reasons on the opposite side, if he does not so much as know what they are, he has no ground for preferring either opinion. The rational position for him would be suspension of judgment, and unless he contents himself with that, he is either led by authority or adopts, like the generality of the world, the side to which he feels most inclination. Nor is it enough that he should hear the arguments of adversaries from his own teachers, presented as they state them, and accompanied by what they offer as refutations. That is not the way to do justice to the arguments or bring them into real contact with his own mind. He must be able to hear them from persons who actually believe them, who defend them in earnest and do their very utmost for them. He must know them in their most plausible and persuasive form; he must feel the whole force of the difficulty which the true view of the subject has to encounter and dispose of, else he will never really possess himself of the portion of truth which meets and removes that difficulty. Ninety-nine in a hundred of what are called educated men are in this condition, even of those who can argue fluently for their opinions. Their conclusion may be true, but it might be false for anything they know; they have never thrown themselves into the mental position of those who think differently from them, and considered what such persons may have to say; and, consequently, they do not, in any proper sense of the word, know the doctrine which they themselves profess. They do not know those parts of it which explain and justify the remainder—the considerations which show that a fact which seemingly conflicts with another is reconcilable with it, or that, of two apparently

strong reasons, one and not the other ought to be preferred. All that part of the truth which turns the scale
and decides the judgment of a completely informed
mind, they are strangers to; nor is it ever really known
but to those who have attended equally and impartially to both sides and endeavored to see the reasons
of both in the strongest light. So essential is this discipline to a real understanding of moral and human subjects that, if opponents of all-important truths do not
exist, it is indispensable to imagine them and supply
them with the strongest arguments which the most
skillful devil's advocate can conjure up.

To abate the force of these considerations, an enemy
of free discussion may be supposed to say that there is
no necessity for mankind in general to know and
understand all that can be said against or for their opinions by philosophers and theologians. That it is not
needful for common men to be able to expose all the
misstatements or fallacies of an ingenious opponent.
That it is enough if there is always somebody capable
of answering them, so that nothing likely to mislead
uninstructed persons remains unrefuted. That simple
minds, having been taught the obvious grounds of the
truths inculcated in them, may trust to authority for the
rest and, being aware that they have neither knowledge
nor talent to resolve every difficulty which can be
raised, may repose in the assurance that all those which
have been raised have been or can be answered by those
who are specially trained to the task.

Conceding to this view of the subject the utmost
that can be claimed for it by those most easily satisfied
with the amount of understanding of truth which
ought to accompany the belief of it, even so, the argument for free discussion is noway weakened. For
even this doctrine acknowledges that mankind ought
to have a rational assurance that all objections have
been satisfactorily answered; and how are they to be
answered if that which requires to be answered is not
spoken? Or how can the answer be known to be satisfactory if the objectors have no opportunity of
showing that it is unsatisfactory? If not the public, at
least the philosophers and theologians who are to resolve the difficulties must make themselves familiar
with those difficulties in their most puzzling form; and
this cannot be accomplished unless they are freely

stated and placed in the most advantageous light
which they admit of.[. . .]

We have now recognized the necessity to the mental well-being of mankind (on which all their other
well-being depends) of freedom of opinion, and freedom of the expression of opinion, on four distinct
grounds, which we will now briefly recapitulate:

First, if any opinion is compelled to silence, that
opinion may, for aught we can certainly know, be true.
To deny this is to assume our own infallibility.

Secondly, though the silenced opinion be an error, it
may, and very commonly does, contain a portion of
truth; and since the general or prevailing opinion on any
subject is rarely or never the whole truth, it is only by
the collision of adverse opinions that the remainder of
the truth has any chance of being supplied.

Thirdly, even if the received opinion be not only true,
but the whole truth; unless it is suffered to be, and actually is, vigorously and earnestly contested, it will, by most
of those who receive it, be held in the manner of a prejudice, with little comprehension or feeling of its rational
grounds. And not only this, but, fourthly, the meaning of
the doctrine itself will be in danger of being lost or en-
feebled, and deprived of its vital effect on the character
and conduct: the dogma becoming a mere formal profession, inefficacious for good, but cumbering the
ground and preventing the growth of any real and heart-
felt conviction from reason or personal experience.

Before quitting the subject of freedom of opinion, it
is fit to take some notice of those who say that the free
expression of all opinions should be permitted on condition that the manner be temperate, and do not pass the
bounds of fair discussion. Much might be said on the
impossibility of fixing where these supposed bounds are
to be placed; for if the test be offense to those whose
opinions are attacked, I think experience testifies that
this offense is given whenever the attack is telling and
powerful, and that every opponent who pushes them
hard, and whom they find it difficult to answer, appears
to them, if he shows any strong feeling on the subject,
an intemperate opponent. But this, though an important consideration in a practical point of view, merges in
a more fundamental objection. Undoubtedly, the manner of asserting an opinion, even though it be a true one,
may be very objectionable and may justly incur severe

censure. But the principal offenses of the kind are such as it is mostly impossible, unless by accidental self-betrayal, to bring home to conviction. The gravest of them is, to argue sophistically, to suppress facts or arguments, to mistake the elements of the case, or misrepresent the opposite opinion. But all this, even to the most aggravated degree, is so continually done in perfect good faith by persons who are not considered, and in many other respects may not deserve to be considered, ignorant or incompetent, that it is rarely possible, on adequate grounds, conscientiously to stamp the misrepresentation as morally culpable, and still less could law presume to interfere with this kind of controversial misconduct. With regard to what is commonly meant by intemperate discussion, namely invective, sarcasm, personality, and the like, the denunciation of these weapons would deserve more sympathy if it were ever proposed to interdict them equally to both sides; but it is only desired to restrain the employment of them against the prevailing opinion; against the unprevailing they may not only be used without general disapproval, but will be likely to obtain for him who uses them the praise of honest zeal and righteous indignation. Yet whatever mischief arises from their use is greatest when they are employed against the comparatively defenseless; and whatever unfair advantage can be derived by any opinion from this mode of asserting it accrues almost exclusively to received opinions. The worst offense of this kind which can be committed by a polemic is to stigmatize those who hold the contrary opinion as bad and immoral men. To calumny of this sort, those who hold any unpopular opinion are peculiarly exposed, because they are in general few and uninfluential, and nobody but themselves feels much interested in seeing justice done them; but this weapon is, from the nature of the case, denied to those who attack a prevailing opinion: they can neither use it with safety to themselves, nor, if they could, would it do anything but recoil on their own cause. In general, opinions contrary to those commonly received can only obtain a hearing by studied moderation of language and the most cautious avoidance of unnecessary offense, from which they hardly ever deviate even in a slight degree without losing ground, while unmeasured vituperation employed on the side of the prevailing opinion really does deter people from professing contrary opinions and from listening to those who profess them. For the interest, therefore, of truth and justice it is far more important to restrain this employment of vituperative language than the other; and, for example, if it were necessary to choose, there would be much more need to discourage offensive attacks on infidelity than on religion. It is, however, obvious that law and authority have no business with restraining either, while opinion ought, in every instance, to determine its verdict by the circumstances of the individual case—condemning everyone, on whichever side of the argument he places himself, in whose mode of advocacy either want of candor, or malignity, bigotry, or intolerance of feeling manifest themselves; but not inferring these vices from the side which a person takes, though it be the contrary side of the question to our own; and giving merited honor to everyone, whatever opinion he may hold, who has calmness to see and honesty to state what his opponents and their opinions really are, exaggerating nothing to their discredit, keeping nothing back which tells, or can be supposed to tell, in their favor. This is the real morality of public discussion; and if often violated, I am happy to think that there are many controversialists who to a great extent observe it, and a still greater number who conscientiously strive toward it.

Karl Marx

Economic and Philosophic Manuscripts of 1844

Alienated Labor

We have proceeded from the presuppositions of political economy. We have accepted its language and its laws. We presupposed private property, the separation of labor, capital and land, hence of wages, profit of capital and rent, likewise the division of labor, competition, the concept of exchange value, etc. From political economy itself, in its own words, we have shown that the worker sinks to the level of a commodity, the most miserable commodity; that the misery of the worker is inversely proportional to the power and volume of his production; that the necessary result of competition is the accumulation of capital in a few hands and thus the revival of monopoly in a more frightful form; and finally that the distinction between capitalist and landowner, between agricultural laborer and industrial worker, disappears and the whole society must divide into the two classes of *proprietors* and propertyless *workers.*

Political economy proceeds from the fact of private property. It does not explain private property. It grasps the actual, *material* process of private property in abstract and general formulae which it then takes as *laws.* It does not *comprehend* these laws, that is, does not prove them as proceeding from the nature of private property. Political economy does not disclose the reason for the division between capital and labor, between capital and land. When, for example, the relation of wages to profits is determined, the ultimate basis is taken to be the interest of the capitalists; that is, political economy assumes what it should develop. Similarly, competition is referred to at every point and explained from external circumstances. Political economy teaches us nothing about the extent to which these external, apparently accidental circumstances are simply the expression of a necessary development. We have seen how political economy regards exchange itself as an accidental fact. The only wheels which political economy puts in motion are *greed* and the *war among the greedy, competition.*

Just because political economy does not grasp the interconnections within the movement, the doctrine of competition could stand opposed to the doctrine of monopoly, the doctrine of freedom of craft to that of the guild, the doctrine of the division of landed property to that of the great estate. Competition, freedom of craft, and division of landed property were developed and conceived only as accidental, deliberate, forced consequences of monopoly, the guild, and feudal property, rather than necessary, inevitable, natural consequences.

We now have to grasp the essential connection among private property, greed, division of labor, capital and landownership, and the connection of exchange with competition, of value with the devaluation of men, of monopoly with competition, etc., and of this whole alienation with the *money*-system.

Let us not put ourselves in a fictitious primordial state like a political economist trying to clarify things. Such a primordial state clarifies nothing. It merely pushes the issue into a gray, misty distance. It acknowledges as a fact or event what it should deduce, namely, the necessary relation between two things for example, between division of labor and exchange. In such a manner theology explains the origin of evil by the fall of man. That is, it asserts as a fact in the form of history what it should explain.

We proceed from a *present* fact of political economy.

The worker becomes poorer the more wealth he produces, the more his production increases in power and extent. The worker becomes a cheaper commodity the more commodities he produces. The *increase in value* of the world of things is directly proportional to the *decrease*

From Karl Marx, *Writings of the Young Marx on Philosophy and Society,* edited and translated by Loyd D. Easton and Kurt H. Guddat. Copyright © 1967 by Doubleday & Company, Inc. Reprinted, with corrections, in 1997 by Hackett Publishing Company. Reprinted by permission of the publisher.

in value of the human world. Labor not only produces commodities. It also produces itself and the worker as a *commodity,* and indeed in the same proportion as it produces commodities in general.

This fact simply indicates that the object which labor produces, its product, stands opposed to it as an *alien thing,* as a *power independent* of the producer. The product of labor is labor embodied and made objective in a thing. It is the *objectification* of labor. The realization of labor is its objectification. In the viewpoint of political economy this realization of labor appears as the *diminution* of the worker, the objectification as the *loss of and subservience to the object,* and the appropriation as *alienation,* as externalization.

So much does the realization of labor appear as diminution that the worker is diminished to the point of starvation. So much does objectification appear as loss of the object that the worker is robbed of the most essential objects not only of life but also of work. Indeed, work itself becomes a thing of which he can take possession only with the greatest effort and with the most unpredictable interruptions. So much does the appropriation of the object appear as alienation that the more objects the worker produces, the fewer he can own and the more he falls under the domination of his product, of capital.

All these consequences follow from the fact that the worker is related to the *product of his labor* as to an *alien* object. For it is clear according to this premise: The more the worker exerts himself, the more powerful becomes the alien objective world which he fashions against himself, the poorer he and his inner world become, the less there is that belongs to him. It is the same in religion. The more man attributes to God, the less he retains in himself. The worker puts his life into the object; then it no longer belongs to him but to the object. The greater this activity, the poorer is the worker. What the product of his work is, he is not. The greater this product is, the smaller is he himself. The *externalization* of the worker in his product means not only that his work becomes an object, an *external* existence, but also that it exists *outside him* independently, alien, an autonomous power, opposed to him. The life he has given to the object confronts him as hostile and alien.

Let us now consider more closely the *objectification,* the worker's production and with it the *alienation* and *loss* of the object, his product.

The worker can make nothing without *nature,* without the *sensuous external world.* It is the material wherein his labor realizes itself, wherein it is active, out of which and by means of which it produces.

But as nature furnishes to labor the *means of life* in the sense that labor cannot *live* without objects upon which labor is exercised, nature also furnishes the *means of life* in the narrower sense, namely, the means of physical subsistence of the *worker* himself.

The more the worker *appropriates* the external world and sensuous nature through his labor, the more he deprives himself of the *means of life* in two respects: first, that the sensuous external world gradually ceases to be an object belonging to his labor, a *means of life* of his work; secondly, that it gradually ceases to be a *means of life* in the immediate sense, a means of physical subsistence of the worker.

In these two respects, therefore, the worker becomes a slave to his objects; first, in that he receives an *object of labor,* that is, he receives *labor,* and secondly that he receives the *means of subsistence.* The first enables him to exist as a *worker* and the second as a *physical subject.* The terminus of this slavery is that he can only maintain himself as a *physical subject* so far as he is a *worker,* and only as a *physical subject* is he a worker.

(The alienation of the worker in his object is expressed according to the laws of political economy as follows: the more the worker produces, the less he has to consume; the more values he creates the more worthless and unworthy he becomes; the better shaped his product, the more misshapen is he; the more civilized his product, the more barbaric is the worker; the more powerful the work, the more powerless becomes the worker; the more intelligence the work has, the more witless is the worker and the more he becomes a slave of nature.)

Political economy conceals the alienation in the nature of labor by ignoring the direct relationship between the worker (labor) *and production.* To be sure, labor produces marvels for the wealthy but it produces deprivation for the worker. It produces palaces, but hovels for the worker. It produces beauty, but mutilation for the worker. It displaces labor through machines, but it throws some workers back into barbarous labor and turns others into machines. It produces intelligence, but for the worker it produces imbecility and cretinism.

The direct relationship of labor to its products is the relationship of the worker to the objects of his production. The relationship of the rich to the objects of production and to production itself is only a *consequence* of this first relationship and confirms it. Later we shall observe the latter aspect.

Thus, when we ask, What is the essential relationship of labor? we ask about the relationship of the *worker* to production.

Up to now we have considered the alienation, the externalization of the worker only from one side: his *relationship to the products of his labor.* But alienation is shown not only in the result but also in the *process of production,* in the *producing activity* itself. How could the worker stand in an alien relationship to the product of his activity if he did not alienate himself from himself in the very act of production? After all, the product is only the résumé of activity, of production. If the product of work is externalization, production itself must be active externalization, externalization of activity, activity of externalization. Only alienation—and externalization in the activity of labor itself—is summarized in the alienation of the object of labor.

What constitutes the externalization of labor?

First is the fact that labor is *external* to the laborer—that is, it is not part of his nature—and that the worker does not affirm himself in his work but denies himself, feels miserable and unhappy, develops no free physical and mental energy but mortifies his flesh and ruins his mind. The worker, therefore feels at ease only outside work, and during work he is outside himself. He is at home when he is not working and when he is working he is not at home. His work, therefore, is not voluntary, but coerced, *forced labor.* It is not the satisfaction of a need but only a *means* to satisfy other needs. Its alien character is obvious from the fact that as soon as no physical or other pressure exists, labor is avoided like the plague. External labor, labor in which man is externalized, is labor of self-sacrifice, of penance. Finally, the external nature of work for the worker appears in the fact that it is not his own but another person's, that in work he does not belong to himself but to someone else. In religion the spontaneity of human imagination, the spontaneity of the human brain and heart, acts independently of the individual as an alien, divine or devilish activity. Similarly,

the activity of the worker is not his own spontaneous activity. It belongs to another. It is the loss of his own self.

The result, therefore, is that man (the worker) feels that he is acting freely only in his animal functions—eating, drinking, and procreating, or at most in his shelter and finery—while in his human functions he feels only like an animal. The animalistic becomes the human and the human the animalistic.

To be sure, eating, drinking, and procreation are genuine human functions. In abstraction, however, and separated from the remaining sphere of human activities and turned into final and sole ends, they are animal functions.

We have considered labor, the act of alienation of practical human activity, in two aspects: (1) the relationship of the worker to the *product of labor* as an alien object dominating him. This relationship is at the same time the relationship to the sensuous external world, to natural objects as an alien world hostile to him; (2) the relationship of labor to the *act of production* in *labor.* This relationship is that of the worker to his own activity as alien and not belonging to him, activity as passivity, power as weakness, procreation as emasculation, the worker's *own* physical and spiritual energy, his personal life—for what else is life but activity—as an activity turned against him, independent of him, and not belonging to him. *Self-alienation,* as against the alienation of the *object,* stated above.

We have now to derive a third aspect of *alienated labor* from the two previous ones.

Man is a species-being not only in that he practically and theoretically makes his own species as well as that of other things his object, but also—and this is only another expression for the same thing—in that as present and living species he considers himself to be a *universal* and consequently *free* being.

The life of the species in man as in animals is physical in that man, (like the animal) lives by inorganic nature. And as man is more universal than the animal, the realm of inorganic nature by which he lives is more universal. As plants, animals, minerals, air, light, etc., in theory form a part of human consciousness, partly as objects of natural science, partly as objects of art—his spiritual inorganic nature or spiritual means of life which he first must prepare for enjoyment and assimilation—so they also form in practice a part of human life and human activity. Man lives physically only by these products of nature; they may appear in the form of food, heat, clothing, housing, etc. The universality of man appears in practice in the universality which makes the whole of nature his *inorganic* body: (1) as a direct means of life, and (2) as the matter, object, and instrument of his life activity. Nature is the *inorganic body* of man, that is, nature insofar as it is not the human body. Man *lives* by nature. This means that nature is his *body* with which he must remain in perpetual process in order not to die. That the physical and spiritual life of man is tied up with nature is another way of saying that nature is linked to itself, for man is a part of nature.

In alienating (1) nature from man, and (2) man from himself, his own active function, his life activity, alienated labor also alienates the *species* from him; it makes *species-life* the means of individual life. In the first place it alienates species-life and the individual life, and secondly it turns the latter in its abstraction into the purpose of the former, also in its abstract and alienated form.

For labor, *life activity,* and *productive life* appear to man at first only as a *means* to satisfy a need, the need to maintain physical existence. Productive life, however, is species-life. It is life begetting life. In the mode of life activity lies the entire character of a species, its species-character; and free conscious activity is the species-character of man. Life itself appears only as a *means of life.*

The animal is immediately one with its life activity, not distinct from it. The animal is *its life activity.* Man makes his life activity itself into an object of will and consciousness. He has conscious life activity. It is not a determination with which he immediately identifies. Conscious life activity distinguishes man immediately from the life activity of the animal. Only thereby is he a species-being. Or rather, he is only a conscious being—that is, his own life is an object for him—since he is a species-being. Only on that account is his activity free activity. Alienated labor reverses the relationship in that man, since he is a conscious being, makes his life activity, his *essence,* only a means for his *existence.*

The practical creation of an *objective world,* the *treatment* of inorganic nature, is proof that man is a conscious species-being, that is, a being which is related to its species as to its own essence or is related to itself as a species-being. To be sure animals also produce. They build themselves nests, dwelling places, like the bees, beavers, ants, etc. But the animal produces only what is immediately necessary for itself or its young. It produces in a one-sided way while man produces universally. The animal produces under the domination of immediate physical need while man produces free of physical need and only genuinely so in freedom from such need. The animal only produces itself while man reproduces the whole of nature. The animal's product belongs immediately to its physical body while man is free when he confronts his product. The animal builds only according to the standard and need of the species to which it belongs while man knows how to produce according to the standard of any species and at all times knows how to apply an intrinsic standard to the object. Thus man creates also according to the laws of beauty.

In the treatment of the objective world, therefore, man proves himself to be genuinely a *species-being.* This production is his active species-life. Through it nature appears as *his* work and his actuality. The object of labor is thus the *objectification of man's species-life:* he produces himself not only intellectually, as in consciousness, but also actively in a real sense and sees himself in a world he made. In taking from man the object of his production, alienated labor takes from his *species-life,* his actual and objective existence as a species. It changes his superiority to the animal to inferiority, since he is deprived of nature, his inorganic body.

By degrading free spontaneous activity to the level of a means, alienated labor makes the species-life of man a means of his physical existence.

The consciousness which man has from his species is altered through alienation, so that species-life becomes a means for him.

(3) Alienated labor hence turns the *species-existence of man,* and also nature as his mental species-capacity, into an existence *alien* to him, into the *means* of his *individual existence.* It alienates his spiritual nature, his *human essence,* from his own body and likewise from nature outside him.

(4) A direct consequence of man's alienation from the product of his work, from his life activity, and from his species-existence, is the *alienation of man* from *man.* When man confronts himself, he confronts *other* men. What holds true of man's relationship to his work, to

the product of his work, and to himself, also holds true of man's relationship to other men, to their labor, and the object of their labor.

In general, the statement that man is alienated from his species-existence means that one man is alienated from another just as each man is alienated from human nature.

The alienation of man, the relation of man to himself, is realized and expressed in the relation between man and other men.

Thus in the relation of alienated labor every man sees the others according to the standard and the relation in which he finds himself as a worker.

We began with an economic fact, the alienation of the worker and his product. We have given expression to the concept of this fact: *alienated, externalized* labor. We have analyzed this concept and have thus analyzed merely a fact of political economy.

Let us now see further how the concept of alienated, externalized labor must express and represent itself in actuality.

If the product of labor is alien to me, confronts me as an alien power, to whom then does it belong?

If my own activity does not belong to me, if it is an alien and forced activity, to whom then does it belong?

To a being *other* than myself.

Who is this being?

Gods? To be sure, in early times the main production, for example, the building of temples in Egypt, India, and Mexico, appears to be in the service of the gods, just as the product belongs to the gods. But gods alone were never workmasters. The same is true of *nature*. And what a contradiction it would be if the more man subjugates nature through his work and the more the miracles of gods are rendered superfluous by the marvels of industry, man should renounce his joy in producing and the enjoyment of his product for love of these powers.

The *alien* being who owns labor and the product of labor, whom labor serves and whom the product of labor satisfies can only be *man* himself.

That the product of labor does not belong to the worker and an alien power confronts him is possible only because this product belongs to *a man other than the worker.* If his activity is torment for him, it must be the *pleasure* and the life-enjoyment for another. Not gods, not nature, but only man himself can be this alien power over man.

Let us consider the statement previously made, that the relationship of man to himself is *objective* and *actual* to him only through his relationship to other men. If man is related to the product of his labor, to his objectified labor, as to an *alien,* hostile, powerful object independent of him, he is so related that another alien, hostile, powerful man independent of him is the lord of this object. If he is unfree in relation to his own activity, he is related to it as bonded activity, activity under the domination, coercion, and yoke of another man.

Every self-alienation of man, from himself and from nature, appears in the relationship which he postulates between other men and himself and nature. Thus religious self-alienation appears necessarily in the relation of laity to priest, or also to a mediator, since we are here now concerned with the spiritual world. In the practical real world self-alienation can appear only in the practical real relationships to other men. The means whereby the alienation proceeds is a *practical* means. Through alienated labor man thus not only produces his relationship to the object and to the act of production as an alien man at enmity with him. He also creates the relation in which other men stand to his production and product, and the relation in which he stands to these other men. Just as he begets his own production as loss of his reality, as his punishment; just as he begets his own product as a loss, a product not belonging to him, so he begets the domination of the non-producer over production and over product. As he alienates his own activity from himself, he confers upon the stranger an activity which is not his own.

Up to this point, we have investigated the relationship only from the side of the worker and will later investigate it also from the side of the non-worker.

Thus through *alienated externalized labor* does the worker create the relation to this work of man alienated to labor and standing outside it. The relation of the worker to labor produces the relation of the capitalist to labor, or whatever one wishes to call the lord of labor. *Private property* is thus product, result, and necessary consequence of *externalized labor,* of the external relation of the worker to nature and to himself.

Private property thus is derived, through analysis, from the concept of *externalized labor,* that is, *externalized man,* alienated labor, alienated life, and *alienated* man.

We have obtained the concept of *externalized labor* (*externalized life*) from political economy as a result of the *movement of private property.* But the analysis of this idea shows that though private property appears to be the ground and cause of externalized labor, it is rather a consequence of externalized labor, just as gods are *originally* not the cause but the effect of an aberration of the human mind. Later this relationship reverses.

Only at the final culmination of the development of private property does this, its secret, reappear—namely, that on the one hand it is the *product* of externalized labor and that secondly it is the *means* through which labor externalizes itself, the *realization of this externalization.*

This development throws light on several conflicts hitherto unresolved.

(1) Political economy proceeds from labor as the very soul of production and yet gives labor nothing, private property everything. From this contradiction Proudhon decided in favor of labor and against private property. We perceive, however, that this apparent contradiction is the contradiction of *alienated labor* with itself and that political economy has only formulated the laws of alienated labor.

Therefore we also perceive that *wages* and *private property* are identical: for when the product, the object of labor, pays for the labor itself, wages are only a necessary consequence of the alienation of labor. In wages labor appears not as an end in itself but as the servant of wages. We shall develop this later and now only draw some conclusions.

An enforced *raising of wages* (disregarding all other difficulties, including that this anomaly could only be maintained forcibly) would therefore be nothing but a *better slave-salary* and would not achieve either for the worker or for labor human significance and dignity.

Even the *equality of wages,* as advanced by Proudhon, would only convert the relation of the contemporary worker to his work into the relation of all men to labor. Society would then be conceived as an abstract capitalist.

Wages are a direct result of alienated labor, and alienated labor is the direct cause of private property. The downfall of one is necessarily the downfall of the other.

(2) From the relation of alienated labor to private property it follows further that the emancipation of society from private property, etc., from servitude, is expressed in its *political* form as the *emancipation of workers,* not as though it is only a question of their emancipation but because in their emancipation is contained universal human emancipation. It is contained in their emancipation because the whole of human servitude is involved in the relation of worker to production, and all relations of servitude are only modifications and consequences of the worker's relation to production.

As we have found the concept of *private property* through *analysis* from the concept of *alienated, externalized labor,* so we can develop all the *categories* of political economy with the aid of these two factors, and we shall again find in each category—for example, barter, competition, capital, money—only a *particular* and *developed expression* of these primary foundations.

Before considering this configuration, however, let us try to solve two problems.

(1) To determine the general *nature of private property* as a result of alienated labor in its relation to *truly human* and *social property.*

(2) We have taken the *alienation of labor* and its *externalization* as a fact and analyzed this fact. How, we ask now, does it happen that *man externalizes* his *labor,* alienates it? How is this alienation rooted in the nature of human development? We have already achieved much in resolving the problem by *transforming* the question concerning the *origin of private property* into the question concerning the relationship of *externalized labor* to evolution of humanity. In talking about *private property* one believes he is dealing with something external to man. Talking of labor, one is immediately dealing with man himself. This new formulation of the problem already contains its solution.

On (1) *The general nature of private property and its relation to truly human property.*

We have resolved alienated labor into two parts which mutually determine each other or rather are only different expressions of one and the same relationship. *Appropriation* appears as *alienation,* as *externalization; externalization* as *appropriation; alienation* as the true *naturalization.*

We considered the one side, *externalized* labor, in relation to the *worker* himself, that is, the *relation of externalized labor to itself.* We have found the *property relation of the non-worker* to the *worker* and *labor* to be the product, the necessary result, of this relationship. *Private property* as the material, summarized expression of externalized labor embraces both relationships—the *relationship of worker to labor, the product of his work, and the non-worker;* and the relationship of the *non-worker to the worker* and *the product of his labor.*

As we have seen that in relation to the worker who *appropriates* nature through his labor the appropriation appears as alienation—self-activity as activity for another and of another, living as the sacrifice of life, production of the object as loss of it to an alien power, an *alien* man—we now consider the relationship of this *alien* man to the worker, to labor and its object.

It should be noted first that everything which appears with the worker as an *activity of externalization* and an ac-

tivity of alienation appears with the non-worker as a *condition of externalization,* a *condition of alienation.*

Secondly, that the *actual, practical attitude* of the worker in production and to his product (as a condition of mind) appears as a *theoretical* attitude in the non-worker confronting him.

Thirdly, the non-worker does everything against the worker which the worker does against himself, but he does not do against his own self what he does against the worker.

Let us consider more closely these three relationships. [Here the manuscript breaks off, unfinished.]

John Rawls

The Original Position and the Principles of Justice

3. The Main Idea of the Theory of Justice

My aim is to present a conception of justice which generalizes and carries to a higher level of abstraction the familiar theory of the social contract as found, say, in Locke, Rousseau, and Kant. In order to do this we are not to think of the original contract as one to enter a particular society or to set up a particular form of government. Rather, the guiding idea is that the principles of justice for the basic structure of society are the object of the original agreement. They are the principles that free and rational persons concerned to further their own interests would accept in an initial position of equality as defining the fundamental terms of their association. These principles are to regulate all further

agreements; they specify the kinds of social cooperation that can be entered into and the forms of government that can be established. This way of regarding the principles of justice I shall call justice as fairness.

Thus we are to imagine that those who engage in social cooperation choose together, in one joint act, the principles which are to assign basic rights and duties and to determine the division of social benefits. Men are to decide in advance how they are to regulate their claims against one another and what is to be the foundation charter of their society. Just as each person must decide by rational reflection what constitutes his good, that is, the system of ends which it is rational for him to pursue, so a group of persons must decide once and for all what is to count among them as just and unjust. The choice which rational men would make in this hypothetical situation of equal liberty, assuming for the present that this choice problem has a solution, determines the principles of justice.

In justice as fairness the original position of equality corresponds to the state of nature in the traditional theory of the social contract. This original position is not, of course, thought of as an actual historical state of affairs, much less as a primitive condition of culture. It is understood as a purely hypothetical situation characterized so as to lead to a certain conception of justice. Among the essential features of this situation is that no one knows his place in society, his class position or social status, nor does any one know his fortune in the distribution of natural assets and abilities, his intelligence, strength, and the like. I shall even assume that the parties do not know their conceptions of the good or their special psychological propensities. The principles of justice are chosen behind a veil of ignorance. This ensures that no one is advantaged or disadvantaged in the choice of principles by the outcome of natural chance or the contingency of social circumstances. Since all are similarly situated and no one is able to design principles to favor his particular condition, the principles of justice are the result of a fair agreement or bargain. For given the circumstances of the original position, the symmetry of everyone's relations to each other, this initial situation is fair between individuals as moral persons, that is, as rational beings with their own ends and capable, I shall assume, of a sense of justice. The original position is, one might say, the appropriate initial status quo, and thus the fundamental agreements reached in it are fair. This explains the propriety of the name "justice as fairness": it conveys the idea that the principles of justice are agreed to in an initial situation that is fair. The name does not mean that the concepts of justice and fairness are the same, any more than the phrase "poetry as metaphor" means that the concepts of poetry and metaphor are the same.

Justice as fairness begins, as I have said, with one of the most general of all choices which persons might make together, namely, with the choice of the first principles of a conception of justice which is to regulate all subsequent criticism and reform of institutions. Then, having chosen a conception of justice, we can suppose that they are to choose a constitution and a legislature to enact laws, and so on, all in accordance with the principles of justice initially agreed upon. Our social situation is just if it is such that by this sequence of hypothetical agreements we would have contracted into the general system of rules which defines it. Moreover, assuming that the original position does deter-

mine a set of principles (that is, that a particular conception of justice would be chosen), it will then be true that whenever social institutions satisfy these principles those engaged in them can say to one another that they are cooperating on terms to which they would agree if they were free and equal persons whose relations with respect to one another were fair. They could all view their arrangements as meeting the stipulations which they would acknowledge in an initial situation that embodies widely accepted and reasonable constraints on the choice of principles. The general recognition of this fact would provide the basis for a public acceptance of the corresponding principles of justice. No society can, of course, be a scheme of cooperation which men enter voluntarily in a literal sense; each person finds himself placed at birth in some particular position in some particular society, and the nature of this position materially affects his life prospects. Yet a society satisfying the principles of justice as fairness comes as close as a society can to being a voluntary scheme, for it meets the principles which free and equal persons would assent to under circumstances that are fair. In this sense its members are autonomous and the obligations they recognize self-imposed.

One feature of justice as fairness is to think of the parties in the initial situation as rational and mutually disinterested. This does not mean that the parties are egoists, that is, individuals with only certain kinds of interests, say in wealth, prestige, and domination. But they are conceived as not taking an interest in one another's interests. They are to presume that even their spiritual aims may be opposed, in the way that the aims of those of different religions may be opposed. Moreover, the concept of rationality must be interpreted as far as possible in the narrow sense, standard in economic theory, of taking the most effective means to given ends. The initial situation must be characterized by stipulations that are widely accepted.

In working out the conception of justice as fairness one main task clearly is to determine which principles of justice would be chosen in the original position. To do this we must describe this situation in some detail and formulate with care the problem of choice which it presents. It may be observed, however, that once the principles of justice are thought of as arising from an original agreement in a situation of equality, it is an open question whether the principle of utility would be acknowledged. Offhand it hardly seems likely that persons who view themselves as equals, entitled to press their claims upon one another, would agree to a principle which may require lesser life prospects for some simply for the sake of a greater sum of advantages enjoyed by others. Since each desires to protect his interests, his capacity to advance his conception of the good, no one has a reason to acquiesce in an enduring loss for himself in order to bring about a greater net balance of satisfaction. In the absence of strong and lasting benevolent impulses, a rational man would not accept a basic structure merely because it maximized the algebraic sum of advantages irrespective of its permanent effects on his own basic rights and interests. Thus it seems that the principle of utility is incompatible with the conception of social cooperation among equals for mutual advantage. It appears to be inconsistent with the idea of reciprocity implicit in the notion of a well-ordered society. Or, at any rate, so I shall argue.

I shall maintain instead that the persons in the initial situation would choose two rather different principles: the first requires equality in the assignment of basic rights and duties, while the second holds that social and economic inequalities, for example inequalities of wealth and authority, are just only if they result in compensating benefits for everyone, and in particular for the least advantaged members of society. These principles rule out justifying institutions on the grounds that the hardships of some are offset by a greater good in the aggregate. It may be expedient but it is not just that some should have less in order that others may prosper. But there is no injustice in the greater benefits earned by a few provided that the situation of persons not so fortunate is thereby improved. The intuitive idea is that since everyone's well-being depends upon a scheme of cooperation without which no one could have a satisfactory life, the division of advantages should be such as to draw forth the willing cooperation of everyone taking part in it, including those less well situated. The two principles mentioned seem to be a fair basis on which those better endowed, or more fortunate in their social position, neither of which we can be said to deserve, could expect the willing cooperation of others when some workable scheme is a necessary condition of the welfare of all. Once we decide to look for a conception of justice that prevents the use of the accidents of natural endowment and the contingencies of social circumstance as counters in a quest for political and economic advantage, we are led to these principles. They express the result of leaving aside those aspects of the social world that seem arbitrary from a moral point of view.

The problem of the choice of principles, however, is extremely difficult. I do not expect the answer I shall suggest to be convincing to everyone. It is, therefore, worth noting from the outset that justice as fairness, like other contract views, consists of two parts: (1) an interpretation of the initial situation and of the problem of choice posed there, and (2) a set of principles which, it is argued, would be agreed to. One may accept the first part of the theory (or some variant thereof), but not the other, and conversely. The concept of the initial contractual situation may seem reasonable although the particular principles proposed are rejected. To be sure, I want to maintain that the most appropriate conception of this situation does lead to principles of justice contrary to utilitarianism and perfectionism, and therefore that the contract doctrine provides an alternative to these views. Still, one may dispute this contention even though one grants that the contractarian method is a useful way of studying ethical theories and of setting forth their underlying assumptions.

Justice as fairness is an example of what I have called a contract theory. Now there may be an objection to the term "contract" and related expressions, but I think it will serve reasonably well. Many words have misleading connotations which at first are likely to confuse. The terms "utility" and "utilitarianism" are surely no exception. They too have unfortunate suggestions which hostile critics have been willing to exploit; yet they are clear enough for those prepared to study utilitarian doctrine. The same should be true of the term "contract" applied to moral theories. As I have mentioned, to understand it one has to keep in mind that it implies a certain level of abstraction. In particular, the content of the relevant agreement is not to enter a given society or to adopt a given form of government, but to accept certain moral principles. Moreover, the undertakings referred to are purely hypothetical: a contract view holds that certain principles would be accepted in a well-defined initial situation.

The merit of the contract terminology is that it conveys the idea that principles of justice may be conceived as principles that would be chosen by rational persons, and that in this way conceptions of justice may be explained and justified. The theory of justice is a part, perhaps the most significant part, of the theory of rational choice. Furthermore, principles of justice deal with conflicting claims upon the advantages won by social cooperation; they apply to the relations among several persons or groups. The word "contract" suggests this plurality as well as the condition that the appropriate division of advantages must be in accordance with principles acceptable to all parties. The condition of publicity for principles of justice is also connoted by the contract phraseology. Thus, if these principles are the outcome of an agreement, citizens have a knowledge of the principles that others follow. It is characteristic of contract theories to stress the public nature of political principles. Finally there is the long tradition of the contract doctrine. Expressing the tie with this line of thought helps to define ideas and accords with natural piety. There are then several advantages in the use of the term "contract." With due precautions taken, it should not be misleading.

A final remark. Justice as fairness is not a complete contract theory. For it is clear that the contractarian idea can be extended to the choice of more or less an entire ethical system, that is, to a system including principles for all the virtues and not only for justice. Now for the most part I shall consider only principles of justice and others closely related to them; I make no attempt to discuss the virtues in a systematic way. Obviously if justice as fairness succeeds reasonably well, a next step would be to study the more general view suggested by the name "rightness as fairness." But even this wider theory fails to embrace all moral relationships, since it would seem to include only our relations with other persons and to leave out of account how we are to conduct ourselves toward animals and the rest of nature. I do not contend that the contract notion offers a way to approach these questions which are certainly of the first importance; and I shall have to put them aside. We must recognize the limited scope of justice as fairness and of the general type of view that it exemplifies. How far its conclusions must be revised once these other matters are understood cannot be decided in advance.

4. The Original Position and Justification

I have said that the original position is the appropriate initial status quo which insures that the fundamental agreements reached in it are fair. This fact yields the name "justice as fairness." It is clear, then, that I want to say that one conception of justice is more reasonable than another, or justifiable with respect to it, if rational persons in the initial situation would choose its principles over those of the other for the role of justice. Conceptions of justice are to be ranked by their acceptability to persons so circumstanced. Understood in this way the question of justification is settled by working out a problem of deliberation: we have to ascertain which principles it would be rational to adopt given the contractual situation. This connects the theory of justice with the theory of rational choice.

If this view of the problem of justification is to succeed, we must, of course, describe in some detail the nature of this choice problem. A problem of rational decision has a definite answer only if we know the beliefs and interests of the parties, their relations with respect to one another, the alternatives between which they are to choose, the procedure whereby they make up their minds, and so on. As the circumstances are presented in different ways, correspondingly different principles are accepted. The concept of the original position, as I shall refer to it, is that of the most philosophically favored interpretation of this initial choice situation for the purposes of a theory of justice.

But how are we to decide what is the most favored interpretation? I assume, for one thing, that there is a broad measure of agreement that principles of justice should be chosen under certain conditions. To justify a particular description of the initial situation one shows that it incorporates these commonly shared presumptions. One argues from widely accepted but weak premises to more specific conclusions. Each of the presumptions should by itself be natural and plausible; some of them may seem innocuous or even trivial. The aim of the contract approach is to establish that taken together they impose significant bounds on acceptable principles of justice. The ideal outcome would be that these conditions determine a unique set of principles; but I shall be satisfied if they suffice to rank the main traditional conceptions of social justice.

One should not be misled, then, by the somewhat unusual conditions which characterize the original position. The idea here is simply to make vivid to ourselves the restrictions that it seems reasonable to impose on arguments for principles of justice, and therefore on these principles themselves. Thus it seems reasonable and generally acceptable that no one should be advantaged or disadvantaged by natural fortune or social circumstances in the choice of principles. It also seems widely agreed that it should be impossible to tailor principles to the circumstances of one's own case. We should insure further that particular inclinations and aspirations, and persons' conceptions of their good do not affect the principles adopted. The aim is to rule out those principles that it would be rational to propose for acceptance, however little the chance of success, only if one knew certain things that are irrelevant from the standpoint of justice. For example, if a man knew that he was wealthy, he might find it rational to advance the principle that various taxes for welfare measures be counted unjust; if he knew that he was poor, he would most likely propose the contrary principle. To represent the desired restrictions one imagines a situation in which everyone is deprived of this sort of information. One excludes the knowledge of those contingencies which sets men at odds and allows them to be guided by their prejudices. In this manner the veil of ignorance is arrived at in a natural way. This concept should cause no difficulty if we keep in mind the constraints on arguments that it is meant to express. At any time we can enter the original position, so to speak, simply by following a certain procedure, namely, by arguing for principles of justice in accordance with these restrictions.

It seems reasonable to suppose that the parties in the original position are equal. That is, all have the same rights in the procedure for choosing principles; each can make proposals, submit reasons for their acceptance, and so on. Obviously the purpose of these conditions is to represent equality between human beings as moral persons, as creatures having a conception of their good and capable of a sense of justice. The basis of equality is taken to be similarity in these two respects. Systems of ends are not ranked in value; and each man is presumed to have the requisite ability to understand and to act upon whatever principles are adopted. Together with the veil of ignorance, these conditions define the principles of justice as those which rational persons concerned to advance their interests would consent to as equals when none are known to be advantaged or disadvantaged by social and natural contingencies.

There is, however, another side to justifying a particular description of the original position. This is to see if the principles which would be chosen match our considered convictions of justice or extend them in an acceptable way. We can note whether applying these principles would lead us to make the same judgments about the basic structure of society which we now make intuitively and in which we have the greatest confidence; or whether, in cases where our present judgments are in doubt and given with hesitation, these principles offer a resolution which we can affirm on reflection. There are questions which we feel sure must be answered in a certain way. For example, we are confident that religious intolerance and racial discrimination are unjust. We think that we have examined these things with care and have reached what we believe is an impartial judgment not likely to be distorted by an excessive attention to our own interests. These convictions are provisional fixed points which we presume any conception of justice must fit. But we have much less assurance as to what is the correct distribution of wealth and authority. Here we may be looking for a way to remove our doubts. We can check an interpretation of the initial situation, then, by the capacity of its principles to accommodate our firmest convictions and to provide guidance where guidance is needed.

In searching for the most favored description of this situation we work from both ends. We begin by describing it so that it represents generally shared and preferably weak conditions. We then see if these conditions are strong enough to yield a significant set of principles. If not, we look for further premises equally reasonable. But if so, and these principles match our considered convictions of justice, then so far well and good. But presumably there will be discrepancies. In this case we have a choice. We can either modify the account of the initial situation or we can revise our existing judgments, for even the judgments we take provisionally as fixed points are liable to revision. By going back and forth, sometimes altering the conditions of the contractual circumstances, at others withdrawing our judgments and conforming them to principle, I assume that eventually we shall find a description of the initial situation that both expresses reasonable conditions and yields principles which match our considered judgments duly pruned and adjusted. This state of affairs I refer to as reflective equilibrium.[1] It is an equilibrium because at last our principles and judgments coincide; and it is reflective since we know to what principles our judgments conform and the premises of their derivation. At the moment everything is in order. But this equilibrium is not necessarily stable. It is liable to be upset by further examination of the conditions which should be imposed on the contractual situation and by particular cases which may lead us to revise our judgments. Yet for the time being we have done what we can to render coherent and to justify our convictions of social justice. We have reached a conception of the original position.

I shall not, of course, actually work through this process. Still, we may think of the interpretation of the original position that I shall present as the result of such a hypothetical course of reflection. It represents the attempt to accommodate within one scheme both reasonable philosophical conditions on principles as well as our considered judgments of justice. In arriving at the favored interpretation of the initial situation there is no point at which an appeal is made to self-evidence in the traditional sense either of general conceptions or particular convictions. I do not claim for the principles of justice proposed that they are necessary truths or derivable from such truths. A conception of justice cannot be deduced from self-evident premises or conditions on principles; instead, its justification is a matter of the mutual support of many considerations, of everything fitting together into one coherent view.

A final comment. We shall want to say that certain principles of justice are justified because they would be agreed to in an initial situation of equality. I have emphasized that this original position is purely hypothet-ical. It is natural to ask why, if this agreement is never actually entered into, we should take any interest in these principles, moral or otherwise. The answer is that the conditions embodied in the description of the original position are ones that we do in fact accept. Or if we do not, then perhaps we can be persuaded to do so by philosophical reflection. Each aspect of the contractual situation can be given supporting grounds. Thus what we shall do is to collect together into one conception a number of conditions on principles that we are ready upon due consideration to recognize as reasonable. These constraints express what we are prepared to regard as limits on fair terms of social cooperation. One way to look at the idea of the original position, therefore, is to see it as an expository device which sums up the meaning of these conditions and helps us to extract their consequences. On the other hand, this conception is also an intuitive notion that suggests its own elaboration, so that led on by it we are drawn to define more clearly the standpoint from which we can best interpret moral relationships. We need a conception that enables us to envision our objective from afar: the intuitive notion of the original position is to do this for us. [. . .]

11. Two Principles of Justice

I shall now state in a provisional form the two principles of justice that I believe would be agreed to in the original position. The first formulation of these principles is tentative. As we go on I shall consider several formulations and approximate step by step the final statement to be given much later. I believe that doing this allows the exposition to proceed in a natural way.

The first statement of the two principles reads as follows.

> First: each person is to have an equal right to the most extensive scheme of equal basic liberties compatible with a similar scheme of liberties for others.

> Second: social and economic inequalities are to be arranged so that they are both (a) reasonably expected to be to everyone's advantage, and (b) attached to positions and offices open to all.

---

1. The process of mutual adjustment of principles and considered judgments is not peculiar to moral philosophy. See Nelson Goodman, *Fact, Fiction, and Forecast* (Cambridge, Mass., Harvard University Press, 1955), pp. 65–68, for parallel remarks concerning the justification of the principles of deductive and inductive inference.

There are two ambiguous phrases in the second principle, namely "everyone's advantage" and "open to all."

These principles primarily apply, as I have said, to the basic structure of society and govern the assignment of rights and duties and regulate the distribution of social and economic advantages. Their formulation presupposes that, for the purposes of a theory of justice, the social structure may be viewed as having two more or less distinct parts, the first principle applying to the one, the second principle to the other. Thus we distinguish between the aspects of the social system that define and secure the equal basic liberties and the aspects that specify and establish social and economic inequalities. Now it is essential to observe that the basic liberties are given by a list of such liberties. Important among these are political liberty (the right to vote and to hold public office) and freedom of speech and assembly; liberty of conscience and freedom of thought; freedom of the person, which includes freedom from psychological oppression and physical assault and dismemberment (integrity of the person); the right to hold personal property and freedom from arbitrary arrest and seizure as defined by the concept of the rule of law. These liberties are to be equal by the first principle.

The second principle applies, in the first approximation, to the distribution of income and wealth and to the design of organizations that make use of differences in authority and responsibility. While the distribution of wealth and income need not be equal, it must be to everyone's advantage, and at the same time, positions of authority and responsibility must be accessible to all. One applies the second principle by holding positions open, and then, subject to this constraint, arranges social and economic inequalities so that everyone benefits.

These principles are to be arranged in a serial order with the first principle prior to the second. This ordering means that infringements of the basic equal liberties protected by the first principle cannot be justified, or compensated for, by greater social and economic advantages. These liberties have a central range of application within which they can be limited and compromised only when they conflict with other basic liberties. Since they may be limited when they clash with one another, none of these liberties is absolute; but however they are adjusted to form one system, this system is to be the same for all. It is difficult, and perhaps impossible, to give a complete specification of these liberties independently from the particular circumstances —social, economic, and technological—of a given society. The hypothesis is that the general form of such a list could be devised with sufficient exactness to sustain this conception of justice. Of course, liberties not on the list, for example, the right to own certain kinds of property (e.g., means of production) and freedom of contract as understood by the doctrine of laissez-faire are not basic; and so they are not protected by the priority of the first principle. Finally, in regard to the second principle, the distribution of wealth and income, and positions of authority and responsibility, are to be consistent with both the basic liberties and equality of opportunity.

The two principles are rather specific in their content, and their acceptance rests on certain assumptions that I must eventually try to explain and justify. For the present, it should be observed that these principles are a special case of a more general conception of justice that can be expressed as follows.

> All social values—liberty and opportunity, income and wealth, and the social bases of self-respect—are to be distributed equally unless an unequal distribution of any, or all, of these values is to everyone's advantage.

Injustice, then, is simply inequalities that are not to the benefit of all. Of course, this conception is extremely vague and requires interpretation.

As a first step, suppose that the basic structure of society distributes certain primary goods, that is, things that every rational man is presumed to want. These goods normally have a use whatever a person's rational plan of life. For simplicity, assume that the chief primary goods at the disposition of society are rights, liberties, and opportunities, and income and wealth. These are the social primary goods. Other primary goods such as health and vigor, intelligence and imagination, are natural goods; although their possession is influenced by the basic structure, they are not so directly under its control. Imagine, then, a hypothetical initial arrangement in which all the social primary goods are equally distributed: everyone has similar rights and duties, and income and wealth are evenly shared. This state of affairs provides a benchmark for judging improvements. If certain inequalities of wealth and differences in authority would make everyone better off than in this hypothetical starting situation, then they accord with the general conception. [. . .]

24. The Veil of Ignorance

The idea of the original position is to set up a fair procedure so that any principles agreed to will be just. The aim is to use the notion of pure procedural justice as a basis of theory. Somehow we must nullify the effects of specific contingencies which put men at odds and tempt them to exploit social and natural circumstances to their own advantage. Now in order to do this I assume that the parties are situated behind a veil of ignorance. They do not know how the various alternatives will affect their own particular case and they are obliged to evaluate principles solely on the basis of general considerations.

It is assumed, then, that the parties do not know certain kinds of particular facts. First of all, no one knows his place in society, his class position or social status; nor does he know his fortune in the distribution of natural assets and abilities, his intelligence and strength, and the like. Nor, again, does anyone know his conception of the good, the particulars of his rational plan of life, or even the special features of his psychology such as his aversion to risk or liability to optimism or pessimism. More than this, I assume that the parties do not know the particular circumstances of their own society. That is, they do not know its economic or political situation, or the level of civilization and culture it has been able to achieve. The persons in the original position have no information as to which generation they belong. These broader restrictions on knowledge are appropriate in part because questions of social justice arise between generations as well as within them, for example, the question of the appropriate rate of capital saving and of the conservation of natural resources and the environment of nature. There is also, theoretically anyway, the question of a reasonable genetic policy. In these cases too, in order to carry through the idea of the original position, the parties must not know the contingencies that set them in opposition. They must choose principles the consequences of which they are prepared to live with whatever generation they turn out to belong to.

As far as possible, then, the only particular facts which the parties know is that their society is subject to the circumstances of justice and whatever this implies. It is taken for granted, however, that they know the general facts about human society. They understand political affairs and the principles of economic theory; they know the basis of social organization and the laws of human psychology. Indeed, the parties are presumed to know whatever general facts affect the choice of the principles of justice. There are no limitations on general information, that is, on general laws and theories, since conceptions of justice must be adjusted to the characteristics of the systems of social cooperation which they are to regulate, and there is no reason to rule out these facts. It is, for example, a consideration against a conception of justice that, in view of the laws of moral psychology, men would not acquire a desire to act upon it even when the institutions of their society satisfied it. For in this case there would be difficulty in securing the stability of social cooperation. An important feature of a conception of justice is that it should generate its own support. Its principles should be such that when they are embodied in the basic structure of society men tend to acquire the corresponding sense of justice and develop a desire to act in accordance with its principles. In this case a conception of justice is stable. This kind of general information is admissible in the original position.

The notion of the veil of ignorance raises several difficulties. Some may object that the exclusion of nearly all particular information makes it difficult to grasp what is meant by the original position. Thus it may be helpful to observe that one or more persons can at any time enter this position, or perhaps better, simulate the deliberations of this hypothetical situation, simply by reasoning in accordance with the appropriate restrictions. In arguing for a conception of justice we must be sure that it is among the permitted alternatives and satisfies the stipulated formal constraints. No considerations can be advanced in its favor unless they would be rational ones for us to urge were we to lack the kind of knowledge that is excluded. The evaluation of principles must proceed in terms of the general consequences of their public recognition and universal application, it being assumed that they will be complied with by everyone. To say that a certain conception of justice would be chosen in the original position is equivalent to saying that rational deliberation satisfying certain conditions and restrictions would reach a certain conclusion. If necessary, the argument to this result could be set out more formally. I shall, however, speak throughout in terms of the notion of the original position. It is more economical and suggestive, and brings out certain essential features that otherwise one might easily overlook.

These remarks show that the original position is not to be thought of as a general assembly which includes at one moment everyone who will live at some time; or, much less, as an assembly of everyone who could live at some time. It is not a gathering of all actual or possible persons. If we conceived of the original position in either of these ways, the conception would cease to be a natural guide to intuition and would lack a clear sense. In any case, the original position must be interpreted so that one can at any time adopt its perspective. It must make no difference when one takes up this viewpoint, or who does so: the restrictions must be such that the same principles are always chosen. The veil of ignorance is a key condition in meeting this requirement. It insures not only that the information available is relevant, but that it is at all times the same.

It may be protested that the condition of the veil of ignorance is irrational. Surely, some may object, principles should be chosen in the light of all the knowledge available. There are various replies to this contention. Here I shall sketch those which emphasize the simplifications that need to be made if one is to have any theory at all. To begin with, it is clear that since the differences among the parties are unknown to them, and everyone is equally rational and similarly situated, each is convinced by the same arguments. Therefore, we can view the agreement in the original position from the standpoint of one person selected at random. If anyone after due reflection prefers a conception of justice to another, then they all do, and a unanimous agreement can be reached. We can, to make the circumstances more vivid, imagine that the parties are required to communicate with each other through a referee as intermediary, and that he is to announce which alternatives have been

suggested and the reasons offered in their support. He forbids the attempt to form coalitions, and he informs the parties when they have come to an understanding. But such a referee is actually superfluous, assuming that the deliberations of the parties must be similar.

Thus there follows the very important consequence that the parties have no basis for bargaining in the usual sense. No one knows his situation in society nor his natural assets, and therefore no one is in a position to tailor principles to his advantage. We might imagine that one of the contractees threatens to hold out unless the others agree to principles favorable to him. But how does he know which principles are especially in his interests? The same holds for the formation of coalitions: if a group were to decide to band together to the disadvantage of the others, they would not know how to favor themselves in the choice of principles. Even if they could get everyone to agree to their proposal, they would have no assurance that it was to their advantage, since they cannot identify themselves either by name or description. The one case where this conclusion fails is that of saving. Since the persons in the original position know that they are contemporaries (taking the present time of entry interpretation), they can favor their generation by refusing to make any sacrifices at all for their successors; they simply acknowledge the principle that no one has a duty to save for posterity. Previous generations have saved or they have not; there is nothing the parties can now do to affect that. So in this instance the veil of ignorance fails to secure the desired result. Therefore, to handle the question of justice between generations, I modify the motivation assumption and add a further constraint.[2] With these adjustments, no generation is able to formulate principles especially designed to advance its own cause and some significant limits on savings principles can be derived. Whatever a person's temporal position, each is forced to choose for all.

The restrictions on particular information in the original position are, then, of fundamental importance. With-

---

2. The constraint is that each person in the original position cares about the well being of some of those in the next generation and that for anyone in the next generation there is someone in the original position who cares about his well being.

out them we would not be able to work out any definite theory of justice at all. We would have to be content with a vague formula stating that justice is what would be agreed to without being able to say much, if anything, about the substance of the agreement itself. The formal constraints of the concept of right, those applying to principles directly, are not sufficient for our purpose. The veil of ignorance makes possible a unanimous choice of a particular conception of justice. Without these limitations on knowledge the bargaining problem of the original position would be hopelessly complicated. Even if theoretically a solution were to exist, we would not, at present anyway, be able to determine it.

The notion of the veil of ignorance is implicit, I think, in Kant's ethics. Nevertheless the problem of defining the knowledge of the parties and of characterizing the alternatives open to them has often been passed over, even by contract theories. Sometimes the situation definitive of moral deliberation is presented in such an indeterminate way that one cannot ascertain how it will turn out. Thus Perry's doctrine is essentially contractarian: he holds that social and personal integration must proceed by entirely different principles, the latter by rational prudence, the former by the concurrence of persons of good will. He would appear to reject utilitarianism on much the same grounds suggested earlier: namely, that it improperly extends the principle of choice for one person to choices facing society. The right course of action is characterized as that which best advances social aims as these would be formulated by reflective agreement, given that the parties have full knowledge of the circumstances and are moved by a benevolent concern for one another's interests. No effort is made, however, to specify in any precise way the possible outcomes of this sort of agreement. Indeed, without a far more elaborate account, no conclusions can be drawn.[3] I do not wish here to criticize others; rather, I want to explain the necessity for what may seem at times like so many irrelevant details.

---

3. See R. B. Perry, *The General Theory of Value* (New York, Longmans, Green and Company, 1926), pp. 674–682.

Now the reasons for the veil of ignorance go beyond mere simplicity. We want to define the original position so that we get the desired solution. If a knowledge of particulars is allowed, then the outcome is biased by arbitrary contingencies. As already observed, to each according to his threat advantage is not a principle of justice. If the original position is to yield agreements that are just, the parties must be fairly situated and treated equally as moral persons. The arbitrariness of the world must be corrected for by adjusting the circumstances of the initial contractual situation. Moreover, if in choosing principles we required unanimity even when there is full information, only a few rather obvious cases could be decided. A conception of justice based on unanimity in these circumstances would indeed be weak and trivial. But once knowledge is excluded, the requirement of unanimity is not out of place and the fact that it can be satisfied is of great importance. It enables us to say of the preferred conception of justice that it represents a genuine reconciliation of interests.

A final comment. For the most part I suppose that the parties possess all general information. No general facts are closed to them. I do this mainly to avoid complications. Nevertheless a conception of justice is to be the public basis of the terms of social cooperation. Since common understanding necessitates certain bounds on the complexity of principles, there may likewise be limits on the use of theoretical knowledge in the original position. Now clearly it would be very difficult to classify and to grade the complexity of the various sorts of general facts. I shall make no attempt to do this. We do however recognize an intricate theoretical construction when we meet one. Thus it seems reasonable to say that other things equal one conception of justice is to be preferred to another when it is founded upon markedly simpler general facts, and its choice does not depend upon elaborate calculations in the light of a vast array of theoretically defined possibilities. It is desirable that the grounds for a public conception of justice should be evident to everyone when circumstances permit. This consideration favors, I believe, the two principles of justice over the criterion of utility.

Robert Nozick

A Libertarian Critique of Rawls

Rawls' Theory

We can bring our discussion of distributive justice into sharper focus by considering in some detail John Rawls' recent contribution to the subject. *A Theory of Justice* is a powerful, deep, subtle, wide-ranging, systematic work in political and moral philosophy which has not seen its like since the writings of John Stuart Mill, if then. [. . .] It is impossible to finish his book without a new and inspiring vision of what a moral theory may attempt to do and unite; how *beautiful* a whole theory can be. I permit myself to concentrate here on disagreements with Rawls only because I am confident that my readers will have discovered for themselves its many virtues.

Social Cooperation

I shall begin by considering the role of the principles of justice. Let us assume, to fix ideas, that a society is a more or less self-sufficient association of persons who in their relations to one another recognize certain rules of conduct as binding and who for the most part act in accordance with them. Suppose further that these rules specify a system of cooperation designed to advance the good of those taking part in it. Then, although a society is a cooperative venture for mutual advantage, it is typically marked by a conflict as well as by an identity of interests. There is an identity of interests since social cooperation makes possible a better life for all than any would have if each were to live solely by his own efforts. There is a conflict of interests since persons are not indifferent as to how the greater benefits produced by their collaboration are distributed, for in order to pursue their ends they each prefer a larger to a lesser share. A set of principles is required for choosing among the various social arrangements which determine this division of advantages and for underwriting an agreement on the proper distributive shares. These principles are the principles of social justice: they provide a way of assigning rights and duties in the basic institutions of society and they define the appropriate distribution of the benefits and burdens of social cooperation. [Rawls, A *Theory of Justice*, p. 4]

Let us imagine n individuals who do not cooperate together and who each live solely by their own efforts. Each person i receives a payoff, return, income, and so forth, S_i; the sum total of what each individual gets acting separately is

$$S = \sum_{i=1}^{n} S_i.$$

By cooperating together they can obtain a larger sum total T. The problem of distributive social justice, according to Rawls, is how these benefits of cooperation are to be distributed or allocated. This problem might be conceived of in two ways: how is the total T to be allocated? Or, how is the incremental amount due to social cooperation, that is the benefits of social cooperation $T - S$, to be allocated? The latter formulation assumes that each individual i receives from the subtotal S of T, his share S_i. The two statements of the problem differ. When combined with the noncooperative distribution of S (each i getting S_i), a " fair-looking" distribution of $T - S$ under the second version may not yield a " fair-looking" distribution of T (the first version). Alternatively, a fair-looking distribution of T may give a particular individual i less than his share S_i. (The constraint $T_i \geq S_i$ on the answer to the first formulation of the problem, where T_i is the share in T of the ith individual, would exclude this possibility.) Rawls, without distinguishing these two formulations of the problem, writes as though his concern is the first one, that is, how the total sum T is to be distributed. One might claim, to support a focus on the first issue, that due to the enormous benefits of social cooperation, the non-cooperative shares S_i are so small in comparison to any cooperative ones T_i that they may be ignored in setting up the problem of social justice. Though we should note that this certainly is not how people entering into co-operation with one another would agree to conceive of the problem of dividing up cooperation's benefits.

Why does social cooperation *create* the problem of distributive justice? Would there be no problem of jus-tice and no need for a theory of justice, if there was no social cooperation at all, if each person got his share solely by his own efforts? If we suppose, as Rawls seems to, that this situation does *not* raise questions of distrib-utive justice, then in virtue of what facts about social cooperation do these questions of justice emerge? What is it about social cooperation that gives rise to issues of justice? It cannot be said that there will be conflicting claims only where there is social cooperation; that in-dividuals who produce independently and (initially) fend for themselves will not make claims of justice on each other. If there were ten Robinson Crusoes, each working alone for two years on separate islands, who discovered each other and the facts of their different al-lotments by radio communication via transmitters left twenty years earlier, could they not make claims on each other, supposing it were possible to transfer goods from one island to the next? Wouldn't the one with least make a claim on ground of need, or on the ground that his island was naturally poorest, or on the ground that he was naturally least capable of fending for himself? Mightn't he say that justice demanded he be given some more by the others, claiming it unfair that he should receive so much less and perhaps be destitute, perhaps starving? He might go on to say that the different indi-vidual noncooperative shares stem from differential nat-ural endowments, which are not deserved, and that the task of justice is to rectify these arbitrary facts and in-equities. Rather than its being the case that no one *will* make such claims in the situation lacking social coop-eration, perhaps the point is that such claims clearly

would be without merit. Why would they clearly be without merit? In the social noncooperation situation, it might be said, each individual deserves what he gets unaided by his own efforts; or rather, no one else can make a claim *of justice* against this holding. It is pellucidly clear in this situation who is entitled to what, so no theory of justice is needed. On this view social cooper-ation introduces a muddying of the waters that makes it unclear or indeterminate who is entitled to what. Rather than saying that no theory of justice applies to this noncooperative case, (wouldn't it be unjust if some-one stole another's products in the noncooperative situ-ation?), I would say that it is a clear case of application of the correct theory of justice: the entitlement theory.

How does social cooperation change things so that the same entitlement principles that apply to the non-cooperative cases become inapplicable or inappropriate to cooperative ones? It might be said that one cannot disentangle the contributions of distinct individuals who cooperate; everything is everyone's joint product. On this joint product, or on any portion of it, each per-son plausibly will make claims of equal strength; all have an equally good claim, or at any rate no person has a distinctly better claim than any other. Somehow (this line of thought continues), it must be decided how this total product of joint social cooperation (to which in-dividual entitlements do not apply differentially) is to be divided up: this is the problem of distributive justice.

Don't individual entitlements apply to parts of the cooperatively produced product? First, suppose that so-cial cooperation is based upon division of labor, spe-cialization, comparative advantage, and exchange; each person works singly to transform some input he re-ceives, contracting with others who further transform or transport his product until it reaches its ultimate con-sumer. People cooperate in making things but they work separately; each person is a miniature firm. The products of each person are easily identifiable, and ex-changes are made in open markets with prices set com-petitively, given informational constraints, and so forth. In such a system of social cooperation, what is the task of a theory of justice? It might be said that whatever holdings result will depend upon the exchange ratios or prices at which exchanges are made, and therefore that the task of a theory of justice is to set criteria for "fair prices." This is hardly the place to trace the serpentine windings of theories of a just price. It is difficult to see why these issues should even arise here. People are choosing to make exchanges with other people and to transfer entitlements, with no restrictions on their freedom to trade with any other party at any mutually acceptable ratio. Why does such sequential social cooperation, linked together by people's voluntary exchanges, raise any special problems about how things are to be distributed? Why isn't the appropriate (a not inappropriate) set of holdings just the one which *actually occurs* via this process of mutually-agreed-to exchanges whereby people choose to give to others what they are entitled to give or hold?

Let us now drop our assumption that people work independently, cooperating only in sequence via voluntary exchanges, and instead consider people who work together jointly to produce something. Is it now impossible to disentangle people's respective contributions? The question here is not whether marginal productivity theory is an appropriate theory of fair or just shares, but whether there is some coherent notion of identifiable marginal product. It seems unlikely that Rawls' theory rests on the strong claim that there is no such reasonably serviceable notion. Anyway, once again we have a situation of a large number of bilateral exchanges: owners of resources reaching separate agreements with entrepreneurs about the use of their resources, entrepreneurs reaching agreements with individual workers, or groups of workers first reaching some joint agreement and then presenting a package to an entrepreneur, and so forth. People transfer their holdings or labor in free markets, with the exchange ratios (prices) determined in the usual manner. If marginal productivity theory is reasonably adequate, people will be receiving, in these voluntary transfers of holdings, roughly their marginal products.

But if the notion of marginal product were so ineffective that factors' marginal products in actual situations of joint production could not be identified by hirers or purchasers of the factors, then the resulting distribution to factors would not be patterned in accordance with marginal product. Someone who viewed marginal productivity theory, where it was applicable, *as a patterned theory of justice,* might think that such sit-

uations of joint production and indeterminate marginal product provided an opportunity for some theory of justice to enter to determine appropriate exchange ratios. But an entitlement theorist would find acceptable whatever distribution resulted from the party's voluntary exchanges. The questions about the workability of marginal productivity theory are intricate ones. Let us merely note here the strong personal incentive for owners of resources to converge to the marginal product, and the strong market pressures tending to produce this result. Employers of factors of productions are not all dolts who don't know what they're doing, transferring holdings they value to others on an irrational and arbitrary basis. Indeed, Rawls' position on inequalities requires that separate contributions to joint products be isolable, to some extent at least. For Rawls goes out of his way to argue that inequalities are justified if they serve to raise the position of the worst-off group in the society, if without the inequalities the worst-off group would be even more worse off. These serviceable inequalities stem, at least in part, from the necessity to provide incentives to certain people to perform various activities or fill various roles that not everyone can do equally well. (Rawls is *not* imagining that inequalities are needed to fill positions that everyone can do equally well, or that the most drudgery-filled positions that require the least skill will command the highest income.) But *to whom* are the incentives to be paid? To which performers of what activities? When it is necessary to provide incentives to some to perform their productive activities, there is no talk of a joint social product from which no individual's contribution can be disentangled. If the product was all that inextricably joint, it couldn't be known that the extra incentives were going to the crucial persons; and it couldn't be known that the additional product produced by these now motivated people is greater than the expenditure to them in incentives. So it couldn't be known whether the provision of incentives was efficient or not, whether it involved a net gain or a net loss. But Rawls' discussion of justifiable inequalities presupposes that these things can be known. And so the claim we have imagined about the indivisible, nonpartitionable nature of the joint product is seen to dissolve, leaving the reasons for the view that social cooperation creates special problems of distributive justice otherwise not present, unclear if not mysterious.

Terms of Cooperation and the Difference Principle

Another entry into the issue of the connection of social cooperation with distributive shares brings us to grips with Rawls' actual discussion. Rawls imagines rational, mutually disinterested individuals meeting in a certain situation, or abstracted from their other features not provided for in this situation. In this hypothetical situation of choice, which Rawls calls "the original position," they choose the first principles of a conception of justice that is to regulate all subsequent criticism and reform of their institutions. While making this choice, no one knows his place in society, his class position or social status, or his natural assets and abilities, his strength, intelligence, and so forth.

> The principles of justice are chosen behind a veil of ignorance. This ensures that no one is advantaged or disadvantaged in the choice of principles by the outcome of natural chance or the contingency of social circumstances. Since all are similarly situated and no one is able to design principles to favor his particular condition, the principles of justice are the result of a fair agreement or bargain. [Rawls, p. 12]

What would persons in the original position agree to?

Persons in the initial situation would choose two . . . principles: the first requires equality in the assignment of basic rights and duties, while the second holds that social and economic inequalities, for example, inequalities of wealth and authority are just only if they result in compensating benefits for everyone, and in particular for the least advantaged members of society. These principles rule out justifying institutions on the grounds that the hardships of some are offset by a greater good in the aggregate. It may be expedient but it is not just that some should have less in order that

others may prosper. But there is no injustice in the greater benefits earned by a few provided that the situation of persons not so fortunate is thereby improved. The intuitive idea is that since everyone's well-being depends upon a scheme of cooperation without which no one could have a satisfactory life, the division of advantages should be such as to draw forth the willing cooperation of everyone taking part in it, including those less well situated. Yet this can be expected only if reasonable terms are proposed. The two principles mentioned seem to be a fair agreement on the basis of which those better endowed, or more fortunate in their social position, neither of which we can be said to deserve, could expect the willing cooperation of others when some workable scheme is a necessary condition of the welfare of all. [Rawls, pp. 14–15]

This second principle, which Rawls specifies as the difference principle, holds that the institutional structure is to be so designed that the worst-off group under it is at least as well off as the worst-off group (not necessarily the same group) would be under any alternative institutional structure. If persons in the original position follow the minimax policy in making the significant choice of principles of justice, Rawls argues, they will choose the difference principle. Our concern here is not whether persons in the position Rawls describes actually would minimax and actually would choose the particular principles Rawls specifies. Still, we should question why individuals in the original position would choose a principle that focuses upon groups, rather than individuals. Won't application of the minimax principle lead each person in the original position to favor maximizing the position of the worst-off *individual?* To be sure, this principle would reduce questions of evaluating social institutions to the issue of how the unhappiest depressive fares. Yet avoiding this by moving the focus to groups (or representative individuals) seems *ad hoc,* and is inadequately motivated for those in the individual position. Nor is it clear which groups are appropriately considered; why exclude the group of depressives or alcoholics or the representative paraplegic?

If the difference principle is not satisfied by some in-stitutional structure J, then under J some group G is worse off than it would be under another institutional structure I that satisfies the principle. If another group F is better off under J than it would be under the I fa-vored by the difference principle, is this sufficient to say that under J "some . . . have less in order that others may prosper"? (Here one would have in mind that G has less in order that F prosper. Could one also make the same statement about I? Does F have less under I in order that G may prosper?) Suppose that in a society the fol-lowing situation prevailed:

1. Group G has amount A and group F has amount B, with B greater than A. Also things could be arranged differently so that G would have more than A, and F would have less than B. (The dif-ferent arrangement might involve a mechanism to transfer some holdings from F to G.)

Is this sufficient to say

2. G is badly off *because* F is well off; G is badly off *in order that* F be well off; F's being well off makes G badly off; G is badly off *on account of* F's being well off; G is not better off *because of* how well off F is.

If so, does the truth of statement 2 depend on G's be-ing in a worse position than F? There is yet another possible institutional structure K that transfers holdings from the worse-off group G to F, making G even more worse off. Does the possibility of K make it true to say that, under J, F is not (even) better off because of how well off G is?

We do not normally hold that the truth of a sub-junctive (as in 1) is alone sufficient for the truth of some indicative causal statement (as in 2). It would improve my life in various ways if you were to choose to become my devoted slave, supposing I could get over the initial discomfort. Is the cause of my present state your not be-coming my slave? Because your enslaving yourself to a poorer person would improve his lot and worsen yours, are we to say that the poor person is badly off because you are as well off as you are; has he less in order that you may prosper? From

3. If P were to do act A then Q would not be in sit-uation S.

we will conclude

4. P's not doing A is responsible for Q's being in sit-uation S; P's not doing A causes Q to be in S.

only if we *also* believe that

5. P ought to do act A, or P has a duty to do act A, or P has an obligation to do act A, and so forth.

Thus the inference from 3 to 4, as in this case, *presup-poses* 5. One cannot argue from 3 to 4 as one step in or-der *to get to* 5. The statement that in a particular situation some have less in order that others may prosper is often based upon the very evaluation of a situation or an in-stitutional framework that it is introduced to support. Since this evaluation does *not* follow merely from the subjunctive (for example, 1 or 3) an *independent* argu-ment must be produced for it.[1]

Rawls holds, as we have seen, that

since everyone's well-being depends upon a scheme of cooperation without which no one could have a satisfactory life, the division of ad-vantages should be such as to draw forth the willing cooperation of everyone taking part in it, including those less well situated. Yet this can be expected only if reasonable terms are pro-posed. The two principles mentioned seem to be a fair agreement on the basis of which those better endowed or more fortunate in their so-cial position . . . could expect the willing coop-eration of others when some workable scheme is a necessary condition of the welfare of all. [Rawls, p. 15]

---

1. Though Rawls does not clearly distinguish 2 from 1 and 4 from 3, I do not claim that he makes the illegitimate step of sliding from the latter subjunctive to the former in-dicative. Even so, the mistake is worth pointing out because it is an easy one to fall into, and it might appear to prop up positions we argue against.

No doubt, the difference principle presents terms on the basis of which those less well endowed would be willing to cooperate. (What *better* terms could they propose for themselves?) But is this a fair agreement on the basis of which those *worse* endowed could expect the *willing* cooperation of others? With regard to the existence of gains from social cooperation, the situation is symmetrical. The better endowed gain by cooperating with the worse endowed, *and* the worse endowed gain by cooperating with the better endowed. Yet the difference principle is not neutral between the better and the worse endowed. Whence the asymmetry?

Perhaps the symmetry is upset if one asks *how much* each gains from the social cooperation. This question might be understood in two ways. How much do people benefit from social cooperation, as compared to their individual holdings in a *non*cooperative scheme? That is, how much is $T_i - S_i$, for each individual *i?* Or, alternatively, how much does each individual gain from general social cooperation, as compared, not with *no* cooperation, but with more limited cooperation? The latter is the more appropriate question with regard to general social cooperation. For failing general agreement on the principles to govern how the benefits of general social cooperation are to be held, not everyone will remain in a noncooperative situation if there is some other beneficial cooperative arrangement involving some, but not all, people, whose participants *can* agree. These people will participate in this more narrow cooperative arrangement. To focus upon the benefits of the better and the worse endowed cooperating together, we must try to imagine less extensive schemes of partitioned social cooperation in which the better endowed cooperate only among themselves and the worse endowed cooperate only among themselves, with no cross-cooperation. The members of both groups gain from the internal cooperation within their respective groups and have larger shares than they would if there were no social cooperation at all. An individual benefits from the wider system of extensive cooperation between the better and the worse endowed to the extent of his incremental gain from this wider cooperation; namely, the amount by which his share under a scheme of general cooperation is greater than it would be under one of limited intragroup (but not crossgroup) cooperation. *General* cooperation will be of more ben-

efit to the better or to the worse endowed if (to pick a simple criterion) the mean incremental gain from general cooperation (when compared with limited intragroup cooperation) is greater in one group than it is in the other.

One might speculate about whether there is an inequality between the groups' mean incremental gains and, if so, which way it goes. If the better-endowed group includes those who manage to accomplish something of great economic advantage to others, such as new inventions, new ideas about production or ways of doing things, skill at economic tasks, and so on, it is difficult to avoid concluding that the *less* well endowed gain *more* than the better endowed do from the scheme of general cooperation. What follows from this conclusion? I do *not* mean to imply that the better endowed should get even more than they get under the entitlement system of general social cooperation. What *does* follow from the conclusion is a deep suspicion of imposing, in the name of fairness, constraints upon voluntary social cooperation (and the set of holdings that arises from it) so that those already benefiting most from this general cooperation benefit even more!

Rawls would have us imagine the worse-endowed persons say something like the following: "Look, better endowed: you gain by cooperating with us. If you want our cooperation you'll have to accept reasonable terms. We suggest these terms: We'll cooperate with you only if we get *as much as possible*. That is, the terms of our cooperation should give us that maximal share such that, if it was tried to give us more, we'd end up with less." How generous these proposed terms are might be seen by imagining that the better endowed make the almost symmetrical opposite proposal: "Look, worse endowed: you gain by cooperating with *us*. If you want our cooperation you'll have to accept reasonable terms. We propose these terms: We'll cooperate with you so long as *we* get as much as possible. That is, the terms of our cooperation should give us the maximal share such that, if it was tried to give us more, we'd end up with less." If these terms seem outrageous, as they are, why don't the terms proposed by those worse endowed seem the same? Why shouldn't the better endowed treat this latter proposal as beneath consideration, supposing someone to have the nerve explicitly to state it?

Rawls devotes much attention to explaining why those less well favored should not complain at receiving less. His explanation, simply put, is that because the inequality works for his advantage, someone less well favored shouldn't complain about it; he receives *more* in the unequal system than he would in an equal one. (Though he might receive still more in another unequal system that placed someone else below him.) But Rawls discusses the question of whether those *more* favored will or should find the terms satisfactory *only* in the following passage, where *A* and *B* are any two representative men with *A* being the more favored:

> The difficulty is to show that *A* has no grounds for complaint. Perhaps he is required to have less than he might since his having more would result in some loss to *B*. Now what can be said to the more favored man? To begin with, it is clear that the well-being of each depends on a scheme of social cooperation without which no one could have a satisfactory life. Secondly, we can ask for the willing cooperation of everyone only if the terms of the scheme are reasonable. The difference principle, then, seems to be a fair basis on which those better endowed, or more fortunate in their social circumstances, could expect others to collaborate with them when some workable arrangement is a necessary condition of the good of all. [Rawls, p. 103]

What Rawls imagines being said to the more favored men does *not* show that these men have no grounds for complaint, nor does it at all diminish the weight of whatever complaints they have. That the well-being of all depends on social cooperation without which no one could have a satisfactory life could also be said to the less well endowed by someone proposing any other principle, including that of maximizing the position of the best endowed. Similarly for the fact that we can ask for the willing cooperation of everyone only if the terms of the scheme are reasonable. The question is: What terms *would be* reasonable? What Rawls imagines being said thus far merely sets up his problem; it doesn't distinguish his proposed difference principle from the almost symmetrical counterproposal that we imag-

ined the better endowed making, or from any other proposal. Thus, when Rawls continues, "The difference principle, then, seems to be a fair basis on which those best endowed, or more fortunate in their social circumstances, could expect others to collaborate with them when some workable arrangement is a necessary condition of the good of all," the presence of the "then" in his sentence is puzzling. Since the sentences which precede it are neutral between his proposal and any other proposal, the conclusion that the difference principle presents a fair basis for cooperation *cannot* follow from what precedes it in this passage. Rawls is merely repeating that it seems reasonable; hardly a convincing reply to anyone to whom it doesn't seem reasonable.

Rawls has not shown that the more favored man *A* has no grounds for complaint at being required to have less in order that another *B* might have more than he otherwise would. And he can't show this, since *A* *does* have grounds for complaint. Doesn't he?

The Original Position and End-Result Principles

How can it have been supposed that these terms offered by the less well endowed are fair? Imagine a social pie somehow appearing so that *no one* has any claim at all on any portion of it, no one has any more of a claim than any other person; yet there must be unanimous agreement on how it is to be divided. Undoubtedly, apart from threats or holdouts in bargaining, an equal distribution would be suggested and found plausible as a solution. (It is, in Schelling's sense, a focal point solution.) If *somehow* the size of the pie wasn't fixed, and it was realized that pursuing an equal distribution somehow would lead to a smaller total pie than otherwise might occur, the people might well agree to an unequal distribution which raised the size of the least share. But in any actual situation, wouldn't this realization reveal something about differential claims on parts of the pie? Who is it that could make the pie larger, and would do it if given a larger share, but not if given an equal share under the scheme of equal distribution? To whom is an incentive to be provided to make this larger contribution? (There's no talk here of inextricably entangled joint product; it's known *to whom* incentives are to be offered, or at least to whom a bonus is to be paid after the fact.) Why doesn't this identifiable differential contribution lead to some differential entitlement?

If things fell from heaven like manna, and no one had any special entitlement to any portion of it, and no manna would fall unless all agreed to a particular distribution, and somehow the quantity varied depending on the distribution, then it is plausible to claim that persons placed so that they couldn't make threats, or hold out for specially large shares, would agree to the difference principle rule of distribution. But is *this* the appropriate model for thinking about how the things people produce are to be distributed? Why think the same results should obtain for situations where there *are* differential entitlements as for situations where there are not?

A procedure that founds principles of distributive justice on what rational persons who know nothing about themselves or their histories would agree to *guarantees that end-state principles of justice will be taken as fundamental.* Perhaps some historical principles of justice are derivable from end-state principles, as the utilitarian tries to derive individual rights, prohibitions on punishing the innocent, and so forth, from *his* end-state principle; perhaps such arguments can be constructed even for the entitlement principle. But no historical principle, it seems, could be agreed to in the first instance by the participants in Rawls' original position. For people meeting together behind a veil of ignorance to decide who gets what, knowing nothing about any special entitlements people may have, will treat anything to be distributed as manna from heaven. [. . .]

It might be objected to our argument that Rawls' procedure is designed to *establish* all facts about justice; there is no independent notion of entitlement, not provided by his theory, to stand on in criticizing his theory. But we do not need any *particular* developed historical-entitlement theory as a basis from which to criticize Rawls' construction. If *any* such fundamental historical-entitlement view is correct, then Rawls' theory is not. We are thus able to make this structural criticism of the type of theory Rawls presents and the type of principles it must yield, without first having formulated fully a particular historical-entitlement theory as an alternative to his. We would be ill advised to accept Rawls'

theory and his construal of the problem as one of which principles would be chosen by rational self-interested individuals behind a veil of ignorance, unless we were sure that no adequate historical-entitlement theory was to be gotten.

Since Rawls' construction doesn't yield a historical or entitlement conception of justice, there will be some feature(s) of his construction in virtue of which it doesn't. Have we done anything other than focus upon the particular feature(s), and say that this makes Rawls' construction incapable in principle of yielding an entitlement or historical conception of justice? This would be a criticism without any force at all, for in this sense we would have to say that the construction is incapable in principle of yielding any conception other than the one it actually yields. It seems clear that our criticism goes deeper than this (and I hope it is clear to the reader); but it is difficult to formulate the requisite criterion of depth. Lest this appear lame, let us add that as Rawls states the root idea underlying the veil of ignorance, that feature which is the most prominent in excluding agreement to an entitlement conception, it is to prevent someone from tailoring principles to his own advantage, from designing principles to favor his particular condition. But not only does the veil of ignorance do this; it ensures that no shadow of entitlement considerations will enter the rational calculations of ignorant, nonmoral individuals constrained to decide in a situation reflecting some formal conditions of morality.[2] Perhaps, in a Rawls-*like* construction, some condition weaker than the veil of ignorance could serve to exclude the special tailoring of principles, or perhaps some other "structural-looking" feature of the choice situation could be

---

2. Someone might think entitlement principles count as specially tailored in a morally objectionable way, and so he might reject my claim that the veil of ignorance accomplishes more than its stated purpose. Since to specially tailor principles is to tailor them *unfairly* for one's own advantage, and since the question of the fairness of the entitlement principle is precisely the issue, it is difficult to decide which begs the question: my criticism of the strength of the veil of ignorance, or the defense against the criticism which I imagine in this note.

formulated to mirror entitlement considerations. But as it stands there is no reflection of entitlement considerations in any form in the situation of those in the original position; these considerations do not enter even to be overridden or outweighed or otherwise put aside. Since no glimmer of entitlement principles is built into the structure of the situation of persons in the original position, there is no way these principles could be selected; and Rawls' construction is incapable in principle of yielding them. This is not to say, of course, that the entitlement principle (or "the principle of natural liberty") couldn't be *written* on the list of principles to be considered by those in the original position. Rawls doesn't do even this, perhaps because it is so transparently clear that there would be no point in including it to be considered *there.*

PHILOSOPHY OF RELIGION

'GOD' IS AT THE core of long-standing answers to fundamental questions: How did the universe begin? What happens to us after death? What purpose is there to our lives? Appeals to God can answer such questions only if God exists and we can rationally believe that God exists. These are distinct. Even if God exists, we may not be in a position to rationally believe that God exists; and given that we are finite and fallible, it may be rational to believe that God exists even if God does not exist. When we inquire into the nature and existence of God, we engage in a metaphysical or ontological search. When we ask whether it is rational to believe that God exists, our question is epistemological.

The conception of God operative in most of these Western readings is of a unique, person-like (rational, intelligent, purposeful) being who is omnipotent (all powerful), omnipresent (present everywhere), omniscient (all knowing), and all-good. Nothing in our ordinary experience—no entity with which we are familiar—has such characteristics. How does one explore a terrain that is so unprecedented within one's ordinary experience?

The heart of Anselm's Ontological Argument—an argument to prove existence—is the conception of God as the most perfect being conceivable. He argues that it follows from the very conception of God that God exists. (A version of the argument is also found in Descartes, pp. 50–76.)

There is something both fishy and intriguing about this argument—the fishy smell is that it seems the intellectual analogue of pulling a real rabbit out of a merely conceptual hat. Conceiving of something—say, a necessary-unicorn—as having to exist cannot make it so. The intriguing part is figuring out where, if at all, the ontological 'trick' takes place. Setting out a version of the argument will clarify the discussion:

1. The concept of God is of a being than which none greater is conceivable.

2. If God does not exist, then there is a different being that is conceivable who has the same attributes as God but who additionally has the attribute of existence.

3. The latter being would then be conceivable as a being greater than God.

4. But that is impossible, since it contradicts the concept of God in (1).

Consequently, 5. The concept of God includes the attribute of existence—that is, God exists by the very nature of the conception of God.

The argument is a *reductio ad absurdum:* it assumes that God does not have the attribute of existence and derives a contradiction (or impossibility) from that assumption. Consequently the assumption (the antecedent of premise 2) is rejected. If the Ontological Argument is sound, the assertion of God's nonexistence is self-contradictory—like 'The tallest student in this class is shorter than the student sitting next to him'.

One objection, which Anselm addresses, claims that the argument proves too much. If for 'God' we substitute a term for another perfect object such as a perfect island, understood as one than which none greater can be conceived, would not the same reductio reasoning prove that the perfect island exists? But is the parallel fair—is perfection of an island akin to the perfection of a rational agent?

Kant objects to the second premise of Anselm's argument on the grounds that existence is not a predicate. It does not describe or attribute a property, characteristic, or feature, such as being tall, strong, or furry. Existence is rather the obtaining or realization of such properties that constitute the individual. Imagine a can of tuna fish. Now look at a can. The can you imagine, like the one you see, is round, flat on top, with words on the wrapper like 'Starkist chunky white tuna in water'. Your imagination might be so good that your imaginary can exactly resembles in visible properties the one on the shelf. The latter exists, not the former, but the properties of the two are the same.

Kant's objection does not address the difference between creatures that have existence accidentally or as a matter of fact (dependent, say, on the tenuous moment of conception and the chance effects on genetic makeup) and an entity that necessarily exists. Is necessary existence a perfection? If a perfect being is possible, must it exist?

Other attempts to prove God's existence begin with observations: A complex universe exists, and it supports life and other systematic processes like the orbiting of the planets. Why and how? If the universe was once empty, must something have intervened to bring the world into existence and set things in motion?

These suggestive thoughts contain the rudiments of Aquinas' 'five ways'. Unlike the Ontological Argument, which attempts to prove a priori that God exists, these arguments attempt to establish the necessity of God's existence on the basis of experience (specifically, on observations of the nature and workings of the universe).

The key claim is that a causal chain—of one event (a cause) bringing about another (the effect)—cannot go on forever. For if it did, there would not be a sufficient cause, or reason, or explanation for the whole process to obtain. But is an absolute starting point—a First Cause, itself uncaused—necessary? Logically and conceptually, it is possible for a sequence to go on infinitely back $(0, -1, -2 \ldots)$ or infinitely forward $(0, 1, 2 \ldots)$. Newton's laws of motion imply that if an object is in motion it will remain in constant motion unless some external force (like friction) intervenes.

Aquinas expresses the demand for a First Cause as a conceptual demand for a sufficient reason or complete explanation of the existence of the universe. Asked why ice floats on (liquid) water, you could cite the effect of lower temperatures on hydrogen bonding. But this leads to further *why* questions, in response to which you might cite fundamental laws of chemistry. But what explains these? What is a sufficient reason for these laws? It seems that the request for empirical or scientific explanation will eventually give out; you will cite the most fundamental of empirical facts and laws, and yet about it the further *why* question can be asked: What ultimately explains or what is a sufficient reason for the universe to be as it is? The Cosmological Argument assumes that the universe cannot contain the answer in itself and that this assumption is not itself an empirical matter. But if you can always continue the causal chain by asking 'and what caused that?' then, having adduced God as the cause of the universe, shouldn't the same 'and what caused that?' question be asked about God?

Our familiar explanations are never ultimate. If you explain why Joe Allen is called on first in taking attendance, it is a sufficient reason or explanation that the roll is in alphabetical order and 'Allen' comes first in the alphabet. The reason or explanation is satisfactory, even if you cannot answer the further question of why he has the last name 'Allen' or why the roll is in alphabetical order. Does the universe or the causal processes in it demand an explanation or reason that is ultimate—sufficient to explain all else, while not subject to the same demand for an explanation of itself?

The other important argument from observation—the Argument from Design—works by analogy. The operation of the universe is taken to be analogous to the harmony, well-functioning, and intricacy of a mechanical device like a watch or a car. We think that such devices must be the product of intelligent and intentional design, dismissing the possibility that they could have been generated by accident or chance. Mix up and throw out the parts of a car or a watch a zillion times, and, it seems, you will never produce a working car or watch. However, at least in the case of living organisms that reproduce and struggle to survive, evolution provides a different explanation for the appearance of design.

Among the natural phenomena that would seem to call for an intentional or intelligent design are the intricate structure of the eye and the forces that maintain planets in orbits around the sun. Natural science can now explain both of these without appeal to God. But recently, the Argument from Design was resurrected to accommodate the fine-tuning of the universe. If certain fundamental constants—like the fine-structure constant, which characterizes electromagnetic interaction—differed by a tiny fraction (one ten-thousandth) of their magnitude, the structure of the universe would be lost or life would be impossible. Parfit's 'Why Anything? Why This?' (231–43) considers whether the fine-tuning issue amounts to anything more than evidence that the conditions for existence are precarious.

Unlike the Cosmological Argument, the Argument from Design is inductive. It attempts to establish its conclusion by a probable inference and so too a conclusion that cannot rule out altogether a chance account. The two basic questions about the Argument from Design are these: How strong is the analogy? How far can nondesign or nonpurposeful explanations reach? Darwin's theory of evolution, which Dennett discusses (285–95), addresses both. To a surprising extent, Hume's discussion (719–51) prefigures Darwin's.

The Argument from Design must rule out chance, randomness, or other nonintentional processes as the source of the appearance of design. Chance or random processes, like rolling dice, produce alternative possibilities. The longer these processes go on, the more possibilities are likely to be realized—in one roll, there is one in thirty-six chance of getting a one on each die; in a hundred rolls, it's a near certainty that 'snake eyes' will occur at least once. Aquinas exploits the role of time in increasing the realization of possibilities. If each natural object has the possibility of not existing, he argues, there is the possibility that they simultaneously fail to exist. At that time there is nothing. If time extends infinitely into the past, then at some past time each possibility, including the nonexistence of everything, has been realized. But we know that there is something. So there must exist a being who brought about that something (the universe) out of nothing. The argument assumes that something cannot come of nothing, requires a being outside the universe, and denies the laws of the conservation of matter and energy. For if the sum of matter and energy is always conserved, although any particular complex of particles might not exist, there is no possibility that nothing exists.

Given vast stretches of time, can we expect design-like arrangements to arise naturally, without divine intervention? Darwin appeals to natural selection to explain how intricately functioning systems arise naturally without purposeful planning and intervention. Evolution does not repeatedly work with the same organisms, but only with those that have features well suited to their environments, though they evolved only by chance mutations from prior surviving organisms. The ones that are well suited are not selected because they are well suited; rather, their closest competitors, which lacked that beneficial, heritable trait, do not survive (to reproduce).

Moreover, since mutation is continuous, evolution is too. Organisms that were light sensitive prevailed over those that were not; those that were able to focus light prevailed over those that were merely light sensitive; and so on until, eventually, over a vast number of generations, eyes evolved. The eye did not arise to help animals see, as the watch was designed to help us tell time. Given, however, that eyes did arise as a heritable mutation, the genes for them were passed on because of the advantage they conferred. The appearance of design results from our biased perspective where we focus on the survivors. Can a similar pattern (random processes, time, selection), except for reproduction, explain other complex patterns in nature?

A further problem for the Argument from Design is that much in nature is not particularly well designed. Most of the universe is dark, cold, empty space. Many species are far from optimally suited to their environments. In *The Panda's Thumb,* Stephen Jay Gould observes that the panda strips bamboo by using an inflexible bone spur that looks like a thumb.[1] The panda would be far better able to strip bamboo, which is crucial for its sustenance, if it had an opposable thumb like ours. An all-powerful designer would presumably have given it one. However, evolution works only with the materials and constraints already in play in the genome, generating a good-enough mechanism for survival, but one that is far from optimal.

Abstract proofs would be unnecessary if we had ordinary evidence for God's existence either by direct observation or through empirical investigation. The mystery of God is one of the two common sources for skepticism about the existence of God or the characteristics attributed to him. The other is the problem of evil, discussed in the selections from Leibniz, Mackie, and van Inwagen.

The problem of evil is how an all-good and all-powerful God can permit the suffering and evil we find both in the moral realm (e.g., the slaughter of the Native Americans) and the natural realm (e.g., the bubonic plague). The problem of evil suggests the following argument:

1. If God exists and he is all good, all knowing, and all powerful, then he could prevent suffering and evil.

2. If he could prevent it, he would.

3. God does not prevent it.

So, 4. Either God does not exist, or he is not all good, or he is not all knowing, or he is not all powerful.

Since the argument is valid, its cogency depends on the truth of its premises. A traditional way to refute it is to offer a 'theodicy' to explain why, contrary to premise 2, God would not act to eliminate evil: Since God gave us free will and his preventing evil, at least moral evil, would interfere with our free will, it is not true that God would prevent it, even though he could. Van Inwagen suggests an extension of this defense to natural evils (evils not involving any exercise of free choice): If God prevented the suffering of some natural evils, he would deceive us into thinking that we were not subject to chance misfortunes, like earthquakes. But God is not a deceiver, a claim for which Descartes famously argued (p. 51).

Another tack denies the implication of premise 3 that there is evil, where evil involves uncompensated suffering. Either the appearance of evil is an illusion we suffer from because we

---

1. Stephen Jay Gould, *The Panda's Thumb.* New York: Norton, 1980.

do not understand the goodness in it according to God's plan, or those who suffer evil in this life will be more than compensated for it by blessing in an eternal life, subsequent to physical death. Even if neither response is credible or comforting to those suffering from evil, each renders this conception of God consistent with the existence of extensive natural and moral evil. Alternatively, premise 1 can be sacrificed by modifying the conception of God—perhaps God is not all good, all knowing, or all powerful. (The Greek gods were not all good, all knowing, or all powerful.)

There remains the epistemic problem of belief. Victims of terrible misfortune often think, 'How can I believe in a God who would permit this to happen?' To understand the force of this question, let's take a closer look at belief.

What you believe, you believe to be true, and you believe it only because you take it to be true. If you believe that the Boston Red Sox won the 2005 World Series, you believe it to be true, and its truth you take to explain why you believe it. If your access to the truth is only via evidence—for example, the reports in the next day's newspapers of the Red Sox victory—you can understand why Clifford boldly concludes:

> It is wrong always, everywhere, and for anyone, to believe anything upon insufficient evidence.

Clifford promotes *evidentialism,* the view that belief ought to be proportioned to the evidence, and his reasoning suggests the following argument:

1. To believe a proposition is to hold that it is true.

So, 2. One only believes a proposition properly if one has evidence or indicators that it is true.

3. There is no evidence or indicators that the proposition that God exists is true.

So, 4. If one is to believe properly, one ought not believe the proposition that God exists.

Defenders of the Argument from Design reject (3). Others reject (3) because they believe there are personal experiences that afford evidence that God exists. How does one know, though, that such experiences are veridical, rather than a psychologically induced reverie?

One kind of personal experience that is thought to provide evidence of God's existence is witnessing a miracle. An isolated experience of what one takes to be a miracle is suspect. But if many witnesses agree, their mutual corroboration is evidence that the experience of each is veridical. That convergence provides strong corroboration is often critical in courts of law. If one witness says that the mugger wore a green jacket, the jurors might not attach much credibility to his report. However, if another witness says so too, the credibility of each report goes up mightily. Why? Because the best way to explain why the two witnesses agree is that they observed the same occurrence, as they now report.

Such agreement provides strong corroboration only if the reports are independent. If jurors subsequently learn that the two witnesses knew each other well, and especially if they shared a reason to want the person in the green jacket to be found guilty, trust in their common report diminishes. For now there is an alternative good explanation for the convergence: The best explanation of why the witnesses agree is not the fact that the mugger wore a green jacket but the fact that they colluded or were influenced by a third party.

Examining cases of testimony for alleged miracles, Hume argues that the reports suffer from a lack of independence. Moreover, he argues, since a miracle involves a violation of the laws of nature (otherwise its explanation is natural, not supernatural), all the evidence for exceptionless laws of nature counts as evidence against testimony that a miracle occurred. Can Hume's argument justify a stance in which one dismisses as not being credible testimony to a miracle without examination?

James effectively rejects Clifford's argument that to believe a proposition requires evidence or indicators that it is true. James defends the right to believe on the basis of faith. Although he accepts the evidence requirement for most empirical propositions, he rejects it for propositions fundamental to living a meaningful life, where, he believes, the evidence is essentially indeterminate. These he thinks include moral and religious beliefs. He maintains that since evidence cannot establish that the belief that God exists is false, one who believes that God exists as an act of faith or decision cannot be shown to have done so irrationally. Is James' assumption that only empirical or scientific beliefs, but not religious or moral ones, are subject to evidentialist demands correct?

The disagreement between James and Clifford presupposes that one can choose one's beliefs. Williams argues that the very concept of belief precludes its being a matter of choice. For my choice is no evidence or indicator of what is true, but only of what I want or desire to be true. I cannot simply choose to believe that a friend will be cured of cancer, because my desire has nothing to do with whether the belief is true. (That's a matter of biology and medicine.)

Evidentialism's origins lie in the rise of science, though its appeal is commonsensical. As more and more of the workings of the world, like the alteration of night and day, came to be explainable by appeal to natural laws, the domain of religious explanation was narrowed. Is belief or faith in God's existence rational, warranted, or reasonable without a scientific basis? Are questions about God's existence or nature even susceptible to scientific testing? Can we formulate testable predictions like 'If Jill is a good, pious person, and she contracts a terrible illness, and many pray for her, God will intervene to cure her'?

Theists typically deny that there are such predictive tests, whose failure could be evidence of the nonexistence of a benevolent God. Flew (751–3) stresses the cognitive cost of this denial. What does the belief that God exists and faith in his goodness come to if there is no real way to derive definite, verifiable consequences from it? Does the lack of verifiability not only weaken one's reason to believe in God but also diminish the content of the would-be belief—from, for example, God answers prayers to God sometimes answers prayers?

There are a number of ways to respond to Flew's concern, one of which we have already noted—that a proposition may be correctly believed without the believer being in a position to defend its truth. James argued for a variant, beginning with a comparison of faith with putting oneself forward to befriend someone—for example, a classmate Bill. In doing so, you risk rejection. But if to protect yourself against embarrassment, you hold back, you miss many opportunities to make friends. You cannot so put yourself forward with any chance of success while also demanding that beliefs, like the belief that Bill seems to want to get to know you too, should be subject to rigorous empirical tests. Initially, in seeking the truth of a religious belief and not just the cautious route of avoiding error, you may have to protect these beliefs against premature falsification. Does the faith-trust analogy go as far as James requires (to justify belief on faith and choice)? When do such beliefs cease to be fragile and falsification cease to be premature?

The Existence and Nature of God

St. Anselm

The Ontological Argument

Chapter 1

A Rousing of the Mind to the Contemplation of God

[…] I acknowledge, Lord, and I thank you, that you have created in me this image of you so that I may remember you, think of you, and love you. Yet this image is so eroded by my vices, so clouded by the smoke of my sins, that it cannot do what it was created to do unless you renew and refashion it. I am not trying to scale your heights, Lord; my understanding is in no way equal to that. But I do long to understand your truth in some way, your truth which my heart believes and loves. For I do not seek to understand in order to believe; I believe in order to understand. For I also believe that "Unless I believe, I shall not understand."

Chapter 2

That God Truly Exists

Therefore, Lord, you who grant understanding to faith, grant that, insofar as you know it is useful to me, I may understand that you exist as we believe you exist, and that you are what we believe you to be. Now we believe that you are something than which nothing greater can be thought. So can it be that no such being exists, since "The fool has said in his heart, 'There is no God' "? (Psalm 14:1; 53:1) But when this same fool

From Anselm, *Monologion and Proslogion,* translated by Thomas Williams (Indianapolis: Hackett Publishing Company, 1996). Reprinted with permission of the publisher.

hears me say "something than which nothing greater can be thought," he surely understands what he hears; and what he understands exists in his understanding, even if he does not understand that it exists [in reality]. For it is one thing for an object to exist in the understanding and quite another to understand that the object exists [in reality]. When a painter, for example, thinks out in advance what he is going to paint, he has it in his understanding, but he does not yet understand that it exists, since he has not yet painted it. But once he has painted it, he both has it in his understanding and understands that it exists because he has now painted it. So even the fool must admit that something than which nothing greater can be thought exists at least in his understanding, since he understands this when he hears it, and whatever is understood exists in the understanding. And surely that than which a greater cannot be thought cannot exist only in the understanding. For if it exists only in the understanding, it can be thought to exist in reality as well, which is greater. So if that than which a greater cannot be thought exists only in the understanding, then that than which a greater cannot be thought is that than which a greater *can* be thought. But that is clearly impossible. Therefore, there is no doubt that something than which a greater cannot be thought exists both in the understanding and in reality.

Chapter 3

That He Cannot Be Thought Not to Exist

This [being] exists so truly that it cannot be thought not to exist. For it is possible to think that something exists that cannot be thought not to exist, and such a being is greater than one that can be thought not to exist. Therefore, if that than which a greater cannot be thought can be thought not to exist, then that than which a greater cannot be thought is *not* that than which a greater cannot be thought; and this is a contradiction. So that than which a greater cannot be thought exists so truly that it cannot be thought not to exist.

And this is you, O Lord our God. You exist so truly, O Lord my God, that you cannot be thought not to exist. And rightly so, for if some mind could think something better than you, a creature would rise above the Creator and sit in judgment upon him, which is completely absurd. Indeed, everything that exists, except for you alone, can be thought not to exist. So you alone among all things have existence most truly, and therefore most greatly. Whatever else exists has existence less truly, and therefore less greatly. So then why did "the fool say in his heart, 'There is no God,'" when it is so evident to the rational mind that you of all beings exist most greatly? Why indeed, except because he is stupid and a fool?

Chapter 4

How the Fool Said in His Heart What Cannot Be Thought

But how has he said in his heart what he could not think? Or how could he not think what he said in his heart, since to say in one's heart is the same as to think? But if he really—or rather, *since* he really—thought this, because he said it in his heart, and did not say it in his heart, because he could not think it, there must be more than one way in which something is 'said in one's heart' or 'thought'. In one sense of the word, to think a thing is to think the word that signifies that thing. But in another sense, it is to understand what exactly the thing is. God can be thought not to exist in the first sense, but not at all in the second sense. No one who understands what God is can think that God does not exist, although he may say these words in his heart with no signification at all, or with some peculiar signification. For God

is that than which a greater cannot be thought. Whoever understands this properly, understands that this being exists in such a way that he cannot, even in thought, fail to exist. So whoever understands that God exists in this way cannot think that he does not exist.

Thanks be to you, my good Lord, thanks be to you. For what I once believed through your grace, I now understand through your illumination, so that even if I did not want to *believe* that you exist, I could not fail to *understand* that you exist.

Chapter 5

That God Is Whatever It Is Better to Be than Not to Be; and That He Alone Exists through Himself, and Makes All Other Things from Nothing

Then what are you, Lord God, than whom nothing greater can be thought? What are you, if not the greatest of all beings, who alone exists through himself and made all other things from nothing. For whatever is not this is less than the greatest that can be thought, but this cannot be thought of you. What good is missing from the highest good, through which every good thing exists? And so you are just, truthful, happy, and whatever it is better to be than not to be. For it is better to be just than unjust, and better to be happy than unhappy. [. . .]

Chapter 15

That God Is Greater than Can Be Thought

Therefore, Lord, you are not merely that than which a greater cannot be thought; you are something greater than can be thought. For since it is possible to think that such a being exists, then if you are not that being, it is possible to think something greater than you. But that is impossible. [. . .]

St. Thomas Aquinas

The Five Ways—Question II, Third Article

Third Article

Whether God Exists?

We proceed thus to the Third Article:—

Objection 1. It seems that God does not exist; because if one of two contraries be infinite, the other would be altogether destroyed. But the name *God* means that He is infinite goodness. If, therefore, God existed, there would be no evil discoverable; but there is evil in the world. Therefore God does not exist.

Obj. 2. Further, it is superfluous to suppose that what can be accounted for by a few principles has been produced by many. But it seems that everything we see in the world can be accounted for by other principles, supposing God did not exist. For all natural things can be reduced to one principle, which is nature; and all voluntary things can be reduced to one principle, which is human reason, or will. Therefore there is no need to suppose God's existence.

On the contrary, It is said in the person of God: *I am Who am* (*Exod.* iii. 14).

I answer that, The existence of God can be proved in five ways.

The first and more manifest way is the argument from motion. It is certain, and evident to our sense, that in the world some things are in motion. Now whatever is moved is moved by another, for nothing can be moved except it is in potentiality to that towards which it is moved; whereas a thing moves inasmuch as it is in act. For motion is nothing else than the reduction of something from potentiality to actuality. But nothing can be reduced from potentiality to actuality, except by something in a state of actuality. Thus that which is ac-

tually hot, as fire, makes wood, which is potentially hot, to be actually hot, and thereby moves and changes it. Now it is not possible that the same thing should be at once in actuality and potentiality in the same respect, but only in different respects. For what is actually hot cannot simultaneously be potentially hot; but it is simultaneously potentially cold. It is therefore impossible that in the same respect and in the same way a thing should be both mover and moved, *i.e.,* that it should move itself. Therefore, whatever is moved must be moved by another. If that by which it is moved be itself moved, then this also must needs be moved by another, and that by another again. But this cannot go on to infinity, because then there would be no first mover, and, consequently, no other mover, seeing that subsequent movers move only inasmuch as they are moved by the first mover; as the staff moves only because it is moved by the hand. Therefore it is necessary to arrive at a first mover, moved by no other; and this everyone understands to be God.

The second way is from the nature of efficient cause. In the world of sensible things we find there is an order of efficient causes. There is no case known (neither is it, indeed, possible) in which a thing is found to be the efficient cause of itself; for so it would be prior to itself, which is impossible. Now in efficient causes it is not possible to go on to infinity, because in all efficient causes following in order, the first is the cause of the intermediate cause, and the intermediate is the cause of the ultimate cause, whether the intermediate cause be several, or one only. Now to take away the cause is to take away the effect. Therefore, if there be no first cause among efficient causes, there will be no ultimate, nor any intermediate, cause. But if in efficient causes, it is possible to go on to infinity, there will be no first efficient cause, neither will there be an ultimate effect, nor any intermediate efficient causes; all of which is plainly false. Therefore it is necessary to admit a first efficient cause, to which everyone gives the name of God.

From Aquinas, *Basic Writings of St. Thomas Aquinas,* edited by Anton C. Pegis (Indianapolis: Hackett Publishing Company, 1997). Reprinted with permission of the publisher.

The third way is taken from possibility and necessity, and runs thus. We find in nature things that are possible to be and not to be, since they are found to be generated, and to be corrupted, and consequently, it is possible for them to be and not to be. But it is impossible for these always to exist, for that which can not-be at some time is not. Therefore, if everything can not-be, then at one time there was nothing in existence. Now if this were true, even now there would be nothing in existence, because that which does not exist begins to exist only through something already existing. Therefore, if at one time nothing was in existence, it would have been impossible for anything to have begun to exist; and thus even now nothing would be in existence—which is absurd. Therefore, not all beings are merely possible, but there must exist something the existence of which is necessary. But every necessary thing either has its necessity caused by another, or not. Now it is impossible to go on to infinity in necessary things which have their necessity caused by another, as has been already proved in regard to efficient causes. Therefore we cannot but admit the existence of some being having of itself its own necessity, and not receiving it from another, but rather causing in others their necessity. This all men speak of as God.

The fourth way is taken from the gradation to be found in things. Among beings there are some more and some less good, true, noble, and the like. But *more* and *less* are predicated of different things according as they resemble in their different ways something which is the maximum, as a thing is said to be hotter according as it more nearly resembles that which is hottest; so that there is something which is truest, something best, something noblest, and consequently, something which is most being, for those things that are greatest in truth are greatest in being, as it is written in *Metaph.* ii. Now the maximum in any genus is the cause of all in that genus, as fire, which is the maximum of heat, is the cause of all hot things, as is said in the same book. Therefore there must also be something which is to all beings the cause of their being, goodness, and every other perfection; and this we call God.

The fifth way is taken from the governance of the world. We see that things which lack knowledge, such as natural bodies, act for an end, and this is evident from their acting always, or nearly always, in the same way, so as to obtain the best result. Hence it is plain that they achieve their end, not fortuitously, but designedly. Now whatever lacks knowledge cannot move towards an end, unless it be directed by some being endowed with knowledge and intelligence; as the arrow is directed by the archer. Therefore some intelligent being exists by whom all natural things are directed to their end; and this being we call God.

Reply Obj. 1. As Augustine says: *Since God is the highest good, He would not allow any evil to exist in His works, unless His omnipotence and goodness were such as to bring good even out of evil.* This is part of the infinite goodness of God, that He should allow evil to exist, and out of it produce good.

Reply Obj. 2. Since nature works for a determinate end under the direction of a higher agent, whatever is done by nature must be traced back to God as to its first cause. So likewise whatever is done voluntarily must be traced back to some higher cause other than human reason and will, since these can change and fail; for all things that are changeable and capable of defect must be traced back to an immovable and self-necessary first principle, as has been shown.

William L. Rowe

The Cosmological Argument and the Principle of Sufficient Reason

The Cosmological Argument began with Plato, flourished in the writings of Aquinas, Leibniz, and Samuel Clarke, and was laid to rest by Hume and Kant. Although I think its death premature, if not unjustified, I shall not here attempt its resurrection. What I have in mind is more in the nature of an autopsy. I wish to uncover, clarify, and examine some of the philosophical concepts and theses essential to the reasoning exhibited in the Cosmological Argument. [. . .]

The Cosmological Argument is an argument for the existence of *God*. As such, the argument has two distinct parts. The first part is an argument to establish the existence of a necessary being, a being that carries the reason of its existence within itself. The second part is an argument to establish that this necessary being is God. A good deal of philosophical criticism has been directed against the first part of the argument. Much less has been directed against the second part. Indeed, some philosophers seem not to have realized that the argument has a second part. For example, in Part IX of his *Dialogues Concerning Natural Religion* Hume has Demea present a summary of only the first part of the Cosmological Argument. Demea appears to *assume* that a necessary being would be God. Thus, after concluding that there exists a necessary being, he simply remarks, "There is consequently such a Being, that is, there is a Deity". But, of course, it is not at all obvious that the necessary being is a Deity. Indeed, Cleanthes quickly asks, "Why may not the material universe be the necessarily existent Being?". Hence, as an argument for the existence of Good, the Cosmological Argument not

only does but must contain a second part in which it is argued that the necessary being possesses the properties—omnipotence, infinite goodness, infinite wisdom, etc.—that God, and only God possesses.

Using the expression 'dependent being' to mean 'a being that has the reason of its existence in the casual efficacy of some other being', and the expression 'independent being' to mean 'a being that has the reason of its existence within its own nature', we may state the argument for the existence of a necessary being (i.e., the first part of the Cosmological Argument) as follows:

1. Whatever exists is either a dependent being or an independent being; therefore,

2. Either there exists an independent being or every being is dependent;

3. It is false that every being is dependent; therefore,

4. There exists an independent being; therefore,

5. There exists a necessary being.

This argument consists of two premises—propositions (1) and (3)—and three inferences. The first inference is from (1) to (2), the second from (2) and (3) to (4), and the third inference is from (4) to (5). Of the premises neither is obviously true, and of the inferences only the first and second are above suspicion. Before discussing the main subject of this paper—namely, proposition (1) and its connection with the Principle of Sufficient Reason—I want to describe the argument in support of premise (3) and the main criticisms of that argument.

Why is it false that every being is dependent? Well, if every being that exists (or ever existed) is dependent then the whole of existing things, it would seem, consists of a collection of dependent beings, that is, a

W. L. Rowe, "The Cosmological Argument and the Principle of Sufficient Reason" from *Man and World,* 1 (1968). Reprinted with kind permission from the author and Springer Science and Business Media.

collection of beings each member of which exists by reason of the casual efficacy of some other being. Now this collection would have to contain an infinite number of members. For suppose it contained a *finite* number, let us say three, *a, b,* and *c.* Now if in Scotus's phrase "a circle of causes is inadmissible" then if *c* is caused by *b* and *b* by *a, a* would exist without a cause, there being no other member of the collection that could be its cause. But in that case *a* would not be what by supposition it is, namely a *dependent* being. Hence, if we grant that a circle of causes is inadmissible it is impossible that the whole of existing this should consist of a collection of dependent beings *finite* in number.

Let us suppose, then, that the dependent beings making up the collection are *infinite* in number. Why is it impossible that the whole of existing things should consist of such a collection? The proponent of the Cosmological Argument answers as follows. The infinite collection *itself,* he argues, requires and explanation for its existence. For since it is true of each member of the collection that it might not have existed, it is true of the whole infinite collection that it might not have existed. But if the entire infinite collection might not have existed there must be some explanation for why it exists rather than not. The explanation cannot lie in the casual efficacy of some being outside of the collection since by supposition the collection includes every being that is or ever was. Nor can the explanation for why there is an infinite collection be found within the collection itself, for since no member of the collection is independent, has the reason of its existence within itself, the collection as a whole cannot have the reason of existence within itself. Thus the conception of an infinite collection of dependent beings is the conception of something whose existence has no explanation whatever. But since premise (1) tells us that whatever exists has an explanation for its existence, either within itself or in the casual efficacy of some other being, it cannot be that the whole of existing things consists of an infinite collection of dependent beings.

Two major criticisms have been advanced against this line of reasoning, criticisms which have achieved some degree of acceptance. According to the first criticism it *makes no sense* to apply the notion of cause or explanation to the totality of things, and the arguments used to show that the whole of existing things must have a cause

or explanation are fallacious. Thus in his B.B.C. debate with Father Copleston, Bertrand Russell took the view that the concept of cause is inapplicable to the universe conceived as the total collection of things. When pressed by Copleston as to how he could rule out "the legitimacy of asking the question how the total, or anything at all comes to be there", Russell responded: "I can illustrate what seems to me your fallacy. Every man who exists has a mother, and it seems to me you argument is that therefore the human race must have a mother, but obviously the human race hasn't a mother—that's a different logical sphere."[1] According to the second major criticism it is intelligible to ask for an explanation of the existence of the infinite collection of dependent beings. But the answer to this question, so the criticism goes, is provided once we learn that each member of the infinite collection has an explanation of its existence. Thus Hume remarks: "Did I show you the particular causes of each individual in a collection of twenty particles of matter, I should think it very reasonable, should you afterwards ask me, what was the cause of the whole twenty. This is sufficiently explained in explaining the cause of the parts."[2]

Although neither criticism is, I think, decisive against the argument given in support of proposition (3), they do draw attention to two crucial steps in the Cosmological Argument. First, it seems that the infinite collection is itself viewed as an existing thing. For only if it is so viewed will it follow from premise (1) that it (the infinite collection) must have a cause or explanation of its existence. Second, the question why each member of the infinite collection exists is felt to be different from the question why the infinite collection exists. For the proponent of the argument admits that each member of the collection has an explanation of its existence— namely, in the casual efficacy of some other member— and yet denies that this explains the existence of the entire infinite collection.

1. 'The Existence of God, A Debate between Bertrand Russell and Father F. C. Copleston', John Hick, (ed.), *The Existence of God* (The Macmillan Company, New York 1964), p. 175. The debate was originally broadcast by the British Broadcasting Corporation in 1948. References are to the debate as reprinted in *The Existence of God.*

2. Hume, *Dialogues,* Part IX.

Perhaps neither of these steps in the argument for proposition (3) is correct. But even if both steps are correct—that is, even if the infinite collection itself may be viewed as an object or thing, and even if to explain each member is not sufficient to explain the collection—it is important to note that it is premise (1) from which it is then inferred that there must be an explanation for the existence of the infinite collection. Thus proposition (1) plays a crucial role not only as a premise in the main argument but also as a premise in the argument for proposition (3). Having seen the crucial role that proposition (1) plays in the Cosmological Argument, we may now examine that proposition in some detail.

Proposition (1) tells us that *whatever exists* must have an explanation for its existence. The explanation may lie either within the nature of the thing itself or in the casual efficacy of some other being. The claim that whatever exists must have an explanation of its existence I shall call the *strong form* of the Principle of Sufficient Reason. This is to be distinguished from the claim that *whatever comes into existence* must have an explanation of its existence. The latter claim I shall call the *weak form* of the Principle of Sufficient Reason. If we imagine a star that has existed from eternity, a star that never came into existence but has always existed, the strong form of the Principle of Sufficient Reason requires, whereas the weak form does not, that there be an explanation for the existence of that star. The Cosmological Argument, as we have seen, employs the strong form of the Principle of Sufficient Reason.

Can the Principle of Sufficient Reason be proved or otherwise known to be true? Some philosophers, it seems, thought that the Principle could be proved. Hume attributes the following argument to Locke.

1. If something exists without a cause, it is caused by nothing;

2. Nothing cannot be the cause of something; therefore,

3. Whatever exists must have a cause.

About this "proof" Hume remarks:

It is sufficient only to observe that when we exclude all causes we really do exclude them, and

neither suppose nothing nor the object itself to be the causes of the existence, and consequently can draw no argument from the absurdity of that exclusion. If everything must have a cause, it follows that upon the exclusion of other causes we must accept of the object itself or of nothing as causes. But it is the very point in question, whether everything must have a cause or not, and therefore, according to all just reasoning, it ought never to be taken for granted.[3]

It is clear from Hume's comment that he rejects premise (1). For he takes the proponent of the argument to mean by premise (1) that if something exists without a cause it, nevertheless, has a cause—although in this case its cause will not be some other thing, it will be *nothing*. But there is a subtlety in this argument that Hume overlooks. In the natural sense of the expression 'caused by nothing' it is *true* that if something exists without a cause it is caused by nothing—to be caused by nothing is simply not to be caused by any thing whatever. Taken in this way, premise (1) is true. Moreover, premise (2) is true as well. For to say that nothing cannot be the cause of something is simply to say that if something has a cause then there must be some *thing* which is its cause. But so interpreted, the premises, although true, do not yield the conclusion that everything has a cause. For from (1) if something exists without a cause then there is no thing which caused it, and (2) if something has a cause then there is a thing which caused it, it in no way follows that everything has a cause. Therefore, if the premises are interpreted so as to be clearly true, the argument is invalid; whereas, if the argument is to appear valid its first premise, as Hume points out, is false or, at the very least, begs the question at issue. In either case the argument fails as a demonstration of the Principle of Sufficient Reason.

Of course, if, as seems likely, the Principle of Sufficient Reason cannot be—at least, has not been—demonstrated, it does not follow that it cannot be *known* to be true. Clearly, if we know any propositions to be true there must be some propositions which we can know to be true without having to *prove* them, without having to derive them from other propositions we know to be true. If this were

---

3. *A Treatise of Human Nature,* Book I, Part III, Section III.

not so, we would have to know an infinite number of propositions in order to know any proposition whatever. Hence, the fact, if it is a fact, that the Principle of Sufficient Reason cannot be demonstrated does not invalidate the view other philosophers seem to take; namely, that the Principle is a necessary truth, known *a priori*.

If the Principle in its strong form is analytically true then the view of these philosophers—namely, that the Principle is a necessary truth, known *a priori,* is probably correct. For every analytically true proposition is necessary and, if known at all, presumably can be known by simply reflecting on it, without relying on empirical evidence. But is the Principle of Sufficient Reason analytically true? Clearly the Principle is not logically true. Nor, it would seem, does the mere notion of the existence of a thing *definitionally* contain the notion of a thing being caused. Kant argued—correctly, I think—that although the proposition 'Every effect has a cause' is analytically true, 'Every event has a cause' is not. The idea of an event, of something happening—a leaf falling, a chair collapsing, etc.—does not seem to contain the idea of something *causing* that event. If this is so then the Principle of Sufficient Reason is certainly not analytically true.

But if the Principle is not analytically true how can it be necessary? Indeed, can any proposition be necessary if it is not analytically true? Many philosophers have held that only analytically true propositions are necessary. But it is, I think, reasonable to argue, as some philosophers have, that, for example, the proposition 'Whatever is red is colored' is necessary but not analytically true. For (i) we do not seem to have a *definition* of 'red' or 'colored' in terms of which the sentence 'Whatever is red is colored' can be reduced to a sentence expressing a logical truth, and yet (ii) it certainly is *impossible* that something be red and not colored. Thus the proposition 'Whatever is red is colored' may well be a synthetic, necessary proposition. Moreover, as Chisholm has argued, there seem to be reasons for the view that the proposition 'Necessarily, whatever is red is colored' is known *a priori*. But even if this is correct, as I am inclined to think it is, it is far from clear that the Principle of Sufficient Reason is a synthetic, necessary proposition known *a priori*.

The difficulty with the view that the Principle, in either its strong or weak form, is *necessary* is that we do

seem able to conceive of things existing, or even of things coming into existence, without having to conceive of those things as having an explanation or cause. Unlike the proposition 'Some red things are not colored', it does seem conceptually possible that something should exist and yet have no cause or explanation of its existence. As Hume remarks, "The separation, therefore, of the idea of a cause from that of a beginning of existence is plainly possible for the imagination, and consequently the actual separation of those objects is so far possible that it implies no contradiction nor absurdity. . . ."[4] Indeed, not only does the denial of the Principle seem to be possible, philosophers have held that the denial of the Principle is *true*.

> . . . many philosophers have maintained that it is not true that everything that exists, or even that everything that has a beginning, has a cause, that is to say, is an effect. The world, they say, contains "spontaneous", free, or uncaused and unoriginated events. In any case they assert very positively that there is no way of proving that such uncaused events do not occur.[5]

In view of this and other difficulties, some contemporary defenders of the Cosmological Argument have retreated from the view that the Principle of Sufficient Reason is a synthetic, necessary proposition known *a priori*. Instead, they have adopted the somewhat more modest view that the Principle is a *metaphysical assumption,* a presupposition we are forced to make in order to make sense of our world. Thus, for example, Father Copleston, in his B.B.C. debate with Russell, argued that something like the Principle of Sufficient Reason is presupposed by science. "I cannot see how science could be conducted on any other assumption than that of order and intelligibility in nature."[6] Another contemporary philosopher, Richard Taylor, has expressed this view as follows:

---

4. *Treatise,* Book I, Part III, Section III.

5. John Laird, *Theism and Cosmology* (Philosophical Library, New York 1942), p. 95. [. . .]

6. 'A Debate', p. 176.

The principle of sufficient reason can be illustrated in various ways, as we have done, and if one thinks about it, he is apt to find that he presupposes it in his thinking about reality, but it cannot be proved. It does not appear to be itself a necessary truth, and at the same time it would be most odd to say it is contingent. If one were to try proving it, he would sooner or later have to appeal to considerations that are less plausible than the principle itself. Indeed, it is hard to see how one could even make an argument for it, without already assuming it. For this reason it might properly be called a presupposition of reason itself. One can deny that it is true, without embarrassment or fear of refutation, but one is apt to find that what he is denying is not really what the principle asserts. We shall, then, treat it here as a datum—not something that is provably true, but as something which all men, whether they ever reflect upon it or not, seem more or less to presuppose.[7]

What are we to make of this view? It must be admitted, I think, that this view is a good deal more plausible than the view that the Principle is a necessary truth, known *a priori*. For the proponent of this more modest view is not contending—or, at least, need not contend—that the Principle states a necessary truth about reality. All he contends is that the Principle is presupposed by us in our dealings with the world. To this he may add that without this presupposition we cannot make any sense of the world. However, there are several critical points pertinent to this view that need discussion.

First, does the scientist in his work really assume that everything that happens has a cause? In the debate between Russell and Copleston, Russell took the view that physicists need not and do not assume that every event has a cause. "As for things not having a cause, the physicists assure us that individual quantum transition in atoms have no cause."[8] Again, he remarks:

... a physicist looks for causes; that does not necessarily imply that there are causes everywhere. A man may look for gold without assuming that there is gold everywhere; if he finds gold, well and good, if he doesn't he's had bad luck. The same is true when the physicist looks for the causes.[9]

How are we to settle this matter? Philosophers who hold that the causal principle is a fundamental assumption reply that the Heisenberg uncertainty principle "tells us something about the success (or lack of it) of the present atomic theory in correlating observations, but not about nature in itself, . . ."[10] Moreover, it is observed that the failure to find causes does not lead anyone to abandon the causal principle. Indeed, it is sometimes argued that it is *impossible* to obtain empirical evidence against the principle. If we don't find gold in a hill after a careful search, we conclude that there's no gold there to be found. But if we don't find the cause of a certain event, we don't conclude that the event has no cause, only that it is extremely difficult to discover. Perhaps, then, there is some reason to think that we do assume that whatever happens has an explanation or cause.

But even if it is granted that in our dealings with the world we presuppose that whatever happens has a cause, there seems to be a serious difficulty confronting the recent defenders of the Cosmological Argument. For what the Cosmological Argument requires—or, more exactly, what the versions argued by Samuel Clarke, Copleston, and Taylor require—is what I have called the strong form of the Principle of Sufficient Reason.

That is, their arguments require as a premise the principle that whatever exists—even an eternal being—has a cause or explanation of its existence. But what we have just granted to be presupposed by us in our dealing with the world is the principle that whatever *happens* has a cause. This latter principle implies that whatever begins to exist has a cause, since the coming into existence of a thing is an event, a happening. Thus the principle we have granted to be presupposed in science and commonsense implies what I have called the weak form of the Principle of Sufficient Reason. But it does not

7. Richard Taylor, *Metaphysics* (Prentice-Hall, Inc., Englewood Cliffs, N.J. 1963), pp. 86–7.

8. 'A Debate', p. 176.

9. *Ibid.*, p. 177.

10. *Ibid.*, p. 176.

imply the strong form of the Principle; it does not imply that whatever exists has a cause. If something comes into existence, its coming into existence is something that happens. But if something exists from eternity, its eternal existence is not one of the things that happen. Hence, even if it be granted that we presuppose a cause for whatever happens, it does not follow that we presuppose a cause or explanation for whatever exists.

Can it reasonably be argued that the strong form of the Principle of Sufficient Reason is, as Taylor suggests, a presupposition that all men make, a presupposition of reason itself? We have granted as a presupposition of reason that there must be a cause or explanation for any thing that comes into existence. Thus if we imagine a star to have come into existence, say, a thousand years ago, it is presupposed that there must be an explanation for its having come into existence. That is, it is assumed by us that there must be a set of prior events that was sufficient to cause the birth of that star. To say, "Nothing caused the birth of the star, it just popped into existence and there is no reason why it came into existence" is, we have granted, to deny a fundamental presupposition of reason itself. But imagine that there is a star in the heavens that never came into existence, a star that has always existed, that has existed from eternity. Do we presuppose that there must be an explanation for the eternal existence of this star? I am doubtful that we do. But short of a metaphysical investigation of mind and its relation to nature, it seems quite impossible to answer this question. Perhaps, then, our most fruitful course here is simply to note the consequences for the Cosmological Argument if the Principle of Sufficient Reason in its strong form is, as Copleston and Taylor maintain, a presupposition all men make.

However, before considering this last question it is, I think, important to clarify the nature of the question concerning a thing's existence to which the Principle of Sufficient Reason demands there be an answer. Of the star that came into existence a thousand years ago, we may ask 'Where did it come from?', 'What brought it into existence?', or 'Why did it come into existence?'. Clearly none of these questions can be asked properly of a star that has existed from eternity. Once we learn that it has always existed we realize that it never came into existence. But there is a simpler question that can be asked both about the eternally existing star and about

the star that came into existence a thousand years ago; namely, 'Why does this thing exist?' Although we may answer—or, at least, show to be improper—the question 'Why did this thing come into existence?' by pointing out that it has always existed, the question 'Why does thing this thing exist rather than not?' cannot be answered or even turned aside by pointing out that it has always existed. As Taylor has noted:

> . . . it is no answer to the question, why a thing exists, to state *how long* it has existed. A geologist does not suppose that he has explained why there should be rivers and mountains merely by pointing out that they are old. Similarly, if one were to ask, concerning the ball of which we have spoken, for some sufficient reason for its being, he would not receive any answer upon being told that it had been there since yesterday. Nor would it be any better answer to say that it had existed since before anyone could remember, or even that it had always existed; for the question was not one concerning its age but its existence.[11]

The question, then, to which the Principle of Sufficient Reason requires that there be an answer is: 'Why does this thing exist?' This question, I am claiming, may be sensibly asked about a star that has existed from eternity, or one that has existed for only a thousand years.

It should be clear that it is one thing to argue, as I have done, that the question 'Why does this thing exist?' makes sense when asked of something that has always existed, and another thing to argue, as I have not done, that all men presuppose that there must be an adequate answer to that question, even when it is asked about something that has existed from eternity. We have granted as a presupposition of reason that there must be an adequate answer to the question when the being of which it is asked has come into existence. But, as I have indicated, it seems at least doubtful that the strong form of the Principle of Sufficient Reason is a presupposition of reason itself.

Suppose, as Taylor, Copleston, and others have claimed, that the Principle of Sufficient Reason in its strong

---

11. Taylor, *Metaphysics,* p. 88.

form is a metaphysical assumption that all men make, whether or not they reflect sufficiently to become aware of the assumption. What bearing would this have on the Cosmological Argument? It would not, of course, show that it is a good argument. For (1) the argument could be invalid, (2) some premise other than the premise expressing the Principle could be false, and (3) even the premise expressing the Principle could be false. The fact, if it is a fact, that all of us presuppose that whatever exists has an explanation of its existence does not imply that nothing exists without a reason for its existence. Nature is not bound to satisfy our presuppositions. As James has remarked in another connection, "In the great boarding-house of nature, the cakes and the butter and the syrup seldom come out so even and leave the plates so clean." However, if we do make such a presupposition we could not *consistently* reject the Cosmological Argument solely because it contains as a premise the Principle of Sufficient Reason. That is, if we reject the

argument it must be for some reason other than its appeal to the Principle of Sufficient Reason.

If, as seems likely, the strong form of the Principle is not a presupposition of reason itself, and if, as I have argued, the Principle is neither analytically true nor a synthetic, necessary truth, known *a priori,* the Cosmological Argument—in so far as it requires the strong form of the Principle as a premise—cannot, I think, reasonably be maintained to be a *proof* of the existence of God. For unless there is a way of knowing the Principle to be true other than those we have explored, it follows that we do not know the Principle to be true. But if we do not know that one of the essential premises of an argument is true then we do not know that it is a good argument for its conclusion. It may, of course, be a perfectly good argument. But if to claim of an argument that it is a *proof* of its conclusion is to imply that its premises are *known* to be true, then we are not entitled to claim that the Cosmological Argument is a proof of the existence of God.

David Hume

Dialogues Concerning Natural Religion

Part II

Demea: I must own, *Cleanthes,* said *Demea,* that nothing can more surprise me than the light in which you have all along put this argument. By the whole tenor of your discourse, one would imagine that you were maintaining the being of a God against the cavils of atheists and infidels, and were necessitated to become a champion for that fundamental principle of all religion. But this, I hope, is not by any means a question among us. No

man; no man, at least of common sense, I am persuaded, ever entertained a serious doubt with regard to a truth so certain and self-evident. The question is not concerning the *being* but the *nature* of God—This I affirm, from the infirmities of human understanding, to be altogether incomprehensible and unknown to us. The essence of that supreme mind, his attributes, the manner of his existence, the very nature of his duration; these and every particular which regards so divine a being are mysterious to men. Finite, weak, and blind creatures, we ought to humble ourselves in his august presence, and, conscious of our frailties, adore in silence his infinite perfections which eye hath not seen, ear hath not heard, neither hath it entered into the heart of man to conceive. They are covered in a deep cloud from human curiosity; it is profaneness to attempt penetrating

From David Hume, *Dialogues Concerning Natural Religion (Second Edition),* edited by Richard H. Popkin (Indianapolis: Hackett Publishing Company, 1998). Reprinted with permission of the publisher.

through these sacred obscurities; and, next to the impiety of denying his existence, is the temerity of prying into his nature and essence, decrees and attributes.

But lest you should think that my *piety* has here got the better of my *philosophy,* I shall support my opinion, if it needs any support, by a very great authority. I might cite all the divines, almost from the foundation of *Christianity,* who have ever treated of this or any other theological subject; but I shall confine myself, at present, to one equally celebrated for piety and philosophy. It is *Father Malebranche* who, I remember, thus expresses himself.[1] "One ought not so much (says he) to call God a spirit in order to express positively what he is, as in order to signify that he is not matter. He is a Being infinitely perfect—of this we cannot doubt. But in the same manner as we ought not to imagine, even supposing him corporeal, that he is clothed with a human body, as the *Anthropomorphites* asserted, under color that that figure was the most perfect of any, so neither ought we to imagine that the spirit of God has human ideas or bears any resemblance to our spirit, under color that we know nothing more perfect than a human mind. We ought rather to believe that as he comprehends the perfections of matter without being material . . . he comprehends also the perfections of created spirits without being spirit, in the manner we conceive spirit: That his true name is *He that is,* or, in other words, Being without restriction, All Being, the Being infinite and universal."

Philo: After so great an authority, *Demea,* replied *Philo,* as that which you have produced, and a thousand more which you might produce, it would appear ridiculous in me to add my sentiment or express my approbation of your doctrine. But surely, where reasonable men treat these subjects, the question can never be concerning the *being* but only the *nature* of the Deity. The former truth, as you well observe, is unquestionable and self-evident. Nothing exists without a cause; and the original cause of this universe (whatever it be) we call *God,* and piously ascribe to him every species of perfection. Whoever scruples this fundamental truth deserves every punishment which can be inflicted among philosophers, to wit, the greatest ridicule, contempt, and disapprobation. But as all perfection is entirely relative, we ought never to imagine that we comprehend the attributes of this divine Being, or to suppose that his perfections have any analogy or likeness to the perfections of a human creature. Wisdom, thought, design, knowledge—these we justly ascribe to him because these words are honorable among men, and we have no other language or other conceptions by which we can express our adoration of him. But let us beware lest we think that our ideas anywise correspond to his perfections, or that his attributes have any resemblance to these qualities among men. He is infinitely superior to our limited view and comprehension; and is more the object of worship in the temple than of disputation in the schools.

In reality, *Cleanthes,* continued he, there is no need of having recourse to that affected skepticism, so displeasing to you, in order to come at this determination. Our ideas reach no farther than our experience: We have no experience of divine attributes and operations. I need not conclude my syllogism: You can draw the inference yourself. And it is a pleasure to me (and I hope to you, too) that just reasoning and sound piety here concur in the same conclusion, and both of them establish the adorably mysterious and incomprehensible nature of the Supreme Being.

Cleanthes: Not to lose any time in circumlocutions, said *Cleanthes,* addressing himself to *Demea,* much less in replying to the pious declamations of *Philo,* I shall briefly explain how I conceive this matter. Look round the world: Contemplate the whole and every part of it: You will find it to be nothing but one great machine, subdivided into an infinite number of lesser machines, which again admit of subdivisions to a degree beyond what human senses and faculties can trace and explain. All these various machines, and even their most minute parts, are adjusted to each other with an accuracy which ravishes into admiration all men who have ever contemplated them. The curious adapting of means to ends, throughout all nature, resembles exactly, though it much exceeds, the productions of human contrivance; of human design, thought, wisdom, and intelligence. Since therefore the effects resemble each other, we are led to infer, by all the rules of analogy, that the causes also resemble, and that the Author of Nature is somewhat similar to the mind of man, though possessed of much larger faculties, proportioned to the grandeur of the work which he has executed. By this argument *a poste-*

---

1. *Recherche de la Vérité,* liv. 3, cap. 9.

riori, and by this argument alone, do we prove at once the existence of a Deity and his similarity to human mind and intelligence.

Demea: I shall be so free, *Cleanthes,* said *Demea,* as to tell you that from the beginning I could not approve of your conclusion concerning the similarity of the Deity to men; still less can I approve of the mediums by which you endeavor to establish it. What! No demonstration of the Being of God! No abstract arguments! No proofs *a priori!* Are these which have hitherto been so much insisted on by philosophers all fallacy, all sophism? Can we reach no farther in this subject than experience and probability? I will say not that this is betraying the cause of a Deity; but surely, by this affected candor, you give advantages to atheists which they never could obtain by the mere dint of argument and reasoning.

Philo: What I chiefly scruple in this subject, said *Philo,* is not so much that all religious arguments are by *Cleanthes* reduced to experience, as that they appear not to be even the most certain and irrefragable of that inferior kind. That a stone will fall, that fire will burn, that the earth has solidity, we have observed a thousand and a thousand times; and when any new instance of this nature is presented, we draw without hesitation the accustomed inference. The exact similarity of the cases gives us a perfect assurance of a similar event, and a stronger evidence is never desired nor sought after. But wherever you depart, in the least, from the similarity of the cases, you diminish proportionably the evidence; and may at last bring it to a very weak *analogy,* which is confessedly liable to error and, uncertainty. After having experienced the circulation of the blood in human creatures, we make no doubt that it takes place in *Titius* and *Maevius;* but from its circulation in frogs and fishes it is only a presumption, though a strong one, from analogy that it takes place in men and other animals. The analogical reasoning is much weaker when we infer the circulation of the sap in vegetables from our experience that the blood circulates in animals; and those who hastily followed that imperfect analogy are found, by more accurate experiments, to have been mistaken.

If we see a house, *Cleanthes,* we conclude, with the greatest certainty, that it had an architect or builder because this is precisely that species of effect which we have experienced to proceed from that species of cause. But surely you will not affirm that the universe bears

such a resemblance to a house that we can with the same certainty infer a similar cause, or that the analogy is here entire and perfect. The dissimilitude is so striking that the utmost you can here pretend to is a guess, a conjecture, a presumption concerning a similar cause; and how that pretension will be received in the world, I leave you to consider.

Cleanthes: It would surely be very ill received, replied *Cleanthes,* and I should be deservedly blamed and detested did I allow that the proofs of a Deity amounted to no more than a guess or conjecture. But is the whole adjustment of means to ends in a house and in the universe so slight a resemblance? The economy of final causes? The order, proportion, and arrangement of every part? Steps of a stair are plainly contrived that human legs may use them in mounting; and this inference is certain and infallible. Human legs are also contrived for walking and mounting; and this inference, I allow, is not altogether so certain because of the dissimilarity which you remark; but does it, therefore, deserve the name only of presumption or conjecture?

Demea: Good God! cried *Demea,* interrupting him, where are we? Zealous defenders of religion allow that the proofs of a Deity fall short of perfect evidence! And you, *Philo,* on whose assistance I depended in proving the adorable mysteriousness of the Divine Nature, do you assent to all these extravagant opinions of *Cleanthes?* For what other name can I give them? or, why spare my censure when such principles are advanced, supported by such an authority, before so young a man as *Pamphilus?*

Philo: You seem not to apprehend, replied *Philo,* that I argue with *Cleanthes* in his own way, and, by showing him the dangerous consequences of his tenets, hope at last to reduce him to our opinion. But what sticks most with you, I observe, is the representation which *Cleanthes* has made of the argument *a posteriori;* and, finding that that argument is likely to escape your hold and vanish into air, you think it so disguised that you can scarcely believe it to be set in its true light. Now, however much I may dissent, in other respects, from the dangerous principle of *Cleanthes,* I must allow that he has fairly represented that argument, and I shall endeavor so to state the matter to you that you will entertain no further scruples with regard to it.

Were a man to abstract from everything which he knows or has seen, he would be altogether incapable, merely from his own ideas, to determine what kind of scene the universe must be, or to give the preference to one state or situation of things above another. For as nothing which he clearly conceives could be esteemed impossible or implying a contradiction, every chimera of his fancy would be upon an equal footing; nor could he assign any just reason why he adheres to one idea or system, and rejects the others which are equally possible.

Again, after he opens his eyes and contemplates the world as it really is, it would be impossible for him at first to assign the cause of any one event, much less of the whole of things, or of the universe. He might set his fancy a rambling, and she might bring him in an infinite variety of reports and representations. These would all be possible; but, being all equally possible, he would never of himself give a satisfactory account for his preferring one of them to the rest. Experience alone can point out to him the true cause of any phenomenon.

Now, according to this method of reasoning, *Demea,* it follows (and is, indeed, tacitly allowed by *Cleanthes* himself) that order, arrangement, or the adjustment of final causes, is not of itself any proof of design, but only so far as it has been experienced to proceed from that principle. For aught we can know *a priori,* matter may contain the source or spring of order originally within itself, as well as mind does; and there is no more difficulty in conceiving that the several elements, from an internal unknown cause, may fall into the most exquisite arrangement, than to conceive that their ideas, in the great universal mind, from a like internal unknown cause, fall into that arrangement. The equal possibility of both these suppositions is allowed. But, by experience, we find, according, to *Cleanthes,* that there is a difference between them. Throw several pieces of steel together, without shape or form; they will never arrange themselves so as to compose a watch. Stone and mortar and wood, without an architect, never erect a house. But the ideas in a human mind, we see, by an unknown, inexplicable economy, arrange themselves so as to form the plan of a watch or house. Experience, therefore, proves that there is an original principle of order in mind, not in matter. From similar effects we infer similar causes. The adjustment of means to ends is alike in the universe, as in a machine of human contrivance. The causes, therefore, must be resembling.

I was from the beginning scandalized, I must own, with this resemblance which is asserted between the Deity and human creatures, and must conceive it to imply such a degradation of the Supreme Being as no sound theist could endure. With your assistance, therefore, *Demea,* I shall endeavor to defend what you justly call the adorable mysteriousness of the Divine Nature, and shall refute this reasoning of *Cleanthes,* provided he allows that I have made a fair representation of it.

When *Cleanthes* had assented, *Philo,* after a short pause, proceeded in the following manner.

That all inferences, *Cleanthes,* concerning fact are founded on experience, and that all experimental reasonings are founded on the supposition that similar causes prove similar effects, and similar effects similar causes, I shall not at present much dispute with you. But observe, I entreat you, with what extreme caution all just reasoners proceed in the transferring of experiments to similar cases. Unless the cases be exactly similar, they repose no perfect confidence in applying their past observation to any particular phenomenon. Every alteration of circumstances occasions a doubt concerning the event; and it requires new experiments to prove certainly that the new circumstances are of no moment or importance. A change in bulk, situation, arrangement, age, disposition of the air, or surrounding bodies; any of these particulars may be attended with the most unexpected consequences. And unless the objects be quite familiar to us, it is the highest temerity to expect with assurance, after any of these changes, an event similar to that which before fell under our observation. The slow and deliberate steps of philosophers here, if anywhere, are distinguished from the precipitate march of the vulgar, who, hurried on by the smallest similitude, are incapable of all discernment or consideration.

But can you think, *Cleanthes,* that your usual phlegm and philosophy have been preserved in so wide a step as you have taken when you compared to the universe houses, ships, furniture, machines; and, from their similarity in some circumstances, inferred a similarity in their causes? Thought, design, intelligence, such as we discover in men and other animals, is no more than one of the springs and principles of the universe, as well as heat or cold, attraction or repulsion, and a hundred others which fall under daily observation. It is an active cause by which some particular parts of nature, we find, produce alterations on other parts. But can a conclusion, with any propriety, be transferred from parts to the whole? Does not the great disproportion bar all comparison and inference? From observing the growth of a hair, can we learn anything concerning the generation of a man? Would the manner of a leaf's blowing, even though perfectly known, afford us any instruction concerning the vegetation of a tree?

But allowing that we were to take the *operations* of one part of nature upon another for the foundation of our judgment concerning the *origin* of the whole (which never can be admitted), yet why select so minute, so weak, so bounded a principle as the reason and design of animals is found to be upon this planet? What peculiar privilege has this little agitation of the brain which we call "thought", that we must thus make it the model of the whole universe? Our partiality in our own favor does indeed present it on all occasions, but sound philosophy ought carefully to guard against so natural an illusion.

So far from admitting, continued *Philo,* that the operations of a part can afford us any just conclusion concerning the origin of the whole, I will not allow any one part to form a rule for another part if the latter be very remote from the former. Is there any reasonable ground to conclude that the inhabitants of other planets possess thought, intelligence, reason, or anything similar to these faculties in men? When nature has so extremely diversified her manner of operation in this small globe, can we imagine that she incessantly copies herself throughout so immense a universe? And if thought, as we may well suppose, be confined merely to this narrow corner, and has even there so limited a sphere of action, with what propriety can we assign it for the original cause of all things? The narrow views of a peasant who makes his domestic economy the rule for the government of kingdoms is in comparison a pardonable sophism.

But were we ever so much assured that a thought and reason resembling the human were to be found throughout the whole universe, and were its activity elsewhere vastly greater and more commanding than it appears in this globe; yet I cannot see why the operations of a world constituted, arranged, adjusted, can with any propriety be extended to a world which is in its embryo-

state, and is advancing towards that constitution and arrangement. By observation we know somewhat of the economy, action, and nourishment of a finished animal; but we must transfer with great caution that observation to the growth of a foetus in the womb, and still more to the formation of an animalcule in the loins of its male parent. Nature, we find, even from our limited experience, possesses an infinite number of springs and principles which incessantly discover themselves on every change of her position and situation. And what new and unknown principles would actuate her in so new and unknown a situation as that of the formation of a universe, we can not, without the utmost temerity, pretend to determine.

A very small part of this great system, during a very short time, is very imperfectly discovered to us; and do we thence pronounce decisively concerning the origin of the whole?

Admirable conclusion! Stone, wood, brick, iron, brass, have not, at this time, in this minute globe of earth, an order or arrangement without human art and contrivance; therefore, the universe could not originally attain its order and arrangement without something similar to human art. But is a part of nature a rule for another part very wide of the former? Is it a rule for the whole? Is a very small part a rule for the universe? Is nature in one situation a certain rule for nature in another situation vastly different from the former?

And can you blame me, *Cleanthes,* if I here imitate the prudent reserve of *Simonides,* who, according to the noted story, being asked by *Hiero, What God was?* desired a day to think of it, and then two days more; and after that manner continually prolonged the term, without ever bringing in his definition or description? Could you even blame me if I had answered, at first, *that I did not know,* and was sensible that this subject lay vastly beyond the reach of my faculties? You might cry out skeptic and raillier, as much as you pleased; but, having found in so many other subjects much more familiar the imperfections and even contradictions of human reason, I never should expect any success from its feeble conjectures in a subject so sublime and so remote from the sphere of our observation. When two *species* of objects have always been observed to be conjoined together, I can *infer,* by custom, the existence of one wherever I *see* the existence of the other; and this I call an argument from experience. But how this argument can have place where the objects, as in the present case, are single, individual, without parallel or specific resemblance, may be difficult to explain. And will any man tell me with a serious countenance that an orderly universe must arise from some thought and art like the human because we have experience of it? To ascertain this reasoning it were requisite that we had experience of the origin of worlds; and it is not sufficient, surely, that we have seen ships and cities arise from human art and contrivance. . . .

Philo was proceeding in this vehement manner, somewhat between jest and earnest, as it appeared to me, when he observed some signs of impatience in *Cleanthes,* and then immediately stopped short. *Cleanthes:* What I had to suggest, said *Cleanthes,* is only that you would not abuse terms, or make use of popular expressions to subvert philosophical reasonings. You know that the vulgar often distinguish reason from experience, even where the question relates only to matter of fact and existence, though it is found, where that *reason* is properly analyzed, that it is nothing but a species of experience. To prove by experience the origin of the universe from mind is not more contrary to common speech than to prove the motion of the earth from the same principle. And a caviller might raise all the same objections to the *Copernican* system which you have urged against my reasonings. Have you other earths, might he say, which you have seen to move? Have . . .

Philo: Yes! cried *Philo,* interrupting him, we have other earths. Is not the moon another earth, which we see to turn round its center? Is not Venus another earth, where we observe the same phenomenon? Are not the revolutions of the sun also a confirmation, from analogy, of the same theory? All the, planets, are they not earths which revolve about the sun? Are not the satellites moons which move round Jupiter and Saturn, and along with these primary planets round the sun? These analogies and resemblances, with others which I have not mentioned, are the sole proofs of the *Copernican* system; and to you it belongs to consider whether you have any analogies of the same kind to support your theory.

In reality, *Cleanthes,* continued he, the modern system of astronomy is now so much received by all inquirers, and has become so essential a part even of our earliest education, that we are not commonly very scrupulous

in examining the reasons upon which it is founded. It is now become a matter of mere curiosity to study the first writers on that subject who had the full force of prejudice to encounter, and were obliged to turn their arguments on every side in order to render them popular and convincing. But if we peruse *Galileo's* famous *Dialogues*[2] concerning the system of the world, we shall find that that great genius, one of the sublimest that ever existed, first bent all his endeavors to prove that there was no foundation for the distinction commonly made between elementary and celestial substances. The Schools, proceeding from the illusions of sense, had carried this distinction very far; and had established the latter substances to be ingenerable, incorruptible, unalterable, impassible; and had assigned all the opposite qualities to the former. But *Galileo,* beginning with the moon, proved its similarity in every particular to the earth: its convex figure, its natural darkness when not illuminated, its density, its distinction into solid and liquid, the variations of its phases, the mutual illuminations of the earth and moon, their mutual eclipses, the inequalities of the lunar surface, etc. After many instances of this kind, with regard to all the planets, men plainly saw that these bodies became proper objects of experience, and that the similarity of their nature enabled us to extend the same arguments and phenomena from one to the other.

In this cautious proceeding of the astronomers you may read your own condemnation, *Cleanthes;* or rather may see that the subject in which you are engaged exceeds all human reason and inquiry. Can you pretend to show any such similarity between the fabric of a house and the generation of a universe? Have you ever seen Nature in any such situation as resembles the first arrangement of the elements? Have worlds ever been formed under your eye, and have you had leisure to observe the whole progress of the phenomenon, from the first appearance of order to its final consummation? If you have, then cite your experience and deliver your theory.

Part III

Cleanthes: How the most absurd argument, replied *Cleanthes,* in the hands of a man of ingenuity and in-

---

2. [Galileo, *Dialogues on the Great World Systems* (1632).]

vention, may acquire an air of probability! Are you not aware, *Philo,* that it became necessary for *Copernicus* and his first disciples to prove the similarity of the terrestrial and celestial matter because several philosophers, blinded by old systems and supported by some sensible appearances, had denied this similarity; but that it is by no means necessary that theists should prove the similarity of the works of nature to those of art, because this similarity is self-evident and undeniable? The same matter, a like form; what more is requisite to show an analogy between their causes, and to ascertain the origin of all things from a divine purpose and intention? Your objections, I must freely tell you, are no better than the abstruse cavils of those philosophers who denied motion, and ought to be refuted in the same manner—by illustrations, examples, and instances rather than by serious argument and philosophy.[3]

Suppose, therefore, that an articulate voice were heard in the clouds, much louder and more melodious than any which human art could ever reach; suppose that this voice were extended in the same instant over all nations and spoke to each nation in its own language and dialect; suppose that the words delivered not only contain a just sense and meaning, but convey some instruction altogether worthy of a benevolent Being superior to mankind—could you possibly hesitate a moment concerning the cause of this voice, and must you not instantly ascribe it to some design or purpose? Yet I cannot see but all the same objections (if they merit that appellation) which lie against the system of theism may also be produced against this inference.

Might you not say that all conclusions concerning fact were founded on experience; that, when we hear an articulate voice in the dark and thence infer a man, it is only the resemblance of the effects which leads us to conclude that there is a like resemblance in the cause; but that this extraordinary voice, by its loudness, extent, and flexibility to all languages, bears so little analogy to any human voice that we have no reason to suppose any analogy in their causes; and, consequently, that a rational, wise, coherent speech proceeded, you know not whence, from some accidental whistling of the winds, not from any divine reason or intelligence? You see clearly your own objections in these cavils; and I hope too, you see clearly that they cannot possibly have more force in the one case than in the other.

But to bring the case still nearer the present one of the universe, I shall make two suppositions which imply not any absurdity or impossibility. Suppose that there is a natural, universal, invariable language, common to every individual of human race, and that books are natural productions which perpetuate themselves in the same manner with animals and vegetables, by descent and propagation. Several expressions of our passions contain a universal language: All brute animals have a natural speech, which, however limited, is very intelligible to their own species. And as there are infinitely fewer parts and less contrivance in the finest composition of eloquence than in the coarsest organized body, the propagation of an *Iliad* or *Aeneid is* an easier supposition than that of any plant or animal.

Suppose, therefore, that you enter into your library thus peopled by natural volumes containing the most refined reason and most exquisite beauty. Could you possibly open one of them and doubt that its original cause bore the strongest analogy to mind and intelligence? When it reasons and discourses; when it expostulates, argues, and enforces its views and topics; when it applies sometimes to the pure intellect, sometimes to the affections; when it collects, disposes, and adorns every consideration suited to the subject; could you persist in asserting that all this, at the bottom, had really no meaning, and that the first formation of this volume in the loins of its original parent proceeded not from thought and design? Your obstinacy, I know, reaches not that degree of firmness; even your skeptical play and wantonness would be abashed at so glaring an absurdity.

But if there be any difference, *Philo,* between this supposed case and the real one of the universe, it is all to the advantage of the latter. The anatomy of an animal affords many stronger instances of design than the perusal of *Livy* or *Tacitus;* and any objection which you start in the former case, by carrying me back to so unusual and extraordinary a scene as the first formation of worlds, the same objection has place on the supposition of our vegetating library. Choose, then, your party, *Philo,*

---

3. [Diogenes was supposed to have listened to Zeno's arguments denying that motion really occurs. Diogenes got up and walked around, and claimed that was sufficient refutation of Zeno's view.]

without ambiguity or evasion; assert either that a rational volume is no proof of a rational cause or admit of a similar cause to all the works of nature.

Let me here observe, too, continued *Cleanthes,* that this religious argument, instead of being weakened by that skepticism so much affected by you, rather acquires force from it and becomes more firm and undisputed. To exclude all argument or reasoning of every kind is either affectation or madness. The declared profession of every reasonable skeptic is only to reject abstruse, remote, and refined arguments; to adhere to common sense and the plain instincts of nature; and to assent, wherever any reasons strike him with so full a force that he cannot, without the greatest violence, prevent it. Now the arguments for natural religion are plainly of this kind; and nothing but the most perverse, obstinate metaphysics can reject them. Consider, anatomize the eye; survey its structure and contrivance, and tell me, from your own feeling, if the idea of a contriver does not immediately flow in upon you with a force like that of sensation. The most obvious conclusion, surely, is in favor of design; and it requires time, reflection, and study, to summon up those frivolous though abstruse objections which can support infidelity. Who can behold the male and female of each species, the correspondence of their parts and instincts, their passions and whole course of life before and after generation, but must be sensible that the propagation of the species is intended by nature? Millions and millions of such instances present themselves through every part of the universe, and no language can convey a more intelligible, irresistible meaning than the curious adjustment of final causes. To what degree, therefore, of blind dogmatism must one have attained to reject such natural and such convincing arguments?

Some beauties in writing we may meet with which seem contrary to rules, and which gain the affections and animate the imagination in opposition to all the precepts of criticism and to the authority of the established masters of art. And if the argument for theism be, as you pretend, contradictory to the principles of logic, its universal, its irresistible influence proves clearly that there may be arguments of a like irregular nature. Whatever cavils may be urged, an orderly world, as well as a coherent, articulate speech, will still be received as an incontestable proof of design and intention.

It sometimes happens, I own, that the religious arguments have not their due influence on an ignorant savage and barbarian; not because they are obscure and difficult, but because he never asks himself any question with regard to them. Whence arises the curious structure of an animal? From the copulation of its parents. And these whence? From *their* parents? A few removes set the objects at such a distance that to him they are lost in darkness and confusion; nor is he actuated by any curiosity to trace them farther. But this is neither dogmatism nor skepticism, but stupidity: a state of mind very different from your sifting, inquisitive disposition, my ingenious friend. You can trace causes from effects; you can compare the most distant and remote objects; and your greatest errors proceed not from barrenness of thought and invention, but from too luxuriant a fertility which suppresses your natural good sense by a profusion of unnecessary scruples and objections.

Pamphilus: Here I could observe, *Hermippus,* that *Philo* was a little embarrassed and confounded. But, while he hesitated in delivering an answer, luckily for him, *Demea* broke in upon the discourse and saved his countenance.

Demea: Your instance, *Cleanthes,* said he, drawn from books and language, being familiar, has, I confess, so much more force on that account; but is there not some danger, too, in this very circumstance, and may it not render us presumptuous, by making us imagine we comprehend the Deity and have some adequate idea of his nature and attributes? When I read a volume, I enter into the mind and intention of the author; I become him, in a manner, for the instant, and have an immediate feeling and conception of those ideas which revolved in his imagination while employed in that composition. But so near an approach we never surely can make to the Deity. His ways are not our ways. His attributes are perfect but incomprehensible. And this volume of nature contains a great and inexplicable riddle, more than any intelligible discourse or reasoning.

The ancient *Platonists,* you know, were the most religious and devout of all the pagan philosophers; yet many of them, particularly *Plotinus,*[4] expressly declare that intellect or understanding is not to be ascribed to

_____

4. [Plotinus, A.D. 205–270, the leading figure in the ancient neoplatonic school of philosophy.]

the Deity, and that our most perfect worship of him consists, not in acts of veneration, reverence, gratitude, or love, but in a certain mysterious self-annihilation or total extinction of all our faculties. These ideas are, perhaps too far stretched; but still it must be acknowledged that, by representing the Deity as so intelligible and comprehensible, and so similar to a human mind, we are guilty of the grossest and most narrow partiality, and make ourselves the model of the whole universe.

All the *sentiments* of the human mind, gratitude, resentment, love, friendship, approbation, blame, pity, emulation, envy, have a plain reference to the state and situation of man, and are calculated for preserving the existence and promoting the activity of such a being in such circumstances. It seems, therefore, unreasonable to transfer such sentiments to a supreme existence or to suppose him actuated by them; and the phenomena, besides, of the universe will not support us in such a theory. All our *ideas* derived from the senses are confessedly false and illusive, and cannot therefore be supposed to have place in a Supreme Intelligence. And as the ideas of internal sentiment, added to those of the external senses, compose the whole furniture of human understanding, we may conclude that none of the *materials* of thought are in any respect similar in the human and in the Divine Intelligence. Now, as to the *manner* of thinking, how can we make any comparison between them or suppose them anywise resembling? Our thought is fluctuating, uncertain, fleeting, successive, and compounded; and were we to remove these circumstances, we absolutely annihilate its essence, and it would in such a case be an abuse of terms to apply to it the name of thought or reason. At least, if it appear more pious and respectful (as it really is) still to retain these terms when we mention the Supreme Being, we ought to acknowledge that their meaning, in that case, is totally incomprehensible; and that the infirmities of our nature do not permit us to reach any ideas which in the least correspond to the ineffable sublimity of the Divine Attributes.

Part IV

Cleanthes: It seems strange to me, said *Cleanthes,* that you, *Demea,* who are so sincere in the cause of religion,

should still maintain the mysterious, incomprehensible nature of the Deity, and should insist so strenuously that he has no manner of likeness or resemblance to human creatures. The Deity, I can readily allow, possesses many powers and attributes of which we can have no comprehension. But, if our ideas, so far as they go, be not just and adequate and correspondent to his real nature, I know not what there is in this subject worth insisting on. Is the name, without any meaning, of such mighty importance? Or how do you *mystics,* who maintain the absolute incomprehensibility of the Deity, differ from skeptics or atheists, who assert that the first cause of all is unknown and unintelligible? Their temerity must be very great if, after rejecting the production by a mind; I mean a mind resembling the human (for I know of no other), they pretend to assign, with certainty, any other specific intelligible cause; and their conscience must be very scrupulous, indeed, if they refuse to call the universal unknown cause a God or Deity, and to bestow on him as many sublime eulogies and unmeaning epithets as you shall please to require of them.

Demea: Who could imagine, replied *Demea,* that *Cleanthes,* the calm philosophical *Cleanthes,* would attempt to refute his antagonists by affixing a nickname to them; and, like the common bigots and inquisitors of the age, have recourse to invective and declamation instead of reasoning? Or does he not perceive that these topics are easily retorted, and that *anthropomorphite* is an appellation as invidious, and implies as dangerous consequences, as the epithet of *mystic* with which he has honored us? In reality, *Cleanthes,* consider what it is you assert when you represent the Deity as similar to a human mind and understanding. What is the soul of man? A composition of various faculties, passions, sentiments, ideas; united, indeed, into one self or person, but still distinct from each other. When it reasons, the ideas which are the parts of its discourse arrange themselves in a certain form or order, which is not preserved entire for a moment, but immediately gives place to another arrangement. New opinions, new passions, new affections, new feelings arise which continually diversify the mental scene and produce in it the greatest variety and most rapid succession imaginable. How is this compatible with that perfect immutability and simplicity which all true theists ascribe to the Deity? By the same act, say they, he sees past, present, and future; his love and hatred, his mercy and justice, are one individual operation: He is entire in every point of space, and complete in every instant of duration. No succession, no change, no acquisition, no diminution. What he is implies not in it any shadow of distinction or diversity. And what he is this moment he ever has been and ever will be, without any new judgment, sentiment, or operation. He stands fixed in one simple, perfect state; nor can you ever say, with any propriety, that this act of his is different from that other, or that this judgment or idea has been lately formed and will give place, by succession, to any different judgment or idea.

Cleanthes: I can readily allow, said *Cleanthes,* that those who maintain the perfect simplicity of the Supreme Being, to the extent in which you have explained it, are complete *mystics,* and chargeable with all the consequences which I have drawn from their opinion. They are, in a word, *atheists,* without knowing it. For though it be allowed that the Deity possesses attributes of which we have no comprehension, yet ought we never to ascribe to him any attributes which are absolutely incompatible with that intelligent nature essential to him. A mind whose acts and sentiments and ideas are not distinct and successive, one that is wholly simple and totally immutable, is a mind which has no thought, no reason, no will, no sentiment, no love, no hatred; or, in a word, is no mind at all. It is an abuse of terms to give it that appellation, and we may as well speak of limited extension without figure, or of number without composition.

Philo: Pray consider, said *Philo,* whom you are at present inveighing against. You are honoring with the appellation of *atheist* all the sound, orthodox divines, almost, who have treated of this subject; and you will at last be, yourself, found, according to your reckoning, the only sound theist in the world. But if idolaters be atheists, as, I think, may justly be asserted, and *Christian* theologians the same, what becomes of the argument, so much celebrated, derived from the universal consent of mankind?

But, because I know you are not much swayed by names and authorities, I shall endeavor to show you, a little more distinctly, the inconveniences of that anthropomorphism which you have embraced, and shall prove that there is no ground to suppose a plan of the world to be formed in the Divine Mind, consisting of distinct ideas, differently arranged, in the same manner as an architect forms in his head the plan of a house which he intends to execute.

It is not easy, I own, to see what is gained by this supposition, whether we judge of the matter by *reason* or by *experience.* We are still obliged to mount higher in order to find the cause of this cause which you had assigned as satisfactory and conclusive.

If *reason* (I mean abstract reason derived from inquiries *a priori*) be not alike mute with regard to all questions concerning cause and effect, this sentence at least it will venture to pronounce; that a mental world or universe of ideas requires a cause as much as does a material world or universe of objects; and, if similar in its arrangement, must require a similar cause. For what is there in this subject which should occasion a different conclusion or inference? In an abstract view, they are entirely alike; and no difficulty attends the one supposition which is not common to both of them.

Again, when we will needs force *experience* to pronounce some sentence, even on these subjects which lie beyond her sphere; neither can she perceive any material difference in this particular between these two kinds of worlds, but finds them to be governed by similar principles, and to depend upon an equal variety of causes in their operations. We have specimens in miniature of both of them. Our own mind resembles the one; a vegetable or animal body the other. Let experience, therefore judge from these samples. Nothing seems more delicate, with regard to its causes, than thought; and as these causes never operate in two persons after the same manner, so we never find two persons who think exactly alike. Nor indeed does the same person think exactly alike at any two different periods of time. A difference of age, of the disposition of his body, of weather, of food, of company, of books, of passions; any of these particulars, or others more minute, are sufficient to alter the curious machinery of thought and communicate to it very different movements and operations. As far as we can judge, vegetables and animal bodies are not more delicate in their motions, nor depend upon a greater variety or more curious adjustment of springs and principles.

How, therefore, shall we satisfy ourselves concerning the cause of that Being whom you suppose the Author of Nature, or, according to your system of anthropomorphism, the Ideal World into which you trace the material? Have we not the same reason to trace that ideal world into another ideal world or new intelligent principle? But if we stop and go no farther, why go so far? Why not stop at the material world? How can we satisfy ourselves without going on *in infinitum?* And, after all, what satisfaction is there in that infinite progression? Let us remember the story of the Indian philosopher and his elephant.[5] It was never more applicable than to the present subject. If the material world rests upon a similar ideal world, this ideal world must rest upon some other, and so on without end. It were better, therefore, never to look beyond the present material world. By supposing it to contain the principle of its order within itself, we really assert it to be God; and the sooner we arrive at that Divine Being, so much the better. When you go one step beyond the mundane system, you only excite an inquisitive humor which it is impossible ever to satisfy.

To say that the different ideas which compose the reason of the Supreme Being fall into order of themselves and by their own nature is really to talk without any precise meaning. If it has a meaning, I would fain know why it is not as good sense to say that the parts of the material world fall into order of themselves and by their own nature? Can the one opinion be intelligible, while the other is not so?

We have, indeed, experience of ideas which fall into order of themselves and without any *known* cause. But, I am sure, we have a much larger experience of matter which does the same, as in all instances of generation and vegetation where the accurate analysis of the cause exceeds all human comprehension. We have also experience of particular systems of thought and of matter which have no order; of the first in madness, of the second in corruption. Why, then, should we think that order is more essential to one than the other? And if it requires a cause in both, what do we gain by your system, in tracing the universe of objects into a similar universe of ideas? The first step which we make leads us on forever. It were, therefore, wise in us to limit all our inquiries to the present world, without looking farther. No satisfaction can ever be attained by these speculations which so far exceed the narrow bounds of human understanding.

It was usual with the *Peripatetics,*[6] you know, *Cleanthes,* when the cause of any phenomenon was demanded, to have recourse to their *faculties* or *occult qualities,* and to say, for instance, that bread nourished by its nutritive faculty, and senna purged by its purgative. But it has been discovered that this subterfuge was nothing but the disguise of ignorance, and that these philosophers, though less ingenuous, really said the same thing with the skeptics or the vulgar who fairly confessed that they knew not the cause of these phenomena. In like manner, when it is asked, what cause produces order in the ideas of the Supreme Being, can any other reason be assigned by you, anthropomorphites, than that it is a *rational* faculty, and that such is the nature of the Deity? But why a similar answer will not be equally satisfactory in accounting for the order of the world, without having recourse to any such intelligent creator as you insist on, may be difficult to determine. It is only to say that such is the nature of material objects, and that they are all originally possessed of a *faculty* of order and proportion. These are only more learned and elaborate ways of confessing our ignorance; nor has the one hypothesis any real advantage above the other, except in its greater conformity to vulgar prejudices.

Cleanthes: You have displayed this argument with great emphasis, replied *Cleanthes:* You seem not sensible how easy it is to answer it. Even in common life, if I assign a cause for any event, is it any objection, *Philo,* that I cannot assign the cause of that cause, and answer every new question which may incessantly be started? And what philosophers could possibly submit to so rigid a rule? Philosophers who confess ultimate causes to be totally unknown, and are sensible that the most refined principles into which they trace the phenomena are still to them as inexplicable as these phenomena themselves are to the vulgar. The order and arrangement of Nature, the curious adjustment of final causes, the plain use and intention of every part and organ; all these bespeak in the clearest language an intelligent cause or author. The

---

5. [This appears in John Locke, *An Essay Concerning Human Understanding,* Book II, chap XIII, sec. 2. The Indian philosopher said the world was resting on the back of an elephant; the elephant on the back of a great tortoise; the great tortoise on the back of he knew not what.]

---

6. [The followers of Aristotle.]

heavens and the earth join in the same testimony: The whole chorus of Nature raises one hymn to the praises of its Creator: You alone, or almost alone, disturb this general harmony. You start abstruse doubts, cavils, and objections; you ask me what is the cause of this cause? I know not; I care not; that concerns not me. I have found a Deity; and here I stop my inquiry. Let those go farther who are wiser or more enterprising.

Philo: I pretend to be neither, replied *Philo;* and for that very reason I should never, perhaps, have attempted to go so far, especially when I am sensible that I must at last be contented to sit down with the same answer which, without further trouble, might have satisfied me from the beginning. If I am still to remain in utter ignorance of causes and can absolutely give an explication of nothing, I shall never esteem it any advantage to shove off for a moment a difficulty which you acknowledge must immediately, in its full force, recur upon me. Naturalists, indeed, very justly explain particular effects by more general causes, though these general causes themselves should remain in the end totally inexplicable; but they never surely thought it satisfactory to explain a particular effect by a particular cause which was no more to be accounted for than the effect itself. An ideal system, arranged of itself, without a precedent design, is not a whit more explicable than a material one which attains its order in a like manner; nor is there any more difficulty in the latter supposition than in the former.

Part V

Philo: But to show you still more inconveniences, continued *Philo,* in your anthropomorphism, please to take a new survey of your principles. *Like effects prove like causes.* This is the experimental argument; and this, you say too, is the sole theological argument. Now it is certain that the liker the effects are which are seen and the liker the causes which are inferred, the stronger is the argument. Every departure on either side diminishes the probability and renders the experiment less conclusive. You cannot doubt of the principle; neither ought you to reject its consequences.

All the new discoveries in astronomy which prove the immense grandeur and magnificence of the works of nature are so many additional arguments for a Deity according to the true system of theism; but, according to your hypothesis of experimental theism, they become so many objections, by removing the effect still farther from all resemblance to the effects of human art and contrivance. For if *Lucretius,* even following the old system of the world, could exclaim:

> Who is strong enough to rule the sum, who to hold in hand and control the mighty bridle of the unfathomable deep? who to turn about all the heavens at one time, and warm the fruitful worlds with ethereal fires, or to, be present in all places and at all times.[7]

If Tully[8] esteemed this reasoning so natural as to put it into the mouth of his Epicurean:

> What power of mental vision enabled your master Plato to descry the vast and elaborate architectural process which, as he makes out, the deity adopted in building the structure of the universe? What method of engineering was employed? What tools and levers and derricks? What agents carried out so vast an understanding? And how were air, fire, water, and earth enabled to obey and execute the will of the architect?[9]

If this argument, I say, had any force in former ages, how much greater must it have at present when the bounds of nature are so infinitely enlarged and such a magnificent scene is opened to us? It is still more unreasonable to form our idea of so unlimited a cause from our experience of the narrow productions of human design and invention.

The discoveries by microscopes, as they open a new universe in miniature, are still objections, according to you; arguments, according to me. The farther we push

---

7. [*On the Nature of Things,* II, 1096–1099 (trans. by W. D. Rouse).]

8. [Tully was a common name for the Roman lawyer and philosopher, Marcus Tullius Cicero, 106–43 B.C.]

9. [Cicero, *The Nature of the Gods,* I, viii, 19 (trans. by H. Rackham).]

our researches of this kind, we are still led to infer the universal cause of all to be vastly different from mankind, or from any object of human experience and observation.

And what say you to the discoveries in anatomy, chemistry, botany? . . .

Cleanthes: These surely are no objections, replied *Cleanthes;* they only discover new instances of art and contrivance. It is still the image of mind reflected on us from innumerable objects. *Philo:* Add a mind *like the human,* said *Philo. Cleanthes:* I know of no other, replied *Cleanthes. Philo:* And the liker, the better, insisted *Philo. Cleanthes:* To be sure, said *Cleanthes.*

Philo: Now, *Cleanthes,* said *Philo,* with an air of alacrity and triumph, mark the consequences. *First,* by this method of reasoning you renounce all claim to infinity in any of the attributes of the Deity. For, as the cause ought only to be proportioned to the effect, and the effect, so far as it falls under our cognizance, is not infinite: What pretensions have we, upon your suppositions, to ascribe that attribute to the Divine Being? You will still insist that, by removing him so much from all similarity to human creatures, we give in to the most arbitrary hypothesis, and at the same time weaken all proofs of his existence.

Secondly, you have no reason, on your theory, for ascribing perfection to the Deity, even in his finite capacity; or for supposing him free from every error, mistake, or incoherence, in his undertakings. There are many inexplicable difficulties in the works of Nature which, if we allow a perfect author to be proved *a priori,* are easily solved, and become only seeming difficulties from the narrow capacity of man, who cannot trace infinite relations. But according to your method of reasoning, these difficulties become all real; and, perhaps, will be insisted on as new instances of likeness to human art and contrivance. At least, you must acknowledge that it is impossible for us to tell, from our limited views, whether this system contains any great faults or deserves any considerable praise if compared to other possible and even real systems. Could a peasant, if the *Aeneid* were read to him, pronounce that poem to be absolutely faultless, or even assign to it its proper rank among the productions of human wit, he who had never seen any other production?

But were this world ever so perfect a production, it must still remain uncertain whether all the excellences

of the work can justly be ascribed to the workman. If we survey a ship, what an exalted idea must we form of the ingenuity of the carpenter who framed so complicated, useful, and beautiful a machine? And what surprise must we feel when we find him a stupid mechanic who imitated others, and copied an art which, through a long succession of ages, after multiplied trials, mistakes, corrections, deliberations, and controversies, had been gradually improving? Many worlds might have been botched and bungled, throughout an eternity, ere this system was struck out; much labor lost; many fruitless trials made; and a slow but continued improvement carried on during infinite ages in the art of world-making. In such subjects, who can determine where the truth, nay, who can conjecture where the probability lies, amidst a great number of hypotheses which may be proposed, and a still greater which may be imagined?

And what shadow of an argument, continued Philo, can you produce from your hypothesis to prove the unity of the Deity? A great number of men join in building a house or ship, in rearing a city, in framing a commonwealth; why may not several deities combine in contriving and framing a world? This is only so much greater similarity to human affairs. By sharing the work among several, we may so much further limit the attributes of each, and get rid of that extensive power and knowledge which must be supposed in one deity, and which, according to you, can only serve to weaken the proof of his existence. And if such foolish, such vicious creatures as man can yet often unite in framing and executing one plan, how much more those deities or demons, whom we may suppose several degrees more perfect?

To multiply causes without necessity is indeed contrary to true philosophy, but this principle applies not to the present case. Were one deity antecedently proved by your theory who were possessed of every attribute requisite to the production of the universe, it would be needless, I own (though not absurd), to suppose any other deity existent. But while it is still a question whether all these attributes are united in one subject or dispersed among several independent beings; by what phenomena in nature can we pretend to decide the controversy? Where we see a body raised in a scale, we are sure that there is in the opposite scale, however concealed from sight, some counterpoising weight equal to it; but it is still allowed to doubt whether that weight be an aggregate of several distinct bodies or one uniform united mass. And if the weight requisite very much exceeds anything which we have ever seen conjoined in any single body, the former supposition becomes still more probable and natural. An intelligent being of such vast power and capacity as is necessary to produce the universe, or, to speak in the language of ancient philosophy, so prodigious an animal, exceeds all analogy and even comprehension.

But further, *Cleanthes,* men are mortal, and renew their species by generation; and this is common to all living creatures. The two great sexes of male and female, says *Milton,* animate the world. Why must this circumstance, so universal, so essential, be excluded from those numerous and limited deities? Behold, then, the theogeny of ancient times brought back upon us.

And why not become a perfect anthropomorphite? Why not assert the deity or deities to be corporeal, and to have eyes, a nose, mouth, ears, etc.? *Epicurus* maintained that no man had ever seen reason but in a human figure; therefore, the gods must have a human figure. And this argument, which is deservedly so much ridiculed by *Cicero,* becomes, according to you, solid and philosophical.

In a word, *Cleanthes,* a man who follows your hypothesis is able, perhaps, to assert or conjecture that the universe sometime arose from something like design: But beyond that position he cannot ascertain one single circumstance, and is left afterwards to fix every point of his theology by the utmost license of fancy and hypothesis. This world, for aught he knows, is very faulty and imperfect, compared to a superior standard; and was only the first rude essay of some infant deity who afterwards abandoned it, ashamed of his lame performance: It is the work only of some dependent, inferior deity, and is the object of derision to his superiors: It is the production of old age and dotage in some superannuated deity; and ever since his death has run on at adventures, from the first impulse and active force which it received from him. . . . You justly give signs of horror, *Demea,* at these strange suppositions; but these, and a thousand more of the same kind, are *Cleanthes'* suppositions, not mine. From the moment the attributes of the Deity are supposed finite, all these have place. And I cannot, for my part, think that so wild and unsettled a

system of theology is, in any respect, preferable to none at all.

Cleanthes: These suppositions I absolutely disown, cried *Cleanthes:* They strike me, however, with no horror, especially when proposed in that rambling way in which they drop from you. On the contrary, they give me pleasure when I see that, by the utmost indulgence of your imagination, you never get rid of the hypothesis of design in the universe, but are obliged at every turn to have recourse to it. To this concession I adhere steadily; and this I regard as a sufficient foundation for religion. [. . .]

Part VII

Philo: But here, continued *Philo,* in examining the ancient system of the soul of the world there strikes me, all on a sudden, a new idea which, if just, must go near to subvert all your reasoning, and destroy even your first inferences on which you repose such confidence. If the universe bears a greater likeness to animal bodies and to vegetables than to the works of human art, it is more probable that its cause resembles the cause of the former than that of the latter, and its origin ought rather to be ascribed to generation or vegetation than to reason or design. Your conclusion, even according to your own principles, is therefore lame and defective.

Demea: Pray open up this argument a little farther, said *Demea,* for I do not rightly apprehend it in that concise manner in which you have expressed it.

Philo: Our friend *Cleanthes,* replied *Philo,* as you have heard, asserts that since no question of fact can be proved otherwise than by experience, the existence of a Deity admits not of proof from any other medium. The world, says he, resembles the works of human contrivance; therefore its cause must also resemble that of the other. Here we may remark that the operation of one very small part of nature, to wit, man, upon another very small part, to wit, that inanimate matter lying within his reach, is the rule by which *Cleanthes* judges of the origin of the whole; and he measures objects, so widely disproportioned, by the same individual standard. But to waive all objections drawn from this topic, I affirm that there are other parts of the universe (besides the machines of human invention) which bear still a greater resemblance to the fabric of the world, and which, therefore, afford a better conjecture concerning the universal origin of this system. These parts are animals and vegetables. The world plainly resembles more an animal or a vegetable than it does a watch or a knitting-loom. Its cause, therefore, it is more probable, resembles the cause of the former. The cause of the former is generation or vegetation. The cause, therefore, of the world we may infer to be something similar or analogous to generation or vegetation.

Demea: But how is it conceivable, said *Demea,* that the world can arise from anything similar to vegetation or generation?

Philo: Very easily, replied *Philo.* In like manner as a tree sheds its seed into the neighboring fields and produces other trees; so the great vegetable, the world, or this planetary system, produces within itself certain seeds which, being scattered into the surrounding chaos, vegetate into new worlds. A comet, for instance, is the seed of a world; and after it has been fully ripened, by passing from sun to sun, and star to star, it is at last tossed into the unformed elements which everywhere surround this universe, and immediately sprouts up into a new system.

Or if, for the sake of variety (for I see no other advantage) we should suppose this world to be an animal; a comet is the egg of this animal; and in like manner as an ostrich lays its egg in the sand, which, without any further care, hatches the egg and produces a new animal, so. . . .

Demea: I understand you, says *Demea:* But what wild, arbitrary suppositions are these? What *data* have you for such extraordinary conclusions? And is the slight, imaginary resemblance of the world to a vegetable or an animal sufficient to establish the same inference with regard to both? Objects which are in general so widely different; ought they to be a standard for each other?

Philo: Right, cries *Philo:* This is the topic on which I have all along insisted. I have still asserted that we have no *data* to establish any system of cosmogony. Our experience, so imperfect in itself and so limited both in extent and duration, can afford us no probable conjecture concerning the whole of things. But if we must needs fix on some hypothesis, by what rule, pray, ought we to determine our choice? Is there any other rule than the great similarity of the objects compared? And

does not a plant or an animal, which springs from vegetation or generation, bear a stronger resemblance to the world than does any artificial machine, which arises from reason and design?

Demea: But what is this vegetation and generation of which you talk? said *Demea.* Can you explain their operations, and anatomize that fine internal structure on which they depend?

Philo: As much, at least, replied *Philo,* as *Cleanthes* can explain the operations of reason, or anatomize that internal structure on which *it* depends. But without any such elaborate disquisitions, when I see an animal, I infer that it sprang from generation; and that with as great certainty as you conclude a house to have been reared by design. These words *generation, reason* mark only certain powers and energies in nature whose effects are known, but whose essence is incomprehensible; and one of these principles, more than the other, has no privilege for being made a standard to the whole of nature.

In reality, *Demea,* it may reasonably be expected that the larger the views are which we take of things, the better will they conduct us in our conclusions concerning such extraordinary and such magnificent subjects. In this little corner of the world alone, there are four principles, *reason, instinct, generation, vegetation,* which are similar to each other, and are the causes of similar effects. What a number of other principles may we naturally suppose in the immense extent and variety of the universe could we travel from planet to planet, and from system to system, in order to examine each part of this mighty fabric? Any one of these four principles above mentioned (and a hundred others which lie open to our conjecture) may afford us a theory by which to judge of the origin of the world; and it is a palpable and egregious partiality to confine our view entirely to that principle by which our own minds operate. Were this principle more intelligible on that account, such a partiality might be somewhat excusable: But reason, in its internal fabric and structure, is really as little known to us as instinct or vegetation; and, perhaps even that vague, undeterminate word "nature" to which the vulgar refer everything is not at the bottom more inexplicable. The effects of these principles are all known to us from experience; but the principles themselves and their manner of operation are totally unknown: Nor is it less intelligible or less conformable to experience to say that the world arose by vegetation, from a seed shed by another world, than to say that it arose from a divine reason or contrivance, according to the sense in which *Cleanthes* understands it.

Demea: But methinks, said *Demea,* if the world had a vegetative quality and could sow the seeds of new worlds into the infinite chaos, this power would be still an additional argument for design in its author. For whence could arise so wonderful a faculty but from design? Or how can order spring from anything which perceives not that order which it bestows?

Philo: You need only look around you, replied *Philo,* to satisfy yourself with regard to this question. A tree bestows order and organization on that tree which springs from it, without knowing the order: An animal in the same manner on its offspring: A bird on its nest; and instances of this kind are even more frequent in the world than those of order which arise from reason and contrivance. To say that all this order in animals and vegetables proceeds ultimately from design is begging the question; nor can that great point be ascertained otherwise than by proving, *a priori,* both that order is, from its nature, inseparably attached to thought, and that it can never of itself or from original unknown principles belong to matter.

But further, *Demea,* this objection which you urge can never be made use of by *Cleanthes,* without renouncing a defence which he has already made against one of my objections. When I inquired concerning the cause of that supreme reason and intelligence into which he resolves everything, he told me that the impossibility of satisfying such inquiries could never be admitted as an objection in any species of philosophy. *We must stop somewhere, says he; nor is it ever within the reach of human capacity to explain ultimate causes or show the last connections of any objects. It is sufficient if any steps, so far as we go, are supported by experience and observation.* Now, that vegetation and generation, as well as reason, are experienced to be principles of order in nature is undeniable. If I rest my system of cosmogony on the former, preferably to the latter, it is at my choice. The matter seems entirely arbitrary. And when *Cleanthes* asks me what is the cause of my great vegetative or generative faculty, I am equally entitled to ask him the cause of his great reasoning principle. These questions we have agreed to forbear on both sides; and it is chiefly his interest on the present occasion to stick to this agreement. Judging by our limited and imperfect experience, generation has some privileges above reason: For we see every day the latter arise from the former, never the former from the latter.

Compare, I beseech you, the consequences on both sides. The world, say I, resembles an animal; therefore it is an animal, therefore it arose from generation. The steps, I confess, are wide; yet there is some small appearance of analogy in each step. The world, says *Cleanthes,* resembles a machine; therefore it is a machine, therefore it arose from design. The steps are here equally wide, and the analogy less striking. And if he pretends to carry on *my* hypothesis a step further, and to infer design or reason from the great principle of generation on which I insist, I may, with better authority, use the same freedom to push further his hypothesis, and infer a divine generation or theogony from his principle of reason. I have at least some faint shadow of experience, which is the utmost that can ever be attained in the present subject. Reason, in innumerable instances, is observed to arise from the principle of generation, and never to arise from any other principle.

Hesiod and all the ancient mythologists were so struck with this analogy that they universally explained the origin of nature from an animal birth, and copulation. *Plato,* too, so far as he is intelligible, seems to have adopted some such notion in his *Timaeus.*

The *Brahmins* assert that the world arose from an infinite spider, who spun this whole complicated mass from his bowels, and annihilates afterwards the whole or any part of it, by absorbing it again and resolving it into his own essence. Here is a species of cosmogony which appears to us ridiculous because a spider is a little contemptible animal whose operations we are never likely to take for a model of the whole universe. But still here is a new species of analogy, even in our globe. And were there a planet wholly inhabited by spiders (which is very possible), this inference would there appear as natural and irrefragable as that which in our planet ascribes the origin of all things to design and intelligence, as explained by *Cleanthes.* Why an orderly system may not be spun from the belly as well as from the brain, it will be difficult for him to give a satisfactory reason.

Cleanthes: I must confess, *Philo,* replied *Cleanthes,* that, of all men living, the task which you have undertaken, of raising doubts and objections, suits you best and seems, in a manner, natural and unavoidable to you. So great is your fertility of invention that I am not ashamed to acknowledge myself unable, on a sudden, to solve regularly such out-of-the-way difficulties as you incessantly start upon me; though I clearly see, in general, their fallacy and error. And I question not, but you are yourself, at present, in the same case, and have not the solution so ready as the objection; while you must be sensible that common sense and reason are entirely against you, and that such whimsies as you have delivered may puzzle but never can convince us. [. . .]

Part X

Demea: It is my opinion, I own, replied *Demea,* that each man feels, in a manner, the truth of religion within his own breast; and, from a consciousness of his imbecility and misery rather than from any reasoning, is led to seek protection from that Being on whom he and all nature are dependent. So anxious or so tedious are even the best scenes of life that futurity is still the object of all our hopes and fears. We incessantly look forward and endeavor, by prayers, adoration, and sacrifice, to appease those unknown powers whom we find, by experience, so able to afflict and oppress us. Wretched creatures that we are! What resource for us amidst the innumerable ills of life did not religion suggest some methods of atonement, and appease those terrors with which we are incessantly agitated and tormented?

Philo: I am indeed persuaded, said *Philo,* that the best and indeed only method of bringing everyone to a due sense of religion is by just representations of the misery and wickedness of men. And for that purpose a talent of eloquence and strong imagery is more requisite than that of reasoning and argument. For is it necessary to prove what everyone feels within himself? It is only necessary to make us feel it, if possible, more intimately and sensibly.

Demea: The people, indeed, replied *Demea,* are sufficiently convinced of this great and melancholy truth. The miseries of life, the unhappiness of man, the general corruptions of our nature, the unsatisfactory enjoyment of pleasures, riches, honors; these phrases have become almost proverbial in all languages. And who can

doubt of what all men declare from their own immediate feeling and experience?

Philo: In this point, said *Philo,* the learned are perfectly agreed with the vulgar; and in all letters, *sacred* and *profane,* the topic of human misery has been insisted on with the most pathetic eloquence that sorrow and melancholy could inspire. The poets, who speak from sentiment, without a system, and whose testimony has therefore the more authority, abound in images of this nature. From *Homer* down to *Dr. Young,*[10] the whole inspired tribe have ever been sensible that no other representation of things would suit the feeling and observation of each individual.

Demea: As to authorities, replied *Demea,* you need not seek them. Look round this library of *Cleanthes.* I shall venture to affirm that, except authors of particular sciences, such as chemistry or botany, who have no occasion to treat of human life, there is scarce one of those innumerable writers from whom the sense of human misery has not, in some passage or other, extorted a complaint and confession of it. At least, the chance is entirely on that side; and no one author has ever, so far as I can recollect, been so extravagant as to deny it.

Philo: There you must excuse me, said *Philo: Leibniz* has denied it, and is perhaps the first who ventured upon so bold and paradoxical an opinion; at least, the first who made it essential to his philosophical system.

Demea: And by being the first, replied *Demea,* might he not have been sensible of his error? For is this a subject in which philosophers can propose to make discoveries especially in so late an age? And can any man hope by a simple denial (for the subject scarcely admits of reasoning) to bear down the united testimony of mankind, founded on sense and consciousness?

And why should man, added he, pretend to an exemption from the lot of all other animals? The whole earth, believe me, *Philo,* is cursed and polluted. A perpetual war is kindled amongst all living creatures. Necessity, hunger, want stimulate the strong and courageous: fear, anxiety, terror agitate the weak and infirm. The first entrance into life gives anguish to the new-born infant and to its wretched parent: weakness, impotence, distress

---

10. [Hume was apparently referring to the prolific poet, Edward Young, 1683–1765.]

attend each stage of that life, and it is, at last, finished in agony and horror.

Philo: Observe, too, says *Philo,* the curious artifices of nature in order to embitter the life of every living being. The stronger prey upon the weaker and keep them in perpetual terror and anxiety. The weaker, too, in their turn, often prey upon the stronger, and vex and molest them without relaxation. Consider that innumerable race of insects, which either are bred on the body of each animal or, flying about, infix their stings in him. These insects have others still less than themselves which torment them. And thus on each hand, before and behind, above and below, every animal is surrounded with enemies which incessantly seek his misery and destruction.

Demea: Man alone, said *Demea,* seems to be, in part, an exception to this rule. For by combination in society he can easily master lions, tigers, and bears, whose greater strength and agility naturally enable them to prey upon him.

Philo: On the contrary, it is here chiefly, cried *Philo,* that the uniform and equal maxims of nature are most apparent. Man, it is true, can, by combination, surmount all his *real* enemies and become master of the whole animal creation: But does he not immediately raise up to himself *imaginary* enemies, the demons of his fancy, who haunt him with superstitious terrors and blast every enjoyment of life? His pleasure, as he imagines, becomes in their eyes a crime: His food and repose give them umbrage and offence; his very sleep and dreams furnish new materials to anxious fear: And even death, his refuge from every other ill, presents only the dread of endless and innumerable woes. Nor does the wolf molest more the timid flock than superstition does the anxious breast of wretched mortals.

Besides, consider, *Demea:* This very society by which we surmount those wild beasts, our natural enemies, what new enemies does it not raise to us? What woe and misery does it not occasion? Man is the greatest enemy of man. Oppression, injustice, contempt, contumely, violence, sedition, war, calumny, treachery, fraud; by these they mutually torment each other, and they would soon dissolve that society which they had formed were it not for the dread of still greater ills which must attend their separation.

Demea: But though these external insults, said *Demea,* from animals, from men, from all the elements, which assault us form a frightful catalogue of woes, they are nothing in comparison of those which arise within ourselves, from the distempered condition of our mind and body. How many lie under the lingering torment of diseases? Hear the pathetic enumeration of the great poet.

> Intestine stone and ulcer, colic-pangs,
> Demoniac frenzy, moping melancholy,
> And moon-struck madness, pining atrophy,
> Marasmus, and wide-wasting pestilence.
> Dire was the tossing, deep the groans: *Despair*
> Tended the sick, busiest from couch to couch.
> And over them triumphant *Death* his dart
> Shook: but delay'd to strike, though oft invok'd
> With vows, as their chief good and final hope.[11]

The disorders of the mind, continued *Demea,* though more secret, are not perhaps less dismal and vexatious. Remorse, shame, anguish, rage, disappointment, anxiety, fear, dejection, despair: who has ever passed through life without cruel inroads from these tormentors? How many have scarcely ever felt any better sensations? Labor and poverty, so abhorred by everyone, are the certain lot of the far greater number: And those few privileged persons who enjoy ease and opulence never reach contentment or true felicity. All the goods of life united would not make a very happy man: But all the ills united would make a wretch indeed; and any one of them almost (and who can be free from every one), nay, often the absence of one good (and who can possess all) is sufficient to render life ineligible.

Were a stranger to drop on a sudden into this world, I would show him, as a specimen of its ills, a hospital full of diseases, a prison crowded with malefactors and debtors, a field of battle strewed with carcases, a fleet foundering in the ocean, a nation languishing under tyranny, famine, or pestilence. To turn the gay side of life to him and give him a notion of its pleasures; whither should I conduct him? to a ball, to an opera, to court? He might justly think that I was only showing him a diversity of distress and sorrow.

Philo: There is no evading such striking instances, said *Philo,* but by apologies which still further aggravate the

---

11. [Milton: *Paradise Lost,* Bk. XI.]

charge. Why have all men, I ask, in all ages, complained incessantly of the miseries of life? . . . They have no just reason, says one: These complaints proceed only from their discontented, repining, anxious disposition. . . . And can there possibly, I reply, be a more certain foundation of misery than such a wretched temper?

But if they were really as unhappy as they pretend, says my antagonist, why do they remain in life? . . .

Not satisfied with life, afraid of death. This is the secret chain, say I, that holds us. We are terrified, not bribed to the continuance of our existence.

It is only a false delicacy, he may insist, which a few refined spirits indulge, and which has spread these complaints among the whole race of mankind. . . . And what is this delicacy, I ask, which you blame? Is it anything but a greater sensibility to all the pleasures and pains of life? And if the man of a delicate, refined temper, by being so much more alive than the rest of the world, is only so much more unhappy, what judgment must we form in general of human life?

Let men remain at rest, says our adversary, and they will be easy. They are willing artificers of their own misery. . . . No! reply I: An anxious languor follows their repose; disappointment, vexation, trouble, their activity and ambition.

Cleanthes: I can observe something like what you mention in some others, replied *Cleanthes;* but I confess I feel little or nothing of it in myself, and hope that it is not so common as you represent it.

Demea: If you feel not human misery yourself, cried *Demea,* I congratulate you on so happy a singularity. Others, seemingly the most prosperous, have not been ashamed to vent their complaints in the most melancholy strains. Let us attend to the great, the fortunate emperor, *Charles V,* when, tired with human grandeur, he resigned all his extensive dominions into the hands of his son. In the last harangue which he made on that memorable occasion, he publicly avowed *that the greatest prosperities which he had ever enjoyed had been mixed with so many adversities that he might truly say he had never enjoyed any satisfaction* or *contentment.* But did the retired life in which he sought for shelter afford him any greater happiness? If we may credit his son's account, his repentance commenced the very day of his resignation.

Cicero's fortune, from small beginnings, rose to the greatest luster and renown; yet what pathetic complaints

of the ills of life do his familiar letters, as well as philosophical discourses, contain? And suitably to his own experience, he introduces *Cato,* the great, the fortunate *Cato* protesting in his old age that had he a new life in his offer he would reject the present.

Ask yourself, ask any of your acquaintance, whether they would live over again the last ten or twenty years of their life. No! but the next twenty, they say will be better:

> And from the dregs of life, hope to receive
> What the first sprightly running could not give.[12]

Thus, at last, they find (such is the greatness of human misery, it reconciles even contradictions) that they complain at once of the shortness of life and of its vanity and sorrow.

Philo: And is it possible, *Cleanthes,* said *Philo,* that after all these reflections, and infinitely more which might be suggested, you can still persevere in your anthropomorphism, and assert the moral attributes of the Deity, his justice, benevolence, mercy, and rectitude, to be of the same nature with these virtues in human creatures? His power, we allow, is infinite; whatever he wills is executed: But neither man nor any other animal is happy; therefore, he does not will their happiness. His wisdom is infinite; He is never mistaken in choosing the means to any end; But the course of nature tends not to human or animal felicity: Therefore, it is not established for that purpose. Through the whole compass of human knowledge there are no inferences more certain and infallible than these. In what respect, then, do his benevolence and mercy resemble the benevolence and mercy of men?

Epicurus' old questions are yet unanswered.

Is he willing to prevent evil, but not able? then is he impotent. Is he able, but not willing? then is he malevolent. Is he both able and willing? whence then is evil?

You ascribe, *Cleanthes,* (and I believe justly), a purpose and intention to nature. But what, I beseech you, is the object of that curious artifice and machinery which she had displayed in all animals? The preservation alone of individuals, and propagation of the species? It seems enough

---

12. [John Dryden, *Aureng-Zebe,* Act IV, sc. 1.]

for her purpose, if such a rank be barely upheld in the universe, without any care or concern for the happiness of the members that compose it. No resource for this purpose: No machinery in order merely to give pleasure or ease: No fund of pure joy and contentment: No indulgence without some want or necessity accompanying it. At least, the few phenomena of this nature are overbalanced by opposite phenomena of still greater importance.

Our sense of music, harmony, and indeed beauty of all kinds, gives satisfaction, without being absolutely necessary to the preservation and propagation of the species. But what racking pains, on the other hand, arise from gouts, gravels, megrims, toothaches, rheumatisms, where the injury to the animal machinery is either small or incurable? Mirth, laughter, play, frolic seem gratuitous satisfactions which have no further tendency; spleen, melancholy, discontent, superstition are pains of the same nature. How then does the divine benevolence display itself, in the sense of you anthropormorphites? None but we mystics, as you were pleased to call us, can account for this strange mixture of phenomena, by deriving it from attributes infinitely perfect but incomprehensible.

Cleanthes: And have you, at last, said *Cleanthes* smiling, betrayed your intentions, *Philo?* Your long agreement with *Demea* did indeed a little surprise me, but I find you were all the while erecting a concealed battery against me. And I must confess that you have now fallen upon a subject worthy of your noble spirit of opposition and controversy. If you can make out the present point, and prove mankind to be unhappy or corrupted, there is an end at once of all religion. For to what purpose establish the natural attributes of the Deity, while the moral are still doubtful and uncertain?

Demea: You take umbrage very easily, replied *Demea,* at opinions the most innocent and the most generally received, even amongst the religious and devout themselves; and nothing can be more surprising than to find a topic like this—concerning the wickedness and misery of man—charged with no less than atheism and profaneness. Have not all pious divines and preachers who have indulged their rhetoric on so fertile a subject; have they not easily, I say, given a solution of any difficulties which may attend it? This world is but a point in comparison of the universe; this life but a moment in comparison of eternity. The present evil phenomena,

therefore, are rectified in other regions, and in some future period of existence. And the eyes of men, being then opened to larger views of things, see the whole connection of general laws, and trace, with adoration, the benevolence and rectitude of the Deity through all the mazes and intricacies of his providence.

Cleanthes: No! replied *Cleanthes,* no! These arbitrary suppositions can never be admitted, contrary to matter of fact, visible and uncontroverted. Whence can any cause be known but from its known effects? Whence can any hypothesis be proved but from the apparent phenomena? To establish one hypothesis upon another is building entirely in the air; and the utmost we ever attain by these conjectures and fictions is to ascertain the bare possibility of our opinion, but never can we, upon such terms, establish its reality.

The only method of supporting divine benevolence (and it is what I willingly embrace) is to deny absolutely the misery and wickedness of man. Your representations are exaggerated; your melancholy views mostly fictitious; your inferences contrary to fact and experience. Health is more common than sickness: Pleasure than pain: Happiness than misery. And for one vexation which we meet with, we attain, upon computation, a hundred enjoyments.

Philo: Admitting your position, replied *Philo,* which yet is extremely doubtful, you must at the same time allow that, if pain be less frequent than pleasure, it is infinitely more violent and durable. One hour of it is often able to outweigh a day, a week, a month of our common insipid enjoyments; and how many days, weeks, and months are passed by several in the most acute torments? Pleasure, scarcely in one instance, is ever able to reach ecstasy and rapture: And in no one instance can it continue for any time at its highest pitch and altitude. The spirits evaporate, the nerves relax, the fabric is disordered, and the enjoyment quickly degenerates into fatigue and uneasiness. But pain often, good God, how often! rises to torture and agony; and the longer it continues, it becomes still more genuine agony and torture. Patience is exhausted, courage languishes, melancholy seizes us, and nothing terminates our misery but the removal of its cause or another event which is the sole cure of all evil, but which, from our natural folly, we regard with still greater horror and consternation.

But not to insist upon these topics, continued *Philo,* though most obvious, certain, and important, I must use the freedom to admonish you, *Cleanthes,* that you have put the controversy upon a most dangerous issue, and are unawares introducing a total skepticism into the most essential articles of natural and revealed theology. What! no method of fixing a just foundation for religion unless we allow the happiness of human life, and maintain a continued existence even in this world, with all our present pains, infirmities, vexations, and follies, to be eligible and desirable! But this is contrary to everyone's feeling and experience; it is contrary to an authority so established as nothing can subvert. No decisive proofs can ever be produced against this authority; nor is it possible for you to compute, estimate, and compare all the pains and all the pleasures in the lives of all men and of all animals: And thus, by your resting the whole system of religion on a point which, from its very nature, must forever be uncertain, you tacitly confess that that system is equally uncertain.

But allowing you what never will be believed, at least, what you never possibly can prove, that animal or, at least, human happiness in this life exceeds its misery, you have yet done nothing; for this is not, by any means, what we expect from infinite power, infinite wisdom, and infinite goodness. Why is there any misery at all in the world? Not by chance, surely. From some cause then. Is it from the intention of the Deity? But he is perfectly benevolent. Is it contrary to his intention? But he is almighty. Nothing can shake the solidity of this reasoning, so short, so clear, so decisive, except we assert that these subjects exceed all human capacity, and that our common measures of truth and falsehood are not applicable to them; a topic which I have all along insisted on, but which you have, from the beginning, rejected with scorn and indignation.

But I will be contented to retire still from this retrenchment, for I deny that you can ever force me in it. I will allow that pain or misery in man is *compatible* with infinite power and goodness in the Deity, even in your sense of these attributes: what are you advanced by all these concessions? A mere possible compatibility is not sufficient. You must *prove* these pure, unmixed and uncontrollable attributes from the present mixed and confused phenomena, and from these alone. A hopeful undertaking! Were the phenomena ever so pure and unmixed, yet, being finite, they would be insufficient for that purpose. How much more, where they are also so jarring and discordant!

Here, *Cleanthes,* I find myself at ease in my argument. Here I triumph. Formerly, when we argued concerning the natural attributes of intelligence and design, I needed all my skeptical and metaphysical subtilty to elude your grasp. In many views of the universe and of its parts, particularly the latter, the beauty and fitness of final causes strike us with such irresistible force that all objections appear (what I believe they really are) mere cavils and sophisms; nor can we then imagine how it was ever possible for us to repose any weight on them. But there is no view of human life or of the condition of mankind from which, without the greatest violence, we can infer the moral attributes or learn that infinite benevolence, conjoined with infinite power and infinite wisdom, which we must discover by the eyes of faith alone. It is your turn now to tug the laboring oar, and to support your philosophical subtilties against the dictates of plain reason and experience.

Part XI

Cleanthes: I scruple not to allow, said *Cleanthes,* that I have been apt to suspect the frequent repetition of the word "infinite," which we meet with in all theological writers, to savor more of panegyric than of philosophy, and that any purposes of reasoning, and even of religion, would be better served were we to rest contented with more accurate and more moderate expressions. The terms "admirable," "excellent," "superlatively great," "wise," and "holy"; these sufficiently fill the imaginations of men, and anything beyond, besides that it leads into absurdities, has no influence on the affections or sentiments. Thus, in the present subject, if we abandon all human analogy, as seems your intention, *Demea,* I am afraid we abandon all religion and retain no conception of the great object of our adoration. If we preserve human analogy, we must forever find it impossible to reconcile any mixture of evil in the universe with infinite attributes; much less can we ever prove the latter from the former. But supposing the Author of Nature to be finitely perfect, though far exceeding mankind, a satisfactory account may then be given of natural and moral evil, and every untoward phenomenon be explained and adjusted. A lesser evil may then be chosen in order to avoid a greater; inconveniences be submitted to in order to reach a desirable end; and, in a word, benevolence, regulated by wisdom and limited by necessity, may produce just such a world as the present. You, *Philo,* who are so prompt at starting views and reflections and analogies, I would gladly hear, at length, without interruption, your opinion of this new theory; and if it deserve our attention, we may afterwards, at more leisure, reduce it into form.

Philo: My sentiments, replied *Philo,* are not worth being made a mystery of; and, therefore, without any ceremony, I shall deliver what occurs to me with regard to the present subject. It must, I think, be allowed that, if a very limited intelligence whom we shall suppose utterly unacquainted with the universe were assured that it were the production of a very good, wise, and powerful being, however finite, he would, from his conjectures, form *beforehand* a different notion of it from what we find it to be by experience; nor would he ever imagine, merely from these attributes of the cause of which he is informed, that the effect could be so full of vice and misery and disorder, as it appears in this life. Supposing now that this person were brought into the world, still assured that it was the workmanship of such a sublime and benevolent being, he might, perhaps, be surprised at the disappointment, but would never retract his former belief if founded on any very solid argument; since such a limited intelligence must be sensible of his own blindness and ignorance, and must allow that there may be many solutions of those phenomena which will forever escape his comprehension. But supposing, which is the real case with regard to man, that this creature is not antecedently convinced of a supreme intelligence, benevolent, and powerful, but is left to gather such a belief from the appearances of things; this entirely alters the case, nor will he ever find any reason for such a conclusion. He may be fully convinced of the narrow limits of his understanding, but this will not help him in forming an inference concerning the goodness of superior powers, since he must form that inference from what he knows, not from what he is ignorant of. The more you exaggerate his weakness and ignorance,

the more diffident you render him, and give him the greater suspicion that such subjects are beyond the reach of his faculties. You are obliged, therefore, to reason with him merely from the known phenomena, and to drop every arbitrary supposition or conjecture.

Did I show you a house or palace where there was not one apartment convenient or agreeable; where the windows, doors, fires, passages, stairs, and the whole economy of the building were the source of noise, confusion, fatigue, darkness, and the extremes of heat and cold, you would certainly blame the contrivance, without any further examination. The architect would in vain display his subtilty, and prove to you that, if this door or that window were altered, greater ills would ensue. What he says may be strictly true: The alteration of one particular, while the other parts of the building remain, may only augment the inconveniences. But still you would assert in general that, if the architect had had skill and good intentions, he might have formed such a plan of the whole, and might have adjusted the parts in such a manner as would have remedied all or most of these inconveniences. His ignorance, or even your own ignorance of such a plan, will never convince you of the impossibility of it. If you find any inconveniences and deformities in the building, you will always, without entering into any detail, condemn the architect.

In short, I repeat the question: Is the world, considered in general and as it appears to us in this life, different from what a man or such a limited being would, *beforehand,* expect from a very powerful, wise, and benevolent Deity? It must be strange prejudice to assert the contrary. And from thence I conclude that, however consistent the world may be, allowing certain suppositions and conjectures with the idea of such a Deity, it can never afford us an inference concerning his existence. The consistency is not absolutely denied, only the inference. Conjectures, especially where infinity is excluded from the divine attributes, may perhaps be sufficient to prove a consistency, but can never be foundations for any inference.

There seem to be *four* circumstances on which depend all or the greatest part of the ills that molest sensible creatures; and it is not impossible but all these circumstances may be necessary and unavoidable. We know so little beyond common life, or even of common life, that, with regard to the economy of a universe, there is no conjecture, however wild, which may not be just; nor any one, however plausible, which may not be erroneous. All that belongs to human understanding, in this deep ignorance and obscurity, is to be skeptical or at least cautious, and not to admit of any hypothesis whatever, much less of any which is supported by no appearance of probability. Now this I assert to be the case with regard to all the causes of evil and the circumstances on which it depends. None of them appear to human reason in the least degree necessary or unavoidable, nor can we suppose them such, without the utmost license of imagination.

The *first* circumstance which introduces evil is that contrivance or economy of the animal creation by which pains, as well as pleasures, are employed to excite all creatures to action, and make them vigilant in the great work of self-preservation. Now pleasure alone, in its various degrees, seems to human understanding sufficient for this purpose. All animals might be constantly in a state of enjoyment; but when urged by any of the necessities of nature, such as thirst, hunger, weariness; instead of pain, they might feel a diminution of pleasure by which they might be prompted to seek that object which is necessary to their subsistence. Men pursue pleasure as eagerly as they avoid pain; at least, they might have been so constituted. It seems, therefore, plainly possible to carry on the business of life without any pain. Why then is any animal ever rendered susceptible of such a sensation? If animals can be free from it an hour, they might enjoy a perpetual exemption from it, and it required as particular a contrivance of their organs to produce that feeling as to endow them with sight, hearing, or any of the senses. Shall we conjecture that such a contrivance was necessary, without any appearance of reason? And shall we build on that conjecture as on the most certain truth?

But a capacity of pain would not alone produce pain were it not for the *second* circumstance, viz., the conducting of the world by general laws; and this seems nowise necessary to a very perfect being. It is true, if everything were conducted by particular volitions, the course of nature would be perpetually broken, and no man could employ his reason in the conduct of life. But might not other particular volitions remedy this inconvenience? In short, might not the Deity exterminate all ill, wherever it were to be found, and produce all good, without any preparation or long progress of causes and effects?

Besides, we must consider that, according to the present economy of the world, the course of nature, though supposed exactly regular, yet to us appears not so, and many events are uncertain, and many disappoint our expectations. Health and sickness, calm and tempest, with an infinite number of other accidents whose causes are unknown and variable, have a great influence both on the fortunes of particular persons and on the prosperity of public societies: And indeed all human life, in a manner, depends on such accidents. A being, therefore, who knows the secret springs of the universe might easily, by particular volitions, turn all these accidents to the good of mankind and render the whole world happy, without discovering himself in any operation. A fleet whose purposes were salutary to society might always meet with a fair wind: Good princes enjoy sound health and long life: Persons born to power and authority be framed with good tempers and virtuous dispositions. A few such events as these, regularly and wisely conducted, would change the face of the world; and yet would no more seem to disturb the course of nature or confound human conduct than the present economy of things, where the causes are secret and variable and compounded. Some small touches given to *Caligula's* brain in his infancy might have converted him into a *Trajan*. One wave, a little higher than the rest, by burying *Caesar* and his fortune in the bottom of the ocean, might have restored liberty to a considerable part of mankind. There may, for aught we know, be good reasons why Providence interposes not in this manner, but they are unknown to us; And, though the mere supposition that such reasons exist may be sufficient to *save* the conclusion concerning the divine attributes, yet surely it can never be sufficient to *establish* that conclusion.

If everything in the universe be conducted by general laws, and if animals be rendered susceptible of pain, it scarcely seems possible but some ill must arise in the various shocks of matter and the various concurrence and opposition of general laws; but this ill would be very rare were it not for the *third* circumstance which I proposed to mention, viz., the great frugality with which all powers and faculties are distributed to every particular being. So well adjusted are the organs and capacities of all animals, and so well fitted to their preservation, that, as far as history or tradition reaches, there appears not to be any single species which has yet been extinguished in the universe. Every animal has the requisite endowments, but these endowments are bestowed with so scrupulous an economy that any considerable diminution must entirely destroy the creature. Wherever one power is increased, there is a proportional abatement in the others. Animals which excel in swiftness are commonly defective in force. Those which possess both are either imperfect in some of their senses or are oppressed with the most craving wants. The human species, whose chief excellence is reason and sagacity, is of all others the most necessitous, and the most deficient in bodily advantages; without clothes, without arms, without food, without lodging, without any convenience of life, except what they owe to their own skill and industry. In short, nature seems to have formed an exact calculation of the necessities of her creatures; and, like a *rigid master,* has afforded them little more powers or endowments than what are strictly sufficient to supply those necessities. An *indulgent parent* would have bestowed a large stock in order to guard against accidents, and secure the happiness and welfare of the creature in the most unfortunate concurrence of circumstances. Every course of life would not have been so surrounded with precipices that the least departure from the true path, by mistake or necessity, must involve us in misery and ruin. Some reserve, some fund, would have been provided to ensure happiness, nor would the powers and the necessities have been adjusted with so rigid an economy. The Author of Nature is inconceivably powerful; his force is supposed great, if not altogether inexhaustible nor is there any reason, as far as we can judge, to make him observe this strict frugality in his dealings with his creatures. It would have been better, were his power extremely limited, to have created fewer animals, and to have endowed these with more faculties for their happiness and preservation. A builder is never esteemed prudent who undertakes a plan beyond what his stock will enable him to finish.

In order to cure most of the ills of human life, I require not that man should have the wings of the eagle, the swiftness of the stag, the force of the ox, the arms of the lion, the scales of the crocodile or rhinoceros; much less do I demand the sagacity of an angel or cherubim. I am contented to take an increase in one single power or faculty of his soul. Let him be endowed with a greater propensity to industry and labor, a more vigorous spring and activity of mind, a more constant bent to business and application. Let the whole species possess naturally an equal diligence with that which many individuals are able to attain by habit and reflection, and the most beneficial consequences, without any allay of ill, is the immediate and necessary result of this endowment. Almost all the moral as well as natural evils of human life arise from idleness; and were our species, by the original constitution of their frame, exempt from this vice or infirmity, the perfect cultivation of land, the improvement of arts and manufactures, the exact execution of every office and duty, immediately follow; and men at once may fully reach that state of society which is so imperfectly attained by the best regulated government. But as industry is a power, and the most valuable of any, nature seems determined, suitably to her usual maxims, to bestow it on men with a very sparing hand; and rather to punish him severely for his deficiency in it than to reward him for his attainments. She has so contrived his frame that nothing but the most violent necessity can oblige him to labor; and she employs all his other wants to overcome, at least in part, the want of diligence, and to endow him with some share of a faculty of which she has thought fit naturally to bereave him. Here our demands may be allowed very humble, and therefore the more reasonable. If we required the endowments of superior penetration and judgment, of a more delicate taste of beauty, of a nicer sensibility to benevolence and friendship, we might be told that we impiously pretend to break the order of Nature, that we want to exalt ourselves into a higher rank of being, that the presents which we require, not being suitable to our state and condition, would only be pernicious to us. But it is hard, I dare to repeat it, it is hard that, being placed in a world so full of wants and necessities, where almost every being and element is either our foe or refuses its assistance; we should also have our own temper to struggle with, and should be deprived of that faculty which can alone fence against these multiplied evils.

The *fourth* circumstance whence arises the misery and ill of the universe is the inaccurate workmanship of all the springs and principles of the great machine of nature. It must be acknowledged that there are few parts of the universe which seem not to serve some purpose, and whose removal would not produce a visible defect and disorder in the whole. The parts hang all together, nor can one be touched without affecting the rest, in a greater or less degree. But at the same time, it must be observed that none of these parts or principles, however useful, are so accurately adjusted as to keep precisely within those bounds in which their utility consists; but they are, all of them, apt, on every occasion, to run into the one extreme or the other. One would imagine that this grand production had not received the last hand of the maker; so little finished is every part, and so coarse are the strokes with which it is executed. Thus the winds are requisite to convey the vapors along the surface of the globe, and to assist men in navigation: But how often, rising up to tempests and hurricanes, do they become pernicious? Rains are necessary to nourish all the plants and animals of the earth: But how often are they defective? how often excessive? Heat is requisite to all life and vegetation, but is not always found in the due proportion. On the mixture and secretion of the humors and juices of the body depend the health and prosperity of the animal: But the parts perform not regularly their proper function. What more useful than all the passions of the mind, ambition, vanity, love, anger? But how often do they break their bounds and cause the greatest convulsions in society? There is nothing so advantageous in the universe but what frequently becomes pernicious, by its excess or defect; nor has nature guarded, with the requisite accuracy, against all disorder or confusion. The irregularity is never perhaps so great as to destroy any species, but is often sufficient to involve the individuals in ruin and misery.

On the concurrence, then, of these *four* circumstances does all or the greatest part of natural evil depend. Were all living creatures incapable of pain, or were the world administered by particular volitions, evil never could have found access into the universe: And were animals endowed with a large stock of powers and faculties, beyond what strict necessity requires, or were the several springs and principles of the universe so accurately framed as to preserve always the just temperament and medium, there must have been very little ill in comparison of what we feel at present. What then shall we pronounce on this occasion? Shall we say that these circumstances are not necessary, and that they might easily have been altered in the contrivance of the universe?

This decision seems too presumptuous for creatures so blind and ignorant. Let us be more modest in our conclusions. Let us allow that, if the goodness of the Deity (I mean a goodness like the human) could be established on any tolerable reasons *a priori,* these phenomena, however untoward, would not be sufficient to subvert that principle, but might easily, in some unknown manner, be reconcilable to it. But let us still assert that, as this goodness is not antecedently established but must be inferred from the phenomena, there can be no grounds for such an inference while there are so many ills in the universe, and while these ills might so easily have been remedied, as far as human understanding can be allowed to judge on such a subject. I am skeptic enough to allow that the bad appearances, notwithstanding all my reasonings, may be compatible with such attributes as you suppose; but surely they can never prove these attributes. Such a conclusion cannot result from skepticism, but must arise from the phenomena, and from our confidence in the reasonings which we deduce from these phenomena.

Look round this universe. What an immense profusion of beings, animated and organized, sensible and active! You admire this prodigious variety and fecundity. But inspect a little more narrowly these living existences, the only beings worth regarding. How hostile and destructive to each other! How insufficient all of them for their own happiness! How contemptible or odious to the spectator! The whole presents nothing but the idea of a blind nature, impregnated by a great vivifying principle, and pouring forth from her lap, without discernment or parental care, her maimed and abortive children!

Here the Manichaean system[13] occurs as a proper hypothesis to solve the difficulty; and, no doubt, in some respects it is very specious and has more probability than the common hypothesis, by giving a plausible account of the strange mixture of good and ill which appears in life. But if we consider, on the other hand, the perfect uniformity and agreement of the parts of the universe, we shall not discover in it any marks of the combat of a malevolent with a benevolent being. There is indeed an opposition of pains and pleasures in the feelings of

---

13. [The ancient Manichean view was that the world is run by both a good force and an evil one.]

sensible creatures; But are not all the operations of nature carried on by an opposition of principles, of hot and cold, moist and dry, light and heavy? The true conclusion is that the original source of all things is entirely indifferent to all these principles, and has no more regard to good above ill than to heat above cold, or to drought above moisture, or to light above heavy.

There may *four* hypotheses be framed concerning the first causes of the universe: *that* they are endowed with perfect goodness; *that* they have perfect malice; *that* they are opposite and have both goodness and malice; *that* they have neither goodness nor malice. Mixed phenomena can never prove the two former unmixed principles; and the uniformity and steadiness of general laws seem to oppose the third. The fourth, therefore, seems by far the most probable.

What I have said concerning natural evil will apply to moral with little or no variation; and we have no more reason to infer that the rectitude of the Supreme Being resembles human rectitude than that his benevolence resembles the human. Nay, it will be thought that we have still greater cause to exclude from him moral sentiments, such as we feel them; since moral evil, in the opinion of many, is much more predominant above moral good than natural evil above natural good.

But even though this should not be allowed, and though the virtue which is in mankind should be acknowledged much superior to the vice; yet, so long as there is any vice at all in the universe, it will very much puzzle you anthropomorphites how to account for it. You must assign a cause for it, without having recourse to the first cause. But as every effect must have a cause, and that cause another, you must either carry on the progression *in infinitum,* or rest on that original principle, who is the ultimate cause of all things. . . .

Demea: Hold! hold! cried *Demea,* Whither does your imagination hurry you? I joined in alliance with you in order to prove the incomprehensible nature of the Divine Being, and refute the principles of *Cleanthes,* who would measure everything by human rule and standard. But I now find you running into all the topics of the greatest libertines and infidels, and betraying that holy cause which you seemingly espoused. Are you secretly, then, a more dangerous enemy than *Cleanthes* himself?

Cleanthes: And are you so late in perceiving it? replied *Cleanthes.* Believe me, *Demea,* your friend *Philo,* from

the beginning, has been amusing himself at both our expense; and it must be confessed that the injudicious reasoning of our vulgar theology has given him but too just a handle of ridicule. The total infirmity of human reason, the absolute incomprehensibility of the Divine Nature, the great and universal misery, and still greater wickedness of men; these are strange topics, surely, to be so fondly cherished by orthodox divines and doctors. In ages of stupidity and ignorance, indeed, these principles may safely be espoused; and perhaps no views of things are more proper to promote superstition than such as encourage the blind amazement, the diffidence, and melancholy of mankind. But at present . . .

Philo: Blame not so much, interposed *Philo,* the ignorance of these reverend gentlemen. They know how to change their style with the times. Formerly, it was a most popular theological topic to maintain that human life was vanity and misery, and to exaggerate all the ills and pains which are incident to men. But of late years, divines, we find, begin to retract this position and maintain, though still with some hesitation, that there are more goods than evils, more pleasures than pains, even in this life. When religion stood entirely upon temper and education, it was thought proper to encourage melancholy; as, indeed, mankind never have recourse to superior powers so readily as in that disposition. But as men have now learned to form principles and to draw consequences, it is necessary to change the batteries, and to make use of such arguments as will endure at least some scrutiny and examination. This variation is the same (and from the same causes) with that which I formerly remarked with regard to skepticism.

Thus *Philo* continued to the last his spirit of opposition, and his censure of established opinions. But I could observe that *Demea* did not at all relish the latter part of the discourse; and he took occasion soon after, on some pretence or other, to leave the company,

Part XII

After Demea's departure, Cleanthes and Philo continued the conversation in the following manner.

Cleanthes: Our friend, I am afraid, said *Cleanthes,* will have little inclination to revive this topic of discourse while you are in company; and to tell the truth, *Philo,* I should rather wish to reason with either of you apart on a subject so sublime and interesting. Your spirit of controversy, joined to your abhorrence of vulgar superstition, carries you strange lengths when engaged in an argument; and there is nothing so sacred and venerable, even in your own eyes, which you spare on that occasion.

Philo: I must confess, replied *Philo,* that I am less cautious on the subject of Natural Religion than on any other; both because I know that I can never, on that head, corrupt the principles of any man of common sense and because no one, I am confident, in whose eyes I appear a man of common sense will ever mistake my intentions. You, in particular, *Cleanthes,* with whom I live in unreserved intimacy; you are sensible that, notwithstanding the freedom of my conversation and my love of singular arguments, no one has a deeper sense of religion impressed on his mind, or pays more profound adoration to the Divine Being, as he discovers himself to reason in the inexplicable contrivance and artifice of nature. A purpose, an intention, a design strikes everywhere the most careless, the most stupid thinker; and no man can be so hardened in absurd systems as at all times to reject it. *That nature does nothing in vain* is a maxim established in all the Schools, merely from the contemplation of the works of nature, without any religious purpose; and, from a firm conviction of its truth, an anatomist who had observed a new organ or canal would never be satisfied till he had also discovered its use and intention. One great foundation of the *Copernican* system is the maxim *that nature acts by the simplest methods, and chooses the most proper means to any end;* and astronomers often, without thinking of it, lay this strong foundation of piety and religion. The same thing is observable in other parts of philosophy; and thus all the sciences almost lead us insensibly to acknowledge a first intelligent Author; and their authority is often so much the greater as they do not directly profess that intention.

It is with pleasure I hear *Galen* reason concerning the structure of the human body. The anatomy of a man, says he,[14] discovers above 600 different muscles; and whoever duly considers these will find that, in each of them, nature must have adjusted at least ten different circumstances in order to attain the end which she proposed: proper figure, just magnitude, right disposition of the several ends, upper and lower position of the whole, the due insertion of the several nerves, veins, and arteries; so that, in the muscles alone, above 6000 several views and intentions must have been formed and executed. The bones he calculates to be 284: The distinct purposes aimed at in the structure of each, above forty. What a prodigious display of artifice, even in these simple and homogeneous parts! But if we consider the skin, ligaments, vessels, glandules, humors, the several limbs and members of the body; how must our astonishment rise upon us, in proportion to the number and intricacy of the parts so artificially adjusted! The further we advance in these researches, we discover new scenes of art and wisdom; but descry still, at a distance, further scenes beyond our reach; in the fine internal structure of the parts, in the economy of the brain, in the fabric of the seminal vessels. All these artifices are repeated in every different species of animal, with wonderful variety, and with exact propriety, suited to the different intentions of nature in framing each species. And if the infidelity of *Galen,* even when these natural sciences were still imperfect, could not withstand such striking appearances, to what pitch of pertinacious obstinacy must a philosopher in this age have attained who can now doubt of a Supreme Intelligence!

Could I meet with one of this species (who, I thank God, are very rare), I would ask him: Supposing there were a God who did not discover himself immediately to our senses, were it possible for him to give stronger proofs of his existence than what appear on the whole face of nature? What indeed could such a Divine Being do but copy the present economy of things; render many of his artifices so plain that no stupidity could mistake them; afford glimpses of still greater artifices which demonstrate his prodigious superiority above our narrow apprehensions, and conceal altogether a great many from such imperfect creatures? Now, according to all rules of just reasoning, every fact must pass for undisputed when it is supported by all the arguments which its nature admits of, even though these arguments be not, in themselves, very numerous or forcible: How much more in the present case where no human imagination can compute their number, and no understanding estimate their cogency.

---

14. *De Formatione Foetus.* [Galen was the most reknowned physician of antiquity.]

Cleanthes: I shall further add, said *Cleanthes,* to what you have so well urged, that one great advantage of the principle of theism is that it is the only system of cosmogony which can be rendered intelligible and complete, and yet can throughout preserve a strong analogy to what we every day see and experience in the world. The comparison of the universe to a machine of human contrivance is so obvious and natural, and is justified by so many instances of order and design in nature, that it must immediately strike all unprejudiced apprehensions, and procure universal approbation. Whoever attempts to weaken this theory cannot pretend to succeed by establishing in its place any other that is precise and determinate: It is sufficient for him if he start doubts and difficulties; and, by remote and abstract views of things, reach that suspense of judgment which is here the utmost boundary of his wishes. But, besides that this state of mind is in itself unsatisfactory, it can never be steadily maintained against such striking appearances as continually engage us into the religious hypothesis. A false, absurd system, human nature, from the force of prejudice, is capable of adhering to with obstinacy and perseverance; but no system at all, in opposition to a theory supported by strong and obvious reason, by natural propensity, and by early education, I think it absolutely impossible to maintain or defend.

Philo: So little, replied *Philo,* do I esteem this suspense of judgment in the present case to be possible that I am apt to suspect there enters somewhat of a dispute of words into this controversy, more than is usually imagined. That the works of nature bear a great analogy to the productions of art is evident; and, according to all the rules of good reasoning, we ought to infer, if we argue at all concerning them, that their causes have a proportional analogy. But as there are also considerable differences, we have reason to suppose a proportional difference in the causes, and, in particular, ought to attribute a much higher degree of power and energy to the Supreme Cause than any we have ever observed in mankind. Here, then, the existence of a DEITY is plainly ascertained by reason; and if we make it a question whether, on account of these analogies, we can properly call him a *mind* or *intelligence,* notwithstanding the vast difference which may reasonably be supposed between him and human minds; what is this but a mere verbal controversy? No man can deny the analogies between the effects: to restrain ourselves from inquiring concerning the causes is scarcely possible. From this inquiry the legitimate conclusion is that the causes have also an analogy: And if we are not contented with calling the first and supreme cause a GOD or DEITY, but desire to vary the expression, what can we call him but MIND or THOUGHT, to which he is justly supposed to bear a considerable resemblance?

All men of sound reason are disgusted with verbal disputes, which abound so much in philosophical and theological inquiries; and it is found that the only remedy for this abuse must arise from clear definitions, from the precision of those ideas which enter into any argument, and from the strict and uniform use of those terms which are employed. But there is a species of controversy which, from the very nature of language and of human ideas, is involved in perpetual ambiguity, and can never, by any precaution or any definitions, be able to reach a reasonable certainty or precision. These are the controversies concerning the degrees of any quality or circumstance. Men may argue to all eternity whether *Hannibal* be a great, or a very great, or a superlatively great man, what degree of beauty *Cleopatra* possessed, what epithet of praise *Livy* or *Thucydides* is entitled to, without bringing the controversy to any determination. The disputants may here agree in their sense and differ in the terms, or *vice versa,* yet never be able to define their terms so as to enter into each other's meaning: Because the degrees of these qualities are not, like quantity or number, susceptible of any exact mensuration, which may be the standard in the controversy. That the dispute concerning theism is of this nature, and consequently is merely verbal, or, perhaps, if possible, still more incurably ambiguous, will appear upon the slightest inquiry. I ask the theist if he does not allow that there is a great and immeasurable, because incomprehensible, difference between the *human* and the *divine* mind: The more pious he is, the more readily will he assent to the affirmative, and the more will he be disposed to magnify the difference: He will even assert that the difference is of a nature which cannot be too much magnified. I next turn to the atheist, who, I assert, is only nominally so and can never possibly be in earnest; and I ask him whether, from the coherence and apparent sympathy in all the parts of this world, there be not a certain degree of analogy among all the operations of nature, in every situation and in every age; whether the rotting of a turnip, the generation of an animal, and the structure of human thought, be not energies that probably bear some remote analogy to each other: It is impossible he can deny it: He will readily acknowledge it. Having obtained this concession, I push him still further in his retreat, and I ask him if it be not probable that the principle which first arranged and still maintains order in this universe bears not also some remote inconceivable analogy to the other operations of nature and, among the rest, to the economy of human mind and thought. However reluctant, he must give his assent. Where then, cry I to both these antagonists, is the subject of your dispute? The theist allows that the original intelligence is very different from human reason: The atheist allows that the original principle of order bears some remote analogy to it. Will you quarrel, Gentlemen, about the degrees, and enter into a controversy which admits not of any precise meaning, nor consequently of any determination? If you should be so obstinate, I should not be surprised to find you insensibly change sides; while the theist, on the one hand, exaggerates the dissimilarity between the Supreme Being and frail, imperfect, variable, fleeting, and mortal creatures; and the atheist, on the other, magnifies the analogy among all the operations of nature, in every period, every situation, and every position. Consider then where the real point of controversy lies; and if you cannot lay aside your disputes, endeavor, at least, to cure yourselves of your animosity.

And here I must also acknowledge, *Cleanthes,* that, as the works of Nature have a much greater analogy to the effects of *our* art and contrivance than to those of *our* benevolence and justice; we have reason to infer that the natural attributes of the Deity have a greater resemblance to those of men than his moral have to human virtues. But what is the consequence? Nothing but this, that the moral qualities of man are more defective in their kind than his natural abilities. For, as the Supreme Being is allowed to be absolutely and entirely perfect, whatever differs most from him departs the farthest from the supreme standard of rectitude and perfection.

These, *Cleanthes,* are my unfeigned sentiments on this subject; and these sentiments, you know, I have ever cherished and maintained. But in proportion to my veneration for true religion is my abhorrence of vulgar superstitions; and I indulge a peculiar pleasure, I confess, in pushing such principles sometimes into absurdity, sometimes into impiety. And you are sensible that all bigots, notwithstanding their great aversion to the latter above the former, are commonly equally guilty of both.

Cleanthes: My inclination, replied *Cleanthes,* lies, I own, a contrary way. Religion, however corrupted, is still better than no religion at all. The doctrine of a future state is so strong and necessary a security to morals that we never ought to abandon or neglect it. For if finite and temporary rewards and punishments have so great an effect, as we daily find: How much greater must be expected from such as are infinite and eternal?

Philo: How happens it then, said *Philo,* if vulgar superstition be so salutary to society, that all history abounds so much with accounts of its pernicious consequences on public affairs? Factions, civil wars, persecutions, subversions of government, oppression, slavery: these are the dismal consequences which always attend its prevalence over the minds of men. If the religious spirit be ever mentioned in any historical narration, we are sure to meet afterwards with a detail of the miseries which attend it. And no period of time can be happier or more prosperous than those in which it is never regarded or heard of.

Cleanthes: The reason of this observation, replied *Cleanthes,* is obvious. The proper office of religion is to regulate the hearts of men, humanize their conduct, infuse the spirit of temperance, order, and obedience; and, as its operation is silent and only enforces the motives of morality and justice, it is in danger of being overlooked and confounded with these other motives. When it distinguishes itself, and acts as a separate principle over men, it has departed from its proper sphere and has become only a cover to faction and ambition.

Philo: And so will all religion, said *Philo,* except the philosophical and rational kind. Your reasonings are more easily eluded than my facts. The inference is not just, because finite and temporary rewards and punishments have so great influence that therefore such as are infinite and eternal must have so much greater. Consider, I beseech you, the attachment which we have to present things, and the little concern which we discover for objects so remote and uncertain. When divines are declaiming against the common behavior and conduct of the world, they always represent this principle as the strongest imaginable (which indeed it is), and describe almost all human kind as lying under the influence of it, and sunk into the deepest lethargy and unconcern about their religious interests. Yet these same divines, when they refute their speculative antagonists, suppose the motives of religion to be so powerful that, without them, it were impossible for civil society to subsist; nor are they ashamed of so palpable a contradiction. It is certain, from experience, that the smallest grain of natural honesty and benevolence has more effect on men's conduct than the most pompous views suggested by theological theories and systems. A man's natural inclination works incessantly upon him; it is forever present to the mind, and mingles itself with every view and consideration: whereas religious motives, where they act at all, operate only by starts and bounds; and it is scarcely possible for them to become altogether habitual to the mind. The force of the greatest gravity, say the philosophers, is infinitely small, in comparison of that of the least impulse, yet it is certain that the smallest gravity will, in the end, prevail above a great impulse because no strokes or blows can be repeated with such constancy as attraction and gravitation.

Another advantage of inclination: It engages on its side all the wit and ingenuity of the mind, and, when set in opposition to religious principles, seeks every method and art of eluding them; in which it is almost always successful. Who can explain the heart of man, or account for those strange salvos and excuses with which people satisfy themselves when they follow their inclinations in opposition to their religious duty? This is well understood in the world; and none but fools ever repose less trust in a man because they hear that, from study and philosophy, he has entertained some speculative doubts with regard to theological subjects. And when we have to do with a man who makes a great profession of religion and devotion, has this any other effect upon several who pass for prudent than to put them on their guard, lest they be cheated and deceived by him?

We must further consider that philosophers, who cultivate reason and reflection, stand less in need of such motives to keep them under the restraint of morals: And that the vulgar, who alone may need them, are utterly incapable of so pure a religion as represents the Deity to be pleased with nothing but virtue in human behavior. The recommendations to the Divinity are generally supposed to be either frivolous observances or rapturous ecstasies or a bigoted credulity. We need not run back into antiquity or wander into remote regions to find instances of this degeneracy. Amongst ourselves, some have been guilty of that atrociousness, unknown to the Egyptian and Grecian superstitions, of declaiming, in express terms, against morality, and representing it as a sure forfeiture of the divine favor if the least trust or reliance be laid upon it.

But even though superstition or enthusiasm should not put itself in direct opposition to morality; the very diverting of the attention, the raising up a new and frivolous species of merit, the preposterous distribution which it makes of praise and blame, must have the most pernicious consequences, and weaken extremely men's attachment to the natural motives of justice and humanity.

Such a principle of action likewise, not being any of the familiar motives of human conduct, acts only by intervals on the temper, and must be roused by continual efforts in order to render the pious zealot satisfied with his own conduct and make him fulfill his devotional task. Many religious exercises are entered into with seeming fervor where the heart, at the time, feels cold and languid. A habit of dissimulation is by degrees contracted: And fraud and falsehood become the predominant principle. Hence the reason of that vulgar observation that the highest zeal in religion and the deepest hypocrisy, so far from being inconsistent, are often or commonly united in the same individual character.

The bad effects of such habits, even in common life, are easily imagined: But, where the interests of religion are concerned, no morality can be forcible enough to bind the enthusiastic zealot. The sacredness of the cause sanctifies every measure which can be made use of to promote it.

The steady attention alone to so important an interest as that of eternal salvation is apt to extinguish the benevolent affections, and beget a narrow, contracted selfishness. And when such a temper is encouraged, it easily eludes all the general precepts of charity and benevolence.

Thus the motives of vulgar superstition have no great influence on general conduct, nor is the operation favorable to morality, in the instances where they predominate.

Is there any maxim in politics more certain and infallible than that both the number and authority of priests should be confined within very narrow limits, and that the civil magistrate ought, for ever, to keep his *fasces* and *axes* from such dangerous hands? But if the spirit of popular religion were so salutary to society, a contrary maxim ought to prevail. The greater number of priests and their greater authority and riches will always augment the religious spirit. And though the priests have the guidance of this spirit, why may we not expect a superior sanctity of life and greater benevolence and moderation from persons who are set apart for religion, who are continually inculcating it upon others, and who must themselves imbibe a greater share of it? Whence comes it then that, in fact, the utmost a wise magistrate can propose with regard to popular religions is, as far as possible, to make a saving game of it, and to prevent their pernicious consequences with regard to society? Every expedient which he tries for so humble a purpose is surrounded with inconveniences. If he admits only one religion among his subjects, he must sacrifice, to an uncertain prospect of tranquility, every consideration of public liberty, science, reason, industry, and even his own independence. If he gives indulgence to several sects, which is the wiser maxim, he must preserve a very philosophical indifference to all of them and carefully restrain the pretensions of the prevailing sect; otherwise he can expect nothing but endless disputes, quarrels, factions, persecutions, and civil commotions.

True religion, I allow, has no such pernicious consequences: But we must treat of religion as it has commonly been found in the world; nor have I anything to do with that speculative tenet of theism which, as it is a species of philosophy, must partake of the beneficial influence of that principle, and, at the same time, must lie under a like inconvenience of being always confined to very few persons.

Oaths are requisite in all courts of judicature, but it is a question whether their authority arises from any popular religion. It is the solemnity and importance of the occasion, the regard to reputation, and the reflecting on the general interests of society, which are the chief restraints upon mankind. Customhouse oaths and political oaths are but little regarded even by some who pretend to principles of honesty and religion: And a *Quaker's* asseveration is with us justly put upon the same

footing with the oath of any other person. I know that *Polybius*[15] ascribes the infamy of Greek faith to the prevalence of the *Epicurean* philosophy; but I know also that Punic faith had as bad a reputation in ancient times as Irish evidence has in modern, though we cannot account for these vulgar observations by the same reason. Not to mention that Greek faith was infamous before the rise of the *Epicurean* philosophy; and *Euripides,*[16] in a passage which I shall point out to you, has glanced a remarkable stroke of satire against his nation, with regard to this circumstance.

Cleanthes: Take care, *Philo,* replied *Cleanthes,* take care; push not matters too far, allow not your zeal against false religion to undermine your veneration for the true. Forfeit not this principle, the chief, the only great comfort in life and our principal support amidst all the attacks of adverse fortune. The most agreeable reflection which it is possible for human imagination to suggest is that of genuine theism, which represents us as the workmanship of a Being perfectly good, wise, and powerful; who created us for happiness; and who, having implanted in us immeasurable desires of good, will prolong our existence to all eternity, and will transfer us into an infinite variety of scenes, in order to satisfy those desires and render our felicity complete and durable. Next to such a Being himself (if the comparison be allowed), the happiest lot which we can imagine is that of being under his guardianship and protection.

Philo: These appearances, said Philo, are most engaging and alluring; and, with regard to the true philosopher, they are more than appearances. But it happens here, as in the former case, that, with regard to the greater part of mankind, the appearances are deceitful, and that the terrors of religion commonly prevail above its comforts.

It is allowed that men never have recourse to devotion so readily as when dejected with grief or depressed with sickness. Is not this a proof that the religious spirit is not so nearly allied to joy as to sorrow?

Cleanthes: But men, when afflicted, find consolation in religion, replied *Cleanthes.*

---

15. [Polybius, *The Histories,* Book VI, chap. 54.]

16. *Iphigenia in Tauris.*

Philo: Sometimes, said *Philo;* but it is natural to imagine that they will form a notion of those unknown beings, suitable to the present gloom and melancholy of their temper, when they betake themselves to the contemplation of them. Accordingly, we find the tremendous images to predominate in all religions; and we ourselves, after having employed the most exalted expression in our descriptions of the Deity, fall into the flattest contradiction in affirming that the damned are infinitely superior in number to the elect.

I shall venture to affirm that there never was a popular religion which represented the state of departed souls in such a light as would render it eligible for human kind that there should be such a state. These fine models of religion are the mere product of philosophy. For as death lies between the eye and the prospect of futurity, that event is so shocking to nature that it must throw a gloom on all the regions which lie beyond it; and suggest to the generality of mankind the idea of *Cerberus* and *Furies,* devils, and torrents of fire and brimstone.

It is true, both fear and hope enter into religion because both these passions, at different times, agitate the human mind, and each of them forms a species of divinity suitable to itself. But when a man is in a cheerful disposition, he is fit for business, or company, or entertainment of any kind; and he naturally applies himself to these and thinks not of religion. When melancholy and dejected, he has nothing to do but brood upon the terrors of the invisible world, and to plunge himself still deeper in affliction. It may indeed happen that, after he has, in this manner, engraved the religious opinions deep into his thought and imagination, there may arrive a change of health or circumstances which may restore his good humor and, raising cheerful prospects of futurity, make him run into the other extreme of joy and triumph. But still it must be acknowledged that, as terror is the primary principle of religion, it is the passion which always predominates in it, and admits but of short intervals of pleasure.

Not to mention that these fits of excessive, enthusiastic joy, by exhausting the spirits, always prepare the way for equal fits of superstitious terror and dejection; nor is there any state of mind so happy as the calm and equable. But this state it is impossible to support where a man thinks that he lies in such profound darkness and uncertainty, between an eternity of happiness and an eternity of misery. No wonder that such an opinion disjoints the ordinary frame of the mind and throws it into the utmost confusion. And though that opinion is seldom so steady in its operation as to influence all the actions; yet it is apt to make a considerable breach in the temper, and to produce that gloom and melancholy so remarkable in all devout people.

It is contrary to common sense to entertain apprehensions or terrors upon account of any opinion whatsoever, or to imagine that we run any risk hereafter, by the freest use of our reason. Such a sentiment implies both an *absurdity* and an *inconsistency.* It is an absurdity to believe that the Deity has human passions, and one of the lowest of human passions, a restless appetite for applause. It is an inconsistency to believe that, since the Deity has this human passion, he has not others also; and, in particular, a disregard to the opinions of creatures so much inferior.

To know God, says *Seneca, is to worship him.* All other worship is indeed absurd, superstitious, and even impious. It degrades him to the low condition of mankind, who are delighted with entreaty, solicitation, presents, and flattery. Yet is this impiety the smallest of which superstition is guilty. Commonly, it depresses the Deity far below the condition of mankind, and represents him as a capricious demon who exercises his power without reason and without humanity! And were that Divine Being disposed to be offended at the vices and follies of silly mortals, who are his own workmanship, ill would it surely fare with the votaries of most popular superstitions. Nor would any of human race merit his *favor* but a very few, the philosophical theists, who entertain or rather indeed endeavor to entertain suitable notions of his divine perfections. As the only persons entitled to his *compassion* and *indulgence* would be the philosophical skeptics, a sect almost equally rare, who, from a natural diffidence of their own capacity, suspend or endeavor to suspend all judgment with regard to such sublime and such extraordinary subjects.

If the whole of natural theology, as some people seem to maintain, resolves itself into one simple, though somewhat ambiguous, at least undefined, proposition, *That the cause or causes of order in the universe probably bear some remote analogy to human intelligence:* If this proposition be not capable of extension, variation, or more particular explication: If it affords no inference that affects

That the cause or causes of order in the universe probably bear some remote analogy to human intelligence: If this proposition be not capable of extension, variation, or more particular explication: If it affords no inference that affects human life, or can be the source of any action or forbearance: And if the analogy, imperfect as it is, can be carried no further than to the human intelligence, and cannot be transferred, with any appearance of probability, to the other qualities of the mind: If this really be the case, what can the most inquisitive, contemplative, and religious man do more than give a plain, philosophical assent to the proposition, as often as it occurs, and believe that the arguments on which it is established exceed the objections which lie against it? Some astonishment, indeed, will naturally arise from the greatness of the object: Some melancholy from its obscurity: Some contempt of human reason that it can give no solution more satisfactory with regard to so extraordinary and magnificent a question. But believe me, *Cleanthes,* the most natural sentiment which a well-disposed mind will feel on this occasion is a longing desire and expectation that heaven would be pleased to dissipate, at least alleviate, this profound ignorance by affording some more particular revelation to mankind, and making discoveries of the nature, attributes, and operations of the divine object of our faith. A person, seasoned with a just sense of the imperfections of natural reason, will fly to revealed truth with the greatest avidity: While the haughty dogmatist, persuaded that he can erect a complete system of theology by the mere help of philosophy, disdains any further aid and rejects this adventitious instructor. To be a philosophical skeptic is, in a man of letters, the first and most essential step towards being a sound, believing *Christian*—a proposition which I would willingly recommend to the attention of Pamphilus; and I hope *Cleanthes* will forgive me for interposing so far in the education and instruction of his pupil.

Pamphilus: Cleanthes and *Philo* pursued not this conversation much further; and as nothing ever made greater impression on me than all the reasonings of that day; so

Antony Flew

Theology and Falsification

Let us begin with a parable. It is a parable developed from a tale told by John Wisdom in his haunting and revelatory article 'Gods'.[1] Once upon a time two explorers came upon a clearing in the jungle. In the clearing were growing many flowers and many weeds. One explorer says, 'Some gardener must tend this plot'. The other disagrees, 'There is no gardener'. So they pitch their tents and set a watch. No gardener is ever seen. 'But perhaps he is an invisible gardener'. So they set up a barbed-wire fence. They electrify it. They patrol it with bloodhounds. (For they remember how H. G. Wells's *The Invisible Man* could be both smelt and touched though he could not be seen.) But no shrieks ever suggest that some intruder has received a shock. No movements of the wire ever betray an invisible climber. The bloodhounds never give cry. Yet still the Believer is not convinced. 'But there is a gardener, invisible, intangible, insensible to electric shocks, a gardener who has no scent and makes no sound, a gardener who comes secretly to look after the garden which he loves'. At last

1. *P.A.S.,* 19445–5, reprinted as Ch. X of *Logic and Language,* Vol I (Blackwell, 1951), and in his *Philosophy and Psychoanalysis* (Blackwell, 1953).

the Sceptic despairs, 'But what remains of your original assertion? Just how does what you call an invisible, intangible, eternally elusive gardener differ from an imaginary gardener or even from no gardener at all?'

In this parable we can see how what starts as an assertion, that something exists or that there is some analogy between certain complexes of phenomena, may be reduced step by step to an altogether different status, to an expression perhaps of a 'picture preference'.[2] The Sceptic says there is no gardener. The Believer says there is a gardener (but invisible, etc.). One man talks about sexual behaviour. Another man prefers to talk of Aphrodite (but knows that there is not really a superhuman person additional to, and somehow responsible for, all sexual phenomena).[3] The process of qualification may be checked at any point before the original assertion is completely withdrawn and something of that first assertion will remain (Tautology). Mr. Wells's invisible man could not, admittedly, be seen, but in all other respects he was a man like the rest of us. But though the process of qualification may be, and of course usually is, checked in time, it is not always judiciously so halted. Someone may dissipate his assertion completely without noticing that he has done so. A fine brash hypothesis may thus be killed by inches, the death by a thousand qualifications.

And in this, it seems to me, lies the peculiar danger, the endemic evil, of theological utterance. Take such utterances as 'God has a plan', 'God created the world', 'God loves us as a father loves his children'. They look at first sight very much like assertions, vast cosmological assertions. Of course, this is no sure sign that they either are, or are intended to be, assertions. But let us confine ourselves to the cases where those who utter such sentences intend them to express assertions. (Merely remarking parenthetically that those who intend or interpret such utterances as crypto-commands, expressions of wishes, disguised ejaculations, concealed ethics, or as anything else but assertions, are unlikely to succeed in making them either properly orthodox or practically effective.)

Now to assert that such and such is the case is necessarily equivalent to denying that such and such is not the case.[4] Suppose then that we are in doubt as to what someone who gives vent to an utterance is asserting, or suppose that, more radically, we are sceptical as to whether he is really asserting anything at all, one way of trying to understand (or perhaps it will be to expose) his utterance is to attempt to find what he would regard as counting against, or as being incompatible with, its truth. For if the utterance is indeed an assertion, it will necessarily be equivalent to a denial of the negation of that assertion. And anything which would count against the assertion, or which would induce the speaker to withdraw it and to admit that it had been mistaken, must be part of (or the whole of) the meaning of the negation of that assertion. And to know the meaning of the negation of an assertion, is as near as makes no matter, to know the meaning of that assertion.[5] And if there is nothing which a putative assertion denies then there is nothing which it asserts either: and so it is not really an assertion. When the Sceptic in the parable asked the Believer, 'Just how does what you call an invisible, intangible, eternally elusive gardener differ from an imaginary gardener or even from no gardener at all?' he was suggesting that the Believer's earlier statement had been so eroded by qualification that it was no longer an assertion at all.

Now it often seems to people who are not religious as if there was no conceivable event or series of events the occurrence of which would be admitted by sophisticated religious people to be a sufficient reason for conceding 'There wasn't a God after all' or 'God does not really love us then'. Someone tells us that God loves us as a father loves his children. We are reassured. But then we see a child dying of inoperable cancer of the throat. His earthly father is driven frantic in his efforts to help, but his Heavenly Father reveals no obvious sign of concern. Some qualification is made—God's love is

---

2. Cf. J. Wisom, 'Other Minds', *Mind*, 1940; reprinted in his *Other Minds* (Blackwell, 1952).

3. C.f. Lucretius, *De Rerum Natura*, II, 655–60,

> His siquis mare Neptunum Cereremque vocare
> Constituet fruges et Bacchi nomine abuti
> Mavolat quam laticis proprium proferre vocamen
> Concedamus ut hic terrarum dictitet orbem
> Esse deum matrem dum vera re tamen ipse
> Religione animum turpi contongere parcat.

---

4. For those who prefer symbolism: $p \equiv \sim\sim p$.

5. For by simply negating $\sim p$ we get $p : \sim\sim p \equiv p$.

'not a merely human love' or it is 'an inscrutable love', perhaps—and we realize that such sufferings are quite compatible with the truth of the assertion that 'God loves us as a father (but, of course,...)'. We are reassured again. But then perhaps we ask: what is this assurance of God's (appropriately qualified) love worth, what is this apparent guarantee really a guarantee against? Just what

would have to happen not merely (morally and wrongly) to tempt but also (logically and rightly) to entitle us to say 'God does not love us' or even 'God does not exist?' I therefore put to the succeeding symposiasts the simple central questions, 'What would have to occur or to have occurred to constitute for you a disproof of the love of, or of the existence of, God?'

Gottfried Leibniz

A Refutation of Arguments from Evil

Summary of the Controversy Reduced to Formal Arguments.

Some persons of discernment have wished me to make this addition. I have the more readily deferred to their opinion, because of the opportunity thereby gained for meeting certain difficulties, and for making observations on certain matters which were not treated in sufficient detail in the work itself.

Objection 1

Whoever does not choose the best course is lacking either in power, or knowledge, or goodness.

God did not choose the best course in creating this world.

Therefore God was lacking in power, or knowledge, or goodness.

Answer

I deny the minor, that is to say, the second premises of this syllogism, and the opponent proves it by this.

From Gottfried Leibniz, *Theodicy,* translated by E. M. Huggard, edited by Austin Farrar (Chicago: Open Court Publishing Company, 1985). Copyright © 1985 by E. M. Huggard. Reprinted with permission of Open Court Publishing Company.

Prosyllogism

Whoever makes things in which there is evil, and which could have been made without any evil, or need not have been made at all, does not choose the best course.

God made a world wherein there is evil; a world, I say, which could have been made without any evil or which need not have been made at all.

Therefore God did not choose the best course.

Answer

I admit the minor of this prosyllogism: for one must confess that there is evil in this world which God has made, and that it would have been possible to make a world without evil or even not to create any world, since its creation depended upon the free will of God. But I deny the major, that is, the first of the two premises of the prosyllogism, and I might content myself with asking for its proof. In order, however, to give a clearer exposition of the matter, I would justify this denial by pointing out that the best course is not always that one which tends towards avoiding evil, since it is possible that the evil may be accompanied by a greater good. For example, the general of an army will prefer a great victory with a slight wound to a state of affairs without this wounds and without victory. I have proved this in further detail in this work by pointing out, through instances taken from mathematics and elsewhere, that an imperfection in the part may be required for a greater perfection in the whole. I have followed therein the opinion of St. Augustine, who said a hundred times that God permitted evil in order to derive from it a good, that is to say, a greater good; and Thomas Aquinas says (in libr. 2, *Sent. Dist.* 32, qu. 1, art. 1) that the permission of evil tends towards the good of the universe. I have shown that among older writers the fall of Adam was termed *felix culpa,* a fortunate sin, because it had been expiated with immense benefit by the incarnation of the Son of God: for he gave to the universe something more noble than anything there would otherwise have been amongst created beings. For the better understanding of the matter I added, following the example of many good authors, that it was consistent with order and the general good for God to grant to certain of his creatures the opportunity to exercise their freedom, even when he foresaw that they would turn to evil: for God could easily correct the evil, and it was not fitting that in order to prevent sin he should always act in an extraordinary way. It will therefore sufficiently refute the objection to show that a world with evil may be better than a world without evil. But I have gone still further in the work, and have even shown that this universe must be indeed better than every other possible universe.

Objection II

If there is more evil than good in intelligent creatures, there is more evil than good in all God's work.

Now there is more evil than good in intelligent creatures.

Therefore there is more evil than good in all God's work.

Answer

I deny the major and the minor of this conditional syllogism. As for the major, I do not admit it because this supposed inference from the part to the whole, from intelligent creatures to all creatures, assumes tacitly and without proof that creatures devoid of reason cannot be compared or taken into account with those that have reason. But why might not the surplus of good in the non-intelligent creatures that fill the world compensate for and even exceed incomparably the surplus of evil in rational creatures? It is true that the value of the latter is greater; but by way of compensation the others are incomparably greater in number; and it may be that the proportion of number and quantity surpasses that of value and quality.

The minor also I cannot admit, namely, that there is more evil than good in intelligent creatures. One need not even agree that there is more evil than good in the human kind. For it is possible, and even a very reasonable thing, that the glory and the perfection of the blessed may be incomparably greater than the misery and imperfection of the damned, and that here the excellence of the total good in the smaller number may exceed the total evil which is in the greater number. The blessed draw near to divinity through a divine Mediator, so far as can belong to these created beings, and make such progress in good as is impossible for the damned to make in evil, even though they should approach as nearly as may be the nature of demons. God is infinite, and the Devil is finite; good can and does go on *ad infinitum,* whereas evil has its bounds. It may be therefore, and it is probable, that there happens in the comparison between the blessed and the damned the opposite of what I said could happen in the comparison between the happy and the unhappy, namely that in the latter the proportion of degrees surpasses that of numbers, while in the comparison between intelligent and non-intelligent the proportion of numbers is greater than that of values. One is justified in assuming that a thing may be so as long as one does not prove that it is impossible, and indeed what is here put forward goes beyond assumption.

But secondly, even should one admit that there is more evil than good in the human kind, one still has every reason for not admitting that there is more evil than good in all intelligent creatures. For there is an inconceivable number of Spirits, and perhaps of other rational creatures besides: and an opponent cannot prove that in the whole City of God, composed as much of Spirits as of rational animals without number and of endless different kinds, the evil exceeds the good. Although one need not, in order to answer an objection, prove that a thing is, when its mere possibility suffices, I have nevertheless shown in this present work that it is a result of the supreme perfection of the Sovereign of the Universe that the kingdom of God should be the most perfect of all states or governments possible, and that in consequence what little evil there is should be required to provide the full measure of the vast good existing there.

Objection III

If it is always impossible not to sin, it is always unjust to punish.

Now it is always impossible not to sin, or rather all sin is necessary.

Therefore it is always unjust to punish.

The minor of this is proved as follows.

First Prosyllogism

Everything predetermined is necessary.

Every event is predetermined.

Therefore every event (and consequently sin also) is necessary.

Again this second minor is proved thus.

Second Prosyllogism

That which is future, that which is foreseen, that which is involved in causes is predetermined.

Every event is of this kind.

Therefore every event is predetermined.

Answer

I admit in a certain sense the conclusion of the second prosyllogism, which is the minor of the first; but I shall deny the major of the first prosyllogism, namely that everything predetermined is necessary; taking 'necessity', say the necessity to sin, or the impossibility of not sinning, or of not doing some action, in the sense relevant to the argument, that is, as a necessity essential and absolute, which destroys the morality of action and the justice of punishment. If anyone meant a different necessity or impossibility (that is, a necessity only moral or hypothetical, which will be explained presently) it is plain that we would deny him the major stated in the objection. We might content ourselves with this answer, and demand the proof of the proposition denied: but I

am well pleased to justify my manner of procedure in the present work, in order to make the matter clear and to throw more light on this whole subject, by explaining the necessity that must be rejected and the determination that must be allowed. The truth is that the necessity contrary to morality, which must be avoided and which would render punishment unjust, is an insuperable necessity, which would render all opposition unavailing, even though one should wish with all one's heart to avoid the necessary action, and though one should make all possible efforts to that end. Now it is plain that this is not applicable to voluntary actions, since one would not do them if one did not so desire. Thus their prevision and predetermination is not absolute, but it presupposes will: if it is certain that one will do them, it is no less certain that one will will to do them. These voluntary actions and their results will not happen whatever one may do and whether one will them or not; but they will happen because one will do, and because one will will to do, that which leads to them. That is involved in prevision and predetermination, and forms the reason thereof. The necessity of such events is called conditional or hypothetical, or again necessity of consequence, because it presupposes the will and the other requisites. But the necessity which destroys morality, and renders punishment unjust and reward unavailing, is found in the things that will be whatever one may do and whatever one may will to do: in a word, it exists in that which is essential. This it is which is called an absolute necessity. Thus it avails nothing with regard to what is necessary absolutely to ordain interdicts or commandments, to propose penalties or prizes, to blame or to praise; it will come to pass no more and no less. In voluntary actions, on the contrary, and in what depends upon them, precepts, armed with power to punish and to reward, very often serve, and are included in the order of causes that make action exist. Thus it comes about that not only pains and effort but also prayers are effective, God having had even these prayers in mind before he ordered things, and having made due allowance for them. That is why the precept *Ora et labora* (Pray and work) remains intact. Thus not only those who (under the empty pretext of the necessity of events) maintain that one can spare oneself the pains demanded by affairs, but also those who argue against prayers, fall into that which the ancients even in their time called 'the Lazy Sophism'. So the predetermination of events by their causes is precisely what contributes to morality instead of destroying it, and the causes incline the will without necessitating it. For this reason the determination we are concerned with is not a necessitation. It is certain (to him who knows all) that the effect will follow this inclination; but this effect does not follow thence by a consequence which is necessary, that is, whose contrary implies contradiction; and it is also by such an inward inclination that the will is determined, without the presence of necessity. Suppose that one has the greatest possible passion (for example, a great thirst), you will admit that the soul can find some reason for resisting it, even if it were only that of displaying its power. Thus though one may never have complete indifference of equipoise, and there is always a predominance of inclination for the course adopted, that predominance does not render absolutely necessary the resolution taken.

Objection IV

Whoever can prevent the sin of others and does not so, but rather contributes to it, although he be fully appraised of it, is accessory thereto.

God can prevent the sin of intelligent creatures; but he does not so, and he rather contributes to it by his co-operation and by the opportunities he causes, although he is fully cognizant of it.

Therefore, etc.

Answer

I deny the major of this syllogism. It may be that one can prevent the sin, but that one ought not to do so, because one could not do so without committing a sin oneself, or (when God is concerned) without acting unreasonably. I have given instances of that, and have applied them to God himself. It may be also that one contributes to the evil, and that one even opens the way to it sometimes, in doing things one is bound to do. And when one does one's duty, or (speaking of God) when,

after full consideration, one does that which reason demands, one is not responsible for events, even when one foresees them. One does not will these evils; but one is willing to permit them for a greater good, which one cannot in reason help preferring to other considerations. This is a *consequent* will, resulting from acts of *antecedent* will, in which one wills the good. I know that some persons, in speaking of the antecedent and consequent will of God, have meant by the antecedent that which wills that all men be saved, and by the consequent that which wills, in consequence of persistent sin, that there be some damned, damnation being a result of sin. But these are only examples of a more general notion, and one may say with the same reason, that God wills by his antecedent will that men sin not, and that by his consequent or final and decretory will (which is always followed by its effect) he wills to permit that they sin, this permission being a result of superior reasons. One has indeed justification for saying, in general, that the antecedent will of God tends towards the production of good and the prevention of evil, each taken in itself, and as it were detached (*particulariter et secundum quid:* Thom., I, qu. 19, art. 6) according to the measure of the degree of each good or of each evil. Likewise one may say that the consequent, or final and total, divine will tends towards the production of as many goods as can be put together, whose combination thereby becomes determined, and involves also the permission of some evils and the exclusion of some goods, as the best possible plan of the universe demands. Arminius, in his *Antiperkinsus,* explained very well that the will of God can be called consequent not only in relation to the action of the creature considered beforehand in the divine understanding, but also in relation to other anterior acts of divine will. But it is enough to consider the passage cited from Thomas Aquinas, and that from Scotus (I, dist. 46, qu. 11), to see that they make this distinction as I have made it here. Nevertheless if anyone will not suffer this use of the terms, let him put 'previous' in place of 'antecedent' will, and 'final' or 'decretory' in place of 'consequent' will. For I do not wish to wrangle about words.

J. L. Mackie

Evil and Omnipotence

The traditional arguments for the existence of God have been fairly thoroughly criticised by philosophers. But the theologian can, if he wishes, accept this criticism. He can admit that no rational proof of God's existence is possible. And he can still retain all that is essential to his position, by holding that God's existence is known in some other, non-rational way. I think, however, that a more telling criticism can be made by way of the traditional problem of evil. Here it can be shown, not that religious beliefs lack rational support, but that they are positively irrational, that the several parts of the essential theological doctrine are inconsistent with one another, so that the theologian can maintain his position as a whole only by a much more extreme rejection of reason than in the former case. He must now be prepared to believe, not merely what cannot be proved, but what can be *disproved* from other beliefs that he also holds.

The problem of evil, in the sense in which I shall be using the phrase, is a problem only for someone who believes that there is a God who is both omnipotent and wholly good. And it is a logical problem, the problem of clarifying and reconciling a number of beliefs: it is not a scientific problem that might be solved by further observations, or a practical problem that might be solved by a decision or an action. These points are obvious; I mention them only because they are sometimes ignored by theologians, who sometimes parry a statement of the problem with such remarks as "Well, can you solve the problem yourself?" or "This is a mystery which may be revealed to us later" or "Evil is something to be faced and overcome, not to be merely discussed".

In its simplest form the problem is this: God is omnipotent; God is wholly good; and yet evil still exists. There seems to be some contradiction between these three propositions, so that if any two of them were true the third would be false. But at the same time all three are essential parts of most theological positions: the theologian, it seems, at once *must* adhere and *cannot consistently* adhere to all three. (The problem does not arise only for theists, but I shall discuss it in the form in which it presents itself for ordinary theism.)

However, the contradiction does not arise immediately; to show it we need some additional premises, or perhaps some quasi-logical rules connecting the terms 'good', 'evil', and 'omnipotent'. These additional principles are that good is opposed to evil, in such a way that a good thing always eliminates evil as far as it can, and that there are no limits to what an omnipotent thing can do. From these it follows that a good omnipotent thing eliminates evil completely, and then the propositions that a good omnipotent thing exists, and that evil exists, are incompatible.

A. Adequate Solutions

Now once the problem is fully stated it is clear that it can be solved, in the sense that the problem will not arise if one gives up at least one of the propositions that constitute it. If you are prepared to say that God is not wholly good, or not quite omnipotent, or that evil does not exist, or that good is not opposed to the kind of evil that exists, or that there are limits to what an omnipotent thing can do, then the problem of evil will not arise for you.

There are, then, quite a number of adequate solutions of the problem of evil, and some of these have been adopted, or almost adopted, by various thinkers. For example, a few have been prepared to deny God's omnipotence, and rather more have been prepared to keep the term 'omnipotence' but severely to restrict its meaning, recording quite a number of things that an omnipotent being cannot do. Some have said that evil is an illusion, perhaps because they held that the whole world of temporal, changing things is an illusion, and that what we

J. L. Mackie, "Evil and Omnipotence" from *Mind,* 56 (1955): 200–212. Copyright © 1955 by the Mind Association. Reprinted with the permission of Oxford University Press.

call evil belongs only to this world, or perhaps because they held that although temporal things *are* much as we see them, those that we call evil are not really evil. Some have said that what we call evil is merely the privation of good, that evil in a positive sense, evil that would really be opposed to good, does not exist. Many have agreed with Pope that disorder is harmony not understood, and that partial evil is universal good. Whether any of these views is *true* is, of course, another question. But each of them gives an adequate solution of the problem of evil in the sense that if you accept it this problem does not arise for you, though you may, of course, have *other* problems to face.

But often enough these adequate solutions are only *almost* adopted. The thinkers who restrict God's power, but keep the term 'omnipotence', may reasonably be suspected of thinking, in other contexts, that his power is really unlimited. Those who say that evil is an illusion may also be thinking, inconsistently, that this illusion is itself an evil. Those who say that "evil" is merely privation of good may also be thinking, inconsistently, that privation of good is an evil. (The fallacy here is akin to some forms of the "naturalistic fallacy" in ethics, where some think, for example, that "good" is just what contributes to evolutionary progress, and that evolutionary progress is itself good.) If Pope meant what he said in the first line of his couplet, that "disorder" is only harmony not understood, the "partial evil" of the second line must, for consistency, mean "that which, taken in isolation, falsely appears to be evil", but it would more naturally mean "that which, in isolation, really is evil". The second line, in fact, hesitates between two views, that "partial evil" isn't really evil, since only the universal quality is real, and that "partial evil" is really an evil, but only a little one.

In addition, therefore, to adequate solutions, we must recognise unsatisfactory inconsistent solutions, in which there is only a half-hearted or temporary rejection of one of the propositions which together constitute the problem. In these, one of the constituent propositions is explicitly rejected, but it is covertly re-asserted or assumed elsewhere in the system.

B. Fallacious Solutions

Besides these half-hearted solutions, which explicitly reject but implicitly assert one of the constituent propositions, there are definitely fallacious solutions which explicitly maintain all the constituent propositions, but implicitly reject at least one of them in the course of the argument that explains away the problem of evil.

There are, in fact, many so-called solutions which purport to remove the contradiction without abandoning any of its constituent propositions. These must be fallacious, as we can see from the very statement of the problem, but it is not so easy to see in each case precisely where the fallacy lies. I suggest that in all cases the fallacy has the general form suggested above: in order to solve the problem one (or perhaps more) of its constituent propositions is given up, but in such a way that it appears to have been retained, and can therefore be asserted without qualification in other contexts. Sometimes there is a further complication: the supposed solution moves to and fro between, say, two of the constituent propositions, at one point asserting the first of these but covertly abandoning the second, at another point asserting the second but covertly abandoning the first. These fallacious solutions often turn upon some equivocation with the words 'good' and 'evil', or upon some vagueness about the way in which good and evil are opposed to one another, or about how much is meant by 'omnipotence'. I propose to examine some of these so-called solutions, and to exhibit their fallacies in detail. Incidentally, I shall also be considering whether an adequate solution could be reached by a minor modification of one or more of the constituent propositions, which would, however, still satisfy all the essential requirements of ordinary theism.

1. "Good cannot exist without evil" or "Evil is necessary as a counterpart to good."

It is sometimes suggested that evil is necessary as a counterpart to good, that if there were no evil there could be no good either, and that this solves the problem of evil. It is true that it points to an answer to the question "Why should there be evil?" But it does so only by qualifying some of the propositions that constitute the problem.

First, it sets a limit to what God can do, saying that God *cannot* create good without simultaneously creating evil, and this means either that God is not omnipotent or that there are *some* limits to what an omnipotent thing can do. It may be replied that these limits are always presupposed, that omnipotence has never meant the power to do what is logically impossible, and on the present view the existence of good without evil would be a logical impossibility. This interpretation or omnipotence may indeed be accepted as a modification of our original account which does not reject anything that is essential to theism, and I shall in general assume it in the subsequent discussion. It is, perhaps, the most common theistic view, but I think that some theists at least have maintained that God can do what is logically impossible. Many theists, at any rate, have held that logic itself is created or laid down by God, that logic is the way in which God arbitrarily chooses to think. (This is, of course, parallel to the ethical view that morally right actions are those which God arbitrarily chooses to command, and the two views encounter similar difficulties.) And *this* account of logic is clearly inconsistent with the view that God is bound by logical necessities—unless it is possible for an omnipotent being to bind himself, an issue which we shall consider later, when we come to the Paradox of Omnipotence. This solution of the problem of evil cannot, therefore, be consistently adopted along with the view that logic is itself created by God.

But, secondly, this solution denies that evil is opposed to good in our original sense. If good and evil are counterparts, a good thing will not "eliminate evil as far as it can". Indeed, this view suggest that good and evil are not strictly qualities of things at all. Perhaps the suggestion is that good and evil are related in much the same way as great and small. Certainly when the term 'great' is used relatively as a condensation of 'greater than so-and-so', and 'small' is used correspondingly, greatness and smallness are counterparts and cannot exist without each other. But in this sense greatness is not a quality, not an intrinsic feature of anything; and it would be absurd to think of a movement in favour of greatness and against smallness in this sense. Such a movement would be self-defeating, since relative greatness can be promoted only by a simultaneous promotion of relative smallness. I feel sure that no theists would be content to regard God's goodness as analogous to this—as if what he supports were not the *good* but the *better,* and as if he had the paradoxical aim that all things should be better than other things.

This point is obscured by the fact that 'great' and 'small' seem to have an absolute as well as a relative sense. I can-

not discuss here whether there is absolute magnitude or not, but if there is, there could be an absolute sense for 'great', it could mean of at least a certain size, and it would make sense to speak of all things getting bigger, of a universe that was expanding all over, and therefore it would make sense to speak of promoting greatness. But in *this* sense great and small are not logically necessary counterparts, either quality could exist without the other. There would be no logical impossibility in everything's being small or in everything's being great.

Neither in the absolute nor in the relative sense, then, of 'great' and 'small' do these terms provide an analogy of the sort that would be needed to support this solution of the problem of evil. In neither case are greatness and smallness *both* necessary counterparts *and* mutually opposed forces or possible objects for support and attack.

It may be replied that good and evil are necessary counterparts in the same way as any quality and its logical opposite: redness can occur, it is suggested, only if non-redness also occurs. But unless evil is merely the privation of good, they are not logical opposites, and some further argument would be needed to show that they are counterparts in the same way as genuine logical opposites. Let us assume that this could be given. There is still doubt of the correctness of the metaphysical principle that a quality must have a real opposite: I suggest that it is not really impossible that everything should be, say, red, that the truth is merely that if everything were red we should not notice redness, and so we should have no word 'red'; we observe and give names to qualities only if they have real opposites. If so, the principle that a term must have an opposite would belong only to our language or to our thought, and would not be an ontological principle, and, correspondingly, the rule that good cannot exist without evil would not state a logical necessity of a sort that God would just have to put up with. God might have made everything good, though *we* should not have noticed it if he had.

But, finally, even if we concede that this *is* an ontological principle, it will provide a solution for the problem of evil only if one is prepared to say, "Evil exists, but only just enough evil to serve as the counterpart of good". I doubt whether any theist will accept this. After all, the *ontological* requirement that non-redness should occur would be satisfied even if all the universe, except for a minute speck, were red, and, if there were a corresponding requirement for evil as a counterpart to good, a minute dose of evil would presumably do. But theists are not usually willing to say, in all contexts, that all the evil that occurs is a minute and necessary dose.

2. "Evil is necessary as a means to good."

It is sometimes suggested that evil is necessary for good not as a counterpart but as a means. In its simple form this has little plausibility as a solution of the problem of evil, since it obviously implies a severe restriction of God's power. It would be a *causal* law that you cannot have a certain end without a certain means, so that if God has to introduce evil as a means to good, he must be subject to at least some causal laws. This certainly conflicts with what a theist normally means by omnipotence. This view of God as limited by causal laws also conflicts with the view that causal laws are themselves made by God, which is more widely held than the corresponding view about the laws of logic. This conflict would, indeed, be resolved if it were possible for an omnipotent being to bind himself, and this possibility has still to be considered. Unless a favourable answer can be given to this question, the suggestion that evil is necessary as a means to good solves the problem of evil only by denying one of its constituent propositions, either that God is omnipotent or that 'omnipotent' means what it says.

3. "The universe is better with some evil in it than it could be if there were no evil."

Much more important is a solution which at first seems to be a mere variant of the previous one, that evil may contribute to the goodness of a whole in which it is found, so that the universe as a whole is better as it is, with some evil in it, than it would be if there were no evil. This solution may be developed in either of two ways. It may be supported by an aesthetic analogy, by the fact that contrasts heighten beauty, that in a musical work, for example, there may occur discords which somehow add to the beauty of the work as a whole. Alternatively, it may be worked out in connexion with the notion of progress, that the best possible organisation of the universe will not be static, but progressive, that the gradual

overcoming of evil by good is really a finer thing than would be the eternal unchallenged supremacy of good.

In either case, this solution usually starts from the assumption that the evil whose existence gives rise to the problem of evil is primarily what is called physical evil, that is to say, pain. In Hume's rather half-hearted presentation of the problem of evil, the evils that he stresses are pain and disease, and those who reply to him argue that the existence of pain and disease makes possible the existence of sympathy, benevolence, heroism, and the gradually successful struggle of doctors and reformers to overcome these evils. In fact, theists often seize the opportunity to accuse those who stress the problem of evil of taking a low, materialistic view of good and evil, equating these with pleasure and pain, and of ignoring the more spiritual goods which can arise in the struggle against evils.

But let us see exactly what is being done here. Let us call pain and misery 'first order evil' or 'evil (1)'. What contrasts with this, namely, pleasure and happiness, will be called 'first order good' or 'good (1)'. Distinct from this is 'second order good' or 'good (2)' which somehow emerges in a complex situation in which evil (1) is a necessary component—logically, not merely causally, necessary. (Exactly *how* it emerges does not matter: in the crudest version of this solution good (2) is simply the heightening of happiness by the contrast with misery, in other versions it includes sympathy with suffering, heroism in facing danger, and the gradual decrease of first order evil and increase of first order good.) It is also being assumed that second order good is more important than first order good or evil, in particular that it more than outweighs the first order evil it involves.

Now this is a particularly subtle attempt to solve the problem of evil. It defends God's goodness and omnipotence on the ground that (on a sufficiently long view) this is the best of all logically possible worlds, because it includes the important second order goods, and yet it admits that real evils, namely first order evils, exist. But does it still hold that good and evil are opposed? Not, clearly, in the sense that we set out originally: good does not tend to eliminate evil in general. Instead, we have a modified, a more complex pattern. First order good (e.g. happiness) *contrasts with* first order evil (e.g. misery): these two are opposed in a fairly mechanical way; some second order goods (e.g. benevolence) try to maximise first order good and minimise first order evil;

but God's goodness is not this, it is rather the will to maximise *second* order good. We might, therefore, call God's goodness an example of a third order goodness, or good (3). While this account is different from our original one, it might well be held to be an improvement on it, to give a more accurate description of the way in which good is opposed to evil, and to be consistent with the essential theist position.

There might, however, be several objections to this solution.

First, some might argue that such qualities as benevolence—and *a fortiori* the third order goodness which promotes benevolence—have a merely derivative value, that they are not higher sorts of good, but merely means to good (1), that is, to happiness, so that it would be absurd for God to keep misery in existence in order to make possible the virtues of benevolence, heroism, etc. The theist who adopts the present solution must, of course, deny this, but he can do so with some plausibility, so I should not press this objection.

Secondly, it follows from this solution that God is not in our sense benevolent or sympathetic: he is not concerned to minimise evil (1), but only to promote good (2); and this might be a disturbing conclusion for some theists.

But, thirdly, the fatal objection is this. Our analysis shows clearly the possibility of the existence of a *second* order evil, an evil (2) contrasting with good (2) as evil (1) contrast with good (1). This would include malevolence, cruelty, callousness, cowardice, and states in which good (1) is decreasing and evil (1) increasing. And just as good (2) is held to be the important kind of good, the kind that God is concerned to promote, so evil (2) will, by analogy, be the important kind of evil, the kind which God, if he were wholly good, and omnipotent, would eliminate. And yet evil (2) plainly exists, and indeed most theists (in other contexts) stress its existence more than that of evil (1). We should, therefore, state the problem of evil in terms of second order evil, and against this form of the problem the present solution is useless.

An attempt might be made to use this solution again, at a higher level, to explain the occurrence of evil (2): indeed the next main solution that we shall examine does just this, with the help of some new notions. Without any fresh notions, such a solution would have little plausibility: for example, we could hardly say that the really important good was a good (3), such as the increase of benevolence in proportion to cruelty, which logically required for its occurrence the occurrence of some second order evil. But even if evil (2) could be explained in this way, it is fairly clear that there would be third order evils contrasting with this third order good: and we should be well on the way to an infinite regress, where the solution of a problem of evil, stated in terms of evil (*n*), indicated the existence of an evil (*n* + 1), and a further problem to be solved.

4. "Evil is due to human freewill."

Perhaps the most important proposed solution of the problem of evil is that evil is not to be ascribed to God at all, but to the independent actions of human beings, supposed to have been endowed by God with freedom of the will. This solution may be combined with the preceding one: first order evil (*e.g.* pain) may be justified as a logically necessary component in second order good (*e.g.* sympathy) while second order evil (*e.g.* cruelty) is not *justified,* but is so ascribed to human beings that God cannot be held responsible for it. This combination evades my third criticism of the preceding solution.

The freewill solution also involves the preceding solution at a higher level. To explain why a wholly good God gave men freewill although it would lead to some important evils, it must be argued that it is better on the whole that men should act freely, and sometimes err, than that they should be innocent automata, acting rightly in a wholly determined way. Freedom, that is to say, is now treated as a third order good, and as being more valuable than second order goods (such as sympathy and heroism) would be if they were deterministically produced, and it is being assumed that second order evils, such as cruelty, are logically necessary accompaniments of freedom, just as pain is a logically necessary pre-condition of sympathy.

I think that this solution is unsatisfactory primarily because of the incoherence of the notion of freedom of the will: but I cannot discuss this topic adequately here, although some of my criticisms will touch upon it.

First I should query the assumption that second order evils are logically necessary accompaniments of freedom. I should ask this: if God has made men such that in their free choices they sometimes prefer what is good and sometimes what is evil, why could he not have made men such that they always freely choose the good? If there is no logical impossibility in a man's freely choosing the good on one, or on several, occasions, there cannot be a logical impossibility in his freely choosing the good on every occasion. God was not, then, faced with a choice between making innocent automata and making beings who, in acting freely, would sometimes go wrong: there was open to him the obviously better possibility of making beings who would act freely but always go right. Clearly, his failure to avail himself of this possibility is inconsistent with his being both omnipotent and wholly good.

If it is replied that this objection is absurd, that the making of some wrong choices is logically necessary for freedom, it would seem that 'freedom' must here mean complete randomness or indeterminacy, including randomness with regard to the alternatives good and evil, in other words that men's choices and consequent actions can be "free" only if they are not determined by their characters. Only on this assumption can God escape the responsibility for men's actions; for if he made them as they are, but did not determine their wrong choices, this can only be because the wrong choices are not determined by men as they are. But then if freedom is randomness, how can it be a characteristic of *will*? And, still more, how can it be the most important good? What value or merit would there be in free choices if these were random actions which were not determined by the nature of the agent?

I conclude that to make this solution plausible two different senses of 'freedom' must be confused, one sense which will justify the view that freedom is a third order good, more valuable than other goods would be without it, and another sense, sheer randomness, to prevent us from ascribing to God a decision to make men such that they sometimes go wrong when he might have made them such that they would always freely go right.

This criticism is sufficient to dispose of this solution. But besides this there is a fundamental difficulty in the notion of an omnipotent God creating men with free will, for if men's wills are really free this must mean that even God cannot control them, that is, that God is no longer omnipotent. It may be objected that God's gift of freedom to men does not mean that he *cannot* control their wills, but that he always *refrains* from controlling their wills. But why, we may ask, should God refrain from controlling evil wills? Why should he not leave men free to will rightly, but intervene when he sees

them beginning to will wrongly? If God could do this, but does not, and if he is wholly good, the only explanation could be that even a wrong free act of will is not really evil, that its freedom is a value which outweighs its wrongness, so that there would be a loss of value if God took away the wrongness and the freedom together. But this is utterly opposed to what theists say about sin in other context. The present solution of the problem of evil, then, can be maintained only in the form that God has made men so free that he *cannot* control their wills.

This leads us to what I call the Paradox of Omnipotence: can an omnipotent being make things which he cannot subsequently control? Or, what is practically equivalent to this, can an omnipotent being make rules which then bind himself? (These are practically equivalent because any such rules could be regarded as setting certain things beyond his control, and *vice versa*.) The second of these formulations is relevant to the suggestions that we have already met, that an omnipotent God creates the rules of logic or causal laws, and is then bound by them.

It is clear that this is a paradox: the questions cannot be answered satisfactorily either in the affirmative or in the negative. If we answer "Yes", it follows that if God actually makes things which he cannot control, or makes rules which bind himself, he is not omnipotent once he has made them: there are *then* things which he cannot do. But if we answer "No", we are immediately asserting that there are things which he cannot do, that is to say that he is already not omnipotent.

It cannot be replied that the question which sets this paradox is not a proper question. It would make perfectly good sense to say that a human mechanic has made a machine which he cannot control: if there is any difficulty about the question it lies in the notion of omnipotence itself.

This, incidentally, shows that although we have approached this paradox from the free will theory, it is equally a problem for a theological determinist. No one thinks that machines have free will, yet they may well be beyond the control of their makers. The determinist might reply that anyone who makes anything determines its ways of acting, and so determines its subsequent behaviour: even the human mechanic does this by his *choice* of materials and structure for his machine, though he does not know all about either of these: the mechanic thus determines, though he may not foresee, his machine's actions. And since God is omniscient, and since his creation of things is total, he both determines and foresees the ways in which his creatures will act. We may grant this, but it is beside the point. The question is not whether God *originally* determined the future actions of his creatures, but whether he can *subsequently* control their actions, or whether he was able in his original creation to put things beyond his subsequent control. Even on determinist principles the answers "Yes" and "No" are equally irreconcilable with God's omnipotence.

Before suggesting a solution of this paradox, I would point out that there is a parallel Paradox of Sovereignty. Can a legal sovereign make a law restricting its own future legislative power? For example, could the British parliament make a law forbidding any future parliament to socialise banking, and also forbidding the future repeal of this law itself? Or could the British parliament, which was legally sovereign in Australia in, say, 1899, pass a valid law, or series of laws, which made it no longer sovereign in 1933? Again, neither the affirmative nor the negative answer is really satisfactory. If we were to answer "Yes", we should be admitting the validity of a law which, if it were actually made, would mean that parliament was no longer sovereign. If we were to answer "No", we should be admitting that there is a law, not logically absurd, which parliament cannot validly make, that is, that parliament is not now a legal sovereign. This paradox can be solved in the following way. We should distinguish between first order laws, that is laws governing the actions of individuals and bodies other than the legislature, and second order laws, that is laws about laws, laws governing the actions of the legislature itself. Correspondingly, we should distinguish two orders of sovereignty, first order sovereignty (sovereignty (1)) which is unlimited authority to make first order laws, and second order sovereignty (sovereignty (2)) which is unlimited authority to make second order laws. If we say that parliament is sovereign we might mean that any parliament at any time has sovereignty (1), or we might mean that parliament has both sovereignty (1) and sovereignty (2) at present, but we cannot without contradiction mean both that the present parliament has sovereignty (2) and that every parliament at every time has sovereignty (1), for if the present parliament has sovereignty (2) it may use it to take away the

sovereignty (1) of later parliaments. What the paradox shows is that we cannot ascribe to any continuing institution legal sovereignty in an inclusive sense.

The analogy between omnipotence and sovereignty shows that the paradox of omnipotence can be solved in a similar way. We may distinguish between first order omnipotence (omnipotence (1)), that is unlimited power to act, and second order omnipotence (omnipotence (2)), that is unlimited power to determine what powers to act things shall have. Then we could consistently say that God all the time has omnipotence (1), but if so no beings at any time have powers to act independently of God. Or we could say that God at one time had omnipotence (2), and used it to assign independent powers to act to certain things, so that God thereafter did not have omnipotence (1). But what the paradox shows is that we cannot consistently ascribe to any continuing being omnipotence in an inclusive sense.

An alternative solution of this paradox would be simply to deny that God is a continuing being, that any times can be assigned to his actions at all. But on this assumption (which also has difficulties of its own) no meaning can be given to the assertion that God made men with wills so free that he could not control them. The paradox of omnipotence can be avoided by putting God outside time, but the freewill solution of the problem of evil cannot be saved in this way, and equally it remains impossible to hold that an omnipotent God *binds himself* by causal or logical laws.

Conclusion

Of the proposed solutions of the problem of evil which we have examined, none has stood up to criticism. There may be other solutions which require examination, but this study strongly suggests that there is no valid solution of the problem which does not modify at least one of the constituent propositions in a way which would seriously affect the essential core of the theistic position.

Quite apart from the problem of evil the paradox of omnipotence has shown that God's omnipotence must in any case be restricted in one way or another, that unqualified omnipotence cannot be ascribed to any being that continues through time. And if God and his actions are not in time, can omnipotence, or power of any sort, be meaningfully ascribed to him?

Peter van Inwagen

The Magnitude, Duration, and Distribution of Evil: A Theodicy

[. . .] It is generally, but not universally, conceded by Christians that the existence of evil has something to do with free will. The theodicy I shall present is of the "free will" type. That is to say, it proceeds by extending and elaborating the following story:

> God made the world and it was very good. An important part of its goodness was that it contained creatures made in His own image—that is, created beings capable of understanding (to some degree) their own nature and their place in the scheme of things entire; creatures, moreover, that were fit to be loved by God and to love Him in return and to love one another. But love implies freedom: for A to love B is for A freely to choose to be united to B in a certain way. Now even an omnipotent being cannot *insure* that some other being *freely* choose x over y. For God to create beings capable of loving Him, therefore, it was necessary for Him to take a risk: to risk the possibility that the beings He created would freely choose to withhold their love from Him. [. . .]

This is the beginning of our theodicy. At its heart is what is a familiar "move" in discussions of the problem of evil, the insistence that even an omnipotent being cannot insure that someone *freely* do one thing rather than some contemplated alternative. [. . .]

I proceed now to elaborate the above very sketchy narrative of the origin of evil. It is obvious that this must be done. As it stands, the narrative accounts for the existence of only, as we might say, "some evil or other." It says nothing about evil of the kinds or in the amounts we actually observe, or anything about its du-

ration—thousands upon thousands of years—or anything about the fact that its worst effects are distributed apparently at random and certainly without regard for desert. I shall elaborate this narrative with certain propositions drawn from Christian theology. [Omitted]

I added the above flesh [omitted] to the skeleton provided by the standard "free-will" account of the origin of evil because it was clear that that skeleton was no theodicy. The skeleton, however, will require more flesh than this. We have still not got a finished theodicy. If we claimed that we had, a sceptic might, quite properly, respond along the following lines.

"God, you say, has set in motion a plan of Atonement. But why is it taking so long for His plan to work out? It's all very well to tell a tale that represents 'the age of evil' as a 'transient flicker at the very beginning of human history.' But every finite period is a mere flicker in Eternity. Nothing has been said to challenge the obvious proposition that God would not allow 'the age of evil' to go on any longer than necessary. Why, then, is 'this long' necessary?

"And why is there so *much* evil at any given time? Evil may be, as you say, the result of the creaturely abuse of free will. But the amount of evil could have been far less. For example, God, without in any way diminishing Cain's free will, could have warned Abel not to turn his back on him. If the implied general policy had been put into effect, a vast amount of evil would have been avoided.

"And why does God allow evil to be so unfairly distributed? Why is it so often the innocent—small children, for example—who suffer? Why is it so often the wicked who prosper?

"And what about 'physical' or 'natural' evil? How can the effects of the Bubonic Plague or the Lisbon earthquake be a result of creaturely free will?

"To roll all of these questions into one, Why has it been for thousands and thousands of years that enor-

Peter van Inwagen, "The Magnitude, Duration, and Distribution of Evil: A Theodicy" from *Philosophical Topics*, 16 (1988). Reprinted with permission of the author and *Philosophical Topics*, University of Arkansas Press.

mous numbers of uncomprehending children have died as a result of epidemic disease and famine and natural disaster—while many a tyrant has died in bed? How could evil of such types and quantity and duration and distribution be necessary to God's plan of Atonement? Or, if all this evil is *not* necessary to God's plan, why does He not eliminate most of it, and make do with that residue of evil that is really necessary?"

II

I will continue to flesh out our skeletal theodicy by attending to the questions posed by our imaginary sceptic. I will address the last of them first.

The question presupposes that if there are evils that are not required by God's plan of Atonement, then there is such a thing as "that residue of evil that is really necessary," the minimum of evil that is required for God's plan to succeed. But this is not a very plausible thesis. It is not very plausible to suppose that there is a way in which evil could be distributed such that (i) that distribution of evil would serve God's purposes as well as any distribution could and (ii) God's purposes would be less well served by *any* distribution involving less evil. (One might as well suppose that if God's purposes require an impressively tall prophet to appear at a certain place and time, there is a minimum height such a prophet could have.) But if there is no minimum of evil that would serve God's purposes, then one cannot argue that God is unjust or cruel for not "getting by with less evil"—any more than one can argue that a law that fines motorists $25.00 for illegal parking is unjust or cruel owing to the fact that a fine of $24.99 would have an identical deterrent effect. The same point can be made in relation to time. If there is a purpose that is served by allowing "the age of evil" to have a certain duration, doubtless the same purpose would be served if the age of evil were cut short by a day or a year or even a century. But we would not call a judge unjust or cruel for imposing on a criminal a sentence of ten years on the ground—doubtless *true*—that a sentence of ten years less a day would have served as well whatever end the sentence was designed to serve. It is obvious that if, for any amount of evil that would have served God's purposes, slightly less evil would have served His purposes just as well—a very plausible assumption—, then the principle

that God should have got by with less evil, if less would have served, entails the *(ex hypothesi* false) conclusion that God should have got by with no evil at all. It may be a difficult problem in philosophical logic correctly to diagnose the defect in illegitimate *sorites* arguments, but it is certainly evident that such a defect exists.

The important things to recognize about these two points are, first, that they are valid and that to ignore them is to court confusion, and, secondly, that, valid though they be, they do not really meet the essence of the difficulty perceived by the sceptic, the difficulty that prompts him to ask, Why so much?, Why so long? To revert to our legal and judicial analogy, there may be no minimum appropriate fine for illegal parking, but (most of us would agree) if a fine of $25.00 would serve whatever purposes a fine for illegal parking is supposed to serve—deterrence, presumably—, then it would be wrong to set the fine at five thousand dollars. Similarly, if an "age of evil" of twenty years' duration, an age during which there were a few dozen broken bones and a score or so of very bad cases of influenza, would have served God's ends as well as the actual evil of human history serves them, then the enormity of His achieving these same ends by allowing the existence of "actual evil" passes all possibility of adequate description.

What the theodicist must do, given the facts of history, is to say what contribution—what essential contribution—to God's plan of Atonement is made by the facts about the types, magnitude, duration, and distribution of evil that are made known to us by historians and journalists (not to mention our own experience).

It will be useful to divide this problem facing the theodicist—and why not call it simply the problem of evil?—into several sub-problems. One division of the problem of evil is well known: the division of the problem into "the problem of moral evil" and "the problem of natural evil." A second division, one that will be particularly useful in our project of fleshing out our skeletal theodicy so as to meet the questions of the imaginary sceptic, cuts across the first. It divides the problem into three:

—the problem of the magnitude of evil

—the problem of the duration of evil

—the problem of the distribution of evil.

III

I assume that we already have an adequate answer to the problem of moral evil. I am not much interested in treating the problem of natural evil; my main interest in the present paper is the sub-problems generated by the second division. I shall, accordingly, treat the problem of natural evil in a rather perfunctory way. I shall suggest the broadest outlines of a solution, and leave the details for another time—or another writer. [. . .]

Natural evil is often cited as a special problem for those who say that evil entered the world through the creaturely abuse of free will, since tornadoes and earthquakes are obviously not caused by the acts—free or unfree—of human beings. The evil that results from tornadoes and earthquakes must nevertheless be treated in any theodicy of the "free will" type as somehow stemming from creaturely free will. One notorious way of doing this is to postulate that tornadoes and earthquakes are caused by malevolent non-human creatures. Another way (the way I shall take) proceeds from the observation that it is not earthquakes and tornadoes *per se* that are evil, but rather the suffering and death that they cause. Consider the following tale.

"Earthquakes all occur in one particular region called Earthquake Country, a region that was uninhabited (because everyone knew about the earthquakes and had no reason to go there) until twenty years ago. At that time, gold was discovered on the borders of Earthquake Country and the geological indications were that there was much more inside. Motivated solely by a desire to get rich, many people—people by no means in want—moved to Earthquake Country to prospect for gold. Many took their families with them. Some of them got rich, but many of them were killed or maimed by earthquakes."

This tale may not be true, but it demonstrates that earthquakes need not be caused by the actions of creatures for the suffering and death caused by earthquakes to be a result of the actions of those creatures.

Our theodicy, as we have so far stated it, entails that at one time—before the Fall—our ancestors lived in a world without evil. This, I suppose, entails that they were not subject to the baleful effects of earthquakes and tornadoes. But why not? Well, for the purposes of a *perfunctory* treatment of the problem of natural evil, we need assume only that there was *some* reason for this, a reason

that became inoperative when our ancestors separated themselves from God. [. . .] A "feral child" is a ruined human being—though he is no less our brother than is Homer or Leonardo—and his ruin entails a grave diminution of his cognitive powers. According to Christianity, we have all been ruined by our separation from God, just as the feral child has been ruined by his separation from the human community. (The feral child's ruin is thus a ruin within a ruin, a second, individual ruin of an already ruined common human nature.) And the ruin of human nature consequent on our separation from God may have involved a grave diminution of our cognitive powers. According to the "just-so story" I am telling, we were designed by God to be able to protect ourselves from earthquakes and tornadoes—if you think that it would be possible to design a planet, and a universe to contain it, that was both capable of supporting human life and contained no earthquakes or tornadoes, I can only point out that you have never tried—and that the loss of this power is as natural a consequence of our ancestors' separation from God as is the loss of the capacity to acquire language a natural consequence of the feral child's separation from the human community. (Expansion of this just-so story to cover tigers and droughts and epidemic disease and so on is left as an exercise for the reader.) [. . .]

This is all I have to say about natural evil, but I wish to remind the reader that if all human beings were wise and good, our sufferings would be vastly less than they are; and it is probably not true that we should be much better off for a complete elimination of natural evil. Doubtless there would be human beings more than willing to take up the slack. Our ancestral ruin is *primarily* a moral, as opposed to a cognitive, ruin. But ruins we are. If two explorers—who have never seen such a thing—come upon a ruined temple in the jungle, and if one of them thinks that it is a natural geological formation and the other that it is a building that is just as it was designed to be, neither will understand its shape. From the Christian point of view, it is impossible for one to understand humanity if one thinks of a human being as either a product of natural forces behind which there is no Mind or as the work that a Mind intended to produce. Both naturalism and deism (Christianity holds) go wrong about our nature right at the outset, and neither can yield an understanding of that nature.

We thus have some basis for understanding both "moral" and "natural" evil. (In a sense, the theodicy I am proposing entails that there is no fundamental distinction between them: natural evil is a special category of moral evil.) That is, we have a basis for understanding why God would allow such things to come to be. [. . .]

I now turn to my primary interests in offering a theodicy: The magnitude, duration, and distribution of evil.

IV

"Our ancestors turned away from God and ruined themselves both morally and intellectually—and thus they began to harm one another and they lost their aboriginal power to protect themselves from the potentially destructive forces of non-human nature. This condition—their wickedness and helplessness—has persisted through all the generations, being somehow hereditary. But God has set a chain of events in motion that will eventually bring this state of affairs to an end."

The theodicist who wishes to add to this story elements that will account for evil as we actually find it must consider the questions about the magnitude, duration, and distribution of evil that we have put into the mouth of our imaginary sceptic. It will aid my order of exposition—and not, I think, unfairly modify the sceptic's case—if we recast the sceptic's three questions as four questions. The first and third have to do with the duration of evil, the second with its magnitude, and the fourth with its distribution.

Question 1. Why didn't God immediately restore His fallen creatures to their original union with Him?

Question 2. Why doesn't God protect His fallen creatures from the worst effects of their separation from Him: the horrible pain and suffering?

Question 3. Why has God allowed "the age of evil" to persist for thousands and thousands of years? [Omitted]

Question 4. Why do the innocent suffer and the wicked prosper?

Question 1

What would doing that actually have involved? Suppose that two brothers quarrel. Suppose that the quarrel becomes violent and then bitter and that finally they come to hate each other. Suppose that their mother prays to God that He restore their mutual love—and not by any gradual process, but immediately, right on the spot. What is she asking God to do? I can think of only one thing: to grant her request, God would have to wipe away all memory of everything that had happened between them since just before the moment they quarreled. Any philosopher worth his salt will probably be able to think of several grave conceptual difficulties that would attend this plan, but (assuming they could be overcome by omnipotence) God would not do such a thing, because, as Descartes has pointed out, God is not a deceiver, and such an act would constitute a grave deception about the facts of history. [. . .] I cannot see how God could simply, by sheer fiat, immediately have restored fallen humanity other than by a similar grave deception. And, we may add, if He did, what would happen next? What would prevent the Fall from immediately recurring?

V

Question 2

Consider the parable of the Prodigal Son. (Those whose memory of this story is dim will find it in the Gospel According to St. Luke, 15:11–32.) Suppose the father of the Prodigal had foreseen the probable effects of his son's rash use of his patrimony, and had hired actors to represent themselves as gamblers and deliberately to lose substantial sums to the Prodigal; and suppose that he had further arranged for his agents to bribe prostitutes to tell the Prodigal that they had fallen in love with him and wanted to give him all their earnings (following which declaration they are to pass on to him monies provided by his father); and suppose that the father's agents, on his instructions, had followed the Prodigal about in secret to protect him from the dangers attendant on the night life of the ancient Middle East.

What would have been the effects of this fatherly solicitude? Certainly the son could have continued to squander his substance indefinitely and with impunity, But here the word impunity must be understood in a rather superficial sense: for the son will be living a life of illusion (and that is a misfortune), and it is hard to see what could ever induce him to consider returning to his father (and I am inclined to think that that would also be a misfortune).

This modification of the story of the Prodigal Son suggests why it is that God does not simply "cancel"—by an almost continuous series of miracles—the pain and suffering that our separation of ourselves from Him has led to. First, if He did so, He would be, no less than in the case of the deleted memories, a deceiver. If He did so, we should be living in a world of illusion. Our lives would be invisibly "propped up" by God, but we should—justifiably—think that we were living successfully simply by the exercise of our native powers. This, it seems to me, would reduce our existence to something worse than meaningless: We should be, every one of us, *comic* figures. (If there were a novel whose plot was the "revised" life of the Prodigal Son sketched above, he could not be its hero or even a sympathetic character. The novel would be a low comedy and he would be the butt of the joke.) Now illusion of this sort is a bad thing in itself, but it would have consequences even worse than its intrinsic badness. If God did what is proposed, we should all be satisfied with our existence—or at least a lot closer to being satisfied than most of us are now. And if we are satisfied with our existence, why should we even consider turning to God and asking for His help? An essential and important component of God's plan of Atonement—this constitutes an addition to our theodicy—is to make us *dissatisfied* with our state of separation from Him; [. . .] Why is it important for human beings to perceive the hideousness of the world? Well, first, because that's how things are. That's what "man on his own" *means*. Look at the world around you—the world of violence, starvation, hatred, the world of the death camps and the Gulag and (quite possibly) thermonuclear or ecological catastrophe. [. . .] These are natural effects of our living to ourselves, just as a literally feral existence is a natural effect of an infant's separation from the human community.

[. . .] The broad psychological outlines of this feature of the plan that our theodicy ascribes to God are not hard to fathom. The realization that undirected human life is bound to be a failure even in secular terms may possibly set people to wondering whether there may not be some direction somewhere. But people who still think that the obvious hideousness of our world is caused by some accidental feature of human life—superstition, technological backwardness, primitive economic organization—, one that we shall presently get round to altering, are probably not going even to consider turning to God. [. . .]

God's refusal to "cancel" the suffering that is a natural consequence of the Fall by providing separated humanity with a vast set of miraculous and invisible props can (according to the theodicy I propose) be understood on the model of a doctor who refuses to prescribe a pain-killer (say, for angina), on the ground that he knows that his patient will curtail some beloved but self-destructive activity—long-distance running, say—only if the patient continues to experience the pain that his condition signals. Now this sort of behavior on the part of a *doctor* may well be morally objectionable. The doctor is the patient's fellow adult and fellow citizen, and, or so it can plausibly be argued, it would be presumptuous of him to act in such a paternalistic way. One might even say that in so acting the doctor would be "playing God." But we can hardly accuse *God* of playing God. God is justifiably paternalistic because He is our Father and because He is perfect in knowledge and wisdom and because, or so I would argue, He has certain rights over us. These rights, as I see it, derive from the following facts: He made up the very idea of there being creatures like us out of the thought of His own mind, and He made us out of nothing to meet the specifications contained in that idea; everything we have—including the intellectual and moral faculties by means of which we make judgments about paternalism—we have received from Him; He made us for a certain purpose (to glorify Him and to enjoy Him forever) and we threaten to prevent that purpose from being fulfilled. [. . .]

Let us formally add these ideas to our theodicy:

The perception by human beings of their incapacity to "live to themselves" is essential to God's plan of Atonement because, first, without this perception few if any human beings would consider turning to God. (If, therefore, God were miraculously to "cancel" the natural consequences of separation from Himself, He would not only be a deceiver but would remove the only motivation fallen human beings have for turning to Him.) And because, secondly, memory of the hideousness of separated human life will be an important, perhaps an essential, component of the final state of restored humanity. Among the natural consequences of separation from God is the vast quantity of pain and suffering that we observe.

VI

Question 3

[Omitted]

Question 4

Let us not discuss cases of the suffering of the innocent that depend on human wickedness or folly or corrupt institutions. Let us instead examine cases in which there are no oppressors but only victims. These would seem to raise all of the difficulties for the theodicist that are raised by cases in which an oppressor is present, and to be amenable to a smaller class of solutions; they are not, for example, amenable to any solution that involves a concern for the ultimate spiritual welfare of the oppressor or respect for his free will or anything of that sort.

A young mother dies of leukemia. A school bus full of children is crushed by a landslide. A child is born without limbs. A wise and good man in the prime of life suffers brain damage and spends the remaining thirty years of his life in a coma. I do not know of a good general term for such events. Journalists often call them tragedies. But this word is properly applied only to events that are in some sense meaningful, and I know of no reason to think that such events *always* have a "meaning." I will call them *horrors.*

Why do horrors happen? I want to suggest that horrors happen for no reason at all, that when, e.g., a child is born without limbs, the only answer to the question, "Why did that happen?" is "There is no reason or ex-

planation; it just happened." Or, at any rate, I want to suggest that this is sometimes the case. (Whether some horrors are brought about by God for special purposes is a question I shall not attempt to answer. If *some* horrors are brought about by God, and thus have a purpose and a meaning known to God but not to us, I have no opinion as to what percentage of the whole they might constitute.) But are not *all* events ordered by God, and must not *all* events therefore have some sort of meaning? Christians and other theists are, I believe, committed to the truth of the following proposition:

> God is the maker of all things, visible and invisible (other than Himself); He sustains all created things in existence from moment to moment, and continuously supplies them with their causal powers.

In a previous paper,[1] in which I presented an account of God's action in the world, I argued that this proposition is consistent with the proposition that there are events having the following feature: If one asks concerning one of these events, "Why did that happen?," the only answer to one's question is, "There is no reason or explanation for that event. God did not cause it to happen or intend it to happen. It is not a part of God's plan for the world or anyone else's plan for anything. It just happened, and that's all there is to say about it." (Let us say of such events that they are *due to chance.*) I will not reproduce my arguments. [...] Now to say that there is no answer to the question, Why did X occur? is not to say that there is no answer to such questions as Why did God allow X to occur? or Why did God not prevent X? I ended the earlier paper with these words:

> If what I have said is true, it yields a moral for students of the Problem of Evil: Do not attempt any solution to this problem that entails that every particular evil has a purpose, or that, with respect

---

1. "The Place of Chance in a World Sustained by God," in *Divine and Human Action: Essays on the Metaphysics of Theism,* Thomas V. Morris, ed. (Ithaca: Cornell University Press, 1988).

to every individual misfortune, or every devastating earthquake, or every disease, God has some special reason for allowing it. Concentrate rather on the problem of what sort of reasons a loving and providential God might have for allowing His creatures to live in a world in which many of the evils that happen to them happen to them for no reason at all.

I will now take my own advice and present my solution to this problem. God's reason for allowing His creatures to live in such a world is that their living in such a world is a natural consequence of their separation from Him. Consider again our earlier sketchy account of natural evil: in separating ourselves from God, we have somehow deprived ourselves of our primordial defenses against such potentially destructive things as tigers and landslides and tornadoes. But if, by our rebellion and folly, we have allowed the destructive potential of these things to become actual, how shall we expect the effects of that actuality to be distributed? At random, surely? That is, with no correlation between these things and the innocence or wickedness of the people they impinge on—since the operations of these things in no way depend upon the moral qualities of the people they interact with? In fact, there is little correlation between the manner in which these things operate and *any* factor under human control (although civilization does what it can to try to induce correlations of this type).

Suppose that a certain man chooses, of his own free will, to stand at spot x at time t. His arrival at that place at that time converges with the arrival of an avalanche. Let us suppose that God did not miraculously cause the avalanche, and that He did not "move" the man to be at that place at that time. And let us also suppose that neither the man's arrival at x at t nor the avalanche's arrival at x at t was determined by the laws of nature and the state of the world, say, one hundred years earlier. [. . .]

The man's death in the avalanche would seem to be in every sense due to chance, even though (the theist must suppose) God knew in advance that he would be killed by the avalanche and could have prevented it. In fact, the theist must suppose that, during the course of that event, God held all of the particles that composed the man and the moving mass of snow and ice in existence and continuously decreed the operation of the laws of nature by which those particles interacted with one another.

Why did God not miraculously save the man? We have seen the answer to this question already. He might very well have. Perhaps He sometimes does miraculously save people in such situations. But if He *always* did so, He would be a deceiver. If He always saved people about to be destroyed by a chance encounter with a violent phenomenon of nature, He would engender an illusion with the following propositional content:

It is possible for human beings to live apart from God and not be subject to destruction by chance.

To live under this illusion would be a bad thing in itself, but, more importantly, it would have harmful effects. This illusion would be, as it were, a tributary of illusion feeding into a great river of illusion whose content was, "Human beings can live successfully in separation from God."

[. . .] It is as if God had had—for some purpose— to cover the earth with a certain number of deep pits. These pits (we may stipulate) were not dangerous, since they could easily be seen and avoided; but we frustrated God's Providence in this matter by deliberately making ourselves blind; and now we complain that some of us—quite often the good and wise and innocent—fall into the pits. God's response, is this: "You are the ones who made yourselves blind. If you make yourselves blind, some of you will fall into the pits, and, moreover, *who* falls into a pit and *when* will be wholly a matter of chance. Goodness and wisdom and innocence have no bearing on this matter. That's part of what being blind means." Or, rather, this is what we might imagine God's response to be in our simple "world of pits." In the real world, we should have to picture God as saying something more complex, something like the following.

"Even I can't make a world that is suitable for human beings but which contains no phenomena that would harm human beings *if* they were in the wrong place at the wrong time. The reasons for this are complicated, but they turn on the fact that the molecular bonds that hold you human beings together must be weaker by many orders of magnitude than the disruptive potential of the surges of energy that must happen here and there in a structurally and nomologically coherent world complex enough to contain you. My Providence dealt with this fact by endowing you with the power never to be in the wrong place at the wrong time, a power you lost when you ruined yourselves by turning away from Me. That is why horrors happen to some of you: you simply blunder into things. If I were to protect you from the consequences of your blindness by guiding you away from potentially destructive phenomena by an unending series of miracles—and I remind you that for all you know I *sometimes* do guide you out of harm's way—I should be deceiving you about the meaning of your separation from Me and seriously weakening the only motivation you have for returning to Me."

We may add the following proposition to our theodicy:

> Among the natural consequences of the Fall is the following evil state of affairs: Horrors happen to people without any relation to desert. They happen simply as a matter of chance. It is a part of God's plan of Atonement that we realize that a natural consequence of our living to ourselves is our living in a world that has that feature.

[. . .] A theodicy is a dialectical enterprise. The present paper, therefore, is best regarded as the "opening move" in such an enterprise, rather than a finished product. In closing, I wish to answer one objection to the theodicy I have presented, an objection that has been raised in conversation and correspondence by Eleonore Stump. Professor Stump objects that the theodicy I have presented represents God as allowing people to suffer misfortunes that do not (even in the long run) benefit *them*. An example may make the point of this objection clear. Suppose that God allows a horrible, disfiguring accident to happen to Alice (a true accident, an event due entirely to chance, but one that God foresaw and could have prevented). And suppose that the only good that is brought out of this accident is embodied in the following state of affairs and certain of its remote consequences: The accident, together with an enormous number of similar horrors, causes various people to realize that one feature of a world in which human beings live to themselves is that in such a world horrors happen to people for no reason at all. But suppose that Alice herself did not need to re-

alize this; suppose that she was already fully aware of this consequence of separation from God. And suppose that many of the people who do come to realize this partly as the result of Alice's accident manage (owing mainly to luck) to get through life without anything very bad happening to them. According to Stump, these suppositions—and it is pretty certain that there *are* cases like this if our theodicy is correct—represent God as violating the following moral principle:

> It is wrong to allow something bad to happen to X—without X's permission—in order to secure some benefit for others (and no benefit for X).

I do not find this principle particularly appealing—not as a *universal* moral principle, one that is supposed to apply with equal rigor to all possible moral agents in all possible circumstances. The circumstances in which it seems most doubtful are these: The agent is in a position of lawful authority over both X and the "others" and is responsible for their welfare (consider, for example, a mother and her children or the state and its citizens); the good to be gained by the "others" is considerably greater than the evil suffered by X; there is no way in which the good for the "others" can be achieved except by allowing the evil in question to happen to X or to someone else no more deserving of it than X; the agent knows these things to be true. By way of example, we might consider cases of quarantine or of the right of eminent domain. Is it not morally permissible for the state to restrict my freedom of movement and action if I am the carrier of a contagious disease, or to force me to move if my house stands in the way of a desperately needed irrigation canal (one that will not benefit *me* in any way)? It is not to the point to protest that these cases are not much like cases involving an omnipotent God, who can cure diseases or provide water by simple fiat. They are counterexamples to the above moral principle, and, therefore, that moral principle is false. What is required of anyone who alleges that the theodicy I have proposed represents God as violating some (correct) moral principle is a careful statement of that moral principle. When we have examined that carefully stated moral principle, and have satisfied ourselves that it is without counterexample, we can proceed with the argument.

Reason and Faith

David Hume

On Miracles

Of Miracles[1]

Part I

There is, in Dr. *Tillotson's* writings, and argument against the *real presence,* which is as concise, and elegant, and strong as any argument can possibly be supposed against a doctrine, so little worthy of a serious refutation. It is acknowledged on all hands, says that learned prelate, that the authority, either of the scripture or of tradition, is founded merely in the testimony of the apostles, who were eye-witnesses to those miracles of our Saviour, by which he proved his divine mission. Our evidence, then, for the truth of the *Christian* religion is less than the evidence for the truth of our senses; because, even in the first authors of our religion, it was no greater; and it is evident it must diminish in passing from them to their disciples; nor can anyone rest such confidence in their testimony, as in the immediate object of his senses. But a weaker evidence can never destroy a stronger; and therefore, were the doctrine of the real presence ever so clearly revealed in scripture, it were directly contrary to the rules of just reasoning to give our assent to it. It con-

tradicts sense, though both the scripture and tradition, on which it is supposed to be built, carry not such evidence with them as sense; when they are considered merely as external evidences, and are not brought home to everyone's breast, by the immediate operation of the Holy Spirit.

Nothing is so convenient as a decisive argument of this kind, which must at least *silence* the most arrogant bigotry and superstition, and free us from their impertinent solicitations. I flatter myself, that I have discovered an argument of a like nature, which, if just, will, with the wise and learned, be an everlasting check to all kinds of superstitious delusion, and consequently, will be useful as long as the world endures. For so long, I presume, will the accounts of miracles and prodigies be found in all history, sacred and profane.

Though experience be our only guide in reasoning concerning matters of fact; it must be acknowledged, that this guide is not altogether infallible, but in some cases is apt to lead us into errors. One who in our climate, should expect better weather in any week of *June* than in one of *December,* would reason justly, and conformably to experience; but it is certain, that he may happen, in the event, to find himself mistaken. However, we may observe, that, in such a case, he would have no cause to complain of experience; because it commonly informs us beforehand of the uncertainty, by that contrariety of events, which we may learn from a diligent observation. All effects follow not with like certainty from their supposed causes. Some events are found, in all countries and all ages, to have been constantly conjoined together. Others are found to have been more variable, and sometimes to disappoint our expectations; so that, in our reasonings concerning matter of fact, there are all

From David Hume, *Enquiry Concerning Human Understanding,* edited by Eric Steinberg (Indianapolis: Hackett Publishing Company, 1993). Reprinted by permission of the publisher.

1. [Dr. John Tillotson, 1630–1694. In his major work, *The Rule of Faith,* first published in 1666, and in his *Discourse against Transubstantiation,* 1684, he attacked the Roman Catholic doctrine that the body and blood of Jesus Christ are really present in the bread and wine at the conclusion of the Eucharist service.]

imaginable degrees of assurance, from the highest certainty to the lowest species of moral evidence.

A wise man, therefore, proportions his belief to the evidence. In such conclusions as are founded on an infallible experience, he expects the event with the last degree of assurance, and regards his past experience as a full *proof* of the future existence of that event. In other cases, he proceeds with more caution: He weighs the opposite experiments: He considers which side is supported by the greater number of experiments: To that side he inclines, with doubt and hesitation; and when at last he fixes his judgment, the evidence exceeds not what we properly call *probability*. All probability, then, supposes an opposition of experiments and observations, where the one side is found to overbalance the other, and to produce a degree of evidence, proportioned to the superiority. A hundred instances or experiments on one side, and fifty on another, afford a doubtful expectation of any event; though a hundred uniform experiments, with only one that is contradictory, reasonably beget a pretty strong degree of assurance. In all cases, we must balance the opposite experiments, where they are opposite, and deduct the smaller number from the greater, in order to know the exact force of the superior evidence.

To apply these principles to a particular instance; we may observe, that there is no species of reasoning more common, more useful, and even necessary to human life, than that which is derived from the testimony of men, and the reports of eye-witnesses and spectators. This species of reasoning, perhaps, one may deny to be founded on the relation of cause and effect. I shall not dispute about a word. It will be sufficient to observe, that our assurance in any argument of this kind is derived from no other principle than our observation of the veracity of human testimony, and of the usual conformity of facts to the reports of witnesses. It being a general maxim, that no objects have any discoverable connection together, and that all the inferences, which we can draw from one to another, are founded merely on our experience of their constant and regular conjunction; it is evident, that we ought not to make an exception to this maxim in favor of human testimony, whose connection with any even seems, in itself, as little necessary as any other. Were not the memory tenacious to a certain degree; had not men commonly an

inclination to truth and a principle of probity; were they not sensible to shame, when detected in a falsehood: Were not these, I say, discovered by *experience* to be qualities, inherent in human nature, we should never repose the least confidence in human testimony. A man delirious, or noted for falsehood and villainy, has no manner of authority with us.

And as the evidence, derived from witnesses and human testimony, is founded on past experience, so it varies with the experience, and is regarded either as a *proof* or a *probability*, according as the conjunction between any particular kind of report and any kind of object has been found to be constant or variable. There are a number of circumstances to be taken into consideration in all judgments of this kind; and the ultimate standard, by which we determine all disputes, that may arise concerning them, is always derived from experience and observation. Where this experience is not entirely uniform on any side, it is attended with an unavoidable contrariety in our judgments, and with the same opposition and mutual destruction of argument as in every other kind of evidence. We frequently hesitate concerning the reports of others. We balance the opposite circumstances, which cause any doubt or uncertainty; and when we discover a superiority on any side, we incline to it; but still with a diminution of assurance, in proportion to the force of its antagonist.

This contrariety of evidence, in the present case, may be derived from several different causes; from the opposition of contrary testimony; from the character or number of the witnesses; from the manner of their delivering their testimony; or from the union of all these circumstances. We entertain a suspicion concerning any matter of fact, when the witnesses contradict each other; when they are but few, or of a doubtful character; when they have an interest in what they affirm; when they deliver their testimony with hesitation, or on the contrary, with too violent asseverations. There are many other particulars of the same kind, which may diminish or destroy the force of any argument, derived from human testimony.

Suppose, for instance, that the fact, which the testimony endeavors to establish, partakes of the extraordinary and the marvelous; in that case, the evidence, resulting from the testimony, admits of a diminution, greater or less, in proportion as the fact is more or less unusual. The reason, why we place any credit in witnesses and historians, is not derived from the *connection*, which we perceive *a priori*, between testimony and reality, but because we are accustomed to find a conformity between them. But when the fact attested is such a one as has seldom fallen under our observation, here is a contest of two opposite experiences; of which the one destroys the other, as far as its force goes, and the superior can only operate on the mind by the force, which remains. The very same principle of experience, which gives us a certain degree of assurance in the testimony of witnesses, gives us also, in this case, another degree of assurance against the fact, which they endeavor to establish; from which contradiction there necessarily arises a counterpoise, and mutual destruction of belief and authority.

I should not believe such a story were it told me by Cato; was a proverbial saying in Rome, even during the lifetime of that philosophical patriot.[2] The incredibility of a fact, it was allowed, might invalidate so great an authority.

The *Indian* prince, who refused to believe the first relations concerning the effects of frost, reasoned justly; and it naturally required very strong testimony to engage his assent to facts, that arose from a state of nature, with which he was unacquainted, and which bore so little analogy to those events, of which he had had constant and uniform experience. Though they were not contrary to his experience, they were not conformable to it.[3]

But in order to increase the probability against the testimony of witnesses, let us suppose, that the fact, which they affirm, instead of being only marvelous, is really miraculous; and suppose also, that the testimony, considered apart and in itself, amounts to an entire proof; in that case, there is proof against proof, of which the strongest must prevail, but still with a diminution of its force, in proportion to that of its antagonist.

A miracle is a violation of the laws of nature; and as a firm and unalterable experience has established these laws, the proof against a miracle, from the very nature of the fact, is as entire as any argument from experience can possibly be imagined. Why is it more than probable, that all men must die; that lead cannot, of itself, remain suspended in the air; that fire consumes wood, and is extinguished by water; unless it be, that these events are found agreeable to the laws of nature, and there is required a violation of these laws, or in other words, a miracle to prevent them? Nothing is esteemed a miracle, if it ever happens in the common course of nature. It is no miracle that a man, seemingly in good health, should die on a sudden: because such a kind of death, though more unusual than any other, has yet been frequently observed to happen. But it is a miracle, that a dead man should come to life; because that has never been observed, in any age or country. There must, therefore, be a uniform experience against every miraculous event, otherwise the event would not merit that appellation. And as a uniform experience amounts to a proof, there is here a direct and full *proof*, from the nature of the fact, against the existence of any mira-

---

2. *Plutarch,* in vita Catonis Min. 19 [*Life of Cato* (the younger)].

3. No *Indian*, it is evident, could have experience that water did not freeze in cold climates. This is placing nature in a situation quite unknown to him; and it is impossible for him to tell *a priori* what will result from it. It is making a new experiment, the consequence of which is always uncertain. One may sometimes conjecture from analogy what will follow; but still this is but conjecture. And it must be confessed, that, in the present case of freezing, the event follows contrary to the rules of analogy, and is such as a rational *Indian* would not look for. The operations of cold upon water are not gradual, according to the degrees of

cold; but whenever it comes to the freezing point, the water passes in a moment, from the utmost liquidity to perfect hardness. Such an event, therefore, may be denominated *extraordinary,* and requires a pretty strong testimony, to render it credible to people in a warm climate: But still is it not *miraculous,* nor contrary to uniform experience of the course of nature in cases where all the circumstances are the same. The inhabitants of *Sumatra* have always seen water fluid in their own climate, and the freezing of their rivers ought to be deemed a prodigy: But they never saw water in *Muscovy* during the winter; and therefore they cannot reasonably be positive what would there be the consequence.

cle; nor can such a proof be destroyed, or the miracle rendered credible, but by an opposite proof, which is superior.[4]

The plain consequence is (and it is a general maxim worthy of our attention), 'That no testimony is sufficient to establish a miracle, unless the testimony be of such a kind, that its falsehood would be more miraculous, than the fact, which it endeavors to establish: And even in that case there is a mutual destruction of arguments, and the superior only gives us an assurance suitable to that degree of force, which remains, after deducting the inferior.' When anyone tells me, that he saw a dead man restored to life, I immediately consider with myself, whether it be more probable, that this person should either deceive or be deceived, or that the fact, which he relates, should really have happened. I weigh the one miracle against the other; and according to the superiority, which I discover, I pronounce my decision, and always reject the greater miracle. If the falsehood of his testimony would be

more miraculous, then the event which he relates; then, and not till then, can he pretend to command my belief or opinion.

Part II

In the foregoing reasoning we have supposed, that the testimony, upon which a miracle is founded, may possibly amount to an entire proof, and that the falsehood of that testimony would be a real prodigy: But it is easy to show, that we have been a great deal too liberal in our concession, and that there never was a miraculous event established on so full an evidence.

For *first,* there is not to be found, in all history, any miracle attested by a sufficient number of men, of such unquestioned good sense, education, and learning, as to secure us against all delusion in themselves; of such undoubted integrity, as to place them beyond all suspicion of any design to deceive others; of such credit and reputation in the eyes of mankind, as to have a great deal to lose in case of their being detected in any falsehood; and at the same time, attesting facts, performed in such a public manner, and in so celebrated a part of the world, as to render the detection unavoidable: All which circumstances are requisite to give us a full assurance in the testimony of men.

Secondly. We may observe in human nature a principle, which, if strictly examined, will be found to diminish extremely the assurance, which we might, from human testimony, have, in any kind of prodigy. The maxim, by which we commonly conduct ourselves in our reasonings, is, that the objects, of which we have no experience, resemble those, of which we have; that what we have found to be most usual is always most probable; and that where there is an opposition of arguments, we ought to give the preference to such as are founded on the greatest number of past observations. But though, in proceeding by this rule, we readily reject any fact which is unusual and incredible in an ordinary degree; yet in advancing farther, the mind observes not always the same rule; but when anything is affirmed utterly absurd and miraculous, it rather the more readily admits of such a fact, upon account of that very circumstance, which ought to destroy all its authority. The

---

4. Sometimes an event may not, *in itself, seem* to be contrary to the laws of nature, and yet, if it were real, it might, by reason of some circumstances, be denominated a miracle; because, in *fact* it is contrary to these laws. Thus if a person, claiming a divine authority, should command a sick person to be well, a healthful man to fall down dead, the clouds to pour rain, the winds to blow, in short, should order many natural events, which immediately follow upon his command; these might justly be esteemed miracles, because they are really, in this case, contrary to the laws of nature. For if any suspicion remain, that the event and command concurred by accident, there is no miracle and no transgression of the laws of nature. If this suspicion be removed, there is evidently a miracle, and a transgression of these laws; because nothing can be more contrary to nature than that the voice or command of a man should have such an influence. A miracle may be accurately defined, *a transgression of a law of nature by a particular volition of the Deity, or by the interposition of some invisible agent.* A miracle may either be discoverable by men or not. This alters not its nature and essence. The raising of a house or ship into the air is a visible miracle. The raising of a feather, when the wind wants ever so little of a force requisite for that purpose, is as real a miracle, though not so sensible with regard to us.

passion of *surprise* and *wonder,* arising from miracles, being an agreeable emotion, gives a sensible tendency towards the belief of those events, from which it is derived. And this goes so far, that even those who cannot enjoy this pleasure immediately, nor can believe those miraculous events, of which they are informed, yet love to partake of the satisfaction at second-hand or by rebound, and place a pride and delight in exciting the admiration of others.

With what greediness are the miraculous accounts of travelers received, their descriptions of sea and land monsters, their relations of wonderful adventures, strange men, and uncouth manners? But if the spirit of religion join itself to the love of wonder, there is an end of common sense; and human testimony, in these circumstances, loses all pretensions to authority. A religionist may be an enthusiast, and imagine he sees what has no reality: He may know his narrative to be false, and yet persevere in it, with the best intentions in the world, for the sake of promoting so holy a cause: Or even where this delusion has not place, vanity, excited by so strong a temptation, operates on him more powerfully than on the rest of mankind in any other circumstances; and self-interest with equal force. His auditors may not have, and commonly have not, sufficient judgment to canvass his evidence: What judgment they have, they renounce by principle, in these sublime and mysterious subjects: Or if they were ever so willing to employ it, passion and a heated imagination disturb the regularity of its operations. Their credulity increases his impudence: And his impudence overpowers their credulity.

Eloquence, when at its highest pitch, leaves little room for reason or reflection; but addressing itself entirely to the fancy or the affections, captivates the willing hearers, and subdues their understanding. Happily, this pitch it seldom attains. But what a *Tully* or a *Demosthenes* could scarcely effect over a *Roman* or *Athenian* audience, every *Capuchin,* every itinerant or stationary teacher can perform over the generality of mankind, and in a higher degree, by touching such gross and vulgar passions.

The many instances of forged miracles, and prophecies, and supernatural events, which, in all ages, have either been detected by contrary evidence, or which detect themselves by their absurdity, prove sufficiently the strong propensity of mankind to the extraordinary and the marvelous, and ought reasonably to beget a suspicion against all relations of this kind. This is our natural way of thinking, even with regard to the most common and most credible events. For instance: There is no kind of report, which rises so easily, and spreads so quickly, especially in country places and provincial towns, as those concerning marriages; insomuch that two young persons of equal condition never see each other twice, but the whole neighborhood immediately join them together. The pleasure of telling a piece of news so interesting, of propagating it, and of being the first reporters of it, spreads the intelligence. And this is so well known, that no man of sense gives attention to these reports, till he find them confirmed by some greater evidence. Do not the same passions, and others still stronger, incline the generality of mankind to believe and report, with the greatest vehemence and assurance, all religious miracles?

Thirdly. It forms a strong presumption against all supernatural and miraculous relations, that they are observed chiefly to abound among ignorant and barbarous nations; or if a civilized people has ever given admission to any of them, that people will be found to have received them from ignorant and barbarous ancestors, who transmitted them with that inviolable sanction and authority, which always attend received opinions. When we peruse the first histories of all nations, we are apt to imagine ourselves transported into some new world; where the whole frame of nature is disjointed, and every element performs its operations in a different manner, from what it does at present. Battles, revolutions, pestilence, famine, and death, are never the effect of those natural causes, which we experience. Prodigies, omens, oracles, judgments, quite obscure the few natural events, that are intermingled with them. But as the former grow thinner every page, in proportion as we advance nearer the enlightened ages, we soon learn, that there is nothing mysterious or supernatural in the case, but that all proceeds from the usual propensity of mankind towards the marvelous, and that, though this inclination may at intervals receive a check from sense and learning, it can never be thoroughly extirpated from human nature.

It is strange, a judicious reader is apt to say, upon the perusal of these wonderful historians, *that such prodigious events never happen in our days.* But it is nothing strange, I hope, that men should lie in all ages. You must surely have seen instances enough of that frailty. You have yourself heard many such marvelous relations started, which, being treated with scorn by all the wise and ju-

dicious, have at last been abandoned even by the vulgar. Be assured, that those renowned lies, which have spread and flourished to such a monstrous height, arose from like beginnings; but being sown in a more proper soil, shot up at last into prodigies almost equal to those which they relate. [. . .]

Richard Price

On the Importance of Christianity and the Nature of Historical Evidence, and Miracles

Section II

The Nature and Grounds of the Regard due to Experience and to the Evidence of Testimony, stated and compared.

"Experience, we have been told, is the ground of the credit we give to *human testimony.* We have found, in past instances, that men have informed us right, and therefore, are disposed to believe them in future instances. But this experience is by no means constant; for we often find that men prevaricate and deceive.—On the other hand: What assures us of those laws of nature, in the violation of which the notion of a miracle consists, is, in like manner, experience. But, this is an experience that has never been interrupted. We have never been deceived in our expectations, that the dead will not come to life, or that the command of a man will not immediately cure a disease. There arises, therefore, from hence, a proof against accounts of miracles which is the strongest of the kind possible, and to believe such ac-

counts on the authority of human testimony, is to prefer a weaker proof to a stronger; to leave a guide that *never* has deceived us, in order to follow one that has *often* deceived us; or to receive, upon the credit of an experience that is *weak* and *variable,* what is contrary to *invariable* experience."

In other words: "A miracle is an event, from the nature of it, inconsistent with all the experience we ever had, and in the highest degree incredible and extraordinary. In the falsehood of testimony, on the contrary, there is no such inconsistency, nor any such incredibility, scarcely any thing being more common. No regard, therefore, can be due to the latter, when it is applied as a proof of the former.—According to this reasoning, we are always to compare the improbability of a fact, with the improbability of the falsehood of the testimony which asserts it, and to determine our assent to that side on which the least improbability lies. Or, in the case of miracles, we are to consider which is most likely, that such events should happen, or that men should either deceive or be deceived. And, as there is nothing more unlikely than the former, or much more common than the latter, particularly, where religion is concerned; it will be right to form a *general resolution, never to lend any*

From Richard Price, *Four Dissertations* (London, 1767).

attention to accounts of miracles, with whatever specious pretexts the may be covered."[1]

"*It is,*" says Mr. Hume, "*a maxim worthy of our attention, that no testimony is sufficient to establish a miracle, unless the testimony be of such a kind, that its falsehood would be more miraculous than the fact which it endeavours to establish. And even in that case, there is a mutual destruction of arguments, and the superior only gives us an assurance suitable to that degree of force, which remains after deducting the inferior. When any one tells me that he saw a dead man restore to life, I immediately consider with myself, whether it be more probable that the person should either deceive or be deceived, or that the fact he relates should really have happened. I weigh the one miracle against the other, and according to the superiority which I discover, I pronounce my decision, and always reject the greater miracle. If the falsehood of his testimony would be more miraculous than the event which he relates, then, and not till then, can he pretend to command my belief or opinion.*"[2] —For such reasons as these, Mr. Hume asserts, "*That the evidence of testimony, when applied to a miracle, carries falsehood upon the very face of it, and is more properly subject of derision than of argument;*[3] and that whoever believes the truth of the Christian religion, *is conscious of a continued miracle in his own person, which subverts all the principle of his understanding, and gives him a determination to believe what is most contrary to custom and experience.*"[4]

This is the objection in its complete force. It has, we see, a plausible appearance, and is urged with much confidence. But I cannot hesitate in asserting that it is founded on false principles; and, I think, this must appear to be true, to any one who will bestow attention on the following observations.

The principles on which this objection is built are chiefly, "That the credit we give to testimony, is derived *solely* from experience;" "that a miracle is a fact *contrary* to experience;" "That the previous improbability of a fact is a proof against it, diminishing, in proportion to

the degree of it, the proof from testimony for it;" and "That no testimony should ever gain credit to an event, unless it is more extraordinary that it should be false, than that the event should have happened." I will, as briefly as possible, examine each of these assertions in order in which they have been now mentioned.

With this view it is necessary first to consider the nature and the foundation of that assurance which experience gives us of the laws of nature. This assurance is nothing but the conviction we have, that future events will be agreeable to what we have hitherto found to be the course of nature, or the *expectation* arising in us, upon having observed that an event has happened in former experiments, that it will happen again in *future* experiments. This expectation has been represented as one of the greatest mysteries, and the result of an ingenious and elaborate disquisition about it is, that it cannot be founded on any reason, and consists only in an association of ideas derived from habit, or a disposition in our imaginations to pass from the idea of one object to the idea of another which we have found to be its usual attendant. But surely, never before were such difficulties raised on a point so plain.—If I was to draw a slip of paper out of a wheel, where I knew there were more white than black papers, I should intuitively see, that there was a probability of drawing a white paper, and therefore should *expect* this; and he who should make a mystery of such an expectation, or apprehend any difficulty in accounting for it, would not deserve to be seriously argued with.—In like manner; if, out of a wheel, the particular contents of which I am ignorant of, I should draw a white paper a hundred times together, I should see that it was probable, that it had in it more white papers than black, and therefore should expect to draw a white paper then next trial. There is no more difficulty in this case than in the former; and it is equally absurd in both cases to ascribe the *expectation,* not to *knowledge,* but to *instinct.*—The case of our assurance of the laws of nature, as far as we are ignorant of the causes that operate in nature, is exactly the same with this. An experiment which has often succeeded, we expect to succeed again, because we perceive intuitively, that such a constancy of event must proceed from something in the constitution of natural causes, disposing them to produce it; [. . .]—In a word: We trust ex-

---

1. See the *Essay on Miracles,* in *Mr. Hume's Philosophical Essays concerning human Understanding,* p. 205, 2nd edition, in the Note. [See pp. 772–7, this volume.]

2. Ib. P 182–P. 206. [See pp. 772–7, this volume.]

3. Page 195. [See pp. 772–7, this volume.]

4. Page 207. [See pp. 772–7, this volume.]

perience, and expect that the future should resemble the past in the course of nature, for the very same reason that, supporting ourselves otherwise in the dark, we should conclude that a die which has turned an ace oftenest in *past* trials is mostly marked with aces, and consequently should expect, that it will go on to turn the same number oftenest in *future* trials.—The ground of the expectation produced by experience being this, it is obvious that it will always be weaker or stronger, in proportion to the greater or less constancy and uniformity of our experience. Thus from the happening of an event in every trial a million of times, we should conclude more confidently, that it will happen again the next trial, than if it had happened less frequently, or if in some of these instances it had failed. The plain reason is, that in the former case it would appear that the causes producing the event are probably of a more fixed-nature, and less liable to be counteracted by opposite causes.— It must, however, be remembered, that the greatest uniformity and frequency of experience will not afford a proper *proof,* that an event will happen in a future trial, or even render it so much as probable, that it will *always* happen in all future trials.—In order to explain this, let us suppose a solid which, for ought we know, may be constituted in any one of an infinity of different ways, and that we can judge of it only from experiments made in throwing it. The oftener we suppose ourselves to have seen it turn the same face, the more we should reckon upon its turning the same face, when thrown next. But though we knew, that it had turned the same face in every trial a million of times, there would be no *certainty,* that it would turn this face again in any particular future trial, nor even the least *probability,* that it would *never* turn any other face. What would appear would be only, that it was *likely,* that it had about a million and a half more of these sides than of all others; [. . .]

But to say no more at present of this. Let us, in the next place, consider what is the ground of the regard we pay to *human testimony.*—We may, I think, see plainly, that it is not experience only; meaning, all along, that kind of experience to which we owe our expectation of natural events, the causes of which are unknown to us. Were this the case, the regard we ought to pay to testimony, would be in proportion to the number of instances, in which we have found, that it

has given us right information, compared with those in which it has deceived us; and it might be calculated in the same manner with the regard due to any conclusions derived from induction. But this is by no means the truth. One action, or one conversation with a man, may convince us of his integrity and induce us to believe his testimony, though we had never, in a single instance, experienced his veracity. His manner of telling his story, its being corroborated by other testimony, and various particulars in the nature and circumstances of it, may satisfy us that it must be true. We feel in ourselves that a regard to truth is one principle in human nature; and we know that there must be such a principle in every reasonable being, and that there is a necessary repugnancy between the perception of moral distinctions and deliberate falsehood. To this, chiefly, is owing the credit we give to human testimony. And from hence, in particular, must be derived our belief of veracity in the Deity.—It might be shown here in many ways, that there is a great difference between the conviction produced by testimony and the conviction produced by experience. But I will content myself with just taking notice, that the one is capable of being carried much higher than the other. When any events, in the course of nature, have often happened, we are sure properly, of nothing but the past fact. Nor, I think, is there in general, antecedently to their happening, any comparison between the assurance we have that they will happen, and that which we have of many facts the knowledge of which we derive from testimony. For example; we are not so certain that the tide will go on to ebb and flow, and the sun to rise and set in the manner they have hitherto done, a year longer, as we are that there has been such a man as *Alexander,* or such an empire as the *Roman.*

From these observations it follows, that to use *testimony* to prove a *miracle* implies no absurdity. 'Tis not using a *feebler* experience to overthrow another of the same kind, which is *stronger:* But, using an argument to establish an event, which yields a direct and positive proof and is capable of producing the strongest conviction to overthrow another founded on different principles, and which, at best, can prove no more than that, previously to the event, there would have appeared to us a presumption against its happening.

What I now mean will be greatly confirmed by observing, that a miracle cannot, with strict propriety, be styled an event *contrary* to experience. This is the second of the assertions in Mr. *Hume's* argument, which I have before mentioned, and to which there is, I think, reason to object. A miracle is more properly an event *different* from experience than *contrary* to it. Were I to see a tempest calmed instantaneously by the word of a man, all my past experience would remain the same; and were I to affirm that I saw what was contrary to it, I could only mean, that I saw what I never before had any experience of. In like manner; was I to be assured by eye witnesses that, on a particular occasion, some event, different from the usual course of things, had happened, testimony, in this case, would afford direct and peremptory evidence for the fact. But what information would experience give?—It would only tell me what happened on other occasions, and in other instances. Its evidence, therefore, would be entirely negative. It would afford no proper proof that the event did not happen, for it can be no part of any one's experience, that the course of nature will continue always the same.—It cannot then be proper to assert (as Mr. *Hume*[5] does) that, in every case of a miracle supported by testimony, there is a contest of two opposite experiences, the strongest of which ought always to determine our judgments.

But this leads me to take notice of the fundamental error in this argument: an error which, I fancy, every person must be sensible of when it is mentioned, and for the sake of pointing out which chiefly this dissertation is written.—The error I mean is contained in the assertion, that "if, previously to an event, there was a greater probability *against* its happening, then there is *for* the truth of the testimony endeavoring to establish it, the former destroys the latter, and renders the event unlikely to have happened in proportion to its superiority." That this is a fundamental point in Mr. *Hume's* objection must be apparent to those who have considered it. By the contest between two opposite experiences in miraculous facts supported by testimony, the greatest of which always destroys the other as far as its force goes; he cannot consistently mean any thing but

this. One of the opposite experiences must be that which acquaints us with the course of nature, and by which, as before explained, it is rendered probable, in proportion to the number of instances in which an event has happened, that it will happen in future trials. The other must be that from whence the credit we give to testimony is derived, which, according to Mr. *Hume,* being our observation of the usual conformity of facts to the reports of witnesses, makes it probable that any event reported by witnesses has happened, in proportion to what we have experienced of this conformity. Now, as in the case of miraculous facts these probabilities oppose one another, and the greatest, according to Mr. Hume, must be the first, because the experience which produces it is constant and invariable; it follows, that there must be always a great overbalance of evidence against their reality. He seems to lay it down as a general maxim, that if it is more improbable that any fact should have really happened, than that men should either deceive or be deceived, it should be rejected by us.—But, it must be needless to take any pains to have mentioned; or, in other words, the principle, that no testimony should engage our belief, except the improbability in the falsehood of it is greater than that in the event which it attests.

In order to make it appear that this is an error, which I desire may be considered is, the degree of improbability which there is against almost all the most common facts, independently of the evidence of testimony for them. In many cases of particular histories which are immediately believed upon the slightest testimony, there would have appeared to us, previously to this testimony, an improbability of almost infinity to one against their reality, as any one must perceive, who will think how sure he is of the falsehood of all facts that have *no* evidence to support them or which he has only *imagined* to himself. It is then very common for the slightest testimony to overcome an almost infinite improbability.

To make this more evident: Let us suppose, that testimony informed us rightly ten times to one in which it deceived us; and that there was nothing to direct our judgments concerning the regard due to witnesses, besides the degree of conformity which we have experienced in past events to their reports. In this case, there

---

5. *Essay on Miracles,* Page 179. [See pp. 772–7, this volume.]

would be the probability of ten to one for the reality of every fact supported by testimony. Suppose then that it informs me of the success of a person in an affair, against the success of which there was the probability of a hundred to one, or of any other even previously improbably in this proportion. I ask, What, on this supposition, would be, on the whole, the probability that the event really happened? Would the right way of computing be, to compare the probability of the truth of the testimony with the probability that the event would not happen, and to reject the event with a confidence proportioned to the superiority of the latter above the former? This Mr. *Hume* directs; but certainly contrary to all reason.— The truth is, that the testimony would give the probability of ten to one to the event, unabated by the supposed probability against it. And one reason this is, that the very experience which teaches us to give credit to testimony, is an experience by which we have found, that it has informed us rightly concerning facts, in which there would have appeared to us, previously, a great improbability.

But to be yet more explicit; Let us suppose the event reported by testimony to be, that a particular side of a die was thrown twice in two trails, and that the testimony is of such a nature that it has as often informed us wrong as right. In this case, there would plainly be an equal chance for the reality of the event, though, previously, there was the probability of thirty-five to one against it: And every one would see, that it would be absurd to say, that there being so considerable a probability against the event, and no probability at all for the truth of the testimony; or, that having had much more frequent experience that two trials have not turned up the same face of a die, than of the conformity of facts to the supposed testimony, therefore, no regard is due to the testimony.—An evidence that is *often* connected with truth, though not *oftener* than with falsehood, is real evidence, and deserves regard. To reject such evidence would be to fall *often* into error, whatever improbabilities may attend the events to which it is applied; and to assert the contrary, would be to assert a manifest contradiction.

The end of a news-paper confines it, in a great measure, to the relation of such facts as are uncommon. Suppose that it reports truth only twice in three times, and

that there are *nine* such uncommon facts reported by it as, that a certain person is alive in his hundredth year, that another was struck dead by lightning, or that a woman has been delivered of three children at a birth; Would it be right to reject *all* these facts, because more extraordinary than the report of falsehood by the news-paper? To say this, would be to say, that what, by supposition, reports truth *six* times in *nine,* does not report truth *once* in nine times.

But let us take a higher case of this kind. The improbability of drawing a lottery in any particular assigned manner, independently of the evidence of testimony, or of our own senses, acquainting us that it *has* been drawn in that manner, is such as exceeds all conception. And yet the most common testimony is sufficient to put us out of doubt about it. Suppose here a person was to reject the evidence offered him on the pretence that the improbability of the falsehood of it is almost infinitely less than that of the event; or, suppose, that universally a person was to reject all accounts which he reads or hears of facts which are more uncommon, than it is that he should read or hear what is false: What would be thought of such a person? How soon would he be made to see and acknowledge his mistake?

In the case I have mentioned of a news-paper supposed to report truth twice in three times, the odds of *two* to *one,* would overcome the odds of *thousands* to *one.* This is no more than saying, that an evidence which, in cases where there were great odds against an event, has been found true twice in three times, *is* true in such cases twice in three times, and communicates the probability of 2 to 1 to the event to which it is applied. Every one will see that this is an assertion so plainly true as to be trifling; and yet the principal part of what I am here asserting may be reduced to it.—The previous improbability of most common facts, that is, the improbability we should see to be in them were they unconnected with all evidence for them, is, I have observed, very great. We have, generally, found testimony right, when applied to such facts. It is therefore reasonable to give credit to it when so applied, tho' not so likely to be true as it was that the facts should not happen: And saying this, is only saying, that an evidence *generally* right ought to be received as being so, notwithstanding improbabilities by which we have found it not to be affected; I will add, and by which too we know that it is *its* nature not to be affected.

What has been last said requires explanation; and it will be proper to dwell a little upon it, in order more fully to show the nature of historical evidence, and the reason and truth of all I have said concerning it.—What I desire may be here attended to is chiefly the following assertion, "that improbabilities *as such* do not lessen the capacity of testimony to report truth."—The only causes of falsehood in testimony are the intention to deceive, and the danger of being deceived. Setting aside the former, let us, for the sake of greater precision, confine our views at present to the latter, or suppose a case where there are no motives to deceive, and where therefore the only source of mis-information from testimony is the danger of being deceived. Let us likewise suppose that this danger is such as makes testimony liable to be wrong once in ten times. Now, I say, that such testimony would communicate its own probability to *every* event reported by it of which sense is *equally* a judge, whether the odds against that event, or the previous improbability in it is more or less.—For instance, a person, who in the dark should take a black-ball out of a heap of 67 white-balls, and 33 black would do what there were the odds of two to one against his doing. He, therefore, who should report this, would report an event which was improbably as two to one; and a person who should affirm that there was no improbability to be removed by the report, would affirm a palpable falsehood. Now, to this fact, the testimony I have supposed, would give the probability of *nine* to one, notwithstanding its previous improbability. Such a testimony would do the same if its report was that a black-ball had been in the same manner taken out of a heap containing 90 white-balls and ten black, or 99 white and one black. That is, it would afford equal evidence whether the improbability of the event was 2 to 1, 10 to 1, or 99 to 1.—The like will appear, if we suppose the reports of such a testimony applied to the particular faces thrown with a set of dies. It would make no difference, whether its reports were applied to the faces thrown with a set of dies of 6 sides or a thousand sides, or to any *different* faces thrown with them, or any *coincidence* of faces. Supposing any considerable number of such reports, the nature of the thing implies, that an equal proportion of them would

be found to be true in either case; because, by supposition, however different the improbabilities are, the only cause of mis-information, namely the danger of a deception of the senses, does not operate more in one case than in the other.—In other words, the improbabilities I mean, being no hindrance to the perceptions of sense, make no opposition to the testimony of a witness who reports honestly from sense; and, therefore, saying that such a testimony, tho' the probability of its own truth is but 9 to 1, will overcome equally an improbability of 2 to 1, 10 to 1, or 99 to 1, is no more saying, that it is equally an over-match for any one of a number of things, by which it is not opposed.—In short, TESTIMONY is truly no more than SENSE at second-hand; and improbabilities, in the circumstances now supposed, can have no more effect on the evidence of the one, than on the evidence of the other.

It is obvious that similar observations might be made on the other cause which I have mentioned of falsehood in testimony. If in any case it cannot be supposed that a witness is deceived, his report will give an event that precise degree of probability which there is of his not intending to deceive, be the event what it will.

A due attention to these observations will, I think, show the reason of the little effect which, in numberless instances, very great previous improbabilities have, when set against the weakest direct testimony. No one can be at a loss to account for this where he has the evidence of *sense*. It appears that there is no greater difficulty in accounting for it, where we have the evidence of *testimony*.

It should be remembered, that nothing I have said implies, that improbabilities ought never to have any influence on our opinion of testimony. Improbabilities, I have observed, *as such,* do not affect the *capacity* of testimony to report truth. They have no *direct* and necessary operation upon it, and should not be considered as a *counter-evidence* invalidating, in proportion to their degree, its reports.—But tho' this is true, it by no means follows, that they may not in many circumstances affect the *credit* of testimony, or cause us to question its veracity. They have sometimes this effect on even the reports on sense, and, therefore, may also on the reports of testimony. This will happen, first, when they are of such a nature as to carry the appearance of *impossibilities*. [. . .]

Thus; if I was to hear a report that a person was in *one* place at a time when I apprehended him to be in *another,* I could not give my assent till it appeared that I had less reason for thinking myself right in this apprehension, than for believing the report. The same is true in all cases where seeming impossibilities or inconsistencies are reported. But, between *impossibilities* and *improbabilities,* however apt we may be to confound them, there is an infinite difference; and no conclusion can be drawn from the one to the other. There are few of the most *incredible* facts that can, with any reason, be called *impossible.* With respect to *miracles,* particularly, there are no arguments which have a tendency to prove this concerning them; or were it even true, that there are such arguments, their utmost effect, agreeably to the observation just made, would be, not to *destroy* the evidence of christianity, but to *counter-balance* it; and there might be still reason to believe christianity, unless is appeared that their force was such as to *outweigh* the force of the evidence for it. Testimony sometimes has convinced men of facts which they judged to be impossible; that is, it has convinced them that they were wrong in this opinion. [. . .]

But, *Secondly,* The chief reason of the effect of improbabilities on our regard to testimony is, their tendency to influence the principle of deceit in the human mind. They have *of themselves,* I have said, no effect on the perceptions of sense, and therefore none on any faithful reports from sense. They may, however, *when perceived,* lead us to question the faithfulness of a report, and give just ground to suspect a design to misrepresent or exaggerate. A *given probability* of testimony communicates itself always entire to an event; but an event may be of such a nature as to lead us to doubt, whether there is that probability or not.—My meaning here will be explained by the following considerations.

Whenever any particular improbabilities appear, or a fact has any thing of the air of the marvelous, the passions are necessarily engaged, and we know that a temptation to deceive takes place in order to draw attention and excite wonder. On the contrary; when a fact is such as not at all to *interest,* or to give any room for imagining that men can intend deceit, we immediately believe it, without minding any previous improbabilities. It is for this reason, that we easily believe any story of a common nature, however complicated, tho' improbable, when the support of testimony is taken from it, almost as infinity to one. But when a story is told us, which is attended with any circumstances not common, or in any way calculated to produce surprize, we place ourselves on our guard, and very reasonably give our assent with caution, because we see that in this case there is room for fearing the operation of the principles of deceit.—Thus; were we to receive an account that number 1500 was the *first* drawn in a lottery, we should immediately believe it; but were we to hear that number 1 was the *first* drawn, we should hesitate and doubt, tho' the improbability of the event gives no more reason for hesitation in the one case than the other; it being certainly no more unlikely, that number 1 should be *first* drawn, than number 1500.

Were we sure in instances of this kind, that the story which surprizes, and the story which does not surprize, came to us from persons who had no more thought of deceiving in one case than in the other, we should in both cases give our assent with equal readiness; and it would be unreasonable to do otherwise. [. . .] If before the beginning of drawing a lottery, we suppose a wager laid in a company, that a particular number shall be first drawn, and if afterwards one who only knows of the wager, without being any way interested in it, should come and report to the company that he had heard that very number first drawn, he would not easily gain credit. But if a stranger, ignorant of the wager, was to come accidentally, and to make the same report, he would be believed. The reason is obvious. It would appear that probably the last of these reporters had nothing but the reality of the fact to lead him to report hits number rather than any other; whereas the contrary would appear to be true of the other.

These observations may be applied to every case in which historical evidence is concerned. A *given* force of testimony never wants ability to produce belief proportioned to its degree; but the situation of reporters and the circumstances of facts may be such as may render us doubtful whether that *given force* is *really* applied. As far as it appears that there is no ground for any doubts of this kind, we are equally forced to believe in all cases. Were we even to receive an account that a lottery had been drawn in the very order of the numbers, in a manner which gave us as little reason to suspect the danger of mistake and deceit, as there is when we are informed that it has been drawn in any other order, we should be obliged to give our assent.

All that has been here asserted may be justly applied to the case of miracles reported by testimony.—Uncommon facts, *as such,* are not less subject to the cognizance of *sense* than the most ordinary. It is as competent a judge, for instance, of a man eight feet high, as of a man five or six feet high, and of the restoration of a withered limb, or the instantaneous cure of a disease, by speaking a word, as of the amputation of a limb, or the gradual cure of a disease by the use of medicines: And were a set of such facts to be related to us by eye- and ear-witnesses, who appeared no more to mean deceit than persons in general do when they relate any thing of a common nature, we should be under a necessity of believing them.—In particular; were there no more reason to question the sincerity of the Apostles when they tell us, that they saw Jesus perform his wonderful works, that they conversed with him familiarly for many days after his resurrection; that he ascended to heaven before their eyes, and that afterwards, in consequence of being endued *with power from on high* agreeably to his promise, they went about thro' all the world preaching the doctrine of *eternal life through him,* and converting men from idolatry and vice, God himself bearing witness with them *by divers miracles, and wonders, and gifts of the Holy Ghost:*[6] [. . .] The *extraordinary* facts they relate are so blended with the *common,* and told with so much of the appearance of a like artless simplicity in both cases, as has, I think, a strong tendency to impress an attentive and impartial mind.

6. Heb. ii. 4.—Rom. xv. 18, 19.

Blaise Pascal

The Wager

[. . .] If there is a God, he is infinitely incomprehensible, since, having neither parts nor limits, he bears no relation to us. We are therefore incapable of knowing either what he is or whether he is. This being so, who will dare undertake to resolve the question? Not we, who bear no relation to him.

Who then will blame Christians for not being able to give rational grounds for their belief, they who profess a religion for which they cannot give rational grounds?

They declare, in proclaiming it to the world, that it is a folly—*stultitiam*[1]—and then you complain that they do not prove it! If they proved it, they would not be keeping their word. It is by lacking proofs that they are not lacking sense. "Yes, but although this excuses those who offer their religion in this way and removes the blame of putting it forward without rational grounds, it does not excuse those who accept it."

Let us then examine this point and say: either God is or he is not. But to which side shall we incline? Reason can determine nothing here. There is an infinite chaos that separates us. At the extremity of this infinite distance,

From Blaise Pascal, *Pensées,* edited and translated by Roger Ariew (Indianapolis: Hackett Publishing Company, 2005). Reprinted by permission of the publisher.

1. Paul, I Corinthians 1:18.

a game is being played in which heads or tails will turn up. How will you wager? You have no rational grounds for choosing either way or for rejecting either alternative.

Do not, then, blame as wrong those who have made a choice, for you know nothing of the matter! "No, but I will blame them for having made, not this choice, but a choice. For although the player who chooses heads is no more at fault than the other one, they are both in the wrong. The right thing is not to wager at all."

Yes; but you must wager. It is not optional. You are committed. Which will you choose, then? Let us see. Since you must choose, let us see what is the less profitable option. You have two things to lose, the true and the good; and two things to stake, your reason and your will, your knowledge and your beatitude; and your nature has two things to avoid, error and wretchedness. Since you must necessarily choose, your reason is no more offended by choosing one rather than the other. This settles one point. But your beatitude? Let us weigh the gain and the loss in calling heads that God exists. Let us assess the two cases. If you win, you win everything; if you lose, you lose nothing. Wager, then, without hesitation that he exists! "This is wonderful. Yes, I must wager. But perhaps I am wagering too much." Let us see: since there is an equal chance of winning and losing, if there were two lives to win for one, you could still wager. But if there were three lives to win, you would have to play (since you must necessarily play), and it would be foolish, when you are forced to play, not to risk your life to win three at a game in which there is an equal chance of losing and winning. But there is an eternity of life and happiness. This being so, if there were an infinity of chances, and only one in your favor, it would still be right to wager one life in order to win two; and, being obliged to play, you would be making the wrong choice if you refused to stake one life against three in a game in which, out of an infinity of chances, there is only one in your favor, if there were an infinite life of infinite happiness to be won. But here there is an infinite life of infinite happiness to be won, there is one chance of winning against a finite number of chances of losing, and what you are staking is finite. All bets are off wherever there is an infinity and wherever there is not an infinite number of chances of losing against the chance of winning. There is no time to hesitate; you must give every-

thing. And thus, when you are forced to play, you must be renouncing reason to preserve life, instead of risking it for an infinite gain, which is as likely to happen as is a loss amounting to nothing.

It is no use saying that it is uncertain whether you will win, that it is certain you are taking a risk, and that the infinite distance between the **certainty** of what you are risking and the **uncertainty** of what you stand to gain makes the finite good you are certainly staking equal to the infinite good that is uncertain. It is not so. All players take a certain risk for an uncertain gain; and yet they take a certain finite risk for an uncertain finite gain without sinning against reason. It is not true that there is an infinite distance between the certain risk and the uncertain gain. Indeed, there is an infinity between the certainty of winning and the certainty of losing. But the uncertainty of winning is proportional to the certainty of the risk, in proportion to the chances of winning and losing. Hence, if there are as many chances on one side as on the other, you are playing for even odds, and then the certainty of what you are risking is equal to the uncertainty of what you may win—so far is it from being infinitely distant. Thus our proposition is infinitely powerful, when the stakes are finite in a game where the chances of winning and losing are even, and the infinite is to be won.

This is conclusive and if people are capable of any truth, this is it.

"I confess it, I admit it. But, still . . . Is there no means of seeing what is in the cards?" Yes, Scripture and the rest, etc. "Yes, but my hands are tied and my mouth is shut; I am forced to wager, and am not free. I have not been released and I am made in such a way that I cannot believe. What, then, would you have me do?" That is true. But at least realize that your inability to believe comes from your passions, since reason brings you to this and yet you cannot believe. Work, then, on convincing yourself, not by adding more proofs of God's existence, but by diminishing your passions. You would like to find faith and do not know the way? You would like to be cured of unbelief and ask for the remedies? Learn from those who were bound like you, and who now wager all they have. These are people who know the way you wish to follow, and who are cured of the illness of which you wish to be cured. Follow the way by which they began: they acted as if they believed, took holy water, had masses said, etc. This will make you believe naturally and mechanically.[2] "But this is what I am afraid of." And why? What do you have to lose? But to show you that this is the way, this diminishes the passions, which are your great obstacles, etc. [. . .]

---

2. Pascal's word is *abêtira*—literally, will make you more like the beasts. Man is in part a beast or machine, and one needs to allow that part its proper function: that is, one needs to act dispassionately or mechanically.

William K. Clifford

The Ethics of Belief

I.—The Duty of Inquiry

A shipowner was about to send to sea an emigrant ship. He knew that she was old, and not over-well built at the first; that she had seen many seas and climes, and often had needed repairs. Doubts had been suggested to him that possibly she was not seaworthy. These doubts preyed upon his mind and made him unhappy; he thought that perhaps he ought to have her thoroughly overhauled and refitted, even though this should put him to great expense. Before the ship sailed, however, he succeeded in overcoming these melancholy reflections. He said to himself that she had gone safely though so many voyages and weathered so many storms that it was idle to suppose she would not come safely home from this trip also. He would put his trust in Providence, which could hardly fail to protect all these unhappy families that were leaving their fatherland to seek for better times elsewhere. He would dismiss from his mind all ungenerous suspicions about the honesty of builders and contractors. In such ways he acquired a sincere and comfortable conviction that his vessel was thoroughly safe and seaworthy; he watched her departure with a

W. K. Clifford, "The Ethics of Belief" from *Contemporary Review* (1877).

light heart, and benevolent wishes for the success of the exiles in their strange new home that was to be; and he got his insurance-money when she went down in mid-ocean and told no tales.

What shall we say of him? Surely this, that he was verily guilty of the death of those men. It is admitted that he did sincerely believe in the soundness of his ship; but the sincerity of his conviction can in no wise help him, because *he had no right to believe on such evidence as was before him*. He had acquired his belief not by honestly earning it in patient investigation, but by stifling his doubts. And although in the end he may have felt so sure about it that he could not think otherwise, yet inasmuch as he had knowingly and willingly worked himself into that frame of mind, he must be held responsible for it.

Let us alter the case a little, and suppose that the ship was not unsound after all; that she made her voyage safely, and many others after it. Will that diminish the guilt of her owner? Not one jot. When an action is once done, it is right or wrong forever; no accidental failure of its good or evil fruits can possibly alter that. The man would not have been innocent, he would only have been not found out. The question of right or wrong has to do with the origin of his belief, not the matter of it; not what it was, but how he got it; not whether it turned out to be true or false, but whether he had a right to believe on such evidence as was before him.

There was once an island in which some of the inhabitants professed a religion teaching neither the doctrine of original sin nor that of eternal punishment. A suspicion got abroad that the professors of this religion had made use of unfair means to get their doctrines taught to children. They were accused of wresting the laws of their country in such a way as to remove children from the care of their natural and legal guardians; and even of stealing them away and keeping them concealed from their friends and relations. A certain number of men formed themselves into a society for the purpose of agitating the public about this matter. They published grave accusations against individual citizens of the highest position and character, and did all in their power to injure these citizens in the exercise of their professions. So great was the noise they made, that a Commission was appointed to investigate the facts; but after the Commission had carefully inquired into all the evidence that could be got, it appeared that the accused were innocent. Not only had they been accused on insufficient evidence, but the evidence of their innocence was such as the agitators might easily have obtained, if they had attempted a fair inquiry. After these disclosures the inhabitants of that country looked upon the members of the agitating society, not only as persons whose judgment was to be distrusted, but also as no longer to be counted honourable men. For although they had sincerely and conscientiously believed in the charges they had made, *yet they had no right to believe on such evidence as was before them.* Their sincere convictions, instead of being honestly earned by patient inquiring, were stolen by listening to the voice of prejudice and passion.

Let us vary this case also, and suppose, other things remaining as before, that a still more accurate investigation proved the accused to have been really guilty. Would this make any difference in the guilt of the accusers? Clearly not; the question is not whether their belief was true or false, but whether they entertained it on wrong grounds. They would no doubt say: "Now you see that we were right after all; next time perhaps you will believe us." And they might be believed, but they would not thereby become honourable men. They would not be innocent, they would only be not found out. Every

one of them, if he chose to examine himself *in foro conscientiæ,* would know that he had acquired and nourished a belief, when he had no right to believe on such evidence as was before him; and therein he would know that he had done a wrong thing.

It may be said, however, that in both of these supposed cases it is not the belief which is judged to be wrong, but the action following upon it. The shipowner might say: "I am perfectly certain that my ship is sound, but still I feel it my duty to have her examined, before trusting the lives of so many people to her." And it might be said to the agitator: "However convinced you were of the justice of your cause and the truth of your convictions, you ought not to have made a public attack upon any man's character until you had examined the evidence on both sides with the utmost patience and care."

In the first place, let us admit that, so far as it goes, this view of the case is right and necessary; right, because even when a man's belief is so fixed that he cannot think otherwise, he still has a choice in regard to the action suggested by it, and so cannot escape the duty of investigating on the ground of the strength of his convictions; and necessary, because those who are not yet capable of controlling their feelings and thoughts must have a plain rule dealing with overt acts.

But this being premised as necessary, it becomes clear that it is not sufficient, and that our previous judgment is required to supplement it. For it is not possible so to sever the belief from the action it suggests as to condemn the one without condemning the other. No man holding a strong belief on one side of a question, or even wishing to hold a belief on one side, can investigate it with such fairness and completeness as if he were really in doubt and unbiased; so that the existence of a belief not founded on fair inquiry unfits a man for the performance of this necessary duty.

Nor is that truly a belief at all which has not some influence upon the actions of him who holds it. He who truly believes that which prompts him to an action has looked upon the action to lust after it, he has committed it already in his heart. If a belief is not realised immediately in open deeds, it is stored up for the guidance of the future. It goes to make a part of that aggregate of beliefs which is the link between sensation and action at every moment of all our lives, and which is so organised and compacted together that no part of it can be isolated from the rest, but every new addition modifies the structure of the whole. No real belief, however trifling and fragmentary it may seem, is ever truly insignificant; it prepares us to receive more of its like, confirms those which resembled it before, and weakens others; and so gradually it lays a stealthy train in our inmost thoughts, which may some day explode into overt action, and leave its stamp upon our character for ever.

And no one man's belief is in any case a private matter which concerns himself alone. Our lives are guided by that general conception of the course of things which has been created by society for social purposes. Our words, our phrases, our forms and processes and modes of thought, are common property, fashioned and perfected from age to age; an heirloom which every succeeding generation inherits as a precious deposit and a scared trust to be handed on to the next one, not unchanged but enlarged and purified, with some clear marks of its proper handiwork. Into this, for good or ill, is woven every belief of every man who has speech of his fellows. An awful privilege, and an awful responsibility, that we should help to create the world in which posterity will live.

In the two supposed cases which have been considered, it has been judged wrong to believe on insufficient evidence, or to nourish belief by suppressing doubts and avoiding investigation. The reason of this judgment is not far to seek: it is that in both these cases the belief held by one man was of great importance to other men. But forasmuch as no belief held by one man, however seemingly trivial the belief, and however obscure the believer, is ever actually insignificant or without its effect on the fate of mankind, we have no choice but to extend our judgment to all cases of belief whatever. Belief, that sacred faculty which prompts the decisions of our will, and knits into harmonious working all the compacted energies of our being, is ours not for ourselves, but for humanity. It is rightly used on truths which have been established by long experience and waiting toil, and which have stood in the fierce light of free and fearless questioning. Then it helps to bind men together, and to strengthen and direct their common action. It is desecrated when given

to unproved and unquestioned statements, for the solace and private pleasure of the believer; to add a tinsel splendour to the plain straight road of our life and display a bright mirage beyond it; or even to drown the common sorrows of our kind by a self-deception which allows them not only to cast down, but also to degrade us. Whoso would deserve well of his fellows in this matter will guard the purity of his belief with a very fanaticism of jealous care, lest at any time it should rest on an unworthy object, and catch a stain which can never be wiped away.

It is not only the leader of men, statesman, philosopher, or poet, that owes this bounden duty to mankind. Every rustic who delivers in the village alehouse his slow, infrequent sentences, may help to kill or keep alive the fatal superstitions which clog his race. Every hardworked wife of an artisan may transmit to her children beliefs which shall knit society together, or rend it in pieces. No simplicity of mind, no obscurity of station, can escape the universal duty of questioning all that we believe.

It is true that this duty is a hard one, and the doubt which comes out of it is often a very bitter thing. It leaves us bare and powerless where we thought that we were safe and strong. To know all about anything is to know how to deal with it under all circumstances. We feel much happier and more secure when we think we know precisely what to do, no matter what happens, than when we have lost our way and do not know where to turn. And if we have supposed ourselves to know all about anything, and to be capable of doing what is fit in regard to it, we naturally do not like to find that we are really ignorant and powerless, that we have to begin again at the beginning, and try to learn what the thing is and how it is to be dealt with—if indeed anything can be learnt about it. It is the sense of power attached to a sense of knowledge that makes men desirous of believing, and afraid of doubting.

This sense of power is the highest and best of pleasures when the belief on which it is founded is a true belief, and has been fairly earned by investigation. For then we may justly feel that it is common property, and holds good for others as well as for ourselves. Then we may be glad, not that *I* have learned secrets by which I am safer and stronger, but that *we men* have got mastery over more of the world; and we shall be strong, not for ourselves, but in the name of Man and in his strength. But if the belief has been accepted on insufficient evidence, the pleasure is a stolen one. Not only does it deceive ourselves by giving us a sense of power which we do not really possess, but it is sinful, because it is stolen in defiance of our duty to mankind. That duty is to guard ourselves from such beliefs as from a pestilence, which may shortly master our own body and the spread to the rest of the town. What would be thought of one who, for the sake of a sweet fruit, should deliberately run the risk of bringing a plague upon his family and his neighbours?

And, as in other such cases, it is not the risk only which has to be considered; for a bad action is always bad at the time when it is done, no matter what happens afterwards. Every time we let ourselves believe for unworthy reasons, we weaken our powers of self-control, of doubting, of judicially and fairly weighing evidence. We all suffer severely enough from the maintenance and support of false beliefs and the fatally wrong actions which they lead to, and the evil born when one such belief is entertained is great and wide. But a greater and wider evil arises when the credulous character is maintained and supported, when a habit of believing for unworthy reasons is fostered and made permanent. If I steal money from any person, there may be no harm done by the mere transfer of possession; he may not feel the loss, or it may prevent him from using the money badly. But I cannot help doing this great wrong towards Man, that I make myself dishonest. What hurts society is not that it should lose its property, but that it should become a den of thieves; for then it must cease to be society. This is why we ought not to do evil that good may come; for at any rate this great evil has come, that we have done evil and are made wicked thereby. In like manner, if I let myself believe anything on insufficient evidence, there may be no great harm done by the mere belief; it may be true after all, or I may never have occasion to exhibit it in outward acts. But I cannot help doing this great wrong towards Man, that I make myself credulous. The danger to society is not merely that it should believe wrong things, though that is great enough; but that it should become credulous, and lose the habit of testing things and inquiring into them; for then it must sink back into savagery.

The harm which is done by credulity in a man is not confined to the fostering of a credulous character in others, and consequent support of false beliefs. Habitual want of care about what I believe leads to habitual want of care in others about the truth of what is told to me. Men speak the truth to one another when each reveres the truth in his own mind and in the other's mind; but how shall my friend revere the truth in my mind when I myself am careless about it, when I believe things because I want to believe them, and because they are comforting and pleasant? Will he not learn to cry, "Peace," to me, when there is no peace? By such a course I shall surround myself with a thick atmosphere of falsehood and fraud, and in that I must live. It may matter little to me, in my cloud-castle of sweet illusions and darling lies; but it matters much to Man that I have made my neighbors ready to deceive. The credulous man is father to the liar and the cheat; he lives in the bosom of this his family, and it is no marvel if he should become even as they are. So closely are our duties knit together, that whoso shall keep the whole law, and yet offend in one point, he is guilty of all.

To sum up; it is wrong always, everywhere, and for anyone, to believe anything upon insufficient evidence.

If a man, holding a belief which he was taught in childhood or persuaded of afterwards, keeps down and pushes away any doubts which arise about it in his mind, purposely avoids the reading of books and the company of men that call in question or discuss it, and regards as impious those questions which cannot easily be asked without disturbing it—the life of that man is one long sin against mankind. [. . .]

III.—The Limits of Inference

The question in what cases we may believe that which goes beyond our experience, is a very large and delicate one, extending to the whole range of scientific method, and requiring a considerable increase in the application of it before it can be answered with anything approaching to completeness. But one rule, lying on the threshold of the subject, of extreme simplicity and vast practical importance, may here be touched upon and shortly laid down.

A little reflection will show us that every belief, even the simplest and most fundamental, goes beyond experience when regarded as a guide to our actions. A burnt child dreads the fire, because it believes that the fire will burn it today just as it did yesterday; but this belief goes beyond experience, and assumes that the unknown fire of today is like the known fire of yesterday. Even the belief that the child was burnt yesterday goes beyond *present* experience, which contains only the memory of a burning, and not the burning itself; it assumes, therefore, that this memory is trustworthy, although we know that a memory may often be mistaken. But if it is to be used as a guide of action, as a hint of what the future is to be, it must assume something about that future, namely, that it will be consistent with the supposition that the burning really took place yesterday; which is going beyond experience. Even the fundamental "I am," which cannot be doubted, is no guide to action until it takes to itself "I shall be," which goes beyond experience. The question is not, therefore, "May we believe what goes beyond experience?" for this is involved in the very great nature of belief; but "How far and in what manner may we add to our experience in forming our beliefs?"

And an answer, of utter simplicity and universality, is suggested by the example we have taken: a burnt child dreads the fire. We may go beyond experience by assuming that what we do not know is like what we do know; or, in other words, we may add to our experience on the assumption of a uniformity in nature. What this uniformity precisely is, how we grow in the knowledge of it from generation to generation, these are questions which for the present we lay aside, being content to examine two instances which may serve to make plainer the nature of the rule.

From certain observations made with the spectroscope, we infer the existence of hydrogen in the sun. By looking into the spectroscope when the sun is shining on its slit, we see certain definite bright lines: and experiments made upon bodies on the earth have taught us that when these bright lines are seen hydrogen is the source of them. We assume, then, that the unknown bright lines in the sun are like the known bright lines of the laboratory, and that hydrogen in the sun behaves as hydrogen under similar circumstances would behave on the earth.

But are we not trusting our spectroscope too much? Surely, having found it to be trustworthy for terrestrial substances, where its statements can be verified by man, we are justified in accepting its testimony in other like cases; but not when it gives us information about things in the sun, where its testimony cannot be directly verified by man?

Certainly, we want to know a little more before this inference can be justified; and fortunately we do know this. The spectroscope testifies to exactly the same thing in the two cases; namely, that light-vibrations of a certain rate are being sent through it. Its construction is such that if it were wrong about this in one case, it would be wrong in the other. When we come to look into the matter, we find that we have really assumed the matter of the sun to be like the matter of the earth, made up of a certain number of distinct substances; and that each of these, when very hot, has a distinct rate of vibration, by which it may be recognised and singled out from the rest. But this is the kind of assumption which we are justified in using when we add to our experience. It is an assumption of uniformity in nature, and can only be checked by comparison with many similar assumptions which we have to make in other such cases.

But is this a true belief, of the existence of hydrogen in the sun? Can it help in the right guidance of human action?

Certainly not, if it is accepted on unworthy grounds and without some understanding of the process by which it is got at. But when this process is taken in as the ground of the belief, it becomes a very serious and practical matter. For if there is no hydrogen in the sun, the spectroscope—that is to say, the measurement of rates of vibration—must be an uncertain guide in recognising different substances; and consequently it ought not to be used in chemical analysis—in assaying, for example—to the great saving of time, trouble, and money. Whereas the acceptance of the spectroscopic method as trustworthy has enriched us not only with new metals, which is a great thing, but with new processes of investigation, which is vastly greater.

For another example, let us consider the way in which we infer the truth of an historical event—say the siege of Syracuse in the Peloponnesian war. Our experience is that manuscripts exist which are said to be and which call themselves manuscripts of the history of Thucydides; that in other manuscripts, stated to be by later historians, he is described as living during the time of the war; and that books, supposed to date from the revival of learning, tell us how these manuscripts had been preserved and were then acquired. We find also that men do not, as a rule, forge books and histories without a special motive; we assume that in this respect men in the past were like men in the present; and we observe that in this case no special motive was present. That is, we add to our experience on the assumption of a uniformity in the characters of men. Because our knowledge of this uniformity is far less complete and exact than our knowledge of that which obtains in physics, inferences of the historical kind are more precarious and less exact than inferences in many other sciences.

But if there is any special reason to suspect the character of the persons who wrote or transmitted certain books, the case becomes altered. If a group of documents give internal evidence that they were produced among people who forged books in the names of others, and who, in describing events, suppressed those things which did not suit them, while they amplified such as did suit them; who not only committed these crimes, but gloried in them as proofs of humility and zeal; then we must say that upon such documents no true historical inference can be founded, but only unsatisfactory conjecture.

We may, then, add to our experience on the assumption of a uniformity in nature; we may fill in our picture of what is and has been, as experience gives it us, in such a way as to make the whole consistent with this uniformity. And practically demonstrative inference—that which gives us a right to believe in the result of it—

is a clear showing that in no other way than by the truth of this result can the uniformity of nature be saved.

No evidence, therefore, can justify us in believing the truth of a statement which is contrary to, or outside of, the uniformity of nature. If our experience is such that it cannot be filled up consistently with uniformity, all we have a right to conclude is that there is something wrong somewhere; but the possibility of inference is taken away; we must rest in our experience, and not go beyond it at all. If an event really happened which was not a part of the uniformity of nature, it would have two properties: no evidence could give the right to believe it to any except those whose actual experience it was; and no inference worthy of belief could be founded upon it at all.

Are we then bound to believe that nature is absolutely and universally uniform? Certainly not, we have no right to believe anything of this kind. The rule only tells us that in forming beliefs which go beyond our experience we may make the assumption that nature is practically uniform so far as we are concerned. Within the range of human action and verification, we may form, by help of this assumption, actual beliefs; beyond it, only those hypotheses which serve for the more accurate asking of questions.

To sum up;—

We may believe what goes beyond our experience, only when it is inferred from that experience by the assumption that what we do not know is like what we know.

We may believe the statement of another person, when there is reasonable ground for supposing that he knows the matter of which he speaks, and that he is speaking the truth so far as he knows it.

It is wrong in all cases to believe on insufficient evidence; and where it is presumption to doubt and to investigate, there it is worse than presumption to believe.

William James

The Will to Believe

I have brought with me tonight something like a sermon on justification by faith to read to you—I mean an essay in justification *of* faith, a defense of our right to adopt a believing attitude in religious matters, in spite of the fact that our merely logical intellect may not have been coerced. "The Will to Believe," accordingly, is the title of my paper.

I have long defended to my own students the lawfulness of voluntarily adopted faith; but as soon as they have got well imbued with the logical spirit, they have as a rule refused to admit my contention to be lawful philosophically, even though in point of fact they were personally all the time chock full of some faith or other themselves. [. . .]

i

Let us give the name of *hypothesis* to anything that may be proposed to our belief; and just as the electricians speak of live and dead wires, let us speak of any hypothesis as either *live* or *dead*. A live hypothesis is one which appeals as a real possibility to him to whom it is proposed. If I ask you to believe in the Mahdi, the notion makes no electric connection with your nature—it refuses to scintillate with any credibility at all. As an hypothesis it is completely dead. To an Arab, however (even if he be not one of the Mahdi's followers), the hypothesis is among the mind's possibilities: it is alive. This shows that deadness and liveness in an hypothesis are not intrinsic properties, but relations to the individual thinker. They are measured by his willingness to act. The maximum of liveness in an hypothesis means willingness to act irrevocably. Practically, that means belief; but

there is some believing tendency wherever there is willingness to act at all.

Next, let us call the decision between two hypotheses an *option*. Options may be of several kinds. They may be—1, *living* or *dead;* 2, *forced* or *avoidable;* 3, *momentous* or *trivial;* and for our purposes we may call an option a *genuine* option when it is of the forced, living, and momentous kind.

1. A living option is one in which both hypotheses are live ones. If I say to you: "Be a theosophist or be a Mohammedan," it is probably a dead option, because for you neither hypothesis is likely to be alive. But if I say: "Be an agnostic or be a Christian," it is otherwise: trained as you are, each hypothesis makes some appeal, however small, to your belief.

2. Next, if I say to you: "Choose between going out with your umbrella or without it," I do not offer you a genuine option, for it is not forced. You can easily avoid it by not going out at all. Similarly, if I say, "Either love me or hate me," "Either call my theory true or call it false," your option is avoidable. You may remain indifferent to me, neither loving nor hating and you may decline to offer any judgment as to my theory. But if I say, "Either accept this truth or go without it," I put on you a forced option, for there is no standing place outside of the alternative. Every dilemma based on a complete logical disjunction, with no possibility of not choosing, is an option of this forced kind.

3. Finally, if I were Dr. Nansen and proposed to you to join my North Pole expedition, your option would be momentous; for this would probably be your only similar opportunity, and your choice now would either exclude you from the North Pole sort of immortality altogether or put at least the chance of it into your hands. He who refuses to embrace a unique opportunity loses the prize as surely as if he tried and failed. *Per contra,* the option is trivial when the opportunity is not unique, when the stake is insignificant, or when the decision is

From an Address to the Philosophical Clubs of Yale and Brown Universities. Published in *New World,* June 1896.

reversible if it later prove unwise. Such trivial options abound in the scientific life. A chemist finds an hypothesis live enough to spend a year in its verification: he believes in it to that extent. But if his experiments prove inconclusive either way, he is quit for his loss of time, no vital harm being done.

It will facilitate our discussion if we keep all these distinctions well in mind.

ii

The next matter to consider is the actual psychology of human opinion. When we look at certain facts, it seems as if our passional and volitional nature lay at the root of all our convictions. When we look at others, it seems as if they could do nothing when the intellect had once said its say. Let us take the latter facts up first.

Does it not seem preposterous on the very face of it to talk of our opinions being modifiable at will? Can our will either help or hinder our intellect in its perceptions of truth? Can we, by just willing it, believe that Abraham Lincoln's existence is a myth, and that the portraits of him in *McClure's Magazine* are all of some one else? Can we, by any effort of our will, or by any strength of wish that it were true, believe ourselves well and about when we are roaring with rheumatism in bed, or feel certain that the sum of the two one-dollar bills in our pocket must be a hundred dollars? We can *say* any of these things, but we are absolutely impotent to believe them; and of just such things is the whole fabric of the truths that we do believe in made up— matters of fact, immediate or remote, as Hume said, and relations between ideas, which are either there or not there for us if we see them so, and which if not there cannot be put there by any action of our own.

In Pascal's Thoughts there is a celebrated passage known in literature as Pascal's wager. In it he tries to force us into Christianity by reasoning as if our concern with truth resembled our concern with the stakes in a game of chance. Translated freely his words are these: You must either believe or not believe that God is— which will you do? Your human reason cannot say. A game is going on between you and the nature of things which at the day of judgment will bring out either heads or tails. Weigh what your gains and your losses would be if you should stake all you have on heads, or God's existence: if you win in such case, you gain eternal beatitude; if you lose, you lose nothing at all. If there were an infinity of chances, and only one for God in this wager, still you ought to stake your all on God; for though you surely risk a finite loss by this procedure, any finite loss is reasonable, even a certain one is reasonable, if there is but the possibility of infinite gain. Go, then, and take holy water, and have masses said; belief will come and stupefy your scruples—*Cela vous fera croire et vous abêtira*. Why should you not? At bottom, what have you to lose?

You probably feel that when religious faith expresses itself thus, in the language of the gaming table, it is put to its last trumps. Surely Pascal's own personal belief in masses and holy water had far other springs; and this celebrated page of his is but an argument for others, a last desperate snatch at a weapon against the hardness of the unbelieving heart. We feel that a faith in masses and holy water adopted wilfully after such a mechanical calculation would lack the inner soul of faith's reality; and if we were ourselves in the place of the Deity, we should probably take particular pleasure in cutting off believers of this pattern from their infinite reward. It is evident that unless there be some preexisting tendency to believe in masses and holy water, the option offered to the will by Pascal is not a living option. Certainly no Turk ever took to masses and holy water on its account; and even to us Protestants these means of salvation seem such foregone impossibilities that Pascal's logic, invoked for them specifically, leaves us unmoved. As well might the Mahdi write to us, saying, "I am the Expected One whom God has created in his effulgence. You shall be infinitely happy if you confess me; otherwise you shall be cut off from the light of the sun. Weigh, then, your infinite gain if I am genuine against your finite sacrifice if I am not!" His logic would be that of Pascal; but he would vainly use it on us, for the hypothesis he offers us is dead. No tendency to act on it exists in us to any degree.

The talk of believing by our volition seems, then, from one point of view, simply silly. From another point of view it is worse than silly, it is vile. When one turns to the magnificent edifice of the physical sciences, and sees how it was reared; what thousands of disinterested moral lives of men lie buried in its mere foundations; what patience and postponement, what choking down of preference, what submission to the icy laws of outer fact are wrought into its very stones and mortar; how absolutely impersonal it stands in its vast augustness—then how besotted and contemptible seems every little sentimentalist who comes blowing his voluntary smoke wreaths, and pretending to decide things from out of his private dream! Can we wonder if those bred in the rugged and manly school of science should feel like spewing such subjectivism out of their mouths? The whole system of loyalties which grow up in the schools of science go dead against its toleration; so that it is only natural that those who have caught the scientific fever should pass over to the opposite extreme, and write sometimes as if the incorruptibly truthful intellect ought positively to prefer bitterness and unacceptableness to the heart of its cup.

> It fortifies my soul to know
> That, though I perish, Truth is so—

sings Clough, while Huxley exclaims: "My only consolation lies in the reflection that, however bad our posterity may become, so far as they hold by the plain rule of not pretending to believe what they have no reason to believe, because it may be to their advantage so to pretend [the word "pretend" is surely here redundant], they will not have reached the lowest depth of immorality." And that delicious *enfant terrible* Clifford writes: "Belief is desecrated when given to unproved and unquestioned statements of the solace and private pleasure of the believer.... Whoso would deserve well of his fellows in this matter will guard the purity of his belief with a very fanaticism of jealous care, lest at any time it should rest on an unworthy object, and catch a stain which can never be wiped away.... If [a] belief has been accepted on insufficient evidence [even though the belief be true, as Clifford on the same page explains] the pleasure is a stolen one.... It is sinful because it is stolen in defiance of our duty to mankind. That duty is to guard ourselves from such beliefs as from a pestilence which may shortly master our own body and then spread to the rest of the town.... It is wrong always,

everywhere, and for every one, to believe anything upon insufficient evidence."

iii

All this strikes one as healthy, even when expressed, as by Clifford, with somewhat too much of robustious pathos in the voice. Free will and simple wishing do seem, in the matter of our credences, to be only fifth wheels to the coach. Yet if any one should thereupon assume that intellectual insight is what remains after wish and will and sentimental preference have taken wing, or that pure reason is what then settles our opinions, he would fly quite as directly in the teeth of the facts.

It is only our already dead hypotheses that our willing nature is unable to bring to life again. But what has made them dead for us is for the most part a previous action of our willing nature of an antagonistic kind. When I say "willing nature," I do not mean only such deliberate volitions as may have set up habits of belief that we cannot now escape from—I mean all such factors of belief as fear and hope, prejudice and passion, imitation and partisanship, the circumpressure of our caste and set. As a matter of fact we find ourselves believing, we hardly know how or why. Mr. Balfour gives the name of "authority" to all those influences, born of the intellectual climate, that make hypotheses possible or impossible for us, alive or dead. Here in this room, we all of us believe in molecules and the conservation of energy, in democracy and necessary progress, in Protestant Christianity and the duty of fighting for "the doctrine of the immortal Monroe," all for no reasons worthy of the name. We see into these matters with no more inner clearness, and probably with much less, than any disbeliever in them might possess. His unconventionality would probably have some grounds to show for its conclusions; but for us, not insight, but the *prestige* of the opinions, is what makes the spark shoot from them and light up our sleeping magazines of faith. Our reason is quite satisfied, in nine hundred and ninety-nine cases out of every thousand of us, if it can find a few arguments that will do to recite in case our credulity is criticized by some one else. Our faith is faith in some one else's faith, and in the greatest matters this is most the case. Our belief in truth itself, for instance, that there is a truth, and that our minds and it are made for each other—what is it but a passionate affirmation of desire, in which our social system backs us up? We want to have a truth; we want to believe that our experiments and studies and discussions must put us in a continually better and better position towards it; and on this line we agree to fight out our thinking lives. But if a pyrrhonistic sceptic asks us *how we know* all this, can our logic find a reply? No! certainly it cannot. It is just one volition against another—we willing to go in for life upon a trust or assumption which he, for his part, does not care to make.

As a rule we disbelieve all facts and theories for which we have no use. Clifford's cosmic emotions find no use for Christian feelings. Huxley belabors the bishops because there is no use for sacerdotalism in his scheme of life. Newman, on the contrary, goes over to Romanism, and finds all sorts of reasons good for staying there, because a priestly system is for him an organic need and delight. Why do so few "scientists" even look at the evidence for telepathy, so called? Because they think, as a leading biologist, now dead, once said to me, that even if such a thing were true, scientists ought to band together to keep it suppressed and concealed. It would undo the uniformity of Nature and all sorts of other things without which scientists cannot carry on their pursuits. But if this very man had been shown something which as a scientist he might *do* with telepathy, he might not only have examined the evidence, but even have found it good enough. This very law which the logicians would impose upon us—if I may give the name of logicians to those who would rule out our willing nature here—is based on nothing but their own natural wish to exclude all elements for which they, in their professional quality of logicians, can find no use.

Evidently, then, our nonintellectual nature does influence our convictions. There are passional tendencies and volitions which run before and others which come after belief, and it is only the latter that are too late for the fair; and they are not too late when the previous passional work has been already in their own direction. Pascal's argument, instead of being powerless, then seems a regular clincher, and is the last stroke needed to make our faith in masses and holy water complete. The state of things is evidently far from simple; and pure insight and logic, whatever they might do ideally, are not the only things that really do produce our creeds.

iv

Our next duty, having recognized this mixed-up state of affairs, is to ask whether it be simply reprehensible and pathological, or whether, on the contrary, we must treat it as a normal element in making up our minds. The thesis I defend is, briefly stated, this: *Our passional nature not only lawfully may, but must, decide an option between propositions, whenever it is a genuine option that cannot by its nature be decided on intellectual grounds; for to say, under such circumstances, "Do not decide, but leave the question open," is itself a passional decision—just like deciding yes or no—and is attended with the same risk of losing the truth.* The thesis thus abstractly expressed will, I trust, soon become quite clear. But I must first indulge in a bit more of preliminary work.

v

It will be observed that for the purposes of this discussion we are on "dogmatic" ground—ground, I mean, which leaves systematic philosophical scepticism altogether out of account. The postulate that there is truth, and that it is the destiny of our minds to attain it, we are deliberately resolving to make, though the sceptic will not make it. We part company with him, therefore, absolutely, at this point. But the faith that truth exists, and that our minds can find it, may be held in two ways. We may talk of the *empiricist* way and of the *absolutist* way of believing in truth. The absolutists in this matter say that we not only can attain to knowing truth, but we can *know when* we have attained to knowing it; while the empiricists think that although we may attain it, we cannot infallibly know when. To *know* is one thing, and to know for certain *that* we know is another. One may hold to the first being possible without the second; hence the empiricists and the absolutists, although neither of them is a sceptic in the usual philosophic sense of the term, show very different degrees of dogmatism in their lives.

If we look at the history of opinions, we see that the empiricist tendency has largely prevailed in science, while in philosophy the absolutist tendency has had everything its own way. The characteristic sort of happiness, indeed, which philosophies yield has mainly consisted in the conviction felt by each successive school or system that by it bottom certitude had been attained. "Other philosophies are collections of opinions, mostly false; *my* philosophy gives standing ground forever"— who does not recognize in this the keynote of every system worthy of the name? A system, to be a system at all, must come as a *closed* system, reversible in this or that detail, perchance, but in its essential features never!

Scholastic orthodoxy, to which one must always go when one wishes to find perfectly clear statement, has beautifully elaborated this absolutist conviction in a doctrine which it calls that of "objective evidence." If, for example, I am unable to doubt that I now exist before you, that two is less than three, or that if all men are mortal then I am mortal too, it is because these things illumine my intellect irresistibly. The final ground of this objective evidence possessed by certain propositions is the *adoequatio intellectûs nostri cum rê.* The certitude it brings involves an *aptitudinem ad extorquendum certum assensum,* on the part of the truth envisaged, and on the side of the subject a *quietem in cognitione,* when once the object is mentally received, that leaves no possibility of doubt behind; and in the whole transaction nothing operates but the *entitas ipsa* of the object and the *entitas ipsa* of the mind. We slouchy modern thinkers dislike to talk in Latin—indeed, we dislike to talk in set terms at all; but at bottom our own state of mind is very much like this whenever we uncritically abandon ourselves: You believe in objective evidence, and I do. Of some things we feel that we are certain: we know, and we know that we do know. There is something that gives a click inside of us, a bell that strikes twelve, when the hands of our mental clock have swept the dial and meet over the meridian hour. The greatest empiricists among us are only empiricists on reflection: when left to their instincts, they dogmatize like infallible popes. When the Cliffords tell us how sinful it is to be Christians on such "insufficient evidence," insufficiency is really the last thing they have in mind. For them the evidence is absolutely sufficient, only it makes the other

way. They believe so completely in an anti-Christian order of the universe that there is no living option: Christianity is a dead hypothesis from the start.

vi

But now, since we are all such absolutists by instinct, what in our quality of students of philosophy ought we to do about the fact? Shall we espouse and indorse it? Or shall we treat it as a weakness of our nature from which we must free ourselves, if we can?

I sincerely believe that the latter course is the only one we can follow as reflective men. Objective evidence and certitude are doubtless very fine ideals to play with, but where on this moonlit and dream-visited planet are they found? I am, therefore, myself a complete empiricist so far as my theory of human knowledge goes. I live, to be sure, by the practical faith that we must go on experiencing and thinking over our experience, for only thus can our opinions grow more true; but to hold any one of them—I absolutely do not care which—as if it never could be reinterpretable or corrigible, I believe to be a tremendously mistaken attitude, and I think that the whole history of philosophy will bear me out. There is but one indefectibly certain truth, and that is the truth that pyrrhonistic scepticism itself leaves standing—the truth that the present phenomenon of consciousness exists. That, however, is the bare starting point of knowledge, the mere admission of a stuff to be philosophized about. The various philosophies are but so many attempts at expressing what this stuff really is. And if we repair to our libraries what disagreement do we discover! Where is a certainly true answer found? Apart from abstract propositions of comparison (such as two and two are the same as four), propositions which tell us nothing by themselves about concrete reality, we find no proposition ever regarded by any one as evidently certain that has not either been called a falsehood, or at least had its truth sincerely questioned by some one else. The transcending of the axioms of geometry, not in play but in earnest, by certain of our contemporaries (as Zöllner and Charles H. Hinton), and the rejection of the whole Aristotelian logic by the Hegelians, are striking instances in point.

No concrete test of what is really true has ever been agreed upon. Some make the criterion external to the moment of perception, putting it either in revelation, the *consensus gentium,* the instincts of the heart, or the systematized experience of the race. Others make the perceptive moment its own test—Descartes, for instance, with his clear and distinct ideas guaranteed by the veracity of God; Reid with his "common sense"; and Kant with his forms of synthetic judgment *a priori.* The inconceivability of the opposite; the capacity to be verified by sense; the possession of complete organic unity or self-relation, realized when a thing is its own other— are standards which, in turn, have been used. The much lauded objective evidence is never triumphantly there; it is a mere aspiration or *Grenzbegriff,* marking the infinitely remote ideal of our thinking life. To claim that certain truths now possess it, is simply to say that when you think them true and they *are* true, then their evidence is objective, otherwise it is not. But practically one's conviction that the evidence one goes by is of the real objective brand, is only one more subjective opinion added to the lot. For what a contradictory array of opinions have objective evidence and absolute certitude been claimed! The world is rational through and through —its existence is an ultimate brute fact; there is a personal God—a personal God is inconceivable; there is an extramental physical world immediately known—the mind can only know its own ideas; a moral imperative exists—obligation is only the resultant of desires; a permanent spiritual principle is in every one—there are only shifting states of mind; there is an endless chain of causes—there is an absolute first cause; an eternal necessity—a freedom; a purpose—no purpose; a primal One—a primal Many; a universal continuity—an essential discontinuity in things; an infinity—no infinity. There is this—there is that; there is indeed nothing which some one has not thought absolutely true, while his neighbor deemed it absolutely false; and not an absolutist among them seems ever to have considered that the trouble may all the time be essential and that the intellect, even with truth directly in its grasp, may have no infallible signal for knowing whether it be truth or no. When, indeed, one remembers that the most striking practical application to life of the doctrine of objective certitude has been the conscientious labors of the Holy Office of the Inquisition, one feels less tempted than ever to lend the doctrine a respectful ear.

But please observe, now, that when as empiricists we give up the doctrine of objective certitude, we do not thereby give up the quest or hope of truth itself. We still pin our faith on its existence, and still believe that we gain an ever better position toward it by systematically continuing to roll up experiences and think. Our great difference from the scholastic lies in the way we face. The strength of his system lies in the principles, the origin, the *terminus a quo* of his thought; for us the strength is in the outcome, the upshot, the *terminus ad quem.* Not where it comes from but what it leads to is to decide. It matters not to an empiricist from what quarter an hypothesis may come to him: he may have acquired it by fair means or by foul; passion may have whispered or accident suggested it; but if the total drift of thinking continues to confirm it, that is what he means by its being true.

vii

One more point, small but important, and our preliminaries are done. There are two ways of looking at our duty in the matter of opinion—ways entirely different, and yet ways about whose difference the theory of knowledge seems hitherto to have shown very little concern. *We must know the truth;* and *we must avoid error* —these are our first and great commandments as wouldbe knowers; but they are not two ways of stating an identical commandment, they are two separable laws. Although it may indeed happen that when we believe the truth A, we escape as an incidental consequence from believing the falsehood B, it hardly ever happens that by merely disbelieving B we necessarily believe A. We may in escaping B fall into believing other falsehoods, C or D, just as bad as B; or we may escape B by not believing anything at all, not even A.

Believe truth! Shun error!—these, we see, are two materially different laws; and by choosing between them we may end by coloring differently our whole intellectual life. We may regard the chase for truth as paramount and the avoidance of error as secondary; or we may, on the other hand, treat the avoidance of error as more imperative, and let truth take, its chance. Clifford, in the instructive passage which I have quoted, exhorts us to the latter course. Believe nothing, he tells us, keep your mind in suspense forever, rather than by closing it on insufficient evidence incur the awful risk of believing lies. You, on the other hand, may think that the risk of being in error is a very small matter when compared with the blessings of real knowledge, and be ready to be duped many times in your investigation rather than postpone indefinitely the chance of guessing true. I myself find it impossible to go with Clifford. We must remember that these feelings of our duty about either truth or error are in any case only expressions of our passional life. Biologically considered, our minds are as ready to grind out falsehood as veracity, and he who says, "Better go without belief forever than believe a lie!" merely shows his own preponderant private horror of becoming a dupe. He may be critical of many of his desires and fears, but this fear he slavishly obeys. He cannot imagine any one questioning its binding force. For my own part, I have also a horror of being duped; but I can believe that worse things than being duped may happen to a man in this world: so Clifford's exhortation has to my ears a thoroughly fantastic sound. It is like a general informing his soldiers that it is better to keep out of battle forever than to risk a single wound. Not so are victories either over enemies or over nature gained. Our errors are surely not such awfully solemn things. In a world where we are so certain to incur them in spite of all our caution, a certain lightness of heart seems healthier than this excessive nervousness on their behalf. At any rate, it seems the fittest thing for the empiricist philosopher.

viii

And now, after all this introduction, let us go straight at our question. I have said, and now repeat it, that not only as a matter of fact do we find our passional nature influencing us in our opinions, but that there are some options between opinions in which this influence must be regarded both as an inevitable and as a lawful determinant of our choice.

I fear here that some of you my hearers will begin to scent danger, and lend an inhospitable ear. Two first steps of passion you have indeed had to admit as necessary—

we must think so as to avoid dupery, and we must think so as to gain truth; but the surest path to those ideal consummations, you will probably consider, is from now onwards to take no further passional step.

Well, of course, I agree as far as the facts will allow. Wherever the option between losing truth and gaining it is not momentous, we can throw the change of *gaining truth* away, and at any rate save ourselves from any chance of *believing falsehood,* by not making up our minds at all till objective evidence has come. In scientific questions, this is almost always the case; and even in human affairs in general, the need of acting is seldom so urgent that a false belief to act on is better than no belief at all. Law courts, indeed, have to decide on the best evidence attainable for the moment, because a judge's duty is to make law as well as to ascertain it, and (as a learned judge once said to me) few cases are worth spending much time over: the great thing is to have them decided on *any* acceptable principle, and got out of the way. But in our dealings with objective nature we obviously are recorders, not makers, of the truth; and decisions for the mere sake of deciding promptly and getting on to the next business would be wholly out of place. Throughout the breadth of physical nature facts are what they are quite independently of us, and seldom is there any such hurry about them that the risks of being duped by believing a premature theory need be faced. The questions here are always trivial options, the hypotheses are hardly living (at any rate not living for us spectators), the choice between believing truth or falsehood is seldom forced. The attitude of sceptical balance is therefore the absolutely wise one if we would escape mistakes. What difference, indeed, does it make to most of us whether we have or have not a theory of the roentgen rays, whether we believe or not in mind stuff, or have a conviction about the causality of conscious states? It makes no difference. Such options are not forced on us. On every account it is better not to make them, but still keep weighing reasons *pro et contra* with an indifferent hand.

I speak, of course, here of the purely judging mind. For purposes of discovery such indifference is to be less highly recommended, and science would be far less advanced than she is if the passionate desire of individuals to get their own faiths confirmed had been kept out of the game. See for example the sagacity which Spencer and Weismann now display. On the other hand, if you want an absolute duffer in an investigation, you must, after all, take the man who has no interest whatever in its results: he is the warranted incapable, the positive fool. The most useful investigator, because the most sensitive observer, is always he whose eager interest in one side of the question is balanced by an equally keen nervousness lest he become deceived. Science has organized this nervousness into a regular *technique,* her so-called method of verification; and she has fallen so deeply in love with the method that one may even say she has ceased to care for truth by itself at all. It is only truth as technically verified that interests her. The truth of truths might come in merely affirmative form, and she would decline to touch it. Such truth as that, she might repeat with Clifford, would be stolen in defiance of her duty to mankind. Human passions, however, are stronger than technical rules. "Le coeur a ses raisons," as Pascal says, "que la raison ne connaît pas"; and however indifferent to all but the bare rules of the game the umpire, the abstract intellect, may be, the concrete players who furnish him the materials to judge of are usually, each one of them, in love with some pet "live hypothesis" of his own. Let us agree, however, that wherever there is no forced option, the dispassionately judicial intellect with no pet hypothesis, saving us, as it does, from dupery at any rate, ought to be our ideal.

The question next arises: Are there not somewhere forced options in our speculative questions, and can we (as men who may be interested at least as much in positively gaining truth as in merely escaping dupery) always wait with impunity till the coercive evidence shall have arrived? It seems *a priori* improbable that the truth should be so nicely adjusted to our needs and powers as that. In the great boarding house of nature, the cakes and the butter and the syrup seldom come out so even and leave the plates so clean. Indeed, we should view them with scientific suspicion if they did.

ix

Moral questions immediately present themselves as questions whose solution cannot wait for sensible proof. A moral question is a question not of what sensibly exists, but of what is good, or would be good if it did exist. Science can tell us what exists; but to compare the *worths,* both of what exists and of what does not exist, we must consult not science, but what Pascal calls our heart. Science herself consults her heart when she lays it down that the infinite ascertainment of fact and correction of false belief are the supreme goods for man. Challenge the statement, and science can only repeat it oracularly, or else prove it by showing that such ascertainment and correction bring man all sorts of other goods which man's heart in turn declares. The question of having moral beliefs at all or not having them is decided by our will. Are our moral preferences true or false, or are they only odd biological phenomena, making things good or bad for *us,* but in themselves indifferent? How can your pure intellect decide? If your heart does not *want* a world of moral reality, your head will assuredly never make you believe in one. Mephistophelian scepticism, indeed, will satisfy the head's play instincts much better than any rigorous idealism can. Some men (even at the student age) are so naturally cool-hearted that the moralistic hypothesis never has for them any pungent life, and in their supercilious presence the hot young moralist always feels strangely ill at ease. The appearance of knowingness is on their side, of naïveté and gullibility on his. Yet, in the inarticulate heart of him, he clings to it that he is not a dupe, and that there is a realm in which (as Emerson says) all their wit and intellectual superiority is no better than the cunning of a fox. Moral scepticism can no more be refuted or proved by logic than intellectual scepticism can. When we stick to it that there *is* truth (be it of either kind), we do so with our whole nature, and resolve to stand or fall by the results. The sceptic with his whole nature adopts the doubting attitude; but which of us is the wiser, Omniscience only knows.

Turn now from these wide questions of good to a certain class of questions of fact, questions concerning personal relations, states of mind between one man and another. *Do you like me or not?*—for example. Whether you do or not depends, in countless instances, on whether I meet you halfway, am willing to assume that you must like me, and show you trust and expectation. The previous faith on my part in your liking's existence is in such cases what makes your liking come. But if I stand aloof, and refuse to budge an inch until I have objective evidence, until you shall have done something apt, as the absolutists say, *ad extorquendum assensum meum,* ten to one your liking never comes. How many women's hearts are vanquished by the mere sanguine insistence of some man that they *must* love him! he will not consent to the hypothesis that they cannot. The desire for a certain kind of truth here brings about that special truth's existence; and so it is in innumerable cases of other sorts. Who gains promotions, boons, appointments, but the man in whose life they are seen to play the part of life hypotheses, who discounts them, sacrifices other things for their sake before they have come, and takes risks for them in advance? His faith acts on the powers above him as a claim, and creates its own verification.

A social organism of any sort whatever, large or small, is what it is because each member proceeds to his own duty with a trust that the other members will simultaneously do theirs. Wherever a desired result is achieved by the cooperation of many independent persons, its existence as a fact is a pure consequence of the percursive faith in one another of those immediately concerned. A government, an army, a commercial system, a ship, a college, an athletic team, all exist on this condition, without which not only is nothing achieved, but nothing is even attempted. A whole train of passengers (individually brave enough) will be looted by a few highwaymen, simply because the latter can count on one another, while each passenger fears that if he makes a movement of resistance, he will be shot before any one else backs him up. If we believed that the whole car-full would rise at once with us, we should each severally rise, and train robbing would never even be attempted. There are, then, cases where a fact cannot come at all unless a preliminary faith exists in its coming. *And where faith in a fact can help create the fact,* that would be an insane logic which should say that faith running ahead of scientific evidence is the "lowest kind of immorality" into which a thinking being can fall. Yet such is the logic by which our scientific absolutists pretend to regulate our lives!

x

In truths dependent on our personal action, then, faith based on desire is certainly a lawful and possibly an indispensable thing.

But now, it will be said, these are all childish human cases, and have nothing to do with great cosmical matters, like the question of religious faith. Let us then pass on to that. Religions differ so much in their accidents that in discussing the religious question we must make it very generic and broad. What then do we now mean by the religious hypothesis? Science says things are; morality says some things are better than other things; and religion says essentially two things.

First, she says that the best things are the more eternal things, the overlapping things, the things in the universe that throw the last stone, so to speak, and say the final word. "Perfection is eternal"—this phrase of Charles Secrétan seems a good way of putting this first affirmation of religion, an affirmation which obviously cannot yet be verified scientifically at all.

The second affirmation of religion is that we are better off even now if we believe her first affirmation to be true.

Now, let us consider what the logical elements of this situation are *in case the religious hypothesis in both its branches be really true.* (Of course, we must admit that possibility at the outset. If we are to discuss the question at all, it must involve a living option. If for any of you religion be a hypothesis that cannot, by any living possibility be true, then you need go no farther. I speak to the "saving remnant" alone.) So proceeding, we see, first, that religion offers itself as a *momentous* option. We are supposed to gain even now, by our belief, and to lose by our nonbelief, a certain vital good. Secondly, religion is a *forced* option, so far as that good goes. We cannot escape the issue by remaining sceptical and waiting for more light, because, although we do avoid error in that way *if religion be untrue,* we lose the good, *if it be true,* just as certainly as if we positively chose to disbelieve. It is as if a man should hesitate indefinitely to ask a certain woman to marry him because he was not perfectly sure that she would prove an angel after he brought her home. Would he not cut himself off from that particular angel possibility as decisively as if he went and married someone else? Scepticism, then, is not avoidance of option; it is option of a certain particular kind of risk. *Better risk loss of truth than chance of error*—that is your faith vetoer's exact position. He is actively playing his stake as much as the believer is; he is backing the field against the religious hypothesis, just as the believer is backing the religious hypothesis against the field. To preach scepticism to us as a duty until "sufficient evidence" for religion be found, is tantamount therefore to telling us, when in presence of the religious hypothesis, that to yield to our fear of its being error is wiser and better than to yield to our hope that it may be true. It is not intellect against all passions, then; it is only intellect with one passion laying down its law. And by what, forsooth, is the supreme wisdom of this passion warranted? Dupery for dupery, what proof is there that dupery through hope is so much worse than dupery through fear? I, for one, can see no proof; and I simply refuse obedience to the scientist's command to imitate his kind of option, in a case where my own stake is important enough to give the right to choose my own form of risk. If religion be true and the evidence for it be still insufficient, I do not wish, by putting your extinguisher upon my nature (which feels to me as if it had after all some business in this matter), to forfeit my sole chance in life of getting upon the winning side—that chance depending, of course, on my willingness to run the risk of acting as if my passional need of taking the world religiously might be prophetic and right.

All this is on the supposition that it really may be prophetic and right, and that, even to us who are discussing the matter, religion is a live hypothesis which may be true. Now, to most of us religion comes in a still further way that makes a veto on our active faith even more illogical. The more perfect and more eternal aspect of the universe is represented in our religions as having personal form. The universe is no longer a mere *It* to us, but a *Thou,* if we are religious; and any relation that may be possible from person to person might be possible here. For instance, although in one sense we are passive portions of the universe, in another we show a curious autonomy, as if we were small active centers on our own account. We feel, too, as if the appeal of religion, to us were made to our own active good will, as if evidence might be forever withheld from us unless we met the hypothesis halfway. To take a trivial illustration: just as a man who in a company of gentlemen made no advances, asked a warrant for every concession, and believed no one's word without proof, would cut himself off by such churlishness from all the social rewards that a more trusting spirit would earn—so here, one who should shut himself up in snarling logicality and try to make the gods extort his recognition willy-nilly, or not get it at all, might cut himself off forever from his only opportunity of making the gods' acquaintance. This feeling, forced on us we know not whence, that by obstinately believing that there are gods (although not to do so would be so easy both for our logic and our life) we are doing the universe the deepest service we can, seems part of the living essence of the religious hypothesis. If the hypothesis *were* true in all its parts, including this one, then pure intellectualism, with its veto on our making willing advances, would be an absurdity; and some participation of our sympathetic nature would be logically required. I, therefore, for one, cannot see my way to accepting the agnostic rules for truth seeking, or wilfully agree to keep my willing nature out of the game. I cannot do so for this plain reason, that *a rule of thinking which would absolutely prevent me from acknowledging certain kinds of truth if those kinds of truth were really there would be an irrational rule.* That for me is the long and short of the formal logic of the situation, no matter what the kinds of truth might materially be.

I confess I do not see how this logic can be escaped. But sad experience makes me fear that some of you may still shrink from radically saying with me, *in abstracto,* that we have the right to believe at our own risk any hypothesis that is live enough to tempt our will. I suspect, however, that if this is so, it is because you have got away from the abstract logical point of view altogether, and are thinking (perhaps without realizing it) of some particular religious hypothesis which for you is dead. The freedom to "believe what we will" you apply to the case of some patent superstition; and the faith you think of is the faith defined by the schoolboy when he said, "Faith is when you believe something that you know ain't true." I can only repeat that this is misapprehension. *In concreto,* the freedom to believe can only cover living options which the intellect of the individual cannot by itself resolve; and living options never seem absurdities to him who has them to consider. When I look at the religious question as it really puts itself to concrete men, and when I think of all the possibilities which both practically and theoretically it involves, then this command that we shall put a stopper on our heart, instincts, and courage, and *wait*—acting of course meanwhile more or less as if religion were *not* true—till doomsday, or till such time as our intellect and senses working together may have raked in evidence enough—this command, I say, seems to me the queerest idol ever manufactured in the philosophic cave. Were we scholastic absolutists, there might be more excuse. If we had an infallible intellect with its objective certitudes, we might feel ourselves disloyal to such a perfect organ of knowledge in not trusting to it exclusively, in not waiting for its releasing word. But if we are empiricists, if we believe that no bell in us tolls to let us know for certain when truth is in our grasp, then it seems a piece of idle fantasticality to preach so solemnly our duty of waiting for the bell. Indeed we *may* wait if we will—I hope you do not think that I am denying that—but if we do so, we do so at our peril as much as if we believed. In either case we *act,* taking our life in our hands. No one of us ought to issue vetoes to the other, nor should we bandy words of abuse. We ought, on the contrary, delicately and profoundly to respect one another's mental freedom: then only shall we bring about the intellectual republic; then only shall we have that spirit of inner tolerance without which all our outer tolerance is soulless, and which is empiricism's glory; then only shall we live and let live, in speculative as well as in practical things.

Bernard Williams

Deciding to Believe

When the subject of belief is proposed for philosophical discussion, one may tend to think of such things as religious and moral beliefs, belief in the sense of conviction of an ideological or practical character. Indeed, many of the most interesting questions in the philosophy of belief are concerned with beliefs of this type. However, this is not in fact what I shall be talking about, though what I say will, I hope, have some relevance to issues that arise in those areas. I wish to start with the question of what it is to believe something, and then go on from that to discuss (rather briefly) how far, if at all, believing something can be related to decision and will. In order to discuss this, I am not going to take religious and moral beliefs, but cases of more straightforward factual belief; the sort of belief one has when one just believes that it is raining, or believes that somebody over there is one's father, or believes that the substance in front of one is salt.

I shall be talking about belief as a psychological state. The word 'belief', of course, can stand equally for the state of somebody who believes something, and for what he believes. And we can talk about beliefs in an impersonal way, when we talk about certain propositions which people believe or might believe. But my principal concern will be with belief as a psychological state: I shall be talking about people believing things.

The ultimate focus of my remarks is going to be on the relations between belief and decision and certain puzzles that arise about the relation between these two ideas. But before we can get into a position to discuss the questions that concern the relations between belief and decision, we must first ask one or two things about what belief is. I shall begin by stating five characteristics—as I take them—of belief. This will not be very accurate; and each of the five things that I am going to mention as a characteristic of belief can itself give rise to a good bit of dispute and philosophical consideration. In the course of mentioning the five features, it will be necessary to mention things which may seem problematic or completely platitudinous.

The first of these features is something which can be roughly summarised as this: beliefs aim at truth. When I say that beliefs aim at truth, I have particularly in mind three things. First: that truth and falsehood are a dimension of an assessment of beliefs as opposed to many other psychological states or dispositions. Thus if somebody just has a habit of a certain kind, or merely has some disposition to action of some kind, it is not appropriate to ask whether this habit of his is true or false, nor does that habit or disposition relate to something which can be called true or false. However, when somebody believes something, then he believes something which can be assessed as true or false, and his belief, in terms of the content of what he believes, is true or false. If a man recognises that what he has been believing is false, he thereby abandons the belief he had. And this leads us to the second feature under this heading: to believe that p is to believe that p is true. To believe that so and so is one and the same as to believe that that thing is true. This is the second point under the heading of 'beliefs aim at truth'.

The third point, closely connected with these, is: to say 'I believe that p' itself carries, in general, a claim that p is true. To say 'I believe that p' conveys the message that p is the case. It is a way, though perhaps a somewhat qualified way, of asserting that p is true. This is connected with the fact that to say 'I believe that p, but p is not true', 'I believe that it is raining but it is not raining' constitutes a paradox, which was famously pointed out by G. E. Moore. This is a paradox but it is not a formal self-contradiction. If it were, then in general 'x believes that p but p is false', would also be a self-contradiction. But this is obviously not so. Thus I can, without any paradox at all, say 'Jones believes that p but p is false'; it is only in the first person, when I say 'I believe that p but p is false', that the paradox arises. The paradox is connected with the fact that I assert these two things; it is connected with this, that 'I believe that p' carries an implied claim to the truth of p.

This trio of points constitutes the first of the features of belief I want to mention, that which I vaguely summed up by saying 'beliefs aim at truth'.

The second feature of belief is that the most straightforward, basic, simple, elementary expression of a belief is an assertion. That is, the most straightforward way of expressing my belief that p, is to make a certain asser-tion. And I think the following is an important point: the assertion that I make, which is the most straightforward or elementary expression of my belief that p, is the assertion *that p*, not the assertion 'I believe that p.' The most elementary and straightforward expression of the belief that it is raining is to say 'it is raining', not to say 'I believe that it's raining.' 'I believe that it's raining' does a rather special job. As a matter of fact, it does a variety of special jobs. In some cases, it makes what is very like an autobiographical remark; but very often in our discourse it does a special job of expressing the belief that p, or asserting that p, in a rather qualifies way. On the whole, if somebody says to me, 'Where is the railroad station?' and I say 'I believe that it's three blocks down there and to the right', he will have slightly less confidence in my utterances than if I just say 'It's three blocks down there and to the right.' We have a near parallel to this in the field of action, in the contrast between saying 'I will do so and so' and saying 'I intend to do so and so.' The direct or primitive expression of an intention to do so and so, is not saying 'I intend to do so and so'; it is saying 'I *will* do so and so.'

This is not to deny that beliefs can be ascribed to non-language-using animals. There are reasons, however, for saying that these are beliefs in a somewhat impoverished sense. There are many interesting questions in this field; I shall refer briefly to one of them. There is a certain conventionality about the ascription of something like a belief to an animal. Suppose that we present to a rabbit or some similar animal, something that looks like the mask of a fox; and that when the animal notices this object it displays characteristic fear behaviour. We might say in this case that the rabbit had *taken* what it was presented with for a fox. We probably would not use the rather pompous phrase of saying that the rabbit *believed* that it was a fox, though even this might not be in every case entirely unnatural. It the case of animals whose behaviour is, in our terms, more obviously sophisticated, and especially in the case of animals such as dogs which perform a very special role for humanity as being things on which we project an enormous amount of anthropomorphic apparatus—in those cases the word 'belief' may come more happily to hand. In any case, we do say about animals that they take things for things, and that they recognise things as things; and in at least certain cases even that they *believe* that something is something. The puzzle about this is: where does this *concept* come from, which, as it were, we pretend the animal is using? We don't think that in an effective sense the animal has the *concept* 'fox'. We have some idea what it is for a human being to have a concept 'fox'; we have a different idea of what it is for him to have the more general concept, for instance, 'predator'. If we were faced with the question: did the rabbit think that it was a fox, or did the rabbit merely think it was a predator that was in front of it? we have some difficulty in deciding this question, indeed, in knowing how to set about deciding this question.

There is an interesting sideline to this. Suppose there is a dog whose master is the President of the United States; a certain figure comes to the door, and this dog wakes up and pricks up his ears when he hears the person crossing the step—we say 'this dog took the person who was coming up the drive for his master'. If this dog's master was the President of the United States, we would hardly say that the dog has taken this figures for the President of the United States. Is this because it is a better shot to say that the dog has got the concept 'master' than it is to say that the dog has got the concept 'President of the United States'? Why? The concept 'master' is as much a concept that embodies elaborate knowledge about human conventions, society, and so forth as does the concept 'President of the United States". There seems to be as much conventionality or artificiality in ascribing to a dog the concept 'master' as there is in ascribing to a dog the concept 'President of the United States'. So why are we happier to say that a dog takes a certain figure for his master than we are to say that the dog takes a certain figure for the President of the United States? I think the answer to this has something to do with the fact, not that the dog really has got an effective concept 'master', which would be an absurd notion, but that so much of the dog's behaviour is in fact conditioned by situations which involve somebody's being his master, whereas very little of the dog's behaviour is conditioned by situations which essentially involve somebody's being President of the United States. That is, the concept 'master' gets into our description of the dog's recognition or quasi-thought or belief because this is a concept we want to use in the course of explaining a great deal of the dog's behaviour.

It is something on those lines, I think, which is going to justify the introduction of certain concepts into an animal's quasi-thoughts or beliefs, and the refusal to introduce other concepts into an animal's quasi-thoughts or beliefs. In the case of human beings, however, the situation is not just like this, because we have other tests for what concepts the human being in fact has.

This, then, was the second feature of belief: that the most straightforward expression of a belief is an assertion, but this does not prevent our using concepts of belief or something rather like belief with regard to animals which are incapable of making assertions and do not possess a language—although we will have to warn ourselves that such beliefs, recognitions and so on, are going to be ascribed to animals in an impoverished and (I think I have said enough to suggest), a somewhat conventionalised sense.

The third feature of belief is that although the most straightforward, simple, and elementary expression of a belief by a language-using creature is an assertion, the assertion of p is neither a necessary nor, and this is the point I want to emphasise, a sufficient condition of having the belief that p. It is not a necessary condition, because I can have beliefs which I do not express, which I shall not utter. In fact it is very plausible to say that most people most of the time have a very large number of beliefs which they are not expressing, never have expressed, and never will express. The point, however, that I want to emphasise is the converse, namely that it is possible for someone to assert that p and try to bring it about that others think that p and think that he believes that p, although he does not; that is to say, assertion can be insincere.

The fact that assertion can be insincere, which is an extremely important fact about assertion, shows, what in any case is obvious, that belief cannot be defined as acceptance, at least if 'acceptance' is taken as the name of an action which we can overtly perform. If you take 'accepting' to be something like accepting an invitation—that is, somebody comes up to me and says 'Will you come to my party tomorrow?' and I accept it if I say something like 'Yes, I will'; then in that sense 'of accepting', 'acceptance' is the name of something like a speech-act, and belief cannot be equated with acceptance in such a sense. Suppose somebody comes up to me and says, 'Do you accept that *p?*'; 'Do you accept that such and such is true?' If I just say 'Yes', then in a speech-act sense of accepting that proposition, in that sense I will have accepted; just like the speech-act of accepting an invitation. But, of course, that is not a sufficient condition of my believing that *p*, because this acceptance may have been insincere. Belief lies at the level of what makes my acceptance sincere or insincere; it does not lie at the level of those acceptances themselves. So we have a picture of belief as of the internal state which my overt assertions may represent or misrepresent. Similarly, statements of intention or promises can be sincere or insincere because they do or do not represent an internal state of intention. Where the expression of a belief is the typical one of an assertion, that assertion itself can be called insincere just in that case in which the man does really believe what he is asserting. This then is the third point; that assertion is not a necessary condition of belief, nor is it a sufficient condition, since assertion can be insincere.

The fourth point is that factual beliefs can be based on evidence. This can mean more than one thing. The weakest sense of this is that the content of a given belief can be probabilified or supported by certain evidential propositions. If I just say that the belief that ancient Crete was occupied by Greek-speaking persons at a certain date is based on, or supported by, the evidence of such and such excavations, I am not, in saying this, talking about any particular person's beliefs: I am talking about a certain proposition which concerns the history of Crete and saying that that proposition is in fact supported by certain evidence which exists. Let us turn from this to a case in which we are referring to a particular person's belief. In saying that his belief is based on particular evidence, we would mean not just that he has the belief and can defend it with the evidence, but that he has the belief just because he has the evidence. This says that if he ceased to believe the evidence, then, other things being equal, he would cease to have that belief. In this case, something that is true of him, namely, that he believes that *p*, depends upon something else being true of him, namely, that he believes these evidential propositions. In this sense of somebody's actual belief being based upon his belief in certain evidential propositions, we have a statement of

the form 'A believes that *p* because he believes that *q*'; and such statements are very often true of most of us.

Where the connexion between *p* and *q* is a rational connexion, that is to say, *q* really is some sort of evidence for *p*, then we can also say '*p* because *q*'; if a man says to me 'Why *p*, why do you believe that *p*?' I can rightly say 'because *q*'. Of course there are other cases in which A believes that *p* because he believes that *q*, which are not cases of rational connexion, or even supposed rational connexion, at all. It is just a fact about him that he believes the one thing because he believes the other, by some kind of irrational association. In this case he cannot rightly say '*p* because *q*', that is, claim a rational connexion between the two propositions. Here we have a case where he believes one thing because he believes another, and that is a pure causal connexion. The point I want to make is that where the connexion is rational—that is, not only does he believe that *p* because he believes that *q*, but we, and he, can also say '*p* because *q*',—that does not stop the 'because' in 'A believes that *p* because he believes that *q*' from being causal. The fact that there is a rational connexion between *p* and *q* does not mean that there is not a causal connexion between A's believing *p* and his believing *q*. We tend to bring out the mere causal connexion between his beliefs in the irrational cases because in those cases there is nothing but a causal connexion between them. But that does not mean that in the case in which the man has one belief rationally grounded on another it is *not* the case that there is a causal connexion between his believing the one thing and his believing the other; in fact I think it is, in general, true that when A believes that *p* because he believes that *q*, this 'because' is a causal 'because'. It is a 'because' of causal explanation, the explanation of how one of his states is causally connected with another.

We do have a genuine and systematic difficulty in the philosophy of mind in filling in the content of that causal 'because', and this is mainly because we have a very shadowy model of the kind of internal state belief is. However, this can be no particular objection to causal connexions between beliefs in the case of evidential connexion; because there are many other cases in which we must invoke a causal connexion between such internal states while we still have only a shadowy notion of what that causal connexion consists in. The most obvious case of this is the case of remembering things that one has experienced in the past. Suppose we say concerning a certain man that he remembers being lost in the park when he was five. What are the necessary conditions for its being the case that he remembers being lost in the park when he was five? The first is that he should, in fact, have been lost in the park when he was five and have experienced that at that time. The second is that he should now know that he was lost in the park, and have some further knowledge of that experience. That is not enough. Suppose it were the case that he was lost in the park when he was five but everything he now knows about it he was told by his mother a few years ago. Then it would not be the case that he remembered being lost in the park when he was five. The further condition which makes it the case that he does remember being lost in the park is that he now knows about it because he experienced it.[1] This necessary condition of event-memory appeals to exactly that kind of indeterminate causal 'because' which we need in the case of one belief being based upon another, of a man's believing that p because he believes that q.

People sometimes argue against the idea that we can have a causal connexion here, on the following ground. It cannot be the case that in rational thought I arrive at one belief causally because I have another belief, since then it would be a perpetual miracle that the laws of nature worked in such a way that we were caused to have beliefs by rational considerations. Granted the different sort of fact that q actually supported p, that q was evidence for p, does it not seem a happy accident or even miraculous that when I believe that q it comes about that I believe that p? This objection is basically an example of what Wisdom has called 'metaphysical double vision', the mistake of taking the same facts twice over and then finding the relation between them mysterious. There are not two facts, first that men are rational creatures who hold beliefs on rational grounds, and second that they have beliefs which quite often cause others in ways which express their rational connexions. On the view in question, the emergence of creatures who are

capable of rational thought just is the emergence of creatures who are capable of having beliefs which are so related. Some may think it a miracle that any such creatures have emerged, but if it is, it is at least not *another* miracle that the required causal connexions obtain in them: if the causal connexions broke down, they would just cease to be rational creatures—and since very many of the beliefs which are held by rational creatures could be held only by rational creatures, they would cease to be capable of holding these beliefs at all.

Not every belief that I have which is *based,* is based on *evidence.* There are some beliefs that I have which are not (relative to the probability of their being true) random or arbitrary, and which are very proper beliefs to have, but which are not based on further evidence; that is, are not based on other beliefs that I have. Indeed, there is a very good reason why it cannot be the case that every belief which one has is based on another belief that one has—namely, one could never stop (or start). Quite evidently there are non-random beliefs which are not based on further evidence. The most notable examples of these, of course, are perceptual beliefs, beliefs that I gain by using my senses around the environment.

In the case of human perception, we have something which we found lacking in the earlier discussion of animals' 'beliefs'. We can understand what it is for somebody to acquire a belief from his environment, and we have a kind of guarantee that the terms in which we describe the cause, that is, the environment which gave rise to his belief, can match the concepts that he uses in describing the environment and therefore, by the same token, in expressing his beliefs. The very condition of having a shared experience, having a shared language and having a common perceived environment which we can know to be such, is this: we share concepts which simultaneously enable us to express our beliefs about our environment, to describe that environment, and to describe other people's perception of the environment. Therefore we get a match between our descriptions of the environment which causes another person's belief, and the concepts which he himself uses in expressing the belief and in describing the environment. This avoids the essentially conventional element which we met in the case of animals, the kind of arbitrariness about which concepts one uses in describing

---

1. On this see Martin and Deutscher, 'Remembering', *Philosophical Review,* LXXV (1966).

their recognitions or beliefs. In the case of a human being we have his own assertions, his own conceptual apparatus, which will make clear how he sees the world. The cause and the effect are described alike from the resources of a common language.

So much for the causality of beliefs; this was the fourth feature of beliefs. Beliefs can be based upon evidence. It is sometimes true that a man believes that *p* because he believes that *q*. I take that to be a causal 'because', and have tried to dispose of at least one objection to thinking that it is so. The fifth, and last point about the nature of belief (and this is something which I shall mention without elaborating at all), is that belief is in many ways an *explanatory* notion; we can, in particular, explain what a man does by saying what he believes. It is important that one cannot explain a man's actions in terms of his beliefs without making an assumption about what his projects are, just as one cannot infer from his actions what his projects are without making assumptions about his beliefs. The trio: project, belief and action, go together. Granted that I know his projects and beliefs, I may be able to predict his actions. Granted that I know his actions and his projects, I may be able to infer his beliefs. And granted that I know his actions and his beliefs I may be able to infer his projects. But I do need basically to know, or to be able to assume, two out of the three in order to be able to get the third. A standard example of this is: I see a man walking with a determined and heavy step onto a certain bridge. We say that it shows he believes that the bridge is safe, but this, of course, is only relative to a project which it is very reasonable to assume that he has, namely to avoid getting drowned. If this were a man who surprisingly had the project of falling in the river, then his walking with firm step onto this bridge would not necessarily manifest the belief that the bridge was safe. This is a fairly obvious point. It is in terms of the trio of project, belief, and action that we offer our explanations.

These, then, are the five characteristics or features of belief that I have wanted to emphasise.

Now I want to consider a certain machine which satisfies, more or less, three of the conditions which I have mentioned: the first, second, and the fourth conditions. In a weak sense, it produces assertions. That is to say, it produces print-out, or, if you like, it has a speech synthesiser in it—though this would be unnecessary luxury. In any case, it produces messages which express propositions, and it has a device which distinguishes between propositions which it asserts, as opposed, for instance, to propositions which it is prepared to hypothesise in the course of an argument. It comes out with something which roughly, it 'claims to be true'. These things that it comes out with can be assessed for truth or falsehood; and so derivatively can be the states of the machine, which issue in these assertions. Further, the states which go with some of these assertions are based in an appropriate way on other states, and the machine arrives at some of these states from others. It goes through a causal process which is at least something like inference. We can add the fact that it gathers information from the environment; it has various sensory bits and pieces which acquire information about the environment and these get represented in the inner states of the machine, which may eventually issue in appropriate assertions.

Now this machine, I claim, would not manifest belief; its states would not be beliefs. They would be instances of a much impoverished notion which I shall call a '*B* state'. Why would a *B* state fall short of the state of a belief? I claim the essential reason for this is that this machine would not offer any satisfaction of the third condition in the list I earlier gave, namely, that it be possible to make insincere assertions, to assert something other than what you believe. In the case of this machine there is a direct route from the state that it is in to what it prints out; or if something goes wrong on this route, it goes mechanically wrong, that is, if something interrupts the connexion between the normal inner state for asserting that *p* and its asserting that *p,* and it comes out with something else, this is merely a case of breakdown. It is not a case of insincere assertion, of its trying to get you to believe that *p* when really all the time it itself believes that not-*p:* we have not yet given it any way of doing that. The fact that we have not yet given it any way of doing that has, I think, deeply impoverished the concept of belief, as applied to this machine. It also, of course, means that when I said this machine made assertions, I should have actually put that in heavy scare-quotes; 'assertion' itself has got to be understood in an impoverished sense here, because our very concept of assertion is tied to the notion of deciding to say something which does or does not mirror what you believe. 'Assertion' in the case of this machine just means, bringing out something in an assertoric mode, without putting qualifications around it.

It is, however, a notable feature of this machine that it could have true *B*-states which were non-accidentally arrived at, that is, which were not randomly turned out but were the product of the environment, the programming and so on; and these might be called 'knowledge'. We could say of this machine that it knows whether so and so is the case, that it knows when the aircraft leaves, that it knows where somebody left something, that it knows where it is itself, that it knows where certain buildings are in the town. I would claim in fact that the use of the word 'know' about this machine is not far away from a lot of uses we make of the word 'know' about human beings, whereas a use of 'believe' to refer to the *B*-states that this machine is in, is quite a long way away from the way in which we use the word 'believe'. There might be *some* machine to which we could properly ascribe beliefs; the point is that a machine to which we properly ascribed knowledge could be a lot more primitive than one to which we properly ascribed beliefs.

This goes against what is a rather deep prejudice in philosophy, that knowledge must be at least as grand as belief, that what knowledge is, is belief plus quite a lot; in particular, belief together with truth and good reasons. This approach seems to me largely mistaken. It is encouraged by concentrating on a very particular situation which academic writings about knowledge are notably fond of, that which might be called the *examiner* situation: the situation in which I know that *p* is true, this other man has asserted that *p* is true, and I ask the question whether this other man really knows it, or merely believes it. I am represented as checking on someone else's credentials for something about which I know already. That of course encourages the idea that knowledge is belief plus reasons and so forth. But this is far from our standard situation with regard to knowledge; our standard situation with regard to knowledge (in relation to other persons) is rather that of trying to find somebody who knows what we don't know; that is, to find somebody who is a source of reliable information about something. In this sense the machine could certainly know something. Our standard question is not

'Does Jones know that *p*?' Our standard question is rather 'Who knows whether *p*?'

As a matter of fact, even with 'Jones knows that *p*', we do not have to have all this elaborate exercise of reasons. Consider the following situation. They are engaged in this illicit love affair; she comes running in, and says 'He knows'. Her lover says: 'You mean he believes it? Well we know it's true. Now has he got good reasons for what he thinks?' She says, 'I think he just picked it up from the gossip next door.' Would her lover then be right in saying 'In that case, he doesn't know'? This would be absurd, basically, because 'he knows' here means 'he's found out', and not that he has very well grounded true beliefs. 'He's found out', however, does express more than 'he's guessed'. What 'he's found out' means is, very roughly, that he has acquired a true belief by an information-chain which starts somewhere near the facts themselves.

In his case, of course, we can speak of a belief. The point is that reflection on this and other common uses of 'know' suggests that much of the point of the concept of knowledge could be preserved if it were applied to things such as our machine which had, not beliefs, but something less.

With regard to the *B*-states, there could be false *B*-states that the machine was in; accidentally or randomly true *B*-states; and non-accidentally true *B*-states, that is *B*-states which were true and which came about in ways which were connected with the fact that they were true, and these last we could call knowledge. But for belief, full-blown belief, we need the possibility of deliberate reticence, not saying what I believe, and of insincerity, saying something other than what I believe. So in a sense we need the will; for it is only with the ability to decide to assert either what I believe or what I do not believe, the ability to decide to speak rather than to remain silent about something, that we get that dimension which is essential to belief, as opposed to the more primitive state, the *B*-state, which we can ascribe to the machine which satisfies the elementary conditions.

From the notion of what belief is, then, we arrive at one connexion between belief and decision, namely, the connexion between full-blown belief and the decision to say or not to say what I believe, the decision to use words to express or not to express what I believe. This is, however, a decision with regard to what we say and do; it is not the decision to believe something. Thus far, belief is connected with decision because belief is connected with the decision to say. It is not the case that belief is connected with any decision to believe. We have not got anything like that yet. Indeed, from what has already been said it seems that we have some rather good reasons for saying that there is not much room for deciding to believe. We might well think that beliefs were things which we, as it were, found we had (to put it very crudely), although we could decide whether to express these or not. In general one feels that this must be on the right track.

It fits in with the picture offered by Hume of belief as a passive phenomenon, something that happens to us. But there is something very peculiar about Hume's account; he seems to think that it is just a contingent fact about belief that it is something that happens to us. He says, in effect: There are some things you can decide and some things you cannot, and that just means that some things happen to respond to the will while others do not. It will be a blank contingent fact if belief does not respond to the will. Now we must agree that there are cases of what we may call contingent limitations on the will. For instance, suppose somebody says that he cannot blush at will. What would it be to blush at will? You could put yourself in a situation which you would guess would make you blush. That is getting yourself to blush —by a route—but it could not possibly count as blushing at will. Consider next the man who brings it about that he blushes by thinking of an embarrassing scene. That is getting a bit nearer to blushing at will, but is perhaps best described as making oneself blush at will. The best candidate of all would be somebody who could just blush in much the way that one can hold one's breath. I do not know whether people can do that, but if they cannot, it will be a contingent fact that they cannot.

Belief cannot be like that; it is not a contingent fact that I cannot bring it about, just like that, that I believe something, as it is a contingent fact that I cannot bring it about, just like that, that I'm blushing. Why is this? One reason is connected with the characteristic of beliefs that they aim at truth. If I could acquire a belief at will, I could acquire it whether it was true or not; moreover I would know that I could acquire it whether it was true or not. If in full consciousness I could will to

acquire a 'belief' irrespective of its truth, it is unclear that before the event I could seriously think of it as a belief, i.e. as something purporting to represent reality. At the very least, there must be a restriction on what is the case after the event; since I could not then, in full consciousness, regard this as a belief of mine, i.e. something I take to be true, and also know that I acquired it at will. With regard to no belief could I know—or, if all this is to be done in full consciousness, even suspect—that I had acquired it at will. But if I can acquire beliefs at will, I must know that I am able to do this; and could I know that I was capable of this feat, if with regard to every feat of this kind which I had performed I necessarily had to believe that it had not taken place?

Another reason stems from our considerations about perceptual belief: a very central idea with regard to empirical belief is that of coming to believe that *p* because it is so, that is, the relation between a man's perceptual environment, his perceptions, and the beliefs that result. Unless a concept satisfies the demands of that notion, namely that we can understand the idea that he comes to believe that *p* because it is so and because his perceptual organs are working, it will not be the concept of empirical belief; it will hardly even be that more impoverished notion which I have mentioned, the *B*-state. But a state that could be produced at will would not satisfy these demands, because there would be no regular connexion between the environment, the perceptions and what the man came out with, which is a necessary condition of a belief or even of a *B*-state.

However, even if it is granted that there is something necessarily bizarre about the idea of believing at will, just like that, it may be said that there is room for the application of decision to belief by more roundabout routes. For we all know that there are causal factors, unconnected with truth, which can produce belief: hypnotism, drugs, all sorts of things could bring it about that I believe that *p*. Suppose a man wanted to believe that *p* and knew that if he went to a hypnotist or a man who gave him certain drugs he would end up believing that *p*. Why could he not use this more roundabout method, granted that he cannot get himself into a state of believing just by lifting himself up by his own shoe straps; why could he not bring it about that he believes that *p* by adopting the policy of going to the hypnotist, the drug man or whatever? Well, in some cases he could and in some cases he could not; I am going to say something about the two sorts of cases. I am not going to discuss the issue of self-deception. The issue of self-deception is an important and complex issue in the philosophy of mind which gives rise to a large number of problems; of course it is true that people can deceive themselves into believing things that they know are false. But I am not going to discuss self-deception; what I am going to raise is rather this question: Why, if we're going to bring it about that we believe something in this kind of way, do we have to use self-deception; that is, what, if anything, is wrong with the idea of a conscious project to make myself believe what I want to believe?

The first thing we have to do is to distinguish between two senses or two applications of the notion of 'wanting to believe' something. I am going to distinguish these under the terms 'truth-centred motives' and 'non-truth-centred motives'. Suppose a man's son has apparently been killed in an accident. It is not absolutely certain he has, but there is very strong evidence that his son was drowned at sea. This man very much wants to believe that his son is alive. Somebody might say: If he wants to believe that his son is alive and this hypnotist can bring it about that he believes that his son is alive, then why should he not adopt the conscious project of going to the hypnotist and getting the hypnotist to make him believe this; then he will have got what he wants—after all, what he wants is to believe that his son is alive, and this is the state the hypnotist will have produced in him. But there is one sense—I think the more plausible one—of 'he wants to believe that his son is alive' in which this means *he wants his son to be alive*—what he essentially wants is the *truth* of his belief. This is what I call a truth-centred motive. The man with this sort of motive cannot conceivably consciously adopt this project, and we can immediately see why the project for him, is incoherent. For what he wants is something about the world, something about his son, namely, that he be alive, and he knows perfectly well that no amount of drugs, hypnotism and so on applied to himself is going to bring that about. So in the case of the 'truth-centred motives', where *wanting to believe* means *wanting it to be the case,* we can see perfectly clearly why this sort of project is impossible and incoherent.

However, he might have a different sort of motive, a non-truth-centred motive. This would be the case if he

said, 'Well, of course what I would like best of all is for my son to be alive; but I cannot change the world in this respect. The point is, though that even if my son isn't alive, I want, I need to believe that he is, because I am so intolerably miserable knowing that he isn't.' Or again a man may want to believe something not caring a damn about the truth of it but because it is fashionable or comfortable or in accordance with the demands of social conformity to believe that thing. Might not such a man, wanting to believe this thing, set out to use the machinery of drugs, hypnotism, or whatever to bring it about that he did? In this case the project does not seem evidently incoherent in the way in which the project was incoherent for the man with the truth-centred motive. What it is, is very deeply irrational, and I think that most of us would have a very strong impulse against engaging in a project of this kind however uncomfortable these truths were which we were having to live with. Why? What is the source of our very strong internalised objection to this kind of project?

I will raise one or two questions which may assist in the discussion of this. First, is the project of trying to get yourself to believe something because it is more comfortable fundamentally different or not from the project (more familiar, and, it might seem, more acceptable) of trying to forget something because it is uncomfortable? That is, if I just wanted to forget what was disagreeable, would this be very different in principle from the project of actually trying to believe something which is untrue? Is the project of trying to forget the true morally or psychologically different from the project of trying to get oneself to believe the false? If so, why? Is one of them easier than the other? If so why? I would add to that question the suggestion that there is almost certainly a genuine asymmetry here, tied in to the asymmetry that while every belief I have ought ideally to be true, it is not the case that every truth ought ideally to be something I believe: belief aims at truth, knowledge does not similarly aim at completeness.

Perhaps, further, one objection to the projects of believing what is false is that there is no end to the amount you have to pull down. It is like a revolutionary movement trying to extirpate the last remains of the *ancien régime*. The man gets rid of this belief about his son, and then there is some belief which strongly implies that his son is dead, and that has to be got rid of. Then there is another belief which could lead his thoughts in the undesired direction, and that has to be got rid of. It might be that a project of this kind tended in the end to involve total destruction of the world of reality, to lead to paranoia. Perhaps this is one reason why we have a strongly internalised objection to it. If we are not going to destroy all the evidence—all consciousness of the evidence—we have to have a project for steering ourselves through the world so as to avoid the embarrassing evidence. That sort of project is the project of the man who is deceiving himself, and he must really know what is true; for if he did not really know what was true, he would not be able to steer around the contrary and conflicting evidence. Whether we should or should not say that he also believes what he really knows to be true, is one of the problems that surround self-deception. But at least the project that leads to that condition, the project of self-deception, is something different from the blank projects of belief-inducement which we were considering.

AESTHETICS

Aʀт is philosophically problematic. Marcel Duchamp took an ordinary urinal, signed it with a fake name, titled it *Fountain,* and displayed it in an art museum. Was it a work of art? If so, what made it art? Paintings by gorillas and chimpanzees were hung in the Field Museum, a museum of natural history in Chicago. Were they art? If not, would they have been art if they had been hung in the Art Institute of Chicago instead? Neolithic paintings have been found in caves in France and Spain. Are they art? What about ritual objects such as elaborate censers or masks? Does it matter whether their creators thought of them, or had the capacity to think of them, as art?

To answer such questions, it seems, we need a definition of 'art'. Any term can be given an arbitrary definition, but that is not what we seek. We want a real definition, one that succeeds in distinguishing between things that are really art and things that are not. Minimally, under such a definition, the term 'art' should apply to all the cases we are confident are works of art, should fail to apply to all the cases we are confident are not works of art, and should decide the hard cases in ways that seem non-arbitrary. Coming up with such a definition is difficult, for artists are creative. They regularly violate established artistic conventions and yet come up with works that we are inclined to classify as art.

Philosophers of art long believed that art imitates life. So they believed that an item's imitating something real is a necessary condition of its being a work of art. They conveniently overlooked how implausible this is as a theory of music. But even in the visual arts it fails, for it cannot accommodate Postimpressionist works—abstracts of various kinds that are not, and do not purport to be, pictures of anything. What then is the definition of art?

Several of the papers that follow attempt to answer this question. Tolstoy maintains that the essence of art is the transmission of feeling from the artist to his audience. The more morally refined the feeling and the wider the audience, the better the art. This makes art essentially intersubjective. Whether something is a work of art depends not just on the object and the artist, but also on the receptivity of the audience. Tolstoy thus considers works that require sensitivity, acuity, experience, or background knowledge to be inferior to works that do not. That his own great works, *War and Peace* and *Anna Karenina,* do not fare well on his account casts doubt on the adequacy of his theory.

Even if we discount the appeals to morality and universality, it is not obvious that all works of art involve the transmission of the artist's feeling. We would not deny Beethoven's ninth symphony the status of art, even if we discovered that he never felt the joy that the work expresses. We are apt to count works like Mondrian's paintings as works of art even though they seem not to express feelings at all. Although Tolstoy's theory captures something important about some art, we may doubt that it yields a real definition of art.

Danto maintains that something is a work of art by virtue of its being accommodated by an aesthetic theory. So there must be aesthetic theories in order for anything to be a work of art. What makes *Fountain* a work of art is the existence of a theory that counts it as art. This raises the question: Does something that already exists become a work of art when a suitable theory is devised? Did the Lescaux painting become art when someone came up with a suitable theory? Or were they art all along? Or were they never art, since they were painted at a time when there was no theory to accommodate them?

Whereas Danto focuses on theories, Dickie focuses on institutions. He argues that the art-world is a social institution that confers the status of art on certain objects. So the gorilla paintings in the natural history museum are not art, but if they were in the art museum, they would be art. For unlike their counterparts in the natural history museum, curators in the art museum have the authority to confer the status of art. (See also the *Euthyphro,* pp. 450–58, and the introduction to the section on ethics, pp. 444–9.) Theories such as Danto's and Dickie's seem to make an object's status as art depend on a framework that surrounds it. Even paradigm cases of art—such as *Hamlet, Swan Lake,* and *The Night Watch*—only merit the status of art because certain institutional or theoretical structures accommodate them. Is this plausible? Or would those works be art even if other institutional or theoretical structures were in place?

Goodman seeks to change the question. 'What is art?' he maintains, assumes that an object either definitely has the status of art or it does not. Instead, we should ask, 'When is art?' That is, under what circumstances does an item function as art? A single item, such as a urinal or a piece of driftwood, might function as a work of art in some circumstances but not in others. Whether an item functions as art is not a matter of what feelings it transmits, or what theories apply to it, or what status an institution confers on it. It is a matter of how the item symbolizes. If it does so in a way that tends to focus attention on the symbol itself, rather than its referent, or its practical function, or its artist, it arguably functions as art. So looked at in a certain way, treated as a symbol of a particular kind, the urinal, the gorilla painting, and the piece of driftwood might all function as art. This does not answer the question of whether something is art, but it does address the question of what it is to treat something as art.

Some people like jazz; others do not. This is, we think, easily explained: They have different tastes in music. Hume agrees. Taste, he maintains, is a matter of feeling or, as he calls it, 'sentiment'. But this raises a problem. There is, we think, no accounting for matters of taste. George likes butterscotch ice cream; Fred does not. But Fred has no basis for saying that George is wrong to like butterscotch ice cream or that pistachio is better than butterscotch ice cream. But when it comes to art, we discriminate between good and bad taste. Anyone who thinks that Clementi is a better composer than Mozart has bad taste in music; anyone who thinks that Longfellow is a better poet than Shakespeare has bad taste in poetry. But if taste is just a feeling—a liking or disliking—what is the basis for such claims?

Hume provides an answer. He recognizes that sentiments are often confounded by irrelevant factors. Since most people cannot disentangle the irrelevancies in their responses to works of art, most people, to one degree or another, lack good taste. If you like a song because it reminds you of your high school sweetheart or a painting because you consider it a good investment, your liking is sincere, but it is not indicative of the aesthetic properties of the works. It is not a manifestation of good taste. An aesthetic response, Hume believes, should be disinterested. It should not be infected with personal or practical concerns. The standard of taste, he believes, is a feeling of liking or disliking. But it is the liking or disliking that would be felt by a disinterested observer. For only such an observer's responses are reflective of the aesthetic properties of a work. Does this resolve the problem? If it works for art, does it also work for ice cream?

Kant does not think that aesthetic reactions are mere expressions of a sentiment. We make aesthetic judgments. Such judgments are subjective in that they are grounded in pleasure or displeasure. But they are judgments; they make a claim on others. If I say, 'This painting pleases me', I announce only that I like it. But if I say, 'This painting is beautiful', I make a universal claim. I contend that everyone else should like it too. The question for Kant is how a subjective reaction can make a claim to universality. His answer, like Hume's, is grounded in such reactions being disinterested. There is nothing special about me or my relation to the painting that accounts for my reaction, so others should have the same reaction. The disinterestedness of my reaction then allows me to claim universal validity for it. Kant cannot prove that aesthetic judgments are in fact universally valid. But he can explain why they are felt as universally valid and can show that it is not impossible that we are right to consider them universally valid.

One question for Hume and Kant is whether all art, or even all good art, is beautiful. If it is not, then not all aesthetic responses are responses to beauty. Another question is whether disinterestedness is sufficient to yield universality. Does the fact that there is nothing idiosyncratic about a response show that everyone else should have the same response?

David Hume

Of the Standard of Taste

The great variety of Taste, as well as of opinion, which prevails in the world, is too obvious not to have fallen under every one's observation. Men of the most confined knowledge are able to remark a difference of taste in the narrow circle of their acquaintance, even where the persons have been educated under the same government, and have early imbibed the same prejudices. But those, who can enlarge their view to contemplate distant nations and remote ages, are still more surprised at the great inconsistence and contrariety. We are apt to call *barbarous* whatever departs widely from our own taste and apprehension: But soon find the epithet of reproach retorted on us. And the highest arrogance and self-conceit is at last startled, on observing an equal assurance on all sides, and scruples, amidst such a contest of sentiment, to pronounce positively in its own favour.

As this variety of taste is obvious to the most careless enquirer; so will it be found, on examination, to be still greater in reality than in appearance. The sentiments of men often differ with regard to beauty and deformity of all kinds, even while their general discourse is the same. There are certain terms in every language, which import blame, and others praise; and all men, who use the same tongue, must agree in their application of them. Every voice is united in applauding elegance, propriety, simplicity, spirit in writing; and in blaming fustian, affectation, coldness, and a false brilliancy: But when critics come to particulars, this seeming unanimity vanishes; and it is found, that they had affixed a very different meaning to their expressions. In all matters of opinion and science, the case is opposite: The difference among men is there oftener found to lie in generals than in particulars; and to be less in reality than in appearance. An explanation of the terms commonly ends the controversy; and the disputants are surprised to find, that they had been quarrelling, while at bottom they agreed in their judgment.

Those who found morality on sentiment, more than on reason, are inclined to comprehend ethics under the former observation, and to maintain, that, in all questions, which regard conduct and manners, the difference among men is really greater than at first sight it appears. It is indeed obvious, that writers of all nations and all ages concur in applauding justice, humanity, magnanimity, prudence, veracity; and in blaming the opposite qualities. Even poets and other authors, whose compositions are chiefly calculated to please the imagination, are yet found from HOMER down to FENELON, to inculcate the same moral precepts, and to bestow their applause and blame on the same virtues and vices. This great unanimity is usually ascribed to the influence of plain reason; which, in all these cases, maintains similar sentiments in all men, and prevents those controversies, to which the abstract sciences are so much exposed. So far as the unanimity is real, this account may be admitted as satisfactory: But we must also allow that some part of the seeming harmony in morals may be accounted for from the very nature of language. The word *virtue,* with its equivalent in every tongue, implies praise; as that of *vice* does blame: And no one, without the most obvious and grossest impropriety, could affix reproach to a term, which in general acceptation is understood in a good sense; or bestow applause, where the idiom requires disapprobation. HOMER's general precepts, where he delivers any such, will never be controverted; but it is obvious, that, when he draws particular pictures of manners, and represents heroism in ACHILLES and prudence in ULYSSES, he intermixes a much greater degree of ferocity in the former, and of cunning and fraud in the latter, than FENELON would admit of. The sage ULYSSES in the GREEK poet seems to delight in lies and fictions, and often employs them without any necessity or even advantage: But his more scrupulous son, in the FRENCH epic writer, exposes himself to the most imminent perils, rather than depart from the most exact line of truth and veracity.

The admirers and followers of the ALCORAN insist on the excellent moral precepts interspersed throughout that wild and absurd performance. But it is to be

From David Hume, *Moral Philosophy*, edited by Geoffrey Sayre-McCord (Indianapolis: Hackett Publishing Company, 2006). Reprinted by permission of the publisher.

supposed, that the ARABIC words, which correspond to the ENGLISH, equity, justice, temperance, meekness, charity, were such as, from the constant use of that tongue, must always be taken in a good sense; and it would have argued the greatest ignorance, not of morals, but of language, to have mentioned them with any epithets, besides those of applause and approbation. But would we know, whether the pretended prophet had really attained a just sentiment of morals? Let us attend to his narration; and we shall soon find, that he bestows praise on such instances of treachery, inhumanity, cruelty, revenge, bigotry, as are utterly in compatible with civilized society. No steady rule of right seems there to be attended to; and every action is blamed or praised, so far only as it is beneficial or hurtful to the true believers.

The merit of delivering true general precepts in ethics is indeed very small. Whoever recommends any moral virtues, really does no more than is implied in the terms themselves. That people, who invented the word *charity,* and used it in a good sense, inculcated more clearly and much more efficaciously, the precept, *be charitable,* than any pretended legislator or prophet, who should insert such a *maxim* in his writings. Of all expressions, those which, together with their other meaning, imply a degree either of blame or approbation, are the least liable to be perverted or mistaken.

It is natural for us to seek a *Standard of Taste;* a rule, by which the various sentiments of men may be reconciled; at least, a decision, afforded, confirming one sentiment, and condemning another.

There is a species of philosophy, which cuts off all hopes of success in such an attempt, and represents the impossibility of ever attaining any standard of taste. The difference, it is said, is very wide between judgment and sentiment. All sentiment is right; because sentiment has a reference to nothing beyond itself, and is always real, wherever a man is conscious of it. But all determinations of the understanding are not right; because they have a reference to something beyond themselves, to wit, real matter of fact; and are not always conformable to that standard. Among a thousand different opinions which different men may entertain of the same subject, there is one, and but one, that is just and true; and the only difficulty is to fix and ascertain it. On the contrary, a thousand different sentiments, excited by the same object, are all right: Because no sentiment represents what

is really in the object. It only marks a certain conformity or relation between the object and the organs or faculties of the mind; and if that conformity did not really exist, the sentiment could never possibly have being. Beauty is no quality in things themselves: It exists merely in the mind which contemplates them; and each mind perceives a different beauty. One person may even perceive deformity, where another is sensible of beauty; and every individual ought to acquiesce in his own sentiment, without pretending to regulate those of others. To seek the real beauty, or real deformity, is as fruitless an enquiry, as to pretend to ascertain the real sweet or real bitter. According to the disposition of the organs, the same object may be both sweet and bitter; and the proverb has justly determined it to be fruitless to dispute concerning tastes. It is very natural, and even quite necessary, to extend this axiom to mental, as well as bodily taste; and thus common sense, which is so often at variance with philosophy, especially with the sceptical kind, is found, in one instance at least, to agree in pronouncing the same decision.

But though this axiom, by passing into a proverb, seems to have attained the sanction of common sense; there is certainly a species of common sense which opposes it, at least serves to modify and restrain it. Whoever would assert an equality of genius and elegance between OGILBY and MILTON, or BUNYAN and ADDISON, would be thought to defend no less an extravagance, than if he had maintained a mole-hill to be as high as TENERIFFE, or a pond as extensive as the ocean. Though there may be found persons, who give the preference to the former authors; no one pays attention to such a taste; and we pronounce without scruple the sentiment of these pretended critics to be absurd and ridiculous. The principle of the natural equality of tastes is then totally forgot, and while we admit it on some occasions, where the objects seem near an equality, it appears an extravagant paradox, or rather a palpable absurdity, where objects so disproportioned are compared together.

It is evident that none of the rules of composition are fixed by reasonings *a priori,* or can be esteemed abstract conclusions of the understanding, from comparing those habitudes and relations of ideas, which are eternal and immutable. Their foundation is the same with that of all the practical sciences, experience; nor are they any thing but general observations, concerning what has been universally found to please in all countries and in all ages. Many of the beauties of poetry and even of eloquence are founded on falsehood and fiction, on hyperboles, metaphors, and an abuse or perversion of terms from their natural meaning. To check the sallies of the imagination, and to reduce every expression to geometrical truth' and exactness, would be the most contrary to the laws of criticism; because it would produce a work, which, by universal experience, has been found the most insipid and disagreeable. But though poetry can never submit to exact truth, it must be confined by rules of art, discovered to the author either by genius or observation. If some negligent or irregular writers have pleased, they have not pleased by their transgressions of rule or order, but in spite of these transgressions: They have possessed other beauties, which were conformable to just criticism; and the force of these beauties has been able to overpower censure, and give the mind a satisfaction superior to the disgust arising from the blemishes. ARIOSTO pleases; but not by his monstrous and improbable fictions, by his bizarre mixture of the serious and comic styles, by the want of coherence in his stories, or by the continual interruptions of his narration. He charms by the force and clearness of his expression, by the readiness and variety of his inventions, and by his natural pictures of the passions, especially those of the gay and amorous kind: And however his faults may diminish our satisfaction, they are not able entirely to destroy it. Did our pleasure really arise from those parts of his poem, which we denominate faults, this would be no objection to criticism in general: It would only be an objection to those particular rules of criticism, which would establish such circumstances to be faults, and would represent them as universally blameable. If they are found to please, they cannot be faults; let the pleasure, which they produce, be ever so unexpected and unaccountable.

But though all the general rules of art are founded only on experience and on the observation of the common sentiments of human nature, we must not imagine, that, on every occasion, the feelings of men will be conformable to these rules. Those finer emotions of the mind are of a very tender and delicate nature, and require the concurrence of many favourable circumstances to make them play with facility and exactness,

according to their general and established principles. The least exterior hindrance to such small springs, or the least internal disorder, disturbs their motion, and confounds the operation of the whole machine. When we would make an experiment of this nature, and would try the force of any beauty or deformity, we must choose with care a proper time and place, and bring the fancy to a suitable situation and disposition. A perfect serenity of mind, a recollection of thought, a due attention to the object; if any of these circumstances be wanting, our experiment will be fallacious, and we shall be unable to judge of the catholic and universal beauty. The relation, which nature has placed between the form and the sentiment, will at least be more obscure; and it will require greater accuracy to trace and discern it. We shall be able to ascertain its influence not so much from the operation of each particular beauty, as from the durable admiration, which attends those works, that have survived all the caprices of mode and fashion, all the mistakes of ignorance and envy.

The same HOMER, who pleased at ATHENS and ROME two thousand years ago, is still admired at PARIS and at LONDON. All the changes of climate, government, religion, and language, have not been able to obscure his glory. Authority or prejudice may give a temporary vogue to a bad poet or orator; but his reputation will never be durable or general. When his compositions are examined by posterity or by foreigners, the enchantment is dissipated, and his faults appear in their true colours. On the contrary, a real genius, the longer his works endure, and the more wide they are spread, the more sincere is the admiration which he meets with. Envy and jealousy have too much place in a narrow circle; and even familiar acquaintance with his person may diminish the applause due to his performances: But when these obstructions are removed, the beauties, which are naturally fitted to excite agreeable sentiments, immediately display their energy; and while the world endures, they maintain their authority over the minds of men.

It appears then, that, amidst all the variety and caprice of taste, there are certain general principles of approbation or blame, whose influence a careful eye may trace in all operations of the mind. Some particular forms or qualities, from the original structure of the internal fabric, are calculated to please, and others to displease; and if they fail of their effect in any particular instance, it is from some apparent defect or imperfection in the organ. A man in a fever would not insist on his palate as able to decide concerning flavours; nor would one, affected with the jaundice, pretend to give a verdict with regard to colours. In each creature, there is a sound and a defective state; and the former alone can be supposed to afford us a true standard of taste and sentiment. If, in the sound state of the organ, there be an entire or a considerable uniformity of sentiment among men, we may thence derive an idea of the perfect beauty; in like manner as the appearance of objects in day-light, to the eye of a man in health, is denominated their true and real colour, even while colour is allowed to be merely a phantasm of the senses.

Many and frequent are the defects in the internal organs, which prevent or weaken the influence of those general principles, on which depends our sentiment of beauty or deformity. Though some objects, by the structure of the mind, be naturally calculated to give pleasure, it is not to be expected, that in every individual the pleasure will be equally felt. Particular incidents and situations occur, which either throw a false light on the objects, or hinder the true from conveying to the imagination the proper sentiment and perception.

One obvious cause, why many feel not the proper sentiment of beauty, is the want of that *delicacy* of imagination, which is requisite to convey a sensibility of those finer emotions. This delicacy every one pretends to: Every one talks of it; and would reduce every kind of taste or sentiment to its standard. But as our intention in this essay is to mingle some light of the understanding with the feelings of sentiment, it will be proper to give a more accurate definition of delicacy, than has hitherto been attempted. And not to draw our philosophy from too profound a source, we shall have recourse to a noted story in DON QUIXOTE.

It is with good reason, says SANCHO to the squire with the great nose, that I pretend to have a judgment in wine: This is a quality hereditary in our family. Two of my kinsmen were once called to give their opinion of a hogshead, which was supposed to be excellent, being old and of a good vintage. One of them tastes it; considers it; and after mature reflection pronounces the wine to be good, were it not for a small taste of leather, which he perceived in it. The other, after using the same precautions, gives also his verdict in favour of the wine;

but with the reserve of a taste of iron, which he could easily distinguish. You cannot imagine how much they were both ridiculed for their judgment. But who laughed in the end? On emptying the hogshead, there was found at the bottom, an old key with a leathern thong tied to it.

The great resemblance between mental and bodily taste will easily teach us to apply this story. Though it be certain, that beauty and deformity, more than sweet and bitter, are not qualities in objects, but belong entirely to the sentiment, internal or external; it must be allowed, that there are certain qualities in objects, which are fitted by nature to produce those particular feelings. Now as these qualities may be found in a small degree, or may be mixed and confounded with each other, it often happens, that the taste is not affected with such minute qualities, or is not able to distinguish all the particular flavours, amidst the disorder, in which they are presented. Where the organs are so fine, as to allow nothing to escape them; and at the same time so exact as to perceive every ingredient in the composition: This we call delicacy of taste, whether we employ these terms in the literal or metaphorical sense. Here then the general rules of beauty are of use; being drawn from established models, and from the observation of what pleases or displeases, when presented singly and in a high degree: And if the same qualities, in a continued composition and in a smaller degree, affect not the organs with a sensible delight or uneasiness, we exclude the person from all pretensions to this delicacy. To produce these general rules or avowed patterns of composition is like finding the key with the leathern thong; which justified the verdict of SANCHO's kinsmen, and confounded those pretended judges who had condemned them. Though the hogshead had never been emptied, the taste of the one was still equally delicate, and that of the other equally dull and languid: But it would have been more difficult to have proved the superiority of the former, to the conviction of every bystander. In like manner, though the beauties of writing had never been methodized, or reduced to general principles; though no excellent models had ever been acknowledged; the different degrees of taste would still have subsisted, and the judgment of one man been preferable to that of another; but it would not have been so easy to silence the bad critic, who might always insist upon his particular sentiment, and refuse to submit to his antagonist. But when we show him an avowed principle of art; when we illustrate this principle by examples, whose operation, from his own particular taste, he acknowledges to be conformable to the principle; when we prove, that the same principle may be applied to the present case, where he did not perceive or feel its influence: He must conclude, upon the whole, that the fault lies in himself, and that he wants the delicacy, which is requisite to make him sensible of every beauty and every blemish, in any composition or discourse.

It is acknowledged to be the perfection of every sense or faculty, to perceive with exactness its most minute objects, and allow nothing to escape its notice and observation. The smaller the objects are, which become sensible to the eye, the finer is that organ, and the more elaborate its make and composition. A good palate is not tried by strong flavours; but by a mixture of small ingredients, where we are still sensible of each part, notwithstanding its minuteness and its confusion with the rest. In like manner, a quick and acute perception of beauty and deformity must be the perfection of our mental taste; nor can a man be satisfied with himself while he suspects, that any excellence or blemish in a discourse has passed him unobserved. In this case, the perfection of the man, and the perfection of the sense or feeling, are found to be united. A very delicate palate, on many occasions, may be a great inconvenience both to a man himself and to his friends: But a delicate taste of wit or beauty must always be a desirable quality; because it is the source of all the finest and most innocent enjoyments, of which human nature is susceptible. In this decision the sentiments of all mankind are agreed. Wherever you can ascertain a delicacy of taste, it is sure to meet with approbation; and the best way of ascertaining it is to appeal to those models and principles, which have been established by the uniform consent and experience of nations and ages.

But though there be naturally a wide difference in point of delicacy between one person and another, nothing tends further to encrease and improve this talent, than *practice* in a particular art, and the frequent survey or contemplation of a particular species of beauty. When objects of any kind are first presented to the eye or imagination, the sentiment, which attends them, is obscure and confused; and the mind is, in a great mea-

sure, incapable of pronouncing concerning their merits or defects. The taste cannot perceive the several excellencies of the performance; much less distinguish the particular character of each excellency, and ascertain its quality and degree. If it pronounce the whole in general to be beautiful or deformed, it is the utmost that can be expected; and even this judgment, a person, so unpractised, will be apt to deliver with great hesitation and reserve. But allow him to acquire experience in those objects, his feeling becomes more exact and nice: He not only perceives the beauties and defects of each part, but marks the distinguishing species of each quality, and assigns it suitable praise or blame. A clear and distinct sentiment attends him through the whole survey of the objects; and he discerns that very degree and kind of approbation or displeasure, which each part is naturally fitted to produce. The mist dissipates, which seemed formerly to hang over the object: The organ acquires greater perfection in its operations; and can pronounce, without danger of mistake, concerning the merits of every performance. In a word, the same address and dexterity, which practice gives to the execution of any work, is also acquired by the same means, in the judging of it.

So advantageous is practice to the discernment of beauty, that, before we can give judgment on any work of importance, it will even be requisite, that that very individual performance be more than once perused by us, and be surveyed in different lights with attention and deliberation. There is a flutter or hurry of thought which attends the first perusal of any piece, and which confounds the genuine sentiment of beauty. The relation of the parts is not discerned: The true characters of style are little distinguished: The several perfections ,and defects seem wrapped up in a species of confusion, and present themselves indistinctly to the imagination. Not to mention, that there is a species of beauty, which, as it is florid and superficial, pleases at first; but being found incompatible with a just expression either of reason or passion, soon palls upon the taste, and is then rejected with disdain, at least rated at a much lower value.

It is impossible to continue in the practice of contemplating any order of beauty, without being frequently obliged to form *comparisons* between the several species and degrees of excellence, and estimating their proportion to each other. A man, who has had no opportunity of comparing the different kinds of beauty, is indeed totally unqualified to pronounce an opinion with regard to any object presented to him. By comparison alone we fix the epithets of praise or blame, and learn how to assign the due degree of each. The coarsest daubing contains a certain lustre of colours and exactness of imitation, which are so far beauties, and would affect the mind of a peasant or Indian with the highest admiration. The most vulgar ballads are not entirely destitute of harmony or nature; and none but a person, familiarized to superior beauties, would pronounce their numbers harsh, or narration uninteresting. A great inferiority of beauty gives pain to a person conversant in the highest excellence of the kind, and is for that reason pronounced a deformity: As the most finished object, with which we are acquainted, is naturally supposed to have reached the pinnacle of perfection, and to be entitled to the highest applause. One accustomed to see, and examine, and weigh the several performances, admired in different ages and nations, can alone rate the merits of a work exhibited to his view, and assign its proper rank among the productions of genius.

But to enable a critic the more fully to execute this undertaking, he must preserve his mind free from all *prejudice,* and allow nothing to enter into his consideration, but the very object which is submitted to his examination. We may observe, that every work of art, in order to produce its due effect on the mind, must be surveyed in a certain point of view, and cannot be fully relished by persons, whose situation, real or imaginary, is not conformable to that which is required by the performance. An orator addresses himself to a particular audience, and must have a regard to their particular genius, interests, opinions, passions, and prejudices; otherwise he hopes in vain to govern their resolutions, and inflame their affections. Should they even have entertained some prepossessions against him, however unreasonable, he must not overlook this disadvantage; but, before he enters upon the subject, must endeavour to conciliate their affection, and acquire their good graces. A critic of a different age or nation, who should peruse this discourse, must have all these circumstances in his eye, and must place himself in the same situation as the audience, in order to form a true judgment of the oration. In like manner, when any work is addressed to the public, though I should have a friendship or enmity with the author, I must depart from this situation; and considering myself as a man in general, forget, if possible, my individual being and my peculiar circumstances. A person influenced by prejudice, complies not with this condition; but obstinately maintains his natural position, without placing himself in that point of view, which the performance supposes. If the work be addressed to persons of a different age or nation, he makes no allowance for their peculiar views and prejudices; but, full of the manners of his own age and country, rashly condemns what seemed admirable in the eyes of those for whom alone the discourse was calculated. If the work be executed for the public, he never sufficiently enlarges his comprehension, or forgets his interest as a friend or enemy, as a rival or commentator. By this means, his sentiments are perverted; nor have the same beauties and blemishes the same influence upon him, as if he had imposed a proper violence on his imagination, and had forgotten himself for a moment. So far his taste evidently departs from the true standard; and of consequence loses all credit and authority.

It is well known, that in all questions, submitted to the understanding, prejudice is destructive of sound judgment, and perverts all operations of the intellectual faculties: It is no less contrary to good taste; nor has it less influence to corrupt our sentiment of beauty. It belongs to *good sense* to check its influence in both cases; and in this respect, as well as in many others, reason, if not an essential part of taste, is at least requisite to the operations of this latter faculty. In all the nobler productions of genius, there is a mutual relation and correspondence of parts; nor can either the beauties or blemishes be perceived by him, whose thought is not capacious enough to comprehend all those parts, and compare them with each other, in order to perceive the consistence and uniformity of the whole. Every work of art has also a certain end or purpose, for which it is calculated; and is to be deemed more or less perfect, as it is more or less fitted to attain this end. The object of eloquence is to persuade, of history to instruct, of poetry to please by means of the passions and the imagination. These ends we must carry constantly in our view, when we peruse any performance; and we must be able to judge how far the means employed are adapted to their respective purposes. Besides, every kind of composition, even the most poetical, is nothing but a chain of propositions and reasonings; not always, indeed, the justest and most exact, but still plausible and specious, however disguised by the colouring of the imagination. The persons introduced in tragedy and epic poetry, must be represented as reasoning, and thinking, and concluding, and acting, suitably to their character and circumstances; and without judgment, as well as taste and invention, a poet can never hope to succeed in so delicate an undertaking. Not to mention, that the same excellence of faculties which contributes to the improvement of reason, the same clearness of conception, the same exactness of distinction, the same vivacity of apprehension, are essential to the operations of true taste, and are its infallible concomitants. It seldom, or never happens, that a man of sense, who has experience in any art, cannot judge of its beauty; and it is no less rare to meet with a man who has a just taste without a sound understanding.

Thus, though the principles of taste be universal, and nearly, if not entirely the same in all men; yet few are qualified to give judgment on any work of art, or establish their own sentiment as the standard of beauty. The organs of internal sensation are seldom so perfect as to allow the general principles their full play, and produce a feeling correspondent to those principles. They either labour under some defect, or are vitiated by some disorder; and by that means, excite a sentiment, which may be pronounced erroneous. When the critic has no delicacy, he judges without any distinction, and is only affected by the grosser and more palpable qualities of the object: The finer touches pass unnoticed and disregarded. Where he is not aided by practice, his verdict is attended with confusion and hesitation. Where no comparison has been employed, the most frivolous beauties, such as rather merit the name of defects, are the object of his admiration. Where he lies under the influence of prejudice, all his natural sentiments are perverted. Where good sense is wanting, he is not qualified to discern the beauties of design and reasoning, which are the highest and most excellent. Under some or other of these imperfections, the generality of men labour; and hence a true judge in the finer arts is observed, even during the most polished ages, to be so rare a character: Strong

sense, united to delicate sentiment, improved by practice, perfected by comparison, and cleared of all prejudice, can alone entitle critics to this valuable character; and the joint verdict of such, wherever they are to be found, is the true standard of taste and beauty.

But where are such critics to be found? By what marks are they to be known? How distinguish them from pretenders? These questions are embarrassing; and seem to throw us back into the same uncertainty, from which, during the course of this essay, we have endeavoured to extricate ourselves.

But if we consider the matter aright, these are questions of fact, not of sentiment. Whether any particular person be endowed with good sense and a delicate imagination, free from prejudice, may often be the subject of dispute, and be liable to great discussion and enquiry: But that such a character is valuable and estimable will be agreed in by all mankind. Where these doubts occur, men can do no more than in other disputable questions, which are submitted to the understanding: They must produce the best arguments, that their invention suggests to them; they must acknowledge a true and decisive standard to exist somewhere, to wit, real existence and matter of fact; and they must have indulgence to such as differ from them in their appeals to this standard. It is sufficient for our present purpose, if we have proved, that the taste of all individuals is not upon an equal footing, and that some men in general, however difficult to be particularly pitched upon, will be acknowledged by universal sentiment to have a preference above others.

But in reality the difficulty of finding, even in particulars, the standard of taste, is not so great as it is represented. Though in speculation, we may readily avow a certain criterion in science and deny it in sentiment, the matter is found in practice to be much more hard to ascertain in the former case than in the latter. Theories of abstract philosophy, systems of profound theology, have prevailed during one age: In a successive period, these have been universally exploded: Their absurdity has been detected: Other theories and systems have supplied their place, which again gave place to their successors: And nothing has been experienced more liable to the revolutions of chance and fashion than these pretended decisions of science. The case is not the same with the beauties of eloquence and poetry. Just expressions of passion and nature are sure, after a little time, to gain public applause, which they maintain for ever. ARISTOTLE, and PLATO, and EPICURUS, and DESCARTES, may successively yield to each other: But TERENCE and VIRGIL maintain an universal, undisputed empire over the minds of men. The abstract philosophy of CICERO has lost its credit: The vehemence of his oratory is still the object of our admiration.

Though men of delicate taste be rare, they are easily to be distinguished in society, by the soundness of their understanding and the superiority of their faculties above the rest of mankind. The ascendant which they acquire, gives a prevalence to that lively approbation, with which they receive any productions of genius, and renders it generally predominant. Many men, when left to themselves, have but a faint and dubious perception of beauty, who yet are capable of relishing any fine stroke, which is pointed out to them. Every convert to the admiration of the real poet or orator is the cause of some new conversion. And though prejudices may prevail for a time, they never unite in celebrating any rival to the true genius, but yield at last to the force of nature and just sentiment. Thus, though a civilized nation may easily be mistaken in the choice of their admired philosopher, they never have been found long to err, in their affection for a favourite epic or tragic author.

But notwithstanding all our endeavours to fix a standard of taste, and reconcile the discordant apprehensions of men, there still remain two sources of variation, which are not sufficient indeed to confound all the boundaries of beauty and deformity, but will often serve to produce a difference in the degrees of our approbation or blame. The one is the different humours of particular men; the other, the particular manners and opinions of our age and country. The general principles of taste are uniform in human nature: Where men vary in their judgments, some defect or perversion in the faculties may commonly be remarked; proceeding either from prejudice, from want of practice, or want of delicacy; and there is just reason for approving one taste, and condemning another. But where there is such a diversity in the internal frame or external situation as is entirely blameless on both sides, and leaves no room to give one the preference above the other; in that case a certain degree of diversity in judgment is unavoidable, and we seek in vain for a standard, by which we can reconcile the contrary sentiments.

A young man, whose passions are warm, will be more sensibly touched with amorous and tender images, than a man more advanced in years, who takes pleasure in wise, philosophical reflections concerning the conduct of life and moderation of the passions. At twenty, OVID may be the favourite author; HORACE at forty; and perhaps TACITUS at fifty. Vainly would we, in such cases, endeavour to enter into the sentiments of others, and divest ourselves of those propensities, which are natural to us. We choose our favourite author as we do our friend, from a conformity of humour and disposition. Mirth or passion, sentiment or reflection; whichever of these most predominates in our temper, it gives us a peculiar sympathy with the writer who resembles us.

One person is more pleased with the sublime; another with the tender; a third with raillery. One has a strong sensibility to blemishes, and is extremely studious of correctness: Another has a more lively feeling of beauties, and pardons twenty absurdities and defects for one elevated or pathetic stroke. The ear of this man is entirely turned towards conciseness and energy; that man is delighted with a copious, rich, and harmonious expression. Simplicity is affected by one; ornament by another. Comedy, tragedy, satire, odes, have each its partizans, who prefer that particular species of writing to all others. It is plainly an error in a critic, to confine his approbation to one species or style of writing, and condemn all the rest. But it is almost impossible not to feel a predilection for that which suits our particular turn and disposition. Such preferences are innocent and unavoidable, and can never reasonably be the object of dispute, because there is no standard, by which they can be decided.

For a like reason, we are more pleased, in the course of our reading, with pictures and characters, that resemble objects which are found in our own age or country, than with those which describe a different set of customs. It is not without some effort, that we reconcile ourselves to the simplicity of ancient manners, and behold princesses carrying water from the spring, and kings and heroes dressing their own victuals. We may allow in general, that the representation of such manners is no fault in the author, nor deformity in the piece; but we are not so sensibly touched with them. For this reason, comedy is not easily transferred from one age or nation to another. A FRENCHMAN or ENGLISHMAN is not pleased with the ANDRIA of TERENCE, or CLITIA of MACHIAVEL; where the fine lady, upon whom all the play turns, never once appears to the spectators, but is always kept behind the scenes, suitably to the reserved humour of the ancient GREEKS and modern ITALIANS. A man of learning and reflection can make allowance for these peculiarities of manners; but a common audience can never divest themselves so far of their usual ideas and sentiments, as to relish pictures which no wise resemble them.

But here there occurs a reflection, which may, perhaps, be useful in examining the celebrated controversy concerning ancient and modern learning; where we often find the one side excusing any seeming absurdity in the ancients from the manners of the age, and the other refusing to admit this excuse, or at least, admitting it only as an apology for the author, not for the performance. In my opinion, the proper boundaries in this subject have seldom been fixed between the contending parties. Where any innocent peculiarities of manners are represented, such as those above mentioned, they ought certainly to be admitted; and a man, who is shocked with them, gives an evident proof of false delicacy and refinement. The poet's *monument more durable than brass,* must fall to the ground like common brick or clay, were men to make no allowance for the continual revolutions of manners and customs, and would admit of nothing but what was suitable to the prevailing fashion. Must we throw aside the pictures of our ancestors, because of their ruffs and fardingales? But where the ideas of morality and decency alter from one age to another, and where vicious manners are described, without being marked with the proper characters of blame and disapprobation; this must be allowed to disfigure the poem, and to be a real deformity. I cannot, nor is it proper I should, enter into such sentiments; and however I may excuse the poet, on account of the manners of his age, I never can relish the composition. The want of humanity and of decency, so conspicuous in the characters drawn by several of the ancient poets, even sometimes by HOMER and the GREEK tragedians, diminishes considerably the merit of their noble performances, and

gives modern authors an advantage over them. We are not interested in the fortunes and sentiments of such rough heroes: We are displeased to find the limits of vice and virtue so much confounded: And whatever indulgence we may give to the writer on account of his prejudices, we cannot prevail on ourselves to enter into his sentiments, or bear an affection to characters, which we plainly discover to be blameable.

The case is not the same with moral principles, as with speculative opinions of any kind. These are in continual flux and revolution. The son embraces a different system from the father. Nay, there scarcely is any man, who can boast of great constancy and uniformity in this particular. Whatever speculative errors may be found in the polite writings of any age or country, they detract but little from the value of those compositions. There needs but a certain turn of thought or imagination to make us enter into all the opinions, which then prevailed, and relish the sentiments or conclusions derived from them. But a very violent effort is requisite to change our judgment of manners, and excite sentiments of approbation or blame, love or hatred, different from those to which the mind from long custom has been familiarized. And where a man is confident of the rectitude of that moral standard, by which he judges, he is justly jealous of it, and will not pervert the sentiments of his heart for a moment, in complaisance to any writer whatsoever.

Of all speculative errors, those, which regard religion, are the most excusable in compositions of genius; nor is it ever permitted to judge of the civility or wisdom of any people, or even of single persons, by the grossness or refinement of their theological principles. The same good sense, that directs men in the ordinary occurrences of life, is not hearkened to in religious matters, which are supposed to be placed altogether above the cognizance of human reason. On this account, all the absurdities of the pagan system of theology must be overlooked by every critic, who would pretend to form a just notion of ancient poetry; and our posterity, in their turn, must have the same indulgence to their forefathers. No religious principles can ever be imputed as a fault to any poet, while they remain merely principles, and take not such strong possession of his heart, as to lay him under the imputation of *bigotry* or *superstition.* Where that happens, they confound the sentiments of moral-ity, and alter the natural boundaries of vice and virtue. They are therefore eternal blemishes, according to the principle abovementioned; nor are the prejudices and false opinions of the age sufficient to justify them.

It is essential to the ROMAN CATHOLIC religion to inspire a violent hatred of every other worship, and to represent all pagans, mahometans, and heretics as the ob-jects of divine wrath and vengeance. Such sentiments, though they are in reality very blameable, are consid-ered as virtues by the zealots of that communion, and are represented in their tragedies and epic poems as a kind of divine heroism. This bigotry has disfigured two very fine tragedies of the FRENCH theatre, POLIEUCTE and ATHALIA; where an intemperate zeal for particular modes of worship is set off with all the pomp imagina-ble, and forms the predominant character of the heroes. "What is this," says the sublime JOAD to JOSABET, find-ing her in discourse with MATHAN, the priest of BAAL, "Does the daughter of DAVID speak to this traitor? Are you not afraid, lest the earth should open and pour forth flames to devour you both? Or lest these holy walls should fall and crush you together? What is his purpose? Why comes that enemy of God hither to poison the air, which we breathe, with his horrid presence?" Such sen-timents are received with great applause on the theatre of PARIS; but at LONDON the spectators would be full as much pleased to hear ACHILLES tell AGAMEMNON, that he was a dog in his forehead, and a deer in his heart, or JUPITER threaten JUNO with a sound drubbing, if she will not be quiet.

RELIGIOUS principles are also a blemish in any po-lite composition, when they rise up to superstition, and intrude themselves into every sentiment, however re-mote from any connection with religion. It is no excuse for the poet, that the customs of his country had bur-thened life with so many religious ceremonies and ob-servances, that no part of it was exempt from that yoke. It must for ever be ridiculous in PETRARCH to com-pare his mistress, LAURA, to JESUS CHRIST. Nor is it less ridiculous in that agreeable libertine, BOCCACE, very seriously to give thanks to GOD ALMIGHTY and the ladies, for their assistance in defending him against his enemies.

Immanuel Kant

The Nature of Aesthetic Judgment

§ 1: A Judgment of Taste Is Aesthetic

If we wish to decide whether something is beautiful or not, we do not use understanding to refer the presenta-tion to the object so as to give rise to cognition; rather, we use imagination (perhaps in connection with un-derstanding) to refer the presentation to the subject and his feeling of pleasure or displeasure. Hence a judgment of taste is not a cognitive judgment and so is not a log-ical judgment but an aesthetic one, by which we mean a judgment whose determining basis *cannot be other* than *subjective.* But any reference of presentations, even of sensations, can be objective (in which case it signifies what is real [rather than formal] in an empirical pre-sentation); expected is a reference to the feeling of pleas-ure and displeasure—this reference designates nothing whatsoever in the object, but here the subject feels him-self, [namely] how he is affected by the presentation.

To apprehend a regular, purposive building with one's cognitive power (whether the presentation is dis-

From Immanuel Kant, *Critique of Judgment,* translated by Werner S. Pluhar (Indianapolis: Hackett Publishing Com-pany, 1987). Reprinted by permission of the publisher.

tinct or confused) is very different form being conscious of this presentation with a sensation of liking. Here the presentation is referred only to the subject, namely, to his feeling of life, under the name feeling of pleasure or displeasure, and this forms the basis of a very special power of discriminating and judging. This power does not contribute anything to cognition, but merely compares the given presentation in the subject with the entire presentational power, of which the mind becomes conscious when it feels its own state. [. . .]

§ 2: The Liking That Determines a Judgment of Taste Is Devoid of All Interest

Interest is what we call the liking we connect with the presentation of an object's existence. Hence such a liking always refers at once to our power of desire, either as the basis that determines it, or at any rate as necessarily connected with that determining basis. But if the question is whether something is beautiful, what we want to know is not whether we or anyone cares, or so much as might care, in any way, about the thing's existence, but rather how we judge it in our mere contemplation of it (intuition or reflection). Suppose someone asks me whether I consider the palace I see before me beautiful. I might reply that I am not fond of things of that sort, made merely to be gaped at. Or I might reply like that Iroquois *sachem* who said that he liked nothing better in Paris than the eating-houses. I might even go on, as *Rousseau* would, to rebuke the vanity of the great who spend the people's sweat on such superfluous things. I might, finally, quite easily convince myself that, if I were on some uninhabited island with no hope of ever again coming among people, and could conjure up such a splendid edifice by a mere wish, I would not even take that much trouble for it if I already had a sufficiently comfortable hut. The questioner may grant all this and approve of it; but it is not to the point. All he wants to know is whether my mere presentation of the object is accompanied by a liking, no matter how indifferent I may be about the existence of the object of his presentation. We can easily see that, in order for me to say that an object is *beautiful,* and to prove that I have taste, what matters is what I do with this presentation within my-

self, and not the [respect] in which I depend on the object's existence. Everyone has to admit that if a judgment about beauty is mingled with the least interest then it is very partial and not a pure judgment of taste. In order to play the judge in matters of taste, we must not be in the least biased in favor of the thing's existence but must be wholly indifferent about it.

There is no better way to elucidate this proposition, which is of prime importance, than by contrasting the pure disinterested[1] liking that occurs in a judgment of taste with a liking connected with interest, especially if we can also be certain that the kinds of interest I am about to mention are the ones there are.

§ 3: A Liking *for the Agreeable* Is Connected with Interest

Agreeable *is what the senses like in sensation.* Here the opportunity arises at once to censure and call attention to a quite common confusion of the two meanings that the word sensation can have. All liking (so it is said or thought) is itself sensation (of a pleasure). Hence whatever is liked, precisely inasmuch as it is liked, is agreeable (and depending on the varying degrees or on the relation to other agreeable sensations, it is *graceful, lovely, delightful, gladdening, etc.*). But if we concede this, then sense impressions that determine inclination, or principles of reason that determine the will, or mere forms of intuition that we reflect on [and] that determine the power of judgment, will all be one and the same insofar as their effect on the feeling of pleasure is concerned, since pleasure would be the agreeableness [found] in the sensation of one's state. And since, after all, everything we do with our powers must in the end aim at the practical and unite in it as its goal, we could not require them to estimate things and their value in any other way than by the gratification they promise; how they provide it

---

1. A judgment we make about an object of our liking may be wholly *disinterested* but still very *interesting,* i.e., it is not based on any interest but it gives rise to an interest; all pure moral judgments are of this sort. But judgments of taste, of themselves, do not even give rise to any interest. Only in society does it become *interesting* to have taste; the reason for this will be indicated later.

would not matter at all in the end. And since all that could make a difference in that promised gratification would be what means we select, people could no longer blame one another for baseness and malice, but only for foolishness and ignorance, since all of them, each according to his own way of viewing things, would be pursuing one and the same goal: gratification.

When [something determines the feeling of pleasure or displeasure and this] determination of that feeling is called sensation, this term means something quite different from what it means when I apply it to the presentation of a thing (through the senses, a receptivity that belongs to the cognitive power.) For in the second case the presentation is referred to the object, but in the first it is referred solely to the subject and is not used for cognition at all, not even for that by which the subject *cognizes* himself.

As I have just explicated it [i.e., for the second case], the word sensation means an objective presentation of sense; and, to avoid constantly running the risk of being misinterpreted, let us call what must always remain merely subjective, and cannot possibly be the presentation of an object, by its other customary name: feeling. The green color of meadows belongs to *objective* sensation, i.e., to the perception of an object of sense; but the color's agreeableness belongs to *subjective* sensation, to feeling, through which no object is presented, but through which the object is regarded as an object of our liking (which is not a cognition of it).

Now that a judgment by which I declare an object to be agreeable expresses an interest in that object is already obvious from the fact that, by means of sensation, the judgment arouses a desire for objects of that kind, so that the liking presupposes something other than my mere judgment about the object: it presupposes that I have referred the existence of the object to my state insofar as that state is affected by such an object. This is why we say of the agreeable not merely that we *like* it but that it *gratifies* us. When I speak of the agreeable, I am not granting mere approval: the agreeable produces an inclination. Indeed, what is agreeable in the liveliest way requires no judgment at all about the character of the object, as we can see in people who aim at nothing but enjoyment (this is the word we use to mark the intensity of the gratification): they like to dispense with all judging.

§ 4: A Liking *for the Good* Is Connected with Interest

Good is what, by means of reason, we like through its mere concept. We call something (viz., if it is something useful) *good for* [this or that] if we like it only as a means. But we call something *intrinsically good* if we like it for its own sake. In both senses of the term, the good always contains the concept of a purpose, consequently a relation of reason to a volition (that is at least possible), and hence a liking for the existence of an object or action. In other words, it contains some interest or other.

In order to consider something good, I must always know what sort of thing the object is [meant] to be, i.e., I must have a [determinate] concept of it. But I do not need this in order to find beauty in something. Flowers, free designs, lines aimlessly intertwined and called foliage: these have no significance, depend on no determinate concept, and yet we like them. A liking for the beautiful must depend on the reflection, regarding an object, that leads to some concept or other (but it is indeterminate which concept this is). This dependence on reflection also distinguishes the liking for the beautiful from [that for] the agreeable, which rests entirely on sensation.

It is true that in many cases it seems as if the agreeable and the good are one and the same. Thus people commonly say that all gratification (especially if it lasts) is intrinsically good, which means roughly the same as to be (lastingly) agreeable and to be good are one and the same. Yet it is easy to see that in talking this way they are merely substituting one word for another by mistake, since the concepts that belong to these terms are in no way interchangeable. Insofar as we present an object as agreeable, we present it solely in relation to sense; but if we are to call the object good [as well], and hence an object of the will, we must first bring it under principles of reason, using the concept of a purpose. [So] if something that gratifies us is also called *good,* it has a very different relation to our liking. This is [also] evident from the fact that in the case of the good there is always the question whether it is good merely indirectly or good directly (i.e., useful, or intrinsically good), whereas in the case of the agreeable this question cannot even arise, since this word always signifies something that we like directly. (What we call beautiful is also liked directly.)

Even in our most ordinary speech we distinguish the agreeable from the good. If a dish stimulates our tasting by its spices and other condiments, we will not hesitate to call it agreeable while granting at the same time that it is not good; for while the dish is directly *appealing* to our senses, we dislike it indirectly, i.e., as considered by reason, which looks ahead to the consequences. Even when we judge health, this difference is still noticeable. To anyone who has it, health is directly agreeable (at least negatively, as the absence of all bodily pain). But in order to say that health is good, we must also use reason and direct this health toward purposes: we must say that health is a state that disposes us to [attend to] all our tasks. [Perhaps in the case of happiness, at least, the agreeable and the good are the same?] Surely everyone believes that happiness, the greatest sum (in number as well as duration) of what is agreeable in life, may be called a true good, indeed the highest good[?] And yet reason balks at this too. Agreeableness is enjoyment. But if our sole aim were enjoyment, it would be foolish to be scrupulous about the means for getting it [i.e.,] about whether we got it passively, from nature's bounty, or through our own activity and our own doing. But reason can never be persuaded that there is any intrinsic value in the existence of a human being who lives merely for *enjoyment* (no matter how industrious he may be in pursuing that aim), even if he served others, all likewise aiming only at enjoyment, as a most efficient means to it because he participated in their gratification by enjoying it through sympathy. Only by what he does without concern for enjoyment, in complete freedom and independently of whatever he could also receive passively from nature, does he give his existence an absolute value, as the existence of a person. Happiness, with all its abundance of agreeableness, is far from being an unconditioned good.[2]

But despite all this difference between the agreeable and the good, they do agree in this: they are always connected with an interest in their object. This holds not only for the agreeable and for what is good indirectly (useful), which we like as the means to something or other that is agreeable, but also for what is good absolutely and in every respect, i.e., the moral good, which carries with it the highest interest. For the good is the object of the will (a power of desire that is determined by reason). But to will something and to have a liking for its existence, i.e., to take an interest in it, are identical.

§ 5: Comparison of the Three Sorts of Liking, Which Differ in Kind

Both the agreeable and the good refer to our power of desire and hence carry a liking with them, the agreeable a liking that is conditioned pathologically by stimuli (*stimuli*), the good a pure practical liking that is determined not just by the presentation of the object but also by the presentation of the subject's connection with the existence of the object; i.e., what we like is not just the object but its existence as well. A judgment of taste, on the other hand, is merely *contemplative,* i.e., it is a judgment that is indifferent to the existence of the object: it [considers] the character of the object only by holding it up to our feeling of pleasure and displeasure. Nor is this contemplation, as such, directed to concepts, for judgment of taste is not a cognitive judgment (whether theoretical or practical) and hence is neither *based* on concepts, nor directed to them as *purposes.*

Hence the agreeable, the beautiful, and the good designate three different relations that presentations have to the feeling of pleasure and displeasure, the feeling by reference to which we distinguish between objects or between ways of presenting them. The terms of approbation which are appropriate to each of these three are also. We call *agreeable* what GRATIFIES us, *beautiful* what we just LIKE, *good* what we ESTEEM, or *endorse,* i.e., that to which we attribute an objective value. Agreeableness holds for nonrational animals too; beauty only for human beings, i.e., beings who are animal and yet rational, though it is not enough that they be rational (e.g., spirits) but they must be animal as well; the good, however, holds for every rational being as such, though I cannot fully justify and explain this proposition until later. We may say that, of all these three kinds of liking, only the liking involved in taste for the beautiful is disinterested

---

2. An obligation to enjoy oneself is a manifest absurdity. So, consequently, must be an alleged obligation to any acts that aim merely at enjoyment, no matter how intellectually subtle (or veiled) that enjoyment may be, indeed, even if it were a mystical so-called heavenly, enjoyment.

and *free,* since we are not compelled to give our approval by any interest, whether of sense of or reason. So we might say that [the term] liking, in the three cases mentioned, refers to *inclination,* or to *favor,* or to *respect.* For FAVOR is the only free liking. Neither an object of inclination, nor one that a law of reason enjoins on us as an object of desire, leaves us the freedom to make an object of pleasure for ourselves out of something or other. All interest either presupposes a need or gives rise to one; and, because interest is the basis that determines approval, it makes the judgment about the object unfree.

Consider, first, the interest of inclination, [which occurs] with the agreeable. Here everyone says: Hunger is the best sauce; and to people with a healthy appetite anything is tasty provided it is edible. Hence if people have a liking of this sort, that does not prove that they are selecting by taste. Only when their need has been satisfied can we tell who in a multitude of people has taste and who does not. In the same way, second, one can find manners without virtue, politeness without benevolence, propriety without integrity, and so on.[3] For where the moral law speaks we are objectively no longer free to select what we must do; and to show taste in our conduct (or in judging other people's conduct) is very different from expressing our moral way of thinking. For this contains a command and gives rise to a need, whereas moral taste only plays with the objects of liking without committing itself to any of them. [. . .]

Taste is the ability to judge an object, or a way of presenting it, by means of liking or disliking *devoid of all interest.* The object of such a liking is called *beautiful.* [. . .]

§ 17: On the Ideal of Beauty

There can be no objective rule of taste, no rule of taste that determines by concepts what is beautiful. For any judgment from this source [i.e., taste] is aesthetic, i.e., the basis determining it is the subject's feeling and not the concept of an object. If we search for a principle of taste that states the universal criterion of the beautiful

by means of determinate concepts, then we engage in a fruitless endeavor, because we search for something that is impossible and intrinsically contradictory. [. . .]

§ 18: What the Modality of a Judgment of Taste Is

About any presentation I can say at least that there is a *possibility* for it (as a cognition) to be connected with a pleasure. About that which I call *agreeable* I say that it *actually* gives rise to pleasure in me. But we think of the *beautiful* as having a *necessary* reference to liking. This necessity is of a special kind. It is not a theoretical objective necessity, allowing us to cognize a priori that everyone *will feel* this liking for the object I call beautiful. Nor is it a practical objective necessity, where, through concepts of a pure rational will that serves freely acting beings as a rule, this liking is the necessary consequence of an objective law and means nothing other than that one absolutely (without any further aim) ought to act in a certain way. Rather, as a necessity that is thought in an aesthetic judgment, it can only be called *exemplary,* i.e., a necessity of the assent of *everyone* to a judgment that is regarded as an example of a universal rule that we are unable to state. Since an aesthetic judgment is not an objective and cognitive one, this necessity cannot be derived from determinate concepts and hence is not apodeictic. Still less can it be inferred from the universality of experience (from a thorough agreement among judgments about the beauty of a certain object). For not only would experience hardly furnish a sufficient amount of evidence for this, but a concept of the necessity of these judgments cannot be based on empirical judgments.

§ 19: The Subjective Necessity That We Attribute to a Judgment of Taste Is Conditioned

A judgment of taste requires everyone to assent; and whoever declares something to be beautiful holds that everyone *ought* to give his approval to the object at hand and that he too should declare it beautiful. Hence the *ought* in an aesthetic judgment, even once we have all

---

3. [I.e., taste, which is free, can manifest itself in manners, politeness, and propriety only where virtue, benevolence, and integrity, with the moral interest they involve, are absent.]

the data needed for judging, is still uttered only conditionally. We solicit everyone else's assent because we have a basis for it that is common to all. Indeed, we could count on that assent, if only we could always be sure that the instance had been subsumed correctly under that basis, which is the rule for the approval.

§ 20 : The Condition for the Necessity Alleged by a Judgment of Taste Is the Idea of a Common Sense

If judgments of taste had (as cognitive judgments do) a determinate objective principle, then anyone making them in accordance with that principle would claim that his judgment is unconditionally necessary. If they had no principle at all, like judgments of the mere taste of sense, then the thought that they have a necessity would not occur to us at all. So they must have a subjective principle, which determines only by feeling rather than by concepts, though nonetheless with universal validity, what is liked or disliked. Such a principle, however, could only be regarded as a *common sense*. This common sense is essentially distinct from the common understanding that is sometimes also called common sense (*sensus communis*); for the latter judges not by feeling but always by concepts, even though these concepts are usually only principles conceived obscurely.

Only under the presupposition, therefore, that there is a common sense (by which, however, we [also] do not mean an outer sense, but mean the effect arising from the free play of our cognitive powers)—only under the presupposition of such a common sense, I maintain, can judgments of taste be made.

§ 21 : Whether We Have a Basis for Presupposing a Common Sense

Cognitions and judgments, along with the conviction that accompanies them, must be universally communicable. For otherwise we could not attribute to them a harmony with the object, but they would one and all be a merely subjective play of the presentational powers, just as skepticism would have it. But if cognitions

are to be communicated, then the mental state, i.e., the attunement of the cognitive powers that is required for cognition in general—namely, that proportion [between them which is] suitable for turning a presentation (by which an object is given us) into cognition—must also be universally communicable. For this attunement is the subjective condition of [the process of] cognition, and without it cognition [in the sense of] the effect [of this process] could not arise. And this [attunement] does actually take place whenever a given object, by means of the sense, induces the imagination to its activity of combining the manifold, the imagination in turn inducing the understanding to its activity of providing unity for this manifold in concepts. But this attunement of the cognitive powers varies in its proportion, depending on what difference there is among the objects that are given. And yet there must be one attunement in which this inner relation is most conducive to the (mutual) quickening of the two mental powers with a view to cognition (of given objects) in general; and the only way this attunement can be determined is by feeling (rather than by concepts). Moreover, this attunement itself, and hence also the feeling of it (when a presentation is given), must be universally communicable, while the universal communicability of a feeling presupposes a common sense. Hence it would seem that we do have a basis for assuming such a sense, and for assuming it without relying on psychological observations, but as the necessary condition of the universal communicability of our cognition, which must be presupposed in any logic and any principle of cognitions that is not skeptical.

§ 22 : The Necessity of the Universal Assent That We Think in a Judgment of Taste Is a Subjective Necessity That We Present as Objective by Presupposing a Common Sense

Whenever we make a judgment declaring something to be beautiful, we permit no one to hold a different opinion, even though we base our judgment only on our feeling rather than on concepts; hence we regard this underlying feeling as a common rather than as a private feeling. But if we are to use this common sense in such as way, we cannot base it on experience; for it seeks to justify us in making judgments that contain an ought: it does not say that everyone *will* agree with my judgment, but that he *ought* to. Hence the common sense, of whose judgment I am at that point offering my judgment of taste as an example, attributing to it *exemplary* validity on that account, is a mere ideal standard. With this standard presupposed, we could rightly turn a judgment that agreed with it, as well as the liking that is expressed in it for some object, into a rule for everyone. For although the principle is only a subjective, it would still be assumed as subjectively universal (an idea necessary for everyone); and so it could, like an objective principle, demand universal assent insofar as agreement among different judging persons is concerned, provided only we are certain that we had subsumed under it correctly.

That we do actually presuppose this indeterminate standard of a common sense is proved by the fact that we presume to make judgments of taste. But is there in fact such a common sense, as a constitutive principle of the possibility of experience, or is there a still higher principle of reason that makes it only a regulative principle for us, [in order] to bring forth in us, for higher purposes, a common sense in the first place? In other words, is taste an original and natural ability, or is taste only the idea of an ability yet to be acquired and [therefore] artificial, so that a judgment of taste with its requirement for universal assent is in fact only a demand of reason to produce such agreement in the way we sense? In the latter case the *ought,* i.e., the objective necessity that everyone's feeling flow along with the particular feeling of each person, would signify only that there is a possibility of reaching such agreement; and the judgment of taste would only offer an example of the application of this principle. These questions we neither wish nor can investigate at this point. For the present our task is only to analyze the power of taste into its elements, and to unite these ultimately in the idea of a common sense. [. . .]

Beautiful is what without a concept is cognized as the object of a *necessary* liking.

Leo Tolstoy

What Is Art?

[. . .] "What is art? What a question! Art is architecture, sculpture, painting, music, and poetry in all its forms," usually replies the ordinary man, the art amateur, or even the artist himself, imagining the matter about which he is talking to be perfectly clear and uniformly understood by everybody. But in architecture, one inquires further, are there not simple buildings which are not objects of art, and buildings with artistic pretensions which are unsuccessful and ugly and therefore cannot be considered as works of art? Wherein lies the characteristic sign of a work of art?

It is the same in sculpture, in music, and in poetry. Art, in all its forms, is bounded on one side by the practically useful, and on the other by unsuccessful attempts at art. How is art to be marked off from each of these? The ordinary educated man of our circle, and even the artist who has not occupied himself especially with aesthetics, will not hesitate at this question either. He thinks the solution has been found long ago and is well known to everyone.

"Art is such activity as produces beauty," says such a man.

If art consists in that, then is a ballet or an operetta art? you inquire.

From Leo Tolstoy, *What Is Art?* translated by Aylmer Maude (Indianapolis: Hackett Publishing Company, 1996). Reprinted by permission of the publisher.

"Yes," says the ordinary man, though with some hesitation, "a good ballet or a graceful operetta is also art in so far as it manifest beauty." [. . .]

What, then, is this conception of beauty so stubbornly held to by people of our circle and day as furnishing a definition of art?

In the subjective aspect, we call beauty that which supplies us with a particular kind of pleasure.

In the objective aspect, we call beauty something absolutely perfect, and we acknowledge it to be so only because we receive, from the manifestation of this absolute perfection, a certain kind of pleasure; so this objective definition is nothing but the subjective conception differently expressed. In reality both conceptions of beauty amount to one and the same thing—namely, the reception by us of a certain kind of pleasure; i.e., we call "beauty" that which pleases us without evoking in us desire. [. . .]

In order to define any human activity it is necessary to understand its sense and importance. And in order to do that it is primarily necessary to examine that activity in itself, in its dependence on its causes and in connection with its effects, and not merely in relation to the pleasure we can get from it.

If we say that the aim of any activity is merely our pleasure, and define it solely by that pleasure, our definition will evidently be a false one. But this is precisely what has occurred in the efforts to define art. Now, if we consider the food question it will not occur to anyone to affirm that the importance of food consists in the pleasure we receive when eating it. Everyone understands that the satisfaction of our taste cannot serve as a basis for our definition of the merits of food, and that we have therefore no right to presuppose that the dinners with cayenne pepper, Limburg cheese, alcohol, etc., to which we are accustomed and which please us, form the very best human food.

And in the same way, beauty, or that which pleases us, can in no sense serve as the basis for the definition of art; nor can a series of objects which afford us pleasure serve as the model of what art should be.

To see the aim and purpose of art in the pleasure we get from it is like assuming (as is done by people of the lowest moral development, e.g., by savages) that the purpose and aim of food is the pleasure derived when consuming it.

Just as people who conceive the aim and purpose of food to be pleasure cannot recognize the real meaning of eating, so people who consider the aim of art to be pleasure cannot realize its true meaning and purpose because they attribute to an activity the meaning of which lies in its connection with other phenomena of life, the false and exceptional aim of pleasure. People come to understand that the meaning of eating lies in the nourishment of the body only when they cease to consider that the object of that activity is pleasure. And it is the same with regard to art. People will come to understand the meaning of art only when they cease to consider that the aim of that activity is beauty, i.e., pleasure. The acknowledgment of beauty (i.e., of a certain kind of pleasure received from art) as being the aim of art not only fails to assist us in finding a definition of what art is, but on the contrary, by transferring the question into a region quite foreign to art (into metaphysical, psychological, physiological, and even historical discussions as to why such a production pleases one person, and such another displeases or pleases someone else), it renders such definition impossible. And since discussions as to why one man likes pears and another prefers meat do not help toward finding a definition of what is essential in nourishment, so the solution of questions of taste in art (to which the discussions on art involuntarily come) not only does not help to make clear in what this particular human activity which we call art really consists, but renders such elucidation quite impossible until we rid ourselves of a conception which justifies every find of art at the cost of confusing the whole matter.

To the question, what is this art to which is offered up the labor of millions, the very lives of men, and even morality itself? we have extracted replies from the existing aesthetics, which all amount to this: that the aim of art is beauty, that beauty is recognized by the enjoyment it gives, and that artistic enjoyment is a good and important thing because it *is* enjoyment. Is a word, enjoyment is good because it is enjoyment. Thus what is considered the definition of art is no definition at all, but only a shuffle to justify existing art. Therefore, however strange it may seem to say so, in spite of the mountains of books written about art no exact definition of art has been constructed. And the reason for this is that the conception of art has been based on the conception of beauty.

[. . .] In order correctly to define art, it is necessary, first of all, to cease to consider it as a means to pleasure and to consider it as one of the conditions of human life. Viewing it in this way we cannot fail to observe that art is one of the means of intercourse between man and man.

Every work of art causes the receiver to enter into a certain kind of relationship both with him who produced, or is producing, the art, and with all those who, simultaneously, previously, or subsequently, receive the same artistic impression.

Speech, transmitting the thoughts and experiences of men, serves as a means of union among them, and art acts in a similar manner. The peculiarity of this latter means of intercourse, distinguishing it from intercourse by means of words, consists in this, that whereas by words a man transmits his thoughts to another, by means of art he transmits his feelings.

The activity of art is based on the fact that a man, receiving through his sense of hearing or sight another man's expression of feeling, is capable of experiencing the emotion which moved the man who expressed it. To take the simplest example: one man laughs, and another who hears becomes merry; or a man weeps, and another who hears feels sorrow. A man is excited or irritated, and another man seeing him comes to a similar state of mind. By his movements or by the sounds of his voice, a man expresses courage and determination or sadness and calmness, and this state of mind passes on to others. A man suffers, expressing his sufferings by groans and spasms, and this suffering transmits itself to other people; a man expresses his feeling of admiration, devotion, fear, respect, or love to certain objects, persons, or phenomena, and others are infected by the same feelings of admiration, devotion, fear, respect, or love to the same objects, persons, and phenomena.

And it is upon this capacity of man to receive another man's expression of feeling and experience those feelings himself, that the activity of art is based.

If a man infects another or others directly, immediately, by his appearance or by the sounds he gives vent to at the very time he experiences the feeling; if he causes another man to yawn when he himself cannot help yawning, or to laugh or cry when he himself is obliged to laugh or cry, or to suffer when he himself is suffering—that does not amount to art.

Art begins when one person, with the object of joining another or others to himself in one and the same feeling, expresses that feeling by certain external indications. To take the simplest example: a boy, having experienced, let us say, fear on encountering a wolf, relates that encounter; and, in order to evoke in others the feeling he has experienced, describes himself, his condition before the encounter, the surroundings, the wood, his own lightheartedness, and then the wolf's appearance, its movements, the distance between himself and the wolf, etc. All this, if only the boy, when telling the story, again experiences the feelings he had lived through and infects the hearers and compels them to feel what the narrator had experienced, is art. If even the boy had not seen a wolf but had frequently been afraid of one, and if, wishing to evoke in others the fear he had felt, he invented an encounter with a wolf and recounted it so as to make his hearers share the feelings he experienced when he feared the wolf, that also would be art. And just in the same way it is art if a man, having experienced either the fear of suffering or the attraction of enjoyment (whether in reality or in imagination), expresses these feelings on canvas or in marble so that others are infected by them. And it is also art if a man feels or imagines to himself feeling of delight, gladness, sorrow, despair, courage, or despondency and the transition from one to another of these feelings, and expresses these feelings by sounds so that the hearers are infected by them and experience them as they were experienced by the composer.

The feelings with which the artist infects others may be most various—very strong or very weak, very important or very insignificant, very bad or very good: feelings of love for one's own country, self-devotion and submission to fate or to God expressed in a drama, raptures of lovers described in a novel, feelings of voluptuousness expressed in a picture, courage expressed in a triumphal march, merriment evoked by a dance, humor evoked by funny story, the feeling of quietness transmitted by an evening landscape or by a lullaby, or the feeling of admiration evoked by a beautiful arabesque—it is all art.

If only the spectators or auditors are infected by the feelings which the author has felt, it is art.

To evoke in oneself a feeling one has once experienced, and having evoked it in oneself, then, by means of movements, lines, colors, sounds, or forms expressed in words, so to transmit that feeling that others may experience the same feeling—this is the activity of art.

Art is a human activity consisting in this, that one man consciously, by means of certain external signs, hands on to others feeling he has lived through, and that other people are infected by these feelings and also experience them.

Art is not, as the metaphysicians say, the manifestation of some mysterious Idea of beauty or God; it is not, as the aesthetical physiologists say, a game in which man lets off his excess of stored-up energy; it is not the expression of man's emotions by external signs; it is not the production of pleasing objects; and, above all, it is not pleasure; but it is a means of union among men, joining them together in the same feelings, and indispensable for the life and progress toward well-being of individuals and of humanity.

As, thanks to man's capacity to express thoughts by words, every man may know all that has been done for him in the realms of thought by all humanity before his day, and can in the present, thanks to this capacity to understand the thoughts of others, become a sharer in their activity and can himself hand on to his contemporaries and descendants the thoughts he has assimilated from others, as well as those which have arisen within himself; so, thanks to man's capacity to be infected with the feelings of others by means of art, all that is being lived through by his contemporaries is accessible to him, as well as the feelings experienced by men thousands of years ago, and he has also the possibility of transmitting his own feelings to others.

If people lacked this capacity to receive the thoughts conceived by the men who preceded them and to pass on to others their own thoughts, men would be like wild beasts, or like Kaspar Hauser.[1]

And if men lacked this other capacity of being infected by art, people might be almost more savage still,

and, above all, more separated from, and more hostile to, one another.

And therefore the activity of art is a most important one, as important as the activity of speech itself and as generally diffused.

We are accustomed to understand art to be only what we hear and see in theaters, concerts, and exhibitions, together with buildings, statues, poems, novels. . . . But all this is but the smallest part of the art by which we communicate with each other in life. All human life is filled with works of art of ever kind—from cradlesong, jest, mimicry, the ornamentation of houses, dress, and utensils, up to church services, buildings, monuments, and triumphal processions. It is all artistic activity. So that by art, in the limited sense of the word, we do not mean all human activity transmitting feelings, but only that part which we for some reason select from it and to which we attach special importance.

This special importance has always been given by all men to that part of this activity which transmits feelings flowing from their religious perceptions, and this small part of art they have specifically called art, attaching to it the full meaning of the word.

That was how men of old—Socrates, Plato, and Aristotle—looked on art. Thus did the Hebrew prophets and the ancient Christians regard art; thus it was, and still is, understood by the Mohammedans, and thus it still is understood by religious folk among our own peasantry.

Some teachers of mankind—as Plato in his *Republic* and people such as the primitive Christians, the strict Mohammedans, and the Buddhists—have gone so far as to repudiate all art.

People viewing art in this way (in contradiction to the prevalent view of today which regards any art as good if only it afford pleasure) considered, and consider, that art (as contrasted with speech, which need not be listened to) is so highly dangerous in its power to infect people against their wills that mankind will lose far less by banishing all art than by tolerating each and every art.

Evidently such people were wrong in repudiating all art, for they denied that which cannot be denied—one of the indispensable means of communication, without which mankind could not exist. But not less wrong are the people of civilized European society of our class and day in favoring any art if it but serves beauty, i.e., gives people pleasure.

---

1. "The foundling of Nuremberg," found in the marketplace of that town on May 26, 1828, apparently some sixteen years old. He spoke little and was almost totally ignorant even of common objects. He subsequently explained that he had been brought up in confinement underground and visited by only one man, whom he seldom saw. –Tr.

Formerly people feared lest among the works of art there might chance to be some causing corruption, and they prohibited art altogether. Now they only fear lest they should be deprived of any enjoyment art can afford, and patronize any art. And I think the last error is much grosser than the first and that its consequences are far more harmful.

[. . .] There is one indubitable indication distinguishing real art from its counterfeit, namely, in infectiousness of art. If a man, without exercising effort and without altering his standpoint on reading, hearing, or seeing another man's work, experiences a mental condition which unites him with that man and with other people who also partake of that work of art, then the object evoking that condition is a work of art. And however poetical, realistic, effectful, or interesting a work may be, it is not a work of art if it does not evoke that feeling (quite distinct from all other feelings) of joy and of spiritual union with another (the author) and with others (those who are also infected by it).

It is true that this indication is an *internal* one, and that there are people who have forgotten what the action of real art is, who expect something else from art (in our society the great majority are in this state), and that therefore such people may mistake for this aesthetic feeling the feeling of diversion and a certain excitement which they receive from counterfeits of art. But though it is impossible to undeceive these people, just as it is impossible to convince a man suffering from "Daltonism"[2] that green is not red, yet, for all that, this indication remains perfectly definite to those whose feeling for art is neither perverted nor atrophied, and it clearly distinguishes the feeling produced by art from all other feelings.

The chief peculiarity of this feeling is that the receiver of a true artistic impression is so united to the artist that he feels as if the work were his own and not someone else's—as if what it expresses were just what he had long been wishing to express. A real work of art destroys, in the consciousness of the receiver, the separation between himself and the artist—not that alone, but also between himself and all whose minds receive this work of art. In this freeing of our personality from its separation and isolation, in this uniting of it with others, lies the chief characteristic and the great attractive force of art.

If a man is infected by the author's condition of soul, if he feels this emotion and this union with others, then the object which has effected this is art; but if there be no such infection, if there be not this union with the author and with others who are moved by the same work—then it is not art. And not only is infection a sure sign of art, but the degree of infectiousness is also the sole measure of excellence in art.

The stronger the infection, the better is the art as art, speaking now apart from its subject matter, i.e., not considering the quality of the feelings it transmits.

And the degree of the infectiousness of art depends on three conditions:

(1) on the greater or lesser individuality of the feeling transmitted;

(2) on the greater or lesser clearness with which the feeling is transmitted;

(3) on the sincerity of the artist, i.e., on the greater or lesser force with which the artist himself feels the emotion he transmits.

The more individual the feeling transmitted the more strongly does it act on the receiver; the more individual the state of soul into which he is transferred, the more pleasure does the receiver obtain, and therefore the more readily and strongly does he join in it.

The clearness of expression assists infection because the receiver, who mingles in consciousness with the author, is the better satisfied the more clearly the feeling is transmitted, which, as it seems to him, he has long known and felt, and for which he has only now found expression.

But most of all is the degree of infectiousness of art increased by the degree of sincerity in the artist. As soon as the spectator, hearer, or reader feels that the artist is infected by his own production, and writes, sings, or plays for himself, and not merely to act on others, this mental condition of the artist infects the receiver; and contrariwise, as soon as the spectator, reader, or hearer

_____

2. [A kind of color blindness discovered by John Dalton. –Ed.]

feels that the author is not writing, singing, or playing for his own satisfaction—does not himself feel what he wishes to express—but is doing it for him, the receiver, a resistance immediately springs up, and the most individual and the newest feelings and the cleverest technique not only fail to produce any infection but actually repel.

I have mentioned three conditions of contagiousness in art, but they may be all summed up into one, the last, sincerity, i.e., that the artist should be impelled by an inner need to express his feeling. That condition includes the first; for if the artist is sincere he will express the feeling as he experienced it. And as each man is different from everyone else, his feeling will be individual for everyone else; and the more individual it is—the more the artist has drawn it from the depths of his nature— the more sympathetic and sincere will it be. And this same sincerity will impel the artist to find a clear expression of the feeling which he wishes to transmit.

Therefore this third condition—sincerity—is the most important of the three. It is always complied with in peasant art, and this explains why such art always acts so powerfully; but it is a condition almost entirely absent from our upper-class art, which is continually produced by artists actuated by personal aims of covetousness or vanity.

Such are the three conditions which divide art from its counterfeits, and which also decide the quality of every work of art apart from its subject matter.

The absence of any one of these conditions excludes a work from the category of art and relegates it to that of art's counterfeits. If the work does not transmit the artist's peculiarity of feeling and is therefore not individual, if it is unintelligibly expressed, or if it has not proceeded from the author's inner need for expression—it is not a work of art. If all these conditions are present, even in the smallest degree, then the work, even if a weak one, is yet a work of art.

The presence in various degrees of these three conditions—individuality, clearness, and sincerity—decides the merit of a work of art as art, apart from subject matter. All works of art take rank of merit according to the degree in which they fulfill the first, the second, and the third of these conditions. In one the individuality of the feeling transmitted may predominate; in another, clearness of expression; in a third, sincerity; while a fourth may have sincerity and individuality but be deficient in clearness; a fifth, individuality and clearness but less sincerity; and so forth, in all possible degrees and combinations.

Thus is art divided from that which is not art, and thus is the quality of art as art decided, independently of its subject matter, i.e., apart from whether the feelings it transmits are good or bad.

But how are we to define good and bad art with reference to its subject matter?

How are we to decide what is good or bad in the subject matter of art?

Art, like speech, is a means of communication, and therefore of progress, i.e., of the movement of humanity forward toward perfection. Speech renders accessible to men of the latest generations all the knowledge discovered by the experience and reflection, both of preceding generations and of the best and foremost men of their own times; art renders accessible to men of the latest generations all the feelings experienced by their predecessors, and those also which are being felt by their best and foremost contemporaries. And as the evolution of knowledge proceeds by truer and more necessary knowledge, dislodging and replacing what is mistaken and unnecessary, so the evolution of feeling proceeds though art—feelings less kind and less needful for the well-being of mankind are replaced by others kinder and more needful for that end. That is the purpose of art. And, speaking now of its subject matter, the more art fulfills that purpose the better the art, and the less it fulfills it, the worse the art.

And the appraisement of feelings (i.e., the acknowledgment of these or those feelings as being more or less good, more or less necessary for the well-being of mankind) is made by the religious perception of the age.

In every period of history, and in every human society, there exists an understanding of the meaning of life which represents the highest level to which men of that society have attained, an understanding defining the highest good at which that society aims. And this understanding is the religious perception of the given time and society. And this religious perception is always clearly expressed by some advanced men, and more or less vividly perceived by all the members of the society. Such a religious perception and its corresponding expression exists always in every society. If it appears to us that in our society there is no religious perception, this is not because there really is none, but only because we do not want to see it. And we often wish not to see it because it exposes the fact that our life is inconsistent with that religious perception.

Religious perception in a society is like the direction of a flowing river. If the river flows at all, it must have a direction. If a society lives, there must be a religious perception indicating the direction in which, more or less consciously, all its members tend.

And so there always has been, and there is, a religious perception in every society. And it is by the standard of this religious perception that the feelings transmitted by art have always been estimated. Only on the basis of this religious perception of their age have men always chosen from the endlessly varied spheres of art that art which transmitted feelings making religious perception operative in actual life. And such art has always been highly valued and encouraged, while art transmitting feelings already outlived, flowing from the antiquated religious perceptions of a former age, has always been condemned and despised. All the rest of art, transmitting those most divers feelings by means of which people commune together, was not condemned, and was tolerated, if only it did not transmit feelings contrary to religious perception. Thus, for instance, among the Greeks art transmitting the feeling of beauty, strength, and courage (Hesiod, Homer, Phidias) was chosen, approved, and encouraged, while art transmitting feelings of rude sensuality, despondency, and effeminacy was condemned and despised. Among the Jews, art transmitting feelings of devotion and submission to the God of the Hebrews and to His will (the epic of Genesis, the prophets, the Psalms) was chosen and encouraged, while art transmitting feelings of idolatry (the golden calf) was condemned and despised. All the rest of art—stories, songs, dances, ornamentation of houses, of utensils, and of clothes—which was not contrary to religious perception was neither distinguished nor discussed. Thus, in regard to its subject matter, has art been appraised always and everywhere, and thus it should be appraised; for this attitude toward art proceeds from the fundamental characteristics of human nature, and those characteristics do not change.

I know that according to an opinion current in our times religion is a superstition which humanity has outgrown, and that it is therefore assumed that no such thing exists as a religious perception, common to us all, by which art, in our time, can be evaluated. I know that this is the opinion current in the pseudo-cultured circles of today. People who do not acknowledge Christianity in its true meaning because it undermines all their social privileges, and who, therefore, invent all kinds of philosophic and aesthetic theories to hide from themselves the meaninglessness and wrongness of their lives, cannot think otherwise. These people intentionally, or sometimes unintentionally, confusing the conception of a religious cult with the conception of a religious perception think that by denying the cult they get rid of religious perception. But even the very attacks on religion and the attempts to establish a life-conception contrary to the religious perception of our times most clearly demonstrate the existence of a religious perception condemning the lives that are not in harmony with it.

If humanity progresses, i.e., moves forward, there must inevitably be a guide to the direction of that movement. And religions have always furnished that guide. All history shows that the progress of humanity is accomplished not otherwise than under the guidance of religion. But if the race cannot progress without the guidance of religion—and progress is always going on, and consequently also in our own times—then there must be a religion of our times. So that, whether it pleases or displeases the so-called cultured people of today, they must admit the existence of religion—not of a religious cult, Catholic, Protestant, or another, but of religious perception—which, even in our times, is the guide always present where there is any progress. And if a religious perception exists among us, then our art should be appraised on the basis of that religious perception; and, as has always and everywhere been the case, art transmitting feelings flowing from the religious perception of our time should be chosen from all the indifferent art, should be acknowledged, highly esteemed, and encouraged, while art running counter to that perception should be condemned and despised, and all the remaining indifferent art should neither be distinguished nor encouraged.

The religious perception of our time, in its widest and most practical application, is the consciousness that our well-being, both material and spiritual, individual and collective, temporal and eternal, lies in the growth of brotherhood among all men—in their loving harmony with one another. This perception is not only expressed by Christ and all the best men of past ages, it is not only repeated in the most varied forms and from most diverse sides by the best men of our own times, but it already serves as a clue to all the complex labor of humanity, consisting as this labor does, on the one hand, in the destruction of physical and moral obstacles to the union of men, and, on the other hand, in establishing the principles common to all men which can and should unite them into one universal brotherhood. And it is on the basis of this perception that we should appraise all the phenomena of our life, and, among the rest, our art also; choosing from all its realms whatever transmits feelings flowing from this religious perception, highly prizing and encouraging such art, rejecting whatever is contrary to this perception, and not attributing to the rest of art an importance not properly pertaining to it. [. . .]

The expression *unite men with God and with one another* may seem obscure to people accustomed to the misuse of these words which is so customary, but the words have a perfectly clear meaning, nevertheless. They indicate that the Christian union of man (in contradiction to the partial, exclusive union of only some men) is that which unites all without exception.

Art, all art, has this characteristic, that it unites people. Every art cause those to whom the artist's feeling is transmitted to unite in soul with the artist, and also with all who receive the same impression. But non-Christian art, while uniting some people together, makes that very union a cause of separation between these united people and others; so that union of this kind is often a source, not only of division, but even of enmity toward others. Such is all patriotic art, with its anthems, poems, and monuments; such is all Church art, i.e., the art of certain cults, with their images, statues, processions, and other local ceremonies. Such art is belated a non-Christian art, uniting the people of one cult only to separate them yet more sharply from the members of other cults, and even to place them in relations of hostility to each other. Christian art is only such as tends to unite all without exception, either by evoking in them the perception that each man and all men stand in like relation toward God and toward their neighbor, or by evoking in them identical feelings which may even be the very simplest, provided only that they are not repugnant to Christianity and are natural to everyone without exception. [. . .]

Whatever the work may be and however it may have been extolled, we have first to ask whether this work is one of real art or a counterfeit. Having acknowledged, on the basis of the indication of its infectiousness even to a small class of people, that a certain production belongs to the realm of art, it is necessary, on the basis of the indication of its accessibility, to decide the next question, Does this work belong to the category of bad, exclusive art, opposed to religious perception, or to Christian art uniting people? And having acknowledged an article to belong to real Christian art, we must then, according to whether it transmits the feelings flowing from love to God and man, or merely the simple feelings uniting all men, assign it a place in the ranks of religious art or in those of universal art.

Only on the basis of such verification shall we find it possible to select from the whole mass of what in our society claims to be art those works which form real, important, necessary spiritual food, and to separate them from all the harmful and useless art and from the counterfeits of art which surround us. Only on the basis of such verification shall we be able to rid ourselves of the pernicious results of harmful art and to avail ourselves of that beneficent action which is the purpose of true and good art and which is indispensable for the spiritual life of man and of humanity.

Nelson Goodman

When Is Art?

1. The Pure in Art

If attempts to answer the question "What is art?" characteristically end in frustration and confusion, perhaps —as so often in philosophy—the question is the wrong one. A reconception of the problem, together with application of some results of a study of the theory of symbols, may help to clarify such moot matters as the role of symbolism in art and the status as art of the 'found object' and so-called 'conceptual art'.

One remarkable view of the relation of symbols to works of art is illustrated in an incident bitingly reported by Mary McCarthy:[1]

> Seven years ago, when I taught in a progressive college, I had a pretty girl student in one of my classes who wanted to be a short-story writer. She was not studying with me, but she knew that I sometimes wrote short stories, and one day, breathless and glowing, she came up to me in the hall, to tell me that she had just written a story that her writing teacher, a Mr. Converse, was terribly excited about. "He thinks it's wonderful," she said, "and he's going to help me fix it up for publication."
>
> I asked what the story was about; the girl was a rather simple being who loved clothes and dates. Her answer had a deprecating tone. It was about a girl (herself) and some sailors she had met on the train. But then her face, which had looked perturbed for a moment, gladdened.

From Nelson Goodman, *Ways of Worldmaking* (Indianapolis: Hackett Publishing Company, 1978). Reprinted by permission of the publisher.

1. "Settling the Colonel's Hash," *Harper's Magazine,* 1954; reprinted in *On the Contrary* (Farrar, Straus and Cudahy, 1961), p. 225.

> "Mr. Converse is going over it with me and we're going to put in the symbols."

Today the bright-eyed art student will more likely be told, with equal subtlety, to keep out the symbols; but the underlying assumption is the same: that symbols, whether enhancements or distractions, are extrinsic to the work itself. A kindred notion seems to be reflected in what we take to be symbolic art. We think first of such works as Bosch's *Garden of Delight* or Goya's *Caprichos* or the Unicorn tapestries or Dali's drooping watches, and then perhaps of religious paintings, the more mystical the better. What is remarkable here is less the association of the symbolic with the esoteric or unearthly than the classification of works as symbolic upon the basis of their having symbols as their subject matter—that is, upon the basis of their depicting rather than of their being symbols. This leaves as nonsymbolic art not only works that depict nothing but also portraits, still-lifes, and landscapes where the subjects are rendered in a straightforward way without arcane allusions and do not themselves stand as symbols.

On the other hand, when we choose works for classification as nonsymbolic, as art without symbols, we confine ourselves to works without subjects; for example, to purely abstract or decorative or formal paintings or buildings or musical compositions. Works that represent anything, no matter what and no matter how prosaically, are excluded; for to represent is surely to refer, to stand for, to symbolize. Every representational work is a symbol; and art without symbols is restricted to art without subject.

That representational works are symbolic according to one usage and nonsymbolic according to another matters little so long as we do not confuse the two usages. What matters very much, though, according to many contemporary artists and critics, is to isolate the work of art as such from whatever it symbolizes or refers to in any way. Let me set forth in quotation marks, since I am offering it for consideration without now expressing any opinion of it, a composite statement of a currently much advocated program or policy or point of view:

> "What a picture symbolizes is external to it, and extraneous to the picture as a work of art. Its subject if it has one, its references—subtle or obvious—by means of symbols from some more or less well-recognized vocabulary, have nothing to do with its aesthetic or artistic significance or character. Whatever a picture refers to or stands for in any way, overt or occult, lies outside it. What really counts is not any such relationship to something else, not what the picture symbolizes, but what it is in itself—what its own intrinsic qualities are. Moreover, the more a picture focuses attention on what it symbolizes, the more we are distracted from its own properties. Accordingly, any symbolization by a picture is not only irrelevant but disturbing. Really pure art shuns all symbolization, refers to nothing, and is to be taken for just what it is, for its inherent character, not for anything it is associated with by some such remote relation as symbolization."

Such a manifesto packs punch. The counsel to concentrate on the intrinsic rather than the extrinsic, the insistence that a work of art is what it is rather than what it symbolizes, and the conclusion that pure art dispenses with external reference of all kinds have the solid sound of straight thinking, and promise to extricate art from smothering thickets of interpretation and commentary.

2. A Dilemma

But a dilemma confronts us here. If we accept this doctrine of the formalist or purist, we seem to be saying that the content of such works as the *Garden of Delight* and the *Caprichos* doesn't really matter and might better be left out. If we reject the doctrine, we seem to be holding that what counts is not just what a work is but lots of things it isn't. In the one case we seem to be advocating lobotomy on many great works; in the other we seem to be condoning impurity in art, emphasizing the extraneous.

The best course, I think, is to recognize the purist position as all right and all wrong. But how can that be? Let's begin by agreeing that what is extraneous is extraneous. But is what a symbol symbolizes always external to it? Certainly not for symbols of all kinds. Consider the symbols:

(a) "this string of words", which stands for itself;

(b) "word", which applies to itself among other words;

(c) "short", which applies to itself and some other words and many other things; and

(d) "having seven syllables", which has seven syllables.

Obviously what some symbols symbolize does not lie entirely outside the symbols. The cases cited are, of course, quite special ones, and the analogues among pictures—that is, pictures that are pictures of themselves or include themselves in what they depict can perhaps be set aside as too rare and idiosyncratic to carry any weight. Let's agree for the present that what a work represents, except in a few cases like these, is external to it and extraneous.

Does this mean that any work that represents nothing meets the purist's demands? Not at all. In the first place, some surely symbolic works such as Bosch's paintings of weird monsters, or the tapestry of a unicorn, represent nothing; for there are no such monsters or demons or unicorns anywhere but in such pictures or in verbal descriptions. To say that the tapestry 'represents and unicorn' amounts only to saying that it is a unicorn-picture, not that there is any animal, or anything at all that it portrays. These works, even though there is nothing they represent, hardly satisfy the purist. Perhaps, though, this is just another philosopher's quibble; and I won't press the point. Let's agree that such pictures, though they represent nothing, are representational in character, hence symbolic and so not 'pure'. All the same, we must note in passing that their being representational involves no representation of anything outside them, so that the purist's objection to them cannot be on that ground. His case will have to be modified in one way or another, with some sacrifice of simplicity and force.

In the second place, not only representational works are symbolic. An abstract painting that represents nothing and is not representational at all may express, and so symbolize, a feeling or other quality, or an emotion or idea. Just because expression is a way of symbolizing something outside the painting—which does not itself sense, feel or think—the purist rejects abstract expressionist as well as representational works.

For a work to be an instance of 'pure' art, of art without symbols, it must on this view neither represent nor express nor even be representational or expressive. But is that enough? Granted, such a work does not stand for anything outside it; all it has are its own properties. But of course if we put it that way, all the properties any picture or anything else has—even such a property as that of representing a given person—are properties of the picture, not properties outside it.

The predictable response is that the important distinction among the several properties a work may have lies between its internal or intrinsic and its external or extrinsic properties; that while all are indeed its own properties, some of them obviously relate the picture to other things; and that a nonrepresentational, nonexpressive work has only internal properties.

This plainly doesn't work; for under any even faintly plausible classification of properties into internal and external, any picture or anything else has properties of both kinds. That a picture is in the Metropolitan Museum, that it was painted in Duluth, that it is younger than Methuselah, would hardly be called internal properties. Getting rid of representation and expression does not give us something free of such external or extraneous properties.

Furthermore, the very distinction between internal and external properties is a notoriously muddled one. Presumably the colors and shapes in a picture must be considered internal; but if an external property is one that relates the picture or object to something else, then colors and shapes obviously must be counted as external; for the color or shape of an object not only may be shared by other objects but also relates the object to others having the same or different colors or shapes.

Sometimes, the terms "internal" and "intrinsic" are dropped in favor of "formal". But the formal in this context cannot be a matter of shape alone. It must include color, and if color, what else? Texture? Size? Material? Of course, we may at will enumerate properties that are to be called formal but the 'at will' gives the case

away. The rationale, the justification, evaporates. The properties left out as nonformal can no longer be characterized as all and only those that relate the picture to something outside it. So we are still faced with the question what if any *principle* is involved—the question how the properties that matter in a nonrepresentational, nonexpressive painting are distinguished from the rest.

I think there is an answer to the question; but to approach it, we'll have to drop all this high-sounding talk of art and philosophy, and come down to earth with a thud.

3. Samples

Consider again an ordinary swatch of textile in a tailor's or upholsterer's sample book. It is unlikely to be a work of art or to picture or express anything. It's simply a sample—a simple sample. But what is it a sample of? Texture, color, weave, thickness, fiber content. . . .; the whole point of this sample, we are tempted to say, is that it was cut from a bolt and has all the same properties as the rest of the material. But that would be too hasty.

Let me tell you two stories—or one story with two parts. Mrs. Mary Tricias studied such a sample book, made her selection, and ordered from her favorite textile shop enough material for her overstuffed chair and sofa—insisting that it be exactly like the sample. When the bundle came she opened it eagerly and was dismayed when several hundred 2" x 3" pieces with zigzag edges exactly like the sample fluttered to the floor. When she called the shop, protesting loudly, the proprietor replied, injured and weary, "But Mrs. Tricias, you said the material must be exactly like the sample. When it arrived from the factory yesterday, I kept my assistants here half the night cutting it up to match the sample."

This incident was nearly forgotten some months later, when Mrs. Tricias, having sewed the pieces together and covered her furniture, decided to have a party. She went to the local bakery, selected a chocolate cupcake from those on display and ordered enough for fifty guests, to be delivered two weeks later. Just as the guests were beginning to arrive, a truck drove up with a single huge cake. The lady running the bake-shop was utterly discouraged by the complaint. "But Mrs. Tricias, you have no idea how much trouble we went to. My husband runs the textile shop and he warned me that your order would have to be in one piece."

The moral of this story is not simply that you can't win, but that a sample is a sample of some of its properties but not others. The swatch is a sample of texture, color, etc. but not of size or shape. The cupcake is a sample of color, texture, size and shape, but still not of all its properties. Mrs. Tricias would have complained even more loudly if what was delivered to her was like the sample in having been baked on the same day two weeks earlier.

Now in general which of its properties is a sample a sample of? Not all its properties; for then the sample would be a sample of nothing but itself. And not its 'formal' or 'internal' or, indeed, any one specifiable set of properties. The kind of property sampled differs from case to case: the cupcake but not the swatch is a sample of size and shape; a specimen of ore may be a sample of what was mined at a given time and place. Moreover, the sampled properties vary widely with context and circumstance. Although the swatch is normally a sample of its texture, etc. but not of its shape or size, if I show it to you in answer to the question "What is an upholsterer's sample?" it then functions not as a sample of the material but as a sample of an upholsterer's sample, so that its size and shape are now among the properties it is a sample of.

In sum, the point is that a sample is a sample of—or *exemplifies*—only some of its properties, and that the properties to which it bears this relationship of exemplification vary with circumstances and can only be distinguished as those properties that it serves, under the given circumstances, as a sample of. Being a sample of or exemplifying is a relationship something like that of being a friend; my friends are not distinguished by any single identifiable property or cluster of properties, but only by standing, for a period of time, in the relationship of friendship with me.

The implications for our problem concerning works of art may now be apparent. The properties that count in a purist painting are those that the picture makes manifest, selects, focuses upon, exhibits, heightens in our consciousness—those that it shows forth—in short, those properties that it does not merely possess but *exemplifies,* stands as a sample of.

If I am right about this, then even the purist's purest painting symbolizes. It exemplifies certain of its proper-

ties. But to exemplify is surely to symbolize—exemplification no less than representation or expression is a form of reference. A work of art, however free of representation and expression, is still a symbol even though what it symbolizes be not things or people or feelings but certain patterns of shape, color, texture that it shows forth.

What, then, of the purist's initial pronouncement that I said facetiously is all right and all wrong? It is all right in saying that what is extraneous is extraneous, in pointing out that what a picture represents often matters very little, in arguing that neither representation nor expression is required of a work, and in stressing the importance of so-called intrinsic or internal or 'formal' properties. But the statement is all wrong in assuming that representation and expression are the only symbolic functions that paintings may perform, in supposing that what a symbol symbolizes is always outside it, and in insisting that what counts in a painting is the mere possession rather than the exemplification of certain properties.

Whoever looks for art without symbols, then, will find none—if all the ways that works symbolize are taken into account. Art without representation or expression or exemplification—yes; art without all three—*no*.

To point out that purist art consists simply in the avoidance of certain kinds of symbolization is not to condemn it but only to uncover the fallacy in the usual manifestos advocating purist art to the exclusion of all other kinds. I am not debating the relative virtues of different schools or types or ways of painting. What seems to me more important is that recognition of the symbolic function of even purist painting gives us a clue to the perennial problem of when we do and when we don't have a work of art.

The literature of aesthetics is littered with desperate attempts to answer the question "What is art?" This question, often hopelessly confused with the question "What is good art?", is acute in the case of found art—the stone picked out of the driveway and exhibited in a museum—and is further aggravated by the promotion of so-called environmental and conceptual art. Is a smashed automobile fender in an art gallery a work of art? What of something that is not even an object, and not exhibited in any gallery or museum—for example, the digging and filling-in of a hole in Central Park as prescribed by Oldenburg? If these are works of art, then are all stones in the driveway and all objects and occurrences works of art? If not, what distinguishes what is from what is not a work of art? That an artist calls is a work of art? That it is exhibited in a museum or gallery? No such answer carries any conviction.

As I remarked at the outset, part of the trouble lies in asking the wrong question—in failing to recognize that a thing may function as a work of art at some times and not at others. In crucial cases, the real question is not "What objects are (permanently) works of art?" but "When is an object a work of art?"—or more briefly, as in my title, "When is art?"

My answer is that just as an object may be a symbol—for instance, a sample—at certain times and under certain circumstances and not at others, so an object may be a work of art at some times and not at others. Indeed, just by virtue of functioning as a symbol in a certain way does an object become, while so functioning, a work of art. The stone is normally no work of art while in the driveway, but may be so when on display in an art museum. In the driveway, it usually performs no symbolic function. In the art museum, it exemplifies certain of its properties—e.g., properties of shape, color, texture. The hole-digging and filling functions as a work insofar as our attention is directed to it as an exemplifying symbol. On the other hand, a Rembrandt painting may cease to function as a work of art when used to replace a broken window or as a blanket.

Now, of course, to function as a symbol in some way or other is not in itself to function as a work of art. Our swatch, when serving as a sample, does not then and thereby become a work of art. Things function as works of art only when their symbolic functioning has certain characteristics. Our stone in a museum of geology takes on symbolic functions as a sample of the stones of a given period, origin, or composition, but it is not then functioning as a work of art.

The question just what characteristics distinguish or are indicative of the symbolizing that constitutes functioning as a work of art calls for careful study in the light of a general theory of symbols. That is more than I can undertake here, but I venture the tentative thought that there are five symptoms of the aesthetic:[2] (1) syntactic

density, where the finest differences in certain respects constitute a difference between symbols—for example, an ungraduated mercury thermometer as contrasted with an electronic digital-read-out instrument; (2) semantic density, where symbols are provided for things distinguished by the finest difference in certain respects—for example, not only the ungraduated thermometer again but also ordinary English, though it is not syntactically dense; (3) relative repleteness, where comparatively many aspects of a symbol are significant—for example, a single-line drawing of a mountain by Hokusai where every feature of shape, line, thickness, etc. counts, in contrast with perhaps the same line as a chart of daily stockmarket averages, where all that counts is the height of the line about the base; (4) exemplification, where a symbol, whether or not it denotes, symbolizes by serving as a sample of properties it literally or metaphorically possesses; and finally (5) multiple and complex reference, where a symbol performs several integrated and interacting referential functions,[3] some direct and some mediated through other symbols.

These symptoms provide no definition, much less a full-blooded description or a celebration. Presence or absence of one or more of them does not qualify or disqualify anything as aesthetic; nor does the extent to which these features are present measure the extent to which an object or experience is aesthetic.[4] Symptoms, after all, are but clues; the patient may have the symptoms without the disease, or the disease without the symptoms. And even for these five symptoms to come somewhere near being disjunctively necessary and conjunctively (as a syndrome) sufficient might well call for some redrawing of the vague and vagrant borderlines of

---

alluded to. The fifth symptom has been added above as the result of conversations with Professors Paul Hernadi and Alan Nagel of the University of Iowa.

3. This excludes ordinary ambiguity, where a term has two or more quite independent denotations at quite different times and in quite different contexts.

4. That poetry, for example, which is not syntactically dense, is less art or less likely to be art that painting that exhibits all four symptoms thus does not at all follow. Some aesthetic symbols may have fewer of the symptoms than some nonaesthetic symbols. This is sometimes misunderstood.

---

2. See Nelson Goodman, *Languages of Art,* Hackett Publishing Co., 1976, pp. 252–55 and the earlier passages there

the aesthetic. Still, notice that these properties tend to focus attention on the symbol rather than, or at least along with, what it refers to. Where we can never determine precisely just which symbol of a system we have or whether we have the same one on a second occasion, where the referent is so elusive that properly fitting a symbol to it requires endless care, where more rather than fewer features of the symbol count, where the symbol is an instance of properties it symbolizes and may perform many interrelated simple and complex referential functions, we cannot merely look through the symbol to what it refers to as we do in obeying traffic lights or reading scientific texts, but must attend constantly to the symbol itself as in seeing paintings or reading poetry. This emphasis upon the nontransparency of a work of art, upon the primacy of the work over what it refers to, far from involving denial or disregard of symbolic functions, derives from certain characteristics of work as a symbol.[5]

Quite apart from specifying the particular characteristics differentiating aesthetic from other symbolization, the answer to the question "When is art?" thus seems to me clearly to be in terms of symbolic function. Perhaps to say that an object is art when and only when it so functions is to overstate the case or to speak elliptically. The Rembrandt painting remains a work of art, as it remains a painting, while functioning only as a blanket; and the stone from the driveway may not strictly become art by functioning as art.[6] Similarly, a chair remains

a chair even if never sat on, and a packing case remains a packing case even if never used except for sitting on. To say what art does is not to say what art is; but I submit that the former is the matter of primary and peculiar concern. The further question of defining stable property in terms of ephemeral function—that what in terms of the when—is not confined to the arts but is quite general, and is the same for defining chairs as for defining objects of art. The parade of instant and inadequate answers is also much the same: that whether an object is art—or a chair—depends upon intent or upon whether it sometimes or usually or always or exclusively functions as such. Because all this tends to obscure more special and significant questions concerning art, I have turned my attention from what art is to what art does.

A salient feature of symbolization, I have urged, is that it may come and go. An object may symbolize different things at different times, and nothing at other times. An inert or purely utilitarian object may come to function as art, and a work of art may come to function as an inert or purely utilitarian object. Perhaps, rather than art being long and life short, both are transient.

The bearing that this inquiry into the nature of works of art has upon the overall undertaking of this book should by now have become quite clear. How an object or event functions as a work explains how, through certain modes of reference, what so functions may contribute to a vision of—and to the making of—a world.

---

5. This is another version of the dictum that the purist is all right and all wrong.

6. Just as what is not red may look or be said to be red *at certain times,* so what is not art may function as or be said to be art at certain times. That an object functions as art at a given time, that it has the status of art at that time, and

that it is art at that time may all be taken as saying the same thing—so long as we take none of these as ascribing to the object any stable status.

Arthur Danto

The Artistic Enfranchisement of Real Objects: The Artworld

Hamlet:
  Do you see nothing there?
The Queen:
  Nothing at all; yet all that is I see.
  Shakespeare: Hamlet, Act III, Scene IV

Hamlet and Socrates, though in praise and deprecation respectively, spoke of art as a mirror held up to nature. As with many disagreements in attitude, this one has a factual basis. Socrates saw mirrors as but reflecting what we can already see; so art, insofar as mirrorlike, yields idle accurate duplications of the appearances of things, and is of no cognitive benefit whatever. Hamlet, more acutely, recognized a remarkable feature of reflecting surfaces, namely that they show us what we could not otherwise perceive—our own face and form—and so art, insofar as it is mirrorlike, reveals us to ourselves, and is, even by Socratic criteria, of some cognitive utility after all. As a philosopher, however, I find Socrates' discussion defective on other, perhaps less profound grounds than these. If a mirror-image of *o* is indeed an imitation of *o,* then, if art is imitation, mirror-images are art. But in fact mirroring objects no more is art than returning weapons to a madman is justice; and reference to mirrorings would be just the sly sort of counterinstance we would expect Socrates to bring forward in rebuttal of the theory he instead uses them to illustrate. If that theory requires us to class *these* as art, it thereby shows its inadequacy: "is an imitation" will not do as a sufficient condition for "is art." Yet, perhaps because artists *were* engaged in imitation, in Socrates' time and after, the insufficiency of the theory was not noticed

until the invention of photography. Once rejected as a sufficient condition, mimesis was quickly discarded as even a necessary one; and since the achievement of Kandinsky, mimetic features have been relegated to the periphery of critical concern, so much so that some works survive in spite of possessing those virtues, excellence in which was once celebrated as the essence of art, narrowly escaping demotion to mere illustrations.

It is, of course, indispensable in Socratic discussion that all participants be masters of the concept up for analysis, since the aim is to match a real defining expression to a term in active use, and the test for adequacy presumably consists in showing that the former analyzes and applies to all and only those things of which the latter is true. The popular disclaimer notwithstanding, then, Socrates' auditors purportedly knew what art was as well as what they liked; and a theory of art, regarded here as a real definition of 'Art', is accordingly not to be of great use in helping men to recognize instances of its application. Their antecedent ability to do this is precisely what the adequacy of the theory is to be tested against, the problem being only to make explicit what they already know. It is *our* use of the term that the theory allegedly means to capture, but we are supposed able, in the words of a recent writer, "to separate those objects which are works of art from those which are not, because . . . we know how correctly to use the word 'art' and to apply the phrase 'work of art.' " Theories, on this account, are somewhat like mirror-images on Socrates' account, showing forth what we already know, wordy reflections of the actual linguistic practice we are masters in.

But telling artworks from other things is not so simple a matter, even for native speakers, and these days one might not be aware he was on artistic terrain without an artistic theory to tell him so. And part of the reason for this lies in the fact that terrain is constituted artistic in virtue of artistic theories, so that one use of theories, in addition to helping us discriminate art from the rest, consists in making art possible. Glaucon and the others could hardly have known what was art and what not: otherwise they would never have been taken by mirror-images.

I

Suppose one thinks of the discovery of a whole new class of artworks as something analogous to the discovery of a whole new class of facts anywhere, viz., as something for theoreticians to explain. In science, as elsewhere, we often accommodate new facts to old theories via auxiliary hypotheses, a pardonable enough conservatism when the theory in question is deemed too valuable to be jettisoned all at once. Now the Imitation Theory of Art (IT) is, if one but thinks it through, an exceedingly powerful theory, explaining a great many phenomena connected with the causation and evaluation of artworks, bringing a surprising unity into a complex domain. Moreover, it is a simple matter to shore it up against many purported counterinstances by such auxiliary hypotheses as that the artist who deviates from mimeticity is perverse, inept, or mad. Ineptitude, chicanery, or folly are, in fact, testable predications. Suppose, then, tests reveal that these hypotheses fail to hold, that the theory, now beyond repair, must be replaced. And a new theory is worked out, capturing what it can of the old theory's competence, together with the heretofore recalcitrant facts. One might, thinking along these lines, represent certain episodes in the history of art as not dissimilar to certain episodes in the history of science, where a conceptual revolution is being effected and where refusal to countenance certain facts, while in part due to prejudice, inertia, and self-interest, is due also to the fact that a well-established, or at least widely credited theory is being threatened in such a way that all coherence goes.

Some such episode transpired with the advent of post-impressionist paintings. In terms of the prevailing artistic theory (IT), it was impossible to accept these as art unless inept art: otherwise they could be discounted as hoaxes, self-advertisements, or the visual counterparts of madmen's ravings. So to get them accepted *as* art, on

a footing with the *Transfiguration* (not to speak of a Landseer stag), require not so much a revolution in taste as a theoretical revision of rather considerable proportions, involving not only the artistic enfranchisement of these objects, but an emphasis upon newly significant features of accepted artworks, so that quite different accounts of their status as artworks would now have to be given. As a result of the new theory's acceptance, not only were post-impressionist paintings taken up as art, but numbers of objects (masks, weapons, etc.) were transferred from anthropological museums (and heterogeneous other places) to *musées des beaux arts,* though, as we would expect from the fact that a criterion for the acceptance of a new theory is that is account for whatever the older one did, nothing had to be transferred out of the *musée des beaux arts*—even if there were internal rearrangements as between storage rooms and exhibition space. Countless native speakers hung upon suburban mantelpieces innumerable replicas of paradigm cases for teaching the expression 'work of art' that would have sent their Edwardian forebears into linguistic apoplexy.

To be sure, I distort by speaking of a theory: historically, there were several, all, interestingly enough, more or less defined in terms of the IT. Art-historical complexities must yield before the exigencies of logical exposition, and I shall speak as though there were one replacing theory, partially compensating for historical falsity by choosing one which was actually enunciated. According to it, the artists in question were to be understood not as unsuccessfully imitating real forms but as successfully creating new ones, quite as real as the forms which the older art had been thought, in its best examples, to be creditably imitating. Art, after all, had long since been thought of as creative (Vasari says that God was the first artist), and the post-impressionists were to be explained as genuinely creative, aiming, in Roger Fry's words, "not at illusion but reality." This theory (RT) furnished a whole new mode of looking at painting, old and new. Indeed, one might almost interpret the crude drawing in Van Gogh and Cézanne, the dislocation of form from contour in Rouault and Dufy, the arbitrary use of color planes in Gauguin and the Fauves, as so many ways of drawing attention to the fact that these were *non-imitations,* specifically intended not to deceive. Logically, this would be roughly like printing "Not Legal Tender" across a brilliantly counterfeited dollar bill, the resulting object (counterfeit *cum* inscription) rendered incapable of deceiving anyone. It is not an illusory dollar bill, but then, just because it is non-illusory it does not automatically become a real dollar bill either. It rather occupies a freshly opened area between real objects and real facsimiles of real objects: it is a non-facsimile, if one requires a word, and a new contribution to the world. Thus, Van Gogh's *Potato Eaters,* as a consequence of certain unmistakable distortions, turns out to be a non-facsimile of real-life potato eaters; and inasmuch as these are not facsimiles of potato eaters, Van Gogh's picture, as a non-imitation, had as much right to be called a real object as did its putative subjects. By means of this theory (RT), artworks re-entered the thick of things from which Socratic theory (IT) had sought to evict them: if no *more* real than what carpenters wrought, they were at least no *less* real. The Post-Impressionist won a victory in ontology.

It is in terms of RT that we must understand the artworks around us today. Thus Roy Lichtenstein paints comic-strip panels, though ten or twelve feet high. These are reasonably faithful to projections onto a gigantesque scale of the homely frames from the daily tabloid, but it is precisely the scale that counts. A skilled engraver might incise *The Virgin and the Chancellor Rollin* on a pinhead, and it would be recognizable as such to the keen of sight, but an engraving of a Barnett Newman on a similar scale would be a blob, disappearing in the reduction. A *photograph* of a Lichtenstein is indiscernible from a photograph of a counterpart panel from *Steve Canyon;* but the photograph fails to capture the scale, and hence is as inaccurate a reproduction as a black-and-white engraving of Botticelli, scale being essential here as color there. Lichtensteins, then, are not imitations but *new entities,* as giant whelks would be. Jasper Johns, by contrast, paints objects with respect to which questions of scale are irrelevant. Yet his objects cannot be imitations, for they have the remarkable property that any intended copy of a member of this class of objects is automatically a member of the class itself, so that these objects are logically inimitable. Thus, a copy of a numeral just *is* that numeral: a painting of 3 is a 3 made of paint. Johns, in addition, paints targets, flags, and maps. Finally, in what I hope are not unwitting footnotes to Plato, two of our pioneers—Robert Rauschenberg and Claes Oldenburg—have made genuine beds.

Rauschenberg's bed hangs on a wall, and is streaked with some desultory housepaint. Oldenburg's bed is a rhomboid, narrower at one end than the other, with what one might speak of as a built-in perspective: ideal for small bedrooms. As beds, these sell at singularly inflated prices, but one *could* sleep in either of them: Rauschenberg has expressed the fear that someone might just climb into his bed and fall asleep. Imagine, now, a certain Testadura—a plain speaker and noted philistine—who is not aware that these are art, and who takes them to be reality simple and pure. He attributes the paintstreaks on Rauschenberg's be to the slovenliness of the owner, and the bias in the Oldenburg bed to the ineptitude of the builder or the whimsy, perhaps, of whoever had it "custom-made." These would be mistakes, but mistakes of rather an odd kind, and not terribly different from that made by the stunned birds who pecked the sham grapes of Zeuxis. They mistook art for reality, and so has Testadura. But it was meant to *be* reality, accord to RT. Can one have mistaken reality for reality? How shall we describe Testadura's error? What, after all, prevents Oldenburg's creation from being a misshapen bed? This is equivalent to asking what makes it art, and with this query we enter a domain of conceptual inquiry where native speakers are poor guides: *they* are lost themselves.

II

To mistake an artwork for a real object is no great feat when an artwork is the real object one mistakes it for. The problem is how to avoid such errors, or to remove them once they are made. The artwork is a bed, and not a bed-illusion; so there is nothing like the traumatic encounter against a flat surface that brought it home to the birds of Zeuxis that they had been duped. Except for the guard cautioning Testadura not to sleep on the artworks, he might never have discovered that this was an artwork and not a bed; and since, after all, one cannot discover that a bed is not a bed, how is Testadura to realize that he has made an error? A certain sort of explanation is required, for the error here is a curiously philosophical one, rather like, if we may assume as correct some well-known views of P. F. Strawson, mistaking a person for a material body when the truth is that a person *is* a material body in the sense that a whole class of predicates, sensibly applicable to material bodies, are sensibly, and by appeal to no different criteria, applicable to persons. So you cannot *discover* that a person is not a material body.

We begin by explaining, perhaps, that the paintstreaks are not to be explained away, that they are *part* of the object, so the object is not a mere bed with—as it happens—streaks of paint spilled over it, but a complex object fabricated out of a bed and some paintstreaks: a paint-bed. Similarly, a person is not a material body with—as it happens—some thoughts superadded, but is a complex entity made up of a body and some conscious states: a conscious-body. Persons, like artworks, must then be taken as irreducible to *parts* of themselves, and are in that sense primitive. Or, more accurately, the paintstreaks are not part of the real object—the bed—which happens to be part of the artwork, but are, *like* the bed, part of the artwork as such. And this might be generalized into a rough characterization of artworks that happen to contain real objects as parts of themselves: not every part of an artwork *A* is part of a real object *R* when *R* is part of *A* and can, moreover, be detached from *A* and seen *merely* as *R*. The mistake thus far will have been to mistake *A* for *part* of itself, namely *R*, even though it would not be incorrect to say that *A* is *R*, that the artwork is a bed. It is the 'is' which requires clarification here.

There is an *is* that figures prominently in statements concerning artworks which is not the *is* of either identity or predication; nor is it the *is* of existence, of identification, or some special *is* made up to serve a philosophic end. Nevertheless, it is in common usage, and is readily mastered by children. It is the sense of *is* in accordance with which a child, shown a circle and a triangle and asked which is him and which his sister, will point to the triangle saying "That is me"; or, in response to my question, the person next to me points to the man in purple and says "That one is Lear"; or in the gallery I point, for my companion's benefit, to a spot in a painting before us and say "That white dab is Icarus." We do not mean, in these instances, that whatever is pointed to stands for, or represents, what it is said to be: yet I would not in the same sense of *is* point to the word and say "That is Icarus." The sentence "That *a* is *b*" is perfectly compatible with "That *a*

is not *b*" when the first employs this sense of *is* and the second employs some other, though *a* and *b* are used nonambiguously throughout. Often, indeed, the truth of the first *requires* the truth of the second. The first, in fact, is incompatible with "That *a* is not *b*" only when the *is* is used nonambiguously throughout. For want of a word I shall designate this the *is of artistic identification;* in each case in which it is used, the *a* stands for some specific physical property of, or physical part of, and object; and, finally, it is a necessary condition for something to be an artwork that some part or property of it be designable by the subject of a sentence that employs this special *is*. It is an *is,* incidentally, which has near-relatives in marginal and mythical pronouncements. (Thus, one *is* Quetzalcoatl; those *are* the Pillars of Hercules.)

Let me illustrate. Two painters are asked to decorate the east and west walls of a science library with frescoes to be respectively called *Newton's First Law* and *Newton's Third Law*. These paintings, when finally unveiled, look, scale apart, as follows:

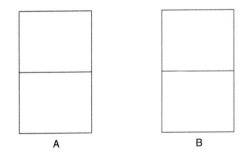

As objects I shall suppose the works to be indiscernible: a black horizontal line on a white ground, equally large in each dimension and element. *B* explains his work as follows: a mass, pressing downward, is met by a mass pressing upward: the lower mass reacts equally and oppositely to the upper one. *A* explains his work as follows: the line through the space is the path of an isolated particle. The path goes from edge to edge, to give the sense of its *going beyond*. If it ended or began within the space, the line would be curved: and it is parallel to the top and bottom edges, for if it were closer to one than to another, there would have to be a force accounting for it, and this is inconsistent with its being the path of an *isolated* particle.

Much follows from these artistic identifications. To regard the middle line as an edge (mass meeting mass) imposes the need to identify the top and bottom half of the picture as rectangles, and as two distinct parts (not necessarily as two masses, for the line could be the edge of *one* mass jutting up—or down—into empty space). If it is an edge, we cannot thus take the entire area of the painting as a single space: it is rather composed of two forms, or one form and a non-form. We could take the entire area as a single space only by taking the middle horizontal as a *line* which is not an edge. But this almost requires a three-dimensional identification of the whole picture: the area can be a flat surface which the line is *above (Jet-flight)*, or *below (Submarine-path)*, or *on (Line)*, or *in (Fissure)*, or *through (Newton's First Law)*—though in this last case the area is not a flat surface but a transparent cross section of absolute space. We could make all these prepositional qualifications clear by imagining perpendicular cross sections to the picture plane. Then, depending upon the applicable prepositional clause, the area is (artistically) interrupted or not by the horizontal element. If we take the line as *through* space, the edges of the picture are not really the edges of the space: the space goes beyond the picture if the line itself does; and we are in the same space as the line is. As *B,* the edges of the picture can be *part* of the picture in case the masses go right to the edges, so that the edges of the picture are *their* edges. In that case, the vertices of the picture would be the vertices of the masses, except that the masses have four vertices more than the picture itself does: here four vertices would be part of the artwork which were not part of the real object. Again, the faces of the masses could be the face of the picture, and in looking at the picture, we are looking at these faces: but *space* has no face, and on the reading of *A* the work has to be read as faceless, and the face of the physical object would not be part of the artwork. Notice here how one artistic identification engenders another artistic identification, and how, consistently with a given identification, we are *required* to give others and *precluded* from still others: indeed, a given identification determines how many elements the work is to contain. These different identifications are incompatible with one another, or generally so, and each might be said to make a different artwork, even though each artwork contains the identical real object as part of itself—or at least parts of the identical real object as part of itself. There are, of course, senseless identifications: no one could, I think, sensibly read the middle horizontal as *Love's Labour's Lost* or *The Ascendency of St. Erasmus.* Finally, notice how acceptance of one identification rather than another is in effect to exchange one *world* for another. We could, indeed, enter a quiet poetic world by identifying the upper area with a clear and cloudless sky, reflected in the still surface of the water below, whiteness kept from whiteness only by the unreal boundary of the horizon.

And now Testadura, having hovered in the wings throughout this discussion, protests that *all he sees is paint:* a white painted oblong with a black line painted across it. And how right he really is: that is all he sees or that anybody can, we aesthetes included. So, if he asks us to show him what there is further to see, to demonstrate through pointing that this is an artwork (*Sea and Sky*), we cannot comply, for he has overlooked nothing (and it would be absurd to suppose he had, that there was something tiny we could point to and he, peering closely, say "So it is! A work of art after all!"). We cannot help him until he has mastered the *is of artistic identification* and so *constitutes* it a work of art. If he cannot achieve this, he will never look upon artworks: he will be like a child who sees sticks as sticks.

But what about pure abstractions, say something that looks just like *A* but is entitled *No. 7?* The 10th Street abstractionist blankly insists that there is nothing here but white paint and black, and none of our literary identifications need apply. What then distinguishes him from Testadura, whose philistine utterances are indiscernible from his? And how can it be an artwork for him and not for Testadura, when they agree that there is nothing that does not meet the eye? The answer, unpopular as it is likely to be to purists of every variety, lies in the fact that this artist has returned to the physicality of paint through an atmosphere compounded of artistic theories and the history of recent and remote painting, elements of which he is trying to refine out of his own work; and as a consequence of this his work belongs in this atmosphere and is part of this history. He has achieved abstraction through rejection of artistic identifications, returning to the real world from which such identifications remove us (he thinks), somewhat in the mode of Ch'ing Yuan, who wrote:

Before I had studied Zen for thirty years, I saw mountains as mountains and waters and waters. When I arrived at a more intimate knowledge, I came to the point where I saw that mountains are not mountains, and waters are not waters. But now that I have got the very substance I am at rest. For it is just that I see mountains once again as mountains, and waters once again as waters.

His identification of what he has made is logically dependent upon the theories and history he rejects. The difference between his utterance and Testadura's "This is black paint and white paint and nothing more" lies in the fact that he is still using the *is* of artistic identification, so that his use of "That black paint is black paint" is not a tautology. Testadura is not at that stage. To see something as art requires something the eye cannot decry—an atmosphere of artistic theory, a knowledge of the history of art: an artworld.

III

Mr. Andy Warhol, the Pop artist, displays facsimiles of Brillo cartons, piled high, in neat stacks, as in the stockroom of the supermarket. They happen to be of wood, painted to look like cardboard, and why not? To paraphrase the critic of the *Times,* if one may make the facsimile of a human being out of bronze, why not the facsimile of a Brillo carton out of plywood? The cost of these boxes happens to be 2×10^3 that of their homely counterparts in real life—a differential hardly ascribable to their advantage in durability. In fact the Brillo people might, at some slight increase in cost, make their boxes out of plywood without these becoming artworks, and Warhol might make *his* out of cardboard without their ceasing to be art. So we may forget questions of intrinsic value, and ask why the Brillo people cannot manufacture art and why Warhol cannot *but* make artworks. Well, his are made by hand, to be sure. Which is like an insane reversal of Picasso's strategy in pasting the label from a bottle of Suze onto a drawing, saying as it were that the academic artist, concerned with exact imitation, must always fall short of the real thing: so why not just *use* the real thing? The Pop artist laboriously reproduces machine-made objects by hand, e.g., painting the

labels on coffee cans (one can hear the familiar commendation "Entirely made by hand" falling painfully out of the guide's vocabulary when confronted by these objects). But the difference cannot consist in craft: a man who carved pebbles out of stones and carefully constructed a work call *Gravel Pile* might invoke the labor theory of value to account for the price he demands; but the question is, What makes it art? And why need Warhol *make* these things anyway? Why not just scrawl his signature across one? Or crush one up and display is as *Crushed Brillo Box* ("A protest against mechanization …") or simply display a Brillo carton as *Uncrushed Brillo Box* ("A bold affirmation of the plastic authenticity of industrial …")? Is this man a kind of Midas, turning whatever he touches into the gold of pure art? And the whole world consisting of latent artworks waiting, like the bread and wine of reality, to be transfigured, through some dark mystery, into the indiscernible flesh and blood of the sacrament? Never mind that the Brillo box may not be good, much less great art. The impressive thing is that it is art at all. But if it is, why are not the indiscernible Brillo boxes that are in the stockroom? Or *has* the whole distinction between art and reality broken down?

Suppose a man collects object (ready-mades), including a Brillo carton; we praise the exhibit for variety, ingenuity, what you will. Next he exhibits nothing but Brillo cartons, and we criticize it as dull, repetitive, self-plagiarizing—or (more profoundly) claim that he is obsessed by regularity and repetition, as in *Marienbad.* Or he piles them high, leaving a narrow path; we tread our way through the smooth opaque stacks and find it an unsettling experience, and write it up as the closing in of consumer products, confining us as prisoners: or we say he is a modern pyramid builder. True, we don't say these things about the stockboy. But then a stockroom is not an art gallery, and we cannot readily separate the Brillo cartons from the gallery they are in, any more than we can separate the Rauschenberg bed from the paint upon it. Outside the gallery, they are pasteboard cartons. But then, scoured clean of paint, Rauschenberg's bed is a bed, just what it was before it was transformed into art. But then if we think this matter through, we discover that the artist has failed, really and of necessity, to produce a mere real object. He has produced an artwork, his use of real Brillo cartons being but an expansion of the resources available to artist, a contribution to *artists' materials,* as oil paint was, or *tuche.*

What in the end makes the difference between a Brillo box and a work of art consisting of a Brillo box is a certain theory of art. It is the theory that takes it up into the world of art, and keeps it from collapsing into the real object which it is (in a sense of *is* other than that of artistic identification). Of course, without the theory, one is unlikely to see it as art, and in order to see it as part of the artworld, one must have mastered a good deal of artistic theory as well as a considerable amount of the history of recent New York painting. It could not have been art fifty years ago. But then there could not have been, everything being equal, flight insurance in the Middle Ages, or Etruscan typewriter erasers. The worlds has to be ready for certain things, the artworld no less than the real one. It is the role of artistic theories, these days as always, to make the artworld, and art, possible. It would, I should think, never have occurred to the painters of Lascaux that they were producing *art* on those walls. Not unless there were neolithic aestheticians.

IV

The artworld stands to the real world in something like the relationship in which the City of God stands to the Earthly City. Certain objects, like certain individuals, enjoy a double citizenship, but there remains, the RT notwithstanding, a fundamental contrast between artworks and real objects. Perhaps this was already dimly sensed by the early framers of the IT who, inchoately realizing the nonreality of art, were perhaps limited only in supposing that the sole way objects had of being other than real is to be sham, so that artworks necessarily had to be imitations of real objects. This was too narrow. So Yeats saw in writing "Once out of nature I shall never take/My bodily form from any natural thing." It is but a matter of choice: and the Brillo box of the artworld may be just the Brillo box of the real one, separated and united by the *is* of artistic identification. But I should like to say some final words about the theories that make artworks possible, and their relationship to one another. In so doing, I shall beg some of the hardest philosophical questions I know.

I shall now think of pairs of predicates related to each other as "opposites," conceding straight off the vagueness of this *demodé* term. Contradictory predicates are not opposites, since one of each of them must apply to every object in the universe, and neither of a pair of opposites need apply to some objects in the universe. An object must first be of a certain kind before either of a pair of opposites applies to it, and then at most and at least one of the opposites must apply to it. So opposites are not contraries, for contraries may both be false of some objects in the universe, but opposites cannot both be false; for of some objects, neither of a pair of opposites *sensibly* applies, unless the object is of the right sort. Then, if the object is of the required kind, the opposites behave as contradictories. If F and non-F are opposites, an object o must be of a certain kind K before either of these sensibly applies; but if o is a member of K, then o either is F or non-F, to the exclusion of the other. The class of pairs of opposites that sensibly apply to the $(\delta)Ko$ I shall designate as the class of K-*relevant predicates.* And a necessary condition for an object to be of a kind K is that at least one pair of K-relevant opposites be sensibly applicable to it. But, in fact, if an object is of kind K, at least and at most one of each K-relevant pair of opposites applies to it.

I am now interested in the K-relevant predicates for the class K of artworks. And let F and non-F be an opposite pair of such predicates. Now it might happen that, throughout an entire period of time, every artwork is non-F. But since nothing thus far is both an artwork and F, it might never occur to anyone that non-F is an artistically relevant predicate. The non-F-ness of artworks goes unmarked. By contrast, all works up to a given time might be G, it never occurring to anyone until that time that something might both be an artwork and non-G; indeed, it might have been though that G was a *defining trait* of artworks when in fact something might first have to be an artwork before G is sensibly predicable of it—in which case non-G might also be predicable of artworks, and G itself then could not have been a defining trait of this class.

Let G be 'is representational' and let F be 'is expressionist'. At a given time, these and their opposites are perhaps the only art-relevant predicates in critical use. Now letting '+' stand for a given predicate P and '−' for its opposite non-*P,* we may construct a style matrix more of less as follows:

F	G
+	+
+	−
−	+
−	−

The rows determine available styles, given the active critical vocabulary: representational expressionistic (e.g., Fauvism); representational nonexpressionistic (Ingres); nonrepresentational expressionistic (Abstract Expressionism); nonrepresentational nonexpressionist (hard-edge abstraction). Plainly, as we add art-relevant predicates, we increase the number of available styles at the rate of 2^n. It is, of course, not easy to see in advance which predicates are going to be added or replaced by their opposites, but suppose an artist determines that *H* shall henceforth be artistically relevant for his paintings. Then, in fact, both *H* and non-*H* become artistically relevant for *all* painting, and if his is the first and only painting that is *H,* every other painting in existence becomes non-*H,* and the entire community of paintings is enriched, together with a doubling of the available style opportunities. It is this retroactive enrichment of the entities in the artworld that makes it possible to discuss Raphael and De Kooning together, or Lichtenstein and Michelangelo. The greater the variety of artistically relevant predicates, the more complex the individual members of the artworld become; and the more one knows of the entire population of the artworld, the richer one's experience with any of its members.

In this regard, notice that, if there are *m* artistically relevant predicates, there is always a bottom row with *m* minuses. This row is apt to be occupied by purists. Having scoured their canvases clear of what they regard as inessential, they credit themselves with having distilled out the essence of art. But this is just their fallacy: exactly as many artistically relevant predicates stand true of their square monochromes as stand true of any member of the Artworld, and they can *exist* as artworks only insofar as "impure" paintings exist. Strictly speaking, a black square by Reinhardt is artistically as rich as Titian's *Sacred and Profane Love.* This explains how less is more.

Fashion, as it happens, favors certain rows of the style matrix: museums, connoisseurs, and others are makeweights in the Artworld. To insist, or seek to, that all artists become representational, perhaps to gain entry into a specially prestigious exhibition, cuts the available style matrix in half: there are then $2^n/2$ ways of satisfying the requirement, and museums then can exhibit all these "approaches" to the topic they have set. But this is a matter of almost purely sociological interest: one row in the matrix is as legitimate as another. An artistic breakthrough consists, I suppose, in adding the possibility of a column to the matrix. Artists then, with greater or less alacrity, occupy the positions thus opened up: this is a remarkable feature of contemporary art, and for those unfamiliar with the matrix, it is hard, and perhaps impossible, to recognize certain positions as occupied by artworks. Nor would these things be artworks without the theories and the histories of the Artworld.

Brillo boxes enter the artworld with that same tonic incongruity the *commedia dell'arte* characters bring into *Ariadne auf Naxos.* Whatever is the artistically relevant predicate in virtue of which they gain their entry, the rest of the Artworld becomes that much the richer in having the opposite predicate available and applicable to its members. And, to return to the views of Hamlet with which we began this discussion, Brillo boxes may reveal us to ourselves as well as anything might: as a mirror held up to nature, they might serve to catch the conscience of our kings.

George Dickie

What Is Art? An Institutional Analysis

The attempt to define "art" by specifying its necessary and sufficient conditions is an old endeavor. The first definition—the imitation theory—despite what now seem like obvious difficulties, more or less satisfied everyone until some time in the nineteenth century. After the expression theory of art broke the domination of the imitation theory, many definitions purporting to reveal the necessary and sufficient conditions of art appeared. In the mid-1950s, several philosophers, inspired by Wittgenstein's talk about concepts, began arguing that there are no necessary and sufficient conditions for art. Until recently, this argument had persuaded so many philosophers of the futility of trying to define art that the flow of definitions had all but ceased. Although I will ultimately try to show that "art" can be defined, the denial of that possibility has had the very great value of forcing us to look deeper into the concept of "art." The parade of dreary and superficial definitions that had been presented was, for a variety of reasons, eminently rejectable. The traditional attempts to define "art," from the imitation theory on, may be thought of as Phase I and the contention that "art" cannot be defined as Phase II. I want to supply Phase III by defining "art" in such a way as to avoid the difficulties of the traditional definitions and to incorporate the insights of the later analysis. I should note that the imitation theory of the fine arts seems to have been adopted by those who held it without much serious thought and perhaps cannot be considered as a self-conscious theory of art in the way that the later theories can be.

The traditional attempts at definition have sometimes failed to see beyond prominent but accidental features of works of art, features that have characterized art at a particular stage in its historical development. For example, until quite recently the works of art clearly recognizable as such were either obviously representational or assumed to be representational. Paintings and sculptures were obviously so, and music was widely assumed in some sense to also be representational. Literature was representational in that is described familiar scenes of life. It was, then, easy enough to think that imitation must be the essence of art. The imitation theory focused on a readily evident relational property of works of art, namely, art's relation to subject matter. The development of nonobjective art showed that imitation is not even an always-accompanying property of art, much less an essential one.

The theory of art as the expression of emotion has focused on another relational property of works of art, the relation of a work to its creator. The expression theory also has proved inadequate, and no other subsequent definition has been satisfactory. Although not fully satisfying as definitions, the imitation and expression theories do provide a clue: both singled out *relational* properties of art as essential. As I shall try to show, the two defining characteristics of art are indeed relational properties, and one of them turns out to be exceedingly complex.

I

The best-known denial that "art" can be defined occurs in Morris Weitz's article "The Role of Theory in Aesthetics."[1] Weitz's conclusion depends upon two arguments which may be called his "generalization argument" and his "classification argument." In stating the "generalization argument" Weitz distinguishes, quite correctly, between the generic conception of "art" and the vari-

1. *Journal of Aesthetics and Art Criticism,* September 1965, pp. 27–35.

ous subconcepts of art such as tragedy, the novel, painting, and the like. He then goes on to give an argument purporting to show that the subconcept "novel" is open, that is, that the member of the class of novels do not share any essential or defining characteristics. He then asserts without further argument that what is true of novels is true of all other subconcepts of art. The generalization from one subconcept to all subconcepts may or may not be justified, but I am not questioning it here. I do question, however, Weitz's additional contention, also asserted without argument, that the generic conception of "art" is open. The best that can be said of his conclusion about the generic sense is that it is unsupported. All or some of the subconcepts of art may be open and the generic conception of art still be closed. That is, it is possible that all or some of the subconcepts of art, such as novel, tragedy, sculpture, and painting, may lack necessary and sufficient conditions and at the same time that "work of art," which is the genus of all the subconcepts, can be defined in terms of necessary and sufficient conditions. Tragedies may not have any characteristics in common which would distinguish them from, say, comedies *within the domain of art,* but it may be that there are common characteristics that works of art have which distinguish them from nonart. Nothing prevents a "closed genus/open species" relationship. Weitz himself has recently cited what he takes to be a similar (although reversed) example of genus-species relationship. He argues that "game" (the genus) is open but that "major league baseball" (a species) is closed.[2]

His second argument, "the classification argument," claims to show that not even the characteristic of artifactuality is a necessary feature of art. Weitz's conclusion here is something of a surprise, because it has been widely assumed by philosophers and nonphilosophers alike that a work of art is necessarily an artifact. His argument is simply that we sometimes utter such statements as "This piece of driftwood is a lovely piece of sculpture," and since such utterances are perfectly intelligible, it follows that some nonartifacts such as certain pieces of driftwood are works of art (sculptures). In other words, something need not be an artifact in or-

der to be correctly classified as a work of art. I will try to rebut this argument shortly.

Recently, Maurice Mandelbaum has raised a question about Wittgenstein's famous contention that "game" cannot be defined and Weitz's thesis about "art."[3] His challenge to both is based on the charge that they have been concerned only with what Mandelbaum calls "exhibited" characteristics and that consequently each has failed to take account of the nonexhibited, relational aspects of games and art. By "exhibited" characteristics Mandelbaum means easily perceived properties such as the fact that a ball is used in a certain kind of game, that a painting has a triangular composition, that an area in a painting is red, or that the plot of a tragedy contains a reversal of fortune. Mandelbaum concludes that when we consider the nonexhibited properties of games, we see that they have in common "the potentiality of . . . [an] . . . absorbing non-practical interest to either participants or spectators."[4] Mandelbaum may or may not be right about "game," but what interests me is the application of his suggestion about nonexhibited properties to the discussion of the definition of art. Although he does not attempt a definition of "art," Mandelbaum does suggest that feature(s) common to all works of art may perhaps be discovered that will be a basis for the definition of "art," if the nonexhibited features of art are attended to.

Having noted Mandelbaum's invaluable suggestion about definition, I now return to Weitz's argument concerning artifactuality. In an earlier attempt to show Weitz wrong, I thought it sufficient to point out that there are two senses of "work of art," an evaluative sense and a classificatory one; Weitz himself distinguishes these in his article as the evaluative and the descriptive senses of art. My earlier argument was that if there is more than one sense of "work of art," then the fact that "This piece of driftwood is a lovely piece of sculpture" is intelligible does not prove what Weitz wants it to prove. Weitz would have to show that "sculpture" is

---

2. "Wittgenstein's Aesthetics," in *Language and Aesthetics,* Benjamin R. Tilghman, ed. (Lawrence, Kans., 1973), p. 14.

3. "Family Resemblances and Generalizations Concerning the Arts," *American Philosophical Quarterly,* July 1965, pp. 219–28; reprinted in *Problems in Aesthetics,* Morris Weitz ed., 2d ed. (London, 1970), pp. 181–97.

4. *Ibid.,* p. 185 in the Weitz anthology.

being used in the sentence in question in the classificatory sense, and this he makes no attempt to do. My argument assumed that once the distinction is made, it is
obvious that "sculpture" is here being used in the evaluative sense. Richard Sclafani has subsequently noted
that my argument shows only that Weitz's argument is
inconclusive and that Weitz might still be right, even
though his argument does not prove his conclusion.
Sclafani, however, has constructed a stronger argument
against Weitz on this point.[5]

Sclafani shows that there is a third sense of "work of
art" and that "driftwood cases" (the nonartifact cases)
fall under it. He begins by comparing a paradigm work
of art, Brancusi's *Bird in Space,* with a piece of driftwood
which looks very much like it. Sclafani says that it seems
natural to say of the piece of driftwood that it is a work
of art and that we do so because it has so many properties in common with the Brancusi piece. He then asks
us to reflect on our characterization of the driftwood
and the *direction* it has taken. We say the driftwood is art
because of its resemblance to some paradigm work of
art or because the driftwood shares properties with several paradigm works of art. The paradigm work or
works are of course always artifacts; the direction of our
move is from paradigmatic (artifactual) works of art to
nonartifactual "art." Sclafani quite correctly takes this to
indicate that there is a primary, paradigmatic sense of
"work of art" (my classificatory sense) and a derivative
or secondary sense into which the "driftwood cases"
fall. Weitz is right in a way in saying that the driftwood
is art, but wrong in concluding that artifactuality is unnecessary for (the primary sense of) art.

There are then at least three distinct senses of "work
of art": the primary or classificatory sense, the secondary or derivative, and the evaluative. Perhaps in most
uses of Weitz's driftwood sentence example, both the
derivative and the evaluative senses would be involved:
the derivative sense if the driftwood shared a number of
properties with some paradigm work of art and the
evaluative sense if the shared properties were found to
be valuable by the speaker. Sclafani gives a case in which
only the evaluative sense functions, when someone says,

"Sally's cake is a work of art." In most uses of such a sentence "work of art" would simply mean that its referent
has valuable qualities. Admittedly, one can imagine
contexts in which the derivative sense would apply to
cakes. (Given the situation in art today, one can easily
imagine cakes to which the primary sense of art could
be applied.) If, however, someone were to say, "This
Rembrandt is a work of art," both the classificatory and
the evaluative senses would be functioning. The expression "this Rembrandt" would convey the information that its referent is a work of art in the classificatory
sense, and "is a work of art" could then only reasonably
be understood in the evaluative sense. Finally, someone
might say of a sea shell or other natural object which
resembles a man's face but is otherwise uninteresting,
"This shell (or other natural object) is a work of art." In
this case, only the derivative sense would be used.

We utter sentences in which the expression "work of
art" has the evaluative sense with considerable frequency, applying it to both natural objects and artifacts.
We speak of works of art in the derived sense with
somewhat less frequency. The classificatory sense of
"work of art," which indicates simply that a thing belongs to a certain category of artifacts, occurs, however,
very infrequently in our discourse. We rarely utter sentences in which we use the classificatory sense, because
it is such a basic notion: we generally know immediately whether an object is a work of art, so that generally no one needs to say, by way of classification, "That
is a work of art," although recent developments in art
such as junk sculpture and found art may occasionally
force such remarks. Even if we do not often talk about
art in this classificatory sense, however, it is a basic concept that structures and guides our thinking about our
world and its contents.

II

It is now clear that artifactuality is a necessary condition (call it the genus) of the primary sense of art. This
fact, however, does not seem very surprising and would
not even be very interesting except that Weitz and
others have denied it. Artifactuality alone, however, is
not the whole story and another necessary condition
(the differentia) has to be specified in order to have a

---

5. "'Art' and Artifactuality," *Southwestern Journal of Philosophy,* Fall 1970, pp. 105–8.

satisfactory definition of "art." Like artifactuality, the second condition is a nonexhibited property, which turns out to be as complicated as artifactuality is simple. The attempt to discover and specify the second condition of art will involve an examination of the intricate complexities of the "artworld." W. E. Kennick, defending a view similar to Weitz's, contends that the kind of approach to be employed here, following Mandelbaum's lead, is futile. He concludes that "the attempt to define Art in terms of what we do with certain objects is as doomed as any other."[6] He tries to support this conclusion by referring to such things as the fact that the ancient Egyptians sealed up paintings and sculptures in tombs. There are two difficulties with Kennick's argument. First, that the Egyptians sealed up paintings and sculptures in tombs does not show that they regarded them differently from the way in which we regard them. They might have put them there for the dead to appreciate or simply because they belonged to the dead person. The Egyptian practice does not establish so radical a difference between their conception of art and ours that a definition subsuming both is impossible. Second, one need not assume that we and the ancient Egyptians share a common conception of art. It would be enough to be able to specify the necessary and sufficient conditions for the concept of art which we have (we present-day Americans, we present-day Westerners, we Westerners since the organization of the system of the arts in or about the eighteenth century—I am not sure of the exact limits of the "we"). Kennick notwithstanding, we are most likely to discover the differentia of art by considering "what we do with certain objects." Of course, nothing guarantees that any given thing we might do or an ancient Egyptian might have done with a work of art will throw light on the concept of art. Not every "doing" will reveal what is required.

Although he does not attempt to formulate a definition, Arthur Danto in his provocative article, "The Artworld," has suggested the direction that must be taken by an attempt to define "art."[7] In reflecting on art and its history together with such present-day developments as Warhol's *Brillo Carton* and Rauschenberg's *Bed*, Danto writes, "To see something as art requires something the eye cannot descry—an atmosphere of artistic theory, a knowledge of history of art: an artworld."[8] Admittedly, this stimulating comment is in need of elucidation, but it is clear that in speaking of "something the eye cannot descry" Danto is agreeing with Mandelbaum that nonexhibited properties are of great importance in constituting something as art. In speaking of atmosphere and history, however, Danto's remark carries us a step further than Mandelbaum's analysis. Danto points to the rich structure in which particular works of art are embedded: he indicates *the institutional nature of art*.

I shall use Danto's term "artworld" to refer to the broad social institution in which works of art have their place. But is there such an institution? George Bernard Shaw speaks somewhere of the apostolic line of succession stretching from Aeschylus to himself. Shaw was no doubt speaking for effect and to draw attention to himself, as he often did, but there is an important truth implied by his remark. There is a long tradition or continuing institution of the theater having its origins in ancient Greek religion and other Greek institutions. That tradition has run very thin at times and perhaps even ceased to exist altogether during some periods, only to be reborn out of its memory and the need for art. The institutions associated with the theater have varied from time to time: in the beginning it was Greek religion and the Greek state; in medieval times, the church; more recently, private business and the state (national theater). What has remained constant with its own identity throughout its history is the theater itself as an established way of doing and behaving, what I shall call the primary convention of the theater. This institutionalized behavior occurs on both sides of the "footlights": both the players and the audience are involved and go to make up the institution of the theater. The roles of the actors and the audience are defined by the traditions of the theater. What the author, management, and players present is art, and it is art because it is presented within the theaterworld framework. Plays are written to have a place in the theater system and they

---

6. "Does Traditional Aesthetics Rest on a Mistake?" *Mind*, 1958, p. 330.

7. *Journal of Philosophy*, October 15, 1964, pp. 571–84. [See pp. 844–851, this volume.]

8. *Ibid.*, p. 580. [See p. 849, this volume.]

exist as plays, that is, as art, within that system. Of course, I do not wish to deny that plays also exist as literary works, that is, as art within the literary system: the theater system and the literary system overlap. Let me make clear what I mean by speaking of the artworld as an institution. Among the meanings of "institution" in *Webster's New Collegiate Dictionary* are the following: "3. That which is instituted as: a. An established practice, law, custom, etc. b. An established society or corporation." When I call the artworld an institution I am saying that it is an established practice. Some persons have thought that an institution must be an established society or corporation and, consequently, have misunderstood my claim about the artworld.

Theater is only one of the systems within the artworld. Each of the systems has had its own origins and historical development. We have some information about the later stages of these developments, but we have to guess about the origins of the basic art systems. I suppose that we have complete knowledge of certain recently developed subsystems or genres such as Dada and happenings. Even if our knowledge is not as complete as we wish it were, however, we do have substantial information about the systems of the artworld as they currently exist and as they have existed for some time. One central feature all of the systems have in common is that each is a framework for the *presenting* of particular works of art. Given the great variety of the systems of the artworld it is not surprising that works of art have no exhibited properties in common. If, however, we step back and view the works in their institutional setting, we will be able to see the essential properties they share.

Theater is a rich and instructive illustration of the institutional nature of art. But it is a development within the domain of painting and sculpture—Dadaism—that most easily reveals the institutional essence of art. Duchamp and friends conferred the status of art on "ready-mades" (urinals, hatracks, snow shovels, and the like), and when we reflect on their deeds we can take note of a kind of human action which has until now gone unnoticed and unappreciated—the action of conferring the status of art. Painters and sculptors, of course, have been engaging all along in the action of conferring this status on the objects they create. As long, however, as the created objects were conventional, given the paradigms of the times, the objects themselves and their fascinating exhibited properties were the focus of the attention of not only spectators and critics but of philosophers of art as well. When an artist of an earlier era painted a picture, he did some or all of a number of things: depicted a human being, portrayed a certain man, fulfilled a commission, worked at his livelihood, and so on. In addition he also acted as an agent of the artworld and conferred the status of art on his creation. Philosophers of art attended to only some of the properties the created object acquired from these various actions, for example, to the representational or to the expressive features of the objects. They entirely ignored the nonexhibited property of status. When, however, the objects are bizarre, as those of the Dadaists are, our attention is forced away from the objects' obvious properties to a consideration of the objects in their social context. As works of art Duchamp's "ready-mades" may not be worth much, but as examples of art they are very valuable for art theory. I am not claiming that Duchamp and friends invented the conferring of the status of art; they simply used an existing institutional device in an unusual way. Duchamp did not invent the artworld, because it was there all along.

The artworld consists of a bundle of systems: theater, painting, sculpture, literature, music, and so on, each of which furnishes an institutional background for the conferring of the status on objects within its domain. No limit can be placed on the number of systems that can be brought under the generic conception of art, and each of the major systems contains further subsystems. These features of the artworld provide the elasticity whereby creativity of even the most radical sort can be accommodated. A whole new system comparable to the theater, for example, could be added in one fell swoop. What is more likely is that a new subsystem would be added within a system. For example, junk sculpture added within sculpture, happenings added within theater. Such additions might in time develop into full-blown systems. Thus, the radical creativity, adventuresomeness, and exuberance of art which Weitz speaks is possible within the concept of art, even though it is closed by the necessary and sufficient conditions of artifactuality and conferred status.

Having now briefly described the artworld, I am in a position to specify a definition of "work of art." The definition will be given in terms of artifactuality and the conferred status of art or, more strictly speaking, the conferred status of candidate for appreciation. Once the definition has been stated, a great deal will still remain to be said by way of clarification: A work of art in the classificatory sense is (1) an artifact (2) a set of the aspects of which has had conferred upon it the status of candidate for appreciation by some person or persons acting on behalf of a certain social institution (the artworld).

The second condition of the definition makes use of four variously interconnected notions: (1) acting on behalf of an institution, (2) conferring of status, (3) being a candidate, and (4) appreciation. The first two of these are so closely related that they must be discussed together. I shall first describe paradigm cases of conferring status outside the artworld and then show how similar actions take place within the artworld. The most clear-cut examples of the conferring of status are certain legal actions of the state. A king's conferring of knighthood, a grand jury's indicting someone, the chairman of the election board certifying that someone is qualified to run for office, or a minister's pronouncing a couple man and wife are examples in which a person or persons acting on behalf of a social institution (the state) confer(s) *legal* status on persons. The congress or a legally constituted commission may confer the status of national park or monument on an area or thing. The examples given suggest that pomp and ceremony are required to establish legal status, but this is not so, although of course a legal system is presupposed. For example, in some jurisdictions common-law marriage is possible— a legal status acquired without ceremony. The conferring of a Ph.D. degree on someone by a university, the election of someone as president of the Rotary, and the declaring of an object as a relic of the church are examples in which a person or persons confer(s) nonlegal status on persons or things. In such cases some social system or other must exist as the framework within which the conferring takes place, but, as before, ceremony is not required to establish status: for example, a person can acquire the status of wise man or village idiot within a community without ceremony.

Some may feel that the notion of conferring status within the artworld is excessively vague. Certainly this notion is not as clear-cut as the conferring of status within the legal system, where procedures and lines of authority are explicitly defined and incorporated into law. The counterparts in the artworld to specified procedures and lines of authority are nowhere codified, and the artworld carries on its business at the level of customary practice. Still there *is* a practice and this defines a social institution. A social institution need not have a formally established constitution, officers, and bylaws in order to exist and have the capacity to confer status—some social institutions are formal and some are informal. The artworld could become formalized, and perhaps has been to some extent in certain political contexts, but most people who are interested in art would probably consider this a bad thing. Such formality would threaten the freshness and exuberance of art. The core personnel of the artworld is a loosely organized, but nevertheless related, set of persons including artists (understood to refer to painters, writers, composers), producers, museum directors, museum-goers, theater-goers, reporters for newspapers, critics for publications of all sorts, art historians, art theorists, philosophers of art, and others. These are the people who keep the machinery of the artworld working and thereby provide for its continuing existence. In addition, every person who sees himself as a member of the artworld is thereby a member. Although I have called the persons just listed the core personnel of the artworld, there is a minimum core within that core without which the artworld would not exist. This essential core consists of artists who create the works, "presenters" to present the works, and "goers" who appreciate the works. This minimum core might be called "the presentation group," for it consists of artist whose activity is necessary if anything is to be presented, the presenters (actors, stage managers, and so on), and the goers whose presence and cooperation is necessary in order for anything to be presented. A given person might play more than one of these essential roles in the case of the presentation of a particular work. Critics, historians, and philosophers or art become members of the artworld at some time after the minimum core personnel of a particular art system get that system into operation. All of these roles are institutionalized and must be learned in one way or another by the participants. For example, a theater-goer is not just someone who happens to enter a theater; he is a person who enters with certain expectations and knowledge about what he will experience and an understanding of how he should behave in the face of what he will experience.

Assuming that the existence of the artworld has been established or at least made plausible, the problem is now to see how status is conferred by this institution. My thesis is that, in a way analogous to the way in which a person is certified as qualified for office, or two persons acquire the status of common-law marriage within a legal system, or a person is elected president of the Rotary, or a person acquires the status of wise man within a community, so an artifact can acquire the status of candidate for appreciation within the social system called "the artworld." How can one tell when the status has been conferred? An artifact's hanging in an art museum as part of a show and a performance at a theater are sure signs. There is, of course, no guarantee that one can always know whether something is a candidate for appreciation, just as one cannot always tell whether a given person is a knight or is married. When an object's status depends upon nonexhibited characteristics, a simple look at the object will not necessarily reveal that status. The nonexhibited relation *may* be symbolized by some badge, for example, by a wedding ring, in which case a simple look will reveal the status.

The more important question is that of how the status of candidate for appreciation is conferred. The examples just mentioned, display in a museum and a performance in a theater, seem to suggest that a number of persons are required for the actual conferring of the status. In one sense a number of persons are required but in another sense only one person is required: a number of persons are required to make up the social institution of the artworld, but only one person is required to act on behalf of the artworld and to confer the status of candidate for appreciation. In fact, many works of art are seen only by one person—the one who creates them—but they are still art. The status in question may be acquired by a single person's acting on behalf of the artworld and *treating an artifact as a candidate for appreciation*. Of course, nothing prevents a group of persons from conferring the status, but it is usually conferred by a single person, the artist who creates the artifact. It may be helpful to compare and contrast the notion of conferring the status of candidate for appreciation with a case in which something is simply presented for appreciation: hopefully this will throw light on the notion of status of candidate. Consider the case of a salesman of plumbing supplies who spreads his wares before us.

"Placing before" and "conferring the status of candidate for appreciation" are very different notions, and this difference can be brought out by comparing the salesman's action with the superficially similar act of Duchamp in entering a urinal which he christened *Fountain* in that now-famous art show. The difference is that Duchamp's action took place within the institutional setting of the artworld and the plumbing salesman's action took place outside of it. The salesman could do what Duchamp did, that is, convert a urinal into a work of art, but such a thing probably would not occur to him. Please remember that *Fountain*'s being a work of art does not mean that it is a good one, nor does this qualification insinuate that it is a bad one either. The antics of a particular present-day artist serve to reinforce the point of the Duchamp case and also to emphasize a significance of the practice of naming works of art. Walter de Maria has in the case of one of his works even gone through the motions, no doubt as a burlesque, of using a procedure used by many legal and some nonlegal institutions—the procedure of licensing. His *High Energy Bar* (a stainless-steel bar) is accompanied by a certificate bearing the name of the work and stating that the bar is a work of art only when the certificate is present. In addition to highlighting the status of art by "certifying" it on a document, this example serves to suggest a significance of the act of naming works of art. An object may acquire the status of art without ever being named but giving it a title makes clear to whomever is interested that an object is a work of art. Specific titles function in a variety of ways—as aides to understanding a work or as a convenient way of identifying it, for example—but any title at all (even *Untitled*) is a badge of status.

The third notion involved in the second condition of the definition is candidacy: a member of the artworld confers the status of candidate for appreciation. The definition does not require that a work of art actually be appreciated, even by one person. The fact is that many, perhaps most, works of art go unappreciated. It is important not to build into the definition of the classificatory sense of "work of art" value properties such as actual appreciation: to do so would make it impossible to speak of unappreciated works of art. Building in value properties might even make it awkward to speak of bad works of art. A theory of art must preserve certain central features of the way in which we talk about art, and we do find it necessary sometimes to speak of unappreciated art and of bad art. Also, not every aspect of a work is included in the candidacy for appreciation; for example, the color of the back of a painting is not ordinarily considered to be something which someone might think it appropriate to appreciate. [. . .] The definition of "work of art" should not, therefore, be understood as asserting that every aspect of a work is included within the candidacy for appreciation.

The fourth notion involved in the second condition of the definition is appreciation itself. Some may assume that the definition is referring to a special kind of *aesthetic* appreciation. [. . .] There is no reason to think that there is a special kind of aesthetic consciousness, attention, or perception. Similarly, I do not think there is any reason to think that there is a special kind of aesthetic appreciation. All that is meant by "appreciation" in the definition is something like "in experiencing the qualities of a thing one finds them worthy or valuable," and this meaning applies quite generally both inside and outside the domain of art. Several persons have felt that my account of the institutional theory of art is incomplete because of what they see as my insufficient analysis of "appreciation." They have, I believe, thought that there are different kinds of appreciation and that the appreciation in the appreciation of art is somehow typically different from the appreciation in the appreciation of nonart. But the only sense in which there is a difference between the appreciation of art and the appreciation of nonart is that the appreciations have different *objects*. The institutional structure in which the art object is embedded, not different kinds of appreciation, makes the difference between the appreciation of art and the appreciation of nonart.

In a recent article[9] Ted Cohen has raised a question concerning (1) candidacy for appreciation and (2) appreciation as these two were treated in my original attempt to define "art."[10] He claims that in order for it to be possible for candidacy for appreciation to be con-

ferred on something that it must be possible for that thing to be appreciated. Perhaps he is right about this; in any event, I cannot think of any reason to disagree with him on this point. The possibility of appreciation is one constraint on the definition: if something cannot be appreciated, it cannot become art. The question that now arises is: is there anything which it is impossible to appreciate? Cohen claims that many things cannot be appreciated; for example, "ordinary thumbtacks, cheap white envelopes, the plastic forks given at some drive-in restaurants."[11] But more importantly, he claims that *Fountain* cannot be appreciated. He says that *Fountain* has a point which can be appreciated, but that it is Duchamp's gesture that has significance (can be appreciated) and not *Fountain* itself. I agree that *Fountain* has the significance Cohen attributes to it, namely, that it was a protest against the art of its day. But why cannot the ordinary qualities of *Fountain*—its gleaming white surface, the depth revealed when it reflects images of surrounding object, its pleasing oval shape—be appreciated? It has qualities similar to those of works by Brancusi and Moore which many do not balk at saying they appreciate. Similarly, thumbtacks, envelopes, and plastic forks have qualities that can be appreciated if one makes the effort to focus attention on them. One of the values of photography is its ability to focus on and bring out the qualities of quite ordinary objects. And the same sort of thing can be done without the benefit of photography by just looking. In short, it seems unlikely to me that any object would not have some quality which is appreciatable and thus likely that the constraint Cohen suggests may well be vacuous. But even if there are some objects that cannot be appreciated, *Fountain* and the other Dadaist creations are not among them.

I should note that in accepting Cohen's claim I am saying that every work of art must have some minimal *potential* value or worthiness. This fact, however, does not collapse the distinction between the evaluative sense and the classificatory sense of "work of art." The evaluative sense is used when the object it is predicated of is deemed *to be* of substantial, actual value, and that object may be a natural object. I will further note that the appreciatability of a work of art in the classificatory

9. "The Possibility of Art: Remarks on a Proposal by Dickie," *Philosophical Review*, January 1973, pp. 69–82.

10. "Defining Art," *American Philosophical Quarterly*, July 1969, pp. 253–6.

11. "The Possibility of Art," p. 78.

sense is *potential* value which in a given case may never be realized.[12]

The definition I have given contains a reference to the artworld. Consequently, some may have the uncomfortable feeling that my definition is viciously circular. Admittedly, in a sense the definition is circular, but it is not viciously so. If I had said something like "A work of art is an artifact on which a status has been conferred by the artworld" and then said of the artworld only that it confers the status of candidacy for appreciation, then the definition would be viciously circular because the circle would be so small and *uninformative*. I have, however, devoted a considerable amount of space to describing and analyzing the historical, organizational, and functional intricacies of the artworld, and if this account is accurate the reader has received a considerable amount of *information* about the artworld. The circle I have run is not small and it is not uninformative. If, in the end, the artworld cannot be described independently of art, that is, if the description contains references to art historians, art reporters, plays, theaters, and so on, then the definition strictly speaking is circular. It is not, however, viciously so, because the whole account in which the definition is embedded contains a great deal of information about the artworld. One must not focus narrowly on the definition alone: for what is important to see is that art is an institutional concept and this requires seeing the definition in the context of the whole account. I suspect that the "problem" of circularity will arise frequently, perhaps always, when institutional concepts are dealt with.

III

The instances of Dadaist art and similar present-day developments which have served to bring the institutional nature of art to our attention suggest several questions. First, if Duchamp can convert such artifacts as a urinal, a snow shovel, and a hatrack into works of art, why can't natural objects such as driftwood also become works of art in the classificatory sense? Perhaps they can if any one

of a number of things is done to them. One way in which this might happen would be for someone to pick up a natural object, take it home, and hang it on the wall. Another way would be to pick up a natural object and enter it in an exhibition. I was assuming earlier, by the way, that the piece of driftwood referred to in Weitz's sentence was in place on a beach and untouched by human hand or at least untouched by any human intention and therefore was art in the evaluative or derivative sense. Natural objects which become works of art in the classificatory sense are artifactualized without the use of tools—artifactuality is conferred on the object rather than worked on it. This means that natural objects which become works of art acquire their artifactuality at the same time that the status of candidate for appreciation is conferred on them, although the act that confers artifactuality is not the same act that confers the status of candidate for appreciation. But perhaps a similar thing ordinarily happens with paintings and poems; they come to exist as artifacts at the same time that they have the status of candidate for appreciation conferred on them. Of course, being an artifact and being a candidate for appreciation are not the same thing—they are two properties which may be acquired at the same time. Many may find the notion of artifactuality being conferred rather than "worked" on an object too strange to accept and admittedly it is an unusual conception. It may be that a special account will have to be worked out for exhibited driftwood and similar cases.

Another question arising with some frequency in connection with discussions of the concept of art and seeming especially relevant in the context of the institutional theory is "How are we to conceive of paintings done by individuals such as Betsy the chimpanzee from the Baltimore Zoo?" Calling Betsy's product paintings is not meant to prejudge that they are works of art, it is just that some word is needed to refer to them. The question of whether Betsy's paintings are art depends upon what is done with them. For example, a year or two ago the Field Museum of Natural History in Chicago exhibited some chimpanzee and gorilla paintings. We must say that these paintings are not works of art. If, however, they had been exhibited a few miles away at the Chicago Art Institute they would have been works of art—the paintings would have been art if the director of the Art Institute had been willing to go out on a limb for his fel-

---

12. I realized that I must make the two points noted in this paragraph as the result of a conversation with Mark Venezia. I wish to thank him for the stimulation of his remarks.

low primates. A great deal depends upon the institutional setting: one institutional setting is congenial to conferring the status of art and the other is not. Please note that although paintings such as Betsy's would remain her paintings even if exhibited at an art museum, they would be the *art* of the person responsible for their being exhibited. Betsy would not (I assume) be able to conceive of herself in such a way as to be a member of the artworld and, hence, would not be able to confer the relevant status. Art is a concept which necessarily involves human intentionality. These last remarks are not intended to denigrate the value (including beauty) of the paintings of chimpanzees shown at natural history museums or the creations of bower birds, but as remarks about what falls under a particular concept.

Danto in "Art Works and Real Things" discusses defeating conditions of the ascriptivity of art.[13] He considers fake paintings, that is, copies of original paintings which are attributed to the creators of the original paintings. He argues that a painting's being a fake prevents it from being a work of art, maintaining that originality is an analytical requirement of being a work of art. That a work is derivative or imitative does not, however, he thinks, prevent it from being a work of art. I think Danto is right about fake paintings, and I can express this in terms of my own account by saying that originality in paintings is an antecedent requirement for the conferring of the candidacy for appreciation. Similar sorts of things would have to be said for similar cases in the arts other than painting. One consequence of this requirement is that there are many works of nonart which people take to be works of art, namely, those fake paintings which are not known to be fakes. When fakes are discovered to be fakes, they do not lose that status of art because they never had the status in the first place, despite what almost everyone had thought. There is some analogy here with patent law. Once an invention has been patented, one exactly like it cannot be patented —the patent for just that invention has been "used up." In the case of patenting, of course, whether the second device is a copy or independently derived is unimportant, but the copying aspect is crucial in the artistic case.

The Van Meegeren painting that was not a copy of an actual Vermeer but a painting done in the manner of Vermeer with a forged signature is a somewhat more complicated case. The painting with the forged signature is not a work of art, but if Van Meegeren had signed his own name the painting would have been.

Strictly speaking, since originality is an analytic requirement for a painting to be a work of art, an originality clause should be incorporated into my definition of "work of art." But since I have not given any analysis of the originality requirement with respect to works other than paintings, I am not in a position to supplement the definition in this way. All I can say at this time is what I said just above, namely, that originality in paintings is an antecedent requirement for the conferring of the candidacy for appreciation and that considerations of a similar sort probably apply in the other arts.

Weitz charges that the defining of "art" or its subconcepts forecloses on creativity. Some of the traditional definitions of "art" *may* have and some of the traditional definitions of its subconcepts probably *did* foreclose on creativity, but this danger is now past. At one time a playwright, for example, may have conceived of and wished to write a play with tragic features but lacking a defining characteristic as specified by, say, Aristotle's definition of "tragedy." Faced with this dilemma the playwright might have been intimidated into abandoning his project. With the present-day disregard for established genres, however, and the clamor for novelty in art, this obstacle to creativity no longer exists. Today, if a new and unusual work is created and it is similar to some members of an established type of art, it will usually be accommodated within that type, or if the new work is very unlike any existing works then a new subconcept will probably be created. Artists today are not easily intimidated, and they regard art genres as loose guidelines rather than rigid specifications. Even if a philosopher's remarks were to have an effect on what artists do today, the institutional conception of art would certainly not foreclose on creativity. The requirement of artifactuality cannot prevent creativity, since artifactuality is a necessary condition of creativity. There cannot be an instance of creativity without an artifact of some kind being produced. The second requirement involving the conferring of status could not inhibit creativity; in fact, it encourages it. Since under

---

13. Arthur Danto, "Art Works and Real Things," *Theoria* parts 1–3, 1973, pp. 12–14.

the definition anything whatever may become art, the definition imposes no restraints on creativity.

The institutional theory of art may sound like saying, "A work of art is an object of which someone has said, 'I christen this object a work of art.'" And it is rather like that, although this does not mean that the conferring of the status of art is a simple matter. Just as the christening of a child has as its background the history and structure of the church, conferring the status of art has as its background the Byzantine complexity of the artworld. Some may find it strange that in the nonart cases discussed, there are ways in which the conferring can go wrong, while that does not appear to be true in art. For example, an indictment might be improperly drawn up and the person charged would not actually be indicted, but nothing parallel seems possible in the case of art. This fact just reflects the differences between the artworld and legal institutions: the legal system deals with matters of grave personal consequences and its procedures must reflect this; the artworld deals with important matters also but they are of a different sort entirely. The artworld does not require rigid procedures; it admits and even encourages frivolity and caprice without losing its serious purpose. Please note that not all legal procedures are as rigid as court procedures and that mistakes made in conferring certain kinds of legal status are not fatal to that status. A minister may make mistakes in reading the marriage ceremony, but the couple that stands before him will still acquire the status of being married. If, however, a mistake cannot be made *in* conferring the status of art, a mistake can be made *by* conferring it. In conferring the status of art on an object one assumes a certain kind of responsibility for the object in its new status—presenting a candidate for appreciation always allows the possibility that no one will appreciate it and that the person who did the conferring will thereby lose face. One *can* make a work of art out of a sow's ear, but that does not necessarily make it a silk purse.

IV

Once the institutional nature of art is noted, the roles of such "theories of art" as the imitation and expression theories played in thinking about art can be seen in an interesting perspective. For example, as long as all art was imitative or thought to be imitative, imitation was thought to be a universal property of art. Not surprisingly, what was though to be the only universal property of art was taken to be the defining property of art. What happened was that an assumed always-accompanying property was mistaken for an essential property, and this mistake led to a mistaken theory of art. Once the imitation theory was formulated, it tended to work in a normative way to encourage artists to be imitative. Of course, philosophical theories do not generally have much effect on the practices of men. The imitation theory in the past may, however, have had more than the usual slight impact, because it was based on a widespread feature of art and therefore reinforced an emphasis on an easily perceived characteristic and because the class of artists was relatively small and contained lines of communication.

The role played by the expression theory was quite different from that of the imitation theory. It was seen as a replacement for the imitation theory and served as its correction. Developments in art had shown that the imitation theory was incorrect and it was quite natural to seek a substitute that focused on another exhibited property of art, in this case its expressive qualities, interpreting them as expressions of the artists. I suspect that the expression theory has a normative role in a way that the imitation theory did not. That is, the expression theory was on the part of many of its proponents an attempt to "reform" art. Whether the expression theorists saw themselves as attempting to influence the creation of art with a certain kind of content or to separate art from something which pretended to be art, they aimed at reform.

From the point of view of the institutional theory, both the imitation theory and the expression theory are mistaken as theories of art. If, however, they are approached as attempts to focus attention on aspects of art (its representative and expressive qualities) which have been and continue to be of great importance, then they have served and continue to serve a valuable function. The institutional definition of "art" does not reveal everything that art can do. A great deal remains to be said about the kinds of thing that art can do, and the imitation and expression theories indicate what *some* of these things are, although not in a perfectly straightforward way. [. . .]

GLOSSARY

accidental.   A property that a thing could gain or lose while still remaining the same thing; an inessential property.

acquired perception.   The acquired ability to judge by means of sense a feature that is not evident to the uneducated sense—e.g., to judge by sight how large a distant object is.

action.   Something that an agent does, as opposed to what merely happens to an agent.

aesthetic.   Pertaining to the arts or to taste.

afterimage.   A visual image that persists after the visual stimulation has ended.

alienated labor.   Separation from ownership, control, and direction of one's work, with the result that work is not an expression of personal creativity.

alienation.   Separation of persons from direct control of their social lives.

allfusion.   The fusion of all members of a set so long as they exist at the same time.

analysis.   The process of breaking down a term or concept into simple parts so that its logical structure is displayed.

analytic.   True (or false) on the basis of meaning alone.

apodictic.   Necessarily true.

a posteriori.   Knowable only on the basis of experience.

appropriation.   To take possession of for one's exclusive use.

a priori.   Knowable independently of experience.

artworld.   The social institution or established practice in which works of art have their place.

association of ideas.   The pattern in which different ideas occur together or in succession.

authority.   The capacity to ensure compliance of others based on their recognition of legitimacy—i.e., based on norms or rules that those affected accept.

autonomy.   Freedom of the will; the capacity to act on the basis of rules one sets for oneself.

axiarchic view.   The view that the world exists because its existence is good.

axiom.   Unquestioned first principle.

behaviorism.   The theory that mental states, such as beliefs and desires, are logical constructs of dispositions to behave.

biconditional.   A proposition with the form 'if x then y and if y then x'.

capitalism.   The economic system in which capital or goods are privately owned and profit is reinvested to generate more capital; the system that underlies a market economy.

causation.   The relation that holds between two items when one brings about the other or when, if the first were not the case, the second would not come to be the case.

certain.   Indubitable.

clear and distinct ideas.   An idea is clear just in case it is possible to distinguish it from every other idea. It is distinct just in case one can tell what ideas compose it. In Descartes, clear and distinct ideas are acceptable.

closure principle.   The principle that knowledge is closed under known logical implication.

coextensive.   Having the same extension or application. 'Vixen' and 'female fox' are coextensive because every vixen is a female fox and every female fox is a vixen.

commodity.   A good or service sold in the marketplace.

commonwealth.   A state governed by the people.

complex idea.   An idea that is composed of simple ideas; the simple ideas must, according to empiricism, originate in sensation, but we can combine them in imagination to form ideas of things we have never experienced.

concept.   A general idea; that which answers to a predicate.

conditional.   A proposition with the form 'if *x* then *y*'.

confirmation.   Support by evidence.

conjunction.   A proposition with the form '*x* and *y*'.

conjunctive fork.   In Salmon, a causal fork in which the common cause screens off one effect from the other.

connotation.   The meaning of a word or phrase.

consciousness.   Awareness, the felt quality of experience.

consistent.   A set of statements is consistent if and only if they can be simultaneously true; it is inconsistent if they cannot be simultaneously true.

constant conjunction.   Types of events are constantly conjoined when events of one type are regularly followed by events of the other type—e.g., events of the clock hands striking twelve are followed by the ringing of the bell. See **causation.**

constitute.   To make up of.

contiguity.   Being placed next to or touching. In Hume, the cause must be contiguous to the effect.

contingent.   Characteristic of a proposition that could be true or could be false.

contradiction.   The conjunction of a proposition and its negation.

contrapositive.   The contrapositive of 'if *x* then *y*' is 'if not-*y* then not-*x*'. A sentence and its contrapositive are logically equivalent.

counterfactual.   A proposition with the form 'if *x* were to happen, *y* would happen' with the implication that the antecedent—the "if" clause—is false or contrary to fact. Sometimes represented A $\square\!\!\rightarrow$ B (see Lewis, 265–73). See **subjunctive conditional.**

covenant.   A binding agreement.

criterion.   A sufficient condition, either logically or in practice. If *x* satisfies the criteria for being *y*, one may safely take *x* to be *y*.

deduction.   An argument whose conclusion follows from some premises by the rules of logic. If the premises of a valid deduction are true, the conclusion is guaranteed also to be true.

defeated justification.   Justification that is discredited by further evidence or reasons.

denotation.   The relation of a term to its referent.

determinism.   The doctrine that every event has a cause.

difference principle.   The principle that states social and economic inequalities are justified only if they benefit the least well off, and only if they attach to offices that are open under fair equality of opportunity.

dignity.   In Kant, the worth of a rational individual.

disinterested.   Having no interest in other people's interests; unbiased.

disjunction.   A proposition with the form '*p* or *q* or both'.

disposition.   A tendency to act in characteristic ways in certain circumstances.

division of labor.   The dividing up of a complex task into smaller subtasks, each of which is performed by an expert.

doxastic.   Pertaining to belief.

dualism.   The doctrine that there are two distinct sorts of things: minds and bodies.

duty.   That which one must do; something required.

effect.   That which is brought about by a cause.

efficient cause.   The agency that brings about an effect.

egoism.   The theory that people are, or ought to be, motivated exclusively by self-interest. Psychological egoism is the view that people are so motivated; ethical egoism is the view that they should be.

eliminativism.   The doctrine that mental terms—such as 'belief', 'desire', 'preference', and so on—are so deeply mistaken that neither they nor anything like them have any place in an adequate theory of mind.

emergent property.   A property at one level of complexity that depends on but cannot be reduced to properties at lower levels of complexity.

eminently.   An effect is eminently in a cause when the cause is more perfect than the effect. Thus, in medieval philosophy, God's perfections are eminently in God.

empirical.   Capable of being confirmed or disconfirmed by experience.

empiricism.   The theory that all knowledge derives from experience.

end state principle.   A principle of justice according to which the outcome of a distribution determines whether that distribution is just.

entailment.   The relation between some premises and a conclusion when the conclusion can be validly inferred from the premises.

entelechy.   The primitive, active force in every monad.

entitlement principle.   A principle of justice that determines who is entitled to what.

entrenchment.   The characteristic of predicates that have, as a matter of fact, been used successfully in predictions.

epiphenomenalism.   The view that physical states cause mental states but that mental states do not cause anything.

epistemology.   The theory of knowledge.

equality.   In political philosophy, the condition in which all persons enjoy exactly the same array of fundamental rights and liberties.

equity.   The state of being just, impartial, and fair.

essence.   A fundamental nature that without which an item would not be the thing or kind of thing it is.

estrangement.   Alienation.

euthanasia.   Mercy killing.

evidence class.   Body of evidence.

evident.   Plain, manifest.

evolution.   The development of all living things from a single source by means of natural selection.

exhausted hypothesis.   A hypothesis that has no remaining undetermined cases.

expressivism.   The ethical theory according to which ethical pronouncements state no facts but rather express favorable or unfavorable attitudes or emotions.

extrinsic.   External.

fact.   An existing state of affairs; that which answers to a true sentence.

fallibility.   The capability to be false or wrong.

falsifiability.   The capacity to be refuted by experience.

final cause.   The end or goal toward which an action is directed or for which an artifact is designed.

first-order desire.   A desire whose object is something other than a desire, belief, or other attitude of the desirer.

fission.   The process of splitting into parts.

forensic.   Pertaining to law. In Locke, capable of being responsible.

form.   The essence of a thing or kind that is knowable by the mind.

formal cause.   The pattern or design of a thing.

formal reality.   The reality of a thing considered in itself and not in relation to anything else.

four-color theorem.   A theorem stating that any plane figure separated into regions can be colored using no more than four colors in such a way that no two adjacent regions are the same color.

freedom.   The absence of constraint.

free will.   The capacity to decide for oneself how to act rather than being made to act by forces beyond one's control.

functionalism.   The theory of mind according to which mental states are functional states, not physical states, so distinct physical states that perform the same function would count as the same mental state.

fusion.   The merging of different elements into a single whole.

genotype.   The genetic constitution of an organism as distinguished from its physical appearance.

grue.   The property shared by green things examined before t and blue things not examined before t.

heteronomy.   The condition of acting on desires that are not legislated by reason.

heuristic. A rule or technique for solving a problem that works pretty well most of the time but is not guaranteed to be successful.

historical principle. A principle of justice maintaining that whether a distribution is just depends on how it came about.

idea. A mental representation of something.

ideal. Perfect.

identity. The set of features that makes a thing the thing it is.

iff. If and only if.

ignoratio elenchi. The fallacy of arguing to an irrelevant conclusion.

imagination. In Descartes, the capacity to form mental images.

immanent causation. In Chisholm (353–9), causation in which an agent causes an event or state of affairs.

imperfect duty. A duty that allows leeway in its execution—e.g., the duty to help others. One has such a duty, but there is a choice of which others to help and how to help them.

impression. A mental effect that is a direct consequence of experience.

induction. An ampliative argument from a body of evidence to a conclusion about a class that is more extensive than the evidence; either from 'Some p are q' to 'All p are q' or from 'Some p are q' to 'Some other p are q'.

inference. The process of reasoning from some propositions to others, with the acceptability of the former being grounds for accepting the latter.

innate. Inborn, not acquired.

intension. Meaning or connotation.

intensionality. The capacity to represent or be about something.

intention. A goal that disposes one to act.

intentional strategy. The strategy of treating the objects whose behavior you want to predict as rational agents with beliefs and desires.

intentional system. A system that can be thought of as a rational agent.

interactionism. The view that the mind and body interact.

interactive fork. In Salmon, a causal fork in which one effect does not screen off the effects of the other.

interpretationism. The view that what a person's beliefs and desires are is always a matter of interpretation.

intersubjective. Shared by different persons or subjects; thus an opinion is intersubjective in that it can be shared.

intrinsic. Inherent, essential.

introspection. Looking into one's own mind to find out what one thinks or how one feels.

intuition. In Kant, that which structures the experience of things in space and time. In contemporary philosophy, an immediate awareness in which one places some credence.

irrational. Contrary to reason, illogical.

justice. The fair distribution of benefits and burdens so that each person is given his due.

language of thought. The mental counterpart of spoken languages, which is believed by some to underlie and explain linguistic competence.

lawlike generalization.   A generalization that has the form of a law of nature and the capacity to sustain counterfactuals but that may not be not true.

law of nature.   (See **natural law.**) In Hobbes, a law that is binding on persons in the state of nature.

leviathan.   In Hobbes, the absolute power of the state and its ruler.

liberty.   The right to act as one chooses; freedom from external control.

light of nature.   In Descartes, the source of fundamental intuitions of the intellect that are inherently reliable.

manifold.   In Kant, the unorganized flux presented to the senses that must be structured by concepts for experience to be possible.

material cause.   The substance or material out of which something is made.

material conditional.   The truth function '$x{\rightarrow}y$' of propositions x and y such that '$x{\rightarrow}y$' is false if x is true and y is false; otherwise it is true.

materialism.   The theory that the world is composed entirely of matter.

material object.   An object composed entirely of matter.

maxim.   A principle according to which an action is performed.

maximin.   A principle according to which one should maximize the minimal outcome; one that makes the worst situation as good as it can be.

meaning.   Connotation, intension.

mentalism.   A theory that recognizes irreducibly mental events or states; a theory that considers beliefs, desires, and the like to be real.

metaphysics.   The study of the fundamental nature of reality.

modality.   The way in which a proposition or sentence describes its subject matter. Necessity and possibility are modal concepts.

modal operator.   Logical operators 'it is necessary that', 'it is possible that', 'it is impossible that'.

mode.   In Locke, a sort of complex idea.

modus ponens.   The rule of logic according to which from p and $p{\rightarrow}q$ it follows that q.

monad.   In Leibniz, unextended, active, indivisible, immaterial entities that compose reality; they do not interact with each other but seem to because of preestablished harmony.

nativism.   The theory that the mind produces ideas that are not derived from external sources; the theory that ideas are innate.

natural law.   A true universal or statistical generalization that sustains counterfactuals and figures in scientific explanations.

natural selection.   The evolutionary process whereby adaptive traits come to dominate in a population because the possession of such traits has survival value.

necessary.   A proposition is necessary if it could not have been false.

necessary condition.   If a is a necessary condition for b, then if a does not obtain, b does not—e.g., oxygen's presence in the air is a necessary condition for a fire to occur. See **sufficient condition.**

negative instance.   A case for which the hypothesis is already determined to be false.

nomic dependence.   A lawlike dependence.

nominalism.   The view that the only entities that exist are individuals; the denial that universals are anything above and beyond their instances.

nomological.   Lawlike.

nomological dangler.   A lawlike connection that appears as a brute contingency that is not explained by other elements in a scientific theory.

objectify.   To externalize; to make something into an object.

objective.   Independent of the attitudes of subjects; an objective truth is true regardless of whether anyone considers it to be true.

objective reality.   In Descartes, reality as an object of thought. Thus a unicorn has objective reality because someone has an idea of a unicorn; the unicorn is the object of her thought.

obligation.   An action required of someone; a duty.

Occam's razor.   The principle: Do not multiply entities beyond necessity.

omniscient.   All knowing.

ontology.   The branch of metaphysics concerned with what exists.

opaque.   Characteristic of a context in which coextensive terms are not intersubstitutable without affecting truth value.

original position.   In Rawls, the position adopted by hypothetical rational agents in framing the social contract.

overdetermination.   An event is overdetermined if there is more than one antecedent event in its causal history that would be sufficient to cause it.

parsimony, principle of.   The principle that the least possible number of assumptions should be made in an explanation of a particular fact.

particular.   An individual; not a universal.

percept.   An immediate deliverance of perception.

percipient.   Perceiver.

perfect duty.   A duty that allows no leeway in its execution, such as the duty to keep one's promises.

perfection, degrees of.   See **reality, degrees of.**

perfectionism.   The ethical position that the goal of life is to perfect oneself.

phenomenological.   Related to consciousness or subjectivity.

phenomenon.   Something that is apparent in experience.

phenotype.   The gross physiological features of an organism produced by the interaction between genes and environment.

physicalism.   The theory that everything that exists is physical.

plastic.   Malleable, capable of being shaped or formed.

positive instance.   A case for which a hypothesis is already determined to be true.

possible world.   A complete, self-consistent set of possibilities; a way the world might be.

power.   The capacity to achieve something or make something happen.

pragmatism.   The theory according to which the practical effects of adopting a theory constitute the whole meaning of the theory.

precept.   A rule or principle of conduct.

preemption.   Event A preempts event B if B would have caused C if A had not occurred and actually caused C—e.g., the poison (preempted cause) would have killed C, except that he was shot first (preempting cause).

preestablished harmony.   In Leibniz, the theory that the order in the world is not due to objects' interacting with each other but to God's creating individual monads and setting them in motion in such a way that their behavior is synchronized.

prejudice.   A judgment made prior to and independent of an examination of the relevant facts.

presentation.   In Kant, an object of direct awareness.

primary goods.   Goods every rational person is presumed to want—e.g., rights and liberties, powers and opportunities, income and wealth, self-respect.

primary quality.   A quality of a perceptible object that is detectable by more than one sense—e.g., size, shape.

principle.   A basic rule.

probabilistic automaton.   A robot whose behavior is not deterministic but is governed by probabilities.

process, brain.   An activity of the brain.

projected.   Actually used in the prediction of an outcome.

projectible.   A property of predicates whose past instances guide valid predictions about future cases.

projection.   An inference from a limited body of cases to a larger body of cases.

projective class.   All the instances of a hypothesis that are neither positive nor negative.

property.   An attribute, trait, or aspect.

proposition.   That which is stated by a declarative sentence; the content of a declarative sentence.

propositional attitude.   An attitude, such as belief or desire, that takes a proposition as an object.

psychophysical law.   A law linking psychological states with physical states.

purposiveness.   In Kant, an adaptation as though to an end.

qualia.   The felt qualities of experience, such as apparent colors or textures.

quality.   Property.

rationalism.   The theory that reason rather than experience plays the dominant role in the acquisition and justification of knowledge.

rationality.   The capacity to use reason; the use of reason.

raw feel.   A deliverance of a sense organ independent of and prior to conceptualization.

realism.   The doctrine that things are as they are regardless of what anyone may believe about how they are.

reality, degrees of.   In Descartes and medieval philosophers, something's degree of reality is inversely proportional to its dependence on other things for its existence. So a shadow has a lesser degree of reality than the thing that casts the shadow, since the thing could exist if the shadow did not, but the shadow would not exist if the thing casting it did not.

realization.   Instantiation.

reason.   A consideration that supports or tells in favor of a claim; rationality.

reduction.   The redefinition of one term by others where the terms in the definition refer to different, more basic elements than the apparent referent of the term being defined. Thus psychophysical reduction defines mental terms in physical terms.

reference.   The relation between a term or other symbol and the thing(s) it symbolizes. A name refers to its bearer.

reflection.   Thought.

reflective equilibrium.   A characteristic of a system of thought in which all elements are mutually supportive and the system as a whole is one that is, on reflection, acceptable.

relation.   A property of two or more places, e.g., 'John is taller than Jim'.

relativism.   The view that truths in a certain subject are not absolute but are relative to something such as a practice or a standpoint.

representation.   In philosophy of mind, the view that the mind contains something like pictures or quasi-linguistic items on which it operates.

resemblance.   Similarity.

responsibility.   Duty, obligation.

retributive view punishment.   The view that punishment is justified only because it is deserved for violation of a moral or legal rule, not because it might either benefit society or improve the violator or criminal.

right.   That which one is free to do.

right of nature.   In Hobbes, the right of a person to do anything in his power to preserve his own life.

rigid designator.   A term that refers to the same thing in all possible worlds or in all possible worlds in which that thing exists.

screen off.   **A** screens off **C** from **B** just in case though **B** raises the probability of **C**, **B** is rendered irrelevant to **C** when another factor, **A**, is present. For example, the probability of **C** = Jones dies by noon is greatly increased by **B** = At 9:30 AM, Smith adds a poison to Jones' drink. However, before the poison has its intended effect, **B** is screened off—rendered causally and probabilistically irrelevant—because of **A** = At 11 AM, White shoots Jones in the heart. See also Salmon, 280 note 15.

secondary quality.   A sensory quality detectable by only one sense.

second-order desires.   Desires concerning what to want or desire.

self-contradiction.   A proposition that is true if and only if it is false.

self-presenting state.   A state such that if one is in it, one knows that one is in it.

semantic.   Pertaining to the relation of a sign or symbol to what it represents.

sensation.   The immediate result of the stimulation of a sense organ.

sense-datum.   An intrinsically private deliverance of the senses; the content of a sensation.

sentiment.   A feeling or emotion.

set.   A collection of zero or more items obeying the laws of set theory.

simple idea.   In Locke, an idea that is not composed of other ideas; rather it derives from impressions of sensation or reflection.

skepticism.   The doctrine that knowledge is impossible.

social contract.   The hypothetical contract that is supposed to underlie a legitimate political regime.

sophistry.   A plausible but fallacious argument.

sovereignty.   Supremacy of political authority or rule.

spirit.   That which animates; a self or soul.

standard.   That against which things are measured; a norm.

state of nature.   The condition in which people were before governments existed or would be in if governments did not exist.

subject, political.   Someone under the political power or authority of another.

subjective.   Depending on an attitude of some subject; thus tastes in ice cream are subjective since the only thing that determines whether mint ice cream tastes good to Joan is whether Joan likes mint ice cream.

subjunctive conditional.   A proposition with the form 'if p were the case, q would be the case'.

sublime.   Great, fearful, and noble; leading to feelings of awe and perhaps dread.

substance.   The bearer of properties.

substratum.   That which underlies properties.

sufficient condition.   If a is a sufficient condition for b, then if a is the case, b is also the case—e.g., Joe's shooting Tom in the head was a sufficient condition for Tom's death. See **necessary condition.**

supported hypothesis.   A hypothesis that has positive instances.

syllogism.   A logically valid argument in which a conclusion follows from two premises.

synonymous.   Having the same meaning.

synthetic.   A proposition whose predicate adds something to what is contained in the subject. Such propositions are thus not true by definition.

taste.   The faculty of discerning aesthetic features.

tautology.   A formula that is true on the basis of its form alone.

teleological.   Having an end, purpose, or function.

thing in itself.   That which lies behind the various ways a thing appears.

tracking truth.   A belief tracks truth just in case the subject would believe it if it were true and would not believe it (at least on his current grounds) if it were not true.

transcendental.   Transcending the senses; a truth is transcendental if it is not a purely mathematical or logical truth and its truth is not discoverable either directly or indirectly by means of the senses.

transeunt causation.   In Chisholm (353–9), causation in which an event or state of affairs causes another event or state of affairs.

transparent.   A sentence is transparent if terms that refer to the same object can be substituted for one another without altering the truth value of the sentence.

truth.   The property a sentence has when things are the way the sentence says that they are.

truth condition.   The condition under which a sentence is true; the way the world must be in order for the sentence to be true.

Turing machine.   An idealized computer that makes precise the concept of an effective computation; a function $f(x)$ is Turing computable if, when a representation of x is inputted, the machine can calculate the value of $f(x)$.

Turing test.   A test to judge whether something has a mind. A person and a machine communicate with an investigator who can ask them questions but cannot see them. If, no matter what questions the investigator asks, she cannot tell which is the person and which is the computer, the computer has a mind.

undefeated justification.   Justification for knowledge that has not been undermined by further evidence.

undetermined instance.   Case that is so far neither a positive nor a negative case.

universal.   A property or relation that can be instantiated by any number of different particular things—e.g., 'red' is a universal since any number of things can be red.

utilitarianism.   The ethical theory according to which the good is that which maximizes utility or happiness; that which promotes the greatest good for the greatest number.

validity.   The property of an argument when its conclusion follows from the premises. In a deductively valid argument, if the premises are true, the conclusion is true. In an inductively valid argument, the conclusion may be false even if the premises are true.

veil of ignorance.   In Rawls, the metaphorical barrier blocking out considerations that would introduce bias into deliberations about the content of the social contract.

veridical.   Expressing or conveying truth.

violated hypothesis.   A hypothesis that has a negative instance.

virtue.   A valuable character trait; virtues may be moral or intellectual or both.

volition.   A mental act of willing or trying required for voluntary action as opposed to mere behavior.

withhold.   To suspend judgment.

BIOGRAPHICAL NOTES

St. Anselm   (1033–1109) was Archbishop of Canterbury and the most prominent Christian theologian and philosopher of the 11th century. He is especially known for his ontological argument, which purports to prove that God exists on the basis of the idea of God alone.

St. Thomas Aquinas   (1225–1274) was a great medieval theologian and philosopher. He was a proponent of natural theology, the view that knowledge of God's existence does not require supernatural revelation but can be ascertained on the basis of reason and experience.

Aristotle   (384–322 BCE), an ancient Greek philosopher, was a student of Plato and a tutor of Alexander the Great. He wrote on a vast array of subjects, including logic, natural science, metaphysics, politics, and ethics. He was one of the most influential philosophers of all time.

Jonathan Bennett   (1930–) was born in New Zealand. He has taught in England, Canada, and the United States. He writes on metaphysics, philosophy of language, ethics, and the history of early modern philosophy.

George Berkeley   (1685–1753) was an Anglican bishop and one of the greatest early modern philosophers. An empiricist, he believed that all knowledge derives from sensation and reflection. This led him to idealism, the view that the only things that exist are minds and ideas.

Albert Camus   (1913–1960) was born in Algeria. He fought in the French resistance during World War II, was editor of an underground newspaper, and wrote novels. He believed that life is absurd and so all action is ultimately pointless.

Roderick Chisholm   (1916–1999) taught at Brown University. He wrote on many topics, notably epistemology, metaphysics, and free will.

William K. Clifford   (1845–1879) was a British philosopher and mathematician who taught at University College, London. He thought that it is immoral to hold beliefs for which one has no evidence.

Arthur Danto   (1924–) is Emeritus Professor of Philosophy at Columbia University and a noted art critic. He specializes in aesthetics, the theory of representations, and philosophical psychology.

Stephen Darwall   (1946–) teaches at the University of Michigan. He works on the foundations of ethics, moral psychology, and the history of moral philosophy.

Daniel Dennett   (1942–) teaches at Tufts University. He writes on cognitive science, philosophy of mind, and evolutionary biology.

René Descartes   (1596–1650) was a French philosopher, mathematician, and scientist. He is known as the founder of modern philosophy. His works framed the central problems in epistemology and philosophy of mind. He invented the Cartesian coordinate system.

George Dickie   (1926–) is Emeritus Professor of Philosophy at the University of Illinois, Chicago. He works on aesthetics and advocates an institutional theory of art.

Antony Flew   (1923–) is a British philosopher who was for many years Professor of Philosophy at the University of Reading. He writes on philosophy of religion, philosophy of education, and philosophy of language.

Jerry Fodor   (1935–) teaches at Rutgers University. He is a major figure in cognitive science and philosophy of mind.

Philippa Foot   (1920–) is a British philosopher who spent many years teaching at Oxford and the University of California, Los Angeles. She specializes in ethics and is a key figure in contemporary virtue theory.

Harry Frankfurt   (1922–) is Professor Emeritus of Philosophy at Princeton University. He works on moral philosophy, philosophy of mind, and 17th-century rationalism.

Edmund L. Gettier   (1927–) is Professor Emeritus of Philosophy at the University of Massachusetts, Amherst. He is best known for his paper "Is Justified True Belief Knowledge?"

Alvin Goldman   (1938–) teaches at Rutgers University. His main interests are epistemology, cognitive science, and philosophy of mind.

Nelson Goodman   (1906–1998) was a prominent American philosopher and logician. He is known especially for his work on aesthetics, metaphysics, and the problem of induction.

Thomas Hobbes   (1588–1679) was a British philosopher best known for his contributions to political philosophy. His *Leviathan* was one of the earliest works on the social contract theory.

David Hume   (1711–1776) was a Scottish philosopher. He was one of the foremost early modern philosophers. He believed that since all knowledge derives from sense impressions, we have no reason to believe in such things as causality, necessity, and God.

Frank Jackson   (1943–) teaches at Australian National University. He works mainly on philosophy of mind, metaphysics, metaethics, and epistemology.

William James   (1842–1910) was an American philosopher and psychologist. He was a leading exponent of pragmatism and was instrumental in the development of the science of psychology.

Immanuel Kant   (1724–1804), a German, was one of the greatest philosophers of all time. He developed a complex system of thought that encompasses metaphysics, epistemology, ethics, aesthetics, and philosophy of religion.

Christine M. Korsgaard   (1952–) teaches at Harvard University. Her main areas of interest are moral philosophy, normativity, and the history of ethics.

Saul Kripke   (1940–) teaches at the Graduate Center, City University of New York. His major contributions have been in logic and philosophy of language.

Gottfried Leibniz   (1646–1716) was a German philosopher and mathematician. His main contributions to philosophy are in metaphysics. His main contribution to mathematics was his invention (simultaneously with Newton) of calculus.

David Lewis   (1941–2001) taught at Princeton University and was a major figure in 20th-century analytic philosophy. His primary work was in metaphysics, philosophy of mind, philosophy of language, and epistemology.

John Locke   (1632–1704), a British philosopher, was one of the major figures in early modern philosophy. His *Essay Concerning Human Understanding* is one of the central works in the history of epistemology. His *Second Treatise on Government* influenced the writers of the U.S. Declaration of Independence and the Constitution.

J. L. Mackie   (1917–1981) was an Australian philosopher who worked on metaphysics, metaethics, and philosophy of religion.

Karl Marx   (1818–1883) was a German philosopher, economist, and historian. He is the author of one of the great systematic critiques of capitalism, *Das Kapital,* and of *The Communist Manifesto.*

John Stuart Mill   (1806–1873) was a British philosopher and political economist. His main works are *Utilitarianism, On Liberty,* and *The Subjection of Women.*

Thomas Nagel   (1937–) teaches at New York University. He works mainly on metaphysics, philosophy of mind, ethics, political philosophy, and philosophy of law.

Friedrich Nietzsche   (1844–1900) was an influential German philosopher known for his critiques of culture, morality, religion, and philosophy.

Robert Nozick   (1938–2002) taught for many years at Harvard University. He wrote on political philosophy, epistemology, metaphysics, and philosophy of mind.

Derek Parfit   (1942–) is a fellow of All Souls College, Oxford. He is known especially for his work on personal identity and ethics.

Blaise Pascal   (1623–1662) was a French thinker who worked primarily on mathematics, physics, and philosophy of religion. He made major contributions to the probability theory, which he investigated to figure out gambling odds.

C. S. Peirce   (1839–1914) was the founder of American pragmatism. His work spans logic, epistemology, the theory of signs, and much else.

John Perry   (1943–) teaches at Stanford University. He works on philosophy of mind and philosophy of language and is especially known for his work on personal identity.

Plato   (c.428–c.348 BCE) was one of the greatest philosophers of all time. He was a student of Socrates and a teacher of Aristotle. His works, written as dialogues, span every branch of philosophy—metaphysics, epistemology, ethics, philosophy of religion, philosophy of art, political philosophy, and so forth. His work is said to have formed the cornerstone of Western culture.

Richard Price   (1723–1791) was a moral and political philosopher from Wales. He argued that reason rather than emotion is the basis of ethics.

Hilary Putnam   (1926–) is Emeritus Professor of Philosophy at Harvard University. He works mainly on metaphysics, philosophy of language, philosophy of science, philosophy of logic, and philosophy of mind.

James Rachels   (1941–2003) taught at the University of Alabama, Birmingham. He specialized in moral philosophy.

John Rawls   (1921–2002) taught at Harvard University. He was the most important and influential political philosopher of the 20th century.

Thomas Reid   (1710–1796) was a philosopher of the Scottish Enlightenment. He is known for his work on personal identity, epistemology, and philosophy of mind.

William L. Rowe   (1931–) is Professor Emeritus of Philosophy at Purdue University. He is known especially for his work on philosophy of religion.

Bertrand Russell   (1872–1970) was a British philosopher and logician and an outspoken advocate of political reform. He made major contributions to modern logic, philosophy of language, epistemology, and philosophy of mind.

Wesley Salmon   (1925–2001) taught philosophy of science at the University of Pittsburgh. His work focused on scientific explanation and probability.

Peter Singer   (1946–) is an Australian philosopher. He teaches at Princeton University and specializes in applied ethics. He is best known for his writings on animal rights.